Theories of
SOCIAL
INEQUALITY

Theories of
SOCIAL INEQUALITY
Classical and Contemporary Perspectives
Second Edition

Edward G. Grabb

HARCOURT
BRACE
CANADA

Harcourt Brace & Company, Canada
Toronto Montreal Fort Worth New York Orlando
Philadelphia San Diego London Sydney Tokyo

Canadian Cataloguing in Publication Data

Grabb, Edward G.
    Theories of social inequality

2nd ed.
First ed. published under title: Social inequality:
classical and contemporary theorists.
ISBN 0-03-922693-X

1. Equality.   2. Social classes.   3. Power (Social
sciences).   I. Title.   II. Title: Social
inequality : classical and contemporary theorists.

HT609.G73 1990   305   C89-094864-X

Publisher: David Dimmell
Developmental Editor: Graeme Whitley
Publishing Services Manager: Karen Eakin
Editorial Co-ordinator: Marcel Chiera
Copy Editor: Judith Turnbull
Cover and Interior Design: Daniel Kewley
Typesetting and Assembly: True to Type Inc.
Printing and Binding: Webcom Ltd.

Printed in Canada

4 5   WC 96 95

For Denise

Preface

This book is the revised second edition of a work first published in 1984 under the title *Social Inequality: Classical and Contemporary Theorists*. In the first edition, my primary goal was to trace and document the major conceptions of social inequality to be found in classical and contemporary sociological theory. My research was based on a relatively close reading of what, in my judgement, were the most promising and prominent perspectives available. My hope was that the book would be of use to two somewhat different audiences: to students at various levels who might see some virtue in a concise assessment of how leading general theorists have dealt with the key conceptual problems in the field of inequality; and to certain colleagues who might share my own interest in, and surprise at, some of the parallels and common ground to be found in a wide range of theoretical approaches, many of which have typically been viewed as essentially distinct and at times even contradictory.

I cannot be an objective judge of whether the first book was completely successful in reaching either or both of these audiences. Perhaps it is fair to say that the decision by Holt, Rinehart and Winston of Canada to produce a second edition is one vote of confidence, and one for which I am genuinely grateful. With the helpful comments of many colleagues and students, I have endeavoured to make this second volume better than the first, by updating and expanding the presentation and by reassessing some of the analyses of classical and contemporary writers from the first edition. Even so, as I had anticipated in preparing the original version, there is truth in the adage that it is impossible to please everyone. Hence, I expect certain readers will argue that too much has been attempted, while others will conclude that much more should have been done.

The changes and additions incorporated into the second edition have not altered the fundamental goals of the original book. I have once again placed considerable emphasis on outlining and clarifying the ideas of Marx and Weber, whose works continue to stand at the core of theoretical developments and debates in the study of inequality. As before, I have included Durkheim among the significant classical thinkers in the area, because of his unquestioned stature as a general theorist in sociology, his insightful and frequently overlooked observations on the particular issue of inequality, and his role as a bridge linking the early theorists' treatments of inequality and the more recent structural-functionalist approach. In this edition, the discussion of Durkheim is not combined with the analysis of structural functionalism but instead is examined in a separate chapter. A brief biographical sketch of Durkheim has also been added, to parallel the presentations of Marx and Weber.

As for the structural-functionalist perspective, it now falls somewhere in the middle of the chronology from early to modern theories, not exactly contemporary but not precisely classical either. Whatever its categorization, however, structural functionalism continues to be of some importance in tracing the main conceptual developments in the study of inequality. Most writers no longer view this perspective as a serious alternative to Marxist or Weberian approaches, and most have been quite critical of its conservative leanings and related difficulties. Nevertheless, several aspects of the structural-functionalist perspective are worthy of note, both in their own right and because of the critical reactions they have stimulated among other theorists. This critical response is illuminating to review, since it marked the start of the contemporary movement back toward Marx and Weber and a revival of interest in debating and reworking the ideas of these two central figures.

The debate over the views of Marx and Weber continues to dominate most current thinking in the study of social inequality and is the principal focus for the material presented in the latter part of the text. For obvious reasons, it is not possible to conduct a thorough assessment of all the contemporary writers who have made a contribution to this debate or to other relevant issues in the theoretical analysis of social inequality. Following the original edition, I have concentrated on a detailed discussion of six recent theorists in the field: Dahrendorf, Lenski, Poulantzas, Wright, Parkin, and Giddens. The initial selection of these writers was guided by the belief, which I continue to hold, that the key ideas embodied in their approaches effectively represent the essential flavour and direction of current views on how social inequality is to be conceived and understood. Therefore, although there are other writers who rival these six and could be examined in their place, I have chosen to retain the original set of recent theorists in this edition. Of course, other analysts will also be considered at appropriate points in the presentation, even though their work is not assessed in detail.

The selection of certain writers, and the consequent exclusion of others, can produce misunderstandings about the intentions of any author who is faced with such choices. A reviewer of the first edition, for example, came away convinced that I was a Marxist, based on my selection of theorists and my interpretation of their writings. In fact, my views on social inequality are clearly more Weberian than Marxist, and I should think this would be apparent from my treatment of the main issues. For example, although the concept of class, which is typically identified as a Marxian concern, receives considerable attention in the book, it is the Weberian idea of power or domination that receives the greatest emphasis and that is used to tie the overall discussion together. Indeed, while some might contend that the concept of class is given undue attention, I suspect that other observers, especially some Marxist scholars, will feel that the opposite is the case, given my stress on the concept of power. In all events, I can only state my own position, which is that class inequalities are pivotal to any complete understanding of social inequality; in addition, however, I argue that class inequalities, like the other key forms of inequality that can be identified in social structures, should also be conceived primarily as consequences of differential access to the major sources of power in society.

It is the recognition of these other forms of inequality that is at the heart of a second point I wish to stress about my goals and intentions in writing this book. My choice of writers to review has been guided by a search for *general* approaches to the study of inequality, as opposed to theories that focus exclusively on *specific* forms or bases of inequality, such as those involving race, gender, region, age, religion, and so on. My contention is that the perspectives examined here are important precisely because they point us toward a more unified approach for analyzing *all* such forms of inequality. This approach centres, as has already been suggested, on the problem of power or domination. This may explain to some readers why I have not devoted space to a detailed exposition of feminist theories or theories of racial oppression, for example, given the specific focus of such analyses in most cases.

I should stress quite strongly, however, that my interest in more general issues does not mean that I believe these specific theories or the topics they address are unimportant or secondary. On the contrary, I would argue that, in certain societies or social settings, inequalities based on gender or race are demonstrably more central than any other forms for understanding the overall pattern of inequality existing in those contexts. At the same time, however, I believe that it is an important and legitimate intellectual task to trace the common threads running through the leading general perspectives on the problem of social inequality, without having to provide a complete exegesis on the many notable issues arising in these more specific areas. A book should be a vehicle for conveying ideas and analysis, but any single book can and should carry only so much cargo. I would also suggest that there are some significant conceptual linkages between the general perspectives I have chosen to investigate, on the one hand, and leading examples of theoretical analyses of specific forms of inequality, on the other. I have tried to illustrate this common ground briefly in the concluding chapter and expect that it may come as some surprise to people working on these more particular concerns. The end product of these efforts is meant to be a more general and macroscopic depiction of how structured inequalities may be conceived in modern societies, incorporating a finite set of crucial themes and issues that most principal theorists, in varying degrees, have already identified.

My greatest reward in writing this book has been the opportunity to learn from and work with a number of outstanding people. I am grateful, first of all, to the support staff in the Sociology Department at the University of Western Ontario, particularly Veronica D'Souza and Denise Statham, for their assistance in preparing the manuscript. My research assistant at Western, Andrea Saunders, also deserves special thanks for her careful and efficient library searches and bibliographic work.

The people at Holt, Rinehart and Winston of Canada have once again provided their consistent support and editorial advice. Dave Dimmell, Heather McWhinney, Steve Payne, Graeme Whitley, and Marcel Chiera have been especially helpful and understanding throughout the process of producing the second edition. I am sincerely grateful to all of them.

Intellectual debts are the most difficult to acknowledge, for it is rarely possible to identify and mention all of those individuals whose work and ideas have helped shape your own. Certainly, the reviewers of the second edition — Lewis A. Coser, formerly of the State University of New York at Stony Brook; S. M. Lipset, Stanford University; Stewart Clegg, University of New England; Wallace Clement, Carleton University; Jill Bystydzienski, Franklin College; Muhammad Fayyaz, Queen's University; Donald Von Eschen, McGill University; Carolyn Howe, College of the Holy Cross; and Jim Curtis, University of Waterloo — are to be thanked for stimulating me to rethink and rework various sections of the manuscript. Equally important are several colleagues, students, and friends, both at Western and elsewhere. These include Anton Allahar, Doug Baer, Sam Clark, George Comninel, Neil Guppy, Bill Johnston, David MacLennan, Kevin McQuillan, Jim Rinehart, Gloria Smith, and Cathy Thorpe. It is people of this calibre who help to ease the burdens of scholarship. Although not all of them will be fully satisfied with the final product, this book has been made immeasurably better by their contributions to it. Writing may indeed be lonely, as some would have it, but any writing worth reading is almost always a collective enterprise.

Edward G. Grabb
London, Canada
July 28, 1989

PUBLISHER'S NOTE TO INSTRUCTORS AND STUDENTS

This textbook is a key component of your course. If you are the instructor of this course, you undoubtedly considered a number of texts carefully before choosing this as the one that will work best for your students and you. The authors and publishers of this book spent considerable time and money to ensure its high quality, and we appreciate your recognition of this effort and accomplishment.

If you are a student, we are confident that this text will help you to meet the objectives of your course. You will also find it helpful after the course is finished, as a valuable addition to your personal library. So hold on to it.

As well, please don't forget that photocopying copyright work means that authors lose royalties that are rightfully theirs. This loss will discourage them from writing another edition of this text or other books, because doing so will simply not be worth their time and effort. If this happens, we all lose — students, instructors, authors, and publishers.

And since we want to hear what you think about this book, please be sure to send us the stamped reply card at the end of the text. This will help us to continue publishing high-quality books for your courses.

Contents

Chapter

1

Theories of Social Inequality: An Introduction

It is a paradox of life that its familiar features are often the most difficult to comprehend. This poses a special problem for sociologists, who are expected to explain these familiar things but who are commonly accused of doing so in unduly complicated ways. And yet, while such accusations are sometimes justified, it is also true, as Randall Collins notes, that obvious social questions may not have obvious or simple answers. Sociology's great strength, in fact, is precisely its potential for penetrating the superficial observation of everyday life and finding the fundamental social processes hidden beneath (Collins, 1982).

These remarks have a particular relevance for the topic of concern in this book — the problem of social inequality. For inequality is one of the most familiar facts of social life, a pervasive element in social relationships that is well known, even to the most casual observer. At the same time, however, social inequality has not been an easy problem to solve or explain. Instead, it has provoked protracted and perplexing arguments over whether it is good or bad, natural or contrived, permanent or transitory in social settings. It has involved many of the most prominent social thinkers in debates about its origins, causes, and what, if anything, should be done to eliminate it. The central purpose of this volume is to review and assess the major elements in these debates, both past and present. In carrying out this purpose, the analysis will highlight the important differences and similarities in the approaches that have been developed, in an effort to trace the main direction that these theoretical exchanges seem to be taking us in understanding the problem of social inequality.

But what is social inequality, exactly? Even this most basic question is unlikely to produce a universally acceptable answer, though most would agree it involves such concerns as the gap between the rich and the poor, or the advantaged and the disadvantaged, in society. More generally, however, social inequality can refer to any of the differences between people (or the socially defined positions they occupy) that are *consequential* for the lives they lead, most particularly for the rights or opportunities they exercise and the rewards or privileges they enjoy. Of greatest importance here are those consequential differences that become *structured*, in the social sense of the term, that are built into the ways that people interact with one another on a recurring basis. Thus, people differ from one another in an infinite number of respects — in everything from height or weight to eye colour or shoe size — but only a finite subset of these differences will be consequential for establishing unequal relations between people, and fewer still will generate structured patterns that are more or less sustained over time and place.

This leads us to a second very basic question: what are the main bases for inequality in society, the key differences between people that affect their rights, opportunities, rewards, and privileges? Once again, a universal answer is far from clear. Complications arise around this question for a variety of reasons.

First of all, some observers argue that the central bases for inequality are *individual differences*, in natural abilities, motivation, willingness to work hard, and so on. In contrast, other analysts contend that inequality is primarily based on the differential treatment people are accorded because of *socially defined characteristics*, such as economic class, race, age, ethnicity, gender, or religion.

A second difficulty in trying to list the main bases for social inequality is the great discrepancy in the importance attached to some criteria across different places and historical periods. Thus, for example, religion was once a major determinant of people's rights and rewards in countries like Canada or the United States but now is of lesser significance. In other nations, however, such as Iran or Northern Ireland, religious affiliation is still a key factor affecting the differences in economic well-being and political influence among the population and continues to provoke grave conflicts between factions.

A third complication to consider is the disagreement that exists over how many bases for inequality are truly important, and which of these are the most consequential in any general portrayal of inequality in society. Opinions on this issue vary; some theorists see a whole spectrum of cross-cutting, individual and socially defined, inequalities, while others stress only one or two key bases as predominant over the rest. Marxist theorists, for example, often emphasize class inequality as the most important above all others, while some writers in feminist theory place much more stress on questions of gender inequality than on any other issue. (For discussion, see Curtis and Scott, 1979; Jeffries and Ransford, 1980; Curtis et al., 1988.)

Finally, the issue of what bases for inequality are most crucial in society is clouded further by the related issue of why some human differences are viewed as significant but not others. As an extreme case, we might wonder, for instance, why eye colour has virtually no impact in creating unequal social relations when something almost as superficial, colour of skin, has been used throughout history as a basis for granting or denying rights and rewards, thereby establishing persistent inequalities among people.

This list of issues provides us with some indication of the challenges involved in attempting to deal with the questions of what social inequality is about and where its major origins and bases should be traced. In subsequent chapters, we shall examine the ways in which leading social theorists have addressed such questions. Although a variety of themes and ideas will be considered, it is helpful at the beginning to be alert to certain topics that will be of particular concern. Hence, in the rest of this opening chapter, we shall briefly introduce four topics around which much of the later discussion revolves. These include the concept of class and its significance for the analysis of social inequality, the part played by the concept of power in theories of inequality, the role of the state in discussions of inequality in modern times, and the outlook for reducing or ending social inequalities in future societies.

Class and Social Inequality

While controversies abound in much of the literature on social inequality, one point that most observers accept is the central importance of the concept of *class* for the original development of theory and research in this area. Some have suggested that sociology itself, not just the analysis of inequality, really began with studies of class, especially in the work of Karl Marx (cf. Dahrendorf, 1969; Giddens, 1973; Hunter, 1986). The term class, of course, is now part of the everyday vocabulary of many people, and there is even some vague agreement in much of the population on how classes are perceived: as social groupings that differ mainly in their command of *economic* or *material resources*, such as money, wealth, or property (e.g., Coleman and Rainwater, 1978; Bell and Robinson, 1980; Grabb and Lambert, 1982; Lambert et al., 1986).

Thus, it is no surprise that class has been central to most discussions of social inequality, since it pertains to that most basic of life's inequalities: the differential access of people to the material means of existence (cf. Carchedi, 1987:79). However, although most social thinkers can agree on the importance of the concept, numerous disputes and questions persist over the more precise meaning of class, how it should best be defined and what its real significance is in the general analysis of inequality. Among the many issues that have been raised, the following should be kept in mind in our review of the major theorists.

First of all, are classes simply *categories* of people in similar economic circumstances, or should the concept of class be reserved solely for those situations in which such categories are also real *groups*, with a common consciousness of membership and some basis for sustained interaction among the people involved? A somewhat related question is whether classes are equivalent to *strata*, to statistical aggregates of people ranked according to criteria such as income, or whether such delineations miss the essential significance of the term class (cf. Stolzman and Gamberg, 1974). Another issue of this sort concerns the distinction between *relational* and *distributive* studies of inequality: are classes most important or interesting for the uneven distribution of income and other rewards among them, or for the relationships of control and subordination that are established in their interactions with one another? (See, for example, Goldthorpe, 1972; Curtis and Scott, 1979; Grabb, 1988.) Fourth, are classes best understood concretely, as sets of real people, or abstractly, as sets of economic *places* or *positions*, filled by people and yet distinct from them, in much the same way that boxes are distinct from their contents? And finally, of course, there is the long-standing dispute over the number of classes that exist in modern societies. Are there just two, a small dominant one and a large subordinate one? Or are there instead some intermediate classes between top and bottom, and if so, how many? Or is it more accurate to say that there are *no* discernible classes, just a finely graded hierarchy without clear breaks? One of the purposes of this analysis is to sort out, if not completely resolve, the debates over these divergent views of class.

Power and Social Inequality

Along with class, *power* has emerged as the other key concept in most major theories of social inequality. Like class, power is recognized as an important idea but at the same time has generated considerable debate over its exact meaning or significance. Largely through the early work of Max Weber, many theorists accept that power occurs where some people are able to control social situations as they see fit, whether other people accept or oppose this control. But many questions continue to arise around the concept. Can power differences between people be dispensed with under the appropriate social conditions, or are relations of control and subordination inherently necessary in any society? Is power unjust and oppressive by definition, or can it be a means for preventing or reducing injustice and oppression? Does power always flow downward from those who command to those who obey, or is there some reciprocal influence back up the chain of command? Such questions of power, of the ability to control social situations, obviously bear on the problem of social inequality, for such control normally has a direct effect in generating and sustaining unequal rights, opportunities, rewards, and privileges among people.

Yet, of all the important questions that have been asked about power, perhaps the most crucial one in recent years has been the following: from what and how many sources does power stem? In other words, does power ultimately originate in a single source or collectivity? Does it lie instead with a few principal factions or interest groups? Or is it widely dispersed to a multitude of individuals and groups in society? While there is still a range of opinion on this question among social theorists, many now seem to believe that power is considerably more concentrated than was once thought. Within this narrower range of viewpoints, the central debate that currently exists is one that pits those, on the one hand, who see power as primarily (even completely) a consequence of class differences against those, on the other hand, who see class as one basis (or the key basis) among a limited but nonetheless multiple set of power differences in society.

As shall be argued later, it is misleading to overstate the disagreements between these two competing viewpoints, since they share more elements in common than is sometimes acknowledged. Still, there are some fundamental distinctions between them that have crucial implications for how we are to think about or conceive of inequality in society. The key difference is mainly in their emphases. The first view contends that social inequality is principally about class inequality and, though it acknowledges non-class inequalities between races or between genders, for example, treats other inequalities as secondary to and largely explicable by class differences. The alternative view contends that while inequality is certainly about class, in some cases first and foremost, it is also about other socially defined characteristics such as race and gender. These traits and others are regularly tied to inequalities in *power* that are at least as significant as class inequalities in many instances, that are not reducible to class differences, and that operate whether or not classes exist in society. It is on this basis that some theorists see power as a more generalizable concept than class, a concept that can be used, at a general level of analysis, to help us understand

and explain social inequality in all its forms. The various disputes, as well as points of agreement, between leading class theorists and prominent power theorists form a major portion of the topics we shall address in this book.

The State and Social Inequality

The choice of placing primary emphasis on class or on power when analyzing social inequality is roughly paralleled by a second debate that has taken on great significance in recent discussions. This is the question of whether the economic structure is the key mechanism through which inequalities develop and are sustained in society, or whether instead it is the political structure, or *state*, that is the central arena for determining the nature of social inequality in modern times.

On the one hand, the economic structure, the system of material production, is the main engine for creating the necessities (and the luxuries) of social life; because of this essential activity, and because control over what is produced and how it is distributed is so closely tied to class differences, there is a case to be made for the view that the economic system and the class relations emerging from it form the crux of any analysis of social inequality. On the other hand, the state is supposed to be the official representative of the general will, at least in nominally democratic societies; hence, it has the responsibility for creating and implementing, by force if necessary, those laws and policies that can either entrench or reduce inequalities in society. This right to legislate and enforce gives to the state leadership ultimate *formal* control, not only over class inequality but over racial, sexual, and other forms of inequality as well. Moreover, the apparent trend toward increased political intervention in economic affairs in contemporary societies has prompted some observers to suggest that the state is also beginning to usurp the essential activities of the economic structure. Such arguments provide the main basis for the view that the state has become the principal player in the modern power struggle and thus the predominant factor to consider in any analysis of social inequality.

The Future of Social Inequality

Probably the main reason why social theorists have devoted so much effort to the problem of social inequality has been their desire to answer one fundamental question: is inequality among people a natural and inevitable feature of society, something that might be reduced but never abolished in social settings, or, on the contrary, is inequality an unnatural and imposed social arrangement, an injustice that can and should be eliminated through social change?

The extensive discussions that have developed around this difficult question have given rise to several important controversies. Some theorists argue, for example, that inequality must be natural, since it is found in all societies. Others counter that its universal existence is no proof that inequality is natural; after all, slavery too was once a universal phenomenon but it is now judged to be an unnatural social arrangement, subject to complete abolition throughout the world. A somewhat related issue is whether people should receive unequal rewards because they contribute different degrees of talent or effort to society, or whether it is possible to develop a social system where such inequality is virtually unnecessary, since people will have subordinated these self-interested motivations to a greater concern with serving the collective good. Still another question along these lines is the problem of the organizational necessity of social inequality: is it possible or not, in any complex society, to establish differences in tasks and administrative responsibilities that do not also promote persistent inequalities in the rights, opportunities, rewards, and privileges of people?

These are just some of the more prominent issues that underlie the general problem of social inequality. Although this introduction is not meant to be exhaustive, it should offer the reader an initial sense of the major topics and questions that theorists in this field have addressed. The points noted here will serve to guide and to structure most of the review and analysis that follow.

We begin in Chapter 2 with the work of Karl Marx, whose original thesis on class structure in capitalist society is an essential backdrop for virtually all of the theories that follow. In Chapter 3, Max Weber's attempt at a constructive critique and extension of Marx's views is the main concern. In Chapter 4, the work of Emile Durkheim is examined and his role in the transition from Marx and Weber to the so-called structural-functionalist school is considered. In Chapter 5, the ideas that structural functionalists have put forth about inequality are assessed. Chapter 6 focuses on more recent theories, most of which involve a critical reaction to, or rejection of, structural functionalism and a resurgence of interest in building from the ideas of Marx and Weber. Six writers have been singled out for discussion in Chapter 6: Dahrendorf, Lenski, Poulantzas, Wright, Parkin, and Giddens. Finally, Chapter 7 provides a summary and evaluation of the major elements in both the classical and contemporary perspectives, and concludes with some speculative observations on the contributions of existing theories to a more unified overview of social inequality in advanced societies.

Karl Marx and the Theory of Class

"Follow your own course and let people talk."
Karl Marx, Introduction to Volume 1 of Capital,
1867

Introduction

We begin our consideration of the major theories of social inequality with the work of Karl Marx. To some, this choice may seem inappropriate, for in a sense Marx was not a theorist of general social inequality at all (cf. Benson, 1978:1). Thus, for example, Marx showed no sustained interest in examining the numerous ways in which people are ranked in societies at any one time. Nevertheless, several aspects of Marx's work do provide the crucial basis from which to build an analysis of social inequality in advanced societies.

First of all, Marx has been characterized by certain analysts as the father of modern sociology itself (e.g., Berlin, 1963:158; Singer, 1980:1), although Comte usually gets credit for this role and others, most notably Saint-Simon, may have an equal claim (Durkheim, 1896:104; Giddens, 1973:23). Because of Marx's central position in the general development of sociology, any of his work that is relevant to the study of social inequality necessarily should be examined and assessed.

A second reason why an examination of Marx's work is essential is that he, more than any other thinker, is responsible for bringing to the forefront of sociology the concept of class. Some have claimed that this concept is now an obsolete one in social theory (e.g., Nisbet, 1959). Others argue, on the contrary, that class continues to be the principal explanatory variable to consider when trying to understand the workings of society (e.g., Giddens, 1973:19; Wright, 1979:3). In either event, it is true that the idea of class has had a significant influence on the way people think about society and their own positions in it. Academics routinely employ the term in their research into the operation of the social structure, while people regularly allude to class or related ideas in their everyday conversation. It is the use, and frequent misuse, of the concept of class that forms the bulk of what until recently has constituted the study of social inequality. Thus, Marx's original formulation of the theory of classes and class structure is a critical starting point for our discussion.

A third reason for Marx's importance is that his analysis of class structure, coupled with his conclusion that future societies will see an end to class-based inequality, has helped to stimulate, or provoke, virtually all of the attempts by subsequent social thinkers to explain social inequality and its transformation over time. Marx shared with later thinkers such as Weber and Durkheim a keen interest in the process by which earlier forms of society, particularly feudalism, eventually gave rise to the contemporary form of society known as advanced capitalism. Marx's view was that the capitalist stage of social development would itself ultimately be superseded by the final and highest form of society, alternately labelled *socialism* or *communism*. It is on the questions of why societies change, and what their ultimate form will be, that many later theorists seem to take issue with Marx.

In fact, what has been called "the debate with Marx's ghost" (Salomon, 1945:596; Zeitlin, 1968:109; cf. Giddens, 1971:185) frequently amounts to a debate with certain *Marxists* — individuals who have adopted Marx's ideas as their own and have interpreted or modified his original work in a variety of ways. As is the case with other schools of social thought, too often these many versions of Marxism have proven internally inconsistent, even contradictory, leading Marx himself to utter his famous remark: "What is certain is that I am no Marxist" (quoted by Engels, 1882:388). The confusion surrounding what Marx really said, or at least really meant, inevitably makes the understanding of his work more difficult. Nevertheless, it will be argued here that the central features of Marx's theory, particularly as they pertain to the study of social inequality, are not always as obscure as certain analysts suggest. If anything, the fact that Marx's work has produced such a wide range of reactions, for and against, says as much about the power of his ideas as it does about their complexity. That nearly four of every ten people in the world currently live under governments that at least claim to follow Marx's principles is perhaps the most telling evidence of his influence (Singer, 1980:1).

Of course, Marx himself did not live to see the birth of any society governed by socialist or communist precepts. He was a nineteenth-century man who devoted his intellectual efforts toward understanding the workings of capitalist society, with the hope that this advanced but flawed form of social organization could be radically transformed to suit the needs of all people. His special concern was European, especially English, capitalism in the 1800s. Hence, some have alleged that his analysis is not totally applicable to present-day societies, societies that have been variously labelled "monopoly capitalist," "state capitalist," or "postcapitalist" (e.g., Dahrendorf, 1959; Baran and Sweezy, 1966). Yet, although the capitalism Marx knew may in some respects no longer exist, in other respects it seems, like the poor and the exploited, to be very much with us still. Capitalism, in its many current guises, continues to be the predominant mode of economic and social organization in the world, though it seems more and more to be rivalled by the numerous varieties of socialism alluded to earlier. The disagreements between proponents of these two types of society, capitalist and socialist, remain fundamental. Marx is such an important figure precisely because his analysis of capitalism and his prognosis that socialism is what the future holds for all of us situate his work at the very centre of this most momentous of global struggles.

For all these reasons, then, Marx's theory of class and class structure in capitalist society is our first concern in this investigation. In order to grasp more fully the origins of Marx's principal ideas, it is instructive to begin with a brief examination of some of the major events and intellectual influences in his life.

Biographical and Intellectual Sketch

Karl Marx was born in Trier, Prussia, in the German Rhineland, in 1818. He died in London, England, in 1883. These 65 years were turbulent ones in Europe, marked by considerable social change, economic development, political upheaval, and intellectual debate. It is not possible here to trace all the numerous people and events that helped shape Marx's ideas; nevertheless, several major influences should be identified for their persistent and deep-seated impact on his thought.

EARLY YEARS

Perhaps the first major influence on Marx's ideas occurred during his adolescence. Marx's father was a moderately prosperous lawyer of Jewish background, well educated and a believer in the liberal ideals of the French Revolution of 1789 — individual freedom and equality in particular. Within his father's circle of intellectual middle-class friends, Marx was exposed to these egalitarian views of humanity and society. As a result, Marx developed a particularly optimistic philosophy about the nature of humanity and the potential of civilization to progress. Later in life, his father would reverse himself and embrace the conservative and reactionary ideas of the Prussian government under which he lived. Part of this reversal included renouncing Judaism for Protestantism, as a means of ingratiating himself with the Prussian authorities. But Marx himself retained throughout his life the belief, learned in these early years, that people are by nature both good and rational. People have, to Marx, the potential to produce a nearly perfect society if only unnatural obstacles, especially oppression by those in economic and political control, are removed from their path (Berlin, 1963:29; McLellan, 1973:87; Singer, 1980:22). As we shall see, Marx's belief in human progress and perfectibility had a significant impact on his expectations for the transformation of the capitalist society in which he lived and for the socialist society of the future that he envisioned.

UNIVERSITY EXPERIENCES

The second important intellectual influence on Marx came into play during his university education. Initially Marx enrolled as a law student at the University of Bonn in 1835. Accounts suggest that the seventeen-year-old Marx started out living the "dissipated life of the ordinary German student" — drinking, writing poetry, getting slightly wounded in a duel, and being arrested occasionally for "riotous behaviour" (Berlin, 1963:33; Singer, 1980:2). After a year of this, Marx's father convinced him to transfer to the University of Berlin; however, this radically changed the course of Marx's life and ended his father's hopes that Marx would become a lawyer.

At Berlin, Marx became absorbed in the ideas of the philosopher Georg Hegel. Hegel had died in 1831, but his thought still dominated the intellectual life of German universities at the time. This was particularly true at Berlin, where Hegel had taught for many years. Marx soon switched from law to the study of Hegelian philosophy. He eventually rejected the *content* of Hegel's theories because of their preoccupation with the abstract world of the mind or the spirit and their tendency to treat ideas as mere mental constructs divorced from the real, concrete world of people and society. Yet Marx was to the end of his life strongly influenced by the *form* or *method* of Hegel's thought. First of all, he accepted completely Hegel's emphasis on the importance of understanding the past, of studying history in order to comprehend the present and project the future (cf. Giddens, 1971:4). Second, Marx employed for his own more concrete purposes the famous and often misunderstood Hegelian notion that change occurs in a *dialectical* fashion. Not all writers agree on the meaning of this idea (cf. Elster, 1985:44). However, put simply, to say that change is dialectical indicates that it is by nature a process of struggle or tension between opposing, incompatible forces. Moreover, in the clash of these forces, neither side comes out in the end unchanged or unscathed. When the struggle is resolved, the resulting victorious force is, in a sense, different from either of the original adversaries, more highly developed and advanced than each predecessor. This dynamic conflict of forces is continual, with newly emerging forces eventually entering the arena to battle the latest victor (cf. Berlin, 1963:55–56).

The problem with this notion, in Marx's view, is that Hegel makes the error of applying it only in the airy realm of ideas — a fact that is consistent with Hegel's general disregard for material, concrete phenomena. Marx's great task at this stage in his life became to "turn Hegel on his head," to take this dialectical method for thinking of change out of the clouds and to apply it to the understanding of how real societies, real human groups, arise, develop, and become transformed over time. Hence, for Marx the key opposing forces to examine are groups, not ideas. Ideas are important social forces, no doubt, but cannot be divorced from the social context in which they emerge or from the people who think them. Marx's application of Hegel's historical and dialectical view of change will become evident later when we consider Marx's analysis of class and class struggle in capitalist society.

POLITICAL ACTIVIST AND REFUGEE

Marx completed a doctoral degree in philosophy in 1841. He hoped to obtain a university teaching post; however, because his political views were already known and unpopular with the conservative Prussian government, the ministry of education ensured that no teaching position was forthcoming. Marx then found alternative employment as a journalist, an occupation that he held on several occasions throughout his life. His first such job, like virtually all the others, was short-lived. As writer and eventual editor of the *Rhenish Gazette (Rheinische Zeitung)*, he published articles that criticized the Prussian government, especially for its treatment of the poor and working classes. This criticism led to the censorship of the paper in 1843. By this time, Marx had become convinced that the same working class he was writing about was destined to be the prime mover in the progress toward a new universal society, where true freedom and full human potential would be realized for all. He now saw himself as playing a key role in awakening the largely unaware labouring masses to their revolutionary task.

In order to express his ideas and fulfil this role more freely, Marx left Germany for France. Initially he attempted to publish a joint French-German journal in Paris, but it met with indifference in France and quick suppression in Germany. Marx lived the years between 1843 and 1849 as a political refugee, first in France, then in Belgium, and briefly in Germany. During this period, Marx was exposed to several crucial influences on his own thought. Out of Feuerbach's critique of religion as an alienating force for humanity, Marx developed the concept of alienation, and, as we shall see, he eventually applied this idea to his analysis of the plight of workers in capitalist society. Marx also read the works of several French socialists. These confirmed in his mind the important role of the working class in transforming capitalism, even though he disagreed with most of these writers on specific issues.

Probably the strongest influence on Marx in this period was Saint-Simon, a French social thinker of the late eighteenth and early nineteenth centuries whose views on social change corresponded closely with those evolving in Marx's own mind. It was largely from Saint-Simon that Marx came to see economic relationships as the key to explaining historical social change. Marx's emphasis on the role of conflict, especially between economic classes, is also in part adopted from Saint-Simon, as is the view that social change occurs because each society bears within it, and generates through its own development, the "germ of its own destruction" (Giddens, 1973:23; cf. Berlin, 1963:90–91). The parallels between this latter idea and Hegel's dialectical view of change were apparent to Marx and served to solidify further his views on this issue.

The most exciting political activities and events of Marx's life also occurred in this turbulent period. By this time, Marx had met his lifelong friend and collaborator, Friedrich Engels, and together they composed a short pamphlet laying out the doctrines of the Communist League, newly formed in 1847. This work was published in 1848 as the now famous *Communist Manifesto.* In that same year, popular revolts against established monarchies occurred in parts of France, Italy, Germany, Austria, and Hungary. Much of Europe was astir with the desire for liberal reform, if not radical change. However, none of these uprisings was completely successful, and any hopes that Marx and others may have had that these events were the forerunners of a socialist revolution were soon quashed. By the middle of 1849, Marx was once again on the move, this time to London, England. Despite occasional glimmers of political upheaval on the continent, the revolution that Marx awaited did not take place, and he was to remain in England for the rest of his life.

ENGLAND AND *CAPITAL*

In the more than 30 years during which Marx lived in England, his principal achievements were those of a scholar. His activities as a radical journalist, political agitator, and organizer of the working class were greatly reduced, although he did take a leading hand in the operation of the first International Workingmen's Association between 1864 and 1872. What consumed most of Marx's energy was his monumental analysis of contemporary capitalism.

Marx, in fact, had contracted to do such a work as early as 1845, but it was repeatedly set aside for his political activities and other writing (Singer, 1980:4). It was both appropriate and somewhat ironic that Marx found himself in England during the writing of this work. England was the most advanced capitalist society in the world at the time and hence served as the most appropriate example or archetype for Marx's analysis. It was ironic, however, that Marx, a radical opponent of capitalism, should find tolerance and refuge within which to express his ideas only in England, the prime example of what he most despised (Berlin, 1963:181).

What Marx found particularly disturbing about capitalism, both in England and elsewhere, was that so much surplus wealth could be produced by this system and yet be distributed to such a small group of people. While the capitalists, the owners of large factories and agricultural lands, were themselves living in splendour and affluence, the workers, who laboured to produce this great wealth, subsisted for the most part in miserable poverty. The contrast between rich and poor was particularly acute in Marx's time, with labourers sometimes working eighteen hours daily. Six-day work weeks were typical, and child labour — employment of children as young as six or seven — was not uncommon. Working conditions themselves were often of the most appalling kind, dirty, cramped, and extremely hazardous (cf. Marx, 1867:Chapters 10 and 15).

Marx's condemnation of the capitalist system in his work *Capital* (*Das Kapital*) was based on the statistical and other evidence made available to him in his laborious daily readings in the British Museum and on his own observations and first-hand experience with poverty. Marx and his family lived in squalor during some of this final stage of his life, although Engels and other friends lightened the burden with occasional financial aid.

One important consequence of Marx's economic plight was that it slowed his progress on the analysis of the capitalist system in England. His emotional strength and resolve to finish the work were also sapped by illness and personal tragedy, including the premature death of his wife and several of his children. Thus, while *Capital* was intended to be the crowning work of his life, only the first volume was really completed, with the second and third volumes compiled and edited by Engels from rough drafts and notes. It would appear that Marx was on the verge of outlining explicitly his most crucial concern, a detailed treatment of the class structure in capitalism, when he died in his study on March 14, 1883.

The incomplete nature of Marx's analysis of capitalism is indeed unfortunate and obviously has only added to the uncertainty and controversy surrounding his work. As noted earlier, however, it is possible to piece together from the existing material, including the

Communist Manifesto and his numerous other writings, a more or less consistent and comprehensible theory of class, class structure, and social change. A discussion of this theory is our main concern in the remainder of this chapter.

Marx's Theory: Class, Class Struggle, and Historical Change

"The history of all hitherto existing society is the history of class struggles" (Marx and Engels, 1848:57). In this straightforward statement at the beginning of the *Communist Manifesto*, Marx provides a key to understanding the essence of his theory. While a massive and complex literature has been generated by both critics and disciples in reaction to Marx, this single assertion captures what may be the most crucial element of his conception of social structure and social change.

In Marx's view, historical epochs are distinguishable from one another primarily by the system of economic organization, or mode of production, that dominates in each era. Thus, the slave-based economies of ancient Greece and Rome are different in key respects from the feudalism of medieval Europe and the capitalist system of Marx's own time. What is similar about all these historical examples of social and economic systems, however, is that according to Marx each one is marked by a basic distinction between classes, between groupings of people who differ in the roles they play in the productive system. In all cases, the most important difference is between those who have property and those who do not. *Property* involves the right of ownership. However, in this context, property refers not to simple personal possessions but to resources that can be used to produce things of value and to generate wealth: land, rental housing, machinery, factories, and the like (Marx and Engels, 1846:230).

The basic split between the owning, propertied class and the nonowning, propertyless class is always present, though it has taken different forms historically: masters versus slaves in ancient times, serfs versus lords in feudalism, the *bourgeoisie* versus the *proletariat* in capitalism. Certainly, more detailed divisions and distinctions might be drawn in each form; nevertheless, the two-class model is for Marx the crucial one to apply in understanding how societies are structured and how they change (Marx and Engels, 1848:58).

Why is the two-class view the key to understanding society? Primarily because, according to Marx, all societies are born of struggle, of the underlying tension or open conflict between the two major economic classes. In fact, social change or development historically has never occurred without it: "No antagonism, no progress. This is the law that civilization has followed up to our days" (Marx, 1847:132). To Marx, owners and nonowners have interests that are naturally opposed to one another. Whenever there is a situation where one group controls the property, the productive apparatus of society, the remaining population is by definition excluded from such control. Nonowners necessarily enter into an exchange relationship with the owning class, giving their labour power to the owners in return for sufficient income to survive and to continue working in the employ of the owning class. The coercive and exploitative aspects of such an arrangement are obvious in the slavery of ancient times and the serfdom of feudalism, since slaves and serfs were legally bound to labour for their masters or manor lords and had virtually no choice in the matter. Coercion and exploitation may seem absent in capitalism, since the exchange of labour for wages between workers and owners occurs between people who are legally free to choose whether or not to accept such a contract. For Marx, however, the propertyless worker in capitalism is no more at liberty to withhold his or her labour from the owner than was the slave or the serf, for the alternative to wage labour is starvation if one possesses no productive property with which to provide food, clothing, and shelter — the simple means of survival.

It is apparent, then, that Marx's theory portrays all societies up to and including his own as arenas for an elemental struggle between "haves" and "have nots," between "oppressor and oppressed" (Marx and Engels, 1848:58, 92). Societies are based on this inherent dichotomy in the productive sphere, and the major force for change in society necessarily involves a conflict of interests between these two groups. We will examine more closely just how Marx envisions the role of conflict in social change. Before doing this, however, we should consider Marx's views on the work process, especially in the capitalist system that was his principal focus. The operation of the capitalist mode of production and its consequences for the people involved in it will be of special concern in the section that follows.

WORK IN CAPITALIST SOCIETY

In our discussion of Marx's background at the beginning of this chapter, we noted his belief in the potential that humans possess for building increasingly better forms of society. Marx sees the best evidence for this in humanity's increasing mastery over nature and the material world throughout history. Human improvement is especially apparent in our ability to produce the means of life for a growing population. Compared to simple tribal societies, for example, modern nations, with their advanced tools and technical knowledge, are far more capable of providing for the needs of people. In fact, modern societies are increasingly able to generate enough goods to accumulate a large surplus of wealth over and above basic needs.

To Marx, it is productive work, not leisure, that under the right conditions is the ideal human activity (cf. Avineri, 1968:104, 107). In fact, it is this creative capacity, this ability to produce things of value, that is essential to human nature and that mainly distinguishes humans from other life forms (Marx and Engels, 1846:31; Marx, 1867:177-78). The ability of modern societies, then, to accumulate a vast surplus of produced wealth is itself a grand accomplishment and a tribute to human potential. That capitalism is the system of economic organization that has been most successful in generating wealth is acknowledged and even applauded by Marx (Marx and Engels, 1848:65-66). The problem with capitalism, however, is that it distorts the structure and meaning of the work process, with negative consequences for society as a whole and for workers in particular. The distortion comes from several characteristics basic to the capitalist mode of economic organization: private property, surplus expropriation, the division of labour, and the alienation of work.

Private Property

Economic production is by definition a social activity, requiring groups of people working together to create things. To Marx, the social character of work is wholly consistent with the general communal nature or "communist essence" of people and belies any claim that each of us is an isolated individual in society (Marx, 1858:84). But the capitalist mode of economic organization artificially creates a situation in which people are individualized and separated in their work, even though, paradoxically, they may be working side by side.

The first factor at the root of the fragmentation of work in capitalism is the existence of private property. As was mentioned earlier, private property is mainly responsible for creating the two-class system in capitalism, the distinction between the owners of property, or bourgeoisie, and those who work for the owners, the proletariat. This initial split immediately erodes the naturally social character of production, to the extent that those involved are not working as a united group toward some common goal but rather are pursuing their own special interests. The principal interest of the bourgeois owners in this context is to maximize their own wealth, rather than the general wealth or that of their workers. The workers themselves also act in their own individual interests in capitalist society and not for the general good (Marx, 1844:238).

In Marx's time, workers lacked bargaining power through unions or legal strikes. As a result, they could not form a united front against employers and their interests were rarely served. Typically, the supply of available labourers exceeded the demand, especially with the development of mechanized production methods. Hence, employers had a ready supply of unemployed workers willing to take any position left vacant by any worker who was fired for making trouble or because of illness or injury. This idle "reserve army of labour," as Marx called it (Marx, 1867:487, 632), ensured that each worker acted primarily as an isolated person, in competition with other workers for a job and unlikely to want to band together with others to see better pay or working conditions. This isolation of workers from one another obviously worked to the advantage of the capitalists, since it assured them of a docile, though frequently discontented, pool of cheap labour.

Expropriation of Surplus Wealth

A second aspect of capitalism that Marx believed distorts the natural work process is the expropriation of surplus wealth by the capitalist at the expense of the worker. One of the great ironies and injustices of capitalism, in Marx's view, is that working people are, through their labour, primarily responsible for the wealth that is generated; yet workers receive only a small portion of this wealth. To Marx, the value that a produced object has is the value of the labour used in its creation. This value should rightly belong to the workers whose labour is expended in making the object. But, under capitalism, workers exchange their labour power for wages that amount to less than the value of the object when it is exchanged or sold in the marketplace. The difference between the wages and the value of the object when it is sold represents a surplus amount that goes to the capitalists as a profit, after their expenses are deducted. The capitalists treat this excess as their own and think of the wages paid out to workers as one of the costs of production.

To Marx, this perception of the process is completely incorrect. It is the workers who have incurred a cost in the exchange of labour for wages, not the capitalists. The workers lose part of the value of their own labour in the surplus the capitalists usurp. This surplus, which is often reinvested by the capitalists, is in fact the accumulated "dead labour" of past workers. *Capital* is really this accumulated past labour, which, in the purchase of new machinery and so on, is used by the capitalist to expand control over and exploitation of "living labour" — that is, the current crop of employed workers (Marx and Engels, 1848:84).

The Division of Labour

To this point we have discussed two characteristics of capitalism that according to Marx have distorted the essentially social nature of people and of work: the role of private property in fragmenting both capitalists and workers into self-interested individuals, and the unjust expropriation of wealth by capitalists at the expense of workers. A third feature of the capitalist mode of production, and one that intensifies these problems still further, is the division of labour.

In its simplest form, the division of labour arises as soon as private property is instituted and the class of owners is separated from the class of workers. Immediately there is a splitting up of the productive process into those who own the means of production and oversee its operation, on the one hand, and those who labour within the production process, on the other hand. As capitalism evolves and develops as a mode of economic organization, this simple division becomes more and more elaborate. It is soon apparent that goods can be produced more quickly and efficiently if all the tasks that go into creating an object are divided into special jobs, each of which is done by a particular worker on a continual basis.

The modern automobile assembly line is perhaps the epitome of how capitalism subdivides the production of an object into a series of small tasks. Capitalist production, based on a complex division of labour, is highly efficient, with far fewer hours of labour required to create the same volume of goods. However, this efficiency benefits the few capitalists at the expense of the many workers, in Marx's view. Workers produce more in the same working time but are paid the same wages. In effect, then, workers have exchanged their labour power for a smaller proportion of the wealth produced. The surplus wealth generated is larger and hence so are the profits of the capitalist.

Not only does the division of labour increase the profits of the capitalist, and thus the rate of exploitation of the workers by the capitalist, but the division of labour also has severe negative effects on the workers' whole orientation to work. We have already noted that Marx believed humanity's essential ability resides in creative labour. Work is an inherently enjoyable activity under natural conditions, since it is the means by which human beings create and shape their own world. But the division of labour into a series of repetitive and routine tasks is destructive of this enjoyable quality of labour. The pleasure of making things is lost to the workers, who find it virtually impossible to identify their productive power in an object to which so little of the creative self has been applied. Hence, for example, putting the same bolts on a series of automobiles all day, every day, provides none of the pride in workmanship and sense of creating something that go into the making of a custom car by a few people.

Alienated Labour

Thus it is that, in the operation of the capitalist mode of production, work becomes something grotesque. Each person's special capability as a creating and producing being is turned into something that divides and separates people from one another, that is used by some people to exploit others, and that, as an activity, is hateful drudgery to be avoided whenever possible.

Marx uses the concept of alienation or alienated labour to signify these negative aspects of work in capitalist society. *Alienation*, unfortunately, is a widely misused term, employed by social scientists to label every imaginable variety of psychological malaise or personal dissatisfaction. In fact, what Marx means by alienation is something quite different. At its most general level, alienation denotes the separation of something from something else (cf. Schacht, 1970). Whenever something that is an attribute or a creation of people is somehow taken away from them or made external to them, in a sense we have a situation of alienation. Marx first encountered this idea in his early studies of Hegel. In particular, Marx was influenced by a critique of Hegel's religious views by the philosopher Feuerbach. Religion, to Feuerbach, involves the attribution of special qualities and powers to a supreme being or god: mercy and compassion, knowledge, the power to create, and so on. In fact, Feuerbach claims, these qualities are humanity's own highest traits and powers, falsely separated or alienated from humans and projected onto this mythical god (cf. Giddens, 1971:3–4).

Marx sees a comparable process of alienation in the field of human labour under capitalism. We have so far discussed three features of capitalist economic organization: the existence of private property, the expropriation of surplus by the capitalist class, and the division of labour. All of these contribute in part to alienation. Marx's view on alienated labour may be summarized in four main points (Giddens, 1971:12–13).

Alienation is apparent, first, in the separation of workers from control over the products they create. These products are the physical embodiment of human labour given by the workers to the capitalist in exchange for wages. This exchange means that labour has itself been alienated from the workers and sold as a *commodity*, no different from the commodities or goods that are created (Marx, 1844:272; Marx, 1867:170; Marx and Engels, 1848:68). In addition, most of the wealth that these products can garner in the market is also taken away from the workers, expropriated by the capitalist and turned into profit.

A second feature of alienation involves the actual work task, which loses its intrinsically enjoyable and rewarding character in capitalism. The division of labour into specialized, repetitive tasks and the lack of control over the work process in such a setting deny the worker the opportunity to "develop freely his mental and physical energy" (Marx, 1844:274). Work does not satisfy the human need to create but becomes an alienated, external means to satisfy other needs. Leisure time and the "animal functions" of "eating, drinking, and procreating" become most important to alienated people, while work, the essential human activity, "is shunned like the plague" (Marx, 1844:274–75).

A third aspect of capitalist production that promotes alienation is also related to the division of labour, especially to the increasing technological complexity that the division of labour entails. Machine technology, for example, is itself an important illustration of how people can harness natural forces and materials to perform useful tasks. Active human mastery of the world is apparent in this mechanization; yet, ironically, the requirement by capitalism that workers must operate this mechanized apparatus on a continual, routine, and repetitive basis means that people are subordinated to the machines they have created (Marx, 1844:273; Marx, 1867:645; Marx and Engels, 1848:69). Once again, then, people's labour takes on a separate, alienated form in the machines that dominate their own creators.

Finally, a fourth sense in which Marx identifies alienation in capitalism concerns money and its power literally to buy anything, even people and human relationships. Marx states: "I am ugly, but I can buy for myself the most beautiful of women, therefore, I am not ugly" — if, that is, I have the power money brings (Marx, 1844:324). The power of money is itself evidence of how human qualities, such as beauty in this example, are externalized from humans, converted into fluid, quantifiable assets like any other commodity. Money is "the alienated *ability of mankind*" (Marx, 1844:325), set apart from people themselves. Here again the idea of externalization or separation is basic to the idea of alienation.

Marx believes alienation in all these forms is inherent in the capitalist mode of economic organization and can be ended only by the overthrow of the capitalist system. Marx is convinced that certain conditions necessary for such a revolutionary overthrow will emerge naturally from the internal logic of capitalist development. In the next section, the major points Marx raises in this regard will be considered.

CAPITALIST DEVELOPMENT AND CHANGE

We have already discussed the importance that Marx places on the struggle between opposing classes throughout history. This emphasis on the conflict between opposites is consistent with the Hegelian dialectical perspective that influenced Marx's early thinking about change. Marx combines this dialectical method with a similar conception borrowed partly from Saint-Simon: the idea that every societal form holds within itself "the germ of its own destruction" — some force or group that eventually arises out of the system that currently exists, opposes the present ruling regime, and thereby changes society in some fundamental way.

Marx applies these two conceptions to his analysis of how capitalism will develop and ultimately be transformed into socialism. Marx begins, however, by examining feudalism, the societal form that preceded capitalism in Europe. In his view, an understanding of how capitalism came to emerge from the ruins of feudalism helps to clarify just how socialist society can develop out of capitalism.

Feudalism and Capitalism

Feudal society in medieval Europe was a highly localized and community-oriented social structure, based on a rural, agricultural economy. Each serf was bonded to a manor lord and worked the lord's land in return for being permitted to live as a tenant on the lord's estate. This system was relatively stable for centuries but gradually evolved and ultimately disintegrated because of a combination of factors.

One factor was the voyages of discovery during this period, which opened up international trade, expanded markets beyond the local communities or feudal estates, and created demands for new goods. The new markets and new demands stimulated the development of new technology and efficient production to meet these requirements. The growth of large-scale manufacturing thus began and with it a demand for labour to work in these settings.

At the same time, the feudal economy was unable to compete in these new markets, and feudal lords saw their resources depleted by wars and civil strife. The impoverished aristocracy became less and less able to afford to retain serfs on their lands. Many serfs were therefore thrown off the land or else, intrigued by the broadening horizons of this new age, sought their own fortunes voluntarily as free people. These freed serfs migrated to the growing urban centres, where they took up employment as workers for the emerging manufacturing interests located in these centres. Such workers were the beginnings of the proletariat, while the merchants, traders, and financiers involved in the manufacturing ventures were the basis for the capitalist bourgeoisie (e.g., Marx and Engels, 1846:33-35, 65-70; Marx and Engels, 1848:59-60; cf. Avineri, 1968:151-56; Giddens, 1971:29-34).

It is apparent in these historical developments how capitalism emerged within the feudal society it was to replace. The transformation, of course, occurred over several centuries and did not happen everywhere at the same pace. Ultimately, however, it occurred throughout Europe. To Marx, the opposition of interests between the developing class of capitalists and the existing feudal aristocracy became increasingly evident at this time. The capitalist class in this era is characterized as a dynamic force for social and economic change, creating new ideas, new production methods, and new wealth. In contrast, the feudal lords are seen as more superfluous to the productive system; yet they continued to reap wealth from it because of the political and other privileges they enjoyed under monarchical governments. Eventually, according to Marx, the capitalist class threw off the feudal yoke that was hindering its progress, sometimes through a combination of confrontation and political accommodation, as in seventeenth-century England, and sometimes through violent revolution, as in eighteenth-century France (Marx and Engels, 1846:72–73).

Modern observers now dispute several aspects of Marx's analysis. They point out, for example, that many of the new capitalists of this period were themselves members of the feudal aristocracy (cf. Wallerstein, 1980:142; Goldstone, 1986:258–67). Nevertheless, such disputes do not alter Marx's basic contention that the process by which capitalism emerged from feudalism will be repeated again in the future. In this same conflict-oriented, dialectical fashion, capitalism will be transformed by a new opposing force growing within itself: the proletariat. Marx's view is that the dynamic and progressive nature of the capitalist class — qualities that played such an important part in overthrowing feudalism — will gradually dissipate as capitalism matures as a system. The entrepreneurial spirit, speculative daring, technical knowledge, and administrative skill displayed by the capitalists will have served their purpose at this point. According to Marx, these qualities will be replaced by increasing entrenchment and resistance to change among the bourgeoisie, who, having taken power, will cling tenaciously to it. During the same period of bourgeois rule, the mass of the population, the working class, will become aware that they themselves, not the bourgeoisie, are the force primarily responsible for the wealth generated in capitalism.

Marx believes it is the destiny of the workers and the producers of society to take the ascendancy and thereby transform the entire economic and social structure. This change will signal the beginning of the final stage of human development, socialist or communist society. This will be a unique achievement in history, for it will be the first successful revolution in which the victors are the majority of the people and not some select minority. It will also mean an end to class divisions and class struggle, since only one class, the universal proletarian class, will remain (Marx and Engels, 1848:77; cf. Avineri, 1968:60–62).

The Factors in Capitalist Transformation

We have not yet specified those processes Marx perceives in capitalism that will promote its demise. Though there are different interpretations and numerous factors that could be noted, seven points in particular seem crucial (cf. Giddens, 1971:52–60; Giddens, 1973:34–37).

First of all, the rise of capitalism, as noted earlier, is closely tied to the growth of large urban centres, which develop as propertyless rural inhabitants flow to the cities in search of employment. This growing concentration of urban labourers is a key initial step toward the development of working-class awareness, since masses of workers are housed in the same neighbourhoods and experience similar living conditions.

A second, related process is the increasing expansion of production into large-scale factories employing many workers. This process makes apparent the basically *social* nature of human production. It also means a concentration of workers in close proximity to one another and a further basis for awareness of their common class position and their common plight (Marx and Engels, 1848:69–70).

Marx suggests a third factor by which workers are made more aware of their shared fate and their separateness from the capitalist class. This factor is the greater suffering that workers face during economic crises. Marx's view is that capitalism is primarily concerned with a rational and efficient, but relentless and self-interested, pursuit of *profits* by the owning class. The drive for more and more profits has frequent and unfortunate consequences for society as a whole, but especially for workers. The bourgeoisie's desire for greater gain often means that it produces more goods than it can sell. This imbalance leads to a loss of money by capitalists, since they must sell their products in order to realize any profit and pay their costs. A common reaction by the capitalist class is to lay off workers in order to reduce costs and save money. But the workers of society are also the main purchasers of goods. Hence, laying off workers means that there are fewer people able to buy products, so that there is an even lower demand for goods and a further loss of money for the capitalists. In this spiral fashion, economic crises tend to occur regularly in the capitalist system and in fact are basic to its operation. Overproduction, followed by higher unemployment, reduced demand, slow economic growth, and depression is the typical pattern. After each crisis, there is a period in which the economy stabilizes and the proletariat may once again find work (Marx, 1844:241, 258–59). Nevertheless, the greater deprivations endured by workers during crises become increasingly apparent to them and underline the basic differences between themselves and the owning class.

Of course, some capitalists also suffer greatly in hard economic times. This brings us to the fourth process in capitalist development that acts to bring about its transformation. It is mainly the small-scale capitalists — what Marx calls the *petty bourgeoisie* — and not the larger-scale owners who are most vulnerable in economic crises. Small owners have fewer reserves of wealth for absorbing losses and less influence for getting bank credit or government subsidies than do large owners. Thus, in economic crises, small capitalists increasingly are forced to sell their businesses or else go bankrupt and are taken over by larger capitalists. It is partly in this way that the economy stabilizes, because the overproduction problem lessens as the number of capitalist producers shrinks. In addition, however, the decline of the petty bourgeoisie means a concentration and centralization of ownership in the hands of an ever-smaller pool of large-scale capitalists. The dispossessed petty bourgeoisie and their descendants eventually join the propertyless working class, and the ranks of the proletariat increase (Marx and Engels, 1848:70–71, 75; Marx, 1867:625–28). At the same time, the disappearance of this middle class of small owners makes it more and more apparent that workers and big capital are the only two classes of consequence in the social structure. This realization promotes the awareness among workers of the clear disparity between the two classes, of the separation between bourgeoisie and proletariat. The process whereby this separation emerges and widens is referred to as *class polarization*.

The fifth feature of capitalism to consider here is its alleged tendency to homogenize the working class as time goes on. In the early stages of capitalism, the proletariat is a varied and divided collection of people with different skill levels. These divisions — between skilled artisans and unskilled manual labourers, for example — are obstacles in the way of proletarian solidarity, since the common interests of workers are less apparent when they perform different tasks and receive different wages. Because of the continual technological advances and mechanization of production as capitalism matures, these distinctions become blurred. Increasingly, all proletarians become the same type of worker: semiskilled minders of machines. This common position is an added impetus toward proletarian class awareness (Marx, 1844:237; Marx and Engels, 1848:71).

A sixth process — one that stimulates class polarization still further — concerns the gap in material well-being and living standards between capitalists and workers. As capitalism matures, *absolute* living standards for workers may improve, or at least not worsen, because of the huge productive capacity of capitalism and the surplus wealth this production generates. However, the *relative* difference in economic rewards between owners and workers continues to widen, in Marx's view, because a larger share of the surplus always goes to the capitalists (Marx, 1867:645). Because of this widening gap and the relative impoverishment of the workers, class polarization once again is promoted.

A seventh and final factor in capitalist development that spurs its overthrow is the rise of stock ownership and the joint stock company. As noted earlier, the capitalist class begins by playing a progressive role in social change. Its innovations and leadership are essential in the push toward the higher stages of society Marx envisions, and its members play an active part in managing the productive process and making administrative decisions. However, under advanced capitalism, businesses increasingly are owned only on paper, with individuals buying stocks in companies. To Marx, such a system makes it patently obvious to the workers that mere ownership of property is entirely superfluous to productive activity. Owners, as stockholders, control the means of production and accumulate rewards from it, yet offer little in return. They may not even be involved in administration, since they can hire managers to perform this task for them. Once again, then, the distinction between proletarian and capitalist is magnified and the dispensability of the bourgeoisie underscored (Marx, 1894:427-29).

Obstacles to Revolution: Ideology and Superstructure

All of these processes and developments in the capitalist system promote the emergence of the fundamental division between bourgeoisie and proletariat. The objective differences in living conditions and the basic opposition of interests are there. Nevertheless, they must be recognized as such by the proletariat before revolutionary change can occur. The proletariat must then organize, mobilize, and act as a class-conscious group to transform society.

Although one might expect Marx to consider both the recognition of the situation and subsequent action to be inevitable occurrences, in fact he sees several important obstacles blocking the path to revolution. These obstacles are sometimes classified under the general term *superstructure*. Superstructure is frequently a confusing concept because it can refer to two separate but related phenomena. First, the superstructure is bound up with the concept of *ideology*, which is essentially the set of ideas or beliefs that govern people's lives. But superstructure can also designate the social structures or organizations people erect to implement these ideas. Thus, for example, religion is a system of beliefs about the world, and the church is the structural embodiment of these religious ideas. The state or political structure is likewise the structural manifestation of the laws, political enactments, rules, and regulations by which society is governed. In many ways, the superstructure concept is like the familiar sociological concept of *institution*, which has a similar dual meaning (cf. Williams, 1960:30-35, 515-20).

Marx seems to use the concept of superstructure in both these senses and rarely distinguishes between them. The state and religion are the major components of the superstructure in Marx's conception, but all "ideological forms," including "the legal, political, religious, aesthetic, or philosophic," are involved (Marx, 1859:52; Marx, 1867:82). Thus, any structure that serves as an embodiment of the ideas that govern us, and moreover is used as a creator and sender of these ideas, is presumably part of this ideological apparatus or superstructure. Hence, the educational system and media of mass communication would be included here, for they play an increasingly important role in modern society as means by which people learn ideas and acquire information (cf. Marx and Engels, 1848:88).

The term superstructure implies that some substructure, or *infrastructure*, also exists. To Marx, this underlying basis to social life is of course the economic system, the "mode of production of material life" (Marx, 1859:52; Marx, 1867:82). What Marx means to convey in the distinction between superstructure and infrastructure is not that the two types of phenomena are entirely unrelated. On the contrary, he is strongly critical of Hegelian philosophy for setting up this artificial separation. Even worse, in Marx's view, is that Hegel then assigns causal priority to ideas over material life, implying that ideas somehow exist before the human reality in which they take shape and are implemented. Marx takes such pains to reject this view that he sometimes seems to make the opposite, and equally tenuous, argument that ideas are totally secondary results of social conditions and have no part in shaping these conditions (e.g., Marx, 1867:19). In fact, Marx's position is for the most part a middle one, lying between the *materialist* and the *idealist* view (Avineri, 1968:69). Ideas and the social conditions in which they operate clearly interact with one another in a continual process of change, and the existence of one is not possible without the other. To argue that ideas in themselves can have no causal impact on material reality is to contradict the great influence of Marx's own ideas on the course of historical social change (Berlin, 1963:284).

The distinction between ideas and material reality is relevant to our discussion because both the ideological and the structural aspects of the superstructure are useful to the capitalist class for maintaining the existing economic system, or infrastructure. To Marx, it is clear that the dominant ideas in any historical epoch are the ideas that the dominant class in that epoch generates (Marx and Engels, 1846:59). While dissenting ideas may find the occasional outlet, as in Marx's own radical journalism, the values, beliefs, and styles of thought that predominate are those created by the ruling class. In capitalism, then, it is the bourgeoisie's values and ideas that are most widely heard and accepted by the population — not only by the members of the bourgeoisie but also by large portions of the working class. This is one of the subtler and more insidious ways in which the path to revolution is obstructed. The bourgeois overthrow of feudalism was for some time impeded by the fact that the bourgeoisie itself accepted or believed in loyalty to higher authority, the divine right of kings, and other tenets of feudal society. In the same way, workers learn through the ideological apparatus of capitalist society that freedom, individualism, and equality are the guiding beliefs of the modern age. The power of ideas is evidenced by the belief among so many workers that these ideas really operate in capitalist society, even though to Marx they only serve the interests of the privileged class. To Marx, the workers are free only to sell their labour power to the bourgeoisie and hence are equal only in their universal exploitation (cf. Marx and Engels, 1846:39-41; Marx and Engels, 1848:84-85; Berlin, 1963:149).

All the segments of the superstructure — the political, legal, religious, educational, and communication systems — disseminate these views. In addition, certain branches of the political or state apparatus, namely the military and the police, play a key part as enforcers of the ideas, especially the laws, enacted and administered in capitalist society. Marx asserts in the *Communist Manifesto* that the state is a mere "committee for managing the common affairs of the whole bourgeoisie" (Marx and Engels, 1848:61). This is partly a polemical exaggeration, in which he purposely understates the role of the state under capitalism. Nevertheless, Marx does believe that the prime purposes of the political system in capitalism are to administer and implement the legal relations of the society and to use force if necessary against those who disobey these laws. At the same time, to the extent that laws are consistent with bourgeois interests for the most part, then the actions of the state are ultimately in the interests of the bourgeoisie. Thus it is that the state leadership can appear to be acting for the general good and enforcing the law in the public interest. State leaders may even believe sincerely that they are doing so, since politicians are equally subject to the seductive appeal of the dominant ideology. Yet, in seeming to serve the general good, the state ultimately works in the overall interest of those who control the economic structure — the bourgeoisie (cf. Jessop, 1982:7-20).

CAPITALISM'S END AND FUTURE SOCIETY

With all these resources at the disposal of the capitalist class, one may wonder that Marx expected a proletarian revolution to occur at all. Indeed, some critics would point to the absence of any current worldwide socialist movement as evidence that Marx's expectations will go unfulfilled. At the same time, however, many of the problems and developments Marx foresaw in the capitalist system have occurred, especially the regular economic crises. This suggests that his views have been at least partly confirmed.

As we have noted, Marx sees the end of capitalism coming about because of the internal problems it generates for itself. He expects the class polarization resulting from these difficulties to override gradually the ideological obstacles standing in the way of the working class's complete awareness of their common position and their revolutionary potential. Marx argues that the proletarians in capitalism share a common class position by the very fact that they are all people excluded from control of the means of production. In Marx's terms, the proletariat forms in this sense a "class in itself" (Marx, 1847:211). The awareness of this common objective position, coupled with a belief in the possibility of change and a concerted desire to seek change, will, despite the repressive power of the state's coercive forces, convert this "class in itself" to a "class for itself" — a revolutionary force that will fundamentally alter capitalist society (Marx, 1847:211).

Marx, however, is not confident in the proletariat's ability to accomplish revolutionary action without the added assistance, organization, and leadership of others (cf. Avineri, 1968:63). He mentions in particular "a small section of the ruling class," presumably revolutionary intellectuals and enlightened members of the bourgeoisie who recognize the destiny of the proletariat and go over to its side (Marx and Engels, 1848:74–75).

Socialism and Dictatorship of the Proletariat

The specific details of how this revolutionary act will come about are never offered by Marx, for, as has been frequently pointed out, Marx is not concerned with providing a blueprint for the revolution or for the structure of the society that will supersede capitalism (e.g., Selsam et al., 1970:20; Singer, 1980:59). Nevertheless, some idea of what Marx envisions for the future can be gleaned from bits and pieces of his writings.

It appears that Marx expects at least two stages in the system that will replace capitalism. The first stage, which may be termed *socialism*, is a temporary one that does not represent the best or highest form of society but is necessary in the transition from capitalism. During this transition, certain residual features of bourgeois society must be retained for a time, particularly some form of state or political apparatus. The state is needed to implement key changes that will eventually make its own existence unnecessary. Political power and decision making will be centralized in this body; however, unlike the state in capitalism, the socialist state will truly represent the interests of all people and not the special interests of any single group.

This "dictatorship of the proletariat," as Marx sometimes refers to it (Marx, 1875:16), will ensure that important initial policies are instituted: abolition of landed property holdings and inheritance rights, centralization of banking in a government bank, institution of a graduated income tax, partial extension of the state ownership of factories and production, abolition of some forms of child labour, and free education for children (Marx and Engels, 1848:94). Many of these ideas seem rather moderate by contemporary standards and in fact have been put into practice by most capitalist democratic governments. The suggestion of only a partial movement of the state to take over production in this first stage seems especially restrained (cf. Avineri, 1968:206).

However, it is clear to Marx that ultimately the entire productive process must be taken out of the hands of private interests. Marx sees the state-directed socialist system as an initial stage that is required while transitional wrinkles are ironed out. During this period, the truly social or communal nature of humanity and the system of material production will gradually become clear to all. The extraction of surplus by a dominant group for its own purposes will no longer occur. Instead, wealth generated in production will be distributed to all workers, after a common fund has first been set aside to provide education, health facilities, social services, and the like. The distribution of wealth during this first stage of socialism will be done on the basis that each worker "receives back from society — after the deductions have been made — exactly what he gives to it" (Marx, 1875:8; cf. Giddens, 1971:61). This policy suggests that all people will be rewarded fairly but not necessarily equally, since individuals will clearly vary in terms of the ability and effort they put into their work. This system, in Marx's words, "tacitly recognizes unequal individual endowment and thus productive capacity as natural privileges" (Marx, 1875:9).

This does not sound like a classless society, at least in the sense that all people are treated exactly the same. Again, however, Marx sees this as a transitional phase in the move toward the final system. In this first stage, people have yet to overcome all the divisive tendencies instilled in them by the ills of capitalist ideology, all the defects of a changing system that "has just emerged after prolonged birth pangs from capitalist society" (Marx, 1875:10). Marx believed that "it was in general incorrect to make a fuss about so-called *distribution* of goods" (Marx, 1875:10). The most important issue for Marx is *relations* between groups, not the *distribution* of wealth to individuals. Marx sees the concern with distribution as a problem stemming from the old bourgeois consciousness and emphasis on individualism. Once the truly social basis of production is recognized, once it is clear that work must be a co-operative enterprise involving every worker and in the interest of every worker, then concerns with the distribution of wealth will dissipate. Differences in ability, effort, responsibility, and so on may continue but will be greatly reduced. People will lose their view of one another as competitors and instead find satisfaction in their differences and in the different roles they play in the collective process of production (Marx, 1847:190; cf. Avineri, 1968:232).

This seems to allow for the continued existence of a division of labour into specific tasks for each worker, despite the fact that elsewhere Marx frequently points to the evils wrought in capitalism by the division of labour (e.g., Marx, 1847:182). It would appear that what will happen as society progresses through the first stage of socialism is a gradual revision and transformation of the division of labour. Two key changes in particular may be noted. First, there will be much greater diversity in the jobs that each worker is able to do. Work may be subdivided into specialized segments, but the same worker will not always perform the same segment. Each worker will be able to "hunt in the morning, fish in the afternoon, rear cattle in the evening, criticise after dinner" (Marx and Engels, 1846:47). This seems to be Marx's quaint way of saying that in the future work will be more varied and workers more versatile. Second, it appears that Marx sees the expansion of mechanized and automated production methods as a means to eliminate the routine drudgery imposed by the division of labour under capitalism. The "progress of technology" and "the application of science to production" under socialism will mean that the worker will be a "regulator" of the production process, "mastering it" rather than being enslaved by it (Marx, 1858:705; also Marx, 1847:190; cf. McLellan, 1971:216; Giddens, 1971:63).

Communism

When these changes in the consciousness of people and in the structure of society are engendered and allowed to flourish, the first stage of socialism will have begun to fade, bringing on the highest societal form, true *communism*. The state's role as central decision maker will have been played out, and the state "will have died away" (Marx, 1875:16). It will be replaced by a decentralized, nonauthoritarian system of administration of the society by all the people. It is not clear what the logistics of this administration are — once again there is no detailed plan — but the new human consciousness, which sees people in their true character, will ensure that the society will function unencumbered by the distorting effects of bourgeois self-interest, greed, and the pursuit of power. Then it will be possible to implement Marx's dictum of equality and selflessness: "From each according to his ability, to each according to his needs" (Marx, 1875:10).

It is essentially Marx's faith in the potential of humans to act as social beings in a universal society that is the basis for his expectations and visions of the future of society. The view of human nature and the belief in the perfectibility of people that Marx acquired early in life and retained throughout his intellectual development are reflected here and seem strangely paradoxical, given his own apparent aloofness toward humanity in general and his reluctance to involve himself personally in the revolution (Avineri, 1968:251-52; Berlin, 1963:1-3).

We will see in the subsequent chapters of this book the tremendous influence that Marx's ideas have had on the study of social inequality and class structure in modern societies. We will also see the skepticism that Marx has provoked in some of those who were to write after him. Both adherents and critics, however, readily acknowledge the deep intellectual debt owed to Marx. His analysis of class structure in capitalist society provides a touchstone against which to compare and assess all subsequent views of social inequality in advanced societies. In the next chapter, we shall consider the second great classical theorist of social inequality, Max Weber. As we shall see, Weber provides a prime example of how both the positive influences of Marx's theory and numerous critical reactions to specific aspects of it can be bound up in the same writer's work.

Summary

In this chapter, we have reviewed the key elements in Marx's theory of class and his analysis of capitalism. We began with an outline of some of the significant experiences in his own life that helped shape his thought. We then considered his contention that class struggle has been the consistent basis for social change and inequality throughout history. The remainder of the chapter dealt with the key issues Marx raises concerning the capitalist form of society. We discussed the distorted nature of work under capitalism; the seven processes inherent in capitalism that promote its transformation from within; the various obstacles in the way of capitalism's revolutionary overthrow; and the ultimate end of capitalism, with a brief sketch of the socialist and communist societal forms that Marx anticipates.

Chapter

3

Max Weber and the Multiple Bases for Inequality

"In the last analysis, the processes of economic development are struggles for power." *Max Weber, Inaugural Lecture at Freiburg University, 1894*

Introduction

Max Weber is the second major classical theorist we shall consider. Weber's analysis is frequently viewed as a distinct alternative to and departure from Marx's theory of class. Indeed, there are significant differences between the ideas of Marx and Weber that cannot be overlooked. At the same time, however, we shall find notable similarities in the interests and conclusions of these two writers. A thorough appreciation of both the similarities and the differences in their work is essential to our understanding of social inequality and of the current state of theory in this field.

Perhaps the most obvious similarity between Marx and Weber is their common concern with examining the origins and development of modern capitalist society using an historical method. In this regard, of course, Marx and Weber share with many nineteenth-century social analysts an interest in how societies have changed or evolved from traditional to modern forms. The two writers are not in total accord about the nature and extent of social inequality, the forces that govern social change, or the likelihood of inequality in future societies. Nevertheless, there can be no doubt that Weber's general conceptions of capitalism, social class, and numerous related ideas are greatly influenced by Marx's writings, virtually all of which preceded his own work. Weber himself identifies Marx as one of the two major intellectual influences (along with Nietzsche) of Weber's time (e.g., Gerth and Mills, 1967:61–62; Giddens, 1972:58; Coser, 1977:249–50).

Sometimes Weber's differences with Marx do not involve substantive issues in sociology so much as they bear on the differing political positions of the two men and their distinct opinions on the likelihood and desirability of socialist revolution. Moreover, often Weber's alleged differences with Marx are really disagreements with certain Marxists of Weber's day, disciples of Marx who interpreted his theories and applied them for their own purposes. Even in these cases it is fair to say that a good deal of Weber's work is a "positive critique" of Marx and Marxism, a "fruitful battle with historical materialism" (Gerth and Mills, 1967:63).

One of the unfortunate parallels between the two writers is that neither one provides a systematic and detailed analysis of social inequality in modern societies. This omission is partly because neither man lived long enough to complete this task and partly because neither thinker is concerned with the issue of social inequality as his principal focus. Indeed, it is somewhat ironic that theoretical developments in the study of social inequality owe so much to two writers for whom the topic was not their primary interest. For Weber as for Marx, then, we must rely on rather short discussions, scattered through his writings, as the means for deciphering his general view of social inequality.

In our analysis of Weber's thought we will take the position that his major contribution to the theory of social inequality lies in his attempt to offer a positive or constructive critique of Marx's ideas, especially as these ideas were interpreted by Marxists of Weber's time. In general, Weber's treatment of Marxist thought can be characterized as "critically respectful" (Collins, 1986a:37). Because of Weber's advantage in living after both Marx and the early Marxists, he is able to draw on a wider and more comprehensive range of sources and evidence, all of which lead him to propose a number of modifications to the Marxist view (cf. Collins, 1986a:38-40).

If there is a common theme in Weber's criticisms, it is that the accurate description and explanation of inequality and other social phenomena involve much greater complexity and variability than some Marxists seem to suggest. This is not to imply that Marxism in its many forms is crude and simplistic, though this charge can be made against specific versions of social theory, Marxist or otherwise. Rather, it is to say that Marxist theory proceeds from the conviction that there is a single, ultimate basis upon which social life is built: the economic, material realm of human activity. Other social phenomena — the political or religious, for example — may be worthy of study, but, in the last analysis, these too are explicable in terms of economic forces. To Marxists, then, the study of these aspects of society should not be allowed to cloud our understanding that the real basis of social structure and inequality is economic.

For Weber, however, the range of noneconomic social forces cannot be dismissed as merely secondary to, or determined by, the economic.

On the contrary, noneconomic considerations, especially the ideas and interests that emerge from politics, religion, and other institutional structures, have a certain autonomy from the economic in many instances. Moreover, these forces sometimes influence economic structures and behaviour as much as they are influenced by them. To many Marxists, such an emphasis on multiple structures only distorts our understanding, because it lays down a smokescreen that masks the underlying material basis for social life. In the Weberian view, these details do not distort our picture of reality. On the contrary, distortion stems from failing to recognize these diverse explanations and multiple causes for social inequality.

A detailed treatment of this general difference between Weber and Marxism, as well as an assessment of the common elements that the works of Marx and Weber share, is the central concern of this chapter. We begin with a brief examination of the life experiences and intellectual influences that affected Weber's thought.

Biographical and Intellectual Sketch

EARLY YEARS

Max Weber was born April 21, 1864, at Erfurt, in the German province of Thuringia. By this time, Karl Marx was a 46-year-old émigré living in England; hence, the two men never met. There are some broad similarities between the backgrounds of Marx and Weber. Like Marx, Weber grew up in a relatively privileged, middle-class German household. Weber's father, like Marx's, was trained in law, though he eventually pursued a career in politics and government at the municipal and later the national level. Like Marx, Weber initially followed his father's wishes and enrolled in law school. This was at the University of Heidelberg in 1882, one year before Marx's death. In the same way that Marx spent his early university days carousing and having a good time, so too did Weber enjoy his initial student life for a time. He joined his father's old fraternity and took a regular part in fencing and drinking bouts. Thus, Weber, who had been a sickly, frail, and bookish child, developed into a hearty, somewhat barrel-shaped young man, complete with duelling scars (Coser, 1977:236; Gerth and Mills, 1967:8). At the same time, Weber managed to be an excellent, conscientious student who was popular with his fellows, partly because of his willingness to help them at examination time.

In contrast to Marx, Weber chose to stick with his legal studies, though, like Marx, he became widely read in other areas, including economics, philosophy, history, and theology. His first year in Heidelberg was followed by a year of compulsory military service at Strasbourg, after which he resumed his legal studies, this time at Marx's old school, the University of Berlin. The move to Berlin was prompted mainly by the wishes of Weber's parents, who had settled there some years before. They were concerned about his boisterous behaviour at Heidelberg and sought to introduce more discipline into his life by having him live at home.

FAMILY INFLUENCES

The family emphasis on discipline was particularly evident in Weber's father, a strict, authoritarian, and brutish man who frequently mistreated his wife. One possible effect on Weber of this family atmosphere was a rejection of arbitrary power and a distrust of authority without accountability. The divergence between Weber and his father is evident in his dislike for his father's political beliefs, which favoured the conservative, reactionary policies of the German kaiser and Chancellor Otto von Bismarck. Like Marx, Weber was a supporter of democracy and human freedom. This is important to recognize because, as Giddens notes, some writers have mistaken Weber's patriotism for Germany and his belief in strong leadership as evidence of right-wing or fascist tendencies (Giddens, 1972:7–8). However, in contrast to Marx, Weber was far less optimistic about the prospects for democracy's survival in future societies. Moreover, despite revealing occasional socialist leanings at different points in his life (Collins, 1988:409), Weber suspected that socialism would be an even greater threat to democracy and freedom than would capitalism. Humanity's best hope, according to Weber, lay in a liberal political system, guided by strong but enlightened leaders and operating within an essentially capitalist economic framework. Weber's political views were influenced in this direction by his uncle, Herman Baumgarten, whom he visited frequently during and after his military service at Strasbourg and who retained a strong belief in the liberal democratic principles Weber's father had forsaken.

Weber's visits with his uncle and other relatives in Strasbourg led to other events that significantly influenced his thought. Although Weber's mother was a devout Protestant, her religious beliefs had not made a notable impression on Weber in his early years. However, in Strasbourg, Weber was in contact with several family members, including his mother's sisters, many of whom were prone to frequent religious and mystical experiences (Gerth and Mills, 1967:9). Thus, Weber witnessed at first hand the power that religious ideas and beliefs can have over people. Though Weber never became a religious man himself, these events helped stimulate his eventual interest in the study of religion and the influence that religious beliefs and other ideas could have in shaping society. Weber's position on this point may be contrasted with that of certain Marxists of his day, who argued that ideas and beliefs are wholly products of social interaction and organization, especially within the sphere of economic production. Weber disagreed with those who adopted this materialist view in the extreme, thereby denying the possibility that ideas could themselves influence and even generate economic structures and behaviour, rather than being mere consequences of these material forces.

SUCCESS AND CRISIS

Weber lived at his parents' Berlin home for almost eight years, beginning in 1884. During this period, he revealed both tremendous scholarly ability and a voracious appetite for work. He completed law school, worked as a junior barrister, and at the same time followed a rigorous course of study leading to a Ph.D. in law in 1889. Unlike Marx, who was denied an academic career because of his political beliefs, Weber enjoyed a meteoric rise in the university community. He began as a lecturer in law at Berlin in 1891. This position was soon followed by a senior professorship in economics at Freiburg in 1894. In 1896, at age 32, Weber became chairman of economics at Heidelberg.

These successes, however, came at the price of a heavy workload that taxed him mentally and physically. Then, in 1897, a crisis triggered some major changes in Weber's life. During a visit by his parents to his home in Heidelberg, Weber argued bitterly with his father over the continued mistreatment of his mother and drove his father from the house. Not long after, Weber's father died. The guilt Weber felt over these events, coupled with the strain of overwork, led to his psychological collapse. Other accounts suggest that Weber's problems also stemmed in part from his dislike for the puritanical tendencies of his mother (Collins, 1986b:20; see also Portis, 1986). In all events, Weber's mental condition was never completely diagnosed and recurred intermittently for the rest of his life. Until just before his death, Weber did not hold another full-time teaching position. Nevertheless, he managed a partial recovery and, with regular pauses for travel and recuperation, was able to continue his research. In fact, most of his famous and important works began to take shape only after this initial breakdown.

AMERICA AND CAPITALISM

An important surge in Weber's work occurred soon after he travelled to the United States in late 1904. His observation of American capitalist society in action made a lasting impression on his thought in a variety of ways. While his reactions were not entirely positive, on the whole Weber admired the United States. He saw in its mass political parties, voluntary citizens' organizations, and other institutions the possibility that freedom and democracy might be sustained in future societies. Weber was a nationalist concerned with the development of his own country, and some have implied that he perceived in the United States the model for a new German society (Gerth and Mills, 1967:17). However, it appears that Weber saw too many contrasts between America and Germany for any direct imitation to be practicable. Moreover, certain aspects of the American system underscored for Weber the paradoxical and even contradictory nature of mass democracy. In particular, Weber noted that bureaucracy — in the form of political-party machines managed by professional politicians and organizers — was at the same time both essential to democratic action in large-scale complex societies and a threat to democratic principles of equality and participation for all.

Weber was also impressed by the large business corporations in the United States. These enterprises were then coming to the forefront as the dominant forces in the world economy. The movement toward bureaucracy was apparent in the corporations as well, contributing to Weber's ultimate conclusion that bureaucratization is a key process in the general trend of modern societies toward *rationalization*. Weber perceived in all spheres of the social structure — politics, economics, religion, education, and so on — this tendency to develop permanent, organized systems for processing problems and people in regular, routine ways. Weber saw bureaucracy as the only organizational form capable of keeping modern, complex societies operating and thus as both inevitable and inescapable. Yet, at the same time, he regretted its destructive impact on the quality of human interaction and on human freedom (e.g., Bendix, 1962:7, 458–59).

After his American travels, in the period up to World War I, Weber made a notable intellectual recovery. His writing began anew, and in 1905 he published perhaps his most famous work, *The Protestant Ethic and the Spirit of Capitalism*. We have already discussed the Protestant background of Weber's mother, the religious experiences of his mother's family, and the subsequent impact of religion on Weber's thought. This impact is most evident in *The Protestant Ethic*. In this analysis, Weber argues that the historical development of modern capitalism was significantly influenced by the ideas and beliefs of certain ascetic Protestant sects, particularly Calvinism. This thesis is consistent with his general critique of materialism, for he seeks to demonstrate how ideas, especially religious beliefs, can and do influence economic and social structures like capitalism, rather than simply reflecting such structures. His views on this point were also affected by his visit to

America, where he observed the tendency for those of ascetic Protestant backgrounds to be overrepresented among the most successful capitalists (cf. Coser, 1977:239).

ACADEMIC AND POLITICAL PROMINENCE

Weber's academic reputation now began to grow anew. His home in Heidelberg became a regular meeting place for prominent German intellectuals. He was soon writing numerous works on a variety of topics, including several essays on method in the social sciences. His key work for the study of social inequality, *Economy and Society*, was begun around this time (1909) and was continued intermittently but unfortunately was never finished (Aron, 1970:305).

One crucial reason for the interruption of Weber's research was the outbreak of World War I. A patriotic German, Weber initially supported the war effort, enlisted as a reserve officer, and served as director of military hospitals around Heidelberg. However, he soon became disillusioned with the war, characteristically, because he questioned the motives and competence of the political regime of the German monarch, Kaiser Wilhelm II (cf. Giddens, 1972:21–22).

Weber had always been interested in his country's political fortunes, and he gradually became directly involved in them. He unofficially sought to convince the German leadership to stop the fighting, without success, and later acted as an advisor to the German delegation to the Versailles peace conference, which ended the war. His political activities also included participation in the drafting of a new German constitution and an increasingly large role in political campaigns. Some even viewed Weber as a potential candidate for the German presidency (Coser, 1977:241). However, his earlier criticisms of the monarchy and of the kaiser's conservative government made support from this quarter unlikely. His dislike of the opposition socialist factions — some of whom he suggested should be in either "the madhouse" or "the zoological gardens" — was also well known (Giddens, 1972:25, 17). Thus, Weber's political prospects eventually dissipated.

Instead of taking up a political career, Weber remained with his academic pursuits and was finally able to resume full-time teaching once again, this time at the University of Munich. It was during this period, as well, that Weber engaged in a series of important and influential lectures, including debates with contemporary Marxists on the nature of capitalism. One series carried the characteristic title "A Positive Critique of Historical Materialism" (Alexander, 1983:55; see also Collins, 1986a:19, 38).

His scholarly eminence and intellectual vigour re-established, Weber seemed on the verge of even greater things when in June 1920 he was stricken with pneumonia and suddenly died, at the age of 56. As with Marx, then, death cut short Weber's career before he was able to complete a thorough and systematic analysis of social inequality. As with Marx again, though, it is possible to piece together the major strands of Weber's work on this topic and identify a more or less coherent basis for his emerging theory. A presentation of these main features of the Weberian perspective and how it compares to that of Marx is our next consideration.

The Weberian Perspective: Complexity and Pluralism in Inequality

In the preceding chapter, we noted that the central point in Marx's theory of social structure is his conviction that, in the last analysis, societies take shape and change through one key process: the struggle between groups for control of the economy, the system of material production. To recognize Marx's singular emphasis on economics is to deny neither his theoretical sophistication nor his obvious awareness of the complex nature of modern societies. Nevertheless, a tendency does exist to view Marx's position as an oversimplified one. In part, this may reflect a failure by certain critics to acknowledge the polemical, and hence purposely exaggerated, nature of some of Marx's statements. In other instances, the responsibility for oversimplifying the original Marxian formulation must fall on the shoulders of certain Marxist disciples, including some who have attempted to put socialist principles into practice in real societies (cf. Avineri, 1968:252).

In either case, it is clear that Weber's alternative view of social structure stems in part from his reaction to an oversimplified or vulgarized Marxism. Thus, a consistent feature of Weber's sociology is his conviction that social processes and forces are always complex and rarely explicable in simple terms. Weber's emphasis on complexity is evident in a variety of ways that, taken together, form the major substance of our discussion in this chapter. There are six areas in particular that we shall examine because of their relevance to the understanding of Weber's general thought and his perspective on social inequality.

First, there is Weber's overall approach to research and sociological method, with its stress on *causal pluralism* and the *probabilistic* nature of social explanation. Second, there is Weber's sense of the often intricate interplay between ideas and material reality, or between the subjective and objective aspects of social life. The third point concerns Weber's multiple conception of the class structure in capitalist society. Fourth is Weber's pluralist view of the bases for hierarchy and group formation in social structures: class, status, and party. The fifth way in which Weber adds complexity to the analysis of inequality is in his outline of the several types of *power* or *domination* in social life. Finally, we shall assess Weber's contention that the control of economic production is just one means by which some people are able to dominate others. Thus, to understand social inequality, we must recognize the several *means of administration*, especially in the form of rationalized bureaucracies, that wield power in modern societies. This last point leads into the concluding discussion, in which we consider Weber's assessment of the prospects for democracy and the socialist alternative in future societies.

WEBER ON METHOD: PROBABILITY AND CAUSAL PLURALISM

Max Weber wrote extensively on the topic of research methods in the social sciences. (See especially the collection of essays in Shils and Finch, 1949.) While it is beyond the purposes of this discussion to consider Weber's methodological orientation in detail, there are certain aspects of his position that are relevant to our analysis. To begin with, we can briefly characterize Weber's approach as a compromise between two opposing schools of thought: those who reject any possibility of applying the techniques of natural science to predict or explain social behaviour and those so-called *positivists* who, on the contrary, contend that the methods and assumptions of sociological research should be essentially identical with those of, say, physics or chemistry (cf. Runciman, 1978:65). Weber locates sociology somewhere between the natural sciences and a discipline like history, in terms of both the generality of explanation and the precision of research techniques. Whereas history concerns itself with the understanding of "important individual events," sociology deals with the observation and explanation of "generalized uniformities" in recurring empirical processes (Weber, 1922:29, 19). Unlike history, sociology can offer theories to account for these empirical regularities. However, social explanations typically will not hold without qualification for all times, all cases, or all conditions. This feature makes sociological explanations distinct from those in natural science to the degree that the latter will hold invariably, assuming appropriate controls for extraneous circumstances.

There are many possible reasons for this essential difference between natural science and social science, including the lesser precision of social concepts and the fact that explanations in social science are subject to constant revision over time, as conditions change (Runciman, 1978:65). Thus, while chemical elements will interact today in the same way as they did centuries ago, individuals or groups in different historical and social contexts may not, and the social scientist must take this possibility into account. For these and other reasons, Weber raises certain restrictions concerning the application of the scientific method in social research. Two of these restrictions or complications are the probabilistic nature of social inquiry and the inherent pluralism in social causation.

Probability

Weber frequently refers to probability when discussing social phenomena (e.g., Weber in Parsons, 1947:99–100, 118–19, 126, 146). In effect, Weber argues that X *may* lead to Y in some, or even most, instances but rarely without exception. This means that we can assess, and sometimes calculate, the probability that X is a cause of Y, but we cannot establish that X will *always* lead to Y, since this is not in the nature of social processes (cf. Weber, 1922:11–12; cf. Giddens, 1971:149, 153). If we take, for example, Marx's contention that the dominant ideas in a society are the ideas of the ruling class, this may be true for some or most of the ideas that predominate in a society but probably not for every dominant idea we could examine. The exceptions do not mean, however, that Marx's claim about the origin of ideas is incorrect. Rather, they indicate that the claim is applicable part of the time and that, within a certain probability, we can predict correctly what ideas predominate in society by examining those generated by the ruling class.

Causal Pluralism

And what of those exceptional cases that do not fit our prediction or explanation? These must be examined to determine, where possible, the reasons for their deviation from our expectations. According to Weber, there are numerous other factors that inevitably are not taken into account when one poses a simple explanation for something. It is conceivable that these additional factors are responsible for deviant cases; hence, it is essential to search for multiple causes for social phenomena, following a strategy of "causal pluralism" (Gerth and Mills, 1967:34, 54, 61). This method seeks social explanation by means of "a pluralistic analysis of factors, which may be isolated and gauged in terms of their respective causal weights" (Gerth and Mills, 1967:65).

If, for example, we wished to understand why some people are rich and others are poor, we might try to explain these differences in wealth in terms of the family class background of the people involved. Perhaps all rich people were born into wealthy families and all poor people were born into poor families, with no other factors playing a part in economic success or failure. In that case, we would be able to explain economic inequality perfectly on the basis of one factor: inheritance of wealth. However, in a complex society, it is probable that other factors also influence one's economic position, not just inheritance. Perhaps an individual's gender or race has an effect on economic well-being, independent of inherited wealth. Even physical beauty or athletic prowess might be related to economic position. Of course, not all of these possible influences would have the same degree of impact. Presumably, for example, inheritance, gender, or race would have a greater effect than beauty in most cases. But, whatever the result of the inquiry, it is imperative that the social scientist look for the several potential causes for social phenomena and assess their relative effects, large or small, by means of empirical observation.

SUBJECTIVE FACTORS AND THE IDEALISM-MATERIALISM DEBATE
Subjective Meanings and Explanation

Another one of the complexities that mark social life, and that to Weber must be considered in any social theory, is the subjective nature of human interaction. This point is related to our previous discussion of Weber's method, since these subjective considerations signify another important distinction between natural and social science. One of the advantages of natural science, and another reason for its greater precision, is that it need deal only with objectively observable and interpretable information. Physics and chemistry, for example, analyze the behaviour of inanimate objects or forces that, under controlled conditions, can be seen to behave in perfectly predictable ways. In social science, however, the units of observation are individual human beings, whose actions are determined not only by objective conditions but also by subjective forces that lie outside the realm of natural science. Thus, social explanations must take into account these additional subjective aspects of social life: the meanings people attach to their actions, the ideas that govern their behaviour, and their consciousness and perceptions of the world around them.

Certain kinds of human behaviour can be readily understood by analyzing subjective phenomena. What Weber calls *rational action*, the calculated pursuit of individual interests, is predictable with a high level of certainty because one can successfully assume what subjective motives are at work in most cases. This kind of behaviour is epitomized in the actions of capitalists in the marketplace, where subjective interests are geared almost completely to the profit motive or the maximization of wealth (cf. Weber, 1922:30).

However, not all human behaviour follows the *ideal type* of rational action. (*Ideal type* refers to a *pure* form here, not necessarily a desirable one.) Some actions are governed by *nonrational* or even irrational considerations — superstition, love, envy, vengeance, and so on — usually in combination with rational concerns. Now, the more that human actions depart from the purely rational type, the more difficult it becomes to discern, in the external acts of people, the subjective intent of their behaviour (Weber, 1922:6). This both adds to the complexity and decreases the precision of social research and social explanation. At the same time, however, this opens up for the sociologist a whole area of inquiry that is closed to the natural scientist and so, in this sense, is an advantage of sociology over natural science. In fact, to Weber, it is this special focus of sociology on subjective meaning and explanation that distinguishes it from other kinds of knowledge (Weber, 1922:15).

Ideas and Material Life

Weber's stress on subjective factors as an integral part of social explanation is consistent once again with his rejection of vulgar Marxist theory. In this case, the point at issue primarily concerns the debate over the relationship between ideas and material reality. As noted in Chapter 2, one of Marx's early tasks was to demonstrate the fallacy in Hegel's idealist philosophy, in which ideas are analyzed without regard for the social conditions in which they emerge and operate. Despite the occasional remark by Marx to the contrary (e.g., Marx, 1867:19), Weber and Marx appear in fact to hold very similar positions on this point (Giddens, 1971:209–10). The problem for Weber, however, is that some of Marx's disciples seem to have replaced Marx's original formulation with an oversimplified and extreme materialist view, which treats ideas and other subjective phenomena as mere by-products of concrete social conditions, totally irrelevant to the explanation of human action.

Thus, Weber takes pains throughout his work to demonstrate that social life is not understood so simply. In his view, those who employ only material, economic factors to explain social action are doomed to failure because the subjective meanings and ideas people live by frequently produce effects different from those that a simple materialist theory would predict. One of Weber's early works points out, for example, that peasants in nineteenth-century Germany chose the freedom (but economic hardship) of wage labour over the relative economic well-being (but servitude) of bonded serfdom (cf. Giddens, 1971:122–23). To Weber, this is but one instance of the tendency for people at times to put a subjective meaning, the idea of freedom in this case, ahead of material conditions when choosing a course of action.

Undoubtedly, the best-known work by Weber that treats this issue is *The Protestant Ethic and the Spirit of Capitalism*. One of the objectives of this study is to show how "ideas become effective forces in history" (Weber, 1905:90). Thus, Weber examines the relationship between the religious ideas and beliefs of ascetic Protestant sects, like Calvinism, and the rise of modern capitalism. Weber observes the Calvinist belief that all people are predestined by God either to salvation or to Hell. He believes that this makes it important to each Calvinist to be successful in this world in whatever *calling* he or she chooses. The action of the Calvinist cannot of course determine whether he or she is saved or damned, since everyone is predestined. However, the psychological need to *appear* to be one of the chosen, to "shew oneself approved unto God" by being a success in this life, is sufficient motivation. This concerted drive for success, when combined with the belief in asceticism, the rejection of worldly pleasures, means that Calvinists tend to accumulate wealth that cannot be spent on frivolities and so is invested in ever-expanding capitalist enterprises. Thus, part of the reason why certain Protestant sects are overrepresented among the capitalist class, and part of the reason why capitalism took the specific direction of development that it did, can be traced to certain dominant ideas in these religions.

It is important to note that Weber never contends that Calvinist religious ideas are the *only* reasons for capitalism's emergence or that capitalism would not have occurred without them. He explicitly rejects such a simplistic explanation as "foolish and doctrinaire" (Weber, 1905:91). His later writings on the subject reveal an even clearer disavowal of strictly idealist explanations and, if anything, put greater stress on the importance of organizational or structural factors in the emergence of modern capitalism (cf. Collins, 1980; Collins, 1986a:19-37). In either case, however, it contributes little to our understanding if we "substitute for a one-sided materialism an equally one-sided spiritualistic causal interpretation" (Weber, 1905:183). One-sided explanations are obviously inconsistent with his sense of the complexity of social processes and his deep-seated belief in causal pluralism. Instead, there is an intricate interplay between objective social conditions and the subjective meanings of individual persons' actions. This combination is responsible for the direction of social action and the shape of social structure.

MULTIPLE CLASSES IN CAPITALISM

To this point, we have attempted to demonstrate the pluralist nature of Weber's assumptions about sociological theory and method. The same characteristics are evident in his views on the specific area of social inquiry of concern to us — social inequality. We can detect these characteristics first of all in Weber's conception of class, the central idea in Marx's analysis of social inequality.

In Chapter 2, we noted that Marx defines class by distinguishing between two key groupings — the owners of the means of economic production, or bourgeoisie, and those nonowners who must work as wage labourers, the proletariat. Weber's formulation has broad similarities to Marx's definition, for both writers treat classes in the most basic sense as economic entities. One difference, however, is that Marx is concerned primarily with the social *relations* between his two classes in the productive sphere, especially the relations of domination and exploitation of the workers by the owners and the inherent conflict these generate between classes. As we have seen, the simple *distribution* of wealth is a secondary consideration for Marx. Weber's emphasis is somewhat the reverse, at least with respect to the concept of economic class. He also speaks of class struggle and relations of class domination, but his main emphasis in defining classes seems to be on the distribution of valued objects and the bases on which some people get more than others.

To understand Weber's view, we must begin by noting that he sees classes as economic categories, developing out of human interaction in a *market*. A market here is basically a system of competitive exchange whereby individuals buy and sell things of value in the pursuit of profit (Weber, 1922:82). These things of value are in effect equivalent to what Weber calls "utilities," which include both material "goods," especially property and possessions, and human "services," namely personal skills and labour power (Weber, 1922:63, 68–69). Essentially, a class is simply an aggregate of people sharing common "situations" in this market and therefore having similar "economic interests" and "life chances" (Weber, 1922:927–28).

We can see that Weber's initial discussion is similar to Marx's because his definition leads to a simple distinction between those who have property and those who have only services to exchange in the marketplace: " 'Property' and 'lack of property' are, therefore, the basic categories of all class situations" (Weber, 1922:927). At this point, however, Weber follows his normal course, and reasserts his disagreement with contemporary Marxism, by pointing out what he believes are other important complexities that the two-class model hides: "Class situations are further differentiated . . . according to the kind of property . . . and the kind of services that can be offered in the market" (Weber, 1922:928). Thus, the existence of different kinds of property makes for additional classes within the broad propertied group, and different types of services and job skills distinguish segments of the working class from one another. Taken to its logical extreme, this definition leads to difficulties because it implies that each of the various kinds of property people own, and each of the numerous job categories that can be identified in the marketplace, may signify a separate class (Weber, 1922:928). Thus, almost every individual in a complex economic system like modern capitalism could in a sense represent a distinct class; hence, the concept of class would be meaningless (cf. Giddens, 1973:78–79).

In actual practice, fortunately, Weber does not apply his formulation in this extreme manner. In the end, his version of the class structure lies between the simple dichotomy of the cruder versions of Marxism and the uncompromising pluralism that his own definition implies. Nevertheless, to present the Weberian view of the structure of classes in capitalism is still difficult because of a disjuncture between two of the sections on class in his unfinished work *Economy and Society* (Weber, 1922:302–7, 926–40). These sections were written at different times and seem inconsistent in places, suggesting that Weber may have revised his initial view after some reconsideration (Giddens, 1973:79).

One solution to these difficulties is to draw a distinction between the idea of class and the related but separate concept of *social class*. As we have already discussed, a class is simply a category, a set of individuals in similar economic circumstances and with similar economic interests. Thus, "a class does not in itself constitute a group [or community]" (Weber, 1922:930); individuals in a simple economic class lack the sense of common position and consciousness of common interests that a true group or community possesses. It is when these subjective qualities are added to the aggregate in question and a process of real group formation emerges that Weber's idea of social class becomes operative. In effect, then, social classes are best understood as economic classes that have acquired in varying degrees some subjective sense of "unity" and "class-conscious organization" (Weber, 1922:302, 305). Here again, the importance Weber attaches to subjective processes is evident.

At the risk of some oversimplification, it is worth pointing out that Weber's distinction between class and social class corresponds broadly to Marx's distinction between a class in itself and a class for itself. That is, just as Marx's class in itself signifies a collectivity that is identifiable on purely economic grounds, without reference to group awareness, so too does Weber's concept of class. And, just as Marx's class for itself possesses a consciousness of common position and interests, so too does Weber's social class. The major difference to be noted here is that Marx uses his formulation primarily with reference to the proletariat in order to indicate the two stages through which the working class must move if it is to become a revolutionary political force for transforming capitalist society. However, Weber's discussion is intended to delineate a whole range of social classes, each of which may differ in the degree of group awareness. Moreover, Weber, as we shall see, believes that the highest degree of group consciousness and the most potential for political action and control lies not with the working class but with those at the top of the social structure.

With this additional element of subjective awareness included, Weber's potentially countless economic class categories in capitalism tend to coalesce into a limited set of four social classes (but see Scott, 1979:182). In effect, Weber's (and Marx's) distinction between the propertied and the propertyless is supplemented by the addition of two other classes (Weber, 1922:305). What this addition amounts to, first, is separating the bourgeoisie into those who control large amounts of property, the big capitalists, and those who have relatively small amounts of productive property, the petty bourgeoisie. Similarly, the propertyless category is subdivided by Weber, this time according to the level of skill and training required of those who sell their services in the marketplace. The key distinction here is between the "working class," who tend to have labour power alone at their disposal, and those who have more marketable skills as "specialists," "technicians," "white-collar employees," or "civil servants" (Weber, 1922:305). Thus, interposed between the large-scale bourgeoisie and the mass of proletarians, we have two middle classes: owners of small, independent shops, businesses, and farms; and a salaried nonmanual class with special education or skills in such areas as law, medicine, and the sciences.

The discussion of middle classes is of extreme importance for our understanding of Marx and Weber and, as we shall see, stands as perhaps the key issue in present debates over the nature of classes in modern societies. If there is one fundamental difference between Marx and Weber on the subject of class structure, it is their discussion of the middle class — more specifically, the salaried nonmanual segment. We should note, to begin with, that the two writers largely agree on the disposition of the petty-bourgeoisie portion of the middle classes. Both writers note the existence of this class in early capitalism but foresee its gradual reduction as capitalism develops. The reader will recall that Marx sees the petty bourgeoisie as a group that would gradually be swallowed up in the growing concentration of productive property in the hands of large-scale capitalists. Weber points out as well how the chance for individuals to become "self-employed small businessmen" has become "less and less feasible" (Weber, 1922:305).

On the question of the salaried nonmanual class, however, Marx and Weber take quite distinct positions. Despite Marx's emphasis on a two-class model of the capitalist class structure, he is aware of this salaried nonmanual group, of "the constantly growing number of the middle classes, those who stand between the workman on the one hand and the capitalist and landlord on the other" (Marx, 1862:573). Because of his emphasis, however, Marx does not deal with them extensively, perhaps because he does not believe they will be a force of consequence in the ultimate shift from capitalism to socialism. To Marx, the salaried middle class is mainly an auxiliary to the bourgeoisie, a set of nonproduction employees who, because of the great surplus wealth generated at this stage of capitalism, can be hired to perform clerical, technical, and minor administrative services for the bourgeoisie (Marx, 1862:571). Their labour may indeed get them more of the distributed rewards than the industrial proletariat. This unjust advantage over regular production workers also makes them a "burden weighing heavily on the working base," while their collaboration with the bourgeoisie increases "the social security and power of the upper ten thousand" (Marx, 1862:573). Nevertheless, they are in key respects akin to the working class, being in a relationship of exploitation by the bourgeoisie and dependent on the capitalist for wages (Marx and Engels, 1848:62).

The Weberian conception differs in that it often stresses the distributive inequalities that Marx downplays. Members of the salaried middle class have better economic life chances and different economic interests that are in themselves sufficient to identify them as a class distinct from the workers, unlikely to take part in fomenting socialist revolution. The salaried middle class, in Weber's view, will continue to expand in numbers and importance as the children of workers and of the petty bourgeoisie move into the market for white-collar posts in the growing bureaucratic organizations of modern society (Weber, 1922:305). Besides, some of the nonmanual middle class, in addition to their distributive advantage over the ordinary workers, occupy jobs in middle management, which places them in relations of domination over other workers. This placement of salaried workers contributes, in Weber's conception, to a clear split between the middle and working classes and sharply reduces the chances that salaried employees will support or identify with the working class in revolutionary action.

MULTIPLE POWER BASES: CLASS, STATUS, AND PARTY

It is clear from our previous review of Weber's conceptions of class and social class that he departs from Marx primarily in his delineation of several, not just two, important class segments. This view of the class structure is but one element in Weber's more general treatment of social inequality as a pluralist phenomenon. Hence, the analysis of class inequality, in Weber's mind, must be interwoven with, and compounded by, the examination of two additional ideas that are conceptually different from class but that can cut across class distinctions in real societies. The two concepts are *status* and *party*.

As a starting point, we should note that Weber's famous treatment of class, status, and party is only part of his larger essay on "political communities" (Weber, 1922:Chapter 9). Thus, underlying the important differences among these three concepts, which we will discuss in the next two subsections, is their common root in Weber's political analysis. A key concern in all of Weber's work is with the "politics" of social life, which broadly speaking is essentially a "struggle" or "conflict" between individuals or groups with opposing interests and different power resources (Weber, 1922:1398, 1414). *Power* here is the chance (or probability) one has to do as one wills, even against the resistance of others (Weber, 1922:53, 926). More will be said on the subjects of power and politics in subsequent sections of this chapter. For now, it is important to be aware of the pivotal roles these two ideas play in Weber's sociology and to recognize that class, status, and party are all aspects of "the distribution of power within the political community" (Weber, 1922:926). Each one represents a potential basis for coalition or organization in the pursuit of personal interests.

Classes versus Status Groups

We have already seen that Weber's classes are categories of individuals differing in economic clout, in "the power . . . to dispose of goods or skills . . . in a given economic order" (Weber in Gerth and Mills, 1967:181). *Status*, however, is something that normally inheres in real *groups*, not simple categories of individuals. In fact, Weber uses the German term *Stände* in this part of his analysis, which is typically translated as "status groups," although some theorists prefer to call such entities "estates" (for debate, see Dahrendorf, 1959:6–7; Bendix, 1960:85; Wenger, 1980, 1987). In either case, however, Weber is clearly speaking of sets of people that are not mere aggregates of individuals but have a subjective sense of common membership and a group awareness that is relatively well defined (Weber, 1922:932). In addition, status groups tend to have a distinctive "style of life," or mode of conduct, that separates them from the rest of the population (Weber, 1922:305, 932). Whereas class membership denotes the extent of one's power in the economic order, status groups are delineated by the power that derives from the "social honor, or prestige" distributed within the "status order" (Weber, 1922:926–27). Thus, the economic-class order and the status order are two distinct hierarchies for representing the relative powers of individuals and groups.

Having drawn this distinction, Weber proceeds to complicate his analysis by indicating conceptual overlaps between class and status. The crucial overlap to clarify is the connection between Weber's idea of status group and his concept of social class. It will be recalled that Weber characterizes social classes as economic classes whose members, to varying degrees, have acquired some sense of group consciousness and a subjective awareness of their common class position. But, as we have noted, subjective awareness is also a basic element in what Weber calls a status group. The key difference here is that status groups are distinguishable from one another not on economic grounds but in terms of social honour. However, whenever economic power is also a basis for both social honour and subjective group awareness, then a social class is also a status group. Thus, Weber asserts that "the status group comes closest to the social class" (Weber, 1922:305). Stripped of its subtler details, what this amounts to is a simple equation: when an economic class, a simple category of people with similar economic power, also takes on the subjective awareness and cohesion of a status group, the result is a *social* class.

It is clear from this interrelation between social class and status group that Weber does not seek to portray the economic and status orders as unrelated in actual societies. In reality, the same people can be, and frequently are, ranked similarly in both orders. Thus, for example, those of the highest economic class also tend to possess high levels of status honour. Property ownership in particular is linked to status honour "with extraordinary regularity" (Weber, 1922:932). The subjective awareness basic to status-group membership typically leads to efforts at closure, or the exclusion of outsiders from interaction with members. This interaction can include everything from social activities and gatherings to marriages within the status circle. Here, too, Weber draws some of his examples of status groups from the economic order. Thus, he suggests, at least partly seriously, that because of group closure "it may be that only the families coming under approximately the same tax class will dance with one another" (Weber, 1922:932).

The purpose, then, of drawing a distinction between classes and status groups is not to assert their total disjuncture but to indicate that they are not necessarily related in a perfect one-to-one correspondence. The power they bestow comes from somewhat different sources, and the extent of their correlation is a matter of empirical investigation in real societies (but see Wenger, 1980). The point is that as long as it is possible for individuals to derive social honour from noneconomic considerations, then the existence of status groups will "hinder the strict carrying through of the sheer market principle" (Weber, 1922:930). Thus, the leaders of the Roman Catholic Church — the Pope and the College of Cardinals — may be said to form a status group, to the extent that their power, or ability to influence the actions of others, does not stem primarily from their market position or economic class, which would be below that of the wealthiest capitalists, for example. Instead, the power of church leaders to exercise their will over others is accorded them largely because many people believe them to be worthy of obedience, as God's representatives on earth. This is just one illustration of how considerations of status can cut across and complicate considerations of class. Such an illustration does not deny the great power of those who control the economy, nor does it disprove the possible empirical connections between those people who dominate each hierarchy. But, for Weber, such examples do reveal that the correlation between the economic order and the status order is not perfect and that, as a consequence, the complexity of social inequality must be acknowledged.

Party

The third concept in Weber's three-pronged treatment of the distribution of power in society is his idea of *party*. Typically, this concept receives far less attention than either class or status. This is probably because Weber himself offers only a brief discussion of party. Some confusion over the significance of party in Weber's scheme has been engendered by the incomplete nature of his discussion. A related difficulty is that Weber identifies power as the specific concern of parties, leading some writers to conclude, erroneously, that *only* parties are concerned with power and that classes and status groups deal with quite different matters. In fact, as has already been noted, all three concepts pertain to the distribution of power (cf. Wenger, 1987:44). Each of the three concepts represents a different base through which power inheres in some groups or individuals more than others.

Parties, in Weber's terminology, are voluntary "associations," systematically organized for the collective "pursuit of interests" (Weber, 1922:284–85). The best-known examples are formal political parties, such as the New Democratic Party in Canada or the Republican Party in the United States. But any organization fitting Weber's definition is a party: pressure groups like the Consumers' Association of Canada, unions such as the United Auto Workers, and professional groups like the American Medical Association.

Like the members of status groups and social classes, members of parties possess some sense of group consciousness and solidarity. In fact, status groups or social classes can also be parties in certain circumstances, provided they develop a rational structure, formal organization, and administrative staff. These organizational qualities are primarily what separates party from the other two concepts (Weber, 1922:285, 938). Thus, not all classes or status groups will be parties, and not all parties will be social classes or status groups, but they *can* and *will* overlap in some cases. The message Weber again conveys here is the pluralist nature of both inequality and the structure of power. Parties, like classes and status groups, are distinct features in the intricate mix of social forces that operate in and shape social structures. In contrast to those Marxists who stress economic power as the single force of consequence in the study of inequality, Weber perceives three major bases for power, according to which different constellations of interests emerge and determine the nature and extent of inequality.

POWER, DOMINATION, AND LEGITIMATE DOMINATION (AUTHORITY)

The complexity of Weber's image becomes more elaborate still when we delve into his analysis of power in social life. Power is probably the most difficult idea to work with and comprehend in Weber's writings. This difficulty is both unfortunate and somewhat ironic, because power is also the central concept in much of his work, particularly that which deals with social inequality. His general view is that inequalities between social actors are traceable primarily to their differential success in the continuing social struggle, the contest between competing or conflicting interests. This struggle is also the essence of what Weber means by politics, in the broadest sense of the term. Essentially, power is the factor that determines the outcome of the social struggle and, hence, the nature and extent of inequality. Power (*Macht*, in German), it will be recalled, is defined as "the probability that one actor within a social relationship will be in a position to carry out his own will despite resistance" (Weber, 1922:53).

The problem with Weber's definition of power is that it is too broad to be very useful. Weber himself concedes that his definition is "amorphous," that "all conceivable qualities of a person" could put that person in a position of power over others (Weber, 1922:53). There also seems to be an allowance here that power relations can be impermanent and sporadic, shifting dramatically on rather short notice.

A key way in which Weber specifies his discussion is to suggest another idea, *domination*, as a "special case of power" (Weber, 1922:53, 941). Domination (*Herrschaft*, in German) refers to those power relations in which *regular patterns* of inequality are established whereby the subordinate group (or individual) *accepts* that position in a sustained arrangement, obeying the commands of the dominant group (or individual). In fact, one could claim that it is just such continuing power arrangements that are most relevant to our analysis of social inequality as a *structured* phenomenon. What the distinction between power and domination allows us to do, then, is to set aside those power relations that are only transient, temporary, or incidental. These situations after all tell us little about the more general, established, and patterned systems of domination that provide most of the framework for inequality at the societal level.

It is important to remember, though, that not all social analysts adopt Weber's distinction between power and domination, either in their scholarly writings or in everyday conversation. Consequently, the term power is frequently employed when discussing situations that, to Weber, are more precisely considered examples of domination. For practical purposes in our analysis, the two terms may be seen as more or less equivalent, since domination, as defined by Weber, is in large measure the key brand of power that students of structured social inequality consider, especially at the macroscopic level.

We have now outlined Weber's distinction between power in general and the more specific variety of power that we are concerned with, domination. In an earlier section of this chapter we discussed Weber's contention that classes, status groups, and parties are the principal bases for exercising power (or domination) in society. In other words, those who are members of dominant classes, status groups, and party associations are able on the whole to exact compliance to their wills, on a regular basis, from the remaining population. To say this, however, is not to provide the reasons why subordinate factions in these spheres accept or endure their subordination.

There are many possible reasons for compliance to domination. In Weber's terms, some of these are based on *legitimacy*, while others are not (Weber, 1922:904). There are essentially three pure types of legitimate domination, or *authority* (*legitime Herrschaft*), that are of note. Subordinates may give compliance because they perceive special charismatic qualities of leadership in those who rule them (*charismatic authority*), because they genuinely believe both in the legality of their subordinate position and in the legal right of those in power to be there (*legal authority*), or because they consciously accept the traditional right of certain groups to lead them (*traditional authority*) (Weber, 1922:215).

In addition, however, there are numerous other reasons for obedience that are not legitimate in this sense. In these cases, domination occurs because, out of unthinking custom, habit, or convention, subjects have always been subordinate and entertain no possibility of change; because of opportunities for personal advantage or self-interest; because of fear of the use of physical force or other reprisals; and so on (cf. Weber, 1922:33–36, 753–58, 946–53).

The question of whether one of these types of domination, legitimate or otherwise, is more prevalent than the others is, as usual for Weber, a matter of empirical investigation. His view is that the predominant type of domination will differ over time and from society to society. But a key underlying reason for compliance in virtually all situations, a sanction that can never be discounted, is the possible application of physical force by the dominant group. The threat of physical force is more prevalent and more blatant, of course, in early, primitive societies, where "violent social action" is "absolutely primordial" (Weber, 1922:904). As societies have evolved, the actual use of force has tended to decrease. This reduction in violence is partly because ruling groups are reluctant to resort constantly to violent means, since these generate resentment and potential rebellion among subordinates. In addition, the actual application of force is less necessary, with periodic exceptions, because the other reasons for compliance gradually come into play.

It is usually a combination of some or all of the reasons listed earlier that promotes acceptance (Weber, 1922:263). In most cases, the rational calculation of self-interest is quite important, especially in the pursuit of economic rewards and social honour (cf. Giddens, 1971:156). As well, the fact that a "legal order" comes into existence is a significant aspect of domination in modern times. It entrenches in law the rights of certain groups relative to others and so can be used by the ruling group both to justify compliance among the willing and to enforce compliance among the unwilling (Weber, 1922:312, 903–4). But the impact of habit and custom, the "unreflective habituation to a regularity of life," is a particularly important, and frequently overlooked, reason for acceptance of domination among the mass of the population (Weber, 1922:312). We shall deal again with many of these ideas about power in subsequent chapters.

Weber's outline of the several reasons that may motivate social actors to accept domination is clearly consistent with his stress on the importance of the subjective meanings that people attach to their behaviour. By elaborating the various types of domination, legitimate and otherwise, that can operate in society, Weber is also providing still more evidence of the complex nature of social processes and the need to take this complexity into account in social explanations. His formulations of power and domination make it clear, as well, that the inequalities between individuals or groups arising out of the economic sphere, or the class structure, are but one means by which power is exercised and one means by which some people are able to dominate others. This last point is worth stressing because, as we shall see, it has been used by some more recent theorists to suggest that power is the pivotal concept for understanding a full range of other inequalities between groups, including those that are differentiated by race, gender, ethnicity, and age, among others. Although Weber says little that explicitly deals with these specific concerns (but see Collins, 1986a:15–16), his recognition that there are multiple non-class bases for power and group formation can be extrapolated to explain or accommodate these other forms of social inequality.

RATIONALIZATION, BUREAUCRACY, AND THE MEANS OF ADMINISTRATION

In our analysis of Marx, we noted that his view of social inequality identifies the dominant people of society as those who control the means of material production. To Marx, the explanation for how systems of inequality arise and change is ultimately rooted in how classes emerge out of the organization of economic activity. It is more difficult to identify in Weber's work the same sense of a single, overriding force shaping social inequality. In fact, the central theme of our discussion of Weber has been to point out his complex view of social inequality and his skepticism about the existence of ultimate social causes.

Nevertheless, there is some basis for the claim that Weber does stress a recurring, if not a singular, process at work in the generation of social inequality. This claim relates to our earlier observation that Weber sees social action generally as a *contested* activity, a struggle between individuals or groups pursuing their own interests. Factions differ in their power to achieve their interests and social inequality, in all its guises, is one major result of this imbalance. The contest or struggle for power, which is the crux of what Weber means by politics, is inherent in social action. Thus, if there is a predominant tendency in Weber's approach, it is to explain social action in terms of politics, defined in this broad sense (cf. Giddens, 1972:34; Giddens, 1973:46–47). Such a perspective differs from Marx's, since Weber views the struggle between economic classes as just one element, albeit a crucial one, in the more universal contest of interests within social structures.

A full appreciation of Weber's power and politics orientation to social inequality requires that we consider three closely connected concepts in his work. These are rationalization, bureaucracy, and the means of administration.

Rationalization

Weber perceives in the historical development of societies a tendency for social action to become increasingly rationalized — that is, to be guided by the reasoned, calculated, or rational pursuit of particular interests. Of course, nonrational actions — those prompted by habit or emotion, for example — do continue to occur in modern societies (Weber, 1922:26). Nevertheless, there is in Weber's view a steady trend toward a predominance of both rationally motivated action and, consequently, rationally organized social structures. This is most obvious in the economic sphere under capitalism, where the calculated pursuit of self-interest reaches an advanced stage (Weber, 1922:71). Economic enterprise becomes geared above all to productive efficiency and its enhancement through the systematic organization of business (Weber, 1905:76). The calculation of profits becomes much more precise with the advent of a money-based economy, accounting procedures, book-keeping, and the retention of records and files (Weber, 1922:107–8). The growth in the specialization of occupations in the workplace and the planned division of labour in large-scale factories and other enterprises are also key features in this economic rationalization (Weber, 1922:436, 1155–56).

As we have seen, Marx is well aware of these processes in capitalist development. However, he believes that such changes as the growing division of labour will provide the ultimate impetus toward class polarization and eventual revolution, whereas Weber sees economic rationalization as but one part of a universal trend toward the systematic organization and administration of social action. Weber notes that a similar process of rationalization has occurred in virtually all the major spheres of social action. In religion, for example, he sees a trend toward *secularization*, whereby religious practice becomes structured, routinized, and administered much like the activities of other organizations, with a formal church hierarchy, standardized ritual, and so forth. This process is accompanied by a decline in the significance of the magical and the mystical aspects of spiritual life. The change in religion is perhaps the best illustration of Weber's idea that there is a progressive "disenchantment of the world" (Weber, 1922:538; cf. Gerth and Mills, 1967:51).

In the same way, Weber points out the development of a rationalized legal order and political system. In early societies, a legal system emerges as a basis for legitimizing the monopoly of physical force by those who control a territory. As this set of laws becomes increasingly elaborate and complex, it eventually comprises rules and regulations for a wide range of social action. Thus, the original ruling group gradually takes on a variety of administrative roles, leading to the establishment of the modern *state*. The functions of the state are numerous: the enactment of new laws; the preservation of "public order"; the protection of "vested rights" such as property ownership; the administration of health, education, and social welfare; and the defence of the territory against outside attack (Weber, 1922:655, 905, 908–9). Each of these activities in any large-scale society requires a permanent, organized system of problem solving, decision making, and policy implementation. In this manner, the trend to rationalization culminates in the system of formal organizations known as bureaucracies.

Bureaucracy

To Weber, it is the rationalized bureaucracies that have become the key players in the power struggle. Bureaucracies of various types have existed from early times. However, the modern bureaucracy is distinguishable from all previous forms by a particular set of traits. We need not examine these characteristics in detail, but they include the existence of specialized occupations, or offices, with designated duties to perform, arranged in a hierarchy of authority or decision-making power. Management of the organization is based on written documents, or files, and the operation is conducted according to an explicit set of rules or administrative regulations (Weber, 1922:956–58).

In Weber's view, such an organization acts almost like a "machine," providing the most rational and efficient means yet devised for administering social activity (Weber, 1922:973). This claim of rational efficiency may seem strange to those who have been caught up in bureaucratic red tape and who thus equate the term bureaucracy with *ir*rationality and *in*efficiency. Certainly Weber himself speaks of the "impediments" that the bureaucratic apparatus can create in individual cases (Weber, 1922:975). Nevertheless, he firmly contends that the administration of modern societies would be much worse, in fact impossible, without the bureaucratic form, given "the increasing complexity of civilization" (Weber, 1922:972). To Weber, this is not a question of preference or a value judgement but a statement of fact. The modern system of rationalized bureaucracies is for Weber a necessary evil: necessary because it is the only practical means for organizing human conduct in the present day, yet evil because it is an "iron cage" that restricts individualism and threatens democracy (cf. Weber, 1905:181–83). We shall return to this point in the concluding section of this chapter.

The Means of Administration

The significance of rationalized bureaucracies for the analysis of social inequality is that they become the key players in the general power struggle. Bureaucracies are the best examples of what Weber means by enduring structures of domination. They provide the means by which social action is governed on a regular basis and through which a system of inequality is established and sustained.

Once again the contrast with the Marxist conception is noteworthy. Whereas Marxism sees control of the means of economic production as the foundation for class structure and inequality in capitalism, Weber contends that differential access to the means of production is just one of the various ways in which power differences and inequality arise. Each of the major institutional structures of capitalist society has its own sphere of influence and its own bureaucratic system of operation. It is the control of all these various *means of administration* that determines social inequality, not just control in the economic sphere. Hence, in addition to the power deriving from control of the economy by bureaucratically organized corporate enterprises, power inheres in those groups that administer the religious system, the communications media, and so forth (Weber, 1922:223–24).

Among the most crucial structures for Weber is the interrelated set of "public organizations" that make up the modern state: the legal structure, the judicial and executive branches of government, the civil-service bureaucracies, the police, and the military (cf. Weber, 1922:980–89). All of these administrative systems hold power in their own right, so that the Marxist emphasis on the economic structure to the exclusion of others is a distortion. Here Weber clearly rejects the notion that the organizations existing outside the economic sphere are merely superstructural props for a ruling class of capitalists. While acknowledging the great power wielded by the bourgeoisie, Weber appears more worried by the threat posed by bureaucratic officials, especially those found in the state, where the means of administration seem to be increasingly concentrated. The modern state has also shown its increasing significance on the international scene, particularly because of its formal power to conduct and control both political and military initiatives in foreign lands (Weber, 1922: 910–25; cf. Collins, 1986a:145–46). It is not surprising that, as we shall discuss later, the power of the state has become a much more prominent concern, even for Marxist scholars, since Weber's time.

THE FUTURE: DEMOCRACY, BUREAUCRACY, AND SOCIALISM

Our outline of Weber's work has revealed a complex, multifaceted conception of social structure and the dynamics of social inequality. Modern society is shaped by an ongoing contest or struggle among self-interested social actors. Through control of economic resources, status honour, and the influence deriving from party associations, power is exercised over others. The power struggle gradually is consolidated into a contest involving formal structures of regular, patterned domination. Increasingly, in modern times, these structures take the form of rational bureaucracies, each headed by its own select group of high administrative officials. Social inequality in this context is firmly established, and power is concentrated in the hands of bureaucratic officials in all spheres of influence, not just the economic. A marked concentration of control over the administration of society falls to the various branches of the state, in particular.

It should be apparent from this description of Weber's position that he does not share Marx's optimism about the transformation of capitalism into a new society of universal human freedom and equality. As has been noted, Weber himself is sympathetic to the cause of political democracy. However, because of the structures of domination that have evolved under capitalism, Weber remains pessimistic about the prospects for democratic action and for any reduction of inequality in future societies. Moreover, for a number of reasons, he is convinced that socialism cannot reduce, and may even intensify, the extent of bureaucratic domination in the future.

Democracy versus Bureaucracy

Democracy, in Weber's definition, is a system of government whose guiding principle is "the 'equal rights' of the governed," a system in which the power of "officialdom" is minimized and the influence of "public opinion" is maximized (Weber, 1922:985). Such a system is most closely approximated in "direct" or "immediate" democracies — those in which persons in authority are obligated to conform to the will of their constituents (Weber, 1922:289). The problem with this brand of democracy is that it cannot function in large-scale systems like a modern society because of the sheer size and complexity of such structures (Weber, 1922:291). The only alternative is to employ what Weber calls "representative democracy," in which constituents elect individuals who are empowered to act in accordance with the general interest. This "representative body" of elected officials in turn typically appoints or elects a subset of their number as a "cabinet," which itself may be overseen by a premier official for purposes of centralized co-ordination of action. Such a system of "parliamentary cabinet government" is the most familiar form of modern democracy at the mass level (cf. Weber, 1922:289–97).

But what, after all, is this system of government? It is clearly another instance of bureaucracy, with the same inherent structure of domination that such a designation implies. The dilemma of democracy in the present and future is that "bureaucracy inevitably accompanies modern mass democracy" (Weber, 1922:983). A bureaucratic form of organization is the only means by which democratic action is feasible in complex societies. It is the one structure that ensures regular, predictable administration while at the same time providing procedures for the protection of constituents against possible abuses of democratic principles by those who govern. That is, governmental powers may themselves be constrained by a democratic system of laws and regulations that includes appeal procedures, explicitly limited terms of office, multiple parties, provision for elections, and so forth.

Unfortunately, government bureaucracy is also a hierarchy of authority, influence, experience, and expertise. Thus, government leaders are a select group with "special expert qualifications" and have access to more information and resources than any other group, even in a democracy (Weber, 1922:985). This means that the very bureaucratic system that is necessary for democracy in modern society creates conditions that could mean undemocratic action by those who rule. Of course, this is not to say that such abuses of democracy *must* occur. On this point, Weber disagrees with his contemporary Robert Michels, who asserts that an "iron law of oligarchy" operates in organizations, ensuring that they always abandon the democratic process in the end (Michels, 1915). Weber's position is more conditional: "democracy inevitably comes into conflict with the bureaucratic tendencies" of modern society (Weber, 1922:985); however, this only means that democracy *may* lose out, not that it always will, with certainty.

This idea comes up again in Weber's observation that political action is always determined by the "principle of small numbers," which gives superior "maneuverability" to "small leading groups" (Weber, 1922:1414). He even says in the same passage that "this is the way it should be," but only as long as leaders are both successful and faithful to essential democratic principles (cf. Weber in Gerth and Mills, 1967:42). For Weber, the key concern in democratic politics is effective leadership (Giddens, 1972:54). His personal preference is for a responsive political democracy, headed by someone possessing special qualities of democratic enlightenment and personal charisma. His fear, however, is that politics in the future will take the form of a "leaderless" democracy, with the mass of the population controlled by a "clique" of bureaucratic officials, a "certified caste of mandarins" (Weber in Gerth and Mills, 1967:113, 71).

The Socialist Alternative

Given all of the previous discussion, Weber's view of the prospects for democracy is, on balance, more pessimistic than optimistic. Even his own preferred version of political democracy contains within it the potential loss of individual autonomy and freedom, because bureaucracy is an "escape-proof" feature of every type of modern society (Weber, 1922:1401). However, any Marxist claim that socialism is both the solution to this dilemma and the means to realize true democracy is, in Weber's view, completely mistaken. The imperative need for systematic organization of social action is universal: "It makes no difference whether the economic system is organized on a capitalistic or socialistic basis" (Weber, 1922:223). If anything, because socialist systems tend to intensify the centralization of decision making in the state and intrude pervasively into all spheres of human activity, "socialism would, in fact, require a still higher degree of formal bureaucratization than capitalism" (Weber, 1922:225). In this way, socialism would further reduce, not increase, human freedom. In other words, any hope for a dictatorship of the proletariat is a delusion. Instead, socialism would be an extreme case of "dictatorship of the official" (Weber in Gerth and Mills, 1967:50).

It appears, therefore, that Weber does not share with Marx the expectation of an eventual end to social conflict and to structured inequality. To Weber, the need for bureaucracy and the factionalism of human interaction make both inequality and competitive struggle inherent features of all societies, socialist or capitalist. One of the key differences between these two great thinkers seems to centre on this point. Both give the idea of struggle a key role in their conception of inequality. But for Marx, on the one hand, struggle is not essential to social life. It is part of society only as long as class systems exist and act to pervert the essentially social and co-operative nature of human interaction. For Weber, on the other hand, struggle is basic to social life and operates generally, not just in the sphere of class relations. In his view, inequality emerges from the continuing contest for power, in which individuals and groups pursue, not the general interest, but their own special interests. One can seek to place checks and balances against the usurpation of power by bureaucratic officials, but such efforts may not be successful and, in any case, will eliminate neither inequality nor the self-interest inherent in human nature.

Which of these images of our present and future is the more accurate one, of course, remains a topic of debate to this day. Ultimately, it is a question with no simple answer. In assessing the future of inequality, some deride Marx for the shortcomings of optimism: his failure to discern all the obstacles to revolution; his omission of a clear guide for his disciples to the universal society; and his perhaps excessive faith in humanity. Still, Weber's hard-nosed pessimism is for some more flawed (cf. Marcuse, 1971). Perhaps in predicting for us a future of bureaucratic cages and embattled democracy, Weber has inadvertently helped contribute, in a self-fulfilling way, to the realization of his own worst fears.

Summary

Our concern in this chapter has been to outline and assess Max Weber's conception of social inequality. Weber's work may be characterized generally as a positive critique of Marx and Marxism. A central theme in Weber's writings is his emphasis on the complex, pluralist nature of inequality. This theme was illustrated by reference to a number of Weber's formulations, especially his conceptions of class, power, and domination. We noted Weber's view of society as an arena for numerous contests among social actors attempting to obtain and exert power, and we examined the important role played by bureaucratic structures in these struggles. Finally, the chapter concluded with Weber's assessment of the chances for democracy in future societies, both socialist and capitalist.

Chapter

4

Durkheim, Social Solidarity, and Social Inequality

"Liberty . . . is itself the product of
regulation. . . . Only rules can prevent abuses of
power." *Emile Durkheim*, The Division of
Labour, *Preface to the second edition, 1902*

Introduction

In this chapter, we consider the work of Emile Durkheim. Durkheim is generally thought to be the third major figure in classical sociological theory. His ideas, along with those of Marx and Weber, are still believed by various writers to lie at the heart of most theoretical developments and debates in sociology today (Wiley, 1987:25; Coser, 1977:174; see also Collins, 1985; Sydie, 1987). However, although Durkheim's contributions to general sociological theory have received wide recognition, the value and relevance of his ideas for the analysis of social inequality have not typically been acknowledged. This relative lack of acknowledgement is partly to be expected, since Durkheim's writings are not primarily concerned with the problem of inequality. Nevertheless, it is also the case that Durkheim has a good deal more to say about inequality than is normally assumed. Moreover, his conceptions share some interesting affinities with the writings of both Marx and Weber. Finally, Durkheim's work serves as a useful bridge between the classical theories of inequality and the more recent structural-functionalist perspective on social stratification, which became prominent after Durkheim's era and which is our major concern in Chapter 5. All of these considerations indicate the importance of examining the ideas put forth by Durkheim on the problem of social inequality.

It is somewhat surprising that, despite being almost exact contemporaries, Durkheim and Weber seem not to have been interested in or influenced by each other's work (Lukes, 1973:397). Durkheim was aware of Weber's writings and occasionally made reference to some of them (Giddens, 1971:119ff.). Even so, Weber stands out as the only major figure of the period whose ideas escaped any substantial critique or evaluation by Durkheim (Lukes, 1973:405). Durkheim did indicate more extensive interest in the theories of Marx. His thought even reveals some broad similarities with Marx's work, partly because of the influence of Saint-Simon on both writers. Nevertheless, the affinities between Marx and Durkheim are rarely direct or explicit ones, as evidenced by the infrequent and incidental citations of Marx in Durkheim's writings (e.g., Durkheim, 1893:393; Durkheim, 1896:12, 14, 59, 221; cf. Giddens, 1971:97).

This shortage of direct links between Durkheim and either Marx or Weber is to some extent the result of Durkheim's specific sociological interests — interests that are largely distinct from those of the other two writers. It is true that the three men share a concern with analyzing and comprehending certain aspects of the origin and development of nineteenth-century capitalism. However, each writer concentrates on a particular feature of this societal form. Marx focuses on class struggle — the opposition between owners and nonowners in the productive sphere — and its role in the emergence, maturation, and anticipated demise of capitalism. In contrast, Weber stresses the more general power struggle, especially with regard to the growth of rationalized bureaucracies, which become the principal structures of domination in modern capitalism but which are allegedly inescapable in socialism as well.

To Durkheim, also, problems of class struggle and power inequities in capitalism are important, but he analyzes them primarily with reference to what for him is the prior and more crucial question: how are the social structures, within which power and class struggle operate, even possible in the first place? By what means does a scattered collection of people coalesce to form the ongoing, enduring entity we call society, when so many conflicting and divisive forces are capable of tearing it asunder? Durkheim's focus, then, is on the cohesiveness, or *solidarity*, of social arrangements.

Durkheim's concern with the question of social solidarity, as well as his general perspective on social inequality, can be more easily comprehended if placed in the historical and intellectual context of his time. As with Marx and Weber, then, our assessment of Durkheim begins with an account of the major life events and other experiences that helped to shape his thought.

Biographical and Intellectual Sketch

EARLY YEARS

Emile Durkheim was born on April 15, 1858, at Epinal, in the Lorraine region of eastern France. His father, grandfather, and great grandfather had all served as rabbis in Lorraine and the nearby province of Alsace. These two areas were home to the largest Jewish community in France at the time (Peyre, 1960:7). This community had been in existence for several centuries but became increasingly well established with the granting of full civil rights to Jews after the French Revolution (Lukes, 1973:39; Coser, 1977:161–62). Durkheim was confirmed into the Jewish faith at age thirteen and showed some initial interest in being a rabbi like his father; however, he soon changed direction and eventually turned away from all religious involvement (Coser, 1977:143). Nevertheless, his interest in religion and its role as a source of social cohesion in both early and modern societies had a lasting impression on much of his sociological thought.

Durkheim appears to have enjoyed a close-knit and supportive family life, but one in which the values of hard work and material austerity were strongly emphasized (cf. Lukes, 1973:39–40). Even in this early period, then, there is evidence that Durkheim developed a sense of duty, diligence, and discipline that was to mark virtually all the other stages of his life (e.g., Coser, 1977:144).

Perhaps the most serious historical event in Durkheim's early years was the defeat of France by Germany in the brief Franco-Prussian War of 1870–71. As a young boy, Durkheim observed some of the grave consequences of this defeat first-hand, including the flaring of anti-Semitism and the tendency by some to blame the Jewish people for the loss of the war. This attitude must have been both hurtful and inexplicable to Durkheim and many other Jews in Alsace-Lorraine, since their community was known for its patriotism and for providing France with many of its career army officers and civil servants (Lukes, 1973:39–41). In spite of such prejudice, however, Durkheim never abandoned his loyalty to his country. He also remained deeply committed to the central ideals of the French Revolution, including the belief in individual liberty and progressive democracy (cf. Lukes, 1973:47, 271, 546; Giddens, 1986:13–15). This point is important to emphasize, since, as Lukes has shown, Durkheim at times has been incorrectly characterized as a reactionary opponent of political liberalism and personal freedom (Lukes, 1973:2–3, 338). On the contrary, Durkheim's contention is that liberty is an essential good in modern societies, provided that it is tempered by a sense of duty and moral obligation to others (cf. Peyre, 1960:21).

DURKHEIM AS A YOUNG SCHOLAR

From the beginning of his scholastic career, Durkheim was recognized as an outstanding student. As a young schoolboy, he was judged to be sufficiently advanced that he skipped two full classes beyond his own age group (Lukes, 1973:41). The one period of academic adversity Durkheim faced occurred in his late adolescence, when he sought admission to the prestigious Ecole Normale Supérieure in Paris.

Accounts suggest that a variety of circumstances, including financial problems, family illness, and the failure of his examiners to appreciate his original mind, contributed to a three-year delay before he was finally accepted into the Ecole in 1879 (Peyre, 1960:10; Lukes, 1973:42). From that point on, however, Durkheim enjoyed virtually total success in his scholastic and academic pursuits.

Life at the Ecole was both spartan and strict, but it apparently suited the serious and severe young Durkheim, who was thought to be rather aloof and stuffy by some of his fellow students (Coser, 1977:144). At the same time, though, the Ecole was an extremely stimulating intellectual environment for Durkheim and rightly deserved its reputation for attracting the brightest and keenest young minds in France (Lukes, 1973:45). Even among this select company, Durkheim was seen as more mature and more able than his classmates, many of whom held him in awe (Lukes, 1973:52).

Durkheim completed his course of study at the Ecole in 1882 and, like other future French intellectuals of the period, spent several years as an instructor at various secondary schools (*lycées*) near Paris (Peyre, 1960:11). He also devoted part of one academic year (1885–86) to a study for the French education ministry, during which he visited and evaluated several German universities, including the University of Berlin (Coser, 1977:145; Lukes, 1973:85). It is interesting that Max Weber, at this same time, was attending Berlin as a student in law. A second parallel of note is that Weber had just returned from his compulsory military service in Alsace-Lorraine, the region of France taken by Germany after the Franco-Prussian conflict and the place where Durkheim was born and his family still lived. Hence, while there is no record that the two men ever knowingly crossed paths, these coincidences make the chance of an unwitting encounter between Durkheim and Weber an intriguing possibility.

In the years that Durkheim served within the *lycées*, he established a reputation as both an exceptional teacher and a promising scholar. His accomplishments ultimately led to his appointment to the University of Bordeaux in 1887, as head of both Social Science and Pedagogy (Education). This post was created especially for Durkheim, who was seen by the education ministry as someone who could create a French social science to rival that which was already flourishing in the German university system (Lukes, 1973:95). His joint involvements, in both social science and pedagogy at Bordeaux in a sense foretold two of his ultimate contributions to French intellectual life: first, as the pioneering figure in the establishment of sociology as a recognized and legitimate field of study and, second, as an active participant in the movement to reshape and modernize the overall system of French education.

THE BORDEAUX PERIOD

Durkheim's time at Bordeaux was an unusually rewarding period, both personally and professionally. He married and settled down to what has been portrayed as a very happy and secure family life. His wife was an important source of support for Durkheim, as a homemaker, as a mother to their two children, and as a collaborator and editor in some of Durkheim's research and writing (Lukes, 1973:99). In the fifteen years he spent at Bordeaux, Durkheim also produced many of his most famous and important works. These include *The Division of Labour in Society*, which was the subject of his doctoral thesis, as well as *The Rules of Sociological Method* and his sociological analysis of *Suicide*. At this time, Durkheim also established the *Année Sociologique*, an annual review of French sociology that soon became the most influential publication of its kind in the country.

Although Durkheim is sometimes viewed as a remote academic, isolated from the conflicts and contentious issues of his day, there is considerable evidence to the contrary. First of all, beginning with his years at Bordeaux, Durkheim showed in his published writings a clear willingness to engage in heated debate or polemical exchange with other leading intellectuals. Many of his contemporaries disagreed fundamentally with his theories and with his promotion of sociology as the discipline best suited to analyzing such diverse concerns as religion, education, suicide, and crime (cf. Lukes, 1973:296, 307, 318–19, 359). Second, although it is true that the pursuit of social or political causes was not a major preoccupation for Durkheim, there are several instances where he was actively involved in the controversial events of his time. The best example from the Bordeaux period was Durkheim's support of the movement to exonerate Alfred Dreyfus, a French army officer of Alsatian Jewish background who had been falsely accused but twice convicted of being a spy for Germany. Durkheim was one of the first academics to speak out and to organize on Dreyfus's behalf; this was characteristic of Durkheim because of his concern with the threat to individual rights and freedoms posed by the case (cf. Lukes, 1973:333, 343, 347). The Dreyfus affair dragged on for many years and was not settled until his eventual acquittal in 1906. At various points throughout this period, Durkheim was among those who showed a readiness and ability to confront powerful adversaries, including right-wing and often anti-Semitic elements within the military, the judiciary, the intelligentsia, and the Catholic Church.

DURKHEIM AT THE SORBONNE

It was almost inevitable that Durkheim's growing reputation as a scholar led, in 1902, to his being called to Paris and the Sorbonne, France's elite university. Durkheim lived out the rest of his life there, as one of the most eminent and formidable figures in French academia.

Not long after moving to the Sorbonne, Durkheim was named Professor of the Science of Education and, later, by special decree of the ministry of education, was made chair in the Science of Education and Sociology (Coser, 1977:147). Just as he had done at Bordeaux, then, Durkheim occupied a dual academic posting that allowed him both to promote sociology as the new science of humanity and to foster important changes in the French education system (Lukes, 1973:409; Coser, 1977:148). Durkheim for several years taught compulsory courses in moral education to many of France's future teachers and also introduced sociology into the French school curriculum (Lukes, 1973:364, 379).

The subject of sociology became increasingly popular and influential in France during the early 1900s, so much so that church leaders and other traditional segments of society feared that the sociological perspective, as presented by Durkheim and his disciples, would come to dominate the minds of an entire generation of French youth. Especially worrisome was Durkheim's secular, nonreligious approach to understanding human values and his apparent preference for the state over the church as the instrument of moral education in modern times (Lukes, 1973:374–75). Durkheim's contention that the growing division of labour in industrial societies would ultimately replace traditional religious beliefs as the main source of social solidarity was also distressing to more conservative thinkers.

While such concerns for the power of sociology were undoubtedly exaggerated, there is little question that this period was a triumphant one for Durkheim's new science of society. Unfortunately, this lively and burgeoning intellectual climate was tragically and irreparably cut short with the outbreak of World War I in 1914. As patriotic as ever, Durkheim immediately turned from his own work to devote most of his energy to the war effort, primarily as an organizer and a researcher for committees publishing studies and other documents on the war (Lukes, 1973:549). Many of Durkheim's most gifted and promising students, including his son, André, enlisted in the military and paid a heavy price for the French cause. Hundreds would be killed before the war finally ended in 1918, among them over half of one graduating class (Peyre, 1960:17; Lukes, 1973:548). For Durkheim, the greatest loss came in April of 1916, when he learned of his son's death on the Bulgarian front. It appears that this personal tragedy was a blow from which Durkheim never recovered. He took great pains to hide his grief and remain busy with his work (Lukes, 1973:558). However, his health steadily deteriorated until late in 1916, when he suffered a stroke. After some brief improvement in his condition, Durkheim's heart gave way, and in November 1917 he died, at the age of 59.

In spite of this unfortunate and untimely end, Durkheim's legacy to sociology has been a rich one. In the remainder of this chapter, we will examine some of this wealth of ideas, particularly those that provide insight into the nature and bases of social inequality. Our initial focus will be on Durkheim's conception of social solidarity and its sources in both early and modern societies. We then consider his views on social inequality, with specific reference to his analysis of the division of labour, the role of the contemporary state, and the special problems posed by the economy. In the concluding sections, we consider Durkheim's views on inequality in future societies and compare some of his projections with those of Marx and Weber.

Durkheim and Social Solidarity

We have already noted that Durkheim's major concern throughout most of his work is with the manner in which societal cohesion or solidarity is made possible. In *The Division of Labour in Society*, Durkheim puts forth his central thesis on social solidarity in human societies. Durkheim's idea of social solidarity suggests an image of society as a set of interconnected groups and individuals, interacting with one another in regular, patterned, and more or less predictable ways. Essential to this interaction is *morality*, or moral regulation, by which Durkheim means the set of rules or norms that guide and govern human conduct. The existence of these guidelines means that individuals interact in accordance with their obligations to others and to society as a whole. In doing so, each person also receives some recognition of his or her own rights and contributions within the collectivity. Morality in this sense is "strictly necessary" for solidarity between people to occur; without morality, "societies cannot exist" (Durkheim, 1893:51). One of Durkheim's prime concerns is to determine how the forces providing morality, and hence solidarity, have changed as society has moved from early forms to modern capitalism (cf. Giddens, 1971:106).

One of Durkheim's essential arguments is that social solidarity stems historically from two sources, one of which prevails in early societies and the second of which predominates in the modern era.

EARLY SOCIETIES AND MECHANICAL SOLIDARITY

Early societies are held together by a "mechanical" or automatic solidarity, a union based on the "likeness" or similarity of people

(Durkheim, 1893:70). Such societies are really aggregations of families or other subunits having certain characteristics in common. These subunits have a structural resemblance to one another, being for the most part economically self-sufficient and capable of providing for their own production and consumption needs. This similarity by itself is not enough to maintain solidarity, since subunits can survive in isolation from one another. In addition, however, early peoples also share a "collective consciousness" (in French, *conscience collective*), a "totality of beliefs and sentiments common to average citizens" (Durkheim, 1893:79). The moral rules necessary for social solidarity in early times are represented in this body of beliefs and sentiments. They provide the social glue that binds together what otherwise would be independent, self-sustaining subgroups. The set of common values is generated within the collectivity and evolves with it over a considerable time, during which adherents presumably come to agree on its central precepts, while dissidents either convert or are excluded.

The collective consciousness, which touches all spheres of life in early societies, finds its principal repository in religion. Early religion embodies not just purely religious beliefs but also a "confused mass" of ideas regarding "law," the "principles of political organization," even "science" (Durkheim, 1893:135). The connection between religion and law is particularly significant for Durkheim. In fact, he believes law is "essentially religious in its origin," representing customs and beliefs similar to those in the collective consciousness, but in a more organized and precise fashion (Durkheim, 1893:65, 92, 110). This link between law and religion is illustrated in the ancient practice of having priests serve as judges and in the medieval concept of the divine right of kings, which granted political and legal powers to monarchs as God's representatives on earth.

In Durkheim's view, then, legal, or *juridical*, rules gradually develop out of the collective consciousness, especially through the influence of religious beliefs. If there is a close correspondence between these legal rules and the collective consciousness, we then have a moral society, one in which individuals acknowledge one another and interact smoothly. However, Durkheim clearly realizes that the formal legal system is not always moral or just. In the course of social change, laws may not change accordingly, making them inappropriate, unjust, and contrary to genuinely moral regulation. Such laws may be maintained only through habit, artificial manipulation, or force (Durkheim, 1893:65, 107–8). Thus, Durkheim recognizes that societies must and will change and that a healthy, or *normal*, society is one in which the regulations that provide the basis for solidarity are suited to the historical period in question.

MODERN SOCIETIES AND ORGANIC SOLIDARITY

The transition of social life from early times to the era of modern capitalism entails fundamental modifications in structural arrangements and, hence, in the form of social solidarity. The old mechanical solidarity, based on likeness and a common set of beliefs and sentiments, is assailed on all sides, most importantly by the expanding division of labour. Here Durkheim reveals that, like Marx and Weber, he perceives the division of labour as a crucial force in the historical evolution of social structures. In contrast to early societies, where subunits resemble one another both in their economic self-sufficiency and in their common belief system, modern societies comprise individuals who tend to be quite dissimilar, engaged in specialized tasks and activities in their daily lives, and guided by distinct norms and values in their personal conduct.

In such a situation, it is difficult to maintain solidarity through the collective consciousness, because a "personal consciousness," with an emphasis on individual distinctiveness, increasingly comes to the forefront in people's minds (Durkheim, 1893:167). This is not to say that the collective consciousness disappears altogether; however, the common beliefs it entails gradually become "very general and indeterminate," acting more as maxims or credos than as detailed guides for conduct (Durkheim, 1893:172). Hence, the collective consciousness provides some integrative force in modern society, but of a vague and general sort. Now "each individual is more and more acquiring his own way of thinking and acting, and submits less completely to the common corporate opinion" (Durkheim, 1893:137, 152, 172).

The weakening of the collective consciousness is paralleled in the declining influence of religious beliefs. Whereas religion "pervades everything" in early society, in the modern era it "tends to embrace a smaller and smaller portion of social life" (Durkheim, 1893:169). Now societies are far more specialized, no longer composed of self-sufficient subgroups but rather of subunits that perform specific "functions" that, taken together, contribute to society's existence (Durkheim, 1893:49). This development of special structures fulfilling particular functions is also evident in the decreasing role of religion: "Little by little, political, economic, and scientific functions free themselves from the religious function, constitute themselves apart, and take on a more and more acknowledged temporal character" (Durkheim, 1893:169). In addition, of course, tasks within each of these special structures or spheres of activity are themselves divided and specialized, producing the complex network of individual positions and roles that is modern society (cf. Durkheim, 1893:40).

It is worth noting here that Durkheim does not mourn the passing of early societies or the decline of the collective consciousness. On the contrary, he views the growing division of labour and specialization of functions as normal aspects of modern life. The new emphasis on individualism and personal distinctiveness in modern societies is also a normal development, something wholly compatible with, even necessary to, the expanding division of labour. Durkheim believes that this "cult" of the individual personality is here to stay and is a positive development, as long as individual goals and interests do not override collective interests or endanger social solidarity (Durkheim, 1893:172, 400). What is needed is some new integrative force to replace the declining collective consciousness — a force that can "come in to take the place of that which has gone" (Durkheim, 1893:173). Otherwise, the individualism of modern life will degenerate into blatant self-interest, or *egoism* — a phenomenon that is destructive of both morality and social solidarity (cf. Giddens, 1986:11, 13).

Durkheim's principal contention in *The Division of Labour in Society,* and one of the most clever twists in his analysis, is that the division of labour is both the main cause for the weakening of the old mechanical solidarity and the key means by which the new form of solidarity emerges. In Durkheim's terms, the function of the division of labour is to provide solidarity on the basis of *dis*similarity, on the fact that highly specialized individuals and subgroups are no longer self-sufficient, but must co-operate and depend on one another for survival (Durkheim, 1893:228). Durkheim calls this form of solidarity "organic" because it portrays modern society as similar in key ways to an advanced biological organism, "a system of different organs, each of which has a special role, and which are themselves formed of differentiated parts" (Durkheim, 1893:181, 190–93).

In addition to providing cohesion through this exchange of interdependent services and functions, "the division of labor produces solidarity . . . because it creates among men an entire system of rights and duties which link them together in a durable way" (Durkheim, 1893:406). Increasingly over time, these rights and duties become established in formal laws because their number and complexity necessitate systematic codification. As noted earlier, Durkheim believes formal law originates with religious beliefs and gradually takes over from religion the task of moral regulation as society evolves. This takeover, however, is never complete. Moral rules, in "a multitude of cases" continue to be based on uncodified and nonlegal precepts, on "usage," "custom," or "unwritten rules" that complement and fill in the gaps left by legal rules (Durkheim, 1893:147, 215).

The nature of these moral and juridical guides for conduct and interaction also changes gradually as society develops. In the past, their prime purpose was to defend and reaffirm the collective consciousness, the common set of beliefs in traditional society. Now, however, they become a complex system of mutual obligations, rights, and duties, which, in ideal circumstances, provide for smooth interaction between individuals, the "pacific and regular concourse of divided functions" (Durkheim, 1893:406).

Durkheim on Social Inequality

At this point, the reader may have the impression that Durkheim's portrayal of modern society is an unrealistically positive one. If social structures are tending toward a new organic solidarity in which people co-operate and depend on one another in a network of rights and obligations, how is it that other analysts perceive so many social problems? What of Marx's concern with class conflict and worker oppression, or Weber's fear of injustice and servitude through bureaucratic domination?

Some critics might suspect Durkheim of ignoring these problems or of considering them unimportant. However, a closer reading of Durkheim reveals his awareness of and interest in such issues. It is true that Durkheim discusses these problems primarily with reference to their effects on social solidarity, which is always his main concern. Nevertheless, his observations provide evidence that he has a clear conception of the nature and consequences of social inequality, one that shows some surprising parallels with the conceptions of both Marx and Weber. We cannot consider Durkheim's views in all their detail, but several key elements should be briefly examined. These include his distinction between the normal division of labour and its *anomic* and *forced* variants, the role of the state as the moral guardian of modern society, the special problem of the economy and the emergence of *occupational groups*, and the prospects for social solidarity and social inequality in future societies.

THE DIVISION OF LABOUR
The Normal Form

When Durkheim stresses the positive functions of the division of labour for modern society, he is speaking of a division of labour that approximates the ideal or normal case. The division of labour is normal if there is genuine moral regulation guiding the interaction between people and if there is justice in the attainment of positions within it. The division of labour is moral if individuals interrelate with restraint, recognizing one another's obligations and contributions, both to other individuals and to the collectivity as a whole. The division of labour is just if each person has an equal opportunity to take on that position most appropriate to his or her capacities and interests. Violation of either of these principles produces an abnormal form of the division of labour, a structure that cannot fulfil the functions Durkheim ascribes to the normal form. Though the distinctions are sometimes blurred, insufficient morality produces an anomic division of labour, whereas insufficient justice leads to a forced division of labour (cf. Durkheim, 1893:Book 3). Let us examine each of these separately.

The Anomic Form

Whenever the division of labour fails to underline and reinforce the ties that bind us, moral deregulation, normlessness, or *anomie* can occur. Rather than producing solidarity, the anomic division of labour can promote "contrary results," a situation in which mutual contributions and obligations are denied or overlooked and a lawless, unconstrained struggle ensues (Durkheim, 1893:353). A prime example is in the economic sphere whenever capitalists and workers become set against each other, with neither side exercising moderation or compromise. The typical consequences are "industrial and commercial crises," marked by "conflict between labor and capital" such that "a sharp line is drawn between masters and workers" (Durkheim, 1893:354–55).

Here Durkheim's discussion sounds very much like Marx's analysis of class polarization in capitalism. Like Marx, Durkheim observes the increasing concentration of capitalist ownership in a few hands, with the result that "enterprises have become a great deal more concentrated than numerous" (Durkheim, 1893:354). This concentration only accentuates the division between owners and workers and makes it even more difficult to build a system based on mutual respect, trust, and moral regulation between classes. The difference between Marx and Durkheim here is that Marx believes such problems are basic to any capitalist division of labour and any class structure. Durkheim, however, believes that class polarization of this sort occurs because the division of labour in this case is anomic — an abnormal form that requires adjustment.

Before proceeding, we should note another interesting parallel between Marxian theory and Durkheim's anomic division of labour. This parallel concerns the working conditions faced by the proletariat in capitalism. We have seen that Marx perceived the capitalist division of labour as a prime cause of alienation in the working class. In a similar way, using similar imagery, Durkheim describes how the anomic division of labour degrades the individual worker, "making him a machine," "an inert piece of machinery" that performs "routine" tasks "with monotonous regularity," "without being interested in them and without understanding them" (Durkheim, 1893:371).

The key difference here between Marx and Durkheim is, again, that Marx apparently believes any division of labour has such consequences, whereas Durkheim identifies this "debasement of human nature" only with the abnormal, anomic division of labour, a system that is itself debased and divested of its moral character (Durkheim, 1893:371). For Durkheim, the solution is not the elimination of the division of labour, which he believes is indispensable to the operation of modern society. Instead, it is essential that each of us perform our roles in the division of labour as best we can, keeping in mind our obligations to our fellows and to society. Not all of us will have equally important parts to play, but such equality is not necessary as long as each person has a sense of obligation and of contribution, a sense that one's labour tends "towards an end that he conceives" and a feeling that one "is serving something" (Durkheim, 1893:372). Moreover, it is not essential that each of us have a similarly broad perspective of how things work. A person "need not embrace vast portions of the social horizon; it is sufficient that he perceive enough of it to understand that his actions have an aim beyond themselves" (Durkheim, 1893:373). These additional elements will alleviate the anomic aspects of the division of labour that have plagued modern capitalism, particularly within the working class.

The Forced Form

The eradication of anomie through moral regulation is for Durkheim basic to any good society. However, regulation alone will not eliminate all the abnormalities that threaten social solidarity. As Durkheim notes, "it is not sufficient that there be rules," for "sometimes the rules themselves are the cause of evil" (Durkheim, 1893:374). This point relates to Durkheim's earlier discussion of the possible lack of correspondence between formal laws or rules and true morality. Rules may exist that are no longer appropriate to the time but are retained because they serve the special interests of those in a position to keep them in operation through force, manipulation, or an appeal to tradition (Durkheim, 1893:65, 107–8).

It is the application of such inappropriate and unjust rules that characterizes the second abnormal division of labour, which Durkheim calls the *forced* form. In modern society, a key basis for morality and social solidarity is the flourishing of individualism, "the free unfolding of the social force that each carries in himself" (Durkheim, 1893:377). A normal division of labour is one in which one's real self, including one's special "aptitudes" and "natural talents," is allowed to develop (Durkheim, 1893:375). Under such a system, people will find their appropriate places in society, thereby satisfying their own desires while at the same time maximizing their ability to fulfil society's needs. However, under the forced division of labour, people in positions of power act out of self-interest, or egoism, implementing rules that protect their favoured positions and that constrain others in roles that are unsuitable and unfair given their abilities and interests. This forced situation still provides a degree of solidarity, but "only an imperfect and troubled solidarity," threatened by strain and eventual collapse (Durkheim, 1893:376). In such a system, the good of society and of most individual citizens is subordinated to the selfish ends of a few.

Here again we can discern significant parallels between Durkheim and Marx. It will be recalled that Marx viewed the division of labour between owners and workers as the basis for an inherent struggle in capitalism, one that occasionally erupts into open conflict but that usually lies below the surface of everyday life. Similarly, Durkheim sees the forced division of labour as conducive to a sustained struggle between classes. It is most obvious in "class-wars," wherein the "lower classes" seek to change the role imposed upon them "from custom or by law," to "dispossess" the ruling class, and to redress "the manner in which labor is distributed" (Durkheim, 1893:374). Typically, however, the struggle is less open, for "the working classes are not really satisfied with the conditions under which they live, but very often accept them only as constrained or forced, since they have not the means to change them" (Durkheim, 1893:356).

It is apparent from these statements that Durkheim's version of functionalism is neither an apology for nor a defence of the existing economic and political arrangements in capitalist society. As long as the division of labour contains these forced elements, through which the powerful employ "express violence" or indirect "shackle," we have an externally imposed structure in which neither the individual nor society is properly served (Durkheim, 1893:377, 380). Such "external inequality" must be eliminated because it "compromises organic sol- idarity" and therefore threatens the very existence of contemporary society (Durkheim, 1893:379). If this elimination means open conflict in some cases, then so be it. The worst injustice in that event would be "the making of conflict itself impossible and refusing to admit the right of combat" (Durkheim, 1893:378). Such statements by Durkheim illustrate, as noted earlier, that he generally held liberal-democratic political views and was not the conservative thinker that some have suggested (see also Lukes, 1973:271; Giddens, 1986:23).

THE ROLE OF THE STATE

Having just noted Durkheim's acceptance of conflict as one means to produce progressive change, we should also acknowledge that his decided preference is for more peaceful solutions. In Durkheim's view, the most serious problems of anomie and forced inequality can be eliminated, or at least reduced, without such radical actions as full-scale revolution or the utter destruction of capitalism (cf. Durkheim, 1896:204). On this point, then, Durkheim and Marx tend to differ.

But what are Durkheim's suggestions for dealing with these abnormal features of modern society? Both anomie and forced inequality are problems over rules, the former a result of insufficient regulation and the latter a consequence of unfair regulation. Hence, Durkheim seeks an initial answer by considering the structure in which most rules and laws are generated and administered: the political system, or state. We discussed earlier the tremendous growth in the number and complexity of rules that accompany the expanding division of labour, and how these rules are increasingly codified as formal laws. The state is in effect the structural embodiment of this modern, sophisticated system of "administrative law" (Durkheim, 1893:219). Durkheim's discussion here has a strong resemblance to Weber's. Like Weber, Durkheim identifies the state as the "central organ" of modern society, expanding, differentiating, taking on a wide range of duties and a "multitude of functions": administering "justice," "educating the young," and managing such diverse services as "public health," "public aid," "transport and communication," and "the military" (Durkheim, 1893:221–22; Durkheim, 1896:43; cf. Weber, 1922:655, 905, 908–9).

It is logical that this state apparatus, which creates and implements the formal rules of conduct in all of these spheres, should also be the key structure for ensuring that these rules are moral and just. The appropriate values of individualism, responsibility, fair play, and mutual obligation can be affirmed through the policies instituted by the state in all these fields. Thus, for example, citizens may be socialized by the education system, the communications media, and so on, to embrace moral precepts and to regulate their behaviour toward others accordingly. Under normal conditions, state leaders will serve as moral examples for the population, underscoring "the spirit of the whole and the sentiment of common solidarity" in their own conduct (Durkheim, 1893:361–62, 227).

Inevitably, of course, not every individual will adopt the moral code. In those presumably rare instances in which criminal or other elements act against the collective interest, the state has the final recourse of physical coercion, through the police or military, with which to exact compliance (cf. Durkheim, 1893:222–23).

THE STATE, THE ECONOMY, AND THE OCCUPATIONAL GROUPS

Interestingly, there is one essential function in society that Durkheim believes cannot be infringed on by the state, and that is the economy. The economy is an exception because it has become so sophisticated and complex under the advanced division of labour that only economic specialists can operate it, people who can deal with the "practical problems" that "arise from a multitude of detail" — problems that "only those very close to the problems know about" (Durkheim, 1893:360). State leaders can remind economic leaders of their moral obligations to society and can moderate excesses or correct abuses in some cases. However, for the most part, the impact of state leaders on economic life is "vague" and "intermittent" (Durkheim, 1893:216, 222, 360-61). The specific everyday operation of the economy "escapes their competence and their action" (Durkheim, 1902:5). Elsewhere Durkheim implies that this situation could change in the future. The growth of economic centralization and big industry, a recent development in Durkheim's time, could provide conditions necessary for state intervention in the economy, if the state apparatus were itself sufficiently developed and sophisticated to take on the task (Durkheim, 1896:42-43). However, barring this uncertain development, the state cannot intercede in industrial or commercial activities in a detailed way "without paralyzing them" and impeding their "vital" function (Durkheim, 1893:239).

This exclusion of the state's moral safeguards from the economic sphere poses serious problems for Durkheim and threatens the prospects for a normal division of labour. For how can we alleviate social injustice and social strife when the economic structure is exempt from moral constraint? How is it possible to eliminate forced inequality and class conflict when the main arena in which such struggles are fought cannot be regulated?

Durkheim's proposed solution to this dilemma is a system of "professional groupings," or "occupational groups" (Durkheim, 1896:203; Durkheim, 1902:28-29). The exact nature of these organizations is not certain, but they are clearly not unions or occupational associations in the usual sense. That is, their role is not to promote the special interests of particular trades or professions; rather, they are to foster the general interest of society at a level that most citizens can understand and accept (Durkheim, 1902:10). The modern state has become "too remote" in many cases, "too external and intermittent to penetrate deeply into individual consciences" (Durkheim, 1902:28). However, the occupational groups are situated between the state and the individual, making them capable of affirming in a more immediate fashion those moral principles that the state can foster in only a general and abstract way.

Their special position means that the occupational groups are also particularly suited to dealing with the problem of moral regulation in the economic sphere. Unlike the state agencies, the occupational groups are able to understand the workings of the economy, because they are a part of it. Thus, they can appreciate the problems of business leaders and individual workers alike. They can therefore play a pivotal intermediate role, impressing on both owners and workers the need to act with moderation and mutual respect in their dealings with each other. The overall effect should be a morally regulated economy, a normal division of labour, and a reduction of class conflict (cf. Durkheim, 1902:10, 14, 31).

FUTURE SOCIETY

It is apparent from the preceding discussion that Durkheim is generally optimistic about the society of the future. His goal of social solidarity based on morality and justice can be accomplished, he believes, provided the capitalist division of labour is adapted to rid itself of anomie, egoism, class conflict, and forced inequality.

In part, Durkheim expects that these abnormalities will be alleviated by the natural evolution of the division of labour. The division of labour, in his view, is already responsible for easing similar problems in traditional feudal and caste societies. Those "prejudices" that once gave favoured rank to people merely because of aristocratic lineage or ascribed religious superiority have gradually been "obliterated" by the division of labour and its need for special, individual talents (Durkheim, 1893:379).

In much the same way, the "special faculties" required for filling important positions in modern capitalism make it increasingly difficult to obtain these positions solely through inherited class privilege (Durkheim, 1893:312). To be sure, some inheritance does still occur and unfairly restricts those who are deserving but are born "bereft of fortune" (Durkheim, 1893:378). Nevertheless, the growing popular sentiment is for the end of such external inequality. People have come to believe that inequality should not arise from any outside force but instead should reflect differences in individual "merits" — the talents and efforts each person contributes in the service of society (Durkheim, 1893:379, 407–8).

The belief in external equality, in what might be called equal opportunity, is so widespread that it "cannot be a pure illusion but must express, in confused fashion, some aspect of reality" (Durkheim, 1893:379). Of course, the agencies of society should not remain passive while this trend emerges but should actively encourage it. The state, in particular, should institute policies that promote external equality. One key means for doing so is to abolish the inheritance of wealth and property. Economic justice, based on "just contract" between free individuals and a "just distribution of social goods," cannot occur "as long as there are rich and poor at birth" (Durkheim, 1902:29; Durkheim, 1893:388). In addition, Durkheim suggests that various kinds of social welfare may be provided to "lighten the burden of the workers," to "narrow the distance separating the two classes," and to "decrease the inequality" (Durkheim, 1896:57).

Such measures, in Durkheim's view, are important if we are to achieve a normal division of labour, one that is free of forced, external inequalities and capable of promoting the solidarity he so fervently seeks. Nevertheless, economic justice alone is not enough. In fact, we may even endanger social solidarity if we become too preoccupied with such issues. That is, even if our future society is one in which "men enter into life in a state of perfect economic equality," we have other, more crucial concerns that cannot be ignored. These are the more pervasive "problems of the environment" — not just our rights within the economic sphere but also our important "duties toward each other, toward the community, etc." (Durkheim, 1902:30).

To harbour an excessive concern with the distribution of economic rewards is to mistake "the secondary for the essential" (Durkheim, 1896:57). Such a concern puts priority on individual interests rather than on the collective good and one's obligations to society as a whole. Here again we see the prime significance that Durkheim attaches to moral regulation of all citizens, by all citizens, and for all citizens. If true morality is heeded, the issue of economic justice will tend to be resolved along with society's other problems. If, however, the concern over economic matters takes precedence, individualism will deteriorate into egoism and self-interest, human desires for gain or power will override moral power, and the "law of the strongest" will be the only law (Durkheim, 1902:3; Durkheim, 1896:57, 199–200). Durkheim's perspective on freedom is particularly significant in this regard. Freedom is *not* the absence of constraint, of moral and legal rules in the economic and other realms: "Quite on the contrary, liberty . . . is itself the product of regulation. I can be free only to the extent that others are forbidden to profit from their physical, economic, or other superiority to the detriment of my liberty. But only rules can prevent [such] abuses of power" (Durkheim, 1902:3; cf. Peyre, 1960:21).

Durkheim's projections and proposals concerning the nature of future society reveal some important similarities to, and equally important differences from, the projections of both Marx and Weber. In the concluding sections on Durkheim, we will consider some of these major points and their significance for the analysis of social inequality.

DURKHEIM AND MARX

There are several aspects of Durkheim's discussion that, on the surface at least, sound intriguingly Marxian. In particular, a comparison of his normal division of labour with Marx's transitional stage of socialism reveals some noteworthy parallels: the elimination of property inheritance, though not of all property ownership; the removal of unequal opportunity from the division of labour, though not necessarily of unequal rewards and positions; and the expansion of the state's role as administrator of social services and guardian of the collective good (cf. Marx and Engels, 1848:94; Marx, 1875:8–9).

Of course, these broad similarities cannot mask certain differences between the two men's views. Marx's future society, even the temporary socialist phase, takes us much further from contemporary capitalism than does Durkheim's normal division of labour. Despite the existence in Marx's socialism of a state administration, unequal rewards, and some private property, the impact of such structures and processes is supposed to be curtailed to a much greater extent than in Durkheim's projected society. Moreover, even these vestiges of capitalist society and the bourgeois consciousness will disappear, for Marx, when we move beyond transitional socialism into true communism. In contrast, Durkheim clearly is less concerned that capitalism be radically restructured. The current system may take on quasi-socialist elements, but primarily through gradual modification and adjustment: "It is not a matter of putting a completely new society in the place of the existing one, but of adapting the latter to the new social conditions" (Durkheim, 1896:204). Besides, in the last analysis, it is not the precise nature of the economic system, but rather the problem of social solidarity, that is Durkheim's primary concern.

It is interesting that, even on this last point, Marx and Durkheim are again somewhat similar. Both writers desire a society of united individuals, where people interact in a spirit of mutual responsibility, contributing in their own way to the collective interest. Both also believe that problems such as the *distribution* of rewards and resources to individuals can be solved if the social *relations* between people are first geared toward the general well-being of society and all its members. Thus, both theorists really embrace the same primary goal of social solidarity and remain hopeful that it will be achieved. Their disagreement concerns mainly the means or preconditions for its achievement. Whereas Durkheim expects that the collective good can be achieved within capitalism, Marx believes it can never be attained without capitalism's prior demise. Hence, as one analyst has observed, Marxism "finds Durkheimian theory much to its taste *after* the revolution" (Parkin, 1979:180).

But an even more basic disagreement arises from their assumptions about human nature. Durkheim's hopes for the good society are always tempered by his conviction that humanity, though not inherently evil, does require the prior constraint of moral regulation to keep egoistic desires in check: "Human passions stop only before a moral power they respect" (Durkheim, 1902:3, 15). Otherwise, in the struggle between egoism and individualism, "the two beings within us," egoism will win out (Durkheim, quoted in Giddens, 1986:11). For Marx, however, the problem is almost the reverse; that is, structural constraints, at least within capitalist society, are the greatest threats to the general well-being of people. Left to develop freely, human nature is essentially good, social, and oriented to the collectivity. It is the removal of unjust constraint through the overthrow of capitalism that will permit this natural condition of humanity eventually to emerge.

DURKHEIM, WEBER, AND THE PROBLEM OF POWER

Any attempt to compare Durkheim and Weber on the subject of social inequality eventually leads to the problem of power. One basic similarity between the two writers is that Durkheim, like Weber, perceives modern society primarily as a pluralist power system, one in which there are several distinct substructures possessing distinct powers and jurisdictions. While this pluralism is not often explicit in Durkheim's work, it may be inferred from at least two points discussed earlier.

First, there is Durkheim's delineation of the several interdependent functions in the modern division of labour. The economic, political, religious, and other functions correspond to the various substructures that compose society, each with its own sphere of influence and duties to discharge.

The second indication of pluralism in Durkheim's analysis is his expectation that certain occupational groups will emerge in future society. These groups will have their own special roles, mediating between the state and individual citizens and arbitrating economic problems, all in the general interest. Moreover, as separate public organizations, they will have powers that are independent both of private economic interests and of state control (Durkheim, 1896:203-4; Durkheim, 1902:7-8). Hence, they would add to the diversity of power bases in modern times, providing some protection against abuses of power, especially by those controlling the state and the economy.

If there is one important difference between Durkheim and Weber on the question of power, it concerns the disposition of the state, or political structure. Like Weber, Durkheim recognizes the increased role of the state in modern life because of the expansion over time of legal rules and the attendant growth of a state apparatus to create and administer these regulations in a wide range of activities. Nevertheless, a crucial divergence between the two writers is Durkheim's relative unconcern with what is Weber's greatest fear: domination and oppression by the state bureaucracy. Here Durkheim resembles Marx somewhat, for both assume that state leaders, under the proper conditions, will be administrators pure and simple, acting out of the same selfless regard for the collectivity as other citizens and posing no threat to democracy or freedom.

For Weber, however, the good will of state bureaucrats cannot be assumed. Those in a legal position to protect the general interest can, instead, use their position to the detriment of the general interest. Like Weber, Durkheim no doubt hoped that the pluralist nature of modern society would provide a set of countervailing forces to control such power abuses. Perhaps the occupational groups, for example, could serve as monitors against improper actions by the state and other structures (cf. Giddens, 1986:28). In a manner similar to that alleged for the free press or for public-interest pressure groups, they could observe wrongdoings, alert the citizenry against them, and mobilize public support to correct them.

In the end, however, Durkheim's discussion of the entire question of state power is incomplete. This is perhaps understandable, given his basic assumption that the struggle for power is not the principal process shaping social life. Such problems as class conflict and the abuse of power clearly exist, but they are really symptoms of more basic ailments caused by insufficient morality and solidarity. Durkheim maintains his conviction that the members of society are united by more than the struggle between interest groups. Interaction based purely on shared interest is inherently unstable: "Today it unites me to you; tomorrow it will make me your enemy" (Durkheim, 1893:203). Society involves more than a contested activity, with shifting alliances competing for power and rewards. If it is not more than this, society will disintegrate, for then "the state of war is continuous" (Durkheim, 1902:6).

Summary

In this chapter, our principal focus has been on the thought of Emile Durkheim. We have seen that Durkheim is keenly interested in identifying the sources of solidarity in human societies and that, in his view, the division of labour serves as the prime mechanism for providing social solidarity in modern times. Our reading of Durkheim's discussion of the division of labour and related issues also has shown that he has a clear understanding of many important concerns in the field of social inequality, including problems of class conflict, injustice, and the potential abuse of power by privileged groups in society. We noted several interesting similarities, as well as certain differences, between Durkheim's views on such questions and those put forth by Marx and Weber. In general, we have found that Durkheim's treatment of the crucial issues in social inequality is an optimistic one, as reflected in his expectation that modern societies will continue to improve and progress as long as we work on removing the various abnormalities in the division of labour as it currently exists. In the next chapter, we shall find that a subsequent school of thought, structural functionalism, not only shares Durkheim's optimism about the prospects for inequality but also argues that the inequalities that do exist in advanced societies can actually serve a positive purpose for the people who live in them.

5

Structural Functionalism and Social Inequality

"The whole social structure, the whole system
of positions, may be viewed as a legitimate
power system." *Kingsley Davis*, Human Society,
1949

Introduction

In this chapter, our task is to assess the fourth major conception of inequality that has emerged from sociological theory. This conception involves the general orientation known as *structural functionalism*. In contrast to Marxian and Weberian theory, structural functionalism is not clearly identified with any single thinker; hence, its origins are not easily traced to one source. Nevertheless, it is apparent that structural functionalism grew primarily out of a general trend toward functionalist analysis in the nineteenth century — a trend that found disciples in such diverse fields as biology, art, law, and architecture (Kallen, 1931:523–25). Among the social sciences, structural functionalism first achieved prominence in anthropology, especially in the work of Radcliffe-Brown (1922, 1935, 1948, 1952) and Malinowski (1926, 1929). Its beginnings in sociology can actually be found somewhat prior to these writers, as evidenced in some of Durkheim's early work near the turn of the century (e.g., Durkheim, 1893, 1895; cf. Lukes, 1973:138, 527–28). However, structural functionalism did not enjoy its greatest prominence until the 1940s and 1950s, with the publication of several influential works by a number of American sociologists, most notably Talcott Parsons (e.g., Parsons, 1940, 1947, 1951, 1953; see also Merton, 1949; Davis, 1949; Davis and Moore, 1945).

Because structural functionalism is a school of thought rather than a single theory, it is difficult both to define it precisely and to review its principles in a manner that everyone will accept. There are many differences in conceptual definitions and theoretical emphases within the rather broad range of writers who make up this school (cf. Alexander,

1985, 1987). As a preliminary statement, however, we can say that structural functionalism is characterized by a particular strategy of inquiry. This strategy entails the investigation of society as if it were a system of parts that are interconnected to form various *structures*, each of which fulfils some *function* for the system.

We will examine the meaning of these two terms in more detail later, but for now we can note that the concept of structure used by structural functionalists is quite similar to that implicit in the formulations of Marx, Weber, and Durkheim: an organized pattern of relationships among individuals or social positions (e.g., Parsons, 1951:21; Johnson, 1960:48; Williams, 1960:20; Levy, 1968:22). In fact, this definition of structure is at least generally akin to that used by most sociologists today (but see Lévi-Strauss, 1968; Giddens, 1979). It is the idea of function that really distinguishes structural functionalism from the rest of sociology. Unfortunately, there are certain disagreements over the precise meaning of function. In Durkheim's early view, a function is the "need" that a structure fulfils for society (Durkheim, 1893:49). Some more recent writers define function as a simple "consequence" or "result" of a particular structure's operating in a system (Parsons, 1951:21; Levy, 1968). This definition leaves unsaid whether or not the function is planned or intentional. Perhaps a more forthright approach is to treat a function as the anticipated or expected "contribution" that a structure makes to society or one of its subsystems (Fallding, 1968:77–78).

The diverse and sometimes vague meanings attached to the idea of function are a primary source of confusion and dispute between structural functionalists and their critics. In fact, this allegation of vagueness and imprecision has been applied to the whole structural-functionalist perspective. Like other grand theorists, it is argued, structural functionalists attempt to fit all social phenomena into one scheme, thereby making their analysis too abstract to be meaningful. Important details and features of society are inevitably excluded or de-emphasized, especially those things not easily explained by the perspective. Thus, in the case of structural functionalism, critics claim that very little is said about such issues as the roles of class and power in social life, the positive part that conflict can play in human interaction, and the beneficial aspects of social change (cf. Mills, 1959:35–42; Lockwood, 1956; Dahrendorf, 1958; Wrong, 1961).

Certain structural functionalists have responded to some of these criticisms in an effort to show that their framework is capable of including such concerns and of seeing beyond vaguely defined functions or general system needs (e.g., Parsons, 1966; Fallding, 1968). Nevertheless, the conviction remains among detractors that structural functionalism ignores essential features of society or pays only lip service to them. (For discussion, see Demerath and Peterson, 1967.) One of the best-known modern thinkers in the functionalist tradition has acknowledged some of the deficiencies of functionalist theory, including its implicit aversion to social instability or change and its insufficient concern with the problem of power differences (Alexander, 1985:14; Alexander, 1987:102, 107). Even so, he also notes that many opponents of functionalist theory engage in manifestly one-sided and ultimately sterile critiques (Alexander, 1987:124).

It is not our purpose in this chapter either to examine this debate in its entirety or to attempt a resolution of it. Yet the great influence that structural functionalism has had on recent social thought makes it essential that we consider the main elements of this perspective and the key criticisms they have raised. Our special concern, of course, is with what structural functionalism has to say about inequality. If the critics are correct, the exclusion of such issues as class, power, conflict, and change would make the structural-functionalist view of social inequality and its causes quite different from the other theories we have already reviewed. At the same time, however, wherever such criticisms are misrepresentations of the structural-functionalist approach, it may be possible to identify similar, or at least compatible, elements in all of these perspectives.

We begin our assessment of structural functionalism with some observations on the links between Durkheim and the modern structural-functionalist school. It will be argued that Durkheim does provide a basis for structural-functionalist sociology in certain general respects but that his conceptions of specific issues are often significantly different from the ideas espoused by current brands of structural functionalism. In the remainder of the chapter, the focus will shift to modern structural functionalism, especially the predominant version developed by Parsons (1937, 1951). This discussion will begin with a review of the basic conceptual scheme of structural functionalism. We will then assess the key criticisms of this approach, especially those concerning the concept of function. This discussion of the general orientation will set the stage for our central task: an examination of the famous structural-functionalist analysis of social inequality, especially as developed by Davis and Moore (1945) and by Parsons (1940, 1953). The important points of similarity and difference between modern structural functionalism and the theories of Marx, Weber, and Durkheim will be of special concern throughout this section of the chapter.

Durkheim and Modern Structural Functionalism

Structural functionalists claim several theorists among their ancestry, including Weber and occasionally even Marx; however, there is little doubt that Durkheim has had a more significant formative influence on modern structural functionalism than either of these two writers (cf. Parsons, 1937; Fallding, 1968:54; Fallding, 1972:94; Collins, 1985:vii–viii). In particular, the tone and emphasis in current structural-functionalist analyses suggest an image of society that generally resembles Durkheim's. Thus, for example, structural functionalists share Durkheim's conception of society as a systematic aggregation of interrelated parts, all fulfilling important tasks for the common good. Structural functionalists likewise retain Durkheim's special interest in organizing and co-ordinating these tasks in order to maximize social integration and the chances for societal survival.

In addition, structural functionalists point to some of the same forces that Durkheim stresses when discussing the integration of modern society. First, integration is aided by the functional interdependence of individual social actors engaged in their own specialized tasks. This phenomenon is similar to Durkheim's idea of solidarity through the division of labour. Second, functionalists see integration stemming from the collective acceptance by individuals of a system of specific norms or rules that guide social relationships and regulate interactions. These norms correspond to the complex set of moral and juridical rules that Durkheim believes will promote the smooth, cohesive operation of modern societies. Finally, structural functionalists argue that integration is enhanced by popular adherence to a body of common values and beliefs. Like Durkheim's collective consciousness, these values are said to pervade social life, providing at least general principles of human conduct and another means for binding society together.

Broad parallels of this sort make it apparent that the similarities between Durkheim's original work and modern structural-functionalist analysis are both noteworthy and genuine. At the same time, however, several important differences are also evident and must be kept in mind (cf. Alexander, 1985:9). While there is no single factor or person responsible for these differences, the principal cause is probably to be found in the work of Talcott Parsons.

Parsons played a pivotal role in bringing the writings of Durkheim to the attention of English-speaking, especially North American, sociologists. In his early work, *The Structure of Social Action*, Parsons attempts a reinterpretation of Durkheim, which, in combination with his views of Weber and others, he uses as a basis for his own theoretical perspective (Parsons, 1937). Much of what is now the core of structural-functionalist sociology is really Parsons's attempt to filter Durkheim, and to some extent Weber, through his own conceptual framework.

In order to grasp the essentials of contemporary structural functionalism, and in order to discern its major departures from Durkheim and its other progenitors, it is important that we briefly consider the basic conceptual scheme employed by Parsons and most subsequent structural functionalists. We will then assess how this scheme gives rise to the structural-functionalist analysis of social inequality. In the process, we will discuss the key ways in which the structural-functionalist perspective diverges from the outlooks of Durkheim, Weber, and Marx.

Structural Functionalism: The Basic Concepts

STRUCTURE

As the name suggests, structural functionalists view society as a system of social *structures*. Structures in this sense are really patterns of relationship or interaction among the various components of society — patterns that are relatively enduring because interactions occur in a regular and more or less organized way.

The structural components of society exist at several levels of generality. At the most general level is society as a whole, which may be viewed as a single, overarching structure. The second level down is a series of more specialized structures that interconnect to form society, rather like the pillars of a building or, following Durkheim, like the organs of a living organism.

Each of these second-level structures is itself characterized by further task specialization. Thus, for example, we can think of the economy as one of these second-level structures. It performs a particular task that is itself a combination of interrelated, even more specialized, tasks: extracting raw materials, such as wood or iron ore; processing these materials into goods, such as lumber or steel; using these goods to manufacture finished products, such as furniture or cars; distributing, selling, and servicing these finished products; and so on. Special economic tasks thus give rise to their own special substructures, and these, taken together, compose the overall economic structure (cf. Parsons, 1953:400).

STATUS AND ROLE

Ultimately, the decomposition of structures in this way leads to the most basic level of analysis: the individual social actor. In the structural-functionalist perspective, each individual occupies a *status* within the various structures of society. Status here does not refer to the prestige of the individual's position, but simply to the position itself. The individual occupying a status is also afforded certain rights and duties, which are the individual's *role* in that status (Williams, 1960:35–36). Thus, status and role tend to go together in what Parsons calls the "status-role bundle" (Parsons, 1951:25; Parsons, 1953:393–94).

Social structure, then, is the interconnection of statuses that results when actors perform their assigned roles in interaction with one another. Thus, when those who fill the various worker, owner, manager, and related statuses of society perform their roles, we have an economic or occupational structure. When those who are voters, legislators, government officials, and so on, fulfil their roles, we have a political structure. The same perspective can be employed to characterize the educational, religious, and other social structures that compose society. One of the unifying aspects of this image of society is that each individual may have a status and a role in all of these structures at the same time. In effect, the individual actor is plugged into numerous structures, rather like a multiple electrical outlet. A related image is to see the individual as segmented into several roles, almost like the slices of an orange (cf. Williams, 1960:517).

NORMS, VALUES, AND INSTITUTIONS

Under the label *social structure*, some structural functionalists include not only the status-role interactions but also the specific rules and general beliefs, the *norms* and *values*, that regulate these interactions (e.g., Johnson, 1960:51). A more prevalent view among structural functionalists, however, is that norms and values are not structural but *cultural*, existing in a different conceptual space that overlays social structures. In other words, norms and values are really ideas or symbols that individuals keep in mind as codes and sanctions for their interactions (cf. Parsons, 1951:327; Williams, 1960:20–30).

This disagreement over whether norms and values are structural or cultural parallels the confusion over the meaning of *superstructure* in Marxian theory, an issue discussed in Chapter 2. Just as superstructure can refer both to sets of ideas and to the structures that embody them, so too are norms and values sometimes equated with the structures that represent them. This equation occurs especially when structural functionalists speak of *institutions*, which are the most permanent, pervasive, and obligatory systems of norms and values in society (Williams, 1960:30–31; cf. Parsons, 1937:407; Parsons, 1951:39; Levy, 1968:27). There is, for example, a common tendency to equate religious institutions, the system of religious rules and beliefs, with the religious structure, the administrative apparatus that has evolved for the nominal purpose of implementing these religious beliefs. The same may be said concerning economic institutions and the economic structure, education and the educational system, or political institutions and the structure of the state (cf. Williams, 1960:517).

This rather loose equation of ideas and realities, of institutions and social structures, is sometimes a useful device, for it aids in organizing one's thinking about social arrangements. However, one must be careful to look for cases where stated values or norms and *actual* structural relations do not correspond. An example would be when a dominant value, such as equal economic opportunity in capitalism, is not served by, or is even impeded by, existing social structures.

FUNCTION

This brings us to the last key concept in structural-functionalist analysis: the idea of *function* itself. We have noted that there is a correspondence between social structures and the institutions that guide their activity. In a similar way, there is a rough correspondence between these two conceptions and the various functions of society. Thus, for example, a structural functionalist would characterize the economy in capitalism as a structure, or system of structures, operating according to a set of corresponding economic institutions, such as private-property owner-ship, in the performance of its main function — the provision of the material means of existence for society's members.

But what, precisely, is meant here by the term function? Is this the economy's intended purpose in society, as planned by some agent or leader, or is it simply an unintended consequence of economic activity? Is the provision of the material means of existence the actual contribution the economy makes to society, or is it merely the stated goal attributed to it by some people and not others? Such questions inevitably arise when the term function is used in sociology. Moreover, as noted at the start of this chapter, structural functionalists and their critics alike cannot agree on how to answer them, because of the confusion and disagreement over the definition of function. Problems are further compounded by the use of several ideas that are related to function but are somehow distinct from it, including "functional requisite," "functional prerequisite," "functional imperative," and "functional prob-lem" (cf. Merton, 1949; Aberle et al., 1950; Parsons, 1951, 1953; Johnson, 1960).

Even if it were possible, it is well beyond our purposes here to sort out the conceptual wrangles involved in the idea of function. And, in any case, most of these disagreements do not undermine at least a basic consistency in the use, if not the definition, of the term. For most structural functionalists, a function is really a *social task*, an activity that must be performed with some degree of adequacy if social groupings are to exist and to sustain their members. Among these tasks are a range of operations: socialization and education of the young, admin-istration of economic and political affairs, regulation of criminal behaviour, and so on.

Presumably, most sociologists would agree that such activities are indeed essential to any society (cf. Giddens, 1979:113–14). Hence, if a straightforward definition along these lines were to be employed consistently, there might be fewer problems with the meaning of the term function. Instead, however, the ambiguity surrounding this central concept in the structural-functionalist scheme has provoked serious suspicions regarding the intentions of structural-functionalist analysis. Among the numerous allegations that have been made, two in particular will be noted here.

First of all, some observers believe that when structural functionalists describe the tasks of society as functions, they are really promoting the view that the existing structures and institutions of society are good or ideal, functioning properly in fulfilling society's needs. The implication is that any alteration in the established arrangements must, in their terms, be *dysfunctional* — that is, disruptive of the stable operation of society. Thus, detractors believe that structural functionalists implicitly adopt an uncritical acceptance of the current social structure, sometimes combined with an outright distrust of social change.

A second key problem involving the idea of function concerns how we decide if something is functional or not. Critics argue that structural functionalists judge structures or institutions solely on the basis of whether they meet the needs of society *as a whole*. To critics, judgement on this basis alone implies that a structure or system of rules will be deemed functional as long as it fulfils some important societal task, regardless of its consequences for particular groups or individuals *within* society.

Thus, for example, an important task for society is to control crime, violence, and other forms of antisocial behaviour. Structures such as the police and the military may be in place to perform this task. However, if the people who command these structures employ policies, official or otherwise, that control crime and violence by means of strict curfews, imprisonment without trial or evidence, and so on, the social-control function may be achieved but at tremendous cost to other segments of society. These organizations and rules could become tools not only to regulate crime but also to eliminate peaceful dissent — to oppress political dissidents, racial minorities, or other legitimate factions who may not hold favour with the society's leadership. Thus, if we were to judge the functionality of a structure *only* in terms of the vague abstraction called society, these dysfunctional aspects of that structure might be ignored, unintentionally or otherwise. Moreover, it would be possible in such a circumstance to hide what are really the *special* goals and interests of certain groups, particularly those in control of the economy or the state, by representing them as society's goals or the general interest.

One important feature of these criticisms is that they result more from what structural functionalists fail to say than from what they actually say, from what they imply more than from what they explicitly advocate. This is not to argue, of course, that all the disagreements between structural functionalism and its critics are simply misunderstandings. As we shall see, there are several fundamental differences, especially in the analysis of social inequality, that seem irreconcilable. However, it *is* contended here that the concept of function in sociology has become a loaded term, detested by some and embraced by others, primarily because of the implied meanings attached to it over the years. There is nothing inherent in the concept that should provoke such feeling, especially if the term is used mainly as a synonym for social task, as discussed earlier.

It is interesting to note in this regard that some Marxist scholars have been among the strongest opponents of the concept of function as employed by the structural-functionalist school; yet there seems to be nothing intrinsic in the term that explains this opposition. In fact, both classical and contemporary Marxists have been known to use the concept of function (or *Funktion*) themselves (e.g., Marx, 1894:379; Engels, 1890a:490; Habermas, 1975; Poulantzas, 1975; Weiss, 1976; Carchedi, 1977; Wright, 1978).

We should also note that at least some structural functionalists have attempted to allay the problems raised by their critics. That is, although structural functionalists admittedly place greater stress on the importance of stability in society, some do try to incorporate a discussion of progressive social change into their scheme. In addition, some structural functionalists do not always judge the functionality of social phenomena in terms of the vaguely defined needs of society as a whole. These writers recognize that one must be explicit about who is being served or not served by particular structures and institutions in a social system (e.g., Johnson, 1960:70; Levy, 1968:25; Fallding, 1968:77–78; cf. Alexander, 1985:14).

ONLY ONE SOCIOLOGY?

As the preceding discussion reveals, the structural-functionalist conceptual scheme portrays society as a complex system of social structures that operate under the guidance of institutionalized norms and values in the performance of special, vital functions for society and its members. Although the terminologies sometimes differ, it should be apparent from the earlier analyses that Marx, Weber, and Durkheim share an interest in these same concerns: how social structures are arranged, how they are regulated or governed, and what they do for (or to) the people who live within them. In fact, it could be argued that virtually all sociologists, past and present, are involved primarily in examining these phenomena.

This very general resemblance between structural-functionalist concerns and those of other sociologists seems to be responsible for a bold claim on the part of some structural-functionalist writers: that there is only one sociology and that it is functionalist. In other words, structural functionalism is not a special version of sociology at all but rather an equivalent term for sociology itself (Davis, 1959; cf. Fallding, 1968:54–55; Fallding, 1972:93; Levy, 1968:22).

Some aspects of this assertion, on the surface, may seem plausible. To begin with, it is true that the basic sociological approach until recent years has been broadly similar to the structural-functionalist strategy. Sociologists do tend to look at society as if it were a system of interconnected parts, of individuals and groups organized in more or less regular interrelationships. Second, this apparent affinity is compounded by the fact that even structural functionalism's critics tend to voice their opposition to it using a functionalist vocabulary (cf. Giddens, 1979:60). A third point that seems to favour the structural-functionalist claim is that a generally similar strategy is used outside the social sciences (cf. Levy, 1968:22). When other scientists wish to understand how something works, they typically perceive the phenomenon in question as if it were a system of interrelated segments. The component pieces can then be separated, analyzed, and mentally reconstructed in an effort to comprehend both the parts and their interconnections. Medical science, for instance, studies the human body as a complex of cells, organs, and subsystems operating in concert to create and sustain life. Biological science examines plants and animals using similar assumptions. The sciences of physics and chemistry likewise proceed from images of chemical and physical matter as composites of elements and particles organized into a systematic whole.

However, a closer look reveals some basic flaws in the argument that structural functionalism is the universal approach in sociology or in science generally. This assertion seems, in particular, to mistake the lesser for the greater. That is, the vaguely similar strategy used by structural functionalists and other sociologists is taken to mean that all sociologists are structural functionalists, whereas it really demonstrates the simple fact that all structural functionalists are sociologists. This reversal introduces some unfortunate misrepresentations. Among structural functionalists, it can produce an unfounded self-assurance, a strong conviction that their particular view is the only one to take. As an aside, we might note that a similar conviction, that their own perspective is the only correct one, sometimes occurs in other theoretical camps as well.

An equally serious misrepresentation in this regard is one that occurs among certain critics of structural functionalism. Some critics automatically assume that any perspective that represents society as a structured system, even in very general terms, is merely another brand of structural functionalism and therefore to be completely dismissed. The point to stress here is that this assumption is just as mistaken as the structural-functionalist assumption that it is the universal approach in sociology. Both views fail to recognize that using a similar strategy of inquiry — one that amounts to sociology itself — does not amount to having the same theory of society. Using this very broad sociological strategy, it is possible to develop numerous theories for how social structures are generated, sustained, and transformed, each of which has a distinct emphasis and draws distinct conclusions. Our task is to determine which of these sociological theories is most useful, or seems most accurate, for explaining the phenomenon under investigation. There are few topics in sociology in which these distinctions between theories are more apparent or more crucial than in the analysis of social inequality. In the remainder of this chapter, we will examine the structural-functionalist approach to social inequality and assess the key ways in which this unique view can be compared with and contrasted to the theories of Marx, Weber, and Durkheim.

Structural Functionalism and Social Inequality

Because there are several variants of the general structural-functionalist perspective in sociology, it is not surprising that there are also several different ways in which structural functionalists have approached the subject of social inequality. Among these formulations, the principal versions are Parsons's early "analytical approach," which he later revised, and the better-known though less comprehensive treatment by Davis and Moore (cf. Parsons, 1940, 1953; Davis and Moore, 1945).

There is no doubt that these analyses diverge on certain points (cf. Münch, 1982:815–16). Nevertheless, the essentials of the various structural-functionalist approaches to the topic of inequality are generally similar. Thus, we will not attempt a detailed review of what, for our purposes, are minor distinctions between these formulations. Instead, we will proceed with an outline of the major themes held in common by the several structural-functionalist discussions of social inequality. In addition to noting these central themes, our second task will be to assess the key areas of similarity and dissimilarity between the modern structural-functionalist perspective on inequality and that posed by each of the three early writers we have considered — Marx, Weber, and Durkheim. Obviously, the number of possible comparisons is very large; therefore, in the interests of clarity and simplicity, only the crucial points of convergence and divergence will be highlighted. The discussion throughout is organized around three principal issues: the differing conceptions of inequality as class structure or as individual *stratification* ranking, the relative importance of consensus and conflict in generating and sustaining social inequality, and the parts played by power and authority in social hierarchies.

SOCIAL INEQUALITY: CLASS STRUCTURE OR STRATIFICATION?

The predominant strategy for studying social inequality over the years has been to focus attention on issues of class. However, as an alternative to the class perspective, researchers will sometimes use a different view, one in which society is perceived as a hierarchy composed of layers, or *strata*. In this stratification perspective, individuals are ranked along a continuum or ladder and divided into discrete categories, which are, in effect, the strata for that particular analysis.

The stratification criterion varies depending on the researcher, but in most cases it is some objective indicator of economic rank, such as income, education, or occupational level. Often researchers will attempt to combine these separate rankings into some overall hierarchy. Perhaps the most common procedure is to calculate a single score for every occupational title, based on the average income and education of those engaged in each occupation. Thus, the occupational structure is transformed into a scale of overall "socio-economic" rank (e.g., Blishen, 1967; Blau and Duncan, 1967; Blishen and McRoberts, 1976; Pineo et al., 1977; Blishen et al., 1987). Another approach is to rely on the *subjective* assessments, by representative samples of the population, of the general *social standing*, or *prestige*, of occupations. These occupational-prestige scores have also been used as indicators of the individual's overall stratification position (e.g., North and Hatt, 1947; Inkeles and Rossi, 1956; Hodge et al., 1964, 1966; Goldthorpe and Hope, 1974; Treiman, 1977).

These various forms of the stratification perspective can be quite useful for students of social inequality. To take a simple illustration, imagine that we wished to determine the degree of income inequality in society. We could proceed by ranking people according to their annual incomes, dividing them into deciles (ten strata of equal size), and then comparing the total amounts of income earned within each stratum. If we determined, for example, that the top tenth of the population receives 50 percent or more of the total and the bottom tenth earns only 1 or 2 percent, this would suggest an extremely unequal society in terms of the distribution of income.

Stratification research along these lines has been done extensively in sociology. In fact, some researchers use this approach almost exclusively; however, it is also common for the same researcher to employ a class view at certain times and a stratification view at other times, depending on the researcher's purposes or interests. Thus, for example, some Marxist scholars, despite being concerned primarily with class issues, will occasionally take a stratification perspective in their empirical investigations (e.g., Kolko, 1962; Johnson, 1979).

The structural-functionalist approach to social inequality is really a special version of this stratification perspective. Structural function-alists also conceive of inequality as a general, continuous hierarchy along which individuals can be ranked (Barber, 1957:77). In their conception, people are stratified on the basis of the various status-roles they perform in society. People tend to fulfil numerous status-roles in life, so that one's ranking is "the general resultant of many particular bases of evaluation" (Parsons, 1951:132). In most cases, however, structural functionalists focus on the status-role the individual adopts in the occupational sphere. Occupation is seen as the best single indicator of general stratification rank, partly because it correlates with many other bases of ranking, such as income and education, but mainly because it is, for most people, the "functionally significant social role" one plays in society (cf. Barber, 1957:171, 184–85).

What this approach means is that, for structural functionalists, the stratification system is really a consequence of collective *judgements* by which society (presumably, people in general) *evaluates* the wor-thiness of a person with regard to his or her importance or contribution to the collectivity (cf. Parsons, 1940:76–77; Parsons, 1953:386–87). This approach corresponds loosely with the occupational-prestige variant of the stratification perspective noted earlier, for both views stratify society in terms of a *subjective* evaluation by others of one's prime social role or status. Of course, it should be emphasized that all prestige researchers are by no means structural functionalists. Nevertheless, this idea of prestige ranking does appear to be the crucial element in structural-functionalist conceptions of stratification (e.g., Davis and Moore, 1945:242; Parsons, 1951:132; Barber, 1957:73; Johnson, 1960:469–70; Williams, 1960:97).

That structural functionalists perceive inequality in terms of one's value to society is, of course, consistent with their general viewpoint, especially their overriding concern with collective sentiments and societal needs. This concern is not in itself particularly objectionable. However, as we shall discuss later in this chapter, one may wonder whether it is possible to achieve collective agreement on which occupations are more important or worthy than others. Furthermore, if collective agreement is not possible, who makes these crucial ranking decisions?

One of the most serious weaknesses in the structural-functionalist conception of inequality as prestige stratification is that it becomes interwoven and confused with questions of class. These prestige strata — ranked categories of people with similar occupational prestige — come to be equated with the class structure. Class is then defined as "a more or less endogamous stratum consisting of families of about equal prestige" (Johnson, 1960:469; cf. Barber, 1957:73; Parsons, 1951:172). The prestige — and hence the "class status" — of all family members is judged by the occupation of the household head, who is usually the "husband-father" (Parsons, 1953:426–27).

Conceptual problems arise when the stratification and class perspectives are confused in this way, when strata are erroneously equated with classes (cf. Stolzman and Gamberg, 1974). While the two perspectives focus on similar topics, especially economic inequality, they differ in certain key respects. For one thing, a stratum, unlike the original idea of class, is not meant to be studied as if it were a real *group*, a set of people interacting with one another or having some sense of common affiliation. Of course, classes are not always real groups either, but there is at least some possibility that classes will form groups in certain circumstances. Thus, for example, a precondition for the overthrow of capitalism in Marxian theory is the development of a revolutionary working class — individuals who, in addition to their common economic position, have a common consciousness, a sense of group solidarity, and a collective will to mobilize for political and social change. In contrast, when stratification analysts examine socioeconomic ranks, income deciles, or other types of strata, these cannot be, and are not intended to be, real groups. Instead, they are statistical aggregates, categories of individuals lumped together for particular research purposes.

Second, class and stratification analysts tend to emphasize different aspects of the inequality they study. On the one hand, class analysts are interested primarily in the *relational* consequences of inequality — that is, in the domination or exploitation of one class by another and the impact of these relations on social structure or social change. Recall, for example, that Marx viewed the relationship between owners and workers in capitalism as the driving force behind social change because of the conflict inherent in this relationship between classes. On the other hand, stratification analysts typically focus on *distributive* inequalities, on the differential allocation of income, prestige, and other rewards or advantages to individuals in society (cf. Goldthorpe, 1972; Curtis and Scott, 1979; Hunter, 1986).

We shall have more to say on these issues later. For now, it is important to note only that the class and stratification perspectives differ and that the structural-functionalist approach tends to blur or ignore the difference. The failure to make this distinction is rather curious. The structural-functionalist view departs completely from Marx's classical treatment of class as defined by relationship to the means of production. Moreover, despite claims by structural functionalists of an affinity between their work and the formulations of both Weber and Durkheim, there is really very little common ground in either case. One structural-functionalist analysis explicitly argues that Weber adopts a prestige-stratum definition of class (Barber, 1957:73). However, as should be clear from Chapter 3, for Weber class is primarily an *economic* concept, related to market position and control over goods and services. In Weber's scheme, the concept closest to the structural-functionalist idea of class as prestige stratum is probably the status group. But the prestige strata in the structural-functionalist scheme are not groups, whereas Weber's status groups obviously are. Besides, Weber goes to great lengths to show that status groups and classes are *not* the same in any case, asserting the conceptual independence of economic class and status honour.

We might expect the structural-functionalist affinity with Durkheim to be very close on this issue of class and stratum, given their broad similarities in general approach, and given the conventional assumption that Durkheim's work is a prototype of modern structural functionalism. However, there are significant disparities. Presumably, Durkheim would agree with the structural-functionalist argument that, ideally, inequality arises through the differential evaluation of what individuals do in and for society. However, this individual stratification has little or no theoretical connection with the idea of class. In fact, in those relatively rare instances where Durkheim speaks of class, his remarks, as we have already seen, are rather close to Marx's and Weber's. His emphasis in discussions of class is, like theirs, on the *economic* differentiation of people, not on their differential prestige or moral worth.

Our intention in this section has been to outline the major differences between the class and stratification perspectives on inequality, especially as these relate to certain conceptual difficulties in the structural-functionalist approach. Structural functionalism's particular view of social inequality seems to comprise selected and modified elements of traditional class-based theories, which have been grafted to the more recent stratification school of social research. This attempted amalgamation has really only confused these two important, but quite separate, formulations. The failure to recognize these distinctions is a serious flaw and underscores our earlier conclusion that structural functionalism, despite its claim to the contrary, is *not* capable of subsuming all of sociology in any satisfactory and complete fashion.

CONFLICT, CONSENSUS, AND SOCIAL INEQUALITY

A second important issue to address in any discussion of structural functionalism is the debate over whether society is characterized primarily by underlying conflict and struggle or by general consensus and agreement among its members. More specifically, we need to examine whether it is mainly through conflict or through consensus that individual and group inequalities become established in social structures.

To understand the structural-functionalist position on this issue, and to compare it with the other theories we have examined, a simple strategy is to locate each approach along a continuum according to the relative importance each attaches to conflict and consensus. On such a scale, Marx probably would fall closest to the conflict end, with Weber nearby. Durkheim would be some distance away from Marx and Weber, but not at the consensus extreme. The modern structural-functionalist school would lie closest to the consensus pole. Let us briefly examine the reasoning behind each of these placements.

Marx, Weber, and Durkheim

Marx's conflict emphasis is most evident in his central premise that unequal relations of power and privilege are the products of a continuous historical struggle for control of the means of production. Although there may be extended periods of time when open social unrest does not occur, this relative stability is not a sign that there is a general consensus on the justice of existing social inequalities. In most cases, this apparent acceptance is a mere illusion and instead reflects a variety of other processes, including successful ideological manipulation of the population by the ruling class, lack of awareness in the lower classes of the causes of and remedies for their subordinate position, or simple despair in the lower classes that inequities can ever be alleviated.

Compared to Marx, Weber seems somewhat more likely to conclude that there is *some* general agreement about the justice of social inequality. To a limited extent, at least, people have conceded that bureaucratic hierarchies and other institutionalized inequalities are a fact of modern life. Nevertheless, claims of consensus should not be overstated on these grounds. First of all, to say that one accepts the inevitability of inequality is not to say that one agrees with how particular hierarchies arise. Moreover, the ultimate origins of this acceptance should not be overlooked. For Weber, from the earliest times it is the monopoly of physical force that has generated inequality and the domination of one group by another. This coercive aspect of inequality may become less obvious as societies develop and power is formally institutionalized, but the ability to force compliance from subordinates nevertheless remains a key underlying basis of social inequality.

Thus, to Weber, considerable conflict and antagonism often lie at the root of what on the surface are stable social hierarchies. Some citizens will actively embrace these existing social arrangements, but others will abide them for a mixture of quite different motives: habit, custom, fear, or a failure to discern alternatives. Such motives have little to do with a general consensus on the justice of the social order.

Moreover, even in those societies where there is evidence of harmony and agreement, social action regularly includes a struggle for advantage among opposing factions and competing interest groups.

Analysts tend to identify Durkheim more with a consensus view of society, and less with a conflict perspective, than either Marx or Weber. This view probably stems from Durkheim's concept of the collective consciousness, the commonly held values and beliefs that he perceives as a unifying force among early peoples. While there is little doubt that Durkheim is interested in such consensual aspects of society, we should not overlook the departures from consensus that he also perceives in social structures. First, we should remember that Durkheim sees the collective consciousness as necessarily weaker in modern times. To be sure, shared sentiments, such as a belief in freedom or equal opportunity, may still set a general moral tone for social action. Beyond this, however, consensus is unlikely, because the growing division of labour makes the legal and moral guides for conduct too specialized, elaborate, and complex for everyone to agree on or even comprehend.

Thus, although Durkheim envisions a just and moral future society, it will not be characterized by some thoroughgoing consensus. What accord there is will stem mainly from *differences* between people in the division of labour, coupled with the recognition by most citizens of the need for mutual co-operation, obligation, and interdependence. We should also note that for Durkheim this differentiated basis for social harmony, the normal division of labour, "is far from being on the verge of realization" (Durkheim, 1893:408). In the interim, forced inequalities and class antagonisms persist beneath the orderly facade of present-day societies, calling into question the view that social hierarchies somehow arise out of a collective consensus among the people.

Structural Functionalism

It is here that structural functionalism enters the discussion. It would be inaccurate to claim that the entire structural-functionalist school ignores the existence of conflict in its portrayal of society (see, for example, Davis, 1949; Fallding, 1968, 1972; Alexander, 1985, 1987). Nevertheless, there is little doubt that structural functionalism deals with conflict mainly as a secondary issue and that, more than any other perspective, it sees consensus as the principal foundation of social structures. On this basis, for example, Parsons disagrees with Durkheim's view that moral consensus, as reflected in collectively held beliefs, has waned in modern times. Instead, Durkheim's collective consciousness has simply changed character and is now embodied in the "ultimate value system" (Parsons, 1937:400–401). This value system is "inculcated from early childhood" into the individual personality and fundamentally shapes even those specific normative rules, rights, and duties that govern social action (Parsons, 1940:73–74).

Hence, as social structures develop, their inherent properties tend, on the whole, to be consistent with a collectively held value system. According to structural functionalism, one such inherent property of society is the existence of inequality or stratification. Stratification is a universal aspect of social life, something that has occurred in virtually all known societies (e.g., Davis and Moore, 1945:242; Davis, 1949:366; Parsons, 1951:188; Williams, 1960:88). To structural functionalists, this prevalence of inequality is evidence of its inevitability and of its acceptability, at least in principle, to social actors.

Even more important to the consensus argument is the claim that there is a high level of agreement in the population about how specific status-roles or occupations should be ranked. At times, of course, structural functionalists concede that people's judgements will not correspond perfectly (e.g., Parsons, 1953:390). Nevertheless, it is argued, consensus on stratification rankings is quite high, at least in stable, democratic societies (e.g., Parsons, 1940:71; Parsons, 1953:388; Davis and Moore, 1945:242; Williams, 1960:93).

And what of the criteria for ranking occupations? What are they, and to what extent is there general agreement on them? As discussed in the section on class versus stratification, structural functionalists envision stratification as a subjective scale of prestige, social standing, or moral evaluation. Various other factors can influence this evaluation of occupations or status-roles, including the power, possessions, or family background of incumbents (Parsons, 1940:75–76; Parsons, 1953:389–90; Davis and Moore, 1945:244–48; Barber, 1957:30–48). For the most part, though, one's worth to society is the key factor, and it is judged by two overriding concerns: the "functional importance" for society of one's occupation and the "differential scarcity" of people with the talent or training needed for its performance (Davis and Moore, 1945:243–44; cf. Davis, 1949:368; Parsons, 1953:403, 410). In other words, because such jobs as doctor or scientist are allegedly more important and harder to fill than such jobs as dishwasher or waiter, they are more highly ranked in the stratification system. Here, too, people are said to be in considerable agreement in their judgements, even for the numerous and complex set of occupations in the modern division of labour (but see Davis and Moore, 1945:244ff.).

One might ask at this point whether there is any evidence to support these allegations of consensus in the stratification rankings that people make. The most commonly cited evidence is the strong correlation (frequently above .90) that various researchers have reported among occupational-prestige rankings done by samples of respondents in different countries or at different times in the same country (e.g., Inkeles and Rossi, 1956; Barber, 1957:105–6; Lipset and Bendix, 1963:14; Hodge et al., 1966; Treiman, 1977).

However, we should note that these results have been criticized on methodological and statistical grounds. For one thing, researchers derive prestige scales by combining the disparate ratings of a sample of respondents, thereby averaging out significant disagreements among respondents in their ratings of some occupations (e.g., Guppy, 1981, 1982; Nosanchuk, 1972; Stehr, 1974; Coxon and Jones, 1978; for debate, see Balkwell et al., 1982; Hodge et al., 1982). Thus, it appears that the high correlations between such scales really mask considerable dissensus in the popular evaluation of status-roles. Therefore, while it is unlikely that the observed correlations are totally the result of such measurement problems, it is also unlikely that, beyond certain obvious distinctions, there exists a general stratification scale that most people will agree on (cf. Parsons, 1940:86).

Before concluding our discussion of conflict and consensus, we should consider one additional point. Let us imagine, for the sake of argument, that there *is* a consensus on the way occupations rank with respect to prestige, moral evaluation, functional importance, or scarcity. We might still wonder why this scale should also give rise to other inequalities — for example, in access to such material advantages as income, wealth, or property. That is, is it not possible that the rewards of prestige and recognition for service to the collectivity might be sufficient distinction for the deserving, thus eliminating the need for material and other inequalities (cf. Tumin, 1953)? The response to this question varies somewhat, depending on which structural functionalist one consults. On the whole, however, the structural-functionalist view is that material inequalities *will* occur and that, in stable societies at least, these differences *should* correspond generally to the scale of evaluation.

This view stems from a particular conception of human nature and motivation (cf. Wrong, 1959:774; Wesolowski, 1966). The structural-functionalist assumption here is that most social actors are oriented to the good of the collectivity, but also to their own "self-interested elements of motivation" (Parsons, 1940:73; Davis, 1953). Stratification serves the function of satisfying both these needs, one collective and one individual, at the same time. However, this is so only if the material and evaluative hierarchies tend to correspond. According to Davis and Moore (1945:244), unequal material rewards motivate the best qualified and most talented to take on those positions that are the toughest, most important, and hardest to fill. Any distribution of economic rewards not based on one's contribution and worth to society will only act as a disincentive to an efficient division of labour, especially because it will discourage rare and able people from assuming the sacrifices and responsibilities of high office (cf. Parsons, 1953:404–5). Note again the implicit assumption of consensus here, this time about the perceived justice of unequal rewards for service and the injustice of alternatives. Especially in Western societies like the United States or Canada, these inequalities are seen as consistent with popularly held beliefs in such values as efficiency, freedom, achievement, and equal opportunity (e.g., Parsons, 1953:395–96; Williams, 1960:415–70).

In the end, however, structural functionalists believe that people see these material incentives and economic rewards as of secondary priority anyway, at least in comparison with the primary rewards of prestige and recognition from others. Wealth, while important in its own right, really has a *symbolic* meaning as an index of achievement and high evaluation in society (Parsons, 1940:83; Parsons, 1953:404–5; Barber, 1957:44). The idea that the distribution of economic advantages is really secondary to recognition for one's contribution to society sounds vaguely like Marx's view that distributive issues will be relatively unimportant in the popular mood that prevails under true communism. Even more, however, this idea resembles Durkheim's image of society under the normal division of labour. In that hypothetical system, there will be an interplay of individual competition for rewards and group co-operation for collective ends. Thus, self-interest exists but is restrained and harnessed for the good of all. Although it involves some exaggeration, one could almost conclude that structural functionalists in North America see Durkheim's future society as an imminent occurrence. The normal division of labour, with equal opportunity and rewards based on merit and contribution, seems to have gone from a nineteenth-century hope to an emerging twentieth-century reality (cf. Parsons, 1953:433–39).

THE CONCEPTION OF POWER IN STRUCTURAL FUNCTIONALISM

So far, we have found that structural functionalists see social inequality as a stratified hierarchy of individual status-roles, ranked primarily by their value, in most people's minds, to society. Individuals compete for access to the higher of these status-roles because of the greater prestige they carry and, secondarily, because of the greater material and other rewards they offer. At least in democratic societies, this competition for rank is relatively open, because people have a reasonable opportunity to excel at what they do best. Such an arrangement is functional in that it ultimately serves both the individual's need to achieve and society's need to have vital positions filled by the most competent and qualified persons. In addition, the resulting stratification system also serves an *integrative* function, by mapping out where people fit in society and by providing a systematic pattern of norms for interaction with others (e.g., Parsons, 1940:73).

But what is to ensure that people either accept where they fit in this structure or agree to the normative rules of the game that place them there? In particular, what is to stop certain individuals or groups from wresting away rewards belonging to others, usurping privileges not rightfully theirs, or otherwise forcing their will on the collectivity? This question really comes down to the role of power in social structures. In this final section, we will examine the approach taken by structural functionalists to the concept of power and the implications it has for their views on social inequality.

Power and the Problem of Social Order

Structural functionalists certainly discuss the idea of power, although their treatments tend to be rather brief and incidental to other issues (cf. Alexander, 1987:107). It is typical of structural functionalists to tie the concept of power directly to the fundamental question noted above: how do we maintain societal stability in the face of internal factions who might disrupt the social structure for their own ends? This so-called *problem of social order* is, in particular, an overriding concern for Parsons, who consistently raises it in his own writings and who attributes a similar preoccupation to Durkheim as well (e.g., Parsons, 1937:89, 307 fn., 314–15, 402–3; Parsons, 1951:36–37, 118–19; cf. Giddens, 1971:106).

The general conclusion reached by Parsons and other structural functionalists is that, apart from isolated incidents, the use of coercive power cannot be the means by which social order is attained, because force itself can only breed disruption and disorder in the end (e.g., Parsons, 1966:246). Thus, to understand how stable societies exist, we must look for the source of social order elsewhere.

According to structural functionalism, social order arises mainly from legitimate and generally accepted bases of social control (e.g., Parsons, 1953:418). A key process here is socialization, whereby most people learn and adopt a set of prescribed rules and norms that permit orderly, mutually beneficial social interaction. This point, of course, relates to the structural-functionalist emphasis on popular consensus discussed earlier in this chapter. The crucial item to stress here is that these rules and norms are obeyed, in the structural-functionalist view, not out of fear of coercion or punishment by those in power, but primarily because the populace is instilled with the need or obligation to do what is right and to eschew what is not (cf. Parsons, 1940:74). Hence, the use of force in stable societies is rare because of the pronounced feeling among the people that both their rules and their rulers are essentially legitimate.

Power and Authority

This sense that legitimacy is the ultimate basis of social order is reflected in structural functionalism's conception of power. On the surface, most structural functionalists appear to employ Weber's classical definition of power: the capacity to exercise one's will, even in the face of opposition (e.g., Parsons, 1966:240; Johnson, 1960:62; Davis, 1949:94–95; cf. Weber, 1922:53). Typically, however, structural functionalists then draw a key distinction. *Power* does not in fact refer to all such instances of exercising one's will despite resistance, but only to those instances that are "illegitimate" or "not institutionally sanctioned." The term *authority* is reserved for those situations where power is legitimate, institutionally recognized, or supported by "social consensus" (Parsons, 1940:76; Parsons, 1953:391–92; Parsons, 1966:240, 249; Barber, 1957:234; Williams, 1960:96). Thus, for example, the government in a democracy exercises authority when it collects property tax, provided that taxation is legally under its jurisdiction; however, the government is exercising power if it seizes a portion of one's property without recourse to legal statutes or some popular mandate.

This distinction between power and authority may seem reasonable enough. But, unfortunately, the tendency is for structural functionalists to believe that the concepts of power and authority exhaust all the situations in which some people hold sway over others. Thus, except for transitory cases of open, illegitimate coercion (power), most social relations are based on legitimate influence (authority), since subordinates must harbour some degree of acceptance if they regularly obey their superiors. Yet such a broad view of what constitutes authority clearly subsumes a wide range of instances in which people obey others out of habit, custom, self-interest, a lack of real or perceived alternatives, and so on. While these situations do not entail coercive power, neither are they examples of truly legitimate control (cf. Habermas, 1975:96). Structural functionalists thus tend to blur important differences in both the intent and the meaning of the influence operating in these cases. It is notable that this failure to acknowledge fully the wide range of situations in which neither power nor authority operates parallels a similar failure, noted earlier in this chapter, to appreciate completely the wide range of situations that involve neither open conflict nor general consensus.

Authority versus Domination

This tendency to emphasize the existence of authority, rather than other forms of influence, in social hierarchies is sometimes presented by structural functionalists as if it were consistent with Weberian theory. However, it is obvious from our discussion in Chapter 3 that this is not the case. The key difference between the structural-functionalist conception and Weber's analysis is that Weber does make an explicit distinction between authority, or genuinely *legitimate* domination, and other forms of domination based on habit, self-interest, and the like.

The failure of structural functionalists and others to discern this crucial difference probably stems from Parsons, whose early translation of Weber's German works incorrectly treats domination (*Herrschaft*) and authority (*legitime Herrschaft*) as equivalent terms (cf. Weber, 1922: 62 ff., 299 ff.; Giddens, 1971:156; Alexander, 1983:20–21).

These concerns over translation and terminology may seem like minor quibbles, but in fact they lead to fundamental difficulties in the way structural functionalists conceive of power and domination in social hierarchies. Of course, we should remind ourselves again that we are dealing with a school of thought, and that not all writers in this school are the same. Nonetheless, the impression given by most structural-functionalist analyses is that virtually all enduring structures of domination are basically legitimate. While this is a view that Weber would never espouse, it occurs rather consistently in structural-functionalist discussions. Thus, for example, Davis (1949:95) asserts that "the whole social structure, the whole system of positions, may be viewed as a legitimate power system." The reasoning here is that "the line of power corresponds roughly with the hierarchy of prestige" — that is, with the popularly held ranking of what are the most important positions in society (Davis, 1949:95). In other words, if the populace agrees that the most powerful positions also have the highest evaluations of importance, then the power structure is legitimate by definition.

However, the crucial question that should be raised here is one we have already noted: who decides what positions are most important and prestigious in society? The structural-functionalist assumption, as discussed earlier, is that society, or everybody in general, makes these decisions. If that were true, then the stratification system and its corresponding power structure would indeed have a legitimate and consensual basis in the popular will. But a plausible alternative is that it is largely the *people in power* who decide which positions are most important and thus most deserving of prestige and other rewards. In that event, the close correspondence among one's power, prestige, and privileges would have little to do with legitimacy or consensus but instead would flow mainly from the capacity of people in positions of domination to establish and maintain their own advantages, through force or other means.

This alternative image of power's role in social hierarchies is generally similar to the views of Weber and Marx, which we reviewed in earlier chapters. It is apparent, then, that structural functionalism departs significantly from these classical perspectives. Although some structural functionalists concede that there are coercive and nonlegit-imate aspects of power at times, there is little doubt that these factors are seen as of secondary importance for generating inequality. Power, in most cases, is not a *zero-sum* relationship wherein people struggle for scarce resources and some win only if others lose. Rather, as modern social structures continue to develop and expand their mastery of the environment, there will really be more power for everyone because of the increased opportunities to exploit and resources to control (see especially Parsons, 1966; also Parsons, 1953:436–37).

The Pluralism of Power

The last element in the structural-functionalist treatment of power that we should briefly discuss is its decidedly pluralist tone. As we have already seen, structural functionalists view modern society as a complex of structures and substructures, each of which performs important tasks for the overall system. This portrayal in itself implies a pluralist power structure, for it suggests numerous centres of jurisdiction, decision making, and control over resources (cf. Alexander, 1985:9; Alexander, 1987:102). As well, each of these structures is in some sense another stratification system, with its own distinct distribution of powers and responsibilities to groups or individuals (e.g., Parsons, 1940:86–87; Davis and Moore, 1945:244 ff.). Thus, while we may speak of "the total 'power' system of a society," it is really made up of multiple components, "a plurality of other systems" that, when co-ordinated, ensure that societal problems are solved and goals achieved (Parsons, 1953:388–89). Moreover, none of these structures by itself is seen as having "monolithic" or "paramount" control. The overall effect is a "separation of powers" so that no one interest group or elite has a "monopoly of influence" (Barber, 1957:241–42; Parsons, 1953:418, 426).

For the individuals and subgroups of society, this pluralism means a great deal of opportunity for mobility into positions of value and authority. If, for example, an individual has little or no power in the political sphere, he or she nonetheless may attain high rank and influence in one or more of the economic, religious, or other substructures. Thus, the overall effect, both on the stratification system and the pattern of power, is considerable "openness," "looseness," and "dispersion" (Parsons, 1940:86–87; Parsons, 1953:407, 430–32).

This portrayal of the modern power structure as fluid and open is of course entirely consistent with the other central tenets of the structural-functionalist perspective we have outlined in this chapter. Equally clear are its departures from Marx's formulation. For Marx, the apparent dispersal of power in modern societies is largely a superstructural illusion, masking the underlying economic basis for all social domination.

The view of power among structural functionalists may seem vaguely similar to Weber's pluralist analysis. Even here, however, Weber's case for the multiple bases of power in society is different, because he sees the dispersion of power as more limited. Moreover, Weber retains a concern over the very real possibility that the domination of social life may eventually be centralized in a massive, omnipotent state bureaucracy. Structural functionalists do not seem to acknowledge the threat that state centralization poses for pluralism, at least with respect to capitalist liberal democracies such as the United States or Canada. It is only with respect to totalitarian societies such as the Soviet Union or Nazi Germany that this threat is identified (cf. Parsons, 1953:407, 418; Barber, 1957:241–42). It is probably no surprise that structural functionalism has achieved its greatest following and its best-known proponents in Western capitalist countries, especially the United States (cf. Wrong, 1959). In these societies, the dominant belief system tends to accept social inequality as legitimate and normal as long as it results from equal opportunity, individual performance, and an absence of coercive power (cf. Alexander, 1987:102, 140).

Thus, we see once again that the structural functionalist view of modern democratic societies seems much closer to Durkheim's vision of the future than it does to the predictions implicit in Marx or Weber. But is the moral, just, and normal division of labour an impending reality? The more skeptical among us may wonder just how close any society, including the United States or Canada, has come to achieving such a system. This is a question that we shall raise again.

Summary

In this chapter we have taken an extensive look at the view of social inequality that has developed out of the so-called structural-functionalist school of sociological theory. In our discussion of modern structural functionalism we reviewed its major concepts and some of the key criticisms that have been levelled against it. Our central concern, however, was to examine the particular manner in which structural functionalists conceive of inequality, especially as it compares with the conceptions of Marx, Weber, and Durkheim. We found that there are significant discrepancies between the structural-functionalist approach and each of these classical writers on most points. Among the crucial differences are the tendency for structural functionalists to see inequality mainly as a matter of individual stratification rank rather than class structure; to depart widely from the classical usage of class when they employ this concept; to perceive far more consensus, and far less conflict, in the processes that lead to inequality; to play down the importance of coercive power, compared to legitimate influence, as the basis for inequality; and to see a significantly more open and equitable system of power and opportunity in present-day societies than is typical in earlier analyses.

The treatment of structural functionalism here has no doubt seemed much more critical and skeptical in tone than was evident in our assessments of the other writers. This critical stance, however, should be partly tempered by the realization that we have had to examine the sometimes diverse school of thought that constitutes structural functionalism as if it were a single, consistent approach. Because of the need to summarize and distil the ideas of so many writers, some oversimplification has been inevitable. Thus, in some instances, the criticisms apply to certain writers more than to others and should not be seen as a categorical rejection of all the ideas and analysts identified with this school. This caution is important to note because of the tendency among some critics to present a mere caricature of structural functionalism and then to dismiss it entirely. The proposal here is to avoid an outright rejection of structural functionalism, at least until we have been able to examine the key issues again. Our final judgement of the structural-functionalist viewpoint, and of the views put forth by the earlier writers as well, should first take into account the most promising recent attempts to conceptualize the problem of social inequality. A review of these efforts is the task to be addressed in the next chapter.

Chapter

6

Recent Perspectives on Social Inequality

"Class power is the cornerstone of power."
Nicos Poulantzas, State, Power, Socialism, 1978

"All social interaction involves the use of
power." *Anthony Giddens*, A Contemporary
Critique of Historical Materialism, *Volume 1, 1981*

"Class structures are the central determinant of
social power," *Erik Olin Wright*, Classes, *1985*

Introduction

We have now examined four of the principal perspectives on social inequality that have emerged from the premodern period: the classical viewpoints of Marx, Weber, and Durkheim, and the more recent structural-functionalist explanation. These views, of course, do not exhaust the theoretical analyses of inequality that we could consider. In particular, there are numerous other formulations that have come to light in recent times. Clearly, it is not possible to review and assess all of these in detail. Moreover, it can be argued that such a thoroughgoing assessment is also unnecessary, provided that we can arrive at a set of contemporary theorists who, taken together, incorporate most of the major conceptual advances to be found in the larger group of writers.

The central goal of this chapter is to conduct a selective assessment of the most promising or prominent of these newer approaches to social inequality. The writers to receive special attention here include Dahrendorf and Lenski, whose works probably are the best-known departures from structural functionalism to come out of the 1950s and 1960s; Poulantzas and Wright, who are arguably the foremost among a range of neo-Marxist thinkers who have achieved distinction in the 1970s and 1980s; and finally Parkin and Giddens, whose efforts represent the best of what has been loosely termed a neo-Weberian upsurge in the 1970s and 1980s.

Inevitably, the selection of these six writers over others is to some extent not a matter on which complete consensus is possible. First of all, these choices reflect an attempt to assess *general* theories of social inequality, rather than a desire to account for any *specific* form of social inequality in isolation from all others. Thus, for example, we will not examine in detail the particular perspectives on gender inequality or racial inequality that currently enjoy favour in sociological accounts of these important phenomena. However, it will be argued later that the general perspectives on social inequality assessed in this chapter provide us with a portrayal of social inequality that is largely consistent with, and in some cases closely corresponds to, the leading perspectives on inequality in these more specific areas. This consistency or correspondence is most apparent in the crucial role that the more specific theories of inequality assign to the concept of class and, even more so, to the concept of power or domination.

A second category of omissions includes several other general perspectives on social inequality that have not been selected for thorough review and discussion. For example, we do not consider earlier Marxists such as Lenin (1917) or Mills (1951, 1956), as well as more recent writers who have been greatly influenced by Marx, such as Wallerstein (1974, 1980), Offe (1974, 1984), and Habermas (1975, 1984), among others. In addition, a whole range of broadly Weberian or non-Marxist theorists is not given detailed consideration (e.g., Blau, 1964, 1977; Lukes, 1974, 1978; Wrong, 1979; Turner, 1984; Collins, 1985, 1986a, 1986b, 1988; Mann, 1986; Runciman, 1989).

The view taken here is that the key insights of these and other writers are, for our purposes, largely represented in the works of the six theorists that have been chosen for detailed review. On specific points, of course, reference to additional theorists will be made when necessary.

Throughout the chapter, the reader should remain alert to the key areas of similarity and dissimilarity, not only among the six selected approaches but also between them and the classical views we have already examined. Obviously, our discussion would be much too involved were we to deal with these comparisons in all their minute aspects. Hence, rather than a comprehensive exposition of all six conceptual schemes, we shall conduct a much more selective investigation, one that critically evaluates each approach but focuses almost exclusively on the four major topics that were outlined in the opening chapter. These four points include each author's stance on the concept of class or class structure; the significance of power for explaining structured inequality generally in society; the interconnection of the state with the economic and other structures of society in modern times; and the prospects for reducing or ending social inequality in the future, through socialist revolution or other means.

The six recent perspectives to be considered in this chapter, combined with the classical views already discussed, occupy a wide theoretical spectrum that, if analyzed in detail, reveals countless subtle

Figure 6.1

The Chronology of Major Theories of Inequality and Approximate
Locations on Loosely Defined Left-Right Continuum

Period of emergence or prominence:				
prior to 1900	Marx, early Marxism			
1900 to 1920		Weber	Durkheim	
				Structural
1920 to 1950				Functionalism
1950 to 1960			Dahrendorf	
1960 to 1970		Lenski		
	Poulantzas			
1970 to present	Wright	Giddens Parkin		

Left _____ **Right**

(inequality based on struggle,   (inequality based on consensus,
rooted in class or economic   has extremely pluralist roots,
power, must be changed by   provides stability and other
radical action)   benefits for society)

differences in conception and emphasis. Yet, when these perspectives are examined on a more general level of analysis, one can argue that their similarities are almost as striking as their differences. The approach taken here is to adopt a middle ground, acknowledging both the essential distinctions and interesting similarities among perspectives, while also simplifying and clarifying the presentation whenever possible. As a step in this direction, it is instructive to array the various theorists along a general continuum between two poles that, for want of more precise terms, are labelled _left_ and _right_. To take the most extreme illustration, those at the left pole see social inequality arising purely out of conflict or struggle between antagonistic groups; trace the root of inequality to the single factor of class location or control of economic power; and stress the major social problems that inequality engenders, problems that can be alleviated only through radical social change. In contrast, those at the right pole see social inequality wholly as the result of consensual interaction between individuals competing with one another according to agreed-upon rules of conduct; believe that inequality flows from an extreme plurality of factors, not from one or a few sources; and stress the positive effects of inequality, especially for societal stability and integration.

Although no theorist under scrutiny here precisely fits either of these two extreme images, we can estimate each one's _relative_ position on the continuum between the poles, as shown in Figure 6.1. Note that each writer's location on the left-right scale is cross-referenced with the approximate time of his emergence or prominence, especially in North American sociological circles. This procedure produces an interesting pattern, one that roughly resembles a *U* laid on its side.

We must avoid grand explanations for this pattern, but one way to make some sense of this apparent trend is to consider the manner in which leading intellectuals respond to the climate of the times in different historical periods. We have already discussed how Weber's work in many respects was a critical reaction to Marx, or at least to the manner in which Marx's main premises were represented by the subsequent groundswell of Marxist thinkers in the late nineteenth and early twentieth centuries. Weber's critique, which is paralleled in Durkheim's writings to some extent, was meant to be a positive, or constructive, one. However, it seems to have set in motion a much wider swing away from the left pole than Weber intended. This swing was accelerated significantly by Parsons's peculiar interpretations of Durkheim and Weber, which eliminated from these writers' works most of the affinities with Marx that we have outlined in previous chapters. The culmination of this trend was the emergence of the structural-functionalist school as the dominant force in sociological thought by the 1950s, especially in the United States.

At about this time, as was noted in Chapter 5, certain influential writers came to react against the inaccuracies they perceived in the more extreme versions of structural functionalism. Dahrendorf was one of the leading critics of what was seen as a false, utopian representation of societal harmony, stability, and consensus by the structural-functionalist school (e.g., Dahrendorf, 1958, 1959, 1968; see also Mills, 1959; Wrong, 1961). The work of Dahrendorf and others provided a catalyst that sent the pendulum swinging back again, away from the right end of the continuum and into a broad middle range of rather diverse viewpoints. Lenski is among the most notable here as someone who himself moved from a structural-functionalist stance to a "synthesizing," partly Weberian position in the 1960s (Lenski, 1966:435).

Although they differ in other respects, writers like Dahrendorf and Lenski share a desire to combine in one perspective key elements from both the left and the right poles, from Marx or Marxism on the one hand and from structural functionalism on the other. There are at least two important developments that have followed in the wake of such efforts. First of all, the changes they have stimulated seem to have come more at the expense of structural functionalism than of Marx. In other words, whereas Marx's ideas have had a continuing influence to the present day, structural functionalism has virtually abandoned the topic of social inequality, at least since the 1960s. This abandonment may be a tacit admission by structural functionalists of fundamental difficulties in their approach to inequality, or it may reflect the simple truth that, after all, the subject is of secondary concern to them and not deserving of sustained attention. Whatever the reason, structural functionalism has been largely supplanted, at least at present, as a serious alternative to Marx in the current literature on social inequality.

The second important consequence of Dahrendorf's and Lenski's work has been a revival of Weberian thought. As we shall see, their focus on power and their plural conception of class and power structures return us to some version of the Weberian perspective. Thus, the pendulum moves back to Weber and the renewal of an old rivalry: the theoretical debate between Weber and Marx. In fact, it has been argued that even now the trend of thought in the study of social inequality oscillates between these two writers, that "the all-pervasive influence of Marx and Weber . . . is, if anything, more pronounced today than at any other stage" (Parkin, 1978:601; see also Collins, 1986a:xi; Wiley, 1987:25). Generally speaking, this is the argument that will be put forth in this chapter. The ideas of Marx and Weber, especially as they have been refurbished in current debates involving Poulantzas, Wright, Parkin, and Giddens, provide the most fruitful basis for examining the general problem of inequality in modern societies.

Depending on the relative emphases of these four writers, it has been typical to classify them as either neo-Marxists or neo-Weberians, with Poulantzas and Wright in the former category and Parkin and Giddens in the latter. Such a classification is not unhelpful, provided it is applied cautiously and at a very general level of discussion. Thus, it is fair to refer to Poulantzas and Wright as neo-Marxists because they provide us with new or fresh analyses based on Marx's first principles. However, it is also the case that, with each succeeding generation, their title as *new* Marxists inevitably must be relinquished to the next cohort of Marx's followers that comes along. We should also note that these categories exhibit wide internal variations. This is well illustrated by Parkin, who readily accepts the neo-Weberian label but disagrees with several other writers to whom he gives the same title (Parkin, 1979:112; Parkin, 1972:29–33).

But probably the greatest difficulty with such simple classifications is that they do not deal precisely with those, like Giddens, who prefer to be allied with neither camp (Giddens, 1981a:296–97; Giddens, 1981b:1; Giddens, 1984:xxxvi). Certainly, although Giddens acknowledges the contributions to his thought from both classical thinkers, some of the subtler elements of his work do not stem from either Marx or Weber. And yet, at a broader level of discussion, there is justification for locating Giddens relatively near the neo-Weberian circle. As we shall see, Giddens, like Weber, is greatly concerned with offering a critical but constructive appraisal of Marx's historical materialism (see especially Giddens, 1981b, 1985). Like Weber, Giddens places considerable stress on the complexity of social inequality and the various forms it can take. Finally, like Weber, Giddens uses as his conceptual centrepiece the idea of power and its role in the structures of domination that shape social interaction in modern societies. For these reasons and others, the neo-Weberian label is not without some provisional foundation.

With this preamble, we are now in a position to review each of the six more recent perspectives on social inequality. We can begin chronologically with the work of Dahrendorf and then Lenski. The neo-Marxist views of Poulantzas and Wright will be considered next, followed by Parkin's neo-Weberian critique of their general position. Finally, Giddens's formulation, which is arguably the most inclusive of the recent perspectives, will be reviewed and assessed.

Ralf Dahrendorf

CLASS CONFLICT IN INDUSTRIAL SOCIETY

In *Class and Class Conflict in Industrial Society* (1959), Ralf Dahrendorf presents his first detailed formulation of the problem of inequality in modern societies. While his later writings also address this same issue, reaffirming many of his original ideas and modifying others, his early work still stands as his most influential and cogent theoretical statement on the nature of social inequality (see also Dahrendorf, 1979, 1988).

A central claim in Dahrendorf's analysis is that neither structural functionalism nor Marxism is adequate by itself as a perspective on society, since the former pays too little attention to the realities of social conflict, while the latter ignores the obvious evidence of consensus and integration in modern social structures (1959:122–24, 158–60). As an alternative, Dahrendorf proposes to "draw from Marx what is still useful" and to incorporate it with certain promising elements of the structural-functionalist viewpoint (1959:118). Hence Dahrendorf contends, following Marx, that conflict is still a basic fact of social life and can have positive consequences for society as a spur to progressive social change. In this way, Dahrendorf seeks to dissociate himself from those structural functionalists and others who saw an "end of ideology" during the 1950s, who proclaimed a complete end to the conflict of ideas and class interests that preoccupied Marx in the nineteenth century (e.g., Riesman et al., 1953; Bell, 1960; for discussion, see Giddens, 1973; Benson, 1978). Dahrendorf's most recent work sustains his essential argument that while we can identify "a wide consensus" in many democratic societies, there is also no question that conflict is still crucial as "a potential for progress" in most cases (Dahrendorf, 1988:xii, 111).

However, despite Dahrendorf's long-standing belief in the fruitful consequences of social conflict, his conceptual affinities with Marx remain rather minor in the end and distinguish him only partially from many of the structural functionalists he criticizes. For Dahrendorf shares with structural functionalism several fundamental ideas, including a general optimism and faith in the political and economic institutions that arose from the prosperity and stability of the post–World War II era. In fact, according to Dahrendorf, several important changes and improvements in the capitalism of Marx's age signal the emergence of a new social structure called "industrial" or "postcapitalist" society (1959:40–41). In general, postcapitalism involves a much more complex system of inequality than can be captured by the simple split between capitalists and workers, the "two great and homogeneous hostile camps with which Marx was concerned" (1959:48). It is marked, first, by a diverse class structure and, second, by a very fluid system of power relations. Moreover, it is a society in which the resolution of class conflict has been "institutionalized" — legitimately incorporated within the state and economic spheres — so that the drastic class strife of Marx's time has been made obsolete. Let us briefly consider each of these points and their relevance to Dahrendorf's views on the future of inequality in postcapitalist society.

Class Structure in Postcapitalism

Dahrendorf rejects Marx's dichotomous, two-class system because it is too simplistic to be applicable in postcapitalist society and because its stress on property ownership as the single distinguishing class characteristic has become outdated. For one thing, the capitalist class has been "decomposed" by the rise of the "joint-stock company," which separates simple ownership from actual control of economic production. Although Marx was certainly aware of this new form of business organization, owned by stockholders and run by managers or corporate executives, Dahrendorf claims that Marx underestimated how much power this arrangement would take from owners and give to executives, who may own no part of the enterprise but still make the crucial business decisions (1959:47).

A second important complication in modern class structures concerns diversification within the working class itself. Like Weber, Dahrendorf criticizes Marx's view that the proletariat will eventually become a homogeneous collection of relatively unskilled machine operators. On the contrary, there are now increasingly elaborate distinctions among workers regarding skill levels, life chances, and prestige, with a need for more, not less, skilled personnel to run and maintain the sophisticated machinery of industry. The result is "a plurality of status and skill groups whose interests often diverge" (1959:51, 277; 1988:77).

The third major factor in this pluralism of classes involves those categories of people who are neither bourgeois nor proletarian precisely but are lumped by various writers under the title "new middle class." To Dahrendorf, some of these people, including salaried white-collar employees, overlap partly with the old working class, while others, including some bureaucrats and the executives noted earlier, may have vague affinities with the old capitalist class. In both cases, however, these intermediate groupings are distinguishable in key respects from capital and labour, confirming once again that "the pleasing simplicity of Marx's view has become a nonsensical construction" (1959:57; 1988:77).

For these reasons and others, Dahrendorf contends that Marx's idea of class can be salvaged only if its entire meaning and definition are altered to reflect the changes in modern social structures. Dahrendorf thus makes an alternative proposal. Because of the separation of ownership and control, the growth of corporate and state bureaucracies, and other manifestations of complex organizational hierarchies, it is apparent that the crux of social inequality is no longer the antagonistic property relations between capital and labour, but the *authority* relations arising within a wide variety of social and organizational settings (1959:136–38). Authority relations are crucial because, while it is possible to imagine an end of inequality in property holdings or in such advantages as income and prestige, it is impossible to conceive of social organization without inequalities in authority (1959:64, 70–71, 219). Moreover, "authority is the more general social relation," with property "but one of its numerous types" (1959:137).

According to Dahrendorf, then, any useful definition of class in postcapitalist society should include the key idea of authority, and the term class relations should refer not only to the conflict between economic groupings but to *all* situations of struggle between those who have authority and those who do not. Hence, Dahrendorf explicitly defines classes as "social conflict groups," distinguished from one another by their "participation in or exclusion from the exercise of authority" (1959:138, 247; 1988:112). These conflicts are most telling within the major institutions and organizations, especially in the economic or industrial sphere and in the political structure or state. In theory, however, they can occur in any hierarchical authority structure, any "imperatively coordinated association" (1959:138–39).

Dahrendorf's redefinition of class in this manner is intriguing and, on the surface, may appear to have merit. His claims that inequalities in authority are inevitable, and that property relations are but one manifestation of such inequalities, seem difficult to deny. Indeed, most analysts, including Marx and Engels, acknowledge both of these points from time to time (e.g., Marx, 1867:300–331; Engels, 1872, 1890b:463–65).

But does the recognition that authority is an important factor in social relations justify its equation with the concept of class? Surely, the answer to this question must be no. Dahrendorf himself concedes that his proposal for defining authority relations as class relations is "pragmatic" and "reversible" (1959:201). Thirty years later, he continues to define class "without undue claims for certainty" and in a manner he admits may seem "cavalier" (1988:47, 112). However, it is difficult to maintain that such temporary or tentative attempts at defining class can serve a useful purpose for our cumulative understanding of theory in this area. Dahrendorf's class definition is inconsistent with the classical views of Marx and Weber in many instances, as well as with established usage. In addition, it has inherent logical problems, for, if every conflict over authority is a class relation, then there are an infinite number of classes, making class virtually meaningless as a concept (cf. 1988:47). As others have pointed out, Dahrendorf's definition also leads to certain ludicrous conclusions, because every confrontation over authority, even between parent and child, for example, is by definition a class conflict (cf. Giddens, 1973:73). Such difficulties are somewhat ironic, since Dahrendorf is critical of theorists who confuse the general with the specific; yet, by seeing all authority relations as class relations, instead of viewing class relations as really one crucial type of authority (or power) relation, Dahrendorf apparently commits precisely the same error himself (1959:137).

Dahrendorf on Power and Authority

It should be clear by now that Dahrendorf's general conceptions of class and inequality are closely tied to his view of authority or power. This emphasis is reminiscent of Weber, with whom Dahrendorf shares certain broad affinities. These include his pluralist view of class and power structures; his belief that authority hierarchies are inevitable in all advanced societies, capitalist or otherwise; and his interest in the growing concentration of influence within formal bureaucracies, especially in politics and industry (1959:299; 1988:25–26).

It is only when we examine Dahrendorf's actual definitions of power and authority that his differences with Weber become apparent. A curious aspect of Dahrendorf's discussion is that he claims to adopt Weber's view of power and authority but, in the end, uses a terminology that is much closer to Parsons and the structural-functionalist school. This inconsistency is most serious in his treatment of Weber's idea of domination (*Herrschaft*). Like Parsons, Dahrendorf generally treats all situations of domination, of patterned or structured power relationships, as if they were legitimate (1959:166). Thus, he fails to distinguish between authority (truly legitimate power) and those cases where subordinates give regular obedience to superiors, not out of a belief in the justice or legitimacy of the relationship, but for a variety of other reasons. At times, Dahrendorf seems to acknowledge the difference between domination and authority, but on the whole he blurs this distinction and so creates considerable confusion (1959:176; 1979:117). In his most recent writing, there is evidence that Dahrendorf now takes a more clearly Weberian position on the idea of power and has altered some of the functionalist overtones in his original conception (1988:26–27). Even so, he does not provide an explicit definition of either power or domination in his current work, so that it is difficult to judge exactly how his use of these concepts has changed, except to note that he tends now to avoid their equation with the idea of authority.

An additional difficulty with Dahrendorf's approach to power is his contention that all situations of conflict must involve two and only two contending parties (1959:126). This means that all class conflicts, and all authority or power relations, must involve a "dichotomy of positions" between those who possess power and those who are deprived of it (1959:170, 238). Such a view obviously departs from Weber, who saw power as a graded phenomenon, varying in degree within bureaucracies and other hierarchies. More important, this dichotomous view is also at odds with social reality. It is not difficult to think of illustrations that run counter to such a perception. The complex authority network of a modern corporation, comprising owners, top executives, middle managers, and salaried employees, among others, cannot be reduced to a simple set of dichotomous relations. The numerous examples of multiparty political systems, as in Canada or Great Britain, are further evidence against the claim that confrontations over power always involve only two factions. Dahrendorf's insistence on the dichotomous nature of power relations seems especially peculiar in the light of his generally pluralist view of social structures and his passing references to "gradations" of power or authority in society (1959:196; 1988:77).

The Institutionalization of Class Conflict

Unlike some of Marx's more extreme critics, Dahrendorf readily accepts that conflict is inherent to social structures and treats it as a definitive feature of all class and power relations. However, what distinguishes him from Marx, and what explains his location toward the structural-functionalist end of our left-right continuum, is Dahrendorf's special conception of modern class conflict. Although he agrees that Marx's "old class conflict is by no means fully played out," he also contends that today's class conflicts are "far removed from the ruthless and absolute class struggle visualized by Marx" (1988:45; 1959:66). Rather than violent class warfare, the contending parties in postcapitalism engage in regulated, or "institutionalized," conflict. In other words, they have "agreed on certain rules of the game and created institutions which [have] provided a framework for the routinization of the process of conflict" (1959:65, 225–27). Dahrendorf maintains the strong conviction that revolutionary conflicts are largely lamentable and "melancholy moments of history" (1988:1, 194). "To be fruitful, conflict has to be domesticated by institutions" and change should be "strategic" and reformist, not revolutionary (1988:xii, 35, 107, 174, 193).

The institutionalization of class struggle is most crucial within the economy and the various legal and political organs of the state. In the economic sphere, it is best illustrated by the spread of unionization and collective bargaining, whereby labour and management pursue their conflicting interests and resolve disputes through conciliation, mediation, or arbitration. In the legal-political sphere, institutionalized conflict is apparent in the settlement of grievances through the law courts and the negotiation of legislation and policy decisions through parliamentary debate (1959:66, 228–31). In this form, conflict is an essential force for social change, as Marx believed, but it also is an important source of coherence and unity, because of its problem-solving function (1959:206–8).

Thus, even though Dahrendorf speaks of conflict at least as much as Marx does, Dahrendorf's stress on the regulated nature and integrative function of conflict reveals that his affinities with Marx are far more tenuous than his ties to structural functionalism. Dahrendorf's closer ties to structural functionalism are evident in his very definition of conflict, which is so broad that it could include everything from outright war to friendly competition, even sports contests and games (1959:135). Such a diluted view of conflict, combined with Dahrendorf's implication that class and power relations are all somehow rooted in authority structures, leads his portrayal of social inequality in quite a different direction from Marx. Social inequality under postcapitalism is a product of the contest for advantage among conflicting interests; however, this contest occurs generally according to institutionalized regulations within both the economy and the state, and under conditions of considerable pluralism and legitimacy. The conflict or struggle that arises is more a means for keeping contemporary industrial society healthy and progressive than a cataclysmic force for the revolutionary overthrow of capitalism (1959:134).

The Future of Inequality

Given Dahrendorf's stress on the constructive and progressive nature of modern social struggle, it is not surprising that he has maintained a generally optimistic view of the future of inequality in postcapitalist society. Not only has class conflict been institutionalized, but equalities of opportunity and condition are themselves becoming part of the established institutions of society. The state has played a key role here through the implementation of public education to increase the mobility chances of the lower strata. Although complete equality of educational opportunity is still to be achieved, sufficient advances have been made that class barriers are gradually weakening and "no social stratum, group, or class can remain completely stable for more than one generation" (1959:59). The state has also acted to narrow the inequalities between top and bottom by establishing social-welfare programs and tax laws that redistribute wealth from the rich to the poor. Thus, Dahrendorf sees a continued reduction of inequality over time, since "the process of levelling social differences cannot be denied" (1959:63, 274).

Since that optimistic interlude of the 1950s, many analysts have despaired that the promised reduction of inequality will ever come true. As recently as the late 1970s, Dahrendorf was among the few observers to claim that the drive for greater equality had *not* waned (1979:128). In fact, although he expressed support for increasing equality in society, he also feared that too much equality could pose problems. In Dahrendorf's view, total equality carries with it many dangers, "for a society in which all are equal in all respects is one devoid of realistic hope and thus of incentives for progress" (1979:123). Since that time, his position has changed once again, for now he agrees with most other analysts that inequalities have become more pronounced in the contemporary period, even in such affluent nations as the United States and the countries of western Europe (1988:x, 149–50). Nonetheless, he also contends that, in the developed societies at least, "the overwhelming majority of the people have found a reasonably cosy existence" (1988:154). Moreover, while he agrees that a more equitable distribution of material wealth and "provisions" is now a higher priority than it was several decades ago, he remains consistent in arguing for the necessity of individual freedom and the hope for personal improvement which that entails, even if it means inequality of condition among citizens (1988:ix, xi, xiv, 8, 18, 73).

Ultimately, then, Dahrendorf sides once again with the structural-functionalist view of inequality, seeing it as necessary to motivate individuals to the pursuit of excellence in a free society. In the end, the real fear for the future is that totalitarian, state-socialist forms of society will predominate (1959:318). Such systems impose equality through a grey sameness that stifles progress and freedom. It is Dahrendorf's fervent belief that hope and liberty are indispensable to any just society but that "hope springs from difference rather than sameness, and liberty from inequality rather than equality" (1979:140; 1988:ix, 8).

Summary Observations

In this section, we have reviewed and evaluated the major elements in Dahrendorf's discussion of class conflict in industrial society, with special reference to his views on social inequality. It is apparent that there are some basic difficulties in Dahrendorf's conceptions of class, power, and conflict. It is also the case that many of his claims concerning the nature of inequality in modern times have had to be revised in the light of recent evidence. Nevertheless, Dahrendorf's analysis is notable as the first prominent attempt to move away from a doctrinaire structural-functionalist perspective by incorporating aspects of Marx and Weber into an alternative orientation to social inequality. The result takes us only part of the way to a more balanced or comprehensive perspective and, apart from some recent shifts to a more clearly Weberian treatment of power, does not relinquish Dahrendorf's basic structural-functionalist leanings. However, Dahrendorf's formulation, especially his original thesis on class and class conflict in the modern era, has been one of the most important stimuli for many of the approaches that we shall examine in the remainder of this chapter.

Gerhard Lenski

SOCIAL INEQUALITY AS POWER AND PRIVILEGE

The second important perspective on social inequality in the more recent literature is Lenski's analysis of *Power and Privilege* (Lenski, 1966). Rather like Dahrendorf before him, Lenski proceeds on the assumption that a comprehensive approach to social inequality must take into account the entire spectrum of views between "radicals" such as Marx on the one hand and "conservatives" like the structural functionalists on the other (cf. Wenger, 1987:45). He portrays his own formulation as an initial step toward a "synthesis of the valid insights of both the conservative and radical traditions," a stance that he readily acknowledges brings him very close to Weber (1966:17-18). The final result is a position roughly midway between the poles of our left-right continuum.

Lenski's proposed synthesis is really a selection of certain basic premises from both the left and the right, moderated and amalgamated in a generally pragmatic fashion. His overall conclusion is that some degree of social inequality is inevitable, as conservatives argue, in part because humans differ in their effort, strength, intelligence, and so on, and tend to use these favoured traits to further their own interests or those of special groups to which they belong. This does not mean that all inequalities result from differences in "natural endowment"; in fact, most do not. Neither does this mean that people are incapable of the altruism and collective orientation that Marx and other radicals have stressed. But partisan interests do normally receive first priority because of natural tendencies in human nature, and a good deal of the apparent co-operation and selflessness that radicals point to occurs more from "enlightened self-interest" or necessity than from a universalistic orientation to the common good (1966:25–32, 441–42; 1988:169–70).

Where Lenski differs markedly from the conservatives is on their insistence that such selfish tendencies in human nature can somehow produce just and legitimate social hierarchies. Thus, Lenski rejects the structural-functionalist view that most people agree on the value or prestige attached to positions in society and that this common evaluation gives rise to differences in both power and material rewards. On the contrary, Lenski argues the reverse view: that differential access to power is ultimately what determines inequalities in material privilege and that power and privilege together determine most of the prestige attached to various groups or individuals in society (1966:44–46). On this crucial point, then, radicals like Marx seem nearer the truth. They recognize that the outward stability of social structures may say little about the extent to which such structures are endorsed by the populace and may instead mask fundamental antagonisms between dominant and subordinate factions. Of course, some level of genuine legitimacy is likely to be accorded the power structure, especially by citizens of Western democratic countries; yet even here legitimacy is often far from complete, and the general acceptance of existing social hierarchies seems to result from at least two additional influences: the potential coercive force of the dominant group; and the "inertia" of custom, habit, or conventional beliefs that holds back the impetus for struggle and change (1966:32–35, 41).

It is clear, then, that Lenski considers differences in power to be the pivotal factor responsible for the structure of inequality in society. Because of this emphasis, it is preferable to begin with a review of Lenski's conception of power and then trace its influence on his discussion of class, the role of the state, and, finally, the prospects for social inequality in the future.

Power and the Multidimensional View of Inequality

It is immediately apparent that Lenski adopts a largely Weberian conception of power, though he reveals certain differences with Weber that should also be noted. Like Weber, he begins by defining power as the capacity to carry out one's will despite opposition. Following Weber, he also maintains that coercive force is "the most effective form of power." Of course, since any enduring system of domination must minimize violent upheaval, it is important that force not be used exclusively or imprudently but should "recede into the background to be used only when other techniques fail." Nevertheless, Lenski echoes Weber's position that force is the "ultimate guarantee" and "the foundation of any system of inequality" (1966:50–51).

Eventually, the factions that control the use of force try to have their power officially entrenched, or formally established, by creating or rewriting laws to protect their general interests. In modern democracies, such laws are not blatantly self-serving in most cases but, on the contrary, are frequently couched in universal terms that give them an air of popular legitimacy. Typically, for example, they not only spell out the powers of those who rule, but also specify the formal rights of subordinates. Thus, a small minority may control the political structure, but there are provisions for the mass of the population to voice their wishes or their grievances through regular elections, referenda, or other means. Still, despite this apparent two-way flow of power between the top and the bottom, the relationship is decidedly *asymmetrical*, with power running more strongly and with far greater effect from the dominant to the subordinate faction (1966:52–53, 58).

Lenski's discussion of power leads him finally to Weber's conclusion that power in modern times stems mainly from the ability to establish, and to enforce if necessary, certain special *rights* relative to others. As already noted, these rights are embedded in legal statutes for the most part, although the informal forces of custom, convention, and traditional beliefs or prejudices frequently supplement the official bases for power differences (cf. 1966:32, 89). The most prominent illustration of the legal basis for power is the formal right to private ownership of productive property. In addition, however, there are numerous examples from societies past and present of the legal establishment or denial of power for different races, sexes, religions, and so on. The supplementary influence of nonlegal conventions and prejudices is also apparent when, for example, certain racial minorities or women are excluded from positions within the ruling faction despite the removal of legal barriers.

From the foregoing discussion, it should be apparent that Lenski shares with Weber a generally pluralist view of both power and inequality. Power derives from a combination of control over coercion and access to legally or conventionally sanctioned rights. Consequently, power differences can generate a wide range of social inequalities, depending on the variety of social categories that come to be accorded or refused such rights. Thus, a fundamental feature of Lenski's approach is that inequality is *multidimensional*, involving multiple criteria for ranking groups or individuals in terms of their power and, thus, their material privilege and prestige. The exact criteria for ranking obviously vary by country and historical period but usually include such diverse bases as property ownership, occupation, education, religion, ethnicity, race, gender, and age.

In many respects, Lenski's multidimensional view is both the key contribution and the most significant difficulty in his overall approach to social inequality. Predictably, Lenski sees Weber as the pioneer of this view, although Sorokin also deserves mention (1966:18; cf. Sorokin, 1927, 1947). However, subsequent critics argue that Lenski's multiple dimensions are different from Weber's delineation of class, status, and party in several key ways (e.g., Parkin, 1972; Giddens, 1973; Hunter, 1986). In particular, Weber's scheme is not explicitly intended to represent different ways for *ranking* people in society but rather to suggest the various bases around which interest groups may coalesce in society's continual power struggle (recall Chapter 3). Another way to express this is to note that Lenski is more clearly a *stratification* theorist than is Weber and that, compared to Weber, he is more concerned with *distributive* inequalities in material and other rewards than with the *relations* between groups that underlie this distribution (1966:2–3, 84–86).

Nevertheless, despite Lenski's apparent confusion of these points, the one undeniable similarity between his multiple dimensions and Weber's ideas of class, status, and party is that they are all derivative from the central concept of power. This makes it possible to conceive of both distributive and relational inequalities in terms of one key idea. It also suggests that our understanding of virtually all social hierarchies, whether they refer to class, race, gender, or any other social criterion, can be tied to the analysis of power, of access to enforceable rights. Whether these multiple forms of inequality are labelled *dimensions* or some other term is, in a sense, immaterial. The important and useful aspect of Lenski's approach is precisely his recognition that such multiple forms exist and that, in one way or another, they are manifestations of power. This modified version of Weber's conception takes us significantly closer than earlier analyses to a *general* strategy for conceiving of social inequality.

Lenski on Class Structure

The one real difficulty with Lenski's multidimensional perspective concerns his conception of class and class structure. At times, his discussion is not unlike Weber's once again, for Lenski visualizes a pluralist class structure, composed of a dominant propertied class, a subordinate working class, and a range of middle classes, as typical of capitalist countries like the United States. If there is a notable difference from Weber at all here, it is Lenski's tendency to be, like Dahrendorf, more convinced of the reduction of class inequality and the dispersion of wealth in modern society (1966:308, 338–82).

Unfortunately, rather than confine his use of the term class to these standard economic concerns and treat class as one of the multiple dimensions of inequality, Lenski introduces confusion by labelling all such dimensions as different types of class systems. In other words, he perceives "property classes," "educational classes," "ethnic classes," "religious classes," and so on, as constitutive of the overall class system (1966:74–82). This strategy is oddly similar to Dahrendorf's view of class, since all power structures come to be defined as class structures, leading to a proliferation of different "classes" in society. Use of this terminology confounds class with power and renders the class concept meaningless. The saving factor here is that we can expunge this weakness from Lenski's approach without abandoning its useful elements.

The Role of the State

Given Lenski's focus on law and the formal institution of power, it is not surprising that, like Weber once again, he places considerable stress on the role of the state in modern systems of inequality. It is the state and its agencies that are responsible for creating, administering, and occasionally imposing by force the laws and formal rights that give power to some and not others. Because of this key role, and because of "the tremendous increase in the functions performed by the state," one might expect that the state's leaders would be central players in the overall power structure. In fact, Lenski does concur with Weber that power has been increasingly concentrated in the government, especially its growing bureaucracies; moreover, he also seems well aware that a dominant economic elite is typically able to turn the power of the state to its advantage on most key issues (1966:304, 310, 342).

And yet, in the end, Lenski is more optimistic than Weber that the cage of state bureaucratic control can be escaped at the same time that exploitation by the ruling class is reduced. To Lenski, the complexities of modern society, and the consequent intervention of the state into numerous spheres of life, have led to a greater, not a lesser, dispersion of power. The elaborate machinery of government has itself created diverse centres of jurisdiction and administration. Of course, the economic elite, as well as other dominant factions or interest groups in the ethnic, racial, gender, religious, and other hierarchies of society, may continue to gain disproportionate advantages from these agencies and the laws they uphold. But there is a limit beyond which such concentration of privilege cannot proceed without provoking public outcry, and it is the state structure itself that is now the key vehicle in this process. The people can oppose the policies of the ruling factions and resolve their own internal disputes through the state government, since it "has become the object of a never ending struggle between a variety of organized groups which, in their totality, represent the special interests of most of the population" (1966:314–18).

Here Lenski seems to share Dahrendorf's confidence that the power struggle can be legitimately institutionalized and acted out, not so much *by* the state as *through* the state, with government a "mere switchboard of authority" (Dahrendorf, 1959:306). We shall encounter this image of the state again in subsequent sections of this chapter.

The Future of Social Inequality

As one might expect, Lenski's projections concerning the future suggest a guarded optimism, the same middle course that characterizes his overall analysis. Lenski devotes much of his discussion to an investigation of the historical trend of inequality. His central conclusion is that social inequality has tended to increase since primitive times but that there is reason to believe the trend is now reversing with the rise of advanced industrial societies. Among the many factors contributing to this alleged reversal are significant improvements in technology, which have made possible a vast increase in surplus wealth, and the spread of democratic ideas, which have captured the imagination of most people. These and other developments make it possible to redistribute both privilege and power to more and more citizens in the modern era (1966:308–17, 428–30; see also Lenski and Nolan, 1984).

Such positive expectations sound in some ways like Dahrendorf's favourable predictions for postcapitalist society. However, Lenski's views are tempered by his conservative assumptions about humanity and social organization, which make the complete elimination of inequalities in power and privilege unlikely in *any* society. Lenski retains his conviction that social rankings are to some degree inevitable because of people's "natural tendency to maximize their personal resources" at the expense of others. In addition, hierarchies seem unavoidable given the importance of co-ordinated decisions in complex social structures and the differences in power or authority that result. Ultimately, then, the reduction of political and economic inequality should continue in the long term but "will stop substantially short of the egalitarian ideal in which power and privilege are shared equally by all members of society." In Lenski's opinion, radical thinkers who see socialism as the path to complete equality are destined to be disappointed (1966:327, 345; cf. 1980:10).

Summary Observations

Our purpose in this portion of the chapter has been to review Lenski's perspective on social inequality as the relationship between power and privilege. Despite certain difficulties in his conception of class, a weakness he shares with Dahrendorf, Lenski's attempted synthesis of radical and conservative views provides some important insights. In particular, his multidimensional strategy suggests an initial means for thinking about social inequality as a generalized phenomenon, a process that is critical for understanding class relations but that arises and endures in numerous other forms as well. Moreover, in stressing that the differential power to enforce rights is the common thread linking all these manifestations of inequality, Lenski achieves a significant advance over Dahrendorf and his contemporaries. As we move through the remainder of this chapter, the importance of Lenski's contribution should become increasingly evident.

Recent Marxist Views

NICOS POULANTZAS

In the century since Marx's death, there have been countless attempts by Marxist scholars to build on the ideas expressed in his extensive, but largely unfinished, writings. Debates continue to arise over which of these attempts represent the best or most promising efforts at reorienting or redirecting Marxian theory in recent years (e.g., Przeworski, 1985; Elster, 1985; Wood, 1986; for reviews, see Therborn, 1986; Levine and Lembcke, 1987; Burris, 1987). However, while not all observers will concur, many argue that the most significant of these recent discussions have primarily been those that connect in some way to Althusser, a Marxist philosopher who has questioned the simplistic readings of Marx by certain early Marxists (cf. Althusser, 1969, 1976; Althusser and Balibar, 1970). Within sociology, Poulantzas and Wright, whose works will be reviewed in the next two sections of this chapter, have been the most successful in applying a broadly similar interpretation (see also Hindess and Hirst, 1975, 1977; Carchedi, 1977, 1987).

Although Poulantzas died in 1979, many contend that the power of his thought endures. He has been described as "the single most influential Marxist political theorist of the post-war period" (Jessop, 1982:153; see also Jessop, 1985:6). His theoretical contributions are said to signify a "turn of the intellectual tide," a "paradigm shift" in the analysis of class structure (Therborn, 1986:97).

Like Althusser, Poulantzas is notable for rejecting the dogmatic economic determinism of some other Marxists, those who completely reduce social analysis to an investigation of capitalist relations of production. While this issue is crucial, in Poulantzas's view there are other forces operating within society that must be grasped if the Marxist goal of revolution is to be realized. Moreover, Poulantzas argues, it is clear that "Marxism alone cannot explain everything," that the decisive role it plays in explaining social processes can still be enhanced by other valid insights (Poulantzas, 1978:23).

With this in mind, Poulantzas seeks to supplement and redirect the traditional Marxist treatment of class, the capitalist state, and several other topics of import for the study of social inequality. Despite certain obscurities and inconsistencies in Poulantzas's formulation, it is instructive to review and evaluate his attempt to accommodate the complications in modern systems of inequality with the essentials of Marx's original analysis. As with the other theorists we have considered, our review will focus on four principal concerns: the concept of class or class structure; the meaning and significance of power in social hierarchies; the role of the state, especially in capitalist society; and the prospects for inequality in the future, with particular reference to the transition to socialism.

Classes in Contemporary Capitalism

Like most recent Marxists, Poulantzas conceives of class primarily as a set of "places" in a structure, although he sometimes uses class to refer to the "men" or "social agents" who fill these places (Poulantzas, 1973b:27; Poulantzas, 1975:14, 203). The distinction between classes as people and classes as structured locations is roughly paralleled in the structural-functionalist insistence that stratification refers mainly to the ranked status-roles individuals occupy rather than to the individuals themselves (Davis and Moore, 1945). While such a distinction is artificial, to Poulantzas and others it is seen as crucial for demonstrating that the *distribution* of people into classes is really a separate problem from the more pressing issue of how the structured *relations* between class locations are generated in the first place. For, even if we could imagine a capitalist society where people have an equal chance to move up or down the class structure, this mobility would do nothing to alter the structure itself or the exploitative relations built into it (Poulantzas, 1975:33).

In any case, both the class places of capitalism and the people within them are defined principally by their location in the productive, or economic, sphere. In addition, however, Poulantzas maintains along with Althusser that both Marx and his more discerning followers recognize how *political* and *ideological* forces can simultaneously act with the central economic factor in the formation of classes. The simultaneous nature of economic, political, and ideological influences on class structure is important to stress here if one is to avoid fruitless "chicken-and-egg" debates over whether the political and ideological superstructures are "caused" by the economic infrastructure or vice versa (recall Chapters 2 and 3). To Poulantzas, it is important to retain

Marx's discovery that economic forces are decisive "in the last analysis" for shaping classes and the other structural relations within capitalism, but such a view is far different from the vulgar Marxist stance that the political and ideological systems operate in perfect co-ordination with the economic and are automatically and completely determined by it (1975:14, 25; 1978:26).

In delimiting the class structure, then, Poulantzas begins with the standard Marxist claim that there are two basic classes in advanced capitalism, the bourgeoisie and the proletariat, and these are divided primarily by their economic relationship, by the fact that the bourgeoisie exploits the productive labour of the proletariat for profit. But the class structure is also sustained over time by political and ideological processes. Like most Marxists, Poulantzas generally identifies the bourgeoisie's political control with the governing and coercive power of the state and sees its ideological influence operating in the religious, educational, and other structures of society. As well, though, Poulantzas uses these two terms in less conventional ways: bourgeois political control is also embedded in the economic system, in the "politics of the workplace" created by capitalist rights of supervision and discipline over labour; bourgeois ideological control is likewise present on the job, in its monopoly of scientific ideas and technical knowledge, which deprives most workers of the means of "mental" production. Poulantzas perceives in Marx's writings this same wider sense of what political and ideological control mean and how these forms of bourgeois domination conjoin with economic relations to reinforce, perpetuate, or "reproduce" the essential class dichotomy (1975:227–36; cf. Marx, 1867:331, 361).

Having affirmed the Marxist view that the essential split between capitalists and workers is not blurred but rather highlighted by political and ideological forces, Poulantzas nevertheless notes that political and ideological factors can act to generate secondary splits *within* the two major classes, in the form of "fractions" or "strata" (1975:23, 198). In the working class, for example, internal fragmentation can arise from skill differences that ultimately cede "political" supervisory power and "ideological" control of special information to a distinct fraction of skilled labourers within the proletariat (1975:15, 245). Even in the bourgeoisie such political and ideological disunities can occur, for, despite their common interest in exploiting the working class, large-, medium-, and small-scale capitalists, as well as industrial, commercial, and finance capitalists, often break ranks because of differences in political clout, policy preferences, or ideological commitment to such beliefs as free enterprise versus monopolistic efficiency. Such divisive tendencies can breed competitive or even antagonistic relations within capital, calling into question "the mythic image of the bourgeoisie as an integrated totality" (1975:139; 1978:143–44). This is not to deny the truth of Marx's two-class system, but to attack any simplistic representations of it.

Still, there is one aspect of Poulantzas's discussion of class fractions that has raised some questions about the dichotomous view of class and caused some controversy with other recent Marxists. Poulantzas identifies various class places near the boundary between bourgeoisie and proletariat that do not fall clearly into either class because they resemble the bourgeoisie on some political, ideological, and economic criteria but resemble the proletariat on others. In the end, he subsumes these intermediate locations under Marx's term the *petty bourgeoisie* to signify that they are, in a sense, linked to the bourgeoisie but play a petty or marginal role relative to this class. This designation does not completely solve the problem of classifying these positions, since they are themselves a heterogeneous mix, fragmented by political, ideological, and economic differentiation. Hence, out of this melange Poulantzas identifies two major subcategories: the "old," or "traditional," petty bourgeoisie, a declining category of independent owners and craftspeople that both Marx and Weber refer to; and the "new" petty bourgeoisie, a growing array of technicians, supervisors, salaried "white-collar" employees, and "tertiary" wage earners (1975:193, 208, 285–89).

It is Poulantzas's designation of a new petty bourgeoisie in advanced capitalism that has generated much of the debate over his work, both inside and outside Marxist circles. His new petty bourgeoisie represents a significant departure from other Marxists, most of whom treat such positions as working class because their occupants are both propertyless and dependent on the capitalists for wages (e.g., Mills, 1951; Braverman, 1974). Poulantzas concedes this dependence to some extent and notes that the new petty bourgeoisie, like the proletariat, is exploited by the capitalist class; nevertheless, the supervisors, engineers, and other segments of the new petty bourgeoisie share considerable political and ideological ties with the capitalists because of their control over workers in the productive setting and their grasp of technical knowledge and expertise denied to the proletariat. Their provisional resemblance to the bourgeoisie is further enhanced by their economic function, which produces no surplus value in Poulantzas's view and is paid for out of the surplus generated by the proletariat. In other words, they share with the capitalist class the bourgeois trait of being "unproductive" (1975:210–16, 235–50).

Other Marxists remain unconvinced by Poulantzas's distinction between productive and unproductive activities because so many class locations are mixtures of both, and because it is not clear that technical knowledge and supervision are irrelevant to the creation of surplus. Besides, all such activities are proletarian to the extent that they place their occupants in a situation of exploitation by capitalist employers. The most distressing aspect of Poulantzas's scheme, for Marxist thinkers, is that his new petty bourgeoisie would form the largest single segment of the class structure and leave a comparatively small and insignificant working class to fight for the overthrow of capitalism (e.g., Wright, 1978:46–53; Wood, 1986:42). Poulantzas himself sees in this no threat to revolutionary action, since the new petty bourgeoisie is likely to increase its proletarian allegiances and weaken its ties to capital with time (1978:242–44).

Poulantzas's overall portrayal of the capitalist class structure nevertheless raises difficulties for any Marxist sympathetic to his analysis. This is primarily because, in the end, Poulantzas comes surprisingly close to an essentially Weberian viewpoint. Like Weber, he wishes to acknowledge both the essential truth of Marx's two-class model and the intricacies that are overlooked if it is taken too literally. Like Weber, he is also faced with an infinite number of classes if he draws all the political, ideological, and economic distinctions possible within each class. Finally, like Weber, he ultimately settles on four key categories: the bourgeoisie, the proletariat, the traditional petty bourgeoisie of small owners, and the new petty bourgeoisie of salaried white-collar, technical, and supervisory personnel (recall Chapter 3). The principal difference, of course, is that Poulantzas rejects Weber's treatment of these latter two categories as distinct *middle classes* in their own right, for this would contradict the basic Marxist precept that there are only two principal classes in advanced capitalism (1975:196–99, 297).

Poulantzas on Power

It has been typical of Marxist discussions to avoid any detailed attempt to conceptualize the notion of power, perhaps because Marx himself devoted little effort to this task. Poulantzas does use the idea of power in his analysis, but in an ambivalent manner. His initial definition treats power solely as the capacity of a *class* "to realize its specific interests in a relation of opposition" to another class (1978:36; 1973a:99; 1975:277). Poulantzas seems to be affirming the conventional Marxist preoccupation with class issues here, since by definition all situations of opposed interests that do not involve class are not worthy of being called power struggles. This usage poses conceptual problems that are almost the reverse of those found earlier in Dahrendorf and Lenski. As we have seen, the latter two writers label all power relations as different types of class relations, thereby making class a meaningless idea. Poulantzas chooses to ignore all power relations that are not class relations and thus makes power the superfluous term.

Yet, on closer inspection, the ambivalence and inconsistency of Poulantzas's view of power is evident, for elsewhere he reveals a wider sense of power that is oddly similar to Weber's conception. First of all, his contention that power is a capacity to realize interests despite opposition is very similar to Weber's, apart from its restriction to class issues (cf. Weber, 1922:53). Moreover, even this restriction appears to disappear at times, since Poulantzas allows that "power relations stretch beyond class relations" to include problems of race, gender, and so on (1978:43–44; 1975:305–6). On these grounds, at least, Poulantzas's neo-Marxist approach to power, like his analysis of class structure, is not incompatible with a limited form of Weberian pluralism. If there is a real quarrel, it is with more extreme pluralists who fail to recognize that economic power is central "in the last instance," that "class power is the cornerstone of power" in the other areas (1973a:113; 1978:44).

The Capitalist State

Poulantzas distinguishes himself from most early Marxists by his attempt to include the state as an important factor in the structure of advanced capitalism. Unfortunately, his discussion is often obscure, primarily because he once again walks a nebulous line between orthodox Marxism and some variant of Weberian pluralism. To begin with, his definition of the state as the "condensation" or "fusion" of class struggle is too cryptic to be very informative. He seems to mean that the state is an organizational *shell* for society, a vast framework of rules and principles that ensure bourgeois domination in all those spheres not immediately part of the economy (1973a:53–55; 1978:26–30; cf. Jessop, 1985:54). At a concrete level, the state thus comprises a network of organizations or "apparatuses" that are of two related types: the political apparatuses, including the executive, legislative, judicial, civil-service, police, and military arms of government; and a range of ideological apparatuses such as education, the mass media, and so on. This portrayal resembles the conventional views of Weber and even Durkheim, except for Poulantzas's curious inclusion of religion, the family, and other structures within the state's ideological apparatuses (1975:24–25). As others have noted, this means that virtually everything but the material production process is subsumed under the capitalist state according to Poulantzas (Giddens and Held, 1982:193).

Given this image of the state as an all-encompassing framework for bourgeois domination, one might suspect that Poulantzas accepts the crude economic determinism of those Marxists who see the state as an appendage or tool of the capitalist class. However, Poulantzas wishes to dissociate himself from this viewpoint while at the same time avoiding charges of pluralism. His compromise is to argue that the state apparatuses are not totally independent operators in the capitalist power structure but nevertheless are *relatively* autonomous from the bourgeoisie (1973a:256; 1975:158; 1978:13). The heads of the state apparatuses are themselves bourgeois for the most part, while the rest of the state personnel are mainly members of the new petty bourgeoisie, white-collar civil servants with varying political and ideological ties to the capitalist class (1975:187; 1978:154–55).

Such inbred allegiances mean that the state will uphold the general interests of the bourgeoisie. Nevertheless, the state is too large and, like the class structure, too fragmented by special interests to exercise a unified political will on all issues. On the contrary, the complex bureaucratic amalgam of state agencies generates an intricate mix of "diversified micropolicies," many of which are "mutually contradictory" (1978:132–35, 194). The overall result is that certain specific policies of the state may produce "short-term material sacrifices" by the bourgeoisie: being required to pay for the improved health and safety conditions of workers; contributing through taxation to public education, social security, or unemployment benefits; and so on (cf. Jessop, 1985:55). Still, these actions by the state really benefit the capitalists in the end, by defusing potential revolt, promoting a compliant and dependable work force, and thus securing the "long-term domination" of the bourgeoisie (1978:30–31, 184–85; cf. Jessop, 1985:61).

Poulantzas's determination to find a middle ground between the state as a tool of capital and the state as an independent force in society ultimately leads to his paradoxical claim that the state, on the one hand, is the very "center" of power in capitalism but, on the other hand, "does not possess any power of its own" (1973a:115; 1975:81; 1978:148). Given his peculiar conception of power as an exclusive aspect of class relations, it does of course follow that the state by definition has no power, since it is not a class (cf. Connell, 1979). And yet Poulantzas must reconcile this with his view that the state is now the prime setting in which power is exercised, because of massive state involvement in social services, public administration, and, increasingly, the operation of the capitalist economy itself (1975:81; 1978:168). His insistence that the state has no power is justified primarily by the fact that the state does not control the means of production, even if it does have an expanded role in taxing and spending the surplus generated. Besides, state incursions into the economy never go beyond certain limits, for fear of eroding the profit motivation of the bourgeoisie on which the state's own funds depend. Often, in fact, state involvement is really a desperate attempt to help the bourgeoisie out of economic crisis or depression. It represents the dilemma state leaders face in trying simultaneously to placate a discontented working class and a capitalist class concerned mainly with its own gains. In short, the state is far from omnipotent under advanced capitalism but instead stands with "its back to the wall and its front poised before a ditch" (1978:191–92, 244).

At least one key difficulty with this assessment of state power should be noted. Poulantzas's own definition of power indicates that it involves the realization of a faction's interests in the face of opposition. But control of material production does not exhaust the means by which interests can be realized or opposition quelled. In particular, one should not overlook the use of coercive force or repression to exact compliance from one's opponents. In fact, Poulantzas follows Weber, Lenski, and others in acknowledging the fundamental role of repression in *all* power relations and notes that power in its most basic form entails physical force, quite literally "the coercion of bodies and the threat of violence or death" (1978:28–29; 1973a:225). But who has the capacity to employ repressive power? Clearly, it is the state that controls this resource, especially through the legalized actions of the police, the military, and the official justice system. In addition, the activities of virtually the entire state bureaucracy enjoy the legal sanction and, if necessary, the coercive aid of these agencies. Poulantzas seems to recognize this point and credits Weber with being the first to establish it (1978:80–81). Yet Poulantzas fails to appreciate fully that this makes state power a distinct force to be reckoned with in society.

Of course, in rejecting Poulantzas's claim that the state has no power, one must not simply take the opposite stance that the state in capitalism has a total monopoly of power. Thus, Poulantzas is correct to note, along with Lenski and others, that organized state repression is subject to limitations, particularly in nominally democratic societies. The laws that establish state powers in modern times can also restrict them, delimiting the state's jurisdictions and spelling out popular rights. Blatant disregard for these limits to power risks public outrage and possible open rebellion against state control (1978:82–83, 31–33). The crucial point to stress is that the state's powers are indeed constrained but that neither these restrictions, nor its ceding of ultimate economic control to the capitalist class, leaves the state's apparatuses without inherent influence. The major weakness in Poulantzas's entire perspective is that he emphasizes the relative autonomy of the state and yet cannot admit the distinct state power that this implies. In addition, his interest in the abstract framework of state apparatuses leads to an insufficient awareness that they are also concrete organizations, run by real people who have considerable say in the running of society.

The Prospects for Socialism

As a committed Marxist, Poulantzas wishes primarily to understand and promote the transformation of capitalism into socialism. Here Poulantzas addresses a question faced by all modern Marxists: why have so many attempts to create an egalitarian society through socialist revolution led to systems bearing little or no resemblance to Marx's version of communism? Interestingly, Poulantzas believes the problem lies with the state (cf. Jessop, 1985:118–19). Such perversions of socialist principles as Stalin's Russia, for example, occurred because of the misguided belief of Lenin and others that an utter smashing of the capitalist state can solve the administrative problems of socialist society. Instead, the administrative void is filled by a "parallel" socialist state, one that does not wither away but too often is more resilient, more bureaucratic, and more repressive than its bourgeois predecessor (1978:252–55).

Poulantzas's alternative strategy is to work within the existing capitalist state to transform it gradually. Briefly, this entails the spread of trade-union activities, workers' political parties, and other new forms of "direct, rank-and-file democracy" (1978:261). In addition to the working class, a key force for change is the new petty bourgeoisie, especially many middle- and lower-level state employees, whom Poulantzas expects to ally with the proletariat as economic crises occur and their material conditions worsen (1978:242–44). To be sure, the eventual use of force cannot be ruled out as necessary to final success. Moreover, it remains to be seen whether current leaders on the left are yet capable of enlisting and organizing mass action. But, in any event, no truly democratic socialism is possible without this base of "broad popular alliances" to counteract totalitarian tendencies (1978:263).

Even in his prescription for the future, then, Poulantzas shares a certain vague similarity with Weber, for both have a distrust of socialism that is really bureaucratic *statism* in disguise, and both advocate working within existing bourgeois structures to change them. Of course, they are unalterably opposed on both the extent and the vehicle of social change. Whereas Weber supports rather minor revisions to bourgeois liberal democracy and sees an enlightened political leadership as the key force to curb bureaucratic domination, Poulantzas desires, like Marx, the fundamental shift from liberal democracy to democratic socialism and considers the mass of the people as the principal factor in this transformation.

Summary Observations

In this section of the chapter, Poulantzas's neo-Marxist perspective has been examined. We have seen that Poulantzas's image of inequality, as reflected in his analyses of class, power, and the capitalist state, falls somewhere between conventional Marxism and a limited form of pluralism broadly suggestive of Weber. In this way, Poulantzas is representative of a large number of modern Marxists who have become engaged in "a prolonged dialogue with the ghost of Weber" (Burris, 1987:67). Although some Marxists worry that this dialogue has resulted in a "Weberianization of Marxist class analysis" (Levine and Lembcke, 1987:6), there are some advantages to building linkages between the two formulations. In Poulantzas's case, the outcome is a perspective that sustains Marx's basic emphasis on control of material production as the key source of power and inequality in society, but that also acknowledges the important political and ideological forces that sometimes escape the notice of other Marxists. Where there are weaknesses in Poulantzas, they arise mainly from his lack of conceptual clarity in some areas and his rather ambivalent handling of the problem of state power. We are left with a contradictory impression of a state that pervades more and more of our lives but somehow has no substantive power of its own. The major omission here is the realization that the state personnel are themselves social actors with powers of legal and physical coercion at their disposal.

ERIK OLIN WRIGHT

The second major neo-Marxist scholar to be considered in this chapter is Erik Olin Wright. Like Poulantzas, and Marx himself, Wright's primary concern has not been to devise a comprehensive theory of social inequality, but rather to investigate the prospects for socialist revolution, given the inherent characteristics of advanced capitalist societies (Wright, 1978:26). Nevertheless, in approaching this task, Wright has also generated several new insights into how inequality can be conceived and understood. Some observers suggest, in fact, that his work represents the most significant and sweeping endeavour of all the current attempts to formulate social class and to make the concept amenable to empirical analysis (e.g., Therborn, 1986:99).

As we shall see, Wright's general conceptualization of class structure in contemporary capitalism has undergone some notable changes since his original formulation (Wright, 1976, 1978, 1979). However, both his early and his revised theoretical schemes are consistent in demonstrating Wright's desire, like that of Poulantzas and Althusser, to provide a revitalized and sophisticated reorientation of early Marxism. Wright devotes his discussion to several of the same issues that are of crucial concern to Poulantzas and that tie closely to the analysis of inequality in advanced societies. For our purposes, the topics of note are the capitalist class structure, especially those anomalous "places" or "locations" that are somehow distinct from the bourgeoisie and proletariat; the origins of power; the role of the capitalist state; and the outlook for a socialist transformation of capitalism in the light of these other considerations. We shall first review his original conception of class and inequality in detail and then examine some of the key changes he has introduced in his most recent writings (Wright, 1985; Wright and Martin, 1987; Steinmetz and Wright, 1989).

The Capitalist Class Structure

Like Poulantzas, Wright wishes to retain the standard two-class model of nineteenth-century Marxism, but in an updated form that incorporates important modifications and extensions of recent times (cf. Wright and Perrone, 1977). However, while Poulantzas sees these developments in terms of "fractions" within the two main classes, Wright uses a more systematic strategy that remains consistent with the classical Marxian concern with ownership and control of the capitalist economy.

According to Wright, capitalism in its most "abstract" or "pure" sense does indeed generate only two classes: those in control of economic production, the bourgeoisie, and those excluded from control of production, the proletariat. However, in real capitalist societies, complications arise, first, because a third class, the old petty bourgeoisie, continues to exist (albeit in a declining form) and, second, because command over the economy is a more complicated issue than it was in the previous stages of capitalism (cf. Wright, 1985:7–8). Wright's earliest attempt to conceptualize classes is based on the premise that control of economic production is now divisible into three key elements: (1) "real economic ownership," which is most crucial and refers to control over all the economic surplus — the profits, products, and other resources of capitalism; (2) command of the physical apparatus of production, which entails supervisory control over the machines, factories, and so on, that are used to make products; and (3) command of labour power, which means supervisory control over workers (1978:73; 1979:24).

Using these three criteria, Wright proposes that the modern bourgeoisie be defined as the set of positions or class locations in which all three types of control are retained, while the proletariat includes those class locations where all three types of control are absent. The third class in capitalism, the petty bourgeoisie, is a carry-over from earlier times and comprises positions filled by people who, as the owners of small businesses, for example, generate and control their own surplus (control 1) and manage their own enterprise (control 2) but do *not* employ workers (control 3).

As for the rest of the class structure, it is composed of positions that, strictly speaking, do not form classes at all because they have some elements of economic control but not others. Wright sees these as "contradictory" locations arrayed between the three main class clusters, as in Figure 6.2. Thus, between the bourgeoisie and proletariat

Figure 6.2
Wright's Original Model of Capitalist Class Relations

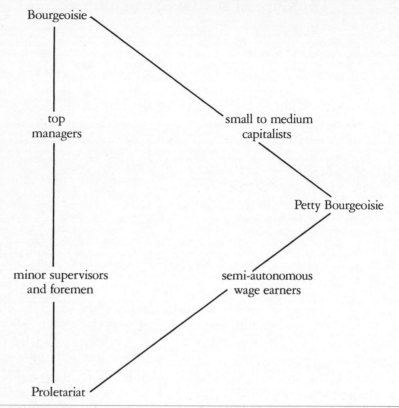

Source: Erik Olin Wright, *Class, Crisis, and the State* (London: New Left Books, 1978), p. 84. Reprinted by permission.

are all those positions filled by people who resemble proletarians in that they do not own or control the economic surplus (control 1) but have varying degrees of supervisory command over both the physical plant and the employees of the enterprise (controls 2 and 3). Along this line, top-level managers are closest to the bourgeoisie, since they control the most workers and large segments of the apparatus, while toward the proletarian end of this continuum are minor supervisors and foremen, who oversee only small sectors of production and a few workers.

The other two ranges of contradictory class locations include small-to medium-scale capitalists, positioned outside the bourgeoisie and toward the petty bourgeoisie primarily because they employ relatively few workers; and "semi-autonomous" wage earners, a mix of scientists, professors, and other salaried professional or technical personnel who are located between the petty bourgeoisie and the proletariat because, like the latter, they employ no workers but, like the former, they have some command over the products of their labour and over the physical means used in their creation (controls 1 and 2) (1978:80–81; 1979:46–47).

In this rather innovative manner, Wright poses an alternative strategy for conceiving of places in the class structure that do not fit precisely into the Marxist two-class model. Wright avoids lumping these positions into a single new middle class like Dahrendorf or a single new petty bourgeoisie like Poulantzas. Instead, he locates them systematically along three separate ranges that vary according to both the type and the degree of economic control enjoyed by their incumbents.

And what of people employed in spheres outside the production process, in the political and ideological structures of society? Here Wright also shuns Poulantzas's simple treatment of all such positions as unproductive elements of the bourgeoisie or petty bourgeoisie. In classifying these locations, Wright's original formulation relies on much the same rationale as that used for the sphere of economic production. That is, within the political and ideological apparatuses of capitalism, class location can also be defined by control of production, but here production refers to political and ideological creations, especially the policies, laws, ideas, and beliefs generated and communicated by such structures. Hence, most of the political and ideological personnel are proletarians, since they are excluded from control over the creation and implementation of policies and ideas. A few at the top — political leaders, supreme magistrates, the heads of education, religion, and so on — control both creation and implementation and therefore are members of the bourgeoisie. The remainder have some partial control over such matters and so occupy contradictory locations between the bourgeoisie and the proletariat. The one apparent difference between these class alignments and those within the economy itself is the absence of any political or ideological counterparts to the petty bourgeoisie (1978:94–97; 1979:54).

Apart from this discrepancy, however, Wright's scheme allows us to envision an entire array of political and ideological apparatuses, running side by side with the economic structure and representing all the major spheres of capitalist society. As depicted in Figure 6.3, the bourgeoisie is really the intersection of positions at the top of all these structures, the proletariat is the intersection along the bottom,

Figure 6.3
The Intersection of Class Relations across Economic, Political, and
Ideological Structures

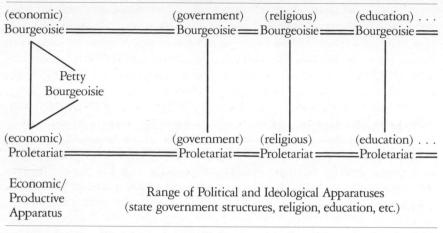

and the various contradictory locations lie between these ends. It is worth noting that this feature of Wright's original formulation bears some resemblance to conventional sociological portrayals of society as a series of interconnected structures, each engaged in a particular task within the larger system. Wright's view enables us to conceive of class structure as a phenomenon that cuts across every sphere of social organization and that, in a sense, joins them all together (cf. Wright, 1980:190).

Wright's Reformulation of Classes (1985)

The conception of classes in contemporary capitalism that Wright first proposed has been a major influence in the thinking of both Marxist and non-Marxist scholars. Apart from the theoretical debate and discussion it has stimulated, Wright's scheme has been widely adopted by other writers as the best available means for measuring or operationalizing class in empirical research (e.g., Grabb, 1980; Johnston and Ornstein, 1982; Hagan and Albonetti, 1982; Hagan and Parker, 1985; Baer et al., 1987, 1990).

Nevertheless, more recently Wright has proposed an alternative formulation to the original version, primarily because of his sensitivity to the claim, which he largely concedes, that his original conception deviates in some key respects from the classical Marxian perspective. Specifically, Wright suggests that his initial scheme tended to depart from the exploitation-based definition of classes, which in his view is fundamental to Marx's treatment. Instead, his first formulation, like most neo-Marxist classifications of the period, put undue emphasis on power or domination as the defining criterion for class differences (1985:15, 56). Thus, his use of various types of *control* over (or domination of) the productive process to define classes leads to a scheme that, in many ways, seems closer to a Weberian than a Marxian conception of class. In place of the old formulation, then, Wright now proposes a classification based on exploitation, where class distinctions arise from the "economically oppressive appropriation of the fruits of the labor of one class by another" (1985:77).

However, rather than produce a set of categories that more closely resembles the simple dichotomy of bourgeoisie and proletariat reminiscent of early Marxism, Wright's latest work generates a more extensive list of class categories than ever before. Building in part on earlier writings by Roemer (1982), Wright concludes that exploitation of one class by another in modern capitalism emerges from three key processes or sources. In addition to the familiar appropriation of resources or assets by owners within the means of production, exploitation also occurs through the differential benefits that some people gain by having higher levels of skill or credentials ("skill/credential assets") or by being more strategically placed in the organizational hierarchy of the productive process ("organization assets") (1985:88). The various combinations of these three different forms of exploitation give rise to a twelve-category typology of class locations in contemporary capitalist society (Figure 6.4).

Ironically, in spite of Wright's desire to develop a scheme that is more faithful to Marx's conception of classes, most contemporary observers, particularly other Marxists, have concluded that Wright's new typology is actually less consistent with classical Marxist thought than was his original formulation (e.g., Meiksins, 1987:51–57; Carchedi, 1987:112–31; Kamolnick, 1988). One major criticism concerns his definition of exploitation, which is said to be distributive in nature and so quite different from Marx's relational view of this concept. Wright's idea of exploitation also implies, for example, that skilled workers somehow exploit less-skilled workers simply because they possess more skill/credential assets. To most other Marxists, this is a conclusion that Marx himself would never accept. It is interesting that Wright himself conceded several of these criticisms but maintains, nonetheless, that the new scheme is a valuable tool for empirical research (Wright, 1989a:10; for debate see Wright, 1989b).

Another difficulty that Wright's new typology poses is that it suggests a much more pluralist, and therefore Weberian, system of classes than does Marx's two-class model and Wright's original analysis. Moreover, the theoretical gains achieved by the new classification seem limited, especially given its added complexity. Essentially, we still have the three main classes that form the triangular pattern in his original

Figure 6.4
Typology of Class Locations in Capitalist Society

Assets in the means of production

	Owners of means of production	Non-owners [wage labourers]			Organization assets
Owns sufficient capital to hire workers and not work	1 Bourgeoisie	4 Expert Managers	7 Semi-Credentialled Managers	10 Uncredentialled Managers	+
Owns sufficient capital to hire workers but must work	2 Small Employers	5 Expert Supervisors	8 Semi-Credentialled Supervisors	11 Uncredentialled Supervisors	>0
Owns sufficient capital to work for self but not to hire workers	3 Petty Bourgeoisie	6 Expert non-managers	9 Semi-Credentialled Workers	12 Proletarians	−
		+	>0	−	

Skill/credential assets

scheme — bourgeoisie, proletariat, and petty bourgeoisie (Figure 6.2). But, in place of the three ranges of "contradictory locations" linking these three classes, we now have nine new categories, all differentiated by whether or not the incumbents in these locations have a great deal, some, or none of the three types of assets (ownership, skills/ credentials, and organization).

The conceptual advantages of this approach are debatable, especially since the practical advantages relative to those of the original also seem questionable. Wright himself notes that the working-class categories in the two schemes "overlap so much that an empirical comparison is difficult to pursue" and that the recent scheme does not represent "a decisive empirical break with the previous approach" (1985:187). For all these reasons, it can be argued that the principal insights and value of Wright's work, as an innovative approach to Marxist class analysis, are largely to be identified with his original rather than with his more recent conception of class structure.

Power, Domination, and the Capitalist State

One aspect of Wright's analysis that receives little explicit attention is the concept of power or domination and its link to social inequality. However, as we have already seen, domination clearly played a significant, if somewhat implicit, role in Wright's original definition and delineation of classes in capitalist society. In addition, although he has attempted to move away from this emphasis in his new typology, there is still evidence that control or domination underlies his views on class, given his contention that people's "assets" and, consequently, their class location stem at least partially from their position in organizational hierarchies or from their designation as having superior skills or credentials over others in the work setting. Hence, although direct references to the structure of power are minimized in much of Wright's analysis, the importance of power in his conception of the class structure seems undeniable (cf. 1985:300).

One reason for the lack of a detailed treatment of power in Wright's writing may be that, for Wright as for Poulantzas, power and class are really inseparable ideas for the most part. On occasion, Wright may seem to give a different impression: for example, he criticizes those Marxists and others who perceive racial, sexual, and other forms of domination as simply class domination in disguise (1979:197, 227–28). At the same time, however, Wright is concerned that the recognition of these other forms of domination or oppression not lead to the "displacement of class from the centre stage" (1985:57). To Wright, as to all Marxist thinkers, class is the crucial idea to understand when analyzing social inequality and is not simply "one of many oppressions, with no particular centrality to social and historical analysis" (1985:57; 1989:7).

In the end, Wright's final position suggests that for him genuine power is virtually indistinct from control over the production and accumulation of economic surplus. This stance is reflected in Wright's essential Marxist assumption that economic domination means control over material resources, without which no other forms of human activity can be sustained. Because of fundamental material needs, those who control the economy ultimately shape all social life, including the political and ideological arrangements of capitalism (1979:15; 1985:98).

It is largely from this perspective that Wright's examination of the state in capitalist society is to be understood. To begin with, we should note that Wright diverges from Poulantzas when defining the state, favouring a more conventional and less inclusive image of the state as mainly the government-run apparatuses of society: the political structure, its civil-service bureaucracies, and certain ideological arms such as public education and any state-administered mass-media organizations. Like Poulantzas, however, Wright generally sees the state structure as one that is severely constrained in its actions by its economic dependence on the capitalist class. Because it generates no surplus of its own, the state relies primarily on taxation of privately accumulated profits and wages for its funds. This is not to say that the state apparatuses are therefore unswerving servants of their capitalist benefactors. Again, Wright parallels Poulantzas in arguing that sectors of the state can and will act against bourgeois wishes at times, out of a commitment to the general welfare or in order to appease discontent within various interest groups in the public at large. Yet these actions rarely threaten bourgeois dominance in the long term, because most state leaders are themselves bourgeois and because the state as a whole requires a contented capitalist class, possessed of the economic incentive necessary to amass profits, employ workers, and thus ensure the state's vital operating revenues.

Hence, the state leadership and the bourgeoisie have a common interest in maintaining a stable, unimpeded capitalist economy. According to Wright, however, the state in advanced capitalism is increasingly required to intervene in the economic sphere, usually against its will, because of the inherent tendencies toward crisis and depression that regularly disrupt the capitalist economy. Such crises are even more serious in advanced capitalism because, as Marx foresaw, economic control has become concentrated in a relatively few giant corporations. Whereas in the past economic depression led to the failure or absorption of small enterprises, now it is these large-scale businesses that are threatened in economic declines. Thus, when Chrysler or Dome Petroleum faces bankruptcy, major portions of the capitalist class are endangered, as well as the jobs of thousands of workers. As a result, the state is compelled to step in to protect capitalist interests, avert popular unrest, and preserve its own tax base. But the state's actions in these cases usually involve short-term solutions that create new problems. Bailing out weak companies, giving preferential treatment to troubled businesses, and increasing taxes to provide more unemployment benefits simply put more burdens on the system, for they subsidize inefficient, unproductive elements at the expense of the healthy sectors and also drain economic surplus through the creation of costly state bureaucracies to administer the programs. In Wright's view, these added burdens eventually engender new crises and force the state to intercede still further in a continuing cycle of intervention that satisfies neither the bourgeoisie nor the majority of workers (1978:156–63, 174–79).

The Prospects for Socialism

Because of the growing inability of the state or the bourgeoisie to ease economic crises, one might expect an increase in popular discontent and in the chance of socialist revolution in future society. Wright contends that a successful shift to socialism is possible, but unlikely as long as two key problems are unresolved. First, the proletariat must come to realize that it has a fundamental interest in the socialist cause; second, the proletariat must become actively involved in changing capitalism from within its own existing structures, especially the state apparatuses. Let us briefly assess each of these points.

Wright argues that workers in most countries continue to be distracted from their fundamental interest in overturning capitalism because of a preoccupation with immediate interests such as wages and job security. Such distraction is understandable, given workers' material deprivation, but Wright is convinced that the proletariat would surely engage in struggles for socialism if only its members had a complete comprehension of their exploitation by the capitalist class (1978:88–90). There are at least two difficulties with such a claim. To begin with, it really assumes, rather than demonstrates, that workers have a fundamental stake in socialism. While such an assumption could be correct, as it stands here it is simply a Marxist axiom, a statement that must be true by definition. Because of this, it ignores other explanations for working-class inaction, including the possibility that workers themselves are capable of judging the merits of socialism and have found them wanting. It is plausible that many workers, on observing the Soviet Union, Poland, China, and other instances of socialism in practice, have chosen capitalism as the lesser of two evils, despite its exploitation and injustice. In that event, capitalism would be more suited to both the immediate *and* the fundamental interests of workers, at least in comparison with current brands of socialism.

The other difficulty in Wright's treatment of class interests is that, whether we use his original or his more recent typology of classes, it is apparent that only a minority of the population is actually located in the working-class proper (1978:84; 1985:195; 1989:9). In the United States, for example, Wright estimates that about 40 to 50 percent of the class structure is proletarian, depending on the criteria of classification and the year in which the estimate is made. Even if all these members of the working class take a strong interest in socialism, a point we have already questioned, a majority or near-majority remain whose class interests partially or completely oppose capitalism's demise. Of these, only 1 or 2 percent are in the bourgeoisie, while another 5 or 6 percent are in the petty bourgeoisie. Thus, the prospects for socialist revolution seem to hinge on those who occupy the numerous contradictory locations or other class categories that form close to half of Wright's class structure (cf. Wright et al., 1982). Of course, if all the people in these positions were to resolve their ambivalent interests in favour of the proletariat, the massive support necessary for a revolutionary overthrow of capitalism could be attainable. In some of Wright's earlier research, he actually perceives signs of "proletarian-ization" among some of the technical, white-collar, and other employees in these locations, for some have seen their objective conditions of labour come more and more to resemble those of the working class. However, compared to Poulantzas and others, Wright seems less certain that all such intermediate positions will become proletarian; instead, it is likely that many will remain distinct for the time being, and new locations of this sort will continue to be created as technology advances (1979:28–32; Wright and Singelmann, 1982; see also Gagliani, 1981). Moreover, subsequent research by Wright himself now suggests that, in the United States, there has been no reduction in these intermediate positions, but rather a significant "expansion of the middle class" in recent decades, even within the traditional petty-bourgeoisie category that both Marxists and non-Marxists have assumed was in decline (Wright and Martin, 1987:25; Steinmetz and Wright, 1989:973). Similar results have also been reported for Canada during the same period (Myles, 1988). The persistence of these other categories, coupled with whatever disaffection exists toward socialism in the proletariat itself, makes it less than probable that a majority desire for the overthrow of capitalism is imminent.

Assuming that the working class is eventually able to overcome these and other impediments to achieving revolutionary consciousness, Wright then raises a second key concern: that workers be allowed a real part in shaping revolutionary change, especially through the political apparatuses of the state. Like Poulantzas, Wright rejects the old view that successful revolution means a sudden and total smashing of the capitalist state, since this typically leads to a totalitarian socialist regime that excludes workers from power and subverts the very principles it is supposed to uphold (cf. 1985:83–84). Wright offers no detailed alternative strategy, but, like Poulantzas, he holds the basic hope that working-class community councils and similar organizations will arise to establish "direct democracy on the fringes of the state administration" (1978:245). Then, as the state increases its involvement in running the economy and the rest of society, workers will be in a position to apply their developing organizational skills and other "capacities" by participating in state programs directly, ultimately achieving their rightful majority influence through democratic means.

Nevertheless, as Wright himself notes, this smooth and democratic achievement of a society ruled by all workers is likely to encounter considerable opposition, depending on whether the state's repressive branches — the police and military — are used against it and on whether possible economic reprisals by the bourgeoisie — the flight of businesses out of the country, for example — are successful in impeding its course (1978:250–51). Apart from these potential obstacles, however, the final hurdle for the universal society of workers may well be organized socialist political parties themselves. To Wright, these are a necessary focal point for concerted proletarian action, and a successful transformation of the capitalist state from within seems inconceivable without them. Yet they are subject to the same pressures for administrative hierarchy and bureaucratic decision making as any other organization and therefore threaten to undermine the broadly based worker involvement in planning and running society that socialism stands for (1978:247, 252; 1985:84–85).

On this final point, then, Wright comes down closer to Weber than many other Marxists would like, for he suggests that even if workers actively seek the socialist transformation, and even if it succeeds, organizational exigencies persist that make a truly democratic socialism difficult (1978:216, 225). Nonetheless, in keeping with Marx, Poulantzas, and Marxist thinkers in general, Wright would rather risk the future on the possibility that workers can overcome these hurdles than on Weber's hope that some enlightened political elite can save capitalism from bureaucratic abuses and its own internal contradictions. Workers must develop and retain the capacity to rule themselves if human societies are to progress, and the chances of this occurring are, in the Marxist view, clearly better under socialism than under any form of capitalism.

Summary Observations

In this section, we have considered Wright's attempt to reorient traditional Marxism to the analysis of modern class structure, the capitalist state, and other topics relevant to the study of social inequality. Overall, Wright's discussion is more clearly conceived and internally consistent than Poulantzas's neo-Marxist formulation, especially with respect to the problem of class structure. While both Poulantzas and Wright provide noteworthy treatments of the state, a topic ignored by most early Marxists, here too Wright's analysis seems preferable to Poulantzas's rather obscure account. The principal weakness in Wright's viewpoint is his omission of any systematic treatment of the concept of power. As a consequence, Wright tends to play down the role of repression and other means of domination that may at times operate separately from economic control. A more thorough treatment of power might also enable Wright to incorporate into his analysis a complete discussion of gender, race, and other non-class forms of inequality.

A second problem in Wright's approach is his failure even to question the assumption that socialism must always be in the fundamental interest of the working class. His certainty on this point is especially surprising in light of his sensitivity to the bureaucratic and totalitarian threats to democratic action that are internal to socialism itself. Skepticism on this issue in particular provides the backdrop for the next perspective to be considered: Parkin's neo-Weberian critique of Marxism.

Frank Parkin

THE BOURGEOIS CRITIQUE OF MARXISM

Parkin's work is the clearest contemporary attempt by an avowed neo-Weberian to provide a renewed perspective on social inequality (1979, 1983). In his analyses, Parkin dissociates himself from certain early Weberians, especially those structural functionalists who have erased from Weber's original analysis his important affinities with Marx (Parkin, 1972:17–18; Parkin, 1978:602–4; Parkin, 1979:48). At the same time, however, Parkin is highly critical of most Marxists as well, because of their inordinate preoccupation with one aspect of social inequality: capitalist economic production and the division between bourgeoisie and proletariat arising within it. Parkin's prime purpose is to act as a non-Marxist or "bourgeois" sociologist and criticize the flaws in this narrow focus. His own position is that there are other important class cleavages in modern society to consider, as well as numerous other forms of exploitation that are distinct from class and that persist independently of the class structure itself. These other forms of exploitation involve a range of social criteria that vary in importance across different societies but typically include race, ethnicity, gender, and religion, among others (1979:9, 89).

To Parkin, it is instructive that whenever Marxists such as Poulantzas and Wright try to incorporate such complications into the conventional two-class model of Marxism, they produce perspectives that invariably resemble Weber's in key respects. This prompts Parkin to note that "inside every neo-Marxist there seems to be a Weberian struggling to get out" (1979:25). Consequently, Parkin concludes that all manifestations of structured inequality can and should be examined using a single, essentially Weberian, conceptual framework. This unified scheme treats power relations, not class relations, as the elemental factor generating inequality but elaborates Weber's original notion of power by linking it to his related but less familiar idea of *social closure*. Because of its central role in Parkin's analysis, we begin with an assessment of his discussion of power as social closure. We then consider Parkin's treatment of class, the modern state, and the outlook for inequality in future society.

Power and Social Closure

Parkin concurs with the view put forward in Chapter 3 that, for Weber, the overall structure of inequality in society stems from a general and continuing struggle for power (1972:46; 1979:44). According to Parkin, however, it is unclear in Weber's discussion precisely what the source or location of power is in society, particularly because his definition of the term is never completely satisfactory (1979:46). Parkin's remedy for this problem is to combine the idea of power with social closure, a less prominent concept in Weber that refers to the various processes by which some social groupings restrict others from "access to resources and opportunities." From this viewpoint, power is really a "built-in attribute" of any closure situation, denoting one's degree of access to these resources and opportunities (1979:44–46).

Parkin suggests two basic forms that social closure can assume: *exclusion*, which is the prime means by which dominant factions deny power to subordinates, and *usurpation*, which is the key means by which subordinates seek to wrest at least some power back from those who dominate them. Of the two, exclusion is by far the more effective form in modern societies, for it is largely established in legal rules and regulations that enjoy the official sanction of the state's justice system and, if necessary, its repressive agencies as well. The obvious example of exclusion in capitalism is the legal right to own private property, which excludes workers from power over the production process. As for usurpation, it is a secondary process for the most part, through which those subordinates denied power by formal exclusion attempt to consolidate themselves and mobilize power in an "upward direction." In its most extreme guise, usurpation could mean a complete overthrow of the ruling faction, as in a proletarian revolution to oust the bourgeoisie from power. Typically, however, usurpation involves more moderate and less potent kinds of action, the most common being a collective withdrawal or disruption of services through strikes or demonstrations. In contrast to exclusion, such usurpationary acts are less often given formal recognition or protection by the state. Such tactics are frequently accorded only grudging or partial legitimation and may even be outlawed in some circumstances. Thus, like Lenski before him, Parkin envisions a two-way flow of power in social hierarchies, but one that is asymmetrical in that the exclusionary powers of the dominant faction generally override the usurpationary responses of subordinates (1979:45, 58, 74, 98).

So far, we have used examples of class relationships to illustrate Parkin's two forms of social closure. However, Parkin stresses that closure processes are the common factor behind all structures of inequality, including ethnic, religious, sexual, and other forms of exploitation in addition to class relations. Once again, Parkin is critical of Marxist analysts here, most of whom ignore these other forms or simply give them passing mention as phenomena that obscure from view the "real" struggle between classes. But, to Parkin, the struggles between blacks and whites in South Africa, Catholics and Protestants in Northern Ireland, or women and men in most every nation are all conflicts over closure, over access to resources and opportunities. Moreover, such antagonisms and the inequalities connected with them occur in both capitalist and socialist societies, regardless of whether class inequality exists or not, so it is incorrect to assume that they are somehow secondary to or derivative from class struggle (1979:113–14). On the contrary, these other bases for inequality are frequently more important than class in explaining social change or collective action in some countries (1978:621–22). What is required, then, is a recognition of these other clashes between interest groups and an analysis of how they reinforce, negate, or otherwise interact with class closure.

Closure and Class Structure

Having noted the general process of social closure and the various systems of power and inequality it can engender, Parkin gives particular attention to the problem of class structure. Despite his criticisms of Marxist analysis, Parkin clearly holds with Marx, as well as Weber, in emphasizing the pivotal role of property relations in defining classes (cf. Murphy, 1988:26). In fact, control of productive property continues to be "the most important form of social closure" in society, since it can mean exclusion from access to the material means of survival itself (1979:53). However, following Weber, Parkin notes that the class system is increasingly being shaped by a second key type of exclusion: the use of formal "credentials," especially educational certification, to close off privileged positions from others (1979:54; Weber, 1922:344; see also Collins, 1979). Particularly in such fields as medicine and law, a few incumbents have gained licence from the state to special forms of knowledge and practice, resulting in a legal monopoly over professional services. Parkin believes these credentials are so important that those who hold them are the second layer of the dominant class, just below those who have exclusive control of productive property (1979:57-58). Parkin's inclusion of educated professionals within the dominant class may be questionable, to the extent that their influence in society would seem clearly to be less significant than that of the most powerful capitalists, for example. Nevertheless, Parkin is correct in recognizing the great advantages that exclusive credentials give to those who possess them. As we have already seen, Marxist scholars like Wright now also lay considerable stress on the significance of credentials or recognized skills for determining class location.

Outside the dominant class, the class structure in Parkin's view seems to form a graded structure of people who have varying degrees of usurpationary influence, occasionally combined with a partial capacity for excluding others. Workers without property or credentials form the subordinate class, although they vary internally according to whether or not they enjoy usurpationary influence because of union affiliation and according to the strength or "disruptive potential" of their union relative to others (1979:80, 93). Between the dominant and subordinate classes, Parkin also notes a range of "intermediate groups" who exercise incomplete forms of both exclusion and usurpation in what Parkin calls "dual closure." The lower end of this middle range includes skilled tradespeople, workers who are unionized and can also invoke limited exclusionary closure through apprenticeship systems and other credential mechanisms. Such certificates are less exclusive than those given doctors and other professions but still provide workers who have these papers some advantages over workers who do not. The remaining intermediate positions primarily involve white-collar "semiprofessions," a mixture of teachers, nurses, social workers, and the like, who may shade into the more established professions at the upper end but normally fall short of the complete exclusionary closure doctors and lawyers have attained. Such semiprofessionals are often state employees, who lack a true monopoly over the knowledge or services they dispense, and who may thus resort to unionization and other usurpationary tactics to defend or improve their position in the collective struggle of interest groups (1979:56-57, 102-8).

In total, then, Parkin's portrayal of the class system comprises a dominant class of people with exclusionary rights to property and to special credentials, a subordinate class of workers with only varying amounts of usurpationary power, and a middle range of semiprofessionals and skilled workers with different mixes of both types of closure at their disposal (cf. 1983). Despite the emphasis on closure, Parkin observes that this structure is open or permeable to some extent. The dominant faction in modern liberal democracies harbours a degree of ideological commitment to individual opportunity, so that some with talent will be allowed and even encouraged to move up from humble origins, while others of privileged background who lack ability must eventually move down. Nevertheless, this sifting process does not alter the closure principles themselves and falls far short of negating the advantages of those who inherit property and other rights of closure. In addition, any commitment to individual opportunity is belied by the tendency of collective or ascriptive criteria, such as race or gender, to become interwoven with considerations of merit and performance. Thus, blacks or women could be denied entry to the dominant class irrespective of their personal qualifications or abilities and could be relegated to the lowest reaches of the subordinate class by white male workers, who may jealously guard what few prerogatives they have themselves (1979:63–68, 90–91). These latter possibilities suggest some of the ways that the other bases of social closure can be overlaid with or embedded in the class structure (cf. Murphy, 1988:80–81). They also illustrate that, in Parkin's view, the idea of social closure provides us with a more powerful conceptual tool for explaining social inequality in *general* than does the idea of class.

The Role of the State

Parkin considers the upsurge of interest in the state the most novel feature of recent discussions of social inequality (1978:617). His own emphasis on exclusionary closure, established and upheld by the legal and repressive branches of the state, suggests that Parkin also sees the state as crucial to contemporary systems of inequality. However, Parkin contends that the concept of the state has been misused or misunderstood by many theorists, especially those on the left. There is an apparent inconsistency in those Marxists such as Poulantzas who argue for the state's relative autonomy, as if it were a separate force in society, and yet claim that it has no power of its own (Parkin, 1978:618; cf. Miliband, 1969). Parkin's own view is generally closer to the latter, for he suggests that it is *people* who have power *through* the state, especially those factions who are most able to infiltrate state positions or influence state personnel from the outside. This means that the state itself is mainly "an instrument of social domination" — in fact, an elaborate cluster of such instruments that subsumes the "administrative, judicial, military, and coercive institutions" of society. These structures are subject to separate and even contradictory manipulation by the various antagonists in the struggle for social closure. Using a different metaphor, Parkin also compares the state to a "mirror" that reflects the overall outcome of conflicts involving classes, races, genders, and the other key interest groups in society (1979:138–39; 1978:619).

Nevertheless, despite this image of a complex contest to acquire power through the state, Parkin also contends that a few dominant factions, particularly the dominant economic class, are typically able to gain majority control over the means of social closure (1972:181–82). In addition, despite Parkin's apparent stance that the state is without power of its own, he seems to allow for one crucial exception: where a single political party is able to take complete control of the state, as occurs in state-socialist systems, for example. In these situations, the will of a single political faction becomes "fused" with the entire state apparatus into one totalitarian, omnipotent "party-state." Under socialism, this means the end of bourgeois class domination, but it can also mean the centralization of all power within the party-state (1979:140). The serious problems Parkin perceives in such a system provide the basis for his assessment of the future of inequality and the relative merits of capitalism, socialism, and social democracy.

Capitalism, Socialism, and Social Democracy

Notwithstanding the acknowledged exploitation, injustice, and other flaws in capitalism, Parkin is not surprised that workers in most developed countries appear to find the prospect of socialism even less palatable. Massive disinterest in the socialist cause in many capitalist countries is less attributable to "false consciousness" or "mystification" within the working class than to the regrettable examples of socialism in action provided by the Soviet Union and other contemporary state-socialist nations. First of all, although organized repression is found in all societies to some extent, the fusion of party and state within totalitarian socialist regimes on the left (and, of course, totalitarian fascist regimes on the right) seems far more conducive to the sustained use of violence and terror than is typical of Western capitalist societies. It is partly because of this spectre of violence on the left, of Stalinist purges and "the possibility that the Red Army might be mobilized for other than purely defensive purposes," that workers in other nations have been suspicious of putting socialist doctrines into practice (1979:201).

A second impediment to popular support for socialism is the evidence that early Marxist revolutionaries, including Stalin, Lenin, Lukacs, and others, placed much greater faith in an elite "vanguard" party than in a general groundswell of workers' involvement in shaping and directing socialist transformation. Certainly, Lenin and others expected this elite dominance to be only temporary, and recent Marxists such as Poulantzas and Wright strongly advocate broad proletarian participation in any future socialist initiatives. Nevertheless, the impression among many workers — that the dictatorship of the proletariat is still a euphemism for totalitarian control by the party-state — is partly responsible for their disavowal of socialist revolution. Even minimal freedoms under capitalism — such as the right of political dissent or the choice of more than one political party to vote for — imply, by comparison, a much more democratic system (1979:153-55, 178-82).

A final factor acting against socialist success is the perception among many workers that the elimination of private control over production has not eradicated inequalities in power or in the distribution of resources and opportunities. Removal of property rights under socialism has meant that other forms of exclusionary closure have become the salient bases for inequality, especially between the mass of the population and an elite category of intellectuals, scientists, officials, and bureaucrats, who have special educational credentials or strategic positions in the party hierarchy with which to exact privilege. As an aside, it is interesting that some Marxists, such as Wright, for example, at times acknowledge this same pattern in state socialism (cf. Wright, 1985:78-79, 83, 122-23). In addition, although the differences between top and bottom are probably smaller under state socialism, workers in capitalist countries still have the perception that there is less wealth to spread around in socialist economies, so that being more equal under socialism may still mean having a more meagre material existence than under capitalism (Parkin, 1979:185-87). If this situation prevails or is perceived to prevail, and if workers put greater stress on distributive issues than some Marxists would prefer, it is unlikely that state socialism can serve as a sufficiently attractive replacement for capitalism.

Although Parkin's assessment implies that neither capitalism nor socialism offers a particularly rosy future, there is at least one other possibility to consider, one that Parkin himself appears to support. Increasingly, in his view, the real choice has become one of state socialism on the one hand and *social democracy*, not pure capitalism, on the other. In the social democracies of Scandinavia, for example, capitalists still retain private control of production and the exclusionary powers that go with it. However, the tensions generated between capitalists and workers can be largely "contained," though never eliminated, through state legislation and other means by which workers get enough usurpationary power that the bourgeoisie retains dominance, but just barely. The trick is to find a balancing point that leaves the capitalist class sufficient incentive to invest and accumulate surplus but that simultaneously reduces the exploitation of workers to the lowest possible level (1979:189). This containment of class struggle need not mean that Dahrendorf's complete legitimation or institutionalization of class conflict is achieved, only that workers and capitalists alike are able to decide how far they can or should go in usurping privilege or excluding others from it.

It is interesting that this social-democratic solution to the problem of inequality returns us to certain basic assumptions about human nature and locates itself somewhere between Marx's belief in the potential selflessness of humanity and the conservative or structural-functionalist insistence on people's inherent motivation to acquire more power or rewards than others. Like Marx, the social-democratic philosophy suggests that all people can flourish under more egalitarian conditions and that, in the proper setting, people are capable of tying personal interest more closely to a concern for the collective good. Yet, as conservative thinkers have argued, no amount of structural change can totally eliminate the "small inner core of human individuality," with its self-interested motives and its belief in differential rewards for differential talent or effort (Parkin, 1979:189–90). From this perspective, some degree of inequality, restricted and reduced though it may be, is perhaps a natural, inevitable, or necessary outcome of social relationships.

Of course, in posing this alternative to state socialism, Parkin is well aware that social democracy has also run into snags when its principles are put into practice. For example, the record of social-democratic governments in western Europe and elsewhere has not been stellar in reducing material inequalities or the concentrated power of capital (1979:200). Yet even modest advances along these lines, when compared to the militarism, totalitarianism, and material shortages of socialist societies, would probably make some form of social democracy the preferred system for most of the working population.

Summary Observations

Parkin's neo-Weberian perspective on social inequality has been the subject in this section of the chapter. Overall, his approach represents a provocative and constructive attempt to reorient Weber's original power perspective by introducing into prominence the concept of social closure. Parkin is able to sustain both Marx's and Weber's stress on class as the crux of social inequality, while also accounting for gender, race, and other important bases of closure or power relations that regularly emerge and become established in social settings. While Parkin's approach thus contributes significantly to a truly general conception of social inequality, there are at least two points that would benefit from additional discussion or elaboration.

First, Parkin's main focus on the legal bases for power or closure, though justifiable, could be expanded to include more-detailed discussion of the nonlegal bases for social domination arising from informal, but equally effective, rules established in traditional beliefs, customs, and habitual practices. Though Parkin is clearly aware of these forms of closure, and the manner in which they can exclude women or racial minorities from power in spite of their *legal* equality, it would be worthwhile to give them greater play, especially since this would be consistent with Weber's original analysis.

Second, Parkin's suggestion that the state has no power, except in such situations as the fusion of party and state under state socialism, seems open to some question (cf. Murphy, 1988:56, 113). Given Parkin's neo-Weberian viewpoint, it stands to reason that he would follow Weber in noting the special power attached to state bureaucrats, power that is not reducible to the class, ethnicity, gender, party, or other external affiliations they possess but that inheres in their roles as bureaucratic administrators and decision makers internal to the state itself. In that sense, heads of state organizations have power in the same way that any other privileged factions do. In a similar vein, one could note that the unique coercive powers of the state's military and police branches also give them special, and in some cases ultimate, control in society.

Anthony Giddens

THE STRUCTURATION OF CLASS, POWER, AND INEQUALITY

The last major approach to social inequality we shall examine is that found in the writings of Anthony Giddens. Giddens is recognized as one of the leading figures in contemporary social thought, both for his insightful analyses of Marx, Weber, Durkheim, and other classical theorists and for his more recent development of a general *theory of structuration* as an alternative perspective in sociology (e.g., Giddens, 1971, 1976, 1977, 1979, 1984). In the process of pursuing both these projects, Giddens has sought to rethink several topics of special relevance to the study of social inequality, especially past and present conceptions of class, power, and the capitalist state (1973, 1981a, 1981b, 1985).

It was noted at the beginning of this chapter that Giddens is often categorized as a neo-Weberian, particularly by Marxist critics of his views (Binns, 1977; Crompton and Gubbay, 1977; Wright, 1978, 1979; Burris, 1987). While there is some validity to this assessment at a very general level of discussion, it should be observed that, as Giddens himself argues, on some issues he owes rather more to Marx than to Weber. Moreover, in generating the finer points of his own perspective, Giddens frequently draws on and builds from a wide range of additional viewpoints that include structuralism and hermeneutics, among others.

These conditions should be kept in mind when noting Giddens's location between the Marxist and Weberian camps on our left-right continuum in Figure 6.1. This position reflects his joint sympathies with basic elements of both Marx and Weber, who, as we have seen, have more in common than many analysts realize. However, Giddens's position on the continuum also signifies his felt need to supplement and modify the views of these classical thinkers. Giddens concurs with Weber's initial attempt to deal with certain points left undeveloped by Marx, especially the pluralist nature of class and power, the importance of bureaucracy in modern systems of domination, and the role of the state as the focus of legal and repressive power in advanced societies. In turn, Giddens has stressed the need to correct and elaborate the manner in which Weber has dealt with these and other issues (1981a:296–300; cf. 1973:100–102; 1984:xxxvi).

The culmination of Giddens's efforts to expand and redirect existing perspectives is his own structuration approach to the analysis of social processes. It is beyond our purposes to explore all the intricacies of this general orientation; nevertheless, its specific application to the problem of social inequality is crucial to consider because, in several respects, it offers the most promising basis for a comprehensive analysis of this area (cf. Turner, 1986:974–75). As with the other perspectives we have examined, the discussion in this section centres on four main issues: the concept of class or class structure, the significance of power in systems of social inequality, the role of the state, and the prospects for inequality in future society.

Class Structure in Advanced Societies

The beginnings of Giddens's overall structuration perspective can be found in his initial analysis of the class structure in advanced societies (1973). Rather like Wright after him, Giddens argues that the two-class system envisioned by Marx, involving bourgeoisie and proletariat, is acceptable primarily as an "abstract" or "pure" model of the capitalist class structure, one that omits certain residual class locations in real societies (1973:27–28). Giddens holds with all Marxists and most Weberians that the crucial factor generating this class system is "ownership or exclusion from ownership of property in the means of production" (1973:100, 271–72). In the end, however, his links to Weber on this issue seem clearer, for he adopts the original Weberian position that classes are largely products of differences in power among groups within the capitalist market. In the economic setting, capitalists enjoy greater power than workers because they retain rights over productive property, while workers have only the right to sell their labour in exchange for a living wage paid by capitalists. Where Giddens reveals his central tie to Weber, and his basic divergence from Marx, is in his contention that there is a third important category of rights that underlies the different economic power, or "market capacity," of people under capitalism. This third factor is the "possession of recognized skills" and "educational qualifications" (1973:101–3).

Using this mixture of Marxian and Weberian precepts, Giddens argues that the three rights, powers, or capacities — property, education or skills, and manual labour — are fundamental to a corresponding "threefold class structure" that is "generic to capitalist society." It is primarily because these three bases of power predominate in the economic sphere that social relationships arise among an "upper" class of those who control most productive property, a "middle" class of those without appreciable property who nonetheless have special education or skills to exchange in the market, and a "lower" or "working" class who have only their manual labour to sell.

Of course, if this three-class scheme is taken too literally, it is subject to the same criticisms as Marx's two-class model, since there are many exceptions that do not fit easily into any of the categories. Giddens himself notes that one cannot draw absolutely clear boundaries between classes, as if they were "lines on a map." This is because some groupings, such as the old petty bourgeoisie or independently employed doctors and other educated professionals, tend to straddle class lines in that they have partial access to more than one of the three types of rights. Using terminology similar to Parkin, Giddens suggests, then, that the degree of "closure" or "exclusion" produced by these rights is not always complete. Besides, the amount that such mixed positions actually blur class lines will vary across different societies, and even different regions within the same society, so that no single model can capture precisely all the detailed differences in class structure that arise in this range of situations.

It is here that Giddens introduces the idea of structuration, primarily as an aid in dealing with these anomalies in real class systems. Rather than speak of classes as if they were discrete groups, explicitly delineated and separated in all instances, Giddens recommends that class structure be construed as a *variable* phenomenon that is generally anchored in a three-class system but that differs in its *degree* of structuration, in the extent to which classes are generated and reproduced over time and place as identifiable, distinct social clusters. In this sense, one can argue that property, educational qualifications, and labour power do act as the major powers or rights that interconnect, or *mediate* between, the economy and the classes arising from it. The three resulting classes will be more clearly defined or structurated in those societies or situations where these three mediate factors tend not to be mixed together in the same occupations or positions (cf. Wright, 1985:106, 112).

In addition, at an immediate, day-to-day, or *proximate* level, Giddens suggests three other factors that can either blur or reinforce the three-class model he outlines. The first proximate factor is the way in which labour is divided in the work setting itself. In some societies, for example, manual labourers are physically separated from specially trained or educated nonmanual workers and invariably perform different tasks. In these cases, the split between middle and working classes is reinforced still further, thus increasing class structuration in such societies.

Similarly, a second proximate factor is the manner in which authority relations are structured in the work setting. Sometimes there is no real difference in the decision-making or supervisory powers of manual workers and specially trained personnel, while in other situations special personnel have authority prerogatives that divide them from manual workers in the same way that their greater education or training does. In the former case there would be some blurring of the boundary between middle and working class, at least on this basis, while in the latter instance the boundary would be enhanced.

The final proximate factor in class structuration is the pattern of *distributive groupings*, by which Giddens means primarily the amount of clustering that occurs because of distinct lifestyles or material consumption habits. The best illustration of this factor is the purchase of housing and the physical segregation or mixing of class clusters that can result. In societies where the upper, middle, and working classes invariably live in clearly designated areas that do not overlap, their pattern of consumption of housing would obviously reinforce the underlying three-class system and make it more readily discernible as a social *reality*. On the other hand, if the predominant pattern in a society or region is a heterogeneous mixing of people in the same neighbourhood, regardless of their market capacities in the economic sphere, then class structuration would be less pronounced and class lines would be more blurred than otherwise (1973:107–10).

What Giddens offers, then, is a basic three-class model that differs from Marx's dichotomous view in two key ways: in its designation of a heterogeneous middle class of educated and skilled personnel, who tend to differ from both capitalists and manual workers; and in its incorporation of a variable element in the conception of class structure, which allows for the possibility that classes in different settings can be more or less distinctly delineated or "structurated," depending on the extent to which these six particular factors act in unison, or against one another, in promoting clear class cleavages. Though there are significant differences in both terminology and focus, Giddens thus shares with many recent theorists a concern with complications that, in contrast to Marx's pure model of classes, are still present in existing capitalist societies.

Perhaps the most telling aspect of Giddens's analysis is his conclusion that these complexities do not negate the truths in Marx but are more significant for understanding capitalist class systems than current Marxists believe. Hence, the middle class is likely to be a persistent reality in advanced capitalism, not some transient fraction or secondary set of contradictory locations. In addition, class affiliations will continue to be elaborate at times, not only because of the variable mix of mediate and proximate divisions, but also because factors such as gender and ethnicity interact with class structuration (1981a:304–7). These views underscore the pluralist image of class and inequality that, more than anything else perhaps, separates Giddens from Marxism (1973:273–74). This pluralism in Giddens carries over into his pivotal analysis of power.

Power and Domination

Giddens's most recent theoretical concerns have centred on refining the concept of power and incorporating it into his more general theory of structuration (1979, 1981b, 1984, 1985). Here, in characteristic fashion, Giddens notes Weber's advances over Marx (who never attempted a complete analysis of power), while at the same time claiming that Weber's view of power is itself in need of elaboration and revision (1981b:4–5).

We shall avoid a detailed review of Giddens's treatment of power, since it involves subtler distinctions and more complex terminology than are appropriate for our discussion. However, in more simplified form, Giddens's formulation is useful here because it connects rather closely with the Weberian view that still prevails on this issue but also because it adds to Weber's conception in certain important respects.

Giddens asserts that power differences are not the only factors linking people together in society but that they do form one such link and are basic to *all* social interaction (1984:32, 227). Power is defined as any "relations of autonomy and dependence between actors in which these actors draw upon and reproduce structural properties of *domination*" 1981b:28–29; 1984:258). Giddens's use of the term domination to define power shows the close connection that he perceives between these two ideas. It is interesting that Weber also ties power and domination together, as we saw in Chapter 3. The interpretation offered there was that power refers to any capacity of an actor (or faction) to exercise his or her will relative to other actors, while domination denotes the regular patterns or structured relations between actors that arise as such power differences are established, routinized, and regenerated over time (cf. Giddens, 1985:7).

Now, while there are undeniable divergences between Giddens and Weber on other points, they share a rough correspondence in this distinction between power as human capacity and domination as a structural manifestation of power. Thus, Giddens sees domination as "structured asymmetries of resources drawn upon and reconstituted in such power relations" (1981b:50; cf. 1979:91–93). What Giddens adds to Weber here is a much more explicit and sophisticated elucidation of this two-sided sense of power, something that is implicit in Weber but must be eked out of his discussion. In fact, Giddens devotes considerable effort to demonstrating that power is "doubled-edged" in a variety of other ways as well: it typically combines some amount of both repression from above and legitimate compliance from below; it can be used to coerce and constrain but also to liberate and transform; it can operate through formal rules and laws or informal customs and traditions; it can involve acts of commission by superiors but also acts of omission or passive resistance by subordinates; and so on (1979:88-94; 1981b:49-51; 1984:257; 1985:10-11). Of course, as we have seen, some of the same points can be found in Weber's writings and also in the more recent analyses of Lenski and Parkin, among others. But Giddens is perhaps most notable for his systematic treatment of this duality in power systems and for his recognition that power exists both as a capacity of persons and as a pattern of relations, sustained or reproduced over time and space (1984:111-12, 1985:7).

It is this same reproductive process, whereby people interact in patterned relations so as to structure (or else change) those relations, that is the essence of what Giddens means by structuration. We have already seen one illustration of this process in the case of class structuration. Class distinctions tend to be solidified or reinforced when people's interactions are determined by their economic capacities (the three mediate factors in capitalism) and by immediate social circumstances related to those capacities (the three proximate factors). The more clearly these bases for interaction separate out clusters of actors from one another, the greater class structuration there is.

The class system also provides the foremost example of how power differences and structures of domination develop in social systems. However, in Giddens's view, capitalist class relations are not the only important case of domination or exploitation in society: "Certain fundamental forms of exploitation do not originate with capitalism, or with class divisions more generally" and "not all forms of exploitation can be explained in terms of class domination." Domination and exploitation also occur in other asymmetrical relations, including those between nation-states — between colonies and imperialistic countries, for example — between ethnic groups, and between the sexes (1981b:25, 60, 242; 1985:256). In other words, the full range of significant social inequalities that can be identified in modern times — not only class inequalities, but those involving gender, ethnicity, international relations, and others — can be understood as manifestations of differences in power or domination and the exploitation these differences entail.

Thus, Giddens leaves no doubt that there is some degree of pluralism in his conception of power. This pluralism is also evident in his overall conception of societal institutions. Although Giddens is highly critical of structural functionalism, and even argues that the term function be banned from sociological discourse, he nonetheless contends that the functionalist perspective is correct to recognize the major institutions of society and their embodiment in large-scale social structures (1981b:16; 1979:97). As was discussed in Chapter 5, structural functionalists conceive of institutions as systems of persistent rules, norms, and values that people tend to live by, or keep in mind, in their interactions with others. These institutions give rise to concrete social structures that roughly correspond to the institutions. An illustration is the formal establishment of a religious structure, or church, in accordance with a particular set of religious values and beliefs.

In a similar fashion, Giddens delineates four basic types of institutions and connects them to a range of concrete social structures. *Political* institutions operate primarily in the political structures of the state and are concerned with "authorization" or the domination of *people*. *Economic* institutions operate mainly in the economic structure and involve "allocation" or the domination of *material phenomena*. Here Giddens suggests that command over people and command over material things are the two key means for establishing power or domination in society (1981:47; 1984:3; cf. 1985:7). Giddens's third category includes *symbolic* institutions, those embodied in religion, education, and the communications media, for example, or in what Poulantzas and Wright would call ideological apparatuses. In his final category, Giddens chooses to distinguish *legal/repressive* institutions from the other three types, although their obvious connections to the legal, military, and police branches of the state suggest they could be included more simply under the political category (1981b:47; 1985:19; cf. Mann, 1986:11; Runciman, 1989:14).

In any case, Giddens's discussion of institutions and structures provides further confirmation of his pluralist view of power and society. This is most obvious, perhaps, in his distinction between political power and economic power, between domination of people and domination of things. In addition, however, the correspondence between institutions and structures is not a simple one-to-one relationship, so that both types of domination operate, at least in secondary form, in the religious and other structures of society as well. It is in this sense that Giddens sees power as a dispersed phenomenon, an integral element of all social life (1981b:28, 49). This does not mean that power can never be disproportionately concentrated in certain structures or factions. On the contrary, it is clear that those who control the economic and political systems are the principal players in the overall power struggle. But it is also the case that any conception that traces power solely to one class, group, or structure is likely to give us an incomplete understanding of the total system of domination in advanced societies.

The Role of the State

Giddens's dualistic view of power as both a human and a structural quality is roughly paralleled in his analysis of the state in advanced societies. In Giddens's opinion, Poulantzas and others are partly correct to represent the state as a structure or framework within which power is exercised by classes (or other interest groups) external to it. However, this does not negate the fact that these structured relations between positions within the state are also occupied by real people as well, by state leaders, bureaucrats, and lesser officials who retain special capacities or powers of their own (1981b:218–20).

Probably the most important sense in which the state is largely a structure for channelling the power of others is in its connections with the economy under capitalism. Giddens accepts the view most closely identified with Offe, but roughly similar to that found in other Marxists such as Poulantzas and Wright, which sees the state as dependent upon the activities of private capitalists for its revenue (cf. Offe, 1974; Offe and Ronge, 1975; Offe, 1984). For this reason, the state structure to some extent is organized by state leaders to facilitate the economic goals of the bourgeoisie. In part, the state personnel are said to be caretakers or managers who, where possible, direct and augment the flow of capitalist economic power in order to aid and maintain both the bourgeoisie's surplus accumulation and the state's tax base. This is seen as the prime reason for the state's growth and its increased intrusion into economic affairs under advanced capitalism (1981b:165, 211; Giddens and Held, 1982:192).

According to Giddens, the state in capitalist society also channels power in a somewhat different sense by "insulating" political power from economic power so that these two means of control seem to the working class to be unrelated. Rather than rally the proletariat to achieve progressive economic change, perhaps even revolution, through political action, the prevailing political parties instituted within most capitalist states keep these issues separate. For the most part, economic struggles are fought as labour-management disputes over wages in the industrial sphere and pose no fundamental threat to the capitalist system itself. Thus, although workers have formal political equality with all other citizens in capitalist democracies, little thought is given to using politics to attain economic equality as well (1981b:127–28; 1985:322).

Nevertheless, in acknowledging these ways in which the state is a structural conduit or framework for the power of external, especially capitalist, interests, Giddens asserts that the state is also a collection of social actors, of leaders and officials with considerable power in their own right. Here Giddens seems to follow Weber to some degree, in that he stresses two bases for domination that are the state's special preserve. First is the monopoly of organized violence inherent in the state's repressive (police and military) branches. Second is the capacity of these branches, as well as various legal and bureaucratic state organizations, to store information and strategic knowledge for surveillance purposes (1985:2, 14–16). These two means for dominating and controlling the populace give those who run the state certain powers that are not subject to the will of the bourgeoisie or any other outside group. It is in this sense that Giddens sees the state's surveillance capabilities and control over the means of violence as "independent influences" in shaping contemporary societies, no less significant for the process of social change than are capitalist class relations and class conflict (1985:2). Moreover, these state powers are evident in virtually all modern societies, capitalist, socialist, or otherwise. Giddens finds it odd that few contemporary analysts, particularly in the structural-functionalist and Marxist camps, have paid much attention to these bases for state power. Clearly, there is ample evidence of their importance and their use in this century by totalitarian regimes on both the left and the right (1981b:94, 175–77, 244; 1985:297–300). The threat posed by these powers of repression and surveillance is one central element in Giddens's assessment of the prospects for future societies.

The Future of Inequality

Giddens's comments concerning the future of social inequality once again reveal his characteristic blend of Marxian and Weberian viewpoints. Like Weber, Giddens is highly critical of current brands of state socialism and extremely doubtful that they can achieve the true transcendence of capitalism they allegedly seek (cf. 1984:32, 227). Nevertheless, like Marx, Giddens retains a personal desire to see a successful transformation of the present exploitation and injustice of capitalist society and harbours some optimism that the possibilities for democratic or "libertarian" socialism do exist (1981b:175; but see 1985:341).

Giddens sees serious flaws in the modern versions of both capitalism and socialism, although like Parkin he apparently finds capitalism, at least the social-democratic variety common in western Europe, to be less objectionable than the state-directed system prevalent in today's socialist countries. Advanced capitalism has been successful on certain counts, most notably the greater political freedoms and material affluence it has provided compared to socialist and other nations. Unfortunately, modern capitalism also fosters fundamental forms of injustice or exploitation that have yet to be alleviated. The relative affluence of people living under capitalism, including workers, has often come at the expense of people in less-developed countries elsewhere as part of the global activity of modern capitalism and the international exploitation of nation-state by nation-state. In addition, within capitalist countries, ethnic and sexual forms of exploitation continue to be significant bases for discrimination and injustice. Finally, of course, advanced capitalism, like all such systems, is premised on the exploitation of one class by another.

Thus, despite providing some measure of material security to workers, capitalism remains a highly unequal form of economic organization, one in which workers have little control over production and in which their labour is itself "commodified" and dehumanized. The political rights and freedoms capitalism offers have failed to compensate for or eliminate these inequities, for capitalism's basic contradiction still remains: it is a system that is impossible without the social or collective production of surplus, and yet it also demands that a select few derive private and disproportionate benefit from that surplus. While this arrangement is not in imminent danger of collapse, in Giddens's view, it is subject to chronic pressures. To Giddens, whether these pressures can be contained, as Parkin and others have argued, depends primarily on the ability of the state to mediate capitalism's basic contradiction, to maintain social conditions that are at least acceptable to the general population without undermining bourgeois domination (1981a:317–19; 1981b:238–39, 250–51; 1985:340–41).

One of the main reasons why capitalism is not immediately threatened by revolution is the general failure of socialism to fulfil its promises. In Giddens's view, current examples of state socialism are at best clumsy prototypes that cannot transcend the capitalist system until they come to grips with their own contradiction. Socialism's contradiction is that it seeks mass equality and participation in social policies and decisions and yet requires a centralized system of production and administration that focuses power in the state. As we have already noted, the concentration of state power, especially through control of surveillance and repression, is a serious threat to equality and freedom that is at least as likely under socialism as under capitalism. Similarly, the bureaucratic domination, sexism, racism, and colonialism common to capitalist systems are also prevalent in current state-socialist regimes.

The crucial lesson here for Marxists is that the abolition of class exploitation by socialist revolution is not enough by itself to bring a just society, since other bases for exploitation still persist. The inability of many Marxists to perceive this stems from their singular concern with class and their consequent failure to note that class relations, though pivotal, are but one manifestation of power differences. Giddens concludes that it is power, conceived along the lines he suggests, that has "universal applicability" to the study of exploitation and inequality. If equality and democracy are to be realized, through socialism or otherwise, it is essential that the use of power in all its forms be examined and understood (1981a:319–20; 1981b:201, 244–48). The unique situation of the modern era, with its trend toward a capitalist "world economy" and its prospect of total nuclear destruction, makes this understanding even more imperative (1981b:196–98, 250; 1985:334–38).

Summary Observations

The purpose of this segment of the chapter has been to outline and assess Giddens's conception of social inequality, with special reference to his structuration approach to class, power, and other related issues. Of the recent perspectives we have examined, Giddens's seems to offer the most comprehensive and inclusive strategy for thinking about social systems and the inequalities that inhere within them. In addition to retaining Marx's classical concern with class and Weber's pluralist revisions and modifications of Marx, Giddens attempts to incorporate what he believes is the central strength of structural functionalism as well: the delineation of major institutions and their attendant concrete structures in advanced societies. The economic, political, religious, and other structures that are identified in this way can all, in varying degrees, be conceived as systems of power, in which patterned relations of domination are established and reproduced over time and space, based on differential control of material ("allocative") and human ("authoritative") resources.

Although there are also clear differences in approach, Giddens's recognition of these distinct structures of domination roughly parallels the separation of economic, political, and ideological apparatuses suggested by Poulantzas, Wright, and other neo-Marxists. The advantage Giddens has over these conceptions stems mainly from his more general concern with analyzing all power relations arising within these structures, as opposed to focusing exclusively on class relations (see also Mann, 1986; Runciman, 1989).

Giddens's stress on the universal role of power in generating all forms of inequality has vague affinities with Dahrendorf, closer connections with Lenski, and even greater similarities with Parkin's social-closure conception. There is a pleasing clarity in Parkin's viewpoint that contrasts with Giddens's rather complex formulation and with Giddens's propensity, as Parkin notes, "to drive conceptual wedges between empirically inseparable things" (Parkin, 1980:892; see also Giddens, 1980). Giddens's attempt to differentiate "locales" from "places" in social space illustrates this tendency to obscure, rather than clarify, his discussion with rather subtle or minor distinctions (1985:12). Another example is his insistence that there is an important conceptual difference between the idea of "structure," on the one hand, and the idea of "structures," on the other (1984:18; cf. Turner, 1986:972). Nevertheless, the complicated nature of Giddens's analysis is also a tribute to its completeness. It would appear that Giddens, more than Parkin, offers us a perspective on inequality that acknowledges the full range of social situations in which power is exercised and inequality established. Giddens also combines Parkin's astute awareness of power as a property of real people with the neo-Marxist (and functionalist) sense of structural arrangements as repositories and channels for power that exist, in a way, apart from the persons that staff them.

For these reasons, then, it could be argued that in several ways Giddens's overall approach provides the most fully developed guide for thinking about and analyzing social inequality that currently exists in social theory. Inevitably, of course, there are specific points raised by Giddens, and by the other theorists for that matter, that remain open to debate and that are unlikely to be reconciled to the satisfaction of every theoretical camp. Nevertheless, it should be evident by now that the writers we have examined are concerned with many of the same issues, and, in different ways, have all contributed to a more complete appreciation of what social inequality is and how it should be conceived. In the closing chapter, we shall briefly summarize and reassess these contributions in an effort to outline the general direction that current thought seems to be moving us in the analysis of social inequality.

Theories of Social Inequality: A Summary and Evaluation

In this concluding chapter, it is important to recapitulate and comment on some of the most crucial contributions and common threads that we have found in examining the various classical and contemporary perspectives on social inequality. Our review will be somewhat selective, for it is intended primarily to underscore the special insights and issues raised by each writer rather than to repeat in detail all of the themes and arguments that have been considered in previous chapters. This summary will enable us to offer some concluding speculations on what key elements should be included in a theoretical overview of social inequality in modern societies. We will also illustrate the feasibility of applying this general overview for the conceptualization of inequality in its more specific forms and manifestations.

The Major Perspectives:
A Selective Review

It should be clear at this stage that Marx's ideas, with which we began our analysis, still stand at the centre of any complete discussion of structured social inequality. Despite the many criticisms levelled against Marx by friend and foe alike, it seems certain that his understanding of the origins of class relations in the sphere of production, and his grasp of the internal workings and contradictions of capitalism, will continue to be unique and lasting contributions to modern social thought.

Marx's work is incomplete as a general perspective on social inequality, in part because the development of such a perspective was not his purpose. Nevertheless, in examining the mechanisms for the revolutionary overthrow of capitalism, the task that required most of his intellectual efforts, Marx also succeeded in identifying what many believe is the principal cleavage, the great divide, in all systems of social inequality: between those who own or control the means of material production and those who survive through their labour power. This essential truth is the point of reference and departure for virtually all the writers who follow.

The second great figure in the study of social inequality is Max Weber. Although several important differences exist between Weber and Marx, there are also fundamental similarities in their thought, especially on the question of class and its pivotal role in the structure of modern society. Those who stress the disagreements in the ideas of Marx and Weber often seem to overlook the affinities between them, as well as Weber's self-professed wish to provide a positive, rather than a destructive, critique of Marxist thought. Many of Weber's major contributions centre on this constructive effort to amplify or modify Marx. These contributions include his recognition in the class system of positions that are neither bourgeois nor proletarian but tend somehow to persist in a middle range between the two main classes; his perception that class relations are best understood as the key type among a more general or plural set of power relations, involving sectional interests and multiple struggles; his delineation of the numerous forms of domination in social structures, including not only legitimate power or authority but also the domination that derives from tradition, habit or custom, fear of repression, and so on; his identification of bureaucratic organizations as the predominant mechanisms for domination in the political, economic, and other spheres of modern life; and his early awareness of the increasing role played by the state in the overall power structure, through its monopoly of repressive force and its connections to the economic system. All these points add immeasurably to the subsequent assessments of social inequality in recent times.

The third classical theorist we considered was Durkheim. The inclusion of Durkheim in an analysis of inequality is perhaps surprising to some, since he is not conventionally seen as a central figure in the field. However, Durkheim's thought offers us an important link between certain basic ideas in Marx and Weber and more recent structural-functionalist formulations. In particular, Durkheim reveals an awareness of such problems as class struggle and alienation under capitalism that is similar to Marx's view in some respects. At the same time, such Weberian concerns as the state and the role of power in society receive more than passing attention. Like Weber, Durkheim sees power, and the social constraints that go with it, arising out of a growing set of legal rules that nonetheless are supplemented at all times by the influence of informal traditions, conventions, habits or customs, and occasionally by coercion. Durkheim also anticipates more recent thinkers like Giddens in a sense, for he too notes the two-sided nature of power, that power can be a positive as well as a limiting force in society, and that rules not only establish power but also prevent its abuse. What separates Durkheim from Marx and Weber, and provides his otherwise tenuous connection to structural functionalism, is his greater stress on the positive, not the negative, consequences of power differences and inequality, specifically within the division of labour.

After Durkheim, we then examined the structural-functionalist school. Among structural functionalists, the predominant strategy is to emphasize Durkheim's sense of the integrative benefits of inequality and to ignore, for the most part, his awareness of the exploitation and injustice that also tend to exist in social hierarchies. This narrow reading of Durkheim is compounded by a peculiar interpretation of Weber, in which any inequalities and power relations that are not based on legitimate authority or consensus go largely unrecognized. The deficiencies in the structural-functionalist approach, which occur because of these omissions, have been discussed earlier. However, in spite of these and other weaknesses, there are at least two elements in structural-functionalist analyses that seem to have a sustained influence in the study of social inequality. First, as Giddens notes, structural functionalism has contributed greatly to the identification of major social institutions and the concrete economic, political, and other structures to which they are tied. Although structural functionalists rarely view them in this way, these structures are a step toward the delineation of a general set of structures of domination in society.

Second, the contention by structural functionalists that there is something inevitable or natural about social inequality is a view that a majority of the population advocates, especially when inequality refers to things like differential rewards for differences in talent or effort (cf. Jasso and Rossi, 1977; Robinson and Bell, 1978; Della Fave, 1980). Of course, popular acceptance of inequality is not a guarantee that it is a natural or inevitable phenomenon. Moreover, as noted in Chapter 1, that social inequality exists in virtually all known societies is not a proof that it must persist in the future. Still, it is difficult to concur with those who simply explain away inequality as some doomed remnant of bourgeois consciousness, a false or distorted form of human relationship that will end with the demise of capitalism. The ready evidence in modern socialist systems of unequal rights, opportunities, rewards, and privileges is sufficient in itself to cast doubt on such claims (e.g., Yanowitch, 1977; Lane, 1982; Giddens and Held, 1982). Hence, until we can achieve some universal shift to an altruistic consciousness among people, there would seem to be at least a kernel of truth in the structural-functionalist view of this question. Even subsequent critics of structural functionalism often appear to agree that such traits as effort, motivation, talent, or training are at least partly responsible for inequality and that, *within certain limits*, most people will perceive this situation as both inescapable and, to some extent, justifiable.

The acknowledgement of these insights and others may partly account for the resurgence of interest in structural functionalism within some academic circles. This new interest seems most apparent in the case of Parsons, whose work has received renewed praise or recognition by such prominent writers as Alexander, Giddens, and Habermas (cf. Antonio, 1989).

Even so, in spite of these considerations, there is little doubt that the structural-functionalist approach, particularly to the study of social inequality, has serious deficiencies. A key difficulty is that *individual* factors like talent and motivation, which are emphasized in the structural-functionalist explanation of inequality, seem in reality to be relatively minor influences, at least in comparison to the *structural* differences in power or class that exist in society. In addition, as many neo-Marxists contend, whatever mobility occurs within these structures because of personal "worth" or effort does little or nothing to change the structures themselves. The point to stress is that established structures tend to define the prospects and life chances of people in most instances, although the roles of individual capacity and human agency should not be overlooked.

After structural functionalism, the first of the more recent theorists we considered was Dahrendorf. Dahrendorf's contributions to the study of inequality mainly involve his rejection of some of the more extreme structural-functionalist accounts. He is most notable for questioning the assumption that all forms of inequality are somehow based on consensus, for calling attention to the inherent conflict in social hierarchies, and for attempting to draw a conceptual connection between class and power (or more precisely, authority). Unfortunately, as we have seen, the third aspect of Dahrendorf's work seems to confuse matters by treating all authority differences as class differences.

The next writer to be assessed, Lenski, also fosters some confusion of class and power. Like Dahrendorf, he also tends to overestimate the extent to which inequalities in class and power have been reduced in the modern era. Nevertheless, Lenski compensates for these problems with his important identification of the multiple bases for power that arise in contemporary societies, and with his suggestion that power in its various forms is primarily responsible for the unequal distribution of material privilege and prestige to groups and individuals. In this manner, Lenski directs us to a more global conception of what social inequality is. In doing so, he also moves us back toward Weber, Marx, and the last theoretical exchange we examined: the continuing debate between neo-Weberian and neo-Marxist views on the problem of social inequality.

A central conclusion of this book is that the most promising basis for developing an adequate conceptualization of social inequality is still to be found in the disputes and discussions growing out of the Marxist class analyses of writers such as Poulantzas and Wright, on the one hand, and the power- or domination-based perspectives of theorists such as Parkin and Giddens, on the other hand. It should also be evident from the previous analysis that the overall thrust of our review generally favours the broadly Weberian views of the latter two writers. The reasons for this choice centre mainly on the greater generalizability of the power concept over the class concept and on the plural inequalities that this allows us to recognize. The existence of some degree of pluralism, and of distinct bases for power in addition to class power, is *explicitly* denied by Poulantzas and other Marxists; yet, as we have seen, these elements are *implicitly* acknowledged in the Marxist delineation of fractions or contradictory locations in the class system and of the economic, political, and ideological apparatuses in capitalist society. The reluctance to give express recognition to this pluralism, or to see any conceptual equivalence in the fact that class, gender, race, and other bases for inequality all involve power relations, seems to stem from a fear that class would thereby be diminished in importance as a concept in this area. Such a fear, however, is unwarranted. It is possible to arrive at a conception of social inequality that maintains the primacy of class analysis but that also appreciates the complex nature of both class relations and the other power relations that are at work in shaping social structures (cf. Miliband, 1987:328). In varying ways, this is what Parkin and especially Giddens have done.

This is not to say that the recent Marxist contributions to the analysis of inequality should be discounted. On the contrary, Wright's work in particular has been valuable for clarifying and redirecting issues first raised by Poulantzas and others. In addition, Wright's conception of the capitalist class structure, especially as outlined in Figures 6.2 and 6.3, appears at present to be the most systematic scheme for portraying class relations and their existence across the various eco-nomic, political, and ideological structures of society. For this to be a more complete picture, however, it also requires that Giddens's duality of social arrangements be incorporated, that this skeleton of class positions be more thoroughly invested with the human content that both Giddens and Parkin favour when discussing classes. In that event, we can accept that relations of productive control form the under-pinnings of the class system, but we can also affirm that clusters of real people will coalesce around the different bases for interaction or closure that are inherent to these relations (for debate, see Burris, 1987).

Such a dual sense of classes as structures and classes as people is useful for avoiding fruitless debates that insist classes must be only one or the other. Similarly empty controversies, over whether power is a capacity of persons or a relation between them and whether the state has power or not, could also be eased if it were seen that both actors and the patterns of interaction between social positions are involved in all these things. Although various writers reveal an awareness of this dual nature of class and power, Giddens has arguably been most successful in incorporating it into his overall perspective on inequality in social systems. His treatment of power is particularly valuable for its assimilation of elements from several other analyses. Included here are his revitalized version of Weber's conception of domination; his use of institutional or structural elaborations similar to those in functionalism and recent Marxism; and his awareness, like Parkin, of the multiple forms of closure and exploitation in society, which contribute not only to class inequality but also to inequalities based on gender, race, and a whole range of other factors.

Social Inequality: A Summary Portrait

Having highlighted the crucial themes in classical and contemporary theories of inequality, we come again to the fundamental questions raised in the opening chapter. We are now in a better position to answer such questions about what social inequality is and how it should be conceived; however, it is also clear that no single set of answers will be universally acceptable, since no single perspective can subsume the others or resolve all the disagreements among theorists. For these reasons, no grand synthesis of viewpoints is either likely or advisable. Nevertheless, there are some views that many, if not most, of the writers do share, at least at a general level of discussion. There should be no surprise in this; given the erudition of the thinkers involved, the surprising outcome would be if they did *not* agree on certain basic points. It can be argued that the broad similarities found in many of the perspectives may at least move us toward some "common vocabulary," as Parkin calls it, for discussing social inequality (Parkin, 1979:42).

As a provisional step in this direction, Figure 7.1 offers a summary picture, or composite scheme, which can aid in the general conceptualization of social inequality in modern societies. This depiction is essentially an abstract representation of the major means for establishing power relations in social settings, the resulting structures of domination

Figure 7.1

The Major Means of Power, Structures of Domination, and Bases for Social Inequality

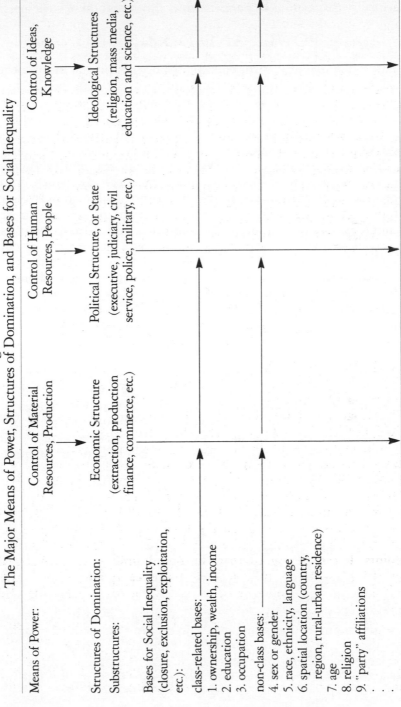

that emerge and are reproduced, and the principal bases for social inequality that typically operate within and across these structures.

POWER AND DOMINATION

First, it is apparent that the concept of power is pivotal in this portrait. In fact, while class and power are the two key concepts in most of the general perspectives on inequality we have reviewed, Figure 7.1 should make it clear that, in this summary portrait, power is employed as the most common or pervasive conceptual element. Power is defined here as a differential capacity to command resources, which gives rise to structured, asymmetric relations of domination and subordination between social actors. There are three key means by which power is normally generated in social systems: control of material resources, of people, and of ideas. The first two means of power correspond roughly to Giddens's concepts of allocation and authorization and to a broadly similar delineation of "human and non-human resources" found in Goldthorpe (1974:218; cf. Grabb, 1982). The third designation of power through ideas is an extension of the twofold scheme. It is reminiscent of Francis Bacon's famous remark that "knowledge is power," that ideas and information can serve as the means (or the medium) of power in the same way that money or people can. The recognition of this third type of power is generally compatible with the work of previous writers we have examined, virtually all of whom, in varying degrees, note the importance of controlling special knowledge and information or the influence that beliefs and ideas can have on social life. In addition, by combining this category of *ideological* power with the other two types, we arrive at a classification that corresponds with the three-way division of social structures (economic, political, and ideological) that most theorists seem to advocate (cf. Mann, 1986; Runciman, 1989).

Thus, below the three means of power shown in Figure 7.1 are three attendant structures: the economic, the political, and the ideological. These social structures could be analyzed in many ways, but because of our specific interest in power and patterned relations of inequality, they are presented here as structures of *domination*. The connections in the diagram are oversimplified in that they imply a simple one-to-one linkage between each type of power and each structure. In fact, the downward arrows indicate only the *primary* linkage, since each form of power can operate in at least a secondary fashion in any of the structures. For example, control of people may be the principal activity within the political structure, but it is also evidenced in the control imposed by owners on workers in the economic structure. Similarly, the political structures that form the state do not derive all their power from the capacity to legislate or coerce human behaviour, for they also control material resources through tax revenues, government ownership of some business enterprises, and so on. As for control of ideas or knowledge, this is most clearly identified with the ideological structures, but it is also a means for retaining power elsewhere, as illustrated by the access to special technical knowledge in the economic structure and the information-gathering powers within the state.

In this manner, then, the vertical dimension in Figure 7.1 signifies the structures (and internal substructures) of domination in the social systems that society comprises. At a more concrete level of discussion, these structures are manifested mainly as bureaucratic or corporate organizations. These organizations are patterned according to formal rules, laws, or rights of office but are also guided by a mix of informal practices, traditions, customs, or habits. It is these formal and informal rules that, taken together, largely determine the nature and extent of inequality in society, what the social bases for inequality will be and how much they will matter.

THE SOCIAL BASES FOR INEQUALITY

The horizontal dimension in Figure 7.1 provides a list of individual and group characteristics that typically have been used as the major bases for inequality in advanced societies. We have noted several times before the dualistic view of power fostered by various writers, most particularly Giddens. One way to look at Figure 7.1 is to think of the vertical dimension as the *structural* part of this duality and to treat the horizontal plane as the second part of the duality, the *human content* of power relations. Along this side of the diagram are the personal attributes and affiliations that inject the structures of domination with their social and human elements. These attributes or affiliations are essentially similar to what a recent theorist has labelled "systacts" (Runciman, 1989:20). They serve as the crucial factors around which group interests coalesce and collective action is organized, in the various competitions or struggles that can arise over access to the three different means of power. In combination, both the structural and the human components of power relations give rise to the multifaceted system of inequality that society comprises, with people processed and located at different levels, depending on the relative share of the major economic, political, and ideological resources at their disposal. It is notable that one of the most recent treatises on social theory also emphasizes the same central role of power in social systems, points to the same three major means or sources of power, and argues for the same duality of structure and human agency in defining power relations. According to this view, "the study of societies is the study of people in roles, and the study of people in roles is the study of the institutional distribution of power" (Runciman, 1989:3, 12).

Class-Related Bases for Inequality

The personal traits, capacities, or criteria for affiliation that are listed in Figure 7.1 can be divided into two main categories. First are three class-related factors: ownership (which also subsumes possession of wealth or income), education, and occupation. Ownership corresponds loosely with the various forms of property ownership that both Marxists and Weberians consider the key mode of economic control or closure in society. Education parallels the credentials basis for inequality that Parkin, Giddens, Wright, and others have stressed. Occupation is almost a residual category here, in that it subsumes such traits as skill level, manual versus nonmanual labour, and so on, that are not captured in the other two class-related bases for inequality. These three factors operate within and across all the structures of domination shown in the vertical dimension. In conjunction, they push capitalist societies toward a class system that is highly complex, that varies in specific details from country to country, but that has at its core three major categories: an upper class composed mainly of the bourgeoisie, large-scale owners and controllers of material production, along with a smaller number of leaders from other spheres, who control political and ideological production and also tend to have sizeable personal fortunes or business holdings; a heterogeneous central category of people who may have limited powers of ownership, such as the ownership of small businesses or financial investments, but who are distinguished in most cases by their access to special education, formal training, recognized skills, or other credentials; and a lower or working class whose members are largely without property or special credentials and rely almost completely on labour power for their material existence (cf. Grabb, 1988:3-8).

Although this image of the class structure seems closest to that of Weber or Giddens, it is also broadly similar to that posed by neo-Marxists such as Wright. Until recently, the most contentious issue has been whether the central category represents a separate middle class all on its own or, instead, a set of contradictory or dual locations that remain secondary to the two main classes. It is interesting that, at least in Wright's case, he now readily refers to these intermediate positions as "the middle class," in spite of the non-Marxist or Weberian connotations of that term (e.g., Wright and Martin, 1987:24-25). It is worth noting, as an aside, that Marx himself had no difficulty with using the middle-class label for such intermediate positions at times (cf. Grabb, 1988:5). In the end, though, the choice of terms is, in a sense, less important than the simple truth that there is something else in addition to the capital-versus-wage-labour distinction that exists in reality and requires explanation or study. That both Marxists and non-Marxists now tend to agree on this third category, if not always on how to label it, seems sufficient grounds for including it here.

Non-Class Bases for Inequality

The second set of human attributes or affiliations shown in the horizontal dimension of Figure 7.1 is a variable list of bases for inequality that are not inherent to class formation, although they are normally correlated with class inequalities in most cases. Whether and to what degree these bases for inequality actually operate will clearly differ from society to society.

One point that should be emphasized is that the reference to these other factors as "non-class" bases for inequality is meant simply to distinguish them analytically from the class-related factors, rather than to imply that they are somehow secondary to or derivative from class inequality. On the contrary, following non-Marxist writers such as Giddens and Parkin, as well as certain Marxist analysts like Wright, it can be argued that any question of the relative primacy or significance of class and non-class factors in the *overall* structure of inequality should be a matter of empirical investigation. The answer to this question, moreover, may well be quite different, depending on which nation or historical period is being considered. For example, it is possible that class inequality may be more crucial or telling in the general pattern of inequality than is gender or race in some instances, but the reverse may be true in other cases.

It should also be noted that the list of non-class bases for inequality is not necessarily exhaustive. There are other traits or affiliations that probably are less obvious or less commonly recognized in the literature as important determinants of people's life chances but that, nonetheless, can play a role in the structure of social inequality. These include physical beauty or disability, for example. Generally, though, the bases listed here appear to be the major factors operating within most modern systems of inequality.

Most of the bases of inequality listed in Figure 7.1 have been noted by several of the writers we have reviewed. This observation is less applicable to the classical theorists who, with the possible exception of Weber, focus most of their attention on class issues and devote little systematic discussion to the other bases for inequality (for some exceptions, see Sydie, 1987; Collins, 1985, 1986a, 1986b, 1988). The contemporary writers deal more explicitly with the key non-class bases. For example, such attributes as sex or gender, ethnicity (including race and language grouping), religion, and age are examined to varying degrees by Lenski, Parkin, Giddens, and Wright. Giddens appears to be the one writer among those we have considered who makes direct reference to the ways in which geographic location can affect patterned relations of inequality. Giddens's key example is the exploitation of one nation-state or country by another. This form of inequality concerns the processes by which developed nations systematically keep less developed nations in situations of subordination in the world economy (cf. Frank, 1969; Wallerstein, 1974, 1980). In addition, however, the inequalities that arise *within* countries can also be delineated, especially between people of different regions or between those who live in rural versus urban settings. These spatial bases for inequality are not always recognized as significant by sociologists, although there appears to be a growing interest in Canada and elsewhere in the problems of regional disparities in economic development and in the more general inequalities involved in "core-periphery" or "metropolis-hinterland" relations (e.g., Innis, 1956; Creighton, 1956; Davis, 1971; Matthews, 1983; Bryan, 1986; Coffey and Polese, 1987).

The final basis for inequality listed in Figure 7.1 concerns access to or exclusion from the power that people experience through their party affiliations. Following Weber, this refers not just to formal political parties. It also serves as a residual term that subsumes all the other organized collectivities or interest groups that people may create in the general contest for power in social settings: trade unions, professional associations, public-interest organizations, various pressure groups, and so on.

It is no coincidence that virtually all of the bases for inequality that are summarized in Figure 7.1 have served as rallying points for collective action among those seeking to reduce or eliminate social injustice in the contemporary period. Among the most prominent examples of such collective attempts to achieve greater equality are the American civil-rights movement, the drive for both francophone and native people's rights in Canada, the fight against apartheid in South Africa, and the women's movement in a wide range of developed nations. While it has not been possible in this book to consider in any detail these and other initiatives for social change, such activities clearly illustrate the continuing, and perhaps increasing, importance of the study of inequality for understanding the general problem of human rights in the modern world (cf. Cairns and Williams, 1985, 1988).

Linking General and Specific Theories of Inequality

Based on the discussion to this point, it can be argued that the theorists we have reviewed provide us with the principal elements necessary for an overall portrait or conceptual apparatus for understanding social inequality in contemporary societies. These elements refer, in particular, to the major forms or sources of power in social structures and to the key class and non-class bases for inequality, around which groups become defined and organized in the competition or struggle over the major power sources. However, because our central concern in this analysis has been to draw out these common elements from leading *general* perspectives on inequality, we have not considered theoretical developments in those bodies of work that address specific forms or manifestations of inequality, such as gender or racial inequality, for example.

It is not within the scope we have set for the current analysis to undertake what would require a series of detailed expositions on theories that target for exclusive consideration each one of the specific bases for inequality noted in Figure 7.1. Nevertheless, it is instructive to take a brief look at some examples of these more focused theories. Such an examination shows that, despite obvious and important differences in the details of these formulations, their conceptual vocabularies and pivotal arguments about the reasons behind these particular forms of inequality are often quite close to what the general theories reviewed here have argued. This suggests an essential linkage or compatibility between these specific theoretical approaches and the overall portrait we have extracted from the general classical and contemporary perspectives. These linkages can be demonstrated, first, with some illustrations from theories of gender and, second, with some instances from studies of race or ethnicity.

THEORIES OF GENDER INEQUALITY

Some of the best examples of conceptual correspondence or compatibility between general and specific approaches are to be found in the area of gender or feminist studies. While the literature in this field has become vast, broad, and diverse in recent decades, there are numerous instances of writers who approach the topic of gender inequality in a manner that is largely similar to that suggested here. That is, most writers in feminist theory trace gender inequality not to innate biological differences, for example, but to socially defined and structured differences between men and women, especially those that arise because of differential access to the means or sources of *power*. Most leading analysts in this area focus, in particular, on the problem of *patriarchy*, which essentially refers to any society, or pattern of social relations in society, in which males have power over and thereby dominate females.

Of course, there are disputes and debates within this range of theorists over which sources of power are more significant or fundamental in determining male dominance. Many theorists, including radical or Marxist feminists but also various non-Marxists, stress the central importance of economic power differences in the sphere of work or material production, and see the intersection of gender and class inequalities as the crux of male ascendancy. Others concur but contend, as well, that male economic power is evident not only in the "public" sphere of productive labour but also in the "private" or domestic division of labour. In the latter setting, women tend to be relegated to subordinate roles within the home and family, providing care and support to male wage earners but living in a situation of dependence on their male partners for their survival or economic well-being. Although there inevitably are many disagreements in emphasis and tone in these accounts, their common element is the acknowledged significance of economic power as a major factor contributing to female subordination and the overall pattern of gender inequality (cf. Friedan, 1963; Millet, 1969; Bernard, 1971; Eisenstein, 1979; Huber and Spitze, 1983; Blumberg, 1978, 1984; Crompton and Mann, 1986; Bologh, 1987; for reviews, see Richardson, 1988; Ritzer, 1988; Collins, 1988).

In addition to economic power, however, many of the leading writers in this field also conceive of political power as a major force accounting for the overall domination of men over women in social structures. Some suggest, in fact, that political (including coercive or military) power has at times played the most crucial role in establishing male dominance historically (Collins, 1975:225–59; Collins, 1988:168–73; see also Millett, 1969). Others acknowledge the importance of political or coercive mechanisms but still see economic power as more significant (Blumberg, 1984:41, 49, 74–75).

Finally, along with economic and political power, most theories that address the problem of gender inequality place considerable weight on what we have called ideological domination, on the power that ideas, beliefs, and cultural values can have in establishing the control of one group or faction by another in social settings. In other words, the teaching and dissemination through society's ideological structures of what roles males and females should occupy can be of major consequence in determining the pattern and extent of gender inequality. Various theorists and students of patriarchy have recognized the part played by ideological power and parallel the classical and contemporary theorists we have reviewed in including this element in their explanations of gender inequality (cf. Ritzer, 1988:306–7; Blumberg, 1984:40–41, 45; Milkman, 1987; Richardson, 1988:156–58).

It should be evident, then, that there are basic affinities and correspondences between the conceptual vocabularies and approaches used by leading theorists of gender inequality and those that we have found in our assessment of more general perspectives. Of course, this does not mean that theories focusing specifically on gender issues are somehow redundant or that gender inequality is just like every other manifestation of inequality we wish to study. Clearly, the explanations for gender inequality are likely to differ from those that might be used to account for class inequality or racial inequality. These differences can arise for many reasons, including possible variations in the relative impact of economic, political, and ideological power in each case. Moreover, explanations for gender inequality will themselves vary because of differences in how these sources of power are distributed to men and women across a range of historical, geographic, and institutional settings. The principal claim here is that gender inequality parallels the other key bases in that it stems primarily from differential access to the three major sources of power (cf. Connell, 1987).

THEORIES OF RACIAL OR ETHNIC INEQUALITY

The study of race and ethnic relations, like the study of gender, has generated an extensive body of research and theory, especially in countries such as the United States and Canada. A review of prominent contributors to this field indicates that, in trying to characterize the nature and causes of inequality, many of them also employ a conceptual approach that focuses primarily on differences in access to power. Probably the best illustration in the Canadian case is Porter's classic study, *The Vertical Mosaic*, which conceives of ethnic (and class) inequality primarily in terms of the relative control that different groups are able to acquire within the country's economic, political, and ideological power structures (Porter, 1965). Once again, there is disagreement on the relative role of each source of power. For example, some writers now are more likely than Porter to stress the importance of economic power over all others; moreover, some also contend that in capitalist societies, at least, ethnic and racial inequalities are best conceived of as secondary fractions within a general system of social inequality that is "primarily based on class relations" (Li, 1988:132, 140). Even so, such debates arise within a context of general agreement on the importance of all three sources of power in creating and sustaining racial and ethnic inequalities (e.g., Ramcharan, 1982:2-4, 97-98; Bolaria and Li, 1985:1-11; Li, 1988:23).

Many of the best-known analyses of racial and ethnic inequality in the United States reveal a similar reliance on the concept of power and its various forms (e.g., Shibutani and Kwan, 1965; Blalock, 1967; Wilson, 1973). Especially in his earlier writings, Wilson has conceived of black subordination in American society primarily as a problem of limited access to various "power resources," including economic, political (or coercive), and ideological (or cultural) components (Wilson, 1973:5, 7, 16-18). Although his stress on power has been supplanted to some extent by a focus on class in his more recent works, the conceptual relevance of power for explaining racial inequality still remains evident (cf. Wilson, 1978, 1987). In these examples from the United States as well, then, it is possible to discern the conceptual links between specific theories of racial inequality, on the one hand, and the overall portrait of inequality we have drawn from the general theorists, on the other. In all cases, the suggestion is that the problem of inequality is largely to be understood with reference to control over the major sources of power by some groups relative to others.

Conclusion

These illustrations complete our discussion and analysis of major theoretical works in the field of social inequality and the applicability of their central ideas to understanding and explaining inequality in all its forms. Any task of this kind, of course, is destined to be unsuccessful, at least in part, since theoretical formulations are continually subject to change. To revise and to elaborate theory is inherently necessary because of the new conceptual developments or discoveries that emerge and ultimately promote the refinement or replacement of existing conceptions about the social world.

Inevitably, then, the establishment of a wholly adequate and comprehensive conceptualization of the sources, structure, and bases of social inequality must remain a distant and elusive goal. For now, our most reasonable hope is that, in this analysis, the key insights of classical and contemporary theory have been made clear and the broad brush-strokes of a general portrait of social inequality have been painted a little more boldly than before.

References

Aberle, D.F., A.K. Cohen, A.K. Davis, M.J. Levy, Jr., and F.X. Sutton
  1950   "The functional prerequisites of society." *Ethics* 60
          (January):100–111.
Alexander, Jeffrey C.
  1983   *Theoretical Logic in Sociology*. Vol. 3, *The Classical Attempt at
          Theoretical Synthesis: Max Weber*. Berkeley: University of
          California Press.
  1987   *Twenty Lectures: Sociological Theory Since World War II*. New
          York: Columbia University Press.
Alexander, Jeffrey C. (ed.)
  1985   *Neofunctionalism*. Beverly Hills: Sage.
Althusser, Louis
  1969   *For Marx*. New York: Pantheon.
  1976   *Essays in Self-Criticism*. London: New Left Books.
Althusser, Louis, and Etienne Balibar
  1970   *Reading Capital*. London: New Left Books.
Antonio, Robert J.
  1989   "The normative foundations of emancipatory theory:
          Evolutionary versus pragmatic perspectives." *American Journal
          of Sociology* 94, no. 4 (January):721–48.
Aron, Raymond
  1970   *Main Currents in Sociological Thought*, Vol. 2. Garden City:
          Anchor Books.
Avineri, Shlomo
  1968   *The Social and Political Thought of Karl Marx*. Cambridge:
          Cambridge University Press.

Baer, Doug, Edward G. Grabb, and William Johnston
    1987   "Class, crisis, and political ideology: recent trends."
            Canadian Review of Sociology and Anthropology 24, no. 1
            (February): 1–22.
    1990   "The values of Canadians and Americans: a critical analysis
            and reassessment." *Social Forces* 68, no. 3 (March):
            (forthcoming).
Balkwell, J.W., F.L. Bates, and A.P. Garbin
    1982   "Does the degree of consensus on occupational status
            evaluations differ by socioeconomic stratum? Response to
            Guppy." *Social Forces* 60 (June):1183–89.
Baran, Paul, and Paul Sweezy
    1966   *Monopoly Capital.* New York: Monthly Review Press.
Barber, Bernard
    1957   *Social Stratification.* New York: Harcourt Brace and World.
Bell, Daniel
    1960   *The End of Ideology.* New York: The Free Press.
Bell, Wendell, and Robert V. Robinson
    1980   "Cognitive maps of class and racial inequalities in England
            and the United States." *American Journal of Sociology* 86
            (September):320–49.
Bendix, Reinhard
    1962   *Max Weber: An Intellectual Portrait.* Garden City: Anchor
            Books.
Benson, Leslie
    1978   *Proletarians and Parties.* London: Methuen.
Berlin, Isaiah
    1963   *Karl Marx: His Life and Environment.* Oxford: Oxford
            University Press.
Bernard, Jessie
    1971   *Women and the Public Interest.* Chicago: Aldine.
Binns, David
    1977   *Beyond the Sociology of Conflict.* London: Macmillan.
Blalock, H.M., Jr.
    1967   *Toward a Theory of Minority Group Relations.* New York:
            Wiley.
Blau, Peter
    1964   *Exchange and Power in Social Life.* New York: Wiley.
    1977   *Inequality and Heterogeneity.* New York: The Free Press.
Blau, Peter, and Otis Dudley Duncan
    1967   *The American Occupational Structure.* New York: Wiley.
Blishen, Bernard
    1967   "A socioeconomic index for occupations in Canada." *Canadian
            Review of Sociology and Anthropology* 4:41–53.

Blishen, B., W. Carroll, and C. Moore
    1987   "The 1981 socioeconomic index for occupations in Canada."
            Canadian Review of Sociology and Anthropology 24, no. 4
            (November):465–88.
Blishen, Bernard, and Hugh McRoberts
    1976   "A revised socioeconomic index for occupations." *Canadian
            Review of Sociology and Anthropology* 13 (February):71–79.
Blumberg, Rae Lesser
    1978   *Stratification: Socioeconomic and Sexual Inequality.* Dubuque:
            William C. Brown Company.
    1984   "A general theory of gender stratification." In R. Collins (ed.),
            Sociological Theory 1984, pp. 23–101. San Francisco: Jossey-
            Bass.
Bolaria, B. Singh, and Peter S. Li
    1985   *Racial Oppression in Canada.* Toronto: Garamond.
Bologh, Roslynn Wallach
    1987   "Marx, Weber, and masculine theorizing." In Norbert Wiley
            (ed.), *The Marx-Weber Debate*, pp. 145–68. Newbury Park,
            California: Sage.
Braverman, Harry
    1974   *Labor and Monopoly Capital.* New York: Monthly Review
            Press.
Bryan, Ingrid
    1986   *Economic Policies in Canada* (second edition). Toronto:
            Butterworths.
Burris, Val
    1987   "The neo-Marxist synthesis of Marx and Weber on class." In
            Norbert Wiley (ed.), *The Marx-Weber Debate*, pp. 67–90.
            Newbury Park, California: Sage.
Cairns, Allan, and Cynthia Williams
    1985   *Constitutionalism, Citizenship, and Society in Canada.* Toronto:
            University of Toronto Press.
    1988   "The state and human rights." In J. Curtis, E. Grabb,
            N. Guppy, and S. Gilbert (eds.), *Social Inequality in Canada:
            Patterns, Problems, Policies,* pp. 385–93. Scarborough: Prentice-
            Hall Canada.
Carchedi, Guglielmo
    1977   *On the Economic Identification of Social Classes.* London:
            Routledge.
    1987   *Class Analysis and Social Research.* Oxford and New York: Basil
            Blackwell.
Coffey, William, and Mario Polese (eds.)
    1987   *Still Living Together.* Halifax: Institute for Research on Public
            Policy.

Coleman, Richard P., and Lee Rainwater
    1978   *Social Standing in America: New Dimensions of Class.* New York: Basic Books.
Collins, Randall
    1975   *Conflict Sociology: Toward an Explanatory Science.* New York: Academic Press.
    1979   *The Credential Society.* New York: Academic Press.
    1980   "Weber's last theory of capitalism: a systematization." *American Sociological Review* 45, no. 6 (December) : 925–42.
    1982   *Sociological Insight: An Introduction to Non-Obvious Sociology.* New York: Oxford University Press.
    1985   *Three Sociological Traditions.* New York and Oxford: Oxford University Press.
    1986a   *Weberian Sociological Theory.* Cambridge: Cambridge University Press.
    1986b   *Max Weber: A Skeleton Key.* Beverly Hills: Sage.
    1988   *Theoretical Sociology.* San Diego: Harcourt Brace Jovanovich.
Connell, R.W.
    1979   "A critique of the Althusserian approach to class." *Theory and Society* 8, no. 3:321–45.
    1987   *Gender and Power: Society, the Person and Sexual Politics.* Cambridge: Polity Press.
Coser, Lewis A.
    1977   *Masters of Sociological Thought.* New York: Harcourt Brace Jovanovich.
Coxon, A., and C. Jones
    1978   *The Images of Occupational Prestige.* London: Macmillan.
Creighton, Donald
    1956   *The Commercial Empire of the St. Lawrence.* Toronto: Macmillan.
Crompton, R., and J. Gubbay
    1977   *Economy and Class Structure.* London: Macmillan.
Crompton, Rosemary, and Michael Mann (eds.)
    1986   *Gender and Stratification.* Cambridge: Polity Press.
Curtis, James E., Edward Grabb, Neil Guppy, and Sid Gilbert (eds.)
    1988   *Social Inequality in Canada: Patterns, Problems, Policies.* Scarborough: Prentice-Hall Canada.
Curtis, James E., and William G. Scott (eds.)
    1979   *Social Stratification: Canada* (second edition). Scarborough: Prentice-Hall Canada.
Dahrendorf, Ralf
    1958   "Out of Utopia: toward a reorientation of sociological analysis." *American Journal of Sociology* 64 (September):115–27.

1959   *Class and Class Conflict in Industrial Society.*
        Stanford: Stanford University Press.
1968   *Essays in the Theory of Society.* London: Routledge and Kegan
        Paul.
1969   "On the origin of inequality among men." In A. Beteille (ed.),
        Social Inequality, pp. 16–44. Middlesex: Penguin.
1979   *Life Chances.* London: Weidenfeld and Nicolson.
1988   *The Modern Social Conflict. An Essay on the Politics of Liberty.*
        London: Weidenfeld and Nicolson.

Davis, A.K.
1971   "Canadian society and history as hinterland versus
        metropolis." In R.J. Ossenberg (ed.), *Canadian Society:
        Pluralism, Change, and Conflict,* pp. 6–32. Scarborough:
        Prentice-Hall Canada.

Davis, Kingsley
1949   *Human Society.* New York: Macmillan.
1953   "Reply to Tumin." *American Sociological Review* 18
        (August):394–97.
1959   "The myth of functional analysis as a special method in
        sociology and anthropology." *American Sociological Review* 24
        (December):757–72.

Davis, Kingsley, and Wilbert E. Moore
1945   "Some principles of stratification." *American Sociological
        Review* 10 (April):242–49.

Della Fave, L. Richard
1980   "The meek shall not inherit the earth: self-evaluation and the
        legitimacy of stratification." *American Sociological Review* 45
        (December):955–71.

Demerath, N.J., and Richard A. Peterson (eds.)
1967   *System, Change, and Conflict.* New York: The Free Press.

Durkheim, Emile
1893   *The Division of Labor in Society* (first edition). New York:
[1964] The Free Press.
1895   *The Rules of Sociological Method.* New York: The Free
[1964] Press.
1896   *Socialism and Saint-Simon.* Yellow Springs, Ohio: Antioch
[1958] Press.
1902   *The Division of Labor in Society. Preface to the Second Edition:*
[1964] *Some Notes on Occupational Groups.* New York: The Free
        Press.

Eisenstein, Zillah
1979   *Capitalist Patriarchy and the Case for Socialist Feminism.* New
        York: Monthly Review Press.

Elster, Jon
    1985   *Making Sense of Marx*. Cambridge: Cambridge University
            Press.
Engels, Friedrich
    1872   "On authority." In R.C. Tucker (ed.), *The Marx-Engels Reader*
    [1978] (second edition), pp. 730–33. New York: Norton.
    1882   Letter from Engels to Bernstein. In *Marx Engels Werke*, Vol.
    [1967] 35. Berlin: Dietz Verlag. Institut für Marxismus-Leninismus
            Beim ZK Der Sed.
    1890a   Letter from Engels to Conrad Schmidt. In *Marx Engels Werke*,
    [1967] Vol. 37, pp. 488–95. Berlin: Dietz Verlag. Institut für
            Marxismus-Leninismus Beim ZK Der Sed.
    1890b   Letter from Engels to J. Bloch. In *Marx Engels Werke*, Vol. 37,
    [1967] pp. 462–65. Berlin: Dietz Verlag. Institut für Marxismus-
            Leninismus Beim ZK Der Sed.
Fallding, Harold
    1968   *The Sociological Task*. Englewood Cliffs: Prentice-Hall.
    1972   "Only one sociology." *British Journal of Sociology* 23
            (March):93–101.
Frank, André Gunder
    1969   *Capitalism and Underdevelopment in Latin America*. New York:
            Monthly Review Press.
Friedan, Betty
    1963   *The Feminine Mystique*. New York: Dell.
Gagliani, Giorgio
    1981   "How many working classes?" *American Journal of Sociology*
            87 (September):259–85.
Gerth, Hans, and C. Wright Mills (eds.)
    1967   *From Max Weber: Essays in Sociology*. Oxford: Oxford
            University Press.
Giddens, Anthony
    1971   *Capitalism and Modern Social Theory*. Cambridge: Cambridge
            University Press.
    1972   *Politics and Sociology in the Thought of Max Weber*. London:
            Macmillan.
    1973   *The Class Structure of the Advanced Societies*. London:
            Hutchinson.
    1976   *New Rules of Sociological Method*. London: Hutchinson.
    1977   *Studies in Social and Political Theory*. London: Hutchinson.
    1979   *Central Problems in Social Theory*. Berkeley: University of
            California Press.
    1980   "Classes, capitalism, and the state." *Theory and Society* 9
            (November):877–90.
    1981a   "Postscript (1979)." In *The Class Structure of the Advanced
            Societies* (second edition), pp. 295–320. London: Hutchinson.

1981b   *A Contemporary Critique of Historical Materialism*. Vol. 1, *Power, Property, and the State*. London: Macmillan.

1984   *The Constitution of Society*. Berkeley and Los Angeles: University of California Press.

1985   *A Contemporary Critique of Historical Materialism*. Vol. 2, *The Nation-State and Violence*. Berkeley and Los Angeles: University of California Press.

Giddens, Anthony (ed.)

1986   *Durkheim on Politics and the State*. Cambridge: Polity Press.

Giddens, Anthony, and David Held (eds.)

1982   *Classes, Power, and Conflict*. Berkeley: University of California Press.

Goldstone, Jack A.

1986   "State breakdown in the English Revolution: a new synthesis." *American Journal of Sociology* 92, no. 2 (September):257–322.

Goldthorpe, John H.

1972   "Class, status, and party in modern Britain." *European Journal of Sociology* 13:342–72.

1974   "Social inequality and social integration in modern Britain." In D. Wedderburn (ed.), *Poverty, Inequality, and Class Structure*, pp. 217–38. London: Cambridge University Press.

Goldthorpe, John H., and Keith Hope

1974   *The Social Grading of Occupations: A New Approach and Scale*. Oxford: Clarendon Press.

Grabb, Edward G.

1980   "Marxist categories and theories of class: the case of working class authoritarianism." *Pacific Sociological Review* 33, no. 4 (October):359–76.

1982   "Social stratification." In J.J. Teevan (ed.), *Introduction to Sociology: A Canadian Focus*, pp. 121–57. Scarborough: Prentice-Hall Canada.

1988   "Conceptual issues in the study of social inequality.' In J. Curtis, E. Grabb, N. Guppy, and S. Gilbert (eds.), *Social Inequality in Canada: Patterns, Problems, Policies*, pp. 1–19. Scarborough: Prentice-Hall Canada.

Grabb, Edward G., and Ronald D. Lambert

1982   "The subjective meanings of social class among Canadians." *Canadian Journal of Sociology* 7, no. 3:297–307.

Guppy, L. Neil

1981   "Occupational prestige and conscience collective: the consensus debate reassessed." Unpublished doctoral dissertation, Sociology Department, University of Waterloo.

1982   "On intersubjectivity and collective conscience in occupational prestige research: a comment on Balkwell-Bates-Garbin and Kraus-Schild-Hodge." *Social Forces* 60 (June):1178–82.

Habermas, Jürgen
    1975   *Legitimation Crisis*. Boston: Beacon Press.
    1984   *The Theory of Communicative Action*. Boston: Beacon Press.
Hagan, John, and Celesta Albonetti
    1982   "Race, class, and the perception of criminal justice in
            America." *American Journal of Sociology* 88, no. 2
            (September):329–55.
Hagan, John, and Patricia Parker
    1985   "White-collar crime and punishment: the class structure and
            legal sanctioning of securities violations." *American Sociological
            Review* 50, no. 3 (June):302–16.
Hindess, B., and P.Q. Hirst
    1975   *Pre-Capitalist Modes of Production*. London: Routledge.
    1977   *Modes of Production and Social Formation*. London: Macmillan.
Hodge, Robert W., V. Kraus, and E.O. Schild
    1982   "Consensus in occupational prestige research: response to
            Guppy." *Social Forces* 60 (June):1190–96.
Hodge, Robert W., Paul M. Siegel, and Peter H. Rossi
    1964   "Occupational prestige in the United States: 1925–1963."
            American Journal of Sociology 70 (November):286–302.
Hodge, Robert W., Donald J. Treiman, and Peter H. Rossi
    1966   "A comparative study of occupational prestige." In R. Bendix
            and S.M. Lipset (eds.), *Class, Status, and Power* (second
            edition), pp. 309–21. New York: The Free Press.
Huber, Joan, and Glenna Spitze
    1983   *Sex Stratification: Children, Housework, and Jobs*. New York:
            Academic Press.
Hunter, Alfred A.
    1986   *Class Tells: On Social Inequality in Canada* (second edition).
            Toronto: Butterworths.
Inkeles, Alex, and Peter Rossi
    1956   "National comparison of occupational prestige." *American
            Journal of Sociology* 61 (January):329–39.
Innis, Harold A.
    1956   *The Fur Trade in Canada*. Toronto: University of Toronto
            Press.
Jasso, G., and P.H. Rossi
    1977   "Distributive justice and earned income." *American Sociological
            Review* 42 (August):639–51.
Jeffries, Vincent, and H. Edward Ransford
    1980   *Social Stratification: A Multiple Hierarchy Approach*. Boston:
            Allyn and Bacon.

Jessop, Bob
    1982   *The Capitalist State*. Oxford: Martin Robertson.
    1985   *Nicos Poulantzas: Marxist Theory and Political Strategy*. New
            York: St. Martin's Press.

Johnson, Harry M.
    1960   *Sociology: A Systematic Introduction*. New York: Harcourt,
            Brace and World.

Johnson, Leo
    1979   "Income disparity and the structure of earnings in Canada,
            1946-74." In J.E. Curtis and W.G. Scott (eds.), *Social
            Stratification: Canada* (second edition), pp. 141-57.
            Scarborough: Prentice-Hall Canada.

Johnston, William, and Michael Ornstein
    1982   "Class, work, and politics." *Canadian Review of Sociology and
            Anthropology* 19, no. 2 (May):196-214.

Kallen, Horace M.
    1931   "Functionalism." In E. Seligman (ed.), *Encyclopedia of the
            Social Sciences*, Vol. 6, pp. 523-26. New York: Macmillan and
            The Free Press.

Kalmonick, Paul
    1988   *Classes: A Marxist Critique*. Dix Hills, New York: General Hall.

Kolko, Gabriel
    1962   *Wealth and Power in America*. New York: Praeger.

Lambert, Ronald D., James Curtis, Steven Brown, and Barry Kay
    1986   "Canadians' beliefs about differences between social classes."
            Canadian Journal of Sociology 11, no. 4 (Winter):379-99.

Lane, David
    1982   *The End of Social Inequality? Class, Status, and Power under
            State Socialism*. Winchester, Mass.: Allen and Unwin.

Lenin, V.I.
    1917   *The State and Revolution*. In *Selected Works*. London:
    [1969]   Lawrence and Wishart.

Lenski, Gerhard E.
    1966   *Power and Privilege: A Theory of Social Stratification*. New
            York: McGraw-Hill.
    1980   "In praise of Mosca and Michels." *Mid-American Review of
            Sociology* 5, no. 2:1-12.
    1988   "Rethinking macrosociological theory." *American Sociological
            Review* 53, no. 2 (April):163-71.

Lenski, Gerhard E., and Patrick Nolan
    1984   "Trajectories of development: a test of ecological-evolutionary
            theory." *Social Forces* 63, no. 1 (September):1-23.

Levine, Rhonda F., and Jerry Lembcke (eds.)
  1987   *Recapturing Marxism: An Appraisal of Recent Trends in Sociological Theory.* New York: Praeger.
Lévi-Strauss, Claude
  1968   *Structural Anthropology.* London: Allen Lane.
Levy, Marion J., Jr.
  1968   "Structural-functional analysis." In D.L. Sills (ed.), *International Encyclopedia of the Social Sciences*, Vol. 6, pp. 21–29. New York: Macmillan and The Free Press.
Li, Peter S.
  1988   *Ethnic Inequality in a Class Society.* Toronto: Wall and Thompson.
Lipset, S.M., and Reinhard Bendix
  1963   *Social Mobility in Industrial Society.* Berkeley: University of California Press.
Lockwood, David
  1956   "Some remarks on 'The Social System.'" *British Journal of Sociology* 7 (June):134–46.
Lukes, S.M.
  1973   *Emile Durkheim: His Life and Work.* Harmondsworth: Penguin Books.
  1974   *Power: A Radical View.* London: Macmillan.
  1978   "Power and authority." In T. Bottomore and R. Nisbet (eds.), *A History of Sociological Analysis*, pp. 633–76. New York: Basic Books.
Malinowski, Bronislaw
  1926   *Crime and Custom in Savage Society.* London: Routledge.
  1929   *The Sexual Life of Savages in Northwest Melanesia.* London: Routledge.
Mann, Michael
  1986   *The Sources of Social Power*, Vol.1. Cambridge: Cambridge University Press.
Marcuse, Herbert
  1971   "Industrialization and capitalism." In O. Stammer (ed.), *Max Weber and Sociology Today*, pp. 133–51. New York: Harper and Row.
Marx, Karl
  1843   Contribution to the Critique of Hegel's Philosophy of Law. In
  [1975] *Marx Engels Collected Works*, Vol. 3. New York: International Publishers.
  1844   Economic and Philosophic Manuscripts of 1844. In *Marx*
  [1975] *Engels Collected Works*, Vol. 3. New York: International Publishers.
  1847   The Poverty of Philosophy. In *Marx Engels Collected Works*,
  [1976] Vol. 6. New York: International Publishers.

1858   *Grundrisse. Foundations of the Critique of Political Economy.*
[1973]   Harmondsworth: Penguin.
1859   A Contribution to the Critique of Political Economy. Excerpt
[1970]   in H. Selsam, D. Goldway, and H. Martel, (eds.), *Dynamics of Social Change.* New York: International Publishers.
1862   *Theories of Surplus Value*, Vol. 2. Moscow: Progress
[1968]   Publishers.
1867   *Capital*, Vol. 1. New York: International Publishers.
[1967]
1875   *Critique of the Gotha Program.* New York: International
[1938]   Publishers.
1894   *Capital*, Vol. 3. New York: International Publishers.
[1967]

Marx, Karl, and Friedrich Engels
1846   The German Ideology. In *Marx Engels Collected Works*, Vol. 5.
[1976]   New York: International Publishers.
1848   *The Communist Manifesto.* New York: Washington Square
[1970]   Press.

Matthews, Ralph
1983   *The Creation of Regional Dependency.* Toronto: University of Toronto Press.

McLellan, David
1971   *The Thought of Karl Marx.* New York: Harper and Row.
1973   *Karl Marx: His Life and Thought.* London: Macmillan.

Meiksins, Peter
1987   "New classes and old theories: the impasse of contemporary class analysis." In R.F. Levine and J. Lembcke (eds.), *Recapturing Marxism: An Appraisal of Recent Trends in Sociological Theory*, pp. 37–63. New York: Praeger.

Merton, Robert K.
1949   *Social Theory and Social Structure.* New York: The Free Press.

Michels, Robert
1915   *Political Parties. A Sociological Study of the Oligarchical*
[1962]   *Tendencies of Modern Democracy.* New York: The Free Press.

Miliband, Ralph
1969   *The State in Capitalist Society.* London: Weidenfeld and Nicolson.
1987   "Classes." In Anthony Giddens and Jonathan Turner (eds.), *Sociological Theory Today*, pp. 325–46. Stanford: Stanford University Press.

Milkman, Ruth
1987   *Gender at Work.* Urbana and Chicago: University of Chicago Press.

Millet, Kate
1969   *Sexual Politics.* Garden City: Doubleday.

Mills, C. Wright
    1951   *White Collar*. New York: Oxford University Press.
    1956   *The Power Elite*. New York: Oxford University Press.
    1959   *The Sociological Imagination*. New York: Oxford University
            Press.
Münch, Richard
    1982   "Talcott Parsons and the theory of action. II. The continuity
            of the development." *American Journal of Sociology* 87
            (January):771–826.
Murphy, Raymond
    1988   *Social Closure: The Theory of Monopolization and Exclusion.*
            Oxford: Clarendon Press.
Nisbet, Robert A.
    1959   "The decline and fall of social class." *Pacific Sociological Review*
            2 (Spring):11–17.
North, Cecil C., and Paul K. Hatt
    1947   "Jobs and occupations: a popular evaluation." *Opinion News*
            (September).
Nosanchuk, T.A.
    1972   "A note on the use of the correlation coefficient for assessing
            the similarity of occupational rankings." *Canadian Review of
            Sociology and Anthropology* 9 (November):357–65.
Offe, Claus
    1974   "Structural problems of the capitalist state." *German Political
            Studies* 1.
    1984   *Contradictions of the Welfare State*. Cambridge, Mass.: MIT
            Press.
Offe, Claus, and Volker Ronge
    1975   "Theses on the theory of the state." *New German Critique*
            6:139–47.
Parkin, Frank
    1972   *Class Inequality and Political Order*. London: Paladin.
    1978   "Social stratification." In T. Bottomore and R. Nisbet (eds.), *A
            History of Sociological Analysis*, pp. 599–632. New York: Basic
            Books.
    1979   *Marxism and Class Theory: A Bourgeois Critique*. London:
            Tavistock.
    1980   "Reply to Giddens." *Theory and Society* 9 (November):891–94.
    1983   "Strategies of social closure in class formation." *Soziale Welt*,
            Supplement 2:121–35.
Parsons, Talcott
    1937   *The Structure of Social Action*, Vol. 1. New York: The Free
            Press.
    1940   "An analytical approach to the theory of social stratification."
    [1964] In T. Parsons, *Essays in Sociological Theory*, pp. 69–88. New
            York: The Free Press.

1947   *Max Weber: The Theory of Social and Economic Organization.*
         New York: The Free Press.
1951   *The Social System.* New York: The Free Press.
1953   "A revised analytical approach to the theory of social
[1964]   stratification." In T. Parsons, *Essays in Sociological Theory,*
         pp. 386–439. New York: The Free Press.
1966   "On the concept of political power." In R. Bendix and S.M.
         Lipset (eds.), *Class, Status, and Power* (second edition),
         pp. 240–65. New York: The Free Press.

Peyre, Henri
1960   "Durkheim: the man, his time, and his intellectual
         background." In Kurt Wolff (ed.), *Emile Durkheim,*
         pp. 3–31. Columbus: Ohio State University Press.

Pineo, Peter, John Porter, and Hugh McRoberts
1977   "The 1971 census and the socioeconomic classification of
         occupations." *Canadian Review of Sociology and Anthropology*
         14 (February):91–102.

Porter, John
1965   *The Vertical Mosaic: An Analysis of Social Class and Power in
         Canada.* Toronto: University of Toronto Press.

Portis, Edward Bryan
1986   *Max Weber and Political Commitment: Science, Politics and
         Personality.* Philadelphia: Temple University Press.

Poulantzas, Nicos
1973a   *Political Power and Social Classes.* London: New Left Books.
1973b   "On social classes." *New Left Review* 78:27–54.
1975   *Classes in Contemporary Capitalism.* London: New Left Books.
1978   *State, Power, Socialism.* London: New Left Books.

Przeworski, Adam
1985   *Capitalism and Social Democracy.* Cambridge: Cambridge
         University Press.

Radcliffe-Brown, A.R.
1922   *The Andaman Islanders.* Cambridge: Cambridge University
         Press.
1935   "On the concept of function in social science." *American
         Anthropologist* 37 (July–September):395–402.
1948   *A Natural Science of Society.* New York: The Free Press.
1952   *Structure and Function in Primitive Society: Essays and Addresses.*
         London: Cohen and West.

Ramcharan, Subhas
1982   *Racism: Non-Whites in Canada.* Toronto: Butterworths.

Richardson, Laurel
1988   *The Dynamics of Sex and Gender: A Sociological Perspective.*
         New York: Harper and Row.

Riesman, David, N. Glazer, and R. Denney
1953   *The Lonely Crowd.* New York: Doubleday.

Ritzer, George
    1988   *Contemporary Sociological Theory* (second edition). New York: Alfred Knopf.
Robinson, Robert V., and Wendell Bell
    1978   "Equality, success, and social justice in England and the United States." *American Sociological Review* 43 (April):125–43.
Roemer, John
    1982   *A General Theory of Exploitation and Class.* Cambridge, Mass.: Harvard University Press.
Runciman, W.G. (ed.)
    1978   *Max Weber: Selections in Translation.* Cambridge: Cambridge University Press.
Runciman, W.G.
    1989   *A Treatise on Social Theory.* Vol. 2, *Substantive Social Theory.* Cambridge: Cambridge University Press.
Salomon, Albert
    1945   "German sociology." In Georges Gurvitch and Wilbert E. Moore (eds.), *Twentieth Century Sociology.* New York: Philosophical Library.
Schacht, Richard
    1970   *Alienation.* Garden City: Doubleday.
Scott, John
    1979   *Corporations, Classes, and Capitalism.* London: Hutchinson.
Selsam, Howard, David Goldway, and Harry Martel (eds.)
    1970   *Dynamics of Social Change.* New York: International Publishers.
Shibutani, T., and K.M. Kwan
    1965   *Ethnic Stratification: A Comparative Approach.* New York: Macmillan.
Shils, Edward, and Henry Finch (eds.)
    1949   *The Methodology of the Social Sciences. Max Weber.* New York: The Free Press.
Singer, Peter
    1980   *Marx.* Oxford: Oxford University Press.
Sorokin, Pitirim A.
    1927   *Social Mobility.* New York: Harper and Row.
    1947   *Society, Culture, and Personality.* New York: Harper and Row.
Stehr, Nico
    1974   "Consensus and dissensus in occupational prestige." *British Journal of Sociology* 25 (December):410–27.
Steinmetz, George, and Erik Olin Wright
    1989   "The fall and rise of the petty bourgeoisie: changing patterns of self-employment in the post-war United States." *American Journal of Sociology* 94, no. 5 (March):973–1018.

Stolzman, James, and Herbert Gamberg
    1974   "Marxist class analysis versus stratification analysis as general
            approaches to social inequality." *Berkeley Journal of Sociology*
            18:105–25.
Sydie, R.A.
    1987   *Natural Women, Cultured Men: A Feminist Perspective on
            Sociological Theory.* Toronto: Methuen.
Therborn, Göran
    1986   "Class analysis: history and defence." In Ulf Himmelstrand
            (ed.), *Sociology: From Crisis to Science*, Vol. 1, pp. 96–132.
            London: Sage.
Treiman, Donald J.
    1977   *Occupational Prestige in Comparative Perspective.* New York:
            Academic Press.
Tumin, Melvin M.
    1953   "Some principles of stratification: a critical analysis." *American
            Sociological Review* 18 (August):387–93.
Turner, Jonathan H.
    1984   *Societal Stratification: A Theoretical Analysis.* New York:
            Columbia University Press.
    1986   "The theory of structuration." *American Journal of Sociology*
            86, no. 4 (January):969–77.
Wallerstein, Immanuel
    1974   *The Modern World-System*, Vol. 1. New York: Academic Press.
    1980   *The Modern World-System*, Vol. 2. New York: Academic Press.
Weber, Max
    1905   *The Protestant Ethic and the Spirit of Capitalism.* New York:
    [1958] Charles Scribner's Sons.
    1922   *Economy and Society*, Vols. 1–3. New York: Bedminster
    [1968] Press.
Weiss, Donald D.
    1976   "Marx versus Smith on the division of labor." In *Technology,
            the Labor Process, and the Working Class*, pp. 104–18. New
            York: Monthly Review Press.
Wenger, Morton G.
    1980   "The transmutation of Weber's *Stand* in American sociology
            and its social roots." In *Current Perspectives in Social Theory*,
            Vol. 1, pp. 357–78.
    1987   "Class closure and the historical/structural limits of the Marx-
            Weber convergence." In Norbert Wiley (ed.), *The Marx-Weber
            Debate*, pp. 43–64. Newbury Park, California: Sage.
Wesolowski, W.
    1966   "Some notes on the functional theory of stratification." In R.
            Bendix and S.M. Lipset (eds.), *Class, Status, and Power* (second
            edition), pp. 64–69. New York: The Free Press.

Wiley, Norbert (ed.)
    1987   *The Marx-Weber Debate.* Newbury Park, California: Sage.
Williams, Robin M., Jr.
    1960   *American Society. A Sociological Interpretation.* New York:
            Knopf.
Wilson, William Julius
    1973   *Power, Racism, and Privilege.* New York: Macmillan.
    1978   *The Declining Significance of Race.* Chicago: University of
            Chicago Press.
    1987   *The Truly Disadvantaged.* Chicago: University of Chicago
            Press.
Wood, Ellen
    1986   *The Retreat from Class. A New 'True' Socialism.* London: Verso.
Wright, Erik Olin
    1976   "Class boundaries in advanced capitalism." *New Left Review*
            98:3–41.
    1978   *Class, Crisis, and the State.* London: New Left Books.
    1979   *Class Structure and Income Determination.* New York:
            Academic Press.
    1980   "Class and occupation." *Theory and Society* 9 (January):
            177–214.
    1985   *Classes.* London: Verso.
    1989a   "The comparative project on class structure and class
            consciousness: an overview." *Acta Sociologica* 32, no. 1:3–22.
    1989b   *The Debate on Classes.* London: Verso.
Wright, Erik Olin, C. Costello, D. Hachen, and J. Sprague
    1982   "The American class structure." *American Sociological Review*
            47 (December):709–26.
Wright, Erik Olin, and Bill Martin
    1987   "The transformation of the American class structure,
            1960–1980." *American Journal of Sociology* 93, no. 1
            (July):1–29.
Wright, Erik Olin, and Luca Perrone
    1977   "Marxist class categories and income inequality." *American
            Sociological Review* 42 (February):32–55.
Wright, Erik Olin, and Joachim Singelmann
    1982   "Proletarianization in the changing American class structure."
            American Journal of Sociology 88 (Supplement):S176–S209.
Wrong, Dennis
    1959   "The functional theory of stratification: some neglected
            considerations." *American Sociological Review* 24
            (December):772–82.
    1961   "The over-socialized conception of man in modern sociology."
            American Sociological Review 26 (April):183–93.
    1979   *Power: Its Forms, Bases and Uses.* New York: Harper and Row.

Yanowitch, Murray
    1977   *Social and Economic Inequality in the Soviet Union.* London:
            Martin Robertson.
Zeitlin, Irving M.
    1968   *Ideology and the Development of Sociological Theory.*
            Englewood Cliffs: Prentice-Hall.

Index

To the owner of this book:

We are interested in your reaction to *Theories of Social Inequality* by
Edward G. Grabb.
1. What was your reason for using this book?

_____university course   _____continuing education course
_____college course   _____personal interest
                                 _____other (specify)
2. In which school are you enrolled? _____
3. Approximately how much of the book did you use?
____¼   ____½   ____¾   ____all
4. What is the best aspect of the book?
5. Have you any suggestions for improvement?
6. Is there anything that should be added?

Fold here

\--

(fold here and tape shut)

- -

MAIL POSTE

Canada Post Corporation / Société canadienne des postes

Postage paid
If mailed in Canada

Port payé
si posté au Canada

Business Reply

Réponse d'affaires

0116870399   01

0116870399-M8Z4X6-BR01

Heather McWhinney
Publisher, College Division
HARCOURT BRACE & COMPANY, CANADA
55 HORNER AVENUE
TORONTO, ONTARIO
M8Z 9Z9

A HANDBOOK OF CONTEMPORARY

SPANISH GRAMMAR

Ana Beatriz Chiquito

Professor, University of Bergen, Norway

Visiting Researcher, MIT

VISTA
HIGHER LEARNING

Boston, Massachusetts

Publisher: José A. Blanco
Managing Editors: Eugenia Corbo, Paola Rios Schaaf (Technology)
Project Manager: Patricia Ravetto
Editors: John DeCarli (Technology), Lauren Krolick, Paula Orrego,
Raquel Rodríguez Muñoz, Carolina Zapata Pérez
Production and Design Director: Marta Kimball
Senior Designer: Sarah Cole
Production and Design Team: María Eugenia Castaño, Oscar Díez, Mauricio Henao,
Jhoany Jiménez, Erik Restrepo, Hamilton Zuleta

Printed in Canada.

ISBN: 978-1-61767-097-8
Library of Congress Card Number: 2010942655

1 2 3 4 5 6 7 8 9 TC 17 16 15 14 13 12 11

Organization

A Handbook of Contemporary Spanish Grammar includes the following sections:

Grammar presentations

- 31 chapters divided into clearly marked sections and subsections
- Complete verb tables for easy reference

Glosario combinatorio

- See pp. xvii and 279 for more details.

Activities

- More than 400 activities
- Immediate feedback provided when practice is done on the Supersite
- Additional practice available online (See p. xviii.)

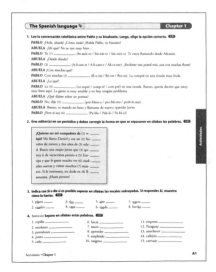

Answer key

- Built-in answer key for checking your work when practice is done manually

Sidebars and icons

- On the first page of every chapter, a sidebar summarizes the chapter's contents.

Chapter 11

A. Overview
B. Comparisons of inequality
C. Comparisons of equality
D. Superlatives

- Clearly marked and numbered headings help you navigate the grammar explanations and easily locate cross-references.

19.B Use of the present perfect

19.B.1 Life experiences – *nunca, alguna vez, hasta ahora*

- A sidebar at the end of the chapter includes the specific activity sequence with its corresponding page numbers. The Supersite icon indicates that these activities are also available online.

Práctica

(S) Actividades 1–16, pp. A18–A20

- In the *Actividades* section, a mouse icon 🖱 indicates when activities are also on the Supersite.

Adverbs 🖱   **Chapter 10**

- Each activity identifies the chapter (**2**) and section(s) (**A–D**) where the material is presented.

   16. Síntesis Elige la palabra que no pertenece al grupo. **2.A–2.D**

- Additional practice on the Supersite, not available in the text, is indicated at the end of each practice section.

   🖱: Practice more at **vhlcentral.com.**

Glosario combinatorio

A Handbook of Contemporary Spanish Grammar features a practical glossary of collocations, or common word combinations. The glossary functions as:

• An invaluable tool for expanding vocabulary and increasing grammatical accuracy

• An excellent reference for improving fluency by learning word combinations commonly used by native speakers

For a detailed description, see p. 279.

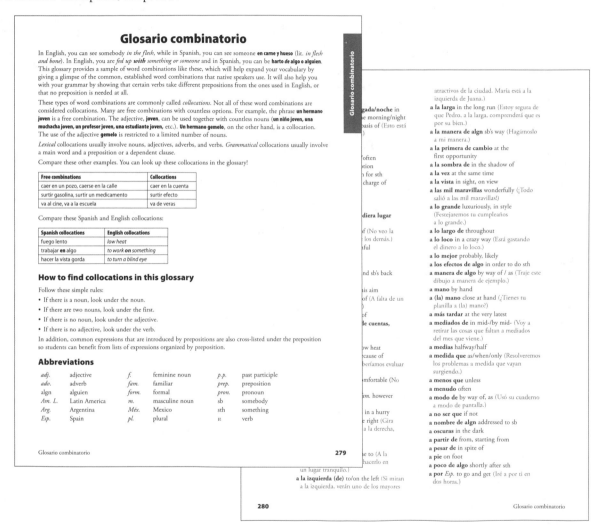

Glosario combinatorio

In English, you can see somebody *in the flesh*, while in Spanish, you can see someone **en carne y hueso** (lit. *in flesh and bone*). In English, you are *fed up* **with** *something or someone* and in Spanish, you can be **harto de algo o alguien**. This glossary provides a sample of word combinations like these, which will help expand your vocabulary by giving a glimpse of the common, established word combinations that native speakers use. It will also help you with your grammar by showing that certain verbs take different prepositions from the ones used in English, or that no preposition is needed at all.

These types of word combinations are commonly called *collocations*. Not all of these word combinations are considered collocations. Many are free combinations with countless options. For example, the phrase **un hermano joven** is a free combination. The adjective, **joven**, can be used together with countless nouns (**un niño joven, una muchacha joven, un profesor joven, una estudiante joven**, etc.). **Un hermano gemelo**, on the other hand, is a collocation. The use of the adjective **gemelo** is restricted to a limited number of nouns.

Lexical collocations usually involve nouns, adjectives, adverbs, and verbs. *Grammatical* collocations usually involve a main word and a preposition or a dependent clause.

Compare these other examples. You can look up these collocations in the glossary!

Free combinations	Collocations
caer en un pozo, caerse en la calle	caer en la cuenta
surtir gasolina, surtir un medicamento	surtir efecto
va al cine, va a la escuela	va de veras

Compare these Spanish and English collocations:

Spanish collocations	English collocations
fuego lento	low heat
trabajar **en** algo	to work **on** something
hacer la vista gorda	to turn a blind eye

How to find collocations in this glossary

Follow these simple rules:
• If there is a noun, look under the noun.
• If there are two nouns, look under the first.
• If there is no noun, look under the adjective.
• If there is no adjective, look under the verb.

In addition, common expressions that are introduced by prepositions are also cross-listed under the preposition so students can benefit from lists of expressions organized by preposition.

Abbreviations

adj.	adjective	*f.*	feminine noun	*p.p.*	past participle
adv.	adverb	*fam.*	familiar	*prep.*	preposition
algn	alguien	*form.*	formal	*pron.*	pronoun
Am. L.	Latin America	*m.*	masculine noun	sb	somebody
Arg.	Argentina	*Méx.*	Mexico	sth	something
Esp.	Spain	*pl.*	plural	*v.*	verb

Glosario combinatorio

279

atractivos de la ciudad. María está a la izquierda de Juana.)

a la larga in the long run (Estoy segura de que Pedro, a la larga, comprenderá que es por su bien.)

a la manera de algn sb's way (Hagámoslo a mi manera.)

a la primera de cambio at the first opportunity

a la sombra de in the shadow of

a la vez at the same time

a la vista in sight, on view

a las mil maravillas wonderfully (¡Todo salió a las mil maravillas!)

a lo grande luxuriously, in style (Festejaremos tu cumpleaños a lo grande.)

a lo largo de throughout

a lo loco in a crazy way (Está gastando el dinero a lo loco.)

a lo mejor probably, likely

a los efectos de algo in order to do sth

a manera de algo by way of / as (Traje este dibujo a manera de ejemplo.)

a mano by hand

a (la) mano close at hand (¿Tienes tu planilla a (la) mano?)

a más tardar at the very latest

a mediados de in mid-/by mid- (Voy a retirar las cosas que faltan a mediados del mes que viene.)

a medias halfway/half

a medida que as/when/only (Resolveremos los problemas a medida que vayan surgiendo.)

a menos que unless

a menudo often

a modo de by way of, as (Usó su cuaderno a modo de pantalla.)

a no ser que if not

a nombre de algn addressed to sb

a oscuras in the dark

a partir de from, starting from

a pesar de in spite of

a pie on foot

a poco de algo shortly after sth

a por *Esp.* to go and get (Iré a por ti en dos horas.)

a la izquierda, verán uno de los mayores

280

Glosario combinatorio

xvii

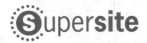

The Supersite for **A Handbook of Contemporary Spanish Grammar** provides a wealth of resources for both students and instructors.

For students

Student resources, available with a Supersite code, are provided free-of-charge with the purchase of a new student text. Here is what you will find at **vhlcentral.com**:

- All activities from the student text, with auto-grading
- Additional practice for each chapter
- Quizzes for self-assessment
- Oxford Spanish Mini Dictionary
- Wimba Voice Board

For instructors

Instructors have access to the entire student site, as well as to these additional resources:

- A robust course management system
- Voice Board capabilities for creating custom oral activities

Supersiteplus

Supersite Plus includes the Supersite for **A Handbook of Contemporary Spanish Grammar**, plus **Wimba Pronto** for online communication and collaboration.

- Audio and video conferencing
- Instant messaging
- Online whiteboard to synchronously view and modify a shared canvas
- Application sharing—perfect for online tutoring
- Online office hours
- Instructor control of Pronto activation/deactivation

To the instructor

A Handbook of Contemporary Spanish Grammar combines thorough, accessible grammar explanations with a unique online component that offers Spanish students an invaluable reference tool. The text's content and organization enable its use as a standalone textbook for grammar courses, as a companion text for language, composition, literature, and culture courses, or as a reference for independent study. The **Handbook** incorporates key updates from the *Nueva gramática* and the *Nueva ortografía,* published in 2010 by the **Real Academia Española**.

Program features

- A topical structure that is flexible and simple to navigate

- Coverage of all major grammar topics, incorporating key updates and revisions from the *Nueva gramática* published by the Real Academia Española

- Concise, comprehensive explanations that include detailed tables and relevant examples

- Presentation of lexical and regional variations

- An abundance of examples of contemporary, real-world usage

- A glossary of collocations (*Glosario combinatorio*)

- Activities that allow students to practice and apply the grammar concepts

- An answer key that allows students to check their work

- Additional online practice and assessment (See p. xviii.)

The *Nueva gramática* and the *Nueva ortografía*

This **Handbook** incorporates key updates from the *Nueva gramática*, published by the **Real Academia Española** (RAE) in conjunction with all the regional Spanish language academies (see p. 18). The nomenclature used by the RAE often differs from that used throughout North America. Though the RAE's nomenclature is standard in this book, other naming conventions are acknowledged and presented.

The same approach has been applied to the grammar explanations. When relevant, both the RAE explanation and the traditional explanation are presented. For an example, see the case of demonstratives on p. 63. As you use the **Handbook**, you will see many instances like this.

The *voseo* conjugations covered correspond to those presented in the verb tables in the *Nueva gramática*. Verb tense presentations and verb tables include the *voseo* form for the present indicative and the affirmative imperative (*salís, salí*). The *voseo* forms for the present subjunctive and the negative imperative that do not match the *tú* forms (*salgás, no salgás*) are acknowledged in the verb presentations, but not included in verb tables.

Reviewers

On behalf of the author and its editors, Vista Higher Learning expresses its sincere appreciation to the many professors nationwide who participated in the preliminary surveys that led to the development of **A Handbook of Contemporary Spanish Grammar**. Their insights, ideas, and detailed comments were invaluable to the final product.

Robert Baah
Seattle Pacific University, WA

Lisa Barboun
Coastal Carolina University, SC

Servio Becerra
Youngstown State University, OH

Karen Berg
College of Charleston, SC

Peggy Buckwalter
Black Hill State University, SD

Vanessa Burch-Urquhart
Western Nevada College, NV

Bonnie Butler
Rutgers University, NJ

Jessie Carduner
Kent State University, OH

Debora Cordeiro Rosa
University of Central Florida, FL

Norma Corrales-Martin
Temple University, PA

Rocío Cortés
University of Wisconsin-Oshkosh, WI

Gerardo Cruz
Cardinal Stritch University, WI

Richard P. Doerr
Metropolitan State College of Denver, CO

Deborah Dougherty
Alma College, MI

Dina A. Fabery
University of Central Florida, FL

Elizabeth Fouts
Saint Anselm College, NH

Jose García
Eastern Washington University, WA

Próspero N. García
Amherst College, MA

Iria González-Liaño
University of Nevada
Las Vegas, NV

Kim Hernandez
Whitworth University, WA

Mary Kempen
Ohio Northern University, OH

Phil Klein
University of Iowa, IA

Iana Konstantinova
Southern Virginia University, VA

Kevin Krogh
Utah State University, UT

Lisa Kuriscak
Ball State University, IN

Joanna Lyskowicz
Drexel University, PA

Jeffrey Mancilla
De Anza College, CA

Francisco Manzo-Robledo
Washington State University, WA

Frank R. Martinez
Lipscomb University, TN

Mark J. Mascia
Sacred Heart University, CT

Collin McKinney
Bucknell University, PA

David Migaj
Wright College, IL

Lee Mitchell
Henderson State University, AR

Evelyn Nadeau
Clarke College, IA

James J. Pancrazio
Illinois State University, IL

Wendy Pilkerton
Linn Benton Community College, OR

Eve Pujol
University of Wisconsin
Madison, WI

George Robinson
Montana State University at Billings, MT

Shelli Rottschafer
Aquinas College, MI

Francisco Salgado-Robles
University of Florida, FL

Rachel Shively
Illinois State University, IL

José I. Suárez
University of Northern Colorado, CO

Sixto E. Torres
Metropolitan State College of Denver, CO

Maria Eugenia Trillo
Western New Mexico University, NM

Dr. Nick Uliano
Cabrini College, PA

Clara L. Vega
Alamance Community College, NC

Mariana Zinni
Queens College CUNY, NY

España y Guinea Ecuatorial

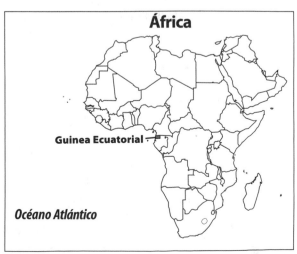

América del Sur

Mar Caribe

Océano Atlántico

Barranquilla
Caracas ✪
VENEZUELA
Cúcuta
San Cristobal
GUAYANA
SURINAME
GUAYANA FRANCESA (FRANCIA)
Medellín
Bogotá ✪
Cali
COLOMBIA
Mitú

Quito ✪
ECUADOR
Guayaquil

ISLAS GALÁPAGOS

Iquitos

Piura
PERÚ

BRASIL

Trujillo

Lima ✪

Cusco
BOLIVIA
Ica
Trinidad

Océano Pacífico
Arequipa
La Paz ✪
Cochabamba
Arica
Santa Cruz
Sucre ✪

PARAGUAY

Antofagasta
Asunción ✪
San Miguel de Tucumán
CHILE
Resistencia

Córdoba

Rosario
Salto
URUGUAY
Mendoza
Montevideo
Valparaíso
Buenos Aires ✪
Santiago ✪
ARGENTINA
Océano Atlántico
Concepción
Mar del Plata

Valdivia

San Carlos de Bariloche

ISLAS MALVINAS (R.U.)

500 km
500 mi.

México, América Central y el Caribe

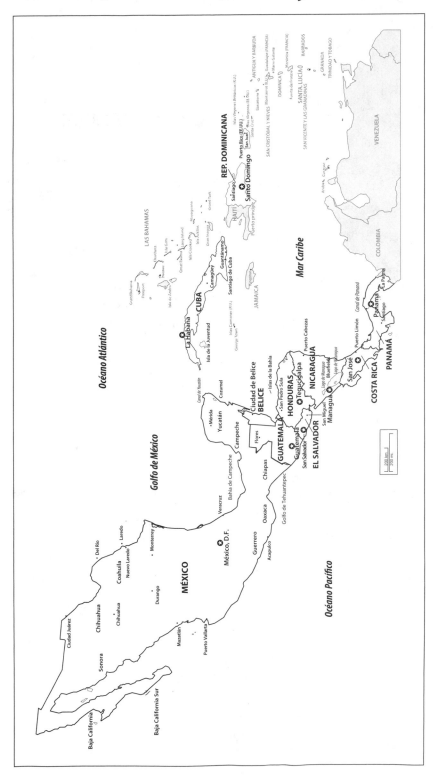

El español en los Estados Unidos

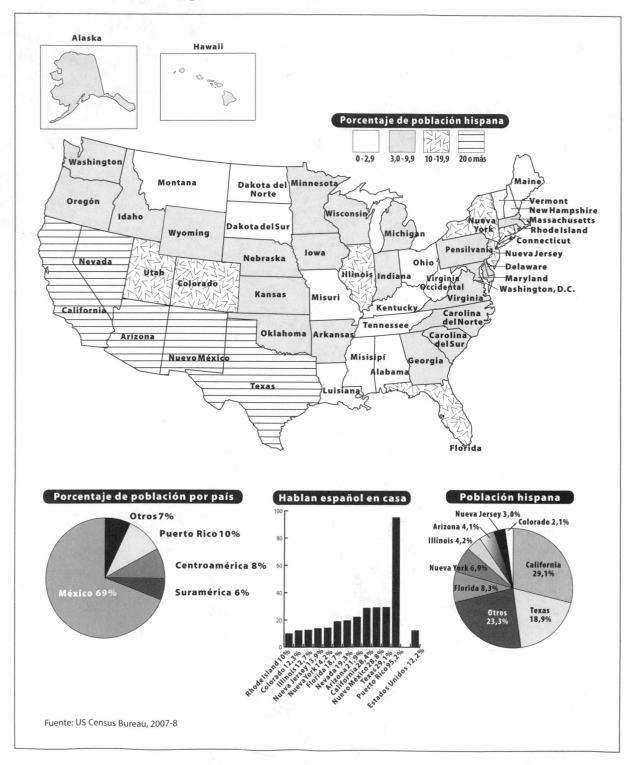

Porcentaje de población hispana

0 - 2,9 | 3,0 - 9,9 | 10 - 19,9 | 20 o más

Alaska

Hawaii

Washington
Oregón
Idaho
Montana
Dakota del Norte
Minnesota
Wisconsin
Michigan
Maine
Vermont
New Hampshire
Massachusetts
Rhode Island
Connecticut
Nevada
Wyoming
Dakota del Sur
Nebraska
Iowa
Illinois
Indiana
Ohio
Pensilvania
Nueva York
Nueva Jersey
Delaware
Maryland
Washington, D.C.
California
Utah
Colorado
Kansas
Misuri
Kentucky
Virginia Occidental
Virginia
Carolina del Norte
Arizona
Oklahoma
Arkansas
Tennessee
Carolina del Sur
Nuevo México
Texas
Misisipí
Alabama
Georgia
Luisiana
Florida

Porcentaje de población por país

- Otros 7%
- Puerto Rico 10%
- Centroamérica 8%
- Suramérica 6%
- México 69%

Hablan español en casa

Rhode Island 10%
Colorado 12,3%
Illinois 12,7%
Nueva Jersey 13,9%
Nueva York 14,2%
Florida 18,7%
Nevada 19,3%
Arizona 21,9%
California 28,4%
Nuevo México 28,8%
Texas 29,1%
Puerto Rico 95,2%
Estados Unidos 12,2%

Población hispana

- Nueva Jersey 3,0%
- Colorado 2,1%
- Arizona 4,1%
- Illinois 4,2%
- Nueva York 6,9%
- Florida 8,3%
- California 29,1%
- Texas 18,9%
- Otros 23,3%

Fuente: US Census Bureau, 2007-8

The Spanish language
La lengua española

1.A Letters

Las letras

Letters represent *phonemes*: distinct sounds in a language which are capable of conveying differences in meaning. One letter can represent multiple phonemes, which in turn can change meanings of words. For example, in English the letter **i** in *wind* (as in weather) and *wind* (the act of twisting, as in winding a clock) represents two different phonemes —sounds— that give the words different meanings. This example shows there is no direct correlation between letters and phonemes.

1.B The alphabet

El alfabeto

The Spanish alphabet, or **abecedario**, has twenty-seven letters. It has five vowels and twenty-two consonants. One of the consonants is silent: **h. Ch** and **ll** are not letters but **dígrafos** (digraphs). Digraphs are combinations of two letters that represent a single sound, like the English *th* in *those*.

a	a	g	ge	m	eme	s	ese
b	be	h	hache	n	ene	t	te
c	ce	i	i	ñ	eñe	u	u
(ch)	(che)	j	jota	o	o	v	uve/ve
d	de	k	ka	p	pe	w	doble uve / doble ve
e	e	l	ele	q	cu	x	equis
f	efe	(ll)	(elle)	r	erre	y	ye (i griega)
						z	zeta

In the past, **ch** and **ll** had their own entries in dictionaries and reference books, just like the other letters. In 1994, the language academies in Spanish-speaking countries voted to follow the international guidelines for alphabetization. Subsequently, **ch** and **ll** were included under **c** and **l**, respectively. The letter **ñ** retained its own entry. Recent reforms have eliminated **ch** and **ll** from the alphabet.

1.C Pronunciation

Pronunciación

In English and Spanish, spelling, sound, and meaning are interconnected. In English, the vowel often differentiates meaning, as in *pop/pope* or *dove* (a bird)/*dove* (past of *to dive*). In Spanish, the stressed syllable can determine the meaning of a word. Most Spanish words carry the stress on the penultimate syllable.

◀ Stress and accents: 1.E

habl**o**   *I speak*   habl**ó**   *he spoke*   cant**o**   *I sing*   cant**ó**   *he sang*

Vowels and consonants

The charts on the next few pages outline how Spanish vowels, consonants, and digraphs are pronounced.

1.C.1 Vowels

The pronunciation of Spanish vowels (**vocales**) is similar to some English vowel sounds. Unlike English, each vowel in Spanish has only one sound.

Spanish vowels	Similar to the following English vowel sounds		Examples	
			Spanish	English meaning
a	**ah** sound	*father*	c**a**sa, **a**la	*house, wing*
e	long **a**	*tell, west*	m**e**sa, p**e**sa	*table, weight*
i	long **e**	*bee, meat*	s**í**, m**i**	*yes, my*
o	long **o**	*more, floor*	y**o**, c**o**c**o**	*I, coconut*
u	long **u**	*food, rude*	l**u**na, t**u**	*moon, your*

1.C.2 Diphthongs

In Spanish, there are strong vowels and weak vowels. **A, e,** and **o** are strong vowels, and **i** and **u** are weak. A diphthong (**diptongo**) is a combination of a strong and a weak vowel, or two weak vowels, in a single syllable. A syllable ending in a vowel + **y** is also considered a diphthong.

Diptongos
ai, ay, au
ia, ua
ei, ey, eu
ie, ue
oi, oy, ou
io, uo
iu, ui, uy

Diphthongs with *a*			Diphthongs with *e*		
ai	b**ai**le	*dance*	ei	s**ei**s	*six*
ay	h**ay**	*there is/are*	ey	r**ey**	*king*
ia	famil**ia**	*family*	ie	c**ie**n	*one hundred*
au	**au**la	*classroom*	eu	**Eu**ropa	*Europe*
ua	c**ua**tro	*four*	ue	b**ue**no	*good*

Diphthongs with *o*			Diphthongs with *u, i*		
oi	**oi**go	*I hear*	iu	c**iu**dad	*city/town*
oy	s**oy**	*I am*	ui	r**ui**do	*noise*
io	qu**io**sco	*kiosk/newsstand*	uy	m**uy**	*very*
ou	b**ou**	*little boat*			
uo	c**uo**ta	*payment/installment*			

Division of words: 1.D.3
Accents on vowel combinations: 1.E.4
Hiatus and accentuation: 1.E.5

1.C.3 Triphthongs

When three vowels are pronounced together as one syllable, they create a triphthong (**triptongo**). Triphthongs begin and end with an unstressed **i** or **u** and have a stressed **a, e,** or **o** in the middle: **buey, guiais.** Most triphthongs with **i** or **u** carry a written accent over the letter in the middle. Most words with triphthongs are verb forms used with **vosotros** (*you, pl.*): **enviáis** (*you send*), **continuáis** (*you continue*).

Division of words: 1.D.3
Accents on vowel combinations: 1.E.4
Hiatus and accentuation: 1.E.5

1.C.4 Combinations: *a, e, o*

When any of the vowels **a, e,** or **o** are paired together, they do not form a diphthong or a triphthong. These combinations always form two syllables: hé-**ro-e**, c**a-o**s, l**e-e**r.

1.C.5 *g, c, d, p,* and *t*

The consonants (**consonantes**) **g** and **c** (both before **a, o,** or **u**), and **d** are pronounced with a short aspiration in English. This aspiration does not occur in Spanish. At the beginning of a phrase or after the letter **n**, the Spanish **g** is pronounced like the *g* in *girl*. In any other position, the Spanish **g** has a somewhat softer sound. The consonants **p** and **t** are also pronounced with a short aspiration in English, but not in Spanish.

Consonants		Examples
b, v	represent the same sound. They are pronounced roughly like the English *b* at the beginning of a word and after **m** and **n.** Between vowels, **b** and **v** are pronounced like a soft English *b* sound; the lips do not close.	**b**ueno (*good*) tam**b**ién (*also*) u**v**a (*grape*)
c	is pronounced like the English *k* in *keep* before **a, o,** and **u,** but without aspiration. In most of Spain, **c** is pronounced like an English *th* before **e** and **i.** In Latin America and southern Spain, it is pronounced like an **s.**	**c**asa (*house*) **c**olonia (*colony*) **c**ielo (*sky*) **c**ena (*dinner*)
d	is pronounced roughly like the English *d* at the beginning of a word and after **l** or **n.** Between vowels and in other positions the **d** has a soft sound (almost like an English *th*).	**d**iez (*ten*) fal**d**a (*skirt*) bo**d**a (*wedding*) Pe**d**ro
f	is pronounced like the English *f.*	**f**in (*end*)
g	is pronounced like the English *g* in *go* before **a, o,** or **u,** and **-ui** or **-ue** (**gue, gui**). Before **e** and **i,** the **g** is pronounced like the Spanish **j.** (See below.)	**g**ato (*cat*) **g**uerra (*war*) **g**igante (*giant*) **g**ente (*folk*)
h	is silent.	**h**ola (*hello*) a**h**ora (*now*)
j	is pronounced in Spanish like a *guttural sound* with varying strength depending on the region. In Latin America, the pronunciation varies from a strong to a very weak English *h.*	**j**efe (*boss*) a**j**o (*garlic*) **j**oven (*young*)
k	is pronounced like the English *k* without aspiration.	**k**ilo (*kilogram*)
l	is pronounced like the English *l.*	**l**indo (*pretty*)
m	is pronounced like the English *m.*	a**m**or (*love*)
n	is pronounced with the tongue a little higher up (towards the back of the teeth) than the English *n,* which is more dental (a little further down).	**n**ada (*nothing*) **n**osotros (*we*) A**n**a
ñ	is pronounced like the *ny* sound in the English word *canyon* or the *ni* sound in the English word *onion.*	ni**ñ**a (*girl*) ma**ñ**ana (*morning*) sue**ñ**o (*dream*)
p	is pronounced like the English *p* without aspiration.	**p**apá (*dad*)
q	is pronounced like the English *k* without aspiration; the letter **q** occurs in Spanish only in the combinations **que** and **qui.**	**q**ueso (*cheese*) a**q**uí (*here*)
r	is pronounced as a strong trill at the beginning of words and after **n, l,** and **s.** Otherwise the **r** is pronounced with a very short, loose, and simple hit of the tongue. Note that a **rr** combination represents a strong trill between vowels. See the digraphs chart on the next page.	**r**osa (*rose*) al**r**ededor (*around*) hon**r**ado (*honest*) co**r**o (*choir*)
s	is pronounced like the English *s* in *summer,* but can vary regionally. In parts of Latin America, southern Spain, and the Caribbean the **s** is aspirated—it is pronounced very soft or it is omitted at the end of a word and before a consonant. In Madrid, the **s** is pronounced with a whistling sound.	**s**ala (*sitting room*) ca**s**a (*house*)
t	is pronounced roughly like the English *t,* but without aspiration.	**t**aza (*cup*)
w	is found only in foreign words and can be pronounced like the English *w* or like the Spanish **b/v.**	**W**ashington

Consonantes

b
v
c
d
f
g
h
j
k
l
m
n
ñ
p
q
r
s
t
w

◀ Omission of the letter **p**: 1.G.3

x	varies in pronunciation regionally. It can be pronounced like an English *ks*, *gs*, or *s* between vowels. Before a consonant, it is usually pronounced like an **s**. When **x** appears in the name of a Mexican town, it is pronounced like the Spanish **j** or English *h*.	e**x**amen (*exam*) e**x**acto (*exact*) me**x**icano (*Mexican*) Mé**x**ico, Oa**x**aca
y	acts as a vowel with the Spanish **i** sound when it is part of a diphthong. At the beginning of words and between vowels, **y** sounds like the English *y* in *yes*. (See also **ll** for regional variations.)	ho**y** (*today*) **y**uca (*yucca*) pla**y**a (*beach*)
z	is pronounced like the English *th* in most parts of Spain. In Latin America, southern Spain, and the Canary Islands, **z** is pronounced like an **s**. Pronouncing the **z** like an **s** is called **seseo**. (See also **c**.)	**z**apato (*shoe*) a**z**ul (*blue*)

Dígrafos

| ch |
| ll |
| rr |

Yeísmo is pronouncing **ll** and **y** like the English *y* in *yes*. It is a common feature in Latin America and in Spain.

	Digraphs	Examples
ch	is pronounced like the English *ch* in chocolate.	**ch**ocolate
ll	is pronounced very much like the English *y* in most parts of Latin America and in many areas of Spain. This is called **yeísmo**. (See also the pronunciation of **y**.) In Argentina, Uruguay, and parts of Paraguay, the **ll** is pronounced similarly to the English *sh*. In central parts of Spain and in some Andean regions of Latin America, the **ll** is pronounced like a continuous **lj** sound.	ca**ll**e (*street*) **ll**ave (*key*)
rr	is a strong rolling **r** sound that occurs between vowels, and it is written with a double **rr**.	ba**rr**o (*mud*) a**rr**oz (*rice*)

1.D Division of words

Separación de las palabras

In writing, it is sometimes necessary to hyphenate words at the end of a line. According to style conventions in Spanish, the words must be divided into syllables; the syllables themselves cannot be divided.

1.D.1 Formation of syllables

a. A consonant between two vowels forms a syllable with the second vowel.

| ca-**m**a-**r**o-**t**e | *boat cabin* | Ca-**t**a-**l**i-**n**a | *Catalina* |
| gra-**m**á-**t**i-**c**a | *grammar* | co-**l**e-**g**io | *school* |

b. The consonants **b, c, f, g,** and **p** followed by **l** or **r** form syllables with the subsequent vowel.

| a-**cr**í-li-co | *acrylic* | en-**cr**ip-ta-do | *encrypted* | an-**gl**o-sa-jo-na | *Anglo-Saxon* |
| a-**br**a-si-vo | *abrasive* | a-**fr**i-ca-no | *African* | em-**pl**e-a-do | *employee* |

c. The consonants **t** and **d** followed by **r** form syllables with the subsequent vowel.

| Pe-**dr**o | *Pedro* | ras-**tr**i-llo | *rake* | a-**tr**o-ci-dad | *atrocity* |

d. The combination **tl** stays united in one syllable in Latin America and the Canary Islands; it is split between two syllables in the rest of Spain.

Latin America	**Spain**	
a-**tl**e-ta	at-**l**e-ta	*athlete*
a-**tl**as	at-**l**as	*atlas*

e. Other consonant pairs are split between two syllables when they occur in the middle of a word.

| pris-**m**a | *prism* | a**c**-ción | *action* | con-**s**o-na**n**-te | *consonant* |

f. When **l** or **r** occur last in a group of three consonants, the last two consonants stay together.

co**m-pro**-mi-so	*compromise*	si**m-ple**	*simple*
si**n-cro**-ni-zar	*to synchronize*	a**m-pli**ar	*to enlarge/extend*

1.D.2 · Diphthongs and triphthongs

Vowel groups which form a diphthong or a triphthong cannot be split.

ja-g**ua**r	*jaguar*	qu**ie**-ro	*I want*	v**iei**-ra	*scallop*
s**ue**l-do	*salary*	d**ue**r-mo	*I sleep/am sleeping*	U-ru-g**uay**	*Uruguay*

1.D.3 · Other vowels

Vowel groups that do not form a diphthong or triphthong can be split into syllables, but stylistically they should stay together.

a-ho-ra	*now*	c**a-o**s	*chaos*	c**a-e**r	*to fall*
l**e-e**r	*to read*	cr**e-o**	*I believe*	ca-c**a-o**	*cocoa*

◄ However, when hyphenating at the end of a line of text, vowel groups that do not form a diphthong should not be divided: **aho-ra, ca-cao**.

1.D.4 · ch, ll, rr

These letter pairs cannot be split.

◄ Digraphs: 1.C.6

an-**ch**o	*wide*	a-**ll**í	*there*	ca-**rr**e-ta	*wagon*
te-**ch**o	*ceiling/roof*	ca-**ll**e	*street*	pe-**rr**o	*dog*

1.D.5 · The letter *x*

X represents two phonemes [ks]. When it occurs between vowels, **x** forms a syllable with the second vowel. If **x** is followed by a consonant, it forms a syllable with the previous vowel.

◄ Variations in the pronunciation of the letter **x**: 1.C.6, 1.G.2a, 3.F.4

Division of words with *x*			
e-**xa**-men	*exam*	tó-**xi**-co	*toxic*
[e-**ksa**-men]		[tó-ksi-ko]	
ex-cep-ción	*exception*	**ex**-plicar	*explain*
[e**ks**-cep-ción]		[e**ks**-pli-kar]	

1.E · Stress and accents

Acentos
(á)
(é)
(í)
(ó)
(ú)

Acentuación

In Spanish, there are two kinds of accents. The accent that indicates the stressed syllable of a word is the **acento prosódico** (*prosodic accent*). The **acento diacrítico** (*diacritical accent*) distinguishes two words that are otherwise spelled the same: **mi** (*my*), **mí** (*me*).

The following rules explain the regular pronunciation of Spanish words, when to use the **tilde** or **acento gráfico**, and the accentuation of diphthongs and triphthongs.

◄ Pronunciation: 1.C

1.E.1 · Stress on the final syllable: *Palabras agudas*

Most words that end in a consonant other than **n** or **s** are stressed on the final syllable. No accent is needed in these cases.

pa-pe**l**	*paper*	ciu-da**d**	*city/town*	es-cri-bi**r**	*to write*

If a word ends in **n, s**, or a vowel and is stressed on the final syllable, a written accent is needed.

ha-bl**é**	*I spoke*	ca-j**ó**n	*box*	qui-z**á**s	*maybe*

One exception is when a word ends in *consonant* + **-s**; a written accent is not needed in this case. This rule usually affects technological or foreign words, such as **robots**.

1.E.2 Stress on the penultimate syllable: *Palabras llanas o graves*

Most words that end in **n, s,** or a vowel are stressed on the penultimate syllable. No accent is needed in these cases.

me-sa   *table*   **can**-ta**n**   *they sing/are singing*   lec-**cio**-ne**s**   *lessons*

If a word ends in any consonant other than **n** or **s**, and is stressed on the penultimate syllable, a written accent is needed.

fá-ci**l**   *easy*   **ál**-bu**m**   *album*   a-**zú**-ca**r**   *sugar*

Words in this group that end in **-s** preceeded by another consonant carry a written accent (**bíceps**), as do plurals of some foreign words, such as **cómics.**

1.E.3 Other cases: *Palabras esdrújulas y sobreesdrújulas*

If the stress falls before the penultimate syllable, the stressed syllable must always be marked with a written accent, regardless of the word's ending or length.

cá-ma-ra   *camera*   ce-**rá**-mi-ca   *ceramic*   e-**léc**-tri-co   *electric*
rá-pi-do   *fast*   **más**-ca-ra   *mask*   **sá**-ba-na   *sheet*

When one or more pronouns are added to an imperative, the number of syllables increases and usually the word will need a written accent on or before the third-to-last syllable.

es**crí**be<u>me</u>   *write to me*   **llá**me<u>los</u>   *call them*
cómpra<u>telos</u>   *buy them for yourself*   ex**plí**ca<u>melo</u>   *explain it to me*
de**mués**tra<u>noslo</u>   *show it to us*   **dí**ga<u>selo</u>   *tell it to him*

1.E.4 Accents on vowel combinations

Diphthongs: 1.C.2
Triphthongs: 1.C.3

Diphthongs and triphthongs follow the accentuation rules of **palabras agudas, palabras llanas,** and **palabras esdrújulas.** When the stress falls on the syllable with the diphthong or triphthong, there are rules that dictate which vowel will carry the accent mark. In these cases, it is useful to remember that the vowels **a, e,** and **o** are considered **fuertes** (*strong*) and the vowels **u** and **i** are **débiles** (*weak*). Diphthongs and triphthongs are either a combination of strong vowels and unstressed weak vowels (**ai, eu,** etc.) or a combination of weak vowels (**ui, uy, iu**). The combination of two strong vowels never forms a diphthong.

a. When a syllable with a diphthong or triphthong requires an accent for stress, the strong vowel carries the written accent and the pronunciation of the diphthong or triphthong is usually maintained. In the following list, we see that <u>**cuen**</u>-ta does not carry a written accent because it ends in a vowel and the stress is on the penultimate syllable (**llana**). **Cuén**-ta-me does have a written accent because the stress is on the third-to-last syllable (**esdrújula**); the accent goes over the strong vowel, **e.**

<u>**cue**</u>n-ta   <u>**cué**</u>n-ta-me   can-<u>tas</u>-t**ei**s   can-**téi**s   U-ru-g**uay**   en-v**iái**s
a-<u>ma</u>-b**ai**s   a-**mái**s   fun-<u>cio</u>-na   fun-**ción**   b<u>uey</u>   a-ve-ri-g**üéi**s

b. If the stress falls on the weak vowel of a *weak vowel + strong vowel* combination that would normally form a diphthong or triphthong, the vowels split to form part of different syllables. This break in the vowels is called **hiato** (*hiatus*). In this case, the stressed weak vowel always carries a written accent.

Hiatus and accentuation: 1.E.5

Regional differences in pronunciation can create a diphthong or hiatus; for example, **mie-do** is pronounced with a diphthong, while the same combination of vowels can be pronounced with a hiatus in some regions of Spain and Latin America: **su-fri-e-ron.** 1.C.2, 1.C.3, 1.E.5

One syllable	Hiatus: Different syllables
La serie es continua. (con-<u>ti</u>-**nua**)	La fiesta continúa. (con-ti-**nú**-a)

When the first weak vowel in a combination of three vowels that would normally form a triphthong is stressed, it stands as a separate syllable while the other two vowels form a diphthong.

oiríais (oi-**rí**-**ai**s)   salíais (sa-**lí**-**ai**s)   comprendíais (com-pren-**dí**-**ai**s)

c. The combination of the weak vowels **i** and **u** forms a diphthong for the purpose of spelling, although it can sometimes be pronounced as either a diphthong or a hiatus.

ciudad (c**iu**-<u>dad</u>)   cuidado (c**ui**-<u>da</u>-do)   ruido (r**ui**-do)
construir (cons-tr**uir**, also pronounced cons-tr**u**-<u>ir</u>)

d. When two weak vowels are combined and the stress falls on the second vowel in the pair, a diphthong is formed and the word follows the regular rules of accentuation. For example, if the diphthong appears in the third-to-last syllable, the second vowel carries a written accent. Note that the accent is always written on the second vowel.

cuídate (<u>c**uí**</u>-da-te)   lingüística (lin-g**üís**-ti-ca)

1.E.5 Hiatus and accentuation

A *hiatus* (**hiato**) is formed when two or more sequential vowels in a word are not pronounced together as one syllable. In Spanish, a hiatus occurs in the following cases:

a. When the vowels **a, e,** and **o** are combined in pairs, they *always* form a hiatus. This also applies when the letter **h** occurs between two of those vowels.

◀ Combinations: *a, e, o*: 1.C.4
Accents on vowel combinations: 1.E.4

ahora	a-<u>ho</u>-ra	*now*		re**a**lidad	re-**a**-li-<u>dad</u>	*reality*
p**oe**ta	po-**e**-ta	*poet*		te**o**rema	te-**o**-<u>re</u>-ma	*theorem*

b. Double vowels or double vowels separated by an **h** also form a hiatus.

alb**ah**aca	al-ba-**ha**-ca	*basil*		micr**oo**ndas	mi-cro-**on**-das	*microwave*
ch**ii**ta	chi-**i**-ta	*Shiite*		pos**ee**r	po-s**e**-**er**	*to own*
c**oo**rdinar	c**o**-**o**r-di-<u>nar</u>	*to coordinate*				

c. The words that appear in the two previous points do not require a written accent according to the rules of accentuation. For example, **poeta** does not carry a written accent because its pronunciation is regular. The stress falls on the vowel **e** (the penultimate syllable) and the word ends in a vowel. The following words, however, require a written accent because they are **esdrújulas** (stress on the third-to-last syllable).

◀ Palabras agudas: 1.E.1
Palabras esdrújulas: 1.E.3

a**é**reo	a-**é**-re-o	*aerial*		cr**é**eme	cr**é**-e-me	*believe me*
ca**ó**tico	ca-**ó**-ti-co	*chaotic*		te**ó**rico	te-**ó**-ri-co	*theoretic*

d. Words that have a strong vowel combined with a weak, stressed vowel always form a hiatus and require a written accent over the stressed vowel. Because the accent is breaking a diphthong, it is required even if other rules for accentuation do not call for it. For example, the word **increíble** is **llana** (stressed on the penultimate syllable) and ends in a vowel, a case which normally does not call for an accent. However, because the **i** is stressed, an accent is required to reflect the correct pronunciation.

◀ Palabras llanas o graves: 1.E.2

ba**ú**l	ba-**ú**l	incre**í**ble	in-cre-**í**-ble	o**í**r	o-**í**r
b**ú**ho	b**ú**-ho	m**í**o	m**í**-o	pa**í**s	pa-**í**s
d**í**a	d**í**-a	proh**í**be	pro-h**í**-be	sonr**í**e	son-r**í**-e

1.E.6 Diacritical marks

The written accent, or **tilde**, indicates the stressed syllable of a word and visually marks the stressed vowel. In speech, the stress on a syllable is called the **acento prosódico** (*prosodic accent*). The **acento diacrítico** (*diacritical accent*) is a written accent mark used to distinguish two words that are otherwise spelled the same.

◀ Spanish relative pronouns: 15.A.2, Question words and exclamations: 1.E.7

a. One-syllable words (**palabras monosílabas**) have only one vowel, or, if they have more than one, they do not have a hiatus (**hiato**). One-syllable words usually do not carry a written accent.

bien   mal   no   si   un   cien   muy   pie   sol   vas

b. A diacritical accent is necessary to differentiate these pairs of words:

de	of, from	dé	imperative of **dar** (to give)
el	definite article	él	he
mi	my	mí	me/myself
se	himself, herself, itself, themselves, yourself (formal)	sé	I know; imperative of **ser** (to be)
si	if	sí	yes; yourself/yourselves/ him/himself/her/herself/ themselves (object of a preposition)
tu	your	tú	you
te	you/yourself	té	tea
mas	but	más	more

Somos **de** Nueva York.	We are from New York.
Por favor, **dé** usted una donación.	Please give a donation.
El chico habla francés y español.	The boy speaks French and Spanish.
Hoy viene **él**, ella no.	He is coming today, but she is not.
Mi padre es Lorenzo.	My father is Lorenzo.
Nora siempre me llama a **mí**.	Nora always calls me.
Viviana **se** mira en el espejo.	Viviana is looking at herself in the mirror.
Sé mucho español.	I know a lot of Spanish.
Sé un buen chico.	Be a good boy.
Si vas a viajar, llámame.	If you're going to travel, call me.
—¿Quieres viajar a Madrid? —¡**Sí**!	—Do you want to go to Madrid? —Yes!
Sólo piensa en **sí** mismo.	He only thinks of himself.
Yo soy **tu** amigo.	I am your friend.
¿Quién eres **tú**?	Who are you?
¿**Te** gusta el **té**?	Do you like tea?
Quiero ir, **mas** no puedo.	I want to go, but I can't.
No hay nada que me guste **más**.	There's nothing I like better.

Aun/aún: 10.B.4, 16.C.6

c. *Aun, aún*

The word **aun** can mean *even, until, also,* or *including,* but the written accent on **aún** changes the meaning to *still* or *yet.*

Estoy cansado, **aun** después de pasar una buena noche.	I am tired even after a good night´s sleep.
¡**Aún** estoy esperando a Luisa!	I am still waiting for Luisa!

d. *Solo, sólo*

The word **solo** can be an adjective or an adverb. As an adjective, it never carries a written accent. The adverb can carry an accent in case of ambiguity; however, according to the *Nueva ortografía*, it is not required. As an adverb, a synonym can also be used: **solamente**, **únicamente**.

¿Estás **solo** en casa?	*Are you home alone?*	**Sólo/Solo** estaré en casa hoy.	*I will only be home today.*

Demonstratives: Ch. 8

e. The demonstratives **este, ese,** and **aquel** and their feminine and plural forms used to carry an accent when they functioned as pronouns and there was risk of ambiguity. It is still possible to use the written accent in case of ambiguity, but it is not required.

Diacritical marks: 1.E.6
Spanish relative pronouns: 15.A.2
Questions and question words: Ch. 14

1.E.7 Question words and exclamations

a. The following words always carry a written accent when their function is interrogative or exclamative:

cómo	how	dónde	where	quién(es)	who	cuánto/a(s)	how much/many
qué	what	cuándo	when	cuál	which	cuáles	which

¿**Cómo** estás?	*How are you?*
¿**Qué** estudias?	*What are you studying?*
¿**Dónde** estudias?	*Where are you studying?*
¿**Cuándo** vas a la clase?	*When are you going to class?*
¿**Quién** es tu profesor?	*Who is your teacher?*
¿**Cuál** es tu asignatura favorita?	*What is your favorite subject?*
¿**Cuánto** pagas en la universidad?	*How much do you pay at the university?*
¿**Cuáles** son tus libros?	*Which books are yours?*
¡**Qué** hermoso día!	*What a beautiful day!*
¡**Cómo** puedes decir eso!	*How can you say that!*
¡**Cuántos** libros tienes!	*You have so many books!*

b. These words also carry a written accent in sentences with an indirect question:

Indirect questions: 31.B.6d

No sé **cuánto** cuesta el libro.	*I don't know how much this book costs.*
Dime **dónde** vives.	*Tell me where you live.*
En las noticias dicen **qué** sucedió.	*They explain what happened on the news.*
En *Google* encuentras **cómo** llegar aquí.	*You can use Google to find out how to get here.*
No recuerdo **cuándo** es su cumpleaños.	*I don't remember when her birthday is.*

1.E.8 Adverbs ending in -mente

Adverbs ending in **-mente**: 10.G

Stress and accents: 1.E

Adverbs ending in **-mente** are formed using the feminine adjective as the base. These words are special in Spanish because they have two prosodic accents: that of the adjective and that of the ending **-mente.** In order to determine whether the adverb needs an accent mark, look at the adjective base. If the adjective has an accent, as in **fácil**, the adverb keeps it: **fácilmente.** If the adjective does not have an accent, as in **tranquila**, the adverb does not either: **tranquilamente.**

bueno	❭	buenamente	cortés	❭	cort**é**smente
claro		claramente	difícil		dif**í**cilmente
preferible		preferiblemente	pésimo		p**é**simamente
terrible		terriblemente	rápido		r**á**pidamente

1.E.9 Accentuation of plurals and compound words

Most nouns and adjectives conserve the accent on the same stressed syllable in both the singular and plural form: **fácil/fáciles, cámara/cámaras.** However, the use of a written accent can also vary when forming the plural.

Plural formation: 2.B

Palabras esdrújulas: 1.E.3

a. Some words gain a syllable in the plural and become **esdrújulas.** The accented syllable remains the same, but a written accent must be added in the plural to reflect the correct stress.

crimen	❭	crímenes	joven	❭	jóvenes
examen		exámenes	orden		órdenes
imagen		imágenes	origen		orígenes

b. The following are examples of words that are irregular because the accented syllable, either written or spoken, is different in the singular and plural.

carácter	caracteres
régimen	regímenes
espécimen	especímenes

c. When a word ends in a stressed syllable with a written accent, as in **televisión, revés,** and **corazón,** the written accent is not necessary in the plural.

revés	reveses	ecuación	ecuaciones
cortés	corteses	nación	naciones
faisán	faisanes	sillón	sillones
confín	confines	fusión	fusiones
delfín	delfines	misión	misiones
jardín	jardines	pensión	pensiones
pequeñín	pequeñines	televisión	televisiones
sillón	sillones	versión	versiones
belén	belenes	corazón	corazones
sartén	sartenes	razón	razones
edición	ediciones	atún	atunes

d. Compound words written as one word follow Spanish rules of accentuation. When the words are separated by a hyphen, they conserve their original accentuation.

tragicómico	político-social
lavaplatos	socio-económico
hispanoamericano	técnico-administrativo

1.E.10 Words with varied accentuation

In Spanish, some words allow for different accentuation without changing meaning. Using one form over the other can be regional or personal preference. Some common examples are:

básquetbol	basquetbol	maníaco/a	maniaco/a
chófer	chofer	olimpíada	olimpiada
cóctel	coctel	paradisíaco/a	paradisiaco/a
fríjol	frijol	período	periodo
fútbol	futbol	policíaco/a	policiaco/a
hipocondríaco/a	hipocondriaco/a	vídeo	video
ícono	icono	zodíaco	zodiaco

1.E.11 Accentuation of capital letters

Capital letters require a written accent according to the rules of accentuation, whether the capital letter is the first letter of the word or the word is written entirely in capitals. Due to past typographical and printing constraints, this rule was not always possible to follow. Therefore, there are still older signs or books that do not follow it.

Él se llama Héctor.   Me llamo Miguel **Á**ngel.   ¡DETÉNGASE!

Puntuación

Punctuation in Spanish is very similar to English. Note these uses:

1.F.1 [.] Period

a. Sentences

As in English, the period (**punto**) marks the end of a sentence. If you are dictating, say **punto [y] seguido** to indicate that sentence should end and the paragraph should continue. To indicate that the sentence and the paragraph should end, say **punto [y] aparte**.

Sentences ending with an abbreviation do not need an additional period.

Visitaremos los EE.UU.	*We will visit the U.S.*

Sentences ending with an ellipsis, or exclamation or question marks, do not need a period unless the sentence is enclosed in parentheses or quotes.

¡Iremos al Cañón del Colorado! Es un sitio majestuoso... Llegaremos allí mañana.	*We will go the Grand Canyon! It's a majestic site... We will arrive there tomorrow.*

b. Abbreviations, acronyms, and symbols

Abbreviations are always followed by a period. Symbols never are; acronyms in all capital letters may or may not be.

◀ Use of capital letters: 1.G.1g

Abbreviation	Symbol	Acronym
Sr. (señor)	kg (kilo)	ONU (Organización de las Naciones Unidas) *UN*
Ud. (usted)	lb (libra, *pound*)	EE. UU. (Estados Unidos de América) *USA*

◀ Abbreviations of ordinal numbers: 6.D.5

Spanish abbreviations of ordinal numbers have a period before the small superscript sign showing the noun's number and/or gender ending.

1.er piso	*first floor*	3.^{a} salida	*third exit*

c. Numbers

Hours and minutes are separated by a period or a colon. Number-only dates are separated by slashes, periods, or hyphens (less common).

◀ The standard date format in Spanish is day/month/year: 6.G.1

La fecha y hora de nacimiento de las gemelas fue: 9.10.2010 a las 5:27 p.m.	*The date and time of the twin girls' birth was: October ninth 2010 at five twenty-seven in the afternoon.*

Thousands and millions are notated by a period in some countries and by a comma in others. The formal rule requires a space to separate the thousands when the number has five or more digits. The comma is the most common sign used to separate decimals in Spanish, although the decimal point is also used in some countries.

◀ Writing styles for numbers: 6.A.1 Numbers and counting expressions: 6.C.2

Current norm		Period	Comma	Decimals	
1000	10 000	10.000	10,000	10,2	10.2
mil		diez mil		diez coma dos	diez punto dos

A period should not be used in the numerical expression of years, page numbers, street numbers, or zip codes, nor in articles, decrees, or laws.

el año 2012	página 2345	calle Príncipe, 1034	28010 Madrid

d. Addresses

Street numbers and postal codes do not have a period, except when there is an abbreviation.

La dirección del Hospital General de México es: Calle Dr. Balmis N.º 148, Col. Doctores, Delegación Cuauhtémoc, C. P. 06726, México, D. F.

Internet URLs and e-mail addresses use periods to separate elements. Note how they are read in Spanish.

Spain: **uve doble** (w) ▶
Lat. Am.: **doble ve** (w)

http://www.whitehouse.gov	*Hache-te-te-pe-dos puntos-barra doble-uve doble-uve doble-uve doble (o triple uve doble)-punto-white house-punto-gov*
minombre.miapellido@miservidor.com	*Mi nombre-punto-mi apellido-arroba-mi servidor-punto-com*

1.F.2 [,] Comma

Non-defining relative ▶
clauses: 15.B.1

a. Inserted clauses that are not essential for the meaning of a sentence start and end with a comma (**coma**), as in English.

El profesor, **que es joven**, trabaja mucho. *The teacher, who is young, works a lot.*

Defining relative clauses: ▶
15.B.2

b. Clauses that are necessary for the meaning of a sentence do not have a comma.

El profesor **que es joven** trabaja mucho; el otro profesor, no. *The young teacher works a lot; the other doesn't.*

c. Use a comma to separate a person's name from an inverted exclamation or question mark.

Hola, **Patricia**, ¿cómo estás? *Hi, Patricia, how are you?*
Martín, ¡bienvenido a casa! *Welcome home, Martin!*

d. Use a comma after a **si** clause at the beginning of a sentence.

Conditional *si* clauses: 23.E.8 ▶

Si vas al mercado, compra manzanas. *If you go to the market, buy apples.*
Compra manzanas si vas al mercado. *Buy apples if you go to the market.*

e. A comma may be used to replace an implied verb.

Ana fue al parque; **Paula**, al cine. *Ana went to the park; Paula, to the movies.*

f. A comma is used before the words **como** and **pero**.

Quiero algo dulce, **como** chocolate. *I want something sweet, like chocolate.*
Tengo sueño, **pero** quiero jugar. *I'm tired, but I want to play.*

g. Commas are used to separate items in enumerated lists. In Spanish, it is incorrect to use a comma before the last item in the series.

Tengo **libros, papel y lápices.** *I have books, paper, and pencils.*

1.F.3 [;] Semicolon

a. The semicolon (**punto y coma**) is used to enumerate groups of things which are separated internally by a comma and/or **y**.

Tengo papel, libros y lápices; cuadernos y computadoras. *I have paper, books, and pencils; notebooks and computers.*

b. A semicolon is used to link two independent clauses without connecting words.

Voy a la fiesta; no me voy a quedar mucho tiempo. *I am going to the party; I am not going to stay long.*

c. A semicolon is used before a dependent clause that begins with a conjunction or phrase such as **sin embargo, por lo tanto, no obstante, por consiguiente, en cambio,** and **en fin.**

Llovió mucho; sin embargo, fuimos al parque. *It rained heavily; however, we went to the park.*

1.F.4 [:] Colon

a. Colons (**dos puntos**) are used after the person's name in a salutation for a letter or e-mail. The colon is more formal than a comma.

Direct discourse: 31.A.1

Querida Paula**:** Espero que estés muy bien.   *Dear Paula: I hope all is well with you.*

b. A colon is also used before the enumeration of several elements.

Tengo muchos amigos: Luis, Marta, Patricia,   *I have many friends: Luis, Marta,*
Frank, Adam y Sarah.   *Patricia, Frank, Adam, and Sarah.*

c. A colon is used to separate a clarification, explanation, cause, consequence, summary, conclusion, or example from a preceding independent clause.

Siempre me dice lo mismo: que busque trabajo.   *He always tells me the same thing: to get a job.*

1.F.5 Questions and exclamations

In Spanish, questions can be asked without changing the sentence structure, as is done in English. The opening question mark conveys the intonation that must be used in order to pronounce the statement as a question. The same occurs with an opening exclamation mark. Opening exclamation marks can be placed anywhere you wish to start an exclamation and where the voice must be raised, even if it is in the middle of the sentence.

Questions and question words: Ch. 14

a. [¿ ?] Question marks – *Signos de interrogación*
The beginning of a question is marked with an inverted question mark. As in English, if the question is part of a longer sentence, a comma separates it.

¿Qué día es hoy**?**   *What day is it today?*   Hace frío, **¿**verdad**?**   *It's cold, isn't it?*

b. [¡ !] Exclamation marks – *Signos de admiración o exclamación*
Exclamation marks are always placed at the beginning and end of an exclamation and follow a comma when placed within a sentence.

¡Qué bonito día**!**   *What a lovely day!*   Me gusta la paella, **¡**es deliciosa**!**   *I like paella. It's delicious!*

1.F.6 [-] Hyphen

The hyphen (**guión corto**) is a short dash that is used in writing to join or separate words.

a. The hyphen joins words to form a compound word. When two adjectives are joined, only the last one agrees with the noun in gender and number; the first is always singular and masculine.

Accentuation of plurals and compound words: 1.E.9d

tareas teórico-prácticas   *theoretical and practical homework*
textos histórico-religiosos   *texts about history and religion*

Words that indicate origin (**gentilicios**) can be written with or without a hyphen.

colombo-irlandés/irlandesa   *of Colombian and Irish origin*
franco-alemán/alemana   *of French and German origin*
afroamericano/a   *Afro-American*

It is also possible to use a hyphen to create new concepts.

¡Luis tiene una **casa-mansión** enorme!   *Luis has a huge mansion-like house!*

b. The hyphen separates syllables of a word when the word does not fit on a line of text. In order to divide the word, it is necessary to follow the Spanish rules for dividing words into syllables.

Division of words: 1.D. Abbreviations, acronyms, and symbols: 1.F.1b

pan-ta-lla   co-rres-pon-den-cia   sal-chi-cha   com-pren-sión   cons-ti-tu-ción
(*screen*)   (*correspondence*)   (*sausage*)   (*comprehension*)   (*constitution*)

Stylistically, it is preferable not to leave one letter alone on a line. Also, abbreviations (**Srta.**) and acronyms (**ONU, EE.UU.**) should not be divided.

c. The hyphen indicates part of a word in grammar texts, word lists, and dictionaries. The position of the hyphen indicates whether the segment goes at the beginning, middle, or end of a word.

El sufijo **-ito** se usa en los diminutivos: libr**ito**.	*The suffix **-ito** is used in diminutives:* libr**ito**.
La palabra **ante**pasado contiene el prefijo **ante-**.	*The word **ante**pasado (ancestor) has the prefix **ante-**.*
Las consonantes **-zc-** aparecen en varios verbos: cono**zc**o.	*The consonants **-zc-** appear in several verbs:* cono**zc**o.

d. Time periods or ranges are specified with a hyphen.

Tenemos que estudiar los capítulos 1-3.	*We have to study chapters 1–3.*
El Quijote fue escrito por Miguel de Cervantes (1547-1616).	El Quijote *was written by Miguel de Cervantes (1547–1616).*
Estudié tres años en la universidad (2011-13).	*I studied three years at the university (2011–2013).*

1.F.7 [—] Dash

The dash (**guión largo** o **raya**) is longer than the hyphen. Its main function is to mark the beginning or end of a segment of text in the following cases:

a. Dashes separate comments that interrupt the text. Commas and parentheses can also serve this function.

Notice that in English there is no space in between the dash and the text. However, in Spanish, the dash is separated by one space from the word that precedes it and attached to the first word of the text that interrupts the sentence.

Celeste —pensativa— contestó mi pregunta.	*Celeste—thoughtful—answered my question.*

b. Dialogues are indicated with a dash at the beginning of each intervention.

—¿Quieres café?	*"Do you want some coffee?"*
—Sí, muchas gracias.	*"Yes, thank you very much."*

c. In narrations with dialogue, the dash separates dialogue from narration.

—Tengo miedo —dijo Pilar cuando escuchó que alguien intentaba abrir la puerta.
—No tengas miedo —le dijo su madre, aunque ella sabía que no podrían escapar.
"I'm scared," said Pilar when she heard someone was trying to open the door.
"Don't be afraid," said her mother, though she knew they could not escape.

1.F.8 Quotation marks

Spanish usually uses a different symbol than English to mark quotation marks (**comillas**): « ». However you may also see single or double straight quotes and smart quotes, as in English: ' ' and " ".

a. The main use of quotation marks is to indicate quotes taken from a text, to tell what a person has said, or to cite titles or names of book chapters, articles, reports, or poems. Punctuation of quotes remains inside the quotation marks, but if punctuation is not part of the quoted text, it falls outside the quotes. The period, however, always appears after the quoted text.

Gabriel García Márquez empieza su autobiografía diciendo «Mi madre me pidió que la acompañara a vender la casa».	*Gabriel García Márquez starts his autobiography saying: "My mother asked me to go sell the house with her."*
Según los estudiantes que han leído el libro, «¡Vale la pena leerlo!».	*According to students who have read the book, "It's worth reading it!"*
¿Leíste el artículo «Náufrago en tierra firme»?	*Have you read the article "Castaway on Land"?*

b. Quotation marks can call attention to a word in a text, for example, to explain a word or indicate that it is foreign, improper, wrong, or said with irony.

«Hablar» es un verbo regular.	*"**Hablar**" (to speak) is a regular verb.*
Las palabras «quiosco» y «kiosco» son igualmente aceptables.	*The words "**quiosco**" and "**kiosco**" are equally acceptable.*
¡Pablo dice que «sabe» escribir!	*Pablo says he "knows" how to write!*

`1.F.9` [...] Ellipsis

Ellipses (**puntos suspensivos**) may indicate that what is expressed in the sentence is uncertain or unknown, but it also has other uses.

a. Ellipses are used to mean *et cetera* in an incomplete list. A capital letter is used if the following phrase is a new sentence, and other punctuation marks may be used if necessary.

En el colegio tenemos que estudiar, escribir, leer… ¡No tengo tiempo para nada más!	*At school we have to study, we have to write, we have to read… I have no time for anything else!*
Tengo amigos mexicanos, peruanos, cubanos… de todas partes.	*I have friends from Mexico, Peru, Cuba… from all over the world.*

b. Ellipses can also express suspense or uncertainty in the message, for example, when writing letters, e-mails, text messages, etc.

Me gané la lotería y… bueno… no sé qué hacer…	*I won the lottery and… well… I don't know what to do…*
Pienso en ti…	*I think of you…*
Estoy esperando tu llamada…	*I'm waiting for your call…*

c. When quoting a text, ellipses in parentheses or brackets indicate that part of the text has been omitted.

Dice García Márquez en su autobiografía: "No nos tuteábamos, por la rara costumbre (…) de tutearse desde el primer saludo y pasar al usted sólo cuando se logra una mayor confianza (…)".

García Márquez says in his autobiography: "We did not use the tú form of address, due to the strange custom (…) of using tú from the first greeting and switching to usted only upon becoming close friends (…)".

`1.F.10` Parentheses and brackets

Parentheses (**paréntesis**) ( ) and brackets (**corchetes**) [ ] have similar functions.

a. Parentheses enclose text that expands on or clarifies what is said in a sentence, for example, data, dates, names, etc.

Me gusta mucho Nueva York (es una metrópoli impresionante) y quiero volver allí. Es extraño que no sea la capital del estado del mismo nombre (la capital es Albany).

I like New York very much (it is an impressive metropolis) and I want to go there again. It is strange it is not the capital of the state of New York (the capital is Albany).

b. When it is necessary to give alternatives in a text, they can be included in parentheses.

Los (Las) estudiantes tendrán vacaciones pronto.	*The students will be on break soon.*

c. Brackets can replace parentheses. They are also used to add comments or clarifications in a sentence that is already in parentheses. Notes about a text, such as notes from a translator or editor, also go in brackets.

El primer presidente afroamericano (se llama Barack Obama [nacido en Hawai] de padre keniano y madre norteamericana) subió al poder en 2009.	*The first Afro-American president (called Barack Obama [born in Hawaii], his father was Kenyan and his mother, American) came into power in 2009.*

1.G Spelling

Ortografía

1.G.1 Use of capital letters

Accentuation of capital letters: 1.E.11

a. Days of the week and months are not capitalized in Spanish as they are in English.

lunes	domingo	viernes	mayo	abril	enero
Monday	*Sunday*	*Friday*	*May*	*April*	*January*

b. All proper nouns begin with a capital letter. Articles or nouns that are part of the proper noun are also capitalized. Adjectives formed from proper nouns are not written with a capital letter. This rule is also valid for names of religions and their followers (adjectives).

Pedro	Luisita	Júpiter	Google	Facebook
Venezuela	**venezolano/a**	La Habana	**habanero/a**	
Cristianismo	**cristiano/a**	Protestantismo	**protestantes**	

c. Prepositions that are part of a Spanish last name are not capitalized except when the last name appears alone. If only the definite article is present, it is always capitalized.

Alejandro de la Hoz	Sr. De la Hoz	Susana la Salle	Sra. La Salle

d. Only the first word in a title is capitalized in Spanish, unless the title includes a proper noun. However, capitals in all words of a title are becoming increasingly used in official settings.

La isla bajo el mar es una novela de Isabel Allende.	*Island Beneath the Sea* is a novel by Isabel Allende.
Instituto Nacional de Salud (Bogotá)	National Institute of Health *(Bogotá)*
Centro Nacional de Educación Básica a Distancia (Cenebad, Madrid)	National Center for Long-Distance Basic Education *(Cenebad, Madrid)*

e. As in English, the first letter of a sentence is always capitalized. After a colon, capitals are normally not used in Spanish. However, capitals are used after a colon in the salutation of a letter or e-mail or if the text that follows a colon is a full quote.

Esta es la primera oración de este párrafo. Continuamos con la segunda oración aquí y terminamos este texto con estas últimas palabras: ¡has leído hasta el final!
This is the first sentence in this paragraph. We continue with the second sentence here and we end this text with these final words: You have read to the end!

f. In Spanish, exclamation marks and question marks can end sentences, in which case the new sentence starts with a capital letter. However, unlike English, a comma can also separate a series of exclamations and/or questions.

¿Sabes cuándo es la fiesta? Creo que será pronto, ¿verdad?	*Do you know when the party is? I think it will be soon, won't it?*
¿Cómo estás?, ¿sigues viviendo en Miami?, ¡cuéntame toda la historia!	*How are you? Still living in Miami? Tell me everything!*

Abbreviations, acronyms, and symbols: 1.F.1b

g. All capitals are used for acronyms of four letters or less. When they are longer, usually only the first letter is capitalized. When acronyms become common nouns, the name is written with lowercase letters.

Insalud	Instituto Nacional de Salud
SIDA (*AIDS*)	Síndrome de Inmunodeficiencia adquirida

1.G.2 Place names

a. The letter **x** in **México** and in other Mexican names and their adjectives, is pronounced like the Spanish **j** when it is the first letter of the word or occurs between vowels. Its pronunciation is /**ks**/ or /**s**/ in consonant combinations.

◀ México: 3.F.4

Name	Adjective	Name	Adjective
México	mexicano/a	Oaxaca	oaxaqueño/a
Xalapa	xalapeño/a / jalapeño/a	San Jerónimo Xayacatlán	xayacateco/a
Tlaxcala	tlaxcalteca	La Mixteca	mixteco/a

b. Names of cities and regions in Spain where other national languages are official may be written in the region's native language.

Catalunya   Euskadi   A Coruña   A Mariña
Cataluña   País Vasco   La Coruña   La Mariña

c. Many cities and geographical places in the world have their own Spanish names or spelling.

Nueva York   Estados Unidos   Venecia   Ginebra   Londres   Holanda   Inglaterra

d. Articles and geographical terms included in the *official* name of a place (city, mountain, river, gulf, etc.) are written in capital letters; otherwise, lowercase is used.

Official name		Description only
el Golfo de México	el Río Bravo	la cordillera de Los Andes
la Ciudad de México	el Río de la Plata	la ciudad de Miami
la Ciudad del Cabo	El Salvador	el río Amazonas
La Paz	El Cairo	la Argentina

e. The names of planets, stars, and constellations are written with a capital letter unless they are used as common nouns.

Los planetas giran alrededor del **Sol**.	Protégete del **sol**.	Los astronautas ven la **Tierra** desde el espacio.	En California, la **tierra** es fértil.
The planets orbit around the Sun.	*Protect yourself from the sun.*	*Astronauts look at the Earth from space.*	*In California, the land is fertile.*

1.G.3 Omission of the letter *p*

a. The letter **p** is silent in words beginning with combination **ps-** (**psicólogo, psiquiatra**). These words may also be spelled without the **p** (**sicólogo**, **siquiatra**). This spelling is accepted, but in formal texts, these words tend to keep the initial **p**. In words containing **-ps-** (**eclipse, cápsula**), the letter **p** is always kept.

b. Among the words that contain the consonant combination **-pt-**, only **septiembre** and **séptimo/a** (*seventh*) can be spelled **setiembre** and **sétimo/a**.

c. The past participles of many verbs ending in **-bir** end in **-to** in most Spanish-speaking countries, except Argentina and Uruguay, where they are spelled with **-pt-**. This is an archaic form that has remained in use in the **Río de la Plata** region.

◀ Irregular past participles: 19.A.2, 25.D.2

Infinitive	English	Past participle	Past participle (Arg./Uru.)
describir	*to describe*	descrito	descripto
inscribir	*to enroll*	inscrito	inscripto
suscribir	*to subscribe*	suscrito	suscripto

La lengua española

In the Spanish-speaking world, the terms **español** (*Spanish*) or **castellano** (*Castilian*) are used to refer to the Spanish language, which today is one of the most widely spoken languages in the world. Castilian was the language in **Castilla** (*Castile*), the powerful kingdom that united with the kingdom of **Aragón** to form **España** and reached the coasts of the New World in 1492. Castile's language spread quickly to the new continent and the word *Castilian,* therefore, demonstrates the origin of the Spanish language. The term is still associated in Spain with the language variant spoken in today's Castile, the government's center. Spain's constitution (1978) declares that **castellano** is the national language, but that the autonomous provinces can have their own official language in addition to **castellano**. Today **catalán** (*Catalan*), **euskera** (*Basque*), **gallego** (*Galician*), and **valenciano** (*Valencian*) are official languages, along with Castilian, in their regions. Furthermore, there are other languages which are not official, such as those spoken in Asturias and Mallorca.

In most parts of Latin America, **español** and **castellano** are used as synonyms, but the term **español** is more common than **castellano.** The Spanish variant, **español americano** or **español de América,** is the mother tongue of over 90% of the nearly 500 million Spanish-speaking people in the world (including the U.S.). Spanish in Latin America also exists in conjunction with other American languages, such as **maya** and **náhuatl** (in Mexico and Guatemala), **quechua** (in Ecuador, Peru, and Bolivia), **guaraní** (in Paraguay), and **English** (in the Caribbean), among others. In many new Latin American constitutions from the 1990s, the majority of countries declared themselves multicultural and multilingual nations, naming Spanish as their official language or as one of their official languages.

Ever since the 1700s, when the Royal Academy for the Spanish Language (**La Real Academia Española, RAE**) published its first standard works—a dictionary, *Diccionario de autoridades* (1726–1739); a text on spelling, *Ortografía* (1741); and one on grammar, *Gramática* (1771)— their rules have played an important role in retaining the Castilian variant as the norm in the whole of the Spanish-speaking world. Eventually, with the formation of the Association of Spanish Language Academies (**Asociación de Academias de la Lengua Española, ASALE**) in 1951, the Spanish-speaking world was finally treated as a whole in terms of the development and use of the Spanish language. A goal was set to maintain the Spanish-speaking community, but also to recognize and make known the different variations of the Spanish language. This goal led to the release of a common description of the Spanish language in the form of a spelling text (1999), a common dictionary, and a common grammar text (approved by the ASALE in 2007 and published in 2010). An updated spelling text, the *Nueva ortografía*, was approved in late 2010. **A Handbook of Contemporary Spanish Grammar** is written from this integral perspective of the Spanish language.

Asociación de Academias de la Lengua Española (ASALE), 1951: http://asale.org	
Real Academia Española (RAE), 1713	Academia Hondureña de la Lengua, 1948
Academia Argentina de Letras, 1931	Academia Mexicana de la Lengua, 1875
Academia Boliviana de la Lengua, 1927	Academia Nacional de Letras del Uruguay, 1943
Academia Chilena de la Lengua, 1885	Academia Nicaragüense de la Lengua, 1928
Academia Colombiana de la Lengua, 1871	Academia Norteamericana de la Lengua Española, 1973
Academia Costarricense de la Lengua, 1923	Academia Panameña de la Lengua, 1926
Academia Cubana de la Lengua, 1926	Academia Paraguaya de la Lengua Española, 1927
Academia Dominicana de la Lengua, 1927	Academia Peruana de la Lengua, 1887
Academia Ecuatoriana de la Lengua, 1874	Academia Puertorriqueña de la Lengua Española, 1945
Academia Filipina de la Lengua Española, 1924	Academia Salvadoreña de la Lengua, 1876
Academia Guatemalteca de la Lengua, 1887	Academia Venezolana de la Lengua, 1883

Práctica

Actividades 1–24, pp. A1–A6

Nouns
Sustantivos

Chapter 2

A. Gender
B. Number
C. Appreciative suffixes
D. Regional variations

2.A Gender

Género

Nouns are words that refer to people, animals, objects, places, events, or abstract concepts. In Spanish, nouns are either feminine or masculine.

2.A.1 People and animals

a. The ending **-a** usually denotes feminine and the ending **-o** denotes masculine.

Masculine		Feminine	
el amig**o**	*the (male) friend*	**la** amig**a**	*the (female) friend*
el chic**o**	*the boy*	**la** chic**a**	*the girl*
el niñ**o**	*the (male) child*	**la** niñ**a**	*the (female) child*
el gat**o**	*the (male) cat*	**la** gat**a**	*the (female) cat*

Determiners and subjects: 4.B.1
Use of definite articles: 5.C

b. An **-a** is added to a noun that ends in **-or** to make it feminine.

Masculine		Feminine	
el profes**or**	*the (male) teacher*	**la** profes**ora**	*the (female) teacher*
el señ**or**	*the man/lord*	**la** señ**ora**	*the lady*

c. Nouns that end in **-ista** and **-al** can be either feminine or masculine. This is determined by the article or context.

el/la art**ista**   *the artist*   **el/la** intelect**ual**   *the intellectual*

el/la electric**ista**   *the electrician*   **el/la** profesion**al**   *the professional*

el/la correspons**al**   *the correspondent*   **el/la** riv**al**   *the rival*

el/la fisc**al**   *the district attorney*

Poeta is both masculine and feminine. The feminine **poetisa** is also used.

d. Nouns that refer to people that end in **-ante**, **-ente** usually can be either masculine or feminine based on the article used.

Masculine	Feminine	
el ag**ente**	**la** ag**ente**	*the agent*
el cant**ante**	**la** cant**ante**	*the singer*
el paci**ente**	**la** paci**ente**	*the patient*
el particip**ante**	**la** particip**ante**	*the participant*
el represent**ante**	**la** represent**ante**	*the representative*

A number of nouns that end in **-ente**, the masculine form, have an **-enta** ending in the feminine form.

Masculine	Feminine	
el asist**ente**	**la** asist**enta**	*the assistant*
el depend**iente**	**la** depend**ienta**	*the shop assistant*
el ger**ente**	**la** ger**enta**	*the manager*
el presid**ente**	**la** presid**enta**	*the president*
el pari**ente**	**la** pari**enta**	*the relative*

e. A number of social roles and professions are either masculine or feminine based on the person's gender.

emperador (*emperor*) →
emperatriz (*empress*)

padrino (*godfather*) →
madrina (*godmother*)

Masculine		Feminine	
el actor	*the actor*	**la** actriz	*the actress*
el caballero	*the gentleman*	**la** dama	*the lady*
el hombre	*the man*	**la** mujer	*the woman*
el padre, **el** papá	*the father*	**la** madre, **la** mamá	*the mother*
el príncipe	*the prince*	**la** princesa	*the princess*
el rey	*the king*	**la** reina	*the queen*
el yerno	*the son-in-law*	**la** nuera	*the daughter-in-law*

f. Some nouns can only be masculine or feminine even though they can refer to both men and women.

Mi padre es **una** buena **persona**.   *My father is a good person.*
¡Tu hija es **un encanto**!   *Your daugher is a very charming girl.*

g. Regarding animals, the *noun* + **macho** is used for masculine, and the *noun* + **hembra** for feminine. Some animal names can be either masculine or feminine, while others can only be one or the other. Pets, such as **el** gat**o** or **el** perr**o**, usually follow gender rules and can take an **-a** in the feminine (**la** gat**a**, **la** perr**a**).

Masculine		Feminine	
la jirafa **macho**	*the male giraffe*	**la** jirafa **hembra**	*the female giraffe*
el os**o**	*the (male) bear*	**la** os**a**	*the (female) bear*
el león	*the lion*	**la** leona	*the lioness*
el caballo	*the horse*	**la yegua**	*the mare*
el toro	*the bull*	**la vaca**	*the cow*
el gallo	*the rooster*	**la gallina**	*the hen*

2.A.2 Things

a. Nouns that denote concrete things or abstract ideas are, with a few exceptions, masculine if they end in **-o** and feminine if they end in **-a**.

Singular feminine nouns that begin with a stressed **a** take the masculine singular article, but take an adjective with a feminine form.
el agua clara, el alma buena: 5.A.3

Masculine		Feminine	
el calendari**o**	*the calendar*	la ros**a**	*the rose*
el florer**o**	*the vase*	la calculador**a**	*the calculator*
el libr**o**	*the book*	la impresor**a**	*the printer*
el pensamient**o**	*the thought*	la ide**a**	*the idea*

Exceptions:

Masculine		Feminine	
el día	*the day*	**la** man**o**	*the hand*
el map**a**	*the map*	**la** fot**o**	*the photo*
el planet**a**	*the planet*	**la** mot**o**	*the motorcycle*
el tranvía	*the tram*	**la** radi**o**	*the radio*

We have La **foto** and la **moto** are feminine because they are short for **la fotografía** and **la motocicleta**.

b. Nouns that end in **-e** can be masculine or feminine. The same applies to the few nouns that end in **-i** or **-u**.

el cin**e**	*the cinema*	**la** gent**e**	*the people*	**el** rub**í**	*the ruby*
la clas**e**	*the class*	**el** puent**e**	*the bridge*	**el** tab**ú**	*the taboo*

c. Nouns that end in **-aje, -al, -és, -in,** and **-or** are usually masculine.

el pas**aje**	*the fare/ticket*	**el** can**al**	*the canal*	**el** estr**és**	*the stress*
el sab**or**	*the taste*	**el** val**or**	*the value/worth*	**el** f**in**	*the end*

Exceptions:

la f**lor**	*the flower*	**la** lab**or**	*the task*

d. Many nouns that end in **-ma** are masculine. Most are of Greek origin and have cognates in English.

el clima	*the climate*	**el** problema	*the problem*
el dilema	*the dilemma*	**el** programa	*the program*
el drama	*the drama*	**el** poema	*the poem*
el enigma	*the enigma*	**el** síntoma	*the symptom*
el idioma	*the language*	**el** sistema	*the system*
el panorama	*the panorama*	**el** tema	*the theme/topic*

e. Nouns that end in **-ción, -sión, -dad, -umbre, -tad, -tud, -is,** and **-z** are usually feminine.

la lec**ción**	*the lesson*	**la** televi**sión**	*the television*
la activi**dad**	*the activity*	**la** liber**tad**	*the freedom*
la sín**tes**is	*the synthesis*	**la** lu**z**	*the light*
la cost**umbre**	*the custom*	**la** juven**tud**	*the youth*

2.A.3 **Other nouns**

a. Names of colors are masculine.

el azul	*blue*	**el** negro	*black*
el amarillo	*yellow*	**el** rojo	*red*
el blanco	*white*	**el** verde	*green*

b. Names of days, months, trees, mountains, rivers, numbers, oceans, and lakes are masculine.

Trabajo **los** lunes.	*I work on Mondays.*
Enero es frí**o**.	*January is cold.*
El pino es bonit**o**.	*The pine tree is beautiful.*
El Aconcagua es alt**o**.	*The Aconcagua Mountain is high.*
El Amazonas es larg**o**.	*The Amazon River is long.*
El 13 no es peligros**o**.	*The number 13 is not dangerous.*
El Atlántico es inmens**o**.	*The Atlantic Ocean is enormous.*
El Titicaca es hermos**o**.	*Lake Titicaca is beautiful.*

City names that begin with **San/Santo** are masculine: San Francisco, Santo Domingo, Santo Tomás. City names that begin with **Santa** are feminine: Santa Marta, Santa Mónica: 3.D.2

c. The gender of town names varies. Names of towns are often feminine if they end in an unstressed **-a**, and if the town is considered a city (**una ciudad**). If you define a town as a place (**un sitio**), masculine is also possible.

la hermosa Barcelona	*beautiful Barcelona*	**la** misteriosa Machu Picchu	*the mysterious Machu Picchu*
la lejana Santiago	*remote Santiago*	**el** inmenso Yucatán	*the immense Yucatán*

d. Names of letters are feminine: **la letra** (*the letter*).

La eñe es española.   *The letter ñ is Spanish.*

e. Infinitives used as nouns are masculine.

el deber   *duty*   **el** atardecer   *dusk*

f. The meaning of some nouns changes based on its masculine or feminine form.

Masculine		Feminine	
el capital	*the capital (funds)*	**la** capital	*the capital (city)*
el cometa	*the comet*	**la** cometa	*the kite*
el cura	*the priest*	**la** cura	*the cure*
el editorial	*the editorial*	**la** editorial	*the publishing house*
el frente	*the front*	**la** frente	*the forehead*
el guía	*the tour guide*	**la** guía	*the tour guide/guide book*
el mañana	*the future*	**la** mañana	*the morning*
el modelo	*the model*	**la** modelo	*the model (fashion)*
el orden	*the order*	**la** orden	*the command; the religious order*
el Papa	*the Pope*	**la** papa/**la** patata	*the potato (Lat. Am.)/the potato (Spain)*
el policía	*the policeman*	**la** policía	*the policewoman/the police*
el pendiente	*the earring*	**la** pendiente	*the slope*

2.B Number

Número

Accentuation of plurals and compound words: 1.E.9

2.B.1 Regular plurals

a. Nouns that end in an *unstressed vowel* form the plural with an **-s**.

Singular		Plural	
el amig**o**	*the friend*	los amig**os**	*the friends*
la cas**a**	*the house*	las cas**as**	*the houses*
el espírit**u**	*the spirit*	los espírit**us**	*the spirits*
la noch**e**	*the night*	las noch**es**	*the nights*

b. Nouns that end in a *stressed* **-a, -o**, or **-e** form the plural with an **-s**.

Singular		Plural	
la mam**á**	*the mother*	las mam**ás**	*the mothers*
el pap**á**	*the father*	los pap**ás**	*the fathers*
el sof**á**	*the sofa*	los sof**ás**	*the sofas*
el caf**é**	*the coffee/cafe*	los caf**és**	*the coffees/cafes*

Singular		Plural	
el pi**e**	*the foot*	los pi**es**	*the feet*
el domin**ó**	*the domino*	los domin**ós**	*the dominoes*
el bur**ó**	*the bureau*	los bur**ós**	*the bureaus*

c. Nouns that end in a *consonant* or a *stressed* **-i** or **-u** form the plural with **-es**. When the noun ends in **-z** in the singular, the **-z** changes to **-c** in the plural.

Singular		Plural	
la actividad	*the activity*	las actividad**es**	*the activities*
el papel	*the paper*	los papel**es**	*the papers*
el monitor	*the monitor*	los monitor**es**	*the monitors*
el esqu**í**	*the ski*	los esqu**íes**	*the skis*
el pe**z**	*the fish*	los pe**ces**	*the fish [pl.]*

d. Words that have an accent on the last syllable and form the plural with **-es** do not have an accent in the plural.

Singular		Plural	
el sal**ón**	*the living room*	**los** sal**ones**	*the living rooms*
la transmis**ión**	*the broadcast*	**las** transmision**es**	*the broadcasts*

Note that there are also nouns that require an accent in the plural to maintain the correct stress, 1.E.9:

joven ⟶ jóvenes

lapiz ⟶ lápices

2.B.2 Irregular plurals

a. Nouns that end in an *unstressed* vowel followed by **-s** do not change form between singular and plural.

el lun**es**	*Monday*	los lun**es**	*Mondays*
el mart**es**	*Tuesday*	los mart**es**	*Tuesdays*
el miércol**es**	*Wednesday*	los miércol**es**	*Wednesdays*
el juev**es**	*Thursday*	los juev**es**	*Thursdays*
el viern**es**	*Friday*	los viern**es**	*Fridays*
el anális**is**	*the analysis*	los anális**is**	*the analyses*
la cris**is**	*the crisis*	las cris**is**	*the crises*
el oas**is**	*the oasis*	los oas**is**	*the oases*
la tes**is**	*the thesis*	las tes**is**	*the theses*

b. Some nouns are only used in the plural.

las afueras	*outskirts*	**los** anteojos	*glasses*
las esposas	*handcuffs*	**los** alrededores	*surroundings*
las gafas	*glasses*	**los** celos	*jealousy*
las nupcias	*wedding*	**los** enseres	*belongings*
las tijeras	*scissors*	**los** prismáticos	*binoculars*
las vacaciones	*vacation*	**los** víveres	*provisions*

The singular **la tijera** is also used.

c. The following nouns have irregular plural forms.

el carácter	*the character*	**los** caracteres	*the characters*
el régimen	*the regime*	**los** regímenes	*the regimes*
el arte	*the art*	**las** artes	*the arts*

Accentuation of plural and compound words: 1.E.9b

2.C | Appreciative suffixes

Sufijos apreciativos

2.C.1 Overview

There are three types of appreciative suffixes: *diminutives* (**diminutivos**), *augmentatives* (**aumentativos**), and *pejoratives* (**despectivos**).They are used to express sentiments or judgements about events, people, and things. While diminutives and augmentatives are generally used to express affection or size, pejorative suffixes attach negative meaning to a word. The use and meaning of appreciative suffixes varies greatly depending on context, intonation of the speaker, and regional differences. The formation of these suffixes also differs from region to region, but the most common rules are described below.

2.C.2 Structure of diminutives

The most common diminutive suffix is **-ito/a**. Other suffixes are **-illo/a, -ico/a,** and **-uelo/a.**

The spelling changes if the word ends in a syllable with **-c-** or **-g-**: jue**go**/ juegu**ito,** bar**co**/barqu**ito.**

a. Generally, in nouns ending with an *unstressed* (**átona**) **-o** or **-a,** the vowel is dropped to add the diminutive **-ito/a.**

gat**o**/gat**ito**   *cat/kitten*   niñ**a**/niñ**ita**   *girl/little girl*

In these cases, the ending **-cito/-cita** is more common in Latin America. Examples of other diminutives of **café**: café**tito,** café**tico,** café**tín,** café**tillo.**

b. If a word ends in a *stressed* vowel, the preferred ending is **-cito/a,** but the diminutive can vary depending on the region.

bebé → bebe**cito,** beb**ito**   papá → papa**cito,** papa**íto,** pap**ito**   café → cafe**cito,** cafe**íto**

c. The most common ending of two-syllable nouns that end in **-e** is **-ecito/a**: madr**ecita.** If the word has more than two syllables, the ending is usually **-ito/a**: compadr**ito,** comadr**ita.**

In general, **-ecito/-ecita** and **-ecillo/-ecilla** are more common in Spain, but they are also used in several parts of Latin America.

d. When the word is a *monosyllable* (**monosílabo**) and ends in a consonant, both **-cito/-cita** and **-ecito/-ecita** can be used: pan**cito,** pan**cillo,** pan**ecito,** pan**ecillo,** flor**cita,** flor**cilla,** flor**ecita,** flor**ecilla.**

Words ending in **-z** have a spelling change:

luz → luce**cita**

Beatriz → Beatri**cita**

e. Words with two or more syllables that end in **-n** or **-r** usually take the ending **-cito/a**: camion**cito,** amor**cito,** cancion**cita.** If they end in any other consonant, the ending is usually **-ito/-ita**: lap**icito,** dificil**ito.**

2.C.3 Structure of augmentatives and pejoratives

Augmentatives (**aumentativos**) and pejoratives (**despectivos**) are formed similarly to diminutives, adding **-ote/a** (**-zote/-zota**), **-azo/a, -ón/ona,** and **-ucho/a, -aco/a, -ote/a, -ajo/a,** respectively.

casa/cas**ona**   *house/big house*   casa/cas**ucha**   *house/ugly house*

2.C.4 Grammatical category, gender, and number

Words with an appreciative suffix follow the rules for forming plurals. They also keep their grammatical category and gender, but some feminine nouns can also be converted to a masculine form with the ending **-ón** for greater emphasis.

noticia → notici**ón**/notici**ona**   lámpara → lampar**ón**/lampar**ona**

2.C.5 Accentuation

Palabras agudas: 1.E.1
Palabras llanas: 1.E.2

The suffix is always the stressed syllable of a word. For this reason, most diminutives form **palabras llanas** (words with the stress on the second-to-last syllable): television**cita,** cama**rita.** The endings **-ón, -ín,** form **palabras agudas** (words with the stress on the last syllable): camis**ón,** pequeñ**ín.**

2.C.6 Grammatical category

Throughout most of the Spanish-speaking world, appreciative suffixes are generally used with just nouns and adjectives. However, in Latin America, diminutives are also used in other grammatical categories such as adverbs, some quantifiers, interjections, and also demonstratives, possessives, plurals, and numbers. The diminutive of the **gerundio** is used mostly in Spain. Some examples of the different grammatical categories are listed in the following table.

Base word	Diminutive	Augmentative	Pejorative
camión *n.*	camion**cito**	camion**ón**, camion**zote**, camion**azo**	camion**ucho**, camion**ete**, camion**aco**
casa *n.*	cas**ita**	cas**ota**, cas**ona**	cas**ucha**
libro *n.*	libr**ito**	libr**ote**, libr**ón**, libr**azo**	libr**ucho**, libr**aco**, libr**ajo**
débil *adj.*	debil**ito/a**, debil**cito/a**	debil**ote/a**	debil**ucho/a**
fuerte *adj.*	fuerte**cito/a**	fuert**ote/a**, fuert**ón/ona**	fuert**ucho/a**
ahora *adv.*	ahor**ita**		
aquí *adv.*	aqui**cito**		
nada *determ.*	nad**ita**		
todo *determ.*	tod**ito/a**		
adiós *interj.*	adios**ito**		
callando *ger.*	calland**ito**		

Adjectives: 3.A.4
Adverbs: 10.J.1

2.C.7 Combinations

Many nouns and adjectives can combine various suffixes (often repeated), but the final result depends on phonetic factors, number of syllables, specific noun or adjective and, of course, on regional and personal preferences.

chico	chiqu**ito**, chiqu**itico**, chiqu**ititito**, chiqu**itiquitico**, chiqu**illo**, chiqu**illito**, chiqu**illico**, chiqu**illote**, chiqu**illazo**, chic**ucho**
joven	joven**citico**, joven**citito**, joven**zotote**
casa	cas**uchita**

2.C.8 Independent words

Some diminutives and augmentatives have been used for so long that they do not change. These are examples of words that are no longer diminutives: **ventanilla, bocadillo.**

2.C.9 Uses of diminutives

a. To indicate smaller size or brevity of events. They can also indicate less intensity when describing physical characteristics of people and things.

Tengo un **autito** muy pequeño.	*I have a very little car.*
Demos un **paseíto cortito.**	*Let's take a very short walk.*
¿Te da **miedito** conducir por esta carretera?	*Aren't you a little scared of driving on this road?*
¿Por qué estás **tristecita** hoy?	*Why are you a little sad today?*

b. To show affection when speaking to loved ones or talking about them: **mamita, papito, amorcito, abuelita, noviecita.** Diminutives are also common with proper names: **Susanita, Eduardito.**

c. To soften requests or orders:

¿Me sirve un **cafecito**, por favor?	*Can I get a coffee, please?*
¿Me haces un **favorcito**?	*Can you do me a little favor?*

d. To soften the meaning of strong words or characteristics:

Esos chicos son unos **ladroncitos**.　　　　*Those boys are just a couple of little thieves.*

e. To diminish the importance of uncomfortable or disagreeable situations:

La **multita** por la infracción es de cien dólares.　　*It's only a little one-hundred dollar fine.*

La **operacioncita** no tiene importancia.　　*The little procedure is nothing.*

2.C.10　Uses of augmentatives

a. To intensify the positive or negative meaning of a noun or adjective:

¡Tu visita me dio un **alegrón** inmenso!　　*Your visit (absolutely) made my day!*

Tenemos un **problemazo**.　　*We have a very/really big problem.*

b. To express an exaggerated size. The ending **-azo/a** can be positive, but context and intonation are crucial for its meaning. When referring to age, the ending **-ón/ona** can be derogatory.

Talking about age: 6.H.3 ▶

Tienes unos **ojazos** que me encantan.　　*I just love your big eyes.*

Él es un **cuarentón** sin futuro.　　*He is a forty-something with no future.*

c. To communicate a "hard hit" with the object described:

machete → **machetazo**　　balón → **balonazo**　　bate → **batazo**　　codo → **codazo**

Adjectives: 3.A.4 ▶

d. Both nouns and adjectives can be pejorative with augmentative suffixes.

¡Has escrito una **novelucha** sin valor!　　*What a trashy piece of pulp fiction you have written!*

Esa pobre familia vive en una **casucha**.　　*That poor family lives in (such) a dump.*

2.D　Regional variations

Variaciones regionales

2.D.1　Gender

The following nouns can be either masculine or feminine depending on the region:

el/la azúcar	*sugar*		**el/la** lente	*the lens*
el/la Internet	*the Internet*		**el/la** maratón	*marathon*
el/la interrogante	*query, question*		**el/la** sartén	*the frying pan*

2.D.2　Job titles for women

a. In Spanish-speaking countries, the masculine form is traditionally used for all job titles, even for women. Use of the feminine form is increasing, especially among young people.

la abogad**a**　　*the lawyer*　　　　**la** médic**a**　　*the doctor*

b. Words referring to people, especially job titles, that have historically had only a masculine form can now be found in the feminine.

For a better understanding of the differences in pronunciation of the **c** and **z** between Spain and Latin America, see Consonants and digraphs: 1.C.6. ▶

el general	**la** general**a**	*the general*	**el** ingeniero	**la** ingenier**a**	*the engineer*
el juez	**la** juez**a**	*the judge*	**el** ministro	**la** ministr**a**	*the minister*

2.D.3　Common word variations

The most common regional variations in Spanish are expressed through vocabulary, especially nouns. For example, *hunting* is called **caza** in Spain, while in Latin America it is called **cacería**. In Latin America, **caza** is pronounced the same as **casa** (*house*) and for that reason a different word is used. The same happens with the word **cocer** (*to cook*), which sounds the same as **coser** (*to sew*). Therefore a different word, **cocinar** (*to cook*), is used in Latin America.

Práctica

 Actividades 1–16, pp. A6–A10.

Adjectives
Adjetivos

3.A Gender and number

Género y número

An adjective describes the characteristics of a noun and agrees with the noun in gender and number.

3.A.1 Endings *-o / -a*

Adjectives that end in **-o** in the masculine form change to **-a** for the feminine form and add **-s** to form the plural.

	Singular		Plural	
Masculine	el libr**o** blanc**o**	*the white book*	los libr**os** blanc**os**	*the white books*
Feminine	la cas**a** blanc**a**	*the white house*	las cas**as** blanc**as**	*the white houses*

3.A.2 Endings *-e / -ista*

Adjectives that end in **-e** or **-ista** do not change in gender, but they do change in number.

	Singular		Plural	
Masculine	**el** libro grand**e**	*the big book*	**los** libros grand**es**	*the big books*
	el país social**ista**	*the socialist country*	**los** países social**istas**	*the socialist countries*
Feminine	**la** casa grand**e**	*the big house*	**las** casas grand**es**	*the big houses*
	la nación social**ista**	*the socialist nation*	**las** naciones social**istas**	*the socialist nations*

If the adjective is augmentative and ends in **-ote,** it forms the feminine with an **-a.**

grandot**ote,** grandot**ota**   *very big*

◀ Diminutives, augmentatives, and pejoratives: 3.A.4

3.A.3 Other endings

a. For adjectives that end in **-or, -án, -ón, -ín,** add **-a** to form the feminine and remove the written accent. To form the plural, add **-es** to the masculine form and **-s** to the feminine form. Bear in mind that in the masculine plural form, the written accent is not needed for the endings **-anes, -ones, -ines.**

conservad**or(es)**	conservad**ora(s)**	*conservative*
encantad**or(es)**	encantad**ora(s)**	*charming*
trabajad**or(es)**	trabajad**ora(s)**	*hard-working*
holgaz**án**/holgaz**anes**	holgaz**ana(s)**	*lazy*
glot**ón**/glot**ones**	glot**ona(s)**	*gluttonous*
pequeñ**ín**/pequeñ**ines**	pequeñ**ina(s)**	*tiny*

b. The following comparative adjectives that end in **-or** do not change in gender, but do take **-es** in the plural.

◀ Comparison of adjectives: 3.E
Comparisons: Ch. 11

anteri**or(es)**	*previous/front*	posteri**or(es)**	*subsequent/back*
mej**or(es)**	*better*	pe**or(es)**	*worse*
interi**or(es)**	*interior*	exteri**or(es)**	*exterior*
may**or(es)**	*older/larger*	men**or(es)**	*younger/smaller*
superi**or(es)**	*superior*	inferi**or(es)**	*inferior*

c. Many adjectives of nationality (**gentilicios**) that end in **-és** take **-a** in the feminine form. The feminine form and both the masculine and feminine plural forms lose the written accent.

Masculine	Feminine	
danés/daneses	danesa(s)	*Danish*
francés/franceses	francesa(s)	*French*
inglés/ingleses	inglesa(s)	*English*
portugués/portugueses	portuguesa(s)	*Portuguese*

Exception:

The adjective **cortés** (*polite*) retains the same form in the feminine. It has the same plural form for both masculine and feminine.

el chico cort**és**	*the polite boy*	**la** chica cort**és**	*the polite girl*
los chicos cort**eses**	*the polite boys*	**las** chicas cort**eses**	*the polite girls*

Many adjectives that form nouns come from art, science, and technology fields.
La **curva** es peligrosa.
La línea es **curva**.

d. Adjectives that end in **í, -a, -ú** do not change in gender, but do have a plural form. Adjectives that end in **-e** or in the consonants **-z, -r, -l, -s** act in the same way.

Singular		Plural	
problema **agrícola**	*agricultural problem*	problemas **agrícolas**	*agricultural problems*
persona **belga**	*Belgian person*	personas **belgas**	*Belgian people*
marinero **bengalí**	*Bengali sailor*	marineros **bengalíes**	*Bengali sailors*
templo **hindú**	*Hindu temple*	templos **hindúes**	*Hindu temples*
estudiante **feliz**	*happy student*	estudiantes **felices**	*happy students*
clase **útil**, libro **útil**	*useful class, useful book*	clases y libros **útiles**	*useful books and classes*
círculo **polar**	*polar circle*	círculos **polares**	*polar circles*

3.A.4 Diminutives, augmentatives, and pejoratives

Appreciative suffixes: 2.C ▶

a. Like nouns, adjectives are very flexible when it comes to adding appreciative suffixes. The most common diminutive endings are **-ito/a(s)** and in some cases **-cito/a(s), -ecito/a(s),** and **-illo/a(s), -ín(es)/ina(s)**.

amarill**ito(s)**	*yellowish*	pequeñ**ín(es)**	*tiny*
gord**ito(s)**	*chubby*	verde**cilla(s)**	*greenish*

b. Augmentatives are less common in adjectives than in nouns. The endings are **-ote/a(s), -zote/a(s), -ón(es)/ona(s)**.

dul**zón**	*"somewhat sweet"*	simpatic**ona**	*very friendly (derogatory)/ "somewhat" nice*
joven**zote**	*handsome young man*	grand**ote**	*very big*

c. The suffix **-ón(ones)/ona(s)** can also be added to nouns to turn them into adjectives. These tend to have a negative connotation.

boca	*mouth*	María, ¡no seas boc**ona**!	*María, don't be a big-mouth!*
barriga	*belly*	Juan es muy barrig**ón**.	*Juan has a big belly.*

d. Some pejorative suffixes are **-acho/a, -ucho/a(s), -ote/a(s), -ajo/a(s)**. In English, the translations may lack the negative connotation the Spanish provides.

fe**úcho**	*quite ugly*	fri**úcha**	*very cold*	pequeñ**ajo**	*very small*
flac**ucho**	*too thin*	gord**ote**	*too fat*	ric**acho**	*filthy rich*

3.B Agreement

Concordancia

3.B.1 Nouns with the same gender

When an adjective describes several nouns of the *same* gender, the adjective takes the same gender in the plural.

un libr**o** y un cuadern**o** nuev**os**	*a new book and notebook*
una lámpar**a** y una mes**a** nuev**as**	*a new lamp and table*

3.B.2 Nouns of different gender

a. When an adjective describes several nouns of *different* gender and is placed *after* the nouns, it takes the masculine form in the plural.

una herman**a** y un herman**o** simpátic**os**	*a nice sister and brother*
un libr**o** y una mes**a** nuev**os**	*a new book and table*

b. When an adjective describes several nouns of *different* gender and is placed *before* the nouns, it agrees with the nearest subsequent noun.

un**os** simpátic**os** amig**os** y amig**as**	*some lovely friends*
un**as** simpátic**as** amig**as** y amig**os**	*some lovely friends*

3.B.3 Nouns used as adjectives

Nouns can be used as adjectives to modify other nouns. In this usage, they are invariable in number.

la palabra **clave**	*the keyword*	las palabras **clave**	*the keywords*
el programa **piloto**	*the pilot program*	los programas **piloto**	*the pilot programs*
el coche **bomba**	*the car bomb*	los coches **bomba**	*the car bombs*

3.B.4 Colors

a. It is common to use names of flowers, plants, minerals, and seeds as color adjectives. In this case, they are normally considered invariable and they are commonly used with **(de) color**. Words in this category include **naranja** (*orange*), **lila** (*lilac*), and **rosa** (*pink*).

la(s) corbata(s) **café/(de) color café**	*the brown tie(s)*
el/los mantel(es) **naranja/(de) color naranja**	*the orange tablecloth(s)*

b. They can also be treated as regular adjectives, in which case they agree with the noun in number but the gender remains invariable: **calcetines lilas**. In the case of **naranja** and **rosa**, the adjectives **anaranjado/a(s)** and **rosado/a(s)** can also be used.

las camisas **rosas**/las camisas **rosadas**	*the pink shirts*

c. When colors are modified by other adjectives (**claro, oscuro, pálido**), both the color and the adjective are usually considered invariable. This usage assumes the omission of the masculine singular noun **color**.

medias **verdes**	*green socks*	medias **(color) verde claro**	*light-green socks*
piel **pálida**	*pale skin*	piel **(color) rosa pálido**	*pale pink skin*

Posición

The adjective is often placed after the noun, but it can also be placed before.

3.C.1 Placement after the noun

a. An adjective placed after a noun distinguishes that particular noun from others within the same group. It is the most common position used in Spanish.

| Me gustan las películas **cómicas.** | *I like funny movies.* |

In this example, the adjective **cómicas** restricts the meaning of the noun by referring only to *funny* movies and excluding all other movies that are not funny.

Adjectives and determiners with fixed placement: 3.C.3c ▶

b. "Relational" adjectives that either derive from a noun or classify a noun are always placed after the noun. Context determines whether an adjective is descriptive or relational. For example, **grave** can be placed before or after **enfermedad** to describe an illness. However, **mental** can only be placed after **enfermedad** because it describes the specific nature of the disease: one related specifically to the brain. These adjectives can usually be paraphrased as "related to" or, in Spanish, as **de** + *noun*: **enfermedad mental = enfermedad de la mente.**

una enfermedad **mental**	una enfermedad **de la mente**
economía **nacional**	economía **de la nación**
actuación **cinematográfica**	actuación **de cine**
ecuación **matemática**	ecuación **de matemáticas**
sitio **web**	sitio **de Internet**
cosas **técnicas**	cosas **de la tecnología**

3.C.2 Placement before the noun

a. Adjectives can be placed before a noun to emphasize or intensify a particular characteristic or suggest that it is inherent to the noun.

| una **oscura** noche de invierno | *a dark winter night* |
| el **horrible** monstruo | *the horrible monster* |

When the adjective is placed before a noun, the noun must be defined by a determiner. See Determiner placement in relation to the noun: 4.B.5 ▶

b. Adjectives that precede a noun can create a certain stylistic effect or tone. They can indicate how the speaker feels toward the person or thing being described.

el **talentoso** autor	*the talented author*
las **feas** casas	*the ugly houses*
unas **pequeñas** calles	*charming streets*
un **amplio** jardín	*a spacious garden*

c. Adjectives are also placed before the noun when we want to communicate that a characteristic is unique to the noun. This mostly happens in poetry and literature for stylistic effect. Such adjectives are called **epítetos** (*epithets*).

| La **famosa** Manhattan con sus **altísimos** rascacielos. | *The famous Manhattan with its very tall skyscrapers.* |

d. Adjectives describing known persons and things precede the noun to highlight an inherent quality or trait.

la **hermosa** ciudad de Madrid	*the beautiful city of Madrid*
mis **queridos** padres	*my dear parents*
el **increíble** hombre araña	*the incredible Spiderman*

3.C.3 **Adjectives and determiners with fixed placement**

a. The following determiners are always placed *before* the noun.

amb**o/a(s)**	*both*	plen**o/a(s)**	*full*
much**o/a(s)**	*a lot (of)/many/much*	poc**o/a(s)**	*little/few*
otr**o/a(s)**	*other/s*	tant**o/a(s)**	*as/so much, as/so many*

b. Adjectives that describe origin, nationality, and noun type are placed *after* the noun.

la casa **alemana**	*the German house*	un chico **cubano**	*a Cuban boy*
una caja **fuerte**	*a safe deposit box*	la calle **principal**	*the main street*

c. Technical and professional characteristics are described by an adjective placed *after* the noun.

◀ Placement after the noun: 3.C.1b

el teléfono **celular**	*the cell phone*	la tesis **doctoral**	*the doctoral thesis*
la página **web**	*the web page*	la impresora **láser**	*the laser printer*

d. Certain adjectives that derive from a noun and convey a direct relationship to it *follow* the noun (**economía → económico; nación → nacional**).

La familia tiene problemas **económicos.**	*The family has economic problems.*
Solo vendemos productos **nacionales.**	*We only sell domestic products.*

e. With comparisons, the adjective is placed *after* the noun.

Quiero un café **caliente,** no un café **frío.**	*I want a hot coffee, not a cold coffee.*

f. Adjectives with appreciative suffixes are placed *after* the noun.

◀ Diminutives, augmentatives, and pejoratives: 3.A.4

Pedro está conduciendo un coche **nuevecito.**	*Pedro is driving a newish car.*
No conozco ciudades **feúchas** en el país.	*I don't know any ugly cities in this country.*

3.C.4 **Placement and meaning**

A number of common adjectives change meaning depending on whether they are placed before or after the noun.

◀ Determiners:
Agreement: 4.B.4
Placement: 4.B.5

Adjectives	Placed before		Placed after	
alto	un **alto** ejecutivo	*a senior executive*	un ejecutivo **alto**	*a tall executive*
bueno	un **buen** amigo	*a good friend*	un chico **bueno**	*a kind boy*
cierto	una **cierta** persona	*a certain person*	una cosa **cierta**	*a sure thing*
diferente	**diferentes** lugares	*several places*	lugares **diferentes**	*different places*
grande	una **gran** casa	*a grand house*	una casa **grande**	*a big house*
medio	**media** hora	*half an hour*	la clase **media**	*the middle class*
nuevo	mis **nuevos** zapatos	*my brand-new shoes*	mis zapatos **nuevos**	*my new shoes*
pobre	un **pobre** pueblo	*unlucky people*	un pueblo **pobre**	*poor/needy people*
puro	**puro** aire	*only air*	aire **puro**	*pure/clean air*
raro	una **rara** cualidad	*a rare quality*	una persona **rara**	*a rare/unusual person*
rico	un **rico** chocolate	*a delicious chocolate*	una familia **rica**	*a rich family*
triste	un **triste** caso	*a sad case*	una historia **triste**	*a sad history*
único	mi **único** amor	*my only love*	un amor **único**	*a unique love*
viejo	un **viejo** amigo	*an old friend*	un amigo **viejo**	*an elderly friend*

◀ **Bueno** is shortened to **buen** when placed before a masculine singular noun. **Grande** is shortened to **gran** before both masculine and feminine singular nouns: 3.D

◀ **mismo, propio**: 7.E.5

3.D Prenominal adjectives

Adjetivos antepuestos

3.D.1 Buen, mal, primer, tercer, algún, ningún

Indefinite quantifiers **algún,
alguno**; **ningún,
ninguno, ninguna**: 7.B.2

The forms **bueno, malo, primero, tercero, alguno, ninguno** drop the final **-o** and become **buen, mal, primer, tercer, algún, ningún** before masculine singular nouns. This does not occur before feminine and plural nouns.

| un **buen** libro | *a good book* | un **mal** ejemplo | *a bad example* |
| el **primer** día | *the first day* | el **tercer** año | *the third year* |

3.D.2 Gran, san

a. The adjective **grande** is shortened before both masculine and feminine singular nouns.

| un **gran** momento | *a big moment* |
| una **gran** fiesta | *a grand party* |

b. The adjective **santo** is shortened to **san** only when it precedes a proper noun that does not begin with *-to* or *-do*.

| **San** Diego | **Santo To**más |
| **San** José | **Santo Do**mingo |

3.E Comparison

Comparación

3.E.1 Structure

Adjectives have gradable inflections. Most adjectives have a basic form, called the *positive* form. The *comparative* form expresses higher and lower grades of a characteristic; the *superlative* form expresses the highest or lowest grades.

Determiners are not inflected:
4.B.3, 4.B.4
Comparison of adverbs: 10.I
Comparisons: Ch. 11

Positive form		Comparative		Superlative	
verde(s)	*green*	**más** verde(s)	*greener*	**el/la/los/las más** verde(s)	*the greenest*
verde(s)	*green*	**menos** verde(s)	*less green*	**el/la/los/las menos** verde(s)	*the least green*

Todo es **más** verde en verano.	*Everything is greener in the summertime.*
La casa blanca es **la más** alta.	*The white house is the tallest.*
Mis jardines son **los más** bonitos.	*My gardens are the most beautiful.*
Esta flor es **menos** roja que esa.	*This flower is less red than that one.*

3.E.2 Irregular inflection

a. Some common adjectives have irregular gradable inflection forms.

Comparative adjectives ending
in **-or**: 3.A.3b

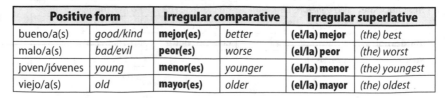

Positive form		Irregular comparative		Irregular superlative	
bueno/a(s)	*good/kind*	**mejor(es)**	*better*	**(el/la) mejor**	*(the) best*
malo/a(s)	*bad/evil*	**peor(es)**	*worse*	**(el/la) peor**	*(the) worst*
joven/jóvenes	*young*	**menor(es)**	*younger*	**(el/la) menor**	*(the) youngest*
viejo/a(s)	*old*	**mayor(es)**	*older*	**(el/la) mayor**	*(the) oldest*

| Rosa es **la mayor** de todos. | *Rosa is the oldest of them all.* |
| Juan es **el menor** de la familia. | *Juan is the youngest in the family.* |

Adjectives • **Chapter 3**

b. The regular comparative forms of **bueno/a** and **malo/a** can be used as well. However, in this case, they exclusively emphasize character judgments.

Mario es **más bueno** que el pan.	*Mario is a very good person.*
Mario es **mejor** deportista que su hermano.	*Mario is a better athlete than his brother.*
Este perro es **más malo** que el diablo.	*This dog is more evil than the devil.*
El problema es **peor** de lo que pensaba.	*The problem is worse than I thought.*

c. Mayor and **menor** are used interchangeably with the regular comparative forms.

Juan es **más viejo** que su hermano.	*Juan is older than his brother.*
Juan es **mayor** que su hermano.	*Juan is older than his brother.*

d. When **pequeño** and **grande** refer to age, their comparative and superlative forms are the same as those for **joven** and **viejo/a**.

Mario es el **más grande/pequeño** de los tres hermanos.	*Mario is the oldest/youngest of the three brothers.*
Mario es el **más viejo/joven** de los tres hermanos.	*Mario is the oldest/youngest of the three brothers.*
Mario es el **mayor/menor** de los tres hermanos.	*Mario is the oldest/youngest of the three brothers.*

e. Grande and **pequeño** also use **mayor** and **menor** as comparative and superlative forms when describing the scope or importance of an issue.

California es el estado con el **mayor** número de hispanohablantes en los EE.UU.
California is the state with the greatest number of Spanish-speakers in the U.S.

3.E.3 Superlatives with -*ísimo/a(s)*

muchísimo, poquísimo: 7.C.1
Adverbs: Superlative
constructions: 10.I.2

a. Spanish also forms superlatives with the endings **-ísimo/a(s).** This form is called the **superlativo absoluto.**

La casa es **alta.**	La casa es **altísima.**	*The house is (very) tall.*
El problema es **fácil.**	El problema es **facilísimo.**	*The problem is (very) easy.*

b. Many **adjectives** have irregular superlatives.

antiguo/a	**antiquísimo/a**	*old/very old*
ardiente	**ardentísimo/a**	*passionate/very passionate*
cruel	**crudelísimo/a** (also **cruelísimo/a**)	*cruel/very cruel*
fiel	**fidelísimo/a**	*loyal/very loyal*

c. Adjectives ending in **-ble** form the superlative with the ending **-bilísimo/a.**

Pedro es **amable.**	Pedro es **amabilísimo.**	*Pedro is (very) kind.*

d. Some adjectives have two absolute superlative forms. However, the regular form is more commonly used.

bueno/a	**buenísimo/a, bonísimo/a**	*good/very good*
fuerte	**fuertísimo/a, fortísimo/a**	*strong/very strong*

e. Some adjectives can take the suffix **-érrimo/a** instead. This is only found in the formal register.

célebre	**celebérrimo/a**	*famous/very famous*
libre	**libérrimo/a**	*free/very free*
mísero/a	**misérrimo/a**	*miserable/very miserable*
pobre	**paupérrimo/a** (also, **pobrísimo/a**)	*poor/very poor*

3.F Regional variations

Variaciones regionales

There are not many grammatical differences in the use of adjectives in the Spanish-speaking world. The differences depend on which adjectives are used in the different regions. A few examples of the variations are illustrated below.

3.F.1 Colors

a. In Spain, it is more common to use **marrón** than **café** for *brown*, and in Latin America **castaño** is used for *dark hair* (**cabello/pelo castaño**).

b. In some regions of the Spanish-speaking world, **morado/a** is used instead of **violeta, colorado/a** is more common than **rojo/a,** and **bordó** is heard instead of **granate**.

3.F.2 Nationality

a. People from India are called **hindú** in Latin America and **indio/a** in Spain. The latter word is used in Latin America to refer to the indigenous people of the region. The adjective **indio/a,** however, also has some negative connotations in Latin America; therefore **indígena** is preferred, especially in written language. **Indiano/a** is used in Spain for the Spaniards who returned home after becoming wealthy in the former Spanish colonies.

b. The adjective **suramericano/a** is more usual in most of Latin America than **sudamericano/a,** which is more common in Spain and Argentina.

3.F.3 ¿Hispano, latino o latinoamericano?

a. In North America, the terms **hispano/a** and **latino/a** are used interchangeably to refer to people from Spanish-speaking countries. Both terms are correct and the preference for one or the other comes from one's personal perception of subtle differences between the two words. Outside of North America, **hispano/a** is used more frequently since one meaning of the term **latino/a** technically refers to all of the peoples, both European and American, that speak any language derived from Latin.

b. Latinoamericano/a refers to anyone from the Americas that speaks Spanish, Portuguese or French, while **hispanoamericano/a** refers exclusively to Spanish-speaking individuals from the Americas. **Iberoamericano/a** describes anyone from Spanish- and Portuguese-speaking countries in the Americas, or from these countries as well as Spain and Portugal.

3.F.4 México

Variations in the pronunciation of the letter **x**: 1.C.6, 1.D.5, 1.G.2a

Although at some point the adjectives **mejicano** and **mexicano** coexisted, the official name of the country is **México** and the official adjective is **mexicano**. This use of the **x** is common in many Mexican place names and in their corresponding adjectives. Although some cities have lost the **x** spelling (such as **Jalisco**), most have retained it. In most cases, this **x** is pronounced like a **j**.

México   mexicano/a   Oaxaca   oaxaqueño/a

Práctica

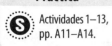

Actividades 1–13, pp. A11–A14.

Determiners
Determinantes

4.A Overview

Aspectos generales

Determiners are words that precede a noun to indicate which object, person, or other entity the noun represents. They can be used to specify if a noun refers to something or someone nonspecific (**un** chico) or to something or someone very specific (like **el** coche or **esta** casa). Determiners can also refer to the quantitative nature of a noun, stating its exact number, as in **tres amigos**, or an indefinite amount: **varias** cosas, **muchas** chicas, **unos** estudiantes. Determiners state and clarify the nature of the noun.

Determiners		
	Groups	**Examples**
Articles *Artículos*	Specific reference: definite articles	**El** parque es grande.
	Non-specific reference: indefinite articles	**Unos** niños juegan.
Quantifiers *Cuantificadores*	Specific quantity: numbers	Hay **tres** árboles.
	Non-specific quantity: affirmative and negative quantifiers	Hay **muchas** personas; **algunos** chicos y **pocas** chicas.
Demonstratives *Demostrativos*	Three-level system for describing relative distance	**Este** árbol y **esas** flores me gustan. **Aquellas** no.
Possessives *Posesivos*	Prenominal and postnominal forms	**Mi** casa es **tuya.**

◀ Articles: Ch. 5

◀ Quantifiers: Numbers: Ch. 6
◀ Indefinite quantifiers and pronouns: Ch. 7

◀ Demonstratives: Ch. 8

◀ Possessives: Ch. 9

It is important to note that many determiners can have several functions in a sentence. For example, quantifiers are especially prone to becoming adverbs. The words **mucho, bastante, más, menos** are determiners that function like adjectives when they support the noun, but they are adverbs when they support the verb.

◀ Most determiners agree in gender and/or number with the noun they modify. Adverbs never change form. Agreement: 4.B.4 Determiners and adverbs: 4.B.7

En verano hay **muchos** conciertos.   *There are many concerts in the summer.*

(**Muchos** is a determiner and modifies **conciertos** by stating its quantity.)

Los conciertos me gustan **mucho.**   *I like concerts very much.*

(**Mucho** is an adverb of quantity and modifies the verb **gustar** by stating how much the speaker likes concerts.)

En la Florida hay **bastantes** playas.   *There are a lot of beaches in Florida.*

(**Bastantes** is a determiner and modifies **playas** by stating its quantity.)

¡Cuando voy allí, nado **bastante**!   *When I go there, I swim a lot!*

(**Bastante** is an adverb of quantity and modifies the verb **nadar** by stating how much the speaker swims.)

¡No digas **más** mentiras!   *Don't tell any more lies!*
No voy a mentir **más**.   *I won't lie any more.*
Debes trabajar **menos**.   *You have to work less.*

◀ Notice that **más** and **menos** do not change form.

Características comunes

4.B.1 Determiners and subjects

a. One of the functions of a determiner is to designate the subject of a sentence.

Tu casa es bonita; **Las** casas son bonitas.

Such sentences without a determiner are grammatically incorrect in Spanish. This does not apply to proper nouns: **La** ciudad es hermosa. (*The city is beautiful.*), Madrid es hermosa. (*Madrid is beautiful.*)

b. When the subject is a *plural* noun, the determiner can be left out in specific written contexts such as newspapers, magazines, and commercials: **Investigadores** encuentran nuevo virus. (*Researchers find new virus.*), **Presos** se amotinan contra guardias. (*Prisoners riot against guards.*)

c. The determiner can be left out when an uncountable noun *follows* a verb that means (*not*) *to exist, to be lacking, to remain*: **Falta** azúcar. (*There's no sugar.*), **No hay** leche. (*There isn't any milk.*)

d. Countable nouns must have determiners when the quantity is specific: Queda **un** pan. (*There is one loaf left.*), Quedan **dos** panes. (*There are two loaves left.*)

e. Plural countable nouns can follow the verb without determiners when they have a non-specific reference. **Faltan** tenedores y cuchillos. (*There aren't any forks or knives.*)

f. The same rule applies to direct objects. A plural noun that functions as a direct object can also follow the verb without a determiner when it has a non-specific reference. Compré libros. (*I bought books.*), Comemos manzanas. (*We are eating apples.*)

g. Indirect objects, however, must always be specified by a determiner: Le compré un libro a **la niña.** (*I bought a book for the girl.*)

h. Personal pronouns and proper nouns can always be the subject without a determiner: **Ella** lee. (*She is reading.*), **Pedro** habla. (*Pedro is talking.*)

4.B.2 Determiners as pronouns

Indefinite pronouns: 7.C.3, 7.D ▶

a. When determiners stand alone, they act as pronouns. This only occurs when a noun is not present. The determiner's reference can often be understood from the context.

Algunos vienen, **otros** se van.	*Some are coming, others are going.*
Esta casa es cara, **esa** no.	*This house is expensive, but not that one.*
Tú tienes amigos; yo no tengo **ninguno.**	*You have friends; I have none.*

Demás: 7.C.10 ▶
Cada: 7.C.8

b. Some determiners can never stand alone as a pronoun and only appear next to other determiners. This applies to **demás,** which must always be preceded by a definite article and is often also used with **todo. Cada** must be followed by a noun.

Dame **las demás** cosas.	*Give me the rest of the things.*
Todo lo demás puede esperar.	*Everything else can wait.*
Cada persona tiene sus ideas.	*Every person has their own ideas.*
Os visitaremos **a cada uno** de vosotros.	*We're going to visit every/each one of you.*

c. The following words are always indefinite pronouns: **algo, alguien, nada, nadie.** They can never act as determiners.

¿Vais a hacer **algo** hoy?	*Are you [pl.] going to do anything today?*
¿Hay **alguien** en casa?	*Is anyone home?*

d. Negative indefinite pronouns and negative determiners require double negation when placed after the verb.

No tenemos **ningún** plan.   *We have no plans./We don't have (any) plans.*
No hay **nadie** en casa.   *There is nobody home.*

4.B.3 Determiners and adjectives

a. An adjective describes a noun and agrees with it in gender and number. Determiners are therefore related to adjectives, but illustrate other aspects of a noun. The main difference between them is that determiners belong to *closed word groups.* This means that there is a limited number of determiners of the same type in each group. It can take hundreds of years for new determiners to develop in a language. New adjectives, on the other hand, are forming continuously in order to describe new things. For example, by following the rules for adjective formation in Spanish, one can create new ones such as: ¡Mi hijo es **hispano-inglés, cibernavegante** y **chateadorcísimo**!

◀ Adjectives: Ch. 3

b. Suffixes and prefixes cannot be added to determiners, with the exception of **mucho** and **poco** (**muchísimo, poquísimo**). Suffixes and prefixes can be added to nouns and adjectives in Spanish: **superitalianísimo** (*unbelievably Italian*), **heladazo** (*gigantic ice-cream*), **colinita** (*little hill*).

◀ Appreciative suffixes: 2.C, 3.A.4

4.B.4 Agreement

The majority of determiners agree in gender and number with the noun they support, (**esta** casa, **algunos** libros, **pocas** chicas), but the determiners **cada, más,** and **menos** never change form (**menos** tiempo, **más** libros).

◀ Comparison of adjectives: 3.E

4.B.5 Placement in relation to the noun

a. It is common for a determiner to be placed before a noun: **este** chico, **el** estudiante. If the noun is described by an adjective preceding it, the determiner must be placed before the adjective: **este** simpático chico, **el** buen estudiante.

◀ Adjective placement before the noun: 3.C.2

b. Some determiners can be placed before or after the noun. Determiners placed after the noun highlight a feature of the noun or create a different emphasis.

◀ Demonstratives after a noun: 8.A.2b

El chico **ese** no es simpático.   *That boy is not nice.*
No soy una persona **cualquiera.**   *I'm not just anyone.*

4.B.6 Combination of two determiners

a. Determiners can be combined in pairs: **estos dos** libros (*these two books*), **mis otras** cosas (*my other things*). Three determiners together are rare, and in such cases the third one is usually a numeral: **los otros cinco** chicos.

b. Of all determiners, only **todo/a(s)** can *precede* a definite article: **todos los** días. The following determiners (with corresponding agreement forms) can *follow* the article: **el mucho** amor, **el poco** dinero, **la otra** vez, **los varios** países, **los tres** amigos.

◀ Use of definite articles: 5.C

c. The indefinite article **un(a)** must be placed after **todo/a** and can only be used in its singular form in this combination. **Un(a)** must be placed before **cierto/a(s),** and can be used in its singular or plural form. **Un(a)** can never be combined with **otro** like in English.

Eres **todo un** caballero.   *You're a real gentleman.*
Ellos pagaron **una cierta** suma.   *They paid a certain amount.*
Ahora vivo en **otra** ciudad.   *Now, I live in another town.*

Demás: 7.C.10

d. Demás always precedes the noun with the definite article in the plural: **los/las demás.** The article agrees with the noun's gender and number. It is common to add **todo/a(s)** to a definite or neuter article: **todas las demás** casas (*all those other houses*), **todo lo demás** (*all the rest*).

4.B.7 Determiners and adverbs

a. Determiners cannot be combined with quantifiers, gradable adverbs, or other expressions of quantity. One can say **muy tranquilo,** but not **muy este.** The exceptions are the determiners **más, menos,** and **poco,** which accept quantifiers: **muy poco** tiempo, **muchos más/menos** estudiantes. On some occasions, possessive pronouns can be placed after and modified by quantifiers or gradable adverbs.

Tiene una risa **muy** suya.   *His laugh is very distinctive.*

Indefinite quantifiers and pronouns: Ch. 7
Quantifying adverbs: 10.D.2

b. The following indefinite determiners which refer to a noun's quantity can also act as adverbs: **bastante, demasiado, más, menos, mucho, poco, tanto, todo.** Like all other adverbs, they can modify verbs, adjectives, or other adverbs.

¡Tú siempre te quejas **tanto**!   *You always complain so much.*
Trabajamos **demasiado**.   *We work too much.*
¡Chateas **bastante** en la red!   *You chat quite a bit online!*
Mi computadora es **un poco** lenta.   *My computer is a bit slow.*

c. Mucho can never be used with adjectives and adverbs; only **muy** can precede them.

El barco navega **muy** rápidamente.   *The boat is sailing very fast.*
El viento está **muy** fuerte hoy.   *The wind is very strong today.*

d. Only **tanto** and **todo** agree in gender and number when they occur before an adjective.

Ella está **toda** entusiasmada.   *She is all excited.*
Mis zapatos están **todos** mojados.   *My shoes are completely soaked.*

e. The abbreviation **tan** can only be used before adjectives and adverbs.

¡El tiempo es **tan** corto y pasa **tan** rápidamente!   *Time is so short and goes so fast!*

Comparisons: Ch. 11

4.B.8 Comparisons with *más, menos, mucho, tanto (tan)*

Comparative structures in Spanish use **que** or **como** and determiners.

El avión es **más** rápido **que** el tren.   *The plane is faster than the train.*
El rock británico es **tan** bueno **como** el estadounidense.   *British rock is just as good as American.*

Práctica

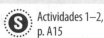

 Actividades 1–2, p. A15

Articles
Artículos

Chapter 5

Determiners (2)
A. Definite and indefinite articles
B. Use of indefinite articles
C. Use of definite articles
D. Regional variations

5.A Definite and indefinite articles

Artículos definidos e indefinidos

5.A.1 Forms of definite and indefinite articles

Both the definite and indefinite articles can be masculine or feminine, singular or plural. They are placed before a noun and take the same gender and number as that noun.

	Definite articles		Indefinite articles	
	Masculine	**Feminine**	**Masculine**	**Feminine**
Singular	**el**	**la**	**un**	**una**
Plural	**los**	**las**	**unos**	**unas**

el amigo	*the friend*	**un** amigo	*a friend*
los amigos	*the friends*	**unos** amigos	*some friends*
la escuela	*the school*	**una** escuela	*a school*
las escuelas	*the schools*	**unas** escuelas	*some schools*

◄ Note that **uno** is an *indefinite pronoun* and it can never be used with a noun: 7.C.4 and 7.D.3

5.A.2 *Lo*

The neuter article **lo** is used before adjectives, possessive pronouns, and gradable adverbs (**mejor, peor**) in order to express abstract concepts. The neuter article **lo** cannot be placed before nouns.

lo bueno	*the good (thing)*	**lo** mío	*my thing*

◄ **Lo mejor, lo peor:** 11.D.3

5.A.3 Use of *el* and *un* with feminine nouns

El and **un** are used before feminine nouns that begin with a stressed **a-** or **ha-**. The noun continues to be feminine in the plural: **el** agua, **las** aguas.

el águila bonit**a**	*the beautiful eagle*	**el ha**cha negr**a**	*the black axe*
un águila bonit**a**	*a beautiful eagle*	**un ha**cha negr**a**	*a black axe*

5.A.4 Abbreviating the article *el*

When the prepositions **a** or **de** precede the definite article **el**, they combine to form a contraction: **a** + **el** = **al** and **de** + **el** = **del**.

Viajo **al** Perú.	*I'm going to Peru.*	el libro **del** chico	*the boy's book*

◄ The article **el** does not form a contraction with the preposition when it is part of a proper name: **Viajo a El Salvador:** 5.C.6

5.B Use of indefinite articles

Uso de los artículos indefinidos

◄ Indefinite determiners: 7.C.4

5.B.1 Placement and agreement of indefinite articles

a. Indefinite articles are always placed before the noun and agree with it in gender and number.

Tengo **un** libro.	*I have a book.*
Escribo **una** carta.	*I'm writing a letter.*

b. Nouns can become subjects accompanied by these determiners.

Unos turistas visitaron la Casa Blanca.	*(Some/A few) Tourists visited the White House.*
Un chico ya la había visitado.	*A boy had already visited it.*

c. No other determiners can appear together with indefinite articles, except for **poco/a(s)** and **cada**.

Tengo **un poco** de café.	*I have some coffee.*
Tengo **unas pocas** amigas mexicanas.	*I have a few Mexican friends.*
Cada uno debe cuidar sus cosas.	*Everyone should look after his/her possessions.*

5.B.2 Reference to quantity

Indefinite determiners: 7.C.4 ▶

a. The singular indefinite articles **un(a)** may refer to exactly one person or object, especially in contrasts and to stress the lack of something countable (*not even one, not a single one*).

No tengo **un** hermano, sino **tres**.	*I don't have **one** brother, but **three**.*
Voy a comprar **una** torta, no **dos**.	*I am going to buy **one** cake, not **two**.*
No hay ni **una** (sola) silla libre.	*There is not a single vacant seat.*

b. The plural indefinite articles **unos/as** refer to an undefined quantity and, with numbers, to an approximate one.

Hay **unas** estudiantes polacas.	*There are **some** Polish students.*
Me quedan **unos cuatro** dólares.	*I have **around** four dollars left.*

5.B.3 Exclamations

In exclamations, to add emphasis, it is common to use an article in cases where it may technically not be required.

Hace frío.	*It's cold.*
¡Hace **un** frío!	*It's so cold!*

5.B.4 *Otro/a(s)*

Uno/a are not used before **otro/a(s)** (*one more, another*).

¡Por favor, **otro** café!	*Another coffee, please!*	**¡Otra** vez!	*One more time!*

5.C Use of definite articles

Uso de los artículos definidos

5.C.1 General uses

Unlike English, Spanish uses the definite article when talking about people, things, or events in general.

Los estudiantes son trabajadores.	*Students are hard-working.*
Me gusta **la** leche.	*I like milk.*

5.C.2 Days and dates

a. The definite article is *not* used with months or to tell which day it is.

Hoy es lunes.	*Today is Monday.*
Ayer fue jueves.	*Yesterday was Thursday.*
Voy a Medellín en noviembre.	*I'm going to Medellín in November.*

b. The definite article is used to refer to something on a specific day or date.

Estudio **los** martes.   *I study on Tuesdays.*
La Nochebuena es **el** 24 de diciembre. *Christmas Eve is December 24.*

5.C.3 Time

Time is indicated by **ser** + **(a) las** + *number* for plurals, and **ser** + **(a) la una** for *one o'clock*.

La clase de español **es a las** tres.   *Spanish class is at three o'clock.*
Son las cuatro de la tarde.   *It is four o'clock in the afternoon.*
La cita es **a la una**.   *The appointment is at one o'clock.*

◀ **Ser** in calendar and time expressions: 29.C.2a

5.C.4 Vocative forms and titles

Articles are not used with titles or proper names when addressing someone directly. However, when talking about someone in the third person, the article is used and matches the person in gender and number. The polite vocative forms **don** and **doña** are used in the singular without an article and are followed by a first name.

Addressing someone	
Señora Gómez, ¿es usted peruana?	*Are you Peruvian, Mrs. Gómez?*
Doctor Medina, ¿cómo está usted?	*How are you, Dr. Medina?*
Don Pedro, ¿habla usted inglés?	*Do you speak English, Pedro?*

Talking about someone	
La señora Gómez es peruana.	*Mrs. Gómez is Peruvian.*
El doctor Medina está bien.	*Dr. Medina is well.*
Don Pedro no habla inglés.	*Pedro doesn't speak English.*

5.C.5 Names of languages

The names of languages take a definite article except after the preposition **en** or with the verbs **hablar** (*to talk*), **aprender** (*to learn*), **comprender** (*to understand*), **enseñar** (*to teach*), **escribir** (*to write*), **leer** (*to read*), and **saber** (*to know*).

El español es fácil.   *Spanish is easy.*
¿Cómo se dice eso **en** español?   *How do you say that in Spanish?*
John, ¿**hablas** español?   *Do you speak Spanish, John?*

5.C.6 Country names

a. The names of some countries and regions are used with the definite article. The article can be left out if it is not a part of the official name.

la Argentina   **los** Estados Unidos   **el** Paraguay
el Brasil   **la** Florida   **el** Perú
el Canadá   **la** India   **la** República Dominicana
el Ecuador   **el** Japón   **el** Uruguay

b. If the article is a part of the official name, it is capitalized. In this case, the masculine article is not abbreviated after the prepositions **a** or **de.**

◀ Abbreviating the article **el**: 5.A.4

Vivo en **El** Salvador.   *I live in El Salvador.*
Llegué a **El** Dorado, en Bogotá.   *I arrived in El Dorado in Bogotá.*

Prenominal possessives: 9.B

5.C.7 Ownership expressions with an article

The definite article replaces prenominal (unstressed) possessive determiners when ownership is obvious, for example, when you talk about parts of the body or personal belongings.

Article instead of possessives: 9.D.4

| Me duelen **los** pies. | ***My*** feet hurt. |
| ¡Ponte **los** zapatos! | Put ***your*** shoes on! |

5.C.8 Position of the definite article

a. The definite article must always be placed before the noun. Adjectives and adjectival phrases (e.g. *adverb* + *adjective*) can come between the article and noun.

Combination of two determiners: 4.B.6

| **la** hermosa Barcelona | *beautiful Barcelona* |
| **los** cada vez más altos precios | *ever-increasing prices* |

b. No determiners other than **todo/a(s)** can be placed before the definite article.

| **todos los** profesores | *all of the professors* |

5.C.9 Articles without nouns

When the noun can be identified from context, the article can be used alone with an adjective, adverb, and/or pronoun.

| No quiero tu bolsa azul; dame **la** roja. | *I don't want your blue bag; give me the red one.* |
| Nos gusta su auto, pero es mejor **el** nuestro. | *We like his car, but ours is better.* |

5.C.10 Articles in exclamations

Lo: 5.A.2

The definite article and the neuter **lo** can be used before an adjective in exclamations. In English, you would normally use *how many/much* or *how* + *adjective*.

| ¡Es increíble **la** gente que hay! | *It's amazing how many people there are!* |
| ¡**Lo** bien que estamos aquí! | *How great life is here!* |

5.C.11 Family names

The definite article in the plural is used before last names (in the singular) to refer to the whole family.

| **Los** Johnson están en Madrid. | *The Johnson family is in Madrid.* |
| Pronto vendrán **los** Romero. | *The Romero family will come soon.* |

5.D Regional variations

Variaciones regionales

5.D.1 Proper names

In some regions of Latin America and Spain, the definite article is used before proper names in spoken language. Normally, it is used only when referring to close friends or family. In regions where this use of the definite article is less common, some native speakers may consider it incorrect.

| Quiero mucho a **la** Juana. | *I'm very fond of Juana.* |
| ¡Debemos visitar **al** Miguel! | *We must visit Miguel!* |

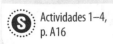

Práctica

Actividades 1–4, p. A16

Quantifiers: Numbers
Cuantificadores: Los números

Chapter 6

Determiners (3)
A. Cardinal numbers
B. Use of cardinal numbers
C. Collective numbers and counting expressions
D. Ordinal numbers
E. Fractions and multiples
F. Time
G. Dates
H. Age
I. Temperature
J. Idiomatic expressions

6.A Cardinal numbers

Números cardinales

0–199 Números del cero al ciento noventa y nueve							
0	cero	10	diez	20	veinte	30	treinta
1	uno/a	11	once	21	veintiuno/a	40	cuarenta
2	dos	12	doce	22	veintidós	50	cincuenta
3	tres	13	trece	23	veintitrés	60	sesenta
4	cuatro	14	catorce	24	veinticuatro	70	setenta
5	cinco	15	quince	25	veinticinco	80	ochenta
6	seis	16	dieciséis	26	veintiséis	90	noventa
7	siete	17	diecisiete	27	veintisiete	100	cien
8	ocho	18	dieciocho	28	veintiocho	101	ciento uno/a
9	nueve	19	diecinueve	29	veintinueve	199	ciento noventa y nueve

200–1000 Números del doscientos al mil			
200	doscientos/as	700	setecientos/as
300	trescientos/as	800	ochocientos/as
400	cuatrocientos/as	900	novecientos/as
500	quinientos/as	1000	mil
600	seiscientos/as		

1001–1 000 000 Números del mil uno a un millón			
1001	mil un(o/a)	100 000	cien mil
1002	mil dos	200 000	doscientos/as mil
2000	dos mil	1 000 000	un millón

2 000 000 Números mayores de dos millones	
2 000 000	dos millones
1 000 000 000	mil millones (*a billion*)
1 000 000 000 000	un billón (*a trillion*)

Spanish	U.S. English	U.K. English								
mil	*thousand*	*thousand*	1000							
un millón	*million*	*million*	1000	000						
mil millones/millardo	*billion*	*thousand million/milliard*	1000	000	000					
un billón	*trillion*	*billion*	1000	000	000	000				
mil billones	*quadrillion*	*billiard*	1000	000	000	000	000			
trillón	*quintillion*	*trillion*	1000	000	000	000	000	000		
mil trillones	*sextillion*	*trilliard*	1000	000	000	000	000	000	000	
cuatrillón	*septillion*	*quadrillion*	1000	000	000	000	000	000	000	000

España tiene alrededor de **cuarenta millones** de habitantes.	Spain has approximately forty million inhabitants.
México tiene más de **cien millones** de habitantes.	Mexico has more than a hundred million inhabitants.
Ecuador tiene **doscientos ochenta y tres mil quinientos sesenta y un** kilómetros cuadrados.	Ecuador is 283,561 km².

6.A.1 Writing styles for numbers

a. Numbers (not decimals) of four digits or fewer are written without a space, period, or comma: **1000; 230.** This also applies to years, pages, postal codes, law paragraphs, and line numbers.

b. Numbers (not decimals) of more than four digits are divided into groups of three, as in English. If the number of digits is not evenly divisible by three, the one or two digits left over form a separate group. Each group is separated by a space: **10 000 000; 23 005; 100 500.** The traditional spelling with a comma or a period as separator every three digits is no longer required. When the number is very large, it can be shortened in the text by writing digits and words: **3 trillones de euros.** Numbers with **mil**, however, cannot be written with both digits and words.

Numbers and counting expressions: 6.C.2
Ordinal numbers: 6.D.2

c. Decimals are marked with a comma, but a period can also be used. The convention varies between Spanish-speaking countries: 0.23 (**cero punto veintitrés**); 0,23 (**cero coma veintitrés**). This figure can also be read as (**cero con**) **veintitrés centésimos** (*zero and twenty-three hundredths*).

6.B Use of cardinal numbers

Uso de los números cardinales

6.B.1 Numbers combined

hay (*there is/are*): 29.B.1

Uno/un	**Un** is used before masculine nouns. *51 books:* cincuenta y **un** libros *541 books:* quinientos cuarenta y **un** libros The term **uno** is only used when it is not followed by a noun. —¿Cuántos estudiantes hay? *How many students are there?* —Hay **uno**. / Hay treinta y **uno**. *There is one. / There are thirty-one.*
Una	**Una** is used before feminine nouns. *31 pounds:* treinta y **una** libras *1001 pounds:* mil (y) **una** libras Note that **uno/una** do not have a plural form even if they are part of a number greater than 1.
Y	**Y** is used between the tens and ones. 1492: mil cuatrocientos noventa **y** dos 2 010 095: dos millones diez mil noventa **y** cinco But: 409 001: cuatrocientos nueve mil uno/a
21–29	Combinations of the number 20 are written as one word. It is less common to use three words. 21: **veintiuno/a** (**veintiún** before masculine nouns) / veinte y uno/a 26: **veintiséis** / veinte y seis 225: doscientos **veinticinco** / doscientos veinte y cinco
31–99	Combinations of numbers between 31 and 99 are written in three words. 32: **treinta y dos**; 92: **noventa y dos** 2255: dos mil doscientos **cincuenta y cinco**

100 **Cien**	**Cien** by itself expresses *a hundred/one hundred*. **Cien** does not agree in gender or number with the noun. *100 books*: **cien** libros *100 boxes*: **cien** cajas El cien es mi número favorito. *One hundred is my favorite number.* ¿Cuántos estudiantes hay? *How many students are there?* Hay **cien** estudiantes. *There are one hundred students.*
101–199 **Ciento**	**Ciento** is used between **101** and **199** before nouns and does not change in gender and number. *103 books*: **ciento** tres libros *169 boxes*: **ciento** sesenta y nueve cajas
200–999 **Cientos/as**	**Cientos/as** is used between **200** and **999** and agrees with the noun's gender. Unlike English, multiple hundreds are expressed in one word (though the subsequent numbers are separate). *200 schools*: **doscientas** escuelas *301 houses*: **trescientas** una casas *999 teachers*: **novecientos noventa y nueve** profesores
1000 **Mil**	**Mil** does not change in gender. In some Latin American countries, the indefinite article **un** can be used before **mil** in financial and legal documents when the number is exactly a thousand. *1000 dollars / girls*: (**un**) **mil** dólares / (**un**) **mil** niñas *2000 dollars / girls*: **dos mil** dólares / **dos mil** niñas
1 000 000 **Millón /** **Millones** **Millón de** **Millones de**	**Millón** is used in the singular when referring to a single million (**un millón, este millón**). When referring to two millions or more, always use **millones** (**dos millones** de personas; *two million people*). *1 021 101 pesos*: **un millón veintiún mil ciento un** pesos *2 100 341 rupees*: **dos millones cien mil trescientas cuarenta y una** rupias Round numbers in *whole millions* are followed by **de.** *1 000 000 pesos*: **un millón de** pesos *131 000 000 dollars*: **ciento treinta y un millones de** dólares But: *131 001 000 dollars*: **ciento treinta y un millones mil** dólares
Cientos de **Miles de** **Millones de**	**Cientos de** and **miles de** are not used for counting. The expressions are used similarly in English and Spanish. **Millones de** can also indicate an unspecified high number of countable nouns. Hay **cientos de / miles de /** *There are hundreds/thousands/* **millones de** personas en las calles. *millions of people on the streets.*

6.B.2 The word *número*

The word **número** is masculine and its article agrees in gender, no matter if the word **número** is explicit or not.

El (**número**) trece me gusta.   *I like the number thirteen.*
El **primer** trece de la lista tiene que ir en color rojo.   *The first (number) thirteen on the list must be in red.*

6.B.3 Plurals

a. Numbers' plural forms follow the same rules as other nouns.

¿Tienes billetes de **cinco** pesos?   *Do you have five-peso bills?*
No, solamente tengo **dieces** y **veintes.**   *No, I only have tens and twenties.*

b. As in English, the number **cero** is used with plural nouns, even with fractions.

Hace cero grados Celsius de temperatura.   *The temprature is zero degrees Celsius.*
El bebé creció solo 0,5 centímetros el último mes.   *Last month the baby grew only 0.5 centimeters.*

Expresiones numéricas colectivas y expresiones para contar

6.C.1 Decena, veintena

Collective numbers are followed by **de** before the noun.

Década and other words for periods of time: 6.J.2

decena(s)	ten(s)	cincuentena	about fifty
docena(s)	dozen(s)	sesentena	about sixty
veintena	about twenty	setentena	about seventy
treintena	about thirty	centenar(es)	a hundred/hundreds
cuarentena	about forty	millar(es)	a thousand/thousands

En la biblioteca hay **millares** de libros.   *There are thousands of books in the library.*

La **docena** de huevos cuesta dos dólares.   *A dozen eggs cost two dollars.*

6.C.2 Numbers and counting expressions

a. Percentages can be preceded by the definite article **el** or the indefinite article **un**.

Los precios suben (el/un) **2%** mañana.   *The prices go up 2% tomorrow.*

Mi casa vale hoy un **diez por ciento** más que cuando la compré.   *My house is worth about 10% more today than when I bought it.*

Writing styles for numbers: 6.A.1

b. In most Spanish-speaking countries, the period is still used after thousands (although it can be left out in newer writing styles) and the comma with decimals.

1.000   mil   **0,5   cero coma cinco**

c. The use of the comma for the thousands is still common in some countries, like México and Perú. The period is used for the decimals.

1,000   mil   **0.5   cero punto cinco**

d. The preposition **con** is used to indicate decimals in prices.

$ 45,60   cuarenta y cinco pesos **con** sesenta centavos   *forty-five pesos and sixty cents*

e. Although done in English, numbers over a thousand can not be read as hundreds in Spanish.

€ 1250   mil doscientos cincuenta euros   *twelve hundred and fifty euros*

f. The verb **ser** (**es/son**) and the following expressions are used to describe calculations in Spanish. The singular form (**es**) is used if the calculation is equal to the numbers 0 or 1 only. The symbols **:** and **/** are also used for division. The symbols **·** or **∗** are also used for multiplication.

	Mathematical operations		Examples
+	La suma	$1 + 2 = 3$	Uno **más/y** dos **es igual a / son** tres.
−	La resta	$2 - 2 = 0$	Dos **menos** dos **es igual a / es** cero.
×	La multiplicación	$3 \times 4 = 12$	Tres **por** cuatro **es igual a / son** doce.
÷	La división	$4 \div 2 = 2$	Cuatro **dividido (por/entre)** dos **es igual a / son** dos.
=	El resultado: *igual a*	$10 - 7 = 3$	Diez menos siete **es igual a / son** tres.

6.D Ordinal numbers

Números ordinales

6.D.1 Ordinal numbers 1—99

a. The ordinal numbers between **1** and **10** are the most used in Spanish. In everyday speech it is also common to use **décimo primero/a** and **décimo segundo/a** instead of **undécimo/a** and **duodécimo/a**, which are not used in many countries. An ordinal number for the number zero does not exist. In most Spanish-speaking countries, the **planta baja** (*ground floor*) is not considered the first floor, whereas in English it is. Therefore, in Spanish the **primer piso** (*first floor*) is usually equivalent to the *second floor* in English, and so on.

Ordinal numbers 1—99			
primer(o/a)	first	**séptimo/a**	seventh
segundo/a	second	**octavo/a**	eighth
tercer(o/a)	third	**noveno/a**	ninth
cuarto/a	fourth	**décimo/a**	tenth
quinto/a	fifth	**undécimo/a**	eleventh
sexto/a	sixth	**duodécimo/a**	twelfth

b. In formal situations, the following ordinal numbers are also used. However, in everyday language there is an increasing trend to avoid the usage of complex ordinal numbers, replacing them with the corresponding cardinal number.

vigésimo/a	twentieth	**sexagésimo/a**	sixtieth
trigésimo/a	thirtieth	**septuagésimo/a**	seventieth
cuadragésimo/a	fortieth	**octogésimo/a**	eightieth
quincuagésimo/a	fiftieth	**nonagésimo/a**	nintieth

Perdí la carrera en la **vigésima** vuelta.	*I lost the race on the twentieth lap.*
Hoy celebramos el **septuagésimo** aniversario de la escuela.	*Today, we're celebrating the school's seventieth anniversary.*

6.D.2 Centésimo, milésimo, millonésimo

The round numbers **centésimo/a(s)** (*hundredth[s]*), **milésimo/a(s)** (*thousandth[s]*), **millonésimo/a(s)** (*millionth[s]*), are mostly used for fractions or used figuratively to mean a large number.

◀ Writing styles for numbers: 6.A.1

Esta es la **milésima** llamada.	*This is the thousandth call.*
1/1000 es un(a) **milésimo/a.**	*1/1000 is a thousandth.*

6.D.3 Milenario, centenario, millonario

Milenario/a and **centenario/a** are terms for age, while **millonario/a** describes wealth, just like in English.

Machu Picchu es una ciudad **milenaria.**	*Machu Picchu is a thousand-year-old city.*
Roberta Martínez es **millonaria.**	*Roberta Martínez is a millionaire.*
Para el **bicentenario** de la Independencia hubo muchos actos oficiales.	*There were many official ceremonies for the bicentennial anniversary of our Independence.*

6.D.4 Agreement

Ordinal numbers are adjectives and agree in gender and number with the noun they modify. In the singular, **primero** and **tercero** are shortened before a masculine noun.

el décimo **tercer** aniversario	*the thirteenth anniversary*
el **tercer** puesto	*the third position*

6.D.5 Abbreviations

In written language, a superscript **a** or **o** is written to the right of the number to indicate the noun's gender and number. The superscript letter is separated from the number with a period. The superscript **-er** is used to abbreviate **primer** and **tercer.**

Viajo en **1.ª** clase.	*I travel in first class.*
Marta vive en el **10.º** piso.	*Marta lives on the tenth floor.*
Está en **3.ᵉʳ** grado.	*She is in third grade.*

6.D.6 Proper names

Royal names and other names in numerical order between **1–10** are written with Roman numerals and are read as ordinal numbers. Starting from the Roman numeral **XI,** the numerals are read as cardinal numbers.

Isabel II	Isabel **segunda**	*Elizabeth II*
Papa Juan Pablo II	Papa Juan Pablo **segundo**	*Pope John Paul II*
Luis XV	Luis **quince**	*Louis XV*
Papa Juan XXIII	Papa Juan **veintitrés**	*Pope John XXIII*

6.D.7 Ordinals used as nouns

With the definite article, ordinals may function as a noun.

Soy la **primera** de la fila y tú, el **tercero.**	*I am the first one in this line; you are the third.*

6.E Fractions and multiples

Números fraccionarios y multiplicativos

6.E.1 Numerators and denominators

a. The *numerator* (**numerador**) in Spanish is read as a cardinal number. *Denominators* (**denominadores**) are read as ordinal numbers, except in the case of 1/2, which is read **un medio**, or **la mitad**, and the masculine form for 1/3 or 2/3, for which the word **tercio(s)** is used. The ordinal number agrees in gender and number with the noun.

1/2	un medio, la mitad	**1/10**	un(a) décimo/a, una décima parte
2/3	dos tercios, dos terceras partes	**1/7**	un sé(p)timo, una sé(p)tima parte
1/4	un cuarto, una cuarta parte	**4/8**	cuatro octavos, cuatro octavas partes
3/5	tres quintos, tres quintas partes	**2/9**	dos novenos, dos novenas partes

b. Starting from 11, **-avo/a** is added to the cardinal numbers in denominators with the exception of **centésimo/a(s)**, **milésimo/a(s)**, **millonésimo/a(s)**.

Tenemos una **doceava** parte de la compañía.	*We own a twelfth of the company.*
Erré la estimación por sólo cinco **centésimas**.	*I misestimated by only five hundredths.*

c. Fractions are followed by **de** before a noun.

El corredor ganó por una **milésima de** segundo.   *The runner won by a thousandth of a second.*
Mil dólares es la **mitad del** precio.   *A thousand dollars is half the price.*

◀ **Medio** is used without **de** before **kilo, litro**, etc. **De** can sometimes be omitted before **cuarto**.
Medio litro de leche.
Un **cuarto (de) kilo** de harina.

6.E.2 Multiples

a. The following words express multiple amounts and can function as nouns or adjectives.

Most used	
doble	*double*
triple	*triple*

Less used	
cuádruple	*cuadruple*
quíntuple	*quintuple*
séxtuple	*sextuple*

En el dormitorio hay una cama **doble.**   *There is a double bed in the bedroom.*
Por favor, dame un café expreso **triple.**   *Please, give me a triple espresso.*
Veinticinco es el **quíntuple** de cinco.   *Twenty-five is five times five.*

b. To express exponential quantities, use *number* + **veces más/menos** (*times more/less*).

Mi auto costó **cinco veces más** que el tuyo.   *My car cost five times more than yours.*

◀ Comparisons with **más/menos**: 11.B

6.F Time

La hora

6.F.1 *Es/son*

a. The time is given with the verb **ser** in the singular (**es**) for one o'clock, and in the plural (**son**) for the rest.

◀ Use of **ser** with the time: 29.C.2

Es la una **en punto.**   *It's one o'clock.*
Son las ocho de la noche.   *It's eight at night.*
Son las cuatro de la mañana.   *It's four in the morning.*

b. It is the norm to ask about the time with the verb **ser** in the singular, but in some parts of Latin America the plural form is also used.

¿Qué hora es? / ¿Qué horas son?   *What time is it?*

6.F.2 Time after the hour

The time that has passed after the hour is expressed with the *hour* plus **y** and the *number of minutes*. **Cuarto** or **quince** can be used for *quarter past* and **media** or **treinta** for *half past*.

Son las ocho **y** diez.   *It's ten past eight.*
Es la una **y cuarto/quince**.   *It's quarter-past one.*
Son las seis **y media/treinta**.   *It's half-past six.*

6.F.3 Time before the hour

The minutes remaining until the next hour are expressed with **menos**, primarily in Spain. In Latin America, the expression **falta(n)** (*it's lacking*) is also used plus the number of minutes which remain until the next hour.

Son las dos **menos** diez.
Faltan diez **para** las dos.   *It's ten to two.*
Es la una **menos** cuarto.
Falta un cuarto **para** la una.   *It's a quarter to one.*

6.F.4 Time (appointments)

The verb **ser** followed by **a** + **la(s)** + *clock time* expresses a time/appointment.

—¿**Es a las** dos de la tarde la cita? *Is the appointment at 2 p.m.?*
—No, es **a la** una de la tarde. *No, it's at 1 p.m.*

ser and **estar** with the calendar ▶ and time: 29.C.2

6.F.5 The 24-hour clock

In Latin America, the 12-hour clock is more commonly used in everyday speech. In Spain, the 24-hour clock sometimes called military time, is also used.

La conferencia es a las **19:30** (diecinueve [y] treinta) **horas.** *The conference is at seven-thirty p.m.*

La boda es a las **15** (quince) **horas.** *The wedding is at three p.m.*

6.F.6 Time expressions: *de la mañana / tarde / noche*

With the 12-hour clock, add whether it is the morning, afternoon, or evening.

Es la una **de la mañana.** *It's one in the morning.*
Son las cinco **de la tarde.** *It's five in the afternoon.*
Son las nueve **de la noche.** *It's nine at night.*

6.G Dates

La fecha

6.G.1 Structure

a. The date is expressed with the verb **ser.** For day, month, and year, cardinal numbers are used with the following structures.

15 de mayo de 2010   Hoy **es** (el) quince de mayo de dos mil diez.   15/05/2010

b. In Spain, the first of the month is expressed with **uno,** but in Latin America, **primero** is used.

Hoy es (el) **uno** de enero.
Hoy es (el) **primero** de enero.   *Today is January first.*

6.G.2 Letters

In letters and other documents, place and date are separated by a comma, like in English. Months can also come before the day's date.

Nueva York, 2 de mayo de 2020   Nueva York, dos de mayo de dos mil veinte
Nueva York, abril 19 de 2010   Nueva York, abril diecinueve de dos mil diez

6.G.3 Years

In Spanish, years are not read as hundreds as they are in English. The year is always read as a cardinal number.

4 de julio de 1776:
Cuatro de julio de mil setecientos setenta y seis   *July fourth, seventeen seventy-six*

6.G.4 The calendar

In Spain, the calendar goes from Monday to Sunday, but in many Latin American countries the calendar starts with Sunday like in the U.S.

6.G.5 Expressions of time for dates

Todo/a(s), **próximo/a(s)**, **dentro de**, and **en** are commonly used in expressions of time.

◀ **todo:** Determiners 7.C.9

todos los días / meses, **todas las** semanas	*every day/month/week*
todos los años	*every year*
dentro de / en **ocho** días dentro de / en **una** semana	*in a week*
dentro de / en **unos** días	*in a few days*
dentro de / en **quince** días dentro de / en **dos** semanas	*in two weeks*
la semana **próxima**; el mes/año **próximo** la **próxima** semana, el **próximo** mes/año	*next week/month/year*
Mi cumpleaños es dentro de **ocho** días.	*My birthday's in a week.*
La escuela empieza dentro de / en **quince** días.	*School begins in two weeks.*

6.H Age

La edad

6.H.1 Structure

In Spanish, age is expressed with the verb **tener**.

◀ **tener** with age: 29.D

Juliana **tiene** tres años.	*Juliana is three years old.*

6.H.2 Birthdays

The verb **cumplir** describes how many years a person is turning or how old a person is.

Juliana **cumple** tres años hoy.	*Juliana is turning three today.* *Juliana is three today.*

6.H.3 Talking about age

In English, it is common to include age when talking about people, for example, in the news (*A sixty-year-old won the lottery.*) In Spanish, it is not so common to use age when talking about people, except when it is of significance to the context. Note the following age expressions.

Expressions of age	Use
quinceañero/a	Terms used to refer to fifteen-year olds. **La fiesta de quinceañera** or **fiesta de quince años** is a celebration for girls who turn fifteen in Latin America to mark their passage into adulthood.
veinteañero/a	A less common term for people around twenty years of age, primarily used to emphasize that they are still young.
cuarentón/cuarentona cincuentón/cincuentona sesentón/sesentona	Derogatory terms used to refer to men or women over forty, fifty, sixty years of age: *forty-year-old, fifty-year-old, sixty-year-old.*
octogenario/a, nonagenario/a, centenario/a	Neutral terms referring to old age for both sexes: *eighty-year-old, ninety-year-old, hundred-year-old.*

◀ Augmentative suffixes: 2.C.10b

6.I Temperature

Temperatura

6.I.1 Structure

a. Temperature can be expressed using the following structures.

Hacer and **estar** with weather expressions 29.C.1

¿**Qué** temperatura **hace**?	*What's the temperature?*
Hace tres grados **bajo cero**.	*It's three degrees below zero.*
¿**Cuántos** grados **hace**?	*How many degrees is it?*
Hace veinte **grados**.	*It's twenty degrees.*
¿**A qué** temperatura **estamos**?	*What's the temperature (now)?*
Estamos a cero **grados**.	*It's freezing (It's zero degrees).*

b. Temperature is measured in degrees Celsius (**grados Celsios/centígrados**) in Spain and Latin America, except in Puerto Rico, which uses both the system used in the U.S., Fahrenheit (**grados Fahrenheit**), and Celsius.

In Spanish, there should be a space between the number and the degree symbol, and no space between the degree symbol and *C* or *F*.

15 °C es aproximadamente 60 °F.   *15 °C is about 60 °F.*

6.I.2 Words and expressions

temperatura **máxima/mínima**	*highest/lowest temperature*
temperatura **media/promedio**	*average temperature*
temperatura **normal**	*normal temperature*

6.J Idiomatic expressions

6.J.1 The expressions *y pico, y tantos*

In order to express *a bit* in relation to quantities (prices, amounts), the expression *number* + **y pico / y tantos** can be used: **treinta y uno y pico**, (*thirty-one and a bit*). In Chile, the latter expression is preferred because the former is considered taboo.

6.J.2 *Década* and other words for periods of time

Collective numbers and counting expressions: 6.C

The periods of time **quinquenio** (*5 years*), **decenio** (*10 years*), and **centenio** (*100 years*) only refer to the numbers of years. **Década** (*decade*), **siglo** (*century*), and **milenio** (*millennium*), on the other hand, are specific periods of years. **Edad** and **era/época** are used to refer to long or remote periods of time: **Edad de Hierro** (*Iron Age*), **Era Moderna** (*Modern Times*). The majority of these terms are formal and are used primarily in written language.

Alejandro y Sara vivieron en la **década de los treinta**, en el **siglo XX**.	*Alejandro and Sara lived in the thirties, in the 20th century.*
El **nuevo milenio** trae muchas incógnitas.	*The new millennium brings many unknowns.*
El presupuesto es solamente para un **quinquenio**. Es **quinquenal**.	*The budget is only for a five-year period. It is every five years.*

Práctica

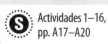

S Actividades 1–16, pp. A17–A20

Indefinite quantifiers and pronouns
Cuantificadores y pronombres indefinidos

Chapter 7

Determiners (4)
A. Determiners and pronouns
B. Positive and negative indefinite quantifiers
C. Indefinite quantifiers with only positive forms
D. Indefinite pronouns
E. Common features of indefinite quantifiers and pronouns
F. Regional variations

7.A Determiners and pronouns

Determinantes y pronombres

Within the grammatical category known as determiners, words like **alguno/a(s)** (*some*) and **muchos/as** (*many*) are considered *indefinite quantifiers*. The indefinite articles **un/una** can also be considered indefinite quantifiers. Just like all other determiners, indefinite quantifiers support the noun and make it indefinite when they refer to identity, quantity, or size. In addition to indefinite quantifiers, this chapter also introduces *indefinite pronouns*; both express indefinite references and have negative forms with double negation. Some indefinite quantifiers can function as *determiners, pronouns,* and *adverbs*.

Había **mucha** gente. *(determiner)*	*There were a lot of people.*
Necesitaba uno pero compré **muchos**. *(pronoun)*	*I needed one but I bought a lot.*
Mi hermano trabaja **mucho**. *(adverb)*	*My brother works a lot.*

◀ Indefinite quantifiers as adverbs: 7.E.4

7.B Positive and negative indefinite quantifiers

Cuantificadores indefinidos con formas afirmativas y negativas

There are two groups of indefinite quantifiers. One group has both negative and positive forms, as shown below, and the other group has only positive forms (see **7.C**). The majority of quantifiers in these groups can agree in gender and number, but none of them have comparative or superlative forms.

◀ Comparisons: 3.E, Ch. 11

Positive		Negative	
algún, alguno/a	*some/any*	**ningún, ninguno/a**	*no/not any/none*
alguno/a(s)	*some [pl.]*	**ninguno/a(s)**	*no/not any [pl.]*

7.B.1 Double negation of *ninguno/a*

The negative forms **ningún** and **ninguno/a** require a double negation when they are placed after the verb; the same applies to the pronouns **nadie** and **nada**.

¡**No** tienes **ningún** perfil personal actualizado en tu sitio web!	*You don't have an updated personal profile on your website!*
No hay **nadie** en el restaurante.	*There is no one in the restaurant.*

◀ Double negation with **ningún** and **tampoco**: 7.E.1

7.B.2 *Algún, alguno/a(s); ningún, ninguno/a*

a. Algún and **ningún** function only as determiners and are only used before singular masculine nouns. Before singular feminine nouns with a stressed **a**, **algún** is commonly used (**algún arma**), but **alguna** is also possible (**alguna arma**). **Alguno(s)** can be both a pronoun and a determiner. As a determiner, the singular form only appears after the noun. **Alguna(s)** can also function as both a pronoun and a determiner. As a determiner, the singular form can be used before or after a noun. The plural forms **algunos/as** can only be used before a noun.

◀ Other short prenominal adjective forms: **buen, mal, primer, tercer**: 3.D

—¿Hay **algún** cine cerca?	*Are there any movie theaters nearby?*
—No, no hay **ningún** cine cerca.	*No, there are no movie theaters nearby.*
¿Tienes **alguna** propuesta?	*Do you have a suggestion?*
Si hay **algún** problema, avísame.	*If there is any problem, let me know.*
No hay problema **alguno**.	*There is no problem.*
Tengo **algunas** dudas.	*I have some doubts.*

ninguno/a in relative
which-clauses: 23.D.2e

b. Alguno/a(s) and **ninguno/a** (but *not* **ningunos/as**) can be used with the preposition **de** or a relative clause (*which*-clauses).

Leímos **algunas de las** nuevas novelas.	*We read some of the new novels.*
No hay **ninguna que** nos guste mucho, pero **algunas de ellas** son muy populares.	*There aren't any that we like in particular, but some of them are very popular.*

c. Alguno/a(s) is always placed after the noun in negative sentences. The following pairs of sentences have the same meaning.

No hay alternativa **alguna**. **No** hay **ninguna** alternativa.	*There isn't an/any alternative.*
No habrá viaje **alguno** este año. **No** habrá **ningún** viaje este año.	*There won't be any trip this year.*

d. The plural forms **ningunos/as** can be used before or after the noun in negative sentences, but the form **ninguno/a de** + *plural article* or *pronoun* is more common.

No he visitado **ninguna de las** plataformas de petróleo.	*I haven't visited any of the oil rigs.*

e. Ninguno/a de + *pronoun* is also used in Spanish to express *none of* in English. In such cases, **nadie** can not be used. However, this concept may be expressed with **nadie** when the **de** + *pronoun* is removed.

Ninguna de nosotras tiene vacaciones.	*None of us has vacation.*
Ninguno de ellos sabe español.	*None of them knows any Spanish.*
Nadie sabe español.	*No one knows Spanish.*

7.C Indefinite quantifiers with only positive forms

Cuantificadores indefinidos solo con formas afirmativas

Quantifying adverbs: 10.D

The group of indefinite quantifiers with only positive forms is large. Some refer to the noun's indefinite identity (**cualquiera**), indefinite quantity (**muchos**), or degree (**más, menos**), while some refer to a whole (**todo**) and others to a part of something (**cada**).

cualquiera que + subjunctive:
23.D.2d
Le venderé mi casa a **cualquiera**
que pague un buen precio.
I will sell my house to whoever
pays the best price.

ambos/as	*both*	**muchos/as**	*many/lots/a lot of*
bastante	*quite/quite a lot/enough*	**otro/a**	*another/another one*
bastantes	*quite/quite a lot/enough [pl.]*	**otros/as**	*other [pl.]*
cada	*each/every*	**poco/a**	*little/bit*
cualquier, cualquiera (de)	*whichever/whoever/any (of)*	**pocos/as**	*few*
cualesquiera (de)	*which/whoever (of)/any*	**tanto/a**	*so much*
demás	*rest/remainder*	**tantos/as**	*so many*
demasiado/a	*too much*	**todo/a**	*all/every/whole/everything*
demasiados/as	*too many [pl.]*	**todos/as**	*all [pl.]*
más	*more*	**un, una**	*a*
menos	*fewer, less*	**unos/as**	*some*
mucho/a	*a lot of/much*	**varios/as**	*various/several*

7.C.1 **Form and agreement**

Indefinite quantifiers that agree in gender and/or number with the noun cannot be compared the way adjectives can. However, the determiners **mucho, poco,** and **tanto** can take the superlative ending **-ísimo/a: muchísimo/a, poquísimo/a, tantísimo/a.**

Ambos novios se han casado **varias** veces.	*Both partners have married several times.*
Ella tiene **muchísimos** hijos y él tiene solo **una** hija.	*She has a lot of children and he has only one daughter.*
Todos son muy felices con **tantísima** gente en casa.	*Everyone is very happy with so many people at home.*
Cada familia es diferente.	*Every family is different.*

◀ mucho - muchísimo:
4.B.3b
Comparison of adjectives: 3.E
Comparison of adverbs: 10.I
Comparisons: Ch. 11

7.C.2 **Positive quantifiers with double placement**

Quantifiers with only positive forms are generally placed before the noun, but the following quantifiers can also be placed after the noun. Note that when following the noun, **cualquiera, más,** and **menos** must be determined with **un/a(os)** or **otro/a(s)** (or a cardinal number).

◀ Combination of two determiners: 4.B.6

◀ **Bastante(s)**: 7.C.7

◀ **Varios**: 7.C.6

bastante(s)	**bastante** dinero	*quite a lot of money*
	dinero **bastante**	*enough money*
vario/a(s)	**varias** galletas	*several cookies*
	galletas **varias**	*an assortment of cookies*
cualquier(a)/ cualesquiera	**cualquier** día	*whichever/any day*
	cualesquiera días	
	un día **cualquiera**	
	unos días **cualesquiera**	
más, menos	**más/menos** pan	*more/less bread*
	un pan **más/menos**	*one more loaf/one loaf less*
	otro pan **más/menos**	*another loaf/another loaf less*
	otros panes **más/menos**	*some more loaves/a few loaves less*

7.C.3 **Indefinite quantifiers as pronouns**

a. With a few exceptions, all quantifiers can function as a pronoun when the noun to which they refer is not explicitly stated.

◀ Determiners as pronouns: 4.B.2

En Argentina **todo** me gusta. Hay **bastante** que ver y **mucho** que hacer.	*I like everything in Argentina. There's quite a lot to see and do.*

b. The shortened forms **un, algún, ningún** and **cualquier** cannot function as pronouns, while the corresponding longer forms in both singular and plural can: **uno/a(s), alguno/a(s), ninguno/a(s), cualquiera, cualesquiera**.

—¿Hay estudiantes franceses aquí?	*Are there French students here?*
—No, este año no hay **ninguno,** pero a veces vienen **algunos**.	*No, there aren't any this year, but sometimes there are some.*

c. In order to function as pronouns, **demás** must be accompanied by an article (**los, las, lo**) and **cada** must always be used with **uno/a** or a noun.

Dos estudiantes de la clase tienen A en todo. **Los demás,** tienen B.	*Two students in the class have an A in everything. The others have a B.*
Cada uno hizo un gran esfuerzo.	*Every one of them tried very hard.*

d. The examples below show **varios/as, otro/a(s),** and **poco/a(s)** used as pronouns.

Varios recibieron un premio, **otros** recibieron dos premios y muy **pocos,** muchos premios.

Some of them received one prize, others received two prizes and very few, a lot of prizes.

7.C.4 *Un, uno/a, unos, unas*

Use of indefinite articles: 5.B
Indefinite pronouns: 7.D

a. Only the forms **un, una,** and **unos/as** can be placed before the noun, while **uno** can be only used as an indefinite determiner in the form **uno de los** (*one of the*) before the noun. In any other context, **uno** is used as a pronoun.

b. Un(a) can usually be omitted in negative sentences (*not any*).

No hay policía en la calle.
There are no policemen on the street.

Ella no tiene familia.
She doesn't have any family.

No tenemos pan en casa.
We don't have any bread in the house.

c. Un poco de (*A little*) is used before the noun.

Hace **un poco de** calor aquí.
It's a little warm here.

d. Unos/as means *about, approximately* when used before numbers.

El boleto de autobús cuesta **unos** cincuenta dólares.
The bus ticket costs about fifty dollars.

7.C.5 *Cualquier, cualquiera, cualesquiera*

a. Before all singular (masculine and feminine) nouns, the shortened form **cualquier** is always used. After both masculine and feminine nouns, only **cualquiera** can be used. When used after the noun, **cualquiera** can also mean *ordinary*.

Cualquier persona puede ser admitida en la universidad.
Any person can be admitted to the university.

Él no es una persona **cualquiera**.
He is not an ordinary person.

Le pediré un favor a **cualquiera de** mis amigos.
I will ask any of my friends a favor.

Cualquiera in relative clauses:
15.B.7, 23.D.2d

Cualquiera que llegue tarde no podrá entrar.
Whoever arrives late will not be allowed in.

b. The plural form, **cualesquiera,** is not commonly used.

Cualesquiera (que) sean tus motivos, no estoy de acuerdo con tu decisión.
Whatever your reasons, I don't agree with your decision.

Traeme dos libros **cualesquiera**.
Bring me any two books.

7.C.6 *Ambos/as, varios/as*

Different meanings of **varios**:
7.C.2

Ambos/as (*Both*) is always plural and can never be followed by **dos**. However, it can be replaced by **los/las dos**. **Ambos/as** can function alone as a pronoun when the noun is not stated. **Varios** expresses a quantity greater than two.

Ambas chicas hablan español.
Both girls speak Spanish.

Las dos chicas estudian mucho.
The two girls study a lot.

Varias personas son suecas.
Several people are Swedish.

Llegaron dos invitados y **ambos** son alemanes.
Two guests arrived and both are German.

7.C.7 *Bastante(s)*

This quantifier must agree in number with the noun, and usually precedes it.

Placement of **bastante** after
the noun: 7.C.2

Hay **bastante** gente en el concierto.
There are quite a lot of people at the concert.

En este libro hay **bastantes** ejemplos de gramática.
In this book there are quite a lot of grammar examples.

7.C.8 *Cada, cada uno/a*

a. Cada does not change form and only indicates a part of a whole. It cannot stand alone without a noun. It is used as a pronoun in the form **cada uno/una (de)**. **Todo** + *singular noun* means *every (single) one* and is a synonym for **cada uno de los/las** + *noun*.

Determiners as pronouns: 4.B.2b
Todo: 7.C.9

Cada estudiante debe hacer el trabajo individualmente.	*Every student should do the work individually.*
Revisaremos el contenido de **cada uno de** los contratos.	*We will go through the contents of every one of the contracts.*
Todo contrato/**Cada uno de** los contratos debe estar firmado.	*Every single contract should be signed.*

b. Cada, cada uno de los/las + *noun* brings attention to each member of a group.

Cada animal es único.	*Each animal is unique.*
Cada uno de los animales es único.	*Each of the animals is unique.*

c. In Spanish, periods of time are expressed with **todo: todos los días, todas las semanas. Cada** is used to convey periodical repetition rather than a whole period of time.

Pienso en ti **cada** segundo del día, **todos** los días.	*I think about you every second of the day, every day.*
Hay que tomar la medicina **cada** dos horas.	*The medicine must be taken every two hours.*
Cada vez suben más los precios.	*The prices keep increasing (each time).*

7.C.9 *Todo*

a. When **todo** indicates something abstract (*everything*), it is an indefinite pronoun.

Todo es muy sencillo.	*It's all very simple.*
¿Lo terminaste **todo**?	*Did you finish everything?*

b. When it refers to an implied noun and appears alone, **todo** is a pronoun and agrees in gender and number with the noun.

—¿Enviaste los paquetes?	*Did you send all the packages?*
—Sí, los envié **todos**.	*Yes, I sent them all.*
Dice que no le gusta la polenta, pero siempre se la come **toda**.	*He says he doesn't like polenta, but he always eats it all.*

c. Todo/a + *singular noun* is a synonym for **todos/as los/las** + *plural noun*.

Todo animal es único.	*Every animal is unique.*
Todos los animales son únicos.	*All animals are unique.*

d. Todo lo, todo el, and **toda la** refer to an entire object or something as a whole.

Eso es **todo lo** que sé.	*That's all/everything I know.*
¡**Todo el** año pasó volando!	*The whole year flew by!*
Te querré **toda la** vida.	*I will love you my whole life.*

e. Todo/a un(a) intensifies the noun.

todo/a un(a): 4.B.6c

Es buenísimo tener **todo un** día libre.	*It's awesome to have a whole day free.*
¡Los glaciares de Alaska son **toda una** maravilla!	*The glaciers in Alaska are all so amazing!*

Determiners as pronouns:
4.B.2b, 4.B.6d

7.C.10 *Demás*

Demás does not change form and usually needs a plural, definite article when it is placed before a noun. It is often used as a noun with the neuter article **lo** to mean *the rest, the remainder* and with **todo** as an intensifier: **todo lo demás** (*everything else*). On rare occasions, **demás** can be used without an article.

Usted debe firmar **los demás** documentos.	*You must sign the rest of the documents.*
Dime **todo lo demás**.	*Tell me about all the rest/everything else.*
Saludos para tu familia y **todos los demás** parientes.	*Greetings to your family and all your other relatives.*
Los jefes y **demás** colegas vendrán a la fiesta de Navidad.	*The bosses and other colleagues will come to the Christmas party.*

7.C.11 *Demasiado/a(s)*

With uncountable nouns (*water, pollution*) **demasiado** means *too much*. With countable nouns, it means *too many*. It can be combined with **poco,** to mean *too little*, but not with **mucho/a(s)**.

Hay **demasiada** contaminación.	*There is too much pollution.*
Tenéis **demasiadas** cosas que hacer.	*You [pl.] have too many things to do.*
Se come mucha carne y **demasiado poco** pescado.	*They eat a lot of meat and not enough fish.*

7.C.12 *Más, menos, mucho/a(s), poco/a(s)*

These quantifiers are very flexible. Their most important function is in comparisons, but they also form many common expressions. Note the use of **un poco más/menos de, varios**.

Expressions with *más, menos, mucho, poco*	
muchas más horas	*many more hours*
muchos menos amigos	*far fewer friends*
un poco más de café	*a little more coffee*
algunos pocos ejemplos **más**	*a few more examples*
bastante más dinero	*quite a lot more money*
bastantes menos cosas	*far fewer/very few things*
otras cosas **más**	*several other things*
varias cosas **menos**	*fewer things*

Invitaron a **mucha más** gente de lo que habían dicho.	*They invited a lot more people than they'd said they would.*
Tendrías que poner **un poco menos de** chocolate y **un poco más de** azucar.	*You should use a little less chocolate and a little more sugar.*
No pienso esperar **muchas** horas **más**.	*I won't wait many more hours.*
Te presto **un** libro **más** y basta.	*I'll lend you one more book and that's it.*

7.C.13 *Otro/a(s)*

a. Unlike English, **otro/a** can never be combined with **un(a)**, but it can be placed after the definite article: **el/la otro/a, los/as otros/as** (*the other, the others*). **Otro** is used in many Spanish expressions.

¡**Otra** pizza, por favor!	*Another pizza, please!*
Te vi **el otro** día.	*I saw you the other day.*
Este café no es bueno; compra **otra** marca.	*This coffee is not good; buy another brand.*
Viajaré el lunes y regresaré **al otro** día.	*I will travel on Monday and return the following day.*

b. Otro/a(s) can be combined with many quantifiers.

Otro/a(s) **with other quantifiers**	
ningún otro estudiante	*no other student*
alguna otra casa	*another house/some other house*
muchos otros países	*many other countries*
cualquier otro día	*any other day*
otro poco de leche	*a little more milk*
otros pocos casos	*a few other cases*
pocas otras personas	*few other people*
varios otros sitios	*several other places*
bastantes otras cosas	*many other things*
todos los otros muebles	*all the other furniture*
todo lo otro	*all the rest*
otra vez **más/menos**	*once more/less*
otras cosas **más/menos**	*some more/fewer things*
otros tres ejemplos	*three other examples*

7.D   Indefinite pronouns

Pronombres indefinidos

7.D.1   Form and placement

Indefinite pronouns can function just like common personal pronouns in a sentence. They do not agree in gender (except **una** for females) and can *never* directly support nouns like the determiners (**algún auto**). **Cada uno/a** (*each one, every*) is included as a compound indefinite pronoun.

◀ **un, uno, una** as indefinite determiners: 7.C.4

Indefinite pronouns			
Positive		**Negative**	
uno (una)	one/someone	**nadie**	no one/nobody
alguien	someone		
algo	something	**nada**	nothing

7.D.2   Features of indefinite pronouns

a. Indefinite pronouns are used with singular verbs. They do not have a plural form. If it is necessary to refer to an indefinite plural group of people, an indefinite quantifier must be used.

◀ Indefinite quantifiers with only positive forms: 7.C

¿Hay **alguien** en casa?	*Is anyone home?*
Tengo que decirte **algo**.	*I have to tell you something.*
Uno no puede saberlo todo.	*One can't know everything.*
Como abogada, **una** trabaja muchas horas diarias.	*As a lawyer, one has to work many hours a day.*

b. The negative forms need double negation when placed after the verb.

◀ Double negation of **ninguno/a**: 7.B.1

No hay **nada**.	*There is nothing/isn't anything.*
No vemos a **nadie** allí.	*We can't see anyone there.*

c. The preposition **a** must be used before indefinite pronouns that refer to a person when they function as objects: **a uno/a, a alguien, a nadie**.

◀ Use of the preposition **a** with direct objects: 12.B.2c, 13.E.2

Ellos no conocen **a nadie**.	*They know no one./They don't know anyone.*
Si **a uno** le gusta el sol, debe ir a Miami.	*Someone who likes the sun ought to go to Miami.*

uno in impersonal se sentences:
28.E.2b

7.D.3 Uno/a

a. Uno/a is used in impersonal expressions that also imply personal experience. Men use **uno** and women use **una**. However, it is also usual for women to use **uno**.

En la playa puede **uno** acostarse y descansar.	On the beach one can lay down and rest.
Uno se siente satisfecho con un trabajo bien hecho.	One feels satisfied after a job well done.
Aquí se siente **uno** muy bien.	One feels very good here.
Como le dije a mi mamá, **una** a veces tiene que quejarse.	As I told my mom, you have to complain sometimes.

b. When the noun is not stated, the determiners **unos** and **unas** also function as pronouns.

¿Tienes **unas** tijeras? Sí, tengo **unas** aquí.	Do you have a pair of scissors? Yes, I've got a pair here.

7.D.4 Nadie más

The expression **nadie más** means *nobody else.*

Nadie más tiene buenas notas.	Nobody else has good grades.
No conocemos a **nadie más** que a ti en la ciudad.	We don't know anyone other than you in the city.

7.D.5 Nada

As a pronoun and an adverb, **nada** forms many idiomatic expressions.

Este aparato **no** sirve para **nada**.	This gadget isn't useful for anything.
Tú **no** sirves para **nada**.	You're completely useless.
Tus notas **no** son **nada** buenas.	Your grades aren't good at all.
Luisa **no** es **nada** simpática.	Luisa is not nice at all.
El príncipe se casó **nada menos que** con una plebeya.	The prince married a commoner, no less.
No queremos **nada más**.	We don't want anything else.
¡Por favor, **nada de** tonterías!	Please, none of that silliness!

7.E Common features of indefinite quantifiers and pronouns

Características comunes de determinantes y pronombres indefinidos

Positive and negative
indefinite quantifiers: 7.B
Indefinite quantifiers with
only positive forms: 7.C

7.E.1 Double negation

A special characteristic in the Spanish language is that the negative indefinite determiners **ningún**, **ninguno/a(s)** and the indefinite pronouns **nadie** and **nada** require *double negation* when they are placed after the verb. In this case, **no** or another negative expression must stand before the verb.

No tengo **nada**.	I don't have anything.
Hoy **no** viene **nadie**.	Nobody is coming today.
Tampoco hay **ninguna** explicación.	There isn't any explanation either.

7.E.2 Reference: person or thing?

The indefinite pronouns **alguien** and **nadie** are *only* used for people, while **algo** and **nada** can *only* be used for things. The indefinite determiners **algún, alguno/a, ningún, ninguno/a, cualquier(a), todo/a(s), un, uno/a** and all the other indefinite quantifiers in tables **7.B** and **7.C** can be used for both people and things.

Hoy **no** trabaja **nadie** porque **no** hay **nada** que hacer.

Nobody is working today because there is nothing to do.

Algunos trabajadores creen que **algo** raro sucede en la fábrica.

Some workers believe that something strange is happening in the factory.

Todos los empleados están seguros de que **alguien** sabe la verdad.

All the employees are sure that someone knows the truth.

7.E.3 The preposition *a* before an indefinite pronoun

The preposition **a** must be placed before all indefinite pronouns and indefinite quantifiers which function as direct or indirect objects and refer to people.

◄ Use of the preposition **a** with direct objects: 12.B.2c, 13.E.2

No conozco **a nadie** en la universidad todavía.

I don't know anyone at the university yet.

Le preguntaré **a algún** estudiante qué actividades hay hoy.

I will ask one of the students what activities there are today.

7.E.4 Indefinite quantifiers and *algo, nada* as adverbs

Algo and **nada** can function as quantifying adverbs. **Tan, tanto, más,** and **menos** are also used as adverbs in comparisons. The adverb **muy** can only be used before adjectives and adverbs, while **mucho** can only be used after the verb.

◄ Comparisons: Ch. 11

◄ Quantifying adverbs: 10.D

Quantifiers and gradable adverbs			
algo	*something*	**nada**	*nothing*
mucho, muy	*a lot/very*	**poco**	*little/few*
demasiado	*too much*	**bastante**	*quite*
tan	*as/very/so*	**tanto**	*so much*
más	*more*	**menos**	*less*

Trabajo **mucho** y **muy** bien.

I work a lot and very well.

¡Los canadienses esquían **tanto** y son **tan** buenos!

Canadians ski a lot and are very good!

A veces esquío **mucho,** otras veces **poco**.

Sometimes I ski a lot, other times not so much.

Me siento **bastante** bien esquiando, pero **algo** insegura porque mis esquíes no son **nada** modernos.

I feel quite good when I ski, but a bit insecure because my skis aren't very new.

Últimamente en Colorado nieva **menos**. Antes nevaba **mucho más**.

Recently, it has been snowing less in Colorado. It used to snow a lot more.

7.E.5 *Mismo, propio*

a. The intensifying forms **mismo/a, mismos/as** (*self/selves*) and **propio/a, propios/as** (*own*) are considered *semi-determiners* (**cuasideterminantes**). They are placed after a personal pronoun or proper noun. Both agree in gender and number but do not have comparative or superlative forms. **Propio/a** intensifies possessive determiners and proper nouns (with the definite article): **mi propio auto** (*my own car*); **el propio Juan,** which means the same as **Juan mismo** (*John himself*). **Propio /a** cannot be used with personal pronouns the same way as **mismo/a.**

◄ Adjectives: **mismo** (*same*), comparisons with **el mismo** (*the same*): 11.C.5
Mismo with reflexives: 27.A.2
Expressions with **propio**: 9.D.3e

¿Quieres tener casa **propia**?

Do you want your own house?

Tú mismo debes decidir sobre tu **propia** vida.

You, yourself, should decide about your own life.

b. In both English and Spanish, *self* must follow the pronoun. Note that *self* cannot always be translated as **mismo/a(s),** which can also be an adjective.

él mismo, ella misma, etcétera	*himself, herself, etc.*
el mismo, la misma, los mismos, las mismas	*the same*
mi propio, mi propia, mis propios, mis propias	*my own*

Por mi parte/Personalmente, me siento rico, pero no tengo ni un centavo.	*I **myself** feel rich, but I don't have a cent to my name.*
Mi blog lo escribo **yo misma/yo sola**.	*I write my blog **myself**.*
Hoy nos visitará el presidente **en persona**.	*Today the president **himself** will visit us.*
Dijo que todo había salido mal, pero **él mismo** se veía contento.	*He said that everything had gone wrong, but he **himself** seemed happy.*
¿Tienes todavía **la misma** dirección?	*Do you still have the same address?*

Use of pronoun in contrasts: 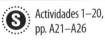 13.A.1b

c. Mismo/a can also intensify a direct or indirect object. **Mismo** can also be used to intensify adverbs such as **ya, ahora, allí**, etc.

Mismo/a with reflexive pronouns: 27.A.2

¿Os veis a vosotros **mismos** como buenos estudiantes?	*Do you see yourselves as good students?*
¿Te darás a ti **misma** un buen regalo?	*Will you give yourself a good present?*
Ven aquí ya **mismo**.	*Come here right now.*

7.E.6 *Sendos*

The determiner **sendos/as** (*each*) can only occur before a plural noun and is used in written, formal language.

Los ganadores recibieron **sendos** premios.	*The winners each received a prize.*
Ellos escribieron **sendas** entradas en sus blogs.	*They each wrote their own blog post.*

7.F Regional variations

Variaciones regionales

7.F.1 *Más*

As an intensifier, **más** is placed after the indefinite pronouns **nada** and **nadie: No hay nada/nadie más**. (*There isn't anything/anyone else.*) In Andalucia, the Caribbean, and in some parts of South America, **más** can occur before **nada** and **nadie** with the same meaning: **No queremos más nada.**

7.F.2 *Poca de, (de) a poco, por poco*

a. In central regions of Spain, **un poco de** can agree in gender: **una poca de sal**.

b. In everyday language, the Mexican expression **a poco** is common for communicating amazement or disbelief: **¿A poco crees que soy tonta?** (*You surely don't think I'm stupid, do you?*)

c. De a poco / de a poquito(s), (*little by little*) is a common adverbial expression in Latin America: **Dame la medicina de a poquitos**. (*Give me the medicine little by little.*)

d. Por poco is often used colloquially to mean *almost*.

Por poco me caigo.   *I almost fell.*

7.F.3 *Con todo y* + **clause or noun**

This expression, which means *despite*, is commonly used in some Latin American countries and in Northeast Spain.

Con todo y tus disculpas, no te perdono.   *Despite your excuses, I don't forgive you.*

Práctica

Actividades 1–20, pp. A21–A26

Demonstratives
Demostrativos

8.A | Demonstrative determiners and pronouns

Determinantes y pronombres demostrativos

8.A.1 | Structure

Demonstrative determiners and pronouns show where people and objects are in relation to the speaker. English has a two-level system: (*this/that, these/those*), which can sometimes be strengthened with *here* and *there*. Spanish has a three-level system which specifies whether the item is close to the person speaking, close to the person being spoken to, or far away from both.

	Determiners				Pronouns
	Masculine		**Feminine**		**Neuter**
Relative placement	**Singular**	**Plural**	**Singular**	**Plural**	**Singular**
close to the person speaking	est**e**	est**os**	est**a**	est**as**	**esto**
close to the person being spoken to	es**e**	es**os**	es**a**	es**as**	**eso**
far away from both people	aquel	aquell**os**	aquell**a**	aquell**as**	**aquello**

8.A.2 | *Este, ese, aquel*

a. Demonstrative determiners in the singular and plural are usually placed before the noun and agree with it in gender and number. These forms can stand after **todo/a(s),** and before cardinal numbers.

Aquella cas**a** es grande.	*That house (over there) is big.*
Estos tres libr**os** son míos.	*These three books are mine.*
No entiendo **todo eso.**	*I don't understand that.*

◀ Cardinal numbers: 6.A

◀ **Todo**: 7.C.9

b. Demonstratives placed after a noun can communicate a condescending or ironic attitude. **Aquel /aquella** has a more neutral attitude than the other forms.

¡No sé qué dice **el** profesor **ese**!	*I don't know what that teacher said!*
El niño **este** no para de hablar.	*That child won't stop talking.*
¡Qué tiempos **aquellos**!	*Those were good times!*

c. Demonstrative determiners with masculine and feminine forms can stand alone (without a noun). In this case, they act as pronouns and they have traditionally carried a written accent to differentiate them from the forms that precede nouns. For years, the written accent was considered a requirement only in cases of ambiguity, such as the one below.

¿Por qué comieron **aquellos** bocadillos?	*Why did they eat those sandwiches?*
¿Por qué comieron **aquéllos** bocadillos?	*Why did they (those people) eat sandwiches?*

The *Nueva ortografía* approved by the RAE in November 2010 still allows the use of the accent in cases of ambiguity. However, it is not a requirement, since the cases of ambiguity are rare and are very easily avoided.

8.A.3 Reference to time and items in a text

a. Demonstrative determiners can also refer to events in the past or near future, or to specific items or ideas in a text. **Este/a** and **estos/as** occur in many expressions to refer to the nearest moment in time within the present time period. **Esta mañana, esta tarde,** and **esta noche** are equivalent to **hoy por la mañana, hoy por la tarde,** and **hoy por la noche.**

esta mañana	*this morning*	esta semana	*this week*
esta tarde	*this afternoon*	este mes	*this month*
esta noche	*tonight*	este año	*this year*

En **estos** días voy a trabajar mucho.   *I'm going to work a lot these days.*
Nos veremos **esta** noche.   *We are meeting up tonight.*
Este año será difícil.   *This year will be difficult.*

b. Ese/a and **aquel/aquella** refer primarily to the past, but can also refer to the future.

En **esa/aquella** época, todo era mejor.   *At that time, everything was better.*
Las ventas empiezan a las ocho y, en **ese** momento, abrirán las puertas.   *The sales start at eight o'clock and, at that moment, the doors will open.*

8.A.4 Esto, eso, aquello

a. The neuter demonstratives **esto, eso,** and **aquello** can only function as neuter pronouns.

Esto que me dijiste me dejó preocupada.   *What you told me made me worried.*
Tengo mucho trabajo y **eso** no me gusta nada.   *I have so much work and I don't like that at all.*
¿**Aquello** te parece bien?   *Does that sound good to you?*

b. The neuter demonstratives are mostly used to refer to objects or concepts. When used to refer to people, they can be derogatory, unless the meaning of the demonstrative is actually explained. They are rarely used to refer to animals.

¡**Esto** es mi equipo de trabajo! (*derog.*)   *This (thing over here) is my work team!*
Mi equipo de trabajo era **eso**, un excelente grupo humano.   *My team was that, a wonderful group of people.*

Lo que: 15.B.7b ▶   **c. Aquello** can replace **lo** in relative clauses. In that case, it does not indicate proximity/distance.

¡Haz **aquello/lo** que te dije!   *Do what I told you!*

Todo: 7.C.9 ▶   **d.** Neuter demonstratives can be used with **todo**.

Todo esto es mentira.   *This is all a lie.*

8.A.5 Aquí, allí

Adverbs of place: 10.E.1 ▶   A few adverbs naturally go with demonstrative pronouns: **acá/aquí, allí/ahí/allá**.

A estas personas que están **aquí** no las conozco.   *These people here, I don't know them.*
Ese señor que está **allí** es Luis.   *That man there is Luis.*

8.B Regional variations

Variaciones regionales

Esto and **este** are often used as fillers in speech, as are expressions such as **pues, ah,** and **eh.**

Este... no sé qué decir...   *Well... I don't know what to say...*
Luisa, ... **esto**... ¿me prestas dinero?   *Luisa, ... um... can I borrow some money?*

Práctica

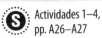 Actividades 1–4, pp. A26–A27

64   Demonstratives • Chapter 8

Possessives
Posesivos

A. Possessive determiners
B. Prenominal possessives
C. Postnominal possessives
D. Features
E. Regional variations

9.A Possessive determiners

Determinantes posesivos

Possessives are determiners that express possession or belonging. The short, unstressed forms (**átonos**) are placed before the noun (*prenominal*). The long, stressed forms (**tónicos**) must always be placed after the noun (*postnominal*), but they can also stand alone as pronouns. Possessives always agree with the noun or object that is owned, regardless of placement.

mi libro	*my book*	el libro **mío**	*my book*
tus amigos	*your friends*	los amigos **tuyos**	*your friends*
nuestra casa	*our house*	la casa **nuestra**	*our house*
vuestro país	*your [pl.] country*	el país **vuestro**	*your [pl.] country*

9.B Prenominal possessives

Determinantes posesivos prenominales

Short possessives are placed before the noun (the object owned) and only agree in number, except **nuestro** and **vuestro,** which agree in both gender and number. **Tú** and **vos** use **tu(s),** and all 3rd persons, including **usted(es),** use **su(s).**

◀ **cuyo:** 15.A.2, 15.B.1-2, 15.B.6

Prenominal possessives			
	Singular	**Plural**	
yo	mi	mis	*my*
tú	tu	tus	*your*
vos	tu	tus	*your*
usted	su	sus	*your*
él	su	sus	*his*
ella	su	sus	*her*
nosotros/as	nuestr**o/a**	nuestr**os/as**	*our*
vosotros/as	vuestr**o/a**	vuestr**os/as**	*your*
ustedes	su	sus	*your*
ellos/as	su	sus	*their*

mi libro	*my book*	**su** escuela	*your/its/his/her/their school*
mis hermanos	*my siblings*	**sus** escuelas	*your/its/his/her/their schools*
tu casa	*your house*	**nuestra** casa	*our house*
tus libros	*your books*	**nuestras** familias	*our families*
nuestro amigo	*our friend*	**nuestros** amigos	*our friends*
vuestros amigos	*your friends*	**vuestras** casas	*your houses*

9.C Postnominal possessives

Determinantes posesivos posnominales

9.C.1 Structure

Like adjectives, postnominal possessives agree in gender and number with the noun to which they refer.

Possessives • **Chapter 9**

65

Postnominal possessives			
	Singular	**Plural**	
yo	mí**o/a**	mí**os/as**	*mine*
tú	tuy**o/a**	tuy**os/as**	*yours*
vos	tuy**o/a**	tuy**os/as**	*yours*
usted	suy**o/a**	suy**os/as**	*yours*
él	suy**o/a**	suy**os/as**	*his*
ella	suy**o/a**	suy**os/as**	*hers*
nosotros/as	nuestr**o/a**	nuestr**os/as**	*ours*
vosotros/as	vuestr**o/a**	vuestr**os/as**	*yours*
ustedes	suy**o/a**	suy**os/as**	*yours*
ellos/as	suy**o/a**	suy**os/as**	*theirs*

Definite article: 5.A.1
Indefinite quantifiers
(determiners): 7.B–7.C

9.C.2 Postnominal forms: use

a. Postnominal forms must be used when a definite article, an indefinite article, or one or more determiners are placed before the noun.

el libro **mío**	*my book (the book of mine)*	**la** casa **mía**	*my house*
los libros **míos**	*my books*	**las** casas **mías**	*my houses*
un amigo **mío**	*my friend*	**varios** libros **vuestros**	*various books of yours*
todas estas cosas **tuyas**	*all these things of yours*	**bastantes** ideas **nuestras**	*quite a lot of our ideas*
el teléfono **tuyo** es mejor que el mío	*your telephone is better than mine*	**un** compañero **nuestro**	*a schoolmate of ours*

Comparisons with postnominal
possessives: 11.B.1f

b. Postnominal possessives can stand alone like pronouns when the noun is not mentioned. They agree in gender and number with the noun they replace and must be used with a definite article.

Este es mi número de teléfono, ¿cuál es **el tuyo**?	*This is my telephone number, what's yours?*
Estos papeles son **los míos** y esos son **los tuyos**.	*These papers are mine and those are yours.*
Haz el pastel con tu receta, no con **la mía**.	*Bake the cake with your recipe, not with mine.*
Esta cámara es **la nuestra**, no **la tuya**.	*This is our camera, not yours.*
Lo tuyo es mío y **lo mío** es tuyo.	*What is yours is mine and what is mine is yours.*
Vuestra casa es muy grande. **La nuestra** es más pequeña.	*Your [pl.] house is very big. Ours is smaller.*

c. With **ser** and **parecer**, postnominal possessives can emphasize ownership without an article or other determiner.

Ese lápiz es **mío**.	*That pencil is mine.*
¿Es **tuyo** todo esto?	*Is all this yours?*
Las demás cosas parecen **mías**.	*The remaining things seem to be mine.*

Combining prenominal and
postnominal possessives:
9.D.7

d. In Spanish, when several possessives are put together such as *yours and mine, your or my friend,* a combination of prenominal and postnominal possessives or a combination of **de** + *subject pronoun* is used.

Mañana vienen **tus** amigos y **los míos**.	*Tomorrow, your friends and mine are coming.*
Las preferencias **de ellos** y **las mías** son iguales.	*Their preferences and mine are the same.*
El carro **de Juan** y **el nuestro** son del mismo modelo.	*Juan's car and ours are the same model.*

e. Postnominal possessives are commonly used instead of compound prepositions made up of *noun + preposition.*

◀ Compound prepositions: 12.A.2b

alrededor de ellos / alrededor **suyo**	*around them*
al lado de ella / al lado **suyo**	*next to her*
en torno a mí / en torno **mío**	*around me*

9.D Features

Características generales

9.D.1 Use of *de + pronoun* to clarify possessor

The possessives **su(s)** and **suyo/a(s)** may refer to something owned by any third person, singular or plural, or by **usted(es).** If the context is ambiguous or to establish contrast, use **de** + *pronoun* or *noun* to identify the owner clearly.

Benito no lavará su auto sino el **de ella**.	*Benito will not wash his car, but hers.*
La familia **de ellos** es muy grande.	*Their family is very large.*
Ellos son los padres **de Leonor**.	*They are Leonor's parents.*
Estos documentos son **de ustedes**.	*These documents are yours.*
¿Este libro es **de usted**?	*Is this book yours?*

9.D.2 Use of *de nosotros/as* in Latin America

In Latin America, **de** + **nosotros/as** frequently replaces **nuestro/a(s)** in oral and written Spanish.

La casa **de nosotros** es en Texas.	*Our home is in Texas.*
Una prima **de nosotras** vive en Miami.	*A cousin of ours lives in Miami.*
El auto **de nosotros** es un modelo viejo.	*Our car is an old model.*

9.D.3 Uses of *propio*

In Spanish, **propio/a(s)** (*own, of one's own*) can be used before or after a noun, with or without a possessive, and can have several meanings.

a. To stress ownership, place **propio/a(s)** *before* a noun and after a possessive, as in English.

◀ Compared with **mismo**: 7.E.5

Mary vio el robo con **sus propios** ojos.	*Mary saw the robbery with her own eyes.*
Prefiero tener **mi propia** habitación.	*I prefer to have my own room.*
Crea **tu propio** blog.	*Create your own blog.*
Juan construyó **su propia** casa.	*Juan built his own house.*

b. Propio/a(s) is used to express characteristics of people and things. Note the use of **de** + *pronoun* or *noun.*

◀ **Ser** with nouns: 30.B.1

Jugar bien es **propio** de campeones.	*Playing well is the way of champions.*
¡Esa risa es **propia** de Luisa!	*That laughter is typical of Luisa!*
El tango es **propio** de Argentina.	*Tango is typical of Argentina.*
La salsa tiene un ritmo muy **propio**.	*Salsa music has a very unique rhythm.*
Las travesuras son **propias** de los niños.	*Pranks are typical of children.*

c. Propio/a can be a synonym of **mismo/a** + *place*. This use is equivalent to the English *proper.*

◀ Vivo en la **misma** capital.

Vivo en la **propia** capital.	*I live in the capital proper.*

d. Propio/a(s) may be a synonym of *adequate, fitting, proper, correct,* or *suitable,* as in the following examples.

Este diccionario es **propio** para estudiantes.	*This dictionary is suitable for students.*
Te daré botas **propias** para el invierno.	*I will give you a pair of adequate winter boots.*

Other meanings of **propio** : 7.E.5 ▶

e. Propio/a appears in many frequent and useful expressions.

Rita vive en su **propio mundo**.	*Rita lives in her own world.*
Estudiamos por **interés propio**.	*We study out of our own interest.*
El acusado actuó en **defensa propia**.	*The accused acted in self-defense.*
Eso lo sé por **experiencia propia**.	*I know that from my own experience.*
Esto lo decides por **cuenta propia**.	*You should decide this on your own.*
Aprendo español a mi **propio ritmo**.	*I learn Spanish at my own pace.*

9.D.4 Article instead of possessives

Ownership expressions with an article: 5.C.7 ▶

a. The definite article is used instead of a possessive with parts of the body or personal belongings. However, with verbs like **ser** and **parecer,** the possessive is used to make ownership clear.

¡Niños, tenéis **las** manos sucias!	*Children, your hands are dirty!*
¿Dónde he dejado **las** gafas?	*Where did I leave my glasses?*
Tengo puestos **los** zapatos nuevos.	*I have my new shoes on.*
Mis zapatos son de cuero.	*My shoes are made of leather.*
Tu piel parece muy seca.	*Your skin looks very dry.*

b. The definite article is used instead of the possessive when the verb is reflexive because the reflexive pronoun already indicates the owner.

Tienes que poner**te los** lentes.	*You have to put in your contacts.*
Voy a lavar**me la** cara.	*I am going to wash my face.*
El perro se rasca **el** lomo.	*The dog is scratching his back.*

Verbs like **gustar**: 13.F.3, 17.B.4 ▶

c. Verbs that express physical reactions and ailments, such as **arder, doler,** and **picar** are used with indirect object pronouns. The affected part of the body, which is the subject of the sentence, uses a definite article, not a possessive.

¿**Te** arden **los** ojos?	*Do your eyes burn?*
A ellos **les** duelen **los** pies.	*Their feet hurt.*

d. When ownership is not obvious, using the possessives helps to clarify who the owner is.

La madre paseaba con **los/sus** hijos.	*The mother was walking with the/her children.*
Hoy visité a **la/mi** vecina.	*I visited the/my neighbor today.*
La/Mi familia me visitará el Día de Acción de Gracias.	*The/My family will visit me on Thanksgiving.*

9.D.5 *Lo* + possessives

With the neuter article **lo**, the postnominal possessives express general ownership or areas of interest.

Lo tuyo es el arte.	*Art is your thing.*
Lo nuestro no es un secreto.	*Our relationship is not a secret.*
Lo mío es tuyo.	*What's mine is yours.*
Y ahora, cada uno a **lo suyo**.	*And now, it's every man for himself.*
Lo vuestro es la literatura.	*Literature is your [pl.] thing.*

9.D.6 Definite and indefinite meaning of possessives

a. Prenominal possessive forms always refer to a definite object: **mis amigos = los amigos míos** (*my friends*). Postnominal possessive forms are much more flexible and may also convey ownership of unspecified objects or unspecified quantity: **unos/muchos/varios/los otros amigos míos** (*some/many/ several/other friends of mine*).

b. Definite articles can never accompany a prenominal possessive because they are already definite, as explained in part **a** above. In this case, postnominal possessives must be used.

Tu trabajo es muy interesante.	*Your work is very interesting.*
El trabajo **tuyo** es muy interesante.	

c. Unlike prenominal possessives, postnominal forms can be used with demonstratives and many indefinite determiners.

◀ Possessive determiners: 9.A

Ese viaje **vuestro** tendrá que esperar.	*That trip of yours will have to wait.*
¡No te diré **ningún** secreto **mío**!	*I won't tell you any of my secrets!*
Olvidamos **varias** cosas **nuestras** en el hotel.	*We forgot several of our things at the hotel.*
¡**Esa** idea **tuya** es fantástica!	*That idea of yours is fantastic!*

d. The verb **estar** is used with definite nouns while **haber** is used with indefinite nouns. This means that prenominal possessive forms (which are definite) are generally used with **estar** and postnominal forms (which are indefinite) with **haber**. When using postnominal possessives with **estar,** you usually need a definite article or another determiner to express definiteness. Compare the following examples:

◀ Uses of **estar** and **haber**: 29.B.1, 30.C.7

Aquí **están los** cinco dólares **tuyos** y **los** cuatro **míos**.	*Here are your five dollars and my four.*
Aquí **están tus** cinco dólares y **mis** cuatro dólares.	*Here are your five dollars and my four dollars.*
Somos tres hermanos: primero **está mi** hermana mayor que tiene veinte años y luego **está mi** hermano menor que tiene quince.	*We are three siblings: first there's my older sister who is twenty years old and then there is my younger brother who is fifteen.*
En el garaje **están mis** libros viejos y hay, además, **varias** cosas **tuyas**.	*In the garage, there are my old books and there are also several things of yours.*
Aquí **hay** cinco dólares **tuyos** y cuatro **míos**.	*Here are five dollars that are yours and four that are mine.*

9.D.7 Combining prenominal and postnominal possessives

Prenominal possessives can be combined with postnominal forms. Several postnominal forms can also be combined, but two prenominal forms can never be combined unless the noun is repeated.

◀ Use of postnominal possessives: 9.C.2d

Los planes **tuyos y míos** son incompatibles.	*Your and my plans are incompatible.*
Hoy vendrán **vuestras** amigas y las **mías**.	*Your friends and mine will come today.*
Mi cumpleaños y **el tuyo** son el mismo día.	*My birthday and yours are on the same day.*
Mi cumpleaños y **tu** cumpleaños son el mismo día.	

9.D.8 Use of possessives in vocatives

a. Postnominal possessives are more common than prenominal possessives in vocatives when addressing someone by name, title, or nickname.

¡Querida Alicia mía, escúchame bien!	*My dear Alicia, listen to me very carefully!*
Amigos míos, ¡la cena está servida!	*Dear friends, dinner is served.*
Cariño mío, te extraño.	*I miss you, my dear.*

b. Particularly in Latin America, the prenominal possessives are commonly used in vocatives.

amor **mío**	**mi** amor	*my love*
cielito **mío**	**mi** cielito	*my darling*
corazón **mío**	**mi** corazón	*my darling*
hijo/a **mío/a**	**mi**jito/**mi**jita, **m'**hijito/**m'**hijita	*my son/daughter*

c. In military circles, the norm is to use prenominal possessives with titles. Kings, nobles, cardinals, and the Pope are addressed in similar ways.

mi capitán	*my captain*	**Su** Alteza Real	*Your Royal Highness*
mi general	*my general*	**Su** Excelencia	*Your Excellence*
mi sargento	*my sargeant*	**Su** Santidad	*Your Holiness*
mi soldado	*my soldier*	**Su** Señoría	*Your Honor*

9.E Regional variations

Variaciones regionales

9.E.1 Adverbs of place used with possessives

Compound prepositions: 12.A.2b ▶

a. The following structure with the adverbs **delante** and **detrás** is common in the Spanish-speaking world:

The agreement of the possessive ▶ with a female owner is *not* accepted in formal speech in most Spanish-speaking countries: ***El perro camina delante** *suya.*

El perro camina **delante de ella**.   *The dog walks in front of her.*

b. Although not as common, the possessive expression can be replaced with a postnominal possessive.

El perro camina **delante suyo**.   *The dog walks in front of her.*

Práctica

S Actividades 1–12, pp. A28–A31

Adverbs
Adverbios

10.A Overview

Aspectos generales

Adverbs describe *when*, *how*, *where*, and *why* something happens or is done. Adverbs can modify a verb, another adverb, an adjective, or a whole sentence. Adverbs always keep the same form and never agree with any noun or other word in the sentence.

Adverbs can be used together with:		
1. Verbs	Camino **rápidamente**.	*I walk **quickly**.*
2. Other Adverbs	Camino **muy** rápidamente.	*I walk **very** quickly.*
3. Adjectives	Estoy **bastante** cansado.	*I am **quite** tired.*
4. Sentences	**Generalmente**, estudio los lunes.	***Usually**, I study on Mondays.*

10.B Adverbs of time

Adverbios de tiempo

10.B.1 *Cuándo, cuando*

Question		Answer	
¿cuándo?	*when?*	**cuando**	*when*

Cuándo with a written accent is used in direct and indirect questions. Without a written accent, **cuando** is used in subordinate clauses.

—¿**Cuándo** hacéis las tareas?   *When do you [pl.] do your homework?*

—Las hacemos **cuando** podemos.   *We do it when we can.*

cuando in subordinate clauses: 23.E.2a
Conjunctions of time: 16.C.3
Relative adverbs: 15.C.1
Indirect questions: 14.B.9, 31.B.6d

10.B.2 Common adverbs of time

ahora	*now*	**entonces**	*then*
antes	*before*	**después**	*after*
		luego	*later*
hoy	*today*	**mañana**	*tomorrow*
		pasado mañana	*day after tomorrow*
		ayer	*yesterday*
		anteayer	*day before yesterday*
		anoche	*last night*
		antenoche	*night before last*
siempre	*always*	**nunca**	*never*
		jamás	*never ever*
tarde	*late*	**temprano**	*early*
todavía, aún	*still*	**todavía no, aún no**	*not yet*
ya	*already, now*	**ya no**	*no longer*
mientras	*while*		

Podemos descansar **después**.	*We can rest **later**.*
Ana viene **mañana**.	*Ana is coming **tomorrow**.*
Siempre estudio mucho.	*I **always** study a lot.*
No estudiaste **ayer**.	*You didn't study **yesterday**.*
Hoy es martes.	***Today** is Tuesday.*
Pronto termino.	*I'll finish **soon**.*
Escribo **mientras** lees.	*I'll write **while** you read.*
Primero trabajamos y **luego/después** descansamos.	***First** we'll work and **later/after** we'll rest.*
Siempre llegas **antes** y yo **después**.	*You always arrive **before** and I arrive **after**.*

10.B.3 *Nunca, jamás*

Nunca and **jamás** mean *never* or, sometimes, *ever*, but **jamás** is more emphatic. They can be used together to make an even stronger negation, **nunca jamás** (*never ever*). These adverbs can come before or after a verb, but both require a double negation when they follow a verb.

Nunca te olvidaré./**No** te olvidaré **nunca**.	*I will **never** forget you.*
Jamás nos diremos adiós./**No** nos diremos adiós **jamás**.	*We will **never** say goodbye.*
Nunca jamás te olvidaré./**No** te olvidaré **nunca jamás**.	*I will **never** (ever) forget you.*

10.B.4 *Ya, ya no; todavía, todavía no; aún, aún no*

a. Note how these adverbs are used in the following sentences:

Ya lo he pagado todo.	*I have **already** paid for everything.*
Ya no estudio literatura.	*I'm **not** studying literature **anymore**.*
Todavía vivo en Nueva York.	*I **still** live in New York.*
Todavía no hablo bien español.	*I **don't** speak Spanish well **yet**.*

b. The following are common expressions used with **ya**.

¡**Ya** voy!	*I'm coming!*	**Ya** (lo) sé.	*I already know that.*
¡**Ya** vengo/regreso!	*I'll be right back!*	**Ya** verás/veremos.	*You'll see. / We'll see.*

Diacritical marks: 1.E.6c ▶

c. Aún is a synonym of **todavía**. **Aun** (without an accent) can mean *even*, *also*, or *including*.

Aún vivo en Nueva York.	*I **still** live in New York.*
Aún no hablo bien español.	*I don't speak Spanish well **yet**.*
Sigo cansado **aun** después de dormir la siesta.	*I am tired **even** after taking a nap.*
Todos, **aun** los que al principio se opusieron, apoyaron la decisión.	*Everyone supported the decision, **including** those who had initially opposed it.*

10.B.5 *Después, luego*

The adverbs **luego** and **después** are synonyms.

Después/Luego vuelvo.	*I'll come back **later**.*

10.B.6 **Adverbs of frequency**

Adverbial phrases: 10.H ▶

a. These adverbs express how often something happens and can be arranged on a scale where **siempre** and **nunca** are opposites, with adverbs of various frequencies in between.

Más frecuencia ←						→ Menos frecuencia	
siempre	*always*	**casi siempre**	*almost always*	**casi nunca**	*almost never*	**nunca, jamás**	*never*
todo/a(s) + def. article + time	*every + time*	**muchas veces**	*many times*	**pocas veces**	*a few times*	**nunca jamás**	*never ever*
		a veces, a menudo	*sometimes, once in a while*	**rara vez**	*seldom, rarely*		
		frecuentemente, con (mucha) frecuencia	*frequently*	**con poca frecuencia**	*not frequently*		

Trabajo **todos los días**.   *I work every day.*

Siempre estudio por la mañana.   *I always study in the morning.*

A veces practico el vocabulario.   *Sometimes I practice the vocabulary.*

Casi siempre escribo en mi blog.   *I almost always write in my blog.*

Nunca me canso de chatear.   *I never get tired of chatting.*

Rara vez vamos a la playa.   *We rarely go to the beach.*

b. In addition to these frequency adverbs and expressions, Spanish uses **cada** + *time expression* to emphasize incremental actions or events.

Cada día aprendo más español.   *I learn more Spanish each day.*

10.C Adverbs of manner

Adverbios de modo

10.C.1 Cómo, como

Question		Answer	
¿Cómo?	*How?*	**como**	*as, like*

Cómo with a written accent is used in direct and indirect questions. **Como** is used without a written accent in comparisons and subordinate clauses that express the manner in which something is done.

El clima está tan bueno hoy **como** ayer.   *The weather is just **as** good today as yesterday.*

Viaja **como** quieras, en avión o en tren.   *Travel **as** you wish, by plane or train.*

—¿**Cómo** quieres el café?   ***How** do you want your coffee?*

—¡Exactamente **como** tú lo preparas!   *Exactly **how** you prepare it!*

Como in subordinate clauses: 23.E.1
Relative adverbs: 15.C.1
Cómo: 14.B.6

Conjunctions of comparison: 16.C.8
Expressing manner - **como**: 16.C.9

10.C.2 Common adverbs of manner

bien	*good*	**mal**	*bad*
mejor	*better*	**peor**	*worse*
así	*this way, like this/that*	**regular**	*so-so*

Quiero el café **así**: ¡caliente!   *I want my coffee **like this**: hot!*

a. The adverbs **bien** and **mal** have their own forms for comparison.

¡Hoy la comida está **peor**!   *The food is **worse** today!*

El clima es **mejor** en verano.   *The climate/weather is **better** in the summer.*

The adverb **bien** can be used as adjective: **Ellos son gente bien.** (*They are good people.*) Also in exclamations: **¡Qué bien!** (*That's great!*)

10.C.3 *Bien*

The adverb **bien** before an adjective acts as an intensifying adverb.

La película es **bien** divertida.	*The film is **quite** funny.*
¡Tienes un auto **bien** bonito!	*You have a **really** nice car!*

10.D Quantifying adverbs

Adverbios de cantidad

10.D.1 *Cuánto, cuanto*

Cuán is a short form of **cuánto** ▶ used mainly in exclamations and can be replaced by **qué**: ¡**Cuán/Qué** listo es este chico! (*What a bright kid he is!*)

Question		Answer	
¿Cuánto?	*How much?*	**cuanto**	*as much (as)*

a. Cuánto with a written accent is used in direct and indirect questions. **Cuanto** without a written accent in subordinate clauses expresses *quantity* or *degree*.

Indirect questions: ▶ 14.B.9, 31.B.6d

—¿**Cuánto** trabajas?	***How much** do you work?*
—Trabajo **cuanto** puedo.	*I work **as much as** I can.*

b. In speech and in less formal texts, it is more common to use **todo lo que** (*as much as*) instead of **cuanto**.

Indefinite quantifiers as ▶ adverbs: 7.E.4

Trabajo **todo lo que** puedo.	*I work **as much as** I can.*

10.D.2 Other common modifiers and quantifying adverbs

Suficiente = bastante ▶

más *(more)*	←	--------------------------------- →	**menos** *(less)*
demasiado *too much*	**mucho, muy** *a lot, very*	**bastante, suficiente** *enough/quite a lot/quite*	**poco** *little*
tanto, tan *so much*	**casi** *almost*	**apenas** *barely, hardly*	**sólo, solamente** *only*

Me comí **casi** todo el paquete.	*I ate **almost** the whole package.*
Apenas tengo dos dólares.	*I **barely** have two dollars.*
Duermes **mucho** y trabajas **poco**.	*You sleep **a lot** and work **little**.*
Solo estudio español.	*I **only** study Spanish.*
Tú trabajas **más** que yo.	*You work **more** than I.*
¡Nieva **tanto** hoy!	*It's snowing **so much** today!*

a. Más, menos, and **tanto** are the most common adverbs used in all types of comparisons.

Comparisons: Ch. 11 ▶

Estudiamos **más que** vosotros.	*We study **more than** you [pl.].*
Tengo **menos** dinero **que** antes.	*I have **less** money **than** before.*
Sabes **tanto como** yo.	*You know **as much** as I do.*

b. Casi is mostly used with the present tense in Spanish, while *almost*, in English, can also be used in the past tense.

Casi compro un auto nuevo.	*I **almost** bought a new car.*

c. The adverb **bastante** can stand alone or be combined with other adjectives or adverbs.

Trabajo **bastante**.	*I work **quite a lot**.*
Mary está **bastante** cansada.	*Mary is **quite** tired.*
Tu trabajo está **bastante** bien.	*Your work is **quite** good.*
No comes **bastante**.	*You don't eat **enough**.*

Bastante placed before and after a noun 7.C.2

d. The adverbs **muy, mucho,** and **demasiado** cannot occur together. Note how they are used in English.

Hablas **mucho**.	*You talk **a lot**.*
Trabajas **demasiado**.	*You work **too much**.*
Estamos **demasiado** cansados.	*We are **too** tired.*
El problema es **muy** difícil.	*The problem is **very** dificult.*

Demasiado: 7.C.11

10.E Adverbs of place

Adverbios de lugar

There are two groups of adverbs that express where an action takes place. One group expresses relative distance from the perspective of the speaker. The other group expresses the location of people and things in a room.

10.E.1 Relative distance

Close to the person speaking		Far from the person speaking	
aquí	*here*	**allí, ahí**	*there*
acá	*here*	**allá**	*there*

a. Aquí and **allí** work similarly to *here* and *there*, and are used primarily to indicate location.

Aquí siempre hace buen tiempo.	*It's always good weather here.*
Allí están tus libros.	*There are your books.*

b. Ahí is more general than **allí** and expresses an indefinite location when used with **por**.

Tus zapatos están **por ahí**.	*Your shoes are somewhere around there.*
—¿Dónde entrenas los domingos?	*Where do you train on Sundays?*
—**Por ahí**, en la ciudad o en el parque.	*Somewhere around there, in the city or the park.*

c. Acá and **allá** are often used with verbs of motion. In contrast to **allí**, the adverb **allá** can be used with **más** and **muy**.

Ven **acá**.	*Come here.*
Isabel va para **allá**.	*Isabel is on her way there.*
El correo está **más allá**.	*The post office is farther away.*

10.E.2 Adverbs of place and direction: *adónde/adonde; dónde/donde*

Donde/adonde: 16.C.10

Adverbs of place can refer to specific locations of people and things and some of them also indicate direction.

a. These adverbs are used to ask and answer a question about a location or direction.

Question		Answer	
¿adónde?	*where?*	**adonde**	*where (in, on, at)*
¿a dónde?	*to where?*	**a donde**	*to where*
¿dónde?	*where?*	**donde**	*where*

b. Dónde (*where*) is a question adverb which refers to location. **Donde** (*where*) can be used to answer a question with **dónde** and refers to a location already mentioned.

Donde in subordinate clauses: 23.E.1
Relative adverb **donde**: 15.C.1

—¿**Dónde** vive tu familia?   *Where does your family live?*
—Vive en la ciudad **donde** nací.   *They live in the city **where** I was born.*

c. It is common to use *preposition* + **la/el/los/las que** in relative clauses as a synonym for **donde**.

—¿**Dónde** estudias?   *Where are you studying?*
—En una escuela **en la que** hay buenos maestros.   *At a school **where** there are good teachers.*

d. Adónde (*To where*) is a question adverb that is used to refer to location with verbs of motion. **Adonde** can be used to answer questions using **adónde**. In this case, **adonde** is a relative adverb referring to a definite location. It can be written as two words: **a dónde, a donde**.

Donde, adonde are used informally for the meaning *at* (*somebody's house*): **Estoy donde Juan.** *I'm at Juan's.*

—¿**Adónde** viajas en verano?   *Where do you travel in the summer?*
—Este año iré a Londres, **adonde** viajé   *This year I'll go to London, **where** I traveled*
el año pasado.   *last year.*
—Viajo **a donde** vive mi familia.   *I'm going **to where** my family lives.*

10.E.3 Other common adverbs of place and direction

Ser, estar with adverbs: 30.C.1, 30.E

The following adverb pairs look similar, but their meanings and uses are different. The adverbs in the *Place* column describe location only. The adverbs in the other column express location relative to a specific *direction*.

Place		**Direction**	
delante	*in front*	**adelante**	*forward, ahead, in front, at the front*
detrás	*in the back*	**atrás**	*behind, back, at the back*
encima	*on top, over*	**arriba**	*above, up*
debajo	*beneath, underneath*	**abajo**	*below, down*
dentro	*within, inside*	**adentro**	*inside*
fuera	*out, outside*	**afuera**	*outside*
cerca	*close (by)*		
lejos	*far (away)*		
alrededor	*around*		
enfrente	*opposite, in front*		

Prepositional phrases: 12.A.2

a. Adverbs of place that describe location usually form prepositional expressions with **de**: **delante de** (*in front of*), **encima de** (*on top of*), **alrededor de** (*around*), etc. The other group of adverbs cannot be used with **de**.

Delante de la iglesia hay una plaza.   *In front of the church there is a square.*
Hay mucha gente **dentro de** la iglesia.   *There are lots of people inside the church.*

b. Only adverbs of place that also convey direction can be used with prepositions indicating movement: **hacia adelante** (*in a forward direction*), **hasta atrás/arriba** (*all the way back/up*), **hacia/para abajo** (*downwards*) and similar expressions.

La chica miraba **para arriba y para abajo**.   *The girl looked up and down.*

Cerca, lejos: 10.E.3h

c. Adverbs of quantity can modify adverbs of place that indicate direction to describe the degree of distance in a specific direction. Adverbs of place that do not indicate direction *do not accept* adverbs of quantity (except **cerca** and **lejos**).

más adelante	*farther on, later*	**muy abajo**	*very far down*
bastante arriba	*very high up*	**un poco atrás**	*a little bit behind*
muy cerca	*very close*	**mucho más lejos**	*much farther away*
demasiado atrás	*too far back*	**nada lejos**	*not very far away*

◀ Prepositional phrases: 12.A.2

d. Delante/detrás express location exclusively, while **adelante/atrás** convey a sense of movement or placement (*forward* and *backward*) in addition to location.

◀ **Delante *de usted:*** see adverbs of place used with possessives: 9.E.1

El parque está allí **delante**.	*The park is there, right in front.*
El parque está allí **adelante**.	*The park is there, farther on.*
La fuente está **detrás**.	*The fountain is in back.*
La fuente está más **atrás**.	*The fountain is farther back.*
Los niños viajan **atrás** y los adultos **adelante**.	*The children ride in the back and the adults in the front.*

e. Arriba and **abajo** express location, but always with a sense of direction, *up* or *down*. Therefore, these two adverbs can be used to mean *upstairs, downstairs* or figuratively as in the expressions: **los de arriba** (*upper class*) and **los de abajo** (*lower class*). **Encima/debajo** express only location.

En el texto, los títulos van **arriba** y las notas van **abajo**.	*In the text, the titles go above and the notes go below.*
En la caja, encuentras los libros **debajo** y los papeles **encima**.	*In the box, you will find the books underneath and the papers on top.*

f. Dentro and **fuera** are not commonly used alone and are usually combined with prepositions to refer to physical or figurative places.

Los rayos X muestran el cuerpo **por dentro**.	*X-rays show the inside of the body.*
Por fuera, la casa se ve chica.	*The house looks small from the outside.*
Hay mucha gente **fuera del** cine.	*There are a lot of people outside the movie theater.*

g. Adentro and **afuera** must be used with an explicit or implied verb of motion.

No te muevas, quédate **afuera**.	*Don't move, stay outside.*
Hace frío, vamos **adentro**.	*It's cold; let's go inside.*

h. Cerca and **lejos** express location only. Adverbs of quantity (**muy, bastante,** etc.) and **de** often accompany these adverbs. They can *never* be used with prepositions of direction.

◀ Adverbs + **hacia, hasta**: 10.E.3b

El centro de la ciudad queda **lejos**.	*The city center is far away.*
Alaska queda **lejos de** Nueva York.	*Alaska is far from New York.*

10.E.4 Adverbs of place and prepositions

There is an important difference between adverbs of place and prepositions. Prepositions must be followed by a noun, while adverbs of place can stand alone.

◀ Compound prepositions: 12.A.2b

Prepositions		Adverbs of place	
El perro está **debajo de** la cama.	*The dog is **under** the bed.*	En la caja encuentras los libros **debajo** y los papeles **encima**.	*In the box, you'll find the books **underneath** and the papers **on top**.*
Las cartas están **encima de** la mesa.	*The letters are **on** the table.*		

Adverbios de afirmación, de negación y de duda

10.F.1 **Common positive and negative adverbs**

¿no?	right (true)?	¿sí?	yes? is it true?
sí	yes	no	no, not
bueno	good, well	también	also
tal vez, quizás	maybe	tampoco	neither

a. In negative sentences, **no** is always placed before the verb. Note how you answer negatively in Spanish: **No, no...** *No... not.* Both **¿sí?** and **¿no?** are placed at the end of the sentence in order to ask a question, which is equivalent to a *tag question* in English.

—Vives en Chicago, **¿no?**   *You live in Chicago, **don't you**?*

—**No, no** vivo en Chicago.   ***No**, I **don't** live in Chicago.*

—**Sí,** vivo en Chicago.   ***Yes**, I live in Chicago.*

b. In spoken language, it is common to add **sí** in order to add emphasis to a positive statement, especially when contrasting negative and positive statements.

¿Tú **no** quieres ir? ¡Yo **sí** quiero!   *You don't want to go? I sure do!*

c. También is used like the English *also.* **Tampoco** is used in negative sentences to mean *neither.*

Gabriel viene y Carolina **también**.   *Gabriel is coming and Carolina too.*

Tú **no** quieres ir y yo **tampoco**.   *You don't want to go and neither do I.*

Use of the subjunctive in
independent clauses:
23.B.1

Ojalá: use of the subjunctive:
23.B.2b

d. Tal vez and **quizás** are synonyms. Both can be used with the indicative and the subjunctive.

Quizás es/sea Luisa.   *It might be Luisa.*

Tal vez viajamos/viajemos pronto.   *We might go soon.*

10.G **Adverbs ending in -*mente***

Adverbios terminados en -*mente*

10.G.1 **Structure**

Adverbs ending in -*mente*: 1.E.8

The most common adverbs in Spanish end in **-mente** and are formed using the feminine form of an adjective. When the adjective does not have a feminine form, the ending **-mente** is added to the basic form. Adjectives keep written accents when they form adverbs.

Adjectives		Adverbs	
Masculine	**Feminine**	**Adjective + -*mente***	
correcto	correc**ta**	correcta**mente**	correctly
fácil	fácil	fácil**mente**	easily
feliz	feliz	feliz**mente**	happily

Felizmente, aprobé el examen.   *Happily, I passed my exam.*

Hablas **correctamente**.   *You speak correctly.*

10.G.2 Adjectives as adverbs

In modern Spanish, a number of common adjectives are also used as adverbs without the
-mente ending. Note that these short forms are always masculine and singular.

Respiro **hondo**.	*I'm breathing deeply.*	Juegan **duro**.	*They play hard.*
Escribes **claro**.	*You write clearly.*	Camino **rápido**.	*I walk quickly.*
Juegas **limpio**.	*You're playing fairly.*	Hablan **raro**.	*They speak in a strange way/strangely.*

10.G.3 Placement of adverbs

a. The placement of an adverb in Spanish is flexible. Adverbs that end in **-mente** are almost
always placed after the verb. Adverbs that support an adjective or other adverbs are usually
placed before the verb.

Laura canta **maravillosamente**.	*Laura sings marvelously.*
Mike **casi siempre** está ocupado.	*Mike is almost always busy.*
La explicación es **poco clara**.	*The explanation is not very clear.*

b. When there are several **-mente** adverbs in a row, only the final adverb keeps the **-mente** ending.

La profesora explica la lección clara, pausada y excelente**mente**.	*The teacher explains the lesson clearly, slowly, and very well.*

10.H Adverbial phrases

Locuciones adverbiales

Adverbial phrases combine adverbs, prepositions, or nouns, and express the same meaning as
adverbs: time, manner, quantity, place, assertion, doubt, and negation.

10.H.1 Adverbial phrases vs. adverbs ending in -*mente*

Some common adverbs ending in **-mente** may be replaced by a prepositional expression with the
same meaning, formed with the corresponding noun.

Adverb ending in -*mente*	Adverbial phrase	
claramente	con claridad	*clearly*
cortésmente	con cortesía	*courteously*
difícilmente	con dificultad	*with difficulty*
firmemente	con firmeza	*firmly*
locamente	con locura	*madly*
rápidamente	con rapidez	*quickly*
repentinamente	de repente	*suddenly*
sinceramente	con sinceridad	*sincerely*
telefónicamente	por teléfono	*by phone*

a la larga	in the long run	**A la larga**, conseguirás trabajo. *You will get a job in the long run.*
a las mil maravillas	wonderfully	¡Se preparó **a las mil maravillas**! *It was prepared wonderfully!*
a lo grande	luxuriously, in style	Celebrarán la boda **a lo grande**. *They will celebrate their wedding in style.*
a (la) mano	close at hand	Lleva tu pasaporte **a (la) mano**. *Have your passport close at hand.*
a menudo	frequently, often	Viajamos en avión **a menudo**. *We travel frequently by plane.*
a veces	sometimes	**A veces** duermo la siesta. *I take naps sometimes.*
al final	at/in the end	**Al final** decidimos irnos en tren. *In the end, we decided to travel by train.*
alguna vez	sometime (ever)	¿Has ido a México **alguna vez**? *Have you ever been to Mexico?*
con frecuencia	frequently, often	Escribo en Twitter **con frecuencia**. *I write on Twitter frequently.*
de primera mano	firsthand	Sé la noticia **de primera mano**. *I know the news firsthand.*
en algún momento	at some point, sometime	**En algún momento** debes decidirte. *You will have to decide sometime.*
en alguna parte	somewhere	He dejado mis gafas **en alguna parte**. *I left my glasses somewhere.*
en buenas manos	in good hands	Este trabajo está **en buenas manos**. *This job is in good hands.*
en fin	finally, well then	**En fin**, tenemos que irnos ya. *Well then, we have to go now.*
por fin	at last, finally	**Por fin** has terminado el trabajo. *You have finished your work at last.*
por las buenas o por las malas	one way or the other	Tendrás que estudiar **por las buenas o por las malas**. *You will have to study one way or the other.*
por necesidad	out of necessity	Trabajamos **por necesidad**. *We work out of necessity.*
por poco	almost	**Por poco** pierdo el autobús. *I almost missed the bus.*

10.I Comparison of adverbs

Comparación del adverbio

10.I.1 Comparative constructions

Comparisons: Ch. 11
Comparison of adjectives: 3.E

a. Adverbs have a basic, positive form, as well as a comparative form. Most adverbs form the comparative using **más** or **menos**. Some have irregular forms.

Adverbs	Positive	Comparative
Regular	eficazmente *efficiently*	más/menos eficazmente *more/less efficiently*
Irregular	bien *well*	mejor *better*
	mal *badly*	peor *worse*
	mucho *much/a lot*	más *more*
	poco *little/a bit*	menos *less*

Actualmente, la gente vive **mejor**.	*Nowadays, people live better.*
El médico cree que como **mal**, pero mi hermano come **peor** que yo.	*The doctor thinks I eat badly, but my brother eats worse than I do.*

b. Comparisons using adverbs can be formed with the following structures:

más/menos + *adverb* + **que** or **tan** + *adverb* + **como**

Viajamos **más frecuentemente que** antes.	*We travel a lot more than before.*
Leemos **tan bien como** vosotros.	*We read as well as you [pl.] do.*

10.I.2 Superlative constructions

a. Absolute superlatives of adverbs can be formed by adding **-mente** to the absolute superlative feminine form of an adjective with an **-ísima** ending. In English, the superlative is reproduced with other intensifying adverbs: *very, unbelievably*, etc.

◄ Superlatives of adverbs: 11.D.2

Adjectives		Adverbs	
Positive	Superlative	Superlative of adjective + *-mente*	
lento	lentísima	lentísimamente	*very slowly*
claro	clarísima	clarísimamente	*very clearly*
fuerte	fuertísima	fuertísimamente	*very strongly/hard*

¡Explicas todo **clarísimamente**!	*You explain everything very clearly!*
Te comportas **tontísimamente**.	*You're behaving really stupidly.*

b. Short adverbs that are identical to masculine singular adjectives take the ending **-ísimo**.

◄ Adjectives as adverbs: 10.G.2

Corre **rápido**.	*He runs fast.*	Corre **rapidísimo**.	*He runs very fast.*

c. Some adverbs that are not derived from adjectives also have absolute superlatives. The absolute superlative keeps the ending of the adverb.

lejos → **lejísimos**	*very far*	cerca → **cerquísima**	*very close*
poco → **poquísimo**	*very little*	mucho → **muchísimo**	*a lot*

Los fines de semana duermo **poquísimo**.	*I sleep very little on weekends.*
Mis primos viven **lejísimos**.	*My cousins live very far away.*

d. Relative superlatives can be formed using a comparative form (sometimes preceded by a definite article).

Fue **la pintura más cuidadosamente** realizada.	*It was **the most carefully** done painting.*
De todas las pinturas, esta es **la más cuidadosamente realizada**.	*Of all the paintings, this is **the most carefully done**.*
Juan es quien **más dedicadamente** trabaja.	*Juan is the one who works the most diligently.*

e. Lo más/menos + *adverb* + *adjective/clause* is usually equivalent to the English *as much as* + *adjective/clause* or *as little as* + *adjective/clause*. The adjective most commonly used in this construction is **posible**.

| Entreno **lo más frecuentemente posible**. | *I train as much as possible.* |
| Trabaja **lo más rápidamente que puede**. | *She works as fast as she can.* |

f. Lo más/menos + *adverb* + *adjective/clause* is also commonly used in time expressions.

| **Lo más tarde que llegué** al trabajo es las diez. | *The latest I arrived to work is ten.* |
| Hazlo **lo más pronto que puedas**. | *Do it as soon as you can.* |

g. When English uses a superlative adverb, Spanish can use either a sentence containing a relative clause or a comparative sentence. Note in the examples below that when using a comparative sentence, the first term is compared with everything/everyone else in the group.

*He runs **the fastest**.*	Él es el que más rápido corre.
	Él corre más rápido que todos.
*We all felt bad, but she felt **the worst**.*	Todos nos sentimos mal, pero ella es la que peor se sintió.
	Todos nos sentimos mal, pero ella se sintió peor que todos.
*She resolved the problem **the most intelligently**.*	Ella es la que resolvió el problema más inteligentemente.
	Ella resolvió el problema más inteligentemente que el resto.

10.J | Regional variations

Variaciones regionales

10.J.1   Diminutives

Diminutives, augmentatives, and pejoratives: 2.C.6, 3.A.4

In Latin America, diminutives of adverbs are common in daily language.

ahora	*now*	**ahorita**	*right now/in a moment*
allá	*there*	**allacito**	*over there*
aquí	*here*	**aquicito**	*exactly here*
después	*later/after*	**despuesito**	*right away/in just a moment*
enseguida	*soon*	**enseguidita**	*in a tiny little bit*

10.J.2   *Vale, bien, de acuerdo, claro que sí*

a. In informal daily language, **vale** is used in Spain for questions with the meaning: *Is that OK?, OK?, Is it alright?* The answer may include the same word.

| —Nos vemos más tarde, **¿vale?** | *We'll meet up later, OK?* |
| —**¡Vale!** | *OK!* |

b. In Latin America, there are many local variations of *OK*. Some of the most common expressions are **está bien, de acuerdo, dale, sí, ok.**

—Regreso pronto, **¿de acuerdo?**	*I'll be back soon, OK?*
—**¡De acuerdo!**	*OK!*
—Nos juntamos más tarde.	*We'll get together later.*
—**Dale.**	*OK.*

c. In the Spanish-speaking world, some of the most common expressions to express agreement or disagreement and to communicate consent are **claro, claro que sí, claro que no, por supuesto que sí, cómo no, por supuesto que no.**

—¿Puedo abrir la ventana?	*Can I open the window?*
—**¡Claro que sí!** ¡Ábrela!	*Of course! Open it!*
—¿Estás irritada?	*Are you irritated/annoyed?*
—**¡Claro que no!**	*Of course not!*

Práctica

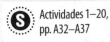
Actividades 1–20,
pp. A32–A37

Comparisons
Comparaciones

Chapter 11

A. Overview
B. Comparisons of inequality
C. Comparisons of equality
D. Superlatives

11.A Overview

Aspectos generales

Some English adjectives have a comparative form in which *-er* is added to the end (*long, longer*), while others use *more* and *less* (*more/less popular*). English adverbs use *more* and *less* for comparative forms (*more slowly*). Nouns are compared using *as many as, more/fewer than*. Spanish uses a much more regular structure to compare differences and inequalities between objects or people (*nouns, pronouns*), characteristics (*adjectives*), actions (*verbs*), and how the actions happen (*adverbs*).

11.B Comparisons of inequality

Desigualdad

11.B.1 Adjectives, adverbs, nouns, and verbs

a. Inequality is expressed in the following way in Spanish.

Comparisons of adjectives, adverbs, nouns, and verbs		
más (*more*) / **menos** (*less*) +	*adjectives/adverbs/nouns/verbs*	+ **que** (*than*)

Note that the subject pronoun is always used in comparisons (**yo, tú, él,** etc.).

Adjectives	Las películas son **más** *largas* **que** las telenovelas.	*Films are longer than soap operas.*
	Antonio es **menos** *famoso* **que** yo.	*Antonio is less famous than I.*
Adverbs	La impresora grande imprime **más** *rápidamente* **que** la pequeña.	*The big printer prints more quickly than the little one.*
	Escribo **mejor** en español **que** en francés.	*I write better in Spanish than in French.*
Nouns	Tengo **más** *libros* **que** Betty.	*I have more books than Betty.*
	Hoy tengo **menos** *dinero* **que** ayer.	*Today I have less money than yesterday.*
Verbs	*Viajas* **más que** yo.	*You travel more than I do.*
	Entreno **menos que** tú.	*I train less than you.*

b. A number of adjectives and adverbs have irregular comparative forms.

Adjectives		Irregular comparatives	
bueno/a(s)	*good*	**mejor(es)**	*better*
malo/a(s)	*bad/evil*	**peor(es)**	*worse*
joven/jóvenes	*young*	**menor(es)**	*younger*
viejo/a(s)	*old*	**mayor(es)**	*older*

Adverbs		Irregular comparatives	
bien	*well*	**mejor**	*better*
mal	*badly*	**peor**	*worse*
mucho	*a lot/very*	**más**	*more*
poco	*little*	**menos**	*less*

Comparison of adjectives: 3.E

Inferior and **superior** are irregular comparatives of **bajo** and **alto**. See table in 11.D.1b.

Comparison of adverbs: 10.I

c. The regular comparative forms of **bueno/a** and **malo/a** can also be used. However, in this case, they exclusively emphasize character judgments.

María es **más buena** que el pan.   *María is a very good person./María is kindness itself.*

María es **mejor** cocinera que su madre.   *María is a better cook than her mother.*

d. Mayor and **menor** are used interchangeably with the regular comparative forms. They are also used as comparative forms of **grande** and **pequeño** when these refer to age.

Carlos es **menor / más joven** que yo.   *Carlos is younger than I am.*

e. Grande and **pequeño** also use **mayor** and **menor** as superlative forms when describing the scope or importance of an issue.

Mi ciudad tiene el **mayor** número de desocupados.   *My city has the largest number of unemployed people.*

f. After **que,** a postnominal possessive always follows a definite article: **el mío, la suya,** etc.

Postnominal possessives: 9.C ▶

Mi auto gasta menos gasolina **que el tuyo**.   *My car consumes less gasoline than yours.*

Nuestras vacaciones son (mucho) más largas **que las vuestras**.   *Our vacations are (much) longer than yours [pl.]*

g. When numbers are compared, **que** is replaced by **de**.

Asisto a **más de** tres clases todos los días.   *I attend more than three classes a day.*

El libro costó **menos de** veinte euros.   *The book cost less than twenty euros.*

Adverbs: **mucho, muy**: 7.E.4 ▶

h. Comparative forms can be strengthened with the help of other adverbs. The most common are **mucho, bastante,** and **(un) poco**. The adverb **muy** cannot be placed before **más** or **menos,** and can only stand before adjectives or adverbs.

El tiempo está hoy **mucho peor** que ayer.   *The weather today is much worse than yesterday.*

Los billetes de avión son **bastante más** caros que los pasajes de tren.   *Plane tickets are quite a lot more expensive than train tickets.*

i. The following comparative expressions indicate that something is different: **diferente a/de, distinto/a(s) + a** (*different from*).

El último libro de Gabo es **diferente a** los otros.   *Gabo's latest book is different from the others.*

Tú eres **distinta a** todas las otras chicas.   *You're different from all the other girls.*

j. In English, comparative forms of an adjective can be used without stating a comparison: *We live in a bigger city in Ecuador. She is married to an older man.* In Spanish this is not possible and such expressions must be said in a different way.

Vivimos en una ciudad **muy/relativamente** grande en Ecuador.   *We live in a very/relatively big city in Ecuador.*

k. In affirmative comparisons, **nadie/ninguno/nunca/nada** express *more/less than anyone, anytime,* etc.

Sois **más** hábiles **que nadie**.   *You [pl.] are more skilled than anyone.*

Podéis bailar **mejor que ninguno**.   *You [pl.] can dance better than anybody.*

Hoy habéis actuado **mejor que nunca**.   *Today you [pl.] have performed better than ever.*

l. The expression **no... más que** in *negative* sentences is not comparative and is equivalent to **no... sino** or **solamente** as in the following examples.

sino: 16.B.1, 16.B.5 ▶

No hablo **más que** español.   *I speak nothing but Spanish.*

No hablo **sino** español.   *I speak nothing but Spanish.*

Solamente hablo español.   *I only speak Spanish.*

11.B.2 **Comparisons with** *de* + ***definite article*** + *que*

a. The second element of a comparison can be a relative clause that refers to the noun in the first term of the comparison. In this case, the second element is introduced by **de** + *definite article* + **que**. The definite article agrees in gender and number with the noun in the first term of the comparison.

más/menos +	*sing. masc. noun* + **del que**	**+ clause**
	sing. fem. noun + **de la que**	
	pl. masc. noun + **de los que**	
	pl. fem. noun + **de las que**	

Gastamos **más *dinero del* que** teníamos.
(gastamos dinero; teníamos dinero)

We spent more money than we had.

Había **más *gente* de *la* que** esperábamos.
(había gente; esperábamos gente)

There were more people than we expected.

Fuimos a **menos *museos* de *los* que** planeábamos visitar. (fuimos a museos; planeábamos visitar museos)

We went to fewer museums than we had planned to visit.

Había **menos *plazas* de *las* que** hay en mi ciudad. (había plazas; hay plazas)

There were fewer squares than there are in my home town.

b. De lo que is used when the second term of a comparison is a clause and the first is a verb, an adjective, or an adverb.

◀ Lo: 5.A.2

Verb	**Trabajó más de lo que** esperábamos.	*He worked more than we expected.*
Adjective	Los precios allí son bastante **más altos de lo que** dice la gente.	*The prices there are a lot higher than people say.*
Adverb	El tiempo pasó **más *rápidamente* de lo que** pensábamos.	*The time passed more quickly than we thought.*

c. De lo que can also be used when the first term of the comparison is a noun. In this case, the verb in the second term of the comparison does not refer specifically to the noun in the first term. This occurs particularly with the noun **vez** or when the first term of the comparison expresses a measurement.

Gasté *cinco dólares* **más de lo que** habíamos acordado.

I spent five dollars more than we had agreed.

Vine de visita *tres veces* **más de lo que** viniste tú.

I came to visit three more times than you.

◀ Multiples: 6.E.2

d. De lo que can also occur when the clause in the second term of the comparison refers to a general concept rather than to the specific noun in the first term of the comparison. In this case, agreement with the noun is also possible.

Gastamos **más *dinero* de lo que/del que** pensábamos. (gastamos dinero; pensábamos gastar menos dinero)

We spent more money than we thought.

Compare with this sentence, in which **de lo que** cannot be used:

Gastamos **más *dinero* del que** teníamos en el banco. (gastamos dinero; teníamos dinero)

We spent more money than we had in the bank.

e. De lo is also used with adjectives like **aconsejable, autorizado, esperado, habitual, justo, necesario, normal, permitido, previsto,** and **requerido.** It is also possible to use **que** in this case.

Trabajé más **de/que lo** esperado.

I worked harder than expected.

Me parece más complicado **de/que lo** previsto.

It seems more complicated than anticipated.

11.C Comparisons of equality

Igualdad

The structures for comparing similar characteristics, people, and objects depend on what is being compared.

11.C.1 Tan

Adjectives and adverbs are compared in the same way when emphasizing similarities.

tan (so) + adjective/adverb + **como** (as)

Adjectives	Las películas no son **tan *cortas* como** las telenovelas.	*Films are not as short as soap operas.*
	Antonio es **tan *famoso* como** yo.	*Antonio is as famous as I am.*
Adverbs	La impresora grande imprime **tan *rápidamente* como** la pequeña.	*The big printer prints just as quickly as the little one.*
	Escribo **tan bien** en español **como** en francés.	*I write as well in Spanish as in French.*

Indefinite quantifiers (determiners): 7.E.4

11.C.2 Tanto/a(s)

Nouns (people and objects) are compared using the word **tanto/a(s),** which agrees with the noun that follows it.

tanto/a(s) (as much/many) + noun + **como** (as)

Nouns	Tengo **tantos libros como** Betty.	*I have as many books as Betty.*
	Hoy, tengo **tanto dinero como** ayer.	*Today, I have just as much money as yesterday.*

11.C.3 Tanto

Verbs are compared using **tanto,** which does not change form and is placed after the verb. The verb is implied after **como** and is normally not repeated.

Tanto... como: 16.B.2d

verb + **tanto** (just as much/as much) + **como** (as)

Verbs	**Viajas tanto como** yo.	*You travel as much as I do.*
	Entreno tanto como tú.	*I train just as much as you.*

11.C.4 Igual/como, tal como

The expression **igual de... que** is used for both adjectives and adverbs. With verbs, **igual que** is used, and with nouns, **igual a** and **(tal) como.**

Adjectives	Rita es **igual de** joven **que** yo. Rita es joven **como** yo.	*Rita is just as young as I.* *Rita is young like me.*
Adverbs	Yo no escribo **igual de** bien **que** tú.	*I don't write as well as you.*
Nouns	Mi camisa es **igual a** / **tal como** la tuya.	*My shirt is just like yours.*
Verbs	Nosotros trabajamos **igual que** / **como** ellos.	*We work just like them.*

11.C.5 *Mismo/a(s)*

Similarity can be expressed using a definite article and **mismo/a(s)** (*the same*).

▶ **Mismo:** Other meanings: 7.E.5 and 27.D

Tengo **la misma** camisa que tú.	*I have the same shirt as you.*
Tenemos **la misma** camisa.	*We have the same shirt.*
Hago **lo mismo** de siempre.	*I'm doing the same as always.*
Siempre ponen **las mismas** películas año tras año.	*They always show the same films year after year.*

11.D Superlatives

El superlativo

Superlatives refer to the highest or lowest grade of a characteristic (adjectives), how something is done (adverbs), or to the greatest or smallest number of people or things (nouns). In English, the superlative is formed with the ending *-est* (*biggest, smallest, youngest*) or with *most, least*.

11.D.1 Adjectives

a. The superlative of adjectives is formed using **el/la/los/las más/menos** + *adjective*.

Me gustan varios deportes, pero el fútbol es **el más interesante**.	*I like many sports, but soccer is the most interesting.*

b. The following adjectives have irregular superlatives.

Adjectives		Comparatives		Superlatives	
alto	*high*	**más alto** superior	*higher*	**el más alto** el superior supremo	*the highest*
bajo	*low*	**más bajo** inferior	*lower*	**el más bajo** el inferior ínfimo	*the lowest*
bueno	*good*	**más bueno** mejor	*better*	**el más bueno** el mejor óptimo	*the best, optimal*
grande	*big*	**más grande** mayor	*bigger*	**el más grande** el mayor máximo	*the biggest, the maximum*
malo	*bad*	**más malo** peor	*worse*	**el más malo** el peor pésimo	*the worst*
pequeño	*small*	**más pequeño** menor	*smaller*	**el más pequeño** el menor mínimo	*the smallest, the minimum*

◀ Comparison of adjectives: 3.E, 11.B.1

◀ **Más bueno** and **más malo** are used exclusively to refer to character traits: 3.E.2b, 11.B.1c

Esta es **la peor** noticia **que** he recibido.	*This is the worst news I've (ever) received.*
Esta película es **la peor que** he visto.	*This film is the worst I've (ever) seen.*
Mario y Carlos son malos diseñadores, pero Pedro es **el peor**.	*Mario and Carlos are bad designers, but Pedro is the worst.*
Mis dos gatitos son buenos como el pan. No muerden ni rasguñan a nadie. Pero el gatito de mi vecino es **el más bueno** de todos.	*My two kittens are very good. They never bite or scratch. But my neighbor's cat is the nicest of all.*
Los resultados no son **óptimos**, pero son aceptables.	*The results are not optimal, but they are acceptable.*

Todo: 7.C.9
c. It is common to add **todos/as** (*all*) in superlative sentences. **Todos/as** is always plural and agrees in gender with the noun that follows it or with the context of the sentence.

Rita es **la** estudiante **más** joven **de todos/as**.	*Rita is the youngest student of all.*

(**todos:** there are male students in the group; **todas:** all students in the group are female)

Rita es **la más** jóven **de todos** los estudiantes.	*Rita is the youngest of all the students.*
¿Cuál es **la mejor** película **de todo** el festival?	*Which is the best film in the whole festival?*

d. De is used if a group is indicated.

Nueva York es **la** ciudad **más** grande **del** país.	*New York is the biggest city in the country.*
Este libro es **el menos** caro **de** estos.	*This book is the least expensive of these.*

Superlatives with **-ísimo**: 3.E.3
Absolute superlative
of adverbs: 11.D.2a-b

e. The endings **-ísimo/a(s)** can be added to adjectives or adverbs to form the *absolute superlative*.

grandísimo	*unbelievably big*	**facilísimo**	*very, very easy*

f. The following superlative adjectives are used in daily language.

Agreement of determiners: 4.B.4

Esa ropa es de **ínfima** calidad.	*Those clothes are of the lowest quality.*
Tu solución no es **óptima**.	*Your solution isn't the best.*
La diferencia es **mínima**.	*The difference is minimal.*
La temperatura **máxima** fue de 3 grados.	*The maximum temperature was 3 degrees.*

g. Comparison of age is made with **mayor/menor,** while peoples' height/size is compared using **alto/bajo** and **grande/pequeño**.

Marcos es **el mayor** de los tres, pero es el más pequeño.	*Marcos is the oldest of the three, but he is the smallest.*
Olivia es **la menor** de la clase pero es la más alta.	*Olivia is the youngest in the class but she is the tallest.*

h. Adjectives can also be strengthened using many adverbs, such as **bien, enormemente, extraordinariamente, terriblemente, impresionantemente, increíblemente, verdaderamente,** and **totalmente.**

Bien as an adverb: 10.C.3
Adverbs ending in **-mente**: 10.G

El problema es **bien** grave.	*The problem is really serious.*
Lucía es **enormemente** rica.	*Lucía is extremely wealthy.*
Eso es **extraordinariamente** extraño.	*That is extraordinarily strange.*
La comida es **terriblemente** mala.	*The food is terribly bad.*
Ella es **impresionantemente** bella.	*She is strikingly beautiful.*
El tráfico está **increíblemente** malo.	*The traffic is incredibly bad.*
Eres **verdaderamente** listo.	*You are truly clever.*
La caja está **totalmente** vacía.	*The box is totally empty.*

11.D.2 **Adverbs**

Comparison of adverbs: 10.I

a. Absolute superlatives of adverbs ending in **-mente** can be formed by adding **-mente** to the absolute superlative feminine form of an adjective with an **-ísima** ending. Short adverbs that are identical to masculine singular adjectives take the ending **-ísimo**.

Adjectives as adverbs: 10.G.2

Ríe **locamente**.	*He laughs wildly.*	Ríe **loquísimamente**.	*He laughs extremely wildly.*
Corre **rápido**.	*He runs fast.*	Corre **rapidísimo**.	*He runs very fast.*

Comparisons • **Chapter 11**

b. Some adverbs that are not derived from adjectives also have absolute superlatives. The absolute superlative keeps the ending of the adverb.

Superlative constructions with adverbs: 10.I.2

lejos → **lejísimos**	*very far*	**cerca** → **cerquísima**	*very close*
poco → **poquísimo**	*very little*	**mucho** → **muchísimo**	*a lot*

Vivo **lejísimos**.   *I live very far.*   Comes **poquísimo**.   *You eat very little.*

c. Superlative constructions can be formed using the comparative form (sometimes preceded by a definite article).

Es el caso **más cuidadosamente** investigado.   *It is the most carefully investigated case.*

De todos los casos, este es **el más cuidadosamente** investigado.   *Of all the cases, this one is the most carefully investigated.*

Es el detective que **más cuidadosamente** investiga.   *He is the detective that most carefully investigates.*

d. Lo más/menos + *adverb* + *adjective/clause* is usually equivalent to the English *as much as* + *adjective/clause* or *as little as* + *adjective/clause*. The adjective most commonly used in this construction is **posible**. This is also used in time expressions.

Entreno **lo más frecuentemente** posible.   *I train as much as possible.*

Trabaja **lo más rápidamente** que puede.   *She works as fast as she can.*

Lo más temprano que llego a la oficina es a las ocho.   *The earliest I get to the office is eight o'clock.*

e. The Spanish equivalent of an English sentence that contains a superlative adverb can be a sentence containing a relative clause or a comparative sentence (in which the first term of the comparison is compared with everything/everyone else in the group).

*He sings **the best**.*   Él es el que mejor canta.
Él canta mejor que todos.

*He worked **the most tirelessly**.*   Él es el que trabajó más incansablemente.
Él trabajó más incansablemente que el resto.

11.D.3   *Lo*

The neuter article **lo** forms abstract noun phrases that can also have a superlative meaning.

Use of neuter article **lo** in order to form nouns: 5.A.2

lo mejor	**Lo mejor** del verano es el calor.	*The best thing about summer is the heat.*
lo más increíble	¡Eso es **lo más increíble** de todo!	*That is the most incredible thing of all!*
lo más posible	Debes decir **lo menos posible**.	*You should say as little as possible.*
lo más romántico	La ceremonia fue **lo más romántico** de la boda.	*The ceremony was the most romantic part of the wedding.*
lo peor	Ese libro es **lo peor que** he leído.	*That book is the worst thing I have (ever) read.*
lo más sensato	Eso es **lo más sensato que** puedes hacer.	*It is the most sensible thing to do.*

The subjunctive in relative clauses: 23.D

11.D.4 Superlatives with *que*

a. Besides **de** + *group*, it is possible to form superlative constructions using **más/menos** and the relative pronoun **que**.

Este libro es **el más interesante de** todos los que he leído.	*This is the most interesting book of all the books I have read.*
Este libro es **el más interesante que** jamás haya leído.	*This is the most interesting book (that) I have ever read.*
Es **el libro que más** me gusta.	*It's the book (that) I like best.*

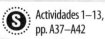 Lo que: 15.B.7b

b. The neutral **lo** is used instead of **el/la/los/las** when it does not refer to a specific noun. The constructions with **lo que más/menos** are usually translated as *the thing that* or *what*.

El que más me gusta es este libro. (**el** = el libro)	*The one I like best is this book.*
Lo que más me gusta es jugar al tenis. (**lo** = jugar al tenis)	*What I like best is to play tennis.*

c. When the comparison focuses on an adjective or adverb, the adjective or adverb is placed between **más/menos** and **que**.

Lo más valioso que tiene mi país es su gente.	*The most valuable thing my country has is its people.*
Lo más rápidamente que puedes viajar allí es en avión.	*The fastest you can travel there is by plane.*

Práctica

Actividades 1–13, pp. A37–A42

The Vista Higher Learning Story

Your Specialized Foreign Language Publisher

Independent, specialized, and privately owned, Vista Higher Learning was founded in 2000 with one mission: to raise the teaching and learning of world languages to a higher level. This mission is based on the following beliefs:

- It is essential to prepare students for a world in which learning another language is a necessity, not a luxury.
- Language learning should be fun and rewarding, and all students should have the tools necessary for achieving success.
- Students who experience success learning a language will be more likely to continue their language studies both inside and outside the classroom.

With this in mind, we decided to take a fresh look at all aspects of language instructional materials. Because we are specialized, we dedicate 100 percent of our resources to this goal and base every decision on how well it supports language learning.

That is where you come in. Since our founding, we have relied on the continuous and invaluable feedback from language instructors and students nationwide. This partnership has proved to be the cornerstone of our success by allowing us to constantly improve our programs to meet your instructional needs.

The result? Programs that make language learning exciting, relevant, and effective through:

- an unprecedented access to resources
- a wide variety of contemporary, authentic materials
- the integration of text, technology, and media, and
- a bold and engaging textbook design

By focusing on our singular passion, we let you focus on yours.

The Vista Higher Learning Team

VISTA
HIGHER LEARNING

31 St. James Avenue Boston, MA 02116-4104 TOLLFREE: 800-618-7375
TELEPHONE: 617-426-4910 FAX: 617-426-5209 **www.vistahigherlearning.com**

Foreword

Spanish is spoken by close to half a billion people around the world and is the official language in most countries in Central and South America, as well as in Mexico and Spain. For a long time, it has also been an important language in teaching institutions around the world.

In 2009, the United States Census Bureau conducted the American Community Survey, which shed some light on the situation of the Spanish language in the United States. According to the survey, there are 45 million people in the United States who speak Spanish as a first or second language. Over 35 million use Spanish as their primary language. The number of students of Spanish in schools and colleges has surpassed six million.

A Handbook of Contemporary Spanish Grammar was developed taking into account the heterogeneous nature of Spanish-language communities in the United States. It provides the support that English speakers and heritage speakers need to master Spanish grammar up to an advanced level.

Grammar topics are presented and reviewed in a clear and logical manner. The text covers basic pronunciation and spelling, parts of speech, verb tenses and moods, tense sequencing, subordinate clauses, and all grammar topics that a student of Spanish needs to master. All concepts and structures are presented in a step-by-step manner, with charts and examples. The handbook also presents regional variations in both the explanations and the examples.

The handbook incorporates significant key updates from the **Real Academia Española**, as presented in the *Nueva gramática de la lengua española* published in 2010. While the *Nueva gramática* targets linguists and scholars, the handbook presents these updates in an accessible, easy-to-follow format.

A glossary of collocations is included to help students improve their vocabulary and deepen their understanding of the subtle differences between terms. The glossary includes grammatical collocations (such as *verb + preposition* combinations), which students will refer to in order to gain mastery over more complex structures.

At the end of the text, hundreds of activities give students ample opportunity to practice and check their understanding.

A Handbook of Contemporary Spanish Grammar is an indispensable tool for anyone with a keen interest in furthering their knowledge of Spanish grammar and achieving a higher level of practical, day-to-day fluency.

Miguel Ángel Quesada Pacheco
Academia Costarricense de la Lengua
Correspondiente de la Real Academia Española

To the student

A Handbook of Contemporary Spanish Grammar is your one-stop source for Spanish grammar reference and practice. Through comprehensive and accessible presentations, detailed charts and diagrams, a *Glosario combinatorio* (glossary of collocations), and substantial auto-gradable practice, this useful reference tool will reinforce and expand your knowledge of Spanish grammatical concepts.

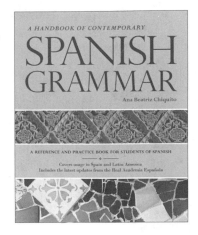

Here are some of the features you will encounter in **A Handbook of Contemporary Spanish Grammar:**

- Grammar presentations that incorporate key updates from the *Nueva gramática*, published in 2010 by the **Real Academia Española**

- Coverage of standard usage in Spain and Latin America, including the use of the *voseo*

- Presentation of regional variations

- An abundance of examples that demonstrate contemporary, real-world usage

- A highly structured, easy-to-navigate design that facilitates the learning of grammar concepts

- A thorough glossary of grammatical and lexical collocations to expand your vocabulary and improve oral and written communication

- Abundant online, auto-gradable activities that practice the concepts

A Handbook of Contemporary Spanish Grammar serves multiple course configurations:

- Stand-alone textbook for advanced Spanish grammar courses

- Companion grammar reference for any advanced Spanish class

- Reference and practice book for heritage speakers and Spanish majors

- Self-study book for students who want to go beyond the grammar taught in introductory and intermediate courses

We hope that **A Handbook of Contemporary Spanish Grammar** will be an invaluable tool as you advance in your study of Spanish.

Table of contents

Prepositions
Las preposiciones

12.A Overview

Aspectos generales

Prepositions are words or word phrases that can be placed before a noun to indicate the semantic relationship between that noun and another word in the sentence. They never change form. The majority of prepositions indicate a relationship between two words in terms of time, location, direction, or origin. The meaning depends on the prepositions used and the words linked.

Since Spanish and English use prepositions in different ways, a preposition used in Spanish may not have a direct English translation.

◀ Use of prepositions: 12.B

Examples		
Location	Roberto está **en** Sevilla.	*Roberto is in Sevilla.*
Time	Mi vuelo es **a** la una.	*My flight is at one.*
Ownership	la casa **de** José María	*José María's house*

12.A.1 Simple prepositions

a. As in English, single-word prepositions in Spanish are a limited set. They are the following:

Simple prepositions			
a	*to —*	**excepto, salvo**	*except, apart from*
ante	*before*	**hacia**	*toward*
bajo	*under*	**hasta**	*until, till*
con	*with*	**mediante**	*through, by means of*
contra	*against*	**para**	*for, to, in order to, by*
de	*of, to, from*	**por**	*for, because of, by*
desde	*from, since*	**según**	*according to*
durante	*during*	**sin**	*without*
en	*on, in, by, at —*	**sobre**	*over, about*
entre	*between*	**tras**	*after, behind*

◀ Verbs with prepositions: 17.B.2

Por favor, siéntate con la espalda **contra** la pared.	*Please sit with your back against the wall.*
Ángel ha estado viajando **desde** ayer.	*Ángel has been traveling since yesterday.*
Según Elisa, va a llover.	*According to Elisa, it is going to rain.*
El perrito corre **tras** su dueño.	*The little dog runs after his owner.*

b. Spanish prepositions always come between two words and can never end a sentence like in English.

◀ Relative pronouns: 15.A.3b

Rita es la chica **con** la que salgo.	*Rita is the girl I go out **with**.*

c. In English two prepositions can be joined using the coordinating conjunctions *and* or *or*, whereas in Spanish, they appear separately in the sentence. The noun or phrase that the preposition refers to is repeated, but the second instance can be replaced by a pronoun.

Tomo el autobús para ir **a** la escuela **y** regresar **de** la escuela.	*I take the bus **to and from** school.*
Plantaremos árboles **delante de** la casa **o detrás de** ella.	*We will plant trees **in front of or behind** the house.*

d. The words **pro**, **versus**, and **vía** are sometimes counted as prepositions. **Pro** precedes nouns: **grupos *pro* derechos humanos** (*pro-human rights groups*). In Spanish, the meaning of **versus (vs.)** is **contra**, **frente a**; it is only used in formal texts: **las grandes economías *versus* las economías de menor escala** (*large economies vs. lower scale economies*). The preposition **vía** indicates how something is done: the medium, the route, etc.: **El viaje es de San Francisco a Nueva York *vía* Chicago.** (*The trip is from San Francisco to New York, via Chicago*).

12.A.2　Compound prepositions and prepositional phrases

Compound prepositions (**locuciones preposicionales**) are formed either by two simple prepositions: **por entre** (*through*), by a combination of preposition(s) and an adverb: **(por) delante de** (*in front of*), **cerca de** (*near*), or combining preposition(s) and a noun: **en contraste con** (*in contrast with*).

a. Below are examples of expressions formed by groups of single prepositions:

a por: 12.C.1

Compound prepositions: *preposition + preposition*		
a por (*Spain*)	Iremos **a por** café.	*We will go **to get** coffee.*
de a	Nos tocan **de a** tres chocolates a cada uno.	*We get three chocolates **each**.*
de entre	Un día **de entre** semana podré trabajar contigo.	*On any **working day**, I will be able to work with you.*
en contra (de)	No actúes **en contra de** tus propios principios.	*Don't act **against** your own principles.*
	¿Estáis **en contra** mía?	*Are you [pl.] **against** me?*
en pro, **en contra de**	¿Estás **en pro** o **en contra** de la propuesta?	*Are you **for** or **against** the proposal?*
para con	Ella es generosa **para con** todos.	*She is generous **with** everyone.*
por entre	El perro se metió **por entre** los arbustos y se escondió.	*The dog squeezed **in between** the bushes and hid.*

b. The prepositions **de** and **por** form many expressions with adverbs. Some adverbs accept **por** when movement is involved (*around the back of, passing by the front of,* etc.).

Adverbs of place with prepositions: 10.E.3

Compound prepositions: *adverb + preposition*			
(por) delante de	*in front of, opposite, across from*	**(por) detrás de**	*behind, in the back of*
enfrente de			
frente a			
al lado de	*beside, next to*	**lejos de**	*far from*
cerca de	*near, close to*		
junto a	*close to, next to*		
encima de	*on top of, on*	**debajo de**	*under, underneath*
por encima de	*over*	**por debajo de**	
dentro de	*in, inside of*	**fuera de**	*out, outside of*
por dentro de		**por fuera de**	
alrededor de	*around*		
antes de	*before*	**después de**	*after*
		luego de	

El autobús pasa **por delante de** la catedral.	The bus passes **in front of** the cathedral.	
La catedral está **enfrente del / frente al** parque.	The cathedral is **opposite** the park.	
En el parque, los niños juegan **al lado de** sus madres.	In the park, the children play **next to** their mothers.	◀ al lado suyo/mío, etc.: 9.C.2e
Vivimos **cerca del** centro de la ciudad.	We live **close to** downtown.	
Mis abuelos viven **junto a** nosotros.	My grandparents live **next to** us.	
Dentro de la casa hay un pequeño patio y **alrededor de** él hay plantas.	**Inside** the house there is a small courtyard and there are plants **around** it.	
La casa se veía vieja **antes de** pintarla. **Después de** pintarla, parece nueva.	The house looked old **before** it was painted. It looks new **after** painting it.	◀ antes de que, después de que: 23.E.2

c. There are many prepositional phrases that are formed with *nouns* and *one or more prepositions*, usually **a**, **de**, **en**, **por**, and **con**. Most of these phrases may function in a sentence as prepositions, adverbs, or adverbial transitions.

Prepositional phrases: *preposition + noun (+ preposition)*		
a base de	Las tortillas se preparan **a base de** maíz.	Tortillas are made **with** corn.
a bordo de	Los pasajeros pasaron **a bordo del** avión.	Passengers got **on board** the plane.
a cargo de	La profesora está **a cargo de** la clase.	The teacher is **in charge of** the class.
a causa de	Nos retrasamos **a causa del** mal tiempo.	We were delayed **because of** bad weather.
a costa de	No hagas nada **a costa de** los demás.	Don't do anything **at the expense of** others.
a eso de	Llegaremos **a eso de** las tres de la tarde.	We will arrive **around** three in the afternoon.
a falta de	**A falta de** computadora, escribiré a mano.	**Lacking** a computer, I will write by hand.
a fondo	Estudiaremos los documentos **a fondo**.	We will study the documents **in depth**.
a fuerza de	**A fuerza de** voluntad, has logrado tener éxito.	**Through** willpower, you have managed to succeed.
a la hora de ⁓	**A la hora de** pagar, ¿no tienes dinero?	**The time comes** to pay the bill, and you don't have money?
a la sombra de	Ese chico creció **a la sombra de** su famoso padre.	That kid grew up **in the shadow of** his famous father.
a la vez	¿Haces todo **a la vez**?	Do you do everything **at the same time**?
a lo largo de	Fue un hombre ejemplar **a lo largo de** toda su vida.	He was an exemplary man **throughout** his whole life.
a lo mejor	**A lo mejor** va a llover hoy.	**Maybe** it will rain today.
a mediados de	Su pedido llegará **a mediados de** mayo.	Your order will arrive **in mid**-May.
a menudo	Estudiamos en la biblioteca **a menudo**.	We study at the library **often**.
a modo de	Leeré un corto texto **a modo de** introducción.	I will read a short text **by way of** introduction.
a partir de	**A partir del** lunes habrá conciertos mensuales.	**Starting** Monday, there will be monthly concerts.
a pesar de	Compraremos la casa **a pesar del** precio.	We will buy the house **in spite of** the price.
a pie	Los estudiantes van a la universidad **a pie**.	Students go to the university **on foot**.
a principios de	El pago se enviará **a principios de** mes.	The payment will be sent **at the beginning of** the month.
a prueba de	Nuestros productos son **a prueba de** golpes.	Our products are shock**proof**.
a raíz de	**A raíz de** la crisis, los precios han subido.	**As a result of** the crisis, prices have risen.

◀ en pie = *standing*

Al menos = por lo menos ▶

De modo que: use of ▶
subjunctive: 16.C.5c

De repente = de pronto ▶

a razón de	Los precios han subido **a razón del** dos por ciento anual.	*Prices have risen **at a rate of** two percent annually.*
a tiempo	Finalmente, todo se hizo **a tiempo**.	*Finally, everything was done **on time**.*
a veces	**A veces** salimos temprano del trabajo.	***Sometimes** we leave work early.*
al menos	¿Me prestas dinero? ¿**Al menos** cinco dólares?	*Can you lend me some money? **At least** five dollars?*
con base en	El informe se realizó **con base en** datos confiables.	*The report was carried out **based on** reliable data.*
con miras a	Los presidentes se reunirán hoy **con miras a** firmar un acuerdo.	*The presidents will meet today **with the purpose of** signing an agreement.*
con motivo de	La cena es **con motivo de** tu visita.	***The reason for** this dinner is your visit.*
con respecto a	No sé nada **con respecto a** este problema.	*I don't know anything **regarding** this problem.*
de acuerdo con	Estoy **de acuerdo con** tu opinión. **De acuerdo con** el profesor, el examen será pronto.	*I **agree with** your opinion. **According to** the teacher, the exam will be soon.*
de lo contrario	Tengo que anotar tu teléfono, **de lo contrario**, lo olvidaré.	*I have to write down your phone number, **if not**, I will forget it.*
de tal modo que, de modo que	Trabajamos mucho **de tal modo que** todo fue un éxito. Trabaja, **de modo que** tengas éxito.	*We worked **in such a way that** everything was a success. Work hard, **so that** you can succeed.*
de nuevo	¡Qué gusto verte **de nuevo**!	*So good to see you **again**!*
de pie	Debes ponerte/estar **de pie** cuando tocan el himno nacional.	*You should **stand up / be standing** when they play the national anthem.*
de regreso a	¿Cuándo estará usted **de regreso a** su trabajo?	*When will you **be back at** work?*
de repente	Hacía sol y **de repente**, empezó a llover.	*It was sunny and **suddenly**, it started to rain.*
de veras	¡**De veras** sabes mucho sobre cine!	*You **really** know a lot about movies!*
de vez en cuando	Vamos al cine **de vez en cuando**.	*We go to the movies **once in a while**.*
en cuanto a	**En cuanto a** películas, me gustan las comedias.	***Regarding** movies, I like comedies.*
en vez de, en lugar de, en cambio de	¿Prefiere usted café **en lugar / cambio / vez de** té?	*Do you prefer coffee **instead of** tea?*
en cambio	La lechuga me gusta, **en cambio** las verduras no.	*I like lettuce; **on the other hand**, I don't like vegetables.*
enseguida	¡Ven **enseguida**!	*Come here **immediately**!*
en torno a	La clase será **en torno a** la literatura moderna.	*The class will be **about** modern literature.*
frente a frente, cara a cara	Los equipos se encontrarán pronto **frente a frente / cara a cara**.	*The teams will soon meet **face to face**.*
para siempre	El petróleo no durará **para siempre**.	*Oil won't last **forever**.*
por eso	Quiero cuidar el ambiente, **por eso** ¡reciclo!	*I want to take care of the environment, **that's why** I recycle!*
por fin	¡**Por fin** acaba de llegar el autobús!	*The bus has **finally** arrived!*
por lo general	**Por lo general**, en España la cena es tarde.	***In general**, dinner in Spain is late.*
por lo menos	Hace mucho frío, pero **por lo menos** hace sol.	*It's cold, but **at least** it's sunny.*
por otra parte, por otro lado	Mi auto es bueno y, **por otra parte / por otro lado**, no es caro.	*My car is nice and **besides**, it's not expensive.*

por poco	¡**Por poco** olvido tu cumpleaños!	I **almost** forgot your birthday!
por supuesto	Este es nuestro mejor precio, **por supuesto**.	This is our best price, **of course**!
sin embargo	Esta novela no es popular y, **sin embargo**, es excelente.	This novel is not very popular. **However**, it's excellent!

◀ **Por poco** is generally used with the present indicative.

◀ **Sin embargo**: 16.B.5

12.B Use of prepositions

Uso de las preposiciones

12.B.1 Overview

a. After a preposition, the pronouns for the first- and second-person singular (**yo**, **tú**) change to **mí**, **ti**, except after the prepositions **entre**, **según**, **excepto**, and **salvo**. After these prepositions, subject pronoun forms are always used: **yo**, **tú**. The pronoun **vos** does not change form after a preposition: **para vos** (*for you*), **con vos** (*with you*).

◀ **Vos:** 13.B.2, 13.B.5
Pronouns after prepositions: 13.C

Ven, siéntate cerca de **mí**.   *Come and sit down close to me.*

Los libros son para **ti**.   *The books are for you.*

Esto queda entre **tú** y **yo**.   *This stays between you and me.*

b. After the preposition **con**, the first-person singular pronoun **mí** changes to **conmigo** and the second-person singular pronoun **ti** changes to **contigo**. These pronouns are invariable.

—¿Quieres ir al cine **conmigo**?   *Do you want to go to the movies with me?*

—Sí, quiero ir al cine **contigo**.   *Yes, I want to go to the movies with you.*

c. The reflexive pronoun **sí** takes the invariable form **consigo** after **con**. **Mismo/misma** can be added for emphasis if the action refers back to the subject.

◀ **Sí:** 13.C.2, 27.A.2
◀ **Mismo:** emphasis: 7.E.5, reflexive: 27.A.2, 27.D.1d

¿Lleva usted su licencia de conducir **consigo**?   *Do you carry your driving license with you?*

Pensé que Lisa hablaba **consigo misma**, pero ¡estaba conversando por su celular!   *I thought that Lisa was talking to herself, but she was talking on her cell phone!*

12.B.2 The preposition *a*

a. The preposition **a** is used in the following cases:

Clues for use	Examples	
Time	La cita es **a las tres**.	*The appointment is at three.*
Time that has passed before something happens/happened	Me **gradúo a** los dos años.	*I'll graduate after two years.*
	Me **gradué a** los dos años.	*I graduated after two years.*
Direction with verbs of motion	**Llegamos a** casa.	*We arrived home.*
	Bajamos al primer piso.	*We went down to the first floor.*
	Vamos a la reunión.	*We are going to the meeting.*
Distance from a location	El correo está **a dos calles** de la iglesia.	*The post office is (located) two streets/blocks from the church.*
al + *infinitive*	**Al contar** el dinero, faltaba un dólar.	*When I counted the money, one dollar was missing.*
	Pagué **al recibir** el paquete.	*I paid upon receiving the package.*

◀ Other verb periphrases with the infinitive: 26.C

b. When the preposition **a** is followed by the article **el**, the two words combine to form the contraction **al**.

Voy **al** mercado.   *I'm going to the market.*
Le di la información **al** profesor.   *I gave the information to the professor.*

c. One of the most important uses of the preposition **a** is to mark the indirect object of the sentence and to indicate that the direct object is a person. This use is called *the personal* **a**.

The preposition **a** with a direct object: 13.E.2 and with an indirect object: 13.F.1

The preposition **a** with indefinite pronouns and quantifiers: 7.D.2c, 7.E.3

Clues for use	Examples	
Precedes the direct object when it is a person (or it is personified).	Conozco **a** mis vecinos.	*I know my neighbors.*
	Quiero mucho **a** mi mascota.	*I love my pet very much.*
Must be used before indefinite pronouns when they refer to people: **nadie**, **alguno**, **todos**, etc.	Admiro **a todos** mis profesores.	*I admire all my teachers.*
	Conozco **a algunos** de mis profesores personalmente.	*I have met some of my teachers personally.*
It is omitted when the direct object does not have a determiner.	Necesitamos ingenieros especializados.	*We need specialized engineers.*
It is omitted after **tener** as long as no indefinite pronouns follow it.	Tenemos muchos amigos. No tenemos **a nadie** para ese trabajo.	*We have many friends.* *We don't have anyone for that job.*
The personal **a** must be used before the indirect object.	Le doy un regalo **a Luis**. Les escribo a **mis amigos**. ¡Agrégale más memoria **a tu PC**!	*I give Luis a gift.* *I write to my friends.* *Add more memory to your PC!*

12.B.3 **The preposition** *con*

Con is used in the following ways:

Estar con: 30.C.4

Clues for use	Examples	
To mean *with/together with*	Pablo está **con** sus amigos.	*Pablo is with his friends.*
Use of tools	Escribo **con** el lápiz.	*I'm writing with the pen.*
With nouns in adverbial phrases of manner	Viajo **con** frecuencia.	*I travel often.*
	Te ayudo **con** gusto.	*I'm happy to help you.*
Condition	**Con** precios tan altos, no puedo comprar nada.	*With such high prices, I can't buy anything.*

12.B.4 **The preposition** *de*

a. De has many uses in Spanish. The most important are shown in the table.

Use of **ser**: 30.B.3

Clues for use	Examples	
Ownership	los zapatos **de** Rita	*Rita's shoes*
	el club **de** los estudiantes	*the students' club*
Nationality	Sois **de** México.	*You [pl.] are from Mexico.*
Direction from a location or origin	El avión llega **de** Vancouver.	*The plane arrives from Vancouver.*
	Salí **de** casa temprano.	*I left home early.*
To express belonging	los estudiantes **de** Washington	*the students from Washington*
	las ventanas **de** la casa	*the windows of the house*
Placed before an infinitive to express purpose	la escoba **de** barrer	*the broom for sweeping*
	la mesa **de** planchar	*the ironing board*
To refer to the material of which an object is made	la caja **de** plástico	*the plastic box*
	la cuchara **de** plata	*the silver spoon*

Clues for use	Examples	
Properties	los estudiantes **de** español	the students of Spanish
	el libro **de** química	the chemistry book
Physical appearance	la persona **de** gafas	the person wearing glasses
	el niño **de** pantalón corto	the child wearing shorts
	la casa **de** ventanas verdes	the house with green windows
estar de + *new or temporal occupation*	**estar de** profesora/enfermero/ayudante	to be a teacher/a nurse/an assistant (for now, currently)
estar de + *noun*: describes conditions	estar **de** mal humor	to be in a bad mood
	estar **de** viaje/vacaciones	to be traveling/on holiday
	estar **de** regreso	to be back
	estar **de** buenas/malas	to be lucky/unlucky
	estar **de** visita	to be visiting
	estar **de** amigos	to be friends

◀ Use of **estar de** to express a temporary profession, work: 30.C.3

b. When the preposition **de** is followed by the article **el**, the two words form the contraction **del**.

El libro **del** que te hablé cuesta 20 dólares.   *The book I talked to you about costs 20 dollars.*

12.B.5 The preposition *en*

En is used to express the following relationships:

Clues for use	Example	
Specifies the location where someone/something is located	Estamos **en** Portugal. Elisa vive **en** la ciudad. El papel está **en** el cajón. Marta está **en** el dormitorio. El país está **en** Europa.	*We're in Portugal.* *Elisa lives in the city.* *The paper is in the drawer.* *Marta is in the bedroom.* *The country is in Europe.*
To mean *on, on top*	La cena está **en** la mesa.	*The dinner is on the table.*
With ordinals and the infinitive in expressions like *the first who...*	Rosa siempre es la primera **en** llegar. Ernesto es el último **en** pagar.	*Rosa is always the first to arrive.* *Ernesto is the last one to pay.*
With months, years, and other time expressions (*not used with days*)	**En** junio hay vacaciones. Lisa llamó **en** ese instante. Estaba feliz **en** esa época.	*There is vacation in June.* *Lisa called just then.* *I was happy during that time.*
Expressions with **estar** + **en**	estar **en** silencio	*to be silent*
	estar **en** la pobreza	*to be poor*
	estar **en** la ignorancia	*to be ignorant*
	estar **en** la cúspide	*to be at the height of fame/wealth/etc.*
	estar **en** la oscuridad	*to be in the dark*

◀ **Estar en** + place: 30.D.1

◀ Llegué **el lunes**.

12.B.6 The prepositions *para* and *por*

Both **para** and **por** mean *to* or *for* but are often used differently in English and Spanish.

Para		
Clues for use	**Examples**	
With a person: refers to the recipient of something	Llegó una carta **para** ti.	*A letter arrived for you.*
	Hay comida **para** todos.	*There's food for everyone.*
With verbs of motion: provides destination	Hoy salimos **para** Chile.	*We're leaving for Chile today.*
	¿Vas **para** la clase?	*Are you going to the class?*
	Ven **para** acá.	*Come here.*
With activity verbs: provides purpose	Trabajo **para** vivir.	*I work to live.*
	Estudiamos **para** aprender.	*We study to learn.*
	Las discotecas son **para** divertirse.	*Nightclubs are for having fun.*
With expressions of time: provides a deadline or a closing date	El documento es **para** el lunes.	*The document is for Monday.*
	Termino el trabajo **para** las tres.	*I'll finish the job by three o'clock.*
With verbs connected to work/tasks: refers to the employer or a client	Trabajo **para** el gobierno. Escribo **para** la televisión.	*I work for the government. I write for TV.*
To express *for being so,* using the formula **para ser tan** + *adjective/ adverb*	**Para** ser tan joven, es muy maduro.	*For a young guy, he's very mature.*
With *tool* + **ser** + **para**: provides area of use	El lápiz es **para** escribir, no **para** jugar.	*Pencils are for writing, not for playing.*
With **estar para** + *infinitive* to express an impending event	Ya estoy **para** salir.	*I'm ready to leave. / I'm about to leave.*

Use of **ser** + **para**: 30.B.4 ▶

See **estar por** in chart below. ▶

Por		
Clues for use	**Examples**	
Refers to cause or justification	Cancelaron el carnaval **por** la lluvia.	*They canceled the carnival because of the rain.*
Describes movements through or around an area	Salimos **por** la puerta principal. Paseáis **por** el parque. Mañana paso **por** tu casa.	*We left through the main door. You stroll through the park. I'll stop by your house tomorrow.*
Provides a time frame	Estaré en Madrid **por** unos días.	*I'll be in Madrid for a few days.*
With communication and transmission: television, telephone, mail, Internet, fax, radio	Envíame el paquete **por** correo. Transmiten los partidos de fútbol **por** radio y televisión. Mi profesor enseña **por** la red. Hablas mucho **por** teléfono.	*Send me the package by mail. They broadcast the soccer games on the radio and TV. My teacher teaches lessons online. You talk a lot on the telephone.*
Describes an exchange	Cambié mi auto viejo **por** uno nuevo. Compramos la bicicleta **por** muy poco dinero.	*I changed my old car for a new one. We bought the bicycle for very little money.*
With **estar** + **por** to express the possibility of doing something in the very near future	**Estoy por** ponerme a estudiar un rato. Ella dice que **está por salir** en cualquier momento.	*I think I'm going to study for a bit. She says she's going to leave at any moment.*

See **estar para** in chart above. ▶

Shows that someone is acting on behalf of someone else	¿Puedes asistir a la reunión **por** mí?	*Can you attend the meeting instead of/for me?*
With percentages	3%: tres **por** ciento	*three percent*
With verbs of motion in the sense of *collecting, getting*	Vamos **por** los niños a las tres. ¿Vas **por** el periódico?	*We'll pick up the children at three o'clock.* *Are you going to go get the newspaper?*
Refers to tasks which are still to be done (with **quedar**, **hay**, **tener**)	Quedan/Hay/Tengo varias cuentas **por** pagar.	*There are/I have several bills left to pay.*

12.B.7 Expressing location, direction, and time with prepositions

The following prepositions convey physical or figurative movement from one point to another, as well as periods of time.

◀ Prepositions used with adverbs of place and direction: 10.E.3

a. The preposition pair **desde-hasta** indicates a precise origin and arrival point, while **de-a** conveys a less concrete *from–to* direction. The preposition **por** conveys a *through* movement, while **hacia** and **para** refer to a *forward* destination without any reference to origin.

¿**Para** dónde vas?	***Where** are you going?*
Voy **de** la biblioteca **al** gimnasio y **desde** allí tomo el autobús **hasta** el teatro.	*I am going **from** the library **to** the gym and **from** there, I take the bus **to** the theater.*
El autobús pasa **por** el centro de la ciudad y sigue **hacia** las afueras.	*The bus passes **through** downtown and continues **toward** the suburbs.*

b. The prepositions above can also refer to *time*. **Desde-hasta** conveys a limit, while **de-a** only describes a direction in time. **Hacia** is used for approximate time, and **por** forms specific time expressions: **por la mañana, por la noche, por la tarde.** The preposition **durante** refers to a progressive period of time, while **a** tells the exact time. **En** is used with months and years (not days of the week) and to express how much time is left for something to be completed: **en un mes** (*within/in a month*), **en tres días** (*within/in three days*).

—¿**Para** cuándo terminarás el proyecto?	*(**For**) when will you finish the project?*
—Lo tendré listo **en** tres días. Hoy martes trabajaré **de** tres **a** cuatro de la tarde y después **desde** mañana **hasta** el viernes. Es decir, trabajaré **durante** tres días.	*I will have it ready **within** three days. Today, Tuesday, I will work **from** three **to** four in the afternoon, and then **from** tomorrow **until** Friday. In other words, I will work **during** three days.*
Terminaré el trabajo **hacia** fines de esta semana.	*I will finish the work **toward** the end of this week.*
¡El viernes **por** la tarde, **a** las tres en punto!	*Friday **in** the afternoon **at** three o'clock!*

c. The preposition pair **ante-tras** describes opposite horizontal locations (*in front of–back of*) and **sobre-bajo** express them vertically (*above–under*), with or without physical contact. **Entre** describes a neutral location *in between* any of these points, also with or without physical contact.

Ante el juez está la acusada y **tras** ella, su familia.	*The accused is **before** the judge and **behind** her, her family.*
Sobre la mesa están las pruebas y **bajo** estas, los documentos del juez.	***On** the table are the exhibits and **under** them, the judge's documents.*
Los guardias están de pie **entre** el juez y la acusada.	*The guards are standing **between** the judge and the accused.*

Compound prepositions: 12.A.2
Adverbs of place and direction:
10.E.3

d. In modern Spanish, the prepositions **ante**, **tras**, and **bajo** are mostly used in idioms, and in formal and figurative language. **Delante de**, **detrás de**, and **debajo de** may replace them if they refer to a *physical* place.

La chica no se rinde **ante** los desafíos.	*The girl doesn't give up when **facing** a challenge.*
Tras la crisis, han aumentado los problemas.	***After** the crisis, the problems have grown.*
Bajo ningún concepto llegues tarde.	*Don't be late **for** any reason at all.*

encima: adverbs of place:
10.E.3

e. Sobre is a synonym of **encima de** only when its reference is a physical place. It can be replaced by **en** only if there is *physical contact* with a horizontal surface. **Contra** implies physical contact *against* a surface (usually vertical) or figuratively, *against* someone or something (a direction, a location, a person, etc.).

La taza de café está **sobre / encima de / en** la mesa.	*The cup of coffee is **on** the table.*
La mesa está **contra** la pared.	*The table is **against** the wall.*
Protégete **contra** el sol.	*Protect yourself **against** the sun.*

f. In addition to location, the preposition **sobre** is often used figuratively. It expresses *about* and *above* or *beyond* a limit (distance, time, quantity, importance, etc.).

El folleto es **sobre** los precios de Internet.	*The brochure is **about** Internet prices.*
Me importas tú **sobre** todas las cosas.	*You matter to me **above** everything else.*

g. The preposition pair **con-sin** (*with–without*) is situational and does not refer to location. **Excepto** and **salvo** (*except*) are synonyms. **Salvo** is formal and used in writing and fixed phrases.

Con mi nuevo teléfono, siempre estoy en la red.	***With** my new phone, I am always online.*
El teléfono es bueno, **excepto** su cámara.	*The phone is good, **except** its camera.*

h. Mediante (*By means of, through*) is formal. Its more common synonyms in Spanish are **con la ayuda de**, **por medio de**, and **a través de**. The preposition **con** may replace it in specific contexts.

Los desacuerdos se resuelven **mediante/con** el diálogo.	*Disagreements are resolved **by means of/through** dialogue.*
Mediante/Con su colaboración, ayudaremos a muchos niños.	***With** your help, we will help many children.*

12.C Regional variations

Variaciones regionales

12.C.1 *A por*

In Spain, **a por** is used with verbs of motion and nouns (*verb* + **a por** + *noun*) to mean *in search of*. It is sometimes used to clarify meaning. For example, **Voy por agua** could mean *I'm going by water*. But **Voy a por agua** means *I'm going to get some water*.

Voy **a por** la escalera.	*I'm going to get the ladder.*
Pronto iremos **a por** Juan.	*We will pick up Juan soon.*

12.C.2 *Entrar en, entrar a*

The verb **entrar** is usually followed by **en** in Spain and **a** in Latin America.

Entro **en** la sala. (*Spain*)	*I'm going into the living room.*
Entro **a la** sala. (*Latin America*)	

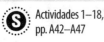

Práctica

Actividades 1–18,
pp. A42–A47

Personal pronouns
Pronombres personales

Chapter 13

A. Subject pronouns
B. Formal and informal address
C. Pronouns after prepositions
D. Direct and indirect objects
E. Direct object pronouns
F. Indirect object pronouns
G. Placement of direct and indirect object pronouns
H. Repetition of direct and indirect objects

13.A Subject pronouns

Pronombres personales sujeto

Pronouns are words that replace nouns, such as *I, you, me, it, him/her, them*. A pronoun has different forms depending on how it is used in a sentence. The subject form is used when a pronoun is the subject of a sentence.

There are two important regional differences for the subject forms of personal pronouns. In Spain, there are two pronouns for the second-person plural: a formal pronoun, **ustedes**, and an informal one, **vosotros/as**. In Latin America, **ustedes** is used both formally and informally. The other difference is the use of **vos** instead of **tú** for the informal second-person singular pronoun in many areas of Latin America.

Map of Spain and Equatorial Guinea: p. xxi
Map of South America: p. xxii
Map of Mexico, Central America and the Caribbean: p. xxiii
Map of **voseo** regions in Latin America: p. 277

Spain			
Singular		**Plural**	
yo	*I*	**nosotros, nosotras**	*we*
tú	*you*	**vosotros, vosotras**	*you*
usted	*you (formal)*	**ustedes**	*you (formal)*
él, ella	*he, she*	**ellos, ellas**	*they*
ello	*it*	(no plural)	

Latin America			
Singular		**Plural**	
yo	*I*	**nosotros, nosotras**	*we*
tú, vos	*you*	**ustedes**	*you*
usted	*you (formal)*		
él, ella	*he, she*	**ellos, ellas**	*they*
ello	*it*	(no plural)	

Ello: 13.A.2b

13.A.1 Use of the pronoun

a. In Spanish, since the verb ending provides information about the subject, the subject pronoun is often omitted in both written and spoken language.

Verb forms: 17.A.2b

Habl**o**.   *I am talking.*   Habl**amos**.   *We are talking.*

b. Subject pronouns are used when the subject is unclear. For example, **él/ella/usted** take the same form and **ellos/ellas/ustedes** do as well, so the pronoun is often needed for clarification. Subject pronouns are also used when comparing and contrasting.

Yo soy profesora y **tú** eres dentista.	*I'm a teacher and you're a dentist.*
Ella es simpática; **él** no lo es.	*She's friendly, he's not.*
Nosotros somos profesores y **vosotros** sois médicos.	*We're teachers and you're [pl.] doctors.*
¿Pagan **ustedes** la cuenta o la pagan **ellos**?	*Are you [pl.] paying the bill or are they?*

c. **Usted** and **ustedes** are often abbreviated in written language as **Ud.** and **Uds.**, respectively.

¿Cómo está **Ud.**?	*How are you?*
Les deseamos a **Uds.** una cordial bienvenida.	*We wish you [pl.] a warm welcome.*

esto, eso, aquello: 8.A.4

a. In order to express a concept or talk about something in general, usually **esto** and **eso** are used.

Eso está bien.	*That is good.*
No comprendemos **esto**.	*We don't understand this.*

b. Ello does not have a plural or other forms. It is a synonym of **eso**.

No pienses en **ello**.	*Don't think about it.*
No pienses en **eso**.	

este/a, ese/a: 8.A.2

c. Este/a and **ese/a** can replace the subject.

—¿Es importante el Premio Nobel?	*Is the Nobel Prize important?*
—Sí, **ese** es importante.	*Yes, that one is important.*

d. Lo can replace a whole sentence or idea.

—¿Es importante el Premio Nobel?	*Is the Nobel Prize important?*
—Sí, **lo** es.	*Yes, it is.*

13.B Formal and informal address

Formas de tratamiento

In Spanish, we can choose between *formal* and *informal* address for one or several people, but the alternatives differ regionally. The differences can be explained through a historical context. When the Spanish language arrived in the Americas at the end of the 15th century, the informal forms of address for one person were **tú** and **vos**, while **Vuestra Merced** (*Your Grace*) was formal. To address several people, **vos** was also used informally and **Vuestras Mercedes** (*Your Graces*) was the respectful form. Later, in the 17th century, the change in pronunciation of **Vuestra(s) Merced(es)** had already generated the modern formal pronouns **usted** and **ustedes**. At the same time, **vosotros/as** had become the plural informal pronoun to avoid confusion with the singular **vos**, which was used less and less frequently in Spain. By the end of the 18th century, **vos** was no longer used in Spain or its political centers across the Atlantic—Mexico, Peru, and the Caribbean—, where **tú** became the preferred form of address for family and friends. The use of **vos** continued in the rest of the Hispanic world, either as the only informal pronoun (as in Argentina) or together with **tú** (as in Colombia). During the same time period, the use of **vosotros/as** became frequent in parts of Spain, but it never took root in the Hispanic regions of Latin America, the Canary Islands, or parts of Andalusia. Today's forms of address in the Hispanic countries reflect this history.

Vuestra merced became **vuesarced**, then **vusted**, and finally, **usted**.

Subject pronoun chart: 13.A

13.B.1 Tú - usted

The use of **tú** for the informal second-person singular is called **tuteo**. In regions that use the **tuteo**, **usted** is the formal address for the second-person singular. In these regions, **tú** is used with close friends and family, while **usted** is used with strangers or those to whom one wishes to show respect. This applies to Spain, Mexico, (except Chiapas), the Caribbean (Puerto Rico, Dominican Republic, most of Cuba, Panama, and the Caribbean coast of Colombia and Venezuela), and many Spanish-speakers in the United States.

Map of Spanish-speakers in the U.S.: p. xxiv

13.B.2 Vos - usted

The use of **vos** for the second-person singular, called **voseo**, occurs in many Latin American countries.

a. There are pure **voseo** regions as well as regions where both **tú** and **vos** are used. Argentina, Uruguay, Paraguay, and parts of Central America, Colombia, and Venezuela are pure **voseo** regions.

b. Regions with both **voseo** and **tuteo** are: Bolivia, Chile, Peru, Ecuador, parts of Colombia and Venezuela, and Chiapas (Mexico). In these regions, **usted** is the formal address for the second-person singular. However, the roles of **tú**, **vos**, and **usted** vary. **Usted** might be used to address children or acquaintances (Central America and parts of Colombia), or **vos** might be used with close friends and family, while **tú** is used with other groups. In Argentina and Uruguay, where only **voseo** is used in informal address, **usted** is used in formal address.

c. The publication of the *Nueva gramática* by the Real Academia Española in 2010 treats **voseo** as an integral part of the Spanish language. The increasing use of informal written language on the Internet, in chat rooms, and in social media has helped to make **voseo** more visible as a characteristic of informal communication in many regions of Latin America. In Argentina, Uruguay, Paraguay, Central America, and the **voseo** regions of Colombia, Venezuela, and Ecuador, the pronoun **vos** is used with its own verb forms, some of which are presented in the verb tables in this book. In Chile, the pronoun **vos** itself is not common and its verb forms are slightly different from those mentioned in the verb tables: **¿Cómo estái?**

◀ Map of **voseo** regions in Latin America: p. 277

◀ Voseo. Present indicative, 17.D

d. In all **voseo** regions, **vos** adopted the direct and indirect object pronouns of **tú** (**Te digo a vos.** *I tell you.*) as well as its possessive and reflexive pronouns (**Vos te sentás en tu silla.** *You sit in your chair.*).

13.B.3 Vosotros/as - ustedes

a. In Spain, there are two plural address forms: the informal **vosotros/as** (for family and friends), and the formal **ustedes** (for strangers and those to whom you wish to show respect).

b. In Latin America, **ustedes**, used with the corresponding **ustedes** verb forms, is the only plural form of address. It is used in both formal and informal contexts. **Vosotros/as** is not used in Latin America except to a very limited degree in specific formal contexts, such as political speeches and religious sermons.

13.B.4 Nosotros/as, vosotros/as, ellos/as

For groups consisting of only women, the feminine forms **nosotras**, **vosotras**, and **ellas** are used. For groups consisting of only men, or both women and men, the masculine form is used.

13.B.5 Tú, vos, usted

Age, gender, and social status play an important role in the choice of address, and it is important to be aware of local variations, especially in formal contexts. Throughout the Spanish-speaking world, **usted(es)** can be used with strangers, even in **voseo** areas. Those who do not use **vos** in their variant of Spanish can use **tú** with friends and acquaintances in **voseo** areas, but it is an advantage to master the **vos** forms for use in pure **voseo** areas.

13.C Pronouns after prepositions

Pronombres preposicionales

13.C.1 Mí, ti, conmigo, contigo

a. The first- and second-person singular pronouns (**yo** and **tú**) take a new form after a preposition: **mí** and **ti**, respectively. The other pronouns (including **vos**) do not change form after a preposition. After the preposition **con**, **mí** and **ti** change to **conmigo** and **contigo**.

conmigo/contigo:
12.B.1b, 27.A.2

Subject pronoun	Pronouns after prepositions			
	After preposition		After preposition *con*	
yo	**mí**	*me*	**conmigo**	*with me*
tú	**ti**	*you*	**contigo**	*with you*

Pronouns after
prepositions: 12.B.1

—**¿Para** quién es el libro? *Who is the book for?*
—Es **para mí**. *It's for me.*

—¿Queréis trabajar **para** nosotros? *Do you [pl.] want to work for us?*
—Sí, queremos trabajar **para** vosotros. *Yes, we want to work for you [pl.].*

—¿Vas al cine **con** tus amigos? *Are you going to the movies with your friends?*
—No, hoy voy **sin** ellos. *No, today I'm going without them.*

—¿Está Isabel **contigo**? *Is Isabel with you?*
—Sí, Isabel está **conmigo**. *Yes, Isabel is with me.*

conmigo/contigo/consigo:
12.B.1b–c, 27.A.2

13.C.2 Sí, consigo

The *reflexive pronoun* **se** changes to **sí** after a preposition, except after the preposition **con**.

Subject pronoun	Reflexive pronoun		Pronoun after prepositions		
			After preposition	After preposition *con*	
él, ella, usted	**se**	*self*	**sí**	**consigo**	*with himself, herself, yourself*
ellos, ellas, ustedes					*with themselves*

13.C.3 With the prepositions *entre, según*

The subject pronouns **yo** and **tú** are used after the prepositions **entre, según, excepto,** and **salvo**.

Entre **tú** y **yo** hay amor. *There is love between you and me.*
Según **tú**, tengo un problema. *According to you, I have a problem.*

13.D Direct and indirect objects

Complementos de objeto directo e indirecto

Sentences consist of a subject and a predicate. The verb is part of the predicate, which says something about what the subject does. In the sentence *I am sleeping,* the verb gives enough information to make the sentence meaningful. In the sentence *I'm giving,* however, more information is needed about the action. An *object* complements the information provided by the verb. In the sentence *I'm giving,* a direct object provides information about *what* is given (for example, *a book*) and an indirect object provides information about *to whom* it is given (for example, *my sister*): *I'm giving* **a book** *to* **my sister**. Direct and indirect objects can be replaced by object pronouns: *I'm giving* **it** *to* **her**.

Transitive and
intransitive verbs: 17.B.1

13.E Direct object pronouns

Pronombres de objeto directo

13.E.1 The direct object

The direct object tells *what* or *who* is directly influenced by the action in the sentence.

Leo **el libro**.	*I am reading the book.*
¿Compraste nuevos **zapatos**?	*Did you buy new shoes?*

13.E.2 The preposition *a* before a person

When the direct object is a person, it must be preceded by the preposition **a**. This also applies to indefinite, possessive, and interrogative pronouns.

The personal **a**: 12.B.2c
Use of the preposition **a** when indefinite pronouns and other determiners are direct objects: 7.D.2c and 7.E.3

Conozco **a Griselda**.	*I know Griselda.*
Esperamos **al Sr. Luis Romero**.	*We are waiting for Mr. Luis Romero.*
Visito **a mis papás**.	*I am visiting my parents.*
¿A **quién** vas a visitar en Nueva York?	*Who are you going to visit in New York?*
Visitaré **a algunos** amigos míos.	*I will visit some friends of mine.*
No espero **a nadie**.	*I am not waiting for anyone.*

13.E.3 Direct object pronouns

a. A direct object can be replaced by a direct object pronoun.

Direct object pronouns		
yo	**me**	*me*
tú, vos	**te**	*you*
usted	**la, lo/le***	*you*
él	**lo/le***	*him*
ella	**la**	*her*
nosotros/as	**nos**	*us*
vosotros/as	**os**	*you*
ustedes	**las, los/les***	*you*
ellos	**los/les***	*them*
ellas	**las**	*them (female)*

*The use of **le/les** as third-person direct object pronouns is called **leísmo**:13.E.4

Me visitan mis amigos.	*My friends are visiting me.*
Te llaman.	*They are calling you.*
Lo espero.	*I am waiting for him/you.*
Las espero.	*I am waiting for you/them.*
Nos invitan.	*They are inviting us.*
Os invito.	*I am inviting you [pl.].*

b. When a preposition is placed before an object pronoun, the pronoun for the first- and second-person singular takes a new form: **mí** and **ti**.

Pronouns after prepositions: 13.C

Nos llaman **a ti** y **a mí**.	*They're calling **you** and **me**.*

13.E.4 *Le/les* **instead of** *lo/los* **as direct object pronouns** - *leísmo*

In Spain, **le/les** is often used as the direct object pronoun for males instead of **lo/los**. In Latin America, **le/les** can occur as the direct object pronoun in some regions, especially with **usted** in sentences that are gender neutral. The use of **le/les** in this case is called **leísmo**.

Conozco **a Juan**.	*I know **Juan**.*
Le conozco. (Spain)	*I know **him**.*
Lo conozco. (Latin America)	

13.F | Indirect object pronouns

Pronombres de objeto indirecto

13.F.1 **The indirect object**

An indirect object is a noun or pronoun that answers the question *to whom* or *for whom* an action is done. Indirect objects can be replaced with the preposition **a** followed by a subject pronoun. The indirect object pronoun is typically used in sentences even when the indirect object also appears.

Le hicimos un favor **a Eric**.	*We did a favor **for Eric**.*
Le hicimos un favor **a él**.	*We did a favor **for him**.*
Le envié una carta **a Eva**.	*I sent a letter **to Eva**.*
Le envié una carta **a ella**.	*I sent a letter **to her**.*

13.F.2 **Indirect object pronouns**

The indirect object can be replaced by an indirect object pronoun.

Indirect object pronouns		
yo	**me**	*me*
tú, vos	**te**	*you*
usted, él, ella	**le (se)**	*you, him, her*
nosotros/as	**nos**	*us*
vosotros/as	**os**	*you*
ustedes, ellos, ellas	**les (se)**	*you, them*

¿**Te** dio Pedro la noticia?	*Did Pedro give you the news?*
La universidad **os** dio las notas.	*The university gave you [pl.] the grades.*
¿**Le** pago la cuenta?	*Shall I pay the bill for him/her/you?*
¿**Me** dices la verdad?	*Are you telling me the truth?*

13.F.3 **Verbs like** *gustar*

a. Many Spanish verbs are conjugated using the indirect object pronouns in a similar way as the English expression *It pleases me*. In this sentence, the *grammatical* subject is *it* and the *logical* subject, *I*, is expressed with its object pronoun: *me*. The corresponding Spanish sentence is **Eso me gusta**. In this sentence, **eso** is the grammatical subject, while the logical subject, **yo**, is expressed with the indirect object pronoun: **me**. In the sentence *I like it.*, the grammatical subject is *I* and the object is *it*.

The subject of each sentence is in *italics* in the following examples. Note that **gustar** is conjugated in the third-person singular, **gusta**, when the subject is a verb or a singular noun and in the plural, **gustan**, when the subject is a plural noun.

Nos gusta mucho *caminar*.	*We really like to walk.*
¿**Os molesta** *el tráfico*?	*Does traffic bother you [pl.]?*
¡**Le encantan** *los paseos*!	*He/She loves excursions!*

b. The indirect object can be spelled out with **a** + *pronoun / proper noun* for emphasis or clarity, especially in the third person since the indirect object pronoun (**le/les**) is sometimes ambiguous.

A Ramiro le aburre *el teatro*.	*Ramiro finds theater boring.*
A todos nos gustan *las buenas noticias*.	*We all like good news.*
¿Les interesa *la música* **a ustedes**?	*Are you [pl.] interested in music?*

13.G Placement of direct and indirect object pronouns

Posición de los pronombres de objeto directo e indirecto

13.G.1 Before finite verbs

Direct and indirect object pronouns are placed before a finite verb, or a verb that can stand alone as the main verb in a sentence.

Placement of pronouns with non-finite verbal forms: 25.B.4, 25.C.8
Finite and non-finite verbal forms: 17.A.2, 25.A

Direct object pronouns	
Nos visitas.	*You're visiting **us**.*

Indirect object pronouns	
Os damos un regalo.	*We're giving **you** [pl.] a present.*

13.G.2 Finite verbs plus an infinitive or a *gerundio*

a. In verbal expressions with a finite verb plus an infinitive or a **gerundio**, direct and indirect object pronouns can be placed either before the finite verb or attached to the infinitive/**gerundio**.

Verb periphrases with infinitives: 26.B-C
Verb periphrases with the **gerundio**: 26.D

Direct object pronouns	
Te voy a invitar.	*I'm going to invite you.*
Voy a invitar**te**.	
Nos estáis esperando.	*You're waiting for us.*
Estáis esperándo**nos**.	

Indirect object pronouns	
Os voy a dar una gran noticia.	*I'm going to give you [pl.] some big news.*
Voy a dar**os** una gran noticia.	
Luisa **nos** está preparando la cena.	*Luisa is preparing dinner for us.*
Luisa está preparándo**nos** la cena.	

b. When an object pronoun is added to the end of a word, a written accent is added, if necessary, to indicate the stressed syllable.

Accents: 1.E.3

es-pe-**ran**-do	*The word ends in a vowel and the stress falls on the penultimate syllable (**llana**). The word is regular and does not need an accent.*
es-pe-**rán**-do-nos	*The stressed syllable is now the third to last (**esdrújula**) and needs a written accent.*

Impersonal expressions
with **ser**: 23.C.8

13.G.3 Impersonal expressions with *ser*

In impersonal expressions with **ser** that are followed by an adjective and the infinitive, the direct and indirect object pronouns are always placed after the infinitive.

Direct object pronouns	
—¿Es bueno estudiar **la lección**?	*Is it good to study **the lesson**?*
—Claro, es bueno estudiar**la**.	*Of course it's good to study **it**.*

Indirect object pronouns	
—¿Es necesario dar**te** instrucciones?	*Is it necessary to give **you** instructions?*
—No, no es necesario dar**me** instrucciones.	*No, it's not necessary to give **me** instructions.*

13.G.4 Compound verb forms with *haber*

Direct and indirect object pronouns must always be placed before the personal forms of **haber** in compound tenses with a past participle.

In all compound forms with
haber, object pronouns
and reflexive pronouns are
placed before **haber**. They
can never be added to the
participle or come after the
participle form.

Direct object pronouns	
—¿Dónde está Lisa?	*Where is Lisa?*
—No **la** he visto.	*I haven't seen **her**.*

Indirect object pronouns	
—¿**Te** han dado el dinero?	*Have they given **you** the money?*
—No, no **me** han dado el dinero.	*No, they haven't given **me** the money.*

Placement of pronouns in
verb periphrases with:
Infinitives: 25.B.4,
Gerundio: 25.C.8
Object and reflexive
pronouns cannot stand
after participles: 19.A.1

13.G.5 Indirect and direct object pronouns in the same sentence

a. When both indirect and direct object pronouns occur together, the indirect object pronoun is always first.

—¿Quién **te** regaló **las flores**?	*Who gave you the flowers?*
—Mis amigos **me las** regalaron.	*My friends gave me them/them to me.*

b. Note that the order of the pronouns also applies when both are placed after the infinitive or the **gerundio**.

—¿Quién **te** va a dar **las flores**?	*Who is going to give you flowers?*
—Mis amigos **me las** van a dar.	*My friends are going to give me them / them to me.*
—Mis amigos van a dár**melas**.	

c. The indirect object pronouns **le/les** change to **se** when followed by the direct object pronouns **la(s)** and **lo(s)**.

—¿**Le** enviaste la carta a Pilar?	*Did you send the letter to Pilar?*
—Sí, **se la** envié.	*Yes, I sent it to her.*
—**Les** diste las galletas a los niños?	*Did you give the cookies to the children?*
—No, no **se las** di.	*No, I didn't give them to them.*

With imperatives

Object pronouns are placed *after* the verb in positive imperatives and *before* the verb in negative imperatives. The indirect object pronoun always precedes the direct object. See the following examples with the formal imperative (**usted**).

◀ Placement of pronouns in imperatives: 24.F

Positive	
¡De**me el libro**, por favor!	*Please give **me the book**!*
¡Dé**melo**, por favor!	*Please give **it to me**!*

Negative	
¡No **nos** mande **los paquetes** todavía, por favor!	*Don't send **the packages to us** yet, please!*
¡No **nos los** mande todavía, por favor!	*Don't send **them to us** yet, please!*

13.H Repetition of direct and indirect objects

Repetición del objeto directo e indirecto

13.H.1 Optional repetition of an object

a. Object pronouns with prepositions (**a mí, a ti, a él**, etc.) can be added after the verb to clarify or emphasize the object. This applies to both the direct and indirect objects and is particularly applicable to **él/ellos, ella(s)**, and **usted(es)**, which have the same indirect object pronouns (**le/les**).

Direct object pronouns	
La respeto.	*I respect **her/you**.*
La respeto **a usted**, Sra. Jones.	*I respect **you**, Mrs. Jones.*

Indirect object pronouns	
Les diré la verdad.	*I'll tell **them/you** [pl.] the truth.*
Les diré la verdad **a ustedes**.	*I'll tell **you** [pl.] the truth.*

b. An object pronoun with a preposition can also be used for all other persons for extra emphasis.

Direct object pronouns	
Me ven **a mí**.	*They see **me**.*
Te llaman **a ti**.	*They're calling **you**.*
Lo espero **a usted**, Sr. Pérez.	*I'm waiting for **you**, Mr. Pérez.*
Las espero **a ellas**.	*I'm waiting for **them**.*
Nos invitan **a nosotros**.	*They're inviting **us**.*
Os invito **a vosotros**.	*I'm inviting **you** [pl.].*

Indirect object pronouns	
¿**Te** dio Miguel la noticia **a ti**?	*Did Miguel tell **you** the news?*
Os envié las notas **a vosotros**.	*I sent the notes to **you** [pl.].*
Le pago la cuenta **a él / a ella / a usted**.	*I'll pay the bill for **him/her/you**.*
¿**Me** dices la verdad **a mí**?	*Are you telling **me** the truth?*
Les pido un favor **a ellos**.	*I'm asking **them** for a favor.*

13.H.2 Necessary repetition of objects

a. When direct or indirect objects in the form of proper nouns or pronouns precede a verb, a corresponding object pronoun is needed *after* the object and *before* the verb.

Direct objects	
A la abuela *la* quiero.	*I love grandma.*
A Juan *lo* visito.	*I am visiting Juan.*
A ti *te* respeto.	*I respect you.*

Indirect objects	
A los chicos *les* doy un regalo.	*I am giving the boys a present.*
A María *le* di mi teléfono.	*I gave María my telephone number.*
A vosotros *os* envío postales.	*I am sending you [pl.] postcards.*

In the examples above, the objects precede the verb: **a la abuela**, **a Juan**, **a ti** (direct objects), and **a los chicos**, **a María**, **a vosotros** (indirect objects). This placement before the verb requires a repetition of the direct or indirect object pronouns.

b. Doubling of object pronouns also applies to things and abstract concepts.

Direct objects	
Esto no **lo** entiendo.	*I don't understand this.*
Tus cartas las recibí ayer.	*I got your letters yesterday.*

Indirect objects	
A la pared le di una capa de pintura.	*I gave the wall a coat of paint.*
A mi cámara le compré más memoria.	*I bought more memory for my camera.*

13.H.3 Indirect objects that communicate personal involvement

In order to communicate that a situation affects someone directly, an indirect object pronoun can be added to the sentence. This object pronoun can be removed without changing the meaning of the sentence.

This use of the indirect object pronoun is common in Spanish and is called **dativo de interés**.

¡Cuída**me** bien la casa!　　　　　*Take good care of the house (for me)!*

13.H.4 *Todo/a(s)*

Object pronouns are usually repeated when the pronoun **todo/a(s)** is the direct or indirect object in the sentence.

Todo: 7.C.9

La policía **lo** sabe **todo**.　　　　　*The police know everything.*
Las invitaron **a todas**.　　　　　*They invited all the girls.*
Les enviamos invitaciones **a todos**.　　　*We sent invitations to everyone.*

13.H.5 Questions and answers

Personal **a**: 12.B.2c, 13.E.2

Note that the preposition **a** must be included when answering a question with an indirect object pronoun or a direct object pronoun that refers to a person.

—¿A quién llamó Viviana?　　　　　*Who did Viviana call?*
—¡**A mí**!　　　　　*Me!*

—¿A quiénes les das el regalo?　　　*Who are you giving the present to?*
—Claro, ¡**a vosotros**!　　　　　*To you [pl.], of course!*

Práctica

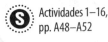 Actividades 1–16, pp. A48–A52

Questions and question words
Preguntas y palabras interrogativas

Chapter 14

A. Direct questions
B. Interrogatives
C. Exclamations with
   question words
D. Regional variations

14.A Direct questions

Preguntas directas

In Spanish, the following structures are used to ask a question that requires a *yes-or-no* answer.

14.A.1 Change of usual word order

The usual structure of a statement in Spanish is *subject + verb*.

Roberto es estudiante.	*Roberto is a student. (statement)*
Roberto está enfermo.	*Roberto is sick. (statement)*

In questions, the verb is usually placed before the subject. Although the intonation may vary, this word order implies a question.

¿**Es** estudiante **Roberto**?	*Is Roberto a student? (question)*
¿**Está Julia** en casa?	*Is Julia home? (question)*

◀ Emphatic constructions (change of the usual sentence structure): 15.B.8

14.A.2 Intonation

A question can also maintain the usual structure of a statement, *subject + verb*. In this case, the intonation indicates that it is a question.

¿**Pedro está** enfermo?	*Pedro is sick?*
¿**Julia está** en casa?	*Julia is home?*

14.A.3 Tag questions

When the usual statement structure is used, a tag question can be added to the end of the sentence, for example: ¿**no**?, ¿**verdad**?, ¿**no es cierto**?, ¿**no es verdad**?, ¿**no es así**?, ¿**ah**?, ¿**eh**?.

—Hace buen tiempo hoy, ¿**no**?	*It's nice weather today, isn't it?*
—Sí, hace muy buen tiempo.	*Yes, it's very nice weather.*
—Te llamas Alberto, ¿**no es cierto**?	*Your name is Alberto, isn't it?*
—No, me llamo Arturo.	*No, my name is Arturo.*
—Vienes mañana, ¿**verdad**?	*You're coming tomorrow, right?*
—Sí, vengo mañana.	*Yes, I'm coming tomorrow.*

14.B Interrogatives

Interrogativos

14.B.1 Structure

a. Questions that require more than a simple *yes-or-no* answer start with an interrogative word. All interrogatives carry an accent.

◀ Relative pronouns: Ch. 15
◀ Adverbs: Ch. 10

Interrogatives		
Qué	*what*	**¿Qué** vas a preparar hoy? *What are you going to prepare today?*
Cuál(es)	*which, what*	**¿Cuál** es tu mejor plato? *Which one is your best dish?*
		¿Cuáles son los ingredientes? *What are the ingredients?*
Quién(es)	*who*	**¿Quiénes** vienen a cenar? *Who is coming to dinner?*
	whom	¿Con **quién** fuiste a la fiesta? *With whom did you go to the party?*
	whose	**¿De quién** es la receta? *Whose recipe is it?*
Cuánto	*how much + verb*	**¿Cuánto** vale la cena? *How much does dinner cost?*
Cuánto/a	*how much + noun*	**¿Cuánta** azúcar quieres? *How much sugar do you want?*
Cuántos/as	*how many + noun*	**¿Cuántos** invitados hay? *How many guests are there?*
Cómo	*how many + noun*	**¿Cómo** está la comida? *How is the food?*
Dónde	*how + verb*	**¿Dónde** está el postre? *Where is the dessert?*
Cuándo	*where*	**¿Cuándo** se sirve la cena? *When is dinner served?*
Por qué	*why*	**¿Por qué** está fría la sopa? *Why is the soup cold?*

Indirect questions:
14.B.9, 31.B.6

b. Interrogatives may also be used with indirect questions.

Van a averiguar **quién** es el chef.　　　*They are going to find out who is the chef.*
Quisiera saber **cuándo** estará lista la cena.　　*I would like to know when dinner will be ready.*

14.B.2　*Qué*

a. Qué (*what, which*) does not change form and can be placed before nouns or verbs.

¿**Qué** plato prefieres?　　　　　*Which dish do you prefer?*
¿**Qué** quieres beber?　　　　　　*What do you want to drink?*
¿**Qué** le pasa a Ramiro?　　　　　*What's happening/wrong with Ramiro?*
¿**Qué** significa eso?　　　　　　*What does that mean?*
¿**Qué** opinas?　　　　　　　　　*What do you think?*

b. Qué is used with the verb **ser** to ask for definitions and explanations.

¿**Qué** es esto?　　　　　　　　*What is this?*
¿**Qué** son estas cosas?　　　　　*What are these things?*
¿**Qué** es *house* en español?　　　*What is* house *in Spanish?*

14.B.3 Cuál, cuáles

a. Cuál(es) is used in questions that require choosing something or someone from several concrete alternatives. The choices are usually preceded by a definite article or demonstrative.

◀ **Cuál(es)** may be followed by a noun, especially in Latin America: 14.D.a

¿**Cuáles** son **tus** amigos?	*Which (ones) are your friends?*
¿**Cuál** era **la** contraseña?	*What was the password?*
¿**Cuál** quieres, **la** sopa o **la** ensalada?	*Which one do you want, the soup or the salad?*
Este es tu postre, ¿**cuál** es **el** mío?	*This is your dessert, which (one) is mine?*

b. If the alternatives in a question are not preceded by a definite article or other determiner (possessive, demonstrative, etc.), the meaning changes and **qué** is more frequent.

◀ Determiners: Ch. 4

¿**Qué** quieres, sopa o ensalada?	*What would you like, soup or salad?*

c. Cuál(es) de followed by *definite article + noun* or *demonstrative* restricts the choices explicitly.

◀ Demonstratives: Ch. 8

¿**Cuál de las** ensaladas prefieres?	*Which one of the salads do you prefer?*
¿**Cuáles de estos** postres son buenos?	*Which of these desserts are good?*

14.B.4 Quién, quiénes

Quién(es) refers only to people. The plural **quiénes** is used if a plural answer is expected.

—¿**Quién** es Luisa?	*Who is Luisa?*
—Luisa es mi hermana.	*Luisa is my sister.*
—¿**Quiénes** vienen a cenar?	*Who is coming to dinner?*
—Vienen Gabi y Rodrigo.	*Gabi and Rodrigo are coming.*
—¿**De quién** son las botas?	*Whose boots are these?*
—Son mías.	*They are mine.*

14.B.5 Cuánto/a(s), cuánto, cuán

a. Cuánto/a (*how much*) and **cuántos/as** (*how many*) agree in gender and number with the noun they modify.

◀ Adverbs: Ch. 10

¿**Cuánto** diner**o** necesitamos?	*How much money do we need?*
¿**Cuánta** agu**a** mineral quieres?	*How much mineral water do you want?*
¿**Cuántas** person**as** vienen hoy?	*How many people are coming today?*
¿**Cuántos** plat**os** vamos a servir?	*How many dishes are we going to serve?*

b. Use **cuántos/as de** to ask explicitly for the quantity of specific countable nouns.

¿**Cuántos de los** estudiantes están aquí hoy?	*How many of the students are here today?*
¿**Cuántas de estas** palabras comprendes?	*How many of these words do you understand?*

c. Cuánto (*how much*) does not change form when it stands alone before a verb.

¿**Cuánto** cuesta la cena?	*How much does the dinner cost?*
¿**Cuánto** pagaste por el postre?	*How much did you pay for the dessert?*

d. Cuánto is abbreviated to **cuán** before *adjectives* and sometimes before *adverbs*. Its use is formal and occurs more commonly in exclamations than in questions, where other structures are generally used instead.

◀ cuánto, cuanto: 10.D.1 cuán = qué tan: 14.B.5e

¿**Cómo son de caros** los pasajes?	
¿**Cuán caros** son los pasajes?	*How expensive are the tickets?*

◀ cómo: 14.B.6

qué tanto, qué tantos: 14.D.c

e. In Latin America, **qué tan**, a common interrogative structure, has the same meaning as **cuán**.

Qué tan + *adjective* or *adverb*	
¿Qué tan *caros* son los boletos?	*How expensive are the tickets?*
¿Qué tan *rápidamente* llegas en tren?	*How fast do you get there by train?*

Adverbs of manner: 10.C
Relative adverbs: 15.C.1

14.B.6 *Cómo*

a. Cómo is invariable and can *only* be followed by verbs.

¿**Cómo** estás?	*How are you?*
¿**Cómo** os parece Barcelona?	*How do you [pl.] like Barcelona?*
¿**Cómo** se enciende la tele?	*How do you turn on the TV?*

b. Unlike the Spanish **cómo**, the English *how* may appear before adjectives and adverbs (usually of manner). English sentences with *how + adjective/adverb* must be rephrased in Spanish with other structures. One of these common structures is shown below.

cuán + *adjective*: 14.B.5d
qué tan + *adjective*:
14.B.5e, 14.D.b

Cómo + **ser** + **de** + *adjective*	
¿**Cómo es de** *difícil* el problema?	*How difficult is the problem?*
¿**Cómo son de** *caros* los libros?	*How expensive are the books?*
¿**Cómo es de** *grande* la ciudad?	*How large is the city?*

Conjunctions of comparison:
16.C.8

c. Cuál es + *noun* or **qué** + *noun* + **tener** are other alternatives. The Spanish noun in these constructions corresponds to the English adjective/adverb in the parallel English structure, *how + adjective/adverb*.

¿**Cómo es de alto** el edificio?	
¿**Cuál es la altura** del edificio?	*How **tall** is the building?*
¿**Qué altura tiene** el edificio?	

¿**Cómo es de importante** la carta?	
¿**Cuál es la importancia** de la carta?	*How **important** is the letter?*
¿**Qué importancia tiene** la carta?	

d. *How* questions concerning weight, height, length, and age are asked with specific verbs, instead of using the English structure *how + adjective*.

¿Cuánto **pesa** el bebé?	*How much does the baby weigh?*
¿Cuánto **pesa** tu portátil?	*How heavy is your laptop?*
¿Cuánto **miden** las ventanas?	*How big are the windows?*
¿Cuánto **mide** usted?	*How tall are you?*
¿Cuántos años **tiene** usted?	*How old are you? (What is your age?)*
¿Qué edad **tiene** usted?	

e. The purpose of the *how* question in English determines which options are used in Spanish: degree of distance (*how far*), frequency of time (*how often*), degree of a quality (*how well, how tired*), etc. Combinations of adverbs and prepositions with interrogatives, **que** + *noun*, and other structures can convey the same meaning in Spanish as a *how* question in English.

cómo de: 14.B.6b
qué tan: 14.B.5e, 14.D.b
cuán: 14.B.5d

¿**Hasta dónde** vas?	***How far** are you going?*
¿**Cada cuánto** visitas a tu familia?	***How often** do you visit your family?*
¿**Con qué frecuencia** para el autobús?	***How often** does the bus stop?*
¿**A qué distancia** queda?	***How far** is it?*
¿**A qué altura** saltas?	***How high** can you jump?*
¿**A qué velocidad** escribes?	***How fast** can you write?*
¿**Cómo** escribes **de rápido**?	

14.B.7 Qué tal

a. Qué tal is a very informal expression equivalent to **cómo**. It is used as a greeting, to inquire about people and daily events, or to make informal invitations.

¡Hola! ¿**Qué tal**?	*Hi! How are you?*
¿**Qué tal** la película?	*How is/was the movie?*
¿**Qué tal** tu familia?	*How is your family?*
¿**Qué tal** por casa?	*How is everyone at home?*
¿**Qué tal** es Juan como médico?	*How good a doctor is Juan?*
¿**Qué tal** un cafecito?	*How about a coffee?*
¿**Qué tal si** vamos al cine hoy?	*How about going to the movies today?*

b. A question with **qué tal** can be rephrased with **cómo** only if it is followed by a verb.

¿**Qué tal** (está) la comida?	*How is the food?*
¿**Cómo está** la comida?	

14.B.8 Dónde, cuándo, por qué

a. Dónde (*where*), **cuándo** (*when*), and **por qué** (*why*) are invariable and their use is similar to English.

¿**Dónde** vives?	***Where** do you live?*
¿**Cuándo** sales para el trabajo?	***When** do you leave for work?*
¿**Por qué** regresaste tarde?	***Why** did you return so late?*

b. Dónde is replaced with **adónde** or **a dónde** with verbs of motion.

¿**Adónde** te mudaste?	*Where did you move to?*

◀ Adverbs of place and direction: 10.E.2

◀ Indirect questions: 31.B.6

14.B.9 Indirect questions

Indirect questions are also asked with question words.

No sé **qué** quieres.	*I don't know what you want.*
Dime **cómo** estás.	*Tell me how you are.*
Avísame **cuándo** llegas.	*Let me know when you arrive.*
Quiero saber **quién** es tu profesor.	*I want to know who your teacher is.*
Queremos saber **cuánto** dinero hay.	*We want to know how much money there is.*

14.B.10 El qué, el cómo, el cuánto, el cuándo, el dónde, el porqué

Some common interrogatives can be used as nouns. These nouns are masculine and singular, and carry an accent mark: **el qué, el cómo, el cuánto, el cuándo, el dónde, el porqué**.

No conocemos **el porqué** de la crisis.	*We don't know the reason for the crisis.*
Sabrás **el cuándo** y **el cómo** de la situación después.	*You will find out the when and the how of the situation later.*

14.C Exclamations with question words

Exclamaciones con expresiones interrogativas

Question words with a written accent are also used in exclamations in the following way:

Qué + noun/ adjective/adverb	¡**Qué** maravilla!	How wonderful!
	¡**Qué** bonito!	How beautiful!
	¡**Qué** bien!	Great! (That's wonderful!)
Cómo + verb	¡**Cómo** te quiero!	I love you so much!
Cómo + verb + **de** + adj.	¡**Cómo** es **de** alto!	It's so tall!
Cuánto + verb	¡**Cuánto** estudias!	You study a lot!
Cuánto/a(s) + noun	¡**Cuánta** gente!	So many people! (There were many...)
	¡**Cuántos** libros!	So many books! (There were many...)
Quién + verb	¡**Quién** fuera rico!	Oh, to be rich!

Exclamations with the subjunctive: 23.B.2

14.D Regional variations

Variaciones regionales

a. Cuál is more frequently followed by a verb than by a noun, but in many Latin American countries, **cuál** precedes the noun when a choice is implied.

¿De **cuál** país hispano eres?	Which Hispanic country are you from?
¿**Cuál** restaurante te gusta más?	Which restaurant do you like the most?
¿**Cuáles** recetas vas a preparar?	Which recipes are you going to prepare?

cuán: 14.B.5e

b. In Latin America, the following expressions can be used for direct and indirect questions, and exclamations. The intonation of the speaker can determine whether he/she is asking a question or making an exclamation.

Qué tan + adjective	¿**Qué tan** bueno es ese café?	How good is that coffee?
	¡**Qué tan** fantástico!	How fantastic!
	Me pregunto **qué tan** caro es.	I wonder how expensive it is.
Qué tan + adverb	¿**Qué tan** bien hablas español?	How well do you speak Spanish?
	¡**Qué tan** bien escribes!	You write so well!
Qué tanto + verb	¿**Qué tanto** tienes que esperar el autobús?	How long do you have to wait for the bus?
	¡**Qué tanto** trabajas!	You work so much!
	Le pregunté **qué tanto** le interesa la política.	I asked him how interested he is in politics.

Indirect questions: 14.B.9, 31.B.6

c. In questions, **cuánto/a(s)** is preferred to **qué tanto/a(s)**, but both expressions can be used in questions and exclamations.

Qué tanto/a(s) + noun	¿**Cuánta** gente hay? ¿**Qué tanta** gente hay?	How many people are there?
	¡**Cuánta** gente hay! ¡**Qué tanta** gente hay!	There are so many people!
	¿**Cuántos** amigos tienes? ¿**Qué tantos** amigos tienes?	How many friends do you have?
	¡**Cuántos** amigos tienes! ¡**Qué tantos** amigos tienes!	You have so many friends!

d. In the Caribbean, primarily the Dominican Republic, Puerto Rico, and Cuba, it is common to put a subject pronoun before the verb in short **qué** questions.

¿**Qué tú** vas a hacer hoy?	What are you going to do today?
¿**Qué tú** quieres?	What do you want?

Práctica

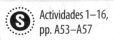

Actividades 1–16, pp. A53–A57

Relative pronouns and adverbs
Pronombres y adverbios relativos

15.A Relative pronouns

Pronombres relativos

15.A.1 Structure

A relative pronoun refers to a noun (person, thing, or idea) and can link two descriptions of the noun into a single, complex sentence, made up of a main clause and a *relative clause* or *adjectival clause*.

El profesor enseña español.	*The professor teaches Spanish.*
El profesor es inglés.	*The professor is English.*
El profesor **que** enseña español es inglés.	*The professor who teaches Spanish is English.*

The noun described, **el profesor**, is called the *antecedent* (**antecedente**). The relative pronoun, **que**, introduces a relative clause (**que enseña español**) that refers to the noun.

15.A.2 Spanish relative pronouns

Que is the most common relative pronoun in spoken Spanish. In written language, many other pronouns are used.

◀ Diacritical marks: 1.E.6

Relative pronouns		Antecedents
que does not change form	*which/who/that*	people, things, ideas
el/la que **el/la cual** article agrees with gender and number of antecedent	*the one/thing* *which/who/that*	people, things, ideas whole sentences, actions, events
los/las que **los/las cuales** article agrees with gender and number of antecedent	*those which/* *who/that*	people, things, ideas, whole sentences, actions, events
lo que, lo cual not used with people, does not change form	*the one/thing* *which/that*	whole sentences, actions, or events
quien, quienes agrees in number with antecedent	*who*	only people
cuyo/a, cuyos/as expresses ownership or connection, agrees in gender and number with item owned	*whose*	people, things

◀ **cualquiera:** *anyone:* Indefinite determiners: 7.C.5 and 15.B.7

◀ **lo que/cual:** Se ofendió mucho, **lo que/cual** me pareció extraño. (*He was very offended, which I thought was strange.*)

◀ **cuyo/a:** El hombre **cuya** voz es melodiosa. (*The man whose voice is melodious.*)

15.A.3 Important differences between Spanish and English

There are three important differences between English and Spanish relative pronouns:

a. In Spanish, relative pronouns are required, whereas in English they are sometimes optional.

El auto **que** tienes es fabuloso.	*The car (that) you have is fabulous.*
¿Es bueno el libro **que** estás leyendo?	*Is the book (that) you're reading good?*
No tengo ningún teléfono **que** funcione bien.	*I don't have a phone that works well.*

◀ Use of the subjunctive in relative clauses: 23.D

Prepositions:12.A.1.b ▶

b. In English, a preposition can be placed after the relative pronoun, usually at the end of the sentence, but in Spanish, the preposition must *always* be placed before the relative pronoun.

Spain: **el ordenador** = ▶
the computer

Esta es la computadora **con la que** siempre escribo.	*This is the computer (**that**) I always write **with**.*
La casa **en la que** vivimos es pequeña.	*The house (**that**) we live **in** is little.*
La chica **con quien / con la que** salgo se llama Anita.	*The girl (**that**) I go out **with** is named Anita.*

Personal **a**: 12.B.2c, 13.E.2 ▶

c. In Spanish, when the relative pronoun relates to a person that is a direct or indirect object in the sentence, the preposition **a** must be placed before the relative pronoun.

Pedro fue **a quien** vi ayer.	*It was Pedro I saw yesterday.*
Camila es la estudiante **a quien** le envié la información.	*Camila is the student I sent the information to.*
Janet, **a quien/a la que/a la cual** conozco bien, está de visita.	*Janet, whom I know well, is visiting.*

15.B Choosing relative pronouns

Elección del pronombre relativo

In order to select an appropriate relative pronoun, the antecedent must first be identified by asking: *Who is the person or what is the thing or idea being described?* In Spanish, the use of the relative pronoun differs depending on whether the clause is *defining* or *non-defining*. If it is non-defining, it is important to note whether the relative pronoun follows a preposition or not.

15.B.1 Non-defining clauses

Comma: 1.F.2 ▶

a. *Non-defining clauses* provide additional information about the antecedent and are always preceded and followed by a comma in Spanish. These clauses are introduced by a relative pronoun (or a relative adverb), sometimes in conjunction with a preposition.

Relative adverbs: 15.C ▶

Mario, **que/quien** siempre llega tarde, no tiene auto.	*Mario, who always arrives late, doesn't have a car.*
Nuestra escuela, **cuya** reputación es excelente, es muy cara.	*Our school, whose reputation is excellent, is very expensive.*

b. When **que** is ambiguous, a *definite article* + **que/cual** can be used to make the antecedent clear.

El señor Juárez y su esposa, **la que/cual** siempre es elegante, llegan hoy.	*Mr. Juárez and his wife, who is always elegant, arrive today.*

15.B.2 Defining clauses

Defining clauses provide information that is necessary for the meaning of a sentence. These are never separated from the antecedent with a comma. Which relative pronoun is used in a defining clause is determined by whether or not a preposition is used.

Choosing relative pronouns in defining clauses		
Relative pronoun	**With a preposition**	**Without a preposition**
que	Yes: after **a, de, en, con**	Yes
el/la/los/las que	Yes	No
el/la/los/las cuales	Yes	No
quien(es)	Yes	No
cuyo/a(s)	Yes	Yes

¿Sabías que cerró el restaurante **en (el) que / en el cual** nos conocimos?	*Did you know that the restaurant where we met has closed?*
El libro **que** me prestaste es muy interesante.	*The book you lent me is very interesting.*
La película **de la cual** hablamos se estrena mañana.	*The movie we talked about opens tomorrow.*

15.B.3 *Que* **in defining clauses**

a. In defining clauses that do not require a preposition, **que** can be used alone (without an article).

Los amigos **que** tengo son estudiantes.	*The friends (that) I have are students.*
La paz **que** hemos logrado es inestable.	*The peace (that) we've attained is unstable.*
Eso **que** me contaste es muy interesante.	*What you told me is very interesting.*
El rock es la música **que** más me gusta.	*Rock is the music (that) I like best.*

b. Que is generally used with an article after all prepositions, but can be used without the article in defining clauses with the prepositions **a**, **de**, **en**, and **con** when the clause does not refer to a person. This usually occurs only in informal speech.

La ciudad **en (la) que** vivo es grande.	*The city (that) I live in is big.*
El aceite **con (el) que** se preparan las tapas es español.	*The oil (that) you make tapas with is Spanish.*
Los problemas **a (los) que** me refiero son graves.	*The problems I'm referring to are serious.*
La causa **por la que** lucho es justa.	*The cause (that/which) I'm fighting for is just.*
El banco **para el que** trabajo es internacional.	*The bank (that) I work for is international.*

15.B.4 *El/la que/cual, los/las que/cuales* **in defining clauses**

In defining clauses, these pronouns must always be used *after a preposition* for both people and things. The article must correspond in gender and number with the antecedent.

El señor **al que** llamé no contestó.	*The man I called didn't answer.*
Los estudiantes **a los que** enseño español son estudiosos.	*The students I teach Spanish to are studious.*
Las carreteras **por las que** conduzco son peligrosas.	*The roads I drive on are dangerous.*
La universidad **en la que** estudio queda en Madrid.	*The university I study at is in Madrid.*
Hoy enviamos las facturas **en las cuales** está toda la información.	*Today we sent the invoices that have all the infomation.*

◀ Personal **a**: 12.B.2c, 13.E.2

15.B.5 *Quien(es)* **in defining clauses**

Quien(es) cannot be used without a preposition in defining clauses. The preposition **a** is placed before **quien** if the antecedent is a direct or indirect object.

Hablé **con quien** contestó el teléfono.	*I talked to the one/person who answered the telephone.*
Le escribí **a quien** tú recomendaste.	*I wrote to the one/person you recommended.*
En Navidad solo les daré regalos **a quienes** más quiero.	*For Christmas, I will only give presents to those I love most.*
Puedes pedirle ayuda **a quien** quieras.	*You can ask whomever you like for help.*
Hay que hablar **con quien** pueda resolver el problema.	*You must talk to someone who is able to solve the problem.*

◀ Use of the subjunctive with unknown antecedent: 23.D.1

15.B.6 *Cuyo/a(s)*

Cuyo/a(s) is sometimes referred to as a *relative adjective.*

Cuyo/a(s) is a formal relative pronoun that is only used in written Spanish. It agrees in gender and number with that which is owned and can be used in defining and non-defining clauses. In speech and in less formal texts, **cuyo** is replaced by **que/cual** and the verb **tener**.

Las personas **cuya** nacionalidad es inglesa…	*People whose nationality is English…*
Las personas **que tienen** nacionalidad inglesa…	*People who have English nationality…*

Cualquiera: 7.C.5

15.B.7   Indefinite antecedents

a. El que (*The one who*) refers to a male or an indefinite person and **la que** refers to an indefinite female (in an all female group). **Cualquiera que/quien** (*Whoever*) refers to anyone, without specifying gender.

El que / Cualquiera que / Quien fume aquí, recibirá una multa.	*Anyone who smokes here will get a fine.*

lo que: 8.A.4c, 11.D.4b

b. Lo que (*what, that which*) is a neutral relative pronoun that refers to an indefinite concept (not a person).

Lo que me interesa es la salud.	*What interests me is health.*
Lo que dices es muy importante.	*What you say is very important.*

15.B.8   Emphatic constructions

In English, the description of an event often uses the following structure, especially in a news context: *It was yesterday when…, There was a four-year-old who…, It was here in the city where…* In Spanish, this sentence structure is rare, and only used to emphasize special aspects of an event (time, person, location, manner, etc.).

Common word order in a sentence: 14.A.1
Other structures using **ser**: 30.B.8
Cuando, donde, and **como** are relative adverbs. See 15.C.

Fue ayer **cuando** Laura Valle resolvió el problema de los robos en la universidad.	*It was yesterday when Laura Valle solved the problem with the robberies at the university.*
Fue en Londres **donde** sucedieron los hechos.	*It was in London where the events took place.*
Fue Laura Valle **quien** / **la que** lo descubrió todo; no fue Felipe, su jefe.	*It was Laura Valle who discovered it all; it wasn't Felipe, her boss.*
Fue así **como** se supo quién era el culpable.	*That was how it was revealed who the culprit was.*
La manera **como/en la que** lo supe es un secreto.	*The way I found it out is a secret.*

15.B.9   Special cases of agreement

a. In emphatic relative clauses similar to **Yo soy el que/quien**, the verb usually agrees with the relative pronoun (**el que/quien**) and not with the subject of **ser** (**yo**). This also happens with the second person singular (**tú, vos**).

Tú eres *quien* más **trabaja**.	*You are the one who works the most.*
Yo soy *el que* **enseña** español.	*I am the one who teaches Spanish.*
Vos sos *la que* **llamó**.	*You are the one who called.*

This is also the case when the relative clause comes first.

La que **sabe** eres tú.	*The one who knows is you.*

b. The verb may agree with the subject of **ser** (first- or second-person singular) only in informal speech.

Tú eres la que **llegas** tarde.	*You are the one who arrives late.*
Yo soy quien **pagaré** la cuenta.	*I am the one who will pay the bill.*
Vos sos la que no **tenés** tiempo.	*You are the one who doesn't have time.*

c. If the expression **uno/a de los que** (*one of those who...*) is the relative clause, the verb normally follows its subject, the relative pronoun **los/las que** (third-person plural). Sometimes the pronoun **uno/a** is omitted, but the verb in the relative clause still agrees with the plural relative pronoun.

Tú eres **uno** de *los que* **escriben** blogs.
Tú eres de *los que* **escriben** blogs.

You are one of those who write blogs.

d. When the subject of **ser** is a plural pronoun (**nosotros**, **vosotros**), the verb always agrees with it.

Vosotros sois los que **habláis** mejor español.
Nosotros somos los que **vendremos**.

You [pl.] are the ones who speak the best Spanish.
We are the ones who will come.

15.C Relative adverbs

Adverbios relativos

15.C.1 *Donde, cuando, como*

a. The adverbs **adonde**, **donde**, **cuando**, and **como** can also introduce a relative clause. They are equivalent to **en el/la que** or **en el/la cual** when referring to the *location*, *time*, or *manner* in which an event occurs. They do not change form and do not have a written accent.

La casa **donde** vivo es grande.
Me gusta la manera **como** trata a los niños.
Extraño la época **cuando** íbamos a la
escuela primaria.

The house I live in is big.
I like the way she treats the kids.
*I miss the times when we were in
elementary school.*

b. In speech and informal texts, **donde** is often replaced with a preposition of place followed by **el/la/los/las que** when a definite location is being discussed.

La universidad (**en**) **donde / en la que** estudio
está en Connecticut.
Paseamos en un parque **donde / en el que** hay
un lago.

*The university where I study
is in Connecticut.*
*We take walks in a park where there
is a lake.*

c. Cuando refers to time in an indicative or subjunctive clause. The subjunctive indicates time in the future.

Use of the subjunctive with
conjunctions of time: 23.E.2

Me alegro **cuando** mi abuela viene de visita.
Volví a casa **cuando** empezó a llover.
Llámame **cuando** tengas tiempo.
Te llamaré **cuando** pueda.

I am glad when my grandmother visits us.
I went back home when it started to rain.
Call me when you have time.
I'll call you when I can.

d. When there is no explicit antecedent, **donde**, **cuando**, and **como** have traditionally been regarded as conjunctions that introduce an adverbial clause. The current interpretation adopted by the RAE also classifies **donde**, **cuando**, and **como** as relative adverbs when there is no antecedent and refers to these clauses as *free relative adverbial clauses*.

Fui **donde** me dijiste.
Llegué **cuando** la película había comenzado.
Lo pinté **como** tú me pediste.

I went where you told me.
I arrived when the film had begun.
I painted it the way you asked me.

e. Como refers to how something is done and can be replaced with **de la manera que / del modo que**. **Como** is a neutral or less specific word in these clauses, but can be emphasized with the word **tal** (*such*).

Vístete **como / de la manera que** quieras.	*Dress as you want.*
Las cosas **como / del modo que** tú las ves no son ciertas.	*Things the way you see them are not true.*
Debéis escribir los textos **tal como / de la manera que** ha dicho el profesor.	*You [pl.] ought to write the texts just as the professor has said.*

15.D Non-specific relative constructions

Relativos inespecíficos

15.D.1 *(A)dondequiera, cuandoquiera, comoquiera*

a. Non-specific relative constructions are formed combining the indefinite quantifiers **(a)dondequiera, cuandoquiera**, and **comoquiera** with a defining relative clause. These indefinite quantifiers are compound words formed by a relative adverb (**donde, cuando, como**) + **-quiera.** They refer to people and things that are not identified.

Te acompañaré **adondequiera** que vayas.	*I'll go with you wherever you go.*
Cuandoquiera que mi jefe tome una decisión, te aviso.	*When my boss makes a decision, I'll let you know.*
Comoquiera que te llames, yo te voy a decir Pepe.	*Whatever your name is, I'm going to call you Pepe.*

b. Cualquiera also belongs to this group when it precedes a defining relative clause.

Cualquiera que sea tu propuesta, la quiero escuchar.	*Whatever your proposal is, I want to hear it.*

Práctica

S Actividades 1–12, pp. A58–A60

Conjunctions
Conjunciones

16.A Overview

Aspectos generales

Conjunctions are words that join elements or clauses together in a sentence. *Coordinating conjunctions* join similar or equal parts of a sentence. *Subordinating conjunctions* make the subordinate clause dependent on the main clause. Conjunctions are invariable and they are a limited set, but two or more words can combine to form conjunctive phrases (**locuciones conjuntivas**).

16.B Coordinating conjunctions

Conjunciones coordinantes

16.B.1 Structure

a. Coordinating conjunctions join together two similar words, expressions, or sentences. Two sentences joined by a coordinating conjunction can each stand alone independently.

Words	En la escuela hay estudiantes **y** profesores.	*At the school there are students **and** teachers.*
Sentences	Podemos ver televisión **o** podemos jugar al ajedrez.	*We can watch TV **or** we can play chess.*

b. The following are the most common coordinating conjunctions in Spanish:

Coordinating conjunctions			
y (e)	*and*	Isabel **y** Ana estudian **y** trabajan.	*Isabel **and** Ana study **and** work.*
o (u)	*or*	¿Quieres café **o** té?	*Do you want coffee **or** tea?*
no... ni **ni... ni**	*neither... nor*	Hoy **no** llueve **ni** nieva.	*It **neither** rains **nor** snows today.*
pero	*but (rather)*	Llueve, **pero** no hace frío.	*It's raining, **but** it's not cold.*
sino		**No** quiero café **sino** té.	*I don't want coffee **but** tea instead / rather tea.*

16.B.2 The conjunction *y*

a. The conjunction **y** expresses sum or addition, and can join words or sentences together.

Tenemos tiempo **y** oportunidad.	*We have time and opportunity.*
Estoy feliz **y** satisfecho	*I am happy and satisfied.*
La profesora enseña **y** corrige las tareas.	*The professor teaches and corrects the homework.*

b. When coordinating more than two elements, a comma is used to separate the elements, except before **y**.

Compré peras, manzanas **y** naranjas.	*I bought pears, apples, and oranges.*

c. The conjunction **y** changes to **e** before words that start with **i-** or **hi-**, except when **hi-** is part of a diphthong.

Ana **e I**sabel conversan por teléfono.	*Ana and Isabel are chatting on the phone.*
Mamá siempre lleva aguja **e hi**lo en su bolso.	*Mom always carries a needle and thread in her bag.*
En la acera hay nieve **y hie**lo.	*On the sidewalk there is snow and ice.*

d. *And* can be expressed with the non-inflected **tanto... como** and **y** in Spanish. This formal structure occurs primarily in written Spanish.

Tanto Lisa **como** Pedro vienen hoy.	*Both Lisa and Pedro are coming today.*
El profesor lo explica todo **tanto** rápido, **como** simple **y** claramente.	*The teacher explains everything quickly, simply, and clearly.*
La casa es **tanto** grande **como** bonita **y** moderna.	*The house is big, nice, and modern.*

Comparisons of equality: 11.C.3 ▶

e. Note the difference when comparisons are made using **tan/tanto... como**.

La casa es **tan** grande **como** bonita **y** moderna.	*The house is as big as it is nice and modern.*
Necesitamos **tantos** libros **como** cuadernos **y** calculadoras.	*We need just as many books as notebooks and calculators.*

16.B.3 **The conjunction** *o*

a. The conjunction **o** expresses two or several alternatives. In Spanish, unlike English, there is no comma before the last element.

Podéis pedir carne, pollo **o** pescado.	*You [pl.] can order beef, chicken, or fish.*

b. The verb is often plural when singular words are joined together with **o**.

Olga **o** Roberto **van** a hablar.	*(Either) Olga or Roberto is going to talk.*

c. Before words that begin with **o** or **ho-**, **u** is used instead.

Tengo siete **u o**cho pesos.	*I have seven or eight pesos.*
¿Regresaste ayer **u ho**y?	*Did you get back yesterday or today?*

d. Traditionally, when **o** appeared between numbers, it was written with an accent mark in order to avoid confusing it with the number zero. According to the RAE's *Nueva ortografía*, modern typography has eliminated the risk of confusing the **o** and the zero. Therefore, the accent mark is no longer used.

Necesitamos 350 **o** 400 pesos.	*We need 350 or 400 pesos.*

e. **Bien... bien** is used instead of **o... o** to indicate that the options are mutually exclusive. This is mostly used in written language.

Podéis viajar, **bien** en auto, **bien** en tren.	*You [pl.] can travel either by car or train.*
Bien me escribes o **bien** me llamas.	*You can either write or call me.*

f. When **bien** is added to **o... o**, the options are mutually exclusive.

Recibió **o bien** un premio, **o bien** una mención especial.	*He received either an award or a special mention.*

16.B.4 The conjunction *ni*

a. The conjunction **ni** joins negative elements together. It always follows another negation.

Pedro **no** llama **ni** escribe.	*Pedro neither calls nor writes.*
Nunca tenemos pan **ni** leche.	*We never have bread nor milk.*

b. **Ni** can be placed before each element or just before the last one.

No tenemos leche **ni** azúcar.	*We don't have milk or sugar.*
¡**No** tenemos **ni** leche **ni** azúcar!	*We don't have milk or sugar!*

c. When the compound conjunction **ni... ni** is used to coordinate nouns in the subject, the verb should be plural.

Ni Juan **ni** Marcos **fueron** a la fiesta.	*Neither Juan nor Marcos went to the party.*

16.B.5 *Pero, sino, mas, sin embargo*

a. **Pero** constrains the meaning of the previous sentence in the same way as *but* in English. **Mas** is a synonym of **pero** that is primarily used in formal texts.

Voy al supermercado, **pero** regreso pronto.	*I'm going to the supermarket, but I'll be back soon.*

b. After a negation, **sino** is used instead of **pero** to indicate and alternate. **Sino que** is used before a finite (conjugated) verb.

La clase **no** es hoy **sino** mañana.	*The class isn't today, but tomorrow.*
No me llamó **sino que** me escribió.	*He didn't call me, but rather he wrote to me.*

c. The expression **sin embargo** has the same meaning as **pero**, but is more formal and mostly used in written language. In formal texts, **sin embargo** is preferred for starting a sentence.

Los precios subieron mucho. **Sin embargo**, los consumidores siguen comprando.	*The prices went up a lot. **However**, consumers continue to buy.*
Los precios subieron mucho, **pero/sin embargo** los consumidores siguen comprando.	*Prices went up a lot, **but/however** consumers continue to buy.*

d. **Pero (que) muy** does not constrain the meaning. It acts as an intensifier.

El libro es muy **pero (que) muy** difícil.	*The book is very very difficult.*

16.B.6 Conjunctions that express consequence or introduce an explanation

Conjunctions that introduce an explanation (**esto es, es decir, o sea**) and conjunctions that express consequence (**por consiguiente, pues, así pues, de manera que**, etc.) are usually grouped with coordinating conjunctions. **Pues** can also be a subordinating conjunction when it expresses cause.

Mi jefe me llamó porque hubo una emergencia. **Por lo tanto/Así pues**, tuve que ir a trabajar el domingo.	*My boss called me because there was an emergency. Therefore, I had to go to work on Sunday.*

16.C Subordinating conjunctions

Conjunciones subordinantes

Subordinate clauses begin with subordinating conjunctions. A subordinate clause (*...if she should come*) is dependent on a main clause (*Nora asked...*) in order to make sense. Subordinating conjunctions form two types of subordinate clauses: **que** clauses (*that* clauses) and adverbial subordinate clauses that are introduced by either simple conjunctions like **porque** (*because*), **aunque** (*although*), or by compound expressions like **tan pronto como** (*as soon as*), **a fin de que** (*in order that*), and others.

16.C.1 · *Que* **clauses (nominal clauses)**

Use of the subjunctive in nominal clauses: 23.C

a. Que is the most common subordinating conjunction in Spanish and is equivalent to *that*. **Que** cannot be left out in Spanish.

Main clause	Subordinate clause	Main clause	Subordinate clause
Creo	**que** va a llover.	*I think*	*(that) it's going to rain.*
Rosita dijo	**que** está cansada.	*Rosita said*	*(that) she's tired.*

Indirect questions, indirect discourse: 31.B.6

b. Que is often used in colloquial Spanish before an interrogative pronoun. This construction is not common in written Spanish.

Main clause	Subordinate clause	Main clause	Subordinate clause
Te preguntan	**que cuál** es tu dirección.	*They're asking you*	*what your address is.*
Me preguntaron	**que dónde** había ido.	*They asked me*	*where I had gone.*

c. In indirect questions without question words, **si** is used. **Que** can precede **si** in colloquial Spanish.

Nos preguntaron (**que**) **si** podíamos ayudar.　　*They asked us if we could help.*

16.C.2 **Adverbial subordinate clauses**

Use of the subjunctive in adverbial subordinate clauses: 23.E

Adverbial subordinate clauses begin with conjunctions that express time, manner, purpose, or other features that elaborate on the action in the main clause.

Main clause	Subordinate clause	Main clause	Subordinate clause
Luis se enferma	**cuando** come helado.	*Luis gets sick*	*when he eats ice cream.*
Luis estaba bien	**hasta que** comió helado.	*Luis was well/fine*	*until he ate ice cream.*
Luis se enfermó	**porque** comió helado.	*Luis got sick*	*because he ate ice cream.*
Luis come helado	**aunque** se enferme.	*Luis eats ice cream*	*even though he gets sick.*

16.C.3 **Conjunctions of time**

These conjunctions describe when the action happens and introduce temporal subordinate clauses.

Use of the subjunctive with conjunctions of time: 23.E.2

Conjunctions of time – *Conjunciones temporales*			
al mismo tiempo que	*at the same time as*	**en cuanto**	*as soon as*
antes de que	*before*	**hasta que**	*until*
apenas	*as soon as*	**mientras (que)**	*while/so long as*
cada vez que	*each time/every time (that)*	**siempre que**	*whenever/always when*
cuando	*when*	**tan pronto como**	*as soon as*
después de que, luego de que	*after/as soon as*	**una vez que**	*as soon as/once*

Siempre visito el Museo del Prado **cuando** estoy en Madrid.　*I always visit the Prado Museum when I'm in Madrid.*

Te llamaré **apenas** termine de estudiar.　*I will call you as soon as I finish studying.*

Leemos el periódico **mientras** desayunamos.　*We read the newspaper while we eat breakfast.*

Cada vez que me olvido el paraguas, ¡llueve!　*Every time I forget my umbrella, it rains!*

Levántate **antes de que** sea tarde.　*Get up before it's too late.*

16.C.4 Conjunctions of cause

a. Cause is primarily expressed with **porque** in Spanish. The indicative is normally used after conjunctions of cause. If the sentence is negative, the subjunctive can be used.

◀ Use of the subjunctive with conjunctions of cause: 23.E.5

Conjunctions of cause – *Conjunciones causales*		
a causa de que / dado que	puesto que	because (of) / given that / since
porque (como)	ya que	

Rita habla bien español **porque** estudió en Madrid.	*Rita speaks Spanish well **because** she studied in Madrid.*
No estudio español **porque** esté de moda, sino porque es el idioma de mis abuelos.	*I don't study Spanish **because** it's popular, but because it is the language my grandparents spoke.*
La casa es cara, **dado que** está en el centro.	*The house is expensive **because** it is downtown.*

b. Subordinate clauses of cause are usually placed after the main clause. When the cause comes first, **como** is used as the conjunction.

Como Rita estudió en Madrid, habla bien español.	***Because/Since** Rita studied in Madrid, she speaks Spanish well.*

16.C.5 Conjunctions of consequence

a. These conjunctions always follow the main clause and express consequence when used with the indicative. The most common conjunction of consequence is **así que**, but there are several others.

◀ Use of the subjunctive with conjunctions of consequence: 23.E.4

Conjunctions of consequence – *Conjunciones consecutivas*	
así que	
de (tal) forma/manera/modo que	so (that)
de (tal) suerte que	

Mi casa está lejos, **así que** tengo que tomar dos autobuses.	*My house is far away, so I have to take two buses.*
El profesor no llegó, **de (tal) modo que** ayer no tuvimos clase.	*The teacher didn't come, so we didn't have class yesterday.*
Ana no tiene trabajo, **de (tal) manera que** tampoco tiene dinero.	*Ana doesn't have a job, so she doesn't have any money either.*

b. **Tal** can also be used after **forma/modo/manera**.

No encuentro el libro, **de manera tal que** no puedo estudiar.	*I can't find the book, so I cannot study.*

c. **De (tal) manera** and **de (tal) modo que** followed by the subjunctive express purpose.

◀ Conjunctions of purpose: 16.C.7

Deben ustedes cumplir la ley, **de tal manera que** no tengan problemas.	*You [pl.] must comply with the law so that you [pl.] won't have any problems.*
Colgó el cuadro **de tal modo que** le dé la luz.	*He hung the painting in such a way that the light would hit it.*

Use of the subjunctive
with conjunctions of
concession: 23.E.6

16.C.6 **Conjunctions of concession**

Clauses introduced by conjunctions of concession express an objection, obstacle, or difficulty for the action in the main clause. This objection or obstacle doesn't alter the action in the main clause as one would expect.

Conjunctions of concession – *Conjunciones concesivas*		
aunque	a pesar de que	although, even though, despite, in spite of
aun cuando	pese a que	

Elena obtiene buenas notas **pese a que** nunca estudia.

Elena gets good grades even though she never studies.

Aunque es joven, Roberto es muy responsable.

Even though he is young, Roberto is very responsible.

A pesar de que la película parece interesante, no sé si la iré a ver.

Despite the fact that the film sounds interesting, I don't know if I'll go see it.

Aun cuando me lo pidiera de rodillas, no iría a la fiesta con él.

Even if he (got down on his knees and) begged me, I wouldn't go to the party with him.

16.C.7 **Conjunctions of purpose**

Use of the subjunctive with
conjunctions of purpose:
23.E.3

a. A fin de que and **para que** always require the subjunctive. **De manera que** and **de modo que** take the subjunctive when they express purpose. The indicative can be used, but the subordinate clause becomes a clause of consequence. Only subordinate clauses of purpose that begin with **para que** can be placed before the main clause.

Conjunctions of purpose – *Conjunciones de finalidad*	
para que	in order that, so (that)
a fin de que, de modo que / de manera que	

Para que tengas buena salud, debes comer bien.

(In order) to have good health, you [pl.] must eat well.

Debéis planear bien **a fin de que** no tengáis problemas más tarde.

You [pl.] should plan well so you don't have problems later.

Te compré entradas para el cine **de modo que** tuvieras algo que hacer el viernes.

I got you movie tickets, so you'd have something to do on Friday.

b. When the indicative is used with **de manera/modo que**, the subordinate clause becomes a clause of consequence. Compare these examples:

Está nevando, **de manera que tienes** que usar botas.

It's snowing, so you have to wear boots.

Te compré un par de botas **de manera que puedas** salir cuando nieva.

I bought you a pair of boots so you can go out when it snows.

16.C.8 Conjunctions of comparison

Comparisons can be made using several structures.

Conjunctions of comparison – *Conjunciones comparativas*			
más... que	*more... than*	**tanto... como**	*as much... as*
menos... que	*less... than*	**igual... que**	*just as much... as*
tan... como	*as/so... as*	**como, como si...**	*as/like, as if...*

Me preocupo **tanto como** te preocupas tú.   *I worry as much as you do.*
Me habla **como si** yo no supiera nada de política.   *He talks to me as if I knew nothing about politics.*

16.C.9 Expressing manner – *como*

a. The relative adverb **como** describes *how* something is done or happens. Followed by the indicative, it refers to past and present actions. The subjunctive is used to express uncertainty about the way in which the action will be performed, or when the action refers to the future.

Subjunctive in adverbial subordinate clauses: 23.E.1

Escribí el ensayo **como** quería el profesor.   *I wrote the essay the way the teacher wanted.*
Escribiré el ensayo **como** quiera el profesor.   *I will write the essay however the teacher wants.*

b. The expression **como si** is used to talk about assumptions and always precedes a form of the past subjunctive.

Beatriz habla español **como si** fuera española.   *Beatriz speaks Spanish as if she were Spanish.*
Te quejas **como si** el examen hubiera sido difícil.   *You're complaining as if the exam had been difficult.*

16.C.10 Expressing location – *donde/adonde*

The relative adverb **donde** can also act as a conjunction.

Iremos **adonde** querráis.   *We'll go where you [pl.] want.*
Vivo **por donde** está la escuela.   *I live around where the school is.*

Adonde is used with verbs of motion: 10.E.2

16.D Conditional conjunctions

Conjunciones condicionales

16.D.1 Conditional clauses

Conditional conjunctions are used to make an assumption about something that will or will not happen. The most important conditional conjunction in Spanish is **si**, although there are others. The subjunctive is used with all conditional conjunctions except with **si**, which has special rules and sometimes takes the indicative, and **siempre que**, which expresses habit (*whenever*) with the indicative and condition with the subjunctive (*as long as*).

Conditional subordinate clauses: 23.E.7

Conditional conjunctions – *Conjunciones condicionales*			
si	*if/whether*	**con tal de que**	*provided that / as long as*
en caso de que	*in case*	**siempre y cuando**	
a menos (de) que	*unless*	**siempre que**	*provided that / as long as / whenever*

Conjunctions • **Chapter 16**   **129**

Lleva el paraguas **en caso de que** llueva.	Carry the umbrella *in case* it rains.
Os escribiré **siempre y cuando** me escribáis.	*I'll write to you [pl.] as long as you [pl.] write to me.*
No podremos ir de paseo **a menos que** tengamos tiempo.	*We will not be able to go for a walk **unless** we have time.*
Siempre que vamos al mercado, compramos demasiado.	***Whenever** we go to the market, we buy too much.*
Iremos al parque, **siempre que** terminemos temprano.	*We will go to the park, **as long as** we finish early.*

16.D.2 Conditional clauses with *si*

a. Spanish distinguishes between real and possible conditional clauses, and *imaginary* (hypothetical) and *counterfactual* (impossible) conditional clauses. Real and possible conditional clauses take the indicative. The subjunctive expresses what is imagined (*If I were rich...*) or impossible (*If the sky were green... ; If I had done it...*).

Conditional clauses with *si*		Result
Real/true	**Si** Luis come helado, *If Luis eats ice cream,*	se enferma. *he gets sick.*
	Si Luis come helado, *If Luis eats ice cream,*	se enfermará. *he will get sick.*
Imagined/hypothetical	**Si** Luis comiera helado, *If Luis ate ice cream,*	se enfermaría. *he would get sick.*
Not fullfilled in the past / impossible	**Si** Luis hubiera comido helado, *If Luis had eaten ice cream,*	se habría enfermado. *he would have gotten sick.*

The past perfect subjunctive with **-era** (but not **-ese**) can also be used to express the unfulfilled/ impossible situation: **Si** Luis hubiera comido helado, se **hubiera** enfermado. Past perfect subjunctive: 22.E

b. When the **si** clause precedes the main clause, a comma is needed. When the **si** clause follows the main clause, no comma is needed.

Si me invitas, allí estaré.	*If you invite me, I'll be there.*
Allí estaré **si me invitas.**	*I will be there if you invite me.*

c. Donde, **como**, and **mientras** can express a condition when they are followed by the subjunctive.

Donde no **encuentre** trabajo, no tendré dinero.	*If I don't find work, I won't have money.*
Como no me **digas** la verdad, les voy a preguntar a tus padres.	*If you don't tell me the truth, I'm going to ask your parents.*
Mientras yo **tenga** salud, trabajaré diariamente.	*As long as I have my health, I'll work every day.*

Práctica

Actividades 1–12, pp. A61–A64

The present indicative
Presente de indicativo

17.A Verbs

Verbos

17.A.1 The sentence

a. A sentence is a self-contained unit that relates a subject to a predicate. The predicate is a grammatical expression that designates states, actions, characteristics, etc., that pertain to the subject. The verb is the main element in the predicate. The other elements of the predicate can be nouns or pronouns that function as *objects*, as in Juan tiene **un libro**; adverbs or adverbial expressions that explain the circumstances around the subject's actions, as in Juan comió **rápidamente** or Juan comió **en la cocina**; prepositions that are required by the verb, as in Juan piensa **en** María; and conjunctions, which link sentences, as in Juan comió **porque** su mamá había preparado su plato favorito.

b. The subject can be represented by a pronoun, a name, a noun, or any expression that can replace it.

Determiners and subjects: 4.B.1

Subject	Predicate	
Ellos **Luis y Ana**	estudian	las lecciones todos los días.
Todos los estudiantes de español **Las personas de las que te hablé**	son	excelentes estudiantes.

17.A.2 Verb forms

a. Verbs describe actions: what you do or what happens. Verb forms are divided into two main groups: personal forms that are conjugated (*finite forms*) and non-personal forms (*non-finite*) that cannot be conjugated: infinitives, present participles (**gerundios**), and past participles.

b. Verbs consist of two parts: a stem and an ending. Spanish verbs are divided into three conjugation groups based on their infinitive endings: **-ar**, **-er**, and **-ir**. What remains after dropping the **-ar**, **-er**, or **-ir** ending is the verb stem. Verbs are conjugated in Spanish by changing the infinitive ending to other endings that indicate person, number, time, and mood. For that reason, in Spanish it is not always necessary to include the subject like in English.

cantar *to sing*			
Stem	**Ending**		*Ending indicates:*
cant-	**-o**	*I sing*	*present indicative, 1st-person singular*
cant-	**-arás**	*you will sing*	*simple future, 2nd-person singular*
cant-	**-ó**	*he/she sang*	*preterite, 3rd-person singular*
cant-	**-aríamos**	*we would sing*	*conditional, 1st-person plural*

17.B Verb objects and complements

Objetos y complementos verbales

17.B.1 Copulative, transitive, and intransitive verbs

a. Verbs are classified into three main categories:

Types	Characteristics	Examples	English
Copulative	links the subject and its complements	María **es** traductora. El agua **está** caliente.	*María is a translator. The water is hot.*
Transitive	takes one or more objects	María **habla** español e inglés con su novio. María **hierve** agua.	*María speaks Spanish and English with her boyfriend. María boils water.*
Intransitive	does not take a direct object	María **habla** demasiado sobre sus amigas. El agua **hierve** desde hace diez minutos.	*María talks too much about her friends. The water has been boiling for ten minutes.*

b. Some verbs can be both transitive and intransitive.

| Carlos **habla** portugués. | *Carlos speaks Portuguese.* |
| Carlos **habla** mucho. | *Carlos speaks a lot.* |

17.B.2 Verbs with prepositions

Glosario combinatorio: ▶
pp. 279–322

a. While some verbs can be followed by a direct object (transitive verbs), others require a prepositional phrase called **complemento de régimen**. Sometimes the same verb can be used with a direct object or with a preposition.

| No **creo en** los fantasmas. | *I don't believe in ghosts.* |
| **Disfruté (de)** las vacaciones. | *I enjoyed my vacation.* |

b. The choice of preposition is not predictable. Verbs with similar meanings might take different prepositions or a direct object. A verb in Spanish might take a preposition that is different from the one required by its English counterpart.

No **confío en** él.	*I don't trust him.*
No **me fío de** él.	*I don't trust him.*
Consiguió diez dólares.	*He got hold of ten dollars.*
Se hizo con diez dólares.	*He got hold of ten dollars.*
Asistí a la conferencia.	*I attended the conference.*

c. The most common prepositions used in **complementos de régimen** are **a, de, en**, and **con**. Verbs that require **por** or **para** are not common.

Preposition	Verb with prepositions			
a	asistir a	*to attend*	jugar a	*to play*
con	encontrarse con	*to meet*	soñar con	*to dream about/of*
de	disfrutar de	*to enjoy*	sufrir de	*to suffer from*
en	confiar en	*to trust*	influir en	*to influence / to have influence on*
por	preocuparse por	*to worry about*	interesarse por	*to be interested in*

¿**Asistió** usted **a** la conferencia?   *Did you attend the conference?*

¡**Disfruta (de)** tu tiempo libre!   *Enjoy your free time!*

Jugaremos al ajedrez profesionalmente.   *We will play chess professionally.*

Ellos sueñan con un mundo mejor.   *They dream of a better world.*

d. In most cases, the preposition is followed by a noun or noun phrase. However, many verbs with prepositions can be followed by infinitives.

Me encontré con **Marcos**.   *I met up with Marcos.*

Soñé con **ella**.   *I dreamt of her.*

Sueño con **ir** a Europa.   *I dream of going to Europe.*

e. Some verbs with prepositions can only be followed by an infinitive. These verbal expressions usually take **a** or **de**.

◀ Verb periphrases with the infinitive: 26.C

verb + preposition + infinitive			
empezar a	*to start*	acabar de	*to finish*
volver a	*to repeat*	tratar de	*to try to*

La película **acaba de empezar**.   *The movie has just begun.*

Traté de alcanzar el autobús.   *I tried to catch the bus.*

17.B.3 Reflexive verbs

◀ Reflexive pronouns and verbs: 27.A

a. Reflexive verbs express the fact that the subject performing the action is also the recipient, directly or indirectly.

Subject	Predicate		
	Reflexive pronoun	**Verb**	**Adverbial expression**
(Yo)	Me	lavo	frecuentemente.

Subject	Predicate			
	Reflexive pronoun	**Verb**	**Direct object**	**Adverbial expression**
(Yo)	Me	lavo	las manos	frecuentemente.

b. Many daily routines are expressed with reflexive verbs.

◀ Reflexive verbs for daily routines: 27.D.1e

Ella **se cepilla** los dientes.   *She brushes her teeth (herself).*

Te pones los zapatos.   *You put on your shoes (yourself).*

c. Verbs that take reflexive pronouns are not always reflexive in meaning.

◀ Reflexive verbs with reciprocal meaning: 27.D.3

◀ Verbs that change meaning: 27.E

◀ Verbs that express change: 27.G

Reciprocal meaning	**Nos** ayuda**mos** siempre.	*We always help each other.*
Change in meaning	Hoy cayeron diez centímetros de nieve. **Se me cayó** el libro.	*Ten centimeters of snow fell today. I dropped the book.*
Physical, social, or mental change	Ana **se casó** con Luis y sus familias **se alegraron**.	*Ana married Luis and their families were happy.*
Verbs of change	Luis **se hizo** ingeniero.	*Luis became an engineer.*

d. Many reflexive verbs require specific prepositions.

Reflexive verbs with prepositions			
atreverse a	*to dare to*	encontrarse con	*to meet up with*
decidirse a	*to decide to*	enojarse con	*to get angry with*
despedirse de	*to say goodbye to*	convertirse en	*to become / turn into*
reírse de	*to laugh at*	interesarse por	*to be/get interested in*

El público **se ríe de** los payasos.   *The audience is laughing at the clowns.*
La chica **se convirtió en** una atleta.   *The girl became an athlete.*
Nos despediremos de ella para siempre.   *We will say goodbye to her forever.*
No **me atrevo a** preguntar qué pasó.   *I don't dare ask what happened.*
¿Dónde **os encontráis con** vuestros amigos?   *Where do you [pl.] meet your friends?*

17.B.4   Verbs like *gustar*

Indirect object pronouns: 13.F
Verbs like **gustar**: 9.D.4, 13.F.3
Reflexive verbs conjugated with an indirect object pronoun: 27.G.2b
Use of the subjunctive in subordinate clauses with verbs like **gustar**: 23.C.3

Pronouns after prepositions: 13.C

a. The Spanish verb **gustar** functions differently from its English counterpart, *to like*. In Spanish, the person or object that is liked is the subject of the sentence and usually appears after the verb. The person that likes something usually appears before the verb and is expressed with an indirect object pronoun. The indirect object is emphasized by adding **a** + *prepositional pronoun*.

Me gusta el helado de chocolate.   *I like chocolate ice cream.*
A mí me gusta el helado de fresa.   *I like strawberry ice cream.*
A mi hermana le gustan los dos.   *My sister likes both.*

b. Since the verb needs to agree with the subject, it agrees with the person or thing that is liked. If the subject is an infinitive, the verb **gustar** is used in the third-person singular form.

A María **le gustan los hombres altos**.   *María likes tall men.*
(**los hombres altos**: *third-person plural subject*; **gustan**: *third-person plural verb*)

A María **le gusta su vecino, Luis**.   *María likes her neighbor, Luis.*
(**su vecino, Luis**: *third-person singular subject*; **gusta**: *third-person singular verb*)

A Marcos y a mí **nos gusta nadar**.   *Marcos and I like swimming / to swim.*
(**nadar** *is an infinitive: third-person singular subject*; **gusta**: *third-person singular verb*)

c. Gustar is most commonly used with third-person singular or plural subjects. However, it is possible to use other subjects.

Me **gustaste** desde el momento en que te vi.   *I liked you from the moment I saw you.*
(*implicit subject:* **tú**, *second-person singular*; **gustaste**: *second-person singular*)

¿Te **gusto**?   *Do you like me?*
(*implicit subject:* **yo**, *first-person singular*; **gusto**: *first-person singular*)

Nos **gustáis** mucho.   *We like you a lot.*
(*implicit subject:* **vosotros**, *second-person plural*; **gustáis**: *second-person plural*)

d. Many other Spanish verbs function like **gustar**. Some of these verbs are shown in the table below:

Verbs like *gustar*			
aburrir	*to bore/tire*	enfadar	*to anger*
agradar	*to please/gratify*	entristecer	*to sadden*
alarmar	*to alarm/startle*	entusiasmar	*to delight / carry away*
alegrar	*to be/make happy*	extrañar	*to miss*
apenar	*to distress*	fascinar	*to fascinate*
asustar	*to scare*	fastidiar	*to annoy/bother/upset*
complacer	*to please*	frustrar	*to frustrate*
convenir	*to suit*	importar	*to be important / care about*
desesperar	*to despair/exasperate*	indignar	*to outrage*
disgustar	*to dislike*	interesar	*to interest / be interested in*
divertir	*to amuse/entertain*	irritar	*to irritate*
doler	*to hurt/ache*	molestar	*to bother/annoy*
emocionar	*to thrill/excite*	preocupar	*to worry*
encantar	*to delight/love*	sorprender	*to surprise*

◀ Article instead of possessives with verbs of physical reactions and ailments: 9.D.4

Los fumadores **me irritan**.	*Smokers irritate me.*
La oscuridad **me asusta**.	*Darkness scares me.*
Nos conviene reunirnos mañana.	*It suits us to meet tomorrow.*
¿**Te divierten** las comedias?	*Do comedies amuse you?*
Me alegra que tengas éxito.	*I am happy that you are successful.*
Nos interesa el español.	*We are interested in Spanish. / Spanish interests us.*
Nuestros clientes **nos importan**.	*Our clients are important to us.*

e. Some of these verbs can also be used reflexively.

Me alegro por tu éxito.	*I am happy for your success.*
Nos interesamos por el español.	*We are interested in Spanish.*

17.C Tense and mood

Tiempo y modo

17.C.1 Verb tense

Verb tense tells when an action takes place: past, present, or future. There is not always a direct correlation between the grammatical verb tense and the time expressed in the sentence. For example, the present indicative can convey future actions in Spanish: **Vengo mañana.** (*I'm coming tomorrow.*)

17.C.2 Verb mood

Verb mood tells how the speaker feels about an action. Spanish has three moods like English. Each mood has its own conjugation form and follows specific rules of use.

a. Indicative: Usually expresses facts.

b. Subjunctive: Expresses doubt or uncertainty, feelings or emotions, wishes, preferences, assumptions, the unknown, and imaginary situations or events.

c. Imperative: Expresses orders and requests.

◀ Subjunctive: Ch. 22–23
Imperative: Ch. 24

Presente de indicativo

17.D.1 **Regular verbs**

a. All three conjugation groups (**-ar**, **-er**, **-ir**) have both regular and irregular verbs. Regular verbs do not have any changes in the stem and each conjugation group has its own conjugation patterns.

Subject pronoun		**cantar** *to sing*	**correr** *to run*	**vivir** *to live*
I	yo	cant**o**	corr**o**	viv**o**
you	tú	cant**as**	corr**es**	viv**es**
you	vos	cant**ás**	corr**és**	viv**ís**
you (formal), he, she	usted, él, ella	cant**a**	corr**e**	viv**e**
we	nosotros/as	cant**amos**	corr**emos**	viv**imos**
you [pl.]	vosotros/as	cant**áis**	corr**éis**	viv**ís**
you [pl.], they	ustedes, ellos/as	cant**an**	corr**en**	viv**en**

Map of the spread of **vos** in Latin America: p. 277
Voseo: 13.B.2 , 13.B.5, 17.D.1c–d

b. Verbs ending in **-ar** are the largest group. New verbs are usually formed in Spanish with the **-ar** ending. The following are some of the most common regular verbs.

Regular verbs, present tense: Verb conjugation tables, p. 261

-*ar* **verbs**					
acabar	*to finish*	ganar	*to win*	pasar	*to pass/spend (time)*
amar	*to love*	investigar	*to investigate*	practicar	*to practice*
bailar	*to dance*	lavar	*to wash*	saltar	*to jump*
buscar	*to look for*	llamar	*to call*	terminar	*to end*
caminar	*to walk*	llegar	*to arrive*	tomar	*to take/drink/eat/have*
comprar	*to buy*	llevar	*to bring/carry*	trabajar	*to work*
desear	*to desire*	mandar	*to order/send*	usar	*to use*
empacar	*to pack*	mirar	*to look*	viajar	*to travel*
escuchar	*to listen*	necesitar	*to need*	visitar	*to visit*

-*er* **verbs**	
aprender	*to learn*
beber	*to drink*
comer	*to eat*
comprender	*to understand*
creer	*to believe*
leer	*to read*
responder	*to answer*
temer	*to fear*
vender	*to sell*

-*ir* **verbs**	
abrir	*to open*
asistir	*to attend (something)*
describir	*to describe*
decidir	*to decide*
escribir	*to write*
insistir	*to insist*
permitir	*to permit/allow*
recibir	*to receive*
subir	*to climb/go up*

—¿Qué deportes **practicas**?   *Which sports do you play/practice?*
—No **practico** deportes.   *I don't play/practice any sports.*
Bailo y **camino** mucho.   *I dance and walk a lot.*

c. The verbal forms of **vos** and **vosotros/as** are similar because these two pronouns share a common origin and their verbal forms are regular, even when the verb is stem-changing or has other irregularities. This regularity is especially striking when **vos** forms are compared to the verbal forms of **tú**, which have many irregularities.

vos: 13.B, 13.B.2, 13.B.5

d. In the present indicative, **vos** is conjugated by adding **-ás** to **-ar** verbs, **-és** to **-er** verbs, and **-ís** to **-ir** verbs. There are very few irregular forms: **vos sos** (*you are*). Note that **-ir** verbs have the same endings for **vos** and **vosotros/as**, except for the verb **ir** (*to go*): **vos vas, vosotros/as vais.**

Vos **and** *vosotros/as*: **regular present indicative**			
Personal pronoun	*-ar* **pensar** *to think*	*-er* **tener** *to have*	*-ir* **decir** *to say*
vos	pens**ás**	ten**és**	dec**ís**
vosotros/as	pens**áis**	ten**éis**	dec**ís**

17.D.2 Verbs with spelling changes in the first-person singular: *yo*

In Spanish, there are a number of verbs that have spelling changes in order to maintain the right sound pattern when conjugating the verb. The spelling changes always occur in the last letters of the verb stem, before adding the endings. The endings usually are regular, but can be irregular in some cases.

Pronunciation of consonants: 1.C.6

a. Verbs that end in **-cer**, **-cir** and **-ger**, **-gir**, **-guir** have spelling changes in the verb stem, but take regular endings.

Verbs with spelling changes: Verb conjugation tables, pp. 257–276. For **c:z**, see verb patterns 32, 72, 75; for **c-zc**, see verb patterns 14, 15, 43.

-cer, -cir **verbs with spelling changes**			
When the verb stem ends in a **vowel**, a **z** is added before the final **c** in the first-person singular.		When the verb stem ends in **n** or **r**, the final **c** becomes a **z** in the first-person singular.	
cono**cer** *to know*	yo cono**zco**	conven**cer** *to convince*	yo conven**zo**
condu**cir** *to drive*	yo condu**zco**	espar**cir** *to spread/sprinkle*	yo espar**zo**

Other *-cer, -cir* **verbs**					
Verbs with **-zco** ending in first-person singular (**yo**)		Verbs with **-zo** ending in first-person singular (**yo**)		Verbs with **-zo** ending in first-person singular with **o → ue** stem change	
agrade**cer**	*to appreciate/thank*	ejer**cer**	*to exercise*	co**cer** → cuezo	*to cook*
apete**cer**	*to fancy / feel like*	ven**cer**	*to beat/defeat*	tor**cer** → tuerzo	*to twist*
condu**cir**	*to drive*				
dedu**cir**	*to deduce*				
desapare**cer**	*to disappear*				
introdu**cir**	*to introduce*				
recono**cer**	*to recognize*				
tradu**cir**	*to translate*				

—Yo **conduzco** limusinas. ¿En qué trabajas tú?   *I drive limousines. What do you do?*

—**Traduzco** del español al inglés para un canal de televisión.   *I translate from Spanish into English for a TV station.*

b. In the first-person singular, **g** is changed to **j**, but the pronunciation remains the same.

-*ger*, -*gir* **verbs with spelling changes**		
Subject pronoun	diri**gir** *to lead/direct/manage/run*	exi**gir** *to claim/demand*
yo	diri**jo**	exi**jo**

Other -*ger*, -*gir* **verbs**			
aco**ger**	*to welcome*	infrin**gir**	*to infringe*
afli**gir**	*to afflict*	prote**ger**	*to protect*
corre**gir**	*to correct*	reco**ger**	*to collect / pick up*
ele**gir**	*to choose/elect*	restrin**gir**	*to restrict*
esco**ger**	*to choose*	sumer**gir**	*to submerge*
fin**gir**	*to pretend*	sur**gir**	*to emerge*

Corregir and **elegir** also have vowel shifts in the stem: **corrijo, elijo:** 17.D.5 Verb conjugation tables, pp. 257–276. See verb patterns 26, 35, 54.

Diri**jo** una organización ecológica.   *I manage an ecological organization.*
Reco**jo** y reciclo la basura.   *I collect and recycle the trash.*
Prote**jo** la naturaleza.   *I protect nature.*
Exi**jo** una ciudad más limpia.   *I demand a cleaner city.*

c. The ending **-guir** changes to **g** in the first-person singular, but the pronunciation remains the same.

-*guir* **verbs with spelling changes**	
Subject pronoun	extin**guir** *to extinguish / put out (fires)*
yo	extin**go**

Other -*guir* **verbs**			
conse**guir**	*to get/obtain/achieve*	prose**guir**	*to continue*
perse**guir**	*to pursue/persecute*	se**guir**	*to follow*

Seguir and **perseguir** also have vowel shifts in the stem: **sigo, persigo:** 17.D.5 Verb Conjugation Tables, pp. 257–276. See verb patterns 36, 64.

Soy policía y persi**go** a los criminales.   *I am a policeman and I chase criminals.*
No extin**go** incendios porque no soy bombero.   *I don't put out fires because I'm not a firefighter.*

17.D.3   **Verbs without spelling changes in** *nosotros/as, vosotros/as, vos*

Some verbs have spelling changes in the present in all persons except **nosotros/as**, **vosotros/as**, and **vos**. The present endings are regular.

a. In **-uir** verbs, **i** changes to **y** before **e** or **i** in all forms except **nosotros/as**, **vosotros/as**, and **vos**.

Conjugation of -*uir* **verbs**	
Subject pronoun	constr**uir** *to build*
yo	constru**yo**
tú	constru**yes**
vos	constru**ís**
usted, él, ella	constru**ye**
nosotros/as	constru**imos**
vosotros/as	constru**ís**
ustedes, ellos/as	constru**yen**

Verbs with spelling changes: Verb conjugation tables, pp. 257–276. See verb pattern 23.

The present indicative • **Chapter 17**

Other -*uir* verbs			
constit**uir**	*to constitute*	h**uir**	*to escape/flee*
constr**uir**	*to build/construct*	incl**uir**	*to include*
contrib**uir**	*to contribute*	infl**uir**	*to influence*
destit**uir**	*to dismiss*	int**uir**	*to sense*
destr**uir**	*to destroy*	recl**uir**	*to imprison/confine*
dismin**uir**	*to diminish*	reconstr**uir**	*to reconstruct*
distrib**uir**	*to distribute*	sustit**uir**	*to substitute/replace*

La gente **huye** cuando hay un huracán. *People flee when there is a hurricane.*

Los huracanes **destruyen** las ciudades. *Hurricanes destroy cities.*

b. Several verbs that end in -**iar** and -**uar** take a written accent on the -**í** and -**ú** except in the **nosotros/as**, **vosotros/as**, and **vos** forms.

-*iar*, -*uar* verbs with spelling changes		
Subject pronoun	env**iar** *to send*	contin**uar** *to continue*
yo	env**í**o	contin**ú**o
tú	env**í**as	contin**ú**as
vos	envi**á**s	continu**á**s
usted, él, ella	env**í**a	contin**ú**a
nosotros/as	enviamos	continuamos
vosotros/as	envi**á**is	continu**á**is
ustedes, ellos/as	env**í**an	contin**ú**an

Verbs that need an accent: Verb conjugation tables, pp. 257–276. For **i:í**, see verb patterns 29, 34, 53; for **u:ú**, see verb patterns 37, 57, 59.

Other -*iar*, -*uar* verbs			
acent**uar**	*to emphasize*	evac**uar**	*to evacuate*
ampl**iar**	*to enlarge/extend*	eval**uar**	*to evaluate*
ans**iar**	*to long for*	grad**uar**se	*to graduate*
conf**iar**	*to confide/trust*	gu**iar**	*to guide*
deval**uar**	*to devalue*	insin**uar**	*to insinuate*
efect**uar**	*to carry out / execute*	perpet**uar**	*to perpetuate*
enfr**iar**	*to cool down / chill*	sit**uar**	*to locate*

Lucía gu**í**a a los turistas. Ellos conf**í**an en ella. *Lucía guides the tourists. They trust her.*

Pronto me grad**ú**o como maestra. *I will graduate as a teacher soon.*

17.D.4 Verbs with diphthongs or vowel shifts in the stem

Several verbs in all three conjugation groups have a systematic vowel shift in the stem. The stressed vowel in the stem becomes a diphthong or the vowel shifts when the verb is conjugated. This happens in all verb forms except for **nosotros/as**, **vosotros/as**, and **vos**. Most verbs with vowel shifts have regular endings, but some are irregular. A few verbs also have an irregular first-person singular (**yo**) conjugation.

Diphthongs: 1.C.2

Spanish verbs have several types of diphthongs in the present indicative: **e → ie**, **o → ue**, **i → ie**, and **u → ue**.

a. Conjugation of verbs with diphtongs: *e → ie*

	empezar *to begin/start*	**perder** *to lose*	**preferir** *to prefer*
yo	empiezo	pierdo	prefiero
tú	empiezas	pierdes	prefieres
vos	empezás	perdés	preferís
usted, él, ella	empieza	pierde	prefiere
nosotros/as	empezamos	perdemos	preferimos
vosotros/as	empezáis	perdéis	preferís
ustedes, ellos/as	empiezan	pierden	prefieren

▶ Verbs with diphtongs:
Verb conjugation tables,
pp. 257–276. See verb
patterns 24, 27, 28, 45,
49, 56, 65.

b. Other verbs with diphthongs: *e → ie*

-ar **verbs**	
atravesar	to cross
calentar	to warm up
cerrar	to close
comenzar	to start/begin
despertar	to wake up
gobernar	to govern
negar	to deny/refuse
pensar	to think
recomendar	to recommend

-er **verbs**	
defender	to defend
descender	to descend
encender	to light / switch on
entender	to understand
querer	to want

-ir **verbs**	
consentir	to consent
divertirse	to have fun
mentir	to lie
sentir	to feel

¿Quieres ir al cine hoy?   *Do you want to go to the movies today?*
Lo siento, hoy prefiero estudiar.   *Sorry, I prefer to study today.*

c. Conjugation of verbs with diphthongs: *o → ue*

	contar *to count*	**volver** *to return*	**dormir** *to sleep*
yo	cuento	vuelvo	duermo
tú	cuentas	vuelves	duermes
vos	contás	volvés	dormís
usted, él, ella	cuenta	vuelve	duerme
nosotros/as	contamos	volvemos	dormimos
vosotros/as	contáis	volvéis	dormís
ustedes, ellos/as	cuentan	vuelven	duermen

▶ Verbs with diphtongs:
Verb conjugation tables,
pp. 257–276. See verb
patterns 6, 9, 16, 25, 44,
50, 61, 67, 72.

d. Other verbs with diphthongs: *o → ue*

-ar **verbs**	
almorzar	to have lunch
costar	to cost
encontrar	to find
mostrar	to show
probar	to try/taste
recordar	to remember
soñar	to dream

-er **verbs**	
devolver	to give back
llover	to rain
mover	to move
poder	to be able
promover	to promote
remover	to remove
resolver	to resolve

-ir **verbs**	
morir	to die

—¿Cuánto **cue**sta el libro?   *How much does the book cost?*

—No re**cue**rdo. Unos veinte dólares.   *I don't remember. About twenty dollars.*

e. Conjugation of verbs with diphthongs: *i → ie*

	adquirir *to acquire*	**inquirir** *to inquire*
yo	adqu**ie**ro	inqu**ie**ro
tú	adqu**ie**res	inqu**ie**res
vos	adquirís	inquirís
usted, él, ella	adqu**ie**re	inqu**ie**re
nosotros/as	adquirimos	inquirimos
vosotros/as	adquirís	inquirís
ustedes, ellos/as	adqu**ie**ren	inqu**ie**ren

Verbs with diphthongs: Verb conjugation tables, pp. 257–276. See verb pattern 4.

En la universidad adqu**ie**ro nuevos conocimientos.   *At college, I gain new knowledge.*

f. Conjugation of verbs with diphthongs: *u → ue*

	jugar *to play*
yo	**jue**go
tú	**jue**gas
vos	jugás
usted, él, ella	**jue**ga
nosotros/as	jugamos
vosotros/as	jugáis
ustedes, ellos/as	**jue**gan

Verbs with diphthongs: Verb conjugation tables, pp. 257–276. See verb pattern 41.

Jugar is the only verb with the **u → ue** vowel shift.

—¿**Jue**gas algún deporte?   *Do you play any sports?*

—Sí, **jue**go al fútbol.   *Yes, I play soccer.*

17.D.5   Vowel shifts

Only **-ir** verbs have an **e → i** vowel shift in the present indicative.

	pedir *to ask for*
yo	p**i**do
tú	p**i**des
vos	pedís
usted, él, ella	p**i**de
nosotros/as	pedimos
vosotros/as	pedís
ustedes, ellos/as	p**i**den

Verbs with vowel shifts: Verb conjugation tables, pp. 257–276. See verb patterns 20, 26, 48, 58, 64.

Other -ir verbs with vowel shift $e \rightarrow i$					
competir	to compete	elegir	to choose	repetir	to repeat
corregir	to correct	impedir	to impede	seguir	to follow
despedir	to dismiss	perseguir	to pursue	servir	to serve

Siempre pido tapas en el restaurante español.   *I always order tapas at the Spanish restaurant.*
Allí nunca repiten los mismos platos.   *They never repeat the same dishes there.*

17.D.6   Irregular verbs in the present indicative

a. Verbs with the ending –go in the first-person singular (yo)

	caer to fall	hacer to do/ make	salir to leave / go out	poner to put	traer to bring	valer to cost / be worth
yo	caigo	hago	salgo	pongo	traigo	valgo
tú	caes	haces	sales	pones	traes	vales
vos	caés	hacés	salís	ponés	traés	valés
usted, él, ella	cae	hace	sale	pone	trae	vale
nosotros/as	caemos	hacemos	salimos	ponemos	traemos	valemos
vosotros/as	caéis	hacéis	salís	ponéis	traéis	valéis
ustedes, ellos/as	caen	hacen	salen	ponen	traen	valen

Irregular verbs are found alphabetically in the Verb conjugation tables, pp. 257–276. See verb patterns 8, 13, 39, 46, 51, 63, 73, 74, 79.

Other verbs like *poner*			
componer	to make up / compose	proponer	to propose
disponer	to dispose/arrange/ prepare/stipulate	suponer	to suppose

Other verbs like *traer*			
atraer	to attract	distraer	to distract

Soy un gran esquiador. ¡No **me caigo** nunca!   *I am a great skier. I never fall!*
Me pongo las botas y los esquíes.   *I'm putting on my boots and skis.*
Salgo de casa muy optimista.   *I leave home in an optimistic mood.*
Traigo muchas fotos del paseo.   *I'm bringing many photos from the outing.*

b. Verbs with the ending -go in the first-person singular (yo), and vowel shifts

	decir $e \rightarrow i$ to say/tell	oír $i \rightarrow y$ to hear	tener $e \rightarrow ie$ to have	venir $e \rightarrow ie$ to come
yo	digo	oigo	tengo	vengo
tú	dices	oyes	tienes	vienes
vos	decís	oís	tenés	venís
usted, él, ella	dice	oye	tiene	viene
nosotros/as	decimos	oímos	tenemos	venimos
vosotros/as	decís	oís	tenéis	venís
ustedes, ellos/as	dicen	oyen	tienen	vienen

Other verbs like *decir*					
desdecir	*to deny*	maldecir	*to curse/swear*	predecir	*to predict*

Other verbs like *tener*					
atenerse	*to abide*	detener	*to detain/stop*	obtener	*to obtain*
contener	*to contain*	mantener	*to maintain*	sostener	*to sustain*

Other verbs like *venir*				
convenir	*to agree/suit*		prevenir	*to prevent*

Verb conjugation tables, pp. 257–276. See verb patterns 11, 20, 46, 69, 76.

—¿Qué **dices**? No te **oigo**.   *What are you saying? I can't hear you.*

—**Digo** que no **vengo** mañana.   *I'm saying that I'm not coming tomorrow.*

—No **tengo** tiempo.   *I don't have time.*

c. Verbs with irregular forms in the first-person singular *(yo)*

Verb conjugation tables, pp. 257–276. See verb patterns 12, 19, 62, 77.

	caber *to fit*	**dar** *to give*	**saber** *to know*	**ver** *to see*
yo	**quepo**	**doy**	**sé**	**veo**
tú	cabes	das	sabes	ves
vos	cabés	das	sabés	ves
usted, él, ella	cabe	da	sabe	ve
nosotros/as	cabemos	damos	sabemos	vemos
vosotros/as	cabéis	dais	sabéis	veis
ustedes, ellos/as	caben	dan	saben	ven

—¡No **quepo** aquí!   *I don't fit here!*

—¿Te **doy** más espacio?   *Shall I give you more room?*

—No **sé**. **Veo** que este escritorio es muy estrecho.   *I don't know. I can see that this desk is very narrow.*

d. Completely irregular verbs

The verb **haber** has two conjugation forms: a personal form like the auxiliary verb, *to have*, and an impersonal form with the meaning *there is/are*.

	estar	**ser**	**haber** *to be, to have*	**ir** *to go*
	to be			
yo	est**oy**	**soy**	**he**	**voy**
tú	est**ás**	**eres**	**has**	**vas**
vos	est**ás**	**sos**	**has**	**vas**
él, ella, usted	est**á**	**es**	**ha**	**va**
nosotros/as	estamos	**somos**	**hemos**	**vamos**
vosotros/as	estáis	**sois**	habéis	**vais**
ustedes, ellos/as	est**án**	**son**	**han**	**van**

Verb conjugation tables, pp. 257–276. See verb patterns 33, 38, 40, 66. Impersonal form of **haber**: 29.B.1

—Hola, ¿dónde **estás**?   *Hello, where are you?*

—Hola, **estoy** en la cafetería.   *Hi, I'm in the cafeteria.*

—Ya **voy**. ¡Espérame!   *I'm coming. Wait for me!*

No **he** cenado todavía.   *I haven't eaten dinner yet.*

En la escuela **hay** muchos estudiantes.   *There are many students in the school.*

17.E Use of the present indicative

Uso del presente de indicativo

17.E.1 Present actions

The present indicative is used for actions that take place in the present: *now, today, this month, this year*.

Estoy aquí.	*I'm here.*
Ahora mismo **salgo**.	*I'm leaving right now.*
Este año **estudio** español.	*I'm studying Spanish this year.*

17.E.2 Habits

Just like in English, the present can be used to express habits. Adverbs or other time expressions emphasize the time period.

Entreno todos los días.	*I train every day.*
Abrimos de 6 de la mañana a 5 de la tarde.	*We open from six in the morning until five in the afternoon.*
Los domingos no **trabajamos**.	*We don't work on Sundays.*

17.E.3 Timeless facts

As in English, the present indicative in Spanish is used in definitions, descriptions, and other timeless statements.

El Sol **es** una estrella.	*The Sun is a star.*
En Chile **se habla** español.	*They speak Spanish in Chile.*
Diez más diez **son** veinte.	*Ten plus ten is twenty.*

The future: Ch. 20

17.E.4 Present with future meaning

The present can express the future with the help of context or time adverbs.

Mañana **te llamo**.	*I'll call you tomorrow.*
Y ahora, ¿qué **hago**?	*And what do I do now?*
Me **caso** el viernes.	*I'm getting married on Friday.*
¡Ya **vamos**!	*We're coming!*

17.E.5 Historical present

Stories in the past with verbs in the present convey involvement. This approach is common in historical texts and in lively oral stories.

Cristobal Colón **llega** al Nuevo Mundo en 1492.	*Christopher Columbus arrives in the New World in 1492.*
México **se independiza** en 1810.	*Mexico becomes independent in 1810.*
España **pierde** su última colonia en 1898.	*Spain loses its last colony in 1898.*

17.E.6 The present with imperative meaning

The use of the present with imperative meaning primarily occurs in spoken language.

¡Os calláis de inmediato!	*Be quiet at once!*
¡Ahora mismo **vienes** aquí!	*Come here at once!*
¡Escribes esa carta hoy mismo!	*Write that letter today!*

17.E.7　Confirming present

In spoken questions, the present is used to convey or confirm wishes or requests. Note the corresponding expressions in English.

¿Te **doy** más espacio?	*Shall I give you / Would you like more room?*
¿**Compramos** un helado?	*Shall we / Would you like to buy an ice cream?*
¿**Os recojo** mañana?	*Shall I / Would you like me to pick you [pl.] up tomorrow?*

17.E.8　Time expressions: *desde, desde hace, hace... que*

◀ hace + *time* + que,
llevar + gerundio
18.E.11

Verbs in the present can refer to actions from the past that continue into the present. The expressions **desde, desde hace,** and **hace** + *time expression* + **que** indicate this continuity in the present.

¿**Desde** cuándo trabajas en el banco?	*How long have you worked at the bank?*
Trabajo en el banco **desde hace** dos años.	*I have worked at the bank for two years.*
Hace dos años **que** trabajo en el banco.	

17.E.9　Conditional clauses

◀ Indicative or subjunctive
in conditional sentences:
16.D.2, 23.E.8

Real and possible conditions in subordinate clauses with **si** are expressed with the present indicative.

Si no **desayuno** bien, siempre me da hambre muy rápido.	*If I don't eat well at breakfast, I always get hungry very quickly.*

17.F　The present progressive

El presente progresivo

17.F.1　Progressive tenses

Spanish can express progressive actions in various ways, but **estar**, in any tense, followed by the present participle (**gerundio**), forms the closest equivalent to the English progressive tenses. The Spanish *present progressive* is formed with the present indicative of **estar: Estoy escribiendo**. (*I am writing*.); the *past progressive* is a verb periphrasis formed with the preterite or the imperfect of **estar: Estuve/Estaba escribiendo**. (*I was writing*.); the *future progressive* is formed with the simple future of **estar: Estaré escribiendo**. (*I will be writing*.) All the other tenses (simple and compound) are formed following the same pattern. Although the structure of the progressive tenses in both languages is similar, they aren't always used in the same way.

◀ Formation of the
gerundio: 25.C

◀ Progressive tenses: 25.C.3,
Verb periphrases with the
gerundio: 26.D

17.F.2　Simple present vs. present progressive

The simple present describes habitual actions. To refer to actions that are not habitual, the present progressive can be used. It is mostly used to emphasize actions that are in progress or are happening *now* or *at this moment*.

Simple present	Present progressive
Elisa **trabaja** desde casa. *Elisa works from home.*	Elisa **está trabajando** desde casa. *Elisa is working from home (lately, now).*
Me duele la rodilla. *My knee hurts.*	**Me está doliendo** la rodilla. *My knee is hurting (right now).*
¿Me **oyes** bien? *Can you hear me well?*	¿Me **estás oyendo** bien? *Can you hear me well (now)?*

17.F.3 Modal verbs

Modal verbs: 26.B

Modal verbs (such as **poder** and **deber**) and **estar** cannot be conjugated in the progressive tenses, but **ser** can, as long as it refers to a temporary situation, usually with passive meaning. This use is limited to formal written language and to current ongoing events.

Passive voice with *ser*	Present progressive
El país **es afectado** por el huracán. *The country is affected by the hurricane.*	El país **está siendo afectado** por el huracán. *The country is being affected by the hurricane.*

17.F.4 Using the present to refer to the future

Progressive tenses: 25.C.3d–f

a. In Spanish, the simple present can be used to refer to the future, while the present progressive is exclusively used to refer to actions that are in progress.

Estoy llegando.	*I am arriving (now).*
Llego mañana.	*I am arriving tomorrow.*
¿Qué estás haciendo?	*What are you doing (now)?*
¿Qué haces mañana?	*What are you doing tomorrow?*

ir a + *infinitive*: 26.C.1

b. The simple present forms of **ir a** + *infinitive* can be used to refer to the future.

| **Voy a comprarme** un carro. | *I am going to buy myself a car.* |
| ¿**Vas a salir** esta noche? | *Are you going out tonight?* |

Práctica

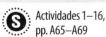

Actividades 1–16,
pp. A65–A69

The preterite and the imperfect
Pretérito perfecto simple e imperfecto

18.A Past-tense forms and verbal aspect

Formas del pasado y aspecto verbal

18.A.1 Past-tense forms

Spanish has two simple tenses to express the past: the *preterite* and the *imperfect*. Both can be similar to the English preterite, but are used differently, depending on the context.

Spanish preterite	Spanish imperfect	English preterite
Hablaste.	Hablabas.	*You spoke.*
Subiste.	Subías.	*You went up.*

18.A.2 Aspect

a. The Spanish preterite and imperfect tenses convey different *aspects* of actions, events, and states of being, and indicate how they are perceived in relation to time. The preterite action has a starting and/or finishing point and clearly shows that an action took place at a definite time or has been completed. On the other hand, the imperfect action does not have a concrete beginning or end; rather, it expresses an ongoing, habitual, repetitive, or frequent action in the past or an action with an indefinite period of time.

Preterite	Imperfect
Al chico le dio frío cuando caminó a la escuela hoy. *The boy got cold when he walked to school today.*	Al chico le daba frío cuando caminaba a la escuela. *The boy used to get cold when he walked to school.*

b. In English, the simple past tense does not always explicitly distinguish between perfect and imperfect actions. Therefore, the Spanish preterite and imperfect tenses can sometimes be translated the same way into English, even though the meaning of preterite and imperfect actions are different.

El perro **saltó** por encima de la cerca.   *The dog jumped over the fence.*

El perro **saltaba** por encima de la cerca.   *The dog jumped over the fence. (over and over again)*

18.B The preterite

Pretérito perfecto simple

18.B.1 Regular verbs

Regular **-er** and **-ir** verbs have the same endings in the preterite. Note that the **yo**, **usted**, **él**, and **ella** forms carry a written accent. The **tú** and **vos** endings are the same.

eterite of regular verbs: p. 261

	-ar **viajar** *to travel*	*-er* **comer** *to eat*	*-ir* **salir** *to go out*
yo	viaj**é**	com**í**	sal**í**
tú/vos	viaj**aste**	com**iste**	sal**iste**
usted, él, ella	viaj**ó**	com**ió**	sal**ió**
nosotros/as	viaj**amos**	com**imos**	sal**imos**
vosotros/as	viaj**asteis**	com**isteis**	sal**isteis**
ustedes, ellos/as	viaj**aron**	com**ieron**	sal**ieron**

18.B.2 Verbs with spelling changes

Some verbs undergo minor spelling changes in the preterite in order to maintain the correct sound pattern. The endings are regular.

a. First-person singular spelling changes:

Verb conjugation tables, pp. 257–276. For **c:qu**, see verb patterns 71, 78; for **g:gu**, see 41, 42, 45, 61; for **g:gü**, see 10; for **z:c**, see 6, 9, 18, 27, 34.

	c → qu **buscar** *to look for*	*g → gu* **jugar** *to play*	*g → gü* **averiguar** *to find out / check*	*z → c* **empezar** *to start/begin*
yo	bus**qu**é	ju**gu**é	averi**gü**é	empe**c**é
tú/vos	buscaste	jugaste	averiguaste	empezaste
usted, él, ella	buscó	jugó	averiguó	empezó
nosotros/as	buscamos	jugamos	averiguamos	empezamos
vosotros/as	buscasteis	jugasteis	averiguasteis	empezasteis
ustedes, ellos/as	buscaron	jugaron	averiguaron	empezaron

Ayer bus**qu**é a Carlos todo el día. *I looked for Carlos all day long yesterday.*
Por la noche averi**gü**é su dirección. *At night I found out his address.*
Visité a Carlos y ju**gu**é ajedrez con él un rato. *I visited Carlos and played chess with him for a while.*

c → qu **Verbs like** *buscar*		*g → gu* **Verbs like** *jugar*	
explicar, expli**qu**é	*to explain*	llegar, lle**gu**é	*to arrive*
practicar, practi**qu**é	*to practice*	pagar, pa**gu**é	*to pay (for)*
tocar, to**qu**é	*to play (an instrument) / to touch*	entregar, entre**gu**é	*to deliver*
sacar, sa**qu**é	*to take (out) / withdraw*	negar, ne**gu**é	*to deny/refuse*
gu → gü **Verbs like** *averiguar*		*z → c* **Verbs like** *empezar*	
apaciguar, apaci**gü**é	*to appease/pacify*	abrazar, abra**c**é	*to hug*
atestiguar, atesti**gü**é	*to attest/testify*	alcanzar, alcan**c**é	*to reach*
desaguar, desa**gü**é	*to drain*	almorzar, almor**c**é	*to have lunch*
santiguarse, me santi**gü**é	*to make the sign of the cross*	comenzar, comen**c**é	*to start/begin*

Ayer comen**c**é mis estudios universitarios. *I began my college studies yesterday.*
Practi**qu**é la pronunciación con Ana. *I practiced my pronunciation with Ana.*
Almor**c**é en la cafetería. *I ate lunch in the cafeteria.*
Por la tarde sa**qu**é dinero del banco y pa**gu**é los libros nuevos. *In the afternoon, I withdrew money from the bank and paid for the new books.*

The preterite and the imperfect • **Chapter 18**

b. Below are the third-person singular and plural spelling changes:

	caer _to fall_	leer _to read_	concluir _to conclude_	oír _to hear_
yo	caí	leí	concluí	oí
tú/vos	caíste	leíste	concluiste	oíste
usted, él, ella	ca**y**ó	le**y**ó	conclu**y**ó	o**y**ó
nosotros/as	caímos	leímos	concluimos	oímos
vosotros/as	caísteis	leísteis	concluisteis	oísteis
ustedes, ellos/as	ca**y**eron	le**y**eron	conclu**y**eron	o**y**eron

Verb conjugation tables, pp. 257–276. See verb patterns 13, 17, 23, 46.

Verbs like _caer_		Verbs like _leer_	
decaer	_to decay/deteriorate_	creer	_to believe_
recaer	_to have a relapse_	poseer	_to have/own_
		proveer	_to provide/supply_
Verbs like _concluir_			
constituir	_to constitute_	huir	_to escape/flee_
construir	_to build/construct_	incluir	_to include_
contribuir	_to contribute_	influir	_to influence_
destituir	_to dismiss/remove_	intuir	_to sense_
destruir	_to destroy_	recluir	_to imprison_
disminuir	_to diminish_	reconstruir	_to reconstruct_
distribuir	_to distribute_	sustituir	_to substitute/replace_

El gobierno constru**y**ó calles nuevas. _The government built new roads._
El ministerio distribu**y**ó los fondos. _The ministry distributed the funds._
Los grupos de presión influ**y**eron en la decisión. _The pressure groups influenced the decision._

18.B.3 Verbs with irregular stems

There are many irregular verbs in the preterite. Many follow predictable patterns.

a. All **-ir** verbs with vowel shifts in the present indicative also have vowel shifts in the third-person singular and plural in the preterite.

Verb conjugation tables, pp. 257–276. See verb patterns 25, 48, 58, 65.

	e → i			o → u
	pedir _to ask for_	reír _to laugh_	sentir _to feel_	dormir _to sleep_
yo	pedí	reí	sentí	dormí
tú/vos	pediste	reíste	sentiste	dormiste
usted, él, ella	p**i**dió	r**i**ó	s**i**ntió	d**u**rmió
nosotros/as	pedimos	reímos	sentimos	dormimos
vosotros/as	pedisteis	reísteis	sentisteis	dormisteis
ustedes, ellos/as	p**i**dieron	r**i**eron	s**i**ntieron	d**u**rmieron

Ayer, en la fiesta, Lisa p**i**dió tapas de jamón. _At the party yesterday, Lisa ordered ham tapas._
Sus amigos p**i**dieron la tortilla española. _Her friends ordered the Spanish omelet._
Todos se r**i**eron mucho y se s**i**ntieron muy bien. _Everyone laughed a lot and felt great._
Nadie d**u**rmió nada. _Nobody slept at all._

b. Irregular stems: **u** group

Verb conjugation tables, pp. 257–276. See verb patterns 7, 12, 33, 38, 50, 51, 62, 69.

Personal form of **haber**: Verb conjugation tables, p. 269 Impersonal form of **haber**: 29.B.1

Infinitive	Stem
andar	and**uv**-
caber	c**up**-
estar	est**uv**-
haber	h**ub**-
poder	p**ud**-
poner	p**us**-
saber	s**up**-
tener	t**uv**-

Endings	
Subject	**andar**
yo	andu**v**e
tú/vos	andu**v**iste
usted, él, ella	andu**v**o
nosotros/as	andu**v**imos
vosotros/as	andu**v**isteis
ustedes, ellos/as	andu**v**ieron

Rita **estuvo** muy poco tiempo en Madrid.   *Rita was in Madrid for a very short time.*
Ella no **pudo** visitar el Museo de Bellas Artes.   *She couldn't visit the Museum of Fine Arts.*
No **tuve** oportunidad de verla.   *I didn't get the chance to see her.*
Nunca **supe** qué pasó.   *I never found out what happened.*

c. Irregular stems: **i** group

Verb conjugation tables, pp. 257–276. See verb patterns 39, 56, 76.

Infinitive	Stem
hacer	h**ic**-
querer	q**uis**-
venir	v**in**-

Endings	
Subject	**hacer**
yo	hic**e**
tú/vos	hic**iste**
usted, él, ella	hiz**o**
nosotros/as	hic**imos**
vosotros/as	hic**isteis**
ustedes, ellos/as	hic**ieron**

Hacer also has a spelling change in the third-person singular: **hizo**.

Patricia no **hizo** nada hoy.   *Patricia didn't do anything today.*
Los invitados no **vinieron** a tiempo.   *The guests didn't arrive on time.*
No **quise** interrumpirte.   *I didn't want to interrupt you.*

d. Irregular stems: **j** group

***Decir** also has vowel changes in the stem.

Note that third-person preterite forms drop the **i** in the ending.

Verb conjugation tables, pp. 257–276. See verb patterns 14, 20, 73.

Infinitive	Stem
conducir	condu**j**-
decir*	di**j**-
introducir	introdu**j**-
producir	produ**j**-
traducir	tradu**j**-
traer	tra**j**-

Endings	
Subject	**decir**
yo	dij**e**
tú/vos	dij**iste**
usted, él, ella	dij**o**
nosotros/as	dij**imos**
vosotros/as	dij**isteis**
ustedes, ellos/as	dij**eron**

—¿**Trajiste** suficiente dinero?   *Did you bring enough money?*
—No, no **traje** dinero.   *No, I didn't bring enough money.*

—¿**Dijisteis** la verdad?   *Did you [pl.] tell the truth?*
—Sí, **dijimos** toda la verdad.   *Yes, we told the whole truth.*

18.B.4 Irregular verbs

Ir, **ser**, and **dar** are irregular in the preterite. Note that the verbs **ser** and **ir** have identical conjugation patterns.

The preterite of *ir, ser,* **and** *dar*		
	ir / ser *to go / to be*	**dar** *to give*
yo	**fui**	**di**
tú/vos	**fuiste**	**diste**
usted, él, ella	**fue**	**dio**
nosotros/as	**fuimos**	**dimos**
vosotros/as	**fuisteis**	**disteis**
ustedes, ellos/as	**fueron**	**dieron**

Verb conjugation tables, pp. 257–276. See verb patterns 19, 40, 66.

—¿**Fuiste** a pasear con Alicia? *Did you go for a walk with Alicia?*
—Sí, **di** un paseo con ella. *Yes, I went for a walk with her.*

18.C Use of the preterite

Uso del pretérito perfecto simple

In Spanish, the preterite is primarily used in the following ways:

18.C.1 To mark the beginning and end of an action

The Spanish preterite indicates the start, the end, or the completion of events and actions in the past. Specific verbs or expressions like *in the end* or *finally* can be used in English to convey this information about the action.

Escribí las cartas.	*I wrote the letters.*
¿Cuándo **empezasteis** el semestre?	*When did you [pl.] start the semester?*
Finalmente **encontré** mis llaves.	*I finally found my keys.*
El perro **se bebió** el agua.	*The dog drank up the water.*

18.C.2 To indicate that an action took place in the past

a. Use of the preterite states that an action or situation actually occurred and ended or did not occur in the past.

Fui a Madrid el año pasado.	*I went to Madrid last year.*
Las clases **me gustaron** mucho.	*I liked the classes a lot.*
Lina no **estuvo** enferma ayer.	*Lina was not sick yesterday.*
Mi abuelo **fue** un gran hombre.	*My grandfather was a great man.*
Ayer no **llovió** en Nueva York.	*Yesterday, it didn't rain in New York.*
Hubo un incendio en un hotel.	*There was a fire in a hotel.*
Nosotros **nos quisimos** mucho.	*We loved each other very much.*
Todo tiempo pasado **fue** mejor.	*In the old days, things were better.*

In the central regions of Spain, Bolivia, and in the north of Argentina, events that have recently occured can be stated using the *present perfect*: **Hoy ha llovido**. *It has rained today.* See Regional variations: 19.C

b. The preterite is used to state historical facts.

La Constitución de Estados Unidos **fue escrita** en 1787.	*The United States Constitution was written in 1787.*
Hernán Cortés **llegó** a México en 1521.	*Hernán Cortés arrived in Mexico in 1521.*
Costó mucho ganar la Segunda Guerra Mundial.	*It cost a lot to win World War II.*
La primera Constitución española **se firmó** en 1812.	*The first Spanish Constitution was signed in 1812.*

Passive voice with **ser**: 28.B

18.C.3 To indicate a sequence of events

a. The preterite can be used to describe actions that were part of a list or chain of events. In this context, the preterite marks the end of one action and the beginning of the next.

Rosa **se levantó** temprano. **Se vistió** rápidamente, no **comió** nada y **salió** corriendo a tomar el autobús.

Rosa got up early. She got dressed quickly, didn't eat anything, and rushed out to catch the bus.

b. Using the imperfect in the same context would indicate habitual or repeated actions in the past.

Rosa **se leventaba** temprano, **se vestía** rápidamente, no **comía** nada y **salía** corriendo a tomar el autobús.

Rosa used to get up early, get dressed quickly, eat nothing, and rush out to catch the bus.

18.D The imperfect tense

El pretérito imperfecto

18.D.1 Regular verbs

Most Spanish verbs have regular forms in the imperfect.

Preterite of regular verbs: p. 261

	-ar **cantar** *to sing*	*-er* **comer** *to eat*	*-ir* **vivir** *to live*
yo	cant**aba**	com**ía**	viv**ía**
tú/vos	cant**abas**	com**ías**	viv**ías**
usted, él, ella	cant**aba**	com**ía**	viv**ía**
nosotros/as	cant**ábamos**	com**íamos**	viv**íamos**
vosotros/as	cant**abais**	com**íais**	viv**íais**
ustedes, ellos/as	cant**aban**	com**ían**	viv**ían**

Flora **vivía** en Bogotá.
Tenía muchos amigos allí.
Se sentía muy contenta.

Flora used to live / lived in Bogotá.
She had many friends there.
She felt very happy.

18.D.2 Irregular verbs

Only three verbs are irregular in the imperfect.

Verb conjugation tables, pp. 257–276. See verb patterns 40, 66, 77.

	ser	**ir**	**ver**
yo	**era**	**iba**	**veía**
tú/vos	**eras**	**ibas**	**veías**
usted, él, ella	**era**	**iba**	**veía**
nosotros/as	**éramos**	**íbamos**	**veíamos**
vosotros/as	**erais**	**ibais**	**veíais**
ustedes, ellos/as	**eran**	**iban**	**veían**

Todo **era** mejor antes.
Íbamos al parque todos los días.
La gente siempre **se veía** feliz.

Everything was better before.
We would / used to go to the park every day.
People always looked happy.

18.E | Use of the imperfect

Uso del pretérito imperfecto

In Spanish, the imperfect is primarily used in the following ways:

18.E.1 | Scene or backdrop

a. The imperfect can be used to *set the scene* for dynamic past actions. For example, it can be used to describe the time of day, how someone felt, or what was happening when another action occurred.

El sol **brillaba**.	*The sun was shining.*
Me sentía optimista.	*I felt optimistic.*
Había paz en el mundo.	*There was peace in the world.*

b. The descriptions above create the backdrop for specific actions that can be expressed using the preterite.

El sol **brillaba** cuando **viajé** ayer.	*The sun was shining when I traveled yesterday.*
Me sentía optimista y todo **salió** bien.	*I felt optimistic and everything went well.*
Había paz en el mundo, pero todo **cambió** en un instante.	*There was peace in the world, but everything changed in an instant.*

c. In stories, the imperfect is used for a description in the past or to tell about what was happening when a specific action occurred. Punctual time expressions like **de pronto** (*suddenly*) and **en ese momento** (*at that moment*) indicate the beginning of a specific past action that interrupts ongoing actions. This interrupting action is expressed with the preterite.

Había paz en el mundo. El sol **brillaba** y **me sentía** optimista, pero ese mismo día **cambió** mi vida para siempre.	*There was peace in the world. The sun was shining and I felt optimistic, but on that same day my life changed forever.*
Anoche **iba** para mi casa. Todo **parecía** muy tranquilo. **Era** tarde y no **se veía** ni un alma, cuando de pronto **escuché** un grito desgarrador.	*I was on my way home last night. Everything seemed very peaceful. It was late and there wasn't a soul to be seen, when suddenly I heard a bloodcurdling scream.*

18.E.2 | Weather

a. Weather can be described using the imperfect as a backdrop for other actions that are expressed in the preterite.

Ayer **nevaba** mucho cuando **salí**.	*It was snowing a lot yesterday when I went out.*

b. When describing the weather during a specific interval in the past, the preterite can be used.

Ayer **nevó** mucho.	*It snowed a lot yesterday.*

18.E.3 | Age

Like the weather, age is a common backdrop for describing past events, and therefore is often expressed using the imperfect. The verb **tener** is used in the imperfect to indicate that someone *was a certain age* when something happened. The verb **cumplir** is used in the preterite to indicate that someone turned a certain age.

Cuando **tenía** dieciocho años, conocí al amor de mi vida.	*When I was eighteen, I met the love of my life.*	◀ **tener** with age: 29.D
Cuando **cumplí** diecinueve años, todo había terminado ya.	*When I turned nineteen, it (our relationship) was over.*	

18.E.4 Characteristics

The imperfect is used to describe the characteristics of people, things, or conditions in the past.

Luis y yo **nos queríamos** mucho.	*Luis and I loved each other a lot.*
Mis abuelos **eran** personas extraordinarias.	*My grandparents were extraordinary people.*

18.E.5 Habits and preferences

With action verbs, the imperfect often describes habits, routines, or events that used to happen repeatedly or at regular intervals in the past. Time expressions such as **todos los días**, **cada año**, **siempre**, etc., are often used to emphasize the repetition of an action.

¿**Ibais** a la escuela todos los días?	*Did you [pl.] go to school every day?*
¿Te **daban** regalos de Navidad?	*Did you use to get Christmas presents?*
Me **gustaba** esquiar.	*I used to like skiing.*

18.E.6 Incomplete action with *ya*

a. After **ya**, the imperfect expresses an action in the past that was about to happen, but was interrupted. **Ir a** + *infinitive* can also be used in the imperfect to express the same thing.

Ya **salía** cuando sonó el teléfono.	*I was on my way out when the phone rang.*
Iban a salir cuando llegaste.	*They were just about to leave when you arrived.*

ir a + infinitive: 26.C.1 ▶

b. The imperfect can be used to express two or more past actions that used to happen at the same time. Note the significant difference with the use of the preterite.

Siempre **me caía** cuando **montaba** en bicicleta.	*I always used to fall when riding my bike.*
Me caí cuando **monté** en bicicleta.	*I fell when I was riding my bike / rode my bike.*

18.E.7 Courtesy

The imperfect can be used to make polite requests.

Quería pedirte una cosa.	*I wanted to ask you for something.*
Venía a solicitar información.	*I came to ask for some information.*

18.E.8 Dreams and children's games

When children invent games based on fantasy or imagination, the context is created using the *imperfect*. When dreams are talked about, the start of the story is often **Soñé que...** and the rest is told in the *imperfect* and other past structures. The *preterite* is rarely used.

Juguemos a que **estábamos** en una nave espacial, que tú **eras** un monstruo y que yo te **perseguía**.	*Let's play that we are in a spaceship, you're a monster and I'm chasing you.*
Soñé que era el día del examen y que no **había estudiado** nada.	*I dreamt that it was exam day and that I hadn't studied anything.*

18.E.9 Completed actions with the imperfect

In news reports and historical texts, the imperfect is sometimes used in place of the preterite to describe a completed action. This stylistic choice lends greater immediacy and a descriptive tone to the narration.

La boda real se realizó ayer en La Almudena. Unas horas después, Madrid **celebraba** la boda del siglo con fiestas en toda la ciudad.	*The royal wedding was held yesterday in La Almudena. Some hours later, Madrid celebrated the wedding of the century with parties all over the city.*

18.E.10   Indirect discourse

a. Indirect discourse is a way to report what someone said without using a direct quote. Indirect discourse is expressed using a subordinate clause with **que**. Quotation marks are not used.

◀ Indirect discourse: Ch. 31

Direct discourse	Indirect discourse
Él **dice**: "No tengo dinero". *He says: "I don't have any money."*	Él **dice/piensa que** no **tiene** dinero. *He says that he doesn't have any money.*
Tú **dijiste**: "Ella **quiere** viajar". *You said: "She wants to travel."*	Tú **dijiste que** ella **quería** viajar. *You said that she wanted to travel.*
Él **decía**: "Ellas no **saben** nada". *He said: "They don't know anything."*	Él **decía que** ellas no **sabían** nada. *He said that they didn't know anything.*
Ellos **dijeron**: "**Esperamos** que no **suban** los precios". *They said: "We hope the prices won't go up."*	Ellos **dijeron que esperaban** que no **subieran** los precios. *They said that they hoped the prices wouldn't go up.*

◀ When the verbs express will or desire, the subjunctive is used in the subordinate clause, but the structure to express indirect discourse is the same.

b. The imperfect is used in indirect discourse when information or questions that were in the present tense in direct discourse are supplied with the preterite of verbs like **decir**, **preguntar**, **comentar**, or other reporting verbs.

Rita dijo que no **tenía** dinero.	*Rita said she didn't have any money.*
Te pregunté que si **querías** cenar.	*I asked you if you wanted to have dinner.*

c. **Ir a** + *infinitive* expresses the future in Spanish. The imperfect of **ir** is often used in indirect discourse to describe what someone *was going to do*.

◀ ir a + *infinitive*: 26.C.1

Jaime me contó que **iba** a viajar.	*Jaime told me that he was going to travel.*
Te pregunté que si **ibas** a cenar.	*I asked you if you were going to have dinner.*

18.E.11   Expressions with *hace/hacía* + **period of time** + *que (no)*

a. **Hace/Hacía** + *period of time* + *que (no)* is used to express *how long since something has (not) been done*. In affirmative sentences, it is equivalent to the verbal periphrasis **llevar** + *time expression* + **gerundio**. In negative sentences, it is equivalent to **llevar** + *time expression* + **sin** + *infinitive*.

◀ llevar + *time expression* + **gerundio**: 26.D

Hace tres años **que vivo** en Madrid. **Llevo** tres años **viviendo** en Madrid.	*I have lived in Madrid for three years.*
Hace un año **que no voy** a Londres. **Llevo** un año **sin ir** a Londres.	*It's been a year since I was last in London. / I haven't been in London for a year.*
¡**Hacía** mucho tiempo **que no** te **veía**! ¡**Llevaba** mucho tiempo **sin verte**!	*I hadn't seen you for ages.*

b. The imperfect is often used when you want to express that a certain amount of time is over.

Llevo mucho tiempo **sin verte**.	*Long time no see. (I still haven't seen you.)*
Llevaba mucho tiempo **sin verte**.	*It's been so long since I've seen you. (But now I've seen you.)*

18.E.12   Impersonal constructions *había, hubo*

When the verb **haber** is used to express existence in the past (*there was/were*), it is always conjugated in the third-person singular. The preterite of **haber**, **hubo**, expresses an action or state that has ended, while the imperfect, **había**, describes the existence of something in the past without stating that it ended.

En el siglo XX **hubo** muchas guerras.	*In the 20th century, there were many wars.*
Casi en ningún país **había** paz en esa época.	*Almost no country had peace during that period.*

Verbos cuyo significado cambia

Some common verbs have different meanings in the preterite and the imperfect. Note that the meaning may also change depending on whether the statement is affirmative or negative.

The examples in this chart describe scenes and narrate events in the story *La siesta del martes* by Gabriel García Márquez.

Saber: 26.B.7

Querer: 26.B.6

Poder: 26.B.5

Verb	Preterite	Imperfect
tener	*to get; to receive* El sacerdote **tuvo** una visita inesperada: la madre y la hermana del difunto. *The priest got an unexpected visit: the mother and the sister of the deceased.*	*to have* La hija **tenía** dificultades para mover la persiana. *The daughter was having a hard time moving the blinds.*
saber	*to find out; to discover* **Supieron** que Carlos se murió el lunes anterior. *They found out that Carlos died the previous Monday.*	*to know* El padre no **sabía** quiénes eran. *The father did not know who they were.*
querer	*to try (without necessarily succeeding)* La mujer **quiso** visitar el cementerio donde estaba enterrado su hijo. *The woman tried to visit the graveyard where her son was buried.*	*to want* La gente del pueblo se asomaba a la ventana porque **quería** ver qué sucedía. *The townspeople looked out their windows because they wanted to see what was happening.*
no querer	*to refuse* La mujer **no quiso** irse de la casa del cura sin verlo. *The woman refused to leave the rectory without seeing him.*	*not to want* La mujer **no quería** despertar al cura. *The woman did not want to wake up the priest.*
conocer	*to meet* Cuando el cura **conoció** a la mujer, se quedó muy sorprendido. *When the priest met the woman, he was very surprised.*	*to know about, to be familiar with* Nadie **conocía** a Carlos en ese pueblo. *Nobody in that town knew Carlos.*
poder	*to manage to do; to succeed in doing* La mujer **pudo** convencer a la hermana del cura de que fuera a buscarlo. *The woman managed to convince the priest's sister to go fetch him.*	*to be able to; to have the ability* En la distancia, **se podía** escuchar la música que tocaba la banda. *The music the band was playing could be heard in the distance.*
no poder	*to be unable to* La chica **no pudo** subir la ventana del tren. *The girl was unable to close the window in the train.*	*to be unable to (in a general sense)* **No se podía** respirar en el tren a causa del calor. *It was so hot inside the train that one could not breathe.*

Práctica

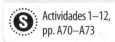
Actividades 1–12, pp. A70–A73

The present perfect and the past perfect
Pretérito perfecto compuesto y pluscuamperfecto

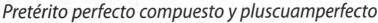

19.A The present perfect

Pretérito perfecto compuesto

The present perfect is formed in Spanish with the present indicative of the auxiliary verb **haber** (see table below) and the past participle of the main verb.

¿**Has leído** este libro?   *Have you read this book?*

19.A.1 Regular past participles

a. To form the past participle, the ending **-ado** is added to regular **-ar** verbs and the ending **-ido** is added to regular **-er** and **-ir** verbs. The **tú** and **vos** forms are the same.

Present perfect					
Subject pronoun	Present indicative of *haber*	+	Regular past participles		
			-ar verbs: *-ado*	*-er* and *-ir* verbs: *-ido*	
			hablar	querer	venir
yo	he				
tú/vos	has				
usted, él, ella	ha	+	habl**ado**	quer**ido**	ven**ido**
nosotros/as	hemos				
vosotros/as	habéis				
ustedes, ellos/as	han				

◀ Compound tenses: Verb conjugation tables, p. 261

◀ The present perfect used to be called the **pretérito perfecto**. Nowadays, it is referred to as **pretérito perfecto compuesto**.

b. In the present perfect, the past participle always ends in **-o**. Unlike in English, in Spanish, words cannot come between **haber** and the past participle. Object and reflexive pronouns must be placed before **haber**.

Siempre **he trabajado** mucho.   *I **have** always **worked** a lot.*

Lo **he buscado** por todos lados.   *I **have looked** for it all over the place.*

Lucas **se ha quedado** dormido.   *Lucas **has overslept.***

◀ The past participle in passive **ser** clauses: 28.B.3
Compound tenses using **haber**: Verb conjugation tables: p. 261

c. When the verb stem of an **-er** or **-ir** verb ends in any vowel except for **-u**, a written accent must be added to the participle, forming the ending **-ído**. The combination of **u** + **i** usually forms a diphthong and does not have a written accent (constr**ui**do, h**ui**do).

◀ Diphthongs: 1.C.2, 1.D.2

Infinitive	Verb stem	Past participle	
creer	cre-	creído	*thought, believed*
leer	le-	leído	*read*
oír	o-	oído	*heard*
sonreír	sonre-	sonreído	*smiled*
traer	tra-	traído	*brought*

¿Has **leído** novelas españolas?   *Have you read Spanish novels?*

a. A number of verbs have an irregular past participle. Most irregular past participles end in **-to**.

Infinitive	Irregular past participles	
abrir	**abierto**	opened
cubrir	**cubierto**	covered
decir	**dicho**	said, told
describir	**descrito**	described
descubrir	**descubierto**	discovered
escribir	**escrito**	written
hacer	**hecho**	done, made
morir	**muerto**	died
poner	**puesto**	placed
resolver	**resuelto**	resolved
romper	**roto**	broken
satisfacer	**satisfecho**	satisfied
ver	**visto**	seen
volver	**vuelto**	returned

Las tiendas no **han abierto** todavía.   *The shops **haven't opened** yet.*

b. The following three verbs have two equally accepted participles, a regular and an irregular form. Both can be used to form compound tenses and passive sentences. The use of **frito**, **impreso**, and **provisto** is increasing in all Spanish-speaking countries as opposed to the regular participles.

Passive voice with **ser**: 28.B ▶

Irregular participles: 25.D.2 ▶

Infinitive	Past participle	
	Regular	Irregular
freír (*to fry*)	fre**ído**	**frito**
imprimir (*to print*)	imprim**ido**	**impreso**
proveer (*to provide*)	prove**ído**	**provisto**

El chef ha **frito (freído)** las cebollas.   *The chef has fried the onions.*
Las cebollas han sido **fritas (freídas)** por el chef.   *The onions have been fried by the chef.*
El secretario **ha impreso (imprimido)** la agenda.   *The secretary has printed the agenda.*
La agenda **ha sido impresa (imprimida)** por el secretario.   *The agenda has been printed by the secretary.*
La agencia de viajes **ha provisto (proveído)** los itinerarios.   *The travel agency has provided the itineraries.*
Los itinerarios **han sido provistos (proveídos)** por la agencia de viajes.   *The itineraries have been provided by the travel agency.*

c. Only the irregular forms can function as adjectives:

las papas *fritas* (*Latin America*)
las patatas *fritas* (*Spain*)   *the potato chips / French fries*
los documentos *impresos*   *the printed documents*
los uniformes *provistos*   *the provided uniforms*

19.B Use of the present perfect

Uso del pretérito perfecto compuesto

The use of the present perfect has regional differences. The following examples show common uses of this tense in most Spanish-speaking regions.

19.B.1 Life experiences – *nunca, alguna vez, hasta ahora, en mi vida*

a. The present perfect can be used to describe life experiences up to the present moment. Adverbs like **alguna vez, nunca, hasta ahora/hoy,** and **en mi vida** (*never before*) are commonly used.

¿Has viajado en barco **alguna vez**?	*Have you ever traveled by boat?*
Nunca he probado el alcohol.	*I have never tried alcohol.*
¡**En mi vida** he estudiado tanto!	*I have never studied so much in my life!*
Hasta ahora, todo **ha salido** bien.	*Everything has gone well until now.*

b. Context usually implies the point in time when the adverb is not explicit.

Amy hace un café delicioso,	*Amy makes a delicious coffee.*
¿lo **has probado** (alguna vez)?	*Have you (ever) tried it?*

19.B.2 Incomplete actions – *todavía no*

The present perfect is used with **todavía no** (*not yet*) to express actions that are not yet complete.

¿**No has salido** todavía?	*Haven't you gone out / left yet?*
No, todavía **no he salido**.	*No, I haven't gone out / left yet.*

19.B.3 Continuous actions – *siempre*

Siempre and other continuous expressions of time like **muchas veces, todos los días,** etc., are used with the present perfect to extend the action into the present. The preterite, in contrast, fixes the action in the past.

Siempre **te he querido**.	*I have always loved you.*
Siempre **te quise**.	*I always loved you.*
Hemos ido al cine todos los días.	*We have been to the movies every day.*
Fuimos al cine todos los días.	*We went to the movies every day.*

19.C Regional variations

Variaciones regionales

The following examples show the major differences when using the present perfect in Spain and Latin America. There are also variations within each of these regions.

19.C.1 Recently completed actions – *ya, por fin, finalmente*

a. Ya (*already*), **por fin** (*in the end*), and **finalmente** (*finally*) indicate completed actions. In Spain, these phrases are usually used with the present perfect, while the preterite is preferred in most parts of Latin America.

Spain	¡Por fin **has llegado**!	*You have finally arrived!*
Latin America	¡Por fin **llegaste**!	

b. Questions and answers with **ya** and **todavía no** are generally used with different verb tenses in Spain and Latin America.

Spain	—¿Ya **has cenado**?	Have you had dinner yet?
	—No, **todavía no he cenado**.	No, I haven't had dinner yet.
	—Sí, **ya he cenado**.	Yes, I have already had dinner.

Latin America	—¿Ya **cenaste**?	Did you eat dinner yet?
	—No, **todavía no he cenado**.	No, I haven't had dinner yet.
	—Sí, **ya cené**.	Yes, I already ate dinner.

c. In central parts of Spain, the present perfect is used to convey actions completed in the near past. The length of this time period in the past can be subjective and is indicated by time expressions such as **hace un momento, este año, hoy,** and so on. This use is also common in the northwest of Argentina and in Bolivia.

Spain (central)	Hace un momento **he visto** a Ernesto.	I saw Ernesto a short time ago.
Latin America	Hace un momento **vi** a Ernesto.	

19.C.2 Interpreting time using the present perfect

When the period of time is specified, the present perfect can be interpreted differently in central parts of Spain and in most parts of Latin America.

Spain (central)	Este verano **hemos ido** mucho al cine.	This summer, we've been to the movies a lot. (The summer is over.)
Latin America		This summer, we've been to the movies a lot. (The summer is not over yet.)

19.C.3 Cause and effect

Cause and effect relationships in the near past are expressed using the present perfect in Spain and the preterite in Latin America.

Spain	—¿Por qué **has llegado** tan tarde hoy? —¡**He perdido** el autobús!	Why did you arrive so late today? I missed the bus!
Latin America	—¿Por qué **llegaste** tan tarde hoy? —¡**Perdí** el autobús!	

19.D The past perfect

Pretérito pluscuamperfecto

The past perfect is formed using the imperfect of **haber** and the past participle of the main verb: **había hablado** (*I had talked*).

Compound tenses: Verb conjugation tables, p. 261
Past participles: 19.A, 25.D

Pluscuamperfecto						
Subject pronoun	Imperfect of *haber*	+	Regular past participles			
			-ar verbs: *-ado*	*-er* and *-ir* verbs: *-ido*		
			hablar	querer	venir	
yo	**había**					
tú/vos	**habías**					
usted, él, ella	**había**	+	habl**ado**	quer**ido**	ven**ido**	
nosotros/as	**habíamos**					
vosotros/as	**habíais**					
ustedes, ellos/as	**habían**					

19.E Use of the past perfect

Uso del pretérito pluscuamperfecto

19.E.1 Past before the past

In Spanish, the past perfect expresses what someone *had done*, or what *had occurred* before another action or condition in the past.

Cuando Lina llamó, Pedro ya **había llamado**.   *When Lina called, Pedro had already called.*

19.E.2 Questions and answers with *ya, todavía no* in the past

Antes, aún, nunca, todavía, and **ya** are often used with the past perfect to indicate the order of past actions. These adverbs, as well as pronouns and the word **no**, cannot come between **haber** and the past participle.

—¿Ya **habías estudiado** español cuando viajaste a Santiago?

Had you already studied Spanish when you traveled to Santiago?

—Claro, ya **había estudiado** español y sabía bastante.

Of course, I had already studied Spanish and I knew quite a lot.

—Cuando llegué a Santiago, no **había estudiado** español todavía.

When I arrived in Santiago, I had not studied Spanish yet.

19.E.3 Indirect discourse

In indirect discourse, the preterite becomes the past perfect.

Camilo dijo: "Vi los fiordos chilenos".   *Camilo said, "I saw the Chilean fjords."*
Camilo me contó que **había visto** los fiordos chilenos.   *Camilo told me that he had seen the Chilean fjords.*

19.F The *pretérito anterior*

The **pretérito anterior** is formed using the preterite of **haber** and the past participle of the main verb. This form of the past perfect is rare in today's spoken Spanish and is generally used only in written language.

Past participles: 19.A, 25.D

			Regular past participles		
Subject pronoun	**Preterite of** *haber*	**+**	***-ar* verbs: *-ado***	***-er* and *-ir* verbs: *-ido***	
			hablar	**querer**	**venir**
yo	**hube**				
tú/vos	**hubiste**				
usted, él, ella	**hubo**	**+**	habl**ado**	quer**ido**	ven**ido**
nosotros/as	**hubimos**				
vosotros/as	**hubisteis**				
ustedes, ellos/as	**hubieron**				

Pretérito anterior (table title)

19.G Use of the *pretérito anterior*

Uso del pretérito anterior

a. The **pretérito anterior** marks the end of an action that happened before another action in the past.

Cuando **se hubo tomado** la decisión, concluyeron la reunión.

When the decision had been made, they ended the meeting.

b. The **pretérito anterior** can be replaced with the preterite (**pretérito perfecto simple**).

Cuando **se tomó** la decisión, concluyeron la reunión.

When the decision was made, they ended the meeting.

Práctica

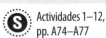
Actividades 1–12, pp. A74–A77

The future
Futuro

20.A Future expressions

Estructuras para expresar el futuro
In Spanish, the future can be expressed using the following structures:

Spanish future expressions		
1. Simple future	Te **devolveré** tus libros muy pronto.	***I will give** you **back** your books very soon.*
2. *ir a + infinitive*	**Vamos a construir** una nueva casa.	***We are going to build** a new house.*
3. Present indicative	**Regreso** el lunes.	***I am coming back** on Monday.* (lit. ***I come back** on Monday.*)

As you can see above, future actions and events can be expressed in Spanish and English using the simple future and *going to + infinitive* expressions. In English, the present progressive may also refer to a future event or action. Note that the Spanish present progressive *cannot* be used to refer to the future. The simple present, however, can be used in Spanish to refer to the future.

◀ Present progressive: 17.F
Present with future meaning: 17.E.4

◀ Other future expressions: 20.D

20.B The simple future

Futuro simple
The future tense of regular verbs is formed by adding future endings to the infinitive ending. Irregular verbs use the same endings, but have changes in the stems. The **tú** and **vos** endings are the same.

20.B.1 Regular verbs

All regular verbs have a written accent in the future tense except the first-person plural, **nosotros/as**.

◀ Regular verbs: verb conjugation tables, p. 261

	-ar	*-er*	*-ir*
yo	trabajar**é**	comer**é**	ir**é**
tú/vos	trabajar**ás**	comer**ás**	ir**ás**
usted, él, ella	trabajar**á**	comer**á**	ir**á**
nosotros/as	trabajar**emos**	comer**emos**	ir**emos**
vosotros/as	trabajar**éis**	comer**éis**	ir**éis**
ustedes, ellos/as	trabajar**án**	comer**án**	ir**án**

20.B.2 Irregular verbs

Few verbs are irregular in the simple future. The verbs that are irregular have a stem change, but take the same endings as regular verbs in the future.

Infinitive	Stem	Infinitive	Stem	Infinitive	Stem
caber	**cabr-**	poder	**podr-**	salir	**saldr-**
decir	**dir-**	poner	**pondr-**	tener	**tendr-**
haber	**habr-**	querer	**querr-**	valer	**valdr-**
hacer	**har-**	saber	**sabr-**	venir	**vendr-**

◀ Verb conjugation tables, pp. 257– 276.

—¿**Vendrás** pronto?   *Will you come soon?*
—Sí, lo **haré**.   *Yes, I will (come).*

20.C Use of the simple future

Uso del futuro simple

20.C.1 Future actions

The simple future is generally used to express future actions and events.

¿**Viajaréis** de vacaciones en julio?	*Will you [pl.] travel / go away on vacation in July?*

20.C.2 Suppositions

The simple future tense can be used to express suppositions or guesses about present or future actions or states. Whether the present or future is referred to depends on the context.

Assumptions about events in the past: 20.F.2

a. Suppositions about the present:

—¿Quién **será** ese hombre?	*I wonder who that man is? / Who may that man be?*
—No lo sé. **Será** alguna persona importante.	*I don't know. He may be an important person.*

b. Suppositions about the future:

—¿Quién **hará** el trabajo? ¿Tú?	*Who will do the job? You?*
—¿Yo? No, lo **hará** Rubén. (Supongo que lo **hará** Rubén.)	*Me? No, Rubén will do it. (I suppose Rubén will do it.)*

20.C.3 Predictions

The simple future is used in forecasts, horoscopes, and predictions.

Mañana **nevará** en las montañas.	*Tomorrow, it will snow in the mountains.*
Las personas de Aries **tendrán** una agradable sorpresa esta semana.	*People born under Aries will have a pleasant surprise this week.*
Predicen que los precios **subirán**.	*They predict that prices will go up.*
Todo **saldrá** bien, ya **verás**.	*Everything will be all right, you'll see.*

20.C.4 Conditional constructions

Conditional conjunctions: 16.D
Conditional **si** clauses: 23.E.8

The simple future can be used to describe something that will happen under certain imagined conditions. When the condition is seen as possible, it is expressed with the present indicative in a **si** clause.

Si nos ganamos la lotería, **compraremos** la casa.	*If we win the lottery, we'll buy the house.*

20.C.5 Decrees

In written language, the simple future is used for laws, regulations, and decrees.

No **matarás**.	*Thou shall not kill.*

20.C.6 Impersonal constructions – *habrá*

When **haber** is used as an impersonal verb in the third-person singular of the future tense, it indicates future existence (*there will [not] be*).

No **habrá** reunión mañana.	*There won't be a meeting tomorrow.*
Habrá vacaciones en julio.	*There will be vacation in July.*
No **habrá** lluvia mañana.	*There won't be rain tomorrow.*
Creo que **habrá** tiempo suficiente.	*I think there will be enough time.*

20.C.7 Contrast – *shall, will*

a. In American English, the simple future is formed by adding the auxiliary *will*, but pay attention to the following uses of *shall* and its Spanish equivalents:

164　　　　　　　　　　　　　　　　　　　　　　　　　　　The future • **Chapter 20**

Communicative function	Spanish	English
Express formal obligation	**Habrá** sanciones.	There **shall** (will) be sanctions.
Express suggestions and requests	¿**Empezamos** (ya)?	**Shall** we start?

b. These Spanish equivalents of *will* are used for making announcements, asking polite questions, offering or refusing to help, ordering in a restaurant, and selecting items in a store.

Se abrirá un nuevo centro comercial.	*A new shopping mall will be opened.*
¿**Asistirá** usted a la reunión?	*Will you attend the meeting?*
¡Yo **abro**!	*I'll get it! (I will open the door.)*
¡Yo no **abro**! (Yo no **abriré**.)	*I won't get it! (I won't open the door.)*
Tráigame una ensalada, por favor.	*I'll have a salad, please.*
Me llevo la blusa roja.	*I'll take the red blouse.*

20.D Other future expressions

Otras expresiones del futuro

20.D.1 *Ir a* + **infinitive**

a. This form is used to express plans or intentions to be carried out immediately or in the very near future.

◀ Ir a + infinitive: 26.C.1

—¿Qué **vas a hacer** esta tarde?	*What are you going to do this afternoon?*
—Estoy rendido y **voy a descansar**.	*I'm exhausted and I'm going to rest.*

b. The form **ir a** + *infinitive* describes events which in all likelihood will happen in the near future.

Es muy tarde. ¡**Vas a perder** el tren!	*It's very late. You are going to miss the train!*

c. **Ir a** + *infinitive* is used in expressions with **ya** to describe an impending event.

Ya **va a empezar** el noticiero.	*The news cast is going to start now.*

20.D.2 The present indicative to express future

The present indicative can only be used to describe future actions if the context refers to the future. Adverbs of time are often part of the sentence.

Las clases **empiezan** mañana.	*School starts tomorrow.*

20.E The future perfect

Futuro compuesto

The future perfect is formed with the simple future of the auxiliary verb **haber** and the past participle of the main verb. **Tú** and **vos** take the same verb form in the future perfect.

◀ Past participles: 19.A.1–2, 25.D

Simple future of *haber*		+	Regular past participles		
			-ar **verbs:** *-ado*	*-er* **and** *-ir* **verbs:** *-ido*	
			hablar	**querer**	**venir**
yo	**habré**				
tú/vos	**habrás**				
usted, él, ella	**habrá**	+	habl**ado**	quer**ido**	ven**ido**
nosotros/as	**habremos**				
vosotros/as	**habréis**				
ustedes, ellos/as	**habrán**				

20.F | Use of the future perfect

Uso del futuro compuesto

20.F.1 A complete action in the future

The future perfect describes an action that will already be complete (*will have happened*) after a specific point in time in the future.

Mañana a esta hora, **habremos regresado** a casa.	*By this time tomorrow, we'll have returned home.*
En junio, ya **habrás terminado** tus estudios.	*By June, you'll have already finished your studies.*

20.F.2 Assumptions about the past

Suppositions about the present or future: 20.C.2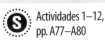

a. The future perfect can express an assumption or guess about the probability of an action or state in the past.

¿Cómo me **habrá ido** en el examen ayer?	*I wonder how I did on the exam yesterday?*
Jaime no vino a trabajar el lunes. ¿Dónde **habrá estado**?	*Jaime didn't come to work on Monday. Where could he have been?*

b. Like the simple future, the future perfect can be used to express distance from past events or reference to other sources.

Según nuestro corresponsal, **habrá habido** muchas personas afectadas por el accidente.	*According to our correspondent, many people will have been affected by the accident.*

20.F.3 Conditional constructions

Conditional conjunctions: 16.D
Conditional clauses: 23.E.8

The future perfect expresses what we believe will have happened if a present condition is fulfilled. The **si** clause describing the condition uses the present indicative.

Si no estudias, **habrás perdido** el tiempo en la escuela.	*If you don't study, you will have wasted your time at school.*

20.F.4 Impersonal constructions – *habrá habido*

The impersonal form of **haber** (*will have been*) can be used to express assumptions about what could have been.

¿**Habrá habido** algún problema?	*Could there have been a problem?*
¿**Habrá habido** buenos resultados en el examen?	*Could there have been good exam results?*

20.G | Regional variations

Variaciones regionales

There are few regional differences in future verb forms in Spanish. It is a bit more common to use **ir a** + *infinitive* in Latin America to refer to both the near and distant future.

Spain	Este año me **graduaré**.	*I'm going to / I will graduate this year.*
Latin America	Este año me **voy a graduar**.	

Práctica

S Actividades 1–12, pp. A77–A80

The conditional
Condicional

21.A The present conditional

Condicional simple

In English, the conditional is expressed with the words *would/should*. In Spanish, the conditional tense is expressed with its own verb forms.

Me alegraría verte de nuevo.   *It would make me happy to see you again.*

Roberto dijo que te **llamaría**.   *Roberto said that he would call you.*

The present conditional of all Spanish verbs is formed by adding the conditional endings to the infinitive endings. The **tú** and **vos** endings are the same.

21.A.1 Regular verbs

All forms have a written accent.

	-ar	**-er**	**-ir**
yo	trabajar**ía**	comer**ía**	subir**ía**
tú/vos	trabajar**ías**	comer**ías**	subir**ías**
usted, él, ella	trabajar**ía**	comer**ía**	subir**ía**
nosotros/as	trabajar**íamos**	comer**íamos**	subir**íamos**
vosotros/as	trabajar**íais**	comer**íais**	subir**íais**
ustedes, ellos/as	trabajar**ían**	comer**ían**	subir**ían**

◀ Regular verbs: Verb conjugation tables, p. 261

21.A.2 Irregular verbs

Irregular verbs have the same stem changes in the conditional as in the simple future tense.

Infinitive	Stem	Infinitive	Stem
caber	**cabr-**	querer	**querr-**
decir	**dir-**	saber	**sabr-**
haber	**habr-**	salir	**saldr-**
hacer	**har-**	tener	**tendr-**
poder	**podr-**	valer	**valdr-**
poner	**pondr-**	venir	**vendr-**

◀ Irregular verbs in the simple future: 20.B.2

◀ Irregular verbs are found alphabetically in the Verb conjugation tables, pp. 257–276.

—¿**Podrías** hacerme un favor?   *Could you do me a favor?*

—Lo **haría** si pudiera.   *I would (do it) if I could.*

21.B Use of the present conditional

Uso del condicional simple

21.B.1 Imagined possibility or characterisitic

The present conditional expresses a possibility in the near future.

Llegaríamos más rápido en avión.   *We would arrive faster by plane.*

Estarías mejor en otro trabajo.   *You would be better off at another job.*

21.B.2   Assumptions about the past

The present conditional can be used to express uncertainties or assumptions about the past.

Jaime no vino a trabajar el lunes. ¿Dónde **estaría**?	*Jaime didn't come to work on Monday. Where could/would he have been?*
Supongo que hace mil años la gente **hablaría** de forma muy distinta.	*I suppose that a thousand years ago people would/could have spoken very differently.*
¿Cómo me **iría** en el examen ayer?	*I wonder how it went (for me) / I did on my exam yesterday.*

21.B.3   Wishes

The present conditional is used with verbs like **gustar, preferir, desear, encantar,** and **alegrar** to express wishes or preferences.

Me encantaría ir al teatro.	*I would love to go to the theater.*
¿**Te gustaría** estudiar español?	*Would you like to study Spanish?*

21.B.4   Courtesy

Imperatives: 24.G.3b

The conditional is used to communicate polite inquiries and requests.

¿**Podrías** ayudarme con esto?	*Could you help me with this?*
¿**Sería** posible realizar la reunión el lunes?	*Could/Would it be possible to hold the meeting on Monday?*

21.B.5   Advice

The conditional is used to give advice with verbs like **deber** and impersonal expressions like **ser bueno, ser mejor,** and **ser conveniente**.

Subjunctive with impersonal expressions: 23.C.8

Deberíais dejar de fumar.	*You [pl.] should stop smoking.*
Sería conveniente que fueras al médico.	*It would be good if you went to the doctor.*
En tu lugar, yo no **haría** eso.	*If I were you / If I were in your shoes, I wouldn't do that.*

Indirect discourse: Ch. 31

21.B.6   Indirect discourse

The conditional is used to express what *would happen* in the future, from the perspective of a past event.

Has prometido varias veces que **iríamos** de compras hoy.	*You have promised several times that we would go shopping today.*
Supe que **habría** una conferencia y he venido para escucharla.	*I found out that there would be a lecture and I've come to listen to it.*

Conditional conjunctions: 16.D
Conditional **si** clauses: 23.E.8

21.B.7   Conditional constructions

The present conditional is used to express what would happen in hypothetical circumstances. The condition is expressed with the imperfect subjunctive in the **si** clause.

The imperfect subjunctive: 22.C

Si no estudiaras, **perderías** el tiempo en la escuela.	*If you didn't study, you would waste your time at school.*
No me **quedaría** en casa el fin de semana si no tuviera que estudiar.	*I wouldn't stay home this weekend if I didn't have to study.*
Si pudierais viajar a cualquier parte, ¿adónde **iríais**?	*If you [pl.] could travel anywhere, where would you go?*

The present conditional form of **haber, habría** (*there would be*), is used to express the possibility that something could happen or could exist.

Con menor velocidad en las carreteras, **habría** menos accidentes.	*With slower speeds on the roads, there would be fewer accidents.*

21.C The conditional perfect

Condicional compuesto

The conditional perfect is formed with **habría** + *past participle*.

<table>
<thead>
<tr>
<th colspan="2" rowspan="3">Conditional of
haber</th>
<th rowspan="3">+</th>
<th colspan="3">Regular past participles</th>
</tr>
<tr>
<th>-ar verbs: -ado</th>
<th colspan="2">-er and -ir verbs: -ido</th>
</tr>
<tr>
<th>hablar</th>
<th>querer</th>
<th>venir</th>
</tr>
</thead>
<tbody>
<tr>
<td>yo</td><td>habría</td>
<td rowspan="6">+</td>
<td rowspan="6">hablado</td>
<td rowspan="6">querido</td>
<td rowspan="6">venido</td>
</tr>
<tr><td>tú/vos</td><td>habrías</td></tr>
<tr><td>usted, él, ella</td><td>habría</td></tr>
<tr><td>nosotros/as</td><td>habríamos</td></tr>
<tr><td>vosotros/as</td><td>habríais</td></tr>
<tr><td>ustedes, ellos/as</td><td>habrían</td></tr>
</tbody>
</table>

◀ Past participles: 19.A.1–2, 25.D

21.D Use of the conditional perfect

Uso del condicional compuesto

21.D.1 Imagined possibility or characterisitic

The conditional perfect can be used to describe an imagined state in contrast to a present situation (what *would [not] have* happened).

Habríamos llegado más rápido en avión.	*We would have arrived faster by plane.*
Habrías estado mejor en otro trabajo.	*You would have been better off at another job.*
Me aseguraste que hoy, a esta hora, ya **habríamos salido** de compras.	*You assured me that today, by this time, we would already have gone out shopping.*
En tu lugar, yo no **habría gastado** tanto dinero en un auto.	*If I were you / If I were in your shoes, I wouldn't have spent so much money on a car.*
La semana pasada **habrías podido** comprar mejores boletos.	*Last week you would have been able to buy better tickets.*

21.D.2 Conditional constructions

The conditional perfect can also be used to express what would have happened in a hypothetical past circumstance. The circumstance or condition is stated in the **si** clause using the past perfect subjunctive.

◀ Conditional conjunctions: 16.D
Conditional **si** clauses: 23.E.8

◀ The past perfect subjunctive: 22.E

Si hubieras estudiado, no **habrías perdido** el tiempo en la escuela.	*If you had studied, you wouldn't have wasted time in school.*
Te **habría invitado** si me hubieras dicho que querías ir.	*I would have invited you if you had told me you wanted to go.*

Modal verb periphrases with
the infinitive: 26.B.2

21.D.3 **English** *should have*

The present conditional of **deber / tener que** + *perfect infinitive* (**haber** + *past participle*) is used to express that something *should have been done*.

Deberías haber estudiado más si querías aprobar el examen.	*You ought to / should have studied more if you wanted to pass the exam.*
Tendrías que haber estudiado más si querías aprobar el examen.	*You should have studied / would have had to study more if you wanted to pass the exam.*

21.D.4 **Impersonal constructions** – *habría habido*

The conditional perfect form of **haber**, **habría** (*there would have been*), is used to express the possibility that something *could have existed* or *could have been*.

Con menor velocidad en las carreteras, **habría habido** menos accidentes.	*With slower speeds on the roads, there would have been fewer accidents.*

Práctica

 Actividades 1–13, pp. A81–A84

The subjunctive
Subjuntivo

22.A Overview

Aspectos generales

Verbs have various grammatical properties. One of the most obvious is *tense*, which tells *when* an action takes place: *past, present*, or *future*. Another important grammatical property is *mood*, which reflects the *intention* of the speaker. Like English, Spanish has three verb moods: *imperative, indicative*, and *subjunctive*. The imperative is used to give commands, the indicative is used to express certainty and objectivity, and the subjunctive is used to express uncertainty and subjectivity, such as doubts, wishes, reactions (i.e., feelings), or imagined realities. The subjunctive mood is rarely used in English, but is essential in Spanish.

The Spanish name for the subjunctive, **subjuntivo**, refers to the dependency of the verb on another element, usually a *governing finite verb*. The governing verb in the sentence generally indicates whether the subjunctive will be used in the dependent clause. When the governing verb communicates a wish (**desear, esperar, necesitar, querer,** etc.), emotion (verbs used with indirect object pronouns, such as **desilusionar, gustar, enojar, encantar, temer,** etc.), impersonal expression (**es bueno que, es fácil que, no conviene que,** etc.), doubt (**dudar, negar,** etc.), or request (**insistir, pedir, prohibir,** etc.), the subjunctive is used.

The governing finite verb: When there is a main clause and a subordinate clause, there are two verbs. The verb in the main clause is the governing finite verb: 23.C

22.B The present subjunctive

Presente de subjuntivo

a. Most of the examples of *subjunctive* used in this chapter appear in groups of three sentences. The first sentence shows the subjunctive in a *nominal* **que**-clause. The second sentence shows the subjunctive in a relative, *adjectival* clause and the third sentence shows the subjunctive in an *adverbial* clause.

Nominal **que**-clause: 23.C
Adjectival clause (relative clause): 23.D
Adverbial clause: 23.E

b. In regions that use **voseo**, the **vos** endings for the present subjunctive can vary. In some areas, the **vos** endings and the **tú** endings are the same: **Quiero que tú/vos salgas de aquí ya mismo.** This is the conjugation presented in this book. The most common **voseo** endings for the present subjunctive are **-és** and **-ás: Quiero que caminés/comás/escribás.** Other regional variations exist as well.

Regional variations: 22.H

Map of **voseo** regions in Latin America: p. 277

22.B.1 Regular verbs

The following endings are added to the verb stem to form the present subjunctive. Note that **-er** and **-ir** verbs have the same endings.

Present subjunctive · regular verbs			
Subject pronoun	**hablar** *to speak/talk*	**comer** *to eat*	**subir** *to go up, to climb*
yo	habl**e**	com**a**	sub**a**
tú/vos	habl**es**	com**as**	sub**as**
usted, él, ella	habl**e**	com**a**	sub**a**
nosotros/as	habl**emos**	com**amos**	sub**amos**
vosotros/as	habl**éis**	com**áis**	sub**áis**
ustedes, ellos/as	habl**en**	com**an**	sub**an**

No es bueno que **hables** cuando comes. *It's not nice to talk with your mouth full (when you're eating).*

Quiero un perrito que no **coma** mucho. *I want a little dog that doesn't eat much.*

¡Compre ya, antes de que **suban** los precios! *Buy now, before the prices go up!*

Verbs with a spelling change

Present indicative verbs
with spelling changes:
17.D.2 and 17.D.3
Verbs with diphthongs or vowel
shifts: 17.D.4 and 17.D.5

Verbs with a spelling change in the first-person singular in the present indicative also have spelling changes in the present subjunctive in order to keep the sound pattern. The verb endings are regular.

a. -ger, -gir, -guir, -uir verbs with spelling changes in the present subjunctive:

Ending	Spelling change	Example	First-person singular: *yo*	
			Present indicative	Present subjunctive
-ger	g → j	escoger	escojo	escoja
-gir	g → j	elegir	elijo	elija
-guir	gu → g	extinguir	extingo	extinga
	e → i	seguir	sigo	siga
-uir	ui → y	construir	construyo	construya

Queremos que **se elija** a un nuevo alcalde.
We want a new mayor to be elected.

Los bomberos necesitan equipos que **extingan** mejor los incendios.
The firemen need equipment that can extinguish fires better.

Necesitamos fondos para que **se construyan** parques.
We need funds to build parks.

b. -car, -gar, -guar, -zar verbs with spelling changes in the present subjunctive

The following verbs do not have spelling changes in the present indicative, but do have spelling changes in the present subjunctive, in order to maintain the verb's pronunciation when it is conjugated. The verb endings are regular. Note that several of these verbs also have a diphthong.

Verbs with a spelling change:
Verb conjugation tables,
pp. 257–276. See verb
patterns 10, 18, 42, 71.

Ending	Spelling change	Infinitive	First-person singular: *yo*	
			Present indicative	Present subjunctive
-car	c → qu	tocar	toco	toque
-gar	g → gu	llegar	llego	llegue
-guar	gu → gü	averiguar	averiguo	averigüe
-zar	z → c	alcanzar	alcanzo	alcance

More examples of **-car, -gar, -guar, -zar** verbs with spelling changes:

-car		*-gar*	
buscar	to look (for)	agregar	to add
machacar	to crush	entregar	to deliver/turn in
picar	to bite/sting	jugar (u → ue)	to play
roncar	to snore	negar (e → ie)	to deny/refuse
sacar	to take (out)	pagar	to pay (for)
salpicar	to splash	rogar (o → ue)	to beg/pray
-guar		*-zar*	
apaciguar	to appease	abrazar	to hug
desaguar	to drain	almorzar (o → ue)	to have lunch
menguar	to fade/wane	empezar (e → ie)	to start/begin
		enderezar	to straighten
		rezar	to pray

The subjunctive • **Chapter 22**

Pídele al pianista que **toque** nuestra canción.

Quiero viajar en un tren que **llegue** al centro de París.

Te ayudaré para que **alcances** tus metas.

Ask the pianist to play our song.

I want to take a train that arrives in downtown Paris.

I will help you so that you reach your goals.

22.B.3 Verbs with accents

Verbs that end in **-iar** and **-uar** take an accent in the present subjunctive just as in the present indicative.

Present indicative: Verb conjugation tables, pp. 257–276. For **i:í**, see verb patterns 29, 34, 53; for **u:ú**, see verb patterns 37, 57, 59.

Ending	Spelling change	Example	First-person singular: *yo*	
			Present indicative	Present subjunctive
-iar	**i → í**	env**iar**	env**í**o	env**í**e
-uar	**u → ú**	contin**uar**	contin**ú**o	contin**ú**e

Other -*iar* and -*uar* verbs			
acent**uar**	*to emphasize*	evac**uar**	*to evacuate*
ampl**iar**	*to enlarge/extend*	eval**uar**	*to evaluate*
ans**iar**	*to long/yearn for*	grad**uar**se	*to graduate*
conf**iar**	*to trust*	gu**iar**	*to guide*
deval**uar**	*to devalue/depreciate*	insin**uar**	*to insinuate*
efect**uar**	*to carry out / execute*	perpet**uar**	*to perpetuate*
enfr**iar**	*to cool down / chill*	sit**uar**	*to situate/locate*

Es necesario que **envíes** tu solicitud a tiempo.

Queremos invertir en monedas que no **se devalúen**.

Cuando **te gradúes**, tendrás mejor sueldo.

It's necessary that you send in your application on time.

We want to invest in currencies that won't depreciate.

When you graduate, you'll get a better salary.

22.B.4 Verbs with consonant changes

When the first-person singular is irregular in the present indicative, the present subjunctive is also irregular. The endings are regular.

a. -cer and **-cir** verbs:

Ending	Spelling change	Example	First-person singular: *yo*	
			Present indicative	Present subjunctive
-cer	**c → zc**	cono**cer**	cono**zc**o	cono**zc**a
-cir	**c → zc**	condu**cir**	condu**zc**o	condu**zc**a

Verb conjugation tables, pp. 257–276. For **c:z**, see verb patterns 32, 72, 75; for **c-zc**, see verb patterns 14, 15, 43

Necesito que **se traduzca** la carta.

No hay nadie que **conduzca** bien.

Ven a la fiesta para que **conozcas** a mis amigos.

I need the letter translated.

There's no one who drives well.

Come to the party so you can meet my friends.

b. Verbs with **-g** in the verb stem:

Irregular verbs are found alphabetically in the verb conjugation tables, pp. 257–276. Irregular verbs in the present indicative: 17.D.6

Infinitive		First-person singular: *yo*	
		Present indicative	**Present subjunctive**
de**c**ir (**e → i**)	*to say/tell*	**dig**o	**dig**a
c**a**er (**a → ai**)	*to fall*	**caig**o	**caig**a
hacer	*to do/make*	**hag**o	**hag**a
oír	*to hear*	**oig**o	**oig**a
poner	*to put/place*	**pong**o	**pong**a
salir	*to go out*	**salg**o	**salg**a
tr**a**er (**a → ai**)	*to bring*	**traig**o	**traig**a
tener	*to have*	**teng**o	**teng**a
valer	*to be worth*	**valg**o	**valg**a
venir	*to come*	**veng**o	**veng**a

¡Espero que **haga** un poco de sol hoy!	*I hope there's some sunshine today!*
Compraremos un auto que no **valga** mucho.	*We will buy a car that doesn't cost much.*
Venid a visitarme cuando **tengáis** tiempo.	*Come and visit me when you [pl.] have time.*

22.B.5 *-ar* **and** *-er* **verbs with diphthongs** *e → ie* **and** *o → ue*

All **-ar** and **-er** verbs that have diphthongs or vowel shifts in the present indicative also have them in the present subjunctive. As with the present indicative, the change occurs in all persons except **nosotros/as,** and **vosotros/as.** The endings stay the same.

a. Conjugation of **-ar** and **-er** verbs with diphthong **e → ie**:

	pensar *to think*	**querer** *to want/love*
yo	p**ie**nse	qu**ie**ra
tú/vos	p**ie**nses	qu**ie**ras
usted, él, ella	p**ie**nse	qu**ie**ra
nosotros/as	pensemos	queramos
vosotros/as	penséis	queráis
ustedes, ellos/as	p**ie**nsen	qu**ie**ran

Verb conjugation tables, pp. 257–276. See verb patterns 24, 27, 28, 45, 49, 56, 65.

Other verbs with diphthong *e → ie*			
-ar verbs		**-er verbs**	
atrave**s**ar	*to cross/go through*	asc**e**nder	*to ascend/rise*
cal**e**ntar	*to warm up / heat*	at**e**nder	*to pay attention*
c**e**rrar	*to close*	def**e**nder	*to defend*
com**e**nzar (**z → c**)	*to start*	desc**e**nder	*to descend/drop*
conf**e**sar	*to confess*	enc**e**nder	*to light / switch on*
desp**e**rtar	*to wake up*	ent**e**nder	*to understand*
emp**e**zar (**z → c**)	*to start*	ext**e**nder	*to extend/spread*
gob**e**rnar	*to govern*	p**e**rder	*to lose/miss*
n**e**gar	*to deny/refuse*	trasc**e**nder	*to become known*
recom**e**ndar	*to recommend*	v**e**rter	*to pour/spill*

	¡Esperamos que nos **entendáis**!	We hope you [pl.] understand us!
	Voy a conseguir un reloj que **me despierte** con música.	I want to get myself a clock that will wake me up with music.
	Enciende la chimenea para que **nos calentemos** un poco.	Light the fire so we can warm up a bit.

b. Conjugation of **-ar** and **-er** verbs with diphthong **o → ue**:

	contar *to relate/count*	**volver** *to return*
yo	c**ue**nte	v**ue**lva
tú/vos	c**ue**ntes	v**ue**lvas
usted, él, ella	c**ue**nte	v**ue**lva
nosotros/as	contemos	volvamos
vosotros/as	contéis	volváis
ustedes, ellos/as	c**ue**nten	v**ue**lvan

Other verbs with diphthong *o → ue*			
-ar **verbs**		*-er* **verbs**	
alm**o**r**z**ar (**z → c**)	*to have lunch*	dev**o**lver	*to give back*
c**o**star	*to cost / be difficult*	ll**o**ver	*to rain*
enc**o**ntrar	*to find*	m**o**ver	*to move*
m**o**strar	*to indicate/show*	p**o**der	*to be able to*
pr**o**bar	*to try/taste*	prom**o**ver	*to promote*
rec**o**rdar	*to remember*	rem**o**ver	*to remove/stir*
s**o**ñar	*to dream*	res**o**lver	*to resolve*
v**o**lar	*to fly*	s**o**ler	*to usually do*

Verb conjugation tables, pp. 257–276. See verb patterns 6, 9, 16, 44, 50, 61, 67, 72.

	Es necesario que **recuerdes** tu contraseña.	You need to remember your password.
	Haré lo que **pueda** para ayudarte.	I'll do what I can to help you.
	Debes tener una buena educación aunque te **cueste** mucho.	You should have a good education even if it's hard work / difficult for you.

c. The verb **oler** (*to smell*) is a unique **o → ue** verb:

h**ue**la, h**ue**las, h**ue**la, **o**lamos, **o**láis, h**ue**lan

Me gusta que la casa **huela** a flores.	I like the house to smell of flowers.

Verb conjugation tables, pp. 257–276. See verb pattern 47.

22.B.6 **-ir verbs with both diphthong and vowel shift**

All **-ir** verbs with a diphthong in the present indicative also have one in the present subjunctive. In addition, these **-ir** verbs also have a vowel shift in the **nosotros/as** and **vosotros/as** forms.

	e → ie **and** *e → i* **preferir** *to prefer*	*o → ue* **and** *o → u* **dormir** *to sleep*
yo	pref**ie**ra	d**ue**rma
tú/vos	pref**ie**ras	d**ue**rmas
usted, él, ella	pref**ie**ra	d**ue**rma
nosotros/as	pref**i**ramos	d**u**rmamos
vosotros/as	pref**i**ráis	d**u**rmáis
ustedes, ellos/as	pref**ie**ran	d**ue**rman

Verb conjugation tables, pp. 257–276. See verb patterns 25, 65.

Other -*ir* verbs with diphthong and vowel shifts			
e → ie and *e → i*		*o → ue* and *o → u*	
di**ve**rtirse	*to have fun*	m**o**rir	*to die*
h**e**rir	*to hurt*		
m**e**ntir	*to lie*		
s**e**ntir	*to feel*		

Me alegra que **te sientas** mejor.   *I'm glad you feel better.*

Prepara el plato que **prefieras**.   *Prepare whichever dish you prefer.*

Acuesta al niño para que **duerma**.   *Put the boy to bed so that he'll sleep.*

22.B.7 ▸ The verbs *adquirir* and *jugar*

Verb conjugation tables, pp. 257–276. See verb patterns 4, 41.

The verb **adquirir** has the diphthong **i → ie**, but does not have a vowel shift like other irregular **-ir** verbs. The verb **jugar** is an **-ar** verb with a **u → ue** diphthong and the spelling change **g → gu** in the stem.

	i → ie **adquirir** *to acquire*	*u → ue* **jugar** *to play*
yo	adqu**ie**ra	j**uegu**e
tú/vos	adqu**ie**ras	j**uegu**es
usted, él, ella	adqu**ie**ra	j**uegu**e
nosotros/as	adquiramos	ju**gu**emos
vosotros/as	adquiráis	ju**gu**éis
ustedes, ellos/as	adqu**ie**ran	j**uegu**en

Es fantástico que mi equipo **juegue** hoy.   *It's fantastic that my team plays/is playing today.*

Apoyaremos al equipo que mejor **juegue**.   *We're going to support the team that plays the best.*

Necesitamos capital para que el equipo **adquiera** más jugadores.   *We need capital so the team acquires/gets more players.*

22.B.8 ▸ Completely irregular verbs in the present subjunctive

Diacritical marks: 1.E.6b

The following verbs are irregular in the present subjunctive. Note that **dé** has an accent in order to distinguish the subjunctive form from the preposition **de**.

Verb conjugation tables, pp. 257–276. See verb patterns 19, 33, 38.

	dar *to give*	**estar** *to be*	**haber** *(auxiliary verb)*
yo	**dé**	**esté**	**haya**
tú/vos	**des**	**estés**	**hayas**
usted, él, ella	**dé**	**esté**	**haya**
nosotros/as	**demos**	**estemos**	**hayamos**
vosotros/as	**deis**	**estéis**	**hayáis**
ustedes, ellos/as	**den**	**estén**	**hayan**

	ir *to go*	**saber** *to know*	**ser** *to be*
yo	**vaya**	**sepa**	**sea**
tú/vos	**vayas**	**sepas**	**seas**
usted, él, ella	**vaya**	**sepa**	**sea**
nosotros/as	**vayamos**	**sepamos**	**seamos**
vosotros/as	**vayáis**	**sepáis**	**seáis**
ustedes, ellos/as	**vayan**	**sepan**	**sean**

Verb conjugation tables, pp. 257–276. See verb patterns 40, 62, 66.

Es estupendo que **seas** profesor.	*It's great that you're a teacher.*
Buscamos a un profesor que **sepa** hablar español.	*We're looking for a teacher who knows how to speak Spanish.*
Puedes empezar en cuanto **estés** listo.	*You can begin as soon as you're ready.*

22.C The imperfect subjunctive

Pretérito imperfecto de subjuntivo

22.C.1 Regular verbs

The following endings are added to the verb stem to form the imperfect subjunctive. The **-ra** and **-se** endings are equal in meaning, but the **-ra** ending is more common, especially in Latin America. Note that **nosotros/as** is the only conjugated form which has a written accent and that **-er** and **-ir** verbs have the same endings.

Regular verbs: Verb conjugation tables, p. 261

	hablar *to talk*	**comer** *to eat*	**subir** *to go up*
yo	habl**ara** habl**ase**	com**iera** com**iese**	sub**iera** sub**iese**
tú/vos	habl**aras** habl**ases**	com**ieras** com**ieses**	sub**ieras** sub**ieses**
usted, él, ella	habl**ara** habl**ase**	com**iera** com**iese**	sub**iera** sub**iese**
nosotros/as	habl**áramos** habl**ásemos**	com**iéramos** com**iésemos**	sub**iéramos** sub**iésemos**
vosotros/as	habl**arais** habl**aseis**	com**ierais** com**ieseis**	sub**ierais** sub**ieseis**
ustedes, ellos/as	habl**aran** habl**asen**	com**ieran** com**iesen**	sub**ieran** sub**iesen**

Me extrañó que nadie **hablara/hablase** español en la clase.	*It was strange that nobody spoke Spanish in the class.*
Quería viajar en un teleférico que me **llevara/llevase** hasta la cima de la montaña.	*I wanted to ride in a cable car that could take me up to the top of the mountain.*
Vimos el menú y salimos de la cafetería sin que nadie **comiera/comiese** nada.	*We looked at the menu and then left the cafe without eating anything.*

22.C.2 Irregular verbs

Many verbs are irregular in the imperfect subjunctive. Irregularities are primarily vowel shifts and consonant changes in the stem. The endings, however, follow a regular pattern. Note that all irregular verbs in the third-person plural of the preterite will also be irregular in the imperfect subjunctive. The most important irregularities are listed in this section.

Irregular verbs in the preterite: 18.B.3 and 18.B.4

a. Verbs with vowel shifts **e** → **i** and **o** → **u**:

	e → i **pedir** to ask for	o → u **dormir** to sleep
yo	p**i**diera/p**i**diese	d**u**rmiera/d**u**rmiese
tú/vos	p**i**dieras/p**i**dieses	d**u**rmieras/d**u**rmieses
usted, él, ella	p**i**diera/p**i**diese	d**u**rmiera/d**u**rmiese
nosotros/as	p**i**diéramos/p**i**diésemos	d**u**rmiéramos/d**u**rmiésemos
vosotros/as	p**i**dierais/p**i**dieseis	d**u**rmierais/d**u**rmieseis
ustedes, ellos/as	p**i**dieran/p**i**diesen	d**u**rmieran/d**u**rmiesen

Verb conjugation tables, pp. 257–276. See verb patterns 25, 48, 58, 65.

Other -ir verbs with vowel shifts		
o → u	m**o**rir	to die
e → i	div**e**rtirse	to have fun
	h**e**rir	to hurt
	m**e**ntir	to lie
	r**e**ír	to laugh
	s**e**ntir	to feel

¡Fue un éxito que la gente **se riera/riese** tanto!	*It was a success to see people laughing so much!*
¡Necesitábamos un espectáculo que **nos divirtiera/divirtiese** de verdad!	*We needed a show that truly entertained us!*
Todo estaba planeado para que **nos sintiéramos/sintiésemos** bien.	*Everything was planned in such a way as to make us feel good.*

b. Verbs with irregular **u**-stem:

Verb conjugation tables, pp. 257–276. See verb patterns 7, 12, 33, 38, 50, 51, 62, 69.

Infinitive	Stem
andar	**anduv-**
caber	**cup-**
estar	**estuv-**
haber	**hub-**
poder	**pud-**
poner	**pus-**
saber	**sup-**
tener	**tuv-**

Endings	
yo	**anduv**iera/**anduv**iese
tú/vos	**anduv**ieras/**anduv**ieses
usted, él, ella	**anduv**iera/**anduv**iese
nosotros/as	**anduv**iéramos/**anduv**iésemos
vosotros/as	**anduv**ierais/**anduv**ieseis
ustedes, ellos/as	**anduv**ieran/**anduv**iesen

¡Me gustaría que **tuviéramos/tuviésemos** más dinero!	*I wish we had more money!*
Necesitábamos un auto que **estuviera/estuviese** en perfecto estado.	*We needed a car in perfect condition.*
Compré un auto grande para que **cupiera/cupiese** toda la familia.	*I bought a big car so the whole family would fit.*

The subjunctive • **Chapter 22**

c. Verbs with irregular **i**-stem:

Infinitive	Stem
dar	**di-**
hacer	**hic-**
querer	**quis-**
venir	**vin-**

Endings	
yo	**hic**iera/**hic**iese
tú/vos	**hic**ieras/**hic**ieses
usted, él, ella	**hic**iera/**hic**iese
nosotros/as	**hic**iéramos/**hic**iésemos
vosotros/as	**hic**ierais/**hic**ieseis
ustedes, ellos/as	**hic**ieran/**hic**iesen

Verb conjugation tables, pp. 257–276. See verb patterns 19, 39, 56, 76.

Fue muy molesto que no **vinieras/ vinieses** a la reunión.
It was very annoying that you didn't come to the meeting.

No había nada que yo **quisiera/quisiese**.
There was nothing that I wanted.

Te llamé para que me **dieras/dieses** una explicación.
I called you to get an explanation.

d. Verbs with irregular **y**-stem: **-caer, -eer, -uir, oír**

Infinitive	Stem
caer	cay-
leer	ley-
concluir	concluy-
oír	oy-

Endings	
yo	**cay**era/**cay**ese
tú/vos	**cay**eras/**cay**eses
usted, él, ella	**cay**era/**cay**ese
nosotros/as	**cay**éramos/**cay**ésemos
vosotros/as	**cay**erais/**cay**eseis
ustedes, ellos/as	**cay**eran/**cay**esen

Verb conjugation tables, pp. 257–276. See verb patterns 13, 17, 23, 46.

Other verbs with the same spelling changes			
Other verbs like *caer*			
decaer	*to decay*	recaer	*to have a relapse*
Other verbs like *leer*			
creer	*to believe/think*	proveer	*to serve/provide*
poseer	*to have/own*	releer	*to read again*
Other verbs like *concluir*			
constituir	*to constitute*	construir	*to build/construct*
contribuir	*to contribute*	incluir	*to include*
destituir	*to dismiss*	influir	*to influence*
destruir	*to destroy*	intuir	*to sense*
disminuir	*to diminish*	recluir	*to imprison*
distribuir	*to distribute*	reconstruir	*to reconstruct*
huir	*to escape/flee*	sustituir	*to substitute/replace*

Fue importante que **reconstruyeran/ reconstruyesen** la ciudad antigua.
It was important to rebuild the ancient part of the city.

No había nada que **disminuyera/ disminuyese** la importancia del proyecto.
There was nothing that would/could diminish the project's significance.

Trabajamos mucho para que el proyecto **concluyera/concluyese** con éxito.
We worked a lot so that the project would be successful.

e. Verbs with irregular **j**-stem:

Verb conjugation tables, pp. 257–276. See verb patterns 14, 20, 73.

Infinitive	Stem
de**c**ir (**e** → **i**)	di**j**-
traer	tra**j**-
conducir	condu**j**-
introducir	introdu**j**-
producir	produ**j**-
reducir	redu**j**-
traducir	tradu**j**-

Endings	
yo	di**j**era/di**j**ese
tú/vos	di**j**eras/di**j**eses
usted, él, ella	di**j**era/di**j**ese
nosotros/as	di**j**éramos/di**j**ésemos
vosotros/as	di**j**erais/di**j**eseis
ustedes, ellos/as	di**j**eran/di**j**esen

Fue un milagro que no **se produjera/produjese** un accidente.

It was amazing that there wasn't an accident.

No había nadie que **condujera/condujese** bien.

There was nobody who could drive well.

No te creería aunque **dijeras/dijeses** la verdad.

I wouldn't believe you even if you were telling the truth.

f. The imperfect subjunctive of **ir** and **ser**:

Verb conjugation tables, pp. 257–276. See verb patterns 40, 66.

yo	**fuera/fuese**
tú/vos	**fueras/fueses**
usted, él, ella	**fuera/fuese**
nosotros/as	**fuéramos/fuésemos**
vosotros/as	**fuerais/fueseis**
ustedes, ellos/as	**fueran/fuesen**

El director nos pidió que **fuéramos/fuésemos** a la reunión de padres de familia.

The principal asked us to go to the parents' meeting.

Yo quería comprar un auto que **fuera/fuese** seguro y confiable.

I wanted to buy a car that was safe and reliable.

Quería llamarte antes de que **fuera/fuese** demasiado tarde.

I wanted to call you before it was too late.

22.D The present perfect subjunctive

Pretérito perfecto de subjuntivo

The present perfect subjunctive is formed with the present subjunctive of the auxiliary verb **haber** and the past participle of the main verb.

Regular and irregular past participles: 19.A.1 and 19.A.2

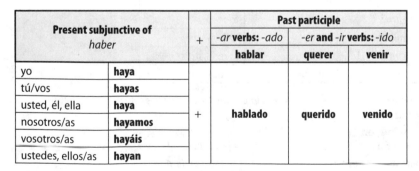

Present subjunctive of *haber*		+	Past participle		
			-ar **verbs:** *-ado*	*-er* **and** *-ir* **verbs:** *-ido*	
			hablar	querer	venir
yo	**haya**	+	**hablado**	**querido**	**venido**
tú/vos	**hayas**				
usted, él, ella	**haya**				
nosotros/as	**hayamos**				
vosotros/as	**hayáis**				
ustedes, ellos/as	**hayan**				

Espero que **hayas tenido** un buen viaje.	*I hope you have had a good trip.*
En mi escuela no hay nadie que **haya reprobado** el examen.	*In my school, there is nobody that has failed the exam.*
Trabajarás mejor cuando **hayas instalado** una buena conexión a Internet.	*You will be able to work better when you have installed a good Internet connection.*

22.E The past perfect subjunctive

Pretérito pluscuamperfecto de subjuntivo

The past perfect subjunctive is formed with the imperfect subjunctive of the auxiliary verb **haber** (**hubiera/hubiese**) and the past participle of the main verb.

◀ Regular and irregular past participles: 19.A.1 and 19.A.2

Past perfect subjunctive *haber*		+	Past participle		
			-ar **verbs:** *-ado*	*-er* **and** *-ir* **verbs:** *-ido*	
			hablar	**querer**	**venir**
yo	**hub**iera/**hub**iese	+			
tú/vos	**hub**ieras/**hub**ieses				
usted, él, ella	**hub**iera/**hub**iese		**hablado**	**querido**	**venido**
nosotros/as	**hub**iéramos/**hub**iésemos				
vosotros/as	**hub**ierais/**hub**ieseis				
ustedes, ellos/as	**hub**ieran/**hub**iesen				

No pensé que **hubieras/hubieses tenido** un buen viaje.	*I didn't think you had had a good trip.*
No hubo nadie que **hubiera/hubiese reprobado** el examen.	*There was nobody who had failed the exam.*
Trabajarías mejor si **hubieras/hubieses instalado** una buena conexión a Internet.	*You would work better if you had installed a good Internet connection.*

22.F The future simple subjunctive

Futuro de subjuntivo

The future simple subjunctive is no longer used in modern Spanish. It is generally only found in legal texts, laws, and regulations.

a. The future simple subjunctive is formed with the same verb stem as the imperfect subjunctive with the following endings:

◀ Imperfect subjunctive: 22.C

	hablar *to talk*	**comer** *to eat*	**subir** *to go up, to climb*
yo	hablar**e**	comier**e**	subier**e**
tú/vos	hablar**es**	comier**es**	subier**es**
usted, él, ella	hablar**e**	comier**e**	subier**e**
nosotros/as	hablár**emos**	comiér**emos**	subiér**emos**
vosotros/as	hablar**eis**	comier**eis**	subier**eis**
ustedes, ellos/as	hablar**en**	comier**en**	subier**en**

b. Irregular verbs have the same irregularities in the verb stems as the imperfect subjunctive. The endings are the same as they are for regular verbs: **fuere, tuviere, hubiere, hiciere**, etc.

c. In everyday speech, the simple future subjunctive only occurs in proverbs or idiomatic expressions, and in formal speeches of a legal nature.

Habrá multa cualquiera que **fuere** el exceso de velocidad.	*There will be a fine whatever the speed limit violation may be.*
Adonde **fueres,** haz lo que **vieres.**	*When in Rome, do as the Romans do.*
Sea quien **fuere** el embajador, la situación no cambiará.	*Whoever the ambassador is, the situation will not change.*

22.G The future perfect subjunctive

Futuro perfecto de subjuntivo

The future perfect subjunctive is formed with the simple future subjunctive of **haber** and the past participle of the verb: **hubiere hablado**, **hubieres hablado**, etc. This verb tense is used in legal texts, but is not common.

Se aceptarán las solicitudes siempre y cuando **hubieren llegado** antes de expirar el plazo.	*Applications will be accepted as long as they have arrived before the deadline.*

22.H Regional variations

Variaciones regionales

Voseo: 22.B.b ▶

The use of **voseo** forms in the present subjunctive varies regionally. Below are the three main forms:

	1. Voseo (using **tú** form)	**2. Voseo** (most **voseo** countries)	**3. Voseo** (Chile)
amar	**ames**	**amés**	**amí(s)**
comer	**comas**	**comás**	**comái(s)**
recibir	**recibas**	**recibás**	**recibái(s)**

Imperative for **vos**: 24.D.1b ▶

Option 2 is common in most **voseo** countries, especially in Central America and the Andean **voseo** countries. In Argentina, it coexists with option 1, while option 2 is the most common for informal negative imperatives (which use the present subjunctive form): **no vayás; no digás.** Option 3 is used primarily in Chile.

Práctica

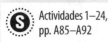

Actividades 1–24, pp. A85–A92

Use of the subjunctive
Uso del subjuntivo

23.A Overview

Aspectos generales

The use of the subjunctive in Spanish follows a fairly regular pattern, depending on the type of clause in which it occurs.

23.A.1 Independent clauses

The use of the subjunctive in independent clauses is very limited and occurs mainly in clauses with adverbs of doubt and possibility (where the indicative is also possible) or in exclamations.

23.A.2 Subordinate clauses

The subjunctive occurs primarily in subordinate clauses governed by a main clause. An understanding of the basic structure of subordinate clauses in Spanish is important for using the subjunctive correctly.

There are three main types of subordinate clauses in which the subjunctive is used:

a. *nominal*, or noun, clauses

b. relative, or *adjectival*, clauses

c. *adverbial* clauses

Since the subjunctive is rarely used in English, the translations of examples in this chapter are written to show the nuances of the subjunctive meaning in Spanish.

23.B The subjunctive in independent clauses

El subjuntivo en oraciones independientes

23.B.1 Probability, doubt

In independent clauses with adverbs or other expressions of doubt or possibility such as **quizás, tal vez, posiblemente**, and **probablemente**, both the indicative and the subjunctive can be used. The verb mood used expresses the degree of probability of the outcome. The indicative expresses a higher probability than the subjunctive.

Expressions of doubt with the subjunctive in **que** clauses: 23.C.6
Tal vez/quizás: 10.F.1d

Subjunctive	Indicative
Posiblemente llegue tarde a casa hoy. *I might arrive/get home late today.*	**Posiblemente** llego tarde a casa hoy. *I'll probably be home late today.*
Quizás fuera gripe lo que tenías. *Maybe you had the flu.*	**Quizás era** gripe lo que tenías. *You probably had the flu.*

A lo mejor (*maybe, perhaps*) is a very common expression for possibility in everyday language.

23.B.2 Exclamations

a. The subjunctive is *always* used in simple wish clauses in the form of exclamations, usually with **vivir**. In English, this is mostly expressed with *hurrah/hooray, come on,* or *long live!*

¡**Viva** el Barcelona!	*Come on, Barcelona!*
¡**Vivan** los nuevos estudiantes!	*Hooray for the new students!*
¡**Viva** España!	*Long live Spain! / Hooray for Spain!*

Such simple exclamations are accompanied by **que** when expressing wishes or requests. These exclamations can be interpreted as containing an implicit verb of wish or desire (**querer, desear, esperar**) that governs what is said.

¡Que se besen los novios!	*The bride and groom may now kiss!*
¡Que llegue pronto mi amigo!	*I hope my friend arrives soon!*

These simple wish clauses are common in social contexts where expressions of good (or bad) wishes are given.

¡Que tengas un feliz viaje!	*Have a good trip!*
¡Que te vaya bien en el examen!	*Hope the exam goes well!*
¡Que os divirtáis mucho!	*Have a lot of fun!*
¡Que cumplas muchos años más!	*Many happy returns!*
¡Que te parta un rayo!	*Damn you!*

b. The exclamation word **ojalá** comes from the Arabic *in sha'a Allah* meaning *if Allah/God wills*. It is used in the same way as *God willing* in English and expresses a strong desire that something happen. **Ojalá** is used in nominal clauses and is *always* followed by a *subjunctive* tense.

Future	**¡Ojalá** (que) tengas un buen viaje!	*Hope you have a good trip!*
Past	**¡Ojalá** (que) hayas tenido un buen viaje!	*Hope you've had a good trip!*
Counter-factual	**¡Ojalá** (que) hubieras tenido un buen viaje!	*Wish you'd had a good trip!*

23.C The subjunctive in nominal clauses

El subjuntivo en cláusulas subordinadas sustantivas

That-clauses are also called *nominal clauses* because they act in the same way that nouns do and can be the *subject, direct object,* or *indirect object* of the sentence. Nominal clauses in Spanish start with the conjunction **que**, which can never be excluded like *that* can in English.

The verb in the main clause is the governing finite verb: **espero**.

Main clause	Subordinate clause
Espero	**que** estés bien.
I hope	*(that) you are well.*

The use of the subjunctive in Spanish nominal clauses is always dependent on the meaning of the main governing verb. This verb can fall into one of various verb groups, each with its own rules for the use of subjunctive. The following are the most important verb groups.

23.C.1 Verbs that express want, wish, influence, or necessity

a. The *subjunctive* is always used in nominal clauses when the main verb either directly or indirectly expresses *want, wish, influence,* or *necessity*. Direct expressions can come in the form of orders and decrees, requirements, permission, and prohibition. Indirect expressions include personal wishes, preferences, prayers, hopes, advice, suggestions, recommendations, and necessities. Examples of this type of verb are shown below.

aconsejar	*to advise*	permitir	*to permit/allow*
desear	*to desire*	preferir	*to prefer*
exigir	*to require*	prohiblr	*to prohibit*
gustar	*to like*	proponer	*to propose*
impedir	*to impede*	querer	*to want*
insistir	*to insist*	recomendar	*to recommend*
mandar	*to order*	requerir	*to require / call for*

necesitar	to need	rogar	to pray/plead
oponerse	to oppose	solicitar	to request
ordenar	to order/arrange	sugerir	to propose/suggest
pedir	to ask (for)	suplicar	to beg/plead

Te aconsejo que no **fumes**.	*I advise you not to smoke.*
Le pido a usted que me **ayude**.	*I'm asking you to help me.*
Te sugiero que no **compres** algo caro.	*I suggest you don't buy something expensive.*
Recomendamos que **revises** tu correo.	*We recommend that you check your mail.*
Le solicito que me **envíe** el cheque.	*I request that you send me the check.*
Os ruego que me **prestéis** dinero.	*I beg you [pl.] to lend me money.*

b. The expression **hacer que** expresses influence and it should be followed by the subjunctive.

La nieve **hará que** el tráfico **se vuelva** imposible.	*The snow will make traffic impossible.*

c. The expression **el (hecho de) que** (*the fact that*) is used mostly with the *subjunctive*. This also applies to the abbreviation **que** (*that*). Note that **el que** in this context is not the same as the relative pronoun **el que** (*the one who/that*).

◀ Relative pronouns: 15.A.2

El (hecho de) que suban los precios es bastante común.	*(The fact) That prices go up is quite common.*
Que todo **sea** tan caro es producto de la globalización.	*That everything is so expensive is a result of globalization.*
El que te gusten los medios sociales es muy positivo.	*(The fact) That you like social media is very positive.*

d. When **el hecho de que** is governed by a main verb that means *to know, to be/become clear,* or *to find out,* the indicative can be used.

Nos damos cuenta **del hecho de que / de que** la gente **está** descontenta.	*We realize that people are unhappy.*

e. The expression **es que** (*it's that*) describes a causal relationship. The *indicative* is used in affirmative clauses and the *subjunctive* in negative subordinate clauses. This expression is an abbreviation of **lo que ocurre/pasa/sucede es que** (*the thing is that*).

◀ lo lógico es que: 23.C.10b

No **es que estemos** aburridos, **es que tenemos** que irnos ya.	*It's not that we are bored, it's just that we have to go now.*
No **es que** yo no **quiera** ayudarte, **es que** no **puedo**.	*It's not that I don't want to help you, I just can't.*

23.C.2 *Decir* **and other reporting verbs**

◀ Indirect discourse: Ch. 31

The verb **decir** and a few others can convey information or express a wish or a request. With these verbs, the *subjunctive* is used when giving an order or when asking for something, and the *indicative* is used when conveying information. The following are examples of reporting verbs.

◀ Direct discourse: 31.A.1 Reporting information and commands: 31.B.2

advertir	to warn	indicar	to indicate
decir	to say/tell	insistir	to insist

Subjunctive	Indicative
Isabel dice que **vengas** pronto. *Isabel says that you must come soon.*	Isabel dice que **vienes** pronto. *Isabel says that you are coming soon.*
La luz roja te indica que **te detengas**. *The red light tells you to stop.*	La luz roja indica que **debes** detenerte. *The red light indicates that you should stop.*
Mis amigos insisten en que **compre** un auto. *My friends insist that I buy a car.*	Mis amigos insisten en que **necesito** un auto. *My friends insist that I need a car.*

23.C.3 **Verbs that express emotions**

Verbs like **gustar**: 17.B.4 ▶

a. The subjunctive is always used in subordinate clauses when the verb in the main clause expresses an emotion or an emotional reaction to something. This happens primarily when a verb expressing emotion (like **gustar**) is inflected with an indirect object pronoun. The subordinate clause describes what a person likes, or finds amazing, frustrating, etc.

Main clause	Subordinate clause
Me alegra	que **tengamos** tantos días libres.
I'm pleased/happy/delighted	*that we have so many free days.*

Other verbs in this group include:

aburrir	*to bore*	enfadar	*to anger*
agradar	*to please*	entristecer	*to sadden*
apenar	*to grieve/sadden*	entusiasmar	*to enthuse/delight*
alarmar	*to alarm*	extrañar	*to surprise*
alegrar	*to please*	fascinar	*to fascinate*
asustar	*to frighten/scare*	fastidiar	*to irritate*
complacer	*to satisfy/please*	frustrar	*to frustrate*
convenir	*to suit*	gustar	*to like*
desesperar	*to exasperate*	importar	*to matter / care about*
disgustar	*to disgust*	indignar	*to infuriate / to make indignant/angry*
divertir	*to amuse*	irritar	*to irritate*
doler	*to hurt/ache*	interesar	*to interest*
emocionar	*to excite*	molestar	*to annoy/bother*
encantar	*to enjoy/love*	sorprender	*to surprise*

Me alegra que nadie **fume** aquí.	*I'm glad that nobody smokes here.*
¿**Os molesta** que **abra** la ventana?	*Do you [pl.] mind if I open the window?*
Nos conviene que la reunión **sea** el martes.	*It's fine with / better for us that the meeting be on Tuesday.*
Me gusta que me **enseñes** a hablar español.	*I like that you teach me to speak Spanish.*

b. Several of the above-mentioned verbs (but not all) can also be used without a subjunctive clause.

Me alegro de/por tu éxito.	*I'm pleased about your success.*
Nos interesamos por el español.	*We're interested in Spanish.*
Nuestros clientes **nos importan**.	*Our clients are important to us.*

23.C.4 **The verb** *sentir* **and other sense verbs**

a. When **sentir** is used with the meaning *to be/feel sorry* in affirmative and negative main clauses, the subjunctive must be used in the subordinate clause. With the indicative, the meaning of **sentir** is *to have a feeling, to feel, to sense*.

Use of the subjunctive • **Chapter 23**

Subjunctive	Indicative
Sentimos que no **puedas** asistir al seminario. *We're sorry that you can't attend the seminar.*	**Siento** que **vamos a tener** problemas. *I sense that we're going to have problems.*

b. When sense verbs like **oír, escuchar, ver, percibir, notar,** and **observar** are used in a negative main clause, the subjunctive is usually used in the subordinate clause. The indicative is rarely used in spoken language to state a real and unequivocal physical state in negative clauses.

Subjunctive	Indicative
No oímos que **se acerque** el autobús. *We can't hear that the bus is approaching/coming.*	**Oímos** que **se acerca** el autobús. *We can hear the bus approaching/coming.*
No veo que **haya** desorden en mi habitación. *I don't see that my room is a mess.*	**Veo** que **hay** desorden en mi habitación. *I see that my room is a mess.*

c. The verbs **temer** (*to fear, to be afraid of*) and **esperar** (*to hope, to expect*) are used with the *subjunctive* in negative and affirmative clauses.

La gente **teme** que **suban** los precios.	*People fear that prices will go up.*
No espero que siempre **tengas** tiempo para todo.	*I don't expect you to always have time for everything.*

d. The verb **temer** can also mean *to believe*. With this meaning, the *indicative* can occur with **temer** in affirmative clauses. The verb **esperar** can also express a thought rather than an intention or expectation. In this case, the *indicative* is used (except the present indicative, which cannot be used in this case).

Subjunctive	Indicative
La gente **teme** que **suban** los precios. *People are worried that prices will go up.*	La gente **teme** que **subirán** los precios. *People believe (fearfully) that prices will go up.*
Esperaba que **tuvierais** tiempo en diciembre. *I hoped you [pl.] would have time in December.*	**Esperaba** que **tendríais** tiempo en diciembre. *I imagined you [pl.] would have time in December.*

e. The expression **esperar a que** (*to wait for something to happen*) always requires the subjunctive in both affirmative and negative clauses.

Espero con alegría **a que llegue** el día de la boda.	*I am very much looking forward to the wedding day.*
No esperaré a que te calmes para darte la noticia.	*I won't wait for you to calm down to give you the news.*

23.C.5 Personal opinions, thoughts, and reviews

a. With verbs that express personal opinions, thoughts, and appraisals in negative main clauses, the *subjunctive* is used in the subordinate clause.

no admitir	to not admit	no parecer	to not seem/look like
no conceder	to not concede	no pensar	to not think
no creer	to not believe	no recordar	to not remember
no opinar	to not think/believe	no suponer	to not suppose

No pienso que la lección **sea** fácil.	*I don't think the lesson is easy.*
No sospecho que aquí **haya** nada raro.	*I don't suspect that there is anything strange here.*

b. When the main verb is affirmative, the *indicative* is used in the subordinate clause.

admitir	to admit	parecer	to seem/look like
conceder	to concede	pensar	to think
creer	to believe	recordar	to remember
opinar	to think/believe	suponer	to suppose

Pienso que la lección **es** fácil. | *I think that the lesson is easy.*
Sospecho que aquí **hay** algo raro. | *I suspect that there is something strange here.*

c. In positive questions, the above-mentioned verbs can be used in spoken language in the *indicative* to signal a desire to confirm or disprove an opinion.

¿Crees que **es** bueno vivir en una ciudad grande? | *Do you think it's good to live in a big city?*

The adverb **sí/no** makes the use of the subjunctive more probable.

¿Tú **sí/no crees** que **sea** bueno vivir en una ciudad tan grande? | *Do you really believe/Don't you believe that it can be good to live in such a big city?*

d. *Parece*

When **parecer** is used to mean *it seems as if*, the *subjunctive* is used. However, with this expression, the present subjunctive cannot be used. The most common verb tenses used are the imperfect and past perfect subjunctive.

como si: 23.E.1e

Parece que **estuviéramos** en Navidad. | *It looks as if / seems like we were in the middle of Christmas.*
No parece que **estuviéramos** en Navidad. | *It doesn't look as if / seem like we were in the middle of Christmas.*
Parece como si **hubiera sido** ayer. | *It seems as though it was yesterday.*

e. *Comprender, entender*

These two verbs convey a meaning of concession or agreement with something previously said when the subjunctive is used in an affirmative clause. However, with the indicative, they retain the meaning *to understand*. They are always used with the *subjunctive* in negative clauses.

Entiendo que **te sientas** mal, ¡tienes fiebre! | *I understand that you feel bad; you have a fever!*
Comprendo que la primera respuesta **es** incorrecta. | *I understand that the first answer is incorrect.*
No **comprendo** que **sea** un error. | *I don't understand how this could be a mistake.*

23.C.6 Verbs of denial or doubt

a. Verbs that express denial and doubt take the *subjunctive* in both affirmative and negative subordinate clauses.

desconfiar de	*to distrust*	ignorar	*to ignore*
dudar	*to doubt*	negar	*to deny*

(No) dudo que **digas** la verdad. | *I (don't) doubt that you're telling the truth.*
(No) niego que **hayamos cometido** un error. | *I (don't) deny that we have made a mistake.*
La policía **(no) desconfía de** que el testigo **diga** la verdad. | *The police (do not) doubt that the witness is telling the truth.*

b. With statements of absolute certainty, however, **no dudar que** takes the indicative. Note this only applies to the negative form.

No dudo que les **dirás** la verdad. | *I don't doubt that you will tell them the truth (and I am certain of that).*
No dudo en absoluto que siempre **pagas** tus cuentas. | *I don't doubt at all that you always pay your bills.*

Impersonal expressions with **ser:** 30.B.6

23.C.7 Impersonal expressions of certainty

Expressions with **ser/estar** + *adjective/noun* and **haber** + *noun* that convey certainty require the *indicative* in affirmative clauses, and generally the *subjunctive* in negative clauses.

Use of the subjunctive • **Chapter 23**

a. Ser (*third-person singular*) + *masculine adjective* + **que**

cierto	*certain*	evidente	*evident*	seguro	*sure*
claro	*clear/obvious*	obvio	*obvious*	verdad	*true*

Es seguro que **habrá** fiesta.   *It's certain that there will be a party.*

No era evidente que **fuera** a ganar el mejor candidato.   *It was not obvious that the best candidate would win.*

b. Estar + *adjective* + **que**

convencido/a de	*convinced (of)*
seguro/a de	*sure (of)*

Estamos seguros de que **lloverá**.   *We're sure it's going to rain.*

¿No estás convencida de que tu decisión   *Aren't you convinced that your decision*
es/sea correcta?   *is the right one?*

c. Haber (*impersonal conjugation*) + *noun* + **de** + **que**

hay certeza de	*it is certain that*	hay evidencia de	*there is evidence that*
no hay (duda de)	*there's no doubt that*	hay seguridad de	*there's assurance/a guarantee that*

Hay certeza de que el tratamiento **es** bueno.   *It's certain that the treatment is good.*

No hay evidencia de que la medicina   *There is no evidence that the medicine*
es/sea efectiva.   *is effective.*

23.C.8 **Impersonal expressions of wishes, preferences, advice, necessity, decisions, and emotions**

After impersonal expressions with **ser, estar**, and other verbs that convey wishes, preferences, advice, necessity, decisions, and emotions, the *subjunctive* is used. This applies both to affirmative and negative clauses. The list below shows some of the most common expressions that indicate the use of the *subjunctive* in the subordinate clause.

Estar with a perfect adjective: 30.C.2

Impersonal expressions with **ser**: 13.G.3, 21.B.5

a. Ser + *singular masculine adjective* + **que**: subjunctive

aconsejable	*advisable*	magnífico	*great, magnificent*
bueno	*good*	malo	*bad*
comprensible	*understandable*	necesario	*necessary*
conveniente	*convenient*	normal	*normal*
dudoso	*doubtful*	peligroso	*dangerous*
esencial	*essential*	probable	*probable/likely*
estupendo	*superb/great/marvelous*	recomendable	*advisable*
fabuloso	*fabulous*	ridículo	*ridiculous*
horroroso	*horrifying*	sospechoso	*suspicious/suspect*
importante	*important*	suficiente	*sufficient*
(in)admisible	*(in)admissible*	terrible	*terrible*
increíble	*incredible*	triste	*sad*
(in)justo	*(un)fair*	urgente	*urgent*
(i)lógico	*(il)logical*	(in)útil	*useful (useless)*

Fue magnífico que nos **dieran** una   *It was great/magnificent that they gave us a*
habitación con vista al mar.   *room with a view of the sea.*

Es probable que **haga** buen tiempo mañana.   *It's likely that it'll be nice out tomorrow.*

No es justo que **tengáis** que trabajar doce horas diarias.   *It's not fair that you [pl.] have to work twelve hours a day.*

b. **Ser** + **mejor/peor /mucho menos/más,** etc. + **que**: subjunctive

mejor	*better*	**peor**	*worse*

Es mejor que **regreses** en avión. — *It's better/best that you take a flight back.*

Fue peor que **mintieras**. — *It was worse that you lied.*

Sería más cómodo que **viajáramos** en tren. — *It would be more comfortable if we traveled by train.*

c. **Ser** + **un(a)** + *noun* + **que**: subjunctive

error	*error/mistake*	lástima	*pity/shame*
fastidio	*nuisance*	lata	*pest/pain*
horror	*horror*	locura	*madness*
peligro	*danger*	milagro	*miracle*
robo	*robbery*	suerte	*luck*
costumbre	*custom*	tontería	*silliness/nonsense*
delicia	*delight/joy*	vergüenza	*shame/embarrassment*

Es una delicia que **nos atiendan** como a reyes. — *It's a delight to be treated as kings.*

¡Fue un milagro que **llamaras**! — *It was a miracle that you called!*

Antes **no era una costumbre** que los hombres **cuidaran** a los niños. — *In the past, it wasn't customary for men to take care of the children.*

d. **Estar** + *adverb/participle* + **que**: subjunctive

bien	*good/fine*	permitido	*permitted/allowed*
decidido	*decided*	prohibido	*prohibited*
mal	*bad*	resuelto	*resolved*

Está bien que **pagues** con tarjeta. — *It's fine to pay with a credit card.*

Está prohibido que **bebamos** aquí. — *It's prohibited to drink here.*

e. **Estar** + *adjective* + *preposition* + **que**: subjunctive

Infinitive or subjunctive: 25.B.5

acostumbrado/a a	*accustomed/used to*	encantado/a de	*glad/delighted to*
asustado/a de	*afraid of*	harto/a de	*fed up with / sick of*
cansado/a de	*tired of*	ilusionado/a con	*hopeful for*
contento/a de	*happy/satisfied/content with*	orgulloso/a de	*proud of*
deseoso/a de	*longing for/eager to*	preocupado/a por	*worried about*
dispuesto/a a	*willing to*	satisfecho/a de	*satisified by/with*

Verb periphrases with the past participle: 26.E

Estamos hartos de que los vecinos **pongan** la música a todo volumen. — *We are fed up with the neighbors playing music so loudly.*

Estoy satisfecha de que todo **haya salido** bien. — *I'm satisfied that everything has gone well.*

f. Other verbs and expressions that take the subjunctive:

basta con que	*it's enough / sufficient that/just*	más vale que	*it had better/it's better that*
da igual que	*it doesn't matter / it's the same as*	puede (ser) que	*it might/could be*
da lo mismo que	*it makes no difference*	vale la pena que	*it's worth*

Basta con que envíes la solicitud. — *Just send the request.*

Más vale que compréis los boletos de avión con tiempo. — *You [pl.] had better buy your plane tickets in advance.*

Use of the subjunctive • **Chapter 23**

23.C.9 Verbs of want: same/different subject

a. When the subject in the main clause and subordinate clause is the same person, the subordinate clause is replaced with the infinitive.

Queremos que **prepares** la cena.	*We want you to prepare dinner.*
Queremos preparar la cena.	*We want to prepare dinner.*
Siento mucho que no **hayas aprobado** el examen.	*I'm so sorry you didn't pass your exam.*
Siento mucho no **haber aprobado** el examen.	*I'm so sorry not to have passed my exam.*

b. In some cases, the subordinate clause can be replaced with the infinitive even when the subjects are different. This happens when an object pronoun in the main clause refers to the same person in the subordinate clause.

La huelga **les impidió** que **viajaran**.	*The strike prevented them from traveling.*
La huelga **les impidió viajar**.	
Te aconsejo que **hagas** más ejercicio.	*I advise you to exercise more.*
Te aconsejo **hacer** más ejercicio.	
Juan **me pidió** que lo **acompañara**.	*Juan asked me to go with him.*
Juan **me pidió acompañarlo**.	
La invité a que **participara** del concurso.	*I invited her to participate in the contest.*
La invité a **participar** del concurso.	

23.C.10 Impersonal expressions with *lo* + adjective/adverb and *lo que*

Lo is a neuter article that is used to form general expressions: **lo bueno** (*the good thing*), **lo mejor** (*the best thing*), **lo que quiero** (*what I want*).

Abstract concepts with **lo:** 5.A.2
Relative pronouns: 15.A.2

a. The *indicative* is used with **lo** expressions that refer to real situations or past events.

Lo + **adjective**	**Indicative**
Lo cierto es	que **estudias** muchísimo.
The fact is	*that you study a lot.*
Lo mejor fue	que **aprobaste** el examen.
The best thing was	*that you passed your exam.*
Lo importante es	que **eres** inteligente.
The important thing is	*that you are intelligent.*

b. The *subjunctive* is used after a number of impersonal expressions that refer to norms, rules, personal reactions, and preferences about what is best, worst, normal, logical, etc.: **lo lógico es que** (*the logical thing [to do] is*), **lo normal es que** (*the normal thing [to do] is*), **lo corriente/común es que** (*the usual thing [to do] is*), and similar expressions. The subjunctive tenses vary based on the tense of **ser**.

Lo + **adjective**	**Subjunctive**
Lo lógico es	que te **llame** yo.
The logical thing (to do) is	*for me to call you.*
Lo más común era	que **fuéramos** a Torrevieja en verano.
The usual thing we did was	*to go to Torrevieja in the summer.*
Lo mejor fue	que te **conociera**.
The best thing was	*meeting you.*

c. In clauses with **lo que** + *verb in the indicative* + **ser**, the subjunctive is used when the verb expresses *a wish, a preference, an order,* or *a necessity*. The indicative is used when referring to something that happens habitually or is a known fact. In these cases, the statement is purely descriptive and there is no wish or necessity on the part of the speaker.

Lo que más me gusta es que nos **sirvas** tapas.	*What I like best is that you serve us tapas.*
Lo que más me gusta es que nunca **hace** frío en Medellín.	*What I like best is that it's never cold in Medellín.*

d. Other common expressions with **lo que** include:

Lo que menos espero es que…	*What I expect least is that…*
Lo único que te pido es que…	*The only thing I ask is that…*
Lo que más necesito es que…	*What I need most is that…*
Lo que no me conviene es que…	*What doesn't suit me is that…*

23.C.11 Tense sequencing

The choice of tense used in a subordinate clause depends on whether the action happened before, at the same time as, or after the action in the main clause.

a. When the *present* or *present perfect subjunctive* appears in the subordinate clause, the present, past, or future is referred to, depending on the tense of the main verb and the context. Some common examples follow.

Main clause		Subordinate clause	
Indicative		**Subjunctive**	
Present	Te **pido** *I ask you*	**Present**	que no **fumes**. *not to smoke.*
Simple future	Siempre te **pediré** *I will always ask you*		
Present perfect	Te **he pedido** *I have asked you*		
	Me **ha molestado** *It has annoyed me*	**Present perfect**	que **hayas fumado/ fumaras** tanto. *that you have smoked so much.*

b. When the main verb is not in the present, present perfect or future, the verb in the subordinate clause can be in the *imperfect subjunctive*. Choice of tense depends on the context. Some common examples follow.

Main clause		Subordinate clause
Indicative		**Imperfect subjunctive**
The preterite	Ayer te **pedí** *Yesterday, I asked you*	que no **fumaras**. *not to smoke.*
The imperfect	Antes te **pedía** *I used to ask you*	
Present conditional	Te **pediría** *I would like to ask you*	
Conditional perfect	Te **habría pedido** *I would have asked you*	

23.D The subjunctive in relative clauses

El subjuntivo en subordinadas relativas

Relative clauses (*adjectival clauses*) start with a relative pronoun: (**el, la, los, las**) **que, quien,** (**el, la**) **cual,** (**los, las**) **cuales, cuya(s)** or with a relative adverb (**cuando, donde, como, cuanto/todo lo que**). Relative clauses provide a description of the antecedent to which they refer.

Relative pronouns and adverbs: Ch. 15

Main clause (antecedent)	Relative clause (characteristic)
Compra **los libros**	**que necesites.**
Buy the books	*you need.*

In the example above, **los libros** is the antecedent for the relative clause **que necesites.**

The use of the *subjunctive* in the relative clause is always determined by the speaker's perspective of the antecedent. This perspective can be subjective or objective.

23.D.1 Unknown/Known antecedent

a. The *indicative* is used in relative clauses to refer to *specific* people, things, ideas, or events that we already know about. The *subjunctive* is used to refer to something or someone *unknown* that has *imagined* or *wished* characteristics.

Subjunctive: unknown	Indicative: known
Vamos a comprar **una casa** que **tenga** tres dormitorios.	Vamos a comprar **una casa** que **tiene** tres dormitorios.
We'd like to buy a house that has three bedrooms.	*We're going to buy a house that has three bedrooms.*
El hotel contratará a **un chef** que **tenga** experiencia.	El hotel contratará a **un chef** que **tiene** experiencia.
The hotel wants to hire a chef who has experience.	*The hotel is going to hire a chef who has experience.*
Iremos a **un restaurante** que **tenga** buena comida.	Iremos a **un restaurante** que **tiene** buena comida.
We want to go to a restaurant that has good food.	*We're going to a restaurant that has good food.*

b. Verbs like **querer, necesitar, buscar**, and **desear** usually occur in relative clauses that describe *imagined* people, things, events, or situations. The indicative is used to describe *specific* or *concrete* people, things, events, or situations.

Subjunctive: imagined	Indicative: specific
Buscamos **un libro** que **explique** bien el subjuntivo.	Buscamos **el libro** que **explica** bien el subjuntivo.
We're looking for a book that can explain the subjunctive well.	*We're looking for the book that explains the subjunctive well.*
Queríamos **una bebida** que no **tuviera** azúcar.	Queríamos **la bebida** que no **tiene** azúcar.
We'd like a drink that doesn't have sugar.	*We wanted the drink that doesn't have sugar.*

c. The subjunctive is also used in relative clauses with a relative adverb that refers to *unknown* and *non-specific* locations, times, or methods of action. The adverb, or **que** and a suitable preposition, starts the relative clause.

Relative adverbs: 15.C

Indefinite pronouns: 7.D

Subjunctive: unknown	Indicative: known
Iremos a un restaurante **donde/en el que haya** sitio para todos.	Iremos a un restaurante **donde/en el que hay** sitio para todos.
We'll go to a restaurant where there is room for everyone. (The speaker does not know of a specific restaurant.)	*We're going to a restaurant where there is room for everyone.* (The speaker knows of a specific restaurant.)
Puedes preparar la cena **como/del modo que quieras**.	Puedes preparar la cena **como/del modo que quieres**.
You can prepare dinner however you want. (The speaker does not know how you want to prepare it.)	*You can prepare dinner however you want.* (The speaker knows how you want to prepare it.)

23.D.2 **Denied / Non-denied and indefinite antecedent**

a. When the main clause indicates or implies that the antecedent does not exist, the subjunctive is used in the subordinate clause.

Negation using *haber*	
Subjunctive: denied/nonexistent	**Indicative: concrete/existing**
En España **no había platos** que **me gustaran** más que el bacalao. *In Spain, there were no dishes I liked more than cod.*	En España **había platos** que **me gustaban** más que el bacalao. *In Spain, there were other dishes I liked more than cod.*
No hay otra persona que me **importe** más que tú. *There is no one more important to me than you.*	**Hay otras personas** que me **importan** más que tú. *There are others who are more important to me than you.*

b. The existence of the antecedent can be denied by negating the whole clause using **nunca, jamás**, or other negative expressions such as **en modo alguno** (*in no way / not in any way*), or **en ninguna parte** (*nowhere*).

Negation using *nunca, jamás*	
Subjunctive	**Indicative**
Nunca/Jamás he sido **una persona** que **lea** mucho. *I have never been a person who reads a lot.*	**Siempre** he sido **una persona** que **lee** mucho. *I have always been a person who reads a lot.*
En ninguna parte hay **plataformas petroleras** que **sean** totalmente seguras. *Nowhere are there oil rigs that are completely safe.*	**En muchas partes** hay **plataformas petroleras** que **son** totalmente seguras. *In many places, there are oil rigs that are completely safe.*

c. Affirmative indefinite pronouns and quantifiers used as antecedents describe something or someone that cannot be identified and require the use of the subjunctive. However, the indicative can be used with affirmative indefinite pronouns and quantifiers to indicate that the speaker knows the antecedent but does not want to identify it.

Affirmative indefinite pronouns	
Subjunctive	**Indicative**
¿Hay **algo** que **quieras** decirme? *Is there something you want to say to me?*	¿Hay **algo** que **quieres** decirme? *Is there something specific you want to say to me?*
Quiero **a alguien** que me **quiera**. *I want someone who loves me.*	Quiero **a alguien** que me **quiere**. *I love someone who loves me.*

Indefinite quantifiers with ▶
only positive forms:
cualquiera, *anyone*: 7.C.5

d. Cualquier(a) is used with the subjunctive whether it occurs before the noun or independently as the pronoun.

Cualquier(a) – ***anybody/who(m)ever/whichever***	
Subjunctive	
Cualquiera que **tenga** visa puede viajar a España. *Whoever has a visa can travel to Spain.*	Puedes preguntarle la dirección a **cualquier** persona que **encuentres**. *You can ask whomever/anybody you find about the address.*

e. The *subjunctive* must be used when an indefinite pronoun or quantifier is negated: **nadie, nada, ninguno/a(s)**, or **ningún/ninguna** + *noun*.

Algún, alguno/a(s); ningún, ninguno/a: 7.B.2b

Negative indefinite pronouns/determiners	Affirmative indefinite pronouns/determiners
Subjunctive	Indicative
No hay **ningún** equipo que **sea** mejor que el nuestro. *There is no other team that is better than ours.*	Hay **otro** equipo que **es** mejor que el nuestro. *There is another team that is better than ours.*
No existe **nadie** que **juegue** mejor que nosotros. *There is no one else who plays better than us.*	Existe **alguien** que **juega** mejor que nosotros. *There is someone who plays better than us.*
La revista no publicó **nada** que me **interesara** mucho. *The magazine didn't publish anything that interested me.*	La revista publicó **algo** que me **interesó** mucho. *The magazine published something that interested me a lot.*

f. The phrase **el/la/los/las que, quien(es)** (*the one[s] that/who*) is used with the *subjunctive* when it refers to someone or something unknown. Note that this applies to defining relative clauses where **lo/el/la cual** cannot be used.

Relative pronouns: 15.A

el/la/los/las que, quien(es) – *the one who / those which*	
Subjunctive	Indicative
Elena irá con **los que deseen** ir al museo. *Elena will go with anyone who wants to go to the museum.*	Elena irá con **los que desean** ir al museo. *Elena will go with those who want to go to the museum.*
Quienes hayan comprado boletos pueden entrar. *Anyone who has bought tickets can get in.*	**Quienes han comprado** boletos pueden entrar. *Those who (already) have bought tickets can get in.*

g. Clauses with **lo que** take the subjunctive when they refer to something non-specific and the indicative when they refer to something specific.

lo que – *what/whatever*	
Subjunctive	Indicative
Lo que digas será muy importante. *Whatever you say will be very important.*	Lo que **dices** es muy importante. *What you say is very important.*

23.D.3 Tense sequencing

The tense of the verbs in the main and relative clauses depends on the context of the sentence. The examples below show some of the most common combinations.

a. When the main verb is in the indicative *present* or *simple future,* the verb in the relative clause is in the *present subjunctive*. When the main verb is in the *present perfect*, the verb in the relative clause is in the *present perfect subjunctive*.

Subjunctive in adverbial clauses: **como, donde, cuando**: 23.E.1

Main clause		Relative clause	
Indicative		Subjunctive	
Present	**Necesito** una impresora *I need a printer*	**Present**	que **funcione** bien. *that works well.*
Simple future	**Necesitaré** una impresora *I will need a printer*		
Present perfect	Jamás **he tenido** una impresora *I've never had a printer*	**Present perfect**	que **haya funcionado** bien. *that has worked well.*

b. When the main verb is in the indicative and refers to the past, the verb in the subordinate clause is in one of the past forms of the subjunctive. The context determines which tense is used.

Main clause		Relative clause	
Indicative		**Subjunctive**	
Preterite	**Necesité** una impresora *I needed a printer*	**Imperfect**	que **funcionara** bien. *that worked well.*
Imperfect	**Necesitaba** una impresora *I needed a printer*		
Present conditional	**Querría** una impresora *I would like a printer*		
Conditional perfect	**Habría querido** una impresora *I would have liked a printer*		

23.E The subjunctive in adverbial clauses

El subjuntivo en oraciones subordinadas adverbiales

Subordinating conjunctions: 16.C Adverbial clauses start with adverbial conjunctions that express time, manner, purpose, concession, cause, condition, and other relationships.

23.E.1 Place, manner, quantity

Relative adverbs: 15.C **a.** In a relative clause, the relative adverbs (**como, donde, cuando**) refer back to the antecedent, which is mentioned and can be identified.

Main clause	Relative clause with antecedent
Estaremos en **un parque** *We'll be in a park*	**donde / en el que podamos** jugar. *where we can play.*

b. When the antecedent is excluded, the adverb does not refer to a specific place, manner, or quantity. These clauses have traditionally been considered adverbial clauses introduced by a conjuction that describe the action (the verb) directly. The *Nueva gramática* regards them as *free relative adverbial clauses* that refer to an implicit antecedent.

Main clause	Adverbial clause
Estaremos *We'll be*	**donde podamos** jugar. *where we can play.*
Vino *He came*	**cuando lo llamamos**. *when we called him.*

c. The *subjunctive* is used in place, manner, and quantity clauses that describe unknown places, methods of action, and quantities/amounts.

como, donde, cuanto, todo lo que	
Subjunctive: unknown	**Indicative: known**
Busca las llaves **donde** las **hayas dejado**. *Look for your keys wherever you left them.*	Busca las llaves **donde** las **dejaste**. *Look for your keys where you left them.*
Resuelvo los problemas **como pueda**. *I resolve problems however I can.*	Resuelvo los problemas **como puedo**. *I resolve problems the way I am able to.*
Ellos harán **cuanto/todo lo que quieran**. *They will do whatever they want.*	Ellos harán **cuanto/todo lo que quieren**. *They will do everything they want.*

d. When the conjunction **como** starts the subordinate clause, the *subjunctive* expresses a condition in a specific context, while the *indicative* expresses a cause.

como	
Subjunctive: condition	**Indicative: cause**
Como no **encuentres** tu pasaporte, no podrás viajar. *If you don't find your passport, you won't be able to travel.*	**Como** no **encuentras** tu pasaporte, no podrás viajar. *Since you can't find your passport, you won't be able to travel.*

e. The conjunctions of manner **como si** and **sin que** always require the *subjunctive* in the subordinate clause. The conjunction **como si** conveys an imagined situation and is used with the *subjunctive* in all tenses except the *present subjunctive*.

como si, sin que	
Subjunctive	
Manuel habla catalán **como si fuera** de Barcelona.	*Manuel speaks Catalan as if he were from Barcelona.*
Manuel aprendió catalán **sin que** nadie le **enseñara**.	*Manuel learned Catalan without anyone teaching him.*

◀ **Parece:** 23.C.5d

◀ Infinitive and **que** –clauses: 23.C.9

f. In exclamations, **ni que** is used with the imperfect subjunctive as an expression of irritation.

No creo lo que dices, ¡**ni que** yo **fuera** tonta!   *I don't believe what you are saying, as if I were stupid!*

23.E.2 Time

Conjunctions of time			
a medida que	*as*	en cuanto	*as soon (as)*
al mismo tiempo que	*at the same time as*	luego (de) que	*after / as soon as*
antes (de) que	*before*	hasta que	*until*
apenas	*as soon as, when just*	mientras (que)	*while (so long as)*
cada vez que	*each time / every time (that)*	según	*according to*
cuando	*when*	siempre que	*whenever (as long as)*
desde que	*since*	tan pronto como	*as soon as / once*
después (de) que	*after / as soon as*	una vez que	*once*

◀ Adverbs of time: 10.B

◀ **mientras** as conditional conjunction: 16.D.2c, 23.E.2b

◀ **cuando** as relative adverb: 15.C.1

a. In general, the *subjunctive* is used in a time clause when the main clause refers to the future. When it does not refer to the future, the *indicative* is used. The examples with **cuando** below illustrate the sequence of time for the majority of time conjunctions. Usually, the subordinate clause comes first.

cuando	
Subjunctive	**Indicative**
Cuando llegue a la oficina, **leeré** mi correo. (Future) *When I get to the office, I'll read my e-mail.*	**Cuando llego** a la oficina, **leo** mi correo. (Present habit) *When I get to the office, I read my e-mail.*
Cuando haya llegado a la oficina, **leeré** mi correo. (Future) *When I have arrived at the office, I'll read my e-mail.*	**Cuando llegué** a la oficina, **leí** mi correo. (Past) *When I got to the office, I read my e-mail.*
Cuando salga de la oficina, **habré leído** mi correo. (Future) *When I leave the office, I will have read my e-mail.*	**Cuando salí** de la oficina, ya **había leído** mi correo. (Past) *When I left the office, I had already read my e-mail.*

Conjunctions of time: 16.C.3

b. Mientras (que) and **siempre que** convey a condition with the *subjunctive* (*if, so/as long as*) and are conjunctions of time with the *indicative*.

mientras, siempre que	
Subjunctive: conditional	**Indicative: time**
Mientras estés enfermo, debes quedarte en casa. *As long as you're sick, you should stay at home.*	**Mientras estás** enfermo, debes quedarte en casa. *While you're sick, you should stay at home.*
Siempre que pidas los boletos con tiempo, pagarás poco. *As long as you book the tickets in advance, you won't pay much.*	**Siempre que pides** tus boletos con tiempo, pagas poco. *When you book the tickets in advance, you don't pay much.*

Antes de que: 16.C.3

c. The conjunction **antes de que** always requires the *subjunctive* in the subordinate clause, but the infinitive can also be used when the subject in the main and subordinate clause is the same. The following conjunctions of time can also be followed by the infinitive: **después de**, **luego de**, and **hasta**. The infinitive follows immediately after conjunctions without **que**.

Infinitive when subject is the same: 23.C.9
Infinitive after a finite verb: 25.B.5

antes de, después/luego de, hasta	
Subjunctive	**Infinitive**
Ven a visitarme **antes de que** yo viaje. *Come and visit me before I travel.*	Ven a visitarme **antes de viajar**. *Come and visit me before you travel.*
¿Podéis quedaros **hasta que terminemos** el trabajo? *Can you [pl.] stay until we've finished the job?*	¿Podéis quedaros **hasta terminar** el trabajo? *Can you [pl.] stay until you've finished the job?*
Os llamaré **después de que regreséis**. *I'll call you [pl.] after you come back.*	Os llamaré **después de regresar**. *I'll call you [pl.] after I come back.*

23.E.3 Purpose, goal

Conjunctions of purpose: 16.C.7

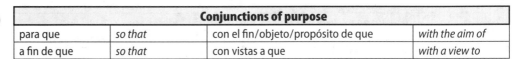

Conjunctions of purpose			
para que	so that	con el fin/objeto/propósito de que	with the aim of
a fin de que	so that	con vistas a que	with a view to

a. Conjunctions of purpose express purpose, intent, goals, and correspond to the English conjunctions *so that, in order that*. The *subjunctive* is used with conjunctions of purpose.

Subjunctive	
La constitución fue modificada **a fin de que** el presidente **pudiera** ser reelecto.	*The constitution was changed so that the president could be re-elected.*

b. Conjunctions of purpose can be followed by the infinitive (without **que**) when the subject in the main and subordinate clause is the same person. Usually a personal pronoun in the main clause will convey who the clause is about.

Subjunctive	Infinitive
Te daré dinero **para que compres** los libros. *I will give you money so that you buy the books.*	Te daré dinero **para comprar** los libros. *I will give you money to buy the books.*

c. With the exception of **para que**, the above-mentioned conjunctions of purpose are mostly used in formal situations and written Spanish.

El gobierno aplicará medidas **con el objeto de que** no **suban** los precios.　　*The government will introduce measures with the objective of keeping prices from rising.*

d. The conjunctions **de (tal) modo que, de (tal) manera que,** and **de (tal) forma que** (*so that, in such a way that*) are used with the *subjunctive* to convey purpose. With the *indicative* they convey consequence.

23.E.4 Consequence

Conjunctions of consequence: 16.C.5

Conjunctions of consequence			
de (tal) forma que	*so that, such that, in such a way that*	tan... que	*so... that*
de (tal) manera que		tal... que	
de (tal) modo que		tanto... que	

a. Conjunctions of consequence express the consequence of a condition using the *indicative*. With the *subjunctive*, they convey purpose.

tal que: 16.C.5b

Mándame un mensaje de texto, **de tal modo que estemos** en contacto.

Text me, so we can keep in touch.

Nos escribimos, **de tal modo que estamos** en contacto.

We write to each other, so we keep in touch.

Subjunctive: purpose	Indicative: consequence
Viaja mucho, **de (tal) modo que conozcas** otras culturas. *Travel a lot, so that you can get to know other cultures.*	Viaja mucho, **de (tal) modo conoces** otras culturas. *Travel a lot, so you get to know other cultures.*
El profesor enseña **de forma que** todos lo/le **entiendan**. *The teacher teaches in a way that allows everyone to understand him.*	El profesor enseña **de forma que** todos lo/le **entienden**. *The teacher teaches in a way that everyone understands him.*

b. After **tan** and **tanto** in an implied comparison, the *indicative* is used. In negative clauses, the *subjunctive* is used.

tan/tanto como: 11.C

Subjunctive: negative	Indicative: affirmative
La nieve no es **tan poca que** no **podamos** esquiar. *There isn't so little snow that we can't ski.*	La nieve es **tan poca que** no **podemos** esquiar. *There's so little snow that we can't ski.*
Los problemas no son **tantos que** yo no **pueda** resolverlos. *The problems are not so many that I can't deal with them.*	Los problemas son **tantos que** no puedo resolverlos. *The problems are so many that I can't deal with them.*

23.E.5 Cause

Conjunctions of cause			
porque	*because*	debido a que	*due to, because*
a causa de que	*because (of)*	puesto que	*since, because*
dado que	*given that*	ya que	*since*

a. Conjunctions of cause in Spanish correspond to the English *because* or *since*. The most common conjunctions of cause are **porque, como,** and **ya que.** In written language, there are more variations.

Conjunctions of cause: 16.C.4

Indicative: affirmative causes	
Cancelaron los vuelos **debido a que / porque nevaba** mucho.	*The flights were canceled because it was snowing a lot.*
No había buenas habitaciones **dado que / porque era** temporada alta.	*There were no good rooms because it was peak season.*

b. Porque, a causa de que, and **debido a que** are followed by the *subjunctive* when the cause is negated.

Subjunctive: negative causes	Indicative: affirmative causes
Estudio español **no porque sea** obligatorio **sino porque** me gusta. *I study Spanish not because it's mandatory, but because I like it.*	Estudio español **porque es** obligatorio. *I study Spanish because it's mandatory.*

23.E.6 **Concession**

Conjunctions of concession		
aunque	pese a que	*even if, despite, in spite of, although, whether*
aun cuando	si bien	
a pesar de (que)	y eso que	

Conjunctions of concession:
16.C.6

a. The most common conjunction of concession is **aunque**. The *subjunctive* is used when the subordinate clause conveys something *imagined, not real,* or *in the future.* The *indicative* expresses a fact. The subordinate clause can be placed before the main clause or after it, and the context determines the tense of the subjunctive (*present, imperfect,* or *past perfect*).

Subjunctive: imagined fact	Indicative: real fact
Siempre hablo español **aunque** me **cueste** mucho. *I always speak Spanish even if it is difficult.*	Siempre hablo español **aunque** me **cuesta** mucho. *I always speak Spanish even though it is difficult.*
Aunque me **hubieras hablado** muy rápido en español, te lo habría entendido todo. *Even if you had spoken very quickly to me in Spanish, I would have understood everything.*	**Aunque** me **has hablado** muy rápido en español, te lo he entendido todo. *Although you have spoken very quickly to me in Spanish, I have understood everything.*

b. The expression **por** + *adjective/adverb/noun* + **que** has a meaning of concession and is used with the *subjunctive.*

Por difícil que parezca, el subjuntivo es realmente fácil.
As hard as it may seem, the subjunctive is really easy.

Por poco que tengas, siempre puedes ser generoso.
As little as you may have, you can always be generous.

Por mucha gente **que venga**, habrá comida para todos.
Even if a lot of people come, there will be plenty of food for everyone.

23.E.7 **Use of the subjunctive in conditional clauses**

Conditional conjunctions: 16.D

Conditional conjunctions			
si	*if*	en caso de que	*in case of*
a no ser que	*if not*	excepto que	*if not*
a menos que	*unless*	siempre y cuando	*if*
con tal (de) que	*provided that / as long as*	siempre que	*provided that / as long as*

a. All conditional conjunctions in the previous table take the subjunctive in the subordinate clause, except the **si** conjunction, which has special rules.

Te llamaré **en caso de que quieras** ir conmigo en el coche.
I'll call you in case you want to go with me in the car.

Iremos al cine **con tal de que** la película **sea** buena.
We'll go to the movies as long as the film is good.

b. The expression **por si acaso** (*in case*) is very common in everyday speech. It can only be used with the *indicative*.

Lleva ropa de abrigo **por si acaso nieva**.

Llevaré la tarjeta de crédito **por si acaso necesito** más dinero.

Take warm clothes in case it snows.

I will bring my credit card in case I need more money.

23.E.8 Conditional *si* clauses

A subordinate **si** (*if*) clause conveys a condition, while the main clause expresses the consequence or the result if the condition is fulfilled. The main clause can express a fact, a probability, a hypothetical situation, or an imperative. Each type of clause carries its own rules.

a. *Facts:* When the condition is real and the consequence is certain, both clauses are in the indicative.

Using the *present indicative* in both clauses indicates that the same result happens every time a condition is fulfilled.

Condition: *present indicative*	Result: *present indicative*
Si **trabajas** mucho,	**ganas** dinero.
If you work a lot,	*you earn money.*

Expressing the condition in the *present indicative* and the result in the *future* (*simple future* or **ir a** + *infinitive*) indicates a clear cause-and-effect relationship.

Condition: *present indicative*	Result: *future indicative*
Si **trabajas** mucho,	**ganarás** / **vas a ganar** dinero.
If you work a lot,	*you will earn money.*

Using the *imperfect indicative* in both clauses indicates that something happened each time a condition was fulfilled.

Condition: *imperfect indicative*	Result: *imperfect indicative*
Si **trabajabas** mucho,	**ganabas** dinero.
If you worked a lot,	*you earned money.*

With the *past* or *present perfect*, conditional clauses with **si** usually communicate an assumption about something that happened, has happened, or will have happened because a condition was fulfilled. These assumptions are often expressed as questions.

Condition: *past/present perfect*	Result: *several possible verb tenses*
Si **trabajaste** / **has trabajado** mucho,	**ganaste** / **has ganado** / **habrás ganado** mucho dinero, ¿no?
If you worked/have worked a lot,	*you earned/have earned/must have earned a lot of money, right?*

b. *Probability:* The condition is an assumption and the result is possible.

When the *present conditional* is used in the main clause to express a probable result (*what would happen*) if a condition were fulfilled, the *imperfect subjunctive* is used in the subordinate **si** clause.

Condition: *imperfect subjunctive*	Result: *present conditional*
Si **trabajaras** mucho,	**ganarías** dinero.
If you worked a lot,	*you would earn money.*

c. *Hypothetical:* Both the condition and the result are only assumptions.

To express what could have happened if an imagined condition had been fulfilled, the *past perfect subjunctive* is used in the subordinate **si** clause and the *conditional perfect* in the main clause.

The past perfect subjunctive:
22.E

Condition: *past perfect subjunctive*	Result: *conditional perfect*
Si **hubieras trabajado** mucho,	**habrías ganado** dinero.
If you had worked a lot,	*you would have earned money.*

Using the past perfect subjunctive in the main clause (**hubieras ganado**) intensifies the assumption that the outcome would have been highly unlikely, but in daily speech the conditional perfect (**habrías ganado**) is preferred. The **-ese** form of the past perfect subjunctive (**hubieses ganado**) is not used in the main clause of a conditional sentence.

Condition: *past perfect subjunctive*	Result: *past perfect subjunctive*
Si **hubieras trabajado** mucho,	**hubieras/habrías ganado** dinero.
If you had worked a lot,	*you could have earned money.*

d. *The imperative in the main clause:* If a condition *is*, *was*, or *will be* fulfilled, the result can be imperative (something that must be done).

Condition: *several possible verb tenses*	Result: *imperative*
Si **trabajas/trabajaste/has trabajado/trabajaras** mucho hoy,	¡**acuéstate** temprano!
If you work/worked/have worked/were going to work a lot today,	*you must go to bed early!*

23.F Regional variations

Variaciones regionales

a. The use of the subjunctive is fairly uniform throughout the Spanish-speaking world. The exception is the use of the *present* subjunctive instead of the *imperfect* subjunctive in nominal clauses in the past. This use occurs mainly in southern parts of Latin America and only when the action in the subordinate clause still pertains to the future.

Indirect discourse: changes in
verb tenses: 31.B.3

Imperfect subjunctive	Present subjunctive
Susana me pidió ayer que **fuera** con ella al centro comercial.	Susana me pidió ayer que **vaya** con ella al centro comercial.
Susana asked me yesterday to go with her to the mall.	

b. The **-ra** and **-se** endings in the imperfect and past perfect subjunctive are equivalent (**hablara, hablase, hubiera/hubiese hablado**), and are used in both Spain and Latin America.

Queríamos una novela que **fuera/fuese** más interesante.	*We wanted a novel that was more interesting.*
No creía que **hubiera/hubiese** problemas.	*I didn't believe that there were problems.*
Habría sido bueno que **hubieras/hubieses dejado** de fumar.	*It would have been good if you had stopped smoking.*

Práctica

 Actividades 1–24, pp. A92–A100

Use of the subjunctive • **Chapter 23**

The imperative
Imperativo

24.A Formal and informal imperative

Imperativo formal e informal

The imperative expresses direct requests or commands with finite (personal) verb forms. Spanish has a formal imperative for **usted** and **ustedes**, an informal imperative for **tú, vos,** and **vosotros**, and reciprocal requests for **nosotros** (*let's*). All negative informal imperatives are the same as the corresponding present subjunctive forms. The affirmative and negative formal imperatives and reciprocal requests for **nosotros** are also formed using the corresponding present subjunctive forms. All conjugation forms that have vowel shifts or diphthongs in the present indicative and the present subjunctive, also have the same changes in the imperative.

24.B Affirmative imperative for *tú*

Imperativo afirmativo de *tú*

24.B.1 Regular affirmative imperatives for *tú*

Regular affirmative forms for **tú** are formed by dropping the **-s** ending in the second-person singular present indicative. Vowel shifts and diphthongs in the present indicative **tú** forms also occur in the imperative.

Regular verbs		Verbs with diphthongs / vowel shifts	
cantar (cantas)	canta	d**o**rmir (d**ue**rmes)	d**ue**rme
comer (comes)	come	p**e**nsar (p**ie**nsas)	p**ie**nsa
escribir (escribes)	escribe	p**e**dir (p**i**des)	p**i**de

¡**Habla** más lento, por favor!   *Speak more slowly, please!*

¡**Escribe** un blog!   *Write a blog!*

¡**Piensa** bien las cosas!   *Think carefully about things!*

24.B.2 Irregular affirmative imperatives for *tú*

There are only a few irregular affirmative imperatives for **tú**.

Completely irregular *tú* imperatives			
decir (*to say*)	**di**	salir (*to leave, to go out*)	**sal**
hacer (*to do*)	**haz**	ser (*to be*)	**sé**
ir (*to go*)	**ve**	tener (*to have*)	**ten**
poner (*to put*)	**pon**	venir (*to come*)	**ven**

¡**Sal** a jugar, pero **ten** cuidado con los autos!   *Go out and play, but watch out for cars!*

¡**Ve** y **pon** las cartas en el buzón!   *Go and put the letters in the mailbox!*

Sé valiente y **di** la verdad.   *Be brave and tell the truth.*

Haz lo que te parezca mejor.   *Do what you think is best.*

The present indicative: 17.D

Verbs with vowel shifts/ diphthongs: verb conjugation tables, pp. 257–276. See verb patterns 25, 48, 49.

Verb conjugation tables, pp. 257–276

Imperativo afirmativo de *vos* y *vosotros*

24.C.1 **Formation of imperatives for** *vos* **and** *vosotros*

The regular affirmative imperative for **vos** and **vosotros** is formed by dropping the **-r** ending from the infinitive and adding an accent to the final vowel for the **vos** imperative (**cantá**), or adding a **-d** to form the **vosotros** imperative (**cantad**). All informal imperatives are regular, with the exception of the **vos** imperative for the verb **ir**, which uses the imperative form of **andar** (**¡Andá!**).

Affirmative imperative for *vos, vosotros*			
Verbs		**vos**	**vosotros**
cant**ar**	canta-	cant**á**	canta**d**
corr**er**	corre-	corr**é**	corre**d**
escrib**ir**	escribi-	escrib**í**	escribi**d**

¡Recordad la contraseña!	*Remember the password!*
Llamá a tu padre.	*Call your father.*
Encendé la luz.	*Turn on the light.*
Andá a buscar a tu hermano.	*Go find your brother.*
Buscad las herramientas.	*Look for the tools.*

24.C.2 **Use of the imperative for** *vos* **and** *vosotros*

a. In Spain, **vosotros** is used with its corresponding imperative forms.

¡Venid a visitarme pronto!	*Come and visit me soon!*
Recordad lo que os dije.	*Remember what I told you.*
Proteged la naturaleza.	*Protect nature.*

b. When **vosotros** is used in Latin America as a formal address (to church congregations and less frequently to voters in political speeches), the **vosotros** pronoun and its imperative forms are also used. The structure is identical to that used in Spain for **vosotros**.

¡Ayudad a vuestra parroquia!	*Help your parish!*

c. In the **voseo** regions of Argentina, Uruguay, Paraguay, Costa Rica, Guatemala, Honduras, Nicaragua, El Salvador, Colombia, Venezuela, and Panama, the above-mentioned **vos** imperative is used.

¡Estudiá bien la propuesta!	*Study the proposal well!*
Recordá lo que te dije.	*Remember what I told you.*
Llamá a tu hermano.	*Call your brother.*
Decí la verdad.	*Tell the truth.*

Voseo with the
subjunctive: 22.B, 22.H
Map of **voseo** regions in
Latin America: p. 277

d. In **voseo** regions in Bolivia, Ecuador, and Chile, the pronoun **vos** is used with the **tú** verb form (**¡Habla, vos!**) in addition to the common form (**¡Hablá, vos!**), or a variant using an **-i** ending (**¡No salgái!**).

24.D Negative imperative for *tú, vos,* and *vosotros*

Imperativo negativo de *tú, vos* y *vosotros*

24.D.1 Regular negative imperatives for *tú, vos,* and *vosotros*

a. All negative imperative **tú**, **vos** and **vosotros** forms are identical to the conjugation forms of the present subjunctive.

The present subjunctive: 22.B

Negative imperative for *tú, vos, vosotros*			
	cantar	**correr**	**subir**
tú/vos	no cantes	no corras	no subas
vosotros	no cantéis	no corráis	no subáis

b. In regions that use **voseo**, the **vos** endings for the present subjunctive can vary. Since the negative imperative matches the present subjunctive form, several negative imperative forms exist for **vos**. In addition to the conjugation presented in the table above (which matches the **tú** form), another common **voseo** ending for the present subjunctive and negative imperative is **-és/-ás**.

Voseo with the subjunctive: 22.B, 22.H

No **cantes/cantés**.   No **corras/corrás**.   No **subas/subás**.

24.D.2 Irregular negative imperatives for *tú, vos,* and *vosotros*

All verbs with vowel shifts and diphthongs keep the irregularities in the informal affirmative and negative imperative forms.

No me **pidas** que mienta.	*Don't ask me to lie.*
No **seas** así conmigo.	*Don't be like that with me.*
Nunca **hagáis** caso de tonterías.	*Never pay attention to such silliness.*

24.E Imperative forms for *usted, ustedes,* and *nosotros*

Imperativo de *usted, ustedes* y *nosotros*

Affirmative imperatives for **usted**, **ustedes**, and **nosotros**, and all their negative imperative forms use the corresponding present subjunctive forms. All verbs with vowel shifts and diphthongs in the present subjunctive keep the irregularities in the affirmative and negative imperative forms for **usted**, **ustedes**, and **nosotros**.

The present subjunctive: 22.B

	cantar	correr	subir
usted	(no) cante	(no) corra	(no) suba
ustedes	(no) canten	(no) corran	(no) suban
nosotros	(no) cantemos	(no) corramos	(no) subamos

No **venga** muy tarde.	*Don't come too late.*
Digan la verdad.	*Tell the truth.*
Nunca **seamos** descorteses.	*Let us never be impolite.*

24.F Placement of pronouns

Posición de los pronombres

Placement of direct and indirect object pronouns: 13.G.6
Placement of reflexive pronouns: 27.A.1

All pronouns (reflexive pronouns, direct and indirect object pronouns) are placed *before* negative imperatives and *after* affirmative imperatives. The other rules of pronoun placement also apply here: a) The indirect object pronoun always comes before the direct object pronoun. b) The indirect object pronoun **le** becomes **se** when it appears with a direct object pronoun.

Necesito tu dirección. ¡Mánda**mela**!	*I need your address. Send it to me!*
Dá**sela** también al profesor y ¡no **se la** des a nadie más!	*Give it to the teacher too, and don't give it to anyone else!*

a. The **-d** ending is dropped from the affirmative **vosotros** imperative when the pronoun **os** is added. This does not happen with other pronouns.

Quita**os** los zapatos antes de entrar.	*Take off your [pl.] shoes before entering.*
Deci**dme** cómo llego allí.	*Tell me how to get there.*

b. In **nosotros** commands, the **-s** ending is dropped before the pronoun **nos**. Also note that **vamos** is generally used instead of **vayamos** (*present subjunctive*).

Sentémo**nos** a descansar.	*Let's sit down and rest.*
Pongámo**nos** a trabajar ya.	*Let's get to work now.*
¡Vámo**nos**!	*Let's go!*

c. The subject pronoun is used with requests only when it is necessary to show a contrast between the people being referred to.

Pon la mesa **tú**, Roberto; ayer la puse **yo**.	*You set the table, Roberto; I did it yesterday.*

24.G Other imperative constructions

Otras expresiones exhortativas

24.G.1 Infinitives

a. In informal everyday language in Spain, the infinitive can also be used with **vosotros** instead of the common imperative.

¡**Ponerse** de pie!	*Stand up!*
¡**Dejaros** de tonterías!	*Stop that nonsense!*

b. Both in Spain and Latin America, an informal request can be strengthened by adding the preposition **a** before the infinitive.

¡**A trabajar**, todo el mundo!	*Everybody, get to work!*
¡**A acostarse**, niños!	*Go to bed, children!*
¡**A entrenarse**, equipo!	*Get training, team!*

24.G.2 Impersonal imperative

a. In contexts where instructions, bans, or commands are expressed to the general public, the *infinitive* is the most common form.

No **fumar**.	*No smoking.*
No **entrar**.	*No entry.*
Leer las instrucciones con cuidado.	*Read the instructions carefully.*
Apagar la luz al salir.	*Turn off the light when you leave.*
¡**Mantener** la calma!	*Stay calm!*

b. Other structures can also be used to express impersonal negative commands. For example, to ban: **Prohibido** + *infinitive* (**Prohibido fumar**) or the imperative for **usted: No fume**. Affirmative impersonal commands can also use the imperative for **usted: Empuje** (*Push*), **Hale** (*Pull*).

24.G.3 The imperative and politeness

The imperative is softened in everyday language using friendly intonation or by using other verb tenses or expressions. Such softening strategies also occur in English.

a. Verb periphrases with infinitives can be used as imperatives.

¡**Ve a traerme** un cafecito!	*Go and get me a coffee!*
¡**Pongámonos a trabajar!**	*Let's get to work!*
¿**Puedes venir** acá, por favor?	*Can you come here, please?*

◀ Modal verb periphrases with the infinitive: 26.B

b. Questions with the present conditional of **poder** and **querer** can also be used as imperatives. Adverbs like **ya, ahora**, and **inmediatamente** can be added to strengthen the command.

¿**Podrías** contestarme ahora?	*Could you answer me now?*
¿**Querría** usted hacerlo ya?	*Could you do that immediately?*

◀ *Present conditional* as a polite form: 21.B.4

c. Questions with verbs in the present and statements starting with **A ver** or ending in interrogatives such as **¿quiere(s)?, ¿puede(s)?, ¿sí?, ¿vale?,** and **¿eh?,** can soften the imperative as well.

¿**Me dices** tu nombre?	*Can you tell me your name?*
¡**A ver** si terminas pronto!	*Let's see if you can get it done soon!*
Llamas ahora, ¿**vale**?	*Call now, okay?*
¿**Puede decirme** qué hora es?	*Could you tell me what time it is?*
Ayúdame, ¿**eh**?	*Help me, will you?*

d. The expression ¿**Por qué no...?** is extremely common in everyday speech as a polite request, but good intonation is important, as it can easily slip into a reproachful exclamation.

¿**Por qué no** me ayudas?	*Would (Why don't) you help me?*
¿**Por qué no** te callas?	*Would (Why don't) you be quiet?*
¿**Por qué no** te acuestas y descansas un poco?	*Would (Why don't) you lie down and get some rest?*

◀ The subjunctive in independent clauses: 23.B

24.G.4 *Que* + subjunctive

Sentences using the structure **que** + *subjunctive* can be classified as requests (¡**Que siga la fiesta**!), but the verb's meaning can also convey an indirect order or request from someone else (*indirect speech*) using an insistent tone.

Que des una explicación.	*You must give an explanation.*
Que vuelvas a llamar.	*You should / have to call again.*
Que me lo **digas** de nuevo.	*Say it to me again.*
¡**Que** te lo **compres**!	*Go ahead and buy it for yourself!*

24.H Imperatives in colloquial expressions

El imperativo en expresiones coloquiales

The imperative is also used in common colloquial expressions such as **oye, no me digas, mira**, and **anda ya**. In this case, its meaning is not that of a command or request, but rather an idiomatic expression.

—**Oye**, tengo que ir al mercado ahora.	*Listen, I have to go to the market now.*
—**¡No me digas** que te olvidaste del postre!	*Don't tell me that you forgot the dessert!*
—**Oye**, ¿sabes que Eva se va a casar?	*Hey, did you know that Eva is getting married?*
—**¡No me digas**!	*You're kidding! / No way!*
Mira que tu opinión me importa.	*Believe me, your opinion is important to me.*
¡Anda! No esperaba verte aquí.	*Goodness! I didn't expect to see you here!*
—Soy la mejor amiga del mundo.	*I am the best friend in the world.*
—**¡Anda ya**!	*Give me a break! / Come on!*

Práctica

 Actividades 1–12, pp. A100–A103

Non-finite verb forms
Formas no personales del verbo

Chapter 25

A. Overview
B. The infinitive
C. The *gerundio*
D. The past participle

25.A Overview

Aspectos generales

In contrast to conjugated personal (*finite*) verb forms, the non-personal (*non-finite*) verb forms are not inflected; they do not change according to the person, number, tense, or mood.

Spanish has three non-finite forms: the *infinitive*, the **gerundio**, and the *past participle*. Although these are verb forms in Spanish, they can have other non-verb functions in a sentence. The infinitive can act as a *noun*, the past participle can act as an *adjective*, and the **gerundio** is primarily used as an *adverb*.

25.A.1 Simple forms

Both the infinitive and the past participle have corresponding forms in English and Spanish, but the **gerundio** does not. The Spanish **gerundio** and the English present participle (the *-ing* form in *I am talking*) are often equated because they form the progressive tense in both languages: **estar leyendo** (*to be reading*). In spite of this similarity, their areas of use are very different. The present participle can be an adjective or an adverb in English (*a **walking** stick; He died **thinking** about his children.*) while the **gerundio** principally functions as an adverb in Spanish. In addition, the words **gerundio** and *gerund* are false cognates. Gerund refers to the nominalization of a verb (***Walking** is good for you.*). In Spanish, the infinitive is used in this case (**Caminar es bueno para la salud**). Therefore, the term **gerundio** is used in this text to refer to this verb form.

◄ Progressive tenses: 17.F.1, 25.C.3, 26.D

Simple forms		
Infinitive	**Past participle**	**Gerundio**
habl**ar** (*to talk / to speak*)	habl**ado** (*spoken*)	habl**ando** (*talking/speaking*)
com**er** (*to eat*)	com**ido** (*eaten*)	com**iendo** (*eating*)
sal**ir** (*to go out / leave*)	sal**ido** (*gone out / left*)	sal**iendo** (*going out / leaving*)

25.A.2 Compound forms

The compound forms of the infinitive and the **gerundio** are formed with **haber** + *past participle*.

◄ Adverbial uses of the **gerundio**: 25.C.5

Perfect infinitive		Gerundio compuesto	
haber (*to have*)	habl**ado** (*spoken*)	**habiendo** (*having*)	habl**ado** (*spoken*)
	com**ido** (*eaten*)		com**ido** (*eaten*)
	sal**ido** (*gone out / left*)		sal**ido** (*gone out / left*)

Deberías **haber comido** antes de salir de casa.   *You should have eaten before you left the house.*
Habiendo salido, pudo hacer la llamada.   *Having stepped out, she was able to make the call.*

25.B The infinitive

El infinitivo

The *infinitive* is the base form of the verb. This form can also act as a noun (where English uses the *-ing* gerund form). The infinitive can be the subject or the object of a sentence; it can be modified with articles and other determiners.

The Spanish infinitive can have three endings: **-ar, -er,** or **-ir**. Only a few other Spanish (non-verb) words have these endings: **bazar, bar, néctar, carácter, revólver, mártir, elixir**, etc. Some infinitives that end in **-ir** (**freír, reír, sonreír**), have an accent mark.

◄ Verbs: 17.A

25.B.1 The infinitive as a noun

a. The infinitive functions as a noun in non-personal clauses with **ser** or with other verbs where an infinitive is the grammatical subject. The real (logical) subject of the infinitive is not mentioned.

Tener salud importa mucho.	*It is very important to have good health.*
Es necesario **trabajar**.	*It is necessary to work.*

b. The use of the article and other determiners with an infinitive is possible, but is usually only common in written language, idiomatic expressions, and formal contexts. An article or other determiner is mandatory when the infinitive is the subject and is modified with an adjective or a prepositional phrase.

Este eterno llover me tiene harta.	*I'm tired of this never-ending rain.*
El hablar de otras personas no me gusta nada.	*I don't like talking about other people at all.*

c. Since the infinitive retains its verbal characteristics, it can be modified by an adverb when it is the subject or object of a sentence. Likewise, it can be modified by a direct object.

> The infinitive with sense verbs: ▶ 25.B.7

Esquiar *bien* es fácil.	*Skiing well is easy.*
Preocuparse *tanto* es totalmente inútil.	*Worrying so much is a complete waste of time.*
Pienso **escribirte** *mucho*.	*I intend to write to you a lot.*
Decirlo es más fácil que **hacerlo**.	*It is easier said than done.*
Estudiar *español* es muy interesante y divertido.	*Studying Spanish is very interesting and fun.*
Quiero recorrer *Latinoamérica* estas vacaciones.	*I want to travel around Latin America over vacation.*

25.B.2 The infinitive with an adverbial function

> Conjunctions: Ch. 16 ▶
> Use of the subjunctive: Ch. 23

a. **Para** + *infinitive* / **sin** + *infinitive* can start adverbial clauses.

Lo hizo **sin pensar**.	*He did it without thinking.*
Para explicarme, hizo un dibujo.	*To explain it to me, he made a drawing.*

> The article **el** after the ▶
> preposition **a** is abbreviated to **al**.

b. **Al** + *infinitive* indicates that an action is happening simultaneously with something else. The order of the clauses can vary and the time of the action is expressed by the conjugated verb.

Al verte, me enamoré.	*Upon seeing you, I fell in love.*

c. The subject of the infinitive must be mentioned explicitly if it is different from the subject in the main clause.

Cierra la puerta al salir **Marta**.	*Close the door when Marta leaves.*
Cierra la puerta al salir.	*Close the door when you leave.*

d. De + *infinitive* is a common expression often used with **ser, seguir**, and **continuar**. It expresses condition or consequence (often negative), assumes a known context, and can have a subject.

De ser tan difíciles las cosas, lo mejor es olvidar el asunto.	*When everything is so difficult, it is best to forget about it.*
De haber continuado así, te habría ido mal.	*If it had continued like that, it would have gone badly for you.*

25.B.3 The infinitive after a noun or adjective

Nouns and adjectives can be modified by a *preposition* + *infinitive:* **problemas por resolver** (*problems to solve*); **trabajo por hacer** (*work to do*).

Vosotros sois **buenos para jugar** al fútbol.	*You [pl.] are good at playing soccer.*
Hay varios **temas a tratar** en la reunión.	*There are several topics to discuss at the meeting.*
Todavía nos queda **mucho por hacer**.	*We still have a lot to do.*

25.B.4 **Placement of pronouns**

a. When the infinitive follows an *adjective + preposition,* object pronouns are added to the infinitive.

Las cartas están **listas para enviár***telas*.	*The letters are ready to be sent to you.*
Estoy **contenta de ver***te*.	*I'm glad to see you.*

b. When the infinitive is clearly governed by a finite verb or forms a verb periphrasis (like **ir a** + *infinitive*), the object or reflexive pronoun is added to the end of the infinitive or before the finite (conjugated) verb.

◀ ir a + *infinitive*: 20.D.1, 26.C.1
Placement of direct and indirect object pronouns: 13.G

La ley tenéis que cumplir**la**.	*The law must be obeyed.*
La ley **la** tenéis que cumplir.	

c. When a reflexive verb is followed by an infinitive, object pronouns are added to the infinitive.

◀ Reflexive pronoun placement: 27.A.1

Me arrepiento de haber**te** mentido.	*I regret lying to you.*
Lina siempre se acuerda de comprar**nos** el diario.	*Lina always remembers to buy us the newspaper.*
¿Te ofreces a ayudar**me**?	*Are you offering to help me?*

25.B.5 **The infinitive after a finite verb**

a. After a main clause that expresses a wish, an infinitive can be used if the subject in the main clause is referring to him/herself. In this case, the infinitive is *self-referential,* i.e. it refers to the same subject in the main clause. When the person in the main clause is expressing a wish about someone else, a nominal **que** clause is necessary.

◀ The subjunctive in nominal clauses: 23.C.8

Infinitive	Nominal clause
Quiero **ser** feliz.	Quiero **que seas** feliz.
I want to be happy.	*I want you to be happy.*

b. After verbs of doubt (**creer, dudar, estimar**), a nominal **que** clause can replace the infinitive in formal spoken language and in written language (newspaper headlines, speeches, laws), even if the same subject performs the action. The combination **dudar** + **poder** + *infinitive* is also common in such contexts.

◀ The subjunctive in nominal clauses: 23.C.9

Infinitive	Nominal clause
Creemos saber la razón del problema.	**Creemos que sabemos** la razón del problema.
We think we know the cause of the problem.	*We think that we know the cause of the problem.*
Estimo ganar más dinero en este puesto.	**Estimo que voy a ganar** más dinero en este puesto.
I estimate I'll make more money in this position.	*I estimate that I'll make more money in this position.*
¿**Dudas poder hacerlo**?	¿**Dudas que puedes** hacerlo?
Do you doubt you can do it?	*Do you doubt that you can do it?*

c. Reporting verbs (**decir, asegurar, informar**) in the third-person singular are often followed by **que** clauses even if the infinitive is self-referential. The use of the self-referential infinitive happens with other persons too, but is less common and more formal than a **que** clause.

◀ Reporting verbs: 23.C.2
Indirect discourse: Ch. 31

Infinitive	Nominal clause
El ministro **afirma decir** la verdad.	El ministro **afirma que dice** la verdad.
The minister claims to tell the truth.	*The minister claims that he's telling the truth.*
Informamos haber terminado el proyecto.	**Informamos que terminamos** el proyecto.
We inform you that we have finished the project.	*We inform you that we finished the project.*

d. Most verbs of command (**dejar, permitir, prohibir, recomendar**) are followed by the infinitive, but a **que** clause followed by the subjunctive is also possible.

Infinitive	Nominal clause
No **dejaré salir** a nadie.	No **dejaré que nadie salga**.
I will not have anyone leaving.	*I will not let anyone leave.*
No se te **permitirá viajar** sin visa.	No se te **permitirá que viajes** sin visa.
You won't be allowed to travel without a visa.	*Traveling without a visa won't be allowed.*

25.B.6 The infinitive with verbs of motion

Verb periphrases: 26.B.2
Use of **para** + *infinitive*: 23.E.3b

Verbs of motion such as **venir, bajar, entrar, llegar** are usually followed by the prepositions **a** or **de** + *infinitive*. In these sentences, the verb retains its original meaning of motion and direction in contrast to verb periphrases where the meaning of the finite verb may be lost (**Voy a estudiar**, *I am going to study*).

Ven **a visitarme**.	*Come and visit me.*
Baja **a abrir** la puerta.	*Go downstairs and open the door.*
Vengo **de trabajar**.	*I'm coming from work.*

25.B.7 The infinitive with sense verbs

Gerundio with sense verbs: 25.C.7

Sense verbs (**ver, oír, sentir**) express a punctual action when followed by the *infinitive* and a progressive action when used with the **gerundio**. In such cases, the infinitive always follows the verb without a preposition.

Infinitive	Gerundio
Os **oí discutir**.	Os **oí discutiendo**.
I heard you [pl.] argue.	*I heard you [pl.] arguing.*
¿Me **viste llegar** a casa?	¿Me **viste llegando** a casa?
Did you see me arrive home?	*Did you see me arriving home?*

25.B.8 The infinitive as an imperative

Infinitive as an imperative: 24.G.1

a. The use of the infinitive in place of the imperative form of **vosotros** is common in informal contexts in Spain: **¡Venir! ¡Callaros!**

Other imperative constructions: 24.G.1 and 24.G.2

b. In the whole Spanish-speaking world, the infinitive is used in commands, instructions, and signs. In spoken language, it is commonly used with the preposition **a**: **¡A venir todos ya!**

Primero, **conectar** el aparato.	*First, connect the device.*	¡A **trabajar**!	*Let's get to work!*
No **cruzar** la calle.	*Do not cross the street.*	¡A **dormir** ya mismo!	*Go to bed now!*

25.B.9 Verb periphrases with infinitives

Verb periphrases: 26.B

The majority of verb periphrases in Spanish are formed with the infinitive and often with the preposition **a** or **de**.

Vamos a viajar.	*Let's travel.*
Hay que **dejar de fumar**.	*You must stop smoking.*

25.C The *gerundio*

The Spanish **gerundio** acts as an adverb of manner with an ongoing meaning and, despite a few exceptions, is rarely used as an adjective. It is also used in many verb periphrases. The **gerundio** has both regular and irregular forms.

25.C.1 Regular forms

The ending **-ando** is added to the verb stem of regular **-ar** verbs, and **-iendo** is added to the stem of regular **-er** and **-ir** verbs.

-*ar* **verbs**	-*er* **verbs**	-*ir* **verbs**
habl**ar**	com**er**	sub**ir**
habl**ando**	com**iendo**	sub**iendo**

25.C.2 Irregular forms

Irregular verbs are often **-er** and **-ir** verbs that form the **gerundio** with **-iendo**, but have vowel shifts or consonant changes in the stem. The list below shows some of the most common examples.

◄ Verb conjugation tables, pp. 257–276. See verb patterns 13, 17, 23, 25, 46, 48, 50, 76.

-*uir*, -*eer*, -*aer* **and other verbs**		$e \to i, o \to u$ **vowel shift**	
Infinitive	*Gerundio*	**Infinitive**	*Gerundio*
constru**ir**	constru**yendo**	p**e**dir	p**i**diendo
le**er**	le**yendo**	v**e**nir	v**i**niendo
ca**er**	ca**yendo**	d**o**rmir	d**u**rmiendo
o**ír**	o**yendo**	p**o**der	p**u**diendo

25.C.3 *Estar + gerundio* (**progressive tenses**)

a. The **gerundio** is combined with the verb **estar** to refer to actions that are ongoing. This verb periphrasis is sometimes referred to as *progressive* or *continuous* tenses.

◄ Progressive tenses: 17.F.1 Verb periphrases with the **gerundio**: 26.D

Estaba trabajando cuando oí la alarma.   *I was working when I heard the alarm.*

b. In Spanish, **estar** + **gerundio** cannot be used to refer to conditions or states.

Está parado ahí.   *He is standing over there.*
Llevaba un suéter rosado.   *She was wearing a pink sweater.*

c. This verb periphrasis can be used in all indicative and subjunctive mood tenses.

Estar + gerundio: **Indicative mood**		
Present	**Estoy trabajando** en este momento.	*I am working right now.*
Simple future	A las ocho **estaré trabajando**.	*I will be working at eight.*
Preterite	**Estuve cocinando** tres horas.	*I was cooking for three hours.*
Imperfect	**Estaba cocinando** cuando sonó el timbre.	*I was cooking when the doorbell rang.*
Present conditional	Si fuera rica, **estaría viajando** por el mundo.	*If I were rich, I would be traveling around the world.*
Future perfect	Para cuando llegue la pizza, **habré estado esperando** más de una hora.	*By the time the pizza arrives, I will have been waiting for over an hour.*
Present perfect	**He estado pensando** mucho en ti.	*I have been thinking a lot about you.*
Past perfect	Cuando me di cuenta de que era el libro equivocado, ya **había estado leyendo** tres horas.	*When I realized it was the wrong book, I had already been reading for three hours.*
Conditional perfect	**Habría estado estudiando** si hubiera sabido que tenía examen.	*I would have been studying if I had known that I had an exam.*

Estar + gerundio: Subjunctive mood		
Present	No creo que **esté durmiendo**.	I don't think he is sleeping.
Imperfect	No podía creer que **estuviera dándole** la mano al presidente.	I couldn't believe I was shaking the president's hand.
Present perfect	Me extraña que **haya estado trabajando** tantas horas.	I think it's strange that he's been working so many hours.
Past perfect	Dudo que **hubiese estado mintiendo**.	I doubt he had been lying.

Present with future meaning: 17.E.4
Using the present to refer to the future: 17.F.4

d. In Spanish, the present form of **estar** + **gerundio** is never used to refer to the future.

Llegan mañana.   They are arriving tomorrow.
(*Not* *Están llegando mañana.)

e. The future form of **estar** + **gerundio** can be used to express probability about the present, while the conditional form can be used to express probability about the past.

—¿Dónde está Carlos?   Where is Carlos?
—**Estará trabajando.**   He must be working.

—¿Por qué no vino Carlos?   Why didn't Carlos come?
—**Estaría trabajando.**   He must have been working.

f. The future perfect of **estar** + **gerundio** can also be used to express probability in the past.

—¿Por qué no atendió el teléfono?   Why didn't he answer the phone?
—**Habrá estado durmiendo.**   He must have been sleeping.

25.C.4 **Other verb periphrases with the** *gerundio*

Verb periphrases with the **gerundio**: 26.D

In addition to **estar**, other verbs can be combined with the **gerundio**. In some cases, the meaning is similar to that of the periphrases with **estar**. In other cases, there are subtle differences.

andar + gerundio	to be + -ing verb	**Andaba pensando** en ir a Punta Cana.	I was thinking of going to Punta Cana.
ir + gerundio	to go + -ing verb	**Voy poniendo** la mesa mientras te preparas.	I'll start setting the table while you get ready.
llevar/pasarse + time expression + gerundio	to be doing something for + time expression	**Llevo** tres años **estudiando** teatro. **Se pasó** todo el verano **estudiando**.	I've been studying drama for three years. She has been studying all summer.
seguir/continuar + gerundio	to keep/continue + -ing verb	**Siguieron planeando** el viaje.	They kept on planning for the trip.
venir + gerundio	to be + -ing verb	**Viene pensando** en cambiar de trabajo.	He has been thinking about changing jobs.
vivir + gerundio	to keep + -ing verb (habitual or repeated action)	**Vive quejándose**.	She keeps complaining all the time.

25.C.5 **Adverbial uses of the** *gerundio*

Adverbial subordinate clauses: 16.C.2

a. The **gerundio** can function like an adverb. The chart that follows describes the main meanings expressed by the **gerundio**.

cause	No **queriendo** escuchar esa conversación, me fui de la reunión.	*Not wanting to listen to that conversation, I left the meeting.*
concession	**Siendo** liberal, sus ideas son un poco conservadoras.	*Being a liberal, his ideas are somewhat conservative.*
condition	**Estando** invitado, sí va.	*If he is invited, he will go.*
manner	Entró **derribando** la puerta.	*He got in by knocking down the door.*
method	Hizo su fortuna **vendiendo** madera.	*He made his fortune selling wood.*
purpose	Me llamó **diciendo** que no iba a venir.	*He called me saying he wasn't going to come.*
simultaneity	Me desperté **queriendo** café.	*I woke up wanting coffee.*

b. To express purpose, the **gerundio** can only be used with verbs of communication. It can be replaced with **para** + *infinitive*.

Le escribió **diciéndole** que la amaba.	*He wrote to her telling her he loved her.*
Le escribió **para decirle** que la amaba.	*He wrote her to tell her that he loved her.*

◀ Conjunctions of purpose: 16.C.7
Adverbial clauses of purpose: 23.E.3
Para + infinitive: 25.B.2b

c. The action expressed by the **gerundio** should happen before, at the same time, or right after the action expressed with the conjugated verb. Although many Spanish speakers use the **gerundio** to refer to an action that happened after (but not *right* after) the action in the main verb, a relative clause is the preferred form in these cases.

Both actions happened at the same time:

Escuchando los anuncios del gobierno, me deprimí.	*Listening to the government announcements, I got depressed.*

The action expressed by the **gerundio** happened before:

Alzando el arco, disparó la flecha.	*Raising the bow, he fired the arrow.*

The action expressed by the **gerundio** happened after:

Aumentaron las tasas de interés **causando** pánico en el mercado.	*Interest rates rose, causing panic in the market.*
Aumentaron las tasas de interés, **lo que causó** pánico en el mercado.	*Interest rates rose, which caused panic in the market.*

d. The **gerundio compuesto** can only refer to actions that happened before the action expressed by the conjugated verb.

Habiendo aprobado el examen, salió a festejar.	*Having passed the exam, he went out to celebrate.*

25.C.6   The *gerundio* vs. the English present participle: adjectival uses

a. Since the **gerundio** normally modifies a verb, the general rule is that it cannot be used as an adjective. Therefore, the English present participle used as an adjective is best replaced by a relative clause, a prepositional phrase, an adjective, or a participle. Sometimes, a completely different structure is needed in Spanish.

there are growing concerns	cada vez preocupa más
suffering people	personas que sufren
growing problems	problemas crecientes / en aumento
swimming pool	pileta de natación / piscina

b. The **gerundio** can be used in picture captions or titles of paintings.

Pablo Picasso, «Mujer **llorando**», 1937.

Pablo Picasso, "Weeping Woman," 1937.

Foto del príncipe heredero **sonriéndoles** a los fotógrafos.

Photo of the crown prince smiling at the photographers.

Mi hermana **enseñándome** a nadar en el verano de 2000.

My sister teaching me to swim, summer 2000.

c. Ardiendo and **hirviendo** can be used as adjectives.

fuego **ardiendo**   *burning fire*   agua **hirviendo**   *boiling water*

25.C.7 Use of the *gerundio* to refer to a direct object

a. With sense verbs like **oír, ver, encontrar, recordar,** and **sentir,** the **gerundio** describes an action performed by the direct object.

Anoche oímos al perro **ladrando**.

Last night we heard the dog barking.

¿No has visto a Sally **bailando**?

Have you not seen Sally dancing?

Hemos encontrado al niño solo y **llorando**.

We found the boy alone and crying.

Placement of the object ▶
pronoun: 13.G

Siempre recordaré a mi profesora **explicándome** el subjuntivo.

I will always remember my teacher explaining the subjunctive to me.

b. The **gerundio** can also be used to refer to the object of a verb that expresses a mental or physical representation (**imaginar, recordar**). The **gerundio** should always express an action, never a state.

Me **lo** imaginé **viajando** por el mundo.

I imagined him traveling around the world.

Los recuerdo **hablando** de sus abuelos.

I remember them talking about their grandparents.

Te hacía **viajando** por Europa.

I thought you were traveling around Europe.

No me puedo imaginar **a Carlos bailando** tango.

I cannot imagine Carlos dancing tango.

Recuerdo que Mario tenía problemas.

I remember Mario having problems.

(*Not* *Recuerdo a Mario teniendo problemas.)

25.C.8 Placement of pronouns

a. When the **gerundio** follows a finite verb, the pronoun is placed before the finite verb or is added to the end of the **gerundio**.

(Te estoy escribiendo la carta.)

(I'm writing the letter to you.)

Te la estoy escribiendo. / Estoy escribiéndo**tela**.

I'm writing it to you.

Gerundio with ▶
sense verbs: 25.C.7

b. Reflexive and object pronouns must be added to the **gerundio** in clauses with sense verbs and objects.

Te vi bajándo**te** del autobús.

I saw you getting off the bus.

Nos oyeron hablándo**les** en francés a los turistas.

They heard us speaking in French to the tourists.

25.D The past participle

El participio

Present and past perfect: ▶
19.A and 19.D
Use of the participle
in passive **ser** clauses: 28.B

The past participle forms all the compound forms with the auxiliary verb **haber** (*to have*): **Has hablado.** (*You have spoken.*). With **ser,** the past participle forms passive sentences: **La carta fue escrita.** (*The letter was written.*). Apart from these verb functions, the participle is generally used as an *adjective*.

25.D.1 Regular forms

a. The ending **-ado** is added to the verb stem of regular **-ar** verbs to form the past participle. The ending **-ido** is added to the stem of regular **-er** and **-ir** verbs. Object and reflexive pronouns must *always* be placed before **haber**.

◀ When used as adjectives, past participles agree in gender and number: 3.A.1

hablar → hablado   comer → comido   subir → subido

b. When the verb stem ends in any vowel except **-u**, a written accent is needed on the past participle ending **-ido** (**-er** and **-ir** verbs). The combination of **u + i** usually forms a diphthong and does not have an accent (**construido, huido**).

◀ Accents on vowel combinations: 1.E.4
Hiatus and accentuation: 1.E.5

Infinitive	Verb stem	Past participle	
creer	**cre-**	creído	*thought*
leer	**le-**	leído	*read*
oír	**o-**	oído	*heard*
sonreír	**sonre-**	sonreído	*smiled*
traer	**tra-**	traído	*brought*

25.D.2 Irregular forms

A number of verbs have an irregular past participle.

◀ Irregular past participles: 19.A.2

Infinitives	Irregular past participles	
abrir	**abierto**	*opened*
cubrir	**cubierto**	*covered*
decir	**dicho**	*said, told*
descubrir	**descubierto**	*discovered*
escribir	**escrito**	*written*
hacer	**hecho**	*done, made*
morir	**muerto**	*died*
poner	**puesto**	*placed*
resolver	**resuelto**	*resolved*
romper	**roto**	*broken*
satisfacer	**satisfecho**	*satisfied*
ver	**visto**	*seen*
volver	**vuelto**	*returned*

25.D.3 Past participles with two forms

a. There are only three Spanish verbs that have two completely equal past participle forms: a regular form and an irregular form that can form all the compound verb tenses with **haber** and passive voice with **ser**.

◀ Passive voice with **ser**: 28.B

Infinitive	Past participle	
	Regular	Irregular
imprimir (*to print*)	imprimido	**impreso**
freír (*to fry*)	freído	**frito**
proveer (*to provide*)	proveído	**provisto**

He **impreso/imprimido** la carta.   *I have printed the letter.*
No hemos **frito/freído** la carne.   *We haven't fried the meat.*
A los viajeros se les ha **provisto/proveído** de todo.   *The travelers have been provided with everything.*

b. In the Spanish-speaking world, **freído** and **provisto** are often used both as a participle and an adjective. The irregular form **impreso** is often used in Latin America both as a participle and an adjective.

El formulario está **impreso**.	*The form is printed.*
Las albóndigas ya están **fritas**.	*The meatballs are already fried.*
La bodega está bien **provista**.	*The wine cellar is well supplied.*

Passive voice with **ser**: 28.B

c. All other Spanish verbs that have two past participle forms use only the regular form in compound tenses with **haber** (**He corregido las cartas.**) and the passive voice with **ser** (**Las cartas han sido corregidas.**). The irregular past participle form is only used as an adjective (**Eso es correcto.**). Below is a list of some of these two-participle verbs with their most common meanings.

Gender and number of adjectives: 3.A

Infinitives	Participles		Adjectives	
absorber	**absorbido**	*absorbed*	**absorto**	*absorbed/engrossed*
atender	**atendido**	*attended/assisted*	**atento**	*attentive/alert/courteous*
bendecir	**bendecido**	*blessed*	**bendito**	*blessed*
confesar	**confesado**	*confessed*	**confeso**	*self-confessed*
confundir	**confundido**	*confused*	**confuso**	*confused/confusing*
despertar	**despertado**	*awakened*	**despierto**	*awake/bright/alert*
elegir	**elegido**	*chosen/elected*	**electo**	*chosen/elected*
maldecir	**maldecido**	*cursed/damned*	**maldito**	*cursed/damned*
prender	**prendido**	*caught*	**preso**	*imprisoned*
presumir	**presumido**	*presumed*	**presunto**	*presumed/alleged*
soltar	**soltado**	*released / let go*	**suelto**	*loose/fluid/fluent*

Electo is mostly used in Latin America as an adjective: **el presidente electo**
el preso: the prisoner
estar preso: to be imprisoned

25.D.4 Use of the past participle

a. The past participle forms all the compound verb forms with **haber** both in the indicative and the subjunctive moods (**ha salido / haya salido**). The participle form always retains the **-ado/-ido** ending in all compound tenses.

Passive voice with **ser**: 28.B
Estar and passive voice with **ser**: 28.C.3

b. The past participle is used in the passive voice with **ser**, where it agrees in gender and number with the subject in the sentence.

La novel**a** **fue escrita** por el escritor.	*The novel was written by the author.*
Las novel**as** **fueron escritas** por el escritor.	*The novels were written by the author.*

Agreement of the past participle in verb periphrases: 26.E

c. With **estar**, the past participle conveys the result of an action. Such sentences often correspond to the passive structure with **ser**.

La carta **fue escrita**. (*passive voice*)	*The letter was written.*
La carta **está escrita**. (**estar** + *past participle*)	*The letter is written.*

Práctica

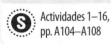

Actividades 1–16, pp. A104–A108

Verb periphrases and modal verbs
Perífrasis verbales y verbos modales

26.A Overview

Aspectos generales

26.A.1 Verb periphrases

a. *Verb periphrases* (**perífrasis verbales**) are verb combinations made up of an auxiliary verb and a main verb. The main verb always uses a non-personal form: *infinitive*, **gerundio**, or *past participle*.

Volvió a hablar con su hermano.	*He spoke with his brother again.*
Siguió hablando durante toda la reunión.	*He continued talking during the entire meeting.*
Llevo ganados diez premios.	*I have won ten awards (so far).*

b. Auxiliary verbs are usually conjugated, but can also appear in non-personal forms.

Volver a hablar con él fue una alegría.	*Talking to him again was a joy.*
No **pudiendo responder** a la pregunta, se echó a llorar.	*Being unable to answer the question, she began to cry.*

c. Most auxiliary verbs can be used as main verbs.

Volvió a su pueblo.	*He returned to his hometown.*
Sigo su blog todas las semanas.	*I follow your blog every week.*
Llevé a los niños a la fiesta.	*I took the children to the party.*

d. There can be another element, such as a preposition or conjunction, joining the two verbs that form the periphrasis.

Tengo *que* **trabajar** el fin de semana.	*I have to work this weekend.*
Debe *de* **haber llovido** mucho.	*It must have rained a lot.*

e. Not all verb combinations are verb periphrases. In a periphrasis, the meaning of the auxiliary verb is totally or partially different from the meaning of the periphrasis as a whole. In addition, the second verb can never be a direct object of the first.

Tengo que trabajar.	*I have to work.*
(periphrasis – **tener** does not express *possession*)	
Debo estudiar.	*I should study.*
(periphrasis – **estudiar** is not the direct object of **debo**)	
Deseo ganar el concurso. Lo deseo.	*I want to win the contest. I want (to win) it.*
(not a periphrasis – **ganar el concurso** is the direct object of **deseo**)	

26.B Modal verb periphrases with the infinitive

◀ The infinitive: 25.B

Perífrasis modales de infinitivo

26.B.1 Modal auxiliaries

a. Modal auxiliaries express possibility, obligation, necessity, and other aspects of the speaker's attitude towards the action expressed by the main verb.

◀ Modal verbs: 17.F.3

Bailo.	*I dance.*
Puedo bailar.	*I can dance.*
Quiero bailar.	*I want to dance.*

Modal verb periphrases can express obligation or necessity, possibility, and doubt.

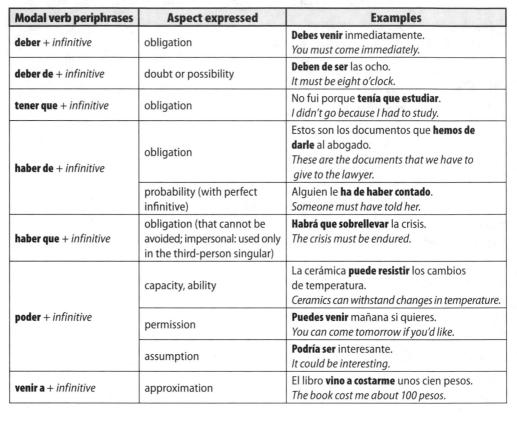

Modal verb periphrases	Aspect expressed	Examples
deber + *infinitive*	obligation	**Debes venir** inmediatamente. *You must come immediately.*
deber de + *infinitive*	doubt or possibility	**Deben de ser** las ocho. *It must be eight o'clock.*
tener que + *infinitive*	obligation	No fui porque **tenía que estudiar**. *I didn't go because I had to study.*
haber de + *infinitive*	obligation	Estos son los documentos que **hemos de darle** al abogado. *These are the documents that we have to give to the lawyer.*
	probability (with perfect infinitive)	Alguien le **ha de haber contado**. *Someone must have told her.*
haber que + *infinitive*	obligation (that cannot be avoided; impersonal: used only in the third-person singular)	**Habrá que sobrellevar** la crisis. *The crisis must be endured.*
poder + *infinitive*	capacity, ability	La cerámica **puede resistir** los cambios de temperatura. *Ceramics can withstand changes in temperature.*
	permission	**Puedes venir** mañana si quieres. *You can come tomorrow if you'd like.*
	assumption	**Podría ser** interesante. *It could be interesting.*
venir a + *infinitive*	approximation	El libro **vino a costarme** unos cien pesos. *The book cost me about 100 pesos.*

Passive constructions with **se** and modal verbs: 28.D.3

26.B.3 **Other modal verb periphrases**

The following verb periphrases are commonly grouped together with modal verb periphrases.

Modal verb periphrases	Aspect expressed	Examples
parecer + *infinitive*	conjecture	**Parece haber** mucha gente en la fiesta. *There seem to be a lot of people at the party.*
querer + *infinitive*	wish, desire	**Quiero escuchar** música. *I want to listen to music.*
saber + *infinitive*	skill	**Sé hablar** español muy bien. *I know how to speak Spanish very well.*

26.B.4 *Deber / deber de*

a. Deber expresses obligation, but is weaker than **tener que**. **Deber de** only expresses assumption or possibility. In everyday speech, the preposition **de** is often dropped and the meaning becomes ambiguous.

Debes cuidar la naturaleza.	*You should take care of nature.*
Deberías gastar menos.	*You should spend less.*
No **debiste** llegar tarde.	*You shouldn't have arrived late.*
Deberás hacerlo aunque no quieras.	*You should/will do it even though you don't want to.*
Este plato **debe de** ser delicioso.	*This dish must be delicious.*
El huracán **debió de** ser muy fuerte porque hizo mucho daño.	*The hurricane must have been very strong because it caused a lot of damage.*

b. The English *should* is usually translated using the present tense or the conditional of **deber**. However, in many cases it can be translated using the future tense or passive constructions with **se** without a modal auxiliary, particularly in handbooks and other instructions.

You **should** go to the doctor.	**Deberías/Debes** ir al médico.
When you press the button, you **should hear** a beep.	Al presionar el botón, **escuchará** un sonido.
	Al presionar el botón, **se escucha** un sonido.

26.B.5 Poder

a. In the preterite, **poder** conveys that someone succeeded in doing something, while the *imperfect* describes whether a person was able to do something or not.

◀ Verbs that change meaning in the preterite and the imperfect: 18.F

La puerta estaba cerrada y no **podíamos** entrar. Finalmente **pudimos** hacerlo.	The door was locked and we couldn't get in. Finally, we managed to do it.

b. The examples below show the use of **poder** in different verb tenses.

Permission or ban	
Todos **podéis** entrar gratis.	All of you [pl.] may go in for free.
¿**Podrías/Puedes** prestarme tu libro?	Could you / Can you lend me your book? / Could I / Can I / May I borrow your book?
No puedes hacer lo que se te ocurra.	You cannot / are not allowed to do whatever you feel like doing.

Possibility/Ability	
¡**No puedo** ponerme las botas!	I can't put my boots on!
Aquí **no se puede** cruzar la calle. ¡Es muy peligroso!	You can't cross the street here. It's very dangerous!
¿**Pudiste** ver la exhibición?	Did you get to see the exhibition?

Assumptions	
Podría ser bueno que vinieras.	It could/might be good if you came.
Eso **pudo/podía** haber sucedido.	It could have happened.
Podrías haber hecho algo.	You could/might have done something.

26.B.6 Querer

Querer is translated differently in the imperfect and the preterite. Notice also the difference in the preterite between **querer** and **no querer**.

◀ Verbs that change meaning in the preterite and the imperfect: 18.F

Quería decirle la verdad, pero no pude.	I wanted to tell him the truth, but I couldn't.
Quise decirle la verdad, pero no pude.	I tried to tell him the truth, but I couldn't.
Me invitaron a salir ayer, pero **no quise**.	I was invited to go out yesterday, but I didn't want to (I refused).

26.B.7 Saber

a. In a verb periphrasis, **saber** indicates that a person has the skills or the knowledge to perform an action. This is independent of being physically, emotionally, or mentally in a state to do it (**poder**).

—¿**Sabes** esquiar?	Can you ski?
—Sí, **sé** esquiar, pero **no puedo** hacerlo. Tengo el pie quebrado.	Yes, I know how to ski, but I can't do it. My foot is broken.
Antes **sabía** hablar bien el español, pero ya **no puedo** hacerlo.	Before I knew how to speak Spanish well, but I can't do it anymore.

b. As a main verb, **saber** is commonly translated as *to know* or *to discover / find out*.

Marcela **sabía** la verdad.	*Marcela knew the truth.*
Marcela **supo** la verdad.	*Marcela discovered / found out the truth.*

Infinitive: 25.B

26.C Other verb periphrases with the infinitive

Otras perífrasis de infinitivo

26.C.1 Verb periphrases that express time

Use of the present to refer to the future: 17.F.4
Use of the imperfect to refer to incomplete actions: 18.E.6, 18.E.10c

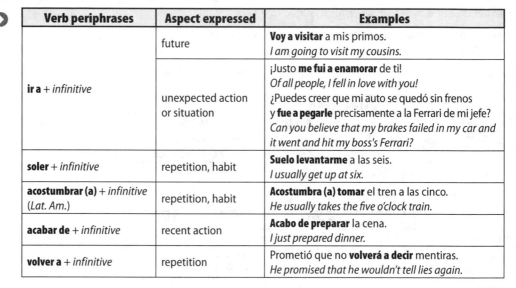

Verb periphrases	Aspect expressed	Examples
ir a + *infinitive*	future	**Voy a visitar** a mis primos. *I am going to visit my cousins.*
	unexpected action or situation	¡Justo **me fui a enamorar** de ti! *Of all people, I fell in love with you!* ¿Puedes creer que mi auto se quedó sin frenos y **fue a pegarle** precisamente a la Ferrari de mi jefe? *Can you believe that my brakes failed in my car and it went and hit my boss's Ferrari?*
soler + *infinitive*	repetition, habit	**Suelo levantarme** a las seis. *I usually get up at six.*
acostumbrar (a) + *infinitive* (*Lat. Am.*)	repetition, habit	**Acostumbra (a) tomar** el tren a las cinco. *He usually takes the five o'clock train.*
acabar de + *infinitive*	recent action	**Acabo de preparar** la cena. *I just prepared dinner.*
volver a + *infinitive*	repetition	Prometió que no **volverá a decir** mentiras. *He promised that he wouldn't tell lies again.*

26.C.2 Verb periphrases that express a phase

Some verb periphrases refer to the preparation, the beginning, the end, or the interruption of an action.

Verb periphrases	Aspect expressed	Examples
estar por + *infinitive*	preparation	**Estaba por preparar** la cena. *I was about to make dinner.*
comenzar/empezar a + *infinitive*	beginning	**Comenzó/Empezó a llover** en cuanto llegamos. *It began to rain as soon as we arrived.*
ponerse a + *infinitive*	beginning	Cuando terminó el espectáculo, todos **se pusieron a aplaudir**. *When the show was over, everyone began to applaud.*
entrar a + *infinitive*	beginning	Todos **entramos a sospechar** de él. *We all started to suspect him.*
dejar/parar de + *infinitive*	interruption	**Dejó de llover** y salió el sol. *It stopped raining and the sun came out.* ¡**Para de llorar**, por favor! *Stop crying, please!*
acabar/terminar de + *infinitive*	end	**Terminé de cocinar** a las ocho. *I finished cooking at eight o'clock.*
pasar a + *infinitive*	transition	Después de estudiar italiano, **pasé a estudiar** ruso. *After studying Italian, I went on to study Russian.*

26.C.3 Verb periphrases that express a hierarchy or scale

a. Some periphrases with infinitives order an action in a series.

Modal verb periphrases	Aspect expressed	Examples
empezar por + *infinitive*	first action in a series	**Empecé por explicarle** que no me gustaba mi trabajo. *I began by explaining to him that I did not like my job.*
acabar/terminar por + *infinitive*	last action in a series	**Terminé por comprar** el vestido violeta. *I ended up buying the purple dress.*
venir a + *infinitive*	result, outcome	En ese caso, ambas opciones **venían a ser** lo mismo. *In that case, both options turned out to be the same.*

b. **Empezar/acabar/terminar por** + *infinitive* can be replaced by **empezar/acabar/terminar** + **gerundio**.

Acabó por irse.
Acabó yéndose.   *He ended up leaving.*

26.D Verb periphrases with the *gerundio*

◄ The **gerundio**: 25.C

Perífrasis de gerundio

All verb periphrases with the **gerundio** express an ongoing action. Most verbs used as auxiliaries in these periphrases are common verbs of movement (**ir, venir, andar, llevar, pasar, seguir,** etc.).

Verb periphrases	Aspect expressed	Examples
estar + **gerundio**	ongoing action	**Estaba trabajando** cuando me llamaste. *I was working when you called me.*
ir + **gerundio**	incremental process with an end limit/result	Sus problemas de salud **fueron aumentando** hasta que finalmente tuvo que dejar de trabajar. *His health problems kept increasing (getting worse) until he finally had to stop working.*
	beginning of an incremental process	¿Podrías **ir pensando** en temas para el último capítulo? *Could you start thinking about topics for the last chapter?*
venir + **gerundio**	process that began in the past and continues up to the current moment	Nos **venía mintiendo**, pero lo descubrimos. *He had been lying to us, but we found out.* ¡Te **vengo diciendo** que comas mejor! *I've been telling you to eat better!*
andar + **gerundio**	current process that usually happens intermittently	El perro **anda olfateando** todos los árboles. *The dog is going around smelling all the trees.*
llevar + *time expression* + **gerundio**	period of time	**Llevo dos años estudiando** español. *I've been studying Spanish for two years.*
pasar(se) + *time expression* + **gerundio**	current process (more emphatic than **estar** + **gerundio**)	**Se pasó la noche llorando** porque extrañaba a su gatito. *He spent the night crying because he missed his kitten.*
vivir + **gerundio** (*Lat. Am.*)	repeated, constant, or habitual action	Mis vecinos **viven gritando**. No me dejan dormir. *My neighbors are always yelling. They don't let me sleep.*
seguir/continuar + **gerundio**	continued process	Ella **sigue estudiando**. *She is still / keeps on studying.*

◄ **Estar** + **gerundio** (Progressive tenses): 25.C.3

Past participle: 19.A.1, 19.A.2, 25.D

26.E Verb periphrases with the past participle

Perífrasis de participio

a. All verb periphrases with the past participle focus on the result of an action or process. The participle agrees in gender and number with the subject, or with the object if there is one.

Estar + *past participle*: 28.C.3

Verb periphrases	Aspect expressed	Examples
estar + *past participle*	resulting state	La carta **está escrita** a mi nombre. *The letter is addressed to me.*
tener + *past participle*	process that has been completed	Eso ya lo **tengo visto**. *I have already looked at that.* Le **tengo prohibido** salir después de las once de la noche. *I have forbidden him to go out after eleven o'clock at night.*
llevar + *past participle*	accumulation up to a certain point in time	**Llevo ganados** cinco premios. *(So far,) I have won five awards.*

The *Nueva gramática* lists only **estar/tener/llevar** + *past participle* as verb periphrases.

b. The following verb phrases are often included with verb periphrases.

dejar + *past participle*	Juan **dejó dicho** que lo llames. *Juan left a message for you to call him.*
encontrarse/hallarse + *past participle*	**Se encuentra muy cansado.** *He is feeling very tired.*
ir + *past participle*	Para marzo ya **iban escritos** cuatro capítulos del libro. *By March, four chapters of the book were already written.*
quedar(se) + *past participle*	**Quedé agotada** después de la fiesta. *I was wiped out after the party.*
resultar + *past participle*	La clase media **resultó beneficiada** por la caída de los precios. *The middle class benefited from the drop in prices.*
seguir + *past participle*	Las calles **siguen vigiladas** por la policía. *The streets continue to be patrolled by the police.*
venir + *past participle*	Las instrucciones **vinieron escritas** en la caja. *The instructions came written on the box.*
verse + *past participle*	Juan **se vio obligado** a partir. *Juan felt obligated to leave.*

Práctica

 Actividades 1–12, pp. A108–A111

Reflexive pronouns and verbs
Pronombres y verbos reflexivos

27.A Structure

Estructura

Reflexive pronouns indicate that the subject is both the doer and the object of the action in a sentence, directly or indirectly: *You* see *yourself* in the mirror. In Spanish, some verbs can only be used reflexively. These verbs are recorded in dictionaries and word lists with the reflexive pronoun **se** after the infinitive ending, like in **lavarse** (*to wash*), **preocuparse** (*to worry*), and **sentirse** (*to feel*). Reflexive pronouns take the same form as object pronouns except for **usted(es)** and the third person: **se**. A different set of pronouns is used after prepositions and is usually followed by the adjective **mismo/a(s)**.

Reflexive verbs: 17.B.3, 27.C
Pronouns after prepositions: 13.C

Subject	Reflexive pronouns	lavarse	Translation	After a preposition
yo	**me**	me lavo	*I wash (myself).*	**mí (conmigo)**
tú	**te**	te lavas	*You wash (yourself).*	**ti (contigo)**
vos	**te**	te lavás	*You wash (yourself).*	**vos**
usted, él, ella	**se**	se lava	*You wash (yourself).* *He/She washes (him/herself).*	**sí, usted/él/ella (consigo)**
nosotros/as	**nos**	nos lavamos	*We wash (ourselves).*	**nosotros/as**
vosotros/as	**os**	os laváis	*You wash (yourselves).*	**vosotros/as**
ustedes, ellos/as	**se**	se lavan	*You/They wash (yourselves/themselves).*	**sí, ustedes/ellos/ellas (consigo)**

Juan **se despierta** temprano.	*Juan wakes up early.*
Mis padres **se preocupan** mucho.	*My parents worry a lot.*
Hazte la pregunta **a ti mismo**.	*Ask the question to yourself.*
Parecía que hablaba **consigo mismo**.	*It seemed he was talking to himself.*

27.A.1 Placement

a. Reflexive pronouns are placed before the conjugated verb. With verb expressions using the infinitive or **gerundio**, the placement is optional, either before the conjugated verb or after the infinitive/**gerundio**.

Ellos **se** lavan.	*They wash (themselves).*
Ellos **se** van a lavar. Ellos van a lavar**se**.	*They are going to wash (themselves).*
Ellos **se** están lavando. Ellos están lavándo**se**.	*They are washing (themselves).*

b. With compound verb forms using **haber** + *past participle*, the pronoun is always placed before the conjugated verb.

—¿**Os** habéis lavado?	*Have you [pl.] washed (yourselves)?*
—No, no **nos** hemos lavado.	*No, we have not washed (ourselves).*

c. Reflexive pronouns are placed after affirmative imperatives and before negative imperatives.

Lávate las manos antes de la cena.	*Wash your hands before dinner.*
No **te** preocupes por nada.	*Don't worry (yourself) about anything.*

Pronouns after
prepositions: 13.C

mismo/a(s): 7.E.5

27.A.2 Reflexive pronouns after a preposition

a. The forms of the reflexive pronouns used after prepositions (**mí, ti, usted/él/ella, nosotros/as, vosotros/as, ustedes/ellos/as**) can convey a reflexive meaning. After prepositions, the form **sí** can also be used instead of **usted, él/ella, ustedes, ellos/as. Sí** is inherently reflexive. When **mí, ti**, and **sí** follow the preposition **con**, they form **conmigo, contigo**, and **consigo**. The adjective **mismo/a(s)** (*self*) usually follows the pronoun to emphasize the reflexive meaning. It agrees in gender and number with the subject.

Pedro sólo piensa en **sí** mism**o**.	*Pedro only thinks about himself.*
Marina habla **consigo** mism**a**.	*Marina is talking / talks to herself.*

b. Compare these reflexive and non-reflexive uses of pronouns after prepositions.

Reflexive use	Non-reflexive use
Habla **consigo misma**. *She talks to herself.*	Habla **con ella**. *She talks to her.*
Llevaba **consigo** un bastón. *He carried a cane with him.*	Fui al parque **con él**. *I went to the park with him.*
Me lo guardé **para mí misma**. *I kept it for myself.*	Lo guardé **para ella**. *I kept it for her.*
Se lo repitió **a sí/ella misma**. *She repeated it to herself.*	Se lo repitió **a ella**. *He repeated it to her.*

27.B Reciprocal pronouns

Pronombres recíprocos

27.B.1 Each other

Different meanings of
reflexive verbs: 27.D

A plural reflexive pronoun may indicate a *reciprocal* meaning corresponding to the English *each other*.

Mis padres y yo **nos queremos** mucho.	*My parents and I love each other very much.*
Vosotros **os llamáis** todos los días.	*You [pl.] call each other every day.*
Los novios **se abrazan**.	*The couple is hugging each other.*
¿**Os habláis** vosotros?	*Are you [pl.] talking to each other?*
¿**Se escriben** tus amigos y tú?	*Do you and your friends write to each other?*

27.B.2 *El uno al otro*

To emphasize a mutual relationship, **el uno al otro / los unos a los otros** can be added after the verb. The preposition changes according to the preposition required by the verb. The adverbs **mutuamente** (*mutually*) and **recíprocamente** (*reciprocally*) are rarely used. They are more common as adjectives in expressions such as: **El respeto entre nosotros es mutuo/recíproco.** (*The respect between us is mutual/reciprocal*).

Los novios se abrazan **el uno al otro**.	*The couple is hugging each other.*
Se pelean todo el tiempo **el uno con el otro.**	*They fight with each other all the time.*
En Navidad nos damos regalos **los unos a los otros**.	*At Christmas, we give each other gifts.*
Los vecinos se ayudan **mutuamente**.	*Neighbors help each other.*

27.C | Reflexive verbs

Verbos reflexivos

Reflexive verbs are conjugated with reflexive pronouns. Many verbs have reflexive and non-reflexive forms. These two conjugation forms for the same verb can result in related or completely different meanings. Spanish verbs that do not have a reflexive meaning but do have a reflexive form are called **verbos pronominales** (*pronominal verbs*).

Reflexive	Non-reflexive
Me **visto** después de bañarme. *I get dressed after taking a bath.*	**Visto** a la bebé después de **bañarla**. *I get the baby dressed after bathing her.*
Te **despiertas** temprano. *You wake up early.*	**Te despierto** temprano. *I wake you up early.*
Las chicas *se* **levantan** tarde. *The girls get up late.*	Las chicas **levantan** pesas. *The girls lift weights.*
No quiero **despedirme** de ti. *I don't want to say goodbye to you.*	Mi jefe me va a **despedir**. *My boss is going to fire me.*

27.D | Different meanings of reflexive verbs

Varios significados de los verbos reflexivos

27.D.1 | Reflexive meaning

a. This is the meaning implied when reflexive verbs are discussed. The subject (which must refer to something living) performs the action and is also subject to it. In this case, the singular reflexive intensifier **a sí mismo/a** (*self*) can be added.

| Ella **se lava** (a sí misma). | She is washing (herself). |
| El perro **se muerde** la cola (a sí mismo). | The dog is biting its tail. |

◀ Reflexive pronouns: 27.A

b. Reflexive verbs and pronouns are used more often in Spanish than in English, although reflexive pronouns are sometimes used in English in a non-reflexive way.

Yo mismo hice la tarea.	I did the homework **myself**.
Me voy a **divorciar**.	I'm going to get divorced.
¿No **te avergüenzas** de eso?	Aren't you ashamed of that?

c. In genuine reflexive verbs, the subject and object refer to the same person. But if an additional object is added to the sentence (for example, **las manos**), the subject is indirectly affected by the action and becomes the indirect object. In this case, the verb is still reflexive.

Los niños **se lavan** las manos.	The children are washing their hands.
¿**Te pintaste** las uñas?	Did you paint your nails?
Ponte el abrigo.	Put on your coat.

◀ Use of article instead of a possessive: 9.D.4

d. In the previous reflexive sentences, it is not common to use the reflexive intensifier (**a mí mismo, a sí mismo**, etc.), but the reflexive action can be emphasized by adding the phrase **por sí mismo/a** or **por sí solo/a** (*himself/herself*).

El abuelo ya no es capaz de levantarse **por sí mismo/solo**.   *Grandpa can't get up by himself anymore.*

e. A number of verbs that describe daily personal care are reflexive. The intensifier **a sí mismo/a** is not needed with these verbs.

Reflexive verbs for daily routines			
acostarse	to go to bed	desvestirse	to get undressed
afeitarse/rasurarse	to shave	maquillarse	to put on makeup
dormirse	to fall asleep	peinarse	to comb one's hair
levantarse	to get/stand up	ponerse	to put on (e.g., clothes)
bañarse, ducharse	to take a bath, to take a shower	quitarse	to take off (e.g., clothes)
cepillarse	to brush (hair or teeth)	vestirse	to get dressed

Nos acostamos tarde.   *We go to bed late.*
Te levantas temprano.   *You get up early.*
Os despertáis a las siete.   *You [pl.] wake up at seven o'clock.*
No puedo **dormirme**.   *I can't fall asleep.*
¿**Te cepillas** los dientes?   *Do you brush your teeth?*
Me ducho y **me visto**.   *I shower and get dressed.*
Ella **se peina** y **se maquilla**.   *She combs her hair and puts on makeup.*

27.D.2 Verbs with only reflexive forms

A few Spanish verbs only have a reflexive form.

Verbs that do not have a reflexive meaning but do have a reflexive form are called **verbos pronominales.**

Verbs with only reflexive forms			
arrepentirse	to regret	quejarse	to complain
atreverse	to dare	jactarse	to boast
abstenerse	to abstain	suicidarse	to commit suicide

El abogado **se jacta** de que nunca ha perdido ni un solo caso. Nadie **se atreve** a **quejarse** de sus servicios.   *The lawyer boasts that he has never lost even a single case. Nobody dares to complain about his services.*

27.D.3 Reciprocal meaning

el uno al otro: 27.B.2

a. When two or more people are doing an action and are also the recipients of that action, the meaning is reciprocal (**recíproco**). The reciprocal meaning is emphasized by adding **el uno al otro**, **la una a la otra**, or **mutuamente**. The following verbs are often used with a reciprocal meaning.

Common verbs with reciprocal meaning	
abrazarse	Los novios **se abrazan**. *The couple hugs (each other).*
amarse/quererse	**Nos queremos** desde siempre. *We have always loved each other.*
ayudarse	Mis amigos y yo **nos ayudamos** (**mutuamente**). *My friends and I help each other.*
besarse	En España **nos besamos** al saludar. *In Spain, we kiss when greeting each other.*
comprometerse	¿Vosotros **os** vais a **comprometer**? *Are you [pl.] going to get engaged?*
escribirse	Deberíamos **escribirnos** más. *We should write to each other more.*
hablarse	Mi madre y yo **nos hablamos** a diario. *My mother and I talk to each other every day.*
llevarse bien/mal	**Nos llevamos** bien. *We get along well (with each other).*
mirarse	La madre y el bebé **se miran** a los ojos. *Mother and child are looking into each other's eyes.*
odiarse	Los perros y los gatos **se odian**. *Dogs and cats hate each other.*
pelearse	Algunas personas **se pelean** por todo. *Some people fight about anything.*
tutearse	Nosotros nunca **nos tuteamos**. *We never address each other informally.*
verse	Mis amigos y yo **nos vemos** los sábados. *My friends and I see each other on Saturdays.*

b. English verbs emphasize reciprocal meaning by adding *each other*. Spanish has similar structures with reflexive verbs.

¿**Nos veremos** mañana?	*Will we see each other tomorrow?*
Los jugadores **se reúnen** hoy para entrenar.	*The players are meeting today for training.*
Algunas personas no **se tratan** bien y **se pelean** mucho.	*Some people don't treat each other well and fight a lot.*

27.D.4 **To get (something) done:** *mandarse a hacer*

When it is obvious that someone other than the subject is doing the action, **hacerse** (*to get* [*something*] *done*), **mandarse a** (*to have* [*something*] *done*), or similar expressions can be used.

Ella **se hizo construir** una gran casa.	*She had a great house built.*

27.D.5 **Verbs that express a complete action**

A number of Spanish verbs use the reflexive form and direct object to express that an action is completely fullfilled in relation to the object.

No sé si **creer** todo lo que dices.	*I don't know whether to believe everything you say.*
No sé si **creerme** todo lo que me dices.	*I don't know if I should believe everything you tell me.*

This meaning is conveyed in all verb tenses and used with verbs that express mental and physical activities, such as *to be able to do something perfectly, to learn something by heart, to know somebody inside out, to eat up, to drink up, to climb to the top, to sink to the bottom,* and similar English expressions.

Reflexive verbs that express a complete action	
andarse	**Nos anduvimos** la ciudad entera. *We walked through the whole city.*
aprenderse	¡La profesora **se aprendió** los nombres de pe a pa! *The teacher learned the names from A to Z!*
beberse	¡Ustedes **se bebieron** la limonada hasta la última gota! *You [pl.] drank all the lemonade to the last drop!*
comerse	Y también **se comieron** todas las tapas y los tacos. *And you also finished off (ate up) all the tapas and tacos.*
conocerse	**Me conozco** las calles de Madrid al derecho y al revés. *I know the streets of Madrid inside out.*
creerse	Ellos **se creyeron** todo lo que les dijeron. *They believed everything they were told.*
fumarse	¿Usted **se fuma** toda una cajetilla en un día? *Do you smoke a whole pack in one day?*
leerse	**Nos leemos** el periódico de principio a fin. *We read the newspaper from cover to cover.*
recorrerse	**Nos recorreremos** el país de un extremo a otro. *We'll travel the country from one end to the other.*
saberse	**Os sabéis** la lección al pie de la letra. *You [pl.] know the lesson by heart.*
tomarse	**Tómate** unas vacaciones, te ves cansado. *Take a vacation, you look exhausted.*
tragarse	¿**Te** puedes **tragar** esas píldoras tan grandes? *Can you swallow such big pills?*
verse	**Nos hemos visto** todas las películas de Almodóvar. *We have seen every single Almodóvar movie.*

27.E Verbs that change meaning in the reflexive form

Verbos que cambian de significado en forma reflexiva

Many Spanish verbs have a slightly different meaning when conjugated with a reflexive pronoun.

Non-reflexive	Meaning	Reflexive	Meaning
animar a	*to encourage (to)*	animarse a	*to motivate oneself (to), to dare*
comer	*to eat*	comerse	*to eat up*
decidir	*to decide*	decidirse a/por	*to decide (for oneself) to*
deshacer algo	*to undo something*	deshacerse de	*to get rid of*
jugar	*to play*	jugarse algo	*to gamble*
saltar	*to jump*	saltarse algo	*to skip, ignore*
unir	*to unite*	unirse a	*to join*

¡**Cómete** todas las verduras!	*Eat up all your vegetables!*
Debes **comer** alimentos sanos.	*You must eat healthy food.*
Deberías **deshacerte** de tu ropa vieja antes de comprarte nueva.	*You should get rid of your old clothes before you buy new ones.*
Lo hice mal, así que tengo que **deshacerlo**.	*I did it wrong, so I need to undo it.*
No **me animo a** contarle la verdad.	*I don't dare tell her the truth.*
¡Hay que **animar a** nuestro equipo!	*We have to encourage our team!*
Se jugó a todo o nada y perdió.	*He put everything on the line and lost.*
Jugó al fútbol toda su vida.	*He played soccer all his life.*

27.F Reflexive verbs that express involuntary actions

Verbos reflexivos que expresan acciones involuntarias

27.F.1 Involuntary actions

a. The pronominal form can be used, particularly with inanimate objects, to express an action without indicating the person or entity responsible for the action.

Se cayó el vaso.	*The glass fell.*
Se cerraron las puertas.	*The doors (were) closed.*
El televisor **se rompió**.	*The TV broke.*
La ventana **se hizo trizas**.	*The window broke into pieces.*

b. When an action is perceived as accidental or involuntary, an indirect object pronoun is used to identify the person performing the action or affected by the action.

Estaba hablando con mi hermano y **se me cayó** el teléfono.	*I was talking to my brother and I dropped the phone.*
Se le rompió su jarrón favorito.	*Her favorite vase broke.*
Se me cerró la puerta en la cara.	*The door (was) closed in my face.*
Cuando escuché lo que dijo, **se me fue** el alma a los pies.	*When I heard what he said, my heart sank.*

c. Constructions like **rompérsele**, **cerrársele**, and **caérsele** can be referred to as *"doubly pronominal,"* since they take both the reflexive pronoun **se** and an indirect object pronoun. Other verbs used in this manner include **ocurrírsele**, **antojársele**, **perdérsele**, **reírsele**, **quedársele**, and **morírsele**.

Se me han ocurrido dos ideas.	*I've thought of two ideas.*
¿Qué **se te antoja** comer hoy?	*What do you feel like eating today?*
Se me murió el pececito.	*My little fish died.*
Cuando le conté la verdad, **se me rio** en la cara.	*When I told her the truth, she laughed in my face.*
Se nos perdió el gato.	*We lost our cat.*
Se nos quedaron las llaves adentro.	*We left the keys inside.*

d. Some of these verbs also have regular pronominal/reflexive uses without the indirect object pronoun. **Antojársele** and **ocurrírsele** can only be used in "doubly pronominal" constructions.

Juan **se rio** mucho.	*Juan laughed a lot.*
Se murió el pececito.	*The little fish died.*
Se perdieron dos niños.	*Two children got lost.*
Las llaves **se quedaron** adentro.	*We left the keys inside. / The keys were left inside.*
Se rompió la llave.	*The key broke.*
Mi hermanita **se cayó**.	*My little sister fell.*

e. Quedar(se) can also be used as a non-pronominal intransitive verb.

Las llaves **quedaron** adentro.	*The keys were left inside.*

27.F.2 *Olvidarse(le)*

The transitive verb **olvidar** can also be used pronominally in two different constructions.

olvidar: **transitive verb**	*olvidarse de:* **intransitive pronominal verb**	*olvidársele algo a alguien:* **doubly pronominal verb**
Olvidé su nombre.	Me olvidé de su nombre.	Se me olvidó su nombre.
I forgot his name.		

27.G Verbs expressing change: *to become*

Verbos de cambio

27.G.1 Change of state

Expressing change and state: 29.E

Verbs that express a shift from one state to another or suggest that a change exists are called *inchoative* verbs. Some of these verbs, such as **emocionarse** (*to get emotional, to be moved*), **envanecerse** (*to become conceited*) and **entristecerse** (*to become sad*), are reflexive, and others, like **envejecer** (*to get old, to age*), **enrojecer** (*to get red, to blush*) are not.

Me emocioné cuando oí las noticias.	*I became emotional when I heard the news.*
La actriz **se entristeció** cuando supo que no había recibido el premio.	*The actress became sad when she found out she had not won the award.*
Juan **envejeció** mucho desde la muerte de su esposa.	*Juan looks a lot older since his wife died.*
Mucha gente **enrojece** cuando la elogian.	*Many people blush when they get compliments.*

27.G.2 Other changes

a. Many reflexive verbs express physical, social, or emotional changes. The table provides some examples. The most important verbs are explained individually after the table.

Reflexive verbs that express change		
Physical position	**Social**	**Emotional**
arrodillarse *to kneel*	**casarse (con)** *to get married (to)*	**alegrarse (de)** *to be happy/glad (about)*
levantarse *to get/ stand up*	**divorciarse (de)** *to get divorced (from)*	**desmotivarse (por)** *to get unmotivated by*
morirse *to die*	**enriquecerse** *to get rich*	**enamorarse (de)** *to fall in love (with)*
moverse *to move*	**graduarse** *to graduate*	**irritarse** *to get irritated*
sentarse *to sit down*	**separarse (de)** *to separate oneself (from)*	**preocuparse (por)** *to worry (about)*

b. Many Spanish verbs that express emotional reactions have two common conjugation forms. One is reflexive and the other is conjugated like **gustar**, with an indirect object pronoun.

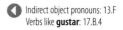 Indirect object pronouns: 13.F
Verbs like **gustar**: 17.B.4

Reflexive form	Conjugation like *gustar*
Me alegro mucho de que vengas.	**Me alegra** mucho que vengas.
I'm so happy that you're coming.	*It makes me happy that you're coming.*
¿Os preocupáis por la economía mundial?	**¿Os preocupa** la economía mundial?
Are you [pl.] worried about the world economy?	*Does the world economy worry you [pl.]?*

27.G.3 Convertirse en + *noun* or *nominal expression*

Convertirse en indicates a change that can happen suddenly or after a process, depending on the context. It expresses a significant change, such as a change from boy to man, from a little city to a big city, and so forth.

Nos convertimos en robots con la tecnología.	*Technology turns us into robots.*
La casa **se convierte en** un manicomio cuando Luis hace fiestas.	*The house turns into a madhouse when Luis has parties.*

27.G.4 Hacerse + *noun* or *adjective*

Hacerse expresses changes that happen as a result of a plan or goal.

Mi hermano **se hizo** cura.	*My brother became a priest.*
Los vikingos **se hicieron** poderosos con su superioridad marítima.	*The Vikings became powerful with their maritime superiority.*
Quiero **hacerme** millonario algún día.	*I want to become a millionaire someday.*
Se están haciendo viejos.	*They are becoming/getting old.*

27.G.5 Ponerse + *adjective*

Ponerse expresses relatively rapid changes that are often emotional or physically visible.

Mis amigos **se pusieron** verdes de la envidia cuando vieron mi nuevo auto.	*My friends became green with envy when they saw my new car.*
¡No **te pongas** triste!	*Don't be sad!*
Nos pusimos furiosos cuando vimos el desorden.	*We became furious when we saw the mess.*
Me pongo tan contento cuando me visita mi hermana.	*I become so happy when my sister visits me.*

27.G.6 Quedarse + *adjective* or *adverb*

Quedarse expresses a long-term result of a change. The reflexive form is more common in Spain, but has the same meaning as the non-reflexive in Latin America.

¿**(Te) has quedado** triste con la noticia?	*Has the news made you sad? (Are you sad because of the news?)*
Con la crisis, **(nos) quedamos** sin nada.	*Because of the crisis, we were left with nothing.*
Te estás quedando calvo.	*You're becoming/going bald.*
Me quedé muy solo cuando mi novia se fue.	*I became very lonely when my girlfriend left.*

27.G.7 *Vol
*Volverse + **adjective** or **noun***

Volverse expresses primarily a mental or physical change of a certain duration and is more permanent than **ponerse**.

Venezuela **se ha vuelto** un país petrolero muy rico.	*Venezuela has become a very rich oil country.*
Uno no **se vuelve** rico de la noche a la mañana.	*One doesn't become rich overnight.*
Se volvió loca.	*She went mad/crazy.*
La leche **se volvió** agria.	*The milk became sour / went bad.*

27.G.8 *Llegar a + **infinitive** + **noun** or **adjective***

This verb periphrasis is the only non-reflexive verb of change. It is used when changes are understood as a longer process and assumes some effort to get to the result.

Nunca **llegaré a ser** famoso.	*I will never become famous.*
Roma **llegó a ser** una gran civilización.	*Rome became a great civilization.*
Es posible que **llegues a tener** éxito.	*It's possible you'll be successful.*

27.G.9 Wishes of change

It is very common to express wishes or plans of change with these verbs.

Ojalá no **se queden** sin casa.	*I hope they are not left without a home.*
Querría que el mundo **llegara a ser** un lugar pacífico.	*I wish the world would become a peaceful place.*
Espero que **nos convirtamos en** grandes amigos.	*I hope that we will become great friends.*

27.G.10 Verb aspect and verbs that express change

a. Verbs that express change are usually used with the perfect tenses (*preterite* and compound perfect tenses), which, like the English *to become*, focus on the end result.

Rosa **se ha vuelto** muy antipática.	*Rosa has become very unfriendly.*
Mi ciudad natal **se ha convertido** en una gran metrópoli.	*My hometown has become a big metropolis.*
Se puso furioso cuando le conté la noticia.	*He became furious when I told him the news.*
En la década de 1950, ya **se había convertido** en el hombre más rico de la ciudad.	*By the 1950s, he had already become the richest man in the city.*
Si hubiera estudiado abogacía, **habría llegado a ser** juez.	*If he had studied law, he would have become a judge.*

b. When verbs that express change are used in the *imperfect* or *present* tense, they usually indicate repetition or a description of something that used to happen. Adverbs such as **cada vez más**, **paulatinamente**, and **progresivamente** or the use of the **gerundio** intensify the verb's meaning.

Me parece que la gramática **se vuelve** cada vez más fácil.	*It seems to me that grammar is becoming easier and easier.*
Me ponía furioso cuando me daban una C en el examen.	*I used to become so angry when they would give me a C on an exam.*
En los cuentos de hadas, las ranas **se convertían en** príncipes.	*In fairy tales, frogs turned into princes.*

Práctica

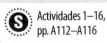
Actividades 1–16, pp. A112–A116

Passive and impersonal constructions
Estructuras pasivas e impersonales

28.A Active, passive, or impersonal

Activa, pasiva o impersonal

28.A.1 Passive constructions

Active constructions emphasize the person or thing that carries out an action. In contrast, passive constructions emphasize the action itself, rather than the agent. The passive voice states that a subject is *receiving* the action, rather than *doing* the action. The direct object of the active sentence becomes the grammatical subject of the passive sentence. Spanish has two ways to express passive actions: the passive voice with **ser** (**voz pasiva con *ser***) and passive constructions with **se** (**pasiva refleja** or **voz pasiva con *se***).

Los aztecas **fundaron** Tenochtitlán. (*active*)	*The Aztecs founded Tenochtitlan.*
Tenochtitlán **fue fundada** por los aztecas. (*passive*)	*Tenochtitlan was founded by the Aztecs.*
¿Sabes en qué año **se fundó** Tenochtitlán? (*passive*)	*Do you know what year Tenochtitlan was founded?*

28.A.2 Impersonal constructions

In Spanish, the impersonal **se** (**se impersonal**) expresses the idea of a non-specific subject performing an action. In English, this idea is often expressed using *they, you, people, one,* etc.

En esta oficina **se trabaja** muchísimo.	*In this office, people work a lot.*
Se habla de su renuncia.	*People are talking about his resignation.*
Si **se está** tranquilo con uno mismo, **se es** feliz.	*If you are at peace with yourself, you are happy.*
Se invitó a mucha gente.	*Many people were invited.*

Unlike the passive constructions with **se**, impersonal constructions with **se** do not have a grammatical subject and the verb is always singular.

28.B Passive voice with *ser*

Voz pasiva con *ser*

28.B.1 The direct object becomes the subject

The passive voice with **ser** can only be formed in Spanish when there is a corresponding active sentence with an *explicit direct object*. The direct object of the active sentence becomes the subject, while the real subject is toned down to *agent* or is removed from the sentence. In the active sentence, the direct object is marked using the preposition **a**. In a passive sentence, this is not necessary since the direct object has become the subject.

◀ Use of **a** with a person as a direct object: 13.E.2

Active voice	Passive voice with *ser*
El rector recibió a los alumnos.	Los alumnos **fueron recibidos** (por el rector).
The principal welcomed the students.	*The students were welcomed (by the principal).*

28.B.2 Verb tenses of *ser* in the passive voice

The verb in the active sentence becomes a *past participle* in the passive sentence and follows **ser** (*to be*), which can generally appear in all verb tenses and moods. However, the passive voice with **ser** is more common in perfect tenses. In the present and imperfect, the passive voice with **ser** expresses repetition or habit.

◀ Regular and irregular *past participle*: 19.A.1, 19.A.2, 25.D

◀ Use of the present indicative: 17.E.2
Use of the imperfect: 18.E.5

Indicative		Subjunctive
El chico es visto	... ha sido visto	Es bueno que el chico sea visto.
... fue visto	... hubo sido visto	Fue bueno que el chico fuera visto.
... era visto	... había sido visto	... fuese visto.
... será visto	... habrá sido visto	... haya sido visto.
... sería visto	... habría sido visto	... hubiera/hubiese sido visto.

Pretérito anterior
(hubo sido visto): 19.F

Infinitive	*Gerundio*
haber sido visto	habiendo sido visto

Una tragedia nuclear como la de Chernóbil no **ha sido vista** nunca.	*A nuclear tragedy like Chernobyl has never been seen.*
Muchos creen que podría **haber sido prevenida**.	*Many believe that it could have been prevented.*
Las señales de peligro nunca **fueron tomadas** en serio.	*The warning signs were never taken seriously.*
Deberían **haberlo sido**.	*They should have been.*

Use of the past participle: 25.D.4
The past participle in
compound tenses: 19.A.1-2

28.B.3 Agreement of past participle

The past participle in the passive voice with **ser** behaves as an adjective and agrees in gender and number with the grammatical subject.

La película fue bien **recibida**.	*The film was well received.*
Las noticias fueron **publicadas** en la red.	*The news was published on the web.*
El problema debe ser **estudiado**.	*The problem should be studied.*
Es necesario que **los gastos** sean **controlados**.	*It is necessary that the expenses be monitored.*

28.B.4 The agent in the passive voice with *ser*

a. In the passive voice with **ser**, the agent, or *logical subject,* is introduced using **por** + *noun*, *pronoun*, or *clause*.

La contaminación es causada **por nosotros**.	*Pollution is caused by us.*
Las reuniones van a ser organizadas **por la ONU**.	*The meetings are going to be organized by the UN.*
Algunas cosas no han sido explicadas **por los responsables**.	*A number of things haven't been explained by those responsible.*
El virus ha sido identificado **por los que conocen su ADN**.	*The virus has been identified by those who recognize its DNA.*

b. It is important to distinguish the agent in passive sentences from causal relationships or other contexts that can also be expressed with **por**. Only the first example below indicates the agent.

La velocidad de los autos es controlada **por la policía** (*agent*).	*The speed limit is monitored by the police.*
La velocidad de los autos es controlada **por seguridad**.	*The speed limit is monitored for safety.*
La velocidad de los autos es controlada **por todo el país**.	*The speed limit is monitored across the country.*

28.C | Limitations of the passive voice with *ser*

Limitaciones de la voz pasiva con *ser*

28.C.1 | Use of passive voice with *ser*

The passive voice occurs primarily in written formal language, such as in professional articles, contracts, legal documents, etc. It is used to a lesser extent in the news. In cases where the actor or doer is still unknown or not mentioned, passive constructions with **se** are preferred.

Passive constructions with **se**: 28.D
Impersonal **se** sentences: 28.E

28.C.2 | The indirect object in the passive voice with *ser*

Only the direct object of an active sentence can become the subject in the passive voice with **ser**. The indirect object can never become the subject. In English, both the direct and indirect object in the active sentence can become the subject in the passive voice.

El premio Nobel de literatura le ha sido otorgado al escritor peruano Mario Vargas Llosa.	*The Noble Prize in Literature was awarded to the Peruvian writer Mario Vargas Llosa.*
Los honorarios me fueron pagados a mí (por el banco).	*The fees were paid to me (by the bank).*
El contrato os será enviado a vosotros (por Marta).	*The contract will be sent to you [pl.] (by Marta).*

28.C.3 | *Estar + past participle*

The passive voice with **ser** can only be formed with the past participle and not with participle-like adjectives such as **electo/a**, or **bendito/a**. However, these adjectives and past participle forms can convey the result of the action of some verbs by using **estar**.

Past participle: 19.A.1, 19.A.2, 25.D
Verb periphrases with the past participle: 26.E
Estar with a perfect adjective: 30.C.2

Passive sentence with *ser*	Resulting state with *estar*
La novela **ha sido escrita** por un gran narrador. *The novel has been/was written by a great storyteller.*	La novela **está escrita** por un gran narrador. *The novel is written by a great storyteller.*
Las tapas **fueron hechas** por el cocinero. *The tapas were made by the cook.*	Las tapas **están hechas** por el cocinero. *The tapas are made by the cook.*
Los parques **fueron diseñados** por un arquitecto. *The parks were designed by an architect.*	Los parques **están diseñados** por un arquitecto. *The parks are designed by an architect.*

28.D | Passive constructions with *se*

Oraciones pasivas reflejas

28.D.1 | The subject in passive constructions with *se*

a. Passive constructions with **se** have an active structure with an *explicit subject* and a *passive meaning*. The subject can be a noun or a clause. The verb agrees with the subject (third-person singular or plural). The verb is always used in the third-person singular if the subject is a clause. Passive constructions with **se** do not have an explicit agent. They are mostly used when the subject (singular or plural) is not a living being. The subjects in the Spanish sentences below are in italics.

El petróleo venezolano **se exporta** a muchos países.	*Venezuelan oil is exported to many countries.*
Los productos **se venden** en todo el mundo.	*The products are sold all over the world.*
Se espera *que la situación mejore.*	*The situation is expected to improve.*

Indefinite quantifiers: 7.C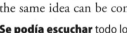

b. Indefinite nouns that refer to people can also be the subject of a sentence. The preposition **a** is not necessary here because the noun is *not* the object, but the subject.

Se prefieren personas con experiencia.	*People with experience are preferred.*
Se necesitaban ayudantes.	*They needed assistants. / Assistants were needed.*
Se busca un buen economista.	*They are looking for a good economist. / A good economist is needed.*
Se admitirán muchos estudiantes.	*They will admit many students. / Many students will be admitted.*

Impersonal **se** sentences: 28.E.2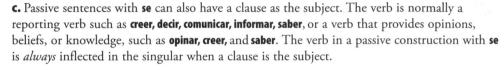

c. Passive sentences with **se** can also have a clause as the subject. The verb is normally a reporting verb such as **creer, decir, comunicar, informar, saber**, or a verb that provides opinions, beliefs, or knowledge, such as **opinar, creer,** and **saber**. The verb in a passive construction with **se** is *always* inflected in the singular when a clause is the subject.

Anteriormente **se creía** *que* los gnomos realmente existían.	*Previously it was thought that gnomes existed.*
No **se sabía** *dónde* vivían.	*It wasn't known where they lived.*
En las leyendas **se narra** *cómo* los gnomos se convertían en montañas.	*In legends, it is told how the gnomes became mountains.*
Nunca **se sabrá** *si* eso era cierto.	*It will never be known if that was true.*

28.D.2 No agent

Passive constructions with **se** have no agent. The real actor or doer of the action is not mentioned and remains unknown.

Las tradiciones **se conservan** de generación en generación.	*Traditions are preserved (passed on) from generation to generation.*
Los documentos **se imprimen** automáticamente.	*The documents are printed automatically.*

28.D.3 Passive constructions with *se* and modal verbs

Modal verb periphrases with the infinitive: 26.B

In English, modal verbs (*can, could, may, might, must, shall, should, will, would*) are often used to express the passive voice using the construction *modal verb + be + past participle*. In Spanish, the same idea can be conveyed using **se** + *modal verb* + *infinitive*.

Se podía escuchar todo lo que decían.	*Everything they said could be heard.*
Se debe hacer algo acerca del problema de la contaminación.	*Something should be done about the pollution problem.*

28.D.4 Placement of *se* with verb periphrases

With verb periphrases, **se** is usually placed before the finite verb, but can also be added after the infinitive or **gerundio**.

Las cartas **se** iban a enviar / iban a enviar**se** por correo.	*The letters were going to be sent in the mail.*
El trabajo **se** tiene que hacer / tiene que hacer**se** bien.	*The work must be done well.*
Se está preparando / Está preparándo**se** una gran cena.	*A great dinner is being prepared.*

28.E Impersonal *se* sentences

Oraciones impersonales con *se*

28.E.1 Impersonal *se* sentences have no subject

Impersonal **se** sentences have a *passive meaning* and *no grammatical subject*, and the verb *always* appears in the third-person singular. The real actor or doer of the action is assumed to be a living being, but is unknown and indefinite. Like passive constructions with **se**, the impersonal **se** is not the subject, but only a structure used to convey that the meaning is impersonal.

28.E.2 General statements

a. Impersonal **se** sentences form general statements with verbs that do not take an object (intransitive verbs) such as **vivir, trabajar,** and **llegar**, and with transitive verbs such as **vender, decir,** and **escribir,** when the object is not mentioned. The verb always appears in the third-person singular. The statement's features are described using an adverb or an adverbial expression.

◀ Intransitive verbs: 17.B.1

¡Aquí **se trabaja** con gusto!	*Here, people work with pleasure!*
Sin buena salud, no **se vive** bien.	*Without good health, one can't live well.*
En los blogs **se escribe** muy francamente.	*In blogs, people write very honestly.*

b. In general statements with reflexive verbs, the indefinite pronoun **uno** is used instead of **se**. Both male and female speakers can use **uno**. Female speakers, however, can also use **una**.

◀ Indefinite pronoun **uno/a**: 7.D.3

Con esta música, **uno se duerme** de inmediato.	*One falls asleep immediately to this music.*
Este mapa impide que **uno se pierda** en la ciudad.	*With this map, you can't get lost in the city.*
No es posible **sentarse uno** a leer sin interrupciones.	*It is impossible to sit down and read without interruptions.*
¿Puede **uno marcharse** de aquí a cualquier hora?	*Can one leave at any time?*

c. Ser and **estar** form general statements with impersonal **se** sentences, but this use is limited. General statements with modal verbs are more common (**poder, deber**).

◀ Modal verb periphrases: 26.B

Se está muy bien en lugares tranquilos.	*A good time is had in calm places.*
No siempre **se es** feliz.	*People are not always happy.*
Se puede salir por esta puerta.	*You can go out this door.*
Puede salirse por esta puerta.	

d. If the implicit actor or doer of the action is a woman, it is possible to use a feminine adjective.

Cuando se es **honrado/a**, se llega más lejos.	*If you are honorable, you will go far.*

28.E.3 Direct objects

a. When the direct object is mentioned and it is a person (proper noun, pronoun), it is preceded by the preposition **a** and the verb is always in the singular.

Se identificará **a los autores** de los robos.	*Those behind the thefts will be identified.*

◀ Use of **a** with a person as a direct object: 13.E.2

Other expressions with
impersonal meaning: 28.H

b. When the direct object is mentioned and preceded by the preposition **a**, it can also be replaced with an object pronoun. In that case, the direct object pronoun will convey information about the agent's gender: **los/las**. It is common to remove the last remnant of the agent's identity by using **le/les** as direct object pronouns in impersonal **se** constructions.

Se identificará **a los autores /** **a las autoras** de los robos.	*Those (male/female) behind the thefts will be identified.*
Se **los/las** identificará.	*They (male/female) will be identified.*
Se **les** identificará.	*They will be identified.*

c. Impersonal **se** sentences can be used with transitive verbs when the direct object is expressed. This use is common in the present tense and appears in signs and ads. **(Se vende casas. Se repara refrigeradores.)** In these cases, the noun is the direct object of the verb and the actor or doer of the action is not stated.

Impersonal *se* **sentence** (*los proyectos:* **direct object**)	
Se aprobó los proyectos.	*The projects were approved.*
Se los aprobó.	*They were approved.*

Passive construction with *se* (*los proyectos:* **subject**)	
Se aprobaron los proyectos.	*The projects were approved.*

28.F The indirect object in passive and impersonal sentences

El objeto indirecto en oraciones pasivas e impersonales

The direct object plays the main role as the grammatical subject in the passive voice with **ser** and in passive constructions with **se**. When the indirect object is explicitly mentioned, it appears in the different sentence types in the following ways.

28.F.1 Active sentence

Placement of direct and indirect
object pronouns before
conjugated verbs: 13.G.1
Object pronouns with
prepositions: 13.H.1b

In a normal active sentence, we can find a subject (**profesor**), a verb (**entregó**), and a direct object (**textos**) as well as an indirect object (**estudiantes**). The objects can be expressed with the corresponding object pronouns.

El profesor les entregó **los textos** a **los estudiantes**.	*The teacher gave the students the texts.*
El profesor **se los** entregó.	*The teacher gave them (to) them.*

28.F.2 Passive voice with *ser*

The real direct object from the sentence above (**textos**) becomes the subject in the passive voice with **ser**. The agent and the references to the indirect object (**les, a los estudiantes**) can be excluded. The indirect object in the active sentence cannot become the subject of the passive voice.

Los textos les fueron entregados a **los estudiantes** (por el profesor).	*The texts were given to the students (by the teacher).*
Los textos les fueron entregados.	*The texts were given to them. (Someone gave them the texts.)*
Los textos fueron entregados.	*The texts were given out. (Someone gave out the texts.)*

Passive constructions with *se*

Passive constructions with **se** have no agent. Information about the indirect object (**les, los estudiantes**) can also be excluded. It is important to note that **se** only indicates that the sentence is impersonal and is not a replacement for the indirect object (**les**), which can be mentioned.

Los textos **se les entregaron** a los estudiantes.	*The texts were given to the students.* *(Someone gave the texts to the students.)*
Los textos **se les entregaron**.	*The texts were given to them.* *(Someone gave them the texts.)*
Los textos **se entregaron**.	*The texts were given out.* *(Someone gave out the texts.)*

28.F.4 **Impersonal** *se* **sentences**

In impersonal **se** sentences, the verb appears in the singular and does not have a subject. In general, impersonal **se** sentences occur with intransitive verbs (without objects). When there are both direct and indirect objects, an impersonal **se** sentence would look like this: **Se entregó los textos a los estudiantes**. Such sentences are not common in Spanish, and other solutions are preferred.

◀ Impersonal **se** sentences with direct objects: 28.E.3c
Intransitive verbs: 17.B.1

Passive construction with *se*	Third-person plural
Se entregaron los textos a los estudiantes. / Los textos **se les entregaron** a los estudiantes.	**Les entregaron** los textos a los estudiantes. / **Se los** entregaron.
The texts were given to the students.	*Someone gave the texts to the students. / The texts were given to the students. / They were given to them.*

28.G Comparison of passive constructions with *se* and impersonal *se* constructions

Passive constructions with *se*		Impersonal *se* constructions	
Can only be formed with transitive verbs.	Se enseña inglés.	*Can be formed with intransitive or transitive verbs.*	Se enseña a hablar mejor. Se vive bien aquí.
The object of the active sentence is the grammatical subject.	Se vendió un cuadro de Picasso. ("un cuadro de Picasso" is the subject of the sentence)	*There is no grammatical subject.*	Nunca se está seguro en el puesto de trabajo.
The verb can be singular or plural (it must agree with the subject).	Se firmará el tratado. / Se firmarán los acuerdos.	*The verb is always singular.*	Se firmará los acuerdos. ("los acuerdos" is a direct object; the sentence has no expressed subject)
The indirect object can be expressed.	Se presentaron los textos al jurado. Se le presentaron.	*The indirect object can be expressed.*	Se presentó los textos al jurado.
Plural direct objects that refer to people and do not have an article can become the subject.	Se buscan nuevos maestros. ("nuevos maestros" is the subject)	*When the direct object is a specific person or group of people, the personal **a** is used. The direct object can be replaced by both direct and indirect object pronouns.*	Se invitó a los/las nuevos/as maestros/as. ("a los/las nuevos/as maestros/as" is the direct object) Se los/las invitó. Se les invitó.

◀ Impersonal **se** sentences with direct objects: 28.E.3c

Passive constructions with *se*		Impersonal *se* constructions	
The passive subject can be a specific person or group of people when it refers to positions/jobs or to something inherent to a position/job.	Se eligieron los nuevos diputados. Se nombró el nuevo embajador.	*If the direct object is a person, it always requires* **a***. The verb is always singular.*	Se eligió a los nuevos diputados. Se nombró al nuevo embajador.
The subject can be a noun clause or a reported question. It can also be an infinitive.	Se dice que habrá despidos. Se ha confirmado cómo sucedió el accidente. Se prohíbe fumar.	(***Note:*** *Due to their impersonal meaning, the examples on the left are sometimes interpreted as impersonal* **se** *constructions. However, this text follows the interpretation of the RAE's* Nueva gramática *regarding these structures.*)	

28.H Other expressions with impersonal meaning

Otras expresiones de impersonalidad

a. The following pronouns can be used in an impersonal sense. The most common is the third-person plural, which refers to an impersonal **ellos**.

Impersonal use of the pronoun	
third-person plural	¿Os **atendieron** bien en el restaurante? *Did you [pl.] get good service / Did they serve you well in the restaurant?*
tú	**Tú** nunca **sabes** a qué hora llega el autobús. *You never know when the bus will come.*
la/mucha gente	Que **la gente** crea lo que quiera. *People can think what they want.*
uno/a	**Uno** nunca sabe con seguridad. *One/You can never know/tell with certainty.*

b. Every expression with the impersonal forms of **haber** is impersonal. The verb is only inflected in the singular: *there is / there are.*

Hay problemas.	*There are problems.*	**Hay** paz/guerra.	*There is peace/war.*
Hay mucho.	*There is a lot.*	**Habrá** algo.	*There will be something.*
Hay poco.	*There isn't much.*	No **habrá** nada.	*There won't be anything.*

c. Hacer, ser, and other verbs in expresssions of time, weather, and climate are impersonal. The verb is only inflected in the singular.

Hace frío/calor.	*It's cold/hot.*	Ya **era** hora.	*It's about time.*
Es de día/noche.	*It's day/night.*	**Llueve.**	*It's raining. / It rains.*
Es Navidad.	*It's Christmas.*	**Nieva.**	*It's snowing. / It snows.*

d. There are many other verbs that function in the same way, such as:

Importa/Conviene hacerlo.	*It's important/useful to do it.*	**Se trata** de estudiar o no estudiar.	*It's about studying or not studying.*

Práctica

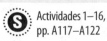

Actividades 1–16,
pp. A117–A122

To be and *to become*
Ser, estar, haber, hacer, tener

Chapter 29

A. Structure: *ser* and *estar*

B. To be: there is, there are

C. Expressing weather and time: *hacer, estar, ser*

D. Expressing age and states: *tener*

E. Expressing change and state

29.A Structure: *ser* and *estar*

Estructura de *ser* y *estar*

29.A.1 To be: *ser*

a. *To be* is expressed in Spanish using **ser** and **estar**, but **haber, hacer,** and **tener** are also used to convey *to be*. **Ser** describes the *essential qualities* of the subject while **estar** describes its *condition* or *state*.

b. The verb **ser** cannot be used on its own with the meaning *to exist*, like in the famous Hamlet question **"¿Ser o no ser? Esa es la cuestión"**. A more appropriate modern Spanish translation would have been **"¿Existir o no existir?"**. In very short yes/no questions and answers, however, **ser** can be used to answer, in the sense *it is* or *it's not*, to confirm or deny the identity of an item.

—Este libro **es** tuyo, ¿verdad?	*This book is yours, isn't it?*
—Sí, sí (lo) **es**. /—No, no (lo) **es**.	*Yes, it is. / No, it isn't.*
—¿**Es** Juan el que va allí?	*Is that Juan over there?*
—Sí, sí (lo) **es**. /—No, no (lo) **es**.	*Yes, it is (him). / No, it isn't (him).*

◀ Use of **ser** and **estar**: Ch. 30

29.A.2 To be: *estar*

The verb **estar** can also appear alone in short yes/no questions and used as an answer in the sense *to be present* in a specific or implied location. For example, when a person asks if someone is home or in the office.

—¿**Está** Juan?	*Is Juan there?*
—No, no **está**. / —Sí, sí **está**.	*No, he isn't. / Yes, he is.*

29.B To be: there is, there are

Haber para expresar existencia

◀ **Ser, estar,** and **haber:** 30.C.7

29.B.1 Impersonal form of *haber*

a. The *impersonal* form of **haber** (*there is / there are*; *is/are present*) is used instead of **estar** to refer to the existence of non-specific people, things, or concepts.

—¿**Hay** conexión a Internet?	*Is there an Internet connection?*
—Sí, sí **hay**. / —No, no **hay**.	*Yes, there is. / No there isn't.*
—¿**Hay** estudiantes alemanes?	*Are there (any) German students?*
—No, no **hay**. /—Sí, sí **hay**.	*No, there aren't./Yes, there are.*

◀ **estar** and **haber** with definite and indefinite possessives: 9.D.6

b. Haber cannot be used with subject pronouns or a noun preceded by a determiner. It can be used with indefinite pronouns, determiners, and numbers, except **ambos, cada, los/las demás**, and **cualquiera**.

—¿**Hay** alguien (en casa)?	*Is anyone home?*
—No, no **hay** nadie.	*No, there's nobody home.*
—¿Cuántos estudiantes **hay**?	*How many students are there?*
—**Hay** uno.	*There's one.*

◀ Use of cardinal numbers: 6.B

c. Subject pronouns and nouns with determiners can be used with **estar** in the same situations.

—¿**Están** Laura y Fernando en casa?	*Are Laura and Fernando home?*
—Ella sí **está**, pero él no.	*She's home, but he isn't.*

—Hola, ¿dónde **estás** tú?	*Hello, where are you?*
—**Estoy** en el parque.	*I'm at the park.*

—¿Cuántos de los estudiantes **están** allí?	*How many of the students are there?*
—Tres de ellos **están** aquí.	*Three of them are here.*

29.B.2   Personal form of *haber*

Haber is conjugated as a finite verb in the compound verb forms of the indicative and subjunctive.

¿**Habéis ido** alguna vez a Costa Rica?	*Have you [pl.] ever been to Costa Rica?*
En Ecuador se **ha hablado** quechua por mucho tiempo.	*In Ecuador, Quechua has been spoken for a long time.*

29.C   Expressing weather and time: *hacer, estar, ser*

Hacer, estar, ser para expresar clima y horas

Expressing temperature: 6.I.1 ▶

29.C.1   Weather expressions

Hacer and **estar** are used in many weather expressions in which English uses *to be*.

Hace frío.	*It's cold.*	**Hace** sol.	*It's sunny.*
Hace calor.	*It's warm.*	**Hace** mal tiempo.	*It's bad weather.*
Está nublado.	*It's cloudy.*	**Está** lloviendo.	*It's raining.*
Está oscuro.	*It's dark.*	**Está** nevando.	*It's snowing.*

29.C.2   Calendar and time

Ser must be used with the noun: 30.B.1
Time: 5.C.3, 6.F ▶

a. Ser is used with the time, days, months, years, and other periods of time.

Son las tres.	*It's three o'clock.*	**Es** verano.	*It's summer.*
Es lunes.	*It's Monday.*	**Es** 2030.	*It's 2030.*

b. Estar can also be used with days, months, years, and times of the year (but not clock time) as long as there is a preposition before the noun (**a, en**). The verb is inflected in the first-person plural: **nosotros**.

Estamos a lunes.	*It's Monday (finally/now).*
Estamos en marzo.	*We're in March now. / It's March (finally/now).*
Estamos en verano.	*It's summer (finally/now).*
Estamos en 2030.	*It's 2030 (finally/now).*

29.D   Expressing age and states: *tener*

Tener para expresar edad y cambios físicos

To turn a certain age: 6.H and 18.E.3 ▶

Tener is used to describe most transient physical states, or to tell age.

Ella **tiene** veinte años.	*She's twenty (years old).*
Él **tiene** hambre/sed/sueño/cansancio/ miedo/calor.	*He is hungry/thirsty/sleepy/ tired/scared/hot.*

Expresar cambio y estado

29.E.1 *To get / to be*: Passive voice with *ser* and *estar* + *past participle*

Passive voice with **ser**: 28.B
Verb periphrases with the past participle: 26.E

a. The passive voice with **ser** is equivalent to the English passive voice with *to be* or *to get*. In this case, the verb expresses a change. The resulting state is described in Spanish with **estar** + *past participle*.

Las cartas **son** escritas.	*The letters are/get written.*
Las cartas **están** escritas.	*The letters are written.*

b. Together with modal verbs, **ser** and **estar** are used as described in **a** above.

Las cartas **deben / tienen que ser** escritas.	*The letters must be/get written.*
Las cartas **deben / tienen que estar** escritas.	*The letters must be written.*

29.E.2 *To be / to become* + infinitive: *es, fue, era*

Verbs expressing change: 27.G

While the *present* and the *imperfect* of **ser** are usually translated as *to be* because they describe states, the *preterite* can sometimes be translated as *to become* because it expresses change.

La situación **es** imposible de entender.	*The situation is impossible to understand.*
La situación **fue** imposible de entender.	*The situation became impossible to understand.*
La situación **era** imposible de entender.	*The situation was impossible to understand.*

29.E.3 *To become / to turn* with weather and time: Spanish equivalents

Changes in weather, time, days, and years that are expressed with *to become* or *to turn* in English can be reproduced in Spanish in several ways.

Dio la una. / Dieron las tres.	*The clock struck one / three.*
Está amaneciendo. (Amaneció.)	*The sun is rising. (The sun rose.)*
Se hace (hizo) de día.	*It's becoming (It became) daylight.*
Se hace (hizo) de noche. /	*It is (was) getting dark. (It got dark.) /*
Anochece. (Anocheció.)	*The sun is setting. (The sun set.)*
Estamos a lunes. / Ya es lunes.	*It's Monday. / Now/Already it's Monday.*
Se está poniendo (volviendo) frío el tiempo.	*It is getting cold.*
Se puso (Se volvió) frío el tiempo.	*It got cold.*
Es verano (Estamos en verano) de nuevo.	*It's summer again. / We are in summer again.*

29.E.4 *To stay* with location: *quedarse*

Verbs expressing change:
volverse, convertirse:
27.G

To stay can be used in English with adverbs of place. In this case, the meaning in Spanish is expressed using **quedarse** (*to remain/stay*).

Hoy **estamos** en la escuela.	*Today, we're at school.*
Hoy **nos quedamos** en la escuela.	*Today, we're staying at school.*

29.E.5 *To become / to go* + adjective: *quedarse* and verbs that express change

Verbs expressing change: 27.G
llegar a ser: 27.G.8

a. Changes can also be conveyed with *to become/go* + *adjective* in English. In Spanish, **quedar(se)**, **ponerse**, and **volverse** can be used.

Ella **(se) quedó** ciega.	*She went (was) blind.*
Ella **se volvió** ciega.	*She became blind.*
Se puso loco.	*He went crazy.*
Me puse pálida.	*I became/went pale.*

b. *To become/get* + *adjective* can be translated using many Spanish reflexive verbs.

alegrarse	*to become happy*	enojarse	*to get angry*
callarse	*to become quiet*	enriquecerse	*to become rich*
cansarse	*to get tired*	entristecerse	*to get sad*
curarse	*to get cured*	mejorarse	*to get better*
empobrecerse	*to become poor*	sonrojarse	*to blush*

Me alegré mucho cuando recibí la noticia.   *I became/got very happy when I got the news.*
No **me canso** de mirar películas.   *I don't get tired of watching movies.*

c. In some cases, both the reflexive and the non-reflexive form can be used.

enloquecer(se)   *to go/become mad*
envejecer(se)   *to get/become old*

d. The verb **quedar(se)** cannot be used with a *noun*. Other verbs, such as **convertirse** and **hacerse**, or verb periphrases, such as **llegar a ser**, are used with a noun to express changes.

Los niños **se quedaron** callados.   *The children remained quiet.*
Ella **se convirtió** en una excelente abogada.   *She became an excellent lawyer.*
Él **llegó a ser** un médico famoso.   *Over time, he became a famous doctor.*
Ellos **se hicieron** políticos.   *They became politicians.*

Práctica

 Actividades 1–7, pp. A123–A124

Use of *ser* and *estar*
Uso de ser y estar

30.A Overview

Aspectos generales

Both **ser** and **estar** mean *to be*, but are used in different ways. In general, **ser** is used to describe the inherent and permanent nature and identity of something. **Estar** is used to describe the condition, state, or location of something; these traits are viewed by the speaker as being circumstantial or temporary, rather than inherent.

Marcos **es** un hombre.	*Marcos is a man.*
Juan **está** cansado.	*Juan is tired.*

30.B Use of *ser*

Usos de ser

30.B.1 Noun: *ser*

Only **ser** can be used with nouns (with or without determiners), proper nouns, possessives, personal and indefinite pronouns, and professions.

Soy **Raquel**. Soy **mujer**.	*I'm Raquel. I'm a woman.*
Soy **estudiante**.	*I'm a student.*
Raquel soy **yo**.	*I'm Raquel.*
Soy **una chica** joven.	*I'm a young girl.*
Julio es **mi primo**.	*Julio is my cousin.*
Somos **muchos**.	*We're many. (There's a lot of us.)*
Esto es **algo** importante.	*This is something important.*

Determiners as subjects/pronouns: 4.B.1–4.B.2
Indefinite pronouns: 7.D
Possessives: 9.C.2c, 9.D.3
Ser with calendar and time: 29.C.2

30.B.2 Adjectives with *ser:* characteristics

Ser describes permanent characteristics that define an individual, an object, or a concept in relation to others of the same kind. The characteristics are perceived as belonging only to the subject. They constitute the subject's identity as an individual or as part of a group.

	Identity: adjective with *ser*		
a.	**Appearance**	Soy alto. Mis ojos son negros.	*I'm tall. My eyes are black.*
b.	**Personality and other qualities**	Soy inteligente y trabajador.	*I'm intelligent and hard-working.*
c.	**Origin, nationality**	Soy español.	*I'm Spanish.*
d.	**Belief, ideology, religion**	Soy creyente. Soy católico.	*I'm a believer. I'm Catholic.*
e.	**Values relating to social norms or constructs**	Soy joven y no soy rico. No soy casado.	*I'm young and not rich. I'm not married.*

De: 12.B.4

30.B.3 Description: *ser + de*

Ser + de followed by nouns or pronouns describes characteristics of people and objects, such as origin, ownership, what they consist of, etc.

Eva **es de** Almería.	*Eva is from Almeria.*
Eva **es de** buen humor. (Tiene buen humor.)	*Eva is good-natured. (She has a good nature.)*
Eva **es de** ojos verdes. (Tiene ojos verdes.)	*Eva is green-eyed. (She has green eyes.)*
La casa **es de** Eva. Es su casa. La casa es suya.	*The house is Eva's. It's her house. The house is hers.*
La casa **es de** madera.	*The house is made of wood.*

30.B.4 Descriptions: *ser para*

Para: 12.B.6

Personal abilities and the purpose of objects can be expressed using **ser** + *adjective* + **para** + *verb*. **Para** + *proper noun* or *pronoun* indicates the receiver.

Ricardo es **bueno para** hablar.	*Ricardo is good at talking.*
La copiadora es **para copiar**.	*The photocopier is for copying.*
La fiesta es **para disfrutarla**.	*The party is for having fun/enjoying.*
El regalo es **para mí/Alejandra**.	*The present is for me/Alejandra.*

30.B.5 Appearance: *ser + con/a/sin*

The appearance of objects is expressed using **ser** + **con/a/sin.**

Mi blusa es **con/sin botones**.	*My blouse has buttons/is without buttons.*
La falda es **a rayas**.	*The skirt is striped.*

30.B.6 Impersonal expressions with *ser*

Impersonal expressions of certainty: 23.C.7

Spanish has many impersonal expressions with **ser** + *noun* or *adjective*.

¿Es cierto que sabes inglés?	*Is it true that you speak English?*
Fue difícil hacerlo.	*It was difficult to do.*
Es una lástima tener que irnos.	*It's a shame that we have to go.*

30.B.7 Personal impression: *ser* with indirect object pronouns

Ser can be used with indirect object pronouns and adjectives to express an opinion.

La situación **nos es indiferente**.	*The situation makes no difference to us.*
Ella **me es** muy **simpática**.	*She seems very nice to me.*
¿**Te fue difícil** llamarme?	*Was it difficult for you to call me?*
No les es fácil pagar de contado.	*It's not easy for them to pay cash.*

30.B.8 Other structures using *ser*

Passive voice with **ser**: 28.B
Emphatic constructions: 15.B.8

Ser is also used in other structures such as the passive voice with **ser: El problema será resuelto.** (*The problem will be solved.*), and emphatic constructions such as **Fue ayer que ocurrió.** (*It was yesterday that it happened.*)

Usos de *estar*

30.C.1   Adjectives and adverbs with *estar*: states

a. Adjectives that describe changeable physical or social states can be used with **estar**. The use of **estar** suggests that the state is temporary or is not a critical part of the subject's identity. Some adjectives about marital status can be used with **ser** or **estar** with the same meaning: **ser/estar casado, soltero, divorciado**.

◀ Adjectives with **ser**: 30.B.2
Gender and number of
adjectives: 3.A

Characteristics: *ser*	**States:** *estar*
El clima **es** inestable. *The weather is unstable.*	El clima **está** inestable. *The weather is (has become) unstable.*
El cielo **es** azul. *The sky is blue.*	El cielo **está** azul. *The sky is blue (today).*
Sandra **es** alegre. *Sandra is a happy person.*	Sandra **está** alegre. *Sandra is happy (at the moment).*
Ella **es** joven. *She is a young person.*	Ella **está** joven. *She is young (still).*
Ella **es** muy pobre. *She is very poor.*	Ella **está** muy pobre. *She is very poor (right now).*

b. Colors, sizes, and other physical characteristics can be described using **estar** when they change in relation to an objective or subjective standard.

Characteristics: *ser*	**States:** *estar*
La esmeralda **es** verde. *The emerald is green.*	Esta pintura **está** muy verde. *This painting is too green.*
El (árbol) bonsái **es** pequeño. *The bonsai (tree) is small.*	Los árboles **están** pequeños. *The trees are (still) small.*
El niño **es** grande y sano. *He is a big and healthy child.*	El niño **está** grande y sano. *The child is big and healthy.*

c. Estar with *adverbs* describes the general state of people and things.

El niño **está** bien ahora. Antes **estaba** peor.   *The child is fine now. He was worse before.*

d. These expressions are used to express how clothes fit:
indirect object pronoun + **está(n)** + *adjective/adverb* (more commonly used in Spain)
indirect object pronoun + **queda(n)** + *adjective/adverb* (more commonly used in the rest of the Spanish-speaking world)

El sombrero **te está / te queda** grande.   *The hat is too big for you.*

e. The expression *indirect object pronoun* + **viene(n)** + *adverb* is used in a similar way.

El lunes **me viene** bien.   *Monday works for me.*

f. Both **ser** and **estar** can be used with the adverb **así**. The choice depends on whether it is an intrinsic characteristic or a temporary state.

Juan **es así**, siempre de mal humor.   *Juan is that way, always in a bad mood.*
Juan **está así** porque perdió su trabajo.   *Juan is that way because he lost his job.*

The past participle in the passive voice with **ser**: 28.B

Reflexive verbs suggesting change: 27.G

Adjectives that convey the result of an action are *perfect* and must be used with **estar**. The most common of such adjectives are the *past participle* forms used in the passive voice with **ser** or those derived from *reflexive verbs* of change (**sentarse, dormirse, despertarse, irritarse**).

estar + *past participle*: 26.E, 28.C.3

Change	State: *estar*
Las casas **son construidas**. *The houses get built.*	Las casas **están construidas**. *The houses are built.*
El problema **ha sido resuelto**. *The problem has been resolved.*	El problema **está resuelto**. *The problem is solved.*
Los niños **se duermen**. *The children are falling asleep.*	Los niños **están dormidos**. *The children are asleep.*
El vaso **se llena**. *The glass is being filled.*	El vaso **está lleno**. *The glass is full.*
Una persona **murió**. *A person died.*	Una persona **está muerta**. *A person is dead.*
El bebé **nació**. *The baby was born.*	El bebé **está vivo**. *The baby is alive.*
Me irrita el ruido. *The noise irritates me.*	**Estoy irritada** por el ruido. *I am irritated by the noise.*
Lisa **se enamoró**. *Lisa fell in love.*	Lisa **está enamorada**. *Lisa is in love.*

30.C.3 *Estar de* + ***noun/adjective***

estar de: 12.B.4

With *nouns* or *adjectives* **estar de** denotes states, moods, jobs, professions, or temporary work. **Andar** is an informal synonym in such sentences, while **encontrarse de** is more formal: **Andrea anda / se encuentra de viaje**. (*Andrea is on a trip*.)

Estoy **de viaje**.	I'm on a trip.
¿Estáis **de vacaciones**?	Are you [pl.] on vacation?
Estamos **de mal humor**.	We're in a bad mood.
¿Está usted **de profesor**?	Are you working as a teacher?

30.C.4 **Idiomatic expressions with** *estar*

Use of prepositions: 12.B

Estar is used in many idiomatic expressions.

estar con	No te preocupes, yo **estoy contigo**.	Don't worry. I'm with you.
	En eso **estoy con** él. Creo que tiene razón.	I agree with him on that. I think he is right.
	Estoy con fiebre.	I have a fever.
estar en	**Estoy en** eso.	I'm working on it.
estar para	No **estoy para** bromas.	I don't feel like listening to your jokes.
estar a punto de	**Estamos a punto de** irnos.	We are about to leave.
estar por	**Estoy por** salir.	I'm about to head out.
estar que + *verb*	La situación **está que** arde.	The situation is very volatile.
	Estoy que no puedo más.	I'm exhausted. / I'm overwhelmed.
estar visto	**Está visto** que de literatura no sabes nada.	It's evident that you don't know anything about literature.
estar por verse	Lo que va a suceder aún **está por verse**.	It is still unclear what's going to happen.

30.C.5 Impersonal expressions with *estar*

Impersonal expressions with **estar** can be formed with *adverbs* and with *adjectives* derived from the *past participle*.

está permitido que	*it is allowed to*	**está mal** que	*it is bad that*
está bien que	*it is good that*	**está visto** que	*it is clear that*

Past participle with **estar**: 25.D.4c Impersonal expressions with **estar**: 23.C.8d-e

30.C.6 *Estar + gerundio*

This *verb periphrasis* refers to continous actions.

Estamos escuchando música.	*We're listening to music.*

estar + gerundio: 25.C.3

30.C.7 *Ser, estar,* **and** *haber*

a. Both **estar** and **haber** can express existence or presence. **Estar** is usually translated as *to be* and refers to the existence or presence of specific objects or people. **Haber** is usually translated as *there is/are* and is used to express existence of an object or person, or occurrence of an event. When using **haber**, the focus is mainly on the existence or occurrence, and the object, person, or event remains unspecified.

Ser, estar, and haber: 29.A-29.C **Estar** and **haber** with definite and indefinite possessives: 9.D.6d

Hay dos personas esperando al abogado.	*There are two people waiting for the lawyer.*
Las dos personas de las que hablamos **están** en la sala de espera.	*The two people we talked about are in the waiting room.*

b. Haber is always used in the singular.

Hubo tres accidentes el fin de semana.	*There were three accidents over the weekend.*
Había mucha nieve.	*There was a lot of snow.*
Dicen que **habrá** tormentas este fin de semana.	*They say there will be storms this weekend.*
Ha habido una pelea.	*There has been a fight.*

c. Both **ser** and **haber** can be used to talk about events. **Haber** points to the occurrence of an unspecified event. **Ser** is used to refer to specific events.

Hubo una fiesta.	*There was a party.*
La fiesta **fue** en un restaurante.	*The party was in a restaurant.*

d. Estar and **haber** are usually interchangeable in relative clauses.

Vi los articulos nuevos que **había/estaban** en la tienda.	*I saw the new items that were in the store.*

30.D *Ser* and *estar* with location

Ser y estar con lugar

30.D.1 *Estar:* **physical location**

Estar implies a concrete physical location or place.

¿Dónde **estarán** mis llaves?	*Where are my keys?*
El auto **está** en el garaje.	*The car is in the garage.*
Las fotos **estaban** en la red.	*The photos were on the web.*
¡Allí **está** el problema!	*There is the problem!*

30.D.2 *Ser* with location: *is (located)*

In conversational Spanish, **ser** describes the location of addresses, buildings, cities, countries, and geographical places. A synonym in Spanish is the verb **quedar**: **¿Dónde queda Nueva York?** (*Where is New York [located]?*).

Mi casa **es** en Connecticut.	*My house is in Connecticut.*
¿Tu boutique **es** en el centro?	*Is your boutique in the center?*
¡Aquí, nada **es** lejos!	*Here, nothing is far!*

30.D.3 *Ser* with location: *to take place*

The location of where events and arrangements *take place* is implied with **ser**. In this case, it is not possible to use **estar**. Corresponding expressions are **tener lugar** (formal) and **celebrar**, which convey a celebration of something.

Quiero que la fiesta **sea** aquí.	*I want the party to be (held) here.*
El partido **será** en Monterrey.	*The match/game will be in Monterrey.*
¿Dónde **va a ser** tu boda?	*Where is your wedding going to be (held)?*
La celebración **fue** en el club.	*The celebration took place at the club.*
Las Fallas **son** en Valencia.	*The Fallas festival is in Valencia.*

30.E Structures with *ser* and *estar*

Estructuras con *ser* y *estar*

		Ser	Estar
Nouns: Ch.2	Nouns	Él es **profesor**. *He is a teacher.*	Only with **estar de** + *profession:* Él **está de profesor**. *He is working as a teacher.*
Adjectives with **ser** and **estar**: 30.B.2, 30.C.1	Adjectives	La silla es **cómoda**. *The chair is comfortable.*	La silla está **cómoda**. *The chair feels comfortable.*
Passive voice with **ser**: 28.B Past participle: 19.A.1, 19.A.2, 25.D	Past participles	Las cuentas **fueron pagadas**. *The bills were paid.*	Las cuentas **están pagadas**. *The bills are paid.*
Prepositions: Ch.12	Prepositional phrases	Somos **de** Inglaterra. *We are from England.* Esto es **para** comer. *This is for eating.*	Estamos **en** la escuela. *We are in school.* Estamos **sin** dinero. *We are without money.*
Adverbs of place: 10.E	Adverbs	Él es **así**. *He is like that.* La fiesta es **aquí**. *The party is being held here.*	Está **así** porque su hermano está enfermo. *He is (being/feeling) like this because his brother is sick.* Estoy **bien**. *I'm fine.* Estamos **aquí**. *We're here.*
Impersonal expressions with **ser**: 23.C.7, 23.C.8	Impersonal expressions	**Es importante que** entrenes. *It's important that you train.*	**Está bien que** entrenes. *It's good that you train.*
Emphatic constructions: 15.B.8	Emphatic constructions	**Es** hoy cuando viajo. *It is today that I travel.* **Fue** eso lo que dije. *That was what I said.*	*Not possible with* **estar**.
estar + gerundio: 25.C.3, 26.D	**Gerundio** (Progressive tenses)	*Not possible with* **ser**.	**Estamos** trabajando. *We're working.*

Práctica

S Actividades 1–12,
pp. A125–A128

Indirect discourse
Discurso indirecto

Chapter 31

A. Overview
B. Indirect discourse:
    necessary changes to
    verb tenses and mood

31.A Overview

Aspectos generales

The ability to relate what we have heard or what we know, think, or believe is important when communicating with other people. Direct and indirect discourse are the strategies used for this purpose.

31.A.1 Direct discourse

Also called *quoted speech*, direct discourse reproduces someone's exact words. In writing, quotation marks indicate that the words enclosed are being reproduced verbatim. Dialogues use a dash for the same purpose. In speech (usually formal), a suitable introductory phrase and proper intonation announces the quotation.

Use of the colon: 1.F.4
Use of the dash: 1.F.7

Direct discourse in writing	Direct discourse in speech
Carlos dice: **"Esta fecha es muy importante para mí"**. *Carlos says: "This date is very important for me."*	Carlos dijo **lo siguiente**: **"Esta fecha es muy importante para mí"**. *Carlos said the following: "This date is very important for me."*

31.A.2 Indirect discourse

Also called *reported speech,* indirect discourse relates someone's statement without quoting their exact words. The structure of the sentence changes to convey the indirect quote. The same structure is used in writing and speech.

Decir and other reporting verbs: 23.C.2

Indirect discourse	
Carlos dijo **que esa fecha era muy importante para él.**	*Carlos said (that) that date was very important for him.*

31.B Indirect discourse: necessary changes to verb tenses and mood

Cambios necesarios en el tiempo o modo verbal

31.B.1 Overview

Several sentence components may have to change when reporting someone's words: personal object and reflexive pronouns, possessives, demonstratives, adverbs of time and place, and *especially* the verb tense and/or mood. These changes are determined by the change of perspective needed when reproducing someone else's words in a different context. Usually if the reporting verb is in the present, the verb tenses stay the same.

Uttered on Monday	Iré al cine **mañana**.	*I'll go to the movies tomorrow.*
Reported on Monday	Dice que irá al cine **mañana**.	*He says he'll go to the movies tomorrow.*
Reported on Tuesday	Dijo / Ha dicho que iría al cine **hoy**.	*He (has) said he'd go to the movies today.*
Reported on Wednesday	Dijo que iría al cine **ayer**.	*He said he'd go to the movies yesterday.*
Reported on Sunday	Dijo que iría al cine **el martes**.	*He said he'd go to the movies on Tuesday.*

31.B.2 Reporting information and commands

The most important thing to keep in mind when reporting your own or someone else's statements is whether the statement conveys *information* or transmits a *command*. When reporting information, the mood of the verb does not change. When reporting commands, the imperative is replaced with the subjunctive.

Decir and other reporting ▶
verbs: 23.C.2

Reporting information	Reporting a command
La profesora dice: "Tú siempre **haces** los deberes". → La profesora dice que tú siempre **haces** los deberes.	La profesora dice: "**Haz** los deberes". → La profesora dice que **hagas** los deberes.
The teacher says: "You always do your homework." → *The teacher says that you always do your homework.*	*The teacher says: "Do your homework." →* *The teacher says that you should do your homework.*

31.B.3 Changes in verb tenses

a. The following verb tenses change in indirect discourse when the reporting verb is used in the past.

	Type of change	Direct discourse	Indirect discourse
Indicative	Present → Imperfect	Ella **dijo:** "**Voy** de compras". *She said: "I am going shopping."*	Ella **dijo** que **iba** de compras. *She said that she was going shopping.*
	Preterite → Past perfect	Ella **dijo:** "**Fui** de compras". *She said: "I went shopping."*	Ella **dijo** que **había ido** de compras. *She said that she had gone shopping.*
	Present perfect → Past perfect	Ella **dijo:** "No **he comprado** nada". *She said: "I haven't bought anything."*	Ella **dijo** que no **había comprado** nada. *She said that she hadn't bought anything.*
	Future → Conditional	Ella **dijo:** "**Compraré** algo". *She said: "I will buy something."*	Ella **dijo** que **compraría** algo. *She said that she would buy something.*
	Future perfect → Perfect conditional	Ella **dijo:** "Esta tarde **habré terminado** mis compras". *She said: "I will have finished my shopping this afternoon."*	Ella **dijo** que esta tarde **habría terminado** sus compras. *She said that she would have finished her shopping this afternoon.*
Subjunctive	Present → Imperfect	Ella **dijo:** "**Quiero** que me **acompañes**". *She said: "I want you to go with me."*	Ella **dijo** que **quería** que la **acompañara**. *She said that she wanted me to go with her.*
	Present perfect → Past perfect	Ella **dijo:** "No creo que me **hayan dado** un buen precio". *She said: "I don't believe they gave me a good price."*	Ella **dijo** que no creía que le **hubieran dado** un buen precio. *She said that she did not believe they had given her a good price.*
	Imperative → Imperfect	Ella **dijo:** "¡**Espérame**!" *She said: "Wait for me!"*	Ella **dijo** que la **esperara**. *She said that I should wait for her.*

Regional variations in ▶
the use of the subjunctive
in nominal clauses: 23.Fa

Ir a: 26.C.1 ▶

b. When reporting a future statement, it is also possible to use the *imperfect* of **ir a** + *infinitive*.

Iré la semana que viene. → Dijo que **iría** la semana siguiente. / Dijo que **iba a ir** la semana siguiente.

I will go next week. → She said she would go next week. / She said she was going to go next week.

31.B.4 Verb tenses that do not change

The following tenses do not change in indirect discourse. However, note that other changes to the sentence may be necessary, such as adding reflexive and object pronouns.

		Direct discourse	Indirect discourse
Indicative	Imperfect	Ella dijo: "**Me gustaban** mucho las tapas". *She said: "I liked tapas a lot."*	Ella dijo que **le gustaban** mucho las tapas. *She said that she used to like tapas a lot.*
	Past perfect	Ella dijo: "Nunca **me había divertido** tanto". *She said: "I'd never had so much fun."*	Ella dijo que nunca **se había divertido** tanto. *She said that she had never had so much fun.*
	Conditional	Ella dijo: "**Tomaría** un crucero". *She said: "I would go on a cruise."*	Ella dijo que **tomaría** un crucero. *She said she would go on a cruise.*
	Conditional perfect	Ella dijo: "**Te habrías divertido** si hubieras venido a la fiesta". *She said: "You would have had fun if you had come to the party."*	Ella dijo que **me habría divertido** si hubiera ido a la fiesta. *She said I would have had fun if I had come to the party.*
Subjunctive	Imperfect	Ella dijo: "Me gustaría que tú **me prepararas** un plato chileno". *She said: "I would like you to prepare a Chilean dish for me."*	Ella dijo que **le** gustaría que **yo le preparara** un plato chileno. *She said that she would like me to prepare a Chilean dish for her.*
	Past perfect	Ella dijo: "**Te** habrías divertido si **hubieras venido** a la fiesta". *She said: "You would have had fun if you had come to the party."*	Ella dijo que **me** habría divertido si **hubiera ido** a la fiesta. *She said I would have had fun if I had come to the party.*

31.B.5 Other necessary changes

a. Retelling and repeating imply a change of perspective and will necessarily require changes in other sentence elements. Spanish and English share these perspectives and the same changes are required.

Direct discourse	Indirect discourse
Ella me dice: "**Te** voy a extrañar mucho". *She tells me: "I am going to miss you a lot."*	Ella dijo que **me** iba a extrañar mucho. *She said she was going to miss me a lot.*
Ella dice: "No puedo poner**me** los zapatos". *She says: "I can't put on my shoes."*	Ella dijo que no podía poner**se** los zapatos. *She said she couldn't put on her shoes.*

b. A change from direct discourse to indirect discourse may also imply a change in time perspective. In addition to changes in verb tenses, adverbs or time expressions may have to change, too.

Direct discourse	Indirect discourse
Fecha: 3 de enero Elena dice: "Publicaré las fotos **mañana**". *Elena says: "I will publish my photos tomorrow."*	Fecha: 15 de enero Elena dijo que publicaría las fotos **al día siguiente**. *Elena said that she would publish her photos the next day.*
Elena dice: "**Anoche** no pude dormir nada". *Elena says: "I couldn't sleep at all last night."*	Elena dijo que no había podido dormir nada **la noche anterior**. *Elena said that she hadn't been able to sleep at all the night before.*

Indirect questions: 14.B.1b, 14.B.9, 16.C.1b-c ▶

a. Questions may be reported indirectly or rephrased to make them more polite. Note that Spanish has the same word order in direct and indirect questions.

	Direct question	**Indirect question**
Present	—Señor, ¿**qué hora es**? *Sir, what time is it?*	—Señor, ¿podría decirme **qué hora es**? *Sir, could you tell me what time it is?*
Past	—¿Qué le **preguntaste** al señor? *What did you ask the man?*	—Le pregunté **qué hora era**. *I asked him what time it was.*

Que before indirect questions: 16.C.1c ▶

b. When reporting *yes/no* questions, **si** introduces the implied question. *If* or *whether* are used in the equivalent construction in English. In informal speech, **que** may be added to the indirect question.

—¿Qué le preguntaste al señor?   *What did you ask the man?*

—Le pregunté (que) **si** sabía la hora.   *I asked him if/whether he knew what time it was.*

Using the future to express conjecture: 20.C.2 ▶

c. Verbs referring to mental activity also form statements with **si**.

Me pregunto **si** este producto es bueno.   *I wonder if/whether this product is good.*

No recuerdo **si** la cita es hoy.   *I don't recall if/whether the appointment is today.*

Question words: 1.E.7 Question formation: 14.A–14.B ▶

d. Question words carry an accent in both direct and indirect questions.

—¿**Cuándo** llegará el avión?   *When will the plane arrive?*

—Nadie sabe **cuándo** llegará.   *No one knows when it will arrive.*

—¿**Cómo** se llamará esa chica?   *What is that girl's name?*

—No sé **cómo** se llama ella.   *I don't know what her name is.*

—¿**Dónde** podrán arreglarme el coche?   *Where can my car be fixed?*

—No sabemos **dónde** podrán arreglártelo.   *We don't know where it can be fixed.*

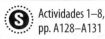

Práctica

S Actividades 1–8, pp. A128–A131

Verb conjugation tables

Pages **261–276** contain verb conjugation patterns. Patterns 1–3 include the simple tenses of three model **-ar, -er,** and **-ir** regular verbs. Patterns 4 to 80 include spell-changing, stem-changing, and irregular verbs. Charts are also provided for the formation of compound tenses (**p. 261**) and **estar + gerundio** periphrases (*progressive tenses*) (**p. 262**). For the formation of reflexive verbs, see **27.A.** To see a list of irregular participles, see **19.A.2** and **25.D.2.**

Spell-changing, stem-changing, and irregular verbs

In patterns 4 to 80, the superscript numbers in parentheses identify the type of irregularity:

[1]Stem-changing verbs (**pensar** → **pienso**)

[2]Verbs with spelling changes (**recoger** → **recojo**)

[3]Verbs with accent changes or verbs that require replacing **u** with **ü** (**reunir** → **reúno; averiguar** → **averigüé**)

[4]Verbs with unique irregularities (sometimes in addition to stem or spelling changes) (**poner** → **puse**)

Note: Any form that deviates from the regular verb patterns is indicated in **bold** font.

Voseo

Voseo conjugations are included in the present indicative and in the second person singular informal imperative. These are the **voseo** forms included in the verb charts in the RAE's *Nueva gramática*. For more information about the **voseo,** see **13.B.2, 22.B.b, 24.C,** and **24.D.1.**

| tú/vos | hablas/hablás | habla/hablá |

Nomenclature

The Spanish names of the verb tenses used in this handbook correspond to the names used in the *Nueva gramática* published by the Real Academia Española.

English terminology used in this handbook	Spanish terminology used in this handbook	Traditional Spanish terminology	Terminology used by Andrés Bello
Simple present	Presente	Presente	Presente
Imperfect	Pretérito imperfecto	Pretérito imperfecto	Copretérito
Preterite	Pretérito perfecto simple	Pretérito indefinido	Pretérito
Present perfect	Pretérito perfecto compuesto	Pretérito perfecto	Antepresente
Past perfect	Pretérito pluscuamperfecto	Pretérito pluscuamperfecto	Antecopretérito
Simple future	Futuro (simple)	Futuro (simple)	Futuro
Future perfect	Futuro compuesto	Futuro compuesto/perfecto	Antefuturo
Present conditional	Condicional (simple)	Condicional simple/presente Potencial simple	Pospretérito
Conditional perfect	Condicional compuesto	Condicional compuesto/perfecto Potencial compuesto/perfecto	Antepospretérito

Tenses not included in the charts

The following tenses are rarely used in contemporary Spanish. They have been excluded from the verb tables in this handbook.

Pretérito anterior (indicativo): See **19.F.**	Cuando **hubo terminado** la fiesta, fuimos a casa.
Futuro simple (subjuntivo): See **22.F.**	Adonde **fueres**, haz lo que vieres.
Futuro compuesto (subjuntivo): See **22.G.**	"Será proclamado Alcalde el concejal que **hubiere obtenido** más votos..."

Negative imperative

The verb forms for the negative imperative are not included in the verb charts. They coincide with the forms of the present subjunctive.

Verb chapters

The following chapters cover verb tense formation and usage.

Indicative			Subjunctive		
	Present	Chapter 17		All tenses – Formation	Chapter 22
	Preterite and Imperfect	Chapter 18			
	Present perfect and Past perfect	Chapter 19		All tenses – Usage	Chapter 23
	Future and Future perfect	Chapter 20			
	Conditional and Conditional perfect	Chapter 21		**Imperative**	Chapter 24

Verbs with stem changes, spelling changes, and irregular verbs

The list below includes common verbs with stem changes, spelling changes, and irregular verbs, as well as the verbs used as models/patterns in the charts on **pp. 261-276**. The number in brackets indicates where in the verb tables you can find the conjugated form of the model verb.

abastecer (*conocer* [15])
aborrecer (*conocer* [15])
abstenerse (*tener* [69])
abstraer (*traer* [73])
acaecer (*conocer* [15])
acentuar (*graduar* [37])
acoger (*proteger* [54])
acontecer (*conocer* [15])
acordar (*contar* [16])
acostar (*contar* [16])
acrecentar (*pensar* [49])
actuar (*graduar* [37])
adherir (*sentir* [65])
adolecer (*conocer* [15])
adormecer (*conocer* [15])
adquirir [4]
aducir (*conducir* [14])
advertir (*sentir* [65])
afligir (*exigir* [35])
ahumar (*rehusar* [57])
airar (*aislar* [5])
aislar [5]
alentar (*pensar* [49])
almorzar [6]
amanecer (*conocer* [15])
amoblar (*contar* [16])
amortiguar (*averiguar* [10])
ampliar (*enviar* [29])
andar [7]
anegar (*negar* [45])
anochecer (*conocer* [15])
apaciguar (*averiguar* [10])
aparecer (*conocer* [15])

apetecer (*conocer* [15])
apretar (*pensar* [49])
aprobar (*contar* [16])
arrepentirse (*sentir* [65])
ascender (*entender* [28])
asentar (*pensar* [49])
asentir (*sentir* [65])
asir [8]
atañer (*tañer* [68])
atardecer (*conocer* [15])
atender (*entender* [28])
atenerse (*tener* [69])
atestiguar (*averiguar* [10])
atraer (*traer* [73])
atravesar (*pensar* [49])
atribuir (*destruir* [23])
aunar (*rehusar* [57])
avergonzar [9]
averiguar [10]
balbucir (*lucir* [43])
bendecir [11]
caber [12]
caer [13]
calentar (*pensar* [49])
cegar (*negar* [45])
ceñir (*teñir* [70])
cerrar (*pensar* [49])
cimentar (*pensar* [49])
cocer (*torcer* [72])
coercer (*vencer* [75])
coger (*proteger* [54])
cohibir (*prohibir* [53])
colgar (*rogar* [61])

comenzar (*empezar* [27])
comer [2]
compadecer (*conocer* [15])
comparecer (*conocer* [15])
competir (*pedir* [48])
comprobar (*contar* [16])
concebir (*pedir* [48])
concernir (*discernir* [24])
concluir (*destruir* [23])
concordar (*contar* [16])
conducir [14]
confesar (*pensar* [49])
confiar (*enviar* [29])
conmover (*mover* [44])
conocer [15]
conseguir (*seguir* [64])
consentir (*sentir* [65])
consolar (*contar* [16])
constituir (*destruir* [23])
construir (*destruir* [23])
contar [16]
contener (*tener* [69])
continuar (*graduar* [37])
contradecir (*predecir* [52])
contraer (*traer* [73])
contrariar (*enviar* [29])
convalecer (*conocer* [15])
convencer (*vencer* [75])
converger (*proteger* [54])
convertir (*sentir* [65])
corregir (*elegir* [26])
corroer (*roer* [60])
costar (*contar* [16])

creer [17]
criar (*enviar* [29])
cruzar [18]
dar [19]
decaer (*caer* [13])
decir [20]
deducir (*conducir* [14])
defender (*entender* [28])
degollar [21]
delinquir [22]
demoler (*mover* [44])
demostrar (*contar* [16])
denegar (*negar* [45])
derretir (*pedir* [48])
desafiar (*enviar* [29])
desaguar (*averiguar* [10])
desalentar (*pensar* [49])
desandar (*andar* [7])
desaparecer (*conocer* [15])
desasir (*asir* [8])
descafeinar (*aislar* [5])
descolgar (*rogar* [61])
desconsolar (*contar* [16])
desdecir (*predecir* [52])
desentenderse (*entender* [28])
desfallecer (*conocer* [15])
desfavorecer (*conocer* [15])
deshacer (*hacer* [39])
deslucir (*lucir* [43])
desmerecer (*conocer* [15])
desoír (*oír* [46])
despedir (*pedir* [48])
despertar (*pensar* [49])
desplegar (*negar* [45])
desteñir (*teñir* [70])
destruir [23]
desvestir (*pedir* [48])
detener (*tener* [69])
diferir (*sentir* [65])
digerir (*sentir* [65])
diluir (*destruir* [23])
dirigir (*exigir* [35])
discernir [24]
disentir (*sentir* [65])
disminuir (*destruir* [23])
distender (*entender* [28])
distinguir (*extinguir* [36])
distraer (*traer* [73])
distribuir (*destruir* [23])
divertir (*sentir* [65])
doler (*mover* [44])
dormir [25]
efectuar (*graduar* [37])
ejercer (*vencer* [75])
elegir [26]
embellecer (*conocer* [15])

embestir (*pedir* [48])
emerger (*proteger* [54])
empalidecer (*conocer* [15])
emparentar (*pensar* [49])
empequeñecer (*conocer* [15])
empezar [27]
empobrecer (*conocer* [15])
encarecer (*conocer* [15])
enceguecer (*conocer* [15])
encender (*entender* [28])
encerrar (*pensar* [49])
encontrar (*contar* [16])
endurecer (*conocer* [15])
enfriar (*enviar* [29])
enfurecer (*conocer* [15])
engullir (*zambullir* [80])
enloquecer (*conocer* [15])
enmendar (*pensar* [49])
enmudecer (*conocer* [15])
enriquecer (*conocer* [15])
ensordecer (*conocer* [15])
entender [28]
enterrar (*pensar* [49])
entorpecer (*conocer* [15])
entrelucir (*lucir* [43])
entreoír (*oír* [46])
entretener (*tener* [69])
entristecer (*conocer* [15])
envejecer (*conocer* [15])
enviar [29]
equivaler (*valer* [74])
erguir [30]
errar [31]
escarmentar (*pensar* [49])
escoger (*proteger* [54])
esforzar (*almorzar* [6])
esparcir [32]
espiar (*enviar* [29])
establecer (*conocer* [15])
estar [33]
estremecer (*conocer* [15])
estreñir (*teñir* [70])
europeizar [34]
evaluar (*graduar* [37])
exceptuar (*graduar* [37])
excluir (*destruir* [23])
exigir [35]
expedir (*pedir* [48])
extender (*entender* [28])
extinguir [36]
extraer (*traer* [73])
fallecer (*conocer* [15])
favorecer (*conocer* [15])
fingir (*exigir* [35])
florecer (*conocer* [15])
fluir (*destruir* [23])

fortalecer (*conocer* [15])
forzar (*almorzar* [6])
fotografiar (*enviar* [29])
fraguar (*averiguar* [10])
fregar (*negar* [45])
freír (*reír* [58])
gobernar (*pensar* [49])
graduar [37]
gruñir (*zambullir* [80])
guiar (*enviar* [29])
haber [38]
habituar (*graduar* [37])
hablar [1]
hacer [39]
helar (*pensar* [49])
hendir (*discernir* [24])
herir (*sentir* [65])
herrar (*pensar* [49])
hervir (*sentir* [65])
homogeneizar (*europeizar* [34])
humedecer (*conocer* [15])
impedir (*pedir* [48])
incluir (*destruir* [23])
inducir (*conducir* [14])
infligir (*exigir* [35])
influir (*destruir* [23])
ingerir (*sentir* [65])
inquirir (*adquirir* [4])
insinuar (*graduar* [37])
instituir (*destruir* [23])
instruir (*destruir* [23])
interferir (*sentir* [65])
introducir (*conducir* [14])
invernar (*pensar* [49])
invertir (*sentir* [65])
investir (*pedir* [48])
ir [40]
judaizar (*europeizar* [34])
jugar [41]
leer (*creer* [17])
liar (*enviar* [29])
llegar [42]
llover (*mover* [44])
lucir [43]
malcriar (*enviar* [29])
maldecir (*bendecir* [11])
malentender (*entender* [28])
malherir (*sentir* [65])
maltraer (*traer* [73])
manifestar (*pensar* [49])
mantener (*tener* [69])
maullar (*rehusar* [57])
mecer (*vencer* [75])
medir (*pedir* [48])
mentir (*sentir* [65])
merecer (*conocer* [15])

merendar (*pensar* [49])
moler (*mover* [44])
morder (*mover* [44])
morir (p.p. muerto) (*dormir* [25])
mostrar (*contar* [16])
mover [44]
mugir (*exigir* [35])
mullir (*zambullir* [80])
nacer (*conocer* [15])
negar [45]
nevar (*pensar* [49])
obedecer (*conocer* [15])
obstruir (*destruir* [23])
obtener (*tener* [69])
ofrecer (*conocer* [15])
oír [46]
oler [47]
oscurecer (*conocer* [15])
padecer (*conocer* [15])
palidecer (*conocer* [15])
parecer (*conocer* [15])
pedir [48]
pensar [49]
perder (*entender* [28])
permanecer (*conocer* [15])
perpetuar (*graduar* [37])
perseguir (*seguir* [64])
plegar (*negar* [45])
poblar (*contar* [16])
poder [50]
poner [51]
poseer (*creer* [17])
predecir [52]
preferir (*sentir* [65])
presentir (*sentir* [65])
prevaler (*valer* [74])
probar (*contar* [16])
producir (*conducir* [14])
prohibir [53]
promover (*mover* [44])
proseguir (*seguir* [64])
proteger [54]
proveer (*creer* [17])
pudrir/podrir [55]
quebrar (*pensar* [49])
querer [56]
recaer (*caer* [13])
recoger (*proteger* [54])
recomenzar (*empezar* [27])
reconducir (*conducir* [14])
recordar (*contar* [16])
recostar (*contar* [16])
reducir (*conducir* [14])
reforzar (*almorzar* [6])
refregar (*negar* [45])
regir (*elegir* [26])

rehusar [57]
reír [58]
releer (*creer* [17])
relucir (*lucir* [43])
remendar (*pensar* [49])
remover (*mover* [44])
rendir (*pedir* [48])
renegar (*negar* [45])
reñir (*teñir* [70])
renovar (*contar* [16])
repetir (*pedir* [48])
replegar (*negar* [45])
reproducir (*conducir* [14])
requerir (*sentir* [65])
resarcir (*esparcir* [32])
resolver (p.p. resuelto) (*mover* [44])
restringir (*exigir* [35])
resurgir (*exigir* [35])
retorcer (*torcer* [72])
retrotraer (*traer* [73])
reunir [59]
reventar (*pensar* [49])
revertir (*sentir* [65])
revolcar (*volcar* [78])
robustecer (*conocer* [15])
rociar (*enviar* [29])
rodar (*contar* [16])
roer [60]
rogar [61]
saber [62]
salir [63]
salpimentar (*pensar* [49])
satisfacer (*hacer* [39])
seducir (*conducir* [14])
seguir [64]
sembrar (*pensar* [49])
sentar (*pensar* [49])
sentir [65]
ser [66]
servir (*pedir* [48])
situar (*graduar* [37])
sobrecoger (*proteger* [54])
sobresalir (*salir* [63])
sobreseer (*creer* [17])
sofreír (*reír* [58])
soler [67]
soltar (*contar* [16])
sonar (*contar* [16])
sonreír (*reír* [58])
soñar (*contar* [16])
sosegar (*negar* [45])
sostener (*tener* [69])
subyacer (*yacer* [79])
sugerir (*sentir* [65])
sumergir (*exigir* [35])
surgir (*exigir* [35])

sustituir (*destruir* [23])
sustraer (*traer* [73])
tañer [68]
tatuar (*graduar* [37])
temblar (*pensar* [49])
tener [69]
tentar (*pensar* [49])
teñir [70]
tocar [71]
torcer [72]
tostar (*contar* [16])
traducir (*conducir* [14])
traer [73]
transferir (*sentir* [65])
trascender (*entender* [28])
traslucirse (*lucir* [43])
trastocar (*volcar* [78])
trocar (*volcar* [78])
tropezar (*empezar* [27])
uncir (*esparcir* [32])
urgir (*exigir* [35])
valer [74]
valuar (*graduar* [37])
variar (*enviar* [29])
vencer [75]
venir [76]
ver [77]
verter (*entender* [28])
vestir (*pedir* [48])
vivir [3]
volar (*contar* [16])
volcar [78]
volver (p.p. vuelto) (*mover* [44])
yacer [79]
zambullir [80]
zurcir (*esparcir* [32])

Verb conjugation tables

Regular verbs: simple tenses

Infinitivo / Gerundio / Participio	Pronombres personales	INDICATIVO					SUBJUNTIVO		IMPERATIVO
		Presente	Pretérito imperfecto	Pretérito perfecto simple	Futuro simple	Condicional simple	Presente	Pretérito imperfecto	
1 hablar hablando hablado	yo tú/vos Ud., él, ella nosotros/as vosotros/as Uds., ellos/as	hablo hablas/hablás habla hablamos habláis hablan	hablaba hablabas hablaba hablábamos hablabais hablaban	hablé hablaste habló hablamos hablasteis hablaron	hablaré hablarás hablará hablaremos hablaréis hablarán	hablaría hablarías hablaría hablaríamos hablaríais hablarían	hable hables hable hablemos habléis hablen	hablara o hablase hablaras o hablases hablara o hablase habláramos o hablásemos hablarais o hablaseis hablaran o hablasen	 habla/hablá hable hablemos hablad hablen
2 comer comiendo comido	yo tú/vos Ud., él, ella nosotros/as vosotros/as Uds., ellos/as	como comes/comés come comemos coméis comen	comía comías comía comíamos comíais comían	comí comiste comió comimos comisteis comieron	comeré comerás comerá comeremos comeréis comerán	comería comerías comería comeríamos comeríais comerían	coma comas coma comamos comáis coman	comiera o comiese comieras o comieses comiera o comiese comiéramos o comiésemos comierais o comieseis comieran o comiesen	 come/comé coma comamos comed coman
3 vivir viviendo vivido	yo tú/vos Ud., él, ella nosotros/as vosotros/as Uds., ellos/as	vivo vives/vivís vive vivimos vivís viven	vivía vivías vivía vivíamos vivíais vivían	viví viviste vivió vivimos vivisteis vivieron	viviré vivirás vivirá viviremos viviréis vivirán	viviría vivirías viviría viviríamos viviríais vivirían	viva vivas viva vivamos viváis vivan	viviera o viviese vivieras o vivieses viviera o viviese viviéramos o viviésemos vivierais o vivieseis vivieran o viviesen	 vive/viví viva vivamos vivid vivan

Compound tenses

INDICATIVO				SUBJUNTIVO	
Pretérito perfecto compuesto	Pretérito pluscuamperfecto	Futuro compuesto	Condicional compuesto	Pretérito perfecto compuesto	Pretérito pluscuamperfecto
he has ha hemos habéis han	había habías había habíamos habíais habían	habré habrás habrá habremos habréis habrán	habría habrías habría habríamos habríais habrían	haya hayas haya hayamos hayáis hayan	hubiera o hubiese hubieras o hubieses hubiera o hubiese hubiéramos o hubiésemos hubierais o hubieseis hubieran o hubiesen
hablado comido vivido	hablado comido vivido	hablado comido vivido	hablado comido vivido	hablado comido vivido	hablado comido vivido

Estar + gerundio (Progressive tenses)

INDICATIVO

Presente		Pretérito imperfecto		Pretérito perfecto simple		Futuro simple		Condicional simple	
estoy		estaba		estuve		estaré		estaría	
estás	hablando	estabas	hablando	estuviste	hablando	estarás	hablando	estarías	hablando
está	comiendo	estaba	comiendo	estuvo	comiendo	estará	comiendo	estaría	comiendo
estamos	viviendo	estábamos	viviendo	estuvimos	viviendo	estaremos	viviendo	estaríamos	viviendo
estáis		estabais		estuvisteis		estaréis		estaríais	
están		estaban		estuvieron		estarán		estarían	

SUBJUNTIVO

Pretérito perfecto		Pretérito imperfecto	
esté		estuviera o estuviese	
estés	hablando	estuvieras o estuvieses	hablando
esté	comiendo	estuviera o estuviese	comiendo
estemos	viviendo	estuviéramos o estuviésemos	viviendo
estéis		estuvierais o estuvieseis	
estén		estuvieran o estuviesen	

Note: Perfect progressive tenses are formed using a conjugated form of **haber** + **estado** + **gerundio**, as in **he estado comiendo, hubiera estado corriendo**, etc.

Verbs with stem changes, spelling changes, and irregular verbs

Infinitivo Gerundio Participio	Pronombres personales	INDICATIVO										SUBJUNTIVO		IMPERATIVO
		Presente	Pretérito imperfecto	Pretérito perfecto simple	Futuro simple	Condicional simple						Presente	Pretérito imperfecto	
4 adquirir [1] (i:ie)	yo	**adquiero**	adquiría	adquirí	adquiriré	adquiriría						**adquiera**	adquiriera o adquiriese	
	tú/vos	**adquieres/ adquirís**	adquirías	adquiriste	adquirirás	adquirirías						**adquieras**	adquirieras o adquirieses	**adquiere/ adquirí**
adquiriendo	Ud., él, ella	**adquiere**	adquiría	adquirió	adquirirá	adquiriría						**adquiera**	adquiriera o adquiriese	**adquiera**
adquirido	nosotros/as	adquirimos	adquiríamos	adquirimos	adquiriremos	adquiriríamos						adquiramos	adquiriéramos o adquiriésemos	adquiramos
	vosotros/as	adquirís	adquiríais	adquiristeis	adquiriréis	adquiriríais						adquiráis	adquirierais o adquirieseis	adquirid
	Uds., ellos/as	**adquieren**	adquirían	adquirieron	adquirirán	adquirirían						**adquieran**	adquirieran o adquiriesen	**adquieran**

5. aislar [3] (i:í) — Gerundio: aislando — Participio: aislado

Pronombres personales	INDICATIVO Presente	Pretérito imperfecto	Pretérito perfecto simple	Futuro simple	Condicional simple	SUBJUNTIVO Presente	Pretérito imperfecto	IMPERATIVO
yo	aíslo	aislaba	aislé	aislaré	aislaría	aísle	aislara o aislase	
tú/vos	aíslas/aislás	aislabas	aislaste	aislarás	aislarías	aísles	aislaras o aislases	aísla/aislá
Ud., él, ella	aísla	aislaba	aisló	aislará	aislaría	aísle	aislara o aislase	aísle
nosotros/as	aislamos	aislábamos	aislamos	aislaremos	aislaríamos	aislemos	aisláramos o aislásemos	aislemos
vosotros/as	aisláis	aislabais	aislasteis	aislaréis	aislaríais	aisléis	aislarais o aislaseis	aislad
Uds., ellos/as	aíslan	aislaban	aislaron	aislarán	aislarían	aíslen	aislaran o aislasen	aíslen

6. almorzar [1, 2] (o:ue) (z:c) — Gerundio: almorzando — Participio: almorzado

Pronombres personales	INDICATIVO Presente	Pretérito imperfecto	Pretérito perfecto simple	Futuro simple	Condicional simple	SUBJUNTIVO Presente	Pretérito imperfecto	IMPERATIVO
yo	almuerzo	almorzaba	almorcé	almorzaré	almorzaría	almuerce	almorzara o almorzase	
tú/vos	almuerzas/almorzás	almorzabas	almorzaste	almorzarás	almorzarías	almuerces	almorzaras o almorzases	almuerza/almorzá
Ud., él, ella	almuerza	almorzaba	almorzó	almorzará	almorzaría	almuerce	almorzara o almorzase	almuerce
nosotros/as	almorzamos	almorzábamos	almorzamos	almorzaremos	almorzaríamos	almorcemos	almorzáramos o almorzásemos	almorcemos
vosotros/as	almorzáis	almorzabais	almorzasteis	almorzaréis	almorzaríais	almorcéis	almorzarais o almorzaseis	almorzad
Uds., ellos/as	almuerzan	almorzaban	almorzaron	almorzarán	almorzarían	almuercen	almorzaran o almorzasen	almuercen

7. andar [4] — Gerundio: andando — Participio: andado

Pronombres personales	INDICATIVO Presente	Pretérito imperfecto	Pretérito perfecto simple	Futuro simple	Condicional simple	SUBJUNTIVO Presente	Pretérito imperfecto	IMPERATIVO
yo	ando	andaba	anduve	andaré	andaría	ande	anduviera o anduviese	
tú/vos	andas/andás	andabas	anduviste	andarás	andarías	andes	anduvieras o anduvieses	anda/andá
Ud., él, ella	anda	andaba	anduvo	andará	andaría	ande	anduviera o anduviese	ande
nosotros/as	andamos	andábamos	anduvimos	andaremos	andaríamos	andemos	anduviéramos o anduviésemos	andemos
vosotros/as	andáis	andabais	anduvisteis	andaréis	andaríais	andéis	anduvierais o anduvieseis	andad
Uds., ellos/as	andan	andaban	anduvieron	andarán	andarían	anden	anduvieran o anduviesen	anden

8. asir [4] — Gerundio: asiendo — Participio: asido

Pronombres personales	INDICATIVO Presente	Pretérito imperfecto	Pretérito perfecto simple	Futuro simple	Condicional simple	SUBJUNTIVO Presente	Pretérito imperfecto	IMPERATIVO
yo	asgo	asía	así	asiré	asiría	asga	asiera o asiese	
tú/vos	ases/asís	asías	asiste	asirás	asirías	asgas	asieras o asieses	ase/así
Ud., él, ella	ase	asía	asió	asirá	asiría	asga	asiera o asiese	asga
nosotros/as	asimos	asíamos	asimos	asiremos	asiríamos	asgamos	asiéramos o asiésemos	asgamos
vosotros/as	asís	asíais	asisteis	asiréis	asiríais	asgáis	asierais o asieseis	asid
Uds., ellos/as	asen	asían	asieron	asirán	asirían	asgan	asieran o asiesen	asgan

9. avergonzar [1, 2] (o:üe) (z:c) — Gerundio: avergonzando — Participio: avergonzado

Pronombres personales	INDICATIVO Presente	Pretérito imperfecto	Pretérito perfecto simple	Futuro simple	Condicional simple	SUBJUNTIVO Presente	Pretérito imperfecto	IMPERATIVO
yo	avergüenzo	avergonzaba	avergoncé	avergonzaré	avergonzaría	avergüence	avergonzara o avergonzase	
tú/vos	avergüenzas/avergonzás	avergonzabas	avergonzaste	avergonzarás	avergonzarías	avergüences	avergonzaras o avergonzases	avergüenza/avergonzá
Ud., él, ella	avergüenza	avergonzaba	avergonzó	avergonzará	avergonzaría	avergüence	avergonzara o avergonzase	avergüence
nosotros/as	avergonzamos	avergonzábamos	avergonzamos	avergonzaremos	avergonzaríamos	avergoncemos	avergonzáramos o avergonzásemos	avergoncemos
vosotros/as	avergonzáis	avergonzabais	avergonzasteis	avergonzaréis	avergonzaríais	avergoncéis	avergonzarais o avergonzaseis	avergonzad
Uds., ellos/as	avergüenzan	avergonzaban	avergonzaron	avergonzarán	avergonzarían	avergüencen	avergonzaran o avergonzasen	avergüencen

10. averiguar (3) (u:ü)

Gerundio: averiguando — Participio: averiguado

Pronombres personales	INDICATIVO Presente	Pretérito imperfecto	Pretérito perfecto simple	Futuro simple	Condicional simple	SUBJUNTIVO Presente	Pretérito imperfecto	IMPERATIVO
yo	averiguo	averiguaba	averigüé	averiguaré	averiguaría	averigüe	averiguara o averiguase	
tú/vos	averiguas/averiguás	averiguabas	averiguaste	averiguarás	averiguarías	averigües	averiguaras o averiguases	averigua/averiguá
Ud., él, ella	averigua	averiguaba	averiguó	averiguará	averiguaría	averigüe	averiguara o averiguase	averigüe
nosotros/as	averiguamos	averiguábamos	averiguamos	averiguaremos	averiguaríamos	averigüemos	averiguáramos o averiguásemos	averigüemos
vosotros/as	averiguáis	averiguabais	averiguasteis	averiguaréis	averiguaríais	averigüéis	averiguarais o averiguaseis	averiguad
Uds., ellos/as	averiguan	averiguaban	averiguaron	averiguarán	averiguarían	averigüen	averiguaran o averiguasen	averigüen

11. bendecir (4)

Gerundio: bendiciendo — Participio: bendecido o bendito

Pronombres personales	INDICATIVO Presente	Pretérito imperfecto	Pretérito perfecto simple	Futuro simple	Condicional simple	SUBJUNTIVO Presente	Pretérito imperfecto	IMPERATIVO
yo	bendigo	bendecía	bendije	bendeciré	bendeciría	bendiga	bendijera o bendijese	
tú/vos	bendices/bendecís	bendecías	bendijiste	bendecirás	bendecirías	bendigas	bendijeras o bendijeses	bendice/bendecí
Ud., él, ella	bendice	bendecía	bendijo	bendecirá	bendeciría	bendiga	bendijera o bendijese	bendiga
nosotros/as	bendecimos	bendecíamos	bendijimos	bendeciremos	bendeciríamos	bendigamos	bendijéramos o bendijésemos	bendigamos
vosotros/as	bendecís	bendecíais	bendijisteis	bendeciréis	bendeciríais	bendigáis	bendijerais o bendijeseis	bendecid
Uds., ellos/as	bendicen	bendecían	bendijeron	bendecirán	bendecirían	bendigan	bendijeran o bendijesen	bendigan

12. caber (4)

Gerundio: cabiendo — Participio: cabido

Pronombres personales	INDICATIVO Presente	Pretérito imperfecto	Pretérito perfecto simple	Futuro simple	Condicional simple	SUBJUNTIVO Presente	Pretérito imperfecto	IMPERATIVO
yo	quepo	cabía	cupe	cabré	cabría	quepa	cupiera o cupiese	
tú/vos	cabes/cabés	cabías	cupiste	cabrás	cabrías	quepas	cupieras o cupieses	cabe/cabé
Ud., él, ella	cabe	cabía	cupo	cabrá	cabría	quepa	cupiera o cupiese	quepa
nosotros/as	cabemos	cabíamos	cupimos	cabremos	cabríamos	quepamos	cupiéramos o cupiésemos	quepamos
vosotros/as	cabéis	cabíais	cupisteis	cabréis	cabríais	quepáis	cupierais o cupieseis	cabed
Uds., ellos/as	caben	cabían	cupieron	cabrán	cabrían	quepan	cupieran o cupiesen	quepan

13. caer (4) (y)

Gerundio: cayendo — Participio: caído

Pronombres personales	INDICATIVO Presente	Pretérito imperfecto	Pretérito perfecto simple	Futuro simple	Condicional simple	SUBJUNTIVO Presente	Pretérito imperfecto	IMPERATIVO
yo	caigo	caía	caí	caeré	caería	caiga	cayera o cayese	
tú/vos	caes/caés	caías	caíste	caerás	caerías	caigas	cayeras o cayeses	cae/caé
Ud., él, ella	cae	caía	cayó	caerá	caería	caiga	cayera o cayese	caiga
nosotros/as	caemos	caíamos	caímos	caeremos	caeríamos	caigamos	cayéramos o cayésemos	caigamos
vosotros/as	caéis	caíais	caísteis	caeréis	caeríais	caigáis	cayerais o cayeseis	caed
Uds., ellos/as	caen	caían	cayeron	caerán	caerían	caigan	cayeran o cayesen	caigan

14. conducir (2) (c:zc)

Gerundio: conduciendo — Participio: conducido

Pronombres personales	INDICATIVO Presente	Pretérito imperfecto	Pretérito perfecto simple	Futuro simple	Condicional simple	SUBJUNTIVO Presente	Pretérito imperfecto	IMPERATIVO
yo	conduzco	conducía	conduje	conduciré	conduciría	conduzca	condujera o condujese	
tú/vos	conduces/conducís	conducías	condujiste	conducirás	conducirías	conduzcas	condujeras o condujeses	conduce/conducí
Ud., él, ella	conduce	conducía	condujo	conducirá	conduciría	conduzca	condujera o condujese	conduzca
nosotros/as	conducimos	conducíamos	condujimos	conduciremos	conduciríamos	conduzcamos	condujéramos o condujésemos	conduzcamos
vosotros/as	conducís	conducíais	condujisteis	conduciréis	conduciríais	conduzcáis	condujerais o condujeseis	conducid
Uds., ellos/as	conducen	conducían	condujeron	conducirán	conducirían	conduzcan	condujeran o condujesen	conduzcan

Infinitivo / Gerundio / Participio	Pronombres personales	INDICATIVO Presente	Pretérito imperfecto	Pretérito perfecto simple	Futuro simple	Condicional simple	SUBJUNTIVO Presente	Pretérito imperfecto	IMPERATIVO
15 **conocer** (1) (c:zc)	yo	**conozco**	conocía	conocí	conoceré	conocería	**conozca**	conociera o conociese	
	tú/vos	conoces/conocés	conocías	conociste	conocerás	conocerías	**conozcas**	conocieras o conocieses	conoce/conocé
	Ud., él, ella	conoce	conocía	conoció	conocerá	conocería	**conozca**	conociera o conociese	**conozca**
conociendo	nosotros/as	conocemos	conocíamos	conocimos	conoceremos	conoceríamos	**conozcamos**	conociéramos o conociésemos	**conozcamos**
conocido	vosotros/as	conocéis	conocíais	conocisteis	conoceréis	conoceríais	**conozcáis**	conocierais o conocieseis	conoced
	Uds., ellos/as	conocen	conocían	conocieron	conocerán	conocerían	**conozcan**	conocieran o conociesen	**conozcan**
16 **contar** (1) (o:ue)	yo	**cuento**	contaba	conté	contaré	contaría	**cuente**	contara o contase	
	tú/vos	**cuentas**/contás	contabas	contaste	contarás	contarías	**cuentes**	contaras o contases	**cuenta**/contá
	Ud., él, ella	**cuenta**	contaba	contó	contará	contaría	**cuente**	contara o contase	**cuente**
contando	nosotros/as	contamos	contábamos	contamos	contaremos	contaríamos	contemos	contáramos o contásemos	contemos
contado	vosotros/as	contáis	contabais	contasteis	contaréis	contaríais	contéis	contarais o contaseis	contad
	Uds., ellos/as	**cuentan**	contaban	contaron	contarán	contarían	**cuenten**	contaran o contasen	**cuenten**
17 **creer** (3, 4) (y)	yo	creo	creía	creí	creeré	creería	crea	**creyera** o **creyese**	
	tú/vos	crees/creés	creías	**creíste**	creerás	creerías	creas	**creyeras** o **creyeses**	cree/creé
	Ud., él, ella	cree	creía	**creyó**	creerá	creería	crea	**creyera** o **creyese**	crea
creyendo	nosotros/as	creemos	creíamos	**creímos**	creeremos	creeríamos	creamos	**creyéramos** o **creyésemos**	creamos
creído	vosotros/as	creéis	creíais	**creísteis**	creeréis	creeríais	creáis	**creyerais** o **creyeseis**	creed
	Uds., ellos/as	creen	creían	**creyeron**	creerán	creerían	crean	**creyeran** o **creyesen**	crean
18 **cruzar** (2) (z:c)	yo	cruzo	cruzaba	**crucé**	cruzaré	cruzaría	**cruce**	cruzara o cruzase	
	tú/vos	cruzas/cruzás	cruzabas	cruzaste	cruzarás	cruzarías	**cruces**	cruzaras o cruzases	cruza/cruzá
	Ud., él, ella	cruza	cruzaba	cruzó	cruzará	cruzaría	**cruce**	cruzara o cruzase	**cruce**
cruzando	nosotros/as	cruzamos	cruzábamos	cruzamos	cruzaremos	cruzaríamos	**crucemos**	cruzáramos o cruzásemos	**crucemos**
cruzado	vosotros/as	cruzáis	cruzabais	cruzasteis	cruzaréis	cruzaríais	**crucéis**	cruzarais o cruzaseis	cruzad
	Uds., ellos/as	cruzan	cruzaban	cruzaron	cruzarán	cruzarían	**crucen**	cruzaran o cruzasen	**crucen**
19 **dar** (4)	yo	**doy**	daba	**di**	daré	daría	**dé**	**diera** o **diese**	
	tú/vos	das	dabas	**diste**	darás	darías	des	**dieras** o **dieses**	da
	Ud., él, ella	da	daba	**dio**	dará	daría	**dé**	**diera** o **diese**	**dé**
dando	nosotros/as	damos	dábamos	**dimos**	daremos	daríamos	demos	**diéramos** o **diésemos**	demos
dado	vosotros/as	**dais**	dabais	**disteis**	daréis	daríais	**deis**	**dierais** o **dieseis**	dad
	Uds., ellos/as	dan	daban	**dieron**	darán	darían	den	**dieran** o **diesen**	den
20 **decir** (1, 4) (e:i)	yo	**digo**	decía	**dije**	**diré**	**diría**	**diga**	**dijera** o **dijese**	
	tú/vos	**dices**/decís	decías	**dijiste**	**dirás**	**dirías**	**digas**	**dijeras** o **dijeses**	**di**/decí
	Ud., él, ella	**dice**	decía	**dijo**	**dirá**	**diría**	**diga**	**dijera** o **dijese**	**diga**
diciendo	nosotros/as	decimos	decíamos	**dijimos**	**diremos**	**diríamos**	**digamos**	**dijéramos** o **dijésemos**	**digamos**
dicho	vosotros/as	decís	decíais	**dijisteis**	**diréis**	**diríais**	**digáis**	**dijerais** o **dijeseis**	decid
	Uds., ellos/as	**dicen**	decían	**dijeron**	**dirán**	**dirían**	**digan**	**dijeran** o **dijesen**	**digan**

Verb conjugation tables

INDICATIVO / SUBJUNTIVO / IMPERATIVO

21 degollar (1, 3) (go:güe) — degollando / degollado

Pronombres personales	Presente	Pretérito imperfecto	Pretérito perfecto simple	Futuro simple	Condicional simple	Subj. Presente	Subj. Pretérito imperfecto	Imperativo
yo	degüello	degollaba	degollé	degollaré	degollaría	degüelle	degollara o degollase	
tú/vos	degüellas/degollás	degollabas	degollaste	degollarás	degollarías	degüelles	degollaras o degollases	degüella/degollá
Ud., él, ella	degüella	degollaba	degolló	degollará	degollaría	degüelle	degollara o degollase	degüelle
nosotros/as	degollamos	degollábamos	degollamos	degollaremos	degollaríamos	degollemos	degolláramos o degollásemos	degollemos
vosotros/as	degolláis	degollabais	degollasteis	degollaréis	degollaríais	degolléis	degollarais o degollaseis	degollad
Uds., ellos/as	degüellan	degollaban	degollaron	degollarán	degollarían	degüellen	degollaran o degollasen	degüellen

22 delinquir (2) (qu:c) — delinquiendo / delinquido

Pronombres personales	Presente	Pretérito imperfecto	Pretérito perfecto simple	Futuro simple	Condicional simple	Subj. Presente	Subj. Pretérito imperfecto	Imperativo
yo	delinco	delinquía	delinquí	delinquiré	delinquiría	delinca	delinquiera o delinquiese	
tú/vos	delinques/delinquís	delinquías	delinquiste	delinquirás	delinquirías	delincas	delinquieras o delinquieses	delinque/delinquí
Ud., él, ella	delinque	delinquía	delinquió	delinquirá	delinquiría	delinca	delinquiera o delinquiese	delinca
nosotros/as	delinquimos	delinquíamos	delinquimos	delinquiremos	delinquiríamos	delincamos	delinquiéramos o delinquiésemos	delincamos
vosotros/as	delinquís	delinquíais	delinquisteis	delinquiréis	delinquiríais	delincáis	delinquierais o delinquieseis	delinquid
Uds., ellos/as	delinquen	delinquían	delinquieron	delinquirán	delinquirían	delincan	delinquieran o delinquiesen	delincan

23 destruir (4) (y) — destruyendo / destruido

Pronombres personales	Presente	Pretérito imperfecto	Pretérito perfecto simple	Futuro simple	Condicional simple	Subj. Presente	Subj. Pretérito imperfecto	Imperativo
yo	destruyo	destruía	destruí	destruiré	destruiría	destruya	destruyera o destruyese	
tú/vos	destruyes/destruís	destruías	destruiste	destruirás	destruirías	destruyas	destruyeras o destruyeses	destruye/destruí
Ud., él, ella	destruye	destruía	destruyó	destruirá	destruiría	destruya	destruyera o destruyese	destruya
nosotros/as	destruimos	destruíamos	destruimos	destruiremos	destruiríamos	destruyamos	destruyéramos o destruyésemos	destruyamos
vosotros/as	destruís	destruíais	destruisteis	destruiréis	destruiríais	destruyáis	destruyerais o destruyeseis	destruid
Uds., ellos/as	destruyen	destruían	destruyeron	destruirán	destruirían	destruyan	destruyeran o destruyesen	destruyan

24 discernir (1) (e:ie) — discerniendo / discernido

Pronombres personales	Presente	Pretérito imperfecto	Pretérito perfecto simple	Futuro simple	Condicional simple	Subj. Presente	Subj. Pretérito imperfecto	Imperativo
yo	discierno	discernía	discerní	discerniré	discerniría	discierna	discerniera o discerniese	
tú/vos	disciernes/discernís	discernías	discerniste	discernirás	discernirías	disciernas	discernieras o discernieses	discierne/discerní
Ud., él, ella	discierne	discernía	discernió	discernirá	discerniría	discierna	discerniera o discerniese	discierna
nosotros/as	discernimos	discerníamos	discernimos	discerniremos	discerniríamos	discernamos	discerniéramos o discerniésemos	discernamos
vosotros/as	discernís	discerníais	discernisteis	discerniréis	discerniríais	discernáis	discernierais o discernieseis	discernid
Uds., ellos/as	disciernen	discernían	discernieron	discernirán	discernirían	disciernan	discernieran o discerniesen	disciernan

25 dormir (1) (o:ue) — durmiendo / dormido

Pronombres personales	Presente	Pretérito imperfecto	Pretérito perfecto simple	Futuro simple	Condicional simple	Subj. Presente	Subj. Pretérito imperfecto	Imperativo
yo	duermo	dormía	dormí	dormiré	dormiría	duerma	durmiera o durmiese	
tú/vos	duermes/dormís	dormías	dormiste	dormirás	dormirías	duermas	durmieras o durmieses	duerme/dormí
Ud., él, ella	duerme	dormía	durmió	dormirá	dormiría	duerma	durmiera o durmiese	duerma
nosotros/as	dormimos	dormíamos	dormimos	dormiremos	dormiríamos	durmamos	durmiéramos o durmiésemos	durmamos
vosotros/as	dormís	dormíais	dormisteis	dormiréis	dormiríais	durmáis	durmierais o durmieseis	dormid
Uds., ellos/as	duermen	dormían	durmieron	dormirán	dormirían	duerman	durmieran o durmiesen	duerman

Verb conjugation tables

Infinitivo / Gerundio Participio	Pronombres personales	INDICATIVO					SUBJUNTIVO		IMPERATIVO
		Presente	Pretérito imperfecto	Pretérito perfecto simple	Futuro simple	Condicional simple	Presente	Pretérito imperfecto	
26 elegir (1,2) (e:i) (g:j) **eligiendo** elegido *o* **electo**	yo	**elijo**	elegía	elegí	elegiré	elegiría	**elija**	**eligiera** *o* **eligiese**	
	tú/vos	**eliges**/elegís	elegías	elegiste	elegirás	elegirías	**elijas**	**eligieras** *o* **eligieses**	elige/elegí
	Ud., él, ella	**elige**	elegía	**eligió**	elegirá	elegiría	**elija**	**eligiera** *o* **eligiese**	**elija**
	nosotros/as	elegimos	elegíamos	elegimos	elegiremos	elegiríamos	**elijamos**	**eligiéramos** *o* **eligiésemos**	**elijamos**
	vosotros/as	elegís	elegíais	elegisteis	elegiréis	elegiríais	**elijáis**	**eligierais** *o* **eligieseis**	elegid
	Uds., ellos/as	**eligen**	elegían	**eligieron**	elegirán	elegirían	**elijan**	**eligieran** *o* **eligiesen**	**elijan**
27 empezar (1,2) (e:ie) (z:c) empezando empezado	yo	**empiezo**	empezaba	**empecé**	empezaré	empezaría	**empiece**	empezara *o* empezase	
	tú/vos	**empiezas**/empezás	empezabas	empezaste	empezarás	empezarías	**empieces**	empezaras *o* empezases	**empieza**/empezá
	Ud., él, ella	**empieza**	empezaba	empezó	empezará	empezaría	**empiece**	empezara *o* empezase	**empiece**
	nosotros/as	empezamos	empezábamos	empezamos	empezaremos	empezaríamos	**empecemos**	empezáramos *o* empezásemos	**empecemos**
	vosotros/as	empezáis	empezabais	empezasteis	empezaréis	empezaríais	**empecéis**	empezarais *o* empezaseis	empezad
	Uds., ellos/as	**empiezan**	empezaban	empezaron	empezarán	empezarían	**empiecen**	empezaran *o* empezasen	**empiecen**
28 entender (1) (e:ie) entendiendo entendido	yo	**entiendo**	entendía	entendí	entenderé	entendería	**entienda**	entendiera *o* entendiese	
	tú/vos	**entiendes**/entendés	entendías	entendiste	entenderás	entenderías	**entiendas**	entendieras *o* entendieses	**entiende**/entendé
	Ud., él, ella	**entiende**	entendía	entendió	entenderá	entendería	**entienda**	entendiera *o* entendiese	**entienda**
	nosotros/as	entendemos	entendíamos	entendimos	entenderemos	entenderíamos	**entendamos**	entendiéramos *o* entendiésemos	**entendamos**
	vosotros/as	entendéis	entendíais	entendisteis	entenderéis	entenderíais	entendáis	entendierais *o* entendieseis	entended
	Uds., ellos/as	**entienden**	entendían	entendieron	entenderán	entenderían	**entiendan**	entendieran *o* entendiesen	**entiendan**
29 enviar (3) (i:í) enviando enviado	yo	**envío**	enviaba	envié	enviaré	enviaría	**envíe**	enviara *o* enviase	
	tú/vos	**envías**/enviás	enviabas	enviaste	enviarás	enviarías	**envíes**	enviaras *o* enviases	**envía**/enviá
	Ud., él, ella	**envía**	enviaba	envió	enviará	enviaría	**envíe**	enviara *o* enviase	**envíe**
	nosotros/as	enviamos	enviábamos	enviamos	enviaremos	enviaríamos	enviemos	enviáramos *o* enviásemos	enviemos
	vosotros/as	enviáis	enviabais	enviasteis	enviaréis	enviaríais	enviéis	enviarais *o* enviaseis	enviad
	Uds., ellos/as	**envían**	enviaban	enviaron	enviarán	enviarían	**envíen**	enviaran *o* enviasen	**envíen**
30 erguir (4) **irguiendo** erguido	yo	**irgo** *o* **yergo**	erguía	erguí	erguiré	erguiría	**irga** *o* **yerga**	**irguiera** *o* **irguiese**	
	tú/vos	**irgues** *o* **yergues**/erguís	erguías	erguiste	erguirás	erguirías	**irgas** *o* **yergas**	**irguieras** *o* **irguieses**	**irgue** *o* **yergue**/ erguí
	Ud., él, ella	**irgue** *o* **yergue**	erguía	**irguió**	erguirá	erguiría	**irga** *o* **yerga**	**irguiera** *o* **irguiese**	**irga** *o* **yerga**
	nosotros/as	erguimos	erguíamos	erguimos	erguiremos	erguiríamos	**irgamos** *o* **yergamos**	**irguiéramos** *o* **irguiésemos**	**irgamos** *o* **yergamos**
	vosotros/as	erguís	erguíais	erguisteis	erguiréis	erguiríais	irgáis *o* yergáis	irguierais *o* irguieseis	erguid
	Uds., ellos/as	**irguen** *o* **yerguen**	erguían	**irguieron**	erguirán	erguirían	**irgan** *o* **yergan**	**irguieran** *o* **irguiesen**	**irgan** *o* **yergan**

Verb conjugation tables

Infinitivo / Gerundio / Participio	Pronombres personales	INDICATIVO Presente	Pretérito imperfecto	Pretérito perfecto simple	Futuro simple	Condicional simple	SUBJUNTIVO Presente	Pretérito imperfecto	IMPERATIVO
31 errar (4) (y) / errando / errado	yo	**yerro** o erro	erraba	erré	erraré	erraría	**yerre** o erre	errara o errase	
	tú/vos	**yerras** o erras/errás	errabas	erraste	errarás	errarías	**yerres** o erres	erraras o errases	**yerra** o erra/errá
	Ud., él, ella	**yerra** o erra	erraba	erró	errará	erraría	**yerre** o erre	errara o errase	**yerre** o erre
	nosotros/as	erramos	errábamos	erramos	erraremos	erraríamos	erremos	erráramos o errásemos	erremos
	vosotros/as	erráis	errabais	errasteis	erraréis	erraríais	erréis	errarais o erraseis	errad
	Uds., ellos/as	**yerran** o erran	erraban	erraron	errarán	errarían	**yerren** o erren	erraran o errasen	**yerren** o erren
32 esparcir (2) (c:z) / esparciendo / esparcido	yo	**esparzo**	esparcía	esparcí	esparciré	esparciría	**esparza**	esparciera o esparciese	
	tú/vos	esparces/esparcís	esparcías	esparciste	esparcirás	esparcirías	**esparzas**	esparcieras o esparcieses	esparce/esparcí
	Ud., él, ella	esparce	esparcía	esparció	esparcirá	esparciría	**esparza**	esparciera o esparciese	**esparza**
	nosotros/as	esparcimos	esparcíamos	esparcimos	esparciremos	esparciríamos	**esparzamos**	esparciéramos o esparciésemos	**esparzamos**
	vosotros/as	esparcís	esparcíais	esparcisteis	esparciréis	esparciríais	**esparzáis**	esparcierais o esparcieseis	esparcid
	Uds., ellos/as	esparcen	esparcían	esparcieron	esparcirán	esparcirían	**esparzan**	esparcieran o esparciesen	**esparzan**
33 estar (4) / estando / estado	yo	**estoy**	estaba	**estuve**	estaré	estaría	**esté**	**estuviera** o **estuviese**	
	tú/vos	**estás**	estabas	**estuviste**	estarás	estarías	**estés**	**estuvieras** o **estuvieses**	**está**
	Ud., él, ella	**está**	estaba	**estuvo**	estará	estaría	**esté**	**estuviera** o **estuviese**	**esté**
	nosotros/as	estamos	estábamos	**estuvimos**	estaremos	estaríamos	estemos	**estuviéramos** o **estuviésemos**	estemos
	vosotros/as	estáis	estabais	**estuvisteis**	estaréis	estaríais	estéis	**estuvierais** o **estuvieseis**	estad
	Uds., ellos/as	**están**	estaban	**estuvieron**	estarán	estarían	**estén**	**estuvieran** o **estuviesen**	**estén**
34 europeizar (2, 3) (z:c) (i:í) / europeizando / europeizado	yo	**europeizo**	europeizaba	**europeicé**	europeizaré	europeizaría	**europeice**	europeizara o europeizase	
	tú/vos	**europeizas/** europeizás	europeizabas	europeizaste	europeizarás	europeizarías	**europeices**	europeizaras o europeizases	**europeiza/** europeizá
	Ud., él, ella	**europeiza**	europeizaba	europeizó	europeizará	europeizaría	**europeice**	europeizara o europeizase	**europeice**
	nosotros/as	europeizamos	europeizábamos	europeizamos	europeizaremos	europeizaríamos	**europeicemos**	europeizáramos o europeizásemos	**europeicemos**
	vosotros/as	europeizáis	europeizabais	europeizasteis	europeizaréis	europeizaríais	**europeicéis**	europeizarais o europeizaseis	europeizad
	Uds., ellos/as	**europeizan**	europeizaban	europeizaron	europeizarán	europeizarían	**europeicen**	europeizaran o europeizasen	**europeicen**
35 exigir (2) (g:j) / exigiendo / exigido	yo	**exijo**	exigía	exigí	exigiré	exigiría	**exija**	exigiera o exigiese	
	tú/vos	exiges/exigís	exigías	exigiste	exigirás	exigirías	**exijas**	exigieras o exigieses	exige/exigí
	Ud., él, ella	exige	exigía	exigió	exigirá	exigiría	**exija**	exigiera o exigiese	**exija**
	nosotros/as	exigimos	exigíamos	exigimos	exigiremos	exigiríamos	**exijamos**	exigiéramos o exigiésemos	**exijamos**
	vosotros/as	exigís	exigíais	exigisteis	exigiréis	exigiríais	**exijáis**	exigierais o exigieseis	exigid
	Uds., ellos/as	exigen	exigían	exigieron	exigirán	exigirían	**exijan**	exigieran o exigiesen	**exijan**
36 extinguir (2) (gu:g) / extinguiendo / extinguido	yo	**extingo**	extinguía	extinguí	extinguiré	extinguiría	**extinga**	extinguiera o extinguiese	
	tú/vos	extingues/ extinguís	extinguías	extinguiste	extinguirás	extinguirías	**extingas**	extinguieras o extinguieses	extingue/ extinguí
	Ud., él, ella	extingue	extinguía	extinguió	extinguirá	extinguiría	**extinga**	extinguiera o extinguiese	**extinga**
	nosotros/as	extinguimos	extinguíamos	extinguimos	extinguiremos	extinguiríamos	**extingamos**	extinguiéramos o extinguiésemos	**extingamos**
	vosotros/as	extinguís	extinguíais	extinguisteis	extinguiréis	extinguiríais	**extingáis**	extinguierais o extinguieseis	extinguid
	Uds., ellos/as	extinguen	extinguían	extinguieron	extinguirán	extinguirían	**extingan**	extinguieran o extinguiesen	**extingan**

Infinitivo / Gerundio / Participio	Pronombres personales	INDICATIVO Presente	Pretérito imperfecto	Pretérito perfecto simple	Futuro simple	Condicional simple	SUBJUNTIVO Presente	Pretérito imperfecto	IMPERATIVO
37 graduar [3] (u:ú)	yo	**gradúo**	graduaba	gradué	graduaré	graduaría	**gradúe**	graduara o graduase	
	tú/vos	**gradúas/graduás**	graduabas	graduaste	graduarás	graduarías	**gradúes**	graduaras o graduases	**gradúa/graduá**
	Ud., él, ella	**gradúa**	graduaba	graduó	graduará	graduaría	**gradúe**	graduara o graduase	**gradúe**
graduando	nosotros/as	graduamos	graduábamos	graduamos	graduaremos	graduaríamos	graduemos	graduáramos o graduásemos	graduemos
graduado	vosotros/as	graduáis	graduabais	graduasteis	graduaréis	graduaríais	graduéis	graduarais o graduaseis	graduad
	Uds., ellos/as	**gradúan**	graduaban	graduaron	graduarán	graduarían	**gradúen**	graduaran o graduasen	**gradúen**
38 haber [4]	yo	**he**	había	**hube**	**habré**	**habría**	**haya**	**hubiera** o **hubiese**	
	tú/vos	**has**	habías	**hubiste**	**habrás**	**habrías**	**hayas**	**hubieras** o **hubieses**	
	Ud., él, ella	**ha**	había	**hubo**	**habrá**	**habría**	**haya**	**hubiera** o **hubiese**	
habiendo	nosotros/as	**hemos**	habíamos	**hubimos**	**habremos**	**habríamos**	**hayamos**	**hubiéramos** o **hubiésemos**	
habido	vosotros/as	habéis	habíais	**hubisteis**	**habréis**	**habríais**	hayáis	**hubierais** o **hubieseis**	
	Uds., ellos/as	**han**	habían	**hubieron**	**habrán**	**habrían**	**hayan**	**hubieran** o **hubiesen**	
39 hacer [4]	yo	**hago**	hacía	**hice**	**haré**	**haría**	**haga**	**hiciera** o **hiciese**	
	tú/vos	haces/hacés	hacías	**hiciste**	**harás**	**harías**	**hagas**	**hicieras** o **hicieses**	**haz/hacé**
	Ud., él, ella	hace	hacía	**hizo**	**hará**	**haría**	**haga**	**hiciera** o **hiciese**	**haga**
haciendo	nosotros/as	hacemos	hacíamos	**hicimos**	**haremos**	**haríamos**	**hagamos**	**hiciéramos** o **hiciésemos**	**hagamos**
hecho	vosotros/as	hacéis	hacíais	**hicisteis**	**haréis**	**haríais**	**hagáis**	**hicierais** o **hicieseis**	haced
	Uds., ellos/as	hacen	hacían	**hicieron**	**harán**	**harían**	**hagan**	**hicieran** o **hiciesen**	**hagan**
40 ir [4]	yo	**voy**	iba	**fui**	iré	iría	**vaya**	**fuera** o **fuese**	
	tú/vos	**vas**	ibas	**fuiste**	irás	irías	**vayas**	**fueras** o **fueses**	**ve/andá**
	Ud., él, ella	**va**	iba	**fue**	irá	iría	**vaya**	**fuera** o **fuese**	**vaya**
yendo	nosotros/as	**vamos**	**íbamos**	**fuimos**	iremos	iríamos	**vayamos**	**fuéramos** o **fuésemos**	**vamos**
ido	vosotros/as	**vais**	ibais	**fuisteis**	iréis	iríais	**vayáis**	**fuerais** o **fueseis**	**id**
	Uds., ellos/as	**van**	iban	**fueron**	irán	irían	**vayan**	**fueran** o **fuesen**	**vayan**
41 jugar [1,2] (u:ue) (g:gu)	yo	**juego**	jugaba	**jugué**	jugaré	jugaría	**juegue**	jugara o jugase	
	tú/vos	**juegas/jugás**	jugabas	jugaste	jugarás	jugarías	**juegues**	jugaras o jugases	**juega/jugá**
	Ud., él, ella	**juega**	jugaba	jugó	jugará	jugaría	**juegue**	jugara o jugase	**juegue**
jugando	nosotros/as	jugamos	jugábamos	jugamos	jugaremos	jugaríamos	**juguemos**	jugáramos o jugásemos	**juguemos**
jugado	vosotros/as	jugáis	jugabais	jugasteis	jugaréis	jugaríais	**juguéis**	jugarais o jugaseis	jugad
	Uds., ellos/as	**juegan**	jugaban	jugaron	jugarán	jugarían	**jueguen**	jugaran o jugasen	**jueguen**
42 llegar [2] (g:gu)	yo	llego	llegaba	**llegué**	llegaré	llegaría	**llegue**	llegara o llegase	
	tú/vos	llegas/llegás	llegabas	llegaste	llegarás	llegarías	**llegues**	llegaras o llegases	llega/llegá
	Ud., él, ella	llega	llegaba	llegó	llegará	llegaría	**llegue**	llegara o llegase	**llegue**
llegando	nosotros/as	llegamos	llegábamos	llegamos	llegaremos	llegaríamos	**lleguemos**	llegáramos o llegásemos	**lleguemos**
llegado	vosotros/as	llegáis	llegabais	llegasteis	llegaréis	llegaríais	**lleguéis**	llegarais o llegaseis	llegad
	Uds., ellos/as	llegan	llegaban	llegaron	llegarán	llegarían	**lleguen**	llegaran o llegasen	**lleguen**

Infinitivo / Gerundio / Participio	Pronombres personales	INDICATIVO Presente	Pretérito imperfecto	Pretérito perfecto simple	Futuro simple	Condicional simple	SUBJUNTIVO Presente	Pretérito imperfecto	IMPERATIVO
43 lucir [1] (c:zc) luciendo lucido	yo	**luzco**	lucía	lucí	luciré	luciría	**luzca**	luciera o luciese	
	tú/vos	luces/lucís	lucías	luciste	lucirás	lucirías	**luzcas**	lucieras o lucieses	luce/lucí
	Ud., él, ella	luce	lucía	lució	lucirá	luciría	**luzca**	luciera o luciese	**luzca**
	nosotros/as	lucimos	lucíamos	lucimos	luciremos	luciríamos	**luzcamos**	luciéramos o luciésemos	**luzcamos**
	vosotros/as	lucís	lucíais	lucisteis	luciréis	luciríais	**luzcáis**	lucierais o lucieseis	lucid
	Uds., ellos/as	lucen	lucían	lucieron	lucirán	lucirían	**luzcan**	lucieran o luciesen	**luzcan**
44 mover [1] (o:ue) moviendo movido	yo	**muevo**	movía	moví	moveré	movería	**mueva**	moviera o moviese	
	tú/vos	**mueves**/movés	movías	moviste	moverás	moverías	**muevas**	movieras o movieses	**mueve**/mové
	Ud., él, ella	**mueve**	movía	movió	moverá	movería	**mueva**	moviera o moviese	**mueva**
	nosotros/as	movemos	movíamos	movimos	moveremos	moveríamos	movamos	moviéramos o moviésemos	movamos
	vosotros/as	movéis	movíais	movisteis	moveréis	moveríais	mováis	movierais o movieseis	moved
	Uds., ellos/as	**mueven**	movían	movieron	moverán	moverían	**muevan**	movieran o moviesen	**muevan**
45 negar [1, 2] (e:ie) (g:gu) negando negado	yo	**niego**	negaba	**negué**	negaré	negaría	**niegue**	negara o negase	
	tú/vos	**niegas**/negás	negabas	negaste	negarás	negarías	**niegues**	negaras o negases	**niega**/negá
	Ud., él, ella	**niega**	negaba	negó	negará	negaría	**niegue**	negara o negase	**niegue**
	nosotros/as	negamos	negábamos	negamos	negaremos	negaríamos	**neguemos**	negáramos o negásemos	**neguemos**
	vosotros/as	negáis	negabais	negasteis	negaréis	negaríais	**neguéis**	negarais o negaseis	negad
	Uds., ellos/as	**niegan**	negaban	negaron	negarán	negarían	**nieguen**	negaran o negasen	**nieguen**
46 oír [3, 4] (y) oyendo oído	yo	**oigo**	oía	oí	oiré	oiría	**oiga**	**oyera** u **oyese**	
	tú/vos	**oyes**/oís	oías	**oíste**	oirás	oirías	**oigas**	**oyeras** u **oyeses**	**oye**/oí
	Ud., él, ella	**oye**	oía	**oyó**	oirá	oiría	**oiga**	**oyera** u **oyese**	**oiga**
	nosotros/as	**oímos**	oíamos	**oímos**	oiremos	oiríamos	**oigamos**	**oyéramos** u **oyésemos**	**oigamos**
	vosotros/as	oís	oíais	**oísteis**	oiréis	oiríais	**oigáis**	**oyerais** u **oyeseis**	**oíd**
	Uds., ellos/as	**oyen**	oían	**oyeron**	oirán	oirían	**oigan**	**oyeran** u **oyesen**	**oigan**
47 oler [1] (o:hue) oliendo olido	yo	**huelo**	olía	olí	oleré	olería	**huela**	oliera u oliese	
	tú/vos	**hueles**/olés	olías	oliste	olerás	olerías	**huelas**	olieras u olieses	**huele**/olé
	Ud., él, ella	**huele**	olía	olió	olerá	olería	**huela**	oliera u oliese	**huela**
	nosotros/as	olemos	olíamos	olimos	oleremos	oleríamos	olamos	oliéramos u oliésemos	olamos
	vosotros/as	oléis	olíais	olisteis	oleréis	oleríais	oláis	olierais u olieseis	oled
	Uds., ellos/as	**huelen**	olían	olieron	olerán	olerían	**huelan**	olieran u oliesen	**huelan**
48 pedir [1] (e:i) pidiendo pedido	yo	**pido**	pedía	pedí	pediré	pediría	**pida**	**pidiera** o **pidiese**	
	tú/vos	**pides**/pedís	pedías	pediste	pedirás	pedirías	**pidas**	**pidieras** o **pidieses**	**pide**/pedí
	Ud., él, ella	**pide**	pedía	**pidió**	pedirá	pediría	**pida**	**pidiera** o **pidiese**	**pida**
	nosotros/as	pedimos	pedíamos	pedimos	pediremos	pediríamos	**pidamos**	**pidiéramos** o **pidiésemos**	**pidamos**
	vosotros/as	pedís	pedíais	pedisteis	pediréis	pediríais	**pidáis**	**pidierais** o **pidieseis**	pedid
	Uds., ellos/as	**piden**	pedían	**pidieron**	pedirán	pedirían	**pidan**	**pidieran** o **pidiesen**	**pidan**

Verb conjugation tables

Infinitivo / Gerundio Participio	Pronombres personales	INDICATIVO Presente	Pretérito imperfecto	Pretérito perfecto simple	Futuro simple	Condicional simple	SUBJUNTIVO Presente	Pretérito imperfecto	IMPERATIVO
49 pensar (1) (e:ie)	yo	**pienso**	pensaba	pensé	pensaré	pensaría	**piense**	pensara o pensase	
	tú/vos	**piensas**/pensás	pensabas	pensaste	pensarás	pensarías	**pienses**	pensaras o pensases	**piensa**/pensá
	Ud., él, ella	**piensa**	pensaba	pensó	pensará	pensaría	**piense**	pensara o pensase	**piense**
pensando	nosotros/as	pensamos	pensábamos	pensamos	pensaremos	pensaríamos	pensemos	pensáramos o pensásemos	pensemos
pensado	vosotros/as	pensáis	pensabais	pensasteis	pensaréis	pensaríais	penséis	pensarais o pensaseis	pensad
	Uds., ellos/as	**piensan**	pensaban	pensaron	pensarán	pensarían	**piensen**	pensaran o pensasen	**piensen**
50 poder (1,4) (o:ue)	yo	**puedo**	podía	**pude**	**podré**	**podría**	**pueda**	**pudiera** o **pudiese**	
	tú/vos	**puedes**/podés	podías	**pudiste**	**podrás**	**podrías**	**puedas**	**pudieras** o **pudieses**	**puede**/podé
	Ud., él, ella	**puede**	podía	**pudo**	**podrá**	**podría**	**pueda**	**pudiera** o **pudiese**	**pueda**
pudiendo	nosotros/as	podemos	podíamos	**pudimos**	**podremos**	**podríamos**	podamos	**pudiéramos** o **pudiésemos**	podamos
podido	vosotros/as	podéis	podíais	**pudisteis**	**podréis**	**podríais**	podáis	**pudierais** o **pudieseis**	poded
	Uds., ellos/as	**pueden**	podían	**pudieron**	**podrán**	**podrían**	**puedan**	**pudieran** o **pudiesen**	**puedan**
51 poner (4)	yo	**pongo**	ponía	**puse**	**pondré**	**pondría**	**ponga**	**pusiera** o **pusiese**	
	tú/vos	pones/ponés	ponías	**pusiste**	**pondrás**	**pondrías**	**pongas**	**pusieras** o **pusieses**	**pon**/poné
	Ud., él, ella	pone	ponía	**puso**	**pondrá**	**pondría**	**ponga**	**pusiera** o **pusiese**	**ponga**
poniendo	nosotros/as	ponemos	poníamos	**pusimos**	**pondremos**	**pondríamos**	**pongamos**	**pusiéramos** o **pusiésemos**	**pongamos**
puesto	vosotros/as	ponéis	poníais	**pusisteis**	**pondréis**	**pondríais**	**pongáis**	**pusierais** o **pusieseis**	poned
	Uds., ellos/as	ponen	ponían	**pusieron**	**pondrán**	**pondrían**	**pongan**	**pusieran** o **pusiesen**	**pongan**
52 predecir (1,4) (e:i)	yo	**predigo**	predecía	**predije**	**predeciré** o **prediré**	predeciría o **prediría**	**prediga**	**predijera** o **predijese**	
	tú/vos	**predices**/predecís	predecías	**predijiste**	**predecirás** o **predirás**	predecirías o **predirías**	**predigas**	**predijeras** o **predijeses**	**predice**/predecí
	Ud., él, ella	**predice**	predecía	**predijo**	**predecirá** o **predirá**	predeciría o **prediría**	**prediga**	**predijera** o **predijese**	**prediga**
prediciendo	nosotros/as	predecimos	predecíamos	**predijimos**	**predeciremos** o **prediremos**	predeciríamos o **prediríamos**	**predigamos**	**predijéramos** o **predijésemos**	**predigamos**
predicho	vosotros/as	predecís	predecíais	**predijisteis**	**predeciréis** o **prediréis**	predeciríais o **prediríais**	**predigáis**	**predijerais** o **predijeseis**	predecid
	Uds., ellos/as	**predicen**	predecían	**predijeron**	**predecirán** o **predirán**	predecirían o **predirían**	**predigan**	**predijeran** o **predijesen**	**predigan**
53 prohibir (3) (i:í)	yo	**prohíbo**	prohibía	prohibí	prohibiré	prohibiría	**prohíba**	prohibiera o prohibiese	
	tú/vos	**prohíbes**/prohibís	prohibías	prohibiste	prohibirás	prohibirías	**prohíbas**	prohibieras o prohibieses	**prohíbe**/prohibís
	Ud., él, ella	**prohíbe**	prohibía	prohibió	prohibirá	prohibiría	**prohíba**	prohibiera o prohibiese	**prohíba**
prohibiendo	nosotros/as	prohibimos	prohibíamos	prohibimos	prohibiremos	prohibiríamos	prohibamos	prohibiéramos o prohibiésemos	prohibamos
prohibido	vosotros/as	prohibís	prohibíais	prohibisteis	prohibiréis	prohibiríais	prohibáis	prohibierais o prohibieseis	prohibid
	Uds., ellos/as	**prohíben**	prohibían	prohibieron	prohibirán	prohibirían	**prohíban**	prohibieran o prohibiesen	**prohíban**

Infinitivo / Gerundio / Participio	Pronombres personales	INDICATIVO Presente	Pretérito imperfecto	Pretérito perfecto simple	Futuro simple	Condicional simple	SUBJUNTIVO Presente	Pretérito imperfecto	IMPERATIVO
54 proteger (2) (g:j) / protegiendo / protegido	yo	**protejo**	protegía	protegí	protegeré	protegería	**proteja**	protegiera o protegiese	
	tú/vos	proteges/protegés	protegías	protegiste	protegerás	protegerías	**protejas**	protegieras o protegieses	protege/protegé
	Ud., él, ella	protege	protegía	protegió	protegerá	protegería	**proteja**	protegiera o protegiese	**proteja**
	nosotros/as	protegemos	protegíamos	protegimos	protegeremos	protegeríamos	**protejamos**	protegiéramos o protegiésemos	**protejamos**
	vosotros/as	protegéis	protegíais	protegisteis	protegeréis	protegeríais	**protejáis**	protegierais o protegieseis	proteged
	Uds., ellos/as	protegen	protegían	protegieron	protegerán	protegerían	**protejan**	protegieran o protegiesen	**protejan**
55 pudrir/podrir (4) / pudriendo / podrido	yo	pudro	pudría o podría	pudrí o podrí	pudriré o podriré	pudriría o podriría	pudra	pudriera o pudriese	
	tú/vos	pudres/pudrís	pudrías o podrías	pudriste o podriste	pudrirás o podrirás	pudrirías o podrirías	pudras	pudrieras o pudrieses	pudre/pudrí o podrí
	Ud., él, ella	pudre	pudría o podría	pudrió o podrió	pudrirá o podrirá	pudriría o podriría	pudra	pudriera o pudriese	pudra
	nosotros/as	pudrimos o podrimos	pudríamos o podríamos	pudrimos o podrimos	pudriremos o podriremos	pudriríamos o podriríamos	pudramos	pudriéramos o pudriésemos	pudramos
	vosotros/as	pudrís o podrís	pudríais o podríais	pudristeis o podristeis	pudriréis o podriréis	pudriríais o podriríais	pudráis	pudrierais o pudrieseis	pudrid o podrid
	Uds., ellos/as	pudren	pudrían o podrían	pudrieron o podrieron	pudrirán o podrirán	pudrirían o podrirían	pudran	pudrieran o pudriesen	pudran
56 querer (1,4) (e:ie) / queriendo / querido	yo	**quiero**	quería	quise	querré	querría	**quiera**	quisiera o quisiese	
	tú/vos	quieres/querés	querías	quisiste	querrás	querrías	**quieras**	quisieras o quisieses	quiere/queré
	Ud., él, ella	quiere	quería	quiso	querrá	querría	**quiera**	quisiera o quisiese	**quiera**
	nosotros/as	queremos	queríamos	quisimos	querremos	querríamos	queramos	quisiéramos o quisiésemos	queramos
	vosotros/as	queréis	queríais	quisisteis	querréis	querríais	queráis	quisierais o quisieseis	quered
	Uds., ellos/as	quieren	querían	quisieron	querrán	querrían	quieran	quisieran o quisiesen	quieran
57 rehusar (3) (u:ú) / rehusando / rehusado	yo	**rehúso**	rehusaba	rehusé	rehusaré	rehusaría	**rehúse**	rehusara o rehusase	
	tú/vos	**rehúsas**/rehusás	rehusabas	rehusaste	rehusarás	rehusarías	**rehúses**	rehusaras o rehusases	**rehúsa**/rehusá
	Ud., él, ella	**rehúsa**	rehusaba	rehusó	rehusará	rehusaría	**rehúse**	rehusara o rehusase	**rehúse**
	nosotros/as	rehusamos	rehusábamos	rehusamos	rehusaremos	rehusaríamos	rehusemos	rehusáramos o rehusásemos	rehusemos
	vosotros/as	rehusáis	rehusabais	rehusasteis	rehusaréis	rehusaríais	rehuséis	rehusarais o rehusaseis	rehusad
	Uds., ellos/as	**rehúsan**	rehusaban	rehusaron	rehusarán	rehusarían	**rehúsen**	rehusaran o rehusasen	**rehúsen**
58 reír (1) (e:i) / riendo / reído	yo	**río**	reía	reí	reiré	reiría	**ría**	riera o riese	
	tú/vos	**ríes**/reís	reías	**reíste**	reirás	reirías	**rías**	rieras o rieses	ríe/reí
	Ud., él, ella	**ríe**	reía	**rio**	reirá	reiría	**ría**	riera o riese	ría
	nosotros/as	**reímos**	reíamos	**reímos**	reiremos	reiríamos	**riamos**	riéramos o riésemos	**riamos**
	vosotros/as	reís	reíais	**reísteis**	reiréis	reiríais	**riáis**	rierais o rieseis	reíd
	Uds., ellos/as	**ríen**	reían	**rieron**	reirán	reirían	**rían**	rieran o riesen	rían

Infinitivo / Gerundio / Participio	Pronombres personales	INDICATIVO					SUBJUNTIVO		IMPERATIVO
		Presente	Pretérito imperfecto	Pretérito perfecto simple	Futuro simple	Condicional simple	Presente	Pretérito imperfecto	
59 reunir [(3)] (u:ú) reuniendo reunido	yo	**reúno**	reunía	reuní	reuniré	reuniría	**reúna**	reuniera o reuniese	
	tú/vos	**reúnes**/reunís	reunías	reuniste	reunirás	reunirías	**reúnas**	reunieras o reunieses	**reúne**/reuní
	Ud., él, ella	**reúne**	reunía	reunió	reunirá	reuniría	**reúna**	reuniera o reuniese	**reúna**
	nosotros/as	reunimos	reuníamos	reunimos	reuniremos	reuniríamos	reunamos	reuniéramos o reuniésemos	reunamos
	vosotros/as	reunís	reuníais	reunisteis	reuniréis	reuniríais	reunáis	reunierais o reunieseis	reunid
	Uds., ellos/as	**reúnen**	reunían	reunieron	reunirán	reunirían	**reúnan**	reunieran o reuniesen	**reúnan**
60 roer [(3, 4)] (y) royendo roído	yo	roo o **roigo** o **royo**	roía	roí	roeré	roería	roa o **roiga** o **roya**	**royera** o **royese**	
	tú/vos	roes/roés	roías	**roíste**	roerás	roerías	roas o **roigas** o **royas**	**royeras** o **royeses**	roe/roé
	Ud., él, ella	roe	roía	**royó**	roerá	roería	roa o **roiga** o **roya**	**royera** o **royese**	roa o **roiga** o **roya**
	nosotros/as	roemos	roíamos	**roímos**	roeremos	roeríamos	roamos o **roigamos** o **royamos**	**royéramos** o **royésemos**	roamos o **roigamos** o **royamos**
	vosotros/as	roéis	roíais	**roísteis**	roeréis	roeríais	roáis o **roigáis** o **royáis**	**royerais** o **royeseis**	roed
	Uds., ellos/as	roen	roían	**royeron**	roerán	roerían	roan o **roigan** o **royan**	**royeran** o **royesen**	roan o **roigan** o **royan**
61 rogar [(1, 2)] (o:ue)(g:gu) rogando rogado	yo	**ruego**	rogaba	**rogué**	rogaré	rogaría	**ruegue**	rogara o rogase	
	tú/vos	**ruegas**/rogás	rogabas	rogaste	rogarás	rogarías	**ruegues**	rogaras o rogases	**ruega**/rogá
	Ud., él, ella	**ruega**	rogaba	rogó	rogará	rogaría	**ruegue**	rogara o rogase	**ruegue**
	nosotros/as	rogamos	rogábamos	rogamos	rogaremos	rogaríamos	**roguemos**	rogáramos o rogásemos	**roguemos**
	vosotros/as	rogáis	rogabais	rogasteis	rogaréis	rogaríais	**roguéis**	rogarais o rogaseis	rogad
	Uds., ellos/as	**ruegan**	rogaban	rogaron	rogarán	rogarían	**rueguen**	rogaran o rogasen	**rueguen**
62 saber [(4)] sabiendo sabido	yo	**sé**	sabía	**supe**	**sabré**	**sabría**	**sepa**	**supiera** o **supiese**	
	tú/vos	sabes/sabés	sabías	**supiste**	**sabrás**	**sabrías**	**sepas**	**supieras** o **supieses**	sabe/sabé
	Ud., él, ella	sabe	sabía	**supo**	**sabrá**	**sabría**	**sepa**	**supiera** o **supiese**	**sepa**
	nosotros/as	sabemos	sabíamos	**supimos**	**sabremos**	**sabríamos**	**sepamos**	**supiéramos** o **supiésemos**	**sepamos**
	vosotros/as	sabéis	sabíais	**supisteis**	**sabréis**	**sabríais**	**sepáis**	**supierais** o **supieseis**	sabed
	Uds., ellos/as	saben	sabían	**supieron**	**sabrán**	**sabrían**	**sepan**	**supieran** o **supiesen**	**sepan**
63 salir [(4)] saliendo salido	yo	**salgo**	salía	salí	**saldré**	**saldría**	**salga**	saliera o saliese	
	tú/vos	sales/salís	salías	saliste	**saldrás**	**saldrías**	**salgas**	salieras o salieses	**sal**/salí
	Ud., él, ella	sale	salía	salió	**saldrá**	**saldría**	**salga**	saliera o saliese	**salga**
	nosotros/as	salimos	salíamos	salimos	**saldremos**	**saldríamos**	**salgamos**	saliéramos o saliésemos	**salgamos**
	vosotros/as	salís	salíais	salisteis	**saldréis**	**saldríais**	**salgáis**	salierais o salieseis	salid
	Uds., ellos/as	salen	salían	salieron	**saldrán**	**saldrían**	**salgan**	salieran o saliesen	**salgan**

Infinitivo / Gerundio / Participio	Pronombres personales	INDICATIVO Presente	Pretérito imperfecto	Pretérito perfecto simple	Futuro simple	Condicional simple	SUBJUNTIVO Presente	Pretérito imperfecto	IMPERATIVO
64 seguir (1,2) (e:i) (gu:g) **siguiendo** seguido	yo	**sigo**	seguía	seguí	seguiré	seguiría	**siga**	**siguiera** o **siguiese**	
	tú/vos	**sigues/seguís**	seguías	seguiste	seguirás	seguirías	**sigas**	**siguieras** o **siguieses**	**sigue/seguí**
	Ud., él, ella	**sigue**	seguía	**siguió**	seguirá	seguiría	**siga**	**siguiera** o **siguiese**	**siga**
	nosotros/as	seguimos	seguíamos	seguimos	seguiremos	seguiríamos	**sigamos**	**siguiéramos** o **siguiésemos**	**sigamos**
	vosotros/as	seguís	seguíais	seguisteis	seguiréis	seguiríais	**sigáis**	**siguierais** o **siguieseis**	seguid
	Uds., ellos/as	**siguen**	seguían	**siguieron**	seguirán	seguirían	**sigan**	**siguieran** o **siguiesen**	**sigan**
65 sentir (1,4) (e:ie) **sintiendo** sentido	yo	**siento**	sentía	sentí	sentiré	sentiría	**sienta**	**sintiera** o **sintiese**	
	tú/vos	**sientes/sentís**	sentías	sentiste	sentirás	sentirías	**sientas**	**sintieras** o **sintieses**	**siente/sentí**
	Ud., él, ella	**siente**	sentía	**sintió**	sentirá	sentiría	**sienta**	**sintiera** o **sintiese**	**sienta**
	nosotros/as	sentimos	sentíamos	sentimos	sentiremos	sentiríamos	**sintamos**	**sintiéramos** o **sintiésemos**	**sintamos**
	vosotros/as	sentís	sentíais	sentisteis	sentiréis	sentiríais	**sintáis**	**sintierais** o **sintieseis**	sentid
	Uds., ellos/as	**sienten**	sentían	**sintieron**	sentirán	sentirían	**sientan**	**sintieran** o **sintiesen**	**sientan**
66 ser (4) siendo sido	yo	**soy**	**era**	**fui**	seré	sería	**sea**	**fuera** o **fuese**	
	tú/vos	**eres/sos**	**eras**	**fuiste**	serás	serías	**seas**	**fueras** o **fueses**	**sé**
	Ud., él, ella	**es**	**era**	**fue**	será	sería	**sea**	**fuera** o **fuese**	**sea**
	nosotros/as	**somos**	**éramos**	**fuimos**	seremos	seríamos	**seamos**	**fuéramos** o **fuésemos**	**seamos**
	vosotros/as	**sois**	**erais**	**fuisteis**	seréis	seríais	**seáis**	**fuerais** o **fueseis**	sed
	Uds., ellos/as	**son**	**eran**	**fueron**	serán	serían	**sean**	**fueran** o **fuesen**	**sean**
67 soler (1) (o:ue) soliendo solido	yo	**suelo**	solía	*soler is a			**suela**		
	tú/vos	**sueles/solés**	solías	defective verb			**suelas**		
	Ud., él, ella	**suele**	solía	(it does not			**suela**		
	nosotros/as	solemos	solíamos	exist in certain			solamos		
	vosotros/as	soléis	solíais	tenses)			soláis		
	Uds., ellos/as	**suelen**	solían				**suelan**		
68 tañer (4) **tañendo** tañido	yo	**taño**	tañía	tañí	tañeré	tañería	**taña**	**tañera** o **tañese**	
	tú/vos	**tañes/tañés**	tañías	tañiste	tañerás	tañerías	**tañas**	**tañeras** o **tañeses**	**tañe/tañé**
	Ud., él, ella	**tañe**	tañía	**tañó**	tañerá	tañería	**taña**	**tañera** o **tañese**	**taña**
	nosotros/as	**tañemos**	tañíamos	tañimos	tañeremos	tañeríamos	**tañamos**	**tañéramos** o **tañésemos**	**tañamos**
	vosotros/as	tañéis	tañíais	tañisteis	tañeréis	tañeríais	**tañáis**	**tañerais** o **tañeseis**	tañed
	Uds., ellos/as	**tañen**	tañían	**tañeron**	tañerán	tañerían	**tañan**	**tañeran** o **tañesen**	**tañan**
69 tener (1,4) (e:ie) teniendo tenido	yo	**tengo**	tenía	**tuve**	**tendré**	**tendría**	**tenga**	**tuviera** o **tuviese**	
	tú/vos	**tienes/tenés**	tenías	**tuviste**	**tendrás**	**tendrías**	**tengas**	**tuvieras** o **tuvieses**	**ten/tené**
	Ud., él, ella	**tiene**	tenía	**tuvo**	**tendrá**	**tendría**	**tenga**	**tuviera** o **tuviese**	**tenga**
	nosotros/as	tenemos	teníamos	**tuvimos**	**tendremos**	**tendríamos**	**tengamos**	**tuviéramos** o **tuviésemos**	**tengamos**
	vosotros/as	tenéis	teníais	**tuvisteis**	**tendréis**	**tendríais**	**tengáis**	**tuvierais** o **tuvieseis**	tened
	Uds., ellos/as	**tienen**	tenían	**tuvieron**	**tendrán**	**tendrían**	**tengan**	**tuvieran** o **tuviesen**	**tengan**

Infinitivo / Gerundio / Participio	Pronombres personales	INDICATIVO Presente	Pretérito imperfecto	Pretérito perfecto simple	Futuro simple	Condicional simple	SUBJUNTIVO Presente	Pretérito imperfecto	IMPERATIVO
70 teñir [1] (e:i) **tiñendo** teñido	yo	**tiño**	teñía	teñí	teñiré	teñiría	**tiña**	**tiñera** o **tiñese**	
	tú/vos	**tiñes**/teñís	teñías	teñiste	teñirás	teñirías	**tiñas**	**tiñeras** o **tiñeses**	**tiñe**/teñí
	Ud., él, ella	**tiñe**	teñía	**tiñó**	teñirá	teñiría	**tiña**	**tiñera** o **tiñese**	**tiña**
	nosotros/as	teñimos	teñíamos	teñimos	teñiremos	teñiríamos	**tiñamos**	**tiñéramos** o **tiñésemos**	**tiñamos**
	vosotros/as	teñís	teñíais	teñisteis	teñiréis	teñiríais	**tiñáis**	**tiñerais** o **tiñeseis**	teñid
	Uds., ellos/as	**tiñen**	teñían	**tiñeron**	teñirán	teñirían	**tiñan**	**tiñeran** o **tiñesen**	**tiñan**
71 tocar [2] (c:qu) tocando tocado	yo	toco	tocaba	**toqué**	tocaré	tocaría	**toque**	tocara o tocase	
	tú/vos	tocas/tocás	tocabas	tocaste	tocarás	tocarías	**toques**	tocaras o tocases	toca/tocá
	Ud., él, ella	toca	tocaba	tocó	tocará	tocaría	**toque**	tocara o tocase	**toque**
	nosotros/as	tocamos	tocábamos	tocamos	tocaremos	tocaríamos	**toquemos**	tocáramos o tocásemos	**toquemos**
	vosotros/as	tocáis	tocabais	tocasteis	tocaréis	tocaríais	**toquéis**	tocarais o tocaseis	tocad
	Uds., ellos/as	tocan	tocaban	tocaron	tocarán	tocarían	**toquen**	tocaran o tocasen	**toquen**
72 torcer [1,2] (o:ue) (c:z) torciendo torcido, **tuerto**	yo	**tuerzo**	torcía	torcí	torceré	torcería	**tuerza**	torciera o torciese	
	tú/vos	**tuerces**/torcés	torcías	torciste	torcerás	torcerías	**tuerzas**	torcieras o torcieses	**tuerce**/torcé
	Ud., él, ella	**tuerce**	torcía	torció	torcerá	torcería	**tuerza**	torciera o torciese	**tuerza**
	nosotros/as	torcemos	torcíamos	torcimos	torceremos	torceríamos	**torzamos**	torciéramos o torciésemos	**torzamos**
	vosotros/as	torcéis	torcíais	torcisteis	torceréis	torceríais	**torzáis**	torcierais o torcieseis	torced
	Uds., ellos/as	**tuercen**	torcían	torcieron	torcerán	torcerían	**tuerzan**	torcieran o torciesen	**tuerzan**
73 traer [4] **trayendo** traído	yo	**traigo**	traía	**traje**	traeré	traería	**traiga**	**trajera** o **trajese**	
	tú/vos	traes/traés	traías	**trajiste**	traerás	traerías	**traigas**	**trajeras** o **trajeses**	trae/traé
	Ud., él, ella	trae	traía	**trajo**	traerá	traería	**traiga**	**trajera** o **trajese**	**traiga**
	nosotros/as	traemos	traíamos	**trajimos**	traeremos	traeríamos	**traigamos**	**trajéramos** o **trajésemos**	**traigamos**
	vosotros/as	traéis	traíais	**trajisteis**	traeréis	traeríais	**traigáis**	**trajerais** o **trajeseis**	traed
	Uds., ellos/as	traen	traían	**trajeron**	traerán	traerían	**traigan**	**trajeran** o **trajesen**	**traigan**
74 valer [4] valiendo valido	yo	**valgo**	valía	valí	**valdré**	**valdría**	**valga**	valiera o valiese	
	tú/vos	vales/valés	valías	valiste	**valdrás**	**valdrías**	**valgas**	valieras o valieses	vale/valé
	Ud., él, ella	vale	valía	valió	**valdrá**	**valdría**	**valga**	valiera o valiese	**valga**
	nosotros/as	valemos	valíamos	valimos	**valdremos**	**valdríamos**	**valgamos**	valiéramos o valiésemos	**valgamos**
	vosotros/as	valéis	valíais	valisteis	**valdréis**	**valdríais**	**valgáis**	valierais o valieseis	valed
	Uds., ellos/as	valen	valían	valieron	**valdrán**	**valdrían**	**valgan**	valieran o valiesen	**valgan**
75 vencer [2] (c:z) venciendo vencido	yo	**venzo**	vencía	vencí	venceré	vencería	**venza**	venciera o venciese	
	tú/vos	vences/vencés	vencías	venciste	vencerás	vencerías	**venzas**	vencieras o vencieses	vence/vencé
	Ud., él, ella	vence	vencía	venció	vencerá	vencería	**venza**	venciera o venciese	**venza**
	nosotros/as	vencemos	vencíamos	vencimos	venceremos	venceríamos	**venzamos**	venciéramos o venciésemos	**venzamos**
	vosotros/as	vencéis	vencíais	vencisteis	venceréis	venceríais	**venzáis**	vencierais o vencieseis	venced
	Uds., ellos/as	vencen	vencían	vencieron	vencerán	vencerían	**venzan**	vencieran o venciesen	**venzan**

Infinitivo Gerundio Participio	Pronombres personales	INDICATIVO Presente	Pretérito imperfecto	Pretérito perfecto simple	Futuro simple	Condicional simple	SUBJUNTIVO Presente	Pretérito imperfecto	IMPERATIVO
76 **venir** (1,4) (e:ie) **viniendo** venido	yo	**vengo**	venía	**vine**	**vendré**	**vendría**	**venga**	**viniera** o **viniese**	
	tú/vos	**vienes**/venís	venías	**viniste**	**vendrás**	**vendrías**	**vengas**	**vinieras** o **vinieses**	**ven**/vení
	Ud., él, ella	**viene**	venía	**vino**	**vendrá**	**vendría**	**venga**	**viniera** o **viniese**	**venga**
	nosotros/as	venimos	veníamos	**vinimos**	**vendremos**	**vendríamos**	**vengamos**	**viniéramos** o **viniésemos**	**vengamos**
	vosotros/as	venís	veníais	**vinisteis**	**vendréis**	**vendríais**	**vengáis**	**vinierais** o **vinieseis**	venid
	Uds., ellos/as	**vienen**	venían	**vinieron**	**vendrán**	**vendrían**	**vengan**	**vinieran** o **viniesen**	**vengan**
77 **ver** (4) viendo **visto**	yo	**veo**	**veía**	**vi**	veré	vería	**vea**	viera o viese	
	tú/vos	ves	**veías**	viste	verás	verías	**veas**	vieras o vieses	ve
	Ud., él, ella	ve	**veía**	**vio**	verá	vería	**vea**	viera o viese	**vea**
	nosotros/as	vemos	**veíamos**	vimos	veremos	veríamos	**veamos**	viéramos o viésemos	**veamos**
	vosotros/as	**veis**	**veíais**	visteis	veréis	veríais	**veáis**	vierais o vieseis	ved
	Uds., ellos/as	ven	**veían**	vieron	verán	verían	**vean**	vieran o viesen	**vean**
78 **volcar** (1,2) (o:ue) (c:qu) volcando volcado	yo	**vuelco**	volcaba	**volqué**	volcaré	volcaría	**vuelque**	volcara o volcase	
	tú/vos	**vuelcas**/volcás	volcabas	volcaste	volcarás	volcarías	**vuelques**	volcaras o volcases	**vuelca**/volcá
	Ud., él, ella	**vuelca**	volcaba	volcó	volcará	volcaría	**vuelque**	volcara o volcase	**vuelque**
	nosotros/as	volcamos	volcábamos	volcamos	volcaremos	volcaríamos	**volquemos**	volcáramos o volcásemos	**volquemos**
	vosotros/as	volcáis	volcabais	volcasteis	volcaréis	volcaríais	**volquéis**	volcarais o volcaseis	volcad
	Uds., ellos/as	**vuelcan**	volcaban	volcaron	volcarán	volcarían	**vuelquen**	volcaran o volcasen	**vuelquen**
79 **yacer** (4) yaciendo yacido	yo	**yazco** o **yazgo** o **yago**	yacía	yací	yaceré	yacería	**yazca** o **yazga** o **yaga**	yaciera o yaciese	
	tú/vos	yaces/yacés	yacías	yaciste	yacerás	yacerías	**yazcas** o **yazgas** o **yagas**	yacieras o yacieses	**yace** o **yaz**/yacé
	Ud., él, ella	yace	yacía	yació	yacerá	yacería	**yazca** o **yazga** o **yaga**	yaciera o yaciese	**yazca** o **yazga** o **yaga**
	nosotros/as	yacemos	yacíamos	yacimos	yaceremos	yaceríamos	**yazcamos** o **yazgamos** o **yagamos**	yaciéramos o yaciésemos	**yazcamos** o **yazgamos** o **yagamos**
	vosotros/as	yacéis	yacíais	yacisteis	yaceréis	yaceríais	**yazcáis** o **yazgáis** o **yagáis**	yacierais o yacieseis	yaced
	Uds., ellos/as	yacen	yacían	yacieron	yacerán	yacerían	**yazcan** o **yazgan** o **yagan**	yacieran o yaciesen	**yazcan** o **yazgan** o **yagan**
80 **zambullir** (4) **zambullendo** zambullido	yo	zambullo	zambullía	zambullí	zambulliré	zambulliría	zambulla	**zambullera** o **zambullese**	zambulle/ zambullí
	tú/vos	zambulles/ zambullís	zambullías	zambulliste	zambullirás	zambullirías	zambullas	**zambulleras** o **zambulleses**	zambulla
	Ud., él, ella	zambulle	zambullía	**zambulló**	zambullirá	zambulliría	zambulla	**zambullera** o **zambullese**	zambulla
	nosotros/as	zambullimos	zambullíamos	zambullimos	zambulliremos	zambulliríamos	zambullamos	**zambulléramos** o **zambullésemos**	zambullamos
	vosotros/as	zambullís	zambullíais	zambullisteis	zambulliréis	zambulliríais	zambulláis	**zambullerais** o **zambulleseis**	zambullid
	Uds., ellos/as	zambullen	zambullían	**zambulleron**	zambullirán	zambullirían	zambullan	**zambulleran** o **zambullesen**	zambullan

El voseo en América Latina

México
Cuba
Honduras
Guatemala
El Salvador
Nicaragua
Costa Rica
Panamá
Venezuela
Colombia
Ecuádor
Perú
Bolivia
Paraguay
Chile
Argentina
Uruguay

N
W E
S

SCALE
0   500   1000 Miles
0   500   1000 Kilometers

Quesada Pacheco, Miguel Ángel (2002):
"El Español de América". San José, Costa Rica,
Editorial Tecnológica de Costa Rica, p.106.

Glosario combinatorio

In English, you can see somebody *in the flesh*, while in Spanish, you can see someone **en carne y hueso** (lit. *in flesh and bone*). In English, you are *fed up **with** something or someone* and in Spanish, you can be **harto *de* algo o alguien**. This glossary provides a sample of word combinations like these, which will help expand your vocabulary by giving a glimpse of the common, established word combinations that native speakers use. It will also help you with your grammar by showing that certain verbs take different prepositions from the ones used in English, or that no preposition is needed at all.

These types of word combinations are commonly called *collocations*. Not all word combinations are considered collocations. Many are free combinations with countless options. For example, the phrase **un hermano joven** is a free combination. The adjective, **joven**, can be used together with countless nouns (**un niño joven, una muchacha joven, un profesor joven, una estudiante joven,** etc.). **Un hermano gemelo**, on the other hand, is a collocation. The use of the adjective **gemelo** is restricted to a limited number of nouns.

Lexical collocations usually involve nouns, adjectives, adverbs, and verbs. *Grammatical* collocations usually involve a main word and a preposition or a dependent clause.

Compare these other examples. You can look up these collocations in the glossary!

Free combinations	Collocations
caer en un pozo, caerse en la calle	caer en la cuenta
surtir gasolina, surtir un medicamento	surtir efecto
va al cine, va a la escuela	va de veras

Compare these Spanish and English collocations:

Spanish collocations	English collocations
fuego lento	*low heat*
trabajar **en** algo	*to work **on** something*
hacer la vista gorda	*to turn a blind eye*

How to find collocations in this glossary

Follow these simple rules:

- If there is a noun, look under the noun.
- If there are two nouns, look under the first.
- If there is no noun, look under the adjective.
- If there is no adjective, look under the verb.

In addition, common expressions that are introduced by prepositions are also cross-listed under the preposition.

Abbreviations

adj.	adjective	*f.*	feminine noun	*p.p.*	past participle
adv.	adverb	*fam.*	familiar	*prep.*	preposition
algn	alguien	*form.*	formal	*pron.*	pronoun
Am. L.	Latin America	*m.*	masculine noun	sb	somebody
Arg.	Argentina	*Méx.*	Mexico	sth	something
Esp.	Spain	*pl.*	plural	*v.*	verb

a *prep.* to, at

a altas horas de la madrugada/noche in the wee/small hours of the morning/night

a base de with/of; on the basis of (Esto está hecho a base de verduras.)

a bordo de onboard

a caballo on horseback

a cada rato every so often/often

a cámara lenta in slow motion

a cambio de algo in return for sth

a cargo de, al cargo de in charge of

a causa de because of

a ciegas blindly

a ciencia cierta for sure

a como dé lugar, ~ como diera lugar however possible

a costa de at the expense of (No veo la gracia de reírse a costa de los demás.)

a cucharadas by the spoonful

a cuenta on account

a dieta on a diet

a escondidas secretly, behind sb's back

a eso de around

a este fin, ~ tal fin with this aim

a falta de lacking/for lack of (A falta de un problema, ¡tenemos diez!)

a fin de with the purpose of

a fin de cuentas, al final de cuentas, al fin y al cabo after all

a fondo in depth

a fuego lento on/at/over low heat

a fuerza de by virtue of/because of

a futuro in the future (Deberíamos evaluar los proyectos a futuro.)

a gusto at ease/at home/comfortable (No me siento a gusto aquí.)

a gusto del consumidor *fam.* however you like

a la carrera, ~ las carreras in a hurry

a la derecha (de) to/on the right (Gira a la derecha. Da un paso a la derecha, por favor.)

a la fuerza by force

a la hora de when it is time to (A la hora de escribir, prefiero hacerlo en un lugar tranquilo.)

a la izquierda (de) to/on the left (Si miran a la izquierda, verán uno de los mayores atractivos de la ciudad. María está a la izquierda de Juana.)

a la larga in the long run (Estoy segura de que Pedro, a la larga, comprenderá que es por su bien.)

a la manera de algn sb's way (Hagámoslo a mi manera.)

a la primera de cambio at the first opportunity

a la sombra de in the shadow of

a la vez at the same time

a la vista in sight, on view

a las mil maravillas wonderfully (¡Todo salió a las mil maravillas!)

a lo grande luxuriously, in style (Festejaremos tu cumpleaños a lo grande.)

a lo largo de throughout

a lo loco in a crazy way (Está gastando el dinero a lo loco.)

a lo mejor probably, likely

a los efectos de algo in order to do sth

a manera de algo by way of / as (Traje este dibujo a manera de ejemplo.)

a mano by hand

a (la) mano close at hand (¿Tienes tu planilla a (la) mano?)

a más tardar at the very latest

a mediados de in mid-/by mid- (Voy a retirar las cosas que faltan a mediados del mes que viene.)

a medias halfway/half

a medida que as/when/only (Resolveremos los problemas a medida que vayan surgiendo.)

a menos que unless

a menudo often

a modo de by way of, as (Usó su cuaderno a modo de pantalla.)

a no ser que if not

a nombre de algn addressed to sb

a oscuras in the dark

a partir de from, starting from

a pesar de in spite of

a pie on foot

a poco de algo shortly after sth

a por *Esp.* to go and get (Iré a por ti en dos horas.)

a primera hora, ~ última hora first thing/
at the last moment

a principios de at the beginning of
(Supongo que nos mudaremos a
principios de año.)

a propósito on purpose, by the way (¡Lo
hiciste a propósito! Ayer me encontré con
Mario; a propósito, me preguntó cuánto
vale tu coche.)

a prueba de impervious to sth, resistant
(¿Tu reloj es a prueba de agua?)

a raíz de as a result of

a rayas striped

a razón de at a rate of

a regañadientes reluctantly

a renglón seguido immediately afterwards
(Las instrucciones se detallan a
renglón seguido.)

a sabiendas knowingly

a salvo safe (Mi familia está a salvo,
gracias a Dios.)

a simple vista to the naked eye

a solas alone (No me gusta quedarme
a solas con ella.)

a su regreso on sb's return

a su vez in turn

a tiempo on time

a todo volumen very loud, at full volume

a tontas y a locas without thinking

a través de through

a trueque de in exchange for

a veces sometimes (A veces me olvido
de hacer las compras.)

a ver all right, now, so; let's see (A ver,
¿qué está pasando acá? Llamémoslo
a ver qué nos dice.)

a vista de pájaro bird's-eye view

al aire libre outdoors

al descubierto exposed

al día up-to-date

al día siguiente, al otro día on the
next day

al efecto, a tal efecto, ~ este efecto for a
particular purpose

al fin at last

al final at/in the end (Al final, ¿qué vas a
hacer en las vacaciones?)

al igual que just as

al lado de beside, next to

al menos at least

al mismo tiempo que at the same time as

al pie de la letra literally, exactly (Siguieron
nuestras instrucciones al pie de la letra.)

**al pie de la montaña, ~ los pies de la
montaña** at the foot of the mountain

al principio at first

al (poco) rato shortly after

al través diagonally

abastecer *v.* to supply

**abastecer a algn de algo, ~ a algn con
algo** to supply sb with sth

abogar *v.* to defend, to fight for

**abogar por algn/algo, ~ en favor de algn/
algo** to defend sb, to fight for sth (El
defensor abogó a favor de los inmigrantes.
Toda su vida abogó por los derechos de
los trabajadores.)

abstenerse *v.* to abstain

abstenerse de algo to refrain/abstain
from sth

abuelo/a *m./f.* grandfather/grandmother

abuelo/a materno/a, ~ paterno/a
maternal/paternal grandfather/mother

abundar *v.* to abound

abundar de algo, ~ en algo to abound in

aburrirse *v.* to be bored

**aburrirse con algo/algn, ~ de algo/algn,
~ por algo** to be bored with sb/sth, to get
tired of sb/sth

abusar *v.* **1** to impose, to take advantage,
to abuse

abusar de algo to impose on sb (Silvia
abusó de mi amabilidad.)

abusar de algn to abuse sb
2 to make excessive use

abusar de algo to make excessive use of sth
(No debes abusar del alcohol.)

abuso *m.* abuse, breach

abuso de autoridad, ~ de confianza abuse
of authority, breach of trust

acabar *v.* to finish, to end

acabar con algo, ~ de hacer algo to finish
sth off, to have just done sth (Acaba con
eso de una vez. Acabo de despertarme.)

acabar por algo to end up by doing sth
(Este niño acabará por volverme loca.)

nunca acabar never-ending (Esto es un asunto de nunca acabar.)

acceder *v.* **1** to gain access, to access

acceder a algo to gain access to sth; to access sth (He podido acceder a los datos.)

2 to obtain

acceder a un cargo/trabajo to obtain/get a position/job

3 to agree

acceder a algo to agree to sth (Lucas accedió a los deseos de Sara.)

acción *f.* action

acción de armas, ~ de guerra military action

acción de gracias thanksgiving

buena/mala acción good/bad deed

novela/película de acción action novel/movie

pasar a la acción, entrar en ~ to go into action

poner algo en acción to put/turn sth into action

aceptar *v.* to accept

aceptar algo, ~ a algn (como algo) to accept sth/sb (Susana aceptó la oferta. ¿Acepta a Sandro como su legítimo esposo?)

acercarse *v.* to approach

acercarse a algo/algn to approach sth/sb

acercarse algo to come closer (Se acercan las fiestas.)

aconsejar *v.* to advise

aconsejar (algo) a algn to advise/give advice to sb

acordar *v.* **1** to agree

acordar algo con algn to agree to sth with sb

2 to award

acordar algo a algn *Am. L.* to award sth to sb (El premio le fue acordado por unanimidad.)

acordarse *v.* to remember

acordarse de algo/algn to remember sth/sb

acostumbrado/a *adj.* **1** used to

estar acostumbrado/a a algo to be used to sth

2 trained

estar bien/mal acostumbrado/a to be well/badly trained (Lo que pasa es que nos tienen mal acostumbrados.)

acostumbrar *v.* **1** to get used (to)

acostumbrar a algn a algo to get sb used to sth

2 to be accustomed

acostumbrar algo, ~ a algo to be accustomed to/in the habit of doing sth

acostumbrarse *v.* to get used (to)

acostumbrarse a algo/algn to get used to sth/sb

acudir *v.* **1** to attend

acudir a algo to attend sth (Debo acudir a la cita.)

2 to come

acudir en ayuda de algn to come to sb's aid/to help sb (Nadie acudió en su ayuda.)

3 to resort to

acudir a algo/algn to resort to sth/sb (No es necesario acudir a la violencia. Tuvo que acudir a su hermano mayor.)

acuerdo *m.* **1** agreement

estar de acuerdo con algo/algn to agree with sth/sb

estar de acuerdo en algo to agree on sth

hacer algo de común acuerdo to do sth by mutual agreement

llegar a un acuerdo, alcanzar un ~, ponerse de ~ to reach an agreement

2 accordance

de acuerdo con according to, complying with (Procederemos de acuerdo con lo hablado.)

acusar *v.* **1** to blame, to charge

acusar a algn de algo to blame/charge sb for sth

2 to show signs of (Su mirada acusaba cansancio.)

3 to acknowledge

acusar recibo de algo to acknowledge receipt of sth

acuse *m.* acknowledgement

acuse de recibo acknowledgement of receipt (¿Me traes el acuse de recibo firmado, por favor?)

adaptarse *v.* to adapt

adaptarse a algo to adapt to sth

adelantado/a *adj.* advanced
  por adelantado in advance

adelante *adv.* forward
  más adelante farther

además *adv.* besides
  además de apart from (Además de feo, es maleducado. Además de ser sabroso, es muy saludable.)

administración *f.* administration; management
  administración de negocios, ~ de empresas business administration
  administración pública civil/public service

admirar *v.* to admire
  admirar algo, ~ a algn to admire sth/sb

admirarse *v.* to be amazed
  admirarse de algo to be amazed at sth

adolecer *v.* to suffer from
  adolecer de algo to suffer from sth

advertir *v.* to warn
  advertir a algn de algo, ~ a algn que to warn sb of sth, to warn sb that (¿Has advertido a Juan de los riesgos? Te advierto que es muy peligroso.)

aficionado/a *m./f.* fan
  ser aficionado a algo to be a fan of sth

agarrarse *v.* **1** to hold on
  agarrarse a algo, ~ de algo to hold on to sth
  2 to have a fight
  agarrarse con algn to have a fight with sb

agencia *f.* agency
  agencia de colocaciones employment agency
  agencia de contactos dating agency
  agencia de prensa/noticias news/press agency
  agencia de publicidad advertising agency
  agencia de viajes travel agency
  agencia inmobiliaria real estate agency

agradar *v.* to appeal
  agradarle algo/algn a algn to be to sb's liking (Me agrada tu actitud. Me agrada la nueva maestra.)

agradecer *v.* to be grateful, to thank
  agradecerle algo a algn, agradecer a algn por algo to thank sb for sth (Te agradezco el regalo. Le agradezco por haberme ayudado.)

agua *f.* water
  agua bendita holy water
  agua corriente running water
  agua de lluvia rainwater
  agua de mar seawater
  agua dulce fresh water
  agua mineral (con/sin gas) sparkling/mineral water (with/without gas)
  agua oxigenada peroxide
  agua potable drinking water
  agua salada salt water
  aguas servidas/residuales sewage
  como agua para chocolate *Méx.* furious
  estar con el agua al cuello to be up to one's neck in problems
  estar más claro que el agua to be crystal clear

ahora *adv.* now
  por ahora for the time being

aire *m.* air
  aire acondicionado air conditioning (Las habitaciones del hotel tienen aire acondicionado.)
  al aire libre outdoors
  en el aire on air
  salir al aire to go out on the air (Nuestro programa sale al aire martes y jueves a las 6 de la tarde.)

alcance *m.* range
  de corto/largo alcance short/long-range

alcanzar *v.* **1** to reach
  alcanzar algo, ~ a algn to reach sth, to catch up with sb
  2 to pass
  alcanzar algo a algn to pass sth to sb
  3 to manage to
  alcanzar a hacer algo to manage to do sth (No alcancé a terminar el trabajo.)

alegrar *v.* to bring happiness
  alegrar a algn to make sb happy

alegrarse *v.* to be glad, to be happy
  alegrarse de algo, ~ por algo/algn to be glad about sth, to be happy for sb

alejarse *v.* to move away
  alejarse de algo/algn to move away from sth/sb

alimentar *v.* to feed
  alimentar a algo/algn to feed sth/sb

alimentar algo to fuel sth (Sus comentarios alimentaron el clima de violencia.)

alimentarse *v.* to live, to run

alimentarse con algo, ~ de algo to live/ run on sth

allí *adv.* there

de allí en adelante from then on

alma *f.* soul

alegrarse en el alma to be overjoyed

alma de la fiesta life/soul of the party

alma gemela soul mate

como (un) alma en pena like a lost soul

con toda el alma with all one's heart

del alma darling/dearest/best (Es mi amigo del alma.)

llegarle a algn al alma to be deeply touched by sth (Las palabras del sacerdote me llegaron al alma.)

sentir algo en el alma to be terribly sorry about sth (Siento en el alma haber sacado ese tema.)

alrededor *adv.* around

alrededor de around

altura *f.* height

estar a la altura de las circunstancias to rise to the occasion

quedar a la altura de algo/algn to be equal to sth/sb

amanecer *v.* to dawn; to wake up/begin at dawn/to start the day (¿A qué hora amanece? ¿Amaneciste bien? Hoy amaneció lloviendo.)

amanecer *m.* dawn, daybreak

amenazar *v.* to threaten

amenazar (a algn) con algo to threaten (sb) with sth

amigo/a *m./f.* friend

amigo/a íntimo/a intimate friend

mejor amigo/a best friend

(no) ser amigo/a de algo to (not) be fond of sth (No soy muy amigo de las fiestas.)

amo/a *m./f.* master/mistress

ama de casa housewife

ama de llaves housekeeper

animarse *v.* to feel like

animarse a hacer algo to feel like doing sth, to dare (to) do sth

aniversario *m.* anniversary

aniversario de boda, ~ de bodas wedding anniversary

ansioso/a *adj.* eager

estar ansioso/a de algo, estar ~ por algo to be anxious/eager to do sth (Estoy ansioso de verlos. Está muy ansiosa por los exámenes.)

anteojos *m.* glasses

anteojos bifocales bifocals

anteojos de sol, ~ oscuros sunglasses

antes *adv.* before

antes de before (Antes de ir a la escuela se detuvo en la plaza.)

antes de Jesucristo, ~ de Cristo BC

antes (de) que before (Llámalo antes de que sea tarde. Lo haré antes que me olvide.)

antes que nada, ~ de nada first of all

antojarse *v.* to feel like

antojársele algo a algn to feel like/crave sth

apartarse *v.* to separate

apartarse de algo/algn to separate from sth/sb

apasionarse *v.* to have a passion for

apasionarse con algo, ~ por algo/algn to have a passion for sth/sb (Mi hijo está apasionado con su nueva guitarra. Marcos está apasionado por esa mujer.)

apetecer *v.* to feel like

apetecerle algo a algn *Esp.* to feel like (Me apetece un paseo.)

apiadarse *v.* to take pity

apiadarse de algo/algn to take pity on sth/sb

apoderarse *v.* to seize

apoderarse de algo/algn to seize sth/sb (El ejército se apoderó del edificio. El miedo se apoderó de todos nosotros.)

apoyar *v.* **1** to rest

apoyar algo en un lugar to rest sth somewhere

2 to support

apoyar a algn (en algo) to support sb (in sth)

apoyar algo to support sth (El presidente apoyó nuestra causa inmediatamente.)

apoyarse *v.* to lean, to base

apoyarse en algo, ~ contra algo to lean on sth (Ellos se apoyan mucho en su familia. Se apoyó contra la pared porque estaba mareado.)

aprender *v.* to learn

aprender a hacer algo to learn to do sth (Debes aprender a escuchar a los demás.)

apresurarse *v.* to hurry

apresurarse a hacer algo to hurry to do sth (Se apresuraron a dejar todo como estaba.)

apresurarse en algo to hurry to do sth (Me parece que se apresuró en su respuesta.)

apropiarse *v.* to appropriate

apropiarse de algo to appropriate sth

aprovechar *v.* to make the best of

aprovecharse *v.* to take advantage

aprovecharse de algo/algn to take advantage of sth/sb

apuro *m.* rush (¿Por qué tanto apuro para terminar el examen?)

poner en un apuro to put in a predicament/tight spot (Su comentario me puso en un apuro.)

tener apuro to be in a hurry; to be urgent (Tengo mucho apuro./El proyecto tiene apuro.)

aquí *adv.* here

por aquí around here

arrepentirse *v.* to regret

arrepentirse de algo to regret sth

arriba *adv.* up

de arriba abajo up and down, from top to bottom

para arriba y para abajo back and forth

arriesgarse *v.* to risk

arriesgarse a algo to risk sth/to take a risk

ascender *v.* to rise

ascender a algo/algn to promote, to be promoted (El grumete ascendió a timonel rápidamente. Parece que van a ascender a Pérez.)

ascender a un lugar to rise to/reach a place or position

asegurarse *v.* to assure, secure

asegurarse de algo to assure oneself of sth

asistir *v.* **1** to attend, to witness

asistir a algo to attend sth, to witness sth (Asistió a la clase. Asistimos a la coronación del rey.)

2 to assist

asistir a algn to assist sb (Asistió al médico durante la operación.)

asombrarse *v.* to be amazed

asombrarse ante algo, ~ con algo, ~ de algo, ~ por algo to be amazed at sth

aspirar *v.* to hope, to seek

aspirar a algo to hope to become sth (Sandra aspira a convertirse en una cantante famosa.)

aspirar a la mano de algn to seek sb's hand in marriage

asustado/a *adj.* afraid

estar asustado/a de to be afraid of

asustar *v.* to frighten

asustar a algn (con algo) to frighten sb (with sth)

asustarse *v.* to get frightened

asustarse ante algo, ~ con algo, ~ de algo, ~ por algo to get frightened about sth

atención *f.* attention

llamar la atención to attract/call attention to

llamarle a algn la atención sobre algo to draw sb's attention to sth

prestar atención a algo/algn to pay attention to sth/sb

atender *v.* to pay attention

atender a algo/algn to pay attention to/ to attend to sth/sb (Debes atender a tus hijos. No atiende a sus deberes.)

atreverse *v.* to dare

atreverse a algo, ~ con algo to dare to do sth

atreverse con algn to dare or take on sb

auge *m.* peak

en auge flourishing

aumento *m.* increase

aumento de algo increase in sth (Estoy preocupada por su aumento de peso. La policía tomará medidas por el aumento de la violencia en los estadios de fútbol.)

pedir un aumento, solicitar un ~ to ask for a pay raise

sufrir un aumento, experimentar un ~ to experience an increase in sth (Los servicios de luz y de gas sufrirán fuertes aumentos. El precio del petróleo experimentó un aumento por tercera semana consecutiva.)

auxilio *m.* help; aid (in an emergency)

acudir en auxilio de algn to go to sb's aid

pedir auxilio to ask for help

prestar auxilio to help

primeros auxilios first aid

avance *m.* advance; news summary

avance científico, ~ de la ciencia scientific breakthrough

avance informativo news summary

ave *f.* bird

ave de mal agüero bird of ill omen

ave de paso bird of passage

ave de rapiña bird of prey

aventurarse *v.* to venture

aventurarse a algo, ~ en algo to venture to do sth

aventurarse por un lugar to venture somewhere

avergonzarse *v.* to be ashamed

avergonzarse de algo/algn, ~ por algo/ algn to be ashamed of sth/sb

avisar *v.* to inform

avisar a algn de algo to let sb know about sth

ayudar *v.* to help

ayudar (a algn) a algo, ~ con algo, ~ en algo to help (sb) with sth

B

bajar *v.* to go down

bajar a hacer algo to come down to do sth (¿Cuándo bajará a saludarnos?)

bajar algo de algo, ~ a algn de algo to get sb/sth down from sth (Baja la muñeca de la repisa, por favor. ¿Bajarías al niño del caballo?)

bajar de algo to get off sth (Los pasajeros ya están bajando del avión.)

banda *f.* strip

banda de sonido, ~ sonora soundtrack

banda magnética magnetic strip

basarse *v.* to base

basarse en algo to be based in/on sth

base *f.* base

a base de with/of; on the basis of (Esto está hecho a base de verduras.)

con base en based on

bastar *v.* to be enough

bastar algo (para), ~ con algo (para), ~ a algn algo to be enough (for) (Basta que yo diga algo para que mis hijos hagan

lo contrario. Basta con marcar 911 para obtener ayuda. A mí me basta con tu palabra.)

bastar y sobrar to be more than enough (Con eso basta y sobra.)

batalla *f.* battle

batalla campal pitched battle

dar batalla to cause a lot of problems/grief (Los problemas de salud le han dado mucha batalla.)

de batalla everyday (Son mis zapatos de batalla.)

beca *f.* grant, scholarship

beca de estudios study grant

beca de investigación research grant

boda *f.* wedding, a special anniversary

bodas de oro golden (wedding) anniversary; golden jubilee

bodas de plata silver (wedding) anniversary; silver jubilee

bolsa *f.* **1** bag

bolsa de agua caliente hot-water bottle

bolsa de (la) basura garbage bag

bolsa de compras, ~ de la compra shopping bag

bolsa de dormir sleeping bag

bolsa de hielo ice pack

2 stock market

bolsa de cereales grain exchange

bolsa de comercio commodities exchange

bolsa de valores stock exchange

bordo *m.* board

a bordo de onboard

bote *m.* boat

bote a remos, ~ de remos rowboat

bote inflable inflatable dinghy/raft

bote salvavidas lifeboat

brecha *f.* breach, opening

abrir brecha to break through

brecha generacional generation gap

estar en la brecha to be in the thick of things

seguir en la brecha to stand one's ground

brindar *v.* **1** to toast

brindar (con algo) por algo/algn, ~ a la salud de algn to toast sb/sth

2 to give, to provide

brindar algo a algn to provide sb with sth
(Le brindaremos toda la información
que necesite.)

broma *f.* joke

celebrar una broma to laugh at a joke

de broma, en ~ as a joke (No le creas,
lo dijo en broma. ¿Te asustaste?
¡Era de broma!)

**fuera de broma, fuera de bromas, bromas
aparte** all joking apart/aside

**hacerle una broma a algn, gastarle una ~
a algn** to play a joke on sb

ni en broma no way

no estar para bromas to not be in the
mood for jokes

bromear *v.* to joke

bromear (con algn) sobre algo to joke
about sth (with sb)

bueno/a *adj.* good

por las buenas o por las malas one way or
the other

burlar *v.* to evade

burlar (a) algo/algn to evade, to get
around, to slip past (El delincuente burló
la vigilancia y huyó. Marcia burló a su
jefe con engaños.)

burlarse *v.* to make fun of

burlarse de algo/algn to make fun
of sth/sb

C

caballo *m.* horse

a caballo on horseback

caballo de carrera, ~ de carreras racehorse

caballo de fuerza horsepower

caber *v.* to fit

caber en algo, ~ por un lugar to fit
somewhere, to fit through sth

no caber en uno/a mismo/a to be
beside oneself

cabo *m.* end

atar los cabos sueltos to tie up the
loose ends

dejar cabos sueltos to leave loose ends

llevar algo a cabo to carry sth out

caer *v.* **1** to fall

caer de bruces to fall on one's face

2 to stoop

caer bajo to stoop low

3 to show up

caer de improviso to show up without
warning

4 caer bien/mal, ~ en gracia to be liked/
disliked, to be fond of

cajero/a *m./f.* cashier

cajero automático, ~ permanente ATM

calidad *f.* quality

calidad de vida standard of living

cámara *f.* camera

cámara de cine film camera

cámara de video video camera

cámara digital digital camera

cámara fotográfica camera

en cámara lenta, a ~ lenta in slow motion

cambiar *v.* to change

cambiar algo a algo, ~ algo en algo to
change sth into sth (Necesito cambiar
estos dólares a pesos. ¿Me puede cambiar
estos bolívares en pesos?)

cambiar algo por algo to change sth
for sth

cambiar de algo to change sth
(¡Cámbiate de ropa!)

cambiarle algo a algo to change sth in sth
(El relojero le cambió la pila a mi reloj.)

cambiarle algo a algn to exchange
sth with sb

cambio *m.* **1** change

a la primera de cambio at the first
opportunity

cambio de aires, ~ de ambiente change
of scenery

2 exchange

a cambio de algo in return for sth

en cambio on the other hand
(El vestido azul es feo; el rojo, en
cambio, es hermoso.)

en cambio de instead of

camino *m.* way; road

**abrir el camino, allanar el ~, preparar
el ~** to pave the way

camino vecinal minor/country road

**estar camino a algo, estar ~ de algo, estar
en el ~ a algo** on the way to (Me crucé
con él camino al dentista. La vi camino
del club. Esa tienda queda en el camino a
la escuela.)

estar en camino to be on sb's way (Ya deben estar en camino, no los llames por teléfono.)

por el camino on the way (Vamos, te lo diré por el camino.)

candelero *m.* candlestick

estar en el candelero to be in the limelight

cansado/a *adj.* tired

estar cansado/a de algo to be tired of sth

cansarse *v.* to get tired

cansarse con algo, ~ de algo/algn to get tired of sth (Mi madre se cansa con la rutina. ¿No te cansas de repetir siempre lo mismo?)

capaz *adj.* capable

ser capaz de algo to be capable of sth

cara *f.* face

cara a cara face to face

echar en cara algo a algn to reproach sth to sb (No me eches en cara lo que has hecho por mí.)

carecer *v.* to lack

carecer de algo to lack sth

cargar *v.* **1** to load

cargar a algn de algo to burden sb with sth

cargar algo con algo to load sth with sth

cargar algo en algo to load sth into/onto sth

2 to carry

cargar con algo to carry sth

3 to charge

cargar contra algn to charge against sb

cargo *m.* **1** charge

a cargo de, al ~ de in charge of

hacerse cargo de algo/algn to take charge of sth, to take care of sb

2 position, job

cargo público public office

desempeñar un cargo to hold a position

carne *f.* **1** flesh

carne de cañón cannon fodder

de carne y hueso quite human

en carne propia by personal experience

en carne y hueso in the flesh

2 meat

carne de res beef/red meat

echar toda la carne al asador, poner

toda la ~ al asador to put all one's eggs in one basket

carrera **1** race

a la carrera, a las carreras in a hurry

carrera armamentista, ~ armamentística, ~ de armamentos arms race

carrera contra reloj race against time

2 degree course

seguir una carrera, hacer una ~ to study for a degree

3 career

hacer carrera to carve out/make a career

casarse *v.* to marry; to get married

casarse con algn to marry sb

casarse en primeras/segundas nupcias to marry/remarry

casarse por poder to get married by proxy

caso *m.* **1** case

caso fortuito misadventure

en caso contrario otherwise

en caso de que in case of

en cualquier caso, en todo ~ in any case

no hay/hubo caso there is/was no way

no tiene caso to be pointless

ser un caso perdido to be a hopeless case

2 attention

hacer caso a algn to pay attention to sb

hacer caso de algo to take notice of sth

hacer caso omiso de algo to ignore (Hizo caso omiso de todas las advertencias de su familia.)

casualidad *f.* chance

de casualidad, por ~ by accident

causa *f.* cause

a causa de, por ~ de because of

causa perdida lost cause

ceder *v.* **1** to hand over

ceder algo a algn to hand sth over to sb

2 to give up

ceder en algo to give sth up

3 to give in

ceder a algo, ~ ante algo/algn to give in to sth/sb

celebrar *v.* to celebrate

celebrar algo, ~ por algo to celebrate sth

ceniza *f.* ash

reducir algo a cenizas to reduce sth to ashes

centro *m.* center

  centro comercial shopping mall

  centro de gravedad center of gravity

  centro de mesa centerpiece

  ser el centro de las miradas to have all
    eyes on sb

ceñirse *v.* to stick to

  ceñirse a algo to stick to sth (Deberías
    ceñirte al reglamento.)

cerca *adv.* close

  cerca de near, close to

cerciorarse *v.* to make certain

  cerciorarse de algo to make certain of sth

cerco *m.* siege

  cerco policial police cordon

  levantar el cerco, alzar el ~ to raise
    the siege

  poner cerco a algo to lay siege to sth

cesar *v.* to cease

  cesar de hacer algo to cease doing sth
    (No cesa de insultarnos.)

  sin cesar nonstop (Se trabajó sin cesar en el
    rescate de los mineros.)

charlar *v.* to chat

  **charlar (con algn) de algo, ~ (con algn)
    sobre algo** to chat about sth (with sb)

cheque *m.* check

  cheque de viaje, ~ de viajero
    traveler's check

  cheque en blanco blank check

  cheque sin fondos, ~ sobregirado
    overdrawn check

chocar(se) *v.* to collide

  **chocarse con algo/algn, ~ contra algo/
    algn** to collide/crash against sth/sb

ciencia *f.* science

  a ciencia cierta for sure

  ciencias ocultas occultism

  de ciencia ficción science fiction

  no tiene ninguna ciencia there is nothing
    difficult about it

cinturón *m.*

  cinturón de seguridad seat belt, safety belt

cita *f.* date, appointment

  cita a ciegas blind date

  concertar una cita to arrange an
    appointment

  darse cita to arrange to meet (Se dieron
    cita en la puerta de la iglesia.)

  pedir cita to make an appointment

  tener una cita con algn to have an
    appointment/date with sb

citarse *v.* to make an appointment

  citarse con algn to make an appointment
    with sb

coincidir *v.* to agree

  coincidir con algn en algo to agree with
    sb on sth

comentar *v.* to discuss

  comentar algo con algn to discuss sth
    with sb

comenzar *v.* to begin

  comenzar a hacer algo to begin to do sth
    (¿Cuándo comenzarás a trabajar?)

  comenzar por algo to begin by sth
    (Puedes comenzar por pedirme disculpas.)

compadecerse *v.* to take pity on

  compadecerse con algn, ~ de algn to take
    pity on sb

comparar *v.* to compare

  **comparar algo con algo, ~ algo/algn
    a algo/algn, ~ a algn con algn** to
    compare sth/sb with sth/sb else (Estuve
    comparando tu camiseta con la mía y
    la tuya es más grande. Si comparas un
    triángulo a un cuadrado, te darás cuenta.
    ¡Deja de compararme con mi hermano!)

compararse *v.* to compare oneself

  compararse con algn to compare oneself
    to sb

compensar *v.* to compensate

  compensar (a algn) con algo to
    compensate (sb) by doing sth (¿Me
    compensarás con un rico pastel?)

  compensar (a algn) por algo to
    compensate (sb) for sth (Decidimos
    compensarlo por su buen desempeño
    en el trabajo.)

competir *v.* **1** to compete

  **competir con algn por algo, ~ contra algn
    por algo** to compete with/against sb for sth
  2 to rival

  competir en algo to compete in sth (Los dos
    artefactos compiten en calidad y precio.)

complacer *v.* to please

  **complacer a algn con algo, ~ a algn en
    algo** to please sb with sth

complacerse *v.* to take pleasure in

complacerse con algo, ~ de algo, ~ en algo to take pleasure in sth (Nos complace con su visita, Su Señoría. Mi hermana se complace en ayudar a los demás.)

completo/a *adj.* complete

por completo completely

componerse *v.* to be made up

componerse de algo to be made up of sth

comprar *v.* to buy

comprar algo a algn to buy sth from/to sb

comprometerse *v.* **1** to commit

comprometerse a algo, ~ en algo to commit to do sth

2 to get engaged

comprometerse con algn to get engaged with sb

comunicar *v.* **1** to inform, to communicate

comunicar algo a algn to communicate sth to sb

por escrito to be notified in writing

2 comunicar algo con algo to connect sth with sth (Este corredor comunica las habitaciones con la sala de estar.)

comunicarse *v.* to communicate

comunicarse (con algn) mediante algo, ~ (con algn) por algo to communicate (with sb) through sth (Ellos se comunican mediante gestos. Trataré de comunicarme por señas.)

con *prep.* with

con base en based on

con buen pie, ~ el pie derecho with a good start (Creo que no comenzaron con buen pie. Nuestra relación comenzó con el pie derecho.)

con dureza harshly

con el fin de with the purpose of

con erguida frente, ~ la frente bien alta, ~ la frente en alto, ~ la frente levantada with one's head held high

con este fin with this aim

con frecuencia frequently, often (¿Vienes a este bar con frecuencia?)

con la guardia baja with one's guard down

con las propias manos with one's own hands

con mal pie, ~ el pie izquierdo badly

con miras a with the purpose of

con motivo de due to, because of

con permiso with your permission/excuse me

con respecto a regarding

con tal (de) que provided that, as long as

con toda el alma with all one's heart

con toda seriedad seriously

con todas las de la ley rightly (No puedes quejarte, ella te ha ganado con todas las de la ley.)

concentrarse *v.* to concentrate

concentrarse en algo to concentrate on sth

condenar *v.* to condemn

condenar a algn a algo to condemn sb to sth (Su mal carácter lo condenó a la soledad.)

condenar a algn por algo to condemn sb for sth (Lo condenaron por robo.)

confiar *v.* **1** to entrust

confiar algo a algn to entrust sb with sth (Le confío la seguridad de mis hijos.)

2 to trust

confiar en algo/algn to trust sth/sb

3 to confide

confiar algo a algn to confide sth to sb (Me confió sus más oscuras intenciones.)

conflicto *m.* conflict

conflicto armado/bélico armed conflict

conflicto de ideas clash of ideas

conflicto de intereses conflict of interests

conflicto laboral labor dispute

conflicto limítrofe border dispute

conformarse *v.* to be happy

conformarse con poco to be happy with very little

confundir *v.* to mix up

confundir algo con algo, ~ a algn con algn to mix sth/sb up with sth/sb else

confundirse *v.* to mistake

confundirse con algo/algn to mistake sth/sb for sth/sb else

confundirse de algo to get sth wrong (Susana se confundió de coche.)

confundirse en algo to make a mistake in sth

conocer *v.* to know

conocer a algn to know sb

conocer de algo to know about sth

consentir *v.* to agree

consentir algo (a algn) to allow (sb) to do sth (Les consienten todo a sus nietos.)

consentir en algo to agree to sth (El ministro consintió en apoyar al candidato.)

consiguiente *adj.* consequent

por consiguiente therefore

consistir *v.* **1** consist

consistir en algo to consist of sth (La prueba consiste en una serie de actividades prácticas.)

2 to consist of/lie in

consistir en algo to consist of sth (¿En qué consiste la gracia?)

constar *v.* **1** to be stated (La edad no consta en el documento.)

constarle a algn algo to be sure that (Me consta que la carta fue enviada.)

hacer constar/que conste to state (Hagamos constar que pagamos la multa.)

que conste for the record, to set the record straight (Que conste que yo nunca le mentí./Jamás le mentí, que conste.)

2 to consist of

constar de algo to consist of sth (El libro consta de una serie de capítulos.)

consultar *v.* to consult

consultar algo a algn, ~ algo con algn, ~ a algn sobre algo to consult about sth with sb

contar 1 to tell

contar algo a algn to tell sth to sb

2 to count

contar con algo/algn to count on sth/sb

contentarse *v.* to be pleased

contentarse con poco to be pleased with very little

contento/a *adj.* happy

estar contento/a con algo, estar ~ de algo, estar ~ por algo to be happy with/about sth (Estamos contentos con los resultados. ¿Estás contenta de haber ido? Están contentos por la visita del gobernador.)

contestar *v.* to answer, to reply

contestar (a) algo, ~ algo a algn to answer sth to sb

contra *prep.* against

contra reembolso cash on delivery

contrario/a *adj.* opposite

de lo contrario if not/otherwise/on the contrary (Termina tu comida; de lo contrario, te quedarás sin postre.)

contribuir *v.* to contribute

contribuir a algo to contribute to sth (Yo contribuí al progreso de la empresa.)

contribuir con algo to contribute sth (Los vecinos contribuyeron con alimentos y ropa.)

control *m.* control

a control remoto, por ~ remoto by remote control (Funciona a control remoto. Eso se maneja por control remoto.)

control antidoping drug test

control de armas gun control

control de calidad quality control

convalecer *v.* to convalesce

convalecer de algo to convalesce from sth

convencer *v.* to persuade

convencer a algn de algo to persuade sb of sth

convencerse *v.* to believe, to accept

convencerse de algo to accept sth (Debes convencerte de que eso terminó.)

convenir *v.* **1** to agree on

a convenir negotiable (La remuneración es a convenir.)

convenir con algn en algo, ~ con algo to agree on sth with sb (Debo convenir con mi exmarido en los horarios de visita. Convenimos con el dictamen de la auditoría.)

2 to be advisable

convenir a uno algo to be good for sb (Me conviene esperar unos días.)

conversar *v.* to talk

conversar (con algn) de algo, ~ (con algn) sobre algo to talk about sth with sb

convertirse *v.* **1** to turn into

convertirse en algo/algn to turn into sth/sb (Se convirtió en una persona despreciable.)

2 to convert

convertirse a algo to convert to sth (Se convirtió al cristianismo.)

convocar v. **to call, to summon**

convocar a algn a algo, ~ a algn para algo to summon sb to sth

coro *m.* chorus

hacerle coro a algn to back sb up

corredor(a) *m./f.* **1** runner

corredor(a) de coches/automóviles race car driver

corredor(a) de fondo long-distance runner

corredor(a) de vallas hurdler

2 agent

corredor(a) de bolsa stockbroker

corredor(a) de seguros insurance broker

cosa *f.* thing

cualquier cosa anything

no ser cosa de broma, no ser ~ de risa to not be a joke

no ser cosa fácil to not be easy (Convencerlo no va a ser cosa fácil.)

poca cosa hardly anything

costa *f.* coast, coastline

a costa de at the expense of (No veo la gracia de reírse a costa de los demás.)

costas expenses (Después del juicio, tuvo que pagar las costas judiciales.)

costar *v.* to cost

costarle a uno algo to lose/to cost one/sb sth (Una pequeña distracción le costó el empleo.)

coste *m.* cost *Esp.*

costo *m.* cost *Am. L.*

costumbre *f.* habit

como de costumbre, para no perder la ~ as always/usual (Olvidaste tu tarea, para no perder la costumbre. Llegó tarde, como de costumbre.)

de costumbre usual (Nos vemos en el lugar de costumbre.)

tener la costumbre de algo, tener algo por ~ to be in the habit of sth

crédito *m.* credit; loan

a crédito on credit

dar crédito a algn/algo to believe (No les dio crédito a mis palabras.)

creer *v.* to believe

creer en algn/algo to believe in sb/sth

creerse *v.* to trust

creerse de algn *Méx.* to trust sb

crisis *f.* crisis

crisis cardíaca heart failure, cardiac arrest

crisis de identidad identity crisis

crisis de los cuarenta midlife crisis

crisis energética energy crisis

crisis nerviosa nervous breakdown

cuando *adv.* when

cada cuando, de ~ en ~ from time to time

cuando más, ~ mucho at the most

cuando menos at the least

cuando quiera whenever (Cuando quiera que llegue el momento.)

cuanto *adv.* as much as

cuanto antes as soon as possible

cuanto más let alone (Es un momento difícil para todos, cuanto más para su esposa.)

en cuanto as soon (as) (Iré en cuanto pueda.)

en cuanto a regarding (En cuanto a la inflación, estamos tomando todas las medidas necesarias.)

por cuanto insofar as

cubierto/a *adj.* covered

estar cubierto/a de algo, estar ~ por algo to be covered with sth

cucharada *f.* spoonful

a cucharadas by the spoonful

cuenta *f.* **1** calculation

a fin de cuentas, al fin de ~ after all

hacer cuentas, sacar ~ to do calculations

2 count

caer en la cuenta de algo, darse ~ de algo to realize sth

llevar la cuenta to keep count

más de la cuenta too much (He comido más de la cuenta.)

3 account

a cuenta on account

abrir/cerrar una cuenta to open/close an account

cuenta a plazo fijo time deposit/fixed-term account

cuenta corriente (de cheques) checking account

cuenta de ahorros savings account

4 consideration

darse cuenta de algo to realize sth

tener algo en cuenta, tomar algo en ~ to take sth into account

cuidar *v.* to look after

  cuidar algo, ~ a algn, ~ de algo/algn to look after sth/sb

cuidarse *v.* **1** to take care

  cuidarse de algo/algn to take care of sth/sb **2** to avoid

  cuidarse de algo to avoid doing sth (Cuídate de lo que dices por ahí.)

culpa *f.* fault

  echarle la culpa de algo a algn to blame sb for sth

  tener la culpa de algo to be sb's fault

culpar *v.* to blame

  culpar a algn de algo, ~ a algn por algo to blame sb for sth

culto *m.* worship

  rendir culto a algo/algn to worship sth/sb

cumplir *v.* to carry out, fulfill, keep

  cumplir con algo/algn to keep (Yo siempre cumplo con mi palabra.)

D

dar *v.* **1** to find

  dar con algo/algn to find sth/sb (No logro dar con él.) **2** to give

  dar algo a algn to give sth to sb

  dar de comer a algn to feed sb **3** to hit

  dar algo contra algo to hit sth against sth **4** to face

  dar a (algo) to face (sth) (Mi ventana da al jardín.)

de *prep.* of, from

  de a each (Nos tocan de a cinco galletas cada una.)

  de a ratos, ~ rato en rato from time to time

  de acuerdo con according to (Procederemos de acuerdo con lo hablado.)

  de allí en adelante from then on

  de broma as a joke (¿Te asustaste? ¡Era de broma!)

  de buen/mal modo, ~ buenos/malos modos in a good/bad way

de buena ley genuine (Es oro de buena ley.)

de buena/mala gana willingly/unwillingly

de buena/mala manera in a good/bad way

de carne y hueso quite human

de casualidad by accident

de ciencia ficción science fiction

de corto/largo alcance short-/long-range

de costumbre usual

de cualquier forma, ~ una u otra forma, ~ todas formas, ~ cualquier manera, ~ todas maneras, ~ cualquier modo, ~ todos modos anyway, in any case

de cuando en cuando from time to time

de derecha right-wing (Jamás votaré a un partido de derecha.)

de enfrente across the street

de entre semana working day (No puedo salir contigo de entre semana, tengo mucho trabajo.)

de esa manera in that way

de frente face-to-face

de golpe, ~ golpe y porrazo suddenly

de gusto for the fun of it

de izquierda left-wing (Sectores de izquierda se opusieron a la medida.)

de la derecha on the right (Me gusta el coche de la derecha.)

de la izquierda on the left (Busca en el cajón de la izquierda.)

de la mano hand in hand

de lo contrario if not/on the contrary/ otherwise (Termina tu comida; de lo contrario, te quedarás sin postre.)

de lujo luxury (Iván y Paola se alojarán en un hotel de lujo durante su luna de miel.)

de mala muerte lousy (No vayas a ese restaurante, es de mala muerte.)

de manera que so (¿De manera que la decisión ya está tomada?)

de modo que in such a way that

de nada you're welcome

de ningún modo no way

de ninguna manera certainly not

de nuevo again

de pie standing (Ponte de pie cuando entre la maestra.)

de plano outright (Se negó de plano a participar en el negocio.)

de primera mano first hand

de pronto suddenly

de propina tip (¿Cuánto has dejado de propina?)

de regreso a to be back at (¿Cuándo estarás de regreso a la oficina?)

de repente suddenly

de rodillas down on one's knees

de tal modo que, ~ modo que in such a way that (Estudió mucho, de tal modo que aprobó el examen. Ya es tarde, de modo que me voy a casa.)

de través *Méx.* diagonally

de un día para el otro overnight

de un golpe all at once

de una vez (por todas) once and for all

de veras really

de vez en cuando once in a while

de vista by sight (A su hermana la conocemos solo de vista.)

del alma darling/dearest/best (Es mi amigo del alma.)

del mismo modo, de igual modo in the same way

debajo *adv.* under

  por debajo de under

debatir *v.* to discuss

  debatir (con algn) sobre algo to discuss sth (with sb)

deber *v.* to owe

  deber algo a algn to owe sth to sb

decidido/a *adj.* determined

  estar decidido a algo to be determined to do sth

decidir *v.* to decide

  decidir sobre algo to make a decision about sth

decidirse *v.* to decide, to dedicate

  decidirse a hacer algo to decide to do sth

  decidirse por algo to decide on sth

dedicar *v.* to devote, to dedicate

  dedicar algo a algn to devote sth to sb (Debes dedicarle más tiempo a tu familia.)

dedicarse *v.* to devote

  dedicarse a algo to devote oneself to sth

defender *v.* to defend

  defender algo, ~ a algn to defend sth/sb

defenderse *v.* to defend oneself

defenderse de algo/algn to defend oneself against sth/sb

degenerar *v.* to degenerate

  degenerar en algo to degenerate/lead into sth

dejar *v.* 1 to stop

  dejar de hacer algo to stop doing sth

  2 to leave

  dejar a algn to leave sb

  dejar algo mucho que desear to leave much to be desired

  3 to let, to allow

  dejar a algn hacer algo to let sb do sth

  4 to fail

  dejar de hacer algo to give up/stop doing sth/to fail to do sth (No dejes de llamarme cuando llegues.)

delante *adv.* ahead

  por delante ahead (Aún nos queda mucho por delante.)

  por delante de in front of, opposite (Ayer pasé por delante de tu casa.)

deliberar *v.* to deliberate

  deliberar sobre algo to deliberate on sth

delito *m.* crime

  cometer un delito, incurrir en un ~ to commit a crime

demandar *v.* 1 to require (Esta tarea demanda mucha concentración.)

  2 to sue

  demandar por daños y perjuicios to sue for damages

demás *pron.* the rest

  estar por demás hacer algo there is no point in doing sth

  lo demás, los/las ~ the rest

  por demás extremely (Te comportas de una manera por demás grosera.)

  por lo demás apart from that

  y demás and the like (Se aceptan perros, gatos y demás.)

demora *f.* delay

  sin demora without delay

dentro *adv.* inside

  por dentro de in, inside of

depender *v.* 1 to depend

  depender de algo/algn to depend on sth/sb

2 to report

depender de algn to report to sb

derecha *f.* right

a la derecha (de) to/on the right (of)
(Gira a la derecha. Da un paso a la
derecha, por favor.)

de derecha right-wing (Jamás votaré a
un partido de derecha.)

de la derecha on the right (Me gusta
el coche de la derecha.)

descansar *v.* **1** to take a break

descansar de algo/algn to take a break
from sth/sb (Necesitaba descansar de
los niños por un día.)

2 to rest upon

descansar en algo, ~ sobre algo to rest
upon sth (Su pierna descansaba sobre
unas almohadas.)

desconfiar *v.* to mistrust

desconfiar de algo/algn to mistrust sth/sb

descubierto/a *adj.* exposed

al descubierto exposed (Sus numerosas
estafas quedaron al descubierto.)

desde *prep.* since

desde el principio, ~ un principio from
the beginning

desear *v.* to wish

desear algo (a algn) to wish sb sth

desembocar *v.* to culminate

desembocar en algo to culminate in sth

deseoso/a *adj.* anxious/eager

estar deseoso/a de to be
anxious/eager about

desgracia *f.* misfortune

por desgracia unfortunately

deshacerse *v.* to get rid

deshacerse de algo/algn to get rid
of sth/sb

desistir *v.* to give up

desistir de algo, ~ en algo to give up
sth (Desistió de vender su casa. Nunca
desistió en su empeño por ser el mejor
de la clase.)

despedir *v.* **1** to see off

despedir a algn to see sb off

2 to fire

despedir a algn to fire sb

despedirse *v.* to say goodbye

despedirse de algo/algn to say goodbye
to sth/sb

desposeer *v.* to strip

desposeer a algn de algo to strip sb of sth

desprenderse **1** to let go

desprenderse de algo/algn to let go of sth/
sb (Deberías desprenderte de los objetos
que ya no usas.)

2 to emerge

desprenderse de algo to emerge from sth
(Los datos se desprenden de una serie
de encuestas.)

después *adv.* later

después de Jesucristo, ~ de Cristo AD

después de todo after all

después (de) que after, as soon as (Después
de que hablé contigo, encendí el televisor.)

destinar *v.* to allocate

destinar algo a algo, ~ algo para algo to
set sth aside for sth

detalle *m.* **1** detail

al detalle retail (Esa tienda vende
al detalle.)

con todo detalle in great detail

dar detalles to go into details

entrar en detalles to go into details

2 little gift; nice gesture (Estuvo en París
y me trajo un detallecito.)

¡Qué detalle! How thoughtful!

tener un detalle con algn to do sth nice
for sb (¿Puedes creer que después
de que lo ayudé tanto no tuvo ningún
detalle conmigo?)

detenerse *v.* **1** to stop

detenerse a hacer algo to stop to do sth

2 to dwell

detenerse en algo to dwell on sth
(Concéntrate en lo importante, no te
detengas en detalles.)

detrás *adv.* behind

(por) detrás de behind, in the back of

devolver *v.* to return

devolver algo a algn to return sth to sb

día *m.* day

al día up-to-date

al día siguiente, al otro ~ on the next day

de un día para otro overnight

día de por medio *Am. L.* every other day

día festivo public holiday

día hábil, ~ laborable working day

día tras día day after day

hoy en día nowadays

diente *m.* tooth

armado hasta los dientes armed to
the teeth

diente de ajo garlic clove

diente de leche baby tooth

salirle los dientes a algn to be teething
(¡Ya le está saliendo el primer dientito!)

dieta *f.* diet

dieta habitual staple diet

estar/ponerse a dieta to be/go on a diet

diferir *v.* **1** to differ

diferir de algo to differ from sth (Su nuevo
trabajo difiere de los anteriores.)

2 to disagree

diferir de algn, ~ entre sí to disagree
with sb

difícil *adj.* difficult

ser algn difícil to be difficult
(Es una persona muy difícil.)

ser difícil de hacer to be difficult to do (Es
una asignatura muy difícil de estudiar.)

Dios *m.* God

Dios mediante God willing

Dios mío/santo for Heaven's sake

por Dios for Heaven's sake

si Dios quiere God willing

dirigir *v.* to address

dirigir algo a algn to address sth to sb

dirigirse *v.* **1** to head for

dirigirse a un lugar to head for a place

2 to address

dirigirse a algn to address sb

discrepar *v.* to disagree

**discrepar (con algn) en algo, ~ (con algn)
sobre algo** to disagree (with sb) on sth

disculparse *v.* to apologize

**disculparse (ante/con algn) de algo, ~
(ante/con algn) por algo** to apologize
(to sb) for sth

discutir *v.* to argue

**discutir con algn por algo, ~ con algn
sobre algo** to argue with sb about sth

discutirle algo a algn to argue sth with sb

disfrutar *v.* to enjoy

disfrutar de algo to enjoy sth

disgustado/a *adj.* annoyed

**estar disgustado/a con algn, estar ~ por
algo** to be annoyed with sb/sth

disgustar *v.* to dislike

disgustarle algo/algn (a algn) to dislike
sth/sb

disgustarse *v.* to get upset

disgustarse con algo, ~ por algo to get
upset because of sth

disponer *v.* to possess

disponer de algo/algn to have sth/sb at
one's disposal

disponerse *v.* to prepare

**disponerse a hacer algo, ~ para hacer
algo** to prepare to do sth

dispuesto/a *adj.* willing

estar dispuesto/a a to be willing to

distanciarse *v.* to distance

distanciarse de algo/algn to distance
oneself from sth/sb

distinguir *v.* **1** to differentiate

distinguir algo de algo to tell sth from
sth else

2 to honor

distinguir a algn con algo to honor sb
with sth

distinguirse *v.* to stand out

distinguirse en algo to stand out in sth

distinguirse por algo to stand out for sth

disuadir *v.* to dissuade

disuadir a algn con algo to dissuade sb
with sth

disuadir a algn de algo to dissuade sb
from sth

divorciarse *v.* to get divorced

divorciarse de algn to get divorced
from sb

doler *v.* to hurt

dolerle a uno/a algo to have a pain
somewhere (Me duele la cabeza.)

dominio *f.* **1** mastery

ser de dominio público to be
public knowledge

tener dominio de uno/a mismo/a to have
self-control

tener el dominio de algo to have
command of sth

2 field

entrar en el dominio de algo to be in the field of sth (Eso entra en el dominio de la Economía.)

duda *f.* doubt

sin duda without (a) doubt

dudar *v.* **1** to doubt

dudar de algo/algn to doubt sth/sb

2 to hesitate

dudar en hacer algo to hesitate in doing sth (No dudes en llamarme si necesitas algo.)

dureza *f.* harshness

con dureza harshly

E

echar *v.* **1** to dismiss/fire

echar a algn to dismiss/fire sb

2 to start

echar a andar algo to start sth

3 to miss

echar de menos algo, ~ de menos a algn to miss sth/sb

echarse *v.* to start

echarse a hacer algo to start to do sth (Los niños se echaron a llorar.)

edad *f.* age

desde temprana edad from an early age

edad adulta, mayoría de ~ adulthood

edad escolar school age

sacarse la edad, quitarse la ~ to make out that sb is younger

ser de edad to be elderly

ser de edad madura, ser de mediana ~ to be middle-aged

efectivo *m.* cash

en efectivo (in) cash

efecto *m.* **1** effect

efecto invernadero greenhouse effect

efecto retroactivo backdated

efecto secundario side effect

efectos especiales/sonoros special/sound effects

en efecto in fact

estar bajo los efectos de algo to be under the influence of sth

hacer efecto, tener ~ to take effect (Esos medicamentos ya no me hacen efecto. La nueva ley tendrá efecto a partir del año próximo.)

surtir efecto to have an effect

2 purpose

a los efectos de algo in order to do sth

al efecto, a tal ~, a este ~ for a particular purpose

ejemplo *m.* example

por ejemplo for example

embargo *m.* seizure/embargo

sin embargo however

empeñarse *v.* to strive, to insist

empeñarse en hacer algo to strive to do sth, to insist on doing sth (Debes empeñarte en lograr tus objetivos. Mi padre se empeñó en que fuera a visitarlo.)

empezar *v.* to begin

empezar a to begin to

empezar por, ~ con to begin with

en *prep.* in, inside, on

en algún momento at some point, sometime

en alguna parte somewhere

en auge flourishing

en broma as a joke (No le creas, lo dijo en broma.)

en buenas manos in good hands (Me marcho, pero los dejo en buenas manos.)

en cámara lenta in slow motion

en cambio however

en carne propia by personal experience

en carne y hueso in the flesh

en caso contrario otherwise

en caso de que in case of

en cierto modo in a way

en contra (de) against (No tengo nada en contra de tus compañeros de trabajo. Te recomiendo no ponerte en su contra.)

en cualquier caso, ~ todo caso in any case

en cuanto as soon (as)

en cuanto a regarding

en cuanto a algo/algn as regards sth/sb (En cuanto a la inflación, estamos tomando todas las medidas necesarias.)

en efectivo (in) cash

en el aire on air

en el futuro, ~ lo futuro in the future (En el futuro, envía los trabajos por correo electrónico. En lo futuro, sé más organizado con los archivos.)

en especie, ~ especies in kind

en fin finally, well then (En fin, creo que eso es todo.)

en frente de in front of

en la margen derecha/izquierda on the right/left bank (En la margen izquierda del río hay más árboles que en la margen derecha.)

en lontananza *form.* in the distance

en (propia) mano hand delivery

en nombre de algo/algn in the name of sth/sb

en pie to be up (awake), to be on one's feet, to be valid (Estuve en pie todo el día. Lo único que quedó en pie fue la antigua capilla. ¿Sabes si la oferta sigue en pie?)

en pie de guerra ready for war

en (un) principio in the beginning

en pro o en contra (de), ~ pro y ~ contra for or against (Hay muchas opiniones en pro y en contra de nuestra propuesta.)

en punto o'clock/on the dot

en razón de because of (No debes discriminar en razón de la edad o la raza de las personas.)

en resumen all in all/in summary

en seguida right away

en suma in short

en torno a about (El argumento de la película gira en torno a las relaciones amorosas.)

en vez de, ~ lugar de, ~ cambio de instead of

en virtud de in virtue of

en vista de que in view of the fact that

enamorado/a *adj.* in love

estar enamorado/a de algn to be in love with sb

enamorarse *v.* to fall in love

enamorarse de algo/algn to fall in love with sth/sb

encantado/a *adj.* glad/enchanted

estar encantado de to be glad about/pleased with

encantar *v.* to love, to really like; to enchant/put a spell on

encantarle a algn algo to love sth (Me encantan tus zapatos.)

encargar *v.* to ask

encargar algo a algn to ask sb to do sth (Me encargó una botella de vino. Le encargamos a José que cuidara de nuestras plantas.)

encargarse *v.* to take care

encargarse de algo to take care of sth

encariñarse *v.* to get attached

encariñarse con algo/algn to get attached to sth/sb

encima *adv.* on top

encima de on top of, on

por encima de over

encomendar *v.* to entrust

encomendar algo a algn to entrust sth to sb (Le encomendaron el sector administrativo.)

encontrar *v.* to find

encontrar algo, ~ a algn to find sth/sb

encontrarse *v.* to meet

encontrarse con algn to find sb

enemigo/a *adj.* enemy

ser enemigo/a de algo to be against sth (Soy enemigo de la violencia.)

enemistado/a *adj.* estranged

estar enemistado/a con algn to be estranged from sb

energía *f.* energy, power

energía atómica atomic power

energía eólica wind energy

energía hidráulica water power

energía nuclear nuclear energy

energía renovable renewable energy

energía solar solar energy

enfadarse *v.* to get angry

enfadarse con algn por algo to get angry at sb for sth

enfermar *v.* **1** to get ill

enfermar de algo *Esp.* to get ill

2 to drive mad *Am. L.* (¡Me enferma esa actitud!)

enfermarse *v.* to get ill

enfermarse de algo *Am. L.* to get ill

enfrentar *v.* to confront

enfrentar a algn con algn to bring sb face-to-face with sb

enfrentar algo, ~ a algn to face sth/sb

enfrentarse *v.* to confront

enfrentarse a algo to face sth

enfrentarse a algn, ~ con algn to confront sb

enfrente *adv.* **1** opposite
de enfrente across the street
enfrente de in front of, opposite
2 in front
enfrente de algo in front of sth

enojar *v.* to anger
enojar a algn algo to make sb angry

enojarse *v.* to get angry
enojarse con algn por algo to get angry at sb for sth

enorgullecerse *v.* to be proud
enorgullecerse de algo/algn, ~ por algo to be proud of sth/sb

enseguida *adv.* immediately
(Te llamaré enseguida.)

enseñar *v.* **1** to teach
enseñar algo a algn to teach sth to sb
2 to show
enseñar algo a algn to show sth to sb

entender *v.* to understand
entender algo, ~ a algn to understand sth/sb
entender de algo to know all about sth
entenderle algo a algn to understand sth sb does (Discúlpame, pero no te entiendo la letra.)

entenderse *v.* **1** to communicate
entenderse con algn to communicate with sb (Se entiende con su primo por señas.)
2 to get along
entenderse con algn to get along with sb (¡Qué suerte que los chicos se entienden!)
3 to deal
entenderse con algn to deal with sb (Es mejor entenderse con el encargado.)

enterarse *v.* to hear, to find out
enterarse de algo to find out about sth

entero/a *adj.* whole
por entero completely

entrar *v.* **1** to go into
entrar a algo *Am. L.* to go into a place (Nunca he entrado a ese cine.)
entrar en algo to go into sth (Entremos en ese banco. No quiere entrar en razón.)
2 to enter
entrar en algo to enter sth (Entramos en una nueva etapa.)

3 to start
entrar a hacer algo to start to do sth (¿A qué hora entras a la escuela?)
entrar como algo to start as sth (Quieren que entre a la editorial como traductora.)

entre *prep.* between
entre horas between meals (No comas golosinas entre horas.)

entregarse *v.* **1** to devote
entregarse a algo/algn to devote oneself to sth/sb
2 to give
entregarse a algo/algn to give oneself over to sth/sb

entristecerse *v.* to grow sad
entristecerse por algo, ~ con algo, ~ a causa de algo to grow sad because of sth

entrometerse *v.* to meddle
entrometerse en algo to meddle in sth

entusiasmarse *v.* to get excited
entusiasmarse por algo, ~ con algo/algn to get excited about sth/sb

enviar *v.* to send
enviar a algn por algo/algn to send sb out for sth/sb
enviar algo a algn to send sth to sb

envidiar *v.* to envy
envidiar algo a algn to envy sb because of sth

equivocarse *v.* to be wrong, to make a mistake
equivocarse en algo, ~ con algo/algn to be wrong/to make a mistake about sth/sb

escalera *f.* ladder, staircase
escalera caracol, ~ de caracol, ~ espiral spiral staircase
escalera de emergencia fire escape
escalera de mano ladder
escalera mecánica escalator

escandalizarse *v.* to be shocked
escandalizarse por algo to be shocked about sth

esconderse *v.* to hide
esconderse de algo/algn to hide from sth/sb

escondido/a *adj.* hidden
a escondidas secretly, behind sb's back

escribir *v.* to write

escribir a máquina to type

escribir algo a algn to write sth to sb

escribir sobre algo to write about sth

escribirse *v.* to write

escribirse con algn to write to each other

escuchar *v.* to hear

escuchar algo de algn, ~ algo sobre algn to hear sth about sb

esforzarse *v.* to strive

esforzarse en algo, ~ por algo to strive to do sth

eso *pron.* that

a eso de around (Llegué a eso de las ocho.)

por eso that's why

especializarse *v.* to major, to specialize

especializarse en algo to major/specialize in sth

especie *f.* **1** kind

en especie, en especies in kind

ser una especie de algo to be a sort of

2 species

especie en peligro (de extinción) endangered species

especie humana human race

especie protegida protected species

especular *v.* to speculate

especular sobre algo to speculate about sth

esperar *v.* **1** to wait

esperar algo, ~ a algn to wait for sth/sb

2 to hope (Espero que no llueva.)

estación *f.* station

estación de autobuses, ~ de ómnibus bus station

estación de bomberos fire station

estación de policía police station

estación de tren, ~ de trenes train station

estación del metro, ~ del subterráneo subway station

estafar *v.* to defraud/con/rip off

estafar (algo) a algn to defraud sb (out of sth)

estrella *f.* star

estrella de cine movie star

estrella de mar starfish

estrella en ascenso rising star

estrella fugaz shooting star

tener buena/mala estrella to be (born) lucky/unlucky

ver (las) estrellas to see stars

estudiar *v.* to study

estudiar algo to study sth

estudiar para algo to study for sth

evitar *v.* to avoid

evitar algo, ~ a algn to avoid sth/sb

exaltarse *v.* to get worked up

exaltarse por algo to get worked up about sth

exhortar *v.* to urge

exhortar a algn a hacer algo to urge sb to do sth (Los exhortó a continuar con su tarea.)

exigir *v.* to demand

exigir algo a algn to demand sth from sb

exponer *v.* **1** to expose

exponer algo a algo, ~ a algn a algo to expose sth/sb to sth (Es una tela muy delicada, no debes exponerla al sol.)

2 to explain, to describe

exponer algo a algn to explain sth to sb (Marcelo le expuso el problema claramente.)

exponerse *v.* to expose oneself

exponerse a algo to expose oneself to sth (No sé por qué te expones a esos peligros.)

extrañar *v.* to miss

extrañar algo, ~ a algn to miss sth/sb

extrañarse *v.* to be surprised

extrañarse de algo to be surprised at sth

F

fácil *adj.* easy

ser fácil de hacer to be easy to do (Es muy fácil de convencer.)

falta *f.* **1** lack

a falta de lacking/for lack of (A falta de un problema, ¡tenemos diez!)

echar algo en falta to be lacking (Aquí lo que se echa en falta es interés por el trabajo.)

falta de algo lack of sth

falta de educación bad manners

falta de pago nonpayment

2 fail

sin falta without fail

3 mistake

falta de ortografía spelling mistake

faltar *v.* to be missing

  faltarle algo a algn, ~ algn a algn to be in want of sth/sb (A ese muchacho le falta un objetivo en la vida. Le falta un amigo que lo aconseje.)

familia *f.* family

  de buena familia from a good family

  familia de acogida foster family

  familia numerosa large family

  familia política in-laws

  sentirse como en familia to feel at home

  tener familia to have children (Mi prima tuvo familia la semana pasada.)

  venirle/ser de familia to run in the family

familiarizarse *v.* to become familiar

  familiarizarse con algo to become familiar with sth

fascinar *v.* to fascinate

  fascinar a algn to fascinate sb (Me fascinan los cuentos de terror.)

felicitar *v.* to congratulate

  felicitar a algn por algo to congratulate sb on sth

fiarse *v.* to trust

  fiarse de algo/algn to trust sth/sb

fijarse *v.* to notice

  fijarse en algo/algn to notice sth/sb

fin *m.* **1** end

  al fin, por ~ at last

  al fin y al cabo after all

  el fin del mundo the end of the world

  en fin finally, well then

  fin de semana weekend

  poner fin a algo to put an end to sth

  por fin finally

  2 purpose

  a este fin, a tal ~, con este ~ with this aim

  con el fin de, a ~ de with the purpose of

  el fin de algo the purpose of sth

  sin fines de lucro, sin fines lucrativos not-for-profit

  un fin en sí mismo an end in itself

final *m.* end

  al final at/in the end

fondo *m.* depth

  a fondo in depth

forma *f.* **1** shape

  en plena forma in top form

  estar en forma, mantenerse en ~ to be/keep fit

  tomar forma to take shape

  2 way

  de cualquier forma, de una ~ o de otra, de todas formas anyway, in any case

  forma de pago method of payment

  forma de ser the way sb is

fortuna *f.* fortune

  amasar una fortuna, hacer una ~ to make a fortune

  por fortuna fortunately

  probar fortuna to try one's luck

frecuencia *f.* frequency

  con frecuencia frequently, often (¿Vienes a este bar con frecuencia?)

frente *f.* **1** forehead

  con erguida frente, con la ~ bien alta, con la ~ en alto, con la ~ levantada with one's head held high

  de frente, frente a ~ face-to-face

  2 front

  el frente de algo the front of sth

  estar al frente de algo to be in charge of sth

  hacer frente a algo/algn to face up to sth/sb

  hacer un frente común to form a united front

  3 *adv.* opposite

  frente a in front of, opposite

fuego *m.* fire

  a fuego lento on/at/over low heat

  abrir fuego contra algo/algn, abrir ~ sobre algo/algn open fire on sth/sb

  estar entre dos fuegos to be between a rock and a hard place

  fuego a discreción fire at will

  fuegos artificiales, ~ de artificio fireworks

  jugar con fuego to play with fire

  prender fuego a algo, pegar ~ a algo to set sth on fire

  sofocar el fuego to put out the fire

fuera *adv.* outside

  fuera de out/outside of

  por fuera de out/outside of

fuerza *f.* strength, force
  a fuerza de by (dint of)
  a la fuerza by force
  fuerza bruta brute force
  fuerza de gravedad force of gravity
  fuerza de trabajo workforce
  fuerza de voluntad willpower
  fuerza pública, fuerzas del orden, fuerzas de orden público police
  por fuerza necessarily
  por fuerza mayor, por causas de ~ mayor force majeure

fundarse *v.* to base
  fundarse en algo to be based on sth (¿En qué se fundan tus sospechas?)

futuro *m.* future
  con/sin futuro sth with good/no prospects (Es una profesión sin futuro. Ese es un muchacho con futuro.)
  en el futuro, en lo ~, a ~ in the future (En el futuro, envía los trabajos por correo electrónico. En lo futuro, sé más organizado con los archivos. Deberíamos evaluar los proyectos a futuro.)
  futuro cercano, ~ próximo near future
  no tener ningún futuro to have no future (Con esta crisis, nuestra empresa no tiene ningún futuro.)

G

gana *f.* desire
  de buena/mala gana willingly/unwillingly
  tener ganas de hacer algo, sentir ~ de hacer algo to feel like doing sth

ganar *v.* to win, to beat
  ganar a algn en algo to beat sb in sth (No quiero jugar contigo, siempre me ganas en todo.)
  ganar a algn para algo to win sb over to sth (Su intención es ganar al directorio para nuestro proyecto.)

general *adj.* general
  por lo general in general

genio *m.* **1** temper
  tener buen/mal genio, estar de buen/mal ~ to be even-/bad-tempered
  2 genius
  ser un genio con algo, ser un genio de

algo to be a genius at/very talented in sth (María es un genio con la pelota. Juan es un genio de las letras.)

gestión *f.* **1** process; procedure (Estoy haciendo las gestiones para abrir una tienda de ropa.)
  2 management
  gestión de proyectos project management
  3 (*pl.*) negotiations

golpe *m.* **1** knock, blow
  de golpe, de ~ y porrazo suddenly
  de un golpe all at once
  2 punch, hit
  golpe bajo hit below the belt
  golpe de efecto dramatic effect
  golpe de estado coup d'état
  golpe de fortuna, ~ de suerte stroke of luck

gozar *v.* to enjoy
  gozar de algo to enjoy sth (Mi abuela goza de buena salud, gracias a Dios.)

gracia *f.* grace
  no verle la gracia a algo to not find sth funny (No le veo la gracia a sus chistes.)

grande *adj.* big, large
  a lo grande luxuriously, in style (Festejaremos tu cumpleaños a lo grande.)

guardia *f.* guard
  bajar la guardia to lower one's guard
  con la guardia baja with one's guard down
  estar de guardia to be on duty/on call
  guardia de seguridad security guard
  guardia municipal, ~ urbana police/municipal guard

guiarse *v.* to follow
  guiarse por algo to follow sth (Nos guiamos por un antiguo mapa.)

gustar *v.* to like
  gustar de algo, ~ a uno algo/algn to like sb/sth

gusto *m.* **1** taste
  a gusto del consumidor *fam.* however you like
  hacer algo a gusto, hacer algo al ~ to do sth as you please
  tener buen/mal gusto to have good/bad taste

tener gusto a algo to taste of sth
2 pleasure
a gusto at ease (No me siento
    a gusto aquí.)
con mucho gusto with pleasure
darle el gusto a algn, hacerle el ~ a
    algn to indulge sb
de gusto, por ~ for the fun of it
mucho gusto, tanto ~ nice to meet you
tener el gusto de algo to be pleased
    to do sth
tomarle el gusto a algo, agarrarle el ~ a
    algo to get to like sth

H

habituarse *v.* to get used to
habituarse a algo to get used to sth
hablar *v.* to talk
hablar a algn to talk to sb
hablar acerca de algo/algn, ~ de algo/
    algn, ~ sobre algo/algn to talk about
    sth/sb
hablar de más to talk too much
ni hablar no way (¿Lo harías? ¡Ni hablar!)
hacer *v.* to do
hacer algo por algn to do sth for sb
hacerse *v.* to become
hacerse de algo/algn to become of sb/sth
    (¿Qué se hizo del coche que tenías? No
    sé qué se hizo de Juan, hace años que no
    lo veo.)
harto/a *adj.* fed up
estar harto/a de to be fed up with
hasta *prep.* until
hasta ahora, ~ la fecha, ~ el momento so far
hasta entonces until then
hasta que until (Hasta que llegue a casa,
    no estaré tranquilo.)
hasta tanto until such time as
no... hasta not until
hermano/a *m./f.* brother/sister
hermano/a gemelo/a, hermano/a
    mellizo/a twin brother/sister
hermano/a mayor/menor older/younger
    brother/sister
medio/a hermano/a half brother/sister
hijo/a *m./f.* son/daughter
como cualquier hijo de vecino, como

todo ~ de vecino like everybody else
hijo/a adoptivo/a adopted son/daughter
hijo/a ilegítimo/a illegitimate
    son/daughter
hijo/a único/a only child
hincapié *m.* emphasis
hacer hincapié en algo to emphasize sth
hora *f.* hour; time
a altas horas de la madrugada/noche in
    the wee/small hours of the morning/night
a la hora de when it is time to
    (A la hora de escribir, prefiero hacerlo en
    un lugar tranquilo.)
a primera hora, a última ~ first thing, at
    the last moment
dar la hora, decir la ~ to tell the time
entre horas between meals (No
    comas golosinas entre horas.)
ser hora de to be time to
ya ser hora de to be about time (Ya era
    hora de que volvieras.)
horario *m.* schedule
horario de trabajo work schedule
horno *m.* oven
horno de microondas microwave oven
huelga *f.* strike
declararse en huelga to go on strike
estar de huelga, estar en ~ to be on strike
huelga de brazos caídos sit-down strike
huelga de hambre hunger strike
huir *v.* to run away, to flee
huir de algo/algn to run away from sth/sb
huirle a algn to avoid sb

I

idea *f.* idea
hacerse a la idea de algo to come to terms
    with sth
idéntico/a *adj.* identical
ser idéntico/a a algn to be identical to sb
igual *adj.* equal
al igual que just as
da igual que doesn't matter
igual a algo/algn, ~ que algo/algn the
    same as sth/sb (Mi brazalete es igual al
    tuyo. Es igual que su madre.)
igual de algo the same as (Está igual de
    alta que la última vez que la vi.)

ser igual algo que algo, dar ~ algo que algo (two or more things) to be equal/the same

ilusionado/a *adj.* hopeful

estar ilusionado/a con to be hopeful for

ilusionarse *v.* to be excited

ilusionarse con algo/algn to be excited about sth/sb

impedir *v.* to prevent

impedir a algn hacer algo to prevent sb from doing sth

importar *v.* to care

importarle algo a algn to care about sth

impuesto *m.* tax

evasión de impuestos tax evasion

impuesto a/sobre la renta income tax

impuesto al valor agregado/añadido, ~ sobre el valor agregado/añadido value-added tax

impuesto directo/indirecto direct/indirect tax

libre de impuestos tax-free

imputar *v.* to attribute/charge/hold responsible

imputarle algo a algn to attribute sth to sb

indemnizar *v.* to compensate

indemnizar a algn con algo to give sth to sb in compensation

indemnizar a algn por algo to compensate sb for sth

indignar *v.* to outrage

indignar algo a algn to be outraged by sth (Esa decisión ha indignado a todos los vecinos.)

indignarse *v.* to be outraged, to become indignant

indignarse con algn por algo to get angry at sb for sth

inducir *v.* to lead

inducir a algn a algo to lead sb to do sth (Las declaraciones del político pueden inducir a la gente a la venganza.)

inferir *v.* to infer

inferir algo de algo to infer sth from sth (Eso es lo que se infiere de las pruebas.)

influir *v.* to influence

influir en algo/algn, ~ a algn en algo to influence sth/sb

informar *v.* to inform

informar a algn de algo, ~ a algn sobre algo to inform sb of sth

informarse *v.* to inquire

informarse de algo, ~ sobre algo to inquire about sth

ingresar *v.* to join, to enter

ingresar en algo, ~ a algo to join sth

inmiscuirse *v.* to interfere, to meddle

inmiscuirse en algo to interfere in sth

inscribirse *v.* to register

inscribirse dentro de algo to register within sth (Esta medida se inscribe dentro de nuestra política de inmigración.)

inscribirse en algo to enroll in/sign up for sth

insistir *v.* to insist

insistir en algo, ~ sobre algo to insist on sth

inspirarse *v.* to be inspired

inspirarse en algo to be inspired by sth

instar *v.* to urge

instar a algn a algo to urge sb to do sth

interés *m.* interest

de interés + [adj.], of + [adj.] + interest (Es un programa de interés humano/político.)

despertar (el) interés to arouse interest (El experimento despertó mucho interés.)

poner interés en algo to take interest in sth

por el interés de algn for sb's own interest (Lo hizo por su propio interés.)

tener interés en algo to be interested in sth

interesar *v.* to concern, to interest

interesar a algn en algo to interest sb in sth (Logré interesarlo en nuestra idea.)

interesar algo/algn a algn to be interested in sth/sb (A mí no me interesa lo que piensan los demás. A Juan no le interesan los chismes.)

interesarse *v.* to take interest

interesarse en algo/algn, ~ por algo/algn to take interest in sth/sb

invitar *v.* to invite

invitar a algn a algo to invite sb to sth

ir *v.* to go

ir a hacer algo to go to do sth

ir (a) por algo/algn to go to get sth/sb

irritar *v.* to annoy

irritar a algn algo to annoy sb (Me irrita su personalidad.)

irritar a algn con algo to annoy sb with sth (Marcela irritó a su hermana con sus insultos.)

irritarse *v.* to get annoyed

irritarse con algo, ~ por algo to get annoyed at sth (Se irritó por lo que dije. Siempre se irrita con las críticas de sus colegas.)

irse *v.* to leave

irse de un lugar to leave a place

izquierda *f.* left

a la izquierda (de) to/on the left (of) (Si miran a la izquierda, verán uno de los mayores atractivos de la ciudad. María está a la izquierda de Juana.)

de izquierda left-wing (Sectores de izquierda se opusieron a la medida.)

de la izquierda on the left (Busca en el cajón de la izquierda.)

J

jactarse *v.* to brag

jactarse de algo to brag about sth

juego *m.* **1** game

estar algo en juego to be at stake (No puedo hacer eso, mi carrera está en juego.)

juego de azar game of chance

juego de ingenio guessing game

juego de mesa, ~ de tablero, ~ de salón board game

juego de palabras pun

poner algo en juego to bring sth to bear (No voy a poner en juego nuestro futuro.)

2 play

juego limpio/sucio fair/foul play

seguirle el juego a algn to play along with sb

ser un juego de niños to be a child's game

3 set

hacer juego con algo to match sth

juego de llaves set of keys

juego de té/café tea/coffee set

jugar *v.* to play

jugar a algo to play sth (¿Quieres jugar al avioncito?)

jugar con algo/algn to play with sth/sb (Estás jugando con tu futuro. ¡Estoy harta de que juegues conmigo!)

jugar contra algo/algn to play against sth/sb (Mañana jugaremos contra un equipo muy bueno.)

jugarse *v.* to risk

jugarse algo to put sth at risk (¿No ves que me estoy jugando el puesto con esto?)

juicio *m.* **1** judgment; sense

estar en su sano juicio to be in one's right mind

juicio de valor value judgement

perder el juicio to go out of one's mind, to go crazy

tener poco juicio to not be very sensible

2 opinion

a juicio de algn in sb's opinion (A mi juicio, lo que hizo está mal.)

dejar algo al juicio de algn to leave sth up to sb (Dejo la decisión a tu juicio.)

3 trial

ir a juicio to go to court

juicio político political trial

llevar a juicio to take to court

junto *adv.* close to

junto a close to, next to

jurar *v.* to swear (Juro que soy inocente.)

jurar por algo/algn to swear to sth/sb (Lo juró por sus hijos. Le juró por Dios que era cierto.)

justificar *v.* to justify, to excuse

justificar a algn to make excuses for sb (No intentes justificarlo, es un irresponsable.)

justificar algo to justify sth (Debes justificar todas tus ausencias.)

juzgar *v.* to judge

a juzgar por algo judging by

juzgar algo, ~ a algn por algo to judge sth/sb for sth

juzgar por uno mismo to judge for oneself

L

lado *m.* side
al lado de beside, next to
por otro lado on the other hand
lamentar *v.* to regret (Lamento lo sucedido.)
lamentarse *v.* to deplore; to complain
lamentarse de algo/algn to deplore sth/sb, to complain about sth/sb (Me lamento de la falta de interés de los jóvenes por la lectura.)
largo/a *adj.* long
a la larga in the long run (Estoy segura de que Pedro, a la larga, comprenderá que es por su bien.)
a lo largo de throughout
lástima *f.* **1** shame, pity
darle lástima a algn to be a shame (Me da lástima dejar esta casa.)
¡Qué lástima! What a pity!
2 sympathy
sentir lástima por algn to feel sorry for sb (Siento lástima por esa pobre madre.)
lejos *adv.* far
lejos de far from
lente *m./f.* lens
lentes de contacto (duro/a(s), blando/a(s)) (hard/soft) contact lenses
ley *f.* law
con todas las de la ley rightly (No puedes quejarte, ella te ha ganado con todas las de la ley.)
conforme la ley, según dispone la ~ in accordance with the law
de buena ley genuine (Es oro de buena ley.)
la ley de la selva, la ~ de la jungla the law of the jungle
ley de la oferta y la demanda law of supply and demand
ley de ventaja advantage
ley seca Prohibition
promulgar/dictar una ley to promulgate/enact a law
violar la ley to break the law
libertad *f.* freedom, liberty
dejar a algn en libertad to free/release sb
libertad bajo fianza, ~ bajo palabra, ~ provisional bail
libertad condicional parole

libertad de cátedra academic freedom
libertad de conciencia freedom of conscience
libertad de cultos, ~ de culto freedom of worship
libertad de expresión, ~ de palabra freedom of expression/speech
libertad de prensa freedom of the press
libre *adj.* free
libre de hacer algo free to do sth (Eres libre de decir lo que quieras.)
limitarse *v.* to merely (do)
limitarse a algo to merely do sth (Por favor, limítese a responder la pregunta.)
limosna *f.* alms
dar limosna to give money (to beggars)
pedir limosna to beg
vivir de limosnas to live off begging
limpio/a *adj.* clean
limpio/a de algo purified of, unblemished by (Es un producto limpio de impurezas.)
pasar algo en limpio, pasar algo a ~ to make a clean copy of sth
sacar algo en limpio to get sth clear
listo/a *adj.* ready
estar listo para algo to be ready to do sth
llanto *m.* crying
romper en llanto to burst into tears
llave *f.* **1** key
bajo siete llaves hidden away
la llave de oro, las llaves de la ciudad the keys to the city
llave de contacto, ~ de encendido ignition key
llave en mano for immediate occupancy (Nos especializamos en construir casas llave en mano.)
llave inglesa monkey wrench
llave maestra master key
2 valve
llave de paso stopcock, main valve
llave del gas gas jet
llegar *v.* **1** to arrive
llegar a un lugar to arrive somewhere
2 to become
llegar a ser algo to become sth/sb (Si sigue así, Agustín llegará a ser un gran escritor.)
llenar *v.* to fill

llenar a algn de algo to fill sb with sth (El embarazo los llenó de alegría.)

llenar algo de algo, ~ algo con algo to fill sth with sth

llenarse *v.* to fill

llenarse de algo, ~ algo de algo to fill with sth (La maceta se llenó de insectos. Los ojos se le llenaron de lágrimas.)

llevar *v.* to bring

llevar algo a algn to bring sth to sb

llevarle... años a algn to be... years older than sb

llevarse *v.* **1** to take away

llevarse algo, ~ a algn to take sth/sb away **2** to get along

llevarse bien/mal con algn to get along/ to not get along with sb

loco/a *adj.* **1** crazy

a lo loco in a crazy way (Está gastando el dinero a lo loco.)

estar loco/a con algo, estar ~ de algo, estar ~ por algo/algn to be crazy with/ from sth/for sth/sb (Está loco con sus novelas. Está loca de alegría. Está loco por su novia.)

loco/a de atar, ~ de remate to be stark raving mad **2** anxious

estar loco/a por algo to be most anxious to do sth (Estamos locos por comenzar a entrenar.)

lograr *v.* to succeed, to achieve sth (Creo que lo lograrás.)

lontananza *f.* distance

en lontananza in the distance

lotería *f.* lottery

ganarse la lotería, sacarse la ~ to win the lottery

sacarse la lotería con algn to strike it lucky with sb

ser una lotería to be a lottery (Comprar un apartamento en ese barrio es una lotería.)

tocarle la lotería a algn to win the lottery

luchar *v.* to fight

luchar contra algo to fight against sth (Está luchando contra una enfermedad muy grave.)

luchar por algo/algn to fight for sth/sb (Luchamos por los derechos de los ciudadanos.)

luego *adv.* after

luego de after

lugar *m.* place

a como dé lugar, a como diera ~ *Am. L.* however possible

dar lugar a algo to provoke sth (Eso dará lugar a disputas.)

dejar a algn en mal lugar to put sb in an awkward position

en lugar de instead of

lugar común cliché (Este discurso está lleno de prejuicios y lugares comunes.)

sin lugar a dudas without a doubt

tener lugar to take place

lujo *m.* luxury

con lujo de detalles with a wealth of detail

darse el lujo de, permitirse el ~ de to have the satisfaction of

de lujo luxury (Iván y Paola se alojarán en un hotel de lujo durante su luna de miel.)

luna *f.* moon

estar con luna, estar de ~ to be in a foul/ bad mood

estar en la luna (de Valencia), vivir en la ~ (de Valencia) to have one's head in the clouds

luna creciente waxing moon

luna de miel honeymoon

luna llena full moon

luna menguante waning moon

luna nueva new moon

luto *m.* mourning

estar de luto por algn to be in mourning for sb

guardar luto a algn to be mourning for sb

ir de luto, llevar ~ to wear mourning clothes

luto riguroso deep mourning

ponerse de luto to go into mourning

quitarse el luto to come out of mourning

M

madrugada *f.* early morning

de madrugada early in the morning (Llegamos de madrugada.)

madrugar *v.* to get/wake up very early

mal *m.* **1** evil

mal menor lesser of two evils **2** illness

echarle el mal de ojo a algn, darle el ~ de ojo a algn to give sb the evil eye

mal de altura, mal de las alturas altitude sickness

mal de Alzheimer/de Chagas/de Parkinson/de San Vito Alzheimer's/Chagas'/Parkinson's/Huntington's disease

mal de amores lovesickness

mal *adj./adv.* bad

estar mal de algo to be short of sth (Desde que Juan se quedó sin trabajo, la familia ha estado muy mal de dinero.)

nada mal not bad at all

malo/a *adj.* bad

mandar *v.* **1** to send

mandar a algn to send sb

mandar algo a algn to send sth to sb

2 to order

mandar a algn a hacer algo to order sb to do sth (¡No me mandes a callar!)

manera *f.* way

a la manera de algn sb's way (Hagámoslo a mi manera.)

a manera de algo by way of (Traje este dibujo a manera de ejemplo.)

de buena/mala manera in a good/bad way

de cualquier manera, de todas maneras anyway, in any case

de esa manera in that way

de manera que so (¿De manera que la decisión ya está tomada?)

de ninguna manera certainly not

manga *f.* sleeve

sacar algo de la manga off the top of one's head

mano *f.* hand

a (la) mano close at hand (¿Tienes tu planilla a (la) mano?)

a mano by hand

con las propias manos with sb's own hands

de la mano hand in hand

de primera mano firsthand

dejar algo en las manos de algn to leave sth in the hands of sb

en buenas manos in good hands (Me marcho, pero los dejo en buenas manos.)

en (propia) mano hand delivery

ir de mano en ~, pasar de ~ en ~ to pass around

irse algo de las manos to get out of hand

levantar la mano to put one's hand up

manos en alto, arriba las manos, manos arriba hands up

tender una mano, ofrecer una ~, dar una ~, echar una ~ to lend a hand

tomarle la mano a algo, agarrarle la ~ a algo to get the hang of sth

maravilla *f.* wonder

a las mil maravillas wonderfully (¡Todo salió a las mil maravillas!)

maravillarse *v.* to be amazed/astonished

maravillarse de algo/algn, ~ con algo/algn, ~ ante algo to be amazed at sth/sb

margen *f.* bank, side *m.* margin

estar al margen de la sociedad/ley to be on the fringes of society/the law

ganar por un amplio/estrecho margen to win by a comfortable/narrow margin

mantenerse al margen de algo to keep out of sth

margen de beneficio, ~ comercial, ~ de ganancias profit margin

margen de error margin of error

margen de tolerancia range of tolerance

nota al margen margin note

mayor *adj.* greater, older

por mayor wholesale

mediados *m.* middle

a mediados de in the middle of (Voy a retirar las cosas que faltan a mediados del mes que viene.)

medida *f.* measure

a medida que as (Resolveremos los problemas a medida que vayan surgiendo.)

medio/a *adj.* half

a medias halfway

meditar *v.* to meditate

meditar sobre algo to meditate on sth

mejor *adj.* better

a lo mejor maybe

menor *adj.* lesser

por menor retail

menos *adj.* less

a menos que unless

al menos at least

por lo menos at least

menudo/a *adj.* small, slight (Es un hombre muy menudo.)

a menudo often

menudo... *Esp.* what a..., such a... (¡Menudo lío! ¡Caí en menuda trampa!)

mercado *m.* market

mercado al aire libre open-air market

mercado cambiario, ~ de divisas foreign exchange market

mercado de abastos, ~ de abasto market

mercado de las pulgas, ~ de pulgas flea market

mercado negro black market

mercado persa bazaar

mesa *f.* table

bendecir la mesa to say grace

levantar la mesa, quitar la ~, recoger la ~ to clear the table

mesa auxiliar side table

mesa de centro, ~ ratona coffee table

mesa de comedor/cocina dining room/ kitchen table

mesa de dibujo drawing board

mesa de negociaciones, ~ negociadora negotiating table

mesa de noche, ~ de luz bedside table

mesa plegable folding table

poner la mesa to set the table

sentarse a la mesa to sit at the table

meta *f.* **1** finish line

llegar a la meta to reach the finish line

2 aim

alcanzar una meta to reach a goal

ponerse algo por meta to set oneself a goal

tener una meta, trazarse una ~ to set a goal for oneself

meterse *v.* **1** to get involved

meterse en algo to get involved in sth

2 to pick on

meterse con algn to pick on sb

3 to become

meterse a algo to become sth (Juan se metió a periodista pero no sabe escribir bien.)

miedo *m.* fear

tener miedo a algo/algn to be afraid of sb/sth

tener miedo de algo to be afraid of sth

mira *f.* view

con miras a with the purpose of

mismo/a *adj.* same

dar lo mismo que to make no difference

misterio *m.* mystery

dejarse de misterio to stop being mysterious (¡Dejaos ya de tanto misterio y contadnos cuándo os vais a casar!)

novela de misterio mystery novel

moda *f.* fashion

estar a la moda, estar de ~, ponerse de ~ to be in fashion

estar de última moda to be very fashionable

estar pasado de moda to be out of fashion

ir a la moda to be trendy

modo *m.* way, manner

a modo de by way of (Usó su cuaderno a modo de pantalla.)

de buen/mal modo, de buenos/malos modos in a good/bad way

de cualquier modo, de todos modos anyway, in any case

de modo que in such a way that

de ningún modo no way

de tal modo que, de ~ que so (that) (Estudió mucho, de tal modo que aprobó el examen. Ya es tarde, de modo que me voy a casa.)

del mismo modo, de igual ~ in the same way

en cierto modo in a way

modo de empleo instructions for use

ni modo not a chance

no es modo de hacer las cosas no way of going about things

molestar *v.* to bother

molestar a algn to bother sb

molestarse *v.* **1** to get upset

molestarse con algn por algo to get upset with sb for sth

2 to take the trouble

molestarse en hacer algo to take the trouble to do sth

momento *m.* moment

en algún momento at some point, sometime

morirse *v.* to die

morirse de algo to die of sth, to be really hungry, thirsty... (Se murió de pulmonía. ¡Me muero de hambre!)

morirse por algo to die for sth (¡Me muero por conocerlo personalmente!)

motivo *m.* reason

  con motivo de the reason for

  por motivos de fuerza mayor force majeure

  por ningún motivo under no circumstances

mozo/a *m./f.* **1** young man/woman

  buen mozo, buena moza good-looking boy/girl

  2 waiter/waitress *Arg.*

muela *f.* molar; back tooth

  muela de juicio wisdom tooth

muerte *f.* death

  amenaza de muerte death threat

  de mala muerte lousy (No vayas a ese restaurante, es de mala muerte.)

  estar condenado a muerte to be sentenced to death

  hacer algo a muerte to do sth to death

  herido de muerte fatally wounded

muerto/a *adj.* dead

  muerto/a de cansancio, ~ de sueño dead-tired

  muerto/a de frío freezing

  muerto/a de hambre starving

  muerto/a de miedo frightened to death

  muerto/a de risa dying of laughter

N

nada *pron.* nothing

  como si nada as if it were nothing

  de nada, por ~ you're welcome

  nada de algo not to need any of sth (No necesitamos nada de combustible.)

  nada de nada not a thing

necesidad *f.* need

  por necesidad out of necessity

negar *v.* to deny

  negar algo a algn to deny sth to sb

negarse *v.* to refuse, to deny

  negarse a hacer algo to refuse to do sth

  negarse algo to deny oneself sth (Se niega todo para que su hija pueda estudiar.)

negociar *v.* to negotiate

  negociar algo con algn to negotiate sth with sb

nombre *m.* name

  a nombre de algn addressed to sb

  en nombre de algo/algn in the name of sth/sb

  no tener nombre to be beyond belief (Lo que has hecho no tiene nombre.)

  nombre artístico stage name

  nombre completo full name

  nombre de guerra, ~ de batalla alias, pseudonym

  nombre de mujer/varón girl's/boy's name

  nombre de pila first name

notar *v.* to notice

  hacerse notar to draw attention to oneself

  notar algo to notice sth

nube *f.* cloud

  por las nubes sky-high (Los precios están por las nubes.)

nuevo/a *adj.* new

  de nuevo again

O

obligar *v.* to force

  obligar a algn a hacer algo to force sb to do sth

obra *f.* work

  obra benéfica, ~ de beneficencia, ~ de caridad act of charity

  obra de arte work of art

  obra de consulta reference book

  obra de teatro theater play

  obra maestra masterpiece

obstinarse *v.* to insist

  obstinarse en algo to insist on sth (Se obstina en dificultar las cosas.)

ocuparse *v.* to be in charge

  ocuparse de algo/algn to be in charge of sth/sb

ofender *v.* to offend

  ofender a algn to offend sb

ofenderse *v.* to be offended

  ofenderse con algn por algo to be offended with sb because of sth

ojo *m.* eye

  a los ojos de la sociedad in the eyes of society

  guiñar el ojo to wink

  ¡Ojo! Be careful!, Watch out!

tener (buen) ojo to be sharp (Mi hermano tiene muy buen ojo para estas cosas.)

oler *v.* to smell

oler a algo to smell like sth (La habitación olía a jazmines.)

oler algo to smell sth (Huele este perfume, es francés.)

olvidarse *v.* to forget

olvidarse de algo/algn to forget about sth/sb

olvidársele algo a algn to forget about sth

opinar *v.* to have an opinion

opinar (algo) de algo/algn, ~ sobre algo/algn to have an opinion about sth/sb (¿Qué opinas de la reforma económica? El ministro opinó sobre las nuevas medidas. Pablo opina que su nuevo jefe es un tirano.)

opinión *f.* opinion

cambiar de opinión to change sb's mind (Mi hermano cambió de opinión sobre las vacaciones.)

oponerse *v.* to oppose

oponerse a algo/algn to oppose sth/sb

optar *v.* to choose

optar por algo to choose sth

ordenar *v.* to order

ordenar algo a algn to order sb to do sth

orgulloso/a *adj.* proud

estar orgulloso/a de to be proud of

oscuro/a *adj.* dark

a oscuras in the dark

P

padecer *v.* to suffer

padecer de algo to suffer from sth

pagar *v.* to pay

pagar al contado, ~ en efectivo to pay in cash

pagar algo a algn to pay sth to sb

pagar algo con algo to pay for sth with sth

pagar (algo) por algo to pay (sth) for sth

para *prep.* for, to

no ser para tanto to not exaggerate/to not be so bad (No te quejes por eso, que no es para tanto.)

para con with (Son muy buenos para con los niños.)

para siempre forever

parada *f.* stop

parada de autobús, ~ de ómnibus bus stop

parada de metro subway stop

parada de taxi taxi stand

parecer *v.* **1** to look like

al parecer, ~ que apparently, evidently, it would seem/appear

2 to have an opinion

a mi parecer in my opinion

parecer mentira to seem impossible

parecerse *v.* to be like

no parecerse en nada a algo/algn not to be/look alike at all

parecerse a algo/algn to be/look like sth/sb

parecido/a *adj.* **1** similar

ser parecido/a a algo/algn to be similar to sth/sb

2 good-looking

ser bien/mal parecido/a to be good-/bad-looking

pareja *f.* **1** couple; pair

formar parejas to get into pairs

vivir en pareja to live together

2 partner

la pareja the other one (No encuentro la pareja de este calcetín.)

tener pareja to have a partner (Después de tanto tiempo de soltería, finalmente tengo pareja.)

parte *f.* part

en alguna parte somewhere

por otra parte besides (La película es interesante y, por otra parte, no tengo nada que hacer.)

participar *v.* to take part

participar en algo to take part in sth

partido *m.* game, match

sacar partido de algo to take advantage of sth

tomar partido to take sides

partir *v.* to leave

a partir de starting

pasaje *m.* ticket

pasaje de ida one-way ticket

pasaje de ida y vuelta round-trip ticket

sacar un pasaje to buy a ticket

paseo *m.* walk

estar de paseo to be visiting

mandar a algn a paseo to tell sb to get lost

paseo marítimo esplanade

paso *m.* **1** passage, passing; path

dicho sea de paso by the way (Dicho sea de paso, te queda muy bien ese color.)

el paso del tiempo the passage of time

2 way

abrir paso to make way

abrirse paso to make one's way

ceder el paso to yield

cerrar el paso to block the way

3 pass

paso fronterizo border crossing

4 step

a pasos agigantados by leaps and bounds

con paso firme firmly, purposefully

dar un paso en falso to stumble; to make a false move

paso a paso step-by-step

5 rate, speed

a este paso at this rate

a paso de hormiga/tortuga at a snail's pace

pata *f.* leg

estirar la pata *fam.* to kick the bucket

meter la pata *fam.* to put one's foot in one's mouth

pata delantera/trasera front/hind leg

patas para arriba *fam.* upside down

saltar en una pata to jump for joy

paz *f.* peace

dejar en paz algo, dejar en ~ a algn, dejar a algn vivir en ~ to let sth/sb alone

descansar en paz rest in peace

estar en paz, quedar en ~ *fam.* to be at peace

firmar la paz to sign a peace agreement

hacer las paces to make up

pedir *v.* to ask; to request

pedir algo a algn to ask sb (for) sth (Pidió un adelanto a su jefe. Pidió a su secretaria que escribiera una carta.)

pedir algo por algo to ask sth for sth (¿Cuánto pide por la bicicleta?)

pedir prestado to borrow

pelearse *v.* to quarrel

pelearse con algn por algo to quarrel with sb over sth

pelo *m.* hair

andar con los pelos de punta, estar con los ~ de punta to be in a real state

caérsele el pelo a algn to lose one's hair

cortarle el pelo a algn to cut sb's hair

cortarse el pelo to have one's hair cut

no tener ni un pelo de tonto to not be a fool

no tener pelos en la lengua to not mince one's words

pelo lacio, ~ liso straight hair

pelo rizado curly hair

ponerle a algn los pelos de punta to make sb's hair stand on end

por un pelo just (¡Nos salvamos por un pelo!)

traído por los pelos, traído de los ~ far-fetched

pena *f.* sorrow

vale la pena que it's worth it that/to (Vale la pena que te esfuerces, tendrás una buena recompensa.)

pensar *v.* to think

pensar algo de algn to think sth of sb (Pienso que Susana es muy cruel.)

pensar en algo/algn to think about sth/sb

percatarse *v.* to notice

percatarse de algo to notice sth

permiso *m.* permission

dar permiso, pedir ~ to give/ask for permission

(con) permiso excuse me

permitir *v.* to allow

permitir algo a algn to allow sb to do sth

persistir *v.* to persist

persistir en algo to persist in sth

pertenecer *v.* to belong

pertenecer a algn to belong to sb (Este reloj le pertenecía a mi bisabuelo.)

pesar *m.* regret, sorrow

a pesar de, pese a in spite of

mal que le pese a algn whether sb likes it or not

pie *m.* foot

a pie on foot

al pie de la letra literally, exactly (Siguieron nuestras instrucciones al pie de la letra.)

al pie de la montaña, a los pies de la montaña at the foot of the mountain

con buen pie, con el ~ derecho to get off to a good start (Creo que no comenzaron con buen pie. Nuestra relación comenzó con el pie derecho.)

con mal pie, con el ~ izquierdo badly

dar pie a algo to give rise to sth

dar pie con bola *fam.* to get sth right (Últimamente todo me sale mal, no doy pie con bola.)

de pie standing (Ponte de pie cuando entre la maestra.)

en pie to be up (awake), to be on one's feet, to be standing (Estuve en pie todo el día. Lo único que quedó en pie fue la antigua capilla. ¿Sabes si la oferta sigue en pie?)

en pie de guerra ready for war

hacer pie to be able to touch the bottom (No puedo hacer pie en esa piscina.)

nacer de pie to be born lucky

nota a pie de página, nota al ~ de página footnote

perder pie, no hacer ~ to get out of one's depth (Si pierdes pie, llámame enseguida.)

pie de fotografía caption

pie de imprenta imprint

pie equino clubfoot

pie plano flat foot

pila *f.* **1** battery

funcionar a pila(s), funcionar con pila(s) to run on batteries

2 pile, loads

pila de algo, pilas de algo mountains of sth

plano *m.* flat

de plano outright (Se negó de plano a participar en el negocio.)

plantado/a *adj.* planted

dejar plantado/a a algn to stand sb up (¡No puedo creer que te dejara plantado!)

plantado de algo planted with sth (El campo está plantado de trigo.)

plazo *m.* **1** period

corto plazo short-term

dar un plazo to give a deadline (Nos dieron un plazo de 30 días para comenzar a pagar.)

largo plazo long-term

medio plazo, mediano ~ middle term

2 installment

pagar a plazos to pay in installments

poco *pron.* little

a poco de algo shortly after sth

dentro de poco soon

poco antes de algo shortly before sth

poco y nada very little, to hardly do sth (Hicieron poco y nada por sus compañeros.)

por poco almost (¡Por poco le creo sus mentiras!)

poder *v.* to be possible

puede (ser) que might/could be (Puede ser que salgamos campeones este año, estamos jugando bien. Puede que mañana llegue tarde a casa, tengo una reunión con mi jefa.)

poner *v.* **1** to put

poner algo en marcha to start sth

poner algo/algn en un lugar to put sth somewhere, to put sb in his/her place

2 to make

poner a algn de una manera to make sb feel some way (Ese poema me pone triste.)

ponerse *v.* to begin

ponerse a hacer algo to begin to (Ponte a hacer la tarea ahora mismo.)

por *prep.* by, for, in

por adelantado in advance

por ahora for the time being

por aquí around here

por casualidad by accident

por causa de because of

por completo, ~ entero completely

por consiguiente, ~ lo tanto therefore

por cuanto insofar as

por delante ahead (Aún nos queda mucho por delante.)

por delante de in front of, opposite (Ayer pasé por delante de tu casa.)

por demás extremely (Te comportas de una manera por demás grosera.)

por dentro de in, inside of

por desgracia unfortunately

por detrás de behind, in the back of

por Dios for heaven's sake

por ejemplo for example

por el camino on the way (Vamos, te lo cuento por el camino.)

por el principio at the beginning

por encima de over

por entre in between (Los niños se metieron por entre los invitados y los perdimos de vista.)

por escrito in writing

por eso that's why

por fin finally

por fortuna fortunately

por fuera de out, outside of

por fuerza necessarily

por fuerza mayor, ~ causas de fuerza mayor, ~ motivos de fuerza mayor force majeure

por gusto for the fun of it

por las buenas o por las malas one way or the other

por las nubes sky-high

por lo demás apart from that

por lo general, ~ regla general in general

por lo menos at least

por lo pronto, ~ de pronto, ~ el pronto for a start

por lo tanto therefore

por lo visto apparently

por mayor wholesale

por menor retail

por nada you're welcome

por necesidad out of necessity

por ningún motivo under no circumstances

por otra parte, ~ otro lado besides (La película es interesante y, por otra parte, no tengo nada que hacer.)

por poco almost (¡Por poco le creo sus mentiras!)

por principio on principle

por siempre jamás forever and ever

por suerte luckily

por supuesto of course

por un pelo just (¡Nos salvamos por un pelo!)

por... vez for the... time

preferir *v.* to prefer

preferir algo a algo to prefer sth to sth

preguntar *v.* to ask

preguntar algo a algn to ask sb sth

preguntar (a algn) por algo/algn to ask (sb) about sth/sb

preocupado/a *adj.* worried

estar preocupado/a por to be worried about

preocupar *v.* to be worried

preocupar a algn to be worried about sth

preocuparse *v.* to worry

preocuparse de algo to take interest in sth (No se preocupó más del tema.)

preocuparse por algo/algn to worry about sth/sb (Estoy preocupada por la educación de mis hijos.)

prescindir *v.* **1** to do without

prescindir de algo/algn to do without sth/sb

prescindir de los servicios de algn to dispense with sb's services

2 to disregard

prescindir de algo to disregard sth

3 to dispense

prescindir de algo to dispense of sth (Decidió prescindir de los detalles.)

presenciar *v.* to witness

presenciar algo to witness sth

prestar *v.* to lend

prestar algo a algn to lend sth to sb

primero/a *adj.* first

ser el/la primero/a en hacer algo to be the first one to do sth (Eres el primero en ocuparse de los niños.)

principio *m.* **1** beginning

a principios de at the beginning of (Supongo que nos mudaremos a principios de año.)

al principio at first

desde el principio, desde un ~ from the beginning

en (un) principio in the beginning

por el principio at the beginning

2 principle

cuestión de principios question of principles

por principio on principle

ser algn de principios to be someone with principles

prisa *f.* haste

  correr prisa to be in a rush

  darse prisa to hurry

privar *v.* to deprive

  privar a algn de algo to deprive sb of sth

privarse *v.* to deprive oneself

  privarse de algo to deprive oneself of sth

procurar *v.* **1** to try, to aim to/at

  procurar hacer algo to try to do sth
    (Procura terminar el proyecto esta semana.)

  2 to obtain

  procurar algo para algn to obtain sth for
    sb (Procuraremos alimentos
    para los refugiados.)

prohibir *v.* to ban/forbid

  prohibirle a algn algo to forbid sb
    to do sth

  prohibirle algo a algn to ban sb from
    doing sth

pronto *adv.* soon

  de pronto suddenly

  ¡hasta pronto! see you soon!

  lo más pronto posible as soon as possible

  por lo pronto, por de ~, por el ~ for
    a start

  tan pronto como as soon as, once

propina *f.* tip

  dar propina to tip

  de propina tip (¿Cuánto has dejado
    de propina?)

  dejar una propina to leave a tip

proponer *v.* to propose, suggest

  **proponer a algn para algo, ~ a algn como
    algo** to propose, suggest sb as sth

  proponer algo a algn to propose sth to sb

proporcionar *v.* to provide

  proporcionar algo a algn to provide sb
    with sth (Me proporcionó todos los
    materiales necesarios.)

propósito *m.* intention

  a propósito on purpose, by the way
    (¡Lo hiciste a propósito! Ayer me encontré
    con Mario; a propósito, me preguntó
    cuánto vale tu coche.)

  propósito de enmienda a promise to
    mend one's ways

  sin propósito aimlessly

  tener buenos propósitos to have
    good intentions

proteger *v.* to protect

  **proteger algo de algo/algn, ~ a algn de
    algo/algn, ~ algo contra algo** to protect
    sth/sb from/against sth/sb

protegerse *v.* to protect oneself

  **protegerse de algo/algn, ~ contra
    algo/algn** to protect oneself from/against
    sth/sb

protestar *v.* to complain

  protestar contra algo/algn to protest
    against sth (Los manifestantes protestan
    contra el gobierno.)

  protestar por algo to complain about sth
    (Protestan por la falta de trabajo.)

provecho *m.* benefit

  sacar provecho de algo to benefit from sth

prueba *f.* proof

  a prueba de impervious to, resistant (¿Tu
    reloj es a prueba de agua?)

punto *m.* point

  **anotarse un punto con algo, marcarse un
    ~ con algo** to get ten out of ten on sth

  en punto o'clock/on the dot

  estar a punto de hacer algo to be about to
    do sth

  poner punto final a algo to end

  punto álgido culminating point, climax
    (La crisis económica alcanzó su
    punto álgido.)

  punto de apoyo fulcrum

  punto decimal decimal point

  punto final period

  punto y aparte period, new paragraph

  punto y coma semicolon

  punto y seguido period

  puntos suspensivos ellipsis

Q

quedar *v.* **1** to fit

  quedarle algo bien/mal a algn to fit well/
    badly (¿Me queda mal el vestido?)

  2 to cause an impression

  quedar bien/mal con algn to make a
    good/bad impression on sb (No quiero
    quedar mal con mis suegros.)

  3 to agree

  quedar en algo con algn to agree to do sth
    with sb (Quedamos en no volver a hablar
    del tema.)

quedarse *v.* to keep

quedarse con algo to keep sth

quedarse dormido to oversleep

quejarse *v.* to complain

quejarse de algo/algn to complain about sb/sth (¿De qué te quejas? No deja de quejarse de sus vecinos.)

quejarse por algo, ~ de algo to complain of sth (Marta se queja por el costo de vida. Tu hijo se queja de un fuerte dolor de muelas.)

quiebra *f.* bankruptcy

declararse en quiebra, irse a la ~ to go bankrupt

quitar *v.* to take off

quitar algo a algn to take sth from sb

R

rabo *m.* tail

con el rabo entre las piernas, con el ~ entre las patas with one's tail between one's legs

raíz *f.* root

a raíz de as a result of

echar raíces to take roots

raíz cuadrada/cúbica square/cube root

rato *m.* while

a cada rato the whole time

al (poco) rato shortly thereafter

de a rato, de a ratos, de ~ en ~ from time to time

hace rato for some time

pasar el rato to spend time/hang out

ratos libres, ~ de ocio spare time

tener para rato to be a while

raya *f.* **1** line

a rayas striped

pasarse de la raya to overstep the mark, to go too far, to push one's luck

tener a algn a raya, mantener a algn a ~ to keep sb under control

2 part

llevar raya al medio/al costado to part one's hair in the middle/to one side

razón *f.* **1** reason

atender razones, atenerse a ~, avenirse a ~ to listen to reason

darle la razón a algn to admit sb is right

en razón de because of (No debes discriminar en razón de la edad o la raza de las personas.)

entrar en razón to see reason

perder la razón to lose one's mind

razón de ser raison d'être/reason for being (¡Esta masacre no tiene razón de ser!)

razón social registered name

tener (la) razón, llevar la ~ to be right

2 rate

a razón de at a rate of

3 information

dar razón de algo/algn to give information about sth/sb

rechazar *v.* to reject

rechazar a algn por algo to reject sb for sth

rechazar algo a algn to reject sth from sb

reclamar *v.* to claim, to demand

reclamar algo de algn to demand sth from sb

recomendar *v.* to recommend

recomendar algo a algn to recommend sth to sb

recompensar *v.* to reward

recompensar a algn por algo to reward sb for sth (Deberías recompensar a tus alumnos por su esfuerzo.)

reconciliarse *v.* to reconcile

reconciliarse con algo to become reconciled to sth (Se reconcilió con su idea de la familia.)

reconciliarse con algn to make up with sb (Marcia se reconcilió con su marido.)

recordar *v.* to remind

recordar algo a algn to remind sb of sth

recuperarse *v.* to recover

recuperarse de algo to recover from sth

recurso *m.* **1** resource

agotar todos los recursos to exhaust all the options

como último recurso as a last resource

recurso natural, recursos naturales natural resource(s)

recursos económicos economic/financial resources

recursos energéticos energy resources

recursos humanos human resources

sin recursos with no means/without resources

2 appeal

interponer/presentar un recurso to file an appeal

red *f.* net

caer en las redes de algn to be trapped by sb

reembolso *m.* refund

contra reembolso cash on delivery

referir *v.* **1** to tell

referir algo a algn to tell sth to sb (Nos refirió sus experiencias como maestro rural.)

2 to refer

referir a algn a algo to refer sb to sth (Nos refirió al segundo párrafo de la nota.)

referirse *v.* to refer

referirse a algo/algn to refer to sth/sb (No entiendo a qué te refieres. No me estaba refiriendo a ti.)

reflexionar *v.* to reflect

reflexionar sobre algo/algn to think about sth/sb

refugiado/a *adj.* refugee

refugiado/a political refugee

refugiado/a de guerra war refugee

regalar *v.* to give as a gift

regalar algo a algn to give sth to sb as a gift

regañadientes *adv.* reluctantly

a regañadientes reluctantly

regla *f.* rule

por regla general in general

regreso *m.* return

a su regreso on sb's return

de regreso a back at/to (¿Cuándo estarás de regreso a la oficina?)

emprender el regreso to set off on the return trip

reírse *v.* to laugh

reírse de algo/algn to laugh at sth/sb

reírse por algo to laugh because of sth

remedio *m.* **1** remedy

santo remedio to do the trick (¿Tienes tos? Prepara un vaso de leche tibia con miel y santo remedio.)

2 solution

no tener remedio to be hopeless/to

have no solution (Olvídalo, nuestro matrimonio no tiene remedio.)

3 option

no tener más remedio que, no quedar más ~ que, no haber más ~ que, no haber otro ~ que to have no option but to

renglón *m.* line

a renglón seguido immediately afterwards (Las instrucciones se detallan a renglón seguido.)

renunciar *v.* **1** to resign

renunciar a algo to resign from sth (Renunció a su trabajo y salió a recorrer el mundo.)

2 to renounce

renunciar a algo to renounce sth (Decidimos renunciar a la lucha armada.)

reñir *v.* to quarrel

reñir con algn to quarrel with sb

reojo *m.* the corner of the eye

mirar de reojo a algn to look at sb out of the corner of one's eye

repente *adv.* suddenly

de repente suddenly

repercutir *v.* **1** to impact

repercutir en algo/algn to have an impact on sth/sb

2 to pass on

repercutir algo en algn, ~ sobre algn to pass sth on to sb

reponerse *v.* to recover

reponerse de algo to recover from sth

reprochar *v.* to reproach

reprochar algo a algn to reproach sb for sth

reputación *f.* reputation

tener reputación de to have a reputation as (Tiene reputación de buen cocinero.)

resentirse *v.* to get upset

resentirse con algn por algo to get upset with sb because of sth

resignarse *v.* to resign oneself

resignarse a algo to resign oneself to sth

resistirse *v.* to be reluctant, to resist

resistirse a algo to resist sth

respecto *m.* matter, regard

con respecto a regarding

respetar *v.* to respect

respetar a algn por algo to respect sb for sth

responder *v.* to answer

responder algo a algn, responder a algo to answer sb about sth

responder por algo/algn to be held responsible

responsabilizar *v.* to blame

responsabilizar a algn de algo to blame sb for sth (La víctima responsabilizó a la policía del fracaso de la operación.)

responsable *adj.* responsible

ser responsable de algo to be responsible for sth

resumen *m.* summary

en resumen all in all

hacer un resumen to summarize

reunirse *v.* to meet

reunirse con algn to meet with sb

revista *f.* **1** magazine

revista de chistes comic book

revista de modas fashion magazine

revista del corazón *Esp.* gossip magazine

2 revue

teatro de revista vaudeville-style comedy

3 review

pasar revista a algo to review sth

rivalizar *v.* to compete

rivalizar con algn por algo to compete with sb on sth

rodilla *f.* knee

de rodillas down on one's knees

hincar la rodilla to go down on one's knee

pedir algo de rodillas to beg on one's knees

rogar *v.* to beg

rogar algo a algn to beg sb for sth

romper *v.* to break

romper algo to break sth

romper con algn to break up with sb

S

saber *v.* **1** to know

(de) haberlo sabido had sb known

saber algo de algo/algn, ~ algo sobre algo/algn to know sth about sth/sb (Mi padre sabe algo de física. ¿Sabes algo de Mariano? ¿Alguien sabe algo sobre la fiesta?)

2 to taste

saber a algo to taste like sth (Esto sabe a nueces.)

sabiendas *adv.* knowingly

a sabiendas knowingly

salida *f.* exit; way out

no verle salida a algo not to see a way out of sth (No le veo la salida a este problema.)

salir *v.* **1** to leave

salir de algo to leave from sth

salir para algo to leave for sth (Salgo para Colombia esta misma noche.)

salir por algo to leave via sth (¡No querrás que salga por la chimenea!)

2 to go

salir a algo to go out onto/into/for (Salieron al balcón. ¿Salimos a comer?)

salir con algn to go out with sb

3 to take after

salir a algn to take after sb (El bebé salió a su padre.)

saludar *v.* to greet

saludar a algn to greet sb

salvo *adv.*

a salvo safe (Mi familia está a salvo, gracias a Dios.)

ponerse a salvo to reach safety

satisfecho/a *adj.* satisfied

estar satisfecho/a de to be satisfied by/with

seguir *v.* to follow

seguir algo, ~ a algn to follow sth/sb

seguro/a *adj.* **1** safe

hacer algo sobre seguro to play safe with sth

2 sure

estar seguro/a de algo to be sure about sth

sentado/a *adj.* seated

esperar sentado/a to not hold sb's breath

sentido *m.* **1** sense

sentido común common sense

sentido de algo sense of sth (Su sentido del deber es admirable.)

sentido de (la) orientación sense of direction

tener sentido to make sense

2 consciousness

perder el sentido to lose consciousness

recobrar el sentido to regain consciousness

sentir *v.* **1** to feel

sentir algo hacia algn, ~ algo por algo/ algn to feel sth for sth/sb

2 to regret

sentir algo to regret sth (Siento mucho haberte dicho eso.)

sentirse 1 to feel

sentirse bien/mal to feel well/ill

2 to be offended

sentirse con algn *Méx.* to be offended with sb (Está sentida con su hermana porque le mintió.)

ser *v.* to be

a no ser que if not, unless

ser de algo/algn to become (¿Qué fue del aumento que te iban a dar? ¿Qué será de nuestros amigos?)

ser *m.* being

el ser y la nada being and nothingness

ser humano human being

ser sobrenatural supernatural being

ser vivo, ~ viviente living being

serie *f.* series

coches/motores de serie production cars/ engines

fuera de serie out of this world

producción en serie, fabricación en ~ mass production

serie numérica numerical sequence

seriedad *f.* seriousness

con toda seriedad seriously

falta de seriedad irresponsibility, lack of seriousness

servir *v.* to serve

servir a algo/algn to serve sth/sb

siempre *adv.* always

casi siempre almost always

como siempre as usual

¡hasta siempre! farewell!

para siempre forever

por siempre jamás forever and ever

siempre que whenever, provided that (Me viene a visitar siempre que puede. Te ayudaré, siempre que prometas contarme toda la verdad.)

siempre y cuando if (Iré siempre y cuando me acompañes.)

silencio *m.* silence

guardar silencio to keep silent

sin *prep.* without

sin cesar nonstop

sin demora without delay

sin embargo however

sin falta without fail

sin fines de lucro, ~ fines lucrativos not-for-profit

sin lugar a dudas, ~ duda without a doubt

sin propósito aimlessly

sobrar *v.* to have in excess

sobrar algo a algn to have sth in excess (Les sobraba el dinero.)

solidarizarse *v.* to support

solidarizarse con algo/algn to support sth/ sb (Nos solidarizamos con su reclamo. La presidenta se solidarizó con los trabajadores despedidos.)

solo/a *adj.* alone

a solas alone (No me gusta quedarme a solas con ella.)

sombra *f.* shadow

a la sombra de in the shadow of

soñar to dream

soñar con algo/algn to dream about sth/sb

sorprender *v.* to surprise

sorprender a algn con algo to surprise sb with sth

sorprenderse *v.* to be surprised

sorprenderse de algo, ~ por algo to be surprised about sth

sospechar *v.* to suspect

sospechar algo, ~ de algn to suspect sth/sb

subasta *f.* auction

sacar algo a subasta to put sth up for auction

subir *v.* to get on

subir a algo to get on/onto sth

suceder *v.* to happen

suceder algo a algn for sth to happen to sb

suerte *f.* **1** chance

caer en suerte, tocar en ~ for something to fall to sb's lot

echar algo a la suerte, echar algo a suertes to toss a coin for sth
la suerte está echada the die is cast
2 luck
buena/mala suerte good/bad luck
desear buena suerte a algn to wish luck to sb
estar de suerte to be in luck
por suerte luckily
probar suerte to try one's luck
traer buena/mala suerte, dar buena/mala ~ to bring good/bad luck
sufrir to suffer
sufrir de algo to suffer from sth
sufrir por algo/algn to suffer because of sth/sb
sugerir *v.* to suggest
sugerir algo a algn to suggest sth to sb
suma *f.* sum
en suma in short
suplicar *v.* to beg, to implore
suplicar a algn por algo/algn to beg sb to do sth
supuesto/a *adj.* so-called
por supuesto of course
sustituir *v.* to replace
sustituir a algn to replace sb
sustituir algo con algo, ~ algo por algo to replace sth with sth

T

tablón *m.* board
tablón de anuncios bulletin board
taller *m.* workshop, garage
taller mecánico, ~ de reparación garage
tanto *pron.* so, so much
otro tanto the same
por (lo) tanto therefore
tanto... como... both... and...
tardar *v.* to take (time)
a más tardar at the very latest
tardar en algo to take a long time to
tarde *adv.* late
hacerse tarde to be getting late
más vale tarde que nunca better late than never
ser tarde para algo to be too late for sth
tarde o temprano sooner or later

tarjeta *f.* card
tarjeta de crédito credit card
tarjeta de débito debit card
tarjeta postal postcard
tasa *f.* **1** tax; fee (Debo pagar las tasas.)
2 rate
tasa de desempleo unemployment rate
tasa de interés interest rate
tasa de mortalidad/natalidad mortality rate/birthrate
telón *m.* curtain
telón de fondo background
temer *v.* to fear
temer a algo/algn to be afraid of sth/sb
temer por algo/algn to fear for sth/sb
tender *v.* to tend
tender a algo to tend to sth (Siempre tiendo a preocuparme por todo.)
tener *v.* to have
tener que ver to pertain/have sth to do (No tiene nada que ver con este asunto.)
terminar *v.* to finish
terminar con algo/algn to finish with sth/sb
terminar de hacer algo to finish sth
tiempo *m.* time
a tiempo on time
al mismo tiempo que at the same time as
tiempo libre free time
tirar *v.* **1** to throw
tirar algo a algn to throw sth to sb, to throw sth at sb
2 to pull
tirar de algo to pull sth
3 to shoot
tirar a dar to shoot to wound
tirar a matar to shoot to kill
tirar a traición to shoot in the back
tomar *v.* to take
tomar a algn por algo to take sb for sth (A nadie le gusta que lo tomen por tonto.)
tono *m.* pitch, tone
estar a tono con to keep up with, to be in tune with
fuera de tono inappropriate, out of place
no venir a tono to be out of place
subido de tono risqué

tonto/a *adj.* silly

  a tontas y a locas without thinking

toparse *v.* to encounter

  toparse con algo/algn to run into sth/sb

torno *m.* about, around

  en torno a around (El argumento
  de la película gira en torno a las
  relaciones amorosas.)

trabajar *v.* to work

  trabajar en algo, ~ con algo to work on/
  in/with sth

  trabajar para algn to work for sb

  trabajar por algo to work for sth

traducir *v.* to translate

  traducir algo a algo to translate sth
  into sth

transformarse *v.* to become

  transformarse en algo/algn to
  become sth/sb

transporte *m.* transportation

  transporte aéreo air freight

  transporte marítimo shipping

  transporte público public transportation

tratar *v.* **1** to try

  tratar de hacer algo to try to do sth

  2 to treat

  tratar bien/mal a algn to treat sb well/bad

  3 to deal

  tratar con algn to deal with sb

  4 to call

  tratar a algn de algo to call sb sth
  (¡Me trató de mentiroso!)

tratarse *v.* **1** to socialize

  tratarse con algn to socialize with sb

  2 to address

  tratarse con respeto to show respect for
  each other, to treat (each) other with
  respect

  tratarse de usted/tú to address each other
  as "usted"/"tú"

  3 to be about

  tratarse de to be about (¿De qué se
  trata la novela?)

través *adv.* across

  a través de through

  al través diagonally

  de través *Méx.* diagonally

trepar *v.* to climb

  trepar a algo, ~ por algo to climb up sth

treparse *v.* to climb

  treparse a algo to climb sth

tropezar *v.* **1** to stumble

  tropezar con algo to stumble over sth
  (Se tropezó con la silla.)

  2 to run into

  tropezar con algo/algn to run into sth/sb
  (¿A que no sabes con quién me
  tropecé hoy?)

trueque *m.* barter

  a trueque de in exchange for

U

último/a *adj.* last

  ser el/la último/a en hacer algo to be
  the last one to do sth (Fue el último en
  dejar el barco.)

V

vacilar *v.* to hesitate

  vacilar en algo to hesitate to do sth
  (No vaciló en la respuesta.)

  vacilar entre algo y algo to hesitate over
  sth (Estoy vacilando entre seguir con este
  empleo y buscar uno nuevo.)

valer *v.* **1** to be worth

  más vale que had better/it's better that
  (Más vale que traigas lo que te pedí la
  semana pasada.)

  valer más/menos to be more/less valuable

  2 to be useful

  valer de algo a algn to be useful
  (Mis protestas no valieron de nada.)

  valer para algo to be good at sth

valerse *v.* **1** to use

  valerse de algo/algn to use sth/sb

  2 to manage

  valerse por uno/a mismo/a to manage on
  one's own (No puede valerse por sí misma.)

vanguardia *f.* vanguard; avant-garde

  estar/ir a la vanguardia (de algo) to be at
  the forefront (of sth)

vengar *v.* to avenge

  vengar algo to avenge sth

vengarse *v.* to take revenge

  vengarse de algo, ~ de algn por algo to
  take revenge (on sb) for sth

ver *v.* to see

a ver all right, now, so; let's see (A ver, ¿qué está pasando acá? Llamémoslo a ver qué nos dice.)

veras *f. pl.* something true (Lo dijo entre veras y bromas.)

de veras really (Te lo digo de veras.)

vestirse *v.* to get dressed; to dress up

vestirse de algo to dress up as sth

vez *f.* time

a la vez at the same time

a su vez in turn

a veces sometimes (A veces me olvido de hacer las compras.)

alguna vez sometime (Deberíamos invitarlos a cenar alguna vez.)

cada vez que each/every time (that)

de una vez (por todas) once and for all

de vez en cuando once in a while

en vez de instead of

por... vez for the... time

una vez que once (Una vez que termines la tarea, podrás jugar con la computadora.)

una y otra vez time after time

vilo *adv.* in the air

estar en vilo, seguir en ~ to be in the air

levantar a algn en vilo to lift sb up off the ground

mantenerse en vilo to be in suspense

virtud *f.* virtue

en virtud de by virtue of

virtudes curativas healing powers

vista *f.* sight

a la vista at sight

a primera vista at first sight

a simple vista to the naked eye

a vista de pájaro bird's-eye view

de vista by sight (A su hermana la conocemos solo de vista.)

en vista de que in view of

estar con la vista puesta en algo/algn, tener la ~ puesta en algo/algn to have one's eye on sth/sb

hacer la vista gorda to turn a blind eye

perder algo de vista, perder a algn de ~ to lose sight of sth/sb

perderse de vista to disappear from view

saltar a la vista the first thing that hits you/stands out

tener algo en vista, tener a algn en ~ to have sth/sb in view/mind

vistazo *m.* look

dar/echar un vistazo a algo to have a quick look at sth (Échale un vistazo al modelo y dime qué te parece.)

visto *p.p.* seen

por lo visto apparently

volumen *m.* volume

a todo volumen at full volume

subir/bajar el volumen to turn the volume up/down

volumen de ventas volume of sales

volver *v.* to do again

volver a hacer algo to do sth again

votar *v.* to vote

votar a algn, ~ por algn to vote for sb

votar a favor de algo, ~ en contra de algo to vote for/against sth

voz *f.* voice

cambiar de voz, mudar de ~ to change one's voice

correr la voz to spread the word

dar la voz de alarma to raise the alarm

1. Lee la conversación telefónica entre Pablo y su bisabuela. Luego, elige la opción correcta. `1.D`

PABLO ¡Hola, abuela! ¿Cómo estás? ¡Habla Pablo, tu bisnieto!

ABUELA ¿Mi qué? No se oye muy bien...

PABLO Tu (1) _____ (bi-snie-to / bis-nie-to / bis-niet-o). Te estoy llamando desde Alicante.

ABUELA ¿Desde dónde?

PABLO (2) _____ (A-li-can-te / A-li-cant-e / Ali-ca-nte). ¿Recibiste una postal mía, una con muchas flores?

ABUELA ¿Con muchas qué?

PABLO Con muchas (3) _____ (fl-o-res / flo-res / flor-es). La compré en una tienda muy linda.

ABUELA ¿La qué?

PABLO La (4) _____ (co-mpré / comp-ré / com-pré) en una tienda. Bueno, quería decirte que estoy muy bien aquí. La gente es muy amable y no hay ningún problema.

ABUELA ¿Qué dijiste sobre un poema?

PABLO No, dije (5) _____ (pro-blem-a / pro-ble-ma / prob-le-ma).

ABUELA Bueno, te mando un beso y llámame de nuevo, querido Javier.

PABLO ¡Pero si soy (6) _____ (Pa-blo / Pab-lo / Pa-bl-o)!

2. Eres editor(a) en un periódico y debes corregir la forma en que se separaron en sílabas las palabras. `1.D`

¿Quieres ser mi compañera de (1) **v-** _____ **iaje?** Me llamo Daniel y soy un (2) ho- _____ mbre de treinta y dos años de (3) eda- _____ d. Busco una mujer joven que (4) qu- _____ iera ir de vacaciones pronto a (5) Eur- _____ opa y que le guste mucho ver (6) ciud- _____ ades nuevas y visitar muchos (7) mus- _____ eos. Si le interesara, no dude en (8) ll- _____ amarme. ¡Hasta pronto!

---

3. Indica con *Sí* o *No* si es posible separar en sílabas las vocales subrayadas. Si respondes *Sí*, muestra cómo lo harías. `1.D`

1. p<u>ia</u>no _____   3. f<u>eo</u> _____   5. <u>ai</u>re _____   7. t<u>ea</u>tro _____

2. c<u>ua</u>dro _____   4. c<u>ao</u>s _____   6. r<u>ue</u>da _____   8. barr<u>io</u> _____

4. Síntesis Separa en sílabas estas palabras. `1.D`

1. cepillo _____   6. hacia _____   11. empresa _____

2. excelente _____   7. suave _____   12. Paraguay _____

3. pantalones _____   8. aprender _____   13. anochecer _____

4. poeta _____   9. empleado _____   14. callejón _____

5. cielo _____   10. oxígeno _____   15. carruaje _____

Actividades

5. ¿Con o sin tilde? Lee esta carta y decide si estas palabras llevan tilde o no. `1.E`

Querida Juana:

(1) _____ (Te / Té) escribo desde Medellín. ¡Estamos tan cerca! No (2) _____ (se / sé) cuántos días me quedaré aquí, pero espero que puedas venir a visitarme. ¿Quieres que te (3) _____ (de / dé) mi número de teléfono? (4) _____ (Si / Sí) quieres, puedes llamarme por las tardes. (5) _____ (Tu / Tú) sí que me has dado tu teléfono, ¿verdad? Hasta pronto.

(6) _____ (Tu / Tú) amiga, Paula

6. Ordena las palabras en esta tabla según sean llanas, agudas o esdrújulas. `1.E`

balón   álbum   silla   ballets   lágrimas   césped   árbol
palabra   razón   ídolos   cómpramelo   estoy   rápido   pasión

Llanas	Agudas	Esdrújulas

7. Forma las palabras. Recuerda colocar o quitar la tilde si es necesario. `1.E`

1. trae + los = _____
2. póster + es = _____
3. devuelve + los = _____
4. récord + s = _____
5. tomate + s = _____
6. inglés + es = _____
7. colección + es = _____
8. come + los = _____

8. En estas oraciones hay palabras que deberían llevar tilde. ¡Corrígelas! `1.E`

1. ¿Hoy es miercoles o jueves? _____
2. Hace ocho dias que nadie me llama. ¡Me siento sola! _____
3. Papá, regalanos camisetas de baloncesto para Navidad. ¡Por favor! _____
4. ¿Quieres venir a tomar un te a casa? _____
5. ¡Cuántos arboles hay en este bosque! _____
6. La profesora me dijo que este calculo estaba mal. ¿Pero dónde está el error? _____

9. En estas palabras, indica dónde está el hiato (si es que lo hay) y qué tipo de vocales lo forman: *fuertes* (F) y *débiles* (D). `1.E`

1. oído _____
2. maíz _____
3. aeroplano _____
4. compañía _____
5. cooperar _____
6. repetía _____
7. Mediterráneo _____
8. reescribir _____
9. Luis _____
10. zanahoria _____
11. león _____
12. tío _____

10. Lee la historia de Martín e indica al menos seis palabras que tengan hiato. `1.E`

Hace poco estuve con Raúl, un gran amigo mío. Siempre lo veo los fines de semana, pero esta vez nos vimos aunque era lunes. Me contó que tuvo una pelea con su novia, María. Dice que incluso le mandó a su casa un ramo de flores con un poema, pero sin buenos resultados. La realidad es que yo tampoco creo que haya una solución. Espero que ella lo llame y se reconcilien un día de estos.

11. ¿Con o sin tilde? En cada oración, hay una palabra con un error. Corrígela. `1.E`

1. Él hermano de Carla todavía no sabe escribir. _____

2. ¡Cuántas veces té he dicho que no tires los papeles al piso! _____

3. Aún si tuviera dinero, no compraría una casa en la playa. _____

4. No debo engordar mas. De lo contrario, podría afectar mi salud. _____

5. ¡Ya se cómo resolver este problema! _____

6. Sí vamos a la playa, debemos llevar sombrero y protección solar. _____

7. ¡Este libro es para tí! _____

8. Señora, la operación de su marido fué exitosa. _____

9. Éstas sillas son muy económicas, ¡no pierda esta oportunidad! _____

10. ¡Te ví ayer en el parque! Estabas con tu amigo José. _____

12. Completa el aviso publicitario con los pronombres interrogativos y exclamativos de la lista. `1.E`

| cómo | como | quién | quien | dónde | donde | que | qué |

¿(1) _____ no soñó alguna vez con una luna de miel (2) _____ sea inolvidable? Podemos ayudarte a planear tu viaje tal (3) _____ lo desees, ¡con (4) _____ hayas elegido para pasar el resto de tu vida! ¿(5) _____ preferirías pasar tu luna de miel? ¿(6) _____ prefieres: playa, montañas o campo? Te damos consejos sobre los mejores lugares (7) _____ podrás disfrutar del romance. ¿(8) _____ puedes comunicarte con nosotros? Llámanos al 435 423 847 o visita nuestra página web (www.lunasllenasdemiel.com).

13. Usa los adjetivos de la lista para reescribir estas oraciones con un adverbio que termine en -*mente*. `1.E`

| atento | frecuente | público | rápido | sincero | teórico |

1. Marta corrió con rapidez hasta la cocina. ¡Su comida se estaba quemando! _____

2. Lee cada frase con atención y encontrarás el error. _____

3. Debes cepillarte los dientes con frecuencia para no tener caries. _____

4. Dímelo con sinceridad, ¿te gusta mi nuevo corte de cabello? _____

5. En teoría, nada debería salir mal. Pero no siempre es así. _____

6. No me gusta que me llames "Juanita" en público, mamá. Dime "Juana", por favor. _____

14. Escribe el singular o el plural de estas palabras. `1.E`

1. _____ → márgenes
2. aborigen → _____
3. _____ → condiciones
4. _____ → manteles
5. árbol → _____
6. _____ → intereses
7. _____ → meses
8. _____ → atunes

15. El señor González es un empresario con muchas actividades. Completa las oraciones con la opción correcta. `1.E`

6:00 a.m. El señor González salió de su casa y su (1) _____ lo llevó al club.
a. chofer   b. chófer   c. Ambas opciones son posibles.

7:30 a.m. Después de hacer ejercicio y jugar al (2) _____, se dio una ducha y se dirigió a su trabajo.
a. fútbol   b. futbol   c. Ambas opciones son posibles.

10:30 a.m. González habló por teléfono con un empleado sobre un reporte (3) _____ de América Latina.
a. economico-social   b. económico-social   c. Ambas opciones son posibles.

1:30 p.m. González le escribe un correo electrónico a su secretaria. El asunto dice: "¿(4) _____ MI ALMUERZO?"
a. DONDE ESTA   b. DÓNDE ESTÁ   c. DONDE ESTÁ

4:00 p.m. González sube al (5) _____ piso del edificio y se reúne con sus empleados.
a. décimoséptimo   b. décimoseptimo   c. decimoséptimo

6:00 p.m. González les comunica a sus empleados que, debido a la mala situación (6) _____, debe despedir al 50% de su plantilla.
a. político-económica   b. politico-economica   c. político-economica

16. Coloca la tilde donde haga falta. Como ayuda, las sílabas tónicas están subrayadas. `1.E`

1. pa_is_
2. _am_plio
3. gra_ma_tica
4. _ha_cia
5. ra_zon_
6. cora_zo_nes
7. _di_melo
8. ac_tuar_
9. _di_me
10. _vi_
11. ac_triz_
12. holan_des_
13. _de_biles
14. _cree_me
15. sutil_men_te
16. poe_si_a
17. _fi_sico-_qui_mico
18. _can_talo
19. veinti_tres_
20. a_que_llo

17. El teclado de la computadora de Julia funciona muy mal. ¡No escribe las comas! Ayuda a Julia a corregir el correo electrónico que escribe a su amiga, Guadalupe. `1.F`

De:	julia@micorreo.com
Para:	guadalupe@micorreo.com
Asunto:	Bienvenida

Hola Guadalupe:

¡Bienvenida a Córdoba amiga! ¡Qué bien que ya estés en la ciudad! No veo la hora de encontrarnos pero estoy un poco ocupada: por las mañanas voy a un curso de cocina. Estoy muy contenta con el curso. La profesora que es tan buena onda resultó ser mi vecina. ¿Puedes creerlo?

¿Te parece que mañana nos veamos? Podemos dar un paseo en barco ir a museos y caminar en el parque. Allá hace frío pero aquí calor. Para mí todo fue tan genial cuando llegué a esta ciudad. ¡Te encantará conocerla!

Un abrazo muy grande

Julia

18. Lee lo que escribió Lucía en su diario de viaje. Completa su relato con la opción correcta. `1.F`

Santiago de Chile_____ (; / . / ,)
(1)
3 de febrero de 2010
Este es mi último día en Santiago y he visto todo
lo que quería ver_____ (: / , / ;) la Plaza de Armas,
(2)
el mercado central, el centro financiero y el teatro
municipal. Para mí_____ (; / , / :)
(3)
lo más increíble de esta ciudad es que tanta
gente vive en ella. Santiago_____ (; / , / :) que fue
(4)

fundada en el siglo XVI_____ (; / , / :) ¡hoy tiene
(5)
6_____ (; / , / :) 6 millones de habitantes!
(6)
Otra cosa que me encantó sobre esta ciudad fue
la gente. ¡Conocí a personas tan amables! Por
ejemplo, a Juanita, la cocinera del hostal _____
(7)
(: / , / ;) a Pablo, el vendedor de periódicos_____
(8)
(: / , / ;) y a Esther, la camarera de un bar.
Espero volver algún día... ¡y pronto!

19. Lee las oraciones y complétalas con los elementos del recuadro. `1.F`

...   ( )   —   —   « »   :   -

1. La asociación franco____alemana de Lima hoy celebra su centenario.

2. Juan me miró a los ojos y me dijo____"Quiero casarme contigo."

3. ____¡Hola, Carlos! Cuánto tiempo sin vernos.
   ____¡Hola, Manuela! Un gusto verte de nuevo.

4. Este año leí muchos poemas, pero el que más me gustó fue ____Al callarse____, de Pablo Neruda.

5. Compramos tantas cosas para la fiesta: dulces, decoración, bebidas, comida____

6. En Buenos Aires____ la capital de Argentina____ hay cada vez más turistas.

20. Corrige la puntuación en estas oraciones. `1.F`

1. Hoy hace tanto calor, ¡verdad!

2. El prefijo —anti significa "contrario".

3. Sara, Paula, Gastón, José, y Pedro fueron al cine el domingo.

4. El jefe de Silvina (que se llama Juan Carlos (igual que el rey de España) no quiere que sus empleados lleguen ni un minuto tarde al trabajo.

5. Lee los capítulos 1.5 y resúmelos en una hoja.

6. Mi hermana que siempre está de mal humor hoy estaba sonriente.

7. —Vienes a la fiesta?
   —Sí si me invitas.

8. Hola. Roberto. Cómo estás?

21. Ricardo visitó con sus compañeros de clase la Ciudad de México. Completa su relato con la opción correcta. `1.G`

El (1) _____ (Lunes / lunes) pasado visité por primera vez el (2) _____ (Distrito Federal / distrito federal), la capital de México. Yo no lo sabía, pero es la octava ciudad más rica del mundo: ¡su (3) _____ (PBI / Pbi) es de 315 000 millones de dólares! Los (4) _____ (Mexicanos / mexicanos) son muy simpáticos y serviciales. El señor (5) _____ (del Valle / Del Valle), el guía de nuestra excursión, no era de México, sino de (6) _____ (el Salvador / El Salvador). Creo que lo que más me interesó de esta excursión fue visitar la (7) _____ (Universidad nacional autónoma de México / Universidad Nacional Autónoma de México). Sí, ¡la famosa (8) _____ (UNAM / Unam)! Ojalá que pueda estudiar allí dentro de unos años.

22. **A estas palabras les falta una letra. Elige la opción correcta para cada palabra.** `1.G`

1. (v/V) _____aca
2. (B/b) _____olivianos
3. (P/p) _____rovincia
4. (O/o) _____toño
5. (a/A) _____mazónico
6. (V/v) _____alencia
7. (t/T) _____ijuana
8. (F/f) _____ebrero

23. **En estas oraciones no se usan correctamente las mayúsculas. Corrige los errores.** `1.G`

1. Mi mamá nació en milán, pero no sabe hablar bien Italiano.
2. La gente fuera de españa no dice "euskadi", sino "país Vasco".
3. El estrecho de Magallanes es un paso marítimo ubicado al sur de sudamérica.
4. El Reino de arabia saudita limita con Jordania y Kuwait, entre otros países.
5. El Río Amazonas tiene un gran caudal de agua.
6. una de las grandes capitales de la moda es parís.
7. La Ciudad de Río De Janeiro es mi ciudad favorita.

24. **Síntesis Une los elementos de las dos columnas para formar oraciones.** `1.D–1.G`

1. En una enumeración, antes de la *y*,
2. Las estaciones del año
3. Para expresar duda, inseguridad o temor,
4. Son ejemplos de palabras con acento diacrítico
5. Los acrónimos de cuatro letras o menos
6. En algunos países, para expresar un decimal,
7. Son ejemplos de palabras con hiato
8. Antes de las citas textuales
9. Son ejemplos de palabras con triptongo

a. *maestro* y *coexistir*.
b. *aún* y *té*.
c. no se usa la coma.
d. se usa la coma.
e. se usan los puntos suspensivos.
f. se usan los dos puntos.
g. *Paraguay* y *Uruguay*.
h. se escriben en mayúscula.
i. se escriben en minúscula.

🖱: Practice more at **vhlcentral.com.**

Nouns 🌿

Chapter 2

1. **Coloca estos sustantivos en la columna adecuada.** `2.A`

fiscal	comediante	representante	malabarista	ciclista	gerenta
profesora	portero	delfín	pájaro	poeta	yegua
artista	nuera	escritor	cirujana	bailarín	toro

Masculino	Femenino	Masculino/Femenino

2. Cambia el género de estos sustantivos. `2.A`

1. el accionista → _____
2. la madrina → _____
3. el periodista → _____
4. el cuñado → _____
5. el joven → _____
6. la yegua → _____

7. la doctora → _____
8. el cocodrilo macho → _____
9. la modelo → _____
10. el emperador → _____
11. el gallo → _____
12. la suegra → _____

3. Lara escribió una composición para la escuela. Complétala con el artículo correspondiente (*la* para femenino, *el* para masculino). `2.A`

Tema: (1) _____ barrio donde vivo

Mi barrio es muy pequeño. Todo (2) _____ vecindario se conoce. Por (3) _____ tarde, todos los niños jugamos en (4) _____ calle. (5) _____ verdad es que todo es muy tranquilo. Solo debemos tener cuidado con (6) _____ tranvía y los coches.

Tenemos muchos lugares para divertirnos. Por ejemplo, (7) _____ cine. Durante (8) _____ fin de semana, en (9) _____ programa hay películas infantiles. Si no hay una película interesante, vemos (10) _____ televisión o escuchamos (11) _____ radio. Pero (12) _____ parque es mi lugar favorito.

En nuestra cuadra, viven muchas familias de distintos países. (13) _____ mitad de ellas viene de Latinoamérica. Lo cierto es que es muy divertido, porque somos todos diferentes, pero (14) _____ comunicación es muy buena siempre.

4. Elige la palabra que no tiene el mismo género que las otras del grupo. `2.A`

1. realidad   mal   poesía   foto
2. dolor   sol   corazón   luz
3. canción   diente   papel   cielo
4. heroína   problema   flor   libertad
5. inteligencia   gente   fantasma   calle
6. día   rol   color   sinceridad

7. muerte   confirmación   ayuda   mapa
8. amor   solicitud   viuda   cara
9. amanecer   poder   lunes   vejez
10. dilema   drama   idea   síntoma
11. rojo   enero   Barcelona   Pacífico
12. tabú   rubí   clase   cine

5. Elige la opción correcta para completar estas oraciones. `2.A`

1. _____ (La orden/El orden) vino directamente del jefe. Debemos obedecerle.

2. En la misa, _____ (la cura/el cura) rezó por la paz en el mundo.

3. Silvio, ¿puedes ayudarme? Tengo solo _____ (una pendiente/un pendiente) y se hace tarde para ir a la fiesta.

4. _____ (La Himalaya/El Himalaya) es una montaña que mide 8 000 metros de altura.

5. Sin dudas, _____ (la rosa/el rosa) es mi color favorito para los vestidos de mis muñecas.

6. Me golpeé y ahora me duelen mucho _____ (la frente/el frente) y los ojos.

Actividades

6. Lee esta descripción sobre la ciudad de Bogotá. Elige la opción correcta. `2.A`

1. La ciudad de Bogotá es _____ capital de la República de Colombia.
   a. la   b. el

2. Está ubicada en _____ centro del país.
   a. la   b. el

3. Tiene _____ población de casi siete millones de habitantes.
   a. una   b. un

4. La ciudad ofrece _____ gran cantidad de museos, teatros y bibliotecas.
   a. una   b. un

5. _____ Bogotá es el río más extenso de los alrededores de la ciudad.
   a. La   b. El

6. _____ orquídea es la flor que se usa como símbolo de Bogotá.
   a. La   b. El

7. Los lugares turísticos más importantes son _____ jardín botánico, el observatorio nacional y el mirador La Calera.
   a. la   b. el

8. _____ azul predomina en la bandera de esta ciudad.
   a. La   b. El

7. Escribe el plural de estas palabras. `2.B`

1. vela _____
2. perro _____
3. canción _____
4. paquete _____
5. emoción _____

6. coche _____
7. papá _____
8. tren _____
9. pez _____
10. mujer _____

11. día _____
12. país _____
13. policía _____
14. reloj _____
15. viernes _____

8. Completa las oraciones con las palabras de la lista. Atención: ¡debes usarlas en plural! `2.B`

| ratón | pared | señor | club | corazón | voz | paz | bus |

1. _____, pueden pasar al salón. La directora los espera.

2. ¡Cuántas historias de _____ rotos!

3. Hay _____ que nos llevan a Buenos Aires por un precio muy económico.

4. Hagamos las _____. No quiero más discusiones.

5. Los _____ de fútbol importantes tienen estadios gigantes.

6. Escucho _____ de niños gritando ¡y no puedo dormir!

7. Ten cuidado. Por la noche, siempre hay _____ en la cocina.

8. Quiero pintar las _____ de color rojo. ¿Qué te parece?

9. Marca los plurales en cada frase e indica si son *regulares* (R) o *irregulares* (I). `2.B`

1. Los miércoles jugamos a las cartas. _____

2. Mi tía compra los mejores tés en la tienda de la esquina. _____

3. En el tribunal, los jueces trabajan hasta la media tarde. _____

4. ¡Quiero comprarme esos pantalones! _____

5. Los paréntesis se usan para encerrar información que amplía la de la oración principal. _____

6. El profesor corrige las tesis de sus alumnos. _____

7. Me encantan los rubíes. _____

8. Con la computadora, puedes contar los caracteres de un texto fácilmente. _____

10. En cada oración, elige la opción correcta. `2.B`

1. El plural de *virus* es _____.
   a. *virus*   b. *viruses*

2. El singular de *cumpleaños* es _____.
   a. *cumpleaño*   b. *cumpleaños*

3. El plural de *crisis* es _____.
   a. *crisises*   b. *crisis*

4. El plural de *compás* es _____.
   a. *compás*   b. *compases*

5. El plural de *comedor* es _____.
   a. *comedores*   b. *comedors*

6. El plural de *régimen* es _____.
   a. *régimenes*   b. *regímenes*

11. Indica si estos sustantivos existen en plural y singular, o solamente en plural. `2.B`

1. oasis _____
2. nupcias _____
3. gafas _____
4. prismáticos _____
5. víveres _____
6. tabúes _____
7. análisis _____
8. imágenes _____
9. jueves _____
10. tijeras _____
11. vacaciones _____
12. afueras _____

12. Corrige este aviso publicitario. Hay 10 errores. `2.B`

> **¡Buscamos jovenes con ganas de aprender!**
>
> ¿Tienes entre 18 y 23 año y eres estudiante de Administración con espíritus emprendedor? ¿Quieres ganar experiencia y trabajar en la vacación? GREA es una empresa que se encuentra en el alrededor de la ciudad de Panamá y ofrece muchos beneficio para sus empleados. El trabajo es de cuatro hora diarias y ofrecemos interesantes condición de contratación. Si te interesa la propuesta, envíanos tu currículums por correo electrónico.

13. Cecilia nos cuenta cómo se sintió la primera vez que viajó en avión. Completa el relato con la opción correcta. `2.C`

Mi primer viaje en avión

El viernes pasado fue la primera vez que viajé en avión. Pero fue un viaje (1) _____ (cortito / cortote), porque duró solo media hora. No puedo mentirles, siempre les tuve algo de (2) _____ (miedito / miedazo) a los aviones.

El avión era enorme. Tenía unas (3) _____ (alitas / alotas) y dos (4) _____ (turbinitas / turbinotas). Pero, por dentro, todo era distinto. En cada fila, había muchos (5) _____ (asientotes / asientitos) donde mi papá casi no podía sentarse y (6) _____ (ventanitas / ventanotas) que no me dejaban ver nada. ¡Parecía un (7) _____ (juguetito / juguetote)!

Cuando despegó, mi mamá me tomó la (8) _____ (manita / manota) y me dijo que me quedara (9) _____ (tranquilita / tranquilota). Mi hermano Daniel, que tiene solo tres años, se comportaba como un verdadero chico (10) _____ (grandote / grandecito). ¡Hasta quería ir a la cabina del piloto! Por suerte, el vuelo estuvo muy bien. Incluso pudimos ver unos (11) _____ (dibujotes / dibujitos) animados en una (12) _____ (pantallita / pantallota) que estaba en frente de cada asiento. ¡No veo la hora de volver a volar!

14. **Gabriela está celosa de su hermana que acaba de nacer. Completa el correo electrónico que le escribe a su amiga Estela.** `2.C`

Hola, Estela:

¿Cómo estás? Te escribo porque tengo un (1) _____ (problemón / problemita) y estoy tan triste. Hace un mes que nació mi (2) _____ (hermanucha / hermanita), Sandra, y, al parecer, ya no le importo a nadie. Es verdad que Sandra nació un poco (3) _____ (debilita / debilota). Ahora está más (4) _____ (fuertucha / fuertecita), pero sigue siendo el centro de atención. Debe ser porque tiene unos (5) _____ (ojitos / ojazos) azules. ¡Son los ojos más grandes que he visto! También sus pequeñas (6) _____ (manitas / manotas) son tan dulces. Quiero que (7) _____ (mamaza / mamita) me preste atención de nuevo. ¿Qué puedo hacer? ¡Gracias por tu (8) _____ (ayudita / ayudota)!

Gabriela

15. **Síntesis Decide si estas afirmaciones son ciertas o falsas. Si son falsas, corrígelas.** `2.A–2.D`

Cierto	Falso	
☐	☐	1. Es correcto decir *la serpiente hembra*.
☐	☐	2. Son despectivos *casucha*, *peliculón* y *flacucho*.
☐	☐	3. *Yerno* es el femenino de *nuera*.
☐	☐	4. En algunos países hispanohablantes, *azúcar* es masculino; y en otros, es femenino.
☐	☐	5. Los diminutivos de *pez*, *carro* y *bebé* son *pezecito*, *carrito* y *bebito*.
☐	☐	6. *Enseres* solamente puede usarse en plural.
☐	☐	7. Es incorrecto usar *parienta* como femenino de *pariente*.
☐	☐	8. El aumentativo **-ito** indica afecto cuando uno se dirige a personas queridas.
☐	☐	9. El aumentativo de *nariz* es *narizota*.
☐	☐	10. *Perrazo* es un aumentativo.

16. **Síntesis Elige la palabra que no pertenece al grupo. ¡Presta atención al género y al número!** `2.A–2.D`

1. solterón   cincuentón   cuarentón   camión
2. viernes   veces   lunes   análisis
3. princesa   suegra   poeta   emperatriz
4. almirante   representante   mariscal   abogado
5. programa   dilema   problema   arena
6. enero   jueves   rojo   flor
7. cita   playita   manchita   pastillita
8. dosis   tesis   crisis   bis
9. baldes   padres   callejones   asistentes
10. clima   panorama   pasaje   madre

Practice more at **vhlcentral.com.**

1. **Reescribe las oraciones colocando las partes subrayadas en femenino.** `3.A`

1. El líder anarquista nació en 1898. _____

2. El niño danzarín salta y salta sin parar. _____

3. El doctor alemán ahora vive en París. _____

4. Un ejecutivo importante renunció a su cargo. _____

5. He perdido mi gato negrote, mi juguete favorito. _____

6. El empleado gentil atiende a los clientes con una sonrisa. _____

7. El niño feliz jugaba en las hamacas del parque. _____

8. El fanático acosador no dejaba tranquila a la cantante. _____

2. **Reescribe los sustantivos y adjetivos según las instrucciones.** `3.A`

1. sabor agradable → (plural) _____

2. perro particular → (femenino) _____

3. profesor conservador → (femenino) _____

4. niño albanés → (femenino) _____

5. político burgués → (femenino, plural) _____

6. salón posterior → (plural) _____

7. rostro paliducho → (plural) _____

8. joven bribón → (femenino) _____

9. plato tentador → (plural) _____

10. coche veloz → (plural) _____

11. publicación periódica → (plural) _____

12. aborigen guaraní → (plural) _____

3. **Julieta y Martina deciden qué vestir para la fiesta de graduación. Completa la conversación con los adjetivos en el género y número adecuados.** `3.B`

JULIETA ¿Tienes una idea (1) _____ (claro) de qué vestirás para la graduación?

MARTINA Sí, tengo una falda y unos zapatos (2) _____ (rojo) que me gustaría combinar con una blusa y una cartera (3) _____ (anaranjado).

JULIETA ¿No te parece que con algo (4) _____ (blanco) quedaría mejor? ¿O unos (5) _____ (bonito) zapatos y falda de color amarillo?

MARTINA No sé, siempre me gustaron las vestimentas (6) _____ (colorido).

JULIETA Mira, yo podría prestarte un vestido con flores (7) _____ (amarillo) claro y tirantes (8) _____ (rojo).

MARTINA ¡Perfecto! Y podría entonces usar mis zapatos y cartera (9) _____ (verde).

JULIETA ¿Puedo verlos?

MARTINA Sí, aquí están. Y, ¿cómo luzco?

JULIETA ¡Como un (10) _____ (impactante) arco iris!

4. **Francisco escribió un poema para su novia, Andrea. Completa el poema con los adjetivos y asegúrate de que el género y el número sean los adecuados.** `3.B`

Tienes unos (1) _____ (hermoso) y (2) _____ (grande) ojos,

y una mirada y sonrisa (3) _____ (bondadoso).

Unas cejas y cabellos (4) _____ (pelirrojo)...

Y una voz tan (5) _____ (fabuloso).

Y yo, un ser (6) _____ (afortunado), como pocos,

miro esas pupilas y pestañas (7) _____ (esplendoroso),

y, con mi corazón en pleno alboroto,

deseo que un buen día seas mi esposa.

5. **En cada oración decide si el adjetivo entre paréntesis debe ir antes o después del sustantivo.** `3.C`

1. Todos dicen que es lindo, pero, para mí, es un _____ perro _____. (feíto)

2. Compré un _____ libro _____ en una feria de artículos usados. (agotado)

3. La _____ revista _____ *Saludables siempre* se publica cada dos meses. (médica)

4. La _____ película _____ del famoso director no tuvo el éxito esperado. (última)

5. Disculpe, señora, ya no tenemos más ese juguete. Se vendió como _____ pan _____. (caliente)

6. La _____ organización _____ lucha por los derechos de los trabajadores. (sindical)

7. La _____ situación _____ de ese país empeora día a día. (social)

8. Juana es una _____ amiga _____. Siempre me ayuda cuando lo necesito. (buena)

6. **Olivia escribió una carta al editor del periódico local. Decide si la ubicación de los adjetivos es adecuada. Si no lo es, corrígela.** `3.C`

Editor estimado:

En la provincia oriental de Recodo, conseguir un digno trabajo es duro. La oficina laboral no ofrece una amable atención. Lo que es peor, los empleados maleducados se ríen de la gente en su cara propia. La realidad cruda es que no hay puestos de trabajo disponibles. Sin embargo, todos están en derecho pleno de ser tratados cordialmente.

Le pido que comunique esta situación a las nacionales autoridades.

Saludos,

Olivia P.

7. **Ordena los elementos para armar una oración que tenga sentido.** `3.C`

1. En realidad, | concurso | tienen posibilidades | ambos | de ganar | participantes | famoso | el
   En realidad, ... _____

2. Pedí | pañuelo | un | expresamente | azul | que me enviaran
   Pedí... _____

3. muchas | romance | que buscan | personas | un | Hay | veraniego
   Hay... _____

4. nocturna | activa | deportistas | tienen | una | vida | Pocos
   Pocos... _____

5. mediterránea | calor | en esta | Hace | playa | tanto
   Hace... _____

6. principal | edificio | en la | El | concurrida | calle Posadas | se encuentra
   El... _____

8. Completa las oraciones con el adjetivo y el sustantivo en el orden correcto. Cada palabra puede usarse una sola vez. **3.C**

menor	buen	ciertas	alta	noticias	lenguas	tensión	gusto
gran	malas	único	santo	padre	hijo	amigo	hermana

1. No sé compartir mis juguetes. Debe ser porque soy _____ _____.

2. ¡Qué bien decorada que está la casa! Ella tiene _____ _____.

3. ¡Cuidado con esos cables! ¡Son de _____ _____!

4. A menudo al Papa se lo denomina _____ _____.

5. No escuches lo que dicen las _____ _____.

6. Un amigo que está a tu lado en momentos difíciles es un _____ _____.

7. Mamá, no puede ser, siempre es lo mismo con mi _____ _____.

8. No te preocupes, no sabemos si son _____ _____.

9. Lee el resumen de un capítulo de la novela *Caballero a caballo* y complétalo. Asegúrate de que el género y el número de los adjetivos sean los adecuados. **3.D**

En el (1) _____ (primero) capítulo de esta (2) _____ (grande) novela, conocemos al (3) _____ (bueno) caballero José de Salamanca, quien emprende un largo viaje en busca de su futura esposa. En la (4) _____ (tercero) jornada, se encuentra con la imagen de (5) _____ (Santo) Diego, quien le aconseja que no siga con su búsqueda, porque podría ser peligroso para su corazón. José de Salamanca no hace caso al supuesto (6) _____ (malo) augurio y sigue adelante. En la (7) _____ (cuarto) jornada de su travesía, recibe una (8) _____ (malo) noticia. Sus (9) _____ (grande) esperanzas se destrozan cuando se entera de que su princesa ya es la esposa del conde de Aranjuez.

10. Dos hermanas discuten sobre sus habitaciones. Completa el diálogo usando comparativos y superlativos. **3.E**

MARIEL Mi ventana es (1) _____ (+ / grande) que la tuya.

CONSTANZA Te equivocas; mi ventana es (2) _____ (+ / grande) de la casa.

MARIEL Mi habitación es (3) _____ (+ / luminosa) que la tuya.

CONSTANZA ¡De ninguna manera! La mía es (4) _____ (+ / luminosa) del primer piso.

MARIEL Y mi cama es (5) _____ (+ / buena) que la tuya.

CONSTANZA ¿En qué mundo vives? Mi cama (6) _____ (+ / buena) de todas.

MARIEL Pero, ¿has visto qué tranquila que es mi habitación? Es (7) _____ (– / ruidosa) que la tuya.

CONSTANZA Imposible. La mía es (8) _____ (– / ruidosa) de la casa.

MARIEL Claro, tú crees que siempre tienes la razón, porque eres la hermana (9) _____ (+ / vieja).

CONSTANZA ¿Ves? Me dices eso porque te aprovechas de ser (10) _____ (+ / joven) de la familia.

MARIEL Uy, ¡qué aburrida que eres, Constanza!

CONSTANZA No, ¡tú eres (11) _____ (+ / aburrida) del mundo!

11. **Elige la opción correcta para completar cada oración.** `3.E`

   1. Juan es _____ de los tres hermanos.
     a. el mayor   b. el más viejo   c. a y b

   2. Carlos es _____ en matemáticas que Marta.
     a. más bueno   b. mejor   c. mayor

   3. El libro es _____ de lo que pensaba.
     a. más bueno   b. mejor   c. menor

   4. El accidente fue _____ de lo que imaginábamos.
     a. más malo   b. peor   c. el peor

   5. Mi hermana es _____ que mi hermano. Ella nunca miente y siempre me ayuda.
     a. mejor   b. la más buena   c. más buena

12. **¡Qué exagerada que es Eloísa!** Completa las oraciones con el superlativo usando el sufijo *-ísimo/a*. `3.E`

   1. Paula dice que su perro es muy flaco, pero el mío es _____.

   2. Concepción me contó que su hermano es muy tonto, pero el mío es _____.

   3. Catalina siempre se queja de que su mochila es muy pesada, pero la mía es _____.

   4. Mi hermana Sara dice que ella es muy ordenada, pero yo soy _____.

   5. Clara cree que su profesora es muy simpática, pero la mía es _____.

   6. A Joan la película le pareció muy triste, pero a mí me pareció _____.

   7. Eva dice que tiene muchos amigos, pero yo tengo _____.

   8. Y mi mamá dice que soy muy exagerada, ¡pero yo digo que soy _____!

13. **Síntesis** Indica qué ejemplo(s) corresponde(n) a cada afirmación. `3.A–3.E`

a. un problema técnico	g. el niño debilucho
b. una gran mujer	h. una forma mejor
c. las niñas y mujeres contentas	i. un hombre narigón
d. la primera vez	j. el caso más importante
e. el defensor ecologista	k. las casas y jardines caros
f. el pobre hombre	l. un diario político-económico

   1. Algunos adjetivos no varían con el género.

   2. Algunos adjetivos se apocopan (abrevian) cuando van delante de un sustantivo.

   3. Algunos adjetivos no se apocopan (abrevian) cuando van delante de un sustantivo femenino.

   4. Algunos adjetivos cambian de significado según estén delante o detrás de un sustantivo.

   5. Algunos adjetivos solo tienen una posición posible.

   6. Algunos adjetivos tienen comparativos irregulares.

   7. La mayoría de los adjetivos tienen superlativos regulares.

   8. Cuando hay varios sustantivos de distinto género antes de un adjetivo, este último toma la forma masculina en plural.

   9. Cuando hay varios sustantivos de igual género, el adjetivo toma el mismo género en plural.

   10. Algunos sustantivos forman adjetivos al agregar un sufijo aumentativo.

   11. Los adjetivos con sufijos apreciativos se colocan después del sustantivo.

Practice more at **vhlcentral.com.**

Actividades

1. Lee el artículo que se publicó en el periódico escolar. Marca los determinantes que aparecen en él. `4.A–4.B`

Amo educado, perro educado

¿Te gustan las mascotas? ¿Siempre quisiste tener una, pero tu mamá piensa que es demasiado trabajo? ¡Tenemos tu solución!

Somos un equipo de veterinarios que trabaja en un albergue con muchos perros abandonados. Algunos perros son cachorros, pero otros son más grandecitos. Estos animalitos buscan amor: ¡sabemos que tú puedes dárselo!

Sabemos que cuidar de un perro no es fácil y muchas madres no quieren encargarse de él. Por eso, te ofrecemos un curso introductorio al cuidado de animales: aprenderás cómo satisfacer todas las necesidades de tu mascota y cómo educarla bien, ¡para que ningún miembro de tu familia se queje! Durante el curso, conocerás a otros niños y jóvenes que te contarán sus experiencias con sus mascotas. Cada uno de ellos tiene historias fantásticas: de amor, de momentos inolvidables, pero también de bastante sacrificio. Por último, cuando hayas acabado el curso y aún tengas muchas ganas de tener un perro, te daremos uno en adopción. El año pasado, cuarenta mascotas encontraron un hogar feliz... ¿Qué esperas? Visita nuestro sitio web www.educaryadoptarperros.com y nos pondremos en contacto contigo.

2. Para cada ejemplo, decide si la palabra subrayada funciona como *determinante*, *pronombre* o *adverbio*. `4.A–4.B`

Ejemplo	Determinante (con sustantivo explícito)	Pronombre (determinante con sustantivo implícito)	Adverbio
1. Las grandes capitales tienen <u>muchos</u> problemas de contaminación.			
2. Comí <u>demasiado</u> esta noche. Mañana debería comer cosas más livianas.			
3. <u>Esta</u> es la última vez que limpio la cocina después de que tú cocinas.			
4. Ya tienes <u>bastantes</u> discusiones con tu jefe... ¡haz las paces de una vez!			
5. Cuando esta casa sea <u>mía</u>, ¡haré fiestas todas las noches!			
6. ¡<u>Alguien</u> me quiere! Tengo una llamada perdida en mi teléfono celular.			
7. ¿Siempre de compras? Tienes que ahorrar. ¡No compres <u>más</u>!			
8. Con <u>tanto</u> humo de cigarrillo, no puedo respirar bien.			
9. Algunos compañeros son amables; pero <u>otros</u>, no.			
10. ¡<u>Esta</u> oportunidad de hacerme famoso es única!			
11. ¿Conoces el trabalenguas que se llama "<u>Tres</u> tristes tigres"?			
12. "<u>Menos</u> televisión y más estudio", me dijo la maestra.			
13. <u>Aquella</u> es mi novia. ¿Acaso no es hermosa?			
14. No hables <u>tanto</u>: ¡estamos en la biblioteca!			
15. <u>Pocas</u> veces me duermo después de las doce de la noche.			
16. ¡Qué hermosa noche! ¡<u>Tantas</u> estrellas!			

Practice more at **vhlcentral.com.**

1. Completa la conversación con el artículo definido adecuado. `5.A`

1. ¡Cuántas veces te dije que no uses mi ropa. ¡Usa _____ tuya!

2. Hoy a _____ cuatro de la tarde podríamos ir al cine, ¿no?

3. En _____ Estados Unidos, la gente no duerme la siesta; pero en _____ Salvador, sí.

4. Me encantan las manzanas, sobre todo _____ verdes.

5. Mis vecinos, _____ Rodríguez, van de vacaciones todos los años a México.

6. Dile a _____ señora Pérez que no podremos ir a la cena _____ jueves.

2. Elige la opción correcta en esta conversación. `5.B`

PABLO ¿Qué podríamos regalarles a tus padres para su aniversario de casados?

MARÍA No sé, no tengo (1) _____ (la/una/otra) idea clara.

PABLO Quizás podríamos comprarles (2) _____ (un/unos/otro) juego de platos; los que les regalamos hace (3) _____ (un/otro/unos) años se rompieron durante la mudanza. ¿Te acuerdas?

MARÍA Sí, es verdad. Pero, ¿cuánto dinero tenemos?

PABLO Creo que (4) _____ (un/otros/unos) ciento cincuenta dólares.

MARÍA Bien, el juego de platos me parece (5) _____ (un/otra/una) buena idea.

3. Completa esta carta con el artículo correspondiente. Si no es necesario usar un artículo, escribe X. `5.B–5.C`

Estimado (1) _____ doctor Pérez:

Quiero hacerle (2) _____ consulta. Estoy de vacaciones con mi hijo Joaquín en (3) _____ Perú desde hace (4) _____ días. Desde ayer, al niño le duele (5) _____ cabeza y tiene fiebre. ¿Puede ser por (6) _____ vacuna que le dio antes del viaje? ¿O tal vez por (7) _____ calurosa que es esta ciudad?

Ayer fuimos a (8) _____ hospital en Lima y (9) _____ médico me dijo que no es nada grave (*serious*). Pero yo quería preguntarle a usted, porque es su pediatra. No hay consejos como (10) _____ suyos.

Muchas gracias por su ayuda,

Paula Sánchez

4. Síntesis Completa el anuncio con las palabras de la lista. `5`

del	el	la	las	los	otra	un	un

Nuevo club escolar de artes marciales

Somos (1) _____ grupo de alumnos (2) _____ noveno año de la escuela Campos Verdes y queremos organizar un club de aficionados a (3) _____ artes marciales.

¿Practicas taekwon-do, karate o alguna (4) _____ arte marcial? ¿Quizás (5) _____ arte marcial que no conocemos?

Estamos en (6) _____ gimnasio de (7) _____ escuela todos (8) _____ jueves por la tarde. ¡Ven, que queremos conocerte!

🪄 Practice more at **vhlcentral.com**.

1. Escribe estos números en letras. `6.A–6.B`

1. 28 _____
2. 132 _____
3. 1200 _____
4. 19 _____
5. 44 _____

6. 102 _____
7. 333 _____
8. 1 000 000 _____
9. 1981 _____
10. 57 _____

2. Reescribe las oraciones usando números. `6.A–6.B`

1. Camila nació el tres de agosto de mil novecientos ochenta y tres.

_____

2. Tardaron ciento tres años en construir este castillo.

_____

3. Para el lunes próximo, tengo que leer doscientas veintiuna páginas.

_____

4. El empresario tiene un millón cuatrocientos mil dólares.

_____

5. Necesitamos vender veintinueve mil unidades este mes.

_____

6. El gobierno dio un subsidio de quinientos ocho dólares a cada vecino por la inundación.

_____

7. Debo devolverte setecientos noventa y un pesos antes del treinta de enero.

_____

8. Debido a la tormenta, se cayeron mil treinta y tres árboles.

_____

3. Reescribe las oraciones usando numerales colectivos. `6.C`

1. Hoy la tienda vendió <u>veinte</u> pares de zapatos en una tarde.

_____

2. En México, hay más de <u>treinta</u> periódicos distintos.

_____

3. Cuando ahorre más dinero, me compraré <u>cien</u> lápices de colores.

_____

4. Si compro <u>diez</u> camisetas, cada una cuesta $8,59.

_____

5. Sí, me llevaré <u>doce</u> rosas.

_____

6. Asistieron al congreso <u>sesenta</u> especialistas.

_____

7. ¡Hay más de <u>mil</u> lugares que quiero visitar!

_____

Actividades

4. Cintia fue al mercado con su madre. Completa la conversación con las palabras de la lista. `6.C`

con   más   es igual a   un   por ciento   y   coma

CINTIA ¿Cuánto costó toda la compra?

MADRE En total, costó diez dólares (1) _____ cincuenta y cinco centavos.

CINTIA Ah, pensé que era más dinero. ¿Estás segura?

MADRE Sí, las verduras costaron ocho dólares; y la carne, cuatro (2) _____ cincuenta (3) _____ cinco centavos.

CINTIA Pero... ocho (4) _____ cuatro (5) _____ cincuenta y cinco (6) _____ doce (7) _____ cincuenta y cinco.

MADRE ¡Qué brillante que es mi hija! Me olvidé del descuento que hizo el verdulero.

CINTIA ¿Quizás (8) _____ veinticinco (9) _____ de descuento?

MADRE Increíble. ¡Ojalá tuviera (10) _____ diez (11) _____ de tu inteligencia!

5. Forma oraciones con elementos de las tres columnas. `6.D`

1. No puede ser: es la	centenario	hombre que se casó en la familia.
2. No sé qué regalarles a los abuelos para su	quinta	vez que lavo los platos.
3. Daniel fue el	milenaria	pieza se encuentra en el Museo Nacional.
4. El 30 de mayo es el	primer	de la fundación de mi pueblo.
5. Luis	trigésimo	era llamado "El Rey Sol".
6. En la actualidad, la	catorce	aniversario de casados.

6. Elige la opción correcta para completar las oraciones. `6.D`

1. El _____ (milenario/millonario) Juan Rodríguez pasa sus vacaciones en Mallorca.

2. La _____ (tercera/tercer) oportunidad es la última.

3. El papa Juan Pablo _____ (dos/segundo) murió en 2005.

4. $\frac{1}{100}$ es un _____ (centésimo/milésimo).

5. En su _____ (trigésimo/treintavo) aniversario, la empresa realizará una gran fiesta.

6. En total, corrí diez vueltas, pero en la _____ (quinta/quincuagésima), paré a descansar un rato.

7. Enrique _____ (ocho/octavo) pertenecía a la casa Tudor.

8. En el _____ (décimo primero/décimo primer) piso, vive mi abuela Porota.

7. Escribe las fracciones en las dos formas posibles. `6.E`

1. 1/2 _____ _____   4. 4/5 _____ _____

2. 1/13 _____ _____   5. 1/8 _____ _____

3. 1/4 _____ _____   6. 2/4 _____ _____

8. Lee la receta y corrígela. En total, hay siete errores. `6.D–6.E`

Cocina rápida: Recetas "en una millonésima segundo"
Hoy: Galletitas navideñas
Mezcle medias taza de azúcar con 250 gramos de harina (es decir, un cuarto kilo de harina). Derrita una quinta del paquete de mantequilla al fuego. Agregue la mantequilla a la primer mezcla. Estire la masa sobre una superficie plana y amásela. Colóquela en la nevera durante un cuarta de hora. Retire la masa y córtela en ocho partes iguales. Tome cada noveno y estírelo con un palo de amasar. Decórelos al gusto y llévelos al horno durante medio hora.

9. ¿Qué hora es? Escríbela de todas las maneras posibles. `6.F`

1. _____
_____
_____
_____

4. _____
_____
_____
_____

2. _____
_____
_____
_____

5. _____
_____
_____
_____

3. _____
_____
_____
_____

6. _____
_____
_____
_____

10. Hoy es lunes y Marcos mira el calendario de esta semana. Escribe respuestas completas de acuerdo con el contenido del calendario. Debes escribir todos los números en letras. `6.F–6.G`

Lunes 1/10	Martes 2/10	Miércoles 3/10	Jueves 4/10	Viernes 5/10
8:40 a.m. Escuela	8.40 a.m. Escuela	8:40 a.m. Escuela	8:40 a.m. Escuela	8:40 a.m. Escuela
4:30 p.m. Natación	6:15 p.m. Regalo para la abuela	11:30 a.m. Examen de español		7:30 p.m. Cumpleaños de la abuela
		2:30 p.m. Dentista		

1. ¿Qué fecha es hoy?

2. ¿Qué sucede el tres de octubre?

3. ¿Qué debe hacer Marcos todos los días?

4. ¿A qué hora debe comprar el regalo para la abuela?

5. ¿A qué hora va a la escuela?

6. ¿Qué debe hacer el miércoles a las dos y media de la tarde?

7. ¿En qué fecha y a qué hora es la fiesta de cumpleaños de la abuela?

8. ¿Qué debe hacer Marcos en la tarde del lunes?

11. Completa la historia de Martina con las palabras de la lista. `6.H`

tenga	cumple	quinceañera	setentón	sesentona
cumplí	ser	sexagenaria	veinteañera	

Un año más

Ayer (1) _____ quince años. La semana que viene, como toda (2) _____, celebro mi cumpleaños con una gran fiesta. Invité a cincuenta personas, entre familiares y amigos. El mismo día de la fiesta, mi abuela (3) _____ sesenta años. En broma, le digo que es una (4) _____, pero ella me dice que es una (5) _____ en perfecto estado físico.

Ella me contó que, cuando ella era una (6) _____, había muchos jóvenes que estaban enamorados de ella. Pero ahora, solo tiene un vecino (7) _____ que la invita todos los domingos a bailar tango. ¡Qué graciosa que es mi abuela! Espero ser igual de divertida cuando (8) _____ su edad.

12. **Lee el pronóstico del tiempo y escribe las preguntas para las respuestas dadas.** `6.I`

Hoy	Mañana	Pasado mañana
Temperatura: 10 °C	Temperatura: −1 °C/4 °C	Temperatura: −3 °C/8 °C

1. ¿_____? Hoy hace 10 °C.

2. ¿_____? Mañana será de −1 °C.

3. ¿_____? Mañana será de 4 °C.

4. ¿_____? Serán de −3 °C y 8 °C.

5. ¿_____? No, aquí medimos la temperatura en grados centígrados.

13. **Síntesis Elige la palabra que no pertenece al grupo.** `6.B–6.J`

1. decenas   docenas   décadas   veintenas

2. tercio   cuarto   quinto   media

3. trigésimo   sexagésimo   décimo   veintiséis

4. máxima   mínima   promedio   próxima

5. cumplir   tener   celebrar   ser

6. sesentón   octogenario   veinteañero   quinceañero

7. décadas   siglos   milenios   millones

8. y veinte   y quince   y medio   y treinta

14. **Síntesis Elige la opción correcta en cada oración.** `6.B–6.J`

1. En la _____ de Hierro, comenzaron a fabricarse armas y herramientas de hierro.
   a. Época   b. Edad

2. Una _____ de huevos son diez huevos.
   a. decena   b. docena

3. Había _____ de personas en el festival.
   a. trescientos   b. cientos

4. _____ una y cuarto, nos encontramos en la estación.
   a. A las   b. A la

5. Debes llegar a las dos _____ diez, porque a las dos en punto sale el tren.
   a. menos   b. y

6. En España, se dice "_____ de enero".
   a. primero   b. uno

7. Hoy estamos a cero _____.
   a. grados   b. grado

8. Un plan quinquenal dura _____ años.
   a. cinco   b. quince

15. **Síntesis Clasifica las palabras de la lista en la categoría apropiada.** `6.B–6.J`

| billón | cuarentena | decena | doceava parte | millar | trescientos | un quinto |
| ciento uno | cuatro octavos | décimo cuarto | mil uno | quinto | trigésimo | la mitad |

Colectivos	Cardinales	Ordinales	Fraccionarios

16. **Síntesis Escribe la palabra que corresponde a cada definición.** `6.B–6.J`

1. período de mil años _____

2. la mitad de algo _____

3. que ocupa el lugar número diez en una serie ordenada de elementos _____

4. persona de más de diecinueve años y menos de treinta _____

5. una parte de las trece iguales en que se divide un todo _____

6. llegar a tener un número entero de años o meses _____

7. que ocupa el lugar número cien en una serie ordenada de elementos _____

8. que ha cumplido ochenta años y aún no ha llegado a los noventa _____

Practice more at **vhlcentral.com**.

1. Escribe las preguntas a estas respuestas. Asegúrate de incluir cuantificadores indefinidos en ellas. `7.A– 7.B`

1. ¿_____? No, ninguna de mis amigas vive en Perú.

2. ¿_____? Sí, hay un parque de diversiones cerca.

3. ¿_____? No, ningún compañero reprobó el examen.

4. ¿_____? No, ninguno de nosotros comerá esta comida.

5. ¿_____? Sí, comeré algunas frutas antes de dormir.

6. ¿_____? Sí, encontraré alguna oficina abierta en este barrio.

2. Completa las oraciones con las palabras de la lista. Atención: hay dos palabras que no debes usar. `7.B`

> algún   alguno   algunos   nada   ningún   ningunas   ninguna   ninguno

1. No tienes _____ posibilidad de ganar la lotería. ¡Mejor ponte a trabajar!

2. _____ de los hombres de esta oficina está casado.

3. ¿Conoces _____ lugar divertido para ir de vacaciones?

4. No tengo _____ gafas de ese color. Mañana me compraré unas.

5. ¿_____ de ustedes podrá ir a la feria medieval? ¡Todos están ocupadísimos!

6. No hay _____ problema, podemos posponer la cita para la semana próxima.

3. Compara las oraciones y decide cuál es correcta. Es posible que ambas oraciones sean correctas. `7.B`

1. _____ a. ¿Conoces el nombre de alguna arma de fuego?
   b. ¿Conoces el nombre de algún arma de fuego?

2. _____ a. Nadie de ellos tiene cabello oscuro.
   b. Ninguno de ellos tiene cabello oscuro.

3. _____ a. No encuentro mis llaves por ningún sitio.
   b. No encuentro mis llaves por ninguno sitio.

4. _____ a. ¿Alguna vez vendrás a visitarme?
   b. ¿Algún vez vendrás a visitarme?

5. _____ a. No había blusa alguna que me gustara.
   b. No había ninguna blusa que me gustara.

4. Reordena las oraciones de forma correcta. `7.B`

1. para mí / No habrá / alguno / regalo / en este cumpleaños

   _____

2. de los / en el sur de Brasil / algunos / campos / Iré a

   _____

3. No, / come / de ellos / carne / ninguno

   _____

4. chico / nos guste / hay / ningún / que / No

   _____

5. Veré / que viven / en Colombia / a / parientes / algunos

   _____

6. ¿? / mexicana / este año / maestra / alguna / Tendremos

   _____

7. vestidos / algunos / mejores / de los / Nos probamos

   _____

5. **Lee la carta que escribió Francisca a su amiga. Indica cuáles son los cuantificadores indefinidos que solo tienen forma positiva.** `7.C`

> Querida Eva:
>
> ¡Te extraño cada día más! ¿Cuándo podremos vernos? Ya sé que tenemos muchas actividades, pero deberíamos encontrarnos cualquier día de estos.
>
> ¿Sería demasiado estrés que nos viéramos el miércoles? Los demás días de la semana trabajo hasta muy tarde. En todo caso, podríamos coordinar para hacer las compras juntas u otra cosa que quieras.
>
> Deberíamos vernos alguna vez antes de fin de año, ¿no?
>
> Espero una respuesta pronto,
> Francisca

6. **Para cada ejemplo, indica si el cuantificador debe concordar en género y/o número con el sustantivo.** `7.C`

Ejemplo	Sí	No
1. Ante **alguna** duda, consulte con su médico de cabecera.		
2. **Cada** uno ordena su habitación.		
3. Tengo **muchísimo** sueño.		
4. Hay **varias** alumnas que son excelentes deportistas.		
5. Habrá **más** contaminación si no cuidamos el planeta.		
6. Compra **menos** dulces la próxima vez.		

7. **Inserta el cuantificador en el lugar adecuado de la oración.** `7.C`

1. En nuestra tienda, le ofrecemos recetas: desde platos elaborados hasta platos rápidos. (varias)

   _____

2. Con dos kilos, me veré mejor. (menos)

   _____

3. Cinco días y comienzan las vacaciones. (más)

   _____

4. Tengo sueño: mejor hablemos mañana. (bastante)

   _____

5. Un día llegarás a casa y estaré esperándote con una gran sorpresa. (cualquiera)

   _____

6. Hay cosas que tenemos que hablar. Necesitamos más tiempo. (varias)

   _____

8. **En estos ejemplos, indica si el cuantificador indefinido funciona como pronombre o no.** `7.C`

1. Quería comprar libros, pero ninguno me pareció interesante. _____
2. Busquemos unas películas buenas y mirémoslas. _____
3. No me decido todavía: cualquiera me viene bien. _____
4. Algunos amigos de Juan viven en México. _____
5. Comunícate con cualquier integrante de nuestro personal. _____
6. ¡Todo me sale mal! _____
7. Al final, me arrepentí de comprar la cámara. No es necesario tener una. _____
8. La vecina de la esquina es amable; las demás, no. _____

9. **Julia y Joaquín hablan sobre su ciudad. Completa la conversación con las palabras de la lista. Si no es necesario agregar una palabra, indícalo con una X.** `7.C`

| cualquier | cualquiera | cualquiera de | un | una | unos |

JULIA ¿Vivirías para siempre en nuestra ciudad?

JOAQUÍN Sí, me encanta. Además, no podría vivir en (1) _____ de los pueblos cercanos.

JULIA Mmm... no sé, nuestra ciudad no tiene (2) _____ playa. Tampoco tiene (3) _____ bosque.

JOAQUÍN Pienso que el clima es ideal aquí. Hace (4) _____ poco de calor en el verano, pero no demasiado.

JULIA Puede ser... De (5) _____ manera, debo quedarme hasta que termine la escuela.

JOAQUÍN Sí, y para eso faltan (6) _____ cuatro años.

JULIA Es verdad, pero podría ir pensando en mudarme a (7) _____ las ciudades que tienen universidades importantes.

JOAQUÍN No es (8) _____ mala idea. Además, ¡tiempo es lo que nos sobra!

10. **Para cada oración, elige la opción correcta. En algunos casos, ambas respuestas son correctas.** `7.C`

1. Carmen y Sandra van a escuelas diferentes, pero _____ (ambas / cada una) juegan en el mismo equipo de hockey.

2. Ya tengo _____ (bastantes/demás) problemas con aprender francés. ¡Aprender también chino sería demasiado!

3. _____ (Todos/Ambos) los estudiantes deben hacer la tarea para el lunes próximo.

4. _____ (Ambos / Los tres) perros deben ir a la veterinaria: Pipo y Colita, hoy; y Huesito, mañana.

5. Estudié _____ (cada una de / todas) las lecciones del libro, de la primera a la última.

6. _____ (Cada semana / Todas las semanas) tengo clases de música.

7. Mi médico dijo que es saludable comer _____ (cada/durante) cuatro horas.

11. **Contesta las preguntas con respuestas completas usando la palabra entre paréntesis.** `7.C`

1. ¿Compraste las cosas que aparecían en la lista? Sí, _____ (todas).

2. ¿Esos pueblos son iguales entre sí? No, _____ (cada).

3. ¿Has estudiado para el examen? Sí, _____ (todo).

4. ¿Eres un experto en motocicletas? Sí, _____ (todo un).

5. ¿Me has contado todos los detalles de la boda? Sí, _____ (todo lo).

12. **Elige la opción correcta para completar estas oraciones.** `7.C`

1. No te preocupes, me encargaré de todo _____ (lo/los) demás.

2. Yo quería ir de viaje de estudios al sur, pero _____ (lo/las) demás eligieron el viaje al norte.

3. Necesito mucho _____ (menos / menos de) tiempo, ¡seis días son más que suficientes!

4. Si hago un poco _____ (más / más de) esfuerzo, me aceptarán en la universidad que quiera.

5. Tengo que arreglar _____ (otros detalles más / otros más detalles) y podremos irnos.

6. ¿Te acuerdas de que _____ (el otro / un otro) día hablamos sobre este tema?

7. Trabajemos _____ (otras tres / tres otras) horas y vámonos al parque.

8. El café no está muy dulce: quiero _____ (otro poco / otro poco de) azúcar.

13. Reemplaza las palabras subrayadas por un pronombre indefinido. `7.D`

1. ¿Hay <u>alguna persona</u> que hable alemán aquí? _____

2. <u>Ninguna persona</u> viene de Colombia. _____

3. Al momento de elegir una playa en toda Latinoamérica, <u>una persona</u> elegiría una playa de Brasil. _____

4. <u>Ninguna persona</u> puede ayudarme. _____

5. No viajes con <u>ninguna cosa</u> que sea de valor. _____

6. Hay <u>una cosa</u> que debes saber. _____

14. Convierte estas oraciones afirmativas en negativas. `7.D`

1. ¿Hay alguien que sea español? _____

2. Yo tenía que decirte algo. _____

3. Escucho algo cuando hablo por teléfono. _____

4. Tú conoces a alguien que puede venir. _____

5. Me cuenta mucho sobre su abuelo, Pedro. _____

15. Reescribe este relato de forma impersonal usando el pronombre _uno_ en lugar del pronombre de la segunda persona del singular. `7.D`

Posibles soluciones para el insomnio

Muchas personas sufren de insomnio ocasionalmente. ¿Pero qué puedes hacer cuando esto se convierte en un problema frecuente?

Puedes hacer ejercicio por la tarde, aunque no demasiado tarde. De lo contrario, al momento de dormir, tienes un ritmo demasiado acelerado y no puedes conciliar el sueño.

Otra opción es no tomar bebidas con mucha cafeína. Cuando tomas mucho café o bebidas energéticas, estás más alerta y no puedes dormirte con tanta facilidad.

Muchos médicos recomiendan que no tengas un televisor en la habitación. Es mejor que la habitación sea un lugar donde solamente duermas.

Y, por último, debes intentar tener horarios regulares, es decir, una rutina.

16. ¿_Nada_ o _nadie_? Completa las oraciones. `7.D`

1. La vendedora de la tienda no fue _____ amable al atenderme.

2. No quiero a _____ más que a ti.

3. No tengo fuerzas para _____. Es mejor que descanse más.

4. El pronóstico no es _____ bueno: el paciente deberá quedarse en el hospital un largo tiempo.

5. ¿Tienes más hambre? Yo no quiero _____ más.

6. ¿Adivina quién me invitó a su cumpleaños? ¡_____ menos que el embajador de México!

17. **Cada vez que Patricia dice algo, Diego la contradice. Escribe los comentarios de Diego usando la palabra entre paréntesis.** `7.E`

1. **PATRICIA** Tu mamá siempre habla mucho.
   DIEGO _____ (poco).

2. **PATRICIA** Es bastante seguro que yo gane una beca.
   DIEGO _____ (nada).

3. **PATRICIA** En el último año, la economía de nuestro país creció mucho menos, en comparación con años anteriores.
   DIEGO _____ (más).

4. **PATRICIA** Este resfriado no es nada grave.
   DIEGO _____ (bastante).

5. **PATRICIA** Hace mucho que dejaste de trabajar.
   DIEGO _____ (tanto).

18. **Completa este folleto con la forma correcta de *mismo* o *propio*.** `7.E`

¡Baje de peso ya!

¿No se siente cómodo con su (1) _____ cuerpo? ¿Tiene unos kilitos de más que lo hacen sentirse inseguro? ¡Siéntase bien consigo (2) _____ en treinta días! Gracias al revolucionario tratamiento que ofrecemos, bajará sus kilos de más de forma fácil y saludable, a su (3) _____ ritmo.

Nuestro método es totalmente distinto de los demás: sin pastillas, sin mentiras, sin recetas mágicas. Se trata de buscar en uno (4) _____ las fuerzas y ganas para darle un rumbo nuevo a su (5) _____ vida. Llame ahora (6) _____ y le regalaremos un video explicativo donde podrá ver testimonios de muchos de nuestros clientes satisfechos.

19. **Síntesis Une los elementos de las dos columnas para formar oraciones.** `7.B–7.E`

1. No tengo ningún _____
2. Algún _____
3. No hay forma _____
4. Creo que hay bastantes _____
5. Ya tengo bastante _____
6. Elige cualquiera de _____
7. Me ha dicho que en todo _____
8. Debes mirar a cada _____
9. Fue mi propia _____
10. Creo que he aprendido _____
11. Mi novio me dijo algo _____

a. con mis problemas. ¡No puedo solucionar los tuyos!
b. lugares donde podríamos festejar tu cumpleaños.
c. momento de tranquilidad.
d. lado de la calle antes de cruzar.
e. madre la que me contó la verdad.
f. día seré rico y dejaré de trabajar.
g. momento estará conmigo.
h. alguna de entrar sin saber el código secreto.
i. mucho esta tarde.
j. las blusas; todas son hermosas.
k. muy dulce.

20. Síntesis Decide a qué ejemplo hace referencia cada explicación. `7.B–7.E`

_____ 1. No tienes ninguna mascota.

_____ 2. ¿Hay algún problema?

_____ 3. Me gusta todo en esta tienda.

_____ 4. Me quedan unos cinco mil dólares en la cuenta.

_____ 5. Ambas sillas pertenecen a Marta.

_____ 6. Cada calle tiene un nombre distinto.

_____ 7. Uno debe cuidar su salud siempre.

_____ 8. Carla y Javier recibieron sendos galardones.

a. Es un cuantificador que se usa siempre en plural y que puede reemplazarse por "los/las dos".

b. Es un cuantificador que se usa en lugar de "aproximadamente" antes de un número.

c. Es un determinante que significa "uno cada uno" y se usa en el lenguaje escrito.

d. Este cuantificador se abrevia antes de sustantivos masculinos en singular.

e. Es un cuantificador que no concuerda en género ni en número con el sustantivo y solo indica una parte de un todo.

f. Esta forma negativa requiere una doble negación cuando se encuentra después del verbo.

g. Se usa cuando el hablante necesita expresarse de una forma impersonal.

h. Es un cuantificador indefinido que, en este caso, se usa como pronombre.

 Practice more at **vhlcentral.com.**

Demonstratives 🌐 | Chapter 8

1. Carlos está en la zapatería y quiere comprarse calzado nuevo. Observa las imágenes y completa las oraciones de la vendedora con determinantes demostrativos. `8.A`

1. _____ zapatos son clásicos y elegantes, ¿le quedan cómodos?

2. Si quiere algo más moderno, tiene _____ zapatos marrones, con rayas marrón claro, que están en el exhibidor.

3. O, si busca algo más informal, puedo ofrecerle _____ zapatillas color beige, están a un precio muy razonable.

4. ¿O prefiere _____ zapatos negros que le ofrecí al principio?

5. Me gustan los zapatos clásicos, llevo _____.

2. **Martín está en la habitación que tenía cuando era niño. Completa la descripción con las palabras de la lista.** `8.A`

aquellos	esas	esos	esta	aquel	eso	este	estas

(1) _____ era mi habitación. Todo (2) _____ espacio de aquí era únicamente para mí, ¿no es genial? (3) _____ repisas que ves aquí están repletas de mis cómics favoritos. En (4) _____ cajones que están detrás de las repisas están mis juguetes de cuando era niño. Y (5) _____ oso gigante que ves al fondo es el primer peluche que me regalaron. Y mira (6) _____ marrón que se ve por la ventana. Es un edificio de oficinas bastante feo. Allí antes había una casa de madera. ¡Qué tiempos (7) _____! Nos pasábamos allí todo el verano. ¡(8) _____ eran aventuras de verdad!

3. **Elige la opción correcta para completar el artículo periodístico.** `8.A`

Accidente automovilístico

(1) _____ (Aquella/Esta) madrugada, alrededor de las 5:30 a.m., dos coches chocaron en la intersección de las calles Colina y San Petersburgo. Según testigos, el conductor del coche azul cruzó la avenida con el semáforo en rojo. Los registros policiales indican que (2) _____ (esto/esta) no es la primera vez que este conductor comete una infracción de (3) _____ (esto/este) tipo. (4) _____ (Este/Aquel) tampoco es el primer accidente en esta intersección.

En la escena del accidente, un vecino, Francisco Gómez, declaró: "(5) _____ (Ese/Esto) ya pasó varias veces antes. (6) _____ (Aquel/Aquello) semáforo no está bien sincronizado con (7) _____ (aquel/aquello)".

Las autoridades de seguridad vial están analizando (8) _____ (eso/este) y otros casos de accidentes por cruzar semáforos en rojo. Sin embargo, afirman que (9) _____ (estas/estos) son casos de negligencia, y no de problemas técnicos.

4. **Síntesis Completa las oraciones con demostrativos.** `8.A–8.B`

1. La niña _____ que está allí no deja de mirarme: ¿qué querrá de mí?

2. _____ tres piedras que tengo en la mano son muy valiosas.

3. ¿Ves _____ que se mueve en el fondo del jardín? ¡Es mi perro!

4. Recibí dos veces la misma factura. Mira aquí: _____ esta semana; y aquella, la semana pasada.

5. ¿Cómo armo _____? No entiendo las instrucciones.

6. _____... no sé la respuesta... no hice la tarea.

7. ¡Ay! ¡Ojalá tuviera tu edad! En _____ tiempos, todo parecía posible.

8. _____ vez no me olvidaré de llevar mi pasaporte.

9. Mira aquí: todo _____ lo gané trabajando... ¡trabajando muchísimo!

Practice more at vhlcentral.com.

Actividades

1. Completa la conversación con los determinantes posesivos correspondientes. `9.B`

MAMÁ ¿Has hecho (1) _____ tarea?

ANDRÉS Por supuesto, mamá. (2) _____ maestro es muy estricto.

MAMÁ ¿Y has ordenado (3) _____ habitación? Mañana viene (4) _____ amigo... ¿cómo se llama?

ANDRÉS Julio. Sí, mamá, hasta guardé todos (5) _____ juegos en el armario.

MAMÁ Bien hecho. Pero, ¿qué hiciste con (6) _____ camiseta de fútbol? Mañana debes llevarla a la escuela.

ANDRÉS No te preocupes, mamita. (7) _____ entrenador tiene todas (8) _____ camisetas en (9) _____ casa.

MAMÁ Así me gusta. ¡Solamente deseo que (10) _____ vidas sean ordenadas!

ANDRÉS ¡Sí, mamá! Y ya lo sabes, ¡(11) _____ deseos son órdenes!

2. Completa las oraciones con los determinantes posesivos correspondientes. `9.C`

1. No encuentro varios cuadernos _____ (yo). ¿Sabes dónde pueden estar?

2. Ayer me llamó una compañera _____ (tú).

3. En el periódico, publicaron muchos artículos _____ (nosotros).

4. ¿Te gustan las novelas de Paulo Coelho? Compré unos libros _____ (él) a un precio muy bueno.

5. ¿Qué haremos con todos estos juguetes _____ (tú) cuando crezcas? Podríamos donarlos.

6. ¡Cómo extraño usar esas zapatillas _____ (yo)! Eran hermosas, ¿te acuerdas?

7. Un profesor _____ (nosotros) nos recomendó esta universidad.

8. En la fiesta, conocí a unos amigos _____ (él).

9. Esas amigas _____ (vosotros) que vinieron de visita son muy simpáticas.

10. ¿Estos libros de contabilidad son _____ (ustedes)?

3. Reescribe estas oraciones cambiando los posesivos según la persona entre paréntesis. `9.B–9.C`

1. Esa compañera tuya no deja de llamar a casa. (vosotros)

_____

2. Varios profesores míos dieron clases en universidades importantes del extranjero. (tú)

_____

3. Nuestras madres hablan tanto. Con razón, nuestros padres miran tanta televisión. (ellos)

_____

4. ¿Puedes alquilar un DVD en la tienda de tu barrio? (yo)

_____

5. Tus zapatos están sucios. Es necesario lavarlos antes de guardarlos en tu armario. (vosotros)

_____

6. Sus perros se llaman Guardián y Sultán, ¿no? Esos nombres no podrían ser más que idea suya. (tú)

_____

4. Completa las oraciones con los posesivos de la lista. `9.B–9.C`

> suya   míos   vuestro   mi   tus   sus   nuestros   tuyos

1. Carla, _____ padres llamaron preocupados. ¡Quieren saber dónde estás!

2. Unos vecinos _____ se quejaron porque mi perro ladra. ¡Qué intolerancia hay en mi barrio!

3. Mis padres son más viejos que los _____.

4. _____ compañera de cuarto, Alicia, estudia toda la noche y no me deja dormir.

5. Estos son _____ derechos como estudiantes. ¡Solamente nosotros podemos defenderlos!

6. ¿Has visto lo linda que es Paula? ¡_____ ojos son impactantes!

7. Es claro que Flavia organizó la fiesta sorpresa. Todo esto es obra _____.

8. Esto es _____, ¿no? Recuerdo que lo habéis dejado en mi casa.

5. Clasifica estos determinantes posesivos según puedan usarse como prenominales, posnominales o ambos. `9.B–9.C`

Determinante	Prenominal	Posnominal	Pre/posnominal
1. su			
2. míos			
3. vuestros			
4. suyos			
5. nuestra			
6. tus			
7. mis			
8. tuya			
9. vuestra			
10. nuestros			

6. Una amiga tuya empezó con sus clases de español hace muy poco. Ayúdala a corregir su tarea. Elige la opción correcta. `9.B–9.C`

> Mis regalos de Navidad
>
> Finalmente llegó la Navidad. (1) _____ (Tus/Mis) papás me dieron muchos regalos.
>
> Bueno, primero, (2) _____ (su/mi) hermano, Pablo, abrió su regalo: un espectacular rompecabezas. Siempre fue (3) _____ (su/mi) sueño tener uno, y se le hizo realidad. Después fue mi turno. A diferencia de Pablo, el único deseo (4) _____ (suyo/mío) era una sencilla muñeca Patsy, ya sabes, la que sale en la televisión. Vi cuatro cajas, que parecían todas cosas (5) _____ (tuyas/mías), porque tenían mi nombre en ellas. En la primera caja, había una muñeca Patsy. Y en las demás, todos (6) _____ (sus/vuestros) accesorios. ¡Sí, y todo era (7) _____ (mío/nuestro)!
>
> En fin, pasé todo (8) _____ (su/mi) fin de semana jugando con mi muñeca Patsy, ¡y con todos (9) _____ (sus/tus) vestidos y zapatos!

7. Reescribe cada frase diciendo exactamente a quién pertenece cada cosa. `9.D`

Regalos para adolescentes
Sugerencia: *Sol y lluvia*

En este libro, encontramos los relatos de Amparo, una hermosa y simpática joven que vive en una pequeña ciudad en el sur de (1) su país natal, Chile. Pero, al cabo de los primeros capítulos, en (2) su diario, es claro que (3) su vida no es de color de rosa: Amparo se encuentra con muchos problemas sin solución.

El autor de *Sol y lluvia*, Facundo Quesada, presentó (4) su libro y dio una conferencia de prensa. En (5) palabras suyas: "Esta historia es ideal para lectores adolescentes, porque pueden identificarse con Amparo. Al leer (6) su diario, ellos se dan cuenta de que no son de otro planeta: que tanto en (7) su vida como en (8) las suyas hay alegrías y tristezas, pero todo tiene una solución". Por esta razón y muchas otras, les recomendamos este libro para (9) sus hijos de entre doce y dieciséis años.

1. _____ 4. _____ 7. _____
2. _____ 5. _____ 8. _____
3. _____ 6. _____ 9. _____

8. Completa las oraciones con *propio, propia, propios* o *propias*. Decide si va antes o después del sustantivo. `9.D`

1. Te lo digo por _____ experiencia _____: cuida tus pertenencias en el aeropuerto.

2. Carina vive en su _____ mundo _____ y nunca presta atención en clase.

3. No puede ser que no me creas: ¡lo he visto con mis _____ ojos _____!

4. Le recomiendo ese abrigo que está en la vidriera: es una _____ chaqueta _____ para el invierno.

5. Yo tengo _____ habitación _____. ¿Y tú? ¿Compartes tu habitación con tu hermana?

6. Ella trabaja por _____ cuenta _____, pero antes era empleada de una tienda.

9. Luciana va al médico. Completa la conversación con determinantes posesivos o artículos definidos. `9.D`

LUCIANA Hola, doctor. Le cuento (1) _____ inquietud: me pica (2) _____ lunar (*mole*) que tengo aquí en (3) _____ brazo. Además, (4) _____ piel es muy blanca.

MÉDICO Bueno, Luciana, primero unas preguntitas. ¿En (5) _____ familia, hay casos de cáncer?

LUCIANA No, nadie tuvo cáncer.

MÉDICO ¿Te duele (6) _____ lunar?

LUCIANA No, no me duele, pero a veces me pica (7) _____ piel de alrededor.

MÉDICO Mmm... Bueno, haremos un examen el lunes que viene.

LUCIANA Bien, déjeme ver (8) _____ agenda... Perfecto, pero, ¿qué puedo hacer para solucionar la picazón?

MÉDICO Es importante que no te rasques (9) _____ piel.

LUCIANA Sí...

MÉDICO Ponte protector solar en (10) _____ brazos antes de salir de (11) _____ hogar.

LUCIANA ¿Solamente allí?

MÉDICO Bueno, lo ideal es que te pongas protector en todo (12) _____ cuerpo.

LUCIANA Perfecto, entonces me cuido (13) _____ lunar hasta la próxima visita.

MÉDICO Luciana, ¡eres (14) _____ mejor paciente!

10. Completa las oraciones con las frases de la lista. `9.D`

mi amiga	mi general	mi papá	auto nuestro
valijas nuestras	tus bufandas	botas tuyas	

1. ¿Recuerdas ese _____ que se descomponía en los días más importantes?

2. Aquí hay unas _____ de color marrón. ¿Las quieres todavía?

3. Para mi cumpleaños, vinieron _____ y la tuya.

4. Estaré listo a las 7 de la mañana, _____, como buen sargento que soy.

5. Mi tía tiene 46 años, y luego está _____, que tiene 43.

6. Aquí están _____ favoritas. ¿Qué hago con ellas?

7. En la casa de Andrea tenemos varias _____ que debemos buscar.

11. Síntesis Decide si estas oraciones son correctas. Corrige las incorrectas. `9.A–9.E`

1. Tengo las gafas siempre sucias. Debería limpiarlas más a menudo. _____

2. Mira, allí están tus libros. Los míos están aquí. _____

3. Sabes que te adoro, mi querida Eva. _____

4. Mi y tu hermano se llaman igual. _____

5. En país tuyo, ¿ahora es invierno o verano? _____

6. Mañana vendrá la tía, ¡no la tuya! _____

7. Me duele mucho mi cabeza. ¿Qué hago? _____

8. El abogado del delincuente declaró que el ataque fue en propia defensa. _____

9. Alteza Real mía, le aseguro que todos los pobladores lo admiran. _____

10. Es posible que recibas alguna carta mía la semana que viene. _____

12. Síntesis Completa la historia con la opción correcta. `9.A–9.E`

De alumno a alumno

¿No consigues (1) _____ (tus/los) libros que te han pedido? ¿No sabes cómo hacer (2) _____ (las tareas tuyas / tus tareas)? No te rompas más (3) _____ (la/tu) cabeza tratando de hacerlas por (4) _____ (propia cuenta / cuenta propia).

¡Ofrecemos (5) _____ (una solución propia / tu solución) para estudiantes de primer año!

Somos un grupo de estudiantes de quinto año a punto de graduarnos y queremos que todos (6) _____ (vuestros compañeros / nuestros compañeros) de escuela tengan el mismo éxito que hemos tenido nosotros. Bajo el lema (*motto*) "Lo (7) _____ (mío/tuyo) es (8) _____ (mío/tuyo)", donamos nuestros libros y apuntes, y ayudamos a quienes tengan dificultades en matemáticas, ciencias y literatura. Puedes encontrarnos en el aula 43, justo enfrente (9) _____ (de la mía / de la tuya).

🪄 Practice more at **vhlcentral.com.**

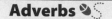

1. Lee este texto e indica si las palabras subrayadas se utilizan como adverbios o adjetivos. `10.A`

El tren en Internet

¡Ahora comprar sus billetes de tren es muy (1) fácil! Ingrese en nuestro sitio web. En el buscador de horarios, elija la hora y el día en el que desea viajar. Luego, busque la tarifa que (2) mejor se adecue a su bolsillo. Cuando la encuentre, haga clic (3) rápidamente sobre la opción escogida. No tiene (4) demasiado tiempo: en cinco minutos deberá concretar su compra. (5) Ahora pague su billete. Le ofrecemos una (6) amplia variedad de medios de pago. No olvide ingresar una dirección de correo electrónico, a la que le enviaremos (7) inmediatamente el billete que deberá imprimir. Preséntese en la estación (8) pocos minutos antes de la salida del tren... ¡y (9) asunto arreglado!

1. _____   4. _____   7. _____

2. _____   5. _____   8. _____

3. _____   6. _____   9. _____

2. Completa las oraciones con las palabras de la lista. `10.B`

> temprano   cuándo   pasado mañana   nunca   antes   cuando   ya (3)   tarde   después

1. Dime _____ estarás en tu casa y pasaré a visitarte.

2. _____ hace frío, uso bufanda y guantes muy abrigados.

3. _____ de los relámpagos, siempre se oye un trueno.

4. _____ de salir del país, verifica que tienes tu pasaporte.

5. Mañana es miércoles y _____ es jueves.

6. ¡Te despiertas demasiado _____! ¡Hoy es domingo y son las 7 a.m.!

7. _____ o temprano verás que tengo razón.

8. _____ no tengo más dinero. ¡Tendré que pedirles un poco a mis padres!

9. _____ jamás adivinarías a quién encontré en la calle.

10. _____ sabes la respuesta... ¡para qué me preguntas!

11. _____ verás qué divertida es esta amiga mía.

3. María Luisa es una chica muy ocupada. Completa su relato con la opción correcta. `10.B`

Todos los días tengo algo para hacer por las tardes, después de la escuela. Es decir, (1) _____ (casi siempre / casi nunca) tengo tiempo libre. (2) _____ (Nunca/Siempre) me encontrarás en casa por las tardes. Si quieres verme, tendrás que ir al club, porque estoy allí (3) _____ (frecuentemente / rara vez).

(4) _____ (A veces / Pocas veces) me gustaría quedarme en casa, pero sé que es importante entrenar y socializar... ¡y no hay nada mejor que el club para eso! Bueno, entonces si quieres que nos veamos, (5) _____ (siempre/nunca) me busques en casa... ¡ya sabes dónde estoy (6) _____ (con poca frecuencia / con mucha frecuencia)!

4. Elige la opción correcta para cada oración. `10.C`

1. _____ (Cómo/Como) me dijiste, compré las flores más lindas para Susana.

2. Cada día me siento _____ (mal/peor): este remedio no cura mi tos.

3. Bate los huevos de esta manera, _____ (cómo/como) te estoy mostrando.

4. Esta carne no está _____ (bien/mejor) cocinada. ¡Parece cruda!

5. La próxima vez elegiré _____ (mejor/así) el destino de mis vacaciones.

6. Tu amiga es _____ (mal/bien) simpática. Invítala a todas nuestras fiestas.

5. Completa la conversación con *bien, mejor, así, cómo* y *como*. `10.C`

REBECA ¡Qué (1) _____! Si te mudas cerca de casa, podremos vernos todas las tardes.

CAMILA Sí… Me encantaría que fuera (2) _____; pero no sé (3) _____ haré para encontrar un apartamento a buen precio y bien ubicado.

REBECA Es verdad, aquí la gente vive (4) _____; por las noches siempre hay movimiento y todos quieren vivir aquí.

CAMILA Quizás sería (5) _____ buscar un apartamento en otro barrio, (6) _____ dijo mi madre.

REBECA No te preocupes, ya encontraremos un apartamento (7) _____ bonito para ti.

CAMILA ¡(8) _____ me gusta! Con esta actitud tan positiva, ¡encontraremos uno genial!

6. Cecilia siempre contradice a su madre. Reescribe las oraciones usando el adverbio adecuado. `10.D`

1. **MADRE** En el supermercado debemos comprar <u>mucho</u>.

   CECILIA _____

2. **MADRE** Tardaremos <u>más</u> que la semana pasada.

   CECILIA _____

3. **MADRE** Nos llevará <u>demasiado</u> tiempo.

   CECILIA _____

4. **MADRE** ¡Tendremos que pagar <u>tanto</u> por un taxi!

   CECILIA _____

5. **MADRE** Será mejor comprar <u>poco</u> para todo el mes.

   CECILIA _____

7. Completa las oraciones con las palabras de la lista. `10.D`

muy	todo lo que	casi	demasiado	cuánto	bastante	cuanto

1. Mi instructor de yoga se entrena _____. Creo que eso no es saludable.

2. _____ rompo mi computadora por llevarla en una mochila inadecuada.

3. No sabes _____ extrañé a mi perro durante las vacaciones.

4. Tu jefa nueva es _____ simpática. Mucho mejor que la anterior, ¿no?

5. _____ más aprendo matemáticas, más mejoro en geometría.

6. Me resulta _____ difícil estudiar más de dos horas seguidas.

7. Te juro que hice _____ pude para comprarte un regalo, pero no encontré nada adecuado para ti.

8. **¿*Aquí, allí* o *allá*? Completa el relato de Cintia.** `10.E`

¡Cómo me gusta mi ciudad nueva! (1) _____ puedo hacer mucho más que en Lobres, mi pueblo anterior. Es verdad que Lobres era más tranquilo. (2) _____ no nos preocupábamos por cerrar con llave las puertas de los carros o cerrar las ventanas por la noche. (3) _____ es diferente: tenemos que tener más cuidado con nuestros bolsos en la calle y estar más atentos. Lo bueno de vivir (4) _____ es que todos los días hay actividades: ir al cine, a museos, ver espectáculos al aire libre, de todo... Y por suerte siempre puedo volver a Lobres cuando quiero. Voy para (5) _____ una vez cada quince días a ver a mis padres. (6) _____ comemos muy rico, dormimos la siesta y disfrutamos de la tranquilidad del pueblo.

9. **Escribe las preguntas para estas respuestas. Debes usar *dónde* o *adónde*.** `10.E`

> **Modelo**
>
> *¿Dónde naciste?*
> Yo nací <u>en Guatemala</u>.

1. _____
   Iremos <u>al centro comercial</u> para comprar regalos.
2. _____
   Nos encontraremos <u>en el restaurante chino</u> a las 10 p.m.
3. _____
   Juana podrá dormir <u>en mi cuarto</u>.
4. _____
   Por la mañana, viajaremos <u>a Jaén</u>.
5. _____
   El avión aterrizará <u>en el aeropuerto internacional</u>.
6. _____
   Iremos a comer <u>a la casa de la abuela</u>.

10. **Elige la opción correcta para cada oración.** `10.E`

1. ¡La camisa azul está _____ (delante/adelante) de tus ojos. ¿Cómo no la ves?
2. ¡Cuidado! Si das dos pasos hacia _____ (detrás/atrás), pisarás al gato.
3. Ven _____ (dentro/adentro). Hace mucho frío para estar allí.
4. _____ (Debajo/Abajo) de esa cama, encontrarás muchas cajas.
5. Mira hacia _____ (encima/arriba): el techo tiene mucha humedad.
6. _____ (Dentro/Adentro) de la tienda, la temperatura es óptima.

11. **Une las oraciones de las columnas para que tengan sentido.** `10.E`

1. Verás que más _____   a. cerca de los carros; es peligroso.
2. No camines muy _____   b. lejos de lo que pensábamos.
3. No estamos nada _____   c. fuera del teatro.
4. El teatro estaba mucho más _____   d. lejos del museo de la ciudad. ¡Tenemos que ir!
5. No te quedes demasiado _____ e. atrás: ¡te perderé de vista!
6. Es verdad: por _____   f. adelante hay una tienda con un cartel anaranjado.
7. Hay mucha gente esperando _____   g. fuera, ella parece una persona dura.

12. Completa las oraciones con adverbios negativos, afirmativos o de duda. `10.F`

| no | quizás | sí | también | tampoco |

1. Qué bien que vendrás al cine. Te gustan las palomitas de maíz, ¿_____?
2. _____ que iremos a la fiesta esta noche.
3. _____ termine de leer el libro este fin de semana… pero no estoy segura.
4. ¡Somos de la misma ciudad! Yo _____ vivo en Nueva York.
5. _____, mi madre vendrá por la tarde. ¿Necesitas hablar únicamente con ella?
6. Camila _____ tendrá vacaciones. Nos quedaremos las dos en la oficina.

13. Reemplaza las palabras subrayadas con adverbios terminados en *-mente*. `10.G–10.H`

1. Me di cuenta de que estaba enamorada de él con locura. _____
2. De repente, todos se habían ido ¡y yo estaba sola! _____
3. Te lo digo con sinceridad: ese vestido no es bonito. _____
4. Podríamos comunicarnos por teléfono, ¿te parece mejor? _____
5. La exhibición salió de maravilla. Ojalá hubieras venido. _____
6. Creo con firmeza en los ideales de nuestro partido. _____
7. Hazlo con tranquilidad y sin apuro. _____
8. Debes tratar a todos con cortesía. _____
9. Ahora sí que lo veo con claridad. _____

14. Decide si estas oraciones son correctas. Si no lo son, corrígelas. `10.G–10.H`

1. Los jugadores corrieron muy rápido detrás de la pelota. _____
2. Julieta increíblemente canta. _____
3. Subimos la montaña lentamente y cuidadosamente. _____
4. Habla más claro, que no te entiendo. _____
5. Debes respirar hondo cuando corres. _____
6. Has respondido correctomente. _____

15. Une las locuciones adverbiales con su significado. `10.H`

_____ 1. a lo grande   a. finalmente

_____ 2. a menudo   b. con todo lujo

_____ 3. en buenas manos   c. a cargo de alguien responsable

_____ 4. por fin   d. bueno…

_____ 5. en fin   e. casi

_____ 6. de primera mano   f. con frecuencia

_____ 7. por poco   g. por experiencia propia

_____ 8. a la larga   h. a largo plazo

Actividades

16. Reescribe las oraciones usando el comparativo. `10.I`

1. Por la tarde, yo trabajo bien. Por la noche, trabajo muy bien.
   Por la noche… _____

2. Claudia dormía mal. Claudia ahora duerme bien.
   Claudia ahora… _____

3. Este año peso poco. El año pasado pesaba mucho.
   Este año… _____

4. Andrés lee rápido. Juan lee muy rápido.
   Andrés… _____

5. En España, se vive bien. En Francia, se vive muy bien.
   En España… _____

6. Mi hermana estudia frecuentemente. Mi hermano estudia muy pocas veces.
   Mi hermana… _____

17. Simón es muy exagerado. Completa las oraciones usando el superlativo. `10.I`

1. Este hombre conduce lento.
   No, este hombre _____.

2. Dormimos tranquilamente toda la noche.
   No, dormimos _____.

3. Ulises comió mucho en casa.
   No, Ulises _____.

4. Isabel respondió las preguntas inteligentemente.
   No, Isabel _____.

5. Como no sabía el camino, Paula llegó tarde.
   No, como _____.

6. Nuestros padres vinieron pronto cuando conocieron la noticia.
   No, nuestros padres _____.

18. Síntesis Clasifica estos adverbios según su clase. `10.A–10.I`

Adverbios	Tiempo	Modo	Cantidad	Lugar
1. nunca				
2. bastante				
3. allí				
4. rápidamente				
5. cerca				
6. rara vez				
7. mañana				
8. mucho				
9. peor				
10. con frecuencia				
11. poco				
12. delante				
13. tranquilamente				

19. Síntesis Completa las oraciones con las palabras de la lista. `10.A–10.B`

allá	jamás	cuándo	suficiente	como
muy	primero	tampoco	bien	dónde

1. No quieres ir al cine y _____ al teatro. ¿Qué quieres hacer entonces?

2. _____ haría una excursión por la montaña. Sabes que tengo fobia a las arañas.

3. _____ cortas la cebolla y luego la fríes.

4. La peluquería está más _____.

5. Estudia _____ bien este tema: seguramente será importante para el examen.

6. He comprado un teléfono _____ pequeño.

7. Ya he comido _____, creo que no comeré postre.

8. ¿A _____ vamos esta noche?

9. Haré la comida _____ tú me digas.

10. La maestra nos dijo exactamente _____ entregar la tarea.

20. Síntesis Corrige el texto. Hay ocho errores. `10.A–10.B`

¿Qué es el mundo laboral?

¿No sabes donde buscar trabajo? ¿No sabes cuanto dinero deberías ganar? Allí te ayudaremos.

_____

Somos un grupo de ex alumnos de tu escuela y queremos ayudarte a conocer un poco menos el mercado laboral. Tampoco queremos contarte sobre nuestros trabajos y como los conseguimos.

_____

_____

Apúntate a las reuniones que realizamos semanal en la sala de conferencias de la escuela. Te esperamos, ¿si?

_____

🎯 Practice more at **vhlcentral.com**.

Comparison 🌀 | Chapter 11

1. Completa las oraciones usando el comparativo. `11.B`

1. El autobús es rápido.
   El tren es muy rápido.
   El tren _____.

2. En Buenos Aires, hace calor.
   En Lima, hace mucho calor.
   En Lima, _____.

3. La maestra de biología es joven.
   La maestra de matemáticas es muy joven.
   La maestra de matemáticas _____.

4. Juana es buena en voleibol.
   Carina es muy buena en voleibol.
   Juana _____.

5. Por la mañana llovió poco.
   Por la tarde llovió mucho.
   Por la mañana _____.

6. *Shrek* es mala.
   Shrek 2 es muy mala.
   Shrek 2 _____.

2. Haz comparaciones entre Martín y Susana. Sigue el modelo. `11.B`

> **Modelo**
>
> Martín comió poco.
> Susana comió mucho.
> *Martín comió más que Susana.*
> *Susana comió menos que Martín.*

1. Martín corre 15 minutos por día.
   Susana corre 30 minutos por día.

   _____

   _____

2. Martín tiene dos perros.
   Susana tiene un perro.

   _____

   _____

3. Martín duerme 8 horas.
   Susana duerme 9 horas.

   _____

   _____

4. Martín tiene un promedio de 8.
   Susana tiene un promedio de 9.

   _____

   _____

5. Martín hizo dos tortas.
   Susana hizo una torta.

   _____

   _____

6. Martín es alto.
   Susana es baja.

   _____

   _____

3. Identifica cuáles de estos adjetivos y adverbios tienen comparativos irregulares. Escribe las formas irregulares. `11.B`

1. malo _____
2. rápido _____
3. poco _____
4. viejo (edad) _____

5. sucio _____
6. oscuro _____
7. llano _____
8. mucho _____

9. alto _____
10. ordenado _____
11. blando _____
12. bueno _____

4. Reescribe las oraciones usando las expresiones entre paréntesis. `11.B`

1. En agosto, tengo aproximadamente dos semanas de vacaciones. (más de)

   _____

2. Durante el verano, voy más seguido al parque. (bastante)

   _____

3. Vivimos en un barrio céntrico. (relativamente)

   _____

4. Cuando estoy a dieta, bebo solamente agua mineral. (más que)

   _____

5. Dormí la siesta y ahora tengo poco sueño. (menos)

   _____

6. Mis manos son más delicadas que tus manos. (tuyas)

   _____

7. Mis horarios actuales son distintos a los que tenía antes. (diferentes)

   _____

Actividades

5. Completa las oraciones con las opciones de la lista. `11.B`

de (2)	de lo que
que (3)	de los que
	de las que

1. Me gusta más _____ pensaba.

2. Tengo más trabajo _____ tú.

3. Asisto a más _____ seis clases en la universidad.

4. Hoy me siento peor _____ ayer.

5. Compré más libros _____ tenía pensado.

6. Fotografié más plazas _____ pensaba.

7. A veces duermo menos _____ lo necesario.

8. No juego más _____ fútbol.

6. Cecilia comenzó las clases y no para de quejarse. Completa su relato con las palabras de la lista. `11.B`

tal como	misma	tanto	mismo	tantas
tan	igual	como	tan	tan

¡Qué día!

Otra vez comenzaron las clases. Debo ir todos los días de 9 a.m. a 12 p.m. y luego de 3 p.m. a 5 p.m. ¡Es increíble tener que estar (1) _____ horas en un mismo lugar! ¡Tengo (2) _____ poco tiempo libre!

La maestra no es la (3) _____ que el año pasado. Ahora tenemos a la señorita Gómez, que es (4) _____ de aburrida que la señorita Albornoz, y nos hace trabajar (5) _____ como quiere. Y lo peor es que siempre nos manda hacer lo (6) _____ que hicimos el año pasado.

Solamente espero que este año no se me haga (7) _____ largo (8) _____ el año pasado. (9) _____ dijo mamá, no debería ser (10) _____ pesimista. Y tiene razón: mirándolo del lado positivo, ya falta un día menos para que terminen las clases.

7. Forma oraciones lógicas combinando elementos de las tres columnas. `11.C`

1. La historia no fue tal	tanto	como sea posible estas vacaciones.
2. Tamara tiene	tantos	de alta que yo.
3. Debo leer	igual	me la contaste. Fue más trágica.
4. Conduce exactamente a la	como	rápido como puedas, antes de que se enfríe.
5. Estela es	misma	mala suerte.
6. No entiendo cómo pude tener	tanta	velocidad que indica el cartel.
7. Come tu tarta	tan	libros que no ha leído aún.

8. Reescribe las oraciones usando el superlativo. `11.D`

> **Modelo**
>
> Este auto es mejor que el resto de los autos. (todos)
> *Este auto es el mejor de todos.*

1. Los productos de nuestra compañía son mejores que los de la competencia. (mercado)

   _____

2. Sebastián es más alto que los compañeros de su clase. (clase)

   _____

3. Este sofá tiene una calidad peor que los demás sofás. (todos)

   _____

4. La música de esta radio es mejor que la de otras radios del país. (país)

   _____

5. Juanito es más pequeño que sus hermanos. (familia)

   _____

6. Mis ensaladas son más deliciosas que las demás. (concurso de cocina)

   _____

7. Mi padre es más viejo que los demás padres. (todos)

   _____

9. Completa este anuncio publicitario con las palabras de la lista. `11.D`

| verdaderamente | novedosísimo | lo más | lo mejor (2) | pequeñísimo |
| óptimo | ínfimo | practiquísimo | extraordinariamente | |

Chaumanchas

En esta oportunidad, le ofrecemos *Chaumanchas*, el (1) _____
quitamanchas de bolsillo. Gracias a su envase (2) _____
pequeño, puede llevarlo con usted adonde vaya. Este quitamanchas es
(3) _____ para madres de niños que se manchan todo el
tiempo o para personas que viajan por negocios. *Chaumanchas* tiene una
efectividad (4) _____ increíble: elimina manchas de aceite,
grasa, tinta, ¡y muchísimas más!

¡Llame ya! ¡Le enviaremos este producto (5) _____ rápido
posible! De esta manera, recibirá (6) _____ del mercado
directamente en su hogar. Y (7) _____ de todo: con la
compra de este (8) _____ producto, recibirá gratis un
(9) _____ cepillo quitamanchas. *Chaumanchas*, el máximo
poder quitamanchas en un (10) _____ envase.

---

10. Isabel contradice a su hermana Eugenia. Completa la conversación con expresiones que indiquen igualdad o desigualdad. `11.B–11.C`

EUGENIA ¿Qué te pareció la fiesta de ayer? Para mí, fue la mejor del año.

ISABEL De ninguna manera, (1) _____.

EUGENIA Pero había más invitados que en la fiesta de Juan. Eso no lo puedes negar...

ISABEL No, había (2) _____ que en esa fiesta.

EUGENIA Y la música era todo el tiempo distinta.

ISABEL No, era siempre (3) _____.

EUGENIA ¡Y bailamos muchísimo!

ISABEL ¡No, (4) _____!

EUGENIA Ay, Isabel, parece que no estuvimos en la misma fiesta. ¡Nunca me divertí tanto!

ISABEL No, ¡nunca (5) _____!

EUGENIA ¿Y la comida? Yo comí muchísimo, ¿y tú?

ISABEL Yo comí (6) _____ y no bebí (7) _____ un vaso de agua.

EUGENIA ¡Qué increíble que seamos hermanas!

ISABEL ¡Sí! Es increíble que seamos de la (8) _____ familia!

11. Cambia las comparaciones usando la palabra entre paréntesis. `11.B–11.C`

1. Catalina es más alta que su madre. (igual)

   _____

2. Tatiana tiene más vestidos que sus amigas. (tantos)

   _____

3. Mis notas son tan buenas como las tuyas. (mejores)

   _____

4. La primera parte de esta película es peor que la segunda. (tan)

   _____

5. Tú no comes más que yo. (tanto)

   _____

6. Mis calcetines son tal como los tuyos. (diferentes)

   _____

12. Síntesis Completa estas oraciones con los comparativos y superlativos que se dan en las opciones. `11.B–11.D`

1. Caminar es _____ agotador que andar en bicicleta.
   a. tan   b. más   c. tanto

2. Cómprate un colchón _____ que el que tienes y dormirás muy bien.
   a. más bueno   b. óptimo   c. mejor

3. Mi reproductor de MP3 es el más pequeño _____ he visto hasta ahora.
   a. que   b. como   c. de

4. Tienes más _____ cien películas en tu mediateca.
   a. que   b. como   c. de

5. Cristina es la empleada que _____ contacto tiene con los clientes.
   a. mejor   b. más   c. buenísimo

6. El fútbol es totalmente distinto _____ los demás deportes.
   a. de   b. a   c. que

7. Esta casa es _____ que las de los alrededores.
   a. mayor   b. más antigua   c. menor

8. Aprender chino es más difícil _____ pensaba.
   a. de los que   b. de lo que   c. que

13. Síntesis **Escribe oraciones a partir de las indicaciones dadas.** `11.B–11.D`

> **Modelo**
>
> Las zapatillas de esta marca son buenas. + / el mercado
> *Las zapatillas de esta marca son las mejores del mercado.*

1. Roma es una ciudad romántica. – / Venecia

   _____

2. El carro azul es muy elegante. = / el carro rojo

   _____

3. Esta vendedora es realmente encantadora. + / el mundo

   _____

4. La tarea de hoy es fácil. – / la tarea de ayer

   _____

5. Este periódico es más conocido que el resto. + / el país

   _____

6. Puedo comprar tantos zapatos como tú. – / tú

   _____

7. Tus tartas son las mejores que he probado. = / tartas de mi madre

   _____

8. Las calles de Madrid son anchísimas. + / toda Europa

   _____

 Practice more at **vhlcentral.com.**

Prepositions   Chapter 12

1. Completa el artículo con las preposiciones de la lista. `12.A`

> para   excepto   durante   de   hasta   desde   entre   tras   sobre

---

Un lugar inolvidable

(1) _____ todos aquellos que desean pasar unas vacaciones de lujo, les recomendamos el hotel *Mar azul*. Este hotel se encuentra (2) _____ la costa del océano Atlántico y posee más de doscientas habitaciones. (3) _____ el siglo XX, allí se hospedaron innumerables famosos (4) _____ la farándula (*show business*) de América Latina; (5) _____ ellos, Luis Miguel y Santana.

(6) _____ 2004 (7) _____ 2006, el hotel permaneció cerrado al público por reformas. (8) _____ las remodelaciones, *Mar azul* reabrió sus puertas, (9) _____ las zonas de sauna y masajes, que se abrieron en 2007.

Desde entonces, el grandioso hotel alberga diariamente a más de 300 huéspedes.

Actividades (sidebar)

2. Reescribe las oraciones usando las palabras de la lista. Haz los cambios necesarios. `12.A`

> pro   vía   versus (2)   o   y

1. Hoy en la televisión podremos ver el partido del Real Madrid <u>contra</u> el Barcelona.
_____

2. Fui a París. <u>Camino a París pasé por</u> Londres.
_____

3. Tobías trabaja para una organización que está <u>a favor de los</u> derechos de los animales.
_____

4. <u>Arriba de</u> la nevera hay suciedad. <u>Debajo de</u> la nevera hay suciedad.
_____

5. Mira el gráfico del precio de alquiler <u>frente al</u> precio de compra.
_____

6. ¿Nos encontramos <u>enfrente del</u> gimnasio? ¿Nos encontramos <u>detrás del</u> gimnasio?
_____

3. Combina elementos de las tres columnas para formar oraciones. `12.A`

1. Yo no tengo nada en	sin	un boleto.
2. Seamos sinceras,	entre	de su cama.
3. Mi casa está muy	contra	él y tú hay problemas.
4. Me encanta dormir la siesta	bajo	de tus amigos.
5. No puedes subir al autobús	sobre	el naranjo.
6. El papel de carta está	debajo	el escritorio.
7. Mi hermana cree que hay monstruos	lejos	del parque de diversiones.

4. Observa el mapa y completa la carta que escribió Yolanda con las preposiciones de la lista. `12.A`

> en   sobre   lejos de   al lado de   cerca de   hasta   delante de   de

Querida Claudia:

¿Cómo estás? Te escribo para contarte sobre mi barrio nuevo... ¡que me encanta!

Vivo en una casa en la esquina (1) _____de_____ la calle Latina y la avenida América. (2) _Al lado de_ mi casita, a la izquierda, está la escuela; y, a la derecha, la biblioteca. (3) _____En_____ la avenida América, no muy (4) _lejos de_ mi casa, está el parque Robles. (5) _delante de_ este parque, está el hospital. La semana pasada fuimos allí con mi mamá porque ella no se sentía muy bien. Mientras ella estaba con el médico, fui (6) _____ el kiosco, que queda justo (7) _____ diagonal al hospital, y me compré un refresco. Y, como estaba tan (8) _cerca de_ la heladería, me compré también un helado.

¿No te parece genial? ¡Es un barrio que tiene todo!

Espero que vengas a visitarme pronto.

Saludos,

Yolanda

5. ✓ **Reordena las oraciones para que tengan sentido.** `12.A`

1. estoy / pro / de la / Yo /reforma constitucional / en _Yo estoy._
2. por / entre / gato / se perdió / El / las malezas _____
3. tu demora, / A / causa / el tren / de / perdimos _____
4. fue / a / Carola / una / por / barra de pan _Carola fue a por una barra de pan_
5. Willy / Tengo / para / con / una obligación _Tengo una obligacion para con Willy_
6. y negra / es roja / fuera / por / dentro / La chaqueta / por _La chaqueta fuera es roja y n...por_
7. cuanto / En / a / deberás comprar / los zapatos, / unos nuevos _En cuanto a deberas comprar_
8. las entrevistas / Son / mejores / cara / cara / a _Son mejores las entrevistas cara a cara_
9. general, / las películas / lo / prefiero / de terror / Por _Por general lo prefiero las peliculas de terror_
10. regreso / leche / Compraremos / de / al hostal _Compraremos leche de regreso al hostal_

6. ✓ **Completa las oraciones con la preposición correcta.** `12.B`

1. Llegamos a Boston __a__ las ocho.
2. Vi __a__ Juan en el parque.
3. Necesito una tabla __para__ planchar nueva.
4. No llegué a horario __por__ tu culpa.
5. Si no tienes el ensayo listo __para__ el jueves, el profesor te quitará un punto.
6. Se movía __con__ mucha lentitud.
7. Parece que este carro estuviera hecho __de__ plástico.

7. **Vuelve a leer las oraciones de la *actividad 6*. Decide a qué preposición hace referencia cada explicación.** `12.B`

1. Se usa para referirse a una causa o justificación. _____
2. Se usa para referirse a una fecha límite. _____
3. Se usa antes de un verbo para expresar propósito. _____
4. Se usa con sustantivos en locuciones adverbiales de modo. _____
5. Se usa con objetos directos cuando refieren a personas. _____
6. Se usa para referirse al material con el que están fabricados los objetos. _____
7. Se usa para referirse a una hora determinada. _____

8. **Reescribe estas oraciones usando la preposición entre paréntesis.** `12.B`

1. Karina cortó el papel usando una tijera. (con)

   _____

2. Isabela tiene nacionalidad española. (de)

   _____

3. Tengo mal humor. (de)

   _____

4. Llegó una carta destinada a ti. (para)

   _____

5. La señora que tiene cabello rubio se quedó dormida. (de)

   _____

6. Debido a este aumento de salario, podré ahorrar un poco más de dinero. (con)

   _____

7. Cuando llegué, tú ya estabas dormida. (a)

   _____

9. **Completa estas oraciones con *a, de, con* y *en*.** 12.B

1. La pescadería está __a__ dos cuadras de mi casa.

2. La cita es __a__ las cuatro de la tarde.

3. Debes estar __en__ silencio. La abuela duerme la siesta.

4. __Con__ gusto, te ayudo a poner la mesa.

5. Todas estas son carteras __de__ Rocío.

6. Deja de hablar por teléfono __con__ tu novio. ¡La factura será carísima!

7. Escríbele un mensaje de texto __a__ Juan y dile que llegaremos tarde.

8. El maestro __de__ español nos da muchísima tarea.

9. __En__ agosto, iremos a las montañas.

10. __A__ los nueve años, viajé por primera vez a *Disneyworld*.

10. **Completa este anuncio con *de, a* o *con*. Incluye el artículo o el pronombre personal si corresponde.** 12.B

Feria (1) _____ **las Naciones**: miles de culturas en un solo lugar
(2) _____ 20 (3) _____ 29 (4) _____ agosto, en el centro (5) _____ exposiciones
de la Ciudad de Buenos Aires, podrás visitar la Feria de las Naciones. Allí podrás comprar
productos (6) _____ todos los países (7) _____ mundo: salchichas (8) _____ Alemania,
perfumes de Francia y mucho más. ¡Es como si estuvieras de viaje por todo el mundo!
Ven ¡y trae (9) _____ tus amigos!

11. **¿*Para* o *por*? Completa las oraciones con la preposición correcta.** 12.B

1. No tengo tiempo __por__ ir de compras contigo.

2. __Por__ las tardes, estudio muchísimo.

3. __Para__ el dolor de garganta, te recomiendo que tomes un té con miel.

4. __Por__ fin, estamos de vacaciones. Necesito descansar de la escuela.

5. Lucía trabaja __para__ una compañía farmacéutica.

6. __Para__ mí, esa película fue la mejor del año.

7. ¿Viajas __por__ placer?

8. La biblioteca es un lugar __para__ leer, ¡silencio!

12. **¿*Con a* o *sin a*? Decide si es necesario usar *a* en cada una de estas oraciones. Si no es necesario, escribe X.** 12.B

1. Julia conoce __X__ todos sus clientes.

2. ¿Por qué le trajiste flores __a__ Paula si no es una ocasión especial?

3. Se buscan __X__ profesores de física.

4. Tengo __X__ demasiados compañeros de trabajo. No puedo invitarlos __a__ todos.

5. Nos dijo el mecánico que debemos ponerle aceite __a__ la motocicleta.

6. ¡Cuánto extraño __X__ mi casa!

7. ¡Cómo me gustaría visitar __a__ Ulises!

13. Elige la opción correcta en cada oración. `12.B`

1. ¿_____ (Para/De) dónde vienes?

2. _____ (Desde/De) mañana, me despertaré todos los días a las 7 a.m.

3. Recuerda pasar _____ (por/entre) la panadería antes de venir a casa.

4. Camina _____ (tras/hasta) la esquina. Cuando estés allí, dobla a la izquierda.

5. La tienda está abierta _____ (de/desde) 3 a 8.

6. ¿_____ (De/Para) dónde vamos esta noche?

7. _En_ (Durante/En) tres días, llegarán mis padres.

8. La bicicleta está apoyada _____ (contra / encima de) la pared.

9. _____ (Salvo/Con) nuestra ayuda, usted podrá conseguir un puesto de trabajo.

10. _____ (Ante/Tras) una tormenta, siempre llega la calma.

14. Síntesis Completa las oraciones con las palabras de la lista. Escribe X si no se necesita una preposición. `12.A–12.C`

| sin | de | desde | hasta | para | entre | en | por |

1. _En_ el momento, no hay pruebas de que los extraterrestres existan.

2. _Sin_ dudas, aprobaremos este examen.

3. _Entre_ la farmacia y la carnicería, está la verdulería.

4. ¿Llegó un correo electrónico _para_ mí?

5. _Por_ estos motivos, no quiero ir de vacaciones con ella.

6. La boda se celebró _____ la iglesia de San Pablo.

7. ¿Se puede vivir _de_ la caridad?

8. ¿Conoces _a_ la casa de Juan?

15. Síntesis Elige la preposición correcta para completar estas oraciones. `12.A–12.C`

1. _____ tu ayuda, no podremos salvar el planeta.
   a. Con   b. Sin   c. En

2. _____ La Habana, verás qué amable que es la gente.
   a. De   b. En   c. Hasta

3. Hay un teléfono _____ la oficina de la directora.
   a. de   b. en   c. entre

4. _____ el año pasado, vivimos en este edificio.
   a. Desde   b. De   c. Entre

5. ¿Cuál es la diferencia _____ *casar* y *cazar*?
   a. en   b. de   c. entre

6. _____ la lluvia, tuvimos que quedarnos en casa.
   a. De   b. Sin   c. Por

7. _____ Guadalajara, hay 1.000 kilómetros.
   a. Hasta   b. Entre   c. De

8. _____ María, todos quieren comer pastel.
   a. Durante   b. Excepto   c. Sin

Actividades

16. Síntesis Completa las oraciones con preposiciones simples o compuestas. `12.A–12.C`

1. _____ regreso a casa, me topé con una manifestación.

2. Los presidentes se reunieron con miras _____ resolver la situación.

3. Aunque este es un país rico, hay mucha gente que vive _____ la pobreza.

4. No sé qué le pasa. Está _____ muy mal humor.

5. Las discrepancias se resuelven _____ el diálogo.

6. Deja la correspondencia _____ la mesa, junto al teléfono.

17. Síntesis Relaciona los ejemplos con las explicaciones. `12.A–12.C`

_____ 1. Se refiere a la ubicación de algo o alguien.

_____ 2. Se refiere al destinatario de algo.

_____ 3. Se usa para expresar un propósito con verbos de actividad.

_____ 4. Se usa para mostrar que alguien hace algo en tu lugar.

_____ 5. Se usa con verbos de movimiento y sustantivos en España.

_____ 6. En España, se usa otra preposición para esta misma frase.

_____ 7. Se usa para expresar posesión.

_____ 8. Se usa con el verbo **estar** para describir condiciones.

_____ 9. Se usa con el verbo **estar** para expresar un trabajo temporario.

a. Aprendo español **para** hablar bien con mis parientes de México.

b. **En** Barcelona, encontrarás gente de todo el mundo.

c. Mis amigos están **de** visita hasta el primero de octubre.

d. Hay un mensaje **para** ti. Léelo.

e. ¿Podrías buscar a Juanito **por** mí?

f. Florencia está **de** camarera en el bar de la esquina.

g. ¿La policía viene **a por** mí? ¡Yo no hice nada!

h. No me interesan las vidas **de** los famosos.

i. Entré **a** la casa y se cortó la luz.

18. Síntesis Completa los espacios en blanco con la preposición (simple o compuesta) adecuada. Como pista, tienes la primera letra de cada una. `12.A–12.C`

1. H_____ la playa, hay dos kilómetros.

2. S_____ mi madre, "al que madruga, Dios lo ayuda".

3. C_____ tu casa, vive la profesora de matemáticas.

4. J_____ mis amigos, organizaré una gran fiesta de cumpleaños.

5. H_____ fines del siglo veinte, se inventó el Bluetooth.

6. E_____ marzo y junio, aquí es otoño.

7. T_____ esa expresión dura, se esconde una persona muy amable.

8. E_____ Juan, todos tienen menos de dieciocho años.

9. E_____ esa época, todos trabajábamos en la misma empresa.

10. Quiero salir c_____ en una cita.

11. C_____ ese vestido, llamarás la atención de todos los invitados.

12. Josefina es siempre la primera e_____ terminar los exámenes.

13. Entré e_____ la estación de metro y compré un boleto.

Practice more at **vhlcentral.com**.

1. Reemplaza el texto subrayado con el pronombre adecuado. `13.A–13.B`

1. Camila y yo jugamos a las cartas toda la tarde. _____

2. ¿Sofía viene a la fiesta de fin de año? _____

3. Sandra y Facundo están durmiendo. _____

4. La abuela vendrá de visita el fin de semana. _____

5. Mi esposa y yo formamos una familia hermosa. _____

6. Romina y Laura son estudiantes de quinto año. _____

7. Mi hermana, mi padre y yo iremos de vacaciones a las montañas. _____

8. No pienses en los costos. La calidad es lo importante. _____

2. ¿Formal o informal? Decide quién dice cada frase. `13.A–13.B`

____ 1. Le prometo que, de ahora en adelante, llegaré temprano todos los días.

____ 2. ¿Podría decirme dónde está la juguetería, por favor?

____ 3. No me molestes más, ¿acaso no ves que estoy estudiando?

____ 4. Vosotros debéis respetar las reglas.

____ 5. Ustedes prometieron organizar competencias deportivas para nosotros.

____ 6. ¿Quieres darme tu teléfono celular?

a. un empleado a su jefe

b. un niño a su hermano

c. una niña a un anciano

d. un director de escuela a los alumnos

e. una amiga a otra

f. un alumno a las autoridades escolares

3. Reescribe las oraciones reemplazando el pronombre subrayado por el pronombre entre paréntesis. `13.A–13.C`

1. Vosotros habéis jugado muy bien esta tarde. (nosotros) _____

2. La empresa está satisfecha con ella. (tú) _____

3. Ustedes siempre tienen muchas vacaciones. (vosotros) _____

4. Para él, las tareas son fáciles. (usted) _____

5. Entre nosotros, hay muy buena comunicación. (ellos) _____

6. Ustedes son estudiantes, ¿verdad? (ellas) _____

4. Completa las oraciones con las palabras de la lista. `13.A–13.C`

vosotros	él	mí	conmigo
yo	tú (2)	ti	consigo

1. ¿Vas _____ o voy yo al supermercado?

2. Para _____, este programa de televisión es muy malo. Pero es solo mi opinión, obviamente.

3. Carlos no está contento _____ mismo.

4. Entre Gabriela y _____ hay muchos conflictos. Debemos hablar sobre eso.

5. Según _____, todos deberíamos trabajar de lunes a lunes.

6. Rita es colombiana y _____ eres venezolano, ¿no?

7. _____ sabéis que es importante mantener la imagen de la empresa.

8. Tengo un regalo hermoso para _____. Te encantará.

9. _____ vivirás tranquila. Verás que soy una persona muy tranquila.

5. Reescribe las oraciones reemplazando el objeto directo por el pronombre correspondiente. `13.E`

1. Roberto compró naranjas en el mercado central. _____

2. Llamamos al abuelo porque lo extrañábamos. _____

3. Julia estudió muy bien la lección de gramática. _____

4. Finalmente la policía atrapó al ladrón. _____

5. Gonzalo buscó sus zapatillas debajo de la mesa. _____

6. Los obreros comen el almuerzo a las dos de la tarde. _____

7. Constanza y Sofía les compran flores a sus madres. _____

8. Traje los libros de la biblioteca. _____

6. Escribe la pregunta o la respuesta según corresponda. `13.E`

> **Modelo**
>
> ¿A quién viste en la fiesta? ¿ _Qué cocinaste_ ?
> _Vi a tu hermana._ (tu hermana) Cociné un pollo al horno.

1. ¿A quién invitamos a nuestra fiesta de aniversario? _____ (todos nuestros amigos)

2. ¿_____ esta noche? Conocí a los padres de Estela.

3. ¿_____ hacer? Prefiero descansar un poco y luego ir a un museo.

4. ¿A quién ama tu hermana? _____ (su novio)

5. ¿Qué tipo de libros lees? _____ (novelas románticas)

6. ¿A quién has llamado por teléfono? _____ (tú)

7. ¿Qué ciudades visitaste? _____ (París y Roma)

8. ¿_____ esta noche? Visitamos a tus primos.

7. Usa los fragmentos para escribir oraciones, reemplazando el objeto indirecto por el pronombre correspondiente. `13.F`

1. Julia / dio / una bufanda / a su hermana _____

2. dijiste / mentiras / a tus compañeros de clase _____

3. ellos / contaron historias de terror / a nuestros hermanos _____

4. el camarero / recomendó / una paella a los turistas _____

5. tu madre / mostró / al cliente / la habitación _____

6. hoy leerás / a tu hermanito / un cuento de hadas _____

7. pedí / dinero / a mis padres _____

8. Lee el relato de Josefina. Primero, marca todos los pronombres de objetos indirectos. Luego indica el sujeto de esas oraciones. `13.F`

Soy una persona un poco complicada. No me gusta salir de casa. Me molesta mucho el ruido de los carros y motocicletas. Por eso, prefiero estar en casa.

Me gusta leer novelas: sobre todo, me interesan las novelas románticas. Además, me encanta ver comedias en la televisión. Ojalá algún día encuentre a mi pareja ideal. Un hombre a quien le guste mirar televisión conmigo, le interesen las noticias de la actualidad y le encante cocinar. ¿Os parecen demasiado grandes mis expectativas?

9. Reordena las oraciones. 13.G

1. la ceremonia / invitaré / a / Los / religiosa _____

2. espera / en / la esquina / Claudia / te _____

3. gran sorpresa / daré / una / Les _____

4. tres entradas / nos / Emilia / para el teatro / compró _____

5. su / me / regalará / Omar / cámara de fotos antigua _____

6. a su casa / Los / de inmediato / llamaré _____

7. ¿? / para armar / das / Me / las instrucciones / la cama _____

10. Reescribe las oraciones. Sigue el modelo como ejemplo. 13.G

> **Modelo**
>
> Te voy a enseñar inglés.
> *Voy a enseñarte inglés.*

1. ¿Nos estás preparando la merienda?

   _____

2. Yo podría ayudarte con tus tareas.

   _____

3. Lucía me va a acompañar hasta la esquina.

   _____

4. El público está alentándolos.

   _____

5. La directora les va a enviar una carta de recomendación.

   _____

6. Estamos dándoles excelentes ideas para hacer un negocio.

   _____

11. Lucas te hace muchas preguntas. Contéstalas usando el pronombre adecuado. 13.G

1. **LUCAS** Falta poco para la fiesta. ¿Has comprado toda la decoración?
   TÚ Sí, _____ .

2. **LUCAS** ¿Sería bueno decorar las ventanas?
   TÚ Sí, _____ .

3. **LUCAS** ¿Has mandado las invitaciones?
   TÚ Sí, _____ .

4. **LUCAS** ¿Has llamado a los invitados para confirmar su presencia?
   TÚ No, aún _____ .

5. **LUCAS** ¿Me darás pronto la lista de invitados?
   TÚ Sí, _____ .

6. **LUCAS** ¿Necesitas mi ayuda?
   TÚ ¡Gracias! Pero no _____ .

12. Matías tiene una lista de quehaceres que le dejó su mamá. Completa los comentarios que escribe Matías junto a cada quehacer usando pronombres para los objetos directos e indirectos. `13.G`

○	HACER TAREA ✓ *Ya la he hecho.*
	LLAMAR TÍA ✓ (1)
	ARREGLAR COMPUTADORA ✗ (2)
	LLEVAR PAQUETE JUANA ✗ (3)
	BUSCAR PERRO ✓ (4)
	DAR COMIDA PERRO ✗ (5)
	DEVOLVER SILLA VECINO ✓ (6)

13. Une los ejemplos con las explicaciones. `13.H`

____ 1. Se repite el objeto para enfatizar su identidad.

____ 2. Se debe repetir el objeto cuando los nombres propios están antepuestos al verbo.

____ 3. Se repite el objeto cuando hace referencia a cosas.

____ 4. Se repite el objeto cuando se hace referencia a conceptos abstractos.

____ 5. Se repite el objeto para indicar que la situación afecta a alguien directamente.

a. ¡Cuídame muy bien a mi perrito!

b. Tienen que comprarle más memoria a mi computadora.

c. A Marta la vemos todos los jueves.

d. Todo esto jamás podremos recordarlo.

e. A mí no me mientes, ¿sí?

14. Síntesis Elige el ejemplo que no se corresponde con los demás. `13.A–13.H`

1. ____
   a. Nosotros somos profesionales.
   b. Ustedes son argentinos.
   c. Vosotros sois extranjeros.

2. ____
   a. Llamé a Francisco ayer.
   b. Invitamos a todos nuestros amigos.
   c. Se la envié la semana pasada.

3. ____
   a. Contigo soy feliz.
   b. Ella no tiene problemas conmigo.
   c. Según ella, yo luzco mayor de lo que soy.

4. ____
   a. A nadie le interesa jugar al póker.
   b. A Juana la quiero mucho.
   c. A mi madre le encanta ir de compras.

5. ____
   a. Se lo daré mañana.
   b. Pronto se venderá la casa.
   c. Se lo he dicho mil veces.

6. ____
   a. No nos despierte muy temprano, por favor.
   b. Llámenme después de las 10 de la mañana.
   c. A mí me quieres, ¿no?

Actividades

15. **Síntesis** **Corrige las oraciones que son incorrectas.** `13.A–13.H`

1. Traje muchas flores para tú.

   _____

2. ¿Te molestan mis ronquidos?

   _____

3. Os daré un regalo si te portas bien, Juana.

   _____

4. Vosotros ya habéis hécholo.

   _____

5. Yo la llevo a ella a su casa, no te preocupes.

   _____

6. A Daniela le conozco de la universidad.

   _____

7. A ti te aprecio mucho.

   _____

8. Mis tíos las me regalaron para Navidad.

   _____

16. **Síntesis** **Completa la carta de Santiago con las palabras de la lista.** `13.A–13.H`

> nos   les (2)   os (2)   me (2)   le   ti   vos

Queridos Juan y Alfredo:

Os escribo porque a mis tíos se (1) _____ ocurrió una idea perfecta para un negocio: ¡un servicio de piscinas móviles! Ya sé que probablemente no (2) _____ parecerá algo viable, pero si tan solo leyerais el plan de negocios que ellos escribieron... ¡es fantástico!

La idea (3) _____ vino a la mente un día de verano, de muchísimo calor. Mi tía (4) _____ dijo a mi tío:

—¿A (5) _____ te gustaría tener una piscina en casa?

Y, mi tío, que es argentino, le contestó con su tono característico:

—A mí (6) _____ parece que a (7) _____ el calor te hace mal... ¿no ves que no tenemos espacio?

Desde ese momento, no dejaron de pensar en tener una piscina, hasta que un día ambos se miraron entre sí, y se dijeron:

—¿Y si (8) _____ trajeran una piscina a nuestra casa?

Bueno, el plan de negocios es muy largo, pero si queréis, (9) _____ lo mando por correo postal.

¿(10) _____ enviaríais vuestras direcciones?

Saludos y hasta pronto,

Santiago

Practice more at **vhlcentral.com.**

Actividades

1. Reordena las oraciones. Usa las mayúsculas como ayuda. `14.A`

1. a comer, / ¿ / no es así / viene / ? / Úrsula

   _____

2. hizo / frío, / verdad / Ayer /¿ / ?

   _____

3. ¿ / Karina / Duerme / todavía / ?

   _____

4. ¿ / toman / ? / Ustedes / el avión / de las 12, / no

   _____

5. Tiene / las notas / el profesor / del examen / ¿ / ?

   _____

6. Sabe / que / Florencia / la llamé / ¿ / ?

   _____

2. Escribe dos tipos de preguntas posibles para estas respuestas, como en el modelo. `14.A`

> **Modelo**
>
> *¿Corrió Juana la maratón?*
> *Juana corrió la maratón, ¿no es cierto?*
> *Sí, Juana corrió la maratón.*

1. _____

   _____

   No, mi hermana no tiene quince años.

2. _____

   _____

   Sí, hoy debo ir a la escuela.

3. _____

   _____

   No, ellos no harán las compras hoy.

4. _____

   _____

   Sí, la primavera en nuestro país comienza el 21 de septiembre.

5. _____

   _____

   No, el edificio no fue construido en 1980.

6. _____

   _____

   No, no quiero pastel.

Actividades

3. Sabrina está en una entrevista de trabajo. Completa las preguntas del entrevistador con *qué, cuál* o *cuáles*. `14.B`

ENTREVISTADOR Buenos días, ¿(1) _____ es su nombre?

SABRINA Me llamo Sabrina Pérez Garrido.

ENTREVISTADOR ¿(2) _____ son sus aptitudes para este trabajo?

SABRINA Bueno... soy estudiante de administración, hablo español e inglés, y tengo un buen dominio de la informática.

ENTREVISTADOR Bien, ¿(3) _____ piensa sobre esta compañía?

SABRINA Pienso que es una compañía de gran nivel, con una buena política de recursos humanos y una gran reputación a nivel mundial.

ENTREVISTADOR ¿(4) _____ son sus pasatiempos?

SABRINA Me gusta leer, hacer deportes y tomar fotografías.

ENTREVISTADOR ¿(5) _____ tipo de trabajo espera hacer para nosotros?

SABRINA Me gustaría ser asistente de directorio.

ENTREVISTADOR Bien, ¿(6) _____ son sus expectativas salariales?

SABRINA No sé exactamente... escucho ofertas.

ENTREVISTADOR Por último, ¿(7) _____ es su número de teléfono?

SABRINA 309-987-0008.

ENTREVISTADOR La llamaremos en cuanto tengamos novedades.

4. En cada pregunta, elige la opción correcta. `14.B`

1. ¿_____ (Quién/Cuál/Quiénes) fue el libertador de Venezuela?
   Simón Bolívar.

2. ¿_____ (Quién/Cuál/Quiénes) es tu fecha de nacimiento?
   El 30 de octubre de 1992.

3. ¿_____ (Qué/Cuál/Quiénes) fueron a tu cumpleaños?
   Mi tía Estela, mis padres y casi todos mis amigos.

4. ¿_____ (Quién/Cuál/Quiénes) era Marilyn Monroe?
   Era una actriz estadounidense.

5. ¿_____ (Quién/Cuál/Qué) estás viendo en la tele?
   Una película de terror.

6. ¿_____ (Quién/Cuál/Quiénes) viven en esta casa?
   Solamente Víctor y su perro.

7. ¿_____ (Quién/Cuál/Qué) llamó por teléfono?
   Tu jefe.

8. ¿_____ (Quién/Cuál/Cuáles) es tu apellido?
   Fernández.

5. Completa las preguntas con el pronombre interrogativo adecuado. `14.B`

1. ¿Cuá_____ kilos de tomates quiere, señora?

2. ¿Cuá_____ días de vacaciones tenemos?

3. ¿Cuá_____ costó la compra en el supermercado?

4. ¿Cuá_____ café has bebido hoy?

5. ¿Cuá_____ empleados tiene la compañía?

6. ¿Cuá_____ lejos está la próxima gasolinera?

7. ¿Cuá_____ trabajaste la semana pasada?

8. ¿Cuá_____ eficaz es este medicamento?

6. Reescribe estas preguntas usando *cómo*. `14.B`

1. ¿Cuán difícil es el problema?
   _____

2. ¿Cuán grande es la habitación?
   _____

3. ¿Qué altura tiene tu padre?
   _____

4. ¿Qué tal te sientes esta tarde?
   _____

5. ¿Qué te parece nuestro apartamento nuevo?
   _____

6. ¿Cuál es el peso de la lavadora?
   _____

7. Completa esta conversación con las palabras de la lista. `14.B`

cuánto	qué	qué tal	cuántos	cómo	cuáles	cuán

VENDEDOR Buenos días. ¿(1) _____?

CLIENTE Muy bien, gracias, ¿y usted?

VENDEDOR Bien, gracias. ¿(2) _____ le puedo ofrecer?

CLIENTE Bueno, quisiera tomates. ¿(3) _____ me recomienda?

VENDEDOR Mire, hoy trajeron unos que están a buen precio. ¿(4) _____ kilos quiere?

CLIENTE ¿(5) _____ son de grandes?

VENDEDOR Son para ensalada, de tamaño medio.

CLIENTE Bien, entonces un kilo, por favor.

VENDEDOR Aquí tiene.

CLIENTE ¿(6) _____ le debo?

VENDEDOR Tres con cincuenta.

CLIENTE Aquí tiene. ¡Hasta luego!

8. Escribe las preguntas indirectas para estas preguntas directas. `14.B`

1. ¿Quién es tu cantante favorito?
   Quiero saber _____.

2. ¿Cuántos años tiene Joaquín?
   Dime _____.

3. ¿Cuánto dinero hay en la cuenta?
   Dile a Carlos _____.

4. ¿Cómo se llama la persona que me espera?
   Recuerda decirme _____.

5. ¿Cuánto tiempo horneas la torta?
   Por favor, dime _____.

6. ¿Cuál es tu número de teléfono?
   Quisiera saber _____.

7. ¿Qué te gustaría beber en la cena?
   Quiero saber _____.

9. Une los elementos de las tres columnas para formar preguntas. `14.B`

1. ¿Qué	años	haces deportes?
2. ¿De qué	altura	debes renovar tu licencia de conducir?
3. ¿Con qué	frecuencia	es tu camiseta?
4. ¿Cada cuántos	talla	de rápido?
5. ¿A qué	nadas	sobre el nivel del mar está la ciudad de Quito?
6. ¿Cómo	distancia	hay entre tu casa y la mía?

10. **Reescribe las oraciones usando la palabra entre paréntesis.** `14.B`

   1. Ismael quiere saber la razón de su despido. (porqué)
   _____

   2. Dime el lugar en que viste tu teléfono por última vez. (dónde)
   _____

   3. ¿A qué hora vendrás a buscarme? (cuándo)
   _____

   4. ¿De qué manera puedo contactar contigo? (cómo)
   _____

   5. ¿Por qué razón no viniste a mi fiesta de cumpleaños? (por qué)
   _____

   6. ¿Cómo está la comida que preparé? (qué tal)
   _____

11. **Elige la opción correcta para cada oración.** `14.B`

   1. ¿_____ (A qué / Cuánta / Cuál) distancia está el hospital?
   2. Realmente no sé _____ (porqué / cuándo / por qué) no me despertaste esta mañana.
   3. ¿_____ (Cuál / Qué tal / Cómo) tus cosas? Hace tanto que no nos vemos.
   4. ¿_____ (Hasta dónde / Dónde / Hasta cuándo) vas? Quizás puedo llevarte con el carro.
   5. ¿_____ (Cómo/Cuán/Cuánto) son de caras esas bicicletas? Me gustaría comprar una nueva.
   6. ¿_____ (Cuáles/Qué/Cuál) son tus zapatos, los verdes o los negros?
   7. Desconozco totalmente el _____ (cuándo/cómo/porqué) del funcionamiento de las redes inalámbricas. Es una tecnología que no logro comprender.

12. **Decide si las siguientes oraciones son correctas. Si no lo son, corrígelas.** `14.B`

   1. Explícame como ir hasta el centro de la ciudad. _____
   2. ¿Qué tal si tomamos un café en este bar? _____
   3. ¿Cuánto años tienes? _____
   4. ¿Que es *alacena* en inglés? _____
   5. ¿Cuánta personas van al cine los fines de semana? _____
   6. ¿Qué grande es la cocina? _____
   7. Dime el por qué de tu visita. _____

13. **Ricardo está de vacaciones y está maravillado con todo lo que ve. Completa las exclamaciones de Ricardo.** `14.C`

   > **Modelo**
   >
   > Ricardo piensa: Los parques de esta ciudad son grandes.
   > Ricardo dice: *¡Qué grandes que son los parques de esta ciudad!*

   1. Ricardo piensa: Hay tantas flores en este parque.
   Ricardo dice: _____

   2. Ricardo piensa: Este barrio es muy elegante.
   Ricardo dice: _____

   3. Ricardo piensa: Los restaurantes son tan caros.
   Ricardo dice: _____

   4. Ricardo piensa: Las calles son tan limpias.
   Ricardo dice: _____

   5. Ricardo piensa: Me gustaría vivir en esta ciudad.
   Ricardo dice: _____

   6. Ricardo piensa: Ojalá fuera rico para vivir aquí.
   Ricardo dice: _____

14. **Une los elementos de las dos columnas para formar oraciones.** `14.D`

1. ¿Qué tanta ____
2. ¡Qué tanto ____
3. ¡Qué tantos ____
4. ¡Qué tanto ____
5. ¿De cuál ____
6. ¿Cuál ____

a. tenemos que esperar para que deje de llover?
b. discoteca te gusta más?
c. animales hay en este zoológico!
d. ciudad vienes?
e. hablas! No te callas un segundo.
f. gente hay en el concierto?

15. Síntesis **Cristina es una famosa cantante. Completa la entrevista que le hicieron con las palabras de la lista.** `14.A–14.D`

| cuántos | cómo | cuál | no es cierto | qué tal | cuándo | qué (3) |

CONDUCTOR Ante todo, Cristina, muchas gracias por darnos esta entrevista. ¿(1) _____ fue tu última entrevista televisiva?

CRISTINA La última fue en agosto de este año. Estuve de gira por todo el país y casi no he tenido tiempo para entrevistas.

CONDUCTOR ¿(2) _____ tu gira? ¿Estás contenta?

CRISTINA La verdad es que fue muy intensa. Muchísimos conciertos, muchas ciudades.

CONDUCTOR ¿(3) _____ fue la reacción del público ante este nuevo espectáculo que presentaste?

CRISTINA Mi público es muy efusivo: cantan, aplauden, bailan. Evidentemente les gustó, pero eso es lo que uno siempre espera, ¿(4) _____?

CONDUCTOR Sí, pero sabemos también que tuviste una convocatoria increíble en tus conciertos. ¿(5) _____ espectadores tuviste?

CRISTINA No sabría decirte... ¡Pero no te imaginas con (6) _____ rapidez se agotaron las entradas!

CONDUCTOR ¡(7) _____ me alegro por ti!

CRISTINA Gracias. Ahora estoy preparando mi nuevo disco.

CONDUCTOR ¿(8) _____ tanto tendremos que esperar para escucharlo?

CRISTINA En dos meses saldrá a la venta. Espero que les guste.

CONDUCTOR Muchas gracias, Cristina. Y no te imaginas con (9) _____ ansias esperamos tu nueva producción.

16. Síntesis **Une los ejemplos con las explicaciones.** `14.A–14.D`

____ 1. Es una estructura afirmativa seguida de una pregunta.

____ 2. Es una pregunta para dar a elegir a alguien entre varias alternativas concretas.

____ 3. Es una pregunta cuyo pronombre interrogativo concuerda en género y número con el sustantivo que modifica.

____ 4. Es una abreviación de *cuánto* y se usa antes de adjetivos.

____ 5. Es una pregunta con estructura afirmativa.

____ 6. Es un pronombre interrogativo que no varía en género ni en número cuando está seguido por verbos.

____ 7. Es una expresión que se usa en Latinoamérica para decir *cuántos*.

a. ¿Cuánto costó la computadora?
b. ¿Cuántos kilos de patatas has comprado?
c. Explícame por qué no llegaste a horario.
d. ¡Qué tantos primos tienes!
e. ¿Qué prefieres beber, agua o jugo?
f. ¿Cuán pesado es tu equipaje?
g. Aquí hace demasiado calor, ¿no?

Practice more at **vhlcentral.com.**

Actividades

1. Marca los antecedentes de los pronombres relativos. En el caso de *cuyo/a*, subraya también la frase con la que concuerda. `15.A`

Mujer busca marido

Me llamo Olivia y tengo 44 años. Busco a un hombre que tenga entre 45 y 55 años y que esté dispuesto a formar una pareja estable.

Me gustaría tener una pareja que no tenga hijos, preferentemente. Me gustan los hombres altos, elegantes y formales.

Soy activa y llevo una vida que podría definir como tranquila. Trabajo durante la semana y los fines de semana hago actividades al aire libre. El estilo de vida que llevo es un poco costoso, por lo tanto, preferiría un hombre cuyo salario sea superior o igual al mío.

Si eres un hombre que tiene estas cualidades, no dudes en llamar al teléfono que aparece abajo.

2. Reordena los elementos para formar oraciones lógicas. `15.A`

1. que / es la mujer / Lucila / las flores / me dio _Lucila es la mujer que me dio las flores_

2. donde / un lugar / puedo comprar / Encontré / productos orgánicos _Encontré un lugar donde puedo comprar productos orgánicos_

3. que / Te / una mujer / ha llamado / se llama Elisa _Te ha llamado que una mujer se llama Elisa_

4. Os gustó / que / os di / ¿ / el regalo / ? _¿Os gustó el regalo que os di_

5. donde / El barrio / está / vivo / muy lejos del centro _El barrio donde vivo está muy lejos del centro_

6. que / en el bar / Nos encontramos / te indiqué _____

3. Une los elementos de las tres columnas para formar oraciones. `15.A`

1. Las tareas	quienes	currículum sea mejor.
2. La tienda	que	puerta es azul es demasiado oscura.
3. Todas las estudiantes	cuyo	hablé me recomendaron el mismo libro.
4. La habitación	con las que	me olvidé el paraguas está cerrada.
5. Contrataremos a la candidata	cuya	cenamos anoche nos han invitado a su casa.
6. Los amigos con los	donde	te encargué deben estar terminadas antes del 20 de junio.

4. Decide si las oraciones son correctas. Si no lo son, corrígelas. `15.A`

1. Le presento al empleado fue contratado la semana pasada. _____

2. La escuela quien está en la esquina es muy buena. _____

3. Los alumnos que tengan buenas calificaciones podrán recibir becas. _____

4. Elige la bufanda donde más te guste. _____

5. Daniela, quien conocí en la escuela, ahora trabaja conmigo. _____

6. Beberé lo que tú bebas. _____

5. Decide si estas proposiciones relativas son explicativas (*non-defining*) (ND) o especificativas (*defining*) (D). `15.B`

_____ 1. Gastón, quien nunca duerme la siesta, siempre se va a dormir a las 8 de la noche.

_____ 2. Las noches que son despejadas son las más frías.

_____ 3. Me encanta la playa a la que fuimos la semana pasada.

_____ 4. Mi bicicleta nueva, la cual compré en el mercado de las pulgas, funciona de maravilla.

_____ 5. Los libros que compré ayer son carísimos.

_____ 6. La niña a la que saludé es nuestra vecina.

6. Completa las oraciones con *que, el que* y *la que*. `15.B`

1. La situación en _____ estoy no es muy agradable.

2. Los colores _____ más me gustan son el rojo y el azul.

3. El banco en _____ estoy sentado es incómodo.

4. Las mujeres _____ trabajan conmigo son súper amables.

5. La discoteca en _____ te conocí es la mejor del pueblo.

6. Te diré el motivo por _____ no vine.

7. No le cuentes a nadie la idea _____ te di.

7. Combina las dos oraciones usando el pronombre relativo entre paréntesis. `15.B`

1. París tiene muchos puentes. París es mi ciudad favorita. (que)

_____

2. La profesora se llama Silvia. Conocí a esta profesora ayer. (quien)

_____

3. Trabajé para una empresa durante 20 años. La empresa está ahora en quiebra. (cual)

_____

4. La semana que viene viajaré a Europa. Europa es mi continente favorito. (cual)

_____

5. Mañana jugaré baloncesto. No he jugado jamás antes al baloncesto. (cual)

_____

8. Completa las oraciones con las palabras de la lista. `15.B`

| lo que | quienes | cualquiera | cuyo | quien | que (2) |

1. Las personas _____ número de documento termine en 8 deberán presentarse el día lunes.

2. _____ quiera comer rico y barato vendrá a nuestro restaurante.

3. El _____ conduzca sin prudencia recibirá una sanción.

4. _____ más me interesa es la historia.

5. Todos los países _____ forman la Unión Europea tienen proyectos en común.

6. Me agradan las personas con _____ puedo hablar sobre literatura.

9. Reescribe las oraciones. Como ayuda, tienes las primeras palabras. `15.B`

1. Yo lavaré los platos. Soy yo _____.

2. El jefe pagará una parte de los despidos. Es el jefe _____.

3. Comimos una exquisita paella en Valencia. Fue en Valencia _____.

4. Cervantes escribió *Don Quijote de la Mancha*. Fue Cervantes _____.

5. Ganamos la competencia el fin de semana pasado. Fue el fin de semana pasado _____.

6. Los estudiantes tienen demasiados reclamos. Son los estudiantes _____.

10. Reescribe las oraciones usando adverbios relativos. `15.C`

1. La ciudad en la que vivo tiene 200.000 habitantes. _____

2. Lo haré del modo en que tú me has dicho._____

3. En la época en que nací, mis padres vivían en el extranjero._____

4. Ella siempre me ha dado todo lo que tenía. _____

5. Me gusta la manera en que crecen esas flores. _____

11. Síntesis Elige la opción correcta para cada oración. `15.A–15.D`

1. No me gusta nada la manera _____ me hablas.
   a. la que   b. en la que   c. que

2. Como dice el dicho: "A _____ madruga, Dios lo ayuda".
   a. los   b. que   c. quien

3. Cecilia _____ es una excelente compañera de trabajo.
   a. , quien es amiga de María,
   b. quien es amiga de María
   c. cuyo cabello es rubio

4. Mañana no tengo que trabajar, _____ me alegra muchísimo.
   a. el que   b. que   c. lo cual

5. El químico _____ se fabricó este material es tóxico.
   a. con quien   b. con el que   c. cuyo

6. Te invitaré _____ que vaya de vacaciones.
   a. donde   b. adondequiera   c. adonde

7. El hombre _____ hablabas es el embajador de China.
   a. con que   b. con quien   c. quien

12. Síntesis Completa las oraciones con el pronombre relativo o el adverbio relativo correcto. `15.A–15.C`

1. Para la época _____ se fundó esta ciudad, la economía era básicamente ganadera.

2. Este periódico, _____ nombre es *La Tribuna*, es uno de los más importantes del país.

3. Ayer conocí a tu padre, de _____ me hablaste tanto.

4. El mismo día _____ choqué con el carro, tú perdiste tu vuelo a Colombia.

5. El doctor _____ me atendió la semana pasada hoy está de vacaciones.

6. La Navidad más divertida _____ pasé fue la de 1998.

7. Te presentaré a las personas con _____ trabajo.

8. La casa _____ vivo es de alquiler.

9. Hoy me levanté muy temprano, _____ es un gran esfuerzo para mí.

10. Mi mejor amiga, _____ es fotógrafa, trabaja mucho.

11. El modo _____ trabaja mi hermano es muy particular.

12. Vimos una casa _____ muros estaban cubiertos de hierba.

Practice more at **vhlcentral.com.**

1. Completa las oraciones con las conjunciones coordinantes de la lista. `16.B`

> ni... ni...　　e　　pues　　sino　　no... ni...　　y　　pero

1. Cuando lleguemos a casa, comeremos frutas _____ chocolates.

2. Mis padres se ducharán _____ irán a hacer las compras.

3. Ese vestido _____ es amarillo _____ naranja: es rosado.

4. _____ crudo, _____ demasiado cocido; quiero que el pavo esté en el punto justo.

5. Llegamos a tiempo a la fiesta, _____ nos olvidamos del regalo para el cumpleañero.

6. No es tu padre _____ tú quien debe hacer la tarea.

7. Voy a ducharme, _____ he hecho deportes ¡y no quiero oler mal!

2. En cada oración, decide cuál es la conjunción coordinante adecuada (*y/o*). `16.B`

1. Tenemos entre cuatro _____ cinco dólares; no sé exactamente cuántos.

2. Bien comes ya mismo _____ esperas hasta las cuatro de la tarde.

3. Mi computadora nueva tiene cámara web _____ pantalla de 17 pulgadas.

4. Por cinco dólares puedes comprar una hamburguesa con patatas fritas, ya sea con un refresco _____ con un zumo, tú eliges.

5. Sara es la cantante; _____ tú, el guitarrista.

6. ¿Cuándo _____ dónde nos encontraremos con Raquel? Pásame la información por mensaje de texto, por favor.

7. Se lo dices tú _____ se lo digo yo.

3. Completa la carta con la opción correcta. `16.B`

> Querida Gabriela:
>
> No sabes cuánto te extraño. Hace apenas un mes que te fuiste a vivir al D.F., (1) _____ (pero/pues) me parece que fue hace un año. (2) _____ (Ni/Tanto) Guadalupe (3) _____ (ni/como) yo te echamos de menos (4) _____ (pues/y) nos gustaría que volvieras pronto; (5) _____ (sin embargo / sino) sabemos que México es tu país favorito (6) _____ (y/e) que eres feliz allí.
>
> Por aquí todo sigue igual: (7) _____ (no/ni) peor (8) _____ (no/ni) mejor. Tenemos siete (9) _____ (o/u) ocho compañeros de clase nuevos, muy simpáticos todos. Uno de ellos habla a la perfección (10) _____ (tan / tanto) inglés como francés (11) _____ (y/o) español, (12) _____ (pero/pues) su madre es francesa, su padre es mexicano y él nació en Estados Unidos.
>
> Recuerda que, si quieres hablar con nosotras, nos puedes contactar (13) _____ (bien/ni) por chat, (14) _____ (sino/bien) por Skype.
>
> ¡Un abrazo fuerte!
>
> Milena

4. En esta conversación indica las conjunciones subordinantes. 16.C

PACIENTE Buenos días, doctor Pérez.

DOCTOR Buenos días. Dígame: ¿qué lo trae por aquí?

PACIENTE A ver... desde hace dos días, cuando me levanto, me duele mucho el estómago.

DOCTOR Me ha dicho que le duele el estómago. ¿Suele comer alimentos poco saludables?

PACIENTE No... pero, pensándolo mejor, aunque no coma nada me duele la barriga. Eso sí, bebo café, me encanta.

DOCTOR Entonces usted no come, pero toma café. ¿Cuántas tazas toma por día?

PACIENTE Tomo solamente dos o tres en cuanto llego al trabajo, dos más una vez que tengo un tiempito libre, y tres más por la tarde porque me da sueño trabajar tanto.

DOCTOR ¡Y después me pregunta que cuál es el motivo de su dolor de estómago!

PACIENTE Creo que tiene razón, doctor. Debería tomar el café con un chorrito de leche, ¿no?

DOCTOR Mire, como usted no mide cuánto café toma, se lo prohibiré totalmente. Siempre que sienta ganas de tomarse un cafecito, tómese un té o, mucho mejor, un vaso de agua, de manera que su estómago no siga empeorando.

PACIENTE Muchas gracias, doctor.

DOCTOR ¡Cuídese! Adiós.

Actividades

5. Reescribe las oraciones para que contengan cláusulas sustantivas (*nominal clauses*). 16.C

Modelo

Tengo frío. (dice/Rosa)
Rosa dice que tiene frío.

1. ¿Cuál es tu número de teléfono? (pregunta/Leonel)

   ____

2. ¿Tienes el correo electrónico de Carla? (pregunta/José)

   ____

3. El lechero vendrá a las nueve. (creen/Juan y Marina)

   ____

4. ¿Has oído el timbre? (pregunta/Estela)

   ____

5. Me gustaría dormir la siesta. (dice/Mirta)

   ____

6. Indica si estas oraciones contienen conjunciones subordinantes temporales o causales. 16.C

1. Antes de que llegaras, estaba hablando por teléfono con Luis. ______________
2. Llegué tarde al trabajo, ya que perdí el tren de las 8. ______________
3. Como no me has llamado, te llamo yo a ti. ______________
4. Tan pronto como empezó la tormenta, la gente se refugió en las tiendas. ______________
5. Cada vez que voy a visitarte, me esperas con una comida riquísima. ______________
6. Dado que no se han cumplido las reglas, todos tendrán sus respectivas sanciones. ______________
7. Puesto que vuestros perros ladran día y noche, deberéis mudaros a otro lugar. ______________
8. Mientras tú cocinas, yo lavo la ropa. ______________

7. En cada oración, elige la opción correcta. `16.C`

1. Compré muchas frutas y verduras, _____ (de manera que / dado que) tendremos la nevera llenísima.

2. Venderemos nuestro carro, _____ (de modo que / puesto que) casi no lo usamos.

3. Tengo muchísimo sueño, _____ (porque / así que) dormiré un rato, ¿sí?

4. Alejandra quiere ir a la playa, _____ (de modo que / porque) quiere disfrutar de este hermoso día.

5. El supermercado está cerrado, _____ (así que / puesto que) tendremos que comer en el restaurante.

6. Mis compañeros de apartamento organizaron una fiesta en el parque, el fin de semana _____ (a causa de que / de modo que) no tengamos que limpiar nuestro apartamento al día siguiente.

8. Une las oraciones usando las conjunciones dadas. `16.C`

Modelo

Mis amigos son muy graciosos. Sin embargo, yo nunca me divierto con ellos.
(aunque) *Aunque mis amigos son muy graciosos, yo nunca me divierto con ellos.*

1. Estudio muchísimo la gramática española. Sin embargo, siempre cometo los mismos errores.
(a pesar de que) _____

2. Trabajaré mucho hoy. Por lo tanto, mañana podré descansar.
(de modo que) _____

3. Martín cocina. Parece un experto.
(como si) _____

4. Julia trabaja mucho. Patricia trabaja las mismas horas que Julia.
(tanto... como) _____

5. Iremos a pasear. Iremos al lugar que tú quieras.
(donde) _____

6. Quieres comer dulces. Antes debes comerte toda la comida.
(para que) _____

7. Yo como una gran cantidad de verduras. Tú comes tantas verduras como yo.
(igual... que) _____

8. Debes ahorrar. Solamente así podrás comprar tu propia casa.
(a fin de que) _____

9. En cada oración, elige la opción correcta. `16.D`

1. _____ dejes de quejarte porque la casa está sucia, mañana limpiaré hasta el último rincón.
a. A menos que   b. En caso de que   c. Con tal de que

2. _____ el precio de los productos orgánicos no suba, seguiré comprándolos.
a. Si   b. Con tal de que   c. Siempre y cuando

3. Los trabajadores no volverán a sus puestos de trabajo _____ les paguen los salarios atrasados.
a. a menos que   b. en caso de que   c. si

4. _____ tengo tiempo, hago deportes.
a. Con tal de que   b. En caso de que   c. Siempre que

5. _____ haya un incendio, baje por las escaleras.
a. En caso de que   b. Siempre y cuando   c. Si

6. _____ no me llamas por mi cumpleaños, me enojaré muchísimo.
a. A menos que   b. Si   c. Siempre que

7. _____ yo pueda trabajar, no te faltará nada.
a. A menos que   b. Mientras   c. Si

8. _____ no elijas algo muy costoso, te compraré un regalo.
a. A menos que   b. Si   c. Siempre que

Actividades

10. Indica si las condiciones son (a) reales/posibles, (b) probables/hipotéticas o (c) imposibles. `16.D`

_____ 1. Si me acompañaras a la fiesta, ganaríamos el premio a la pareja de la noche.

_____ 2. Te invitaremos a cenar solamente si nos prometes que serás puntual.

_____ 3. Si tuvieras una mascota, comprenderías la responsabilidad de tener un animal a tu cargo.

_____ 4. Los abuelos no te habrían regalado ese CD si hubieran sabido que ya lo tenías.

_____ 5. Si saliera el sol, iríamos a patinar al parque.

_____ 6. Si mis hijos tienen clases por la mañana, podré anotarme en el curso de cerámica.

_____ 7. Nunca se lo habría contado a Silvia si me hubieras dicho que era un secreto.

_____ 8. Si haces ejercicio, te mantienes en forma.

11. Síntesis Une las frases para formar oraciones lógicas. `16.B–16.D`

1. Aunque odio los teléfonos móviles, _____

2. Siempre que hago una pausa, _____

3. Para que mi jefe no se enfade, _____

4. Me quedé sin batería en el teléfono, _____

5. Sin querer borré todos los contactos, _____

6. Como borré todos los contactos, _____

7. Ahora sé cómo usar el teléfono, _____

a. en mi trabajo me piden que tenga uno.

b. de modo que mi jefe no pudo comunicarse conmigo.

c. así que no tengo excusas para no estar en contacto con mi jefe.

d. porque no sabía usar el teléfono.

e. mi jefe me dio un papel con todos los teléfonos.

f. mi jefe me llama por teléfono.

g. debo devolver sus llamadas de inmediato.

12. Síntesis Completa las oraciones con las conjunciones de la lista. Hay dos conjunciones que no debes usar. `16.B–16.D`

al mismo tiempo que	cada vez que	ni	pero	que si	sino
antes de que	cuando	o	pues	si	tanto... como
así que	en caso de que	para que	que	sin embargo	y

1. Mamá me aseguró _____ Papá Noel vendría si me portaba bien.

2. El señor González no es tu amigo, _____ tu profesor, _____ háblale con respeto.

3. El secretario no redactó la carta _____ organizó las reuniones, _____ lo despidieron.

4. _____ dieran las doce, Cenicienta debía volver a su casa.

5. _____ la fiesta sea un éxito, debemos hacer mucha publicidad.

6. _____ no puedas venir, por favor, avísanos con antelación.

7. _____ hace frío, me gusta quedarme en casa y ver películas.

8. _____ pones atención, verás que aprenderás más rápido.

9. _____ te vas de vacaciones, la oficina es un caos.

10. No sé si reír _____ llorar.

11. Mis padres no llegaron aún. _____, avisaron que vendrían temprano.

12. No puedo salir esta tarde, _____ debo trabajar.

13. Adriana lavó la ropa, limpió la casa _____ preparó la cena.

14. Tengo muchos días de vacaciones, _____ me tomaré solamente una semana.

15. _____ Melisa _____ Romina y Mariela son maestras.

Practice more at **vhlcentral.com.**

1. Indica si los verbos en este texto son *copulativos*, *transitivos* o *intransitivos*. Escríbelos en la columna correcta. `17.B`

El famoso actor Julio Suárez, quien **protagonizó** telenovelas como *Amar **es** vivir* y *Enamorados siempre*, **sufrió** ayer un accidente de tránsito cuando **conducía** por el centro de Bogotá. Aunque Suárez no **tuvo** lesiones graves, el acompañante del artista aún **está** en el Hospital Central.

El accidente **sucedió** a las 20 horas del lunes 3 de agosto, cuando otro conductor **hizo** un giro peligroso para **ingresar** a una gasolinera y **chocó** el vehículo del prestigioso actor.

Suárez **está** preocupado por la salud de su amigo, a quien **conoció** cuando **era** aún un actor desconocido. "Les **pido** a los conductores que **sean** más prudentes al **conducir**", exclamó el artista.

Copulativo	Transitivo	Intransitivo

2. En cada oración, elige la opción correcta. `17.B`

1. ¡Cuántas veces soñé _____ (por/con) una fiesta como esta!

2. Horacio siempre se interesó _____ (por/en) la arquitectura de la ciudad.

3. ¿Confirmaste que asistiremos _____ (a/en) la reunión escolar?

4. ¡Ojalá quisieras jugar _____ (con/a) las cartas conmigo!

5. Volveremos _____ (a/en) vernos la semana que viene.

6. Mis padres se han encontrado _____ (en/con) los tuyos en el supermercado.

7. ¿Habéis disfrutado _____ (de/con) la playa?

3. En cada oración, elige la opción correcta. `17.B`

1. Juliana _____ de las escaleras y tuvo que ir al hospital.
   a. cayó   b. se cayó

2. No _____ despertarte: ¡dormías tan plácidamente!
   a. me atreví   b. me atreví a

3. Ayer _____ demasiado tarde.
   a. despertamos   b. nos despertamos

4. Quiero que _____ a la abuela hasta que yo vuelva.
   a. cuides   b. te cuides

5. Por favor, ¡_____ esa barba! ¡No te queda bien!
   a. afeita   b. aféitate

6. Estaba preparando la comida y _____ el dedo con un cuchillo.
   a. corté   b. me corté

7. No _____ la ropa y ahora no tenemos ni un par de calcetines limpios.
   a. lavamos   b. nos lavamos

4. Reescribe las oraciones usando el verbo entre paréntesis. `17.B`

1. Los alumnos detestan hacer la tarea. (disgustar)

   _____

2. ¿No te sientes triste por la despedida de Flor? (entristecer)

   _____

3. Adoro ir a las montañas en invierno. (fascinar)

   _____

4. ¡Qué sorpresa tu visita! (sorprender)

   _____

5. Tengo miedo de los fantasmas. (asustar)

   _____

6. Para mí, es muy divertido ir de compras. (divertir)

   _____

5. Conjuga estos verbos en presente de indicativo. `17.D`

1. completar (nosotros) _____   5. insistir (ella) _____

2. cumplir (vosotros) _____   6. leer (yo) _____

3. beber (tú) _____   7. responder (él) _____

4. viajar (ellos) _____   8. investigar (vos) _____

6. Completa las oraciones usando los verbos de la lista conjugados en presente de indicativo. `17.D`

| conseguir | cocer | ejercer | exigir | introducir | traducir | recoger |

1. ¿_____ (yo) la moneda en esta ranura?

2. ¿Cuánto tiempo _____ (yo) esta pasta?

3. Te _____ que me ayudes a limpiar la casa.

4. _____ (yo) la profesión desde hace veinte años.

5. Yo _____ los juguetes y tú los guardas en el armario.

6. No _____ (yo) olvidarte: sueño contigo todas las noches.

7. ¿Cómo _____ (yo) esta palabra? No se me ocurre cómo hacerlo.

7. Reescribe las oraciones usando el pronombre indicado. `17.D`

1. ¿Por qué incluyes a Juana en tu lista de invitados, pero no a mí? (vos)

   _____

   _____

2. ¿Continuáis con las clases de guitarra? (tú)

   _____

3. No confiamos en el criterio de Emiliano. (yo)

   _____

4. Siempre perdéis el hilo de la conversación. (ellos)

   _____

5. Nosotros te defendemos si pasa algo. (yo)

   _____

6. Volvemos a las nueve y media de la noche. (ellos)

   _____

7. Te pedimos un gran favor. (yo)

   _____

8. Completa el texto con los verbos conjugados en presente de indicativo. `17.D`

decidir	convertirse	comenzar	recordar	afligir	acostarse	repetirse
situarse	perseguir	soñar	contar	empezar	deducir	

El martes que viene se estrenará en todas las salas del país la película *La escuela*. Este drama
(1) _____ con la participación de estrellas, como el joven actor Tomás Rapal y la ya
consagrada Gabriela Perotti.

La historia (2) _____ en un pequeño pueblo y es protagonizada por un niño llamado Juan
que (3) _____ el año en una escuela nueva. Ese primer día de clases (4) _____
en una pesadilla, porque sus compañeros lo maltratan y lo (5) _____ por los pasillos de
la escuela.

Esa noche, cuando Juan (6) _____ en la cama, (7) _____ hacer todo lo posible
para que sus compañeros lo acepten. Sin embargo, al día siguiente, Juan nota que la situación
del día anterior (8) _____. Al final del día, Juan (9) _____ que no será fácil
enfrentarse a sus compañeros y que debe hacer algo para adaptarse a la nueva escuela.

Así (10) _____ esta magnífica historia: un niño que (11) _____ con ser
aceptado. Sin duda, esta situación nos (12) _____ nuestra niñez y los problemas que
(13) _____ a los más pequeños en esta difícil etapa de la vida. Una película totalmente
recomendable para ver en familia.

9. Completa las oraciones según lo que dice el calendario con los verbos conjugados en presente de indicativo. `17.D`

○	**Lunes**
	9:30 poner a lavar ropa
	11:00 salir de paseo con la abuela
	15:00 traer al perro de la veterinaria
	17:00 hacer resumen de literatura
	20:00 componer canción para Paola
	22:00 proponer casamiento a Paola

Bueno, hoy es un día muy especial y complicado, pero
ya tengo todo organizado en mi mente. Si a las 9:30
(1) _____ a lavar la ropa, a las 10:30 puedo colgarla,
justo cuando (2) _____ de paseo con la abuela.
Después de una larga caminata con ella, (3) _____
a casa al perro que está en la veterinaria. Duermo una breve
siesta y a las 17:00 (4) _____ el resumen de literatura.
Después, me baño y me visto bien elegante con mi ropa
recién lavada. A las 20:00, uso toda mi inspiración y le
(5) _____ una canción a Paola. Con esa canción, le
(6) _____ casamiento. ¡No hay forma de que diga que no!

10. Completa las oraciones con los verbos conjugados en presente de indicativo. `17.D`

1. No te _____ (oír) bien si no hablas claro.

2. La escultura _____ (tener) más de trescientos años.

3. ¿Finalmente _____ (venir) tu familia a visitarte?

4. Tú siempre _____ (maldecir) cuando conduces. No debes hacerlo frente a los niños.

5. O te _____ (atener) a las reglas de la casa o te buscas otro lugar donde vivir.

6. Cuando _____ (decir, yo) algo, quiero que me escuches.

7. ¿Los bebés _____ (oír) también cuando están en la panza de su mamá?

11. Escribe oraciones completas siguiendo el modelo. `17.D`

> **Modelo**
>
> Yo – dar – flor / Tú – dar – beso
> *Yo te doy una flor si tú me das un beso.*

1. Yo – decir – la verdad / Tú – decir – la verdad – también

   _____

2. Ellos – ver – el documental / Yo – ver – también

   _____

3. Yo – estar – de buen humor / Vosotros – estar – de buen humor – también

   _____

4. Yo – ir – a la fiesta / Tú – ir – también

   _____

5. Yo – traer – torta / Vosotros – traer – un regalo

   _____

12. Para cada oración, indica por qué se utiliza el presente de indicativo. `17.E`

Ejemplos	Acciones presentes	Costumbres	Hechos intemporales
1. Este mes hago ejercicios en el parque.			
2. La Luna es un satélite de la Tierra.			
3. Cuatro más ocho son doce.			
4. A las 7 abre la panadería.			
5. Por la noche, comemos en el salón.			
6. En Argentina, se habla español.			
7. Ahora mismo llamo a la tía.			

13. Para cada oración, indica por qué se utiliza el presente de indicativo. `17.E`

_____ 1. En 1916, se declara la independencia de Argentina.
        a. presente histórico   b. hechos intemporales

_____ 2. El domingo cocino un riquísimo pollo.
        a. presente para dar órdenes   b. presente para referirse al futuro

_____ 3. ¿Te doy dinero para el metro?
        a. presente para dar órdenes   b. presente de confirmación

_____ 4. Si duermo mal, estoy cansadísimo al día siguiente.
        a. cláusulas condicionales   b. hechos intemporales

_____ 5. ¡Ya mismo dejas lo que haces y vienes aquí!
        a. presente para dar órdenes   b. presente para referirse al futuro

_____ 6. ¿Tomamos un café?
        a. presente de confirmación   b. presente para referirse al futuro

14. Une las frases para formar oraciones lógicas. `17.F`

1. Gonzalo trabaja en una fábrica _____
2. Los niños leen cuentos de terror _____
3. Ulises está trabajando _____
4. Estoy llegando a tu casa, _____
5. Los profesores están leyendo tu examen _____
6. Llego tarde, _____
7. Mis colegas están viajando a Europa _____
8. Te escribo por correo electrónico _____
9. Estoy trabajando en mi tesis _____

a. y no quiere que lo molesten ahora.
b. y siempre tienen miedo a la hora de dormir.
c. baja a abrirme la puerta.
d. y además estudia ingeniería.
e. no me esperes para comer.
f. y no pueden creer los errores ortográficos que tiene.
g. la semana que viene.
h. y espero terminarla pronto.
i. en este momento porque tienen que ir a una conferencia en Madrid.

15. Síntesis Completa las oraciones con el verbo conjugado en presente o presente progresivo. `17.A–17.F`

1. A Elena le _____ (encantar) las flores rojas.
2. Roberto _____ (casarse) con Susana en mayo.
3. _____ (llamar, yo) a la puerta, ¡pero no me abres! ¿Por qué?
4. Por el contexto, _____ (deducir, yo) que ese término está relacionado con la física.
5. Todavía _____ (elegir, yo) qué voy a comer. ¿Tú ya elegiste?
6. Tu recuerdo me _____ (perseguir) día y noche.
7. Mi esposa y yo _____ (construir) una casa en el bosque. En noviembre, estará terminada.
8. ¿Por qué no _____ (empezar, tú) a cocinar mientras yo limpio el comedor?
9. En este momento no _____ (poder, yo) atenderte.
10. Mi amiga _____ (llegar) de Australia la semana que viene.
11. No puede atender el teléfono porque en este instante _____ (domir).
12. Si no _____ (descansar), te vas a enfermar.

16. Síntesis Conjuga estos verbos en presente y presente progresivo. Si no es posible conjugar el verbo en presente progresivo, coloca una X. `17.A–17.F`

1. perder (ellos) _____ _____
2. atravesar (yo) _____ _____
3. querer (ellos) _____ _____
4. costar (él) _____ _____
5. poder (vos) _____ _____
6. promover (yo) _____ _____
7. confesar (nosotros) _____ _____
8. estar (vosotros) _____ _____
9. destruir (tú) _____ _____
10. oír (ella) _____ _____
11. deber (tú) _____ _____
12. salir (yo) _____ _____

Practice more at **vhlcentral.com.**

Actividades

Actividades

1. Lee el texto e indica los verbos conjugados en pretérito perfecto simple. `18.B`

Libros perdidos

Me llamo Francisco y el día lunes 23 de agosto tuve una clase en el aula 213. Estuve allí desde las 9 a.m. hasta las 12 p.m. Cuando salí, me olvidé un bolso con libros debajo de la silla. Son un libro de Matemáticas, otro de Física y uno de Química; los compré en la librería universitaria y escribí mi nombre en la primera hoja.

Si alguien los encontró, les pido que me escriban o me llamen al teléfono que aparece abajo.

¡Muchas gracias!
Teléfono: 932 80 394
Correo electrónico: francisco_gutierrez@universidad.edu

2. Completa las oraciones usando el pretérito perfecto simple. `18.B`

1. Ayer yo __jugué__ (jugar) al fútbol durante tres horas.
2. Yo ya te __expliqúe__ (explicar) tres veces el argumento de la película.
3. El lunes yo __toqué__ (tocar) el timbre de tu casa, pero nadie __contestó__ (contestar).
4. __Se cayó__ (caerse) aceite al piso. Ten cuidado.
5. Es increíble lo rápido que __se reconstruyó__ (reconstruirse) la ciudad después de la inundación.
6. Carolina _____ (sentirse) mal todo el día y ahora está en el hospital.
7. ¿Quién __puso__ (poner) un calcetín en la nevera?
8. El chofer __condujo__ (conducir) a una velocidad superior a la permitida.

3. Reescribe las oraciones con el pronombre entre paréntesis. `18.B`

1. Cristina averiguó el teléfono del chico que vio en el autobús. (yo)
   _____
2. ¿Por qué llegaron tarde tus compañeros? (tú)
   __llegaste_____
3. ¿Oíste tú también un ruido fuerte? (él)
   _____
4. Dormimos muy bien anoche. (ellos)
   _____
5. Nunca supimos el motivo del incendio. (yo)
   __supe_____
6. Carla y Juan hicieron la comida. (ella)
   __hizo_____
7. Ayer fui a la estación de tren para comprar los boletos. (nosotros)
   __fuimos_____

4. Escribe estos verbos en pretérito imperfecto. `18.D`

1. (yo) estuve	_estaba_	6. (nosotros) vemos	_v._
2. (yo) duermo	_dormía_	7. (vosotros) fuisteis	____
3. (tú) comiste	_comías_	8. (ellos) compraron	~~comean~~ compraban
4. (nosotros) vivimos	_vivimos_	9. (nosotros) estamos	_estabamos_
5. (nosotros) somos	_fuimos_	10. (yo) supe	_sabía_

5. **Decide si las explicaciones hacen referencia al pretérito perfecto simple (PPS) o al pretérito imperfecto (PI). Luego une las explicaciones con los ejemplos.** `18.B–18.E`

Explicación	Ejemplo
1. Se usa para constatar datos históricos. _____	a. Ya iba a llamarte cuando sonó el timbre.
2. Se usa para expresar cómo solía ser una persona en el pasado. _____	b. El famoso pintor nació el 3 de mayo de 1599.
3. Se usa para expresar una acción en el pasado que no sucedió debido a una interrupción. _____	c. El autobús se descompuso en el medio de la ruta.
4. Se usa para enfatizar la simultaneidad de dos acciones en el pasado. _____	d. Mi novio siempre me regalaba flores cuando venía a visitarme.
5. Se usa para expresar cortesía. _____	e. Mi bisabuelo era amable, simpático y muy culto.
6. Se usa para indicar que algo sucedió en el pasado. _____	f. Quería pedirle un favor.
7. Se usa para enfatizar el fin de una acción y el comienzo de otra. _____	g. Hace cinco años que vivo en este barrio.
8. Se usa como perífrasis del verbo *llevar + gerundio*. _____	h. Ese día salí de casa a las 10, tomé el autobús a las 11 y llegué al trabajo a tiempo.

6. **Elige la opción correcta.** `18.B–18.E`

1. ¿Qué día _visitaste_ (visitabas/visitaste) el museo? Me pareció haberte visto.
2. Cuando _cumplía_ (cumplí/cumplía) ocho años, me regalaron mi primera bicicleta.
3. Cuando era estudiante, _me despertaba_ (me desperté / me despertaba) temprano y _desayunaba_ (desayuné/desayunaba) con mucha tranquilidad.
4. El día _fue_ (fue/estaba) soleado, pero de repente _se nubló_ (se nublaba / se nubló) y _comenzó_ (comenzaba/comenzó) a llover.
5. Juguemos a que _teníamos_ (teníamos/tuvimos) una gran mansión para nosotras y que _éramos_ (fuimos/éramos) millonarias.
6. Cuando _fui_ (fui/iba) a salir de casa _me acordé_ (me acordé / me acordaba) de que era el cumpleaños de mi madre.
7. Mi primera maestra _se llamaba_ (se llamó / se llamaba) Claudia.
8. A las ocho de la mañana, _había_ (hubo/había) sol, pero igualmente _decidía_ (decidí/decidía) no ir al parque.
9. _Iba_ (Fui/Iba) camino a casa cuando _me encontré_ (me encontré / me encontraba) con Pedro.

7. **¿Pretérito perfecto simple o pretérito imperfecto? Decide qué tiempo verbal debes usar y completa las oraciones con los verbos de la lista.** `18.B–18.E`

aliviar	decir	haber	ir (2)	sacar	ser
dar	doler	hacer	llegar	sentarse	

El martes pasado (1) _____ al dentista, porque me (2) _____ la muela. ¡(3) _____ tanto que no (4) _____ al dentista! Por suerte, no (5) _____ mucha gente en la sala de espera. En cuanto (6) _____ en el sillón, el dentista me (7) _____ una inyección con anestesia que (8) _____ totalmente el dolor. Después, me (9) _____ que abriera bien grande la boca ¡y me (10) _____ la muela! ¡Todo (11) _____ tan rápido que no (12) _____ a tener miedo!

8. **Escoge la forma correcta de los verbos en la composición de Eduardo.** `18.B–18.E`

Mi escuela nueva

El 7 de septiembre de 2010 (1) _fui_ (**iba/fui**) por primera vez a mi escuela nueva. Me (2) _impactó_ (**impactaba/impactó**) la belleza del edificio: tiene tres pisos, dos jardines gigantes y una cancha de fútbol propia. Cuando (3) _entré_ (**entraba/entré**) en la clase, todos mis compañeros me saludaron con una sonrisa. La directora incluso me (4) _dio_ (**daba/dio**) un regalo de bienvenida. Cuando (5) _terminó_ (**terminaba/terminó**) la clase, mis compañeros me (6) _invitaron_ (**invitaban/invitaron**) a tomar un helado. En mi escuela anterior, mis compañeros (7) _eran_ (**eran/fueron**) aburridos y antipáticos. ¡Qué suerte que (8) _decidía_ (**decidía/decidí**) cambiarme de escuela! Estoy contentísimo.

9. **Catalina está enojada con su mejor amigo, Tomás. Completa las oraciones.** `18.E`

> **Modelo**
>
> Tomás dijo: "Quiero que vengas a visitarme".
> Catalina: Me dijiste que *querías que fuera a visitarte*, pero después no parecías tan contento de verme.

1. Tomás dijo: "Es muy importante que seas puntual".
   Catalina: Me dijiste que _____,
   pero cuando llegué a tu casa, ¡no estabas!

2. Tomás dijo: "Tengo una sorpresa para ti".
   Catalina: Me dijiste que _____,
   pero todo era una mentira.

3. Tomás dijo: "Prefiero estar a solas contigo porque hace mucho que no nos vemos".
   Catalina: Me dijiste que _____,
   pero invitaste a tres amigos más.

4. Tomás dijo: "Espero ver todas las fotos de tus últimas vacaciones".
   Catalina: Me dijiste que _____,
   ¡pero te aburriste a la segunda foto!

5. Tomás dijo: "Hace tres meses que no paso tiempo con amigos".
   Catalina: Me dijiste que _____,
   ¡pero un amigo tuyo me dijo que diste una fiesta el sábado pasado!

6. Tomás dijo: "Eres mi mejor amiga".
   Catalina: Me dijiste que _____,
   ¡pero tus acciones dicen lo contrario!

10. **Completa las oraciones con el verbo conjugado en pretérito perfecto simple o pretérito imperfecto.** `18.F`

1. Finalmente, el caballo _____ (poder) adelantarse y ganó la carrera.

2. Nuestros vecinos no _____ (querer) hacer un fondo común para las reparaciones del edificio.

3. Ayer discutimos con Fernando, porque él _____ (querer) ir al cine y yo, no.

4. Cuando conocí a Marta, en 2010, ella _____ (tener) un novio que se llamaba Omar.

5. ¿Recuerdas el club del barrio? Allí siempre se _____ (poder) jugar al baloncesto y al fútbol incluso sin ser socio.

6. Ayer _____ (saber, yo) que me contrataron para trabajar en la tienda de juguetes más grande del país.

7. ¿Recuerdas cuántos años _____ (tener, nosotros) cuando nos mudamos a esta casa?

11. Síntesis Completa las oraciones con los verbos de la lista en el tiempo verbal indicado. `18.A–18.F`

Pretérito perfecto simple	Pretérito imperfecto
haber	ir
traducir	saber
oír	ser
pedir	haber
hacer	preparar

1. La directora nos ____iba____ que nos comportáramos bien durante la ceremonia escolar.

2. Yo no ~~hacía~~ era que tenías 18 años. ¡Pareces mayor!

3. ¿Quiénes ____hacihiciste____ esta torta? ¡Está riquísima!

4. Graciela _____ al inglés este libro sobre historia sudamericana.

5. Cuando _____ a llamarte, se cortó la luz.

6. La abuela siempre nos _____ el desayuno.

7. De pronto, _____ un ruido y salté de la cama.

8. Soñé que _____ una famosísima actriz.

9. En los años sesenta, _____ un gran movimiento de liberación femenina.

10. En esa época, _____ mucha gente que no sabía leer.

12. Síntesis Completa el relato de Diego con el pretérito perfecto simple o el pretérito imperfecto. `18.A–18.F`

Pilar y yo (1) _____ (conocerse) en el primer año de la escuela primaria cuando (2) _____ (tener) seis años y desde ese momento no nos separamos nunca. Este año (3) _____ (decidir) festejar nuestros cumpleaños juntos. Pilar (4) _____ (enviar) todas las invitaciones y yo (5) _____ (comprar) las comida y las bebidas.

En el día de la fiesta el sol (6) _____ (brillar) y casi no (7) _____ (hacer) frío. (8) _____ (Parecer) que todo iba a salir perfecto. Sin embargo, nadie (9) _____ (aparecer) a la hora esperada. Pilar y yo no (10) _____ (saber) por qué la gente no había venido.

De pronto, ambos (11) _____ (correr) a buscar las invitaciones. Cuando las (12) _____ (leer), ¡no (13) _____ (poder) creerlo! ¡La hora (14) _____ (ser) incorrecta!

Por suerte, dos horas después (15) _____ (comenzar) a llegar los invitados. La fiesta (16) _____ (estar) genial. (17) _____ (Hacer) mucho tiempo que no (18) _____ (divertirse) tanto en una fiesta de cumpleaños.

 Practice more at **vhlcentral.com.**

1. Completa las oraciones con los verbos conjugados en pretérito perfecto compuesto. 19.A

1. Magdalena _____ (estudiar) toda la tarde.

2. Todavía no _____ (terminar) mis tareas.

3. ¡Por fin los trabajadores _____ (recibir) un aumento de sueldo!

4. Vosotros ya _____ (esperar) demasiado.

5. Las autoridades _____ (actuar) de forma muy responsable.

6. Roberto _____ (llegar) hace un momento.

7. Nuestro jefe nos _____ (invitar) a una conferencia en Las Bahamas.

2. Reordena las oraciones y conjuga los verbos en pretérito perfecto compuesto. 19.A

1. ¿ / comer (tú) / Alguna vez / paella / ?

_____

2. no / vender / Lucía / todavía / su bicicleta

_____

3. Este año / en / esta zona / transformarse / un centro financiero

_____

4. En mi vida / un carro / tener / rojo

_____

5. ¿ / cuál será / mostrarte / tu oficina / Tus jefes / ?

_____

6. ¡ / te / de mí / Tan pronto / olvidar / !

_____

3. Indica qué verbos tienen participios regulares y cuáles tienen participios pasados irregulares o las dos opciones. Escribe los participios. 19.A

comprar	sonreír	concurrir	ver	crecer	resolver
estar	leer	descubrir	freír	aumentar	morir

Regulares	Irregulares

4. Completa las oraciones conjugando los verbos en pretérito perfecto compuesto. 19.A

1. El músico aún no _____ (componer) la canción que le pidió el director de cine.

2. ¿_____ (Leer, vosotros) bien qué dice ese cartel?

3. Veo que ya _____ (volver, tú).

4. ¿Quién _____ (abrir) la puerta?

5. Mi madre _____ (traer) unas flores hermosas.

6. ¿Dónde _____ (poner) Olivia el azúcar?

7. Hasta ahora, los estudiantes no _____ (resolver) el problema matemático.

5. Decide por qué en estas oraciones se utiliza el pretérito perfecto compuesto. Indica *acción continua*, *acción incompleta* o *experiencia*, según el caso. `19.B`

Ejemplos	Explicación
1. ¿Has dormido alguna vez en una tienda de campaña?	
2. Hemos ido al centro comercial todos los días.	
3. Todavía no he conseguido hablar con mi abuela.	
4. ¡En mi vida he comido tanto como hoy!	
5. Juana está realmente bella hoy, ¿la has visto?	
6. Siempre he querido tener un pececito.	
7. Hasta hoy, no hemos tenido problema alguno.	
8. Muchas veces nos hemos ido a dormir sin comer.	
9. Lorena está haciendo dieta, pero aún no ha podido bajar de peso.	

6. Une las oraciones con sus contextos. `19.B`

_____ 1. He olvidado cerrar la ventana de mi habitación.

_____ 2. La semana pasada olvidé cerrar la ventana de mi habitación.

_____ 3. Mamá ha ido a sus clases de guitarra esta mañana.

_____ 4. Mamá fue a clases de guitarra la semana pasada.

_____ 5. La alumna nueva ha llegado hace unos minutos.

_____ 6. La alumna nueva llegó a la escuela.

a. Me ha dicho que está feliz con su profesor nuevo.

b. No le gustaron y ahora quiere ir a clases de piano.

c. Ahora llueve y seguramente ha entrado agua.

d. Sería bueno saludarla y darle la bienvenida a la escuela.

e. Ahora sé que debo asegurarme de que esté cerrada.

f. Unos minutos después, ya tenía varios amigos.

7. Señala en la conversación telefónica los casos en que los latinoamericanos usarían el pretérito simple. Luego escribe esos verbos en pretérito simple al final de cada párrafo. `19.C`

LUPE ¿Hola?

ANDREA Hola, Lupe, soy Andrea. ¡Por fin te he encontrado en casa! ¿Cómo estás? _____

LUPE Bien, un poco ocupada, pero dime.

ANDREA Hace unos minutos he visto a Tomás en la estación de tren. Me contó que jamás ha tomado un avión en su vida. No entiendo cómo puede viajar siempre en tren o en autobús... ¡se tarda tanto en llegar! Por ejemplo, este año, ¡que ya se acabó! con mi madre hemos viajado en más de ocho ocasiones desde Lima hasta Buenos Aires en avión. ¿Te imaginas un viaje así en autobús? _____

LUPE No, no podría imaginármelo.

ANDREA ¿Y ya te he contado que hace unos días vi en el aeropuerto a tu profesora de música? Nunca he hablado con ella, pero tampoco lo haría: no parece muy simpática. _____

LUPE Andrea, lamento interrumpirte, pero todavía no he cocinado, ni me he duchado y tengo que irme a las clases de cerámica. _____

ANDREA Sí, sí, no te preocupes. Yo ya he cocinado, he lavado los platos y ahora estoy mirando un programa de chismes sobre famosos. _____

LUPE En serio, Andrea. ¡Tengo que irme!

ANDREA Bueno, bueno. Te mando un beso y nos vemos. ¡Chau!

8. Completa las oraciones usando el pluscuamperfecto. `19.D`

1. Cuando llegué, todos los autobuses ya _había salido_ (salir).

2. Nunca _había imaginado_ (imaginar) que algo así podía sucederme.

3. Una semana antes, nosotros _habíamos recibido_ (recibir) una carta de la tía, en la que decía que estaba muy bien de salud.

4. Mi hermanito no _había entendido_ (entender) la letra de la canción hasta que yo se la expliqué.

5. No pudimos viajar porque _habíamos olvidado_ (olvidar) el pasaporte en casa.

6. Roberto nos dijo que su perro _____ (comerse) su tarea de matemáticas.

7. Hasta ese momento, jamás _____ (probar, nosotros) el helado con sabor a café.

9. Indica por qué se utiliza el pluscuamperfecto en estas oraciones. Escribe el número de la oración en la columna correcta. `19.E`

Pasado antes del pasado	Discurso indirecto

1. El cliente llamó al camarero y le dijo que había visto una mosca en su sopa.

2. No, todavía no había recibido tu mensaje cuando me llamaste.

3. Nos preguntaron si habíamos notado algún cambio en la casa.

4. Llegaste justo cuando yo había salido de casa.

5. ¿Ya habías conocido a Francisco cuando te graduaste?

6. Invitamos a Eduardo a una fiesta, pero nos dijo que la noche anterior no había dormido mucho y estaba cansado.

7. ¿Vosotros os habíais mudado ya cuando vine a vivir a Chile?

10. Modifica las oraciones usando el pluscuamperfecto. `19.E`

Modelo

Me fui de casa y luego tú llegaste. (cuando)
Cuando llegaste a casa, yo ya me había ido.

1. Apagué mi teléfono móvil y luego tú me llamaste. (cuando)
_____

2. Nos levantamos de la cama y luego sonó el despertador. (cuando)
_____

3. Laura estudió mucho y luego aprobó el examen. (porque)
_____

4. Natalia dejó la dieta y luego subió de peso. (porque)
_____

5. Terminamos de comer y luego llegó Raúl. (cuando)
_____

6. Pablo se rompió la pierna esquiando y luego no pudo ir a la fiesta. (porque)
_____

11. Síntesis Une las frases para armar oraciones lógicas. `19.A–19.D`

1. Todavía no me _____

2. Sin duda, este último año _____

3. Al buscar mi bolso, me di cuenta de que _____

4. Le pregunté al camarero si _____

5. Me contestó que, cuando ocurrió el hecho, él todavía no _____

6. Hasta ahora, nadie _____

7. Jamás me _____

a. me lo habían robado.

b. había empezado su turno.

c. he sentido tan indefensa como hoy.

d. ha encontrado mi bolso o al ladrón.

e. he tenido mucha mala suerte.

f. he recuperado de esta amarga situación por la que pasé.

g. había visto a alguien sospechoso.

12. Síntesis Completa las oraciones con pretérito perfecto compuesto o pluscuamperfecto. `19.A–19.D`

1. Todavía no _____ (encontrar) al amor de mi vida. ¿Lo encontraré algún día?

2. Siempre _____ (anhelar) tener un carro; pero, ahora que lo tengo, no lo uso.

3. El doctor me dijo que yo _____ (cometer) un error al no consultar antes por mi dolor de espalda.

4. ¿No _____ (terminar) tu tarea todavía? Ya llega el profesor.

5. _____ (dormir, nosotros) todos los días hasta las once de la mañana. Deberíamos despertarnos más temprano.

6. _____ (nevar) muchísimo y por eso no podíamos usar las bicicletas.

7. Ella solamente quería saber si tú _____ (limpiarse) los pies antes de entrar a la casa.

8. Hasta ahora, ya _____ (tomar, yo) cinco clases de salsa.

9. Julián no me _____ (devolver) el libro de matemáticas. Lo llamaré para pedírselo.

10. Todos _____ (imprimir) sus ensayos, ¡pero yo no! Por suerte, corrí a casa y lo imprimí de inmediato.

Practice more at **vhlcentral.com.**

1. Completa las oraciones con el futuro simple. `20.B`

1. El famoso artista _____ (dar) un gran concierto en México.

2. ¿La abuela _____ (cocinar) para nosotros el domingo?

3. ¿Quién me _____ (ayudar) con la mudanza?

4. Los periodistas dicen que el pueblo _____ (elegir) al candidato conservador.

5. Si te comes toda la comida, te _____ (regalar, yo) un riquísimo chocolate.

6. Las reuniones se _____ (cancelar) hasta nuevo aviso.

7. Según los expertos, los precios de los alimentos _____ (subir) un tres por ciento este año.

2. Para cada verbo, indica cuál es la raíz usada para conjugarlo en futuro simple. `20.B`

1. hacer _____
2. salir _____
3. valer _____
4. tener _____
5. venir _____
6. saber _____
7. caber _____
8. poner _____
9. haber _____
10. querer _____

Actividades

3. **Completa el texto con los verbos de la lista conjugados en futuro simple.** `20.B`

> querer   poder   hacer   venir   salir   tener   valer

Cuando sea grande, (1) _____ muchísimo dinero y compraré una casa que (2) _____ millones de dólares. (3) _____ fiestas a las que (4) _____ muchísimas personas de todas partes del mundo. Seré tan famoso que (5) _____ en las portadas de todas las revistas y todos los medios (6) _____ hacerme entrevistas. Pero la gran pregunta es: ¿cómo (7) _____ ganar tanto dinero?

4. **En cada oración, indica por qué se usa el futuro simple.** `20.C`

> a. acciones futuras   b. suposiciones sobre el presente   c. leyes/reglas
> d. suposiciones sobre el futuro e. pronósticos   f. consecuencias en el futuro

1. ¿Quién será esa chica que nos está saludando? _____
2. Seguramente Estela será nuestra profesora de matemáticas este año. _____
3. Si trabajáis mucho, tendréis muy buenas notas. _____
4. Los trabajadores dispondrán de un día de vacaciones por cada veinte días trabajados. _____
5. Este fin de semana, lloverá en el norte del país. _____
6. ¿Volverás a Chile algún día? _____

5. **En estas oraciones, indica por qué se emplea el futuro simple.** `20.C`

1. Creo que mañana entregarán las notas del examen.
   a. suposición sobre el futuro   b. acción en el futuro
2. Las personas de este signo conocerán a mucha gente este año.
   a. predicción   b. consecuencia en el futuro
3. No robarás.
   a. acción en el futuro   b. leyes/reglas
4. No habrá trenes mañana debido a la huelga general.
   a. suposición sobre el presente   b. acción en el futuro
5. Este año iré de vacaciones al Caribe.
   a. acción en el futuro   b. suposición sobre el futuro
6. Alicia estará en la plaza. Ve y fíjate.
   a. suposición sobre el presente   b. suposición sobre el futuro

6. **Une los elementos de las dos columnas para formar oraciones lógicas.** `20.C`

1. Hoy yo _____   a. estaré invitado a la boda?
2. Por favor, tráigame _____ b. un hospital nuevo en 2021.
3. ¿Le compramos _____   c. un vaso de agua.
4. Seré _____   d. penas de hasta ocho años por ese delito.
5. Habrá _____   e. lavo los platos, ¿sí?
6. ¿Yo también _____   f. un regalo?
7. Me llevo _____   g. rico algún día, sin duda.
8. Se construirá _____   h. esa bufanda colorida.

7. En cada oración, indica la opción que refleja el uso más frecuente en español. `20.D`

1. a. Ya empezará la película.
   b. Ya va a empezar la película.

2. a. Llámame más tarde; ahora voy a comer.
   b. Llámame más tarde; ahora comeré.

3. a. ¿Qué harás después del trabajo?
   b. ¿Qué vas a hacer después del trabajo?

4. a. No te apoyes contra la pared recién pintada. Te vas a manchar la ropa.
   b. No te apoyes contra la pared recién pintada. Te mancharás la ropa.

5. a. Apaga tu teléfono celular. Ya empezará la función.
   b. Apaga tu teléfono celular. Ya va a empezar la función.

6. a. Mañana tengo una cita con Cristina.
   b. Mañana tendré una cita con Cristina.

8. Une las oraciones con las explicaciones. `20.D`

_____ 1. ¿Vas a comerte toda la ensalada?

_____ 2. Casi no hay más helado. Si no te apuras, vas a quedarte sin nada.

_____ 3. Mañana a las doce viene la abuela.

_____ 4. Ya vendrá tu madre, no llores más.

_____ 5. Ya van a abrir los negocios.

a. Se describe una acción explicitándose mediante adverbios que tendrá lugar en el futuro.

b. Se expresa una suposición.

c. Se expresa una intención de algo que se hará inmediatamente.

d. Se describe un evento con gran probabilidad de suceder de inmediato.

e. Se describe una acción o un hecho inminente.

9. Completa las oraciones con los verbos conjugados en futuro perfecto. `20.E`

1. El lunes a esta hora, _____ (terminar, nosotros) la mudanza.

2. ¿Dónde _____ (quedar) mi cepillo de dientes? No lo veo por ningún lado.

3. ¿_____ (Haber) disturbios después del partido de fútbol?

4. Si no asistes a las clases de francés, _____ (desperdiciar) el dinero que pagaste.

5. ¡Qué increíble! Dentro de un mes, _____ (graduarse, nosotros).

6. ¿_____ (Llamar) alguien mientras no estuvimos en casa?

7. Mario _____ (cansarse) de esperar. Por eso, se fue sin nosotros.

8. Cuando me vieron con esa camiseta, _____ (pensar) que soy fanático de Boca Juniors.

9. Ana ya _____ (conseguir) entradas. Por eso no te llamó para comprar tu entrada extra.

10. Si trabajais este verano, antes de graduaros ya _____ (obtener) experiencia laboral.

11. Para cuando lleguemos, ya _____ (acabarse) la fiesta.

12. No sé exactamente cuántos kilos de carne compré, pero _____ (comprar) unos cinco o seis kilos.

Actividades

10. En cada oración, elige la opción correcta. `20.F`

1. Ya _____ (comeremos / habremos comido) en cualquier momento.

2. ¿A Lucas le _____ (habrá gustado / gustará) realmente mi regalo? No parecía demasiado sorprendido al abrirlo.

3. Según las encuestas, el candidato liberal _____ (habrá obtenido / obtendrá) un cincuenta por ciento de los votos.

4. ¿Quién _____ (se encargará / se habrá encargado) de la decoración del salón? Es realmente una obra de arte.

5. Según el periódico, mañana _____ (lloverá / habrá llovido) por la tarde.

6. Si haces ejercicio, _____ (tendrás / habrás tenido) una vida más saludable.

7. Creo que _____ (habrá / habrá habido) muchísimo para ver en la exposición de mañana.

8. ¿Dónde _____ (irá / habrá ido) tu hermana? Hace un ratito estaba aquí.

11. Completa las oraciones con el futuro simple o el futuro compuesto. Hay tres verbos que no debes usar. `20.F`

| inventar | dormir | nacer | saber | valer | contar | estar | jugar | venir | subir |

1. ¿Te das cuenta de que dentro de una hora ya _____ más de cuatro horas seguidas? En lugar de eso, deberías estudiar más.

2. ¿Cuánto _____ esa hermosa blusa?

3. ¿_____ tu hermana a cenar? Ya lleva una hora de retraso.

4. Si el doctor está en lo cierto, en agosto _____ tu hermanita; por lo que tendrás compañera de cuarto.

5. ¿Piensas que los precios _____ en diciembre por la Navidad?

6. ¿Vanesa le _____ la verdad a su madre sobre sus malas calificaciones? Yo no lo creo, porque su madre dice a todos que su hija es la mejor alumna de la clase.

7. Si nos acostamos temprano, mañana _____ más descansados.

12. Síntesis Lee el texto y elige la forma verbal más apropiada. `20.B–20.F`

Planes para estas vacaciones

Si todo sale bien, dentro de quince días (1) _____ (estaré / habré estado) en Río de Janeiro, disfrutando de la playa y de la compañía de mis amigos. Pero primero tengo que hacer varias cosas.

Esta semana (2) _____ (tengo / tendré) una reunión con mi jefe para pedirle que me aumente el sueldo y me dé algunos días más de vacaciones. Seguramente me (3) _____ (habrá dicho / dirá) que no al principio; pero después de una hora, (4) _____ (acepta / aceptará) mi pedido. Pensándolo bien, ahora mismo lo (5) _____ (llamaré / voy a llamar) para adelantar la reunión.

La semana que viene ya (6) _____ (habré recibido / recibiré) mi aumento de sueldo y con ese dinero (7) _____ (podré / puedo) comprar los pasajes de avión y los regalos para mis amigos. A Juanita quiero comprarle un libro con fotos de San Francisco; y a Pablo, una camiseta de béisbol. Estoy segura de que (8) _____ (quedarán / van a quedar) boquiabiertos con los regalos.

Por último, espero que el tiempo sea bueno. Según el pronóstico, (9) _____ (habrá llovido / lloverá) muy poco. Espero que así sea, porque de lo contrario (10) _____ (habré gastado / gastaré) muchísimo dinero para estar todo el día dentro del hotel.

Practice more at **vhlcentral.com**.

1. Completa las oraciones con los verbos conjugados en el condicional simple. `21.A`

1. ¿_____ (Tener, tú) una manta de más? No encuentro la mía y tengo frío.

2. Si hiciéramos ejercicio, _____ (poder, nosotros) ir de excursión a las montañas.

3. ¿Te _____ (gustar) venir a cenar a mi casa?

4. Si me preguntaras a mí, no _____ (saber) qué decirte.

5. La mujer policía nos dijo que el tren _____ (pasar) a las 17 horas.

6. ¿Crees que _____ (valer) la pena comprar una bicicleta nueva?

7. _____ (Deber, tú) trabajar menos horas. Luces muy cansado.

8. _____ (Querer) vender mi carro. ¿Cuánto dinero me _____ (dar, usted) por él?

2. Completa las oraciones con los verbos de la lista conjugados en el condicional simple. `21.A`

| saber | vivir | ser | decir | poner | caber | querer | valer |

1. ¿Crees que este sofá _____ en mi habitación?

2. Si supieras la verdad, ¿me la _____?

3. Si tuviera más espacio en el comedor, _____ aquí una mesa para ocho personas.

4. _____ conveniente que no gastaras tanto dinero en tecnología.

5. Constanza _____ tener más tiempo libre para hacer deportes.

6. ¿Crees que tus padres _____ en un pueblo pequeño?

7. Me robaron el canasto de la bicicleta. ¿Quién _____ un canasto tan viejo y roto?

8. ¿_____ acompañarme a la fiesta el viernes? Puedo pasarte a buscar.

9. Si estuviéramos en tu situación, no _____ qué hacer.

10. ¿Crees que _____ la pena invertir en acciones de esa compañía?

11. ¿Qué le _____ a vuestro actor favorito?

12. Acabo de comprar este cuadro y no sé dónde se vería mejor. ¿Usted dónde lo _____?

3. ¿Consejo, suposición o deseo? Decide por qué Juanita usa el condicional presente en estas oraciones. `21.B`

1. ¿Te gustaría que te regalara una planta para tu graduación? _____

2. ¿Cómo le iría a Tamara en su primer día de clases? _____

3. Preferiría quedarme en casa. _____

4. Deberíais ordenar vuestras habitaciones: vendrán los abuelos este fin de semana. _____

5. Sería mejor que llegues temprano. Necesito ayuda en la cocina. _____

6. Se cree que los griegos tendrían un sistema de comunicación eficiente. _____

7. A nosotros nos gustaría pintar la cocina de color verde. ¿Qué te parece la idea? _____

8. Yo en tu lugar, seguiría con las clases de pintura. ¡Eres un genio para las artes! _____

4. Lucas piensa mucho sobre su vida. Completa las oraciones de forma lógica y conjuga el verbo entre paréntesis. `21.B`

1. Si estudiara más español, _____

2. Si tuviera más dinero, _____

3. Si mis amigos fueran más deportistas, _____

4. Si mi madre me diera más libertad, _____

5. Si tuviera videojuegos nuevos, _____

6. Si no tuviera que ir a la escuela tan temprano, _____

7. Si me encontrara con mi banda de música favorita, _____

a. _____ (armar) un equipo de fútbol.

b. _____ (poder) viajar a México.

c. _____ (comprar) más videojuegos.

d. _____ (dormir) más horas.

e. _____ (salir) hasta tarde con mis amigos.

f. _____ (venir) más amigos a visitarme.

g. les _____ (decir) que me encanta su música.

5. Estela le da consejos a su hermanita que está enferma. Completa las oraciones con los verbos conjugados en el condicional simple. `21.B`

> **Modelo**
>
> (mejor / ponerse una bufanda)
> *Sería mejor que te pusieras una bufanda.*

1. (en tu lugar / tomar mucho té)

   _____

2. (yo que tú / quedar en cama)

   _____

3. (deber / dormir más por la noche)

   _____

4. (en tu lugar / ir al médico)

   _____

5. (yo que tú / no tomar medicamentos)

   _____

6. (en tu lugar / estar contenta por no ir a la escuela)

   _____

6. Une las explicaciones sobre el condicional simple con los ejemplos. `21.B`

1. Se usa para expresar deseos. _____

2. Se usa para dar consejos y sugerencias. _____

3. Se usa para expresar cortesía. _____

4. Se usa para expresar duda o probabilidad en el pasado. _____

5. Se usa para expresar un futuro desde un punto de vista pasado. _____

6. Se usa para hacer una invitación. _____

a. No sé a qué hora nos acostamos anoche. Serían las dos de la mañana.

b. Deberías hablar más español que inglés. Así aprenderás más rápido.

c. Me gustaría viajar al Congo.

d. Nos prometiste que nos llamarías al mediodía.

e. ¿Querrías ir al cine conmigo?

f. ¿Te importaría cerrar la ventana?

7. **Completa las oraciones con los verbos conjugados en condicional compuesto.** `21.C`

   1. Si hubiera tenido más tiempo, _____ (hacer) las compras.

   2. Si nos hubiéramos conocido antes, quizás _____ (ser) marido y mujer.

   3. Si Olivia no se hubiera mudado a otro barrio, _____ (compartir) muchas más tardes juntas.

   4. Me _____ (ir) mejor en el examen si me hubiera preparado mejor.

   5. Yo en tu lugar, no _____ (comer) tanto. Ahora te duele la barriga.

   6. Con tu ayuda, _____ (tardar, nosotros) mucho menos en hacer la mudanza.
      ¡Pero no nos ayudaste!

   7. Me _____ (gustar) pasar más tiempo con vosotros; pero tuve que trabajar muchísimo.

8. **Decide si el condicional compuesto se usa para expresar (a)** *una situación imaginaria que contrasta con el presente* o **(b)** *una circunstancia hipotética del pasado.* `21.D`

   1. Sin el cinturón de seguridad, el accidente habría sido mucho más grave. _____

   2. Te habría invitado a la fiesta si hubiera sabido que estabas en la ciudad. _____

   3. Si hubiera estado en tu lugar, yo habría visitado más museos. _____

   4. Me aseguraste que, para esta fecha, tendrías el trabajo terminado. _____

   5. Si Pamela hubiera llevado una vianda para el viaje, no habría tenido
      que pagar ocho dólares por un chocolate. _____

   6. Si Pedro hubiera sabido que estaba enferma, me habría llamado. _____

   7. Seguramente tú habrías cenado en casa si sabías que había comida. _____

9. **Escoge la forma correcta del verbo en el aviso publicitario.** `21.D`

   ¿Qué (1) _____ (pasaría / habría pasado) si usted hubiera sabido los números de la pasada lotería de Navidad? ¿Se imagina cómo habría sido su vida? Piense cuántas casas (2) _____ (compraría / habría comprado) con ese dinero.

   Pero, claro, usted jamás (3) _____ (ganaría / habría ganado) la lotería porque no tenía... ¡la fabulosa BOLA DE CRISTAL®! El revolucionario producto que adivina el futuro.

   Usted que ahora está solo, si hubiera tenido la BOLA DE CRISTAL®, (4) _____ (sabría / habría sabido) dónde encontrar al amor de su vida. ¡Incluso (5) _____ (habría tenido / tendría) al alcance de su mano todas las técnicas para conquistarlo!

   Por eso, no siga perdiendo el tiempo. Deje atrás su pasado lleno de tristezas ¡y compre ya la BOLA DE CRISTAL®! ¡Debería (6) _____ (haberlo hecho / hacerlo) hace tiempo!

   Llame ya al teléfono que aparece en pantalla y termine con sus incertidumbres.

10. **Síntesis Completa las oraciones con los verbos conjugados en condicional simple o condicional compuesto, según corresponda.** `21.A–21.D`

    1. Si hubieras llevado el teléfono móvil, no _____ (tener, nosotros) este desencuentro.

    2. Si fuera de vacaciones a Chile, me _____ (gustar) conocer Valparaíso.

    3. Yo te _____ (regalar) otro libro si hubiera sabido que este ya lo tenías.

    4. Con un mayor control del tránsito, la gente _____ (conducir) a la velocidad permitida.

    5. ¿_____ (Votar) a ese candidato si hubieras sabido que solamente decía mentiras?

    6. ¿_____ (Votar, tú) de nuevo por Justo Juárez si se presentara a elecciones?

    7. Tú _____ (deber) dicho la verdad desde un principio, las cosas serían más claras entre nosotros ahora. ¡Pero no lo son!

11. Síntesis En cada oración, elige la opción correcta. `21.A–21.D`

1. No te preocupes, de todas maneras, ellos no _____ nuestra propuesta. Tenían muchas otras mejores.
   a. habrían aceptado   b. aceptarían

2. ¿_____ volver a casa ahora o más tarde? Haremos lo que tú quieras.
   a. Habrías preferido   b. Preferirías

3. Si me hubieras avisado, _____ una comida vegetariana.
   a. habría cocinado   b. cocinaría

4. ¿_____ estudiar más tiempo español antes de ir a Guatemala? Yo creo que fue el momento ideal para ti.
   a. Habrías preferido   b. Preferirías

5. Si hubiera sabido que dormías, no _____ la puerta.
   a. habría tocado   b. tocaría

6. Otra vez llegamos tarde. _____ menos en metro.
   a. Tardaríamos   b. Habríamos tardado

7. Supe que _____ una exposición de tu pintor favorito y corrí a decírtelo.
   a. habría   b. habría habido

8. ¡_____ prestarte dinero si tanta falta te hacía!
   a. Podría   b. Habría podido

9. ¿Dónde _____ Natalia ayer por la tarde? No estaba en la oficina.
   a. estaría   b. habría estado

12. Síntesis Decide si debes usar el condicional simple o el condicional compuesto. `21.A–21.D`

1. Si supieras el esfuerzo que me costó aprender español, ¡no _____ (decir) que hablo mal!

2. ¿Te _____ (gustar) casarte conmigo? ¡Te amo tanto!

3. Nuestras mascotas _____ (ser) más obedientes si les hubiéramos enseñado modales a tiempo.

4. ¿_____ (ser) posible reservar una habitación para dos personas?

5. Las autoridades confirmaron que _____ (solucionar) la crisis energética para comienzos de 2019.

6. ¿Cuánto crees que _____ (valer) el alquiler de un apartamento como este?

7. Con una buena política de salud, este invierno _____ (haber) menos enfermos de gripe. Pero como ves, no fue así.

8. En tu lugar, yo no _____ (escribir) en los bancos de la escuela. Ahora te castigarán por ello.

13. Síntesis Explica qué habrías hecho tú en estas situaciones. Usa las frases de la lista. `21.A–21.D`

| echarle la culpa a otro camarero | llamar al cerrajero |
| pedir disculpas | decirle que la pintura era buena |

1. _____ 2. _____ 3. _____ 4. _____

_____

Practice more at **vhlcentral.com.**

1. Lee el texto e indica si los verbos subrayados están en modo indicativo (I) o subjuntivo (S). `22.A`

Querida Lucía:

Te escribo porque (1) _____ tengo un gran dilema. (2) _____ Me gustaría tener una mascota, ya sea un gato o un perro. Probablemente (3) _____ busque un gato, porque son más independientes y no (4) _____ necesitan tanto cuidado.

En todo caso, dudo que mis padres (5) _____ acepten mi propuesta. Por eso, (6) _____ voy a buscar la forma de convencerlos. ¿Se te (7) _____ ocurren buenos argumentos que (8) _____ puedan convencerlos?

También pensé en llegar un día a casa con un gato o perro sin hacer muchas preguntas antes. Pero no (9) _____ quiero que mi mamá (10) _____ se enoje y (11) _____ me grite durante todo un día. ¿Qué (12) _____ me recomiendas que (13) _____ haga? Quiero tener una mascota y sé que (14) _____ podré hacerme cargo de ella.

Hasta pronto,
Raúl

2. Completa las oraciones con los verbos de la lista conjugados en presente de subjuntivo. `22.B`

ladrar   escribir   vivir   correr   desempeñarse   charlar   transmitir

1. El entrenador espera que el equipo _____ mejor en este partido.
2. Por más que _____ (tú), no podrás escaparte de mí.
3. ¿Hay algún canal de televisión que _____ el partido en directo?
4. Me gustaría que _____ (nosotros) con más tranquilidad.
5. ¿Conoces algún animal que _____ más de cien años?
6. La dueña del apartamento no quiere un perro que _____ si está solo.
7. Mi hermana me pide siempre que le _____ un correo electrónico cada semana.

3. Silvina le explica a su amiga las actividades que deben hacer para la próxima clase. Completa las oraciones siguiendo el modelo. `22.B`

> **Modelo**
>
> **PROFESORA** Mañana deberán llegar temprano a clase.
> **SILVINA** La profesora quiere que *mañana lleguemos temprano a clase.*

1. **PROFESORA** Deberán aprender de memoria el himno nacional.
   SILVINA La profesora quiere que _____.
2. **PROFESORA** Cada uno pasará al frente y lo cantará.
   SILVINA Ella quiere que cada uno _____.
3. **PROFESORA** Si lo desean, pueden cantar el himno en parejas.
   SILVINA Nos ha permitido que _____.
4. **PROFESORA** No deberán cometer ni un solo error al cantar la letra.
   SILVINA Ella no admitirá que _____.
5. **PROFESORA** Posiblemente la directora los escuchará cantar.
   SILVINA Dijo que es posible que _____.
6. **PROFESORA** Si todo sale bien, los mejores cantantes formarán parte del coro.
   SILVINA Ella espera que _____.

4. **Completa las oraciones con el verbo conjugado en presente de subjuntivo.** `22.B`

   1. Antes de que _____ (empezar) la función, deberán apagar sus teléfonos móviles.

   2. Es mejor que tú _____ (escoger) el regalo que prefieras. No conozco realmente tus gustos.

   3. Espero que el pueblo _____ (elegir) bien a su futuro presidente.

   4. Tu padre y yo no queremos que tus amigos _____ (seguir) llamando a la hora de comer.

   5. Los profesores nos recomiendan que _____ (buscar, nosotros) la bibliografía en sitios de Internet confiables.

   6. Estela no cree que Julia _____ (tener) las llaves de nuestra casa. ¿Quién podría tenerlas entonces?

   7. Los jueces no permiten que sus vidas privadas _____ (influir) en sus trabajos.

   8. Una posibilidad es que _____ (dedicarse) a dar clases de matemáticas. Así podrás ganar dinero extra.

5. **Completa la nota que escribió Renata a su hermanita menor con los verbos conjugados en presente de subjuntivo.** `22.B`

   | destruir | cargar | agregar | salir | seguir | apagar | conseguir | alcanzar | tocar |

   Querida hermanita:

   Sé que ya sabes cómo cuidar a mi tortuga, pero quiero asegurarme de que todo (1) _____ bien.

   Ante todo, te ruego que no (2) _____ el plato de Manuelita con demasiada lechuga. Ella come muy poco. Otra cosa importante: te sugiero que (3) _____ agua fresca al bebedero todas las mañanas.

   Recuerda que a ella no le gusta que la (4) _____ demasiado. No es muy cariñosa y además se asusta cuando viene alguien nuevo. Por la noche, es mejor que (5) _____ la luz, así ella duerme mejor.

   Sobre las puertas, mantenlas cerradas para que ella no (6) _____ las plantas que me regaló la abuela. Sé que quizás exagero, pero no quiero que Manuelita (7) _____ esas plantas con flores tan lindas.

   Ojalá que (8) _____ recordar todo lo que te expliqué y te agradezco muchísimo tu ayuda. Sé que es mucho pedir que (9) _____ mis instrucciones al pie de la letra, pero sabes que Manuelita es como mi hija y quiero que siempre esté bien.

   ¡Nos vemos el lunes!
   Renata

6. **Conjuga estos verbos irregulares en presente de subjuntivo en la persona indicada.** `22.B`

   Modelo

   salir – 1.ª persona del singular: *salga*

   1. traer – 2.ª persona del singular _____
   2. insinuar – 3.ª persona del plural _____
   3. enviar – 3.ª persona del singular _____
   4. guiar – 1.ª persona del plural _____
   5. conocer – 1.ª persona del singular _____
   6. decir – 3.ª persona del singular _____
   7. valer – 3.ª persona del plural _____
   8. tener – 2.ª persona del plural _____

7. **Completa las oraciones con los verbos que sean irregulares o tengan cambios ortográficos en presente de subjuntivo.** `22.B`

oír	mencionar	conducir	prestar	escuchar	decir
agrandar	evaluar	poner	ampliar	determinar	manejar

1. Ojalá _____ (ellos) esta carretera. Es muy angosta y hay muchos accidentes de tránsito.

2. Es mejor que le _____ al pintor que vienes de parte mía. Así te hará un descuento.

3. Esperemos que el gobierno pronto _____ los daños producidos por la catástrofe y _____ en marcha un plan de recuperación de los bosques quemados.

4. No estoy seguro de que la abuela _____ bien la música. Quizás deberíamos subir el volumen.

5. Necesito que _____ atención a lo que te digo.

6. Te prohíbo que _____ a una velocidad mayor a la permitida.

8. **Juancito contradice siempre a su amiga, Teresa. Completa lo que dice, siguiendo el modelo.** `22.B`

> **Modelo**
>
> **TERESA** Las clases comenzarán a las doce.
> **JUANCITO** No es verdad que *las clases comiencen a las doce.*

1. **TERESA** Empieza a estudiar veinte días antes del examen.
   JUANCITO No es necesario que _____.

2. **TERESA** Te contaré una historia increíble.
   JUANCITO No quiero que me _____.

3. **TERESA** Seguramente la comida costará unos veinte dólares.
   JUANCITO No creo que _____.

4. **TERESA** Llueve muchísimo.
   JUANCITO No puede ser que _____.

5. **TERESA** Te despertaré a las nueve con el desayuno.
   JUANCITO No quiero que me _____.

6. **TERESA** Probablemente te devolveré los libros a fin de mes.
   JUANCITO Es poco probable que me _____.

9. **Reescribe las oraciones usando la persona indicada entre paréntesis.** `22.B`

1. Es mejor que no pensemos en cosas negativas.
   (yo) _____

2. Cuando descendáis las escaleras, veréis a la derecha una gran puerta. Esa es la cocina.
   (tú) _____

3. Los profesores no pretenden que entiendas todo el texto; solo la idea principal.
   (nosotros) _____

4. La niña insiste en que sus padres le cuenten un cuento cada noche.
   (vos) _____

5. Haremos todo lo que podamos para recaudar dinero para los pobres.
   (tú) _____

6. Quiero que oláis el nuevo perfume que me compré.
   (tú) _____

10. **Completa las oraciones con los verbos de la lista.** `22.B`

> dormir (2)   morir   divertirse   herir   preferir

1. Es posible que Lucas _____ volver a casa más temprano. Mejor dale las llaves a él.

2. Quiero que _____ tiempo suficiente, así podréis estar atentos en el seminario de mañana.

3. Le pusimos un bozal al perro para que no _____ a los niños.

4. Ojalá que _____ en la fiesta de Guido.

5. Otra posibilidad es que _____ (nosotros) en una tienda de campaña. Creo que sería lo más económico.

6. El día que mi perro _____ será el día más triste de mi vida.

11. **Completa las tablas con los verbos conjugados en presente de subjuntivo.** `22.B`

Pronombre	adquirir	jugar
yo	(1)	juegue
tú, vos	(2)	(6)
usted, él, ella	(3)	(7)
nosotros/as	(4)	juguemos
vosotros/as	adquiráis	(8)
ustedes, ellos/as	(5)	(9)

12. **Construye oraciones negativas usando el presente de subjuntivo.** `22.B`

> **Modelo**
>
> Creo que Juan tiene miedo a las arañas.
> No creo que Juan *tenga miedo a las arañas.*

1. Me parece que llueve.

   No me parece que _____.

2. La policía piensa que el asesino todavía está en los alrededores de la escena del crimen.

   La policía no piensa que _____.

3. Creo que Luis recuerda el día en que nos conocimos.

   No creo que Luis _____.

4. Estoy segura de que ellos prefieren ir de vacaciones a la playa.

   No estoy segura de que ellos _____.

5. Sandra se sabe de memoria toda la lección.

   No creo que Sandra _____.

6. Creo que hoy llego a tiempo para ver la telenovela.

   No creo que _____.

7. Me parece que Juan y Carlos van a venir a la fiesta.

   No creo que _____.

8. Estoy segura que vosotros podéis participar en el evento.

   No creo que _____.

13. Completa el artículo con los verbos conjugados en presente de subjuntivo. `22.B`

| adquirir | divertirse | enfriarse | volver | pensar | guiar | costar | organizar | querer | dormir |

"Acampar es incómodo"

Aquí ofrecemos consejos sobre cómo acampar, justamente para quienes (1) _____ que acampar es un sufrimiento.

- Es importante que realmente (2) _____ (ustedes) ir de campamento. Ir a regañadientes (*reluctantly*) o porque no tienen reserva de hotel es un mal comienzo.

- Si eligen un campamento libre, hablen con un guardaparques que los (3) _____ y siempre tengan a mano un mapa de la zona.

- Les recomendamos que (4) _____ (ustedes) un equipamiento adecuado para el clima del lugar al que vayan. Quizás el equipo (5) _____ más de lo que habían presupuestado; pero un equipamiento bueno es siempre una buena inversión.

- Es fundamental que (6) _____ (ustedes) el campamento: separar las áreas donde comerán, dormirán o descansarán.

- Cuando (7) _____ (ustedes), les recomendamos abrigarse bien la cabeza y los pies. No queremos que estas zonas (8) _____, porque luego es muy difícil recuperar el calor.

Esperamos que (9) _____ (ustedes) en su próximo campamento ¡y que (10) _____ (ustedes) a hacerlo una y otra vez!

14. Indica qué oraciones incluyen verbos conjugados en pretérito imperfecto de subjuntivo. Subráyalos. `22.C`

1. Espero que la temperatura sea agradable este fin de semana. No quiero llevar mucho abrigo.

2. Me pareció raro que no te comieras toda tu comida.

3. Me gustaría que hablásemos a solas sobre este tema.

4. Si los trabajadores pidieran un aumento de sueldo, con gusto se lo daría.

5. Es mejor que no haya postre. Ya comimos demasiado.

6. ¡Ojalá pudiéramos ir de vacaciones a Cusco este verano!

7. No creo que sepas todas las respuestas. ¡Solamente el profesor las sabe!

8. Te pedí que te cambiases la camisa. ¡Esa está sucia!

15. El pretérito imperfecto de subjuntivo tiene dos formas. Escribe junto a cada verbo las dos formas correspondientes a la primera persona del singular. `22.C`

1. subir _____ _____
2. pedir _____ _____
3. caber _____ _____
4. ser _____ _____
5. poner _____ _____
6. lastimar _____ _____
7. hacer _____ _____

8. concluir _____ _____
9. desear _____ _____
10. querer _____ _____
11. poseer _____ _____
12. decir _____ _____
13. ir _____ _____

16. Completa las oraciones con los verbos conjugados en pretérito imperfecto de subjuntivo. `22.C`

1. Si yo _____ (hablar) quechua, podría ser traductor en una comunidad indígena.

2. ¡Cómo me gustaría que _____ (viajar, nosotros) a la India!

3. Hasta ayer necesitaba un empleado que _____ (trabajar) por las tardes.

4. Habíamos preparado todo para que los agasajados _____ (sorprenderse) al entrar.

5. Compré comida para que _____ (cocinar, nosotros) juntos.

6. Fue fundamental para el rescate que los bomberos _____ (llegar) de inmediato.

17. Conjuga estos verbos en pretérito imperfecto de subjuntivo. `22.C`

1. divertir (yo) _____

2. saber (nosotros) _____

3. tener (ellos) _____

4. caer (vosotros) _____

5. leer (tú) _____

6. producir (ella) _____

7. ser (ustedes) _____

8. distribuir (ellos) _____

9. dar (yo) _____

10. hacer (él) _____

18. Reescribe las oraciones usando el pretérito imperfecto de subjuntivo. `22.C`

1. Te pido que me prestes atención.
   Te pedí que _____.

2. Podemos ir al cine si realmente quieres.
   Podríamos ir al cine si realmente _____.

3. Te llamo para que me incluyas en tu lista de invitados.
   Te llamé para _____

4. No quiero que destruyan ese edificio antiguo tan hermoso.
   No quería _____

5. Me alegra que puedas venir a nuestra fiesta.
   Me alegró _____

6. Quiero que te sientas como en casa.
   Quería que _____

7. Julia nos recomienda que tengamos cuidado con nuestros bolsos.
   Julia nos recomendó _____

8. Le recomiendo que vaya a esa panadería y que pruebe las galletas de limón.
   Le recomendé _____

19. Escribe los verbos en pretérito perfecto de subjuntivo. `22.D`

1. tardar (ellos) _____

2. ser (nosotros) _____

3. compartir (vosotros) _____

4. pedir (ustedes) _____

5. beber (yo) _____

6. escribir (tú) _____

7. probar (ella) _____

8. descubrir (nosotros) _____

9. traducir (ellos) _____

10. jugar (vos) _____

20. Completa las oraciones conjugando los verbos en el pretérito perfecto de subjuntivo. `22.D`

1. No es verdad que _____ (querer) leer tu diario íntimo. Jamás lo haríamos.

2. Nos alegra tanto que _____ (venir, ustedes).

3. Esperamos que _____ (pasar, usted) un día estupendo en nuestro spa.

4. No dudo que Julieta _____ (preguntar) por Martín. Todos sabemos que ella está enamorada de él.

5. En mi familia no hay nadie que _____ (divorciarse).

6. Verás que la escuela te parecerá más fácil una vez que _____ (aprobar) los primeros exámenes.

21. Indica qué oraciones incluyen verbos conjugados en pretérito pluscuamperfecto de subjuntivo. Subráyalos. `22.E`

1. Si hubieras llegado temprano a casa, no te habrías perdido el exquisito postre que hizo Camila.

2. No sabía que hoy era tu cumpleaños.

3. Cuando hayan aprendido todas las palabras, les haré una pequeña prueba.

4. Entre mis amigos, no encontré a nadie que hubiera ido a Quito.

5. Me habría bastado con que me hubieras mandado un mensaje de texto. Estuve esperándote dos horas bajo la lluvia.

6. Si hubiésemos salido antes, no habríamos perdido el tren.

7. No pensé que hubieses disfrutado la fiesta tanto como yo.

8. Nunca pensé que pudiese haber tanta gente allí.

9. Te habría invitado a la fiesta si hubiera sabido que ya habías vuelto de tu viaje.

22. Completa las oraciones con el verbo conjugado en el pretérito pluscuamperfecto de subjuntivo. `22.E`

1. Si tan solo _____ (saber) que querías ir a la playa, te habría invitado.

2. Si _____ (conocer) antes a tu hermana, la habría invitado a mi casamiento.

3. ¡Ojalá _____ (poder, nosotros) trabajar en esta escuela!

4. Si vosotros _____ (subir) a la torre, habríais visto toda la ciudad.

5. Si _____ (cerrar, tú) la puerta, el gato no se habría escapado.

6. En toda la universidad no encontré a dos profesores que _____ (graduarse) después de 1990.

23. Completa las oraciones conjugando los verbos en el tiempo verbal indicado. `22.F–22.G`

1. Cualquiera _____ (ser) la nacionalidad de los turistas, se deberán solicitar los pasaportes en todos los casos. (futuro del subjuntivo)

2. Se tendrán en cuenta aquellos currículos que se _____ (recibir) antes del 20 de agosto. (futuro perfecto del subjuntivo)

3. A donde _____ (ir), haz lo que _____ (ver). (futuro del subjuntivo)

4. Quien _____ (tener) algo en contra de esta unión, ya no podrá evitarla. (futuro perfecto del subjuntivo)

5. Sea quien _____ (ser) el culpable de este delito, deberá pagar por ello. (futuro del subjuntivo)

24. **Síntesis** Identifica los verbos en subjuntivo e indica en qué tiempo están conjugados. `22.A–22.H`

1. Que te haya invitado a comer a casa no significa que no tengas que ayudarme a cocinar. _____

2. Vaya a donde fuere, el fantasma de mis pesadillas me persigue. _____

3. Ojalá nos divirtamos en la casa de Paula. _____

4. Hicimos muchísimo para que todo saliera tal como lo planeamos. _____

5. Si tu hermana nos pidiera ayuda, seríamos los primeros en ayudarla. _____

6. Hicimos comidas sin carne para que los vegetarianos pudiesen disfrutar del banquete. _____

7. Me pareció tan extraño que Tamara no fuera a clase. _____

8. Quien hubiere desobedecido a las autoridades será castigado con ocho años de prisión. _____

9. Por más que hayas sido elegido como mejor compañero, deberás estudiar muchísimo para pasar de año. _____

🪄 Practice more at **vhlcentral.com.**

Use of the subjunctive 🍃   **Chapter 23**

1. **Completa las oraciones con los verbos de la lista conjugados en subjuntivo.** `23.B`

cambiar	cumplir
avisar	venir
divertir	llegar
regalar	reconciliarse

1. ¡Que te _____ muchísimo en la fiesta!

2. ¡Ojalá me _____ la muñeca que tanto quiero! Creo que ellos ya saben qué quiero.

3. ¡Ojalá nos _____ antes sobre el retraso del tren! Habríamos aprovechado para ver más la ciudad.

4. ¡Que _____ muchísimos años más, hermanita!

5. Posiblemente _____ de visita la tía Carolina. Ábrele la puerta, ¿sí?

6. Quizás el gobierno _____ su política económica en los próximos años.

7. Ojalá que _____ . Hacen muy buena pareja.

8. Posiblemente (nosotros) _____ tarde mañana a causa del tráfico.

2. **Une las frases para formar oraciones lógicas.** `23.B`

1. Ojalá Roberto no traiga postre de chocolate; ____   a. así que yo no compraré nada.
2. Ojalá Roberto no hubiera traído una tarta de limón: ____   b. de la cena que hice.
3. Probablemente Roberto compre algo de postre, ____   c. el que trajo la torta de naranja.
4. Quizás fuera Roberto ____   d. siempre estar conmigo.
5. Ojalá Roberto haya disfrutado ____   e. yo ya compré uno.
6. Ojalá Roberto disfrute ____   f. me la comí toda y ahora me duele la barriga.

3. Sofía le da consejos a su amiga Elena. Escribe oraciones siguiendo el modelo. `23.C`

> **Modelo**
>
> Estudia después de cada clase. (insistir)
> *Insisto en que estudies después de cada clase.*

1. Sé puntual. (sugerir)
   _____

2. Ayuda a tus compañeros. (aconsejar)
   _____

3. Siempre haz los ejercicios de matemáticas. (recomendar)
   _____

4. Llámame por la tarde si tienes preguntas. (pedir)
   _____

5. ¡Presta atención a mis consejos! (rogar)
   _____

6. Recuerda todo lo que te digo. (necesitar)
   _____

4. Completa las oraciones con un elemento de cada lista. `23.C`

que	elegir
el que	retrasarse
es que	tener
hace que	aprobar
el hecho de que	bajar

1. La huelga del transporte _____ todos los vuelos _____.
2. _____ no _____ el examen no es excusa para bajar los brazos. ¡Te queda medio año por delante!
3. _____ te _____ "mejor compañero" habla muy bien de ti.
4. _____ _____ los precios no es algo muy frecuente en este país.
5. No _____ yo _____ poco dinero, es que todo aquí es muy caro.

5. Lee estas oraciones y decide si en cada caso se expresa deseo o se brinda información. `23.C`

1. Agustina insistió en que le trajeran un café. _____
2. Manuela le gritó a su hermana que se quedara tranquila. _____
3. Mi novia insiste en que soy el chico más lindo del mundo. _____
4. El policía me indicó que estacionara. _____
5. Las autoridades afirmaron que los pasajeros están a salvo. _____
6. Insisto en que me dejen hablar con un abogado. _____
7. Te advierto que no me hagas enojar. _____
8. Mi padre sostiene que él tiene la razón. _____

6. Reescribe las oraciones siguiendo el modelo. `23.C`

> **Modelo**
>
> ¿Te visitan tus padres? ¡Cuánto me alegra!
> *Me alegra que te visiten tus padres.*

1. ¿Te robaron la maleta? ¡Qué indignante! _____

2. ¿Estás fumando? ¡Cómo me molesta! _____

3. ¿Los vecinos están haciendo una fiesta? ¡Cómo me enfada eso! _____

4. ¿Has perdido el tren? ¡Cuánto lo lamento! _____

5. ¿Has ganado la lotería? ¡Qué sorpresa! _____

7. En cada oración, elige la opción correcta. `23.C`

1. Ya no oímos cuando _____ los vecinos. Usamos protectores en los oídos por la noche.
   a. griten   b. gritan

2. Temo que la inyección me _____. ¡Mira lo grande que es la aguja!
   a. duele   b. dolerá

3. Esperaba con ansias a que me _____ sobre la beca.
   a. contestan   b. contestaran

4. Creo que la camarera _____ muy amable.
   a. es   b. sea

5. No pienso que la profesora nos _____ buenas notas.
   a. da   b. dé

6. Parece como si _____ ocho grados bajo cero.
   a. hace   b. hiciera

7. ¿Piensas que _____ mejor esperar a que bajen los precios?
   a. es   b. sea

8. Presiento que esto _____ en un gran problema pronto.
   a. se convierta   b. se convertirá

8. Fabián es un chico que lo cuestiona todo. Completa las oraciones con los verbos conjugados en indicativo o subjuntivo según corresponda. `23.C`

1. Desconfío de que me _____ (has contado / hayas contado) la verdad sobre tus calificaciones.

2. Pero no dudo en absoluto que _____ (seas/eres) una buena persona.

3. Aunque no niego que _____ (haya pensado / he pensado) lo contrario.

4. Es cierto también que esto ya _____ (ha sucedido / haya sucedido) antes.

5. No hay certeza alguna de que _____ (vayas/vas) a cambiar de actitud.

6. Pero, al fin y al cabo, estoy convencido de que nuestra amistad _____ (sobreviva/sobrevivirá) a este conflicto.

7. Te aconsejo que _____ (dejas/dejes) de fumar.

8. Admito que no _____ (haya leído / he leído) ese libro.

9. Fue muy importante que nos _____ (dijeras/dijiste) la verdad.

10. Estoy muy acostumbrada a que los vecinos _____ (hagan/hacen) mucho ruido.

9. **Tomás critica la forma de actuar de sus compañeros de grupo. Completa las oraciones con los verbos conjugados en subjuntivo.** `23.C`

De:	tomasito@email.com
Para:	leandroj@email.com, vanesam@email.com
Asunto:	El trabajo en grupo

Fue increíble que se (1) _____ (comportar) de esa manera la clase pasada. No es justo que yo siempre (2) _____ (tener) que hacer las tareas por ustedes. ¡Es terrible que (3) _____ (pensar) de esa manera!

Tú, Leandro. Fue un error que no (4) _____ (venir) a la reunión del sábado pasado. No era el trato que solo un miembro del grupo (5) _____ (trabajar) por todos. Está bien que ahora (6) _____ (querer) compensar tu error, pero ya es demasiado tarde.

Y tú, Vanesa, ¿acaso estás acostumbrada a que la gente te (7) _____ (esperar)? Estoy harto de que (8) _____ (llegar) tarde a todas las reuniones.

A los dos, les repito lo que ya les dije la semana pasada: más vale que (9) _____ (cambiar) de actitud. Me da igual que la profesora los (10) _____ (desaprobar): si esto no cambia, le contaré todo.

10. **Une las frases para formar oraciones lógicas.** `23.C`

1. Queríamos _____
2. Te aconsejamos _____
3. A tus padres les ha molestado _____
4. A los empleados les molesta _____
5. Es la tercera vez que les pido _____
6. Ayer Julio nos pidió dos veces _____
7. La lluvia les impidió _____

a. que no hayamos limpiado la casa después de la reunión.
b. que no descuides tu bolso.
c. que limpien la sala después de usarla.
d. ir de excursión a la montaña.
e. ir al cine y ver la película nueva de vampiros.
f. que los clientes no saluden al entrar.
g. que no habláramos muy alto.

11. **Reescribe las oraciones usando *lo + adjetivo/adverbio* y *lo que*.** `23.C`

1. Pasa a buscarme tú. Eso es lo lógico.

_____

2. Eres realmente hermosa. Eso es lo cierto.

_____

3. La gente es simpática. Eso es lo más común.

_____

4. El tren llegó a horario. Eso fue lo más normal.

_____

5. Por suerte, no nos robaron. Eso habría sido lo peor.

_____

6. El sistema de transporte funciona muy mal. Eso es lo que veo.

_____

7. Has aprobado el examen. Eso es lo bueno.

_____

8. Escribes inglés perfectamente aunque no es tu primer idioma. Eso es lo más interesante.

_____

12. Para cada oración, elige la opción correcta. `23.D`

1. La junta directiva elegirá a un delegado que es muy responsable.
   a. La junta también tomará en cuenta la experiencia de los candidatos en esa área.
   b. Se llama Juan Carlos Gómez y tiene experiencia en esa área.

2. Buscamos un sillón que tenga dos metros de largo.
   a. En el comedor, no nos entraría uno más grande.
   b. Lo vimos la semana pasada en un catálogo.

3. Los niños quieren un muñeco que dice frases en español.
   a. Se llama "Sr. Caballín", pero no lo encuentro en ninguna juguetería.
   b. Les compraré el primero que vea.

4. Te llevaré a un museo donde haya una exposición de arte.
   a. He estado allí antes y he visto exposiciones súper interesantes.
   b. Seguramente encontraremos uno por aquí cerca.

5. Necesito un diccionario que tenga imágenes.
   a. Lo vi en Internet y ahora no recuerdo el nombre.
   b. Creo que me ayudaría a memorizar las palabras más rápido.

13. En cada oración, elige la opción correcta. `23.D`

1. _____ (Jamás/Siempre) he sido una alumna que tiene buenas notas.

2. _____ (En ninguna parte / En muchas partes) del mundo hay aeropuertos donde se pueda fumar.

3. En tu casa _____ (no había / había) un par de cuadros que me encantaban.

4. _____ (No existe nadie / Existe alguien) que pueda resolver este acertijo.

5. Quiero una bufanda. Cómprame _____ (cualquiera/una) que cuesta menos de 8 dólares y que vi ayer en la vidriera.

6. Contrata a cualquiera que _____ (pueda trabajar / puede trabajar) los fines de semana.

7. Busco a la persona que _____ (quiera/quiere) alquilar mi habitación. Su nombre es Manuel, pero no recuerdo su apellido.

14. Completa las oraciones con los verbos conjugados en indicativo o subjuntivo. `23.C–23.D`

1. Lo que _____ (decidir) Marta será respetado por todos.

2. Ahora lo que más _____ (necesitar, nosotros) es un buen colchón.

3. A mi cumpleaños estarán invitados los que me _____ (llamar) para saludarme.

4. Quienes _____ (hacer) la reserva del asiento tienen una plaza asegurada.

5. Lo que no me conviene es que _____ (subir) la tasa de interés.

6. Lo que más nos gusta es que nos _____ (regalar) videojuegos.

7. Quienes te _____ (acabar) de saludar son los vecinos del primer piso.

8. Me gustaría tener una casa que _____ (tener) una piscina climatizada en la sala, pero no creo que exista.

9. Nunca he conocido a nadie que le _____ (gustar) comer comida picante en el desayuno.

10. En Argentina, no había comida que me _____ (encantar) más que el asado.

15. Reescribe las oraciones siguiendo el modelo. `23.D`

> **Modelo**
>
> Necesito un par de tijeras que corten bien.
> Jamás he tenido *un par de tijeras que hayan cortado bien.*

1. Busco a un hombre que sea cariñoso.
   Buscaba _____.

2. Quiero estudiar una profesión que me haga feliz.
   Habría querido _____.

3. Necesito un par de lentes que cuesten menos de 90 dólares.
   Necesitaba _____.

4. Quiero tener amigos que sean sociables.
   Habría querido _____.

5. Busco un libro que sea en inglés.
   Buscaba _____.

16. Une los elementos de las tres columnas para formar oraciones lógicas. `23.E`

1. Nos encontraremos en un bar	como	podamos conectarnos a Internet.
2. Dinos un nombre	cuanto	la dejó el conserje.
3. Estaré en la plaza	en el que	tú quieras.
4. Haz las cosas	donde	quieren.
5. Ellos comen	que	te guste mucho.
6. Busca la maleta	en la que	nos conocimos.

17. Reescribe las oraciones usando la conjunción entre paréntesis. `23.E`

1. Juan Manuel habla castellano como un español. (como si fuera)
   _____

2. Hice la tarea y nadie me ayudó. (sin que)
   _____

3. Si no llegas a horario, me habré ido. (como)
   _____

4. Dado que no tienes dinero, te prestaré un poco. (como)
   _____

5. ¡Ni loca te presto dinero! (ni que)
   _____

18. Lee la carta de Joaquín y elige la opción correcta. `23.E`

Querida Alicia:

¿Cómo estás? Luego de (1) _____ (que reciba/recibir) tu mensaje de texto, me quedé un poco preocupado. Imagínate que, tan pronto como lo (2) _____ (leyera/leí), corrí hasta este cibercafé para comunicarme contigo.

¿Estás más tranquila? ¡Qué mala suerte con estos ladrones! Pero cuántas veces te dije que, cada vez que (3) _____ (camines/caminas) por el centro, lleves tu bolso delante de ti. Estas son las cosas que pasan cuando (4) _____ (descuidas/descuides) tus pertenencias. Te recomiendo que vayas a la comisaría ya mismo. Después de que (5) _____ (hagas/haces) la denuncia, la policía comenzará a buscar tus documentos. Hasta que (6) _____ (recuperes/recuperas) tu pasaporte, usa tu documento de identidad mexicano. Por favor, apenas (7) _____ (lees/leas) mi mensaje, llámame por teléfono.

Un abrazo,
Joaquín

19. Completa las oraciones con las conjunciones de la lista. `23.E`

| tanto que | a causa de que | para | tan … que | porque (2) | a fin de que |

1. Ando en bicicleta no _____ me guste, sino _____ no perjudica el medio ambiente.

2. _____ no haya desempleo, el gobierno puso en marcha un plan de generación de puestos de trabajo.

3. Llovía _____ no pudimos ir al concierto.

4. La probabilidad de ganar el concurso no es _____ baja _____ debamos desanimarnos.

5. _____ perdimos el autobús, ahora tenemos que esperar dos horas.

6. Tengo que pedir un crédito _____ comprar la casa.

20. Reescribe las oraciones usando la conjunción entre paréntesis. `23.E`

1. No tengo hambre, pero comeré una porción de pizza. (si bien)

   _____

2. No me invitaron a la fiesta. De todas maneras, no habría ido a esa fiesta. (aunque)

   _____

3. Podría venir mucha gente a la fiesta. Sin embargo, habrá lugar para todos. (por + *sustantivo* + que)

   _____

4. Hacía mucho calor. Sin embargo, los niños jugaron en el parque. (pese a que)

   _____

5. No compraría esa casa aún teniendo el dinero. (aunque)

   _____

6. Ni siquiera viviendo en Barcelona me sería fácil aprender catalán. (aun cuando)

   _____

21. **Escribe oraciones a partir de las frases dadas. Conjuga los verbos en subjuntivo o indicativo, según corresponda.** `23.E`

1. Podrías venir a cenar a casa _____.
   (a no ser que / ya / tener / planes)

2. Lleva el paraguas _____.
   (por si acaso / llover)

3. Compré bebida de más _____.
   (en caso de que / esta noche / venir / más invitados)

4. Solo serás exitoso _____.
   (si / esforzarte)

5. Habrías llegado a tiempo _____.
   (si / el metro / funcionar / bien)

6. Si anoche saliste hasta las 4 de la madrugada, _____.
   (hoy / no / deber / quejarte)

7. Si me dijeras que ganaste la lotería, _____.
   (yo / no / creerte)

22. **Síntesis Completa el texto con la opción correcta.** `23.A–23.E`

¿Que cuáles (1) _____ (son/sean) mis sueños? ¡Qué pregunta! Bueno, esperaba que me (2) _____ (hagas/hicieras) una pregunta más concreta.

A ver... No es que (3) _____ (haya/hay) algo con lo que sueñe en realidad. Me gusta vivir el momento y disfrutar del día a día. Pero, para ser sincera, a veces sueño con encontrar a un hombre que me (4) _____ (quiere/quiera) y a quien yo (5) _____ (quiera/quiero). Sería tan romántico estar en pareja ¡y para toda la vida! Quizás yo (6) _____ (sea/soy) un poco ingenua, pero para mí es muy importante saber que la otra persona se (7) _____ (compromete/comprometa) a tener una relación de muy largo plazo.

Y hablando de sueños o ambiciones... ¡ojalá (8) _____ (tenga/tuviera) un trabajo mejor! Deseo estar en una empresa donde me (9) _____ (paguen/pagaran) más y (10) _____ (tenga/tuviera) que trabajar menos. ¡Eso sí que no creo que se (11) _____ (haga/hace) realidad! Pero soñar no cuesta nada.

23. **Síntesis Completa las oraciones con las palabras o frases de la lista.** `23.A–23.E`

No siento	Que	Es aconsejable	Comprendo	Estoy convencido
Es sorprendente	El que	Siento	Parece como si	

1. ¡_____ duerman bien!

2. _____ que no gasten dinero en hoteles caros.

3. _____ hayas sido amable conmigo hoy no me dice nada.

4. _____ que hoy será un gran día.

5. _____ que nos espere un futuro brillante.

6. _____ la gente no tuviera ganas de trabajar.

7. _____ que no hayas llegado a tiempo. El tránsito en esta ciudad es un caos.

8. _____ de que seremos los vencedores.

9. _____ que una actriz tan mala recibiera un Oscar.

24. Síntesis Une los ejemplos con las explicaciones. `23.A–23.E`

_____ 1. Dormiré en una cama que sea cómoda.

_____ 2. Lo lógico es que durmamos en una tienda de campaña.

_____ 3. No había una sola persona que hablara español.

_____ 4. Mientras sigas comportándote mal en clase, jamás tendrás buenas notas.

_____ 5. Los precios son tan altos que no podemos comprar ni un café.

_____ 6. Por si acaso no me despierto, llámame por teléfono por la mañana.

_____ 7. Si tocas el fuego, te quemarás.

_____ 8. El pueblo desconfía de que el gobernador sea honesto.

a. Usamos el subjuntivo con expresiones que hacen referencia a normas, reglas o preferencias consideradas las mejores, las peores, etc.

b. Usamos el subjuntivo en proposiciones temporales cuando la oración hace referencia a una acción futura.

c. Usamos el subjuntivo en proposiciones relativas cuando nos referimos a algo cuyas características imaginamos o deseamos.

d. Usamos el indicativo para expresar una condición cuando la relación condición-resultado es segura.

e. Usamos el indicativo siempre con esta expresión.

f. Usamos el subjuntivo cuando afirmamos que el antecedente de la proposición relativa no existe.

g. Usamos el indicativo en comparaciones implícitas.

h. Usamos el subjuntivo con verbos que expresan duda, tanto en proposiciones subordinadas afirmativas como negativas.

Practice more at **vhlcentral.com.**

The imperative   Chapter 24

1. Completa las oraciones con el verbo conjugado en imperativo afirmativo de _tú_. `24.B`

1. _____ (descansar) unas horas y te paso a buscar a las 8.

2. _____ (limpiar) tus gafas. ¡Están muy sucias!

3. _____ (comer) toda tu comida si quieres el postre.

4. _____ (esperar) hasta que venga la abuela.

5. _____ (leer) en voz alta las primeras frases del libro.

6. _____ (ordenar) la habitación: ¡es un desastre!

7. _____ (ir) a visitar a tus abuelos.

8. _____ (poner) las bolsas sobre la mesa.

9. _____ (tener) bien a mano el pasaporte.

10. _____ (comprar) este libro. Te lo recomiendo.

2. Reescribe las oraciones con el verbo conjugado en imperativo afirmativo de tú. `24.B`

1. Tienes que venir a casa a buscar el DVD. ¡_____!

2. Tienes que ser amable con tus compañeros de clase. ¡_____!

3. Tienes que poner cada libro en su lugar. ¡_____!

4. Tienes que hacer todo lo que yo te digo. ¡_____!

5. Tienes que ir a la farmacia ya mismo. ¡_____!

6. Tienes que decir "permiso" antes de entrar. ¡_____!

3. Eres jefe de redacción del periódico escolar. Contesta las preguntas de tus compañeros. `24.C`

> **Modelo**
>
> **COMPAÑEROS** ¿Debemos escribir artículos?
> (No, corregir | artículos | redactados)
> **TÚ** *No, corregid los artículos redactados.*

1. **COMPAÑEROS** ¿Debemos entrevistar al director?
   (No, entrevistar | profesor de música)
   TÚ _____

2. **COMPAÑEROS** ¿Llamamos por teléfono al profesor de música?
   (No, enviar | mensaje electrónico)
   TÚ _____

3. **COMPAÑEROS** ¿Debemos pensar en preguntas sobre música contemporánea?
   (No, hacer | preguntas | música clásica)
   TÚ _____

4. **COMPAÑEROS** ¿Debemos escribir el artículo para el lunes?
   (No, escribir | artículo | miércoles)
   TÚ _____

5. **COMPAÑEROS** ¿Podemos hacer un descanso ahora?
   (Sí, descansar | una hora)
   TÚ _____

4. Una amiga argentina te da consejos para cuando llegues a Buenos Aires. Escribe sus mandatos usando el imperativo afirmativo de *vos*. `24.C`

1. (tener cuidado con tus maletas) _____

2. (comprar un mapa en la estación) _____

3. (preguntar dónde tomar el autobús 152) _____

4. (ser simpática con el chofer del autobús) _____

5. (buscar la calle Juramento) _____

6. (tocar el timbre del apartamento 1B) _____

5. Reescribe las oraciones en imperativo negativo. `24.D`

1. Haz ejercicio cuatro veces por semana. _____

2. Leed todos los libros de la biblioteca. _____

3. Tirad los periódicos viejos a la basura. _____

4. Sé cordial con los turistas. _____

5. Aparca tu carro enfrente de mi casa. _____

6. Venid a cenar a casa. _____

7. Sal de ahí. _____

8. Ayudad a vuestros amigos. _____

6. Completa las oraciones con los verbos de la lista conjugados en imperativo de *usted*, *ustedes* o *nosotros*. `24.E`

> decir   jugar   hacer   pedir   respetar   subir   tomar

1. Hoy no _____ a la pelota. Ayer practicamos demasiadas horas.

2. _____ el tren de las 8:50, profesor. Lo esperaré en la estación.

3. Alumnos, _____ las normas de la escuela; de lo contrario, habrá sanciones para todos.

4. No _____ que somos estudiantes. Es mejor que crean que somos profesionales.

5. _____ lo que quiera, señor Juárez. La empresa pagará la cuenta del restaurante.

6. _____ hasta el quinto piso. Allí los estará esperando la coordinadora.

7. Jamás _____ trampa en la competencia deportiva. El entrenador se enojaría muchísimo con nosotros.

7. Escribe las oraciones siguiendo el ejemplo. `24.F`

> **Modelo**
>
> ¿Me traes una bebida?
> *Tráeme una bebida.*
> *Tráemela.*

1. ¿Nos das un abrazo?

_____

_____

2. ¿Os quitáis el abrigo?

_____

_____

3. ¿Me cortas el cabello?

_____

_____

4. ¿Nos regalas unas rosas?

_____

_____

5. ¿Me manda una postal, señorita Álvarez?

_____

_____

8. Completa los consejos de salud que da el Doctor Salvador a sus televidentes. `24.B–24.F`

Buenos días, damas y caballeros. Hoy hablaremos sobre cómo llevar una vida saludable.

Si quieren vivir durante mucho tiempo y gozar de buena salud, sigan mis consejos. Primero, no (1) _____ (fumar) más. El cigarrillo causa cáncer de pulmón a ustedes y a quienes los rodean. ¡(2) _____ (Decidirse) de una vez y (3) _____ (terminar) con ese vicio! Segundo, (4) _____ (olvidarse) de las comidas con gran contenido graso y, además, ¡(5) _____ (hacer) deporte! (6) _____ (Caminar), (7) _____ (correr), lo que ustedes quieran... ¡y no (8) _____ (mirar) tanta televisión! Por último, (9) _____ (dormir), como mínimo, ocho horas diarias.

¡(10) _____ (Ser) inteligentes y (11) _____ (cuidarse)! ¡Hasta la próxima!

9. Completa los mandatos del cocinero español a sus empleados. `24.B–24.F`

Julia y Lucía, (1) _____ (cortar) la zanahoria en tiritas muy finas. Tú, Marcelo, (2) _____ (tener) más cuidado cuando lavas las patatas: tienen tierra todavía. Y tú, Ester, (3) _____ (ir) al depósito y (4) _____ (traer) dos kilos de cebollas. (5) _____ (Deber, vosotros) prestar atención a lo que os digo. ¡No (6) _____ (distraerse, vosotros)!

¡(7) _____ (Hacer, nosotros) de este restaurante el mejor de toda España! Y ahora, (8) _____ (poner) manos a la obra.

10. **Reescribe las oraciones usando la estructura indicada entre paréntesis.** `24.G`

1. ¡Venid a casa ya mismo!
   (infinitivo) _____

2. Lea el prospecto del medicamento.
   (imperativo impersonal) _____

3. ¡Trabajen duro!
   (A + infinitivo) _____

4. ¡Tomad un plato cada uno!
   (infinitivo) _____

5. Prohibido adelantarse.
   (imperativo negativo de tú) _____

6. ¡Poner más empeño!
   (imperativo afirmativo de vosotros) _____

11. **Eres nuevo en la oficina y quieres ser muy amable. Reescribe las oraciones usando los comienzos indicados.** `24.G`

1. ¡Hagan silencio!
   ¿Podrían_____?

2. ¡A trabajar, todos!
   ¡Pongámonos_____!

3. ¡Dame el teléfono de este cliente!
   ¿Me_____?

4. ¡Cállate la boca!
   ¡A ver_____!

5. ¡Ayúdame con los paquetes!
   ¿Por qué_____?

6. ¡Paga el café que te compré!
   Que_____.

12. **Síntesis** **La directora, Tomás y sus padres tienen una reunión. Completa los mandatos informales (dirigidos a Tomás) y formales (dirigidos a sus padres).** `24.B–24.G`

> ayudarlo con las tareas para el hogar
> enseñarle buenos modales
> llegar puntualmente
>
> molestar a tus compañeros
> prestar atención a la clase
> recompensarlo con dinero

Tomás, (1) _____ o te quedarás fuera de la escuela. Y a ustedes, les pido por favor, (2) _____ a Tomás. Le contesta mal a todos los profesores y eso es inadmisible. Otra cosa, Tomás, (3) _____. La profesora Menéndez se queja de que no sabes ni siquiera en qué asignatura estás.

Y, usted, señor Pérez, no (4) _____. Es evidente que Tomás no es el autor de frases como "La situación político-financiera de Azerbaiján es inverosímil".

Ah, me olvidaba: ¡no (5) _____ cuando aprueba un examen, señores padres! Él tiene el deber de estudiar... ¡sin recibir nada a cambio!

Por último, Tomás, ¡no (6) _____! Te quedarás sin amigos en poco tiempo.

Practice more at **vhlcentral.com.**

1. Completa la tabla clasificando las formas no personales de los verbos que aparecen en el texto. `25.A`

> Querida Natalia:
>
> Desde hace dos años, mi familia viene festejando Halloween, también llamada "Noche de Brujas". Nos encanta disfrazarnos de personajes que dan miedo. Claro, tener el mejor disfraz no es fácil. El año pasado estuve diseñando mi traje durante una semana. Pero al probármelo, me quedaba demasiado ajustado, por lo que terminé comprando un disfraz ya confeccionado en una tienda.
>
> Este año tengo mucho por hacer. ¿Quieres ayudarme? Por lo visto, deberé tener más cuidado cuando haga mi disfraz. Si estás decidida a ayudarme, todas las sugerencias serán bien recibidas.
>
> Avísame qué te parece lo que te he propuesto.
>
> ¡Hasta pronto!
>
> Leandro

Infinitivo	Gerundio	Participio

2. Reemplaza el texto subrayado por una frase con infinitivo. `25.B`

1. El sonido de las campanas no me dejó dormir.
   _____

2. La caminata es una buena forma de ejercicio.
   _____

3. La compra de la casa nos llenó de deudas.
   _____

4. No es bueno que beba refrescos.
   _____

5. El baile me divierte.
   _____

6. Te recomiendo que comas frutas y verduras.
   _____

3. Reescribe las oraciones usando el infinitivo. `25.B`

1. Me alegré tanto cuando te vi.
   Al _____.

2. Si hubieras estudiado más, hoy tendrías mejores calificaciones.
   De _____.

3. Cuando amaneció, la playa estaba desierta.
   Al _____.

4. Si es tan complicado el viaje, mejor nos quedamos aquí.
   De _____.

5. Cuando llegue Juan, llámame por teléfono.
   Al _____.

6. Si hubiéramos seguido caminando, habríamos llegado al muelle.
   De _____.

Actividades

4. En cada oración, elige la opción correcta. `25.B`

1. Me gustaría _____ alegre.
   a. estar   b. que yo esté   c. Ambas opciones son posibles.

2. No permitiremos _____ sin entrada.
   a. que ingresen   b. ingresar   c. Ambas opciones son posibles.

3. Lucía está cansada y quiere _____ la siesta.
   a. dormir   b. que ella duerma   c. Ambas opciones son posibles.

4. El delincuente se declaró inocente. El testigo asegura _____.
   a. mentir   b. que miente   c. Ambas opciones son posibles.

5. No se te permitirá _____ con tanto equipaje.
   a. que viajes   b. viajar   c. Ambas opciones son posibles.

6. Tenemos muchos asuntos _____.
   a. por discutir   b. que debemos discutir   c. Ambas opciones son posibles.

5. Une las frases para formar oraciones lógicas. `25.B`

1. Te dije que salieras ____   a. de correr.
2. Eran las seis cuando vine ____   b. gritar y vinimos corriendo.
3. Te oímos ____   c. caminando de la mano.
4. Por favor, no ____   d. a cerrar el negocio.
5. Nos vieron ____   e. molestar.
6. Vamos ____   f. a abrirme la puerta cuando llegara.

6. Completa las oraciones combinando los verbos de ambas listas. `25.C`

andar	seguir	bajar	necesitar
llevar	terminar	comer	pensar
quedar	venir	ir	trabajar

1. Por más que me digas que es malo para la salud, yo _____ _____ carne.
2. Ayer me _____ _____ en lo que me dijiste. ¿De veras te quieres mudar?
3. Mi padre _____ treinta años _____ en la misma compañía. ¡Es increíble!
4. Emilio _____ _____ de peso desde el verano pasado. ¡Parece que va a desaparecer!
5. Al final, los estudiantes _____ _____ a Cancún en su viaje de estudios.
6. Mi hermana _____ _____ una bicicleta nueva. Le regalaré una para su cumpleaños.

7. Clasifica los ejemplos de gerundio según los usos mencionados en la lista. `25.C`

| a. causa | b. concesión | c. condición | d. método | e. modo | f. propósito | g. simultaneidad |

1. Siendo tan jóvenes, parecen muy responsables. ___   5. Me dormí pensando en el problema. ___
2. Lloviendo mañana, iremos al cine en vez de al parque. ___   6. No queriendo ver a Juan, me fui de la fiesta. ___
3. Los alumnos salieron corriendo de la escuela. ___   7. Pablo se hizo famoso cantando boleros. ___
4. Nos llamaron diciendo que había huelga. ___

8. Reescribe las oraciones usando el gerundio. `25.C`

1. El jefe nos llamó para decirnos que estábamos despedidos.
_____

2. Como no te encontré, me fui a casa.
_____

3. Mientras caminábamos, cantábamos.
_____

4. Como vi que no había comida, decidí irme al mercado.
_____

5. Si presionas el botón de ese modo, lo romperás.
_____

6. Me quebré la pierna mientras practicaba esquí.
_____

9. En cada oración, elige la opción correcta. `25.C`

1. En la tienda, había dos cajas _____ (conteniendo/que contenían) rompecabezas de mil piezas.
2. ¿No me ves? ¡Estoy _____ (parando/parado) frente a ti!
3. El autobús chocó contra un árbol _____ (resultando heridos los pasajeros/habiendo esquivado una vaca).
4. Cocina la pasta en agua _____ (que hierve/hirviendo) durante cinco minutos.
5. No me puedo imaginar a mi abuelo _____ (cantando/cantar) en una banda de rock.
6. Me encanta la foto de tu madre _____ (abrazando/que abraza) a tu padre.
7. La policía salió en busca del delincuente _____ (capturándolo/y lo capturó) unos minutos después.

10. Completa el relato de Cristina con el participio adecuado del verbo entre paréntesis. `25.D`

Hoy me he (1) _____ (despertar) muy (2) _____ (confundir). Soñé que era (3) _____ (elegir) presidente del país. Sí, como has (4) _____ (oír). Lo más (5) _____ (confundir) de todo era que yo nunca me había (6) _____ (presentar) a elecciones. Después de haber (7) _____ (asumir) el cargo, me acusaban de ser una gobernante (8) _____ (corromper), que había (9) _____ (robar) millones de dólares al pueblo. Después de un juicio de cinco minutos y sin prueba alguna, estaba (10) _____ (prender) de por vida.
Por suerte, en cuanto estuve lo suficientemente (11) _____ (despertar), me di cuenta de que estaba (12) _____ (sanar) y (13) _____ (salvar).

11. Escribe oraciones siguiendo el modelo. `25.D`

> **Modelo**
> Se ha cocinado un pollo.
> *El pollo está cocinado.*

1. Se ha redactado la renuncia.
_____

2. Se ha divorciado Julia.
_____

3. Se han casado Juan y Paula.
_____

4. Se ha soltado al perro.
_____

5. Se ha corregido el ensayo.
_____

6. Se ha resuelto el problema.
_____

12. En cada oración, elige la opción correcta. `25.D`

1. Los comentarios _____ realizados por usuarios anónimos.
   a. son   b. están

2. El enigma _____ resuelto por el famoso científico Juan Carlos Luz.
   a. será   b. estará

3. La tienda _____ abierta de 8 a 12.
   a. está   b. fue

4. La paciente _____ atendida por la doctora Pérez.
   a. ha sido   b. ha estado

5. La ciudad _____ conquistada por los indígenas en 1450.
   a. ha estado   b. ha sido

6. El templo _____ construido de piedras y lodo.
   a. está   b. es

7. Las clases _____ suspendidas hasta nuevo aviso.
   a. han estado   b. han sido

13. Síntesis Completa el artículo con la forma no personal adecuada de los verbos de la lista. `25.A–25.D`

| decidir | golpear | liberar | presumir | quedarse | recibir | ser |

Carlos Castaño, el (1) _____ asesino de la cantante Úrsula Gómez, ha sido (2) _____ en el día de ayer. (3) _____ declarado inocente por el jurado, Castaño ahora ha (4) _____ hacerle juicio al Estado. Dos días antes, el jurado había (5) _____ una carta de una vecina de Gómez. En ella, la vecina describe que vio a una mujer (6) _____ a Gómez la noche del 8 de diciembre. Al (7) _____ sin sospechosos, la policía ha reanudado la búsqueda.

14. Síntesis Completa las oraciones con la forma no personal del verbo entre paréntesis. `25.A–25.D`

1. Nadie se hace rico _____ (vender) artesanías.
2. De _____ (continuar) la huelga, no podremos viajar a Alicante.
3. Segundo, _____ (desconectar) el suministro eléctrico.
4. Quiero comprar el cuadro que se llama "Mujer _____ (tejer)".
5. Me encanta el refrán que dice "A lo _____ (hacer), pecho".
6. _____ (pagar) con la tarjeta de crédito, te endeudarás sin saberlo.
7. Juan camina _____ (mover) los brazos de un lado al otro.
8. Al _____ (oír) la puerta, el gato se escondió debajo del sofá.

15. Síntesis Une las frases para formar oraciones lógicas. `25.A–25.D`

1. No soy capaz _____
2. Compré fresas _____
3. Vimos una película _____
4. A la tienda, entró una mujer _____
5. Cómo me gusta _____
6. Me quedé dormida _____
7. Luciana estaba _____

a. acordándome de cuánto te gustan.
b. comiendo palomitas de maíz.
c. de dormir en una tienda de campaña.
d. al sentarme en la silla.
e. el cantar de los pájaros.
f. atenta a las palabras de su amiga.
g. dando gritos y saltando.

16. Síntesis Une los ejemplos con las explicaciones. `25.A–25.D`

1. Para expresar propósito, el gerundio solamente puede usarse con verbos de comunicación.

2. Los verbos de movimiento como este siempre llevan la preposición **a** o **de**.

3. Por lo general, se usa el infinitivo junto a verbos de deseo para indicar que el sujeto de la acción deseada es quien expresa el deseo.

4. Solo hay tres verbos en español que permiten formar tiempos compuestos con el participio regular o el irregular. Solo la forma irregular se usa como adjetivo.

5. Se puede usar el gerundio para referirse al objeto de los verbos que expresan una representación, ya sea mental o física.

6. Esta estructura funciona como un adverbio para indicar que la acción está ocurriendo paralelamente a otra.

7. Los sustantivos y adjetivos pueden ser modificados por una preposición más infinitivo.

8. Hay verbos que al parecer tienen dos formas de participio pasado, pero se emplea el participio regular para formar tiempos compuestos con **haber**.

a. Baja a recibir el pedido del supermercado, por favor.

b. He impreso el pasaje del tren en la casa de Irma.

c. Al salir, cerré la puerta.

d. Nuestra prima nos escribió contándonos que se casaba.

e. Quiero ganar la lotería.

f. ¡Tenemos tantas cosas por hacer!

g. Me imagino a Marina patinando sobre hielo ¡y me da risa!

h. Nunca he sido tan bien atendido en un restaurante.

 Practice more at **vhlcentral.com.**

1. Completa las oraciones con los verbos modales de la lista. `26.B`

> deber (2)   tener (2)   haber (3)   poder (2)   venir (2)

1. Esta mesa no _____ a costar más de 300 dólares, ¿la compramos?

2. ¿_____ probar la ensalada? Se ve tan rica y tengo tanta hambre.

3. No tenemos otra opción: _____ de sacar esa muela, aunque no quieras.

4. Lucía _____ de haberse quedado dormida. Son las 10 y todavía no ha llegado al trabajo.

5. Los alumnos _____ de asistir, como mínimo, a un 75% de las clases.

6. Como las habitaciones de todos los hoteles estaban reservadas, mis padres _____ que dormir en el auto.

7. _____ de ser tres o cuatro los que aún no han pagado la cuota del club. No estoy segura.

8. Elisa y tú _____ hacer la presentación de Historia para el miércoles próximo.

9. Al final, los arreglos de la casa _____ a costarnos más de dos mil pesos.

10. Me quedé en casa porque _____ que estudiar para el examen.

11. ¿Sabías que las bolsas de plástico _____ causar la muerte de muchas mascotas que se meten en ellas y se asfixian?

2. En cada oración, elige la opción correcta. `26.B`

1. No _____ (deberías/debes de) salir tan desabrigada si tienes tos.

2. ¿Finalmente _____ (pudiste/podías) hablar con María? Yo la llamé varias veces y me atendió el contestador.

3. ¡Esta bici es el mejor regalo! Siempre _____ (quería/quise) tener una bicicleta amarilla.

4. ¿_____ (Debes/Sabes) hablar alemán? Hay una clienta que necesita ayuda ¡y no habla ni un poquito de español!

5. Cuando encienda la lavadora, _____ (debería titilar/titilará) una luz verde.

6. No _____ (debías/debiste) haberle puesto tanta sal a la ensalada. ¡Es imposible comerla!

7. En las montañas, _____ (parece/puede) haber mucha nieve. Es un día perfecto para esquiar.

8. Por supuesto que sé andar en bicicleta, pero hoy no _____ (puedo/debo de) hacerlo. ¡Me duele la rodilla!

3. Decide si estos ejemplos de perífrasis verbales expresan *tiempo*, una *fase* o una *serie*. `26.C`

1. Juana se puso a llorar en cuanto vio a su hija en el traje de novia. _____

2. Empezaremos por meter toda la ropa en cajas. Luego, las rotularemos. _____

3. No acostumbramos beber café por las mañanas. _____

4. ¡Deja de llamarme por teléfono! _____

5. Volveremos a vernos pronto, ¿no? _____

6. Todo nuestro trabajo vino a resultar en vano. ¡Todo por no leer bien las instrucciones! _____

7. Cuando llegaste, estaba por escribirte un mensaje de texto. _____

8. ¡Justo vengo a olvidarme el trabajo de historia en casa! _____

4. Completa la carta con las perífrasis verbales del cuadro. `26.C`

volveré a	fui a	para de	puso a	acababa de	empiezo por	suelo	terminaré por

Querida hermana:

¿Cómo estás? (1) _____ decirte que te extraño muchísimo. Bien sabes que yo no (2) _____ quejarme, pero estos primeros días aquí en Chile no han sido fáciles.

No te imaginas qué frío que es el clima aquí. ¡No (3) _____ llover! Ayer (4) _____ salir de casa, muy bien vestida para ir a una entrevista y, de pronto, se (5) _____ llover a cántaros. Por supuesto, no (6) _____ salir sin paraguas.

Otra cosa, mi compañera de cuarto es muy maleducada. Nunca limpia, tampoco cocina y me trata mal. ¡Qué mala suerte que tengo! ¿Cómo (7) _____ parar a esta habitación?

Bueno, veré qué hago en las próximas semanas. Seguramente (8) _____ mudarme a otra habitación.

Un gran abrazo,

Tu hermana menor

5. Une los elementos de las tres columnas para formar oraciones lógicas. `26.C`

1. Después de probar con el canto,	volvería a	estudiar pintura.
2. En esas dos horas, el profesor no	dejó de	robar en la tienda.
3. Me juró que no	iría a	comer dulces, ¡pero este bombón es tentador!
4. Un rato después de salir el sol,	suelo	hablar ni un segundo.
5. Es verdad que no	pasé a	hacer las compras por iniciativa propia.
6. Natalia nunca	entró a	nublarse y a la media hora llovía sin parar.

6. Usa los verbos de la lista para formar perífrasis verbales de gerundio de los verbos entre paréntesis. `26.D`

andar   estar   ir   venir   llevar   seguir   vivir   pasarse

1. ¿Te das cuenta de que _____ (hablar) por teléfono desde que llegué?

2. Mi madre _____ (criticar) a todas sus vecinas. ¡Es insoportable!

3. El perro _____ toda la tarde _____ (ladrar) y los vecinos se quejaron.

4. Los impuestos _____ (aumentar) hasta que fue casi imposible pagarlos.

5. ¡Hace cuánto que te _____ (pedir) que arregles el grifo de la cocina!

6. Mi padre _____ (necesitar) una corbata nueva. Se la regalaré para su cumpleaños.

7. Juana _____ (vivir) dos años en Ecuador.

8. Yo _____ (trabajar) hasta las 8 de la noche. ¿Tú qué quieres hacer?

7. En cada oración, elige la opción correcta. `26.D`

1. Finalmente, _____ (terminé/anduve) comprando la chaqueta amarilla. La azul no me convencía del todo.

2. La falta de agua potable _____ (anda/continúa) siendo el problema más grave de las zonas más pobres del país.

3. Tomás _____ (sigue/lleva) buscando trabajo unos cuatro meses.

4. La paciente _____ (va/está) recuperándose de la operación. Por favor, déjenla dormir.

5. _____ (Sigo/Llevo) esperando el llamado de Pablo.

6. El niñito ese _____ (está/vive) molestando en clase. Hablaré con sus padres.

8. Une las explicaciones con los ejemplos. `26.D`

1. Expresa un proceso en aumento que tiene un límite o resultado.

2. Expresa una acción constante, habitual o que se repite.

3. Expresa una acción referida a un período de tiempo.

4. Expresa un proceso en curso que se da intermitentemente.

5. Expresa un proceso que comenzó en el pasado y continúa hasta ahora.

6. Expresa un proceso en curso, pero es más enfático que **estar** + **gerundio**.

a._____ Llevo tres horas esperándote en la esquina. ¿Dónde te metiste?

b._____ La humedad de esa pared fue creciendo hasta que finalmente el dueño decidió repararla.

c._____ Mi prima se pasó toda la tarde llorando por su mamá.

d._____ Ya nos venía pareciendo que faltaba dinero de la caja y ahora descubrimos que el vendedor nos robaba.

e._____ Juan y su novia viven peleándose por cualquier cosa.

f._____ Lucas anda preguntando por ti. ¿Por qué no lo llamas?

9. **Reescribe las oraciones usando perífrasis de participio.** `26.E`

1. Mamá le prohibió a Luisito que use vasos de vidrio. (tener) _____
2. Gonzalo ha ganado tres carreras. (llevar) _____
3. Mis amigos han comprado las entradas para mañana. (tener) _____
4. Este director ha dirigido más de veinte películas. (llevar) _____
5. La carta se escribió con tinta roja. (estar) _____
6. Ya escribí veinte capítulos del libro. (llevar) _____

10. **Completa las oraciones con perífrasis verbales usando los verbos de la lista.** `26.E`

> tener (2)   ver   seguir   quedar (2)   estar   venir

1. La profesora _____ encantada con tu trabajo final. Seguramente te pondrá una buena nota.
2. Ya _____ preparado todo para el concierto de esta noche.
3. El nombre de la empresa _____ impreso en los sobres. No hace falta escribir nada.
4. _____ decidido que se cerrará el restaurante hasta el verano próximo.
5. Federica _____ preocupada por la salud de su perrito. Hace una semana que está enfermo.
6. Mis padres _____ pensado ir de vacaciones al Caribe.
7. Te _____ dicho que me llames con tiempo antes de pasar por casa.
8. Al final, nos _____ obligados a tomar una decisión drástica.

11. **Síntesis Completa las perífrasis con el infinitivo, participio o gerundio de los verbos de la lista.** `26.B–26.E`

> tener   perjudicar   gastar   ver   despertarte   dormir (2)

1. Perdona, no quería _____. ¡Te llamaré más tarde!
2. Marta está _____ desde las 2 de la tarde.
3. Todos resultamos _____ por la crisis económica.
4. No suelo _____ la siesta, ¡pero hoy estaba tan cansada!
5. Sigo _____ pesadillas con fantasmas. ¡Todo por ver esa película!
6. Llevamos _____ demasiado dinero en este negocio.
7. Acabo de _____ a la chica más linda del mundo.

12. **Síntesis Une las explicaciones con los ejemplos.** `26.B–26.E`

___ 1. Indica una acción que está a punto de empezar.

___ 2. Indica una acción que se está desarrollando.

___ 3. Indica una acción acabada.

___ 4. Indica una acción considerada como resultado.

___ 5. Indica una acción que se repite varias veces.

___ 6. Indica una obligación.

___ 7. Indica una posibilidad.

___ 8. Indica el punto justo de conclusión de una acción.

a. Nadia dejó de leer, porque le dolía la cabeza.

b. Estaba por cocinar algo cuando apareciste con una pizza.

c. Suelo comer un yogur como cena.

d. Puedo comerme tres platos de sopa cuando tengo hambre.

e. Hemos de vender más de veinte productos por día.

f. Me estoy rompiendo la cabeza con este crucigrama.

g. Terminamos de tomar el café y nos vamos, ¿sí?

h. Tengo estudiada toda la lección uno.

$: Practice more at **vhlcentral.com.**

1. Indica los pronombres y verbos reflexivos. `27.A`

> Juan:
>
> Hoy me desperté a las siete de la mañana. Apenas escuché el despertador, me senté en la cama y te llamé por teléfono para despertarte. El teléfono sonó, sonó y sonó, pero no atendiste.
>
> Como todavía era temprano, no me preocupé y decidí darme un baño largo. Después, me cepillé los dientes y me peiné.
>
> Dos minutos después de salir de la ducha, me di cuenta de mi error: ¡me había equivocado de número de teléfono! Ahora me siento tan mal por esta situación. Llegaste tarde al trabajo, tu jefe se enojó contigo y casi pierdes tu trabajo.
>
> ¡Espero que sepas disculparme!
>
> Lucas

2. Escribe las oraciones usando pronombres y verbos reflexivos. `27.A`

Modelo

> dormirse / yo / 8.00 p.m.
> *Me duermo a las 8.00 p.m.*
> *Me voy a dormir/Voy a dormirme a las 8.00 p.m.*

1. afeitarse / Oscar / 9.00 a.m.
   _____
   _____

2. reunirse / ellos / miércoles
   _____
   _____

3. reírse / vosotros / mucho
   _____
   _____

4. pelearse / nosotros / nunca
   _____
   _____

5. ponerse / Gabriela / tacones
   _____
   _____

3. Reescribe las oraciones usando *el uno al otro, los unos a los otros*, etc. `27.B`

1. Juan e Isabel se apoyan mutuamente.
   _____

2. Los alumnos y los profesores siempre se critican mutuamente.
   _____

3. Federica y su amiga se respetan mutuamente.
   _____

4. Los trabajadores se ayudan mutuamente.
   _____

5. Mi madre y mi hermana se miraron entre sí con tristeza.
   _____

4. Indica si estos ejemplos contienen verbos reflexivos. Escribe *sí* o *no*. `27.C–27.D`

1. Me he maquillado demasiado, ¿no? _____

2. Juan durmió al niño y comenzó a estudiar. _____

3. ¿Te manchaste la camisa otra vez? _____

4. Despiértenme a las nueve. _____

5. Quita tus cosas de mi armario. _____

6. Los invitados deberán vestirse de etiqueta. _____

5. En cada oración, elige la opción correcta. `27.C–27.D`

1. Florencia se bañó _____ rápidamente y salió al cine.
   a. a sí misma   b. X

2. El pobre perrito ya no puede levantarse _____.
   a. por sí mismo   b. X

3. Mi hermano no sabe defenderse _____.
   a. X   b. por sí solo

4. Me acosté _____ muy temprano.
   a. a mí mismo   b. X

5. ¿El niño ya es capaz de ducharse _____?
   a. por sí mismo   b. X

6. ¿A qué hora te despiertas _____ para ir a trabajar?
   a. X   b. a ti misma

7. Una vez que crezca, la niña podrá vestirse _____.
   a. X   b. por sí sola

6. Clasifica los verbos según sean únicamente reflexivos o no. `27.C–27.D`

arrepentirse	cansarse	desvivirse
jactarse	lavarse	quemarse
comportarse	conocerse	dignarse
odiarse	quejarse	rebelarse

Únicamente reflexivos	Reflexivos/No reflexivos

Actividades

7. Completa las oraciones con los verbos de la lista. Agrega el pronombre adecuado a cada verbo. `27.C–27.D`

apoyar	aprender	casar		confesar	duchar	reunir	odiar
abrazar	arrepentir	comprometer		conocer	escribir (2)	mirar	pelear

1. Los enamorados _____ a los ojos y _____ su amor.

2. Estamos tan contentos. _____ el 20 de octubre y _____ el 1.º de diciembre.

3. Los hermanos siempre _____ mutuamente.

4. María y Julia _____ todo el día y sin ningún motivo.

5. Es algo muy raro, pero mi perro y mi gato no _____.

6. Quiero que _____ más seguido. Sé que vivimos lejos, pero queremos estar comunicados, ¿no es así?

7. Las amigas _____ cuando se reencontraron después de tantos años.

8. Aníbal _____ con agua fría porque se había acabado el agua caliente.

9. No es verdad que Ana _____ todos los nombres la primera vez que los oyó.

10. Los directivos _____ la semana próxima para analizar las nuevas propuestas.

11. Ellos _____ cuando eran niños y _____ cartas desde entonces.

12. No _____ de haberle dicho la verdad, aunque no le haya gustado oírla.

8. Completa las oraciones usando los verbos de la lista para expresar una acción "completa". `27.C–27.D`

andar	comer	conocer	creer	saber

1. _____ todos los restaurantes vegetarianos de la ciudad.

2. ¿De veras _____ lo que dice mi hermanita? ¡No seas tonta!

3. Cuando tienen hambre, esos niños _____ tres platos de sopa cada uno.

4. Andrea _____ de memoria los nombres de todas las actrices de la telenovela.

5. ¿_____ toda Barcelona? Supongo que estás cansada.

9. Une los ejemplos con las explicaciones. `27.C–27.D`

_____ 1. Es un verbo que implica reciprocidad.

_____ 2. Es un verbo que solamente puede ser reflexivo.

_____ 3. Es un verbo que expresa una acción "completa".

_____ 4. Es un verbo que implica que uno mismo no realizó la acción.

_____ 5. Es un verbo cuyo sujeto es afectado indirectamente por la acción y, por lo tanto, se convierte en objeto indirecto.

a. ¡De qué color más raro te teñiste el cabello!

b. Me aprendí todo el vocabulario para el examen.

c. Las mujeres no nos llevamos bien entre nosotras.

d. ¡Te quejas y te quejas todo el día!

e. ¡Qué lindo vestido que me mandé a hacer!

10. En cada oración, elige la opción correcta. `27.E`

1. _____ (Anima/Anímate) a tu amiga a que venga a la fiesta.

2. _____ (Me decidí/Decidí) no comprar una casa en las montañas.

3. Josefina _____ (se saltó/saltó) el almuerzo: piensa que así podrá adelgazar más rápido.

4. _____ (Jugamos/Nos jugamos) el pellejo en este partido. ¡Debemos ganarlo sí o sí!

5. No _____ (te deshagas/deshagas) el trabajo que con tanto esfuerzo logramos hacer.

6. ¡_____ (Cómanse/Coman) todo el chocolate! A mí no me gusta.

11. Escribe las respuestas usando reflexivos que expresan acciones involuntarias. `27.F`

> **Modelo**
>
> ¿Qué le pasó a la botella? (romper)
> *Se rompió.*

1. ¿Qué le pasó a tu motocicleta? (descomponer)

   _____

2. ¿Qué le pasó a la batería de tu teléfono? (descargar)

   _____

3. ¿Qué les pasó a los adornos que te regalé? (caer)

   _____

4. ¿Qué le pasó al ovillo de lana? (enredar)

   _____

5. ¿Qué les pasó a los edificios? (derrumbar)

   _____

12. Escribe oraciones siguiendo el modelo. `27.F`

> **Modelo**
>
> Se descompuso la radio. (yo)
> *Se me descompuso la radio.*

1. Se quebró la madera. (tú)

   _____

2. Se cerró la puerta. (él)

   _____

3. Se rompió la tetera. (yo)

   _____

4. Se derramó la leche. (nosotros)

   _____

5. Se agotó la batería. (mi auto)

   _____

6. Olvido siempre los nombres.

   _____

7. Esos hermanitos siempre pierden las llaves.

   _____

13. Completa las oraciones con verbos que expresen cambio. Como pista, tienes los adjetivos que corresponden a dichos verbos. `27.G`

> emocionado/a   enamorado/a   muerto/a   rico/a   rojo/a   separado/a

1. Cuando se dio cuenta de que todos lo miraban, Juan _____.
2. Mi madre _____ tanto cuando nos graduamos.
3. Mi gato _____ en 2005.
4. Los empresarios _____ a raíz del aumento de los bienes inmuebles.
5. Las adolescentes pronto _____ de la estrella de la música pop.
6. La diputada _____ de su marido y ahora se ve más feliz.

14. Reescribe las oraciones usando el verbo entre paréntesis. `27.G`

1. La oficina es un caos cuando tú no estás. (convertirse)

_____

2. Tu pececito se entristece apenas sales de la sala. (ponerse)

_____

3. Mi prima se enriqueció con su tienda de perfumes. (hacerse)

_____

4. La mala noticia me preocupa todavía. (quedarse)

_____

5. Ahora Madrid es una ciudad muy cara. (volverse)

_____

6. Algún día, seré muy rico. (llegar a ser)

_____

15. Síntesis En cada oración, elige la opción correcta. `27.A–27.G`

1. El ladrón _____ de los objetos robados.
   a. se deshizo   b. deshizo

2. El cabello _____ cada día más.
   a. se cae   b. se me cae

3. ¡Qué tonta soy! _____ los libros en casa.
   a. Se me olvidaron   b. Se olvidaron

4. Juan es tan ingenuo. _____ todo lo que le dicen.
   a. Cree   b. Se cree

5. _____ que vendrías más temprano.
   a. Se me ocurrió   b. Me ocurrió

6. Isabela _____ al bebé y se puso a leer.
   a. se acostó   b. acostó

16. Síntesis Decide qué oración es la intrusa. `27.A–27.G`

1. a. Me leí el libro en una tarde.
   b. Me caí de las escaleras.
   c. Me conozco Venezuela de cabo a rabo.

2. a. No te atreviste a llamarme.
   b. El jefe se dignó a subir los salarios.
   c. La empresa se declaró en quiebra.

3. a. Luisa se operó el lunes.
   b. La ventana se abrió.
   c. El vidrio se rompió.

4. a. Has avergonzado a tu hermana.
   b. El delincuente burló la guardia policial.
   c. ¿Te has burlado de mí?

5. a. Nos casamos en junio.
   b. Te irritaste un poco, ¿no?
   c. Se me olvidó traer dinero.

6. a. ¡Se hizo demasiado tarde!
   b. Se volvió para decirme algo.
   c. El barrio se ha vuelto un lugar concurrido.

Practice more at **vhlcentral.com.**

1. Convierte las oraciones en oraciones pasivas con ser. `28.B–28.C`

1. El Senado aprobó hoy la ley de alimentos orgánicos.

   _____

2. Miles de fanáticos vieron el partido.

   _____

3. La crítica elogió el documental *La selva hoy*.

   _____

4. Los arqueólogos chilenos descubrieron tres tumbas egipcias.

   _____

5. La policía controló la identidad de los pasajeros.

   _____

6. Ambos países firmarán un acuerdo de cooperación.

   _____

2. En cada oración, elige la opción correcta. `28.B–28.C`

1. La prensa de los Estados Unidos _____ muy _____ por no ser imparcial.
   a. fueron/criticados   b. fue/criticada

2. Las cartas que escribió la niña _____ hace dos semanas.
   a. fue enviada   b. fueron enviadas

3. La habitación ya _____ por el señor vestido de azul.
   a. ha sido pagada   b. ha sido pagado

4. Carina _____ mejor compañera por todos sus compañeros.
   a. fue elegida   b. fue electa

5. El contrato de trabajo y el acuerdo de confidencialidad _____ por todas las partes interesadas.
   a. será firmado   b. serán firmados

6. La fila de prioridad de embarque _____ por todos los pasajeros.
   a. deberá ser respetada   b. deberá ser respetado

3. Reordena los elementos para formar oraciones completas. `28.B–28.C`

1. cruelmente / por / fueron / Los animalitos / tratados / el cazador / . *Los animalitos se tratado*

   Los animalitos Fueron tratados

2. información / serán / con 50.000 dólares / Quienes den / recompensados / .

   Quienes den

3. los lectores / fueron / enviados / Los periódicos / a / esta tarde / . *Los periodicos se envidan a los lectores*

   Los periódicos fueron enviados a los lectores esta tarde

4. El problema / el jefe del departamento / había sido / por / resuelto / . *El problema*

   El problema había sido resuelto por el jefe del departamento

5. por / diseñado y confeccionado / El vestido de novia / fue / el afamado diseñador / .

   El vestido de novia fue diseñado y confeccionado por el afamado diseñada

6. fue / El conserje / despertado / los visitantes / por / .

   El conserje fue despertado por los visitantes

   El conserje se desperto por los visitantes

4. Reescribe las oraciones en voz pasiva siguiendo el modelo. `28.B–28.C`

> **Modelo**
>
> Juan cambiará la lámpara de la cocina.
> *La lámpara de la cocina será cambiada por Juan.*
> *La lámpara ya está cambiada.*

1. La policía prenderá al delincuente.

   _____

   _____

2. Mi madre hará el pastel para mi cumpleaños.

   _____

   _____

3. Ulises redactará una carta de queja.

   _____

   _____

4. Todos los trabajadores pagarán los aportes jubilatorios.

   _____

   _____

5. El directorio de la compañía publicará la revista *Novedades empresariales*.

   _____

   _____

5. Escribe las oraciones siguiendo el modelo. `28.D`

> **Modelo**
>
> Café: hacer - servir
> *Primero, se hace el café. Luego, se lo sirve.*

1. Papas: pelar - cortar

   _____

2. Tarta: hornear - probar

   _____

3. Casa: construir - pintar

   _____

4. Bombilla de luz: apagar - cambiar

   _____

5. Paciente: llamar - examinar

   _____

6. Cabello: lavar - cortar

   _____

7. Galletas: decorar - hornear

   _____

Actividades

6. Lee las tareas que tienen los cadetes de primer año de la academia militar y completa las oraciones. `28.D`

Lunes	Martes	Miércoles	Jueves	Viernes	Sábado
limpiar el pasillo	ordenar las habitaciones	lavar la ropa	preparar la cena	planchar las camisas	disfrutar el día

1. El lunes se debe _____.
2. El martes _____.
3. _____.
4. _____.
5. _____.
6. _____.

7. Completa las oraciones con los verbos de la lista. Deberás elegir entre oraciones pasivas con ser y oraciones pasivas reflejas. `28.B–28.D`

> detener   saber   mojar   firmar   reparar   aceptar   agregar

1. La antena de mi casa está rota y _____ por un profesional la semana que viene.
2. _____ todas las solicitudes que cumplan con los requisitos.
3. La lavadora no funciona sin detergente. Antes de encenderla, _____ las pastillas en este recipiente.
4. Ayer dejé abierta la ventana de la habitación y _____ todos mis apuntes con la lluvia.
5. Las prescripciones de medicamentos siempre _____ por los médicos.
6. Según la policía, _____ a los responsables del crimen en el transcurso de esta semana.
7. No _____ aún dónde está el dinero robado.

8. Elige la opción correcta para completar cada oración. `28.B–28.D`

1. Ayer vi que, en el restaurante de la esquina, _____ camareros. ¿Te interesa?
   a. se buscan   b. se busca   c. Ambas opciones son posibles.
2. _____ que al final del cuento el príncipe siempre conquista el corazón de la mujer de sus sueños.
   a. Se supone   b. Se suponen   c. Ambas opciones son posibles.
3. Esta enfermedad ya _____ por los expertos de nuestro país.
   a. ha sido estudiada   b. se ha estudiado   c. Ambas opciones son posibles.
4. Los detalles de la reunión _____ durante esta semana.
   a. se prepararán   b. serán preparados   c. Ambas opciones son posibles.
5. La naranja es la fruta que más _____ en España.
   a. se exporta   b. se exportan   c. Ambas opciones son posibles.
6. Las instrucciones _____ con antelación.
   a. deberían comunicarse   b. se deberían comunicar   c. Ambas opciones son posibles.
7. Las cuentas del hogar _____ por correo electrónico a la brevedad.
   a. se envía   b. se envían   c. Ambas opciones son posibles.

9. Escribe oraciones siguiendo el modelo. `28.E`

> **Modelo**
>
> pincel - pintar. *Con el pincel, se pinta.*
> oficina - trabajar. *En la oficina, se trabaja.*

1. cuchillo - cortar

_____

2. pimienta - condimentar

_____

3. cuchara - probar

_____

4. tenedor - comer

_____

5. lápiz - escribir

_____

6. ayuntamiento - debatir

_____

7. escuela - aprender

_____

8. comedor - comer

_____

10. Reescribe las construcciones impersonales subrayadas usando el pronombre indefinido *uno/a* o el pronombre *se*, según corresponda. `28.E`

1. "¡En esta cama, se puede dormir tan bien!", dijo Juan. _____
2. "Si se está tranquilo, se puede trabajar mejor", dijo Lucas. _____
3. En esta tienda una puede comprar lo que quiera. _____
4. "¡Qué bien que se vive en esta ciudad!", dijo Sara. _____
5. "A la estación, se llega en veinte minutos", dijo mi hermana. _____
6. "En la clase de baile, se transpira muchísimo", dijo Julio. _____

11. Escribe oraciones siguiendo el modelo. `28.E`

> **Modelo**
>
> Los pasajeros serán controlados al subir al autobús.
> *Se controlará a los pasajeros al subir al autobús.*
> *Se los controlará al subir al autobús.*

1. Las mujeres son maltratadas en ese país.

_____

_____

2. Los peatones deben ser respetados.

_____

_____

3. Las enfermeras son contratadas por un año.

_____

_____

4. Todo el pueblo es encuestado cada diez años.

_____

_____

5. Los trabajadores son evaluados cada trimestre.

_____

_____

12. En el siguiente texto, indica dónde está expresado el objeto indirecto. `28.F`

Primero, se redactaron las normas de seguridad. Una vez redactadas, la gerencia se las enseñó a los miembros del departamento de documentación. Cuando estaban listas, se las enviaron a todos los trabajadores de la planta.

Hubo diversas reacciones de parte de los trabajadores. Se le informó a la gerencia que muchas de las normas eran obsoletas y se le advirtió que debían hacerse modificaciones con urgencia.

Ahora se han reformado las normas. Mañana por la tarde se las presentará al gerente general. Esta vez seguramente se las aprobará sin objeciones.

13. Decide si estas oraciones son construcciones pasivas con *se* o impersonales con *se*. `28.G`

1. En el instituto que está cerca de casa se enseñan más de veinte idiomas. _____

2. Jamás se supo el origen de esa donación. _____

3. Se contratan camareros con experiencia. _____

4. Cuando se estudia, se aprueba sin problemas. _____

5. Se dicen muchas mentiras en la prensa amarilla. _____

6. Se elogió a nuestra directora en el discurso de inauguración. _____

7. Se vendieron más de cuarenta videojuegos en un día. _____

8. Se cree cada vez menos en los gobernantes. _____

9. Nunca se supo el porqué de su decisión. _____

10. Aquí se trabaja muchísimo. _____

14. Reescribe las oraciones usando la pista entre paréntesis. `28.H`

1. Nunca se sabe cómo estará el tiempo al día siguiente. (uno)

_____

2. Se hace lo que se puede. (gente)

_____

3. Es conveniente tener un botiquín de primeros auxilios. (convenir)

_____

4. No se puede respirar en esta habitación llena de humo. (una)

_____

5. Se te han enviado dos postales. (tercera persona del plural)

_____

6. Ha caído muchísima lluvia en la última semana. (llover)

_____

7. Abundan los libros sobre historia medieval en esta biblioteca. (haber)

_____

8. El clima está frío en esa época. (hacer)

_____

9. Te recomiendo que estudies mucho para el examen. (convenir)

_____

15. Completa las oraciones con las palabras de la lista. `28.H`

habían	es	había	han	hay	hubo	era

1. _____ demasiada nieve y no podemos salir de casa.

2. ¿_____ problemas entre Martín y tú? Veo que ya no se hablan.

3. Este mes, se _____ vendido más de mil ejemplares de la novela.

4. Mis artículos _____ sido publicados en la revista *Lugares* ¡y yo no me había enterado!

5. _____ tanto sol que tuve que ponerme a la sombra.

6. _____ invierno, pero parece primavera.

7. ¡Ya _____ hora de que me llamaras!

16. Síntesis Elige la opción con construcción pasiva o impersonal que tenga el mismo significado que la oración original. `28.B–28.H`

1. Reformaron los hoteles por los festejos de fin de año.
   a. Los festejos de fin de año reformaron los hoteles.
   b. Se reformaron los hoteles por los festejos de fin de año.

2. La película fue galardonada con ocho estatuillas.
   a. Se galardonó la película con ocho estatuillas.
   b. Ocho estatuillas galardonaron la película.

3. Uno se puede perder muy fácilmente en este bosque.
   a. En este bosque, uno puede ser perdido fácilmente.
   b. Puedes perderte fácilmente en este bosque.

4. Los investigadores persiguieron al asesino día y noche.
   a. El asesino fue perseguido por los investigadores día y noche.
   b. Se persiguió al asesino día y noche.

5. Los mejores deportistas serán premiados por su desempeño.
   a. Se premiará por su desempeño a los mejores deportistas.
   b. Los mejores deportistas premiarán por su desempeño.

6. El titular deberá firmar los cheques de viajero.
   a. Los cheques de viajero deberán ser firmados por el titular.
   b. Se deberá firmar los cheques de viajero.

7. Lo condenaron injustamente.
   a. Se lo condenó injustamente.
   b. Uno se condenó injustamente.

8. Los conductores fueron multados por exceso de velocidad.
   a. Se multó a los conductores por exceso de velocidad.
   b. El exceso de velocidad multó a los conductores.

Practice more at **vhlcentral.com.**

1. Completa la conversación con los verbos *haber* o *estar*. `29.B`

LUCIANO Hola, soy Luciano, ¿(1) _____ Paula?

JOSEFINA Aquí no (2) _____ ninguna Paula, debes haberte equivocado de número de teléfono.

LUCIANO Seguramente (3) _____ un malentendido.

JOSEFINA Mira, yo vivo aquí y puedo asegurarte que no (4) _____ nadie en esta casa que se llame así.

LUCIANO ¿(5) _____ alguna posibilidad de que estés confundida?

JOSEFINA ¡No (6) _____ posibilidad alguna! Vivo con mi compañera de piso ¡y no se llama Paula!

LUCIANO ¿Y (7) _____ tu compañera contigo ahora?

JOSEFINA No, ahora (8) _____ en la universidad.

LUCIANO Bueno, dile que llamó Luciano y que se (9) _____ olvidado unos libros con su nombre en el aula.

JOSEFINA ¿Paula? ¿No será Laura?

LUCIANO "Laura", "Paula", ¡qué más da! ¡(10) _____ una letra de diferencia!

2. En cada oración, elige la opción correcta. `29.C`

1. _____ (Está/Es) oscuro y _____ (es/son) las 4 de la tarde. ¡Qué feo es el invierno!

2. ¿_____ (Será/Estará) nevando en la montaña ahora?

3. _____ (Es/Estamos) a martes y Juan todavía no ha pagado el alquiler.

4. ¡Esas camisas ya no se usan! _____ (Estamos/Es) en 2010, ¡no en 1980!

5. Ayer _____ (estuvo/fue) nublado y las fotos salieron muy oscuras.

6. _____ (Es/Son) la una: ¿dónde está Carlos?

7. ¿Hoy _____ (estamos/es) lunes o martes?

3. Julián lleva un diario donde escribe sobre las cosas que le pasan todos los días. Completa el diario con las palabras de la lista. `29.C`

| está | hizo | estuvo | estamos | son |
| es | hace | hubo (2) | hará | es |

Hoy (1) _____ 8 de julio y (2) _____ las tres de la tarde. A pesar de que (3) _____ verano, (4) _____ mucho frío afuera y (5) _____ lloviendo a cántaros.

Ayer también (6) _____ mal tiempo. (7) _____ nublado y (8) _____ mucho viento.

¡Qué mal! Hoy (9) _____ a viernes y en toda la semana no (10) _____ ni un solo día lindo.

¿(11) _____ menos frío mañana? Me fijaré ya mismo en el pronóstico.

4. Completa las oraciones con la conjugación apropiada de *ser*, *estar* o *tener*. `29.D`

1. Ayer no dormí bien y ahora _____ muchísimo sueño.

2. Ema _____ veinte años menor que Graciela.

3. El perro seguramente _____ hambriento. Dale un poco de comida.

4. ¿Los niños les _____ miedo todavía a los payasos?

5. Este edificio _____ más de doscientos años, ¿puedes creerlo?

6. ¡Qué cansada que _____! Mejor me quedaré en casa.

7. ¿_____ calor? Si os parece, bajaré la calefacción un poco.

5. Traduce las siguientes oraciones usando como ayuda la palabra entre paréntesis. `29.E`

1. It's becoming night.

_____ (hacer).

2. It turned cold.

_____ (ponerse).

3. The clock struck five.

_____ (dar).

4. It's winter again.

_____ (de nuevo).

5. Now it's Friday.

_____ (ya).

6. It became day.

_____ (hacer).

6. Traduce las siguientes oraciones siguiendo el modelo. `29.E`

Modelo

He went crazy.
Se enloqueció.
Se volvió loco / Se puso loco.

1. She blushed.

_____

_____

2. She became happy.

_____

_____

3. My grandfather became rich.

_____

_____

4. I got better.

_____

_____

5. They got sad.

_____

_____

6. We became quiet.

_____

_____

7. He went crazy.

_____

_____

7. Síntesis En cada oración, elige la opción correcta. `29.B–29.E`

1. ¿_____ (Está/Hay) alguien que se llame Ángela en tu clase?

2. José ya _____ (tiene/es) veinticuatro años.

3. Mi hermanito _____ (es/está) cansado.

4. Las lámparas _____ (están/fueron) destruidas por vándalos.

5. En verano, _____ (se hace/anochece) de noche muy tarde.

6. _____ (Estamos/Es) en abril y todavía los árboles no tienen hojas.

7. Hoy _____ (estuve/me quedé) en casa, porque me dolía la barriga.

8. Sara se _____ (volvió/puso) tan triste cuando vio que te habías ido.

9. La música _____ (fue/era) tan alta que no podíamos hablar entre nosotros.

10. ¿_____ (Están/Hay) Silvia y Susana en la escuela?

Practice more at **vhlcentral.com.**

Actividades • **Chapter 29**

1. Completa las oraciones con las preposiciones de la lista. `30.B`

> a   de   sin   para   con

1. Me llamo Juliana y soy _____ Medellín, Colombia.
2. Esta casa es ideal _____ hacer una fiesta, ¿no te parece?
3. Como dice mi abuela, mi hermanita es _____ buen comer.
4. ¡Todos esos regalos son _____ ti!
5. ¿Viste un bolso azul? Es _____ lunares blancos.
6. No me gustan los bolsos que son _____ cremallera. ¡Son un imán para los ladrones!
7. El mantel que me regalaron es _____ cuadros.

2. Reescribe estas oraciones usando *ser* y las palabras entre paréntesis. `30.B`

1. La hermana de Juan me parece muy amable. (me)

   _____

2. ¿De veras sabes andar a caballo? (cierto)

   _____

3. ¡Siento tanto que no nos hayamos visto! (lástima)

   _____

4. Profesora, nos pareció muy difícil hacer la tarea. (nos)

   _____

5. Para mí, no es fácil dormir con la luz del día. (me)

   _____

6. Nací en Bogotá y viví ahí hasta los quince años. (de)

   _____

7. Marcos habla muy bien inglés. (bueno)

   _____

8. Construyeron la casa con madera. (de)

   _____

3. Une las frases para formar oraciones lógicas. `30.C`

1. Luis está _____
2. En este restaurante, no está _____
3. En Alemania, está _____
4. La directora está _____
5. Guillermo, estoy _____
6. En la oficina, la cosa está _____
7. Solo por dos meses, Romina está _____

a. que arde... mejor hablaré con mi jefe mañana.
b. por llegar a tu casa. ¿Bajas a abrirme la puerta?
c. permitido fumar, ¿no ves el cartel?
d. de camarera en el bar de la esquina.
e. con mucha tos. Le llevaré un té.
f. mal visto saludar con un beso a alguien que acabas de conocer.
g. de vacaciones durante todo enero. Llámala por teléfono si es algo urgente.

4. Reescribe las oraciones usando *estar* y la preposición indicada. `30.C`

1. Nos acompaña nuestro queridísimo Presidente. (con)

   _____

2. Tengo dolor de garganta desde hace una semana. (con)

   _____

3. Casi salgo de casa sin las llaves. (a punto de)

   _____

4. Pronto comenzarán las obras del metro nuevo. (por)

   _____

5. Mi padre siempre fue partidario de los liberales. (con)

   _____

6. Justo iba a comprarte una camisa del mismo color. (por)

   _____

5. *¿Ser* o *estar*? En cada oración, elige la opción correcta. `30.B–30.C`

1. Mira, los dedos de mis manos _____ azules por el frío.

   a. son   b. están

2. Ese pantalón te _____ muy grande. ¿No ves que se te cae cuando caminas?

   a. es   b. está

3. Las cosas en esta casa _____ así. Si no te gusta, puedes irte a otro lado.

   a. son   b. están

4. Natalia _____ de muy mal humor ahora. Mejor habla con ella mañana.

   a. está   b. es

5. ¡_____ cansado de ser el único que limpia en esta casa!

   a. Soy   b. Estoy

6. ¡Qué grande que _____ tu hija! ¡Cuánto ha crecido en el último verano!

   a. es   b. está

7. Te conviene comprar una cama que _____ de madera aunque cueste más que las de metal.

   a. sea   b. esté

6. Completa el texto con *ser* o *estar* según corresponda. `30.B–30.C`

¡Qué linda que (1) _____ (es/está) Barcelona! Sin duda, ahora (2) _____ (está/es) entre mis ciudades favoritas para vivir.

El clima (3) _____ (está/es) caluroso en verano, pero no muy frío en invierno. Además, (4) _____ (es/está) la playa ahí nomás. ¿Qué más se puede pedir?

También me encanta la gente, que siempre (5) _____ (está/es) de buen humor para atendernos. (6) _____ (Es/Está) como estar en casa. ¡(7) _____ (Estoy/Soy) muerta de ganas de mudarme a esta ciudad!

7. En cada oración, elige entre *ser* o *estar*, según corresponda. `30.B–30.C`

1. Hace un rato que no escucho las voces de Juanito y Pedrito. Ya _____ (serán/estarán) dormidos.

2. ¿Sabes de quién _____ (está/es) enamorada Isabel?

3. La decisión _____ (fue/estuvo) aceptada por toda la empresa.

4. ¿Creías que _____ (era/estaba) satisfecha con mis notas? ¡De ninguna manera!

5. ¡Qué triste que _____ (es/está) el perrito! ¿Le pasa algo?

6. ¡Hoy sí que _____ (estás/eres) trabajadora, Paula! No paras ni un minuto.

7. ¿_____ (Es/Está) verdad que lanzarás un disco nuevo el año que viene?

8. **¿*Haber* o *estar*? Completa la conversación con la opción correcta.** `30.C`

SABRINA Sabes que en la esquina (1) _____ (está/hay) un parque gigante, ¿no?

TERESA ¿Estás segura? ¿En qué esquina (2) _____ (está/hay)?

SABRINA En la esquina de la avenida Naciones Unidas y Terrazas.

TERESA Ah, sí, ¿a qué venía eso?

SABRINA Allí (3) _____ (hay/está) un concierto esta tarde.

TERESA Genial. ¿(4) _____ (Habrá/Habrán) bandas conocidas?

SABRINA No lo sé, pero el año pasado (5) _____ (hubo/estuvo) muy bien.

TERESA ¿Y sabes si (6) _____ (estará/habrá) lluvia?

SABRINA Mmm... dicen que (7) _____ (habrá/estará) nuboso, pero no muy frío.

TERESA Perfecto. ¿Y tienes entradas? (8) _____ (Hay/Están) dos compañeras de la uni que vendrán a casa a comer y me gustaría ir con ellas.

SABRINA ¡Por supuesto! La entrada es libre y (9) _____ (está/hay) abierto a todo el público.

9. **Une las frases para formar oraciones lógicas.** `30.D`

1. Mi casa está _____

2. Dime dónde será _____

3. Lucía, estoy _____

4. Los sanfermines son _____

5. Las flores están _____

a. la fiesta de aniversario de los abuelos.

b. en Pamplona, en junio. ¿Quieres que vayamos?

c. muy lejos de la tuya.

d. aquí en la esquina, ¿no me ves?

e. en el auto. Tráelas, por favor.

10. **Síntesis En cada oración, elige la opción correcta.** `30.B–30.E`

1. La cama _____ (está/es) muy cara ahora. La semana pasada el precio era menor.

2. _____ (Es/Está) importante que vengas a la reunión del jueves.

3. ¿_____ (Estabas/Eras) durmiendo? ¡Discúlpame!

4. _____ (Fue/Estuvo) Francisco quien te llamó ayer, no Federico.

5. Por suerte, la comida ya _____ (está/es) hecha. En un minuto podremos comer.

6. Quiero que _____ (seamos/estemos) felices para toda la vida.

7. _____ (Es/Está) perfecto que estudies mucho, pero también tienes que descansar un poco.

11. **Síntesis Completa las oraciones con los verbos de la lista.** `30.B–30.E`

estábamos	están	fue	son (2)	estuvo
ha	está (2)	será	hubo	es

1. Marina _____ abogada, pero ahora _____ de profesora de historia en una escuela.

2. _____ evidente que _____ problemas de organización en el desfile del mes pasado. Este mes será diferente.

3. ¿El perro _____ en mi habitación? Las paredes _____ llenas de barro.

4. Aunque los novios _____ de Buenos Aires, la boda _____ en Córdoba.

5. _____ en el cine cuando nos llamaste. _____ prohibido usar el teléfono celular allí.

6. _____ habido muchas peleas entre ellos, pero hoy _____ muy amigos.

12. Rodrigo no sabe bien cuándo usar *ser* y *estar*. Ayúdalo a terminar su texto con los verbos adecuados. `30.B–30.E`

> Mi equipo de fútbol favorito
>
> (1) _____ (Está/Es) sabido que en España hay dos equipos de fútbol muy importantes:
> el Real Madrid y el F.C. Barcelona. El problema (2) _____ (es/está) que yo (3) _____
> (soy/estoy) del F.C. Real Madrid, a pesar de (4) _____ (estar/ser) de la ciudad de Barcelona.
> Me (5) _____ (es/está) tan difícil vivir en Barcelona ¡y ver cómo las banderas del Barcelona
> (6) _____ (son/están) hasta en la sopa! Por eso, (7) _____ (soy/estoy) a punto de lanzar
> una campaña para reclutar más fanáticos del Real en Barcelona. Si, (8) _____ (eres/estás)
> conmigo, envíame un mensaje electrónico a mejormadrid@barcelona.es

Practice more at **vhlcentral.com**.

Indirect discourse ✎ⵛ | Chapter 31

1. Escribe las oraciones en discurso indirecto siguiendo el modelo. `31.B`

Modelo

> (viernes) Lucía dijo: "No iré a la fiesta de mañana".
> (Hoy es sábado.) *Lucía dijo que no irá a la fiesta de hoy.*

1. (martes) Tu hermana dijo: "Anoche dormí doce horas".
   (Hoy es viernes.) _____

2. (viernes) La profesora nos dijo: "Estudien para el examen de la semana que viene".
   (Hoy es sábado.) _____

3. (lunes) El presidente dijo: "Me entrevistaré con el presidente ecuatoriano pasado mañana".
   (Hoy es miércoles.) _____

4. (domingo) Juana me dijo: "Nos veremos el martes por la noche".
   (Hoy es lunes.) _____

5. (viernes) Mi tutor me dijo: "Mañana no tendremos clases".
   (Hoy es domingo.) _____

2. Decide si en estas oraciones se da información (I) o una orden (O). Luego, escribe las oraciones en discurso indirecto. `31.B`

1. "Pase y mire sin compromiso". _____ _____

2. "Por favor, no se siente allí". _____ _____

3. "Los pantalones están en oferta". _____ _____

4. "Llévese dos pantalones por 20 dólares". _____ _____

5. "La tienda cierra a las nueve". _____ _____

6. "Apúrese a comprar". _____ _____

7. "Le agradezco su visita". _____ _____

3. **Lee el mensaje electrónico que escribió Daniela y completa la nota de Emilio a Juan reescribiendo las oraciones en discurso indirecto.** `31.B`

¡Hola!
¡Estoy tan feliz porque nos vemos mañana! Llegaré a las nueve y media a la Estación del Sur.
Te esperaré en las escaleras del edificio principal. ¡No te olvides de pasar a buscarme!
No he tenido vacaciones con amigos desde 2006. Quiero que disfrutemos lo máximo posible.
Llama a Juan y avísale sobre mi llegada.
Daniela

Juan:
Hoy recibí un correo electrónico de Daniela.
1. Dijo que _____.
2. Me confirmó que _____.
3. Dijo que _____ y que _____.
4. Luego explicó que _____ y que _____ lo máximo posible.
5. Por último, me pidió _____ y que _____.
Saludos,
Emilio

4. **En cada oración, elige la conjugación apropiada del verbo.** `31.B`

1. Andrés dijo: "Quiero que me ayudes con la tarea".
Andrés dijo que quería que lo _____ (ayudar/ayudara) con la tarea.

2. Los niños dijeron: "Iremos al parque por la tarde".
Los niños dijeron que _____ (irían/iríamos) al parque por la tarde.

3. José y Roberto me dijeron: "Haz la presentación por nosotros".
José y Roberto me dijeron que _____ (hiciste/hiciera) la presentación por ellos.

4. Sandra nos dijo: "He olvidado las llaves dentro de mi casa".
Sandra nos dijo que se _____ (hubiera olvidado/había olvidado) las llaves dentro de su casa.

5. La directora dijo: "No me parece que ustedes se hayan comportado bien".
La directora dijo que no le parecía que ustedes se _____ (habían/hubieran) comportado bien".

6. Mi madre dijo: "Voy a la peluquería y vuelvo en una hora".
Mi madre dijo que _____ (iría/iba) a la peluquería y que _____ (volvería/volvía) en una hora.

7. Mi hermano me dijo: "Son las seis. Te llamo en una hora".
Mi hermano me dijo que _____ (serían/eran) las seis y que me _____ (llamaría/llamaba) en una hora.

8. El doctor me dijo: "Toma el jarabe".
El doctor me dijo que _____ (tomara/hubiese tomado) el jarabe.

5. Elige la opción correcta para transcribir cada oración en discurso indirecto. `31.B`

1. Él dijo: "Nunca había desaprobado un examen".
   a. Él dijo que nunca había desaprobado un examen.
   b. Él dijo que nunca hubiera desaprobado un examen.

2. Tú me dijiste: "Me encantaría que me fueras a buscar al aeropuerto".
   a. Tú me dijiste que te encantaría que te vaya a buscar al aeropuerto.
   b. Tú me dijiste que te encantaría que te fuera a buscar al aeropuerto.

3. El vecino nos dijo: "No hagan más ruido: no puedo dormir".
   a. El vecino nos dijo que no hagan más ruido porque no podía dormir.
   b. El vecino nos dijo que no hiciéramos más ruido porque no podía dormir.

4. Laura nos dijo: "Me caí de la bicicleta".
   a. Laura nos dijo que se había caído de la bicicleta.
   b. Laura nos dijo que se cayó de la bicicleta.

5. Los clientes de la mesa dos dijeron: "Nos gustaban más los platos del cocinero anterior".
   a. Los clientes de la mesa dos dijeron que les habían gustado más los platos que hacía el cocinero anterior.
   b. Los clientes de la mesa dos dijeron que les gustaban más los platos que hacía el cocinero anterior.

6. Él dijo: "En una hora habré terminado de trabajar y estaré de vacaciones".
   a. Él dijo que en una hora habría terminado de trabajar y estará de vacaciones.
   b. Él dijo que en una hora habría terminado de trabajar y estaría de vacaciones.

7. Juan me explicó: "No te puedo contar la verdad porque me voy a meter en problemas".
   a. Juan me explicó que no me podría contar la verdad porque se metería en problemas.
   b. Juan me explicó que no me podía contar la verdad porque se iba a meter en problemas.

8. Mariela me dijo: "Si no quieres venir, no vengas".
   a. Mariela me dijo que, si no quería ir, no fuese.
   b. Mariela me dijo que, si no quisiera ir, no fuera.

6. Une las oraciones en discurso directo con las oraciones en discurso indirecto. Hay tres oraciones en discurso indirecto que no debes usar. `31.B`

_____ 1. Él dijo: "Me duelen los pies".

_____ 2. Ella dijo: "Quisiera una sopa".

_____ 3. Él dijo: "Mañana nos despertaremos temprano".

_____ 4. Ella dijo: "Anoche escuché ruidos raros".

_____ 5. Él dijo: "Aún no se ha secado mi ropa".

_____ 6. Ella dijo: "Ahora quiero una sopa".

a. Él dijo que había escuchado ruidos raros la noche anterior.

b. Él dijo que le dolían los pies.

c. Él dijo que aún no se había secado su ropa.

d. Ella dijo que había escuchado ruidos raros la noche anterior.

e. Él dijo que mañana se despertarían temprano.

f. Ella dijo que quería una sopa.

g. Ella dijo que en ese momento quería una sopa.

h. Él dijo que al día siguiente se despertarían temprano.

i. Él dijo que aún no se había secado mi ropa.

7. Reordena los elementos para formular preguntas indirectas. `31.B`

1. ¿ / está / podría / dónde / el correo más cercano / decirme / Señora, / ?

_____

2. mi papá / me pasa a buscar / si / a las cinco / No recuerdo / o / a las seis / .

_____

3. ¿ / cumple /cuándo / años / Sabes / Cristina / ?

_____

4. si / Me pregunto / es / esta película / divertida / .

_____

5. si / no / tenía calor / Le / con esa chaqueta / pregunté / .

_____

6. era / el nombre / supe / cuál / Nunca / de esa chica tan bonita / .

_____

7. ¿ / hora / decirme / a qué / Puedes / comeremos / ?

_____

8. Completa las oraciones para transformar el discurso directo en indirecto. `31.A–31.B`

1. ¿Cuánto tiempo se tarda para llegar en tren a Barcelona?
   Me gustaría saber _____.

2. ¡He perdido mi cartera!
   Marina me dijo _____.

3. ¡No me molestes más!
   Cecilia me pidió _____.

4. Señor, ¿cómo será el tiempo mañana?
   Le pregunté al señor _____.

5. Señora, ¿tiene cambio de veinte dólares?
   Señora, quisiera saber _____.

6. Ayer trabajé hasta las diez de la noche.
   Mi hermana me contó _____.

7. Nunca había tenido un accidente de tránsito.
   Mi tío me dijo _____.

8. Nos gustaría que nos mostraras las fotos de tu viaje.
   Mis padres me pidieron _____.

9. Si hubiéramos tenido tiempo, te habríamos visitado.
   Mis primos me dijeron _____.

10. Compraría una computadora nueva si tuviera dinero ahorrado.
    Le expliqué a mi jefe _____.

Practice more at **vhlcentral.com.**

1. 1. bis-nie-to 2. A-li-can-te 3. flo-res 4. com-pré 5. pro-ble-ma 6. Pa-blo

2. 1. via-je 2. hom-bre 3. e-dad 4. quie-ra 5. Eu-ro-pa 6. ciu-dades 7. muse-os 8. lla-marme

3. 1. No 2. No 3. Sí, fe-o 4. Sí, ca-os 5. No 6. No 7. Sí, te-a-tro 8. No

4. 1. ce-pi-llo 2. ex-ce-len-te 3. pan-ta-lo-nes 4. po-e-ta 5. cie-lo 6. ha-cia 7. sua-ve 8. a-pren-der 9. em-ple-a-do 10. o-xí-ge-no 11. em-pre-sa 12. Pa-ra-guay 13. a-no-che-cer 14. ca-lle-jón 15. ca-rrua-je

5. 1. Te 2. sé 3. dé 4. Si 5. Tú 6. Tu

6. Llanas: césped, silla, árbol, palabra, álbum; Agudas: balón, razón, ballets, estoy, pasión; Esdrújulas: ídolos, cómpramelo, rápido, lágrimas

7. 1. tráelos 2. pósteres 3. devuélvelos 4. récords 5. tomates 6. ingleses 7. colecciones 8. cómelos

8. 1. miércoles 2. días 3. regálanos 4. té 5. árboles 6. cálculo

9. 1. oído (F, D) 2. maíz (F, D) 3. aeroplano (F, F) 4. compañía (D, F) 5. cooperar (F, F) 6. repetía (D, F) 7. Mediterráneo (F, F) 8. reescribir (F, F) 9. No hay hiato. (D, D) 10. zanahoria (F, F) 11. león (F, F) 12. tío (D, F)

10. Raúl, mío, veo, pelea, María, poema, realidad, creo, día

11. 1. El 2. te 3. Aun 4. más 5. sé 6. Si 7. ti 8. fue 9. Estas 10. vi

12. 1. Quién 2. que 3. como 4. quien 5. Dónde 6. Qué 7. donde 8. Cómo

13. 1. rápidamente 2. atentamente 3. frecuentemente 4. sinceramente 5. teóricamente 6. públicamente

14. 1. margen 2. aborígenes 3. condición 4. mantel 5. árboles 6. interés 7. mes 8. atún

15. 1. c 2. c 3. b 4. b 5. c 6. a

16. 1. país 2. (correcto) 3. gramática 4. (correcto) 5. razón 6. (correcto) 7. dímelo 8. (correcto) 9. (correcto) 10. (correcto) 11. (correcto) 12. holandés 13. débiles 14. créeme 15. (correcto) 16. poesía 17. físico-químico 18. cántalo 19. (correcto) 20. veintitrés 20. (correcto)

17. Hola, Guadalupe:
¡Bienvenida a Córdoba, amiga! ¡Qué bien que ya estés en la ciudad! No veo la hora de encontrarnos, pero estoy un poco ocupada: por las mañanas, voy a un curso de cocina. Estoy muy contenta con el curso. La profesora, que es tan buena onda, resultó ser mi vecina. ¿Puedes creerlo? ¿Te parece que mañana nos veamos? Podemos dar un paseo en barco, ir a museos y caminar en el parque. Allá hace frío, pero aquí, calor. Para mí, todo fue tan genial cuando llegué a esta ciudad. ¡Te encantará conocerla!
Un abrazo muy grande,
Julia

18. 1. , 2. : 3. , 4. , 5. , 6. , 7. ; 8. ;

19. 1. - 2. : 3. — — 4. « » 5. ... 6. ( ) or — —

20. 1. Hoy hace tanto calor, ¿verdad? 2. El prefijo -anti significa "contrario". 3. Sara, Paula, Gastón, José y Pedro fueron al cine el domingo. 4. El jefe de Silvina (que se llama Juan Carlos [igual que el Rey de España]) no quiere que sus empleados lleguen ni un minuto tarde al trabajo. 5. Lee los capítulos 1-5 y resúmelos en una

hoja. 6. Mi hermana (que siempre está de mal humor)/ —que siempre está de mal humor—/, que siempre está de mal humor, / que siempre está de mal humor hoy estaba sonriente. 7. —¿Vienes a la fiesta? —Sí, si me invitas. 8. Hola, Roberto. ¿Cómo estás?

21. 1. lunes 2. Distrito Federal 3. PBI 4. mexicanos 5. Del Valle 6. El Salvador 7. Universidad Nacional Autónoma de México 8. UNAM

22. 1. vaca 2. bolivianos 3. provincia 4. otoño 5. amazónico 6. Valencia 7. Tijuana 8. febrero

23. 1. Milán, italiano 2. España, Euskadi, País 3. Estrecho, Sudamérica 4. Arabia Saudita 5. río Amazonas 6. Una, París 7. ciudad, de

24. 1. c 2. i 3. e 4. b 5. h 6. d 7. a 8. f 9. g

1. Masculino: portero, delfín, escritor, pájaro, poeta, bailarín, toro; Femenino: profesora, nuera, cirujana, gerenta, yegua; Masculino/Femenino: fiscal, artista, comediante, representante, malabarista, ciclista

2. 1. la accionista 2. el padrino 3. la periodista 4. la cuñada 5. la joven 6. el caballo 7. el doctor 8. la cocodrilo hembra 9. el modelo 10. la emperatriz 11. la gallina 12. el suegro

3. 1. El 2. el 3. la 4. la 5. La 6. el 7. el 8. el 9. el 10. la 11. la 12. el 13. La 14. la

4. 1. mal 2. luz 3. canción 4. problema 5. fantasma 6. sinceridad 7. mapa 8. amor 9. vejez 10. idea 11. Barcelona 12. clase

5. 1. La orden 2. el cura 3. un pendiente 4. El Himalaya 5. el rosa 6. la frente

6. 1. a 2. b 3. a 4. a 5. b 6. a 7. b 8. b

7. 1. velas 2. perros 3. canciones 4. paquetes 5. emociones 6. coches 7. papás 8. trenes 9. peces 10. mujeres 11. días 12. países 13. policías 14. relojes 15. viernes

8. 1. Señores 2. corazones 3. buses 4. paces 5. clubes 6. voces 7. ratones 8. paredes

9. 1. miércoles (I), cartas (R) 2. tés (R) 3. jueces (R) 4. pantalones (R) 5. paréntesis (I) 6. tesis (I), alumnos (R) 7. rubíes (R) 8. caracteres (I)

10. 1. a 2. b 3. b 4. b 5. a 6. b

11. 1. plural y singular 2. plural 3. plural 4. plural 5. plural 6. plural y singular 7. plural y singular 8. plural y singular 9. plural y singular 10. singular y plural 11. plural 12. plural

12. jóvenes, ganas, años, espíritu, las vacaciones, los alrededores, beneficios, horas, condiciones, currículum

13. 1. cortito 2. miedito 3. alotas 4. turbinotas 5. asientitos 6. ventanitas 7. juguetito 8. manita 9. tranquilita 10. grandote 11. dibujitos 12. pantallita

14. 1. problemón/problemita 2. hermanita 3. debilita 4. fuertecita 5. ojazos 6. manitas 7. mamita 8. ayudita

15. 1. Cierto. 2. Falso. *Peliculón* no es despectivo. 3. Falso. *Yerno* es el masculino de *nuera*. 4. Cierto. 5. Falso. El diminutivo de *pez* es *pececito*. 6. Cierto. 7. Falso. Es correcto usar *parienta*. 8. Falso. El diminutivo -**ito** indica afecto. 9. Cierto. 10. Cierto.

16. 1. camión 2. veces 3. poeta 4. abogado 5. arena 6. flor 7. cita 8. bis 9. callejones 10. madre

Chapter 3

1. 1. La líder anarquista nació en 1898. 2. La niña danzarina salta y salta sin parar. 3. La doctora alemana ahora vive en París. 4. Una ejecutiva importante renunció a su cargo. 5. He perdido mi gata negrota, mi juguete favorito. 6. La empleada gentil atiende a los clientes con una sonrisa. 7. La niña feliz jugaba en las hamacas del parque. 8. La fanática acosadora no dejaba tranquila a la cantante.

2. 1. sabores agradables 2. perra particular 3. profesora conservadora 4. niña albanesa 5. políticas burguesas 6. salones posteriores 7. rostros paliduchos 8. joven bribona 9. platos tentadores 10. coches veloces 11. publicaciones periódicas 12. aborígenes guaraníes

3. 1. clara 2. rojos 3. anaranjadas 4. blanco 5. bonitos 6. coloridas 7. amarillo 8. rojos 9. verdes 10. impactante

4. 1. hermosos 2. grandes 3. bondadosas 4. pelirrojos 5. fabulosa 6. afortunado 7. esplendorosas

5. 1. perro feíto 2. libro agotado 3. revista médica 4. última película 5. pan caliente 6. organización sindical 7. situación social 8. buena amiga

6. Estimado editor:
En la provincia oriental de Recodo, conseguir un trabajo digno es duro. La oficina laboral no ofrece una atención amable. Lo que es peor, los maleducados empleados se ríen de la gente en su propia cara. La cruda realidad es que no hay puestos de trabajo disponibles. Sin embargo, todos están en pleno derecho de ser tratados cordialmente.
Le pido que comunique esta situación a las autoridades nacionales.
Saludos,
Olivia P.

7. 1. En realidad, ambos participantes tienen posibilidades de ganar el famoso concurso. 2. Pedí expresamente que me enviaran un pañuelo azul. 3. Hay muchas personas que buscan un romance veraniego. 4. Pocos deportistas tienen una vida nocturna activa. 5. Hace tanto calor en esta playa mediterránea. 6. El edificio principal se encuentra en la concurrida calle Posadas.

8. 1. hijo único 2. buen gusto 3. alta tensión 4. santo padre 5. malas lenguas 6. gran amigo 7. hermana menor 8. noticias ciertas

9. 1. primer 2. gran 3. buen 4. tercera 5. San 6. mal 7. cuarta 8. mala 9. grandes

10. 1. más grande 2. la más grande 3. más luminosa 4. la más luminosa 5. mejor 6. la mejor 7. menos ruidosa 8. la menos ruidosa 9. mayor 10. la más joven/la menor 11. la más aburrida

11. 1. c 2. b 3. b. 4. b. 5. c

12. 1. flaquísimo 2. tontísimo 3. pesadísima 4. ordenadísima 5. simpatiquísima 6. tristísima 7. muchísimos 8. exageradísima

13. 1. b, e, f, h, j 2. b 3. d 4. b, f 5. a, e, l 6. h 7. j 8. k 9. c 10. i 11. g

Chapter 4

1. 1. **las** mascotas 2. **tu** mamá 3. **demasiado** trabajo 4. **tu** solución 5. **un** equipo 6. **un** albergue 7. **muchos** perros 8. **Algunos** perros 9. **Estos** animalitos 10. **un** perro 11. **muchas** madres 12. **un** curso 13. **todas las** necesidades 14. **tu** mascota 15. **ningún** miembro 16. **tu** familia 17. **el** curso 18. **otros** niños y jóvenes 19. **sus** experiencias 20. **sus** mascotas 21. **Cada** uno 22. **bastante** sacrificio 23. **el** curso 24. **muchas** ganas 25. **un** perro 26. **El** año 27. **cuarenta** mascotas 28. **un** hogar 29. **nuestro** sitio

2. 1. determinante 2. adverbio 3. pronombre 4. determinante 5. pronombre 6. pronombre 7. adverbio 8. determinante 9. pronombre 10. determinante 11. determinante 12. determinante 13. pronombre 14. adverbio 15. determinante 16. determinante

Chapter 5

1. 1. la 2. las 3. los; El 4. las 5. los 6. la; el
2. 1. una 2. un/otro 3. unos 4. unos 5. una
3. 1. X 2. una 3. el/X 4. unos 5. la 6. la 7. lo 8. un 9. el 10. los
4. 1. un 2. del 3. las 4. otra 5. un 6. el 7. la 8. los

Chapter 6

1. 1. veintiocho 2. ciento treinta y dos 3. mil doscientos 4. diecinueve 5. cuarenta y cuatro 6. ciento dos 7. trescientos treinta y tres 8. un millón 9. mil novecientos ochenta y uno 10. cincuenta y siete

2. 1. Camila nació el 3 de agosto de 1983. 2. Tardaron 103 años en construir este castillo. 3. Para el lunes próximo, tengo que leer 221 páginas. 4. El empresario tiene 1 400 000 dólares. 5. Necesitamos vender 29 000 unidades este mes. 6. El gobierno dio un subsidio de 508 dólares a cada vecino por la inundación. 7. Debo devolverte 791 pesos antes del 30 de enero. 8. Debido a la tormenta, se cayeron 1033 árboles.

3. 1. una veintena de 2. una treintena de 3. una centena de 4. una decena de 5. una docena de 6. una sesentena de 7. un millar de

4. 1. con 2. con 3. y 4. más 5. con 6. es igual a 7. con 8. un 9. por ciento 10. un 11. por ciento

5. 1. No puede ser: es la quinta vez que lavo los platos. 2. No sé qué regalarles a los abuelos para su trigésimo aniversario de casados. 3. Daniel fue el primer hombre que se casó en la familia. 4. El 30 de mayo es el centenario de la fundación de mi pueblo. 5. Luis catorce era llamado "El Rey Sol". 6. En la actualidad, la milenaria pieza se encuentra en el Museo Nacional.

6. 1. millonario 2. tercera 3. segundo 4. centésimo 5. trigésimo 6. quinta 7. octavo 8. décimo primer

7. 1. un medio; la mitad 2. un treceavo; una treceava parte 3. un cuarto; una cuarta parte 4. cuatro quintos; cuatro quintas partes 5. un octavo; una octava parte 6. dos cuartos; dos cuartas partes

8. millonésima de segundo, media taza, un quinto/una quinta parte, la primera mezcla, un cuarto de hora, octavo, media hora

9. 1. Son las ocho y cuarto. Son las ocho y quince. 2. Son las nueve y media. Son las nueve y treinta. 3. Son las doce menos cuarto. Falta un cuarto para las doce. Son las once y cuarenta y cinco. 4. Son las cuatro menos cinco. Faltan cinco para las cuatro. Son las tres y cincuenta y cinco. 5. Son las siete menos veinte. Faltan veinte para las siete. Son las seis y cuarenta. 6. Son las seis menos diez. Faltan diez para las seis. Son las cinco y cincuenta.

10. 1. Hoy es primero/uno de octubre. 2. El tres de octubre, Marcos debe ir a la escuela, hacer su examen de español e ir al dentista. 3. Marcos debe ir a la escuela todos los días. 4. Marcos debe comprar el regalo para la abuela a las seis y cuarto/quince de la tarde. 5. Marcos va a la escuela a las nueve menos veinte/ocho y cuarenta de la mañana. 6. El miércoles a las dos y media/treinta de la tarde, Marcos debe ir al dentista. 7. La fiesta de cumpleaños de la abuela es el cinco de octubre a las siete y media/treinta de la tarde. 8. En la tarde del lunes, Marcos debe ir a natación.

11. 1. cumplí 2. quinceañera 3. cumple 4. sesentona 5. sexagenaria 6. veinteañera 7. setentón 8. tenga

12. 1. ¿Cuántos grados hace hoy? / ¿Qué temperatura hace hoy? 2. ¿Cuál será la temperatura mínima mañana? 3. ¿Cuál será la temperatura máxima mañana? 4. ¿Cuáles serán las temperaturas mínima y máxima pasado mañana? 5. ¿Aquí miden la temperatura en grados Fahrenheit?

13. 1. décadas 2. media 3. veintiséis 4. próxima 5. ser 6. sesentón 7. millones 8. y medio

14. 1. b 2. a 3. b 4. b 5. a 6. b 7. a 8. a

15. Colectivo: decena, cuarentena, millar; Cardinal: ciento uno, billón, trescientos, mil uno; Ordinal: décimo cuarto, trigésimo, quinto; Fraccionario: la mitad, doceava parte, un quinto, cuatro octavos

16. 1. milenio 2. medio 3. décimo 4. veinteañero 5. treceavo 6. cumplir 7. centésimo 8. octogenario

Chapter 7

1. 1. ¿Alguna de tus amigas vive en Perú? 2. ¿Hay algún/un parque de diversiones cerca? 3. ¿Algún compañero reprobó el examen? 4. ¿Alguno de ustedes/vosotros comerá esta comida? 5. ¿Comerás algunas/unas frutas antes de dormir? 6. ¿Encontrarás alguna/una oficina abierta en este barrio?

2. 1. ninguna 2. Ninguno 3. algún 4. ningunas 5. Alguno/Ninguno 6. ningún

3. 1. a y b 2. b 3. a 4. a 5. a y b

4. 1. No habrá regalo alguno para mí en este cumpleaños. 2. Iré a algunos de los campos en el sur de Brasil. 3. No, ninguno de ellos come carne. 4. No hay ningún chico que nos guste. 5. Veré a algunos parientes que viven en Colombia. 6. ¿Tendremos alguna maestra mexicana este año? 7. Nos probamos algunos de los mejores vestidos.

5. cada, muchas, cualquier, demasiado, demás, todo, otra, una

6. 1. sí 2. no 3. sí 4. sí 5. no 6. no

7. 1. En nuestra tienda, le ofrecemos recetas varias/varias recetas: desde platos elaborados hasta platos rápidos. 2. Con dos kilos menos, me veré mejor. 3. Cinco días más y comienzan las vacaciones. 4. Tengo bastante sueño: mejor hablemos mañana. 5. Un día cualquiera llegarás a casa y estaré esperándote con una gran sorpresa. 6. Hay varias cosas que tenemos que hablar. Necesitamos más tiempo.

8. 1. ninguno: pronombre 2. unas: no es pronombre 3. cualquiera: pronombre 4. Algunos: no es pronombre 5. cualquier: no es pronombre 6. todo: pronombre 7. una: pronombre 8. demás: pronombre

9. 1. cualquiera 2. X/una 3. X/un 4. un 5. cualquier 6. unos/X 7. cualquiera de 8. una/X

10. 1. ambas 2. bastantes 3. Todos 4. Los tres 5. cada una de / todas 6. Cada semana / Todas las semanas 7. cada

11. Answers will vary slightly. Suggested answers: 1. Sí, compré todas las que aparecían en la lista. 2. No, cada pueblo es distinto. 3. Sí, he estudiado todo para el examen. 4. Sí, soy todo un experto en motocicletas. 5. Sí, te he contado todo lo que sé sobre la boda.

12. 1. lo 2. las 3. menos 4. más de 5. otros detalles más 6. el otro 7. otras tres 8. otro poco de

13. 1. alguien 2. Nadie 3. uno/alguien 4. Nadie/Ninguno 5. nada 6. algo

14. 1. ¿No hay nadie que sea español? 2. Yo no tenía que decirte nada. / Yo no tenía nada que decirte. 3. No escucho nada cuando hablo por teléfono. 4. Tú no conoces a nadie que pueda venir. 5. No me cuenta nada sobre su abuelo, Pedro.

15. Answers may vary slightly.
Posibles soluciones para el insomnio
Muchas personas sufren de insomnio ocasionalmente. ¿Pero qué puede hacer uno/a cuando esto se convierte en un problema frecuente?
Uno/a puede hacer ejercicio por la tarde, aunque no demasiado tarde. De lo contrario, al momento de dormir, uno/a tiene un ritmo demasiado acelerado y (uno/a) no puede conciliar el sueño.
Otra opción es no tomar bebidas con mucha cafeína. Cuando uno/a toma mucho café o bebidas energéticas, (uno/a) está más alerta y no puede dormirse con tanta facilidad.
Muchos médicos recomiendan que uno/a no tenga un televisor en la habitación. Es mejor que la habitación sea un lugar donde (uno/a) solamente duerma.
Y, por último, uno/a debe intentar tener horarios regulares, es decir, una rutina.

16. 1. nada 2. nadie 3. nada 4. nada 5. nada 6. Nada

17. 1. Mi mamá siempre habla poco. 2. No es nada seguro que ganes una beca. / No es (nada) seguro que ganes nada. 3. En el último año, la economía de nuestro país creció mucho más, en comparación con años anteriores. 4. Este resfriado es bastante grave. 5. No hace tanto que dejé de trabajar.

18. 1. propio 2. mismo/misma 3. propio 4. mismo 5. propia 6. mismo

19. 1. c 2. f 3. h 4. b 5. a 6. j 7. g 8. d 9. e 10. i 11. k

20. 1. f 2. d 3. h 4. b 5. a 6. e 7. g 8. c

1. 1. Esos 2. esos/aquellos 3. esas/aquellas 4. esos 5. estos
2. 1. Esta 2. este 3. Estas 4. esos 5. aquel 6. eso
7. aquellos 8. Esas
3. 1. Esta 2. esta 3. este 4. Este 5. Esto 6. Aquel
7. aquel 8. este 9. estos
4. 1. esa 2. Estas 3. aquello 4. ésta 5. esto/eso
6. Este/Esto 7. aquellos 8. Esta 9. esto

1. 1. tu 2. Nuestro/Mi 3. tu 4. tu 5. mis 6. tu
7. Nuestro/Mi 8. nuestras 9. su 10. nuestras 11. tus
2. 1. míos 2. tuya 3. nuestros 4. suyos 5. tuyos 6. mías
7. nuestro 8. suyos 9. vuestras 10. suyos
3. 1. Esa compañera vuestra no deja de llamar a casa.
2. Varios profesores tuyos dieron clases en universidades
importantes del extranjero. 3. Sus madres hablan tanto.
Con razón, sus padres miran tanta televisión. 4. ¿Puedes
alquilar un DVD en la tienda de mi barrio? 5. Vuestros
zapatos están sucios. Es necesario lavarlos antes de
guardarlos en vuestro armario. 6. Tus perros se llaman
Guardián y Sultán, ¿no? Esos nombres no podrían ser
más que idea tuya.
4. 1. tus 2. míos/nuestros 3. tuyos 4. Mi 5. nuestros/sus
6. Sus 7. suya 8. vuestro
5. **Prenominal:** su, tus, mis **Posnominal:** suyos, tuya, míos
Pre/posnominal: vuestros, nuestra, vuestra, nuestros
6. 1. Mis 2. mi 3. su 4. mío 5. mías 6. sus 7. mío
8. mi 9. sus
7. Possible answers: 1. el país natal de Amparo/ella
2. el diario de Amparo/ella 3. la vida de Amparo/ella
4. el libro de Facundo Quesada / de él 5. palabras de
Facundo Quesada / de él / del autor 6. el diario de
Amparo/ella 7. la vida de Amparo/ella 8. las vidas de
los lectores adolescentes / de ellos 9. los hijos de los
lectores/ustedes
8. 1. experiencia propia 2. propio mundo 3. propios ojos
4. chaqueta propia 5. habitación propia
6. cuenta propia
9. 1. mi 2. el 3. el 4. mi 5. tu 6. el 7. la 8. mi
9. la 10. los 11. tu 12. el/tu 13. el 14. mi/la
10. 1. auto nuestro 2. botas tuyas 3. mi amiga 4. mi
general 5. mi papá 6. tus bufandas 7. valijas nuestras
11. 1. Correcta 2. Correcta 3. Correcta 4. Incorrecta: Mi
hermano y el tuyo se llaman igual. 5. Incorrecta: En tu
país, ¿ahora es invierno o verano? 6. Incorrecta: Mañana
vendrá mi/su/nuestra tía, ¡no la tuya! 7. Incorrecta: Me
duele mucho la cabeza. ¿Qué hago? 8. Incorrecta: El
abogado del delincuente declaró que el ataque fue en
defensa propia. 9. Incorrecta: Mi Alteza Real, le aseguro
que todos los pobladores lo admiran. 10. Correcta
12. 1. los 2. tus tareas 3. la 4. cuenta propia 5. una
solución propia 6. nuestros compañeros 7. mío
8. tuyo 9. de la tuya

1. 1. fácil, adjetivo 2. mejor, adverbio 3. rápidamente,
adverbio 4. demasiado, adjetivo 5. ahora, adverbio
6. amplia, adjetivo 7. inmediatamente, adverbio
8. pocos, adjetivo 9. arreglado, adjetivo
2. 1. cuándo 2. Cuando 3. Después 4. Antes 5. pasado
mañana 6. temprano 7. Tarde 8. Ya 9. Nunca 10. Ya
11. Ya
3. 1. casi nunca 2. Nunca 3. frecuentemente 4. A veces
5. nunca 6. con mucha frecuencia
4. 1. Como 2. peor 3. como 4. bien 5. mejor 6. bien
5. 1. bien 2. así 3. cómo 4. bien 5. mejor 6. como
7. bien 8. Así
6. 1. En el supermercado debemos comprar poco.
2. Tardaremos menos que la semana pasada.
3. Nos llevará poco tiempo. / Apenas nos llevará tiempo.
4. ¡Tendremos que pagar (tan) poco por un taxi!
5. Será mejor comprar mucho para todo el mes.
7. 1. demasiado 2. Casi 3. cuánto 4. bastante/muy
5. Cuanto 6. muy/bastante/demasiado 7. todo lo que
8. 1. Aquí 2. Allí/Allá 3. Aquí 4. aquí 5. allá 6. Allí/Allá
9. 1. ¿Adónde iremos/irán/iréis para comprar regalos?
2. ¿Dónde nos encontraremos / se encontrarán / os
encontraréis a las 10 p.m.? 3. ¿Dónde podrá dormir
Juana? 4. ¿Adónde viajaremos/viajarán/viajaréis por la
mañana? 5. ¿Dónde aterrizará el avión? 6. ¿Adónde
iremos/irán/iréis a comer?
10. 1. delante 2. atrás 3. adentro 4. Debajo 5. arriba
6. Dentro
11. 1. f 2. a 3. d 4. b 5. e 6. g 7. c
12. 1. no 2. Sí 3. Quizás 4. también 5. Sí 6. tampoco
13. 1. locamente 2. Repentinamente 3. sinceramente
4. telefónicamente 5. maravillosamente 6. firmemente
7. tranquilamente 8. cortésmente 9. claramente
14. 1. Correcta 2. Incorrecta: Julieta canta increíblemente.
3. Incorrecta: Subimos la montaña lenta y
cuidadosamente. 4. Correcta 5. Correcta 6. Incorrecta:
Has respondido correctamente.
15. 1. b 2. f 3. c 4. a 5. d 6. g 7. e 8. h
16. 1. Por la noche trabajo mejor que por la tarde.
2. Claudia ahora duerme mejor (que antes). 3. Este año
peso menos que el año pasado. 4. Andrés lee más lento /
menos rápido que Juan. 5. En España se vive peor que
en Francia. 6. Mi hermana estudia más frecuentemente
/ con más frecuencia que mi hermano.
17. 1. conduce lentísimo 2. tranquilísimamente toda la
noche 3. comió muchísimo en casa 4. respondió las
preguntas inteligentísimamente 5. no sabía el camino,
Paula llegó tardísimo 6. vinieron prontísimo cuando
conocieron la noticia
18. 1. Tiempo 2. Cantidad 3. Lugar 4. Modo 5. Lugar
6. Tiempo 7. Tiempo 8. Cantidad 9. Modo
10. Tiempo 11. Cantidad 12. Lugar 13. Modo
19. 1. tampoco 2. Jamás 3. Primero 4. allá 5. muy
6. bien/muy 7. suficiente 8. dónde 9. como
10. cuándo/dónde
20. ¿Qué es el mundo laboral?
¿No sabes dónde buscar trabajo? ¿No sabes cuánto dinero
deberías ganar? Aquí te ayudaremos. Somos un grupo de

ex alumnos de tu escuela y queremos ayudarte a conocer un poco más el mercado laboral. También queremos contarte sobre nuestros trabajos y cómo los conseguimos. Apúntate a las reuniones que realizamos semanalmente en la sala de conferencias de la escuela. Te esperamos, ¿sí?

Chapter 11

1. 1. es más rápido que el autobús 2. hace más calor que en Buenos Aires 3. es más joven / menor que la maestra de biología 4. es peor que Carina en voleibol 5. llovió menos que por la tarde 6. es peor que *Shrek*

2. 1. Martín corre menos que Susana. Susana corre más que Martín. 2. Martín tiene más perros que Susana. Susana tiene menos perros que Martín. 3. Martín duerme menos que Susana. Susana duerme más que Martín. 4. Martín tiene peor promedio que Susana. Susana tiene mejor promedio que Martín. 5. Martín hizo más tortas que Susana. Susana hizo menos tortas que Martín. 6. Martín es más alto que Susana. Susana es más baja que Martín.

3. 1. irregular: peor 2. regular 3. irregular: menos 4. irregular: mayor 5. regular 6. regular 7. regular 8. irregular: más 9. regular 10. regular 11. regular 12. irregular: mejor

4. 1. En agosto, tengo más de dos semanas de vacaciones. 2. Durante el verano, voy bastante más seguido al parque. / Durante el verano, voy bastante al parque. 3. Vivimos en un barrio relativamente céntrico. 4. Cuando estoy a dieta, no bebo más que agua mineral. 5. Dormí la siesta y ahora tengo menos sueño. 6. Mis manos son más delicadas que las tuyas. 7. Mis horarios actuales son diferentes de/a los que tenía antes.

5. 1. de lo que 2. que 3. de 4. que 5. de los que 6. de las que 7. de 8. que

6. 1. tantas 2. tan 3. misma 4. igual 5. tanto 6. mismo 7. tan 8. como 9. Tal como/Como 10. tan

7. 1. La historia no fue tal como me la contaste. Fue más trágica. 2. Tamara tiene tantos libros que no ha leído aún. / Tamara tiene tan/tanta mala suerte. 3. Debo leer tanto como sea posible estas vacaciones. 4. Conduce exactamente a la misma velocidad que indica el cartel. 5. Estela es igual de alta que yo. 6. No entiendo cómo pude tener tanta/tan mala suerte. 7. Come tu tarta tan rápido como puedas, antes de que se enfríe.

8. 1. Los productos de nuestra compañía son los mejores del mercado. 2. Sebastián es el más alto de su/la clase. 3. Este sofá tiene la peor calidad de todos. 4. La música de esta radio es la mejor del país. 5. Juanito es el menor / el más pequeño de la/su familia. 6. Mis ensaladas son las más deliciosas del concurso de cocina. 7. Mi padre es el mayor / más viejo de todos.

9. 1. practiquísimo/óptimo/novedosísimo 2. extraordinariamente/verdaderamente 3. óptimo/practiquísimo 4. verdaderamente 5. lo más 6. lo mejor 7. lo mejor 8. novedosísimo/pequeñísimo 9. pequeñísimo/ínfimo 10. ínfimo/pequeñísimo

10. 1. fue la peor (del año) 2. menos invitados 3. la misma / igual 4. bailamos poquísimo / no bailamos muchísimo 5. me aburrí tanto / me divertí tan poco 6. poquísimo 7. más que 8. misma

11. 1. Catalina es igual de alta que su madre. 2. Tatiana tiene tantos vestidos como sus amigas. 3. Mis notas son mejores que las tuyas. 4. La primera parte de esta película es tan mala como la segunda. 5. Tú no comes tanto como yo. 6. Mis calcetines son diferentes de/a los tuyos.

12. 1. b 2. c 3. a 4. c 5. b 6. b 7. b 8. b

13. 1. Roma es menos romántica que Venecia. 2. El carro azul es tan elegante como el carro rojo. / El carro azul es igual de elegante que el carro rojo. 3. Esta vendedora es la más encantadora del mundo. 4. La tarea de hoy es menos fácil que la de ayer. 5. Este periódico es el más conocido del país. 6. Puedo comprar menos zapatos que tú. 7. Tus tartas son igual de buenas que las de mi madre. / Tus tartas son tan buenas como las de mi madre. 8. Las calles de Madrid son las más anchas de toda Europa.

Chapter 12

1. 1. Para 2. sobre 3. Durante 4. de 5. entre 6. Desde 7. hasta 8. Tras 9. excepto

2. Answers may vary. Suggested answers: 1. Hoy en la televisión podremos ver el partido del Real Madrid versus el Barcelona. 2. Fui a París vía Londres. 3. Tobías trabaja para una organización pro derechos de los animales. 4. Arriba y debajo de la nevera hay suciedad. 5. Mira el gráfico del precio de alquiler versus el precio de compra. 6. ¿Nos encontramos enfrente o detrás del gimnasio?

3. 1. Yo no tengo nada en contra de tus amigos. 2. Seamos sinceras, entre él y tú hay problemas. 3. Mi casa está muy lejos del parque de diversiones. 4. Me encanta dormir la siesta bajo el naranjo. 5. No puedes subir al autobús sin un boleto. 6. El papel de carta está sobre el escritorio. 7. Mi hermana cree que hay monstruos debajo de su cama.

4. 1. de 2. Al lado de / Cerca de 3. En/Sobre 4. lejos de 5. Delante de / Cerca de 6. hasta 7. en 8. cerca de

5. 1. Yo estoy en pro de la reforma constitucional. 2. El gato se perdió por entre las malezas. 3. A causa de tu demora, perdimos el tren. 4. Carola fue a por una barra de pan. 5. Tengo una obligación para con Willy. 6. La chaqueta es roja por dentro/fuera y negra por fuera/dentro. 7. En cuanto a los zapatos, deberás comprar unos nuevos. 8. Son mejores las entrevistas cara a cara. 9. Por lo general, prefiero las películas de terror. 10. Compraremos leche de regreso al hostal.

6. 1. a 2. a 3. de 4. por 5. para 6. con 7. de

7. 1. por 2. para 3. de 4. con 5. a 6. de 7. a

8. 1. Karina cortó el papel con una tijera. 2. Isabela es de España. 3. Estoy de mal humor. 4. Llegó una carta para ti. 5. La señora de cabello rubio se quedó dormida. 6. Con este aumento de salario, podré ahorrar un poco más de dinero. 7. Al llegar (yo), tú ya estabas dormida.

9. 1. a 2. a 3. en 4. Con 5. de 6. con 7. a 8. de 9. En 10. A

10. 1. de 2. Del 3. al 4. de 5. de 6. de 7. del 8. de 9. a/contigo a

11. 1. para 2. Por 3. Para 4. Por 5. para 6. Para 7. por 8. para

12. 1. a 2. a 3. X 4. X; a 5. a 6. X 7. a

13. 1. De 2. Desde 3. por 4. hasta 5. de 6. Para 7. En 8. contra 9. Con 10. Tras

14. 1. Hasta/Por 2. Sin 3. Entre 4. para 5. Por 6. en 7. de 8. X

15. 1. b 2. b 3. b 4. a 5. c 6. c 7. a 8. b

16. 1. De 2. a 3. en 4. de 5. a través de / mediante / con 6. sobre / encima de / en

17. 1. b 2. d 3. a 4. e 5. g 6. i 7. h 8. c 9. f

18. 1. Hasta 2. Según 3. Cerca de 4. Junto a / Junto con 5. Hacia 6. Entre 7. Tras 8. Excepto 9. En 10. contigo 11. Con 12. en 13. en

Chapter 13

1. 1. Nosotros/as 2. Ella 3. Ellos 4. Ella 5. Nosotros 6. Ellas 7. Nosotros 8. ello/eso

2. 1. a 2. c 3. b 4. d 5. f 6. e

3. 1. Nosotros hemos jugado muy bien esta tarde. 2. La empresa está satisfecha contigo. 3. Vosotros siempre tenéis muchas vacaciones. 4. Para usted, las tareas son fáciles. 5. Entre ellos, hay muy buena comunicación. 6. Ellas son estudiantes, ¿verdad?

4. 1. tú 2. mí 3. consigo 4. yo/tú/él/vosotros 5. él/tú/vosotros 6. tú 7. Vosotros 8. ti 9. Conmigo/Tú

5. 1. Roberto las compró en el mercado central. 2. Lo/Le llamamos porque lo extrañábamos. 3. Julia la estudió muy bien. 4. Finalmente la policía lo atrapó. 5. Gonzalo las buscó debajo de la mesa. 6. Los obreros lo comen a las dos de la tarde. 7. Constanza y Sofía se las compran a sus madres. 8. Los traje de la biblioteca.

6. 1. Invitamos a todos nuestros amigos. 2. ¿A quiénes conociste esta noche? 3. ¿Qué prefieres hacer? 4. Mi hermana ama a su novio. 5. Leo novelas románticas. 6. Te he llamado a ti. 7. Visité París y Roma. 8. ¿A quiénes visitamos/visitasteis/visitaron esta noche?

7. 1. Julia le dio una bufanda. 2. Les dijiste mentiras. 3. Ellos les contaron historias de terror. 4. El camarero les recomendó una paella. 5. Tu madre le mostró la habitación. 6. Hoy le leerás un cuento de hadas. 7. Les pedí dinero.

8. Soy una persona un poco complicada. No **me** gusta salir de casa. **Me** molesta mucho <u>el ruido de los carros y</u> <u>motocicletas</u>. Por eso, prefiero estar en casa. **Me** gusta leer novelas: sobre todo, **me** interesan <u>las</u> <u>novelas románticas.</u> Además, **me** encanta <u>ver comedias</u> <u>en la televisión.</u> Ojalá algún día encuentre a mi pareja ideal. Un hombre a quien **le** guste <u>mirar televisión</u> <u>conmigo,</u> **le** interesen <u>las noticias de la actualidad</u> y **le** encante <u>cocinar.</u> ¿**Os** parecen demasiado grandes <u>mis expectativas?</u>

9. 1. Los invitaré a la ceremonia religiosa. 2. Claudia te espera en la esquina. 3. Les daré una gran sorpresa. 4. Emilia nos compró tres entradas para el teatro. 5. Omar me regalará su cámara de fotos antigua. 6. Los llamaré de inmediato a su casa. 7. ¿Me das las instrucciones para armar la cama?

10. 1. ¿Estás preparándonos la merienda? 2. Yo te podría ayudar con tus tareas. 3. Lucía va a acompañarme hasta la esquina. 4. El público los está alentando.

5. La directora va a enviarles una carta de recomendación. 6. Les estamos dando excelentes ideas para hacer un negocio.

11. 1. la he comprado 2. sería bueno decorarlas 3. las he mandado 4. no los he llamado 5. te la daré pronto 6. la necesito

12. 1. Ya la he llamado. 2. No la he arreglado. 3. No se lo he llevado. 4. Ya lo he buscado. 5. No se la he dado. 6. Ya se la he devuelto.

13. 1. e 2. c 3. b 4. d 5. a

14. 1. a 2. c 3. c 4. b 5. b 6. c

15. 1. Incorrecta: Traje muchas flores para ti. 2. Correcta 3. Incorrecta: Te daré un regalo si te portas bien, Juana. 4. Incorrecta: Vosotros ya lo habéis hecho. 5. Correcta 6. Incorrecta: A Daniela la conozco de la universidad. 7. Correcta 8. Incorrecta: Mis tíos me las regalaron para Navidad.

16. 1. les 2. os 3. les 4. le 5. ti 6. me 7. vos 8. nos 9. os 10. Me

Chapter 14

1. 1. Úrsula viene a comer, ¿no es así? 2. Ayer hizo frío, ¿verdad? 3. ¿Duerme Karina todavía? 4. Ustedes toman el avión de las 12, ¿no? 5. ¿Tiene el profesor las notas del examen? 6. ¿Sabe Florencia que la llamé?

2. Answers will vary. Sample answers: 1. Tu hermana tiene quince años, ¿no es así? / ¿Tiene tu hermana quince años? 2. ¿Debes ir hoy a la escuela? / Debes ir a la escuela hoy, ¿no? 3. ¿Harán ellos las compras hoy? / Ellos harán las compras hoy, ¿verdad? 4. ¿Comienza la primavera el 21 de septiembre en nuestro/su país? / La primavera comienza el 21 de septiembre en nuestro/su país, ¿no es así? 5. ¿Fue construido el edificio en 1980? / El edificio fue construido en 1980, ¿no? 6. ¿Quieres pastel? / No quieres pastel, ¿verdad?

3. 1. cuál 2. Cuáles 3. qué 4. Cuáles 5. Qué 6. cuáles 7. cuál

4. 1. Quién 2. Cuál 3. Quiénes 4. Quién 5. Qué 6. Quiénes 7. Quién 8. Cuál

5. 1. Cuántos 2. Cuántos 3. Cuánto 4. Cuánto 5. Cuántos 6. Cuán 7. Cuánto 8. Cuán

6. 1. ¿Cómo es de difícil el problema? 2. ¿Cómo es de grande la habitación? 3. ¿Cómo es de alto tu padre? 4. ¿Cómo te sientes esta tarde? 5. ¿Cómo te parece nuestro apartamento nuevo? 6. ¿Cómo es de pesada la lavadora?

7. 1. Qué tal 2. Qué 3. Cuáles 4. Cuántos 5. Cómo 6. Cuánto

8. 1. quién es tu cantante favorito 2. cuántos años tiene Joaquín 3. cuánto dinero hay en la cuenta 4. cómo se llama la persona que me espera 5. cuánto tiempo horneas la torta 6. cuál es tu número de teléfono 7. qué te gustaría beber en la cena

9. 1. ¿Qué distancia hay entre tu casa y la mía? 2. ¿De qué talla es tu camiseta? 3. ¿Con qué frecuencia haces deportes? 4. ¿Cada cuántos años debes renovar tu licencia de conducir? 5. ¿A qué altura sobre el nivel del mar está la ciudad de Quito? 6. ¿Cómo nadas de rápido?

10. 1. Ismael quiero saber el porqué de su despido. 2. Dime dónde viste tu teléfono por última vez. 3. ¿Cuándo vendrás a buscarme? 4. ¿Cómo puedo contactar contigo?

5. ¿Por qué no viniste a mi fiesta de cumpleaños?
6. ¿Qué tal (está) la comida que preparé?

11. 1. A qué 2. por qué 3. Qué tal 4. Hasta dónde
5. Cómo 6. Cuáles 7. cómo

12. 1. Incorrecta: Explícame cómo ir hasta el centro de la
ciudad. 2. Correcta 3. Incorrecta: ¿Cuántos años tienes?
4. Incorrecta: ¿Qué es *alacena* en inglés?
5. Incorrecta: ¿Cuántas personas van al cine los fines de
semana? 6. Incorrecta: ¿Cuán grande es la cocina?
7. Dime el porqué de tu visita.

13. 1. ¡Cuántas flores hay en este parque! 2. ¡Qué elegante
es este barrio! 3. ¡Qué caros son los restaurantes!
4. ¡Qué limpias son las calles! 5. ¡Cuánto/Cómo me
gustaría vivir en esta ciudad! 6. ¡Quién fuera rico para
vivir aquí!

14. 1. f 2. e 3. c 4. a 5. d 6. b

15. 1. Cuándo 2. Qué tal 3. Cuál 4. no es cierto
5. Cuántos 6. qué 7. Cómo 8. Qué 9. qué

16. 1. g 2. e 3. b 4. f 5. c 6. a 7. d

Chapter 15

1. Mujer busca marido

Me llamo Olivia y tengo 44 años. Busco a <u>un hombre</u>
que tenga entre 45 y 55 años y que esté dispuesto a
formar una pareja estable.
Me gustaría tener <u>una pareja</u> que no tenga hijos,
preferentemente. Me gustan los hombres altos,
elegantes y formales.
Soy activa y llevo <u>una vida</u> que podría definir como
tranquila. Trabajo <u>durante</u> la semana y los fines de semana
hago actividades al aire libre. El <u>estilo de vida</u> que llevo es
un poco costoso, por lo tanto, preferiría <u>un hombre</u> cuyo
salario sea superior o igual al mío.
Si eres un <u>hombre</u> que tiene estas cualidades, no dudes en
llamar al <u>teléfono</u> que aparece abajo.

2. 1. Lucila es la mujer que me dio las flores. 2. Encontré
un lugar donde puedo comprar productos orgánicos.
3. Te ha llamado una mujer que se llama Elisa. 4. ¿Os
gustó el regalo que os di? 5. El barrio donde vivo está
muy lejos del centro. 6. Nos encontramos en el bar que
te indiqué.

3. 1. Las tareas que te encargué deben estar terminadas
antes del 20 de junio. 2. La tienda donde me olvidé
el paraguas está cerrada. 3. Todas las estudiantes con
las que hablé me recomendaron el mismo libro. 4. La
habitación cuya puerta es azul es demasiado oscura.
5. Contrataremos a la candidata cuyo currículum sea
mejor. 6. Los amigos con los que cenamos anoche nos
han invitado a su casa.

4. 1. Incorrecta: Le presento al empleado **que** fue
contratado la semana pasada. 2. Incorrecta: La escuela
que está en la esquina es muy buena. 3. Correcta
4. Incorrecta: Elige la bufanda **que** más te guste.
5. Incorrecta: Daniela, **a quien** conocí en la escuela,
ahora trabaja conmigo. 6. Correcta

5. 1. ND 2. D 3. D 4. ND 5. D 6. D

6. 1. la que 2. que 3. el que 4. que 5. la que 6. el que
7. que

7. 1. París, que es mi ciudad favorita, tiene muchos
puentes. / París, que tiene muchos puentes, es mi ciudad

favorita. 2. La profesora a quien conocí ayer se llama
Silvia. 3. La empresa para la cual trabajé durante 20
años está ahora en quiebra. 4. La semana que viene
viajaré a Europa, el cual es mi continente favorito.
5. Mañana jugaré baloncesto, al cual jamás antes
he jugado.

8. 1. cuyo 2. Quien 3. que 4. Lo que 5. que 6. quienes

9. 1. Soy yo quien / el/la que lavará los platos. 2. Es el jefe
quien / el que pagará una parte de los despidos. 3. Fue
en Valencia donde comimos una exquisita paella.
4. Fue Cervantes el que/quien escribió *Don Quijote de la
Mancha*. 5. Fue el fin de semana pasado cuando ganamos
la competencia. 6. Son los estudiantes quienes / los que
tienen demasiados reclamos.

10. 1. La ciudad donde vivo tiene 200.000 habitantes.
2. Lo haré (del modo) como tú me has dicho. 3. En la
época cuando nací, mis padres vivían en el extranjero.
4. Ella siempre me ha dado todo cuanto tenía. 5. Me
gusta la manera como crecen esas flores.

11. 1. b 2. c 3. a 4. c 5. b 6. b 7. b

12. 1. en la que / cuando 2. cuyo 3. quien 4. en (el) que
5. que 6. que 7. quienes / las que / las cuales 8. en la
que / donde 9. lo que / lo cual 10. que/quien 11. como /
en el que / en el cual 12. cuyos

Chapter 16

1. 1. y 2. e 3. no... ni.../ni... ni... 4. Ni... ni... 5. pero
6. sino 7. pues

2. 1. y 2. o 3. y 4. o 5. y 6. y 7. o

3. 1. pero 2. Tanto 3. como 4. y 5. sin embargo 6. y
7. ni 8. ni 9. u 10. tanto 11. y 12. pues 13. bien
14. bien

4. PACIENTE Buenos días, doctor Pérez.
DOCTOR Buenos días. Dígame: ¿qué lo trae por aquí?
PACIENTE A ver... desde hace dos días, **cuando** me
levanto, me duele mucho el estómago.
DOCTOR Me ha dicho **que** le duele el estómago.
¿Suele comer alimentos poco saludables?
PACIENTE No... pero, pensándolo mejor, **aunque**
no coma nada me duele la barriga. Eso sí, bebo café,
me encanta.
DOCTOR Entonces usted no come, pero toma café.
¿Cuántas tazas toma por día?
PACIENTE Tomo solamente dos o tres **en cuanto**
llego al trabajo, dos más **una vez que** tengo un tiempito
libre, y tres más por la tarde **porque** me da sueño
trabajar tanto.
DOCTOR ¡Y después me pregunta **que** cuál es el
motivo de su dolor de estómago!
PACIENTE Creo **que** tiene razón, doctor. Debería
tomar el café con un chorrito de leche, ¿no?
DOCTOR Mire, **como** usted no mide cuánto café toma,
se lo prohibiré totalmente. **Siempre que** sienta ganas de
tomarse un cafecito, tómese un té o, mucho mejor, un
vaso de agua, **de manera que** su estómago
no siga empeorando.
PACIENTE Muchas gracias, doctor.
DOCTOR ¡Cuídese! Adiós.

5. 1. Leonel pregunta que cuál es tu número de teléfono.
2. José pregunta que si tienes el correo electrónico de

Carla. 3. Juan y Marina creen que el lechero vendrá a las nueve. 4. Estela pregunta que si has oído el timbre. 5. Mirta dice que le gustaría dormir la siesta.

6. 1. temporal 2. causal 3. causal 4. temporal 5. temporal 6. causal 7. causal 8. temporal

7. 1. de manera que 2. puesto que 3. así que 4. porque 5. así que 6. de modo que

8. 1. A pesar de que estudio muchísimo la gramática española, siempre cometo los mismos errores. 2. Trabajaré mucho hoy de modo que mañana pueda descansar. 3. Martín cocina como si fuera un experto. 4. Patricia trabaja tanto como Julia. 5. Iremos a pasear donde tú quieras. 6. Para que comas dulces, antes debes comerte toda la comida. 7. Yo como igual cantidad de verduras que las que comes tú. 8. Debes ahorrar a fin de que puedas comprar tu propio piso.

9. 1. c 2. c 3. a 4. c 5. a 6. b 7. b 8. c

10. 1. b 2. a 3. b 4. c 5. b 6. a 7. c 8. a

11. 1. a 2. f 3. g 4. b 5. d 6. e 7. c

12. 1. que 2. sino; así que 3. ni, así que 4. Antes de que 5. Para que 6. En caso de que 7. Cuando/Si/Cada vez que 8. Si 9. Cada vez que/Cuando 10. o 11. Sin embargo, 12. pues 13. y 14. pero 15. Tanto; como

Chapter 17

1. **Copulativo:** es, está, era, sean; **Transitivo:** protagonizó, sufrió, tuvo, hizo, chocó, conoció, pido; **Intransitivo:** conducía, sucedió, ingresar, conducir

2. 1. con 2. por 3. a 4. a 5. a 6. con 7. de

3. 1. b 2. b 3. b 4. a 5. b 6. b 7. a

4. 1. A los alumnos les disgusta hacer la tarea. 2. ¿No te entristece la despedida de Flor? 3. Me fascina ir a las montañas en invierno. 4. ¡Me sorprende tu visita! 5. Me asustan los fantasmas. 6. Me divierte (mucho) ir de compras.

5. 1. completamos 2. cumplís 3. bebes 4. viajan 5. insiste 6. leo 7. responde 8. investigás

6. 1. Introduzco 2. cuezo 3. exijo 4. Ejerzo 5. recojo 6. consigo 7. traduzco

7. 1. ¿Por qué incluís a Juana en tu lista de invitados, pero no a mí? 2. ¿Continúas con las clases de guitarra? 3. No confío en el criterio de Emiliano. 4. Siempre pierden el hilo de la conversación. 5. Yo te defiendo si pasa algo. 6. Vuelven a las nueve y media de la noche. 7. Te pido un gran favor.

8. 1. cuenta 2. se sitúa 3. empieza/comienza 4. se convierte 5. persiguen 6. se acuesta 7. decide 8. se repite 9. deduce 10. comienza/empieza 11. sueña 12. recuerda 13. afligen

9. 1. pongo 2. salgo 3. traigo 4. hago 5. compongo 6. propongo

10. 1. oigo 2. tiene 3. viene 4. maldices 5. atienes 6. digo 7. oyen

11. 1. Yo digo la verdad si tu dices la verdad también. 2. Ellos ven el documental si yo lo veo también. 3. Yo estoy de buen humor si vosotros estáis de buen humor también. 4. Yo voy a la fiesta si tú vas también. 5. Yo traigo la torta si vosotros traéis un regalo.

12. Acciones presentes: 1, 7
Costumbres: 4, 5
Hechos intemporales: 2, 3, 6

13. 1. a 2. b 3. b 4. a 5. a 6. a

14. 1. d 2. b 3. a 4. c 5. f 6. e 7. i 8. g 9. h

15. 1. encantan 2. se casa 3. Estoy llamando / Llamo 4. deduzco 5. estoy eligiendo 6. persigue 7. estamos construyendo 8. empiezas 9. puedo 10. llega 11. está durmiendo 12. descansas/descansás

16. 1. pierden, están perdiendo 2. atravieso, estoy atravesando 3. quieren, están queriendo 4. cuesta, está costando 5. podés, X 6. promuevo, estoy promoviendo 7. confesamos, estamos confesando 8. estáis, X 9. destruyes, estás destruyendo 10. oye, está oyendo 11. debes, X 12. salgo; estoy saliendo

Chapter 18

1. **Libros perdidos**
Me llamo Francisco y el día lunes 23 de agosto tuve una clase en el aula 213. Estuve allí desde las 9 a.m. hasta las 12 p.m. Cuando salí, me olvidé un bolso con libros debajo de la silla. Son un libro de Matemáticas, otro de Física y uno de Química; los compré en la librería universitaria y escribí mi nombre en la primera hoja. Si alguien los encontró, les pido que me escriban o me llamen al teléfono que aparece abajo.

2. 1. jugué 2. expliqué 3. toqué; contestó 4. Se cayó 5. se reconstruyó 6. se sintió 7. puso 8. condujo

3. 1. (Yo) averigüé el teléfono del chico que vi en el autobús. 2. ¿Por qué llegaste tarde? 3. ¿Oyó él también un ruido fuerte? 4. Ellos durmieron muy bien anoche. 5. Nunca supe el motivo del incendio. 6. Ella hizo la comida. 7. Ayer fuimos a la estación de tren para comprar los boletos.

4. 1. estaba 2. dormía 3. comías 4. vivíamos 5. éramos 6. veíamos 7. ibais/erais 8. compraban 9. estábamos 10. sabía

5. 1. pretérito perfecto simple, b 2. pretérito imperfecto, e 3. pretérito imperfecto, a 4. pretérito imperfecto, d 5. pretérito imperfecto, f 6. pretérito perfecto simple, c 7. pretérito perfecto simple, h 8. pretérito perfecto simple, g

6. 1. visitaste 2. cumplí 3. me despertaba; desayunaba 4. estaba; se nubló; comenzó 5. teníamos; éramos 6. iba; me acordé 7. se llamaba 8. había; decidí 9. Iba; me encontré

7. 1. fui 2. dolía 3. Hacía 4. iba 5. había 6. me senté 7. dio 8. alivió 9. dijo 10. sacó 11. fue 12. llegué

8. 1. fui 2. impactó 3. entré 4. dio 5. terminó 6. invitaron 7. eran 8. decidí

9. 1. era muy importante que yo fuera puntual 2. tenías una sorpresa para mí 3. preferías estar a solas conmigo porque hacía mucho tiempo que no nos veíamos 4. esperabas ver todas las fotos de mis últimas vacaciones 5. hacía tres meses que no pasabas tiempo con amigos 6. yo era tu mejor amiga

10. 1. pudo 2. quisieron 3. quería 4. tenía 5. podía 6. supe 7. teníamos

11. 1. pidió 2. sabía 3. hicieron 4. tradujo 5. iba
6. preparaba 7. oí 8. era 9. hubo 10. había

12. 1. nos conocimos 2. teníamos 3. decidimos 4. envió
5. compré 6. brillaba 7. hacía 8. Parecía 9. apareció
10. sabíamos 11. corrimos 12. leímos 13. podíamos
14. era 15. comenzaron 16. estuvo 17. Hacía
18. nos divertíamos

Chapter 19

1. 1. ha estudiado 2. he terminado 3. han recibido
4. habéis esperado 5. han actuado 6. ha llegado
7. ha invitado

2. 1. ¿Alguna vez has comido paella? 2. Lucía todavía no
ha vendido su bicicleta. 3. Este año esta zona se ha
transformado en un centro financiero. 4. En mi vida he
tenido un carro rojo. 5. ¿Tus jefes te han mostrado cuál
será tu oficina? 6. ¡Tan pronto te has olvidado de mí!

3. **Regulares:** comprado, estado, sonreído, leído,
concurrido, freído, crecido, aumentado
Irregulares: descubierto, visto, frito, resuelto, muerto

4. 1. ha compuesto 2. Habéis leído 3. has vuelto 4. ha
abierto 5. ha traído 6. ha puesto 7. han resuelto

5. 1. experiencia 2. acción continua 3. acción incompleta
4. experiencia 5. experiencia 6. acción continua
7. experiencia 8. acción continua 9. acción incompleta

6. 1. c 2. e 3. a 4. b 5. d 6. f

7. he encontrado: encontré, he visto: vi, hemos viajado:
viajamos, he contado: conté, he cocinado: cociné, he
lavado: lavé

8. 1. habían salido 2. había imaginado 3. habíamos
recibido 4. había entendido 5. habíamos olvidado
6. se había comido 7. habíamos probado

9. Pasado antes del pasado: 2, 4, 5, 7
Discurso indirecto: 1, 3, 6

10. 1. Cuando tú me llamaste, ya había apagado mi teléfono
móvil. 2. Cuando sonó el despertador, ya nos habíamos
levantado de la cama. 3. Laura aprobó el examen,
porque había estudiado mucho. 4. Natalia subió de
peso, porque había dejado la dieta. 5. Cuando llegó
Raúl, ya habíamos terminado de comer. 6. Pablo
no pudo ir a la fiesta porque se había roto la
pierna esquiando.

11. 1. f 2. e 3. a 4. g 5. b 6. d 7. c

12. 1. he encontrado 2. había anhelado 3. había cometido
4. has terminado 5. Hemos dormido 6. Ha nevado/
Había nevado 7. te habías limpiado 8. he tomado
9. ha devuelto 10. habían impreso/imprimido

Chapter 20

1. 1. dará 2. cocinará 3. ayudará 4. elegirá 5. regalaré
6. cancelarán 7. subirán

2. 1. har- 2. saldr- 3. valdr- 4. tendr- 5. vendr- 6. sabr-
7. cabr- 8. pondr- 9. habr- 10. querr-

3. 1. tendré 2. valdrá 3. Haré 4. vendrán 5. saldré
6. querrán 7. podré

4. 1. b 2. d 3. f 4. c 5. e 6. a

5. 1. a 2. a 3. b 4. b 5. a 6. a

6. 1. e 2. c/h 3. f 4. g 5. d/b 6. a 7. h 8. b

7. 1. b 2. a 3. b 4. a 5. b 6. a

8. 1. c 2. d 3. a 4. b 5. e

9. 1. habremos terminado 2. habrá quedado 3. Habrá
habido 4. habrás desperdiciado 5. nos habremos
graduado 6. Habrá llamado 7. se habrá cansado
8. habrán pensado 9. habrá conseguido 10. habréis
obtenido 11. se habrá acabado 12. habré comprado

10. 1. comeremos 2. habrá gustado 3. obtendrá 4. se habrá
encargado 5. lloverá 6. tendrás 7. habrá 8. habrá ido

11. 1. habrás jugado 2. valdrá / habrá valido 3. Vendrá
4. habrá nacido/nacerá 5. subirán 6. habrá contado
7. estaremos

12. 1. estaré 2. tengo/tendré 3. dirá 4. aceptará 5. voy a
llamar 6. habré recibido 7. podré/puedo 8. quedarán
9. lloverá 10. habré gastado

Chapter 21

1. 1. Tendrías 2. podríamos 3. gustaría 4. sabría
5. pasaría 6. valdría 7. Deberías 8. Querría; daría

2. 1. cabría 2. dirías 3. pondría 4. Sería 5. querría
6. vivirían 7. querría 8. Querrías 9. sabríamos
10. valdría 11. diríais 12. pondría

3. 1. deseo 2. suposición 3. deseo 4. consejo 5. consejo
6. suposición 7. deseo 8. consejo

4. 1. b, podría 2. c, compraría 3. a, armaría 4. e, saldría
5. f, vendrían 6. d, dormiría 7. g, diría

5. 1. En tu lugar, yo tomaría mucho té. / Yo en tu lugar,
tomaría mucho té. 2. Yo que tú, me quedaría en cama.
3. Deberías dormir más por la noche. 4. Yo en tu lugar,
iría al médico. 5. Yo que tú, no tomaría medicamentos.
6. Yo en tu lugar, estaría contenta por no ir a la escuela.

6. 1. c 2. b 3. f 4. a 5. d 6. e

7. 1. habría hecho 2. habríamos sido 3. habríamos
compartido 4. habría ido 5. habría comido
6. habríamos tardado 7. habría gustado

8. 1. a 2. b 3. b 4. a 5. b 6. b 7. b

9. 1. habría pasado 2 habría comprado 3. habría ganado
4. habría sabido 5. habría tenido 6. haberlo hecho

10. 1. habríamos tenido 2. gustaría 3. habría regalado
4. conduciría 5. Habrías votado 6. Votarías
7. deberías haber

11. 1. a 2. b 3. a 4. a 5. a 6. b 7. a 8. b 9. a

12. 1. dirías 2. gustaría 3. serían 4. Sería 5. solucionarían
6. valdría 7. habría habido 8. habría escrito

13. 1. Yo habría llamado al cerrajero. 2. Yo habría culpado
a otro camarero. 3. Yo (le) habría pedido disculpas.
4. Yo le habría dicho que la pintura era buena.

Chapter 22

1. 1. indicativo 2. indicativo 3. subjuntivo 4. indicativo
5. subjuntivo 6. indicativo 7. indicativo 8. subjuntivo
9. indicativo 10. subjuntivo 11. subjuntivo
12. indicativo 13. subjuntivo 14. indicativo

2. 1. se desempeñe 2. corras 3. transmita 4. charlemos
5. viva 6. ladre 7. escriba

3. 1. La profesora quiere que aprendamos de memoria el
himno nacional 2. Ella quiere que cada uno pase al
frente y lo cante 3. Nos ha permitido que cantemos el
himno en parejas 4. Ella no admitirá que cometamos

ni un solo error al cantar la letra 5. Dijo que es posible que la directora nos escuche cantar 6. Ella espera que los mejores cantantes formen parte del coro

4. 1. empiece 2. escojas 3. elija 4. sigan 5. busquemos 6. tenga 7. influyan 8. te dediques

5. 1. salga 2. cargues 3. agregues 4. toques/toquen 5. apagues 6. alcance 7. destruya 8. consigas 9. sigas

6. 1. traigas/traiga 2. insinúen 3. envíe 4. guiemos 5. conozca 6. diga 7. valgan 8. tengáis/tengan

7. 1. amplíen 2. digas 3. evalúe; ponga 4. oiga 5. pongas 6. conduzcas

8. 1. empiece a estudiar veinte días antes del examen 2. cuentes una historia increíble 3. la comida cueste (unos) veinte dólares 4. llueva muchísimo 5. despiertes a las nueve con el desayuno 6. devuelvas los libros a fin de mes

9. 1. Es mejor que no piense en cosas negativas. 2. Cuando desciendas las escaleras, verás a la derecha una gran puerta. Ésa es la cocina. 3. Los profesores no pretenden que entendamos todo el texto; solo la idea principal. / Nosotros no pretendemos que entiendas todo el texto; solo la idea principal. 4. Vos insistís en que tus padres te cuenten un cuento cada noche. / La niña insiste en que vos le contés/cuentes un cuento cada noche. 5. Harás todo lo que puedas para recaudar dinero para los pobres. 6. Quiero que huelas el nuevo perfume que me compré.

10. 1. prefiera 2. durmáis 3. hiera 4. nos divirtamos 5. durmamos 6. muera

11. 1. adquiera 2. adquieras 3. adquiera 4. adquiramos 5. adquieran 6. juegues 7. juegue 8. juguéis 9. jueguen

12. 1. llueva 2. el asesino todavía esté en los alrededores de la escena del crimen 3. recuerde el día en que nos conocimos 4. prefieran ir de vacaciones a la playa 5. se sepa de memoria toda la lección 6. hoy llegue a tiempo para ver la telenovela 7. Juan y Carlos vengan a la fiesta / Juan y Carlos vayan a venir a la fiesta 8. (vosotros) podáis participar en el evento

13. 1. piensen 2. quieran 3. guíe 4. adquieran 5. cueste 6. organicen 7. duerman 8. se enfríen 9. se diviertan 10. vuelvan

14. 2. te comieras 3. hablásemos 4. pidieran 6. pudiéramos 8. te cambiases

15. 1. subiera; subiese 2. pidiera; pidiese 3. cupiera; cupiese 4. fuera; fuese 5. pusiera; pusiese 6. lastimara; lastimase 7. hiciera; hiciese 8. concluyera; concluyese 9. deseara; desease 10. quisiera; quisiese 11. poseyera; poseyese 12. dijera; dijese 13. fuera; fuese

16. 1. hablara/hablase 2. viajáramos/viajásemos 3. trabajara/trabajase 4. se sorprendieran / se sorprendiesen 5. cocináramos/cocinásemos 6. llegaran/llegasen

17. 1. divirtiera/divirtiese 2. supiéramos/supiésemos 3. tuvieran/tuviesen 4. cayerais/cayeseis 5. leyeras/leyeses 6. produjera/produjese 7. fueran/fuesen 8. distribuyeran/distribuyesen 9. diera/diese 10. hiciera/hiciese

18. 1. me prestaras/prestases atención 2. quisieras/quisieses 3. que me incluyeras/incluyeses en tu lista de invitados 4. que destruyeran/destruyesen ese edificio antiguo tan hermoso 5. que pudieras/pudiesen venir a nuestra fiesta

6. te sintieras/sintieses como en casa 7. que tuviéramos/tuviésemos cuidado con nuestros bolsos 8. que fuera/fuese a esa panadería y que probara/probase las galletas de limón

19. 1. hayan tardado 2. hayamos sido 3. hayáis compartido 4. hayan pedido 5. haya bebido 6. hayas escrito 7. haya probado 8. hayamos descubierto 9. hayan traducido 10. hayas jugado

20. 1. hayamos querido 2. hayan venido 3. haya pasado 4. haya preguntado 5. se haya divorciado 6. hayas aprobado

21. 1. hubieras llegado 4. hubiera ido 5. hubieras mandado 6. hubiésemos salido 7. hubieses disfrutado 9. hubiera sabido

22. 1. hubiera/hubiese sabido 2. hubiera/hubiese conocido 3. hubiéramos/hubiésemos podido 4. hubierais/hubieseis subido 5. hubieras/hubieses cerrado 6. se hubieran/hubiesen graduado

23. 1. fuere 2. hubieren recibido 3. fueres, vieres 4. hubiere tenido 5. fuere

24. 1. haya invitado, pretérito perfecto; tengas, presente 2. vaya, presente; fuere, futuro 3. nos divirtamos, presente 4. saliera, pretérito imperfecto 5. pidiera, pretérito imperfecto 6. pudiesen, pretérito imperfecto 7. fuera, pretérito imperfecto 8. hubiere desobedecido, futuro perfecto 9. hayas sido elegido, pretérito perfecto

Chapter 23

1. 1. diviertas 2. regalen 3. hubieran avisado 4. cumplas 5. venga 6. cambie 7. se reconcilien 8. lleguemos

2. 1. e 2. f 3. a 4. c 5. b 6. d

3. 1. Te sugiero que seas puntual. 2. Te aconsejo que ayudes a tus compañeros. 3. Te recomiendo que siempre hagas los ejercicios de matemáticas. 4. Te pido que me llames por la tarde si tienes preguntas. 5. Te ruego que prestes atención a mis consejos. 6. Necesito que recuerdes todo lo que te digo.

4. 1. hace que, se retrasen 2. Que/El que/El hecho de que, hayas aprobado 3. Que/El que/El hecho de que, hayan elegido 4. Que/El que/El hecho de que, bajen 5. es que, tenga

5. 1. deseo 2. deseo 3. información 4. deseo 5. información 6. deseo 7. deseo 8. información

6. 1. Me indigna que te hayan robado/robaran/robasen la maleta. 2. Me molesta que estés fumando. 3. Me enfada que los vecinos estén haciendo una fiesta. 4. Lamento que hayas perdido/perdieras/perdieses el tren. 5. Me sorprende que hayas ganado/ganaras/ganases la lotería.

7. 1. b 2. b 3. b 4. a 5. b 6. b 7. a 8. b

8. 1. hayas contado 2. eres 3. he pensado 4. ha sucedido 5. vayas 6. sobrevivirá 7. dejes 8. he leído 9. dijeras 10. hagan

9. 1. comportaran/hayan comportado 2. tenga 3. piensen 4. vinieras/hayas venido 5. trabajara 6. quieras 7. espere 8. llegues 9. cambien 10. desapruebe

10. 1. e/d 2. b 3. a 4. f 5. c 6. g 7. d

11. 1. b 2. a 3. a 4. b 5. b

12. 1. Siempre 2. En ninguna parte 3. había 4. No existe nadie 5. una 6. pueda trabajar 7. quiere

13. 1. Lo lógico es que tú pases a buscarme. 2. Lo cierto es que eres realmente hermosa. 3. Lo más común es que la gente sea simpática. 4. Lo más normal fue que el tren llegara a horario. 5. Lo peor habría sido que nos robaran. 6. Lo que veo es que el sistema de transporte funciona muy mal. 7. Lo bueno es que hayas aprobado el examen. 8. Lo más interesante es que escribas inglés perfectamente aunque no sea tu primer idioma.

14. 1. decida 2. necesitamos 3. llamen 4. hayan hecho 5. suba 6. regalen 7. acaban 8. tuviera 9. guste 10. encantara

15. 1. Buscaba a un hombre que fuera cariñoso. 2. Habría querido estudiar una profesión que me hiciera feliz. 3. Necesitaba un par de lentes que costaran menos de 90 dólares. 4. Habría querido tener amigos que fueran sociables. 5. Buscaba un libro que fuera en inglés.

16. 1. Nos encontraremos en un bar en el que podamos conectarnos a Internet. 2. Dinos un nombre que te guste mucho. 3. Estaré en la plaza en la que nos conocimos. 4. Haz las cosas como tú quieras. 5. Ellos comen cuanto quieren. 6. Busca la maleta donde la dejó el conserje.

17. 1. Juan Manuel habla castellano como si fuera español. 2. Hice la tarea sin que nadie me ayudara. 3. Como no llegues a horario, me habré ido. 4. Como no tienes dinero, te prestaré un poco. 5. ¡Ni que fuera/estuviera loca te prestaría dinero!

18. 1. recibir 2. leí 3. camines 4. descuidas 5. hagas 6. recuperes 7. leas

19. 1. porque, porque 2. A fin de que 3. tanto que 4. tan, que 5. A causa de que 6. para

20. 1. Si bien no tengo hambre, comeré una porción de pizza. 2. Aunque me hubieran invitado a la fiesta, no habría ido. 3. Por más/mucha gente que venga a la fiesta, habrá lugar para todos. 4. Pese a que hacía mucho calor, los niños jugaron en el parque. 5. No compraría esa casa aunque tuviera el dinero. 6. Aun cuando viviera en Barcelona, no me sería fácil aprender catalán.

21. 1. a no ser que ya tuvieras planes 2. por si acaso llueve 3. en caso de que esta noche vengan más invitados 4. si te esfuerzas 5. si el metro hubiera funcionado bien 6. hoy no debes quejarte/hoy no te debes quejar 7. yo no te creería

22. 1. son 2. hicieras 3. haya 4. quiera 5. quiera 6. sea 7. compromete 8. tuviera 9. paguen 10. tenga 11. haga

23. 1. Que 2. Es aconsejable/Comprendo 3. El que/Que 4. Siento/Comprendo 5. No siento 6. Parece como si 7. Comprendo/Siento 8. Estoy convencido 9. Es sorprendente/Siento

24. 1. c 2. a 3. f 4. b 5. g 6. e 7. d 8. h

Chapter 24

1. 1. Descansa 2. Limpia 3. Come 4. Espera 5. Lee 6. Ordena 7. Ve 8. Pon 9. Ten 10. Compra

2. 1. Ven a casa a buscar el DVD 2. Sé amable con tus compañeros de clase 3. Pon cada libro en su lugar 4. Haz todo lo que yo te digo 5. Ve a la farmacia ya mismo 6. Di "permiso" antes de entrar

3. 1. No, entrevistad al profesor de música. 2. No, enviadle un correo electrónico. 3. No, haced preguntas sobre música clásica. 4. No, escribid el artículo para el miércoles. 5. Sí, descansad una hora.

4. 1. Tené cuidado con tus maletas. 2. Comprá un mapa en la estación. 3. Preguntá dónde tomar el autobús 152. 4. Sé simpática con el chofer del autobús. 5. Buscá la calle Juramento. 6. Tocá el timbre del departamento 1B.

5. 1. No hagas ejercicio cuatro veces por semana. 2. No leáis todos los libros de la biblioteca. 3. No tiréis los periódicos viejos a la basura. 4. No seas cordial con los turistas. 5. No aparques tu carro enfrente de mi casa. 6. No vengáis a cenar a casa. 7. No salgas de ahí. 8. No ayudéis a vuestros vecinos.

6. 1. juguemos 2. Tome 3. respeten 4. digamos 5. Pida 6. Suban 7. hagamos

7. 1. Danos un abrazo. Dánoslo. 2. Quitaos el abrigo. Quitáoslo. 3. Córtame el cabello. Córtamelo. 4. Regálanos unas rosas. Regálanoslas. 5. Mándeme una postal, señorita Álvarez. Mándemela, señorita Álvarez.

8. 1. fumen 2. Decídanse 3. terminen 4. olvídense 5. hagan 6. Caminen 7. corran 8. miren 9. duerman 10. Sean 11. cuídense

9. 1. cortad 2. ten 3. ve 4. trae 5. Debéis 6. os distraigáis 7. Hagamos 8. pongamos/poned

10. 1. ¡Venir a casa ya mismo! 2. Leer el prospecto del medicamento. 3. ¡A trabajar duro! 4. ¡Tomar un plato cada uno! 5. No te adelantes. 6. ¡Poned más empeño!

11. 1. hacer silencio 2. a trabajar (todos) 3. das/darías el teléfono de ese cliente 4. si te callas la boca 5. no me ayudas con los paquetes 6. pagues el café que te compré

12. 1. llega puntualmente 2. enséñenle buenos modales 3. presta atención a la clase 4. lo ayude con las tareas para el hogar 5. lo recompensen con dinero 6. molestes a tus compañeros

Chapter 25

1. **Infinitivo:** disfrazarnos, tener, probármelo, hacer, ayudarme, tener, ayudarme **Gerundio:** festejando, diseñando, comprando **Participio:** llamada, ajustado, confeccionado, visto, decidida, recibidas, propuesto

2. 1. El sonar de las campanas 2. Caminar 3. Comprar la casa 4. beber refrescos 5. Bailar 6. comer frutas y verduras.

3. 1. Al verte, me alegré tanto. 2. De haber estudiado más, hoy tendrías mejores calificaciones. 3. Al amanecer, la playa estaba desierta. 4. De ser tan complicado el viaje, mejor nos quedamos aquí. 5. Al llegar Juan, llámame por teléfono. 6. De seguir caminando, habríamos llegado al muelle.

4. 1. a 2. c 3. a 4. b 5. c 6. c

5. 1. f 2. a/d 3. b 4. e 5. c 6. d

6. 1. sigo comiendo 2. quedé pensando 3. lleva, trabajando 4. viene bajando 5. terminaron yendo 6. anda necesitando

7. 1. b 2. c 3. e 4. f 5. g 6. a 7. d

8. 1. El jefe nos llamó diciendo/diciéndonos que estábamos despedidos. 2. No habiéndote encontrado, me fui a casa. 3. Caminábamos cantando. 4. Viendo que no había comida, decidí irme al mercado. 5. Presionando el botón de ese modo, lo romperás. 6. Me quebré la pierna practicando esquí.

9. 1. que contenían 2. parado 3. habiendo esquivado una vaca 4. hirviendo 5. cantando 6. abrazando 7. y lo capturó

10. 1. despertado 2. confundida 3. electa/elegida 4. oído 5. confuso 6. presentado 7. asumido 8. corrupta 9. robado 10. presa 11. despierta 12. sana 13. salva

11. 1. La renuncia está redactada. 2. Julia está divorciada. 3. Juan y Paula están casados. 4. El perro está suelto. 5. El ensayo está corregido. 6. El problema está resuelto.

12. 1. a 2. a 3. a 4. a 5. b 6. a 7. b

13. 1. presunto 2. liberado 3. Habiendo sido 4. decidido 5. recibido 6. golpeando 7. quedarse

14. 1. vendiendo 2. continuar 3. desconectar 4. tejiendo 5. hecho 6. Pagando 7. moviendo 8. oír

15. 1. c 2. a 3. b 4. g 5. e 6. d 7. f

16. 1. d 2. a 3. e 4. b 5. g 6. c 7. f 8. h

Chapter 26

1. 1. viene 2. Puedo 3. hemos/he 4. ha/debe 5. han 6. tuvieron 7. Deben/Han 8. deben 9. vinieron 10. tuve/tenía 11. pueden

2. 1. deberías 2. pudiste 3. quise 4. Sabes 5. titilará 6. debiste 7. parece 8. puedo

3. 1. fase 2. serie 3. tiempo 4. fase 5. tiempo 6. serie 7. fase 8. serie

4. 1. Empiezo por 2. suelo 3. para de 4. acababa de 5. puso a 6. volveré a 7. fui a 8. terminaré por

5. 1. Después de probar con el canto, pasé a estudiar pintura. 2. En esas dos horas, el profesor no dejó de hablar ni un segundo. 3. Me juró que no volvería a robar en la tienda. 4. Un rato después de salir el sol, entró a nublarse y a la media hora llovía sin parar. 5. Es verdad que no suelo comer dulces, ¡pero este bombón es tentador! 6. Natalia nunca iría a hacer las compras por iniciativa propia.

6. 1. estás hablando 2. vive criticando 3. se pasó, ladrando 4. fueron aumentando 5. vengo pidiendo 6. anda necesitando 7. lleva viviendo 8. seguiré trabajando

7. 1. terminé 2. continúa 3. lleva 4. está 5. Sigo 6. vive

8. 1. b 2. e 3. a 4. f 5. d 6. c

9. 1. Mamá le tiene prohibido a Luisito usar vasos de vidrio. 2. Gonzalo lleva ganadas tres carreras. 3. Mis amigos tienen compradas las entradas para mañana. 4. Este director lleva dirigidas más de veinte películas. 5. La carta está escrita con tinta roja. 6. Llevo escritos veinte capítulos del libro.

10. 1. quedó/está 2. está 3. viene/está 4. Quedó/Está 5. sigue/está 6. tienen 7. tengo 8. vimos

11. 1. despertarte 2. durmiendo 3. perjudicados 4. dormir 5. teniendo 6. gastado 7. ver

12. 1. b 2. f 3. a 4. h 5. c 6. e 7. d 8. g

Chapter 27

1. Juan:
Hoy **me desperté** a las siete de la mañana. Apenas escuché el despertador, **me senté** en la cama y te llamé por teléfono para despertarte. El teléfono sonó, sonó y sonó, pero no atendiste.
Como todavía era temprano, no **me preocupé** y decidí **darme** un baño largo. Después, **me cepillé** los dientes y **me peiné**.
Dos minutos después de salir de la ducha, **me di cuenta** de mi error: ¡me **había equivocado** de número de teléfono! Ahora **me siento** tan mal por esta situación. Llegaste tarde al trabajo, tu jefe **se enojó** contigo y casi pierdes tu trabajo.
¡Espero que sepas disculparme!
Lucas

2. 1. Oscar se afeita a las 9.00 a.m. Oscar se va a afeitar/va a afeitarse a las 9.00 a.m. 2. Ellos se reúnen el miércoles. Ellos se van a reunir/van a reunirse el miércoles. 3. Vosotros os reís mucho. Vosotros os vais a reír mucho/vais a reíros mucho. 4. Nosotros nunca nos peleamos. Nosotros nunca nos vamos a pelear/vamos a pelearnos. 5. Gabriela se pone tacones. Gabriela se va a poner tacones/va a ponerse tacones.

3. 1. Juan e Isabel se apoyan el uno al otro. 2. Los alumnos y los profesores siempre se critican los unos a los otros. 3. Federica y su amiga se respetan la una a la otra. 4. Los trabajadores se ayudan los unos a los otros. 5. Mi madre y mi hermana se miraron la una a la otra con tristeza.

4. 1. Sí 2. No 3. Sí 4. No 5. No 6. Sí

5. 1. b 2. a 3. b 4. b 5. a 6. a 7. b

6. **Solo reflexivos:** comportarse, desvivirse, jactarse, rebelarse, arrepentirse, dignarse, quejarse **Reflexivos/No reflexivos:** lavarse, odiarse, conocerse, quemarse, cansarse

7. 1. se miran, se confiesan 2. Nos comprometimos, nos casamos / nos casaremos / nos vamos a casar / vamos a casarnos 3. se apoyan 4. se pelean 5. se odian 6. nos escribamos 7. se abrazaron 8. se duchó 9. se aprendió 10. se reunirán/se reunen 11. se conocieron, se escriben/escribieron/se han escrito 12. me arrepiento

8. 1. Me conozco 2. te crees 3. se comen 4. se sabe 5. Te anduviste

9. 1. c 2. d 3. b 4. e 5. a

10. 1. Anima 2. Decidí 3. se saltó 4. Nos jugamos 5. deshagas 6. Cómanse

11. 1. Se descompuso. 2. Se descargó. 3. Se cayeron. 4. Se enredó. 5. Se derrumbaron.

12. 1. Se te quebró la madera. 2. Se le cerró la puerta. 3. Se me rompió la tetera. 4. Se nos derramó la leche. 5. Se le agotó la batería a mi auto. 6. Se me olvidan siempre los nombres. 7. Siempre se les pierden las llaves a esos hermanitos.

13. 1. se enrojeció/se puso rojo 2. se emocionó 3. se murió 4. se enriquecieron/se volvieron/se hicieron ricos 5. se enamoraron 6. se separó

14. 1. La oficina se convierte en un caos cuando tú no estás. 2. Tu pececito se pone triste apenas sales de la sala. 3. Mi prima se hizo rica con su tienda de perfumes. 4. Me quedé preocupado/a con la mala noticia.

5. Madrid se volvió/ha vuelto una ciudad muy cara.
6. Algún día, llegaré a ser rico.
15. 1. a 2. b 3. a 4. b 5. a 6. b
16. 1. b 2. c 3. a 4. c 5. c 6. b

Chapter 28

1. 1. La ley de alimentos orgánicos fue aprobada hoy por el Senado. 2. El partido fue visto por miles de fanáticos. 3. El documental *La selva hoy* fue elogiado por la crítica. 4. Tres tumbas egipcias fueron descubiertas por los arqueólogos chilenos. 5. La identidad de los pasajeros fue controlada por la policía. 6. Un acuerdo de cooperación será firmado por ambos países.
2. 1. b 2. b 3. a 4. a 5. b 6. a
3. 1. Los animalitos fueron tratados cruelmente por el cazador. 2. Quienes den información serán recompensados con 50.000 dólares. 3. Los periódicos fueron enviados a los lectores esta tarde. 4. El problema había sido resuelto por el jefe del departamento. 5. El vestido de novia fue diseñado y confeccionado por el afamado diseñador. 6. El conserje fue despertado por los visitantes.
4. 1. El delincuente será prendido por la policía. El delincuente ya está preso. 2. El pastel de cumpleaños será hecho por mi madre. El pastel de cumpleaños ya está hecho. 3. Una carta de queja será redactada por Ulises. La carta de queja ya está redactada. 4. Los aportes jubilatorios serán pagados por todos los trabajadores. Los aportes jubilatorios ya están pagados/pagos. 5. La revista *Novedades empresariales* será publicada por el directorio de la compañía. La revista *Novedades empresariales* ya está publicada.
5. 1. Primero, se pelan las papas. Luego, se las corta. 2. Primero, se hornea la tarta. Luego, se la prueba. 3. Primero, se construye la casa. Luego, se la pinta. 4. Primero, se apaga la bombilla de luz. Luego, se la cambia. 5. Primero, se llama al paciente. Luego, se lo examina. 6. Primero, se lava el cabello. Luego, se lo corta. 7. Primero, se decoran las galletas. Luego, se las hornea.
6. 1. limpiar el pasillo. 2. se deben ordenar las habitaciones. 3. El miércoles se debe lavar la ropa. 4. El jueves se prepara la cena./El jueves se debe preparar la cena. 5. El viernes se planchan las camisas./El viernes se deben planchar las camisas. 6. El sábado se disfruta el día.
7. 1. será reparada 2. Se aceptarán/Se aceptan 3. se deben agregar/se agregan 4. se mojaron 5. son firmadas/deben ser firmadas 6. se detendrá 7. se sabe
8. 1. a 2. a 3. a 4. c 5. a 6. c 7. b
9. 1. Con el cuchillo, se corta. 2. Con la pimienta, se condimenta. 3. Con la cuchara, se prueba. 4. Con el tenedor, se come. 5. Con el lápiz, se escribe. 6. En el ayuntamiento, se debate. 7. En la escuela, se aprende. 8. En el comedor, se come.
10. 1. uno puede dormir 2. uno está tranquilo, puede trabajar 3. se puede comprar 4. vive una 5. una llega 6. uno transpira
11. 1. Se maltrata a las mujeres en este país. Se las maltrata en este país. 2. Se debe respetar a los peatones. Se debe

respetarlos/Se los debe respetar. 3. Se contrata a las enfermeras por un año. Se las contrata por un año. 4. Se encuesta al pueblo cada diez años. Se lo encuesta cada diez años. 5. Se evalúa a los trabajadores cada trimestre. Se los evalúa cada trimestre.
12. Primero, se redactaron las normas de seguridad. Una vez redactadas, la gerencia **se** las enseñó **a los miembros del departamento de documentación**. Cuando estaban listas, **se** las enviaron **a todos los trabajadores de la planta**. Hubo diversas reacciones de parte de los trabajadores. **Se le** informó **a la gerencia** que muchas de las normas eran obsoletas y se **le** advirtió que debían hacerse modificaciones con urgencia.
Ahora se han reformado las normas. Mañana por la tarde un grupo de especialistas **se** las presentará **al gerente general**. Esta vez seguramente se las aprobará sin objeciones.
13. 1. pasiva 2. impersonal 3. pasiva 4. impersonal 5. pasiva 6. impersonal 7. pasiva 8. impersonal 9. pasiva 10. impersonal
14. 1. Uno nunca sabe cómo estará el tiempo al día siguiente. 2. La gente hace lo que puede. 3. Conviene tener un botiquín de primeros auxilios. 4. Una no puede respirar en esta habitación llena de humo. 5. Han enviado dos postales para ti. 6. Ha llovido muchísimo en la última semana. 7. Hay muchos libros sobre historia medieval en esta biblioteca. 8. Hace mucho frío en esa época del año. 9. Conviene estudiar mucho para el examen.
15. 1. Hay 2. Hubo/Hay 3. han 4. habían 5. Había 6. Es 7. era
16. 1. b 2. a 3. b 4. a 5. a 6. a 7. a 8. a

Chapter 29

1. 1. está 2. hay 3. hay 4. hay 5. Hay 6. hay 7. está 8. está 9. ha 10. Hay
2. 1. Está, son 2. Estará 3. Estamos 4. Estamos 5. estuvo 6. Es 7. es
3. 1. es 2. son 3. es 4. hace 5. está 6. hizo 7. estuvo 8. hubo 9. estamos 10. hubo 11. Hará
4. 1. tengo 2. es 3. está/estará 4. tienen 5. tiene 6. estoy 7. Tenéis
5. 1. Se está haciendo de noche. 2. Se puso frío. 3. Dieron las cinco. 4. Es invierno de nuevo. 5. Ya es viernes. 6. Se hizo de día.
6. 1. Ella se enrojeció. Ella se puso colorada/roja. 2. Ella se alegró. Ella se puso contenta/alegre. 3. Mi abuelo se enriqueció. Mi abuelo se hizo rico. 4. Me mejoré. Me puse mejor. 5. Ellos se entristecieron. Ellos se pusieron tristes. 6. Nos callamos. Nos quedamos callados. 7. Él (se) enloqueció. Se puso/volvió loco.
7. 1. Hay 2. tiene 3. está 4. fueron 5. se hace 6. Estamos 7. me quedé 8. puso 9. era 10. Están

Chapter 30

1. 1. de 2. para 3. de 4. para 5. con/a 6. sin 7. a/de
2. 1. La hermana de Juan me es muy amable. 2. ¿Es cierto que sabes andar a caballo? 3. ¡Es una lástima que no nos hayamos visto! 4. Profesora, nos fue muy difícil hacer

la tarea. 5. No me es fácil dormir con la luz del día.
6. Soy de Bogotá y viví ahí hasta los quince años.
7. Marcos es muy bueno para/con el inglés. 8. La casa
es de madera.

3. 1. e 2. c 3. f 4. g 5. b 6. a 7. d

4. 1. Estamos con nuestro queridísimo Presidente.
2. Estoy con dolor de garganta desde hace una semana.
3. Estuve a punto de salir de casa sin las llaves.
4. Están por comenzar las obras del metro nuevo.
5. Mi padre siempre estuvo/estaba con los liberales.
6. Estaba/Estuve por comprarte una camisa del
mismo color.

5. 1. b 2. b 3. a 4. a 5. b 6. b 7. a

6. 1. es 2. está 3. es 4. está 5. está 6. Es 7. Estoy

7. 1. estarán 2. está 3. fue 4. estaba 5. está 6. estás
7. Es

8. 1. hay 2. está 3. hay 4. Habrá 5. estuvo 6. habrá
7. estará 8. Hay 9. está

9. 1. c 2. a 3. d 4. b 5. e

10. 1. está 2. Es 3. Estabas 4. Fue 5. está 6. seamos
7. Está

11. 1. es, está 2. Fue/Es, hubo 3. estuvo, están 4. son, será/
es 5. Estábamos, Está 6. Ha, son

12. 1. Es 2. es 3. soy 4. ser 5. es 6. están 7. estoy
8. estás

Chapter 31

1. 1. Tu hermana dijo que había dormido doce horas
en la noche del lunes. 2. La profesora nos dijo que
estudiáramos/estudiemos para el examen de la semana
que viene. 3. El presidente dijo que hoy se entrevistaría
con el presidente ecuatoriano. 4. Juana me dijo que nos
veríamos mañana/el martes por la noche. 5. Mi tutor
me dijo que el sábado/ayer no tendríamos clases.

2. 1. orden; Me dijo que pasara y mirara sin compromiso.
2. orden; Me dijo que (por favor) no me sentara allí.
3. información; Me dijo que los pantalones estaban en
oferta. 4. orden; Me dijo que me llevara dos pantalones
por 20 dólares. 5. información; Me dijo que la tienda
cerraba a las nueve. 6. orden; Me dijo que me apurara a
comprar. 7. información; Me dijo que me agradecía la
visita/agradecía mi visita.

3. 1. estaba muy feliz porque nos veríamos al día siguiente
2. llegaría a las nueve y media a la Estación del Sur
3. me esperaría en las escaleras del edificio principal;
no me olvidara de pasar a buscarla 4. no había tenido
vacaciones con amigos desde 2006; quería que lo
disfrutáramos 5. te llamara; te avisara sobre su llegada

4. 1. ayudara 2. irían 3. hiciera 4. había olvidado
5. hubieran 6. iba, volvía 7. eran, llamaba 8. tomara

5. 1. a 2. b 3. b 4. a 5. b 6. b 7. b 8. a

6. 1. b 2. f 3. h 4. d 5. c 6. g

7. 1. Señora, ¿podría decirme dónde está el correo más
cercano? 2. No recuerdo si mi papá me pasa a buscar
a las cinco o a las seis. 3. ¿Sabes cuándo cumple años
Cristina? 4. Me pregunto si esta película es divertida.
5. Le pregunté si no tenía calor con esa chaqueta.
6. Nunca supe cuál era el nombre de esa chica tan
bonita. 7. ¿Puedes decirme a qué hora comeremos?

8. 1. cuánto tiempo se tarda para llegar en tren a Barcelona
2. que había perdido su cartera 3. que no la molestara/
moleste más 4. cómo sería el tiempo al día siguiente
5. si tiene cambio de veinte dólares 6. que el día
anterior había trabajado hasta las diez de la noche
7. que nunca había tenido un accidente de tránsito
8. que les mostrara las fotos de mi viaje 9. que, si
hubieran tenido tiempo, me habrían visitado
10. que compraría una computadora nueva si
tuviera dinero ahorrado

Index

Index

S

Image credits

Image credits

About the author

Ana Beatriz Chiquito is a Professor of Spanish at the University of Bergen, Norway, and for nearly twenty years has been affiliated with the Center for Educational Computing Initiatives at MIT as a Visiting Research Engineer. Professor Chiquito holds degrees in Linguistics, Social Sciences, and Teacher Education, and has been a Visiting Professor at the University of Massachusetts, Boston; the Universidad Católica de Quito; the Universidad de Costa Rica; the Norwegian School of Economics and Business Administration; and at the UNDP Program in Public Administration in Ecuador. Professor Chiquito has extensive international experience designing and developing e-learning applications for language education at all levels and for over thirty years has led research projects in Spanish linguistics, sociolinguistics, and e-learning in Latin America, Spain, Norway, and the United States. She has also co-authored several textbooks and e-learning applications for Spanish as a foreign language for the U.S. and European markets. A native of Colombia, she now divides her time between the Boston area and Norway.